Economics
Principles and Tools
Second Edition

PRENTICE HALL SERIES IN ECONOMICS

Adams/Brock, *The Structure of American Industry*, 10/e
Blanchard, *Macroeconomics*, 2/e
Blau/Ferber/Winkler, *The Economics of Women, Men, and Work*, 3/e
Boardman/Greenberg/Vining/Wiemer, *Cost Benefit Analysis: Concepts and Practice*, 2/e
Bogart, *The Economics of Cities and Suburbs*
Case/Fair, *Principles of Economics*, 5/e
Case/Fair, *Principles of Macroeconomics*, 5/e
Case/Fair, *Principles of Microeconomics*, 5/e
Caves, *American Industry: Structure, Conduct, Performance*, 7/e
Collinge/Ayers, *Economics by Design: Principles and Issues*, 2/e
DiPasquale/Wheaton, *Urban Economics and Real Estate Markets*
Feiner, *Race and Gender in the American Economy: Views Across the Spectrum*
Folland/Goodman/Stano, *Economics of Health and Health Care*, 3/e
Froyen, *Macroeconomics: Theories and Policies*, 6/e
Greene, *Econometric Analysis*, 4/e
Heilbroner/Milberg, *The Making of an Economic Society*, 10/e
Heyne, *The Economic Way of Thinking*, 9/e
Hirschleifer/Hirschleifer, *Price Theory and Applications*, 6/e
Keat/Young, *Managerial Economics*, 3/e
Milgrom/Roberts, *Economics, Organization, and Management*
O'Sullivan/Sheffrin, *Economics: Principles and Tools*, 2/e
O'Sullivan/Sheffrin, *Macroeconomics: Principles and Tools*, 2/e
O'Sullivan/Sheffrin, *Microeconomics: Principles and Tools*, 2/e
Petersen/Lewis, *Managerial Economics*, 4/e
Pindyck/Rubinfeld, *Microeconomics*, 5/e
Reynolds/Masters/Moser, *Labor Economics and Labor Relations*, 11/e
Roberts, *The Choice: A Fable of Free Trade and Protectionism*, Revised
Sachs/Larrain, *Macroeconomics in the Global Economy*
Schiller, *The Economics of Poverty and Discrimination*, 8/e
Weidenbaum, *Business and Government in the Global Marketplace*, 6/e

Economics
Principles and Tools
Second Edition

Arthur O'Sullivan

Oregon State University

Steven M. Sheffrin

University of California, Davis

Upper Saddle River, New Jersey

Library of Congress Cataloging-in-Publication Data

O'Sullivan, Arthur.
　Economics: principles and tools/Arthur O'Sullivan, Steven M. Sheffrin.—2nd ed.
　　p. cm.
　Includes bibliographical references and index.
　ISBN 0-13-027383-X
　　1. Economics.　I. Sheffrin, Steven M.　II. Title.

HB171.5.O84 2000
330—dc21　　　　　　　　　　　　　　　　　　　　　　　00-032632

Senior Editor: Rod Banister
Senior Development Editor: Michael Elia
Managing Editor (Editorial): Gladys Soto
Vice-President/Editorial Director: James C. Boyd
Editor-in-Chief: PJ Boardman
Editorial Assistant: Marie McHale
Assistant Editor: Holly Brown
Media Project Manager: Bill Minick
Senior Marketing Manager: Lori Braumberger
Managing Editor (Production): Cynthia Regan
Senior Production Editor: Richard DeLorenzo
Production Coordinator: Elena Barnett
Manufacturing Buyer/Supervisor: Paul Smolenski
Senior Prepress/Manufacturing Manager: Vincent Scelta
Design Manager: Patricia Smythe
Photo Researcher: Abby Reip
Cover Design/Interior Design: Lee Goldstein
Associate Director, Multimedia Production: Karen Goldsmith
Manager, Multimedia Production/Composition: Christy Mahon
Multimedia Artist: Brian Staples

10 9 8 7 6 5 4 3 2
ISBN 0-13-027383-X

To Our Children: Conor, Maura, Meera, and Kiran

About the Authors

Arthur O'Sullivan

Arthur O'Sullivan is a professor of economics at Oregon State University. After receiving his B.S. Degree in economics at the University of Oregon, he spent two years in the Peace Corps, working with city planners in the Philippines. He received his Ph.D. in economics from Princeton University in 1981, and then spent 11 years at the University of California, Davis, where he won several teaching awards. At Oregon State University, he teaches microeconomics at different levels, from the introductory course to advanced courses for doctoral students. He is the author of the best-selling textbook, *Urban Economics*, currently in its fourth edition.

Professor O'Sullivan's research explores economic issues concerning urban land use, environmental protection, and public finance. His articles appear in many economics journals, including *Journal of Urban Economics*, *Journal of Environmental Economics and Management*, *National Tax Journal*, and *Journal of Public Economics*.

 Professor O'Sullivan lives with his family in Corvallis, Oregon. He enjoys outdoor activities, including the kids' sport du jour (soccer, basketball, baseball, badminton, lawn hockey, or tackle the guy with the ball). Indoors, he is learning how to play the fiddle, much to the dismay of his family and the delight of the neighborhood dogs.

Steven M. Sheffrin

Steven M. Sheffrin is dean of the division of social sciences and professor of economics at the University of California, Davis. He has been a visiting professor at Princeton University, Oxford University, and the London School of Economics, and served as a financial economist with the Office of Tax Analysis of the United States Department of Treasury. He has been on the faculty at Davis since 1976 and served as the chairman of the department of economics. He received his B.A. from Wesleyan University and his Ph.D. in economics from the Massachusetts Institute of Technology.

Professor Sheffrin is the author of seven other books and monographs and over 80 articles in the fields of macroeconomics, public finance, and international economics. His most recent books include *Rational Expectations* (Second Edition) and *Property Taxes and Tax Revolts: The Legacy of Proposition 13* (with Arthur O'Sullivan and Terri Sexton), both from Cambridge University Press.

Professor Sheffrin has taught macroeconomics at all levels, from large lectures of principles (classes of 400) to graduate classes for doctoral students. He is the recipient of the Thomas Mayer Distinguished Teaching Award in economics.

He lives with his wife Anjali (also an economist) and his two children in Davis, California. In addition to a passion for current affairs and travel, he plays a tough game of tennis.

Brief Contents

Contents

A CLOSER LOOK

Features

Features

Preface

Our Story

When we set out to write an economics text, we were driven by the vision of the sleeping student. A few years ago, one of the authors was in the middle of a fascinating lecture on monopoly pricing when he heard snoring. It wasn't the first time a student had fallen asleep in one of his classes, but this was the loudest snoring he had ever heard—it sounded like a sputtering chain saw. The instructor turned to Bill, who was sitting next to the sleeping student and asked, "Could you wake him up?" Bill looked at the sleeping student and then gazed theatrically around the room at the other students. He finally looked back at the instructor and said, "Well professor, I think you should wake him up. After all, you put him to sleep."

That experience changed the way we taught economics. It highlighted for us a basic truth—for many students, economics isn't exactly exciting. We took this as a challenge—to get first-time economics students to see the *relevance* of economics to their *lives*, their *careers*, and their *futures*.

In order to get students to see the relevance of economics we knew that we had to *engage* them. With the first edition of *Economics: Principles and Tools*, we helped professors to do that by emphasizing an active learning approach. We engaged students by teaching them how to do something—economic analysis. We kept the book brief, lively, and to the point, and used the five key principles of economics as an organizing theme.

The first edition was a success in classrooms across the country, but it wasn't enough because we knew that we could do even better.

Our Mission

Our objective was to make the sequel even better than the original. Although the first edition of the book was successful, we set ourselves a higher standard: *to make it better*. We knew that students and other instructors would provide the most important help, so we began an extensive review process. We had dozens of professors and students review the first edition, encouraging them to give us lots of constructive criticism. We gave them free rein to tell us what they liked and disliked about the book—and asked them to suggest ways to make the text a better teaching instrument. In addition, several focus groups took a critical look at the first edition and suggested ways to improve the book.

Armed with the comments and suggestions from the reviewers, student users, and focus groups, we locked ourselves up in a hotel for 48 hours with the top-notch editorial staff from Prentice Hall. We examined, discussed, debated, and reexamined all of the information we had gathered. The end result was a clearly defined revision plan for the second edition. Our plan carefully incorporated the comments and suggestions of professors and students. After thoroughly revising the manuscript based on this feedback, we sent the revised manuscript for another set of peer reviews. We were pleased that the second round of reviews confirmed our belief that we had achieved our goal of improving an already good book.

At the end of this process, we met our goal: We wrote a better textbook. We are proud to present *Economics: Principles And Tools, Second Edition*. Over the next few pages, we will show you exactly what we have done to make it better. At the same time, we will point out what made this book such a success in its first edition.

Key Improvements

We knew that our text's **brevity and student accessibility** were strengths, so we made it even more focused and accessible by streamlining chapters. In particular, we made these key changes:

We thoroughly revised the chapter on production cost (now called Production and Cost) to integrate the concepts of production and cost. We use key ideas from production theory to explain the shapes of the firm's short-run and long-run cost curves. The reviewers asked for a more detailed discussion of the link between production and cost, and we delivered.

We reorganized the chapters on different market structures along more traditional lines. In addition, we wrote two applied chapters on market structure: Using Market Power: Price Discrimination and Advertising (Chapter 13) and Controlling Market Power: Antitrust Policy and Deregulation (Chapter 14).

We reorganized the first two chapters on macroeconomics, with Chapter 20 devoted to production and income, and Chapter 21 focusing on unemployment and inflation. Our original version put these two concepts together. Our peer reviewers wanted two separate chapters in order to add depth.

The chapter on **supply and demand** (Chapter 4) has been reorganized to provide a more thorough and methodical presentation of the basics of supply and demand.

We undertook an unprecedented review of our test bank to ensure accuracy. We hired an outside team of economists, writers, and fact checkers to check and double-check the over 7,000 test questions in both the Microeconomics and Macroeconomics Test Bank manuals. We also had the questions thoroughly reviewed by educational psychologists to evaluate the effectiveness of the format and wording of the questions. The questions were then tested on a group of dedicated honors students at Oregon State University.

Brief Contents

viii

Teaching Philosophy

We began with the idea that an introductory economics course should be taught as if it is the last economics class a student will ever take. Because this is true for most students, we have just one opportunity to teach them how to use economics. The best way to teach economics is to focus on a few key concepts and ideas and apply them repeatedly in different circumstances.

We start the book with the five key principles of economics and then apply them throughout the book. This approach provides students with the big picture—the framework of economic reasoning. We make the key concepts unforgettable by using them repeatedly, illustrating them with intriguing examples, and giving students many opportunities to practice what they've learned.

Our book is designed to be accessible to students. We have kept the writing lean, the examples lively and topical, and the visuals exciting.

Principles And Tools

In keeping with the themes of relevance and student accessibility, we have once again organized our text around the **five key principles** of economics. Throughout the text, every point of theory is tied back to the five key principles and is indicated by the 🔑 symbol.

1. **The Principle of Opportunity Cost.** The opportunity cost of something is what you sacrifice to get it.
2. **The Marginal Principle.** Pick the level of an activity at which the marginal benefit equals the marginal cost.
3. **The Principle of Diminishing Returns.** If we increase one input while holding the other inputs fixed, output will increase, but at a decreasing rate.
4. **The Spillover Principle.** In some circumstances, decision makers do not bear all the cost or experience all the benefits from their decision.
5. **The Reality Principle.** What matters to people is the real value of money or income—its purchasing power—not the face value of money or income.

We use these principles to explain the logic underpinning the most important tools of economics. By using these five principles repeatedly, we reveal the logic of economic reasoning and demystify the tools of economics. Students see the big picture and also learn how to use the tools of economics properly.

"What I Do, I Understand" – *Confucius*

Our book is based on **Active Learning**, a teaching approach based on the idea that students learn best by doing. Our book engages students by letting them do activities as they read. We implement **Active Learning** with the following features:

- **Economic Detective** exercises provide a few clues and then ask the student to solve the economic mystery.

The Case of the Cheap Pet Salon

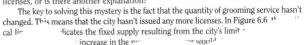

ECONOMIC DETECTIVE

After 20 years of dog haircuts, perms, and pedicures, Doug wants to sell his pet-grooming salon. Several months earlier, a similar pet salon sold for $50,000. But Doug hasn't found anyone willing to buy his for more than $20,000. He suspects that the city has quietly increased the number of pet-grooming licenses, and that's why the price of grooming services dropped, pulling down the market price of pet salons like his. According to the local pet-grooming association, the quantity of grooming services (the number of haircuts, perms, and pedicures) has not changed in recent years. Why has the market price of a pet salon decreased so much? Has the city issued more licenses, or is there another explanation?

The key to solving this mystery is the fact that the quantity of grooming service hasn't changed. This means that the city hasn't issued any more licenses. In Figure 6.6 th_ cal li~ ~dicates the fixed supply resulting from the city's limit ~
increase in the n~ ~~e would ~
~f s~

Using the **TOOLS**

This chapter introduced several new tools of economics, including four different elasticities and a formula that can be used to predict the change in price resulting from a change in supply or demand. Here are some opportunities to use these tools to do your own economic analysis.

1. Projecting Transit Ridership
As a transit planner, you must predict how many people ride commuter trains and how much money is generated from train fares. According to a recent study,[7] the short-run price elasticity of demand for commuter rail is 0.62 and the long-run elasticity is 1.59. The current ridership is 100,000 people per day. Suppose fares increase by 10%.

a. Predict the changes in train ridership over a one-month period (short run) and a five-year period (long run).

b. Over the one-month period, will total revenue increase or decrease? What will happen in the five-year period?

2. Bumper Crops
job is to predict the total revenue generated by th   last year's
       100 million bus   price   er

TEST Your Understanding

1. Money solves the problem of double coincidence of wants that would regularly occur under a system of _____.

2. Why is money only an imperfect store of value?

3. What is the problem associated with the double coincidence of wants?

4. Because we measure all prices in monetary units, money serves as a unit of account. True or false? Explain.

5. Why are checks includ   definition of money?

- **Using the Tools** questions at the end of each chapter give students opportunities to do their own economic analysis. Complete answers appear at the end of each chapter.

- **Economic Experiments** actively involve the student in role-playing as consumers, producers, and policy makers. All these activities are designed to be fun for students and easy for professors, who decide when and how to use them.

- **Test Your Understanding** questions help students determine whether they understand the preceding material before continuing. These are straightforward questions that ask students to review and synthesize what they have read. Complete answers appear at the end of each chapter.

- **Chapter-opening stories** open each chapter and motivate the chapter's subject matter.

- Each chapter starts with a list of **practical questions** that are answered in the chapter.

- **Lively Examples** are integrated throughout the text and help bring economic concepts to life. We have hundreds of fresh, new examples in this edition.

- **A Closer Look** boxes are featured throughout the text and provide brief, interesting examples of the tools and concepts discussed in the text.

A CLOSER LOOK   Foreign Sweatshops and Codes of Conduct

Several widely publicized reports have documented poor working conditions and low wages in foreign factories that produce shoes, clothing, and toys for U.S. corporations. In 1996, a report revealed that part of Wal-Mart's Kathie Lee Collection was produced in Honduras by people working 20 hours per day for 31 cents per hour.[9] Similar reports suggested that goods sold by Nike, Disney, and Mattel were produced in overseas sweatshops. Some human-rights activists have organized protests to publicize what they consider unethical business practices and have organized consumer boycotts.

The corporations have responded to the uproar by monitoring the firms that produce their goods and establishing codes of conduct for foreign suppliers.[10] The Council on Economic Priorities, an interest grou   New York, inspects workplaces and a   cial Accountability   " to

- How much more are consumers willing to pay for "No Sweat" products?
- Will firms selling "No Sweat" products lose customers to firms selling products pr
  tories that don't meet the codes of conduct?

Macro Organization

Because the U.S. economy has performed so well in recent years—low inflation, low unemployment—and our last recession in the early 1990's, economists have been increasingly interested in economic growth. In fact, most of our students do not even remember living through a recession, which is why we cover long-run growth early in the macroeconomics chapters. We are living in a new world where we no longer tell students that low inflation and full employment are incompatible because the real world is telling us that it *is* possible. Our theories of economic growth address the fundamental question of how long-term living standards are determined and why some countries prosper while others do not. This is the essence of economic growth. As one noted economist says, "Once you start thinking about growth, its hard to think about anything else."

A key dilemma confronting economics professors has always been how much time to devote to classical topics such as growth and production, versus more Keynesian topics such as economic fluctuations. Our book is designed to let professors *choose*. It works like this: to pursue a classical approach, professors should initially concentrate on the first four chapters, followed by the first four chapters in the macroeconomics section. To focus on Keynesian themes, start with Chapters 1–4, cover the first two chapters in macroeconomics, and then turn to the chapter on aggregate demand and supply.

The Teaching And Learning Package

Each component of the teaching and learning package has been carefully crafted to ensure that the introductory economics course is a rewarding experience for both students and instructors.

Test Banks

We've assembled a team of dedicated educators to edit, write, review, and accuracy check the over 7,000 multiple-choice questions in both the microeconomics and macroeconomics test banks.

Each Test Bank, *Microeconomics: Principles and Tools*, prepared by Sheryl Ball and Mark McLeod, both of Virginia PolyTechnic Institute and State University, and *Macroeconomics: Principles and Tools*, prepared by Mary Lesser of Iona College, offers approximately 3,500 multiple-choice, true/false, short answer, and problem questions. Each question is keyed by degree of difficulty (easy, moderate, or challenging), page reference, and type of question (definitional, conceptual, or applied). The second edition contains a wealth of new questions and totally new graphs.

The authors of both test banks worked together and with a team of technical reviewers to follow a strict formula of screening, analysis, and assessment of every test question. Linda Ghent of East Carolina University, Peggy Crane of Southwestern College, and James Swofford of University of South Alabama, contributed to a continuous technical review and numerous accuracy checks of both test banks.

Prentice Hall Test Manager, Version 4.1

The Test Banks are designed for use with the Prentice Hall Test Manager, a computerized package that allows instructors to custom design, save, and generate classroom tests. The test program (in PC Windows and Macintosh formats) permits instructors to edit, add, or delete questions from the test banks; edit existing graphics and create new graphics; analyze test results; and organize a database of tests and student results.

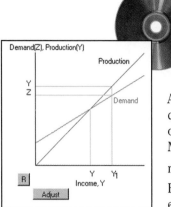

Active Learning CD-ROM

This interactive student CD-ROM, prepared by Stephen J. Perez of Washington State University, in conjunction with Gregory M. Werner, Inc., includes, for each chapter, a tutorial walk-through, which incorporates a detailed summary of key concepts with hot links to Chapter-Opening Questions, Test Your Understanding, key tables and graphs, pop-up glossary terms, Active Graphs, and end-of-chapter self-assessment quizzes. The end-of-chapter quizzes, prepared by Rashid Al-Hmoud of Texas Tech University and Fernando Quijano of Dickinson State University, contain twenty original multiple-choice questions. More than sixty Active Graphs are featured on the CD-ROM, which correspond to the most important figures in the text. Active Graphs are referenced with this icon: .

Each Active Graph allows students to change the value of a variable and look at the effects on the equilibrium. The Active Learning CD-ROM also links the student to myPHLIP Web site.

Prentice Hall's Learning on the Internet Partnership/Companion Website
(http://www.prenhall.com/osullivan)

myPHLIP is a content-rich, multidisciplinary Web site with Internet exercises, activities, and resources related specifically to the second edition of *Economics: Principles and Tools*. New Internet resources are added every two weeks by a team of economics professors to provide both the student and the instructor with the most current, up-to-date resources available.

Current Events Articles and Exercises, related to topics in each chapter, are fully supported by group activities, critical-thinking exercises, and discussion questions. These articles, from current news publications to economics-related publications, help show students the relevance of economics in today's world.

The Online Study Guide, prepared by Leonie Stone of SUNY, Geneseo, offers students another opportunity to sharpen their problem-solving skills and to assess their understanding of the text material. The Online Study Guide for O'Sullivan/Sheffrin contains two levels of quizzes: definitional and applied. Each level includes 15 to 20 multiple-choice and true/false questions, and 2 essay questions per chapter. The Online Study Guide grades each question submitted by the student, provides immediate feedback for correct and incorrect answers, and allows students to e-mail results to up to four e-mail addresses. The myPHLIP site also links the student to the Take it to the Net exercises featured in the textbook. These Web-destination exercises are keyed to each chapter and direct the student to an appropriate, updated, economics related Web site to gather data and analyze a specific economic problem. In addition to these features, an additional book chapter, Interest Rates and Present Value, will be available to students at this Web site.

For the instructor, myPHLIP offers resources such as the Syllabus Manager, answers to Current Events and Internet exercises, and a Faculty Lounge area including teaching resources and faculty chat rooms. From the myPHLIP web site, instructors can also download supplements and lecture aids, including the Instructor's Manuals and PowerPoint Presentations. Instructors should contact their Prentice Hall sales representative to get the necessary username and password to access the faculty resources on myPHLIP.

On-line Course Offerings

WebCT

Developed by educators, WebCT provides faculty with easy-to-use Internet tools to create on-line courses. Prentice Hall provides the content and enhanced features to help instructors create a complete on-line course. For more information, please visit our Web site, located at http://www.prenhall.com/webct.

Blackboard

Easy to use, Blackboard's simple templates and tools make it easy to create, manage and use on-line course materials. Prentice Hall provides the content and instructors can create on-line courses using the Blackboard tools which include design, communication, testing, and course management tools. For more information, please visit our website located at http://www.prenhall.com/blackboard.

The Wall Street Journal Print and Interactive Editions

Prentice Hall has formed a strategic alliance with *The Wall Street Journal*, the most respected and trusted daily source for information on business and economics. For a small additional charge, Prentice Hall offers your students a 10-week subscription to The Wall Street Journal print edition and The Wall Street Journal Interactive Edition. Adopting professors will receive a free subscription of both the print and interactive version as well as weekly subject-specific Wall Street Journal educators' lesson plans.

Instructor's Manuals

Two Instructor's Manuals, *Macroeconomics: Principles and Tools*, prepared by Stephen Perez of Washington State University, *and Microeconomics: Principles and Tools*, prepared by Leonie Stone of SUNY, Geneseo, reflect the textbook's organization, incorporating policy problems in case studies, exercises, extra questions, and useful Internet links. The manuals also provide detailed outlines (suitable for use as lecture notes) and solutions to all questions in the textbook.

Each Instructor's Manual contains by chapter: a summary, an outline, opening questions, examples for class discussion, teaching tips, extended examples, problems and discussion questions, test your understanding questions, Internet exercises, and tips for classroom experiments. A combined Instructor's Manual is available for *Economics: Principles and Tools*.

Instructor's Resource CD-ROM

This Instructor's Resource CD-ROM includes the computerized test banks, instructor's manuals, PowerPoint Presentation, and transparency masters of all the figures and tables from the text. It is dual platform for both PC and Macintosh.

PowerPoint Presentation

This lecture presentation tool, prepared by Fernando Quijano of Dickinson State University, offers outlines and summaries of important text material, tables and graphs that build, and additional exercises. The PowerPoint Presentation is included in the instructor's resource CD-ROM and is downloadable from the O'Sullivan/Sheffrin Web site.

Using Economic Experiments in the Classroom

Prepared by Dirk Yandell of the University of San Diego, this manual contains experiments that illustrate topics such as positive vs. normative economics and monopoly. The experiments include tables and charts, in addition to an overview, learning objectives, a list of preparations and materials needed, a detailed What to Do section, an analysis of the results, and questions that require students to interpret and analyze the material.

ABC/Prentice Hall Video Library

Prentice Hall and ABC News have combined their experience in academic publishing and global reporting to provide a comprehensive video ancillary to enhance our principles of economics texts. Through its wide variety of award-winning programs, such as *Nightline, This Week With David Brinkley, World News Tonight,* and *20/20,* ABC offers a resource for feature and documentary-style videos related to the chapters in the text. The programs have extremely high production quality, present substantial content, and are hosted by well-versed, well-known anchors. A new ABC/PH Economics Video Library is available every two years.

Video Guide

The integrated Video Guide prepared by Mary Lesser at Iona College, provides a summary of each of the clips in the Video Library. For each video, the guide also supplies running time, teaching notes, and discussion questions, as well as useful tips on how to use the clip in class. Each video is keyed to the appropriate topic in the text.

Study Guides

Both Study Guides, *Macroeconomics: Principles and Tools* and *Microeconomics: Principles and Tools*, prepared by Janice Boucher Breuer of University of South Carolina, emphasize the practical application of theory. Each Study Guide is a practicum designed to promote comprehension of economic principles and develop each student's ability to apply them to different problems.

Each Study Guide contains by chapter: an overview of the corresponding chapter in the textbook, a checklist to provide a quick summary of material covered in the textbook and lectures, a list of key terms, practice exams, and the detailed answer keys. Integrated throughout each Study Guide are Performance Enhancing Tips (PETs), which are designed to help students understand economics by applying the principles and promoting analytical thinking.

Two practice exams, featuring both multiple-choice and essay questions, are included at the end of each chapter. Both exams require students to apply one or more economic principles to arrive at each correct answer. Full solutions to the multiple-choice questions are included, not only listing each correct answer but also explaining in detail why one answer is correct and the others are not. Detailed answers to the essay questions are also provided.

A combined Study Guide to accompany *Economics: Principles and Tools* is also available for this edition.

A Word Of Thanks

There is a long distance between the initial vision of an innovative principles text and the final product. Along the way we participated in a structured process to reach our goal.

We wish to acknowledge the assistance of the many individuals who participated in this process. First we want to thank the participants who took part in the focus groups for the first and second editions, they helped us see the manuscript from a fresh perspective:

Carlos Aquilar, El Paso Community College

Jim Bradley, University of South Carolina

Thomas Collum, Northeastern Illinois University

David Craig, Westark College

Jeff Holt, Tulsa Junior College

Thomas Jeitschko, Texas A & M University

Gary Langer, Roosevelt University

Mark McCleod, Virginia Polytechnic Institute and State University

Tom McKinnon, University of Arkansas

Amy Meyers, Parkland Community College

Hassan Mohammadi, Illinois State University

John Morgan, College of Charleston

Norm Paul, San Jacinto Community College

Nampeang Pingkarawat, Chicago State University

Scanlan Romer, Delta Community College

Barbara Ross-Pfeiffer, Kapiolani Community College

Virginia Shingleton, Valparaiso University

Zahra Saderion, Houston Community College

Jim Swofford, University of South Alabama

Linda Wilson, University of Texas–Arlington

Janet West, University of Nebraska–Omaha

Michael Youngblood, Rock Valley Community College

Many people read all or parts of the manuscript at various stages. For their helpful criticisms, we thank:

Christine Amsler, Michigan State University

Karijit K. Arora, Le Moyne College

Alex Azarchs, Pace University

Kevin A. Baird, Montgomery County Community College

Donald Balch, University of South Carolina

Sheryl Ball, Virginia Polytechnic Institute and State University

Mahamudu Bawumia, Baylor University

Charles Scott Benson Jr. Idaho State University

John Payne Bigelow, Louisiana State University

Scott Bloom, North Dakota State University

Janice Boucher Breuer, University of South Carolina

Kathleen K. Bromley, Monroe Community College

Cindy Cannon, North Harris College

Katie Canty, Cape Fear Community College

David L. Coberly, Southwest Texas State University

John L. Conant, Indiana State University

Ana-Maria Conley, DeVry Institute of Technology

Ed Coulson, Penn State University

Lee Craig, North Carolina State University

Peggy Crane, Southwestern College

Albert B. Culver, California State University, Chico

Norman Cure, Macomb Community College

Irma de Alonso, Florida International University

Sel Dibooglu, Southern Illinois University

Martine Duchatelet, Barry University

Mousumi Duttaray, Indiana University

Ghazi Duwaji, University of Texas, Arlington

David Eaton, Murray State University

Duane Eberhardt, Missouri Southern State College

Carl Enomoto, New Mexico State University

David Figlio, University of Florida

E.B. Gendel, Woodbury University

Dan Georgianna, University of Massachusetts–Dartmouth

Linda Ghent, East Carolina University

Hossein Gholami, Fayetteville Tech Community College

Randy R. Grant, Linfield College

Paul C. Harris, Jr., Camden County College

James E. Hartley, Mount Holyoke College

Rowland Harvey, DeVry Institute of Technology

John Henry, California State University, Sacramento

Robert Herman, Nassau Community College

Charles W. Haase, San Francisco State University

Charlotte Denise Hixson, Midlands Technical College

Jeff Holt, Tulsa Community College

Brad Hoppes, Southwest Missouri State University

Calvin Hoy, County College of Morris

Jonathan O. Ikoba, Scott Community College

John A. Jascot, Capital Community Technical College

Thomas Jeitschko, Texas A & M University

George Jensen, California State University, Los Angeles

Taghi T. Kermani, Youngstown State University

Rose Kilburn, Modesto Junior College

Philip King, San Francisco State University

James T. Kyle, Indiana Sate University

Gary Langer, Roosevelt University

Susan Linz, Michigan State University

Marianne Lowery, Erie Community College

Melanie Marks, Longwood College

Jessica McCraw, University of Texas, Arlington

Thomas J. Meeks, Virginia State University

Jeannette Mitchell, Rochester Institute of Technology

Rahmat Mozayan, Heald College

William Neilson, Texas A & M University

Alex Obiya, San Diego City College

Paul Okello, University of Texas, Arlington

Charles M. Oldham, Jr., Fayetteville Technical Community College

Jack W. Osman, San Francisco State University

Carl Parker, Fort Hays State University

Randall Parker, East Carolina University

Stephen Perez, Washington State University

Stan Peters, Southeast Community College

Chirinjev Peterson, Greenville Technical College

Nampeang Pingkarawat, Chicago State University

L. Wayne Plumly, Jr., Valdosta State University

Dan Rickman, Oklahoma State University

John Robertson, University of Kentucky

Barbara Ross-Pfeiffer, Kapiolani Community College

George Schatz, Maine Maritime Academy

Kurt Schwabe, University of California, Riverside

Mark Siegler, Williams College

Terri Sexton, California State University, Sacramento

Dennis Shannon, Belleville Area College

Virginia Shingleton, Valparaiso University

Ed Sorensen, San Francisco State University

Abdulwahab Sraiheen, Kutztown University

James Swofford, University of South Alabama

Evan Tanner, Thunderbird, The American Graduate School of International Management

Robert Tansky, St. Clair County Community College

Denise Turnage, Midlands Technical College

Fred Tyler, Fordham University

James R. VanBeek, Blinn College

Daniel Villegas, Cal Polytechnic State University

Chester Waters, Durham Technical
    Community College, Shaw University
Irvin Weintraub, Towson State University
Donald Wells, University of Arizona

James Wheeler, North Carolina State
    University
Gilbert Wolfe, Middlesex Community
    College

A special acknowledgment goes to the instructors who were willing to class-test drafts of the manuscript in different stages of development. They provided us with instant feedback on parts that worked and parts that needed changes:

John Constantine, University of
    California, Davis
John Farrell, Oregon State University
James Hartley, Mt. Holyoke College
Kailash Khandke, Furman College
Peter Lindert, University of California,
    Davis

Louis Makowski, University of California,
    Davis
Stephen J. Perez, Washington State
    University
Barbara Ross-Pfeiffer, Kapiolani
    Community College

From the start, Prentice Hall provided us with first-class support and advice. Jim Boyd, PJ Boardman, Lori Braumberger, Marie McHale, Gladys Soto, Holly Brown, and Rick DeLorenzo of Prentice Hall contributed in myriad ways to the project. We want to single out two people for special mention. Our Development Editor, Mike Elia, worked with us patiently to make our prose clean and lively, and our presentation utterly clear. Finally, we are deeply indebted to Rod Banister, Economics Editor at Prentice Hall, who used a combination of great organizational skill and a good sense of humor to guide the project from start to finish.

Last but not least, we must thank our families, who have seen us disappear, sometimes physically and other times mentally, to spend hours wrapped up in our own world of principles of economics. A project of this magnitude is very absorbing, and our families have been particularly supportive in this endeavor.

ARTHUR O'SULLIVAN

STEVEN SHEFFRIN

CHAPTER

1

Introduction:
What Is Economics?

Picture the following scenes:

- Betsy was studying for a midterm when someone invited her to a party. Should she go to the party or stay home and study?
- The Rentz family is tired of paying rent every month to the landlord. Should they buy their own home?
- The young entrepreneurs who started scour.com, an Internet search engine for video and music, have been offered $4 million for a 51% share in their company. Should they accept the offer?
- The California legislature is discussing the governor's proposed budget. Should the legislators accept it or should they give more money to the state's universities?
- The Federal Reserve Board is meeting in Washington, D.C. Should the board cut interest rates?

What do the people in these scenes have in common? Each person or group will make a decision, and each decision will require some economic reasoning.

conomic reasoning involves a careful evaluation of alternative actions. Betsy can have some party fun, but she might get a lower grade on the midterm as a result. The Rentz family can buy a home, but to come up with the down payment, they may sacrifice a family vacation or a new car. The young entrepreneurs can take $4 million now or they can continue to operate on their own and wait for a better offer. The California legislature can give more money to universities, but that means there will be less money for other programs such as prisons. The Federal Reserve Board can cut interest rates and help people who want to borrow money, but the lower interest rates might heat up the economy and cause inflation. Because there are alternative courses of action, people face trade-offs, and economic reasoning helps people think carefully about these trade-offs and then make decisions.

What Is Economics?

Economics: The study of the choices made by people who are faced with scarcity.

Scarcity: A situation in which resources are limited and can be used in different ways, so one good or service must be sacrificed for another.

Economics is the study of the choices made by people when there is scarcity, that is, when there are limits to what they can get. **Scarcity** is a situation in which resources—the things we use to produce goods and services—are limited in quantity and can be used in different ways. Because resources are limited, we must sacrifice one good or service for another. Here are some examples of scarcity:

- Like everyone else, you have a limited amount of time today. If you play video games for an hour, you have one less hour to spend on other activities such as studying, exercising, or working.

- A city has a limited amount of land. If the city uses an acre of land to build a park, there is one less acre for apartments, office buildings, or factories.

- A nation has a limited number of people, so if it forms an army, it has fewer people to serve as teachers, scientists, and police officers.

Because of scarcity, people must make choices. You must decide how to spend your time; the city must decide how to use its land; and we as a nation must decide how to divide our people among teaching, science, law enforcement, and the military.

Decisions are made at every level in society. Individuals decide what products to buy, what occupation to pursue, and how much money to save. Firms decide what products to produce and how to produce them. Governments decide what projects and programs to complete and how to pay for them. The choices made by individuals, firms, and governments answer three basic questions:

1. What products do we produce? There are trade-offs in the choice among alternative products. For example, if a hospital devotes its resources to producing more heart transplants, it has fewer resources for caring for premature infants.

2. How do we produce these products? There are alternative ways to produce the products we desire. For example, utility companies can produce electricity with oil, solar power, or nuclear power. Professors can teach college students in large lectures or in small sections.

3. Who consumes the products? We must decide how the products of society are distributed among people. If some people earn more money than others, should they consume more goods? How much money should be taken from the rich and given to the poor?

Scarcity and Production Possibilities

Let's take a closer look at the first question, What products do we produce? The resources that are used to produce products are known as the **factors of production**. Economists have identified five factors of production:

1. **Natural resources** are created by acts of nature. Natural resources—for example, arable land, mineral deposits, oil and gas deposits, and water—are used to produce goods and services. Some economists refer to all types of natural resources as land.

2. **Labor** is the human effort—including both physical and mental effort—used to produce goods and services. Labor is scarce because there are only 24 hours in each day: If we spend time in one activity, such as work, we have less time for other activities, such as recreation.

3. **Physical capital** is made by human beings and is used to produce goods and services; some examples of physical capital are machines, buildings, equipment, roads, pencils, computers, and trucks.

4. **Human capital** is the knowledge and skills a worker acquires through education and experience; human capital, like physical capital, is used to produce goods and services, although not in the same way. Every job requires some human capital: To be a surgeon, you must learn anatomy and acquire surgical skills; to be an accountant, you must learn the rules of accounting and acquire computer skills; to be a taxi driver, you must know the city's streets; to be a musician, you must know how to play an instrument well enough to be paid for playing it. One of the reasons for getting a college degree is to increase your human capital, widening your employment opportunities.

5. **Entrepreneurship** is the effort used to coordinate the production and sale of goods and services. An entrepreneur comes up with an idea for a good or a service and decides how to produce it. The entrepreneur takes risks, committing money and time without any guarantee of profit, hoping of course for success and big profits.

Before we can decide what products to produce, we must determine which combinations of products are possible, given our productive resources and our technological know-how. A production possibilities graph shows an economy's production options, the different combinations of products the economy can produce. The two-dimensional graph can show the production options with two general categories of goods, such as farm goods and factory goods or capital goods and consumer goods. The graph can also show the production options for any pair of specific goods, such as guns and butter, computers and space missions, or houses and automobiles.

Figure 1.1 shows a production possibilities graph for an economy that produces farm goods and factory goods. The possible or feasible combinations of these two types of goods are shown on the curve and in the shaded area. For example, one option is point *b*, with 700 tons of factory goods and 10 tons of farm goods. Another option is point *i*, with 300 tons of factory goods and 20 tons of farm goods. The set of points on the border between the shaded and unshaded area is called the **production possibilities curve** (or production possibilities frontier) because it separates the combinations that are attainable (the shaded area within the curve and the curve itself) from the combinations that are not attainable (the unshaded area outside the curve).

Factors of production: The resources that are used to produce goods and services.

Natural resources: Things created by acts of nature and used to produce goods and services.

Labor: Human effort, including both physical and mental effort, used to produce goods and services.

Physical capital: Objects made by human beings to produce goods and services.

Human capital: The knowledge and skills acquired by a worker through education and experience and used to produce goods and services.

Entrepreneurship: Effort used to coordinate the production and sale of goods and services.

Production possibilities curve: A curve that shows the possible combinations of goods and services available to an economy, given that all productive resources are fully employed and efficiently used.

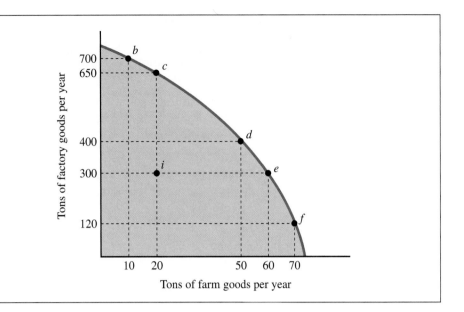

Figure 1.1

Scarcity and the Production Possibilities Curve

The production possibilities curve (or frontier) illustrates the notion of scarcity: With a given amount of resources, an increase in farm goods comes at the expense of factory goods. The curve is bowed outward because resources are not perfectly adaptable to the production of the two goods.

What is the difference between points inside the curve and points on the curve? For any point inside the curve, we can find a point on the curve that generates more of both goods. For example, at point *i* the economy can produce 300 tons of factory goods and 20 tons of farm goods. But we know from point *d* that the economy could produce more of both products: 400 tons of factory goods and 50 tons of farm goods. Producing at point *i* is clearly inferior to producing at point *d*. In general, an economy that is producing at a point inside the production possibilities curve could do better: It could produce more of both goods.

An economy might be at a point below the curve for the following reasons:

- Resources are not fully employed. For example, some workers could be idle, or some production facilities could be idle or underused.

- Resources are used inefficiently. Products can be produced with different mixtures of inputs, and some mixtures produce more output than others. If businesses pick the wrong input mixture, the economy won't produce as much output as it could.

In contrast, when an economy reaches a point on the production possibilities curve, it would be impossible to increase the production of both goods. For every point on the curve, the society's resources are fully employed and used in an efficient manner.

The production possibilities curve illustrates the notion of scarcity. At a given time, an economy has a fixed amount of each factor of production. That means we can produce more of one product only if we produce less of another product. To produce more farm goods, we take resources away from factories. As we move resources out of factory production, the quantity of factory goods will decrease. For example, if we move from point *b* to point *c* on the production possibilities curve in Figure 1.1, we sacrifice 50 tons of factory goods (700 tons − 650 tons) to get 10 more tons of farm goods (20 tons − 10 tons).

Compare the move from point *b* to point *c* with the move from point *e* to point *f*. Starting at point *b*, a 10-ton increase in farm goods decreases factory goods by 50 tons. Starting at point *e*, a 10-ton increase in farm goods decreases factory goods by 180 tons.

On the lower part of the curve, we sacrifice more factory goods to get the same 10-ton increase in farm goods. Why?

The answer is that resources are not perfectly adaptable for the production of both goods. Some resources are more suitable for factory production, while others are more suitable for farming. Starting at point *b*, the economy uses its most fertile land to produce farm goods. A 10-ton increase in farm goods reduces the quantity of factory goods by only 50 tons because plenty of fertile land is available for conversion to farming. As the economy moves downward along the production possibilities curve, farmers will be forced to use land that is progressively less fertile. To increase farm output by 10 tons, farmers will need more land and more of the other inputs. As progressively larger quantities of resources are diverted from factory goods, the sacrifice of factory goods becomes larger and larger. In the move from point *e* to point *f*, the land converted to farming is so poor that to increase farm output by 10 tons, so much land and other resources are diverted to farms that factory output drops by 180 tons.

What sort of changes would shift the entire production possibilities curve? The curve shows the production options available with a given set of productive resources, so an increase in an economy's resources will shift the entire curve outward. If an economy acquires more resources—natural resources, labor, physical capital, human capital, or entrepreneurial ability—the economy can produce more of both products. As a result, the production possibilities curve will shift outward, as shown in Figure 1.2. For example, if we start at point *d* and the economy's resources increase, we can produce more factory goods (point *g*), more farm goods (point *h*), or more of both goods (points between *g* and *h*). The curve will also shift outward as a result of technological innovations that allow us to produce more output with a given quantity of resources.

The production possibilities frontier could shift inward as well. Suppose a hurricane destroys factories, roads, and train tracks. The economy will have fewer resources available for production, so the production possibilities curve will shift inward. That means the nation will produce fewer factory goods, fewer farm goods, or fewer of both. Similarly, recent wars in Iraq and Kosovo—which caused widespread destruction of

Figure 1.2

Shifting the Production Possibilities Curve
The production possibilities curve will shift outward as a result of an increase in the economy's resources (natural resources, labor, physical capital, human capital, and entrepreneurship) or a technological innovation that increases the output from a given amount of resources.

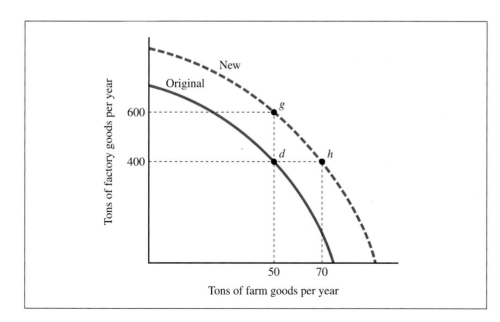

roads, factories, bridges, electricity generation facilities, and housing—shifted the production possibilities frontiers of those economies inward.

Markets and the Invisible Hand

Let's look at how a market-based economy answers the three basic economic questions. A **market** is an arrangement that allows buyers and sellers to exchange things, trading what they have for what they want. For example, the labor market allows workers and firms to exchange time and money. A software firm has money and wants workers to design programs, while the worker has time and wants income to support the family. Similarly, the car market allows consumers and producers to exchange cars and money. A consumer has money and wants a car, while a producer has a car and wants money. By providing opportunities to trade goods and services, markets help society to answer the three basic questions of what to produce, how to produce it, and who gets the products produced.

> **Market:** An arrangement that allows buyers and sellers to exchange things: A buyer exchanges money for a product; a seller exchanges a product for money.

Markets determine the prices of goods and services, and these prices guide decisions about what and how much to buy and sell. Consider a hurricane in Florida that disrupts the electric power supply and disables refrigerators, so people must use ice to preserve their food. The sudden increase in the demand for ice will increase its price. The higher price will cause consumers to use ice wisely and to switch to foods that don't require refrigeration. At the same time, the higher price will encourage profit-seeking firms to produce more ice to accommodate the greater demand. On both sides of the market, the higher price helps the state to deal with the power disruption caused by the hurricane.

The decisions made in markets result from the interactions of millions of people, each acting in his or her own self-interest. Adam Smith used the metaphor of the invisible hand to explain that people acting in their own self-interest may actually promote the interest of society as a whole.

> *It is not from the benevolence of the butcher, the brewer, or the baker that we expect our dinner, but from their regard to their own interest. We address ourselves, not to their humanity but to their self-love, and never talk to them of our own necessities but of their advantages. [Man is] led by an invisible hand to promote an end which was no part of his intention. . . . By pursuing his own interest he frequently promotes that of the society more effectually than when he really intends to promote it.*

Adam Smith, *Wealth of Nations* (New York: Modern Library, 1994)

In the last sentence Smith said "frequently," not "always." Smith recognized that individuals pursuing their own self-interest will not necessarily promote the social interest. Later in the book we'll discuss situations in which the pursuit of self-interest will be contrary to the interest of society as a whole. In these cases it is sensible for the government to guide people's decisions to promote the social interest.

In modern economies, most of the decisions about how much to produce, how to produce it, and who gets the products are made in markets. Of course, no economy relies exclusively on markets to make these economic decisions. Later in the book we'll look at how government regulates markets, provides goods and services, imposes taxes to pay for the goods and services it provides, and redistributes income.

1. List the three basic questions that we can ask about a society's economy.

2. Which of these three questions does the production possibilities curve help to answer?

The Economic Way of Thinking

How do economists think about problems and decision-making? This economic way of thinking is best summarized by noted economist John Maynard Keynes: "The Theory of Economics does not furnish a body of settled conclusions immediately applicable to policy. It is a method rather than a doctrine, an apparatus of the mind, a technique of thinking which helps its possessor to draw correct conclusions." Let's look at some of the elements of the economic way of thinking.

Use Assumptions to Simplify

Economists use assumptions to make things simpler and to focus on what really matters. Most people use simplifying assumptions in their everyday thinking and decision-making. For example, suppose you want to travel from Seattle to San Francisco by automobile. If you use a road map to pick a travel route, you are using two assumptions to simplify your decision-making:

- The earth is flat: The flat road map does not show the curvature of the earth.

- The highways are flat: The standard road map does not show hills and mountains.

These two assumptions are abstractions from reality. But they are useful because they simplify your decision-making without affecting your choice of a travel route. You could plan your trip with a globe that shows all the topographical features of the alternative travel routes between Seattle and San Francisco, but you would probably pick the same travel route because the curvature of the earth and the topography of the highways are irrelevant for your trip. In this case, the assumptions underlying the standard road map are harmless.

What if you decide to travel by bicycle instead of by automobile? Now the two assumptions are not harmless unless you want to pedal up mountains. If you use the standard road map and assume that there are no mountains between Seattle and San Francisco, you are likely to pick a mountainous route instead of a flat one. In this case, the simplifying assumption makes a difference. The lesson from this example is that we must think carefully about whether an assumption is truly harmless.

In this book, we use simplifying assumptions to help make it easier to learn a concept or to analyze something. Most of the assumptions will be harmless in the sense that they simplify the analysis by eliminating irrelevant details. Although many of the assumptions are unrealistic, that does not mean that the analysis based on the assumption is incorrect. Just as we can use an unrealistic road map to plan a trip, we can use unrealistic assumptions to do economic analysis. When we use an assumption that actually affects the analysis, we'll alert you to this fact and explore the implications of alternative assumptions.

Most of the economic analysis in this book is based on two assumptions, both of which are realistic in most circumstances:

- **Self-interest.** We'll assume that people act in their own self-interest, without considering the effects of their actions on other people. We assume that a pizza consumer doesn't care about other people who might want to buy the pizza, but only about his or her own well-being. Similarly, we assume that a pizzeria owner doesn't care about how his or her decisions affect other people, but only about the owner's profit. There is solid evidence that most people act in their own self-interest in most situations, so the economic analysis in this book is relevant for a wide range of decisions.

- **Informed decisions.** We'll assume that people make informed decisions. We assume that a consumer deciding what to eat for lunch knows the price of pizza, the prices of alternative foods, and the relevant characteristics of the foods (taste, amount of fat, number of calories). With this information, the consumer can make an informed decision about what to eat. Similarly, the manager of a pizzeria knows the cost of producing pizza, and this information leads to an informed decision about how many pizzas to produce and what price to charge. In most cases, consumers and producers have enough information to make informed decisions. Later in the book, we'll discuss situations in which one side of the market is poorly informed.

Explore the Relationship Between Two Variables

Variable: A measure of something that can take on different values.

Economic analysis often involves variables and how they affect each other. A **variable** is a measure of something that can have different values. For example, consider a student who has a part-time job and also receives a fixed weekly allowance from her parents. Her weekly income is a variable whose value is determined by the values of the other variables: the number of hours she works, the hourly wage she is paid, and the weekly allowance she gets from her parents.

To explore the relationship between any two variables, such as the hours worked and weekly income, we must assume that the other variables do not change. For example, the student might say, "If I work one more hour this week, my income will increase by $4." In making this statement, the student is exploring the relationship between two variables (work time and income), assuming that the other two variables (wage and allowance) do not change. To be complete, the statement must say, "If I work one more hour this week, my income will increase by $4, assuming that my wage and my allowance do not change."

This book contains many statements about the relationship between two variables. For example, the number of pizzas a person eats depends on the price of pizza, the price of burgers, and that person's income. Suppose we say, "A decrease in the price of pizzas, increases the quantity of pizzas consumed." This is a statement about the relationship between two variables—the price of pizzas and the quantity of pizzas—implicitly assuming that the other two variables, the price of burgers and the person's income, do not change in value. Sometimes we will make this assumption explicit by adding a warning label: "A decrease in the price of pizzas increases the quantity of pizzas consumed, **ceteris paribus.**" The Latin words mean "other things being equal to what they were before." In the present context, the phrase means "other variables being fixed." From now on, whenever we refer to a relationship between two variables, we assume that the other relevant variables are held fixed.

Ceteris paribus: Latin, meaning "other things being equal." In economics, the phrase indicates that all other variables are held fixed.

Think Marginal

Economists often need to consider how a small change in one variable causes a change in another variable. A small change in value is called a marginal change. The marginal question is, If we increase one variable by one unit, by how much will the other variable change? The key feature of this marginal question is that one variable increases by a single unit. For the student who is concerned about income, the marginal question is, If I work one more hour per week, by how much will my income increase?

You will encounter marginal thinking throughout this book. Here are some other marginal questions:

- If I spend one more year in school, by how much will my lifetime income increase?
- If I buy one more CD, how many tapes will I sacrifice?
- If a table producer hires one more carpenter, how many more tables will be produced?
- If national income increases by $1 billion, by how much will spending on consumer goods increase?

Answering a marginal question like any of these is the first step in deciding whether or not to pursue a particular activity. You will see more about this as we move along in this book.

Preview of Coming Attractions: Microeconomics

There are two types of economic analysis: microeconomics and macroeconomics. **Microeconomics** is the study of the choices made by households, firms, and government and of how these choices affect the markets for goods and services. Let's look at three ways we can use microeconomic analysis.

Microeconomics: The study of the choices made by consumers, firms, and government and of how their choices affect the market for a particular good or service.

Understand Markets and Predict Changes

One reason for studying microeconomics is to understand better how markets work. Once you know how markets operate, you can use economic analysis to predict changes in the price of a particular good and changes in the quantity of the good sold. In this book we answer dozens of practical questions about markets and how they operate. Let's look at a practical question that can be answered with some simple economic analysis.

How would a tax on beer affect the number of highway deaths among young adults? A tax on beer will make it more expensive, and young adults, like other beer consumers, will consume less of it. Alcohol consumption contributes to highway accidents, and the number of highway fatalities among young adults is roughly proportional to the total beer consumption by young adults. Therefore, a tax that decreases beer consumption by 10% will decrease highway deaths among young adults by about 10%.

Make Personal and Managerial Decisions

We use economic analysis, on the personal level, to decide how to spend our time, what career to pursue, and how to spend and save the money we earn. As workers, we use economic analysis to decide how to produce goods and services, how much to produce, and how much to charge for them. Let's use some economic analysis to look at a practical question confronting someone considering starting a business.

If the existing music stores in your city are profitable and you have enough money to start your own music store, should you do it? If you enter this market, the competition between the stores for consumers will heat up, leading to lower prices for tapes and CDs. In addition, your costs may be higher than the costs of the stores that are already established. It will be sensible to enter the market only if you expect a small drop in price and a small difference in cost. Of course, there is the risk that the existing stores may try to protect their market shares by cutting prices and increasing their advertising. Indeed, entering what appears to be a lucrative market may turn out to be a financial disaster.

Evaluate Public Policies

Although modern societies use markets to make most of the decisions concerning production and consumption, the government has several important roles in a market-based society. We can use economic analysis to determine how well the government performs its roles in the market economy. We can also explore the trade-offs associated with various public policies. Let's look at a practical question about public policy.

Is it sensible for the government to pay part of the cost of your college education? Think about who benefits from your education. You get many benefits yourself, including higher lifetime income, more career options, and the thrill of learning. But other people also benefit from your education. In the modern workplace, teamwork is important, and the productivity of a team of workers depends in part on the education level of the team members. A college education is likely to make you a better team worker, allowing your fellow workers to be more productive and earn more income. In addition, your college education will make you a more intelligent citizen, which means that you'll make better choices on election day. It is sensible for the government to help pay for your college education because taxpayers (your fellow workers and citizens) benefit from your education.

Preview of Coming Attractions: Macroeconomics

Macroeconomics: The study of the nation's economy as a whole.

Macroeconomics is the study of the nation's economy as a whole. In macroeconomics we learn about important topics that are regularly discussed in newspapers and on television, including unemployment, inflation, the budget deficit, and the trade deficit. Macroeconomics explains why economies grow and change, and why economic growth is sometimes interrupted.

In the 1930s, over 25% of the workers in the United States could not find jobs. Many banks were closed, thousands of factories were shut down, and the economy nearly ground to a halt. In terms of the production possibilities curve described earlier in the chapter, the U.S. economy was inside the production possibilities curve: Our resources were not fully employed, and we didn't produce as many goods and services as we could. Macroeconomics explains the forces that cause the economy to malfunction in this way and provides insights into how we might fix the economy to allow it to grow.

John Maynard Keynes (pronounced "Canes"), known as the father of "Keynesian" economics, was a renowned economist who taught at Cambridge University in England. During the dismal 1930s, Keynes wrote a book, *The General Theory of Employment, Interest, and Money*. Writing at a time of massive unemployment, Keynes emphasized the short-run benefits of government spending to stimulate the

The standard of living has increased dramatically in the last several decades. We eat better food and live in better houses.

economy and put people back to work. Some examples of government spending that could decrease unemployment are building highways and hiring more public-school teachers.

Modern macroeconomics goes beyond dealing with short-term crises such as high unemployment and considers the issue of growth over the long term. Because of economic growth in the last several decades, people in the United States today enjoy a much higher living standard than that experienced by their grandparents. We drive better cars and live in houses with more amenities, and even many middle-class Americans travel routinely across the country and around the world. We can consume more of all goods and services because the economy has more of the resources needed to produce these goods and services, as indicated by an outward shift of the possibilities frontier. Macroeconomics explains why some of these resources increase over time and how an increase in these resources translates into a higher standard of living.

Macroeconomic issues are at the heart of many national political debates. Every candidate for president of the United States must convince voters that he or she understands the concepts of macroeconomics. Once elected, the prospects for reelection depend crucially on how well the economy performs during his or her term as president. If the public believes that the economy has performed well, the president is likely to be reelected. But if the public thinks that the economy has not performed well, they are unlikely to support the incumbent. In recent years, several presidents—including Jimmy Carter and George Bush—were not reelected because the economy performed poorly during their terms as president.

For a preview, let's think about three ways we can use macroeconomic analysis.

Understand How a National Economy Operates

One purpose of studying macroeconomics is to understand how the entire economy works. We can answer the following question with some macroeconomic analysis: Why do some countries grow much faster than others?

In the fastest-growing countries, citizens save a large fraction of the money they earn, and the workforce is well educated. Saving money provides funds that firms can use to purchase machines and equipment. An economy with a well-equipped workforce will grow faster than an economy whose workers are poorly equipped. A country with a well-educated workforce is able to quickly adopt new technologies that increase the productivity of its workforce.

Understand the Grand Debates over Economic Policy

Macroeconomics developed as a separate branch of economics during the 1930s, when the entire world suffered from massive unemployment. With a knowledge of macroeconomics, you can make sense of all sorts of policy debates, including the debate over the wisdom of policies designed to reduce the unemployment rate.

Should Congress and the President do something to reduce the unemployment rate? If unemployment is very high, the Congress and the President may want to reduce it. However, it is important not to reduce the unemployment rate too much, because as we'll see later in the book, a low unemployment rate will cause inflation. Moreover, unemployment can't be reduced overnight. Therefore, it is sensible to take action only if we believe that inaction will lead to persistent unemployment. In macroeconomics, we study the trade-offs associated with policies designed to combat unemployment and inflation.

Make Informed Business Decisions

A third reason for studying macroeconomics is to make informed business decisions. A manager who understands how the national economy operates will make better decisions involving interest rates, exchange rates, the inflation rate, and the unemployment rate. A manager who intends to borrow money for a new production facility could use her knowledge of macroeconomics to predict the effects of current public policies on interest rates and then decide whether to borrow the money now or later. Similarly, a manager must keep an eye on the inflation rate to help decide how much to charge for his firm's products and how much to pay workers. A manager who studies macroeconomics will be better equipped to understand the complexities of unemployment, interest rates and inflation.

TEST Your Understanding

3. Two simplifying assumptions are used extensively in economics. What are they?

4. Suppose your grade on an economics exam is affected by the number of lectures you attend. What is the marginal question you should ask yourself about this relationship?

Summary

This chapter explains what economics is and why it is useful. Economics is about choices made by individuals, organizations, governments, and society as a whole. We can use economic analysis to understand how these choices affect the world around us. We can also use economics to make our own choices as consumers, workers, managers, and voters. Here are the main points of the chapter.

1. The production possibilities curve shows the combinations of goods and services available to an economy and illustrates the notion of scarcity: the production of one product comes at the expense of another. The curve will shift outward as a result of an increase in the economy's productive resources or an improvement in technology.

2. We use microeconomics to understand how markets work, predict changes in prices and quantities, make personal or managerial decisions, and evaluate the merits of public policies.

3. Macroeconomics explains how an economy works and helps us to understand the grand debates over economic policy.

4. To think like an economist, we (a) use assumptions to simplify what we are analyzing; (b) explore the relationship between the values of two variables, holding fixed the values of any other related variables; and (c) think in marginal terms.

5. Two assumptions are used extensively in economics: People act in their own self-interest, and people make informed choices.

Key Terms

ceteris paribus, 8
economics, 2
entrepreneurship, 3
factors of production, 3
human capital, 3

labor, 3
macroeconomics, 10
market, 6
microeconomics, 9
natural resources, 3

physical capital, 3
production possibilities curve, 3
scarcity, 2
variable, 8

Problems and Discussion Questions

1. For some goods and services, the assumption that people have enough information to make informed choices is unrealistic. Provide a brief list of some of these goods and services.

2. For some decisions, you act altruistically rather than acting in your own self-interest. Provide a brief list of such decisions.

3. "If I study one more hour for my economics exam, I expect my grade to increase by 3 points." List the variables that are implicitly assumed to be fixed in that statement.

4. It's your first day on your job in the advertising department of a baseball team. Your boss wants to know whether it is sensible to run one more television advertisement encouraging people to attend an upcoming game. List the relevant marginal questions.

5. Complete the statement: As we switch resources from the production of one good to another, we _____ the production possibilities curve; as we add resources to an economy, we _____ the curve.

6. Web Exercise. Visit the Web site for the CIA's World Fact Book (*http://www.odci.gov/cia/publications/ factbook/*). Pick a country and get some data about its factors of production (labor, human capital, natural resources).

7. Web Exercise. Visit the Web site of the IndUS Entrepreneurs, a nonprofit organization for entrepreneurs (*http://www.tie.org*). Access the page describing the organization's programs (*http:// www.tie.org/prog.html*). What does this organization do and how might it be helpful for aspiring entrepreneurs?

Model Answers for Questions

Test Your Understanding

1. What goods and services do we produce? How do we produce the goods and services we select? Who consumes the goods and services we produce?

2. The production possibilities curve shows the combinations of goods that are available to the economy, so it helps us to answer the first question.

3. People act in their own self-interest; people make informed decisions.

4. "If I attend one more lecture, by how much will my exam grade increase?"

Using Graphs and Formulas

In this appendix, we review the mechanics of graphing. You'll recognize most of the simple graphs and formulas in this appendix, because they were covered in your high-school mathematics. We'll review them here to prepare you to use them as you begin your own economic analysis.

Using Graphs to Show Relationships

A graph is a visual representation of the relationship between two variables. As we saw earlier in Chapter 1, a variable is a measure of something that can take on different values. For example, suppose that you have a part-time job and you are interested in the relationship between the number of hours you work and your weekly income. The relevant variables are the hours you work per week and your weekly income.

We can use a table of numbers such as Table 1A.1 to show the relationship between time worked and income. Let's assume that your weekly allowance from your parents is $20 and your part-time job pays $4 per hour. For example, if you work 10 hours per week, your weekly income is $60 ($20 from your parents and $40 from your job). The more you work, the higher your weekly income: If you work 22 hours, your weekly income is $108; if you work 30 hours, it is $140.

Drawing a Graph

A graph makes it easier to see the relationship between time worked and income. To draw a graph, we perform seven simple steps.

1. Draw a horizontal line to represent the first variable. In Figure 1A.1 we measure time worked along the horizontal axis (also known as the x axis). As we move to the right along the horizontal axis, the number of hours worked increases, from zero to 30 hours. The numbers along the horizontal axis are spaced equally.

2. Draw a vertical line intersecting the first line to represent the second variable. In Figure 1A.1 we measure income along the vertical axis (also known as the y axis). As we move up along the vertical axis, income increases from zero to $140.

3. Pick a combination of time worked and income from the table of numbers. From the second column, for instance, time worked is 10 hours and income is $60.

4. Find the point on the horizontal axis with that number of hours worked—10 hours worked—and draw a dashed line vertically straight up from that point.

Table 1A.1 Relationship Between Work Time and Income

Hours worked per week	0	10	22	30
Income per week	$20	$60	$108	$140

Figure 1A.1

Relationship Between Hours Worked and Total Income

There is a positive relationship between the amount of work time and income. The slope of the curve is $4: Each additional hour of work increases income by $4.

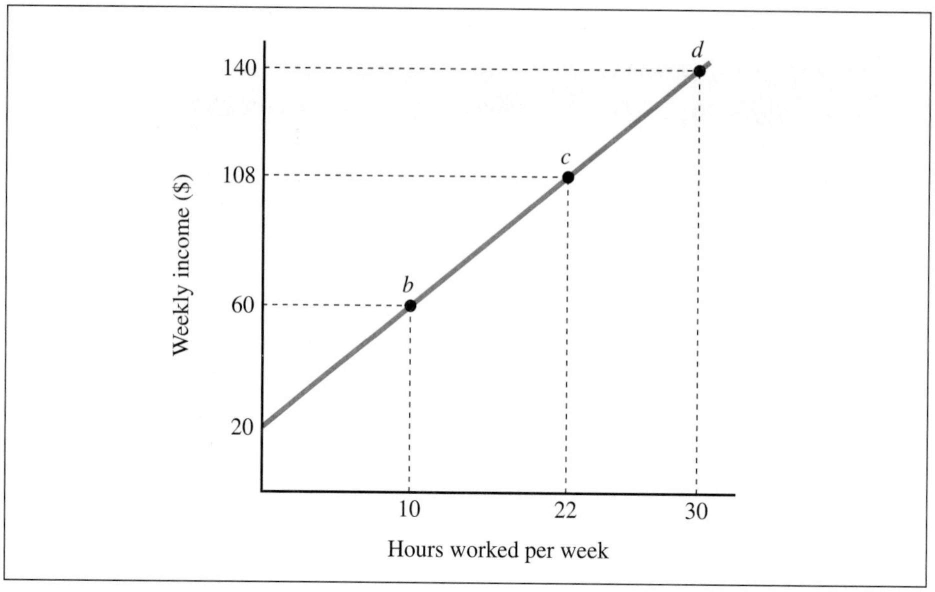

5. Find the point on the vertical axis with the income corresponding to those hours worked ($60) and draw a dashed line horizontally straight to the right from that point.

6. The intersection of the dashed lines shows the combination of those hours worked and the income for working those hours. Point *b* shows the combination of 10 hours worked and $60 income.

7. Repeat steps 3 through 6 for different combinations of work time and income from the table of numbers. Once you have a series of points on the graph (*b*, *c*, and *d*), you can connect them to draw a curve that shows the relationship between hours worked and income.

Positive relationship: A relationship in which an increase in the value of one variable increases the value of another variable.

There is a **positive relationship** between two variables if an increase in the value of one variable increases the value of the other variable. An increase in the time you work increases your income, so there is a positive relationship between the two variables. As you increase the time you work, you move upward along the curve shown in Figure 1A.1 to higher income levels.

Negative relationship: A relationship in which an increase in the value of one variable decreases the value of another variable.

There is a **negative relationship** between two variables if an increase in the value of one variable decreases the value of the other variable. For example, there is a negative relationship between the amount of time you work and your performance in school. Some people refer to a positive relationship as a direct relationship and to a negative relationship as an inverse relationship.

Computing the Slope

Slope of a curve: The change in the variable on the vertical axis resulting from a one-unit increase in the variable on the horizontal axis.

How sensitive is one variable to changes in the other variable? We can use the slope of the curve to measure this sensitivity. The **slope of a curve** is the change in the variable on the vertical axis resulting from a one-unit increase in the variable on the horizontal axis. Once we pick two points on a curve, we can compute the slope as follows:

$$\text{slope} = \frac{\text{vertical difference between two points}}{\text{horizontal difference between two points}}$$

To compute the slope of a curve, we take four steps:

1. Pick two points on the curve: for example, points *b* and *c* in Figure 1A.1.
2. Compute the vertical distance between the two points (also known as the rise). For points *b* and *c*, the vertical distance between the points is $48 ($108 – $60).
3. Compute the horizontal distance between the same two points (also known as the run). For points *b* and *c*, the horizontal distance between the points is 12 hours (22 hours – 10 hours).
4. Divide the vertical distance by the horizontal distance to get the slope. The slope between points *b* and *c* is $4 per hour:

$$\text{slope} = \frac{\text{vertical difference}}{\text{horizontal difference}} = \frac{48}{12} = 4$$

In this case, a 12-hour increase in time worked increases income by $48, so the increase in income per hour of work is $4, which makes sense because this is the hourly wage.

Because the curve is a straight line, the slope is the same at all points along the curve. You can check this yourself by using the values between points *c* and *d* to calculate the slope.

Moving Along the Curve Versus Shifting the Curve

Up to this point, we've explored the effect of change in variables that cause movement along a given curve. In Figure 1A.1 we see the relationship between a student's hours of work (on the horizontal axis) and her income (on the vertical axis). The student's income also depends on her allowance and her wage, so we can make two observations about the curve in Figure 1A.1.

1. To draw this curve, we must specify the weekly allowance ($20) and the hourly wage ($4).
2. The curve shows that an increase in time worked increases the student's income, assuming that her allowance and her wage are fixed.

A change in the student's weekly allowance will shift the curve showing the relationship between time worked and income. In Figure 1A.2, when the allowance increases from $20 to $35, the curve shifts upward by $15. For a given time worked, the student's income increases by $15. Now the income associated with 10 hours of work and the higher allowance is $75 (point *z*), compared to $60 with 10 hours of work and the original allowance (point *b*). In general, an increase in the allowance shifts the curve upward and leftward: For a given amount of time worked, the student will have more income (an upward shift as a result of the increased allowance). To reach a given amount of income, the student needs fewer hours of work (a leftward shift).

This book uses dozens of two-dimensional curves, each of which shows the relationship between only two variables. That is all a single curve can show. A common error is to forget that a single curve tells only part of the story. In Figure 1A.2 we needed two curves to show what happened when we looked at three variables (work time, allowance, and income). Here are some simple rules that will help to avoid this error:

- A change in one of the variables shown on the graph causes movement along the curve. In Figure 1A.2 an increase in work time causes movement along the curve from point *b* to point *c*.

Figure 1A.2

Shifting the Curve

To draw a curve showing the relationship between hours worked and total income, we assume that the weekly allowance ($20) and the wage ($4) are fixed. An increase in the weekly allowance from $20 to $35 shifts the curve upward by $15: For each quantity of work hours, income is $15 higher.

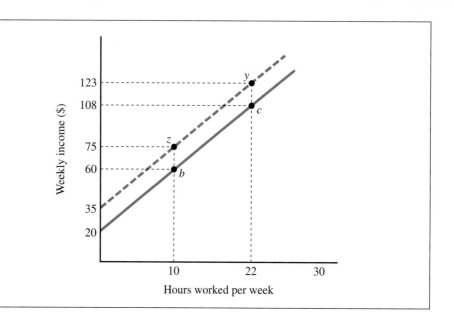

- A change in one of the variables that is not shown on the graph (one of the variables held fixed in drawing the curve) shifts the entire curve. In Figure 1A.2 an increase in the allowance causes the entire curve to shift upward.

Negative and Nonlinear Relationships

We can use a graph to show a negative relationship between two variables. Consider a consumer who has a monthly budget of $150 to spend on CDs (at a price of $10 per CD) and cassette tapes (at a price of $5 per tape). Table 1A.2 shows the relationship between the number of CDs purchased and the number of tapes purchased. If the consumer buys 5 CDs in a certain month, he will spend a total of $50 on CDs, leaving $100 to spend on tapes. With the $100 he can buy 20 tapes at a price of $5 per tape. As the number of CDs increases, the number of tapes decreases, from 20 tapes and 5 CDs, to 10 tapes and 10 CDs, to 0 tapes and 15 CDs.

Using the seven-step process outlined earlier, we can use the numbers in Table 1A.2 to draw a curve showing this negative relationship. In Figure 1A.3 the curve is negatively sloped: The more the consumer spends on CDs, the fewer tapes he can buy. We can use points e and f to compute the slope of the curve. The slope is -2 tapes per CD: A five-unit increase in CDs (the horizontal difference, or the run) decreases the number of tapes by 10 (the vertical difference, or the rise):

$$\text{slope} = \frac{\text{vertical difference}}{\text{horizontal difference}} = \frac{-50}{5} = -10$$

Table 1A.2   Relationship Between CDs and Tapes

Number of CDs purchased	0	5	10	15
Number of tapes purchased	30	20	10	0

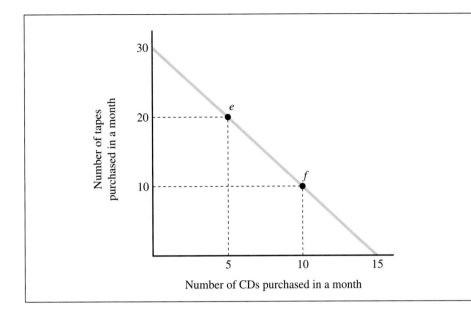

A Negative Relationship Between CD Purchases and Tape Purchases
There is a negative relationship between the number of CDs purchased and the number of cassette tapes purchased. Because the price of CDs is $10 and the price of tapes is $5, the slope of the curve is −2 tapes per CD: Each additional CD decreases the number of tapes by 2.

The curve is a straight line with a constant slope of −2 tapes per CD.

We can use a graph to show a nonlinear relationship between two variables. Panel A of Figure 1A.4 shows the relationship between study time and the exam grade that results from study time. Although the exam grade increases as study time increases, the grade increases at a decreasing rate; that means the increase in grade is smaller and smaller for each additional hour of study. For example, the second hour of study increases the grade by 4 points (from 6 points to 10 points), but the ninth hour of study increases the grade by only 1 point (from 24 points to 25 points). This is a nonlinear relationship: The slope of the curve changes as we move along the curve. In Figure 1A.4 the slope decreases as we move to the right along the curve: The slope is 4 between points g and h but only 1 between points i and j.

Another possibility for a nonlinear curve is that the slope increases (the curve becomes steeper) as we move to the right along the curve. This is shown in panel B of Figure 1A.4. The slope of the curve increases as the amount of grain increases, meaning that total production cost increases at an increasing rate. If the producer increases production from 2 tons to 3 tons, the total cost increases by $5 (from $10 to $15). On the upper portion of the curve, if the producer increases production from 10 to 11 tons, the total cost increases by $25 (from $100 to $125).

Using Formulas to Compute Values

Economists often use formulas to compute the values of the relevant variables. Here is a brief review of the mechanics of formulas.

Computing Percentage Changes

In many cases, the formulas that economists use involve percentage changes. In this book we use the simple approach to computing percentage changes: We divide the change in the variable by the initial value of the variable and then multiply by 100. For example, if the price of pizzas increases from $20 to $22, the percentage change is 10%:

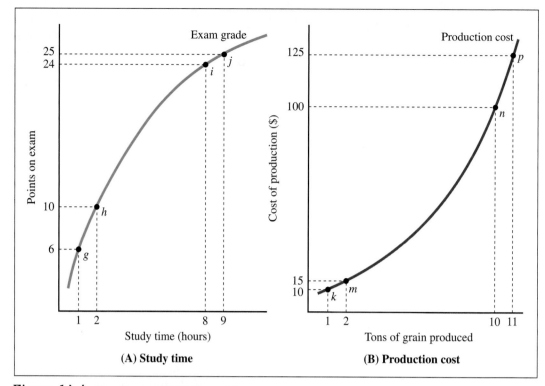

Figure 1A.4 **Nonlinear Relationships**

(A) Study Time There is a positive and nonlinear relationship between study time and the grade on an exam. As study time increases, the exam grade increases at a decreasing rate. For example, the second hour of study increases the grade by 4 points (from 6 points to 10 points), but the ninth hour of study increases the grade by only 1 point (from 24 points to 25 points).

(B) Production Cost There is a positive and nonlinear relationship between the quantity of grain produced and total production cost. As the quantity increases, total cost increases at an increasing rate. For example, to increase production from 1 ton to 2 tons, production cost increases by $5 (from $10 to $15), but to increase production from 10 to 11 tons, total cost increases by $25 (from $100 to $125).

The change ($2) divided by the initial value ($20) is 0.10; multiplying this number by 100 generates a percentage change of 10%:

$$\text{percentage change} = \frac{\text{absolute change}}{\text{initial value}} = \frac{2}{20} = 0.10 = 10\%$$

Going in the other direction, if the price decreases from $20 to $19, the percentage change is –5%: The change (–$1) divided by the initial value ($20) is –0.05, or –5%. The alternative to the simple approach is the midpoint approach, under which the percentage change equals the absolute change in the variable divided by the average value or the midpoint of the variable. For example, if the price of pizza increases from $20 to $22, the computed percentage change under the midpoint approach would be 9.52381%:

$$\text{percentage change} = \frac{\text{absolute change}}{\text{average value}} = \frac{2}{(20+22)/2}$$

$$= \frac{2}{21} = 0.0952381 = 9.52381\%$$

If the change in the variable is relatively small, the extra precision associated with the midpoint approach is usually not worth the extra effort. The simple approach allows us to spend less time doing tedious arithmetic and more time doing economic analysis. In this book we use the simple approach to compute percentage changes: If the price increases from $20 to $22, the price has increased by 10%.

If we know a percentage change, we can translate it into an absolute change. For example, if a price has increased by 10% and the initial price is $20, then we add 10% of the initial price ($2 is 10% of $20) to the initial price ($20), for a new price of $22. If the price decreases by 5%, we subtract 5% of the initial price ($1 is 5% of $20) from the initial price ($20), for a new price of $19.

Using Formulas to Compute Missing Values

It will often be useful to compute the value of the numerator (the top half of a fraction) of a particular formula. To do so, we must have values for the other two parts of the formula. For example, consider the relationship between time worked and income. Suppose the slope of the curve showing this relationship is $4 per hour. If you decide to work 7 more hours per week, how much more income will you earn? In this case we can compute the change in income by looking at the formula for the slope of the curve:

$$\text{slope} = \frac{\text{difference in income}}{\text{difference in work time}}$$

$$4 = \frac{\text{difference in income}}{7}$$

Because we know two of the three parts of the slope formula (the slope is $4 and the difference in work time is 7 hours), we can figure out the third part (the difference in income) by plugging in different numbers for the numerator until we find the value that satisfies the formula. In this case the answer is $28: Plugging $28 into the numerator, the difference in income is four times the difference in work time, which is consistent with a slope of $4.

There is a more direct approach to computing the value of the numerator or denominator of a formula. We can rearrange the three parts of the formula to put the missing variable on the left side. For example, to compute the difference in income resulting from a change in work time, we can rearrange the slope formula as follows:

$$\text{difference in income} = \text{slope} \times \text{difference in work time}$$

When we plug in the slope (4) and the difference in work time (7 hours), the change in income is $28 = $4 times 7 hours. We can use the same process to compute the value of the denominator, given values for the two other variables.

negative relationship, 16   positive relationship, 16   slope of a curve, 16

Exercises and Discussion Questions

1. Suppose you belong to a tennis club that has a monthly fee of $100 and a charge of $5 per hour for court time to play tennis.
   a. Use a curve to show the relationship between the monthly bill from the club and the hours of tennis played.
   b. What is the slope of the curve?
   c. If you increase your monthly tennis time by 3 hours, by how much will your monthly bill increase?

2. Suppose that to make pizza, Terry uses three ingredients: tomato sauce, dough, and cheese. Terry initially uses 100 gallons of tomato sauce per day, and the cost of other ingredients (dough, cheese) is $500 per day.
   a. Draw a curve to show the relationship between the price of tomato sauce and the daily cost of producing pizza (for prices between $1 and $5).
   b. To draw the curve, what variables are assumed to be fixed?
   c. What sort of changes would cause movement upward along the curve?
   d. What is the slope of the curve?
   e. What sort of changes would cause the entire curve to shift upward?

3. Compute the percentage changes for the following changes:

Initial Value	New Value	Percentage Change
10	11	_____
100	98	_____
50	53	_____

4. The price of jeans decreases by 15%. If the original price was $20, what is the new price?

5. Suppose the slope of a curve showing the relationship between the number of burglaries per month (on the vertical axis) and the number of police officers (on the horizontal axis) is −0.50 burglaries per police officer. Use the slope formula to compute the change in the number of burglaries resulting from hiring eight additional police officers.

6. Complete the statement: A change in one of the variables shown on a graph causes movement _____ a curve, while a change in one of the variables that is not shown on the graph _____ the curve.

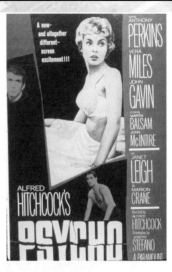

Key Principles of Economics

Your student film society is looking for an auditorium to use for an all-day Hitchcock film program and is willing to pay up to $200 for one. Your college has a new auditorium that would be perfect for your event. According to the campus facility manager, "The daily rent on the auditorium is $450, an amount that includes $300 to help pay for the cost of building the auditorium, $50 to help pay for insurance, and $100 to cover the extra costs of electricity and jan- itorial services for a one-day event." How should you respond to the facility manager? As we'll see, if you could persuade the facility manager to use the marginal principle—one of the five key principles of economics—you could rent the facility for only $101.

Principle: A simple truth that most people understand and accept.

I n this chapter, we introduce five key principles that provide a foundation for economic analysis. The dictionary defines a **principle** as a simple, self-evident truth that most people readily understand and accept. For example, most people readily accept the principle of gravity. The five principles of economics provide the underlying logic of economic analysis and also help explain the tools of economic analysis. As you go through the book, you will see these principles again and again as you do your own economic analysis. Here are some practical questions we answer in this chapter:

1. **What is the cost of producing military goods such as bombs and warships?**
2. **When is it sensible to tighten the emissions standards on cars, reducing the allowable volume of pollution per mile driven?**
3. **As a firm hires more workers, what happens to the total output of its factory?**
4. **If a paper producer dumps chemical waste into a river, what is the true cost of paper?**
5. **Suppose your wage doubles and at the same time the prices of consumer goods double, too. Are you better off, worse off, or equally well off?**

The Principle of Opportunity Cost

The principle of opportunity cost incorporates the notion that no matter what we do, there is always a trade-off. We must trade off one thing for another because resources are limited and can be used in different ways: By acquiring something, we use up resources that could have been used to acquire something else. The notion of opportunity cost allows us to measure this trade-off.

PRINCIPLE OF OPPORTUNITY COST

The opportunity cost of something is what you sacrifice to get it.

Opportunity cost: What you sacrifice to get something.

Most decisions involve several alternatives. For example, if you spend an hour studying for an economics exam, you have one less hour to pursue other activities. To determine the opportunity cost of something, we look at what you consider the best of these other activities. For example, suppose the alternatives to studying economics are studying for a history exam and playing a video game. If you consider studying for history a better use of your time than video play, then the opportunity cost of studying economics is what you sacrifice by not studying history. We ignore the video game because that is not the best alternative use of your time.

How can we measure the opportunity cost of an hour spent studying for an economics exam? Suppose an hour of studying history—instead of economics—would increase your grade on a history exam by 4 points. In this case the opportunity cost of an hour studying economics is 4 points lost on the history exam. If the best alternative to studying economics were playing video games, then the opportunity cost would be the pleasure you would get from an hour in the video arcade.

The principle of opportunity cost can be applied to decisions about how to spend a fixed money budget. For example, suppose that you have a fixed budget to spend on recorded music and CDs cost twice as much as audio tapes. If you buy a CD, you must sacrifice two tapes: The opportunity cost of one CD is two audio tapes. A hospital with a fixed salary budget can increase the number of doctors only at the expense of nurses or physician's assistants. If a doctor costs five times as much as a nurse, the opportunity cost of a doctor is five nurses.

In some cases, a good that appears to be free actually has a cost. That's why economists are fond of saying, "There's no such thing as a free lunch." Suppose someone offers to buy you lunch if you agree to listen to a sales pitch for a time-share condominium. Although you don't pay any money for the lunch, there is an opportunity cost because you could spend that time in another way. The lunch isn't free because you sacrifice an hour of your time to get it. For another example of a good that isn't really free, read "A Closer Look: There's No Such Thing as a Free PC."

Opportunity Cost and Production Possibilities

The production possibilities curve illustrates the principle of opportunity cost for an entire economy. As you saw in Chapter 1, this curve shows all the possible combinations of goods and services available to an economy, assuming that all its productive resources are fully employed. The principle of opportunity cost explains why the production possibilities curve is negatively sloped. At a given time an economy has fixed amounts of productive resources, so the production of one product comes at the expense of another product.

Using the Principle: Military Spending, Collectibles

We can use the principle of opportunity cost to explore the cost of military spending. Malaysia bought two warships in 1992, paying a price equal to the cost of providing safe drinking water for the 5 million Malaysians who lacked it.[1] In other words, the opportunity cost of the warships was safe drinking water for 5 million people. When the Soviet Union fell apart and military tensions around the world diminished, citizens in the United States and Western Europe called for massive cuts in defense spending, with the idea of spending the "peace dividend" on social programs. The French cut their annual defense budget by billions of dollars and withdrew 50,000 troops stationed on German soil.[2] In the United States, the number of people employed by the military has decreased,

A CLOSER LOOK | There's No Such Thing as a Free PC

In 1999, a new company called Free-PC shocked the personal computer industry by giving computers away. The free computers weren't slow-computing dinosaurs with old technology. They were 333-MHz machines that came with a keyboard and a monitor. Were they really free?

Here's the catch. Before you get your machine, you provide Free-PC with lots of personal information, such as your occupation, your household income, and a list of the magazines and newspapers you read. The folks at Free-PC also want to know your birthday and the birthdays of your friends and family. They are also interested in your leisure interests—Do

you like sports, gardening, hiking, stamp collecting, knitting, or reading? The information that you provide will help to determine what sorts of advertisements will constantly occupy the bottom and right side of your computer screen. If you find the endless parade of advertisements annoying, you sacrifice annoyance-free computing to get your computer, so there is a cost associated with the "free" computer. You could use masking tape to cover up the ads, but then the cost of the PC is the price of the masking tape—and the loss of screen space for viewing documents, spreadsheets, and Web pages. What appears to be a free good isn't really free.

For many developing countries, the opportunity cost of military spending is safe drinking water

and the Pentagon developed a new program, "Troops to Teachers," to help former soldiers get jobs teaching in local schools.[3] The switch from army duty to teaching reminds us that the opportunity cost of a soldier may be a teacher.

What is the cost of buying a collectible good such as a baseball card, an antique Barbie doll, a Beanie Baby, or a work of art? Suppose you buy an antique Barbie doll for $1,000, intending to resell it for more money a year later. If the price doesn't change and you resell it for $1,000, does that mean that having the doll for a year didn't cost you anything? Applying the principle of opportunity cost, you could have invested the $1,000 in a bank account earning 5% interest, so the cost of having the Barbie doll for the year is the $50 you could have earned in a bank account during the year.

Using the Principle: The Opportunity Cost of a College Degree

What is the opportunity cost of a college degree? Consider a student who spends four years in college, paying $10,000 per year for tuition and books. Part of the opportunity cost of college is the $40,000 worth of other goods the student must sacrifice to pay for tuition and books. Instead of going to college, the student could spend this money on a car, stereo equipment, or ski trips. If instead of going to college, the student could have worked as a bank clerk for $20,000 per year, the other part of the opportunity cost of college is $80,000 that could have been earned during the four years. That makes the total opportunity cost of the student's college degree $120,000:

Tuition and books (4 years at $10,000 per year)	$ 40,000
Opportunity cost of college time (4 years at $20,000 per year)	80,000
Total opportunity cost	$120,000

We haven't included the costs of food or housing in our computations of opportunity cost. That's because a student must eat and live somewhere even if he or she doesn't go to college. But if housing and food are more expensive in college, then we would include the *extra costs* of housing and food in our calculations of opportunity cost.

There are other things to consider in a person's decision to attend college. As we'll see later, a college degree can increase a person's earning power, so there are benefits from a college degree. In addition, there is the thrill of learning and the pleasure of meeting new people. To make an informed decision about whether to attend college, we must compare the benefits to the opportunity costs.

The Marginal Principle

The marginal principle provides a simple decision-making rule that helps individuals, firms, and governments make decisions. Economists think in marginal terms, considering how a one-unit change in one variable affects the value of another variable. When we say marginal, we're considering a small change or an incremental change.

MARGINAL **PRINCIPLE**

> **Increase the level of an activity if its marginal benefit exceeds its marginal cost; reduce the level of an activity if its marginal cost exceeds its marginal benefit. If possible, pick the level at which the activity's marginal benefit equals its marginal cost.**

The marginal principle enables us to fine-tune our decisions. We can use the principle to determine whether a one-unit increase in a variable would make us better off. For example, a barber could decide whether to keep his or her shop open for one more hour. You could decide whether to study one more hour for a psychology midterm.

The marginal principle is based on a comparison of the marginal benefits and marginal costs of a particular activity. The **marginal benefit** of some activity is the extra benefit resulting from a small increase in the activity, for example, the extra revenue generated by keeping a barbershop open for one more hour. Similarly, the **marginal cost** is the additional cost resulting from a small increase in the activity, for example, the additional costs incurred by keeping a shop open for one more hour. According to the marginal principle, you should continue to increase the activity as long as the marginal benefit is greater than the marginal cost. When you've reached the level where the marginal benefit equals the marginal cost, your fine-tuning is done. It's worth emphasizing that the marginal principle is based on marginal benefits and costs, not total benefits and total costs.

Marginal benefit: The extra benefit resulting from a small increase in some activity.
Marginal cost: The additional cost resulting from a small increase in some activity.

Example: Operating a Barbershop

Consider a problem facing Edward Scissorhands the barber. Suppose that on a particular day, Edward must decide whether to keep his shop open for an extra hour, for 4 hours instead of 3. To use the marginal principle, Edward must compare the marginal benefit of staying open to its marginal cost: If the marginal benefit exceeds the marginal cost, he will be better off if he stays open for the extra hour.

- The marginal benefit of remaining open is the revenue generated during the extra hour—the fourth hour. If Edward charges $10 for a haircut and expects to give 4 haircuts per hour, the marginal benefit of remaining open for one more hour is $40.

- The marginal cost of remaining open is the extra cost incurred during the fourth hour. Suppose the cost of the barbershop itself doesn't change with the number of hours it is open: Edward pays the same amount for rent, insurance, and electricity no matter how many hours the shop is open. Then the marginal cost is simply the opportunity cost of Edward's time. If Edward's opportunity cost for the fourth hour spent in the barbershop is $30, the marginal cost of remaining open is $30.

Because the marginal benefit ($40 in haircut revenue) exceeds the marginal cost ($30), it would be sensible for Edward to remain open for the extra hour.

The marginal principle suggests that Edward should increase his hours of operation until the marginal benefit equals the marginal cost. He should consider staying open for more than four hours, looking at the marginal benefits and marginal costs of staying open the fifth hour, the sixth hour, and so on. Suppose the marginal benefit is constant at $40 per hour: no matter how many hours he stays open, Edward can cut 4 heads of hair per hour and charge $10 per head. In Figure 2.1 the marginal-benefit curve is horizontal at $40 per hour.

Figure 2.1 shows the marginal-cost curve for the barbershop. The longer Edward stays open, the higher the opportunity cost of an hour spent in the shop. As Edward spends more and more time in the barbershop, he sacrifices activities that are progressively more valuable to him. For example, the fourth hour in the barbershop may come at the expense of rollerblading, which he values at $30 per hour, but the fifth hour comes at the expense of doing artistic shrubbery clipping, which he values at $35 per hour. In Figure 2.1 the marginal cost curve is positively sloped, reflecting Edward's rising opportunity cost of time spent in the barbershop.

In Figure 2.1, the marginal benefit equals the marginal cost at 6 hours (shown by point *e*). For the first 5 hours, the $40 marginal benefit exceeds the marginal cost, so Edward should remain open for at least 5 hours. For the sixth hour, the marginal benefit equals the marginal cost, so Edward is indifferent between operating the barbershop and doing something else during that hour. We'll assume that Edward, like other people using the marginal principle, will go to the point where the marginal benefit equals the marginal cost. Edward stops at 6 hours because the

Figure 2.1

Marginal Principle and the Barbershop

The marginal principle suggests that Edward should operate his barbershop 6 hours per day. The marginal benefit is constant at $40 per hour. The marginal cost increases as the number of hours increases, reflecting higher opportunity costs as Edward spends more and more time in the barbershop. The marginal cost equals the $40 marginal benefit at 6 hours per day.

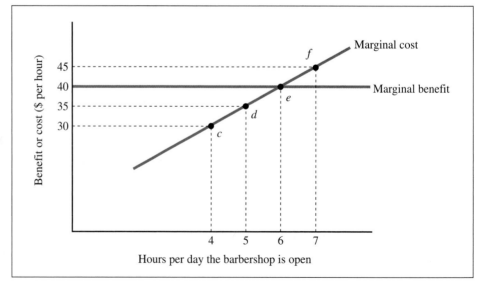

marginal cost for the seventh hour is $45 (shown by point *f*), which exceeds the $40 marginal benefit.

To use the marginal principle properly, Edward must measure his costs carefully. It is worth noting two important ideas about costs.

- Edward ignores **fixed costs**, defined as costs that do not change as the level of an activity changes. Edward's fixed costs are the costs that do not change when he remains open for a longer time. Edward ignores the monthly rent on his barbershop because the rent is fixed: It does not change if he keeps the shop open 4 hours instead of 3 hours. A common error is to include fixed costs in the calculation of marginal cost.

Fixed costs: Costs that do not change as the level of an activity changes.

- Edward includes his opportunity costs. Although Edward does not pay himself an hourly wage, he does incur a cost because instead of cutting hair, he could be doing something else. A common error is to include only **explicit costs**, defined as the firm's actual cash payments for purchased inputs, and to ignore **implicit costs**, defined as the opportunity cost of nonpurchased inputs. Edward avoids this error by including the opportunity cost of his time.

Explicit costs: Costs in the form of actual cash payments.
Implicit costs: The opportunity cost of nonpurchased inputs.

The marginal principle has been part of the economic way of thinking for a long time. Read "A Closer Look: Alfred Marshall on the Marginal Principle," for a simple explanation from a classic book.

Using the Marginal Principle: Renting College Facilities, Emissions Standards

Many colleges rent their facilities to student groups for events such as film showings, dances, and musical performances. In the example from the beginning of the chapter, a student group is willing to pay $200 to use a campus auditorium for a day. To decide whether to accept the group's offer, the college should determine the marginal cost of renting out the auditorium. The marginal cost equals the extra costs the college incurs by allowing the student group to use an otherwise vacant auditorium. In our example, the extra cost is $100 for extra electricity and janitorial service. It would be sensible for the college to rent the auditorium because the marginal benefit ($200 from the student

A CLOSER LOOK | Alfred Marshall on the Marginal Principle

Alfred Marshall's *Principles of Economics*, published in 1890, was used for decades as a classroom text. Here is Marshall's explanation of the marginal principle: "When a boy picks blackberries for his own eating . . . the pleasure of eating is more than enough to repay the trouble of picking. But after he has eaten a good deal, the desire for more diminishes; while the task of picking begins to cause weariness. . . . Equilibrium is reached when at last his eagerness to play and his disinclination for the work of picking counterbalances the desire for eating. The satisfaction which he can get from picking fruit has arrived at its maximum: for up to that time every fresh picking has added more to his pleasure than it has taken away; and after that time any further picking would take away from his pleasure more than it would add."

Source: Alfred Marshall, *Principles of Economics*, 8th ed. (London: Macmillan, 1920), p. 330.

group) exceeds the marginal cost ($100). In fact, the college should be willing to rent the facility for any amount greater than $100.

Most colleges do not use this sort of logic. Instead, they use complex formulas to compute the perceived cost of renting out a facility. In most cases, the perceived cost includes some of the fixed costs of the college, costs that are unaffected by renting out the facility for the day. In our example, the facility manager included $300 worth of construction cost and $50 worth of insurance cost as part of the cost of the auditorium, computing a cost of $450 instead of $100. Because many colleges include costs that aren't affected by the use of a facility, they overestimate the actual cost of renting out their facilities, missing opportunities to serve student groups and make some money at the same time.

We can use the marginal principle to analyze emissions standards for automobiles. The government specifies how much of each pollutant a new car is allowed to emit. For example, the rules specify the maximum volume of carbon monoxide to be emitted per mile of travel. The marginal question is, Should the standard be stricter, with fewer units of carbon monoxide allowed? On the benefit side, a stricter standard reduces the health costs resulting from pollution: If the air is cleaner, people whose respiratory ailments are worsened by air pollution will have fewer visits to doctors and hospitals, lower medication costs, and will lose fewer work days. On the cost side, a stricter standard requires more expensive control equipment on the cars and may also reduce fuel efficiency. Using the marginal principle, the government would make the emissions standard stricter as long as the marginal benefit (savings in health costs) exceeds the marginal cost (the cost of additional equipment and extra fuel).

TEST Your Understanding

1. The cost of a master's degree in engineering equals the tuition plus the cost of books. True or false? Explain.

2. Suppose a nation picks 1,000 young adults at random to serve in the army. What information do you need to determine the cost of using these people in the army?

3. Explain the logic behind the economist's quip "There is no such thing as a free lunch."

4. If a bus company adds a third daily bus between two cities, the company's total costs will increase from $500 to $600 per day and its total revenue will increase by $150 per day. Should the company add the third bus?

5. Suppose you can save $50 by purchasing your new car in a different city. If the trip requires only $10 in gasoline, is the trip worthwhile?

The Principle of Diminishing Returns

Principle of diminishing returns: As one input increases while the other inputs are held fixed, output increases but at a decreasing rate.

Xena has a small copy shop, with one copying machine and one worker. When the backlog of orders piled up, she decided to hire a second worker, expecting that doubling her workforce would double the output of her copy shop, from 500 pages per hour to 1000. She was surprised when output increased to only 800 pages per hour. If she had known about the **principle of diminishing returns**, she would not have been surprised.

PRINCIPLE OF DIMINISHING RETURNS

> **Suppose output is produced with two or more inputs and we increase one input while holding the other input or inputs fixed. Beyond some point—called the point of diminishing returns—output will increase at a decreasing rate.**

Xena added a worker (one input) while holding the number of copying machines (the other input) fixed. Because the two workers shared a single copying machine, each worker spent some time waiting for the machine to be available. As a result, although adding the second worker increased the output of the copy shop, output did not double. With a single worker and a single copy machine, Xena has reached the point of diminishing returns: As she increases the number of workers, output increases but at a decreasing rate. The first worker increases output by 500 pages (from zero to 500), but the second worker increases output by only 300 pages (from 500 to 800).

This principle of diminishing returns is relevant when we try to produce more output in an existing production facility (a factory, a store, an office, or a farm) by increasing the number of workers sharing the facility. When we add a worker to the facility, each worker becomes less productive because he or she works with a smaller piece of the facility: There are more workers to share the machinery, equipment, and factory space. As we pack more and more workers into the factory, total output increases, but at a decreasing rate.

Table 2.1 shows fictitious but convenient data for representing the production of pizza at a particular facility. The production facility is the pizzeria premises, the pizza oven, and all the machines and equipment used to produce pizza. If the pizzeria has a single worker, the single worker assembles 12 uncooked pizzas per hour and pops them into the oven as soon as they are assembled. Suppose he is joined by a second worker, who could also assemble 12 pizzas per hour. Because this second worker shares the pizza oven with the first worker, he will occasionally have to wait before he can pop his assembled pizzas into the oven. Similarly, once the second worker's pizzas are in the oven, the first worker will have to wait to get another batch of his assembled pizzas into that oven. Therefore, we wouldn't expect output to double just because the number of workers has doubled. If total output is only 18 pizzas, adding workers increases output, but at a decreasing rate: Hiring the first worker increased output by 12 pizzas (from zero to 12); hiring the second increased output by only 6 pizzas.

Figure 2.2 shows the pizzeria's **total product curve**, which shows how many pizzas are produced with different quantities of labor. As the pizzeria adds workers, total product increases but at a decreasing rate. Hiring a second worker increases output by 6 pizzas,

Total product curve: A curve showing the relationship between the quantity of labor and the quantity of output.

Table 2.1 Diminishing Returns for Pizza

Number of workers	Total product: pizzas produced	Marginal product
1	12	12
2	18	6
3	21	3
4	22	1

Figure 2.2

Total Product Curve and Diminishing Returns

As the number of workers increases, the number of pizzas produced per hour increases but at a decreasing rate. The second worker increases output by 6 pizzas (from 12 pizzas to 18 pizzas), but the fourth worker increases output by only 1 pizza (from 21 pizzas to 22 pizzas). Diminishing returns occurs because workers share a pizza oven.

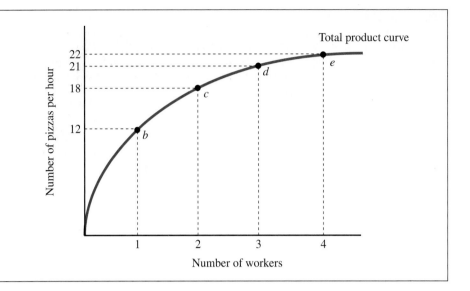

while hiring a third worker increases output by only 3 pizzas, and hiring a fourth worker increases output by only 1 pizza. It's possible that hiring a fifth worker would not increase output at all or may even reduce output because the workers will get into each others' way.

Marginal product of labor: The change in output from one additional worker.

The **marginal product of labor** is defined as the change in output from one additional worker. As shown in the third column in Table 2.1, the marginal product of the first pizza worker is 12 pizzas, and the marginal product of the second worker is 6 pizzas. In a three-worker pizzeria even more time would be spent waiting for an empty oven, and the marginal product of the third worker is only 3 pizzas. When there are diminishing returns, the marginal product of labor decreases as the number of workers increases.

Diminishing Returns in the Short Run

Short run: A period of time over which one or more factors of production is fixed; in most cases, a period of time over which a firm cannot modify an existing facility or build a new one.

Later in the book, we use the principle of diminishing returns to explore the decisions made by a firm in the short run. The **short run** is a period of time over which one or more factors of production is fixed. In most cases, the short run is defined as a period of time over which a firm cannot modify an existing facility or build a new one. The length of the short run varies across industries, depending on how long it takes to build a production facility. The short run for a hot-dog stand lasts just a few days: That's how long it takes to get another hot-dog cart. In contrast, if it takes a year to build a computer factory, the short run for a computer manufacturer is one year. Diminishing returns occur in the short run because adding workers to an existing facility means that each worker gets a smaller piece of the facility, and each becomes less productive.

What About the Long Run?

Long run: A period of time long enough that a firm can change all the factors of production, meaning that a firm can modify its existing production facility or build a new one.

The principle of diminishing returns is not relevant in the long run. The **long run** is defined as a period of time long enough for a firm to change all its factors of production, meaning that it can modify its existing facility or build a new one. To increase output in the long run, a firm can build an additional production facility and hire workers for the new facility. In the long run, the firm will not suffer from diminishing returns because workers won't have to share a production facility with more and more workers. For example, if the firm builds a second factory that is identical to the first and hires the same number of workers, the firm's output will double. Because firms can duplicate or replicate their production facilities in the long run, the principle of diminishing returns is irrelevant for long-run decisions.

The Spillover Principle

In Chapter 1, we discussed the role of markets in determining what goods are produced, how they are produced, and who gets what is produced. The metaphor of the invisible hand suggests that the decisions of millions of consumers and producers, each acting in his or her own self-interest, will frequently promote the interests of society as a whole. Let's consider some circumstances under which we cannot rely on individuals to make choices that are socially desirable.

The **spillover** principle suggests that the costs or benefits of some decisions "spill over" onto people who are not involved in making those decisions. A spillover occurs when people who are external to a decision are affected by the decision. Another word for spillover is *externality*.

Spillover: A cost or benefit experienced by people who are external to the decision about how much of a good to produce or consume.

SPILLOVER **PRINCIPLE**

> **For some goods the costs or benefits associated with produc-ing or consuming those goods are not confined to the person or organization producing or consuming them.**

Let's examine spillover costs first and then turn to spillover benefits. Consider a paper mill that dumps chemical waste into a river, and these wastes make the water unhealthy for drinking. The manager of the paper firm decides how much paper to produce, but some of the costs of producing paper are incurred by people who live in a city downstream from the mill. For example, the city might spend extra money to clean the water before its citizens can safely drink the water. Suppose for each ton of paper produced, the city's water-treatment costs increase by $10. In this case, the spillover cost of paper is $10 per ton. In deciding how much paper to produce, the paper firm will consider the cost of the inputs it buys—for example, it may pay $30 per ton for labor and raw materials—but won't consider the $10 spillover cost incurred by people downstream.

Here are some other examples of spillover costs:

- When Freon leaks from a car air conditioner, it is released into the atmosphere, where it depletes the protective ozone layer and increases the number of cases of skin cancer. A person deciding whether to repair a leaky air conditioner might not consider the effects of releasing freon on the number of cancer cases.
- Your neighbor throws a loud party while you are trying to study. In deciding whether to have the party, the neighbor doesn't consider the consequences for your exam grade.
- Secondhand smoke from cigarettes is bothersome and causes health problems for people who breathe it in.

In each example, the decision-maker incurs some—but not all—of the costs associated with the decision. As we'll see later in the book, the challenge for policymakers is to ensure that everyone who bears the costs of a decision is involved in the decision-making process.

Some goods generate spillover benefits instead of spillover costs. Suppose a farmer is thinking about building a dike or small flood-control dam on a river, at a cost of $100,000. If the farmer's benefit from the dike is only $40,000, he or she won't build it. If three other farmers would experience the same benefit, the total benefit would be $160,000, and it would be sensible for them to get together and build the dike. To make the right decision, we must get all the potential beneficiaries to participate in the decision-making process. If each of the four farmers contributed $25,000 to a dike-building fund, the dike could be built.

There are many goods that generate spillover benefits. Here are some examples:

- If a person contributes money to public television, everyone who watches public television benefits from that contribution. A person deciding whether to contribute doesn't necessarily consider the benefits experienced by others.

- If a scientist discovers a new way to treat a common disease, everyone suffering from the disease will benefit. In deciding what problem to work on, the scientist doesn't necessarily consider the benefits experienced by society as a whole.

- If you get a college degree, you may become a better team worker, so your fellow workers will be more productive and earn more income. In your decision to complete college, you probably didn't consider the benefits to be experienced by your fellow workers.

- If you buy a fire extinguisher, it is less likely that a fire that starts in your apartment will spread to other apartments. In deciding whether to buy an extinguisher, you probably don't consider the benefits to your neighbors.

In each case, some of the benefits spill over onto people who are not involved in the decision-making process, so a decision-maker might decide against taking an action that would be beneficial to society. For example, scientists might not spend their time on a

There are spillover benefits from scientific research. In considering what problems to work on, scientists don't necessarily consider the spillover benefits from their research.

project that could reduce disease. Your high-school friends might decide to forgo college because the cost they incur exceeds the benefits they will experience.

If people do not face the full costs and benefits of their actions—including the spillover costs and spillover benefits—we cannot rely on unregulated markets to make decisions that are in the general interests of society. But there are ways for the government to intervene in markets to ensure that decision-makers bear the full costs or experience the full benefits of their actions. Later in the book, we'll discuss some of the ways in which government can solve spillover problems.

TEST Your Understanding

6. When a table producer hired its twentieth worker, the output of its factory increased by five tables per month. If the firm hires two more workers—a twenty-first and a twenty-second worker—would you expect output to increase by ten tables per month?

7. According to the principle of diminishing returns, an additional worker decreases total output. True or False? Explain.

8. For each of the following examples, is there a spillover benefit or a spillover cost?

- Your roommate plays loud, obnoxious music.
- Strip mining causes oil and gas to enter the underground water system, making smoking in your bathtub hazardous to your health.
- A person in a residential neighborhood collects and restores old cars on his front lawn.
- A family contributes $5,000 to an organization that provides holiday meals to the poor.
- A landowner preserves a large stand of ancient trees and thus provides a habitat for the spotted owl (an endangered species).

The Reality Principle

One of the key ideas in economics is that people are interested not just in the amount of money they have, but also in how much their money will buy.

REALITY **PRINCIPLE**

> **What matters to people is the real value of money or income—its purchasing power—not the face value of money or income.**

To illustrate this principle, suppose you work in the college bookstore to earn extra money to pay for movies and newspapers. If your take-home pay is $10 per hour, is this a high wage or a low wage? The answer depends on the prices of the goods you buy. If a movie costs $4 and a newspaper costs $1, with one hour of work you could afford to see two movies and buy two papers. The wage may seem high enough for you. But if a movie costs $8 and a newspaper costs $2, an hour of work would buy only one movie and one paper, and the same $10 wage doesn't seem so high. This is the reality principle in action: What matters is not how many dollars you earn but what those dollars will purchase.

The reality principle can explain how people choose the amount of money to carry around with them. Suppose you typically withdraw $40 per week from an ATM to cover your normal expenses. If the prices of all the goods you purchase during the week double, you would have to withdraw $80 per week to make the same purchases. The amount of money people carry around depends on the prices of the goods and services they buy.

Economists use special terms to express the ideas behind the reality principle:

Nominal value: The face value of an amount of money.

- The **nominal value** of an amount of money is simply its face value. For example, the nominal wage paid by the bookstore is $10 per hour.

Real value: The value of an amount of money in terms of the quantity of goods the money can buy.

- The **real value** of an amount of money is measured in terms of the quantity of goods the money can buy. For example, the real value of your bookstore wage would fall as the prices of movies and newspapers increase even though your nominal wage stayed the same.

Using the Reality Principle: Government Programs and Statistics

Government officials use the reality principle when they design public programs. For example, Social Security payments are increased each year to ensure that the checks received by the elderly and other recipients will purchase the same amount of goods and services even if prices have increased.

The government also uses the reality principle when it publishes statistics about the economy. For example, when the government issues reports about changes in "real wages" in the economy over time, these statistics take into account the prices of the goods purchased by workers. Therefore the real wage is stated in terms of its buying power, rather than its face value or nominal value.

TEST Your Understanding

9. Average hourly earnings in the United States increased between 1970 and 1993, but real wages fell. How could this occur?

10. Suppose your wage doubles and so do the prices of all consumer goods. Are you better off, worse off, or just as well off?

11. Suppose your bank pays you 4% per year on your savings account: Each $100 in the bank grows to $104 over a one-year period. If prices increase by 3% per year, how much do you really gain by keeping $100 in the bank for a year?

Using the **TOOLS**

We've explained the five key principles of economics, which provide the foundation of economic analysis. Here are some opportunities to use the principles to do your own economic analysis.

1. ECONOMIC EXPERIMENT: Producing Foldits

Here is a simple economic experiment that takes about 15 minutes to run. The instructor places a stapler and a stack of paper on a table. Students produce "foldits" by folding a page of paper in thirds and stapling both ends of the folded page. There is an inspector who checks each foldit to be sure that it is produced correctly. The experiment starts with a single worker, who has one minute to produce as many foldits as possible. After the instructor records the number of foldits produced, the process is repeated with two students, three students, four students, and so on. The question is, "How does the number of foldits produced change as the number of workers increases?"

2. What's the Cost?

Consider the following statements about costs. Are they correct? If not, provide a correct statement about the relevant cost.

- One year ago, I loaned $100 to a friend, and she just paid me back the whole $100. The loan didn't cost me anything.
- Our sawmill bought five truckloads of logs a year ago for $20,000. Today we'll use the logs to make picnic tables. The cost of using the logs is $20,000.
- Our new football stadium was built on land that a wealthy alum donated to our university. The university didn't have to buy the land, so the cost of the stadium equals the amount the university pays to the construction company that builds the stadium.

3. How Much RAM?

You are about to buy a personal computer and must decide how much random-access memory (RAM) to have in the computer. Suppose each 32-megabyte block of RAM costs $40. For example, a computer with two blocks of memory (64 MB) costs $40 more than a computer with one block (32 MB). The marginal benefit of memory is $320 for the first block and decreases by half for each additional block, to $160 for the second block, $80 for the third block, and so on. How many blocks of memory should you get in your computer? Illustrate your answer with a graph.

Summary

This chapter covers five key principles of economics, defined as simple, self-evident truths that most people would readily accept. If you understand these principles, you are ready for the rest of the book, which will show you how to do your own economic analysis. In fact, if you've done the exercises in this chapter, you're already doing economic analysis.

1. **Principle of opportunity cost.** The opportunity cost of something is what you sacrifice to get it.

2. **Marginal principle.** Increase the level of an activity if its marginal benefit exceeds its marginal cost; reduce the level if its marginal cost exceeds its marginal benefit. If possible, pick the level at which the marginal benefit equals the marginal cost.

3. **Principle of diminishing returns.** Suppose that output is produced with two or more inputs and that we increase one input while holding the other inputs fixed. Beyond some point—called the point of diminishing returns—output will increase at a decreasing rate.

4. **Spillover principle.** For some goods, the costs or benefits associated with the good are not confined to the person or organization that decides how much of the good to produce or consume.

5. **Reality principle.** What matters to people is the real value of money or income—its purchasing power—not the face value of money or income.

Key Terms

explicit costs, 29
fixed costs, 29
implicit costs, 29
long run, 32
marginal benefit, 27

marginal cost, 27
marginal product of labor, 32
nominal value, 36
opportunity cost, 24
principle, 24

principle of diminishing returns, 30
real value, 36
short run, 32
spillover, 33
total product curve, 31

Problems and Discussion Questions

1. Suppose another year of college will increase your lifetime earnings by $30,000. The costs of tuition and books add up to only $8,000 for an additional year. Comment on the following statement: "Because the benefit of $30,000 exceeds the $8,000 cost, you should complete another year of college."

2. To celebrate its fiftieth anniversary, a gasoline station sells gasoline at the price it charged on its first day of operation: $0.10 per gallon. As you drive by the gasoline station, you notice a long line of people waiting to buy gasoline. What types of people would you expect to join the line?

3. You are the mayor of a large city, and you must decide how many police officers to hire. Explain how you could use the marginal principle to help make the decision.

4. Consider a city that must decide how many mobile cardiac arrest units (specially equipped ambulances designed to treat people immediately after a heart attack) to deploy. Explain how you could use the marginal principle to help make the decision.

5. Explain why the principle of diminishing returns does not occur in the long run.

6. You are the manager of a firm that makes computers. If you had to decide how much output to produce in the next week, would you use the principle of diminishing returns? If you had to decide how much output to produce ten years from now, would you use the principle of diminishing returns?

7. Your coffee shop has a single espresso machine. As the firm adds more and more workers, would you expect output (espressos per hour) to increase at a constant rate? Why or why not?

8. Use the spillover principle to discuss the following examples. Are there spillover costs or spillover benefits?
   - Logging causes soil erosion and stream degradation, harming fish.
   - An environmental group buys 50 acres of wetlands to provide a habitat for migrating birds.
   - Your office mate smokes cigarettes.
   - A person buys a dilapidated house in your neighborhood and fixes it up.

9. Explain this statement: The salaries of baseball players have increased in both real and nominal terms.

10. **Web Exercise.** Visit the Web site of the U.S. Environmental Protection Agency, accessing the page with answers to frequently asked questions (*http://www.epa.gov/history/faqs/index.htm*). What is the EPA's mission, what are its goals, and how does it try to achieve these goals? Why do we need an organization like the EPA?

11. **Web Exercise.** The price of a gallon of gasoline was $0.42 in 1973 and had risen to $1.33 by 1999. How does the change in the price of gasoline compare to the cost of other goods? To answer, go to the Web site of the Bureau of Labor Statistics *(http://www.bls.gov/cpihome.htm)* and get information on the consumer price index (CPI). The CPI measures the cost of a standard market basket of goods in different years. The value of the CPI is 100 in the base year, and as prices increase, the value of the CPI increases. For example, a value of 123 means that prices have risen to the point where the cost of the standard market basket of goods is 23% higher than it was in the base year. How does the CPI figure for 1973 compare to that of 1999? Has the price of gasoline increased or decreased compared to the cost of other consumer goods?

Take It to the Net

We invite you to visit the O'Sullivan/Sheffrin page on the Prentice Hall Web site at:
http://www.prenhall.com/osullivan/
for additional World Wide Web exercises for this chapter.

Model Answers to Questions

Chapter-Opening Questions

1. To get a warship, we sacrifice something else, such as safe drinking water for 2.5 million Malaysians.

2. According to the marginal principle, the standard should be made stricter if the marginal benefit (the savings in health costs from a cleaner environment) exceeds the marginal cost (the cost of additional equipment and extra fuel).

3. According to the principle of diminishing returns, output will eventually increase at a decreasing rate.

4. The true cost (or what economists refer to as the economic cost) of paper equals the firm's cost (for material, labor, and the paper mill) and the cost associated with the pollution generated as a byproduct of paper.

5. Your income will buy the same quantity of goods and services, so you will be equally well off.

Test Your Understanding

1. False. This statement ignores the opportunity cost of time spent in school.

2. We need the opportunity cost of using the people in the army instead of in the civilian economy. One measure of the opportunity cost is the wages the people could have earned as engineers, teachers, doctors, lawyers, or factory workers.

3. One of the costs of a lunch is the time spent eating it. Even if someone else pays for your lunch, it is not truly free.

4. The marginal benefit is $150, and the marginal cost is only $100 (equal to $600 − $500), so it would be sensible to add the third bus.

5. It will be worthwhile if the opportunity cost of the time spent traveling is less than $40.

6. No. If the factory experiences diminishing returns, the additional output from the twenty-first worker

will be smaller than the output from the additional output from the twentieth worker, and the extra output from the twenty-second worker will be even smaller than the output from the twenty-first worker. Therefore, hiring two more workers will increase total output by less than 10 tables.

7. False. The principle says that output increases but at a decreasing rate. Its does not say that hiring another worker decreases output, although this is a possibility with a very crowded factory.

8. *Obnoxious music:* Spillover cost. You must listen to what you consider awful music chosen by your roommate.

Contaminated water: Spillover cost. People who bathe in the contaminated water risk being burned.

Yard cars: Spillover cost. For most people, a bunch of partly restored cars (cars jacked up on the street or on the front lawn) is an eyesore.

Food for the poor: Spillover benefit. Even noncontributors are happy if the poor receive holiday meals.

Endangered species: Spillover benefit. Many people like the idea of preventing a species from becoming extinct.

9. The price of consumer goods increased faster than wages.

10. Your real wage hasn't changed, so you are just as well off.

11. A set of goods that cost you $100 will cost you $103 today, so you must use $3 of your $4 interest earnings to cover the higher costs, leaving you with only $1 as actual interest earnings.

Using the Tools

2. What's the Cost? The opportunity cost of the loan to the friend is the interest the person could have earned if the $100 were in a bank account instead. The opportunity cost of the logs is the amount of money the firm could get by selling the logs on the log market today. The opportunity cost of the land is the value of land in its next-best alternative, for example, a classroom building, a library, or a student center.

3. How Much RAM? See Figure 2.A. The marginal benefit of RAM equals the marginal cost at 4 blocks (128 MB).

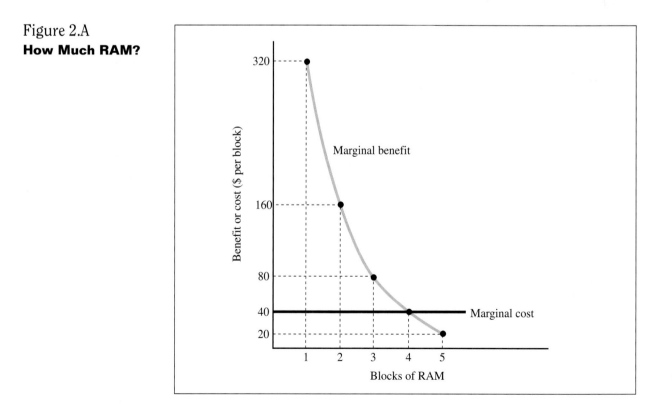

Figure 2.A
How Much RAM?

 **Notes**

1. United Nations Development Program, *Human Development Report 1994* (New York: Oxford University Press, 1994).

2. Alan Riding, "The French Seek Their Own 'Peace Dividend,'" *New York Times*, July 15, 1990, p. 6.

3. Eric Schmitt, "Peace Dividend: Troops Turn to Teaching," *New York Times*, November 30, 1994, p. B1.

3

Markets in the Global Economy

The Barbie doll, the most profitable doll in history, is sold in 140 countries at a rate of two dolls per second, with annual sales of between $1 billion and $2 billion.[1] Barbie dolls are designed in the United States, but most of the production occurs elsewhere. Saudi Arabia provides the oil used in Taiwanese factories to produce the vinyl plastic pellets that become the doll's body. Japan supplies the nylon hair, and China provides the doll's cotton clothes. The machinery used in Barbie factories in China and Indonesia comes from Japan, Europe, and the United States. The United States provides the molds used to form the dolls and the pigments and oils used to paint them. The Barbie doll, a symbol of American culture and commerce, is an international product. Most Barbie dolls come in a box labeled "Made in China," but only about $0.33 of the $10 retail price goes to the factories in China that assemble the dolls. The rest goes to input suppliers around the world and to Mattel, which collects a $1 profit on each Barbie sold.

n Chapter 1, we saw that a society makes three types of economic decisions: what products to produce, how to produce them, and who gets the products. In modern economies, most of these decisions are made in markets. In this chapter, we provide an overview of a modern market-based economy, explaining why markets exist, how they operate, and the role government plays in markets. We'll explain what the term *global economy* means, and we'll discuss the rationale for thinking in global terms.

The material we cover in this chapter will help you to understand how a market-based economy operates in today's global environment. Here are some of the practical questions we answer:

1. **Why do markets exist?**
2. **Why do both rich and poor nations benefit from trade?**
3. **How do governments restrict international trade?**
4. **What are GATT, NAFTA, and the World Trade Organization?**

Why Do Markets Exist?

In Chapter 1, we saw that a market is an arrangement that allows buyers and sellers to exchange things. A buyer exchanges money for a product (a good or service), while a seller exchanges a product for money. Before we explore how a market operates, let's think about why markets exist in the first place.

In the words of Adam Smith, "Man is the only animal that makes bargains; one dog does not exchange bones with another dog." We use markets to make our bargains, exchanging what we have for what we want. If each person were self-sufficient, producing everything he or she consumed, there would be no need for markets. Markets exist because we aren't self-sufficient but instead consume many products produced by other people. To get the money to pay for these products, each of us produces something to sell. Some people grow food; others produce goods such as cloth-

The typical person is not self-sufficient but instead specializes by working at a particular job and uses his or her income to purchase goods and services.

ing and bicycles; and others provide services such as medical care or legal advice. Because each of us specializes in one or two products, we need markets to sell what we produce and to buy other products. Most of us use the labor market to sell our work time to employers and then use our labor income to buy food, housing, appliances, and other products.

Specialization and the Gains from Trade

Why do people specialize and trade? We can explain the rationale for specialization and trade with an example involving two people and two products: bread and shirts. The first two rows of Table 3.1 show how much of each good Brenda and Sam can produce in one hour. Brenda can produce either six loaves of bread or two shirts, while Sam can produce either one loaf of bread or one shirt.

We can use the principle of opportunity cost to explain the benefits from specialization and trade.

PRINCIPLE OF OPPORTUNITY COST

The opportunity cost of something is what you sacrifice to get it.

Opportunity cost is defined in terms of one unit of the good or, in our example, in terms of one shirt or one loaf of bread. The opportunity costs are shown in the third and fourth rows of Table 3.1.

1. Brenda's opportunity cost of one shirt is three loaves of bread; that's how many loaves of bread she could produce in the time it takes her to produce one shirt. She needs half an hour to produce a shirt, and during that half hour, she could produce three loaves of bread instead.

2. Brenda's opportunity cost of a loaf of bread is one third of a shirt; that's how many shirts she could produce in the time it takes her to produce a loaf of bread. She needs one sixth of an hour to produce a loaf of bread, and during that one sixth of an hour, she could produce one third of a shirt instead.

3. Sam's opportunity cost of a shirt is one loaf of bread.

4. Sam's opportunity cost of a loaf of bread is one shirt.

Each person could be self-sufficient. Brenda could produce all the bread and shirts she wants to consume, and Sam could produce everything for himself too. But what would happen if they decided to specialize and trade? Suppose they agree to trade at the rate of two loaves of bread for each shirt.

Table 3.1 Production per Hour and Opportunity Cost

	Brenda	Sam
Bread produced per hour	6	1
Shirts produced per hour	2	1
Opportunity cost of one loaf of bread	1/3 shirt	1 shirt
Opportunity cost of one shirt	3 loaves of bread	1 loaf of bread

- Brenda could specialize in bread and trade for shirts. Instead of producing one shirt for herself, Brenda could use the time it would take to produce one shirt to produce three loaves of bread; that's her opportunity cost of a shirt. If she then trades two loaves of bread for one shirt, she will have one loaf of bread left over. Specialization and trade make Brenda better off because she gets the same number of shirts and one extra loaf of bread.

- Sam could specialize in shirts and trade for bread. Instead of producing one loaf of bread for himself, Sam could use the time it would take to produce a loaf of bread to produce one shirt; that's his opportunity cost of a loaf of bread. If he trades the shirt for two loaves of bread, he will have two loaves of bread instead of the one he could have produced himself. Specialization and trade make Sam better off because he gets the same number of shirts and one extra loaf of bread.

This example shows the benefit of specialization and trade. By specializing and trading, each person can consume more.

Opportunity Cost and Comparative Advantage

Comparative advantage: The ability of one person or nation to produce a good at an opportunity cost that is lower than the opportunity cost of another person or nation.

We say that a person has a **comparative advantage** in producing a particular good if he or she has a lower opportunity cost than another person in producing that good. It is sensible for each person to produce the good for which he or she has a comparative advantage.

- **Shirts.** Sam's opportunity cost for shirts (one loaf) is lower than Brenda's (three loaves), so it is sensible for Sam to specialize in shirts and trade for bread.

- **Bread.** Brenda's opportunity cost for bread (one-third shirt) is lower than Sam's (one shirt), so Brenda should specialize in bread and trade for shirts.

As we saw in Table 3.1, specialization and trade—with each person producing the good for which he or she has a comparative advantage—allows each person to consume more.

Absolute advantage: The ability of one person or nation to produce a particular good at a lower absolute cost than that of another person or nation.

You may have noticed that Brenda is more productive than Sam in producing both goods. Economists say that she has an **absolute advantage** in producing both goods. Despite her absolute advantage, Brenda gains from specializing in bread and trading some of her bread for shirts produced by Sam. In an hour Brenda can produce twice as many shirts as Sam, but she can produce *six* times as many loaves of bread. Brenda relies on Sam to make some of her shirts because that frees her to spend more time producing bread, the good for which she has the greatest productivity advantage over Sam and therefore a comparative advantage. The lesson is that trade results from comparative advantage (lower opportunity costs), not from absolute advantage.

TEST Your Understanding

1. Tim's opportunity cost of producing one chair is five tables, while Carla's opportunity cost of producing one chair is one table. Compute each person's opportunity cost of tables. Which person should produce chairs, and which should produce tables?

2. In an hour, a financial planner can either produce three financial statements or answer twelve phone calls. What is the opportunity cost of a financial statement? What is the opportunity cost of a phone call?

3. Wally is the manager of a car wash and is more productive at washing cars than are any of the potential workers he could hire. Does that mean he should wash all the cars himself?

How Do Markets Operate?

Now that we know why markets exist, we're ready to discuss how they operate. In a modern economy, direct trade between two individuals is rare. Rather than producing one consumer good and trading directly with other consumers/producers, most exchanges occur in markets involving firms and other organizations. Markets allow us to exchange what we have for what we want. Most of us work in firms or other organizations for a paycheck, which we then use to buy goods and services from other firms.

The Circular Flow

Figure 3.1 is a **circular flow diagram** of a simple market-based economy. Exchanges occur in two markets:

Circular flow diagram: A diagram showing the flow of money and goods between markets.

- **Factor or input market.** The owners of the factors of production—natural resources, labor, physical capital (machines, buildings, and equipment), and human capital (the knowledge and skills acquired by a worker)—sell these inputs to organizations that use the inputs to produce goods and services.

- **Product or output market.** The organizations that produce goods and services sell their products to consumers.

There are two types of decision-makers in the circular flow model: households and firms.

Households as Sellers and Buyers

Households own the factors of production (inputs) and firms have the knowledge and the ability required to transform inputs into outputs. As shown by arrows B and C in Figure 3.1, the factor markets allow households and firms to exchange inputs and

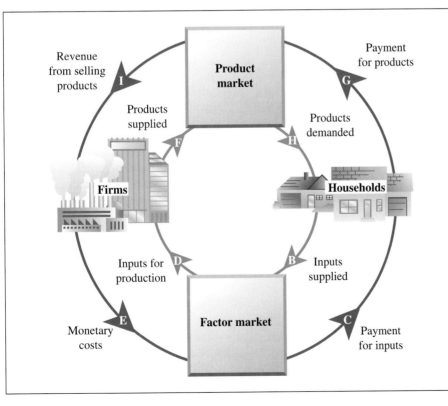

Figure 3.1
Circular Flow Diagram
The circular flow diagram shows the interactions between households (the suppliers of factors of production, or inputs) and firms (the producers of products) in the factor and product markets.

money: Households supply inputs to the factor market (arrow B), and firms pay households for these inputs (arrow C). There are three types of factor markets:

- In the labor market, firms hire workers, paying them wages or salaries in exchange for the output produced by the workers. In the United States, about three-fourths of the income earned by households comes from wages and salaries.

- In the capital market, households use their savings—money in bank accounts, mutual funds, and stock investments—to provide the funds that firms use to buy physical capital, for example, machines, buildings, and equipment. In exchange for the use of their savings, households receive interest payments or some portion of the firm's profits. In the United States, about 20% of the income earned by households comes from interest payments and profits.

- In the natural resource market, households own natural resources (for example, land, minerals, or oil) or own the firms that control the natural resources. These natural resources are sold to firms to use as inputs in the production process.

Households are also involved in the product market, where they purchase goods and services from firms. This interaction between households and firms is shown by arrows H and G in Figure 3.1: Households consume the products produced by firms (arrow H) and pay firms for these products (arrow G). To summarize, households are sellers in factor markets and buyers in product markets.

Firms as Sellers and Buyers

The purpose of a firm is to transform inputs into outputs—products—and then sell the products. Before a firm can produce anything, it must get the inputs required for production. As shown by arrow D in Figure 3.1, inputs flow from the factor markets to the firm, where they're used to produce output. As shown by arrow E, the money to pay for the inputs flows from the firm to the factor market on its way to households. In other words, the firm is a buyer in the factor markets. Once the firm produces a product, it brings it to the product market (shown by arrow F) and receives money when consumers buy it (arrow I).

Figure 3.1 shows that economic activity is circular. The inner circle shows physical flows (products and inputs), and the outer circle shows monetary flows (money exchanged for inputs or products). Firms pay money to households for their inputs. In the other direction, households pay money to firms when they buy the firms' products.

This circular flow diagram is a starting point for describing how an economy works, but it is incomplete for two reasons. First, the diagram does not show the role of government in the economy. As we'll see throughout the book, the government is a big part of a market-based economy: Government provides some goods and services, redistributes income, collects taxes, and regulates firms. Second, the diagram does not show the effects of international trade, which, as we'll see later in the chapter, is a large and growing part of most modern economies.

The Global Economy and Interdependence

In today's global economy, many products are produced in one country and sold in another. International trade is one component of the global economy. After introducing some of the language of international trade, we discuss the foreign-exchange market, which allows people to exchange currency, facilitating trade between nations with different currencies. Then we'll discuss global interdependence, exploring some of the economic ripple effects of changes in individual nations.

Markets and International Trade

Recall how Brenda and Sam benefited from specialization and trade. We saw that specialization and trade are beneficial if there are differences in opportunity costs that generate comparative advantages. Although our example consisted of two individuals, the same ideas apply to nations, which differ in their natural resources, climate, public infrastructure, physical capital, and labor forces. The resulting differences in productivity mean that, like an individual, a nation has a comparative advantage in the production of particular products. When a nation specializes in production and engages in trade, it gives its citizens an opportunity to consume larger quantities of goods and services.

A nation will specialize in the product for which it has a comparative advantage. Like trade between individuals, international trade results from comparative advantage, not absolute advantage. This explains why a rich nation trades with a poor nation, even though a rich nation is more productive and has an absolute advantage in all products. For example, suppose the United States is more efficient than India in producing both computers and clothing but that the United States has a comparative advantage in computers while India has a comparative advantage in clothing. Both countries would be better off if each country specialized—the United States in computers and India in clothing—and traded. Remember, it is comparative advantage that matters. Even if the United States were absolutely more efficient in producing clothing, both countries would still benefit from specialization and trade.

International Trade: Exports and Imports

From the perspective of the United States, an **export** is a good produced in the United States and sold in another country, while an **import** is a good produced elsewhere and purchased in the United States. As shown in Figure 3.2, the leading U.S. exports are agricultural commodities, electrical machinery, and chemicals, while the leading imports are automated data-processing equipment (ADP) and office machinery, electrical

Export: A good produced in the "home" country (for example, the United States) and sold in another country.

Import: A good produced in a foreign country and purchased by residents of the "home" country (for example, the United States).

A proposal to lift trade restrictions is often met with opposition from people employed in protected domestic industries. French farmers protested against GATT.

Figure 3.2
Major Imports and Exports of the United States

Source: Statistical Abstract of the United States (Washington, DC: U.S. Government Printing Office, 1997).

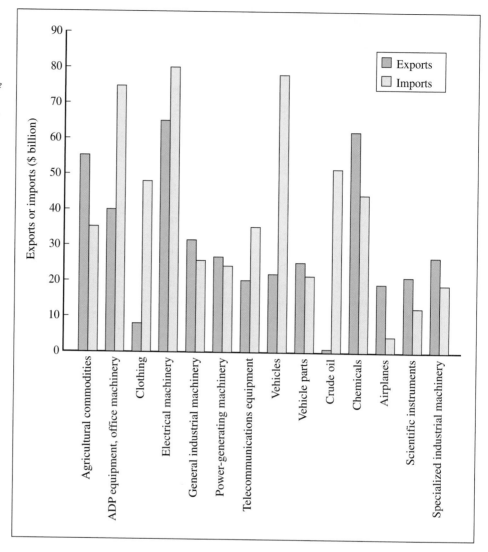

machinery, vehicles, and crude oil. Figure 3.3 shows the volumes of trade between the United States and its major trading partners. The three largest partners are Canada, Japan, and Mexico.

We began this chapter by explaining why a Barbie doll is a global product. As explained in "A Closer Look: Multinational Confusion: Imports or Domestic Products?," the global nature of production makes it difficult to distinguish between domestic products and foreign products.

Currency Markets and Exchange Rates

Foreign exchange market: A market in which people exchange one currency for another.

Exchange rate: The price at which currencies trade for one another.

The **foreign exchange market** allows people to exchange one nation's currency for another nation's currency, such as U.S. dollars for Japanese yen. Because each nation uses a different currency, international trade would not be possible without a foreign exchange market. A U.S. firm that sells computers in Japan is paid in yen but must pay its U.S. workers with dollars. The foreign exchange market allows the U.S. firm to exchange the yen it receives for dollars. The **exchange rate** is defined as the rate at which we can

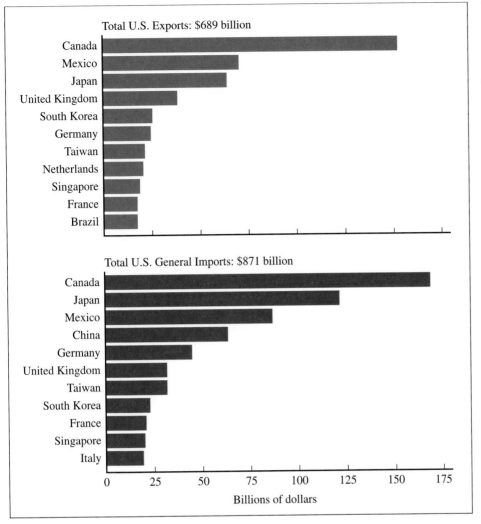

Figure 3.3

Major Trading Partners of the United States

Source: Statistical Abstract of the United States (Washington, DC: U.S. Government Printing Office, 1998).

Total U.S. Exports: $689 billion

Canada
Mexico
Japan
United Kingdom
South Korea
Germany
Taiwan
Netherlands
Singapore
France
Brazil

Total U.S. General Imports: $871 billion

Canada
Japan
Mexico
China
Germany
United Kingdom
Taiwan
South Korea
France
Singapore
Italy

0   25   50   75   100   125   150   175

Billions of dollars

exchange one currency for another. At an exchange rate of 90 yen per dollar, if the U.S. firm sells a computer in Japan for 90,000 yen, it can exchange the yen for 1,000 U.S. dollars.

Many newspapers publish information on foreign exchange rates. As shown in Table 3.2, exchange rates are quoted in two equivalent ways. First, the "value in dollars" indicates how many dollars a single unit of the foreign currency will buy. For example, the value in dollars of a German mark was $0.4894, meaning that 1 mark could be exchanged for $0.4894. Second, "the units per dollar" indicates how many units of the foreign currency are needed to buy 1 dollar. To get 1 dollar, you needed 2.0434 marks.

We can use the exchange rate between two currencies to determine the actual cost of a good produced in another nation. Suppose you are planning a trip to Mexico and want to determine the cost of staying in a hotel. If a hotel room in Mexico costs 450 pesos per night and the exchange rate is 9 pesos per dollar, the hotel room will cost you $50: To get the 450 pesos to pay for the room, you must sacrifice $50. If the exchange rate were 10 pesos per dollar instead, the hotel room would cost you only $45 a night: To get the 450 pesos, you would need only $45. The greater the exchange rate (pesos per dollar), the cheaper the hotel room in Mexico.

Table 3.2 Exchange Rates in April 2000

Nation	Currency	Value in Dollars (U.S. $ equivalent)	Units per Dollar (Currency per U.S. $)
Australia	Dollar	0.6083	1.6438
Brazil	Real	0.5741	1.7420
Britain	Pound sterling	1.5985	0.6256
Canada	Dollar	0.6898	1.4498
France	Franc	0.1459	6.8532
Germany	Mark	0.4894	2.0434
Hong Kong	Dollar	0.1248	7.7868
Ireland	Punt	1.2154	0.8228
Israel	Shekel	0.2467	4.0531
Japan	Yen	0.009537	104.86
Mexico	Peso	0.1076	9.2905
Saudi Arabia	Rial	0.2666	3.7507

Source: Wall Street Journal, April 14, 2000, page C23.

Multinational corporation: An organization that produces and sells goods and services throughout the world.

Worldwide sourcing: The practice of buying components for a product from nations throughout the world.

Global Interdependence

In the modern global economy, the nations of the world are intertwined. The fortunes of one nation affect those of its trading partners. Suppose the German economy goes through a bad spell and faces severe economic difficulties, including a high unemployment rate. As a result, German consumers will purchase fewer goods and services,

A CLOSER LOOK

Multinational Confusion: Imports or Domestic Products?

Multinational corporations design, manufacture, and market their products around the globe. For example, U.S. automobile firms design their cars in the United States but import parts and components from Asia, assemble many of the cars in Canada and Mexico, and then sell them in the United States. According to some estimates, U.S. automakers buy over one-third of the Japanese auto parts imported into the United States. The practice of using inputs (raw materials or components) from other parts of the world is known as **worldwide sourcing**, and the phenomenon means that an automobile purchased from a U.S. firm is not a purely domestic product. Many other goods are produced on a global basis, including high-priced athletic shoes (designed in the United States but produced in the Far East) and personal computers (designed in the United States but assembled overseas with parts and components from the United States and other nations). Worldwide sourcing blurs the distinction between domestic products and foreign products.

Source: Valerie Reitman, "At the Roots of the U.S.–Japan Trade Gap," *Wall Street Journal*, October 10, 1994, p. A10.

including fewer imported goods from countries like Belgium. Firms in Belgium will produce less output and will hire fewer workers. The unemployment that began in Germany thus spreads to Belgium. Through international economic linkages, Germany's bad times can be transmitted to Belgium.

While trade brings the advantages of world specialization, it also creates vulnerabilities. The benefits of increased world productivity come at the cost of increased reliance on the economic fortunes of economic neighbors. Large economic powers such as the United States, Germany, and Japan can have a large effect on the economies of other nations. The saying "When the U.S. sneezes, Canada catches a cold" expresses this idea. Countries that produce key raw materials, such as oil, can also have very large effects. During the 1970s, the oil-producing countries raised the world price of oil and inflicted much economic hardship on large countries such as the United States, Japan, and the countries of Western Europe.

The economies of the world are linked through the financial system as well as through trade in goods and services. One of the most important developments of the last decade has been the increase in the financial linkages between countries. For example, the residents of the United States can now routinely invest in firms in Asia and Latin America. A firm in Thailand that wants to undertake a major new venture might borrow funds in Western Europe, Japan, or the United States. Large banks in Japan have routinely made loans to firms throughout the world. In the past, many governments limited the ability of their citizens and businesses to borrow or lend in foreign countries. But in recent years, many economies have undergone a process of **financial liberalization**, opening up their financial markets to participants from foreign countries.

> **Financial liberalization:** The opening of financial markets to participants from foreign countries.

Financial liberalization creates many new opportunities for countries. They no longer need to rely on their own residents to finance important projects but instead can tap the resources from the entire world. Similarly, financial liberalization allows investors to scout the world for new and profitable investment opportunities and does not restrict them to their own country. In general, financial liberalization facilitates global specialization and leads to a more efficient world economy.

Financial liberalization creates opportunities and creates new vulnerabilities. Suppose investors have a bad experience in one developing country and become convinced that the economic prospects of that country have deteriorated. They begin to cut back on their loans to that country, slowing down economic activity there. At the same time, they may conclude, perhaps inaccurately, that similar difficulties plague a neighboring country, causing them to pull funds from that country too, also causing economic difficulties in the neighboring country. Before financial liberalization, neither country would have attracted the funds necessary to grow as rapidly as they did. But they would not have been subject to the changing opinions of the international financial markets either.

Because of the tighter linkages in product and financial markets, the economies of the world are becoming more and more interdependent. The greater flow of products across national boundaries and the increases in international financial transactions have increased the need for international institutions to help make the system work. The **International Monetary Fund**, headquartered in Washington, D.C., works closely with the governments of the world to promote efficient and effective financial policies to facilitate the growth in world trade and commerce.

> **International Monetary Fund:** An organization that works closely with national governments to promote financial policies that facilitate world trade.

TEST Your Understanding

4. What fraction of household income comes from wages and salaries?

5. What do firms do?

6. Nation T can produce either 3 tons of wheat or 9 tons of steel, while nation H can produce either 4 tons of wheat or 8 tons of steel. Which nation has a comparative advantage in wheat? Which has a comparative advantage in steel?

7. Complete the statement with *more* or *less*: If the exchange between U.S. dollars and French francs went from 5 francs per dollar to 3 francs per dollar, this would tend to make French goods _____ expensive to U.S. citizens.

Government in a Market Economy

What is the role of government in a market-based economy? Later in the book, we'll discuss the various roles of government, including the provision of public goods and services (such as highways and national defense), income redistribution programs (such as cash assistance and subsidizes for medical care), and taxation. In this chapter, we focus on government policies that regulate markets and control international trade.

Government Regulation of Markets

It is possible to imagine a world in which the government plays no role in the economy. In such a world, all economic decisions (what products to produce, how to produce them, and who gets the products) would be made in unregulated markets. This is referred to as laissez-faire, which translates from French roughly as "let it happen." In modern economies, however, the government plays an important role in many markets.

The government establishes a legal system to enforce property rights. If you buy land to build a house, you must register your purchase with the appropriate government agency and ensure that you are buying the land from the rightful owner and that no one else has a claim on that property. The government's legal system also makes it possible for one person to write a binding contract with another. A contract facilitates a transaction because each person involved in the transaction can be confident that the other person will fulfill his or her part of the deal. Without the legal system to enforce contracts, it would be nearly impossible to conduct business.

Governments at all levels also regulate economic activity. At the national level, the government regulates the purchase and sale of stocks and bonds, promotes competition among firms by blocking some corporate mergers, promotes safety in food products and workplaces, and limits air and water pollution. The states regulate banking, transportation, education, land use, and many professions (physicians, lawyers, pharmacists, and house builders). Local governments use zoning and other regulations to control land use. It is difficult to think of a single area in which the government does not influence markets.

Mixed economy: A market-based economic system in which government plays an important role, including the regulation of markets, where most economic decisions are made.

Because government plays such an important role in most modern market-based economies, most countries have what economists call **mixed economies**. Although most economic decisions are made in markets, these markets are regulated by the government, and the regulations differ from nation to nation and from state to state.

Alternative Economic Systems

An alternative to a market-based economy is a **centrally planned economy**, an economic system under which production and consumption decisions are made by a central government, not by individual producers and consumers in markets. In a pure centrally planned economy, there is no private property; everything is owned by the government.

In a centrally planned economy, a central bureaucracy makes all the decisions about what products to produce, how to produce them, and who gets the products. Bureaucrats tell each firm how much it should produce. One challenge for bureaucrats is to ensure that each firm has enough raw materials and workers to meet the firm's production goals. Another challenge for bureaucrats is to accurately assess the preferences of consumers so that the goods that are produced are actually desired by consumers.

Until the late 1980s, central planners ran the economies of the Soviet Union, most nations in Eastern Europe, and China. While some of these economies were effective in developing heavy industry, there were several major problems. The fundamental problem was that the bureaucrats lacked the information needed to make the millions of decisions required to allocate raw materials and other inputs to thousands of production facilities in the economy. The result was inefficiency and waste. Moreover, these economies lacked the flexibility of market economies. As computers and the information revolution transformed market economies throughout the world, planned economies were slow to adapt.

Many nations that had relied on centrally planned economies have recently shifted to mixed economic systems, with prices and private property. Two challenges are associated with the **transition** to economic systems in which markets play a much greater role in making economic decisions about production and consumption: the establishment of property rights and privatization of state-run firms.

The first challenge is to establish clear property rights and the rule of law. If property rights are uncertain, entrepreneurs will not be willing to make large investments and take risks because there will be no guarantee that they will benefit from successful projects. Entrepreneurs need law and order to prevent criminals from stealing the profits from legitimate enterprises. Russia has had severe problems with organized crime, making it difficult for ordinary businesses to exist without paying large sums for "protection." Entrepreneurs also need a legal system that prevents the government from unduly interfering with their everyday business activities. It will take time to develop the legal culture necessary to support a market-based economy.

A second challenge in the transition to a mixed economy is to **privatize** state-owned firms, that is, to sell the firms to individuals. Once a firm is sold off, it is allowed to compete with other firms in the marketplace. One problem with privatizing is that only the profitable production facilities will continue to operate. No one will want to buy unprofitable facilities, so many people will lose their jobs. Of course, other job opportunities will eventually appear as successful operations are expanded, but there may be a period when total employment drops. Another problem with privatizing is that there may be only one or two firms in a certain market, so even after the firms are privatized, there will be little competition between the privatized firms.

The difficulties for societies making the transition to a mixed economy make one thing clear. To have a successful market-based economy, the government must establish property rights, enforce laws, and provide a framework of regulation. Modern Western market economies have developed the roles of government gradually over many decades. Economies making the transition need to develop these roles more rapidly.

Centrally planned economy: An economy in which a government bureaucracy decides how much of each good to produce, how to produce the goods, and how to allocate the products among consumers.

Transition: The process of shifting from a centrally planned economy toward a mixed economic system, with markets playing a greater role in the economy.

Privatizing: The process of selling state firms to individuals.

Transition in Russia

The Soviet Union arose out of a pair of revolutions in Russia in 1917, followed by three years of civil war in which the Communists, led by Vladimir Lenin, won control of the government. Under the repressive control of the Communist party, central planning was introduced during the 1920s.

In the late 1980s, a new leader, Mikhail Gorbachev, began a series of radical political and economic reforms. Because Gorbachev believed that economic prosperity could not happen without political freedom, he introduced **glasnost**. A policy of "openness," *glasnost* encouraged Soviet citizens to say what they wished without fear of government persecution.

Gorbachev's economic reform was a plan for economic restructuring, called **perestroika**. *Perestroika* called for a gradual change from a centrally planned system to free enterprise. Gorbachev's main desire was to incorporate the use of markets and incentives into the existing structure of communism.

Under *perestroika*, the government began to allow factory managers, rather than central planners, to decide what goods to produce and how much to charge for them. It converted several factories from the production of military goods to the production of consumer goods. Many factories set goals to improve the quality of goods produced. For the first time in decades, people were allowed to start their own businesses.

With little experience in democracy and free enterprise, however, the transition to a market economy proved difficult. Economic reform produced some initial hardships. People lost secure government jobs, benefits, and pensions. Many people, especially the elderly, were hurt financially. Other Russians, however, quickly began to make the new system work for them, starting their own businesses. Many prospered.

In 1991, Russians voted in their first democratic election. They chose Boris Yeltsin as president of the Russian Republic. Yeltsin came to power by promising rapid progress towards a market-based economy. Under Yeltsin's administration, there were improvements in the economy. But many hardships continued. Prices of goods in the Soviet Union were kept artificially low by the government. In 1992, Yeltsin lifted price controls. Now that prices were controlled not by the government, but by the workings of supply and demand, many prices increased rapidly.

Transition in China

In the first half of the twentieth century, China struggled with civil war. In 1949, the supporters of communism, led by Mao Zedong, defeated the anticommunist nationalists. The Nationalist party retreated to what is now Taiwan. The communists took power in China's capital city, Beijing. Since then, China developed its own version of communism.

In 1958, Mao introduced an ambitious development plan called the Great Leap Forward. The Great Leap Forward was intended to turn China into a world economic power in the shortest time possible. All of the country's land was taken over by the central government. The people were organized into self-sufficient settlements called People's Communes.

These communes, sometimes with as many as 25,000 people, contained both farms and industries. Life in a People's Commune resembled life in the military. Communist party officials made all the decisions about what goods were made and who received them. The people's task was simply to work in the fields or factories. They received the same rewards no matter how much or how little they produced.

The Great Leap Forward was a disaster. Without incentives for workers, production fell. In the ensuing famine, about 20 million people starved to death under this development plan.

Glasnost: A policy of political "openness" introduced into the Soviet Union in the late 1980s.

Perestroika: Soviet leader Gorbachev's plan for economic restructuring.

In the 1960s, Mao instituted a Cultural Revolution. His intention was for China to further embrace communism by destroying all traces of the past. Mao organized an army of radical young men and women called the Red Guards, to carry out his policy. The Red Guards persecuted people in their attempt to eradicate what Mao called "the Four Olds": old ideology, old thought, old habits, and old customs. Mao succeeded only in further damaging the Chinese economy.

Mao died in 1976 and was succeeded by Deng Xiaoping. Deng introduced a new approach that not only shifted more power to local government, but also used the tools of the free market to improve productivity.

Deng began a program of economic reform called the Four Modernizations. The goals of the program were to improve agriculture, industry, science and technology, and defense as quickly as possible. Deng was not afraid to use free enterprise as a means of accomplishing these goals.

Deng replaced the People's Communes with the contract responsibility system. Under this arrangement, the government rented land to individual farm families. Each family then decided for themselves what to produce. The families contracted with the government to provide a certain amount of crops at a set price. Once the contract was fulfilled, they were free to sell any extra crops at markets for whatever prices they could get. Farmers increased their production, and in the first eight years of the program, their incomes tripled.

Deng had two goals for industry. First, he wanted people to spend more money on consumer goods. Therefore he changed the focus on production to the production of small consumer goods such as clothing, appliances, and bicycles. He also wanted factories to increase production. To accomplish this, Deng gave more decision-making power to factory managers. He started a system of rewards for managers and workers who found ways to make factories more productive.

In addition, Deng set up four **special economic zones** along China's east coast. In these zones, local governments are allowed to offer tax incentives to foreign investors. Businesses are allowed to make most of their own investment and production decisions. Foreign companies are allowed to operate in these zones. Deng located these first four zones near Hong Kong and Taiwan. He hoped to attract foreign investment, companies, and technology from these economic giants. The zones have proved so successful that China now has hundreds of these special zones.

Special economic zones: Designated regions in China where foreign investment is encouraged, businesses can make most of their own investment and production decisions, and foreign companies are allowed to operate.

Most of China's rapid economic growth has taken place in the special economic zones of the coastal cities. The interior regions lag far behind. The population has also shifted dramatically. About 120 million people have left the interior villages to seek their fortunes in the booming cities. Rapid urban growth has resulted in an increase in crime that the weak and sometimes corrupt police force has trouble handling.

Despite these negative effects, the economy has benefited. Since the start of Deng's reforms, China's economy has quadrupled in size.

Protectionist Policies

Despite the advantages from global specialization, most nations use trade barriers to restrict international trade. Why? Trade barriers are often designed to protect domestic firms from competition from foreign firms and to protect the jobs of workers in industries that would be adversely affected by trade. These industries are often very successful in lobbying politicians to obtain protections from trade. Policies that restrict trade are known as **protectionist policies**.

There are three common forms of protection:

- A quota is an absolute limit on the volume of a particular good that can be imported into a country. If a country imposed a quota on steel imports of 200,000 tons, only 200,000 tons of steel could enter that country.

Protectionist policies: Rules that restrict the free flow of goods between nations, including tariffs (taxes on imports), quotas (limits on total imports), voluntary export restraints (agreements between governments to limit imports), and nontariff trade barriers (subtle practices that hinder trade).

- Under a voluntary export restraint, one country agrees to limit the volume of exports to another country. For example, the Japanese government agreed to limit the number of Japanese cars sold in the United States and Europe. Many nations use voluntary export restraints to avoid explicit quotas, which are often prohibited by treaties.

- A tariff is a special tax on imported goods. For example, a 10% tariff on imported television sets means that the tax on a $300 imported TV set is $30.

There are other ways a nation can limit imports without an official trade barrier. One way is to target imports for extra-strict enforcement of health and safety laws. A foreign firm that is faced with stricter standards than domestic firms may decide to stay out of the market. Another way a country can restrict imports is to design or allow its customs system to be inefficient and sluggish. If it takes a lot of time and effort to pass imported goods through customs, foreign firms may drop out of the market. These are examples of nontariff trade barriers, practices that do not show up as official laws but have the same effects as tariffs and quotas.

History of Tariff and Trade Agreements

Since 1980, the average U.S. tariff has been about 5% of the value of imported goods, a rate that is close to the average tariffs in Japan and most European nations but very low by historical standards. Under the Smoot-Hawley tariffs of the 1930s, the average tariff in the United States was a whopping 59% of value. Tariffs are lower today because of several international agreements that reduce tariffs.

The first major trade agreement following World War II was the **General Agreement on Tariffs and Trade (GATT)**. This agreement was initiated in 1947 by the United States and 23 other nations and now has over 100 member nations. There have been eight rounds of GATT negotiations over tariffs and trade regulations, resulting in progressively lower tariffs for the member nations. The last set of negotiations, the Uruguay round, completed in 1994, decreased tariffs by about one-third of the previous level. In 1995 the **World Trade Organization (WTO)** was formed to enforce GATT and other international trade agreements.

In recent years, various groups of nations have formed trade associations to lower trade barriers and promote international trade.

- The **North American Free Trade Agreement (NAFTA)**. This agreement took effect in 1994 and will be implemented over a 15-year period. The agreement will eventually eliminate all tariffs and other trade barriers between Canada, Mexico, and the United States. NAFTA may soon be extended to other nations in the Western Hemisphere.

- A total of 15 nations have joined the **European Union (EU)**, an organization designed to remove all trade barriers within Europe and create a single market. Eleven of these nations have already committed to using a single currency, called the euro.

- The leaders of 18 Asian nations formed an organization called **Asian Pacific Economic Cooperation (APEC)** and in 1994 signed a nonbinding agreement to reduce trade barriers between their nations.

General Agreement on Tariffs and Trade (GATT): An international agreement that has lowered trade barriers between the United States and other nations.

World Trade Organization (WTO): An organization that oversees GATT and other international trade agreements.

North American Free Trade Agreement (NAFTA): An international agreement that lowers barriers to trade between the United States, Mexico, and Canada (signed in 1994).

European Union (EU): An organization of European nations that has reduced trade barriers within Europe.

Asian Pacific Economic Cooperation (APEC): An organization of 18 Asian nations that attempts to reduce trade barriers between their nations.

8. Match each trade restriction with its description.

Restriction	Description
A. Tariffs	**1.** Limits on total imports.
B. Quotas	**2.** Hidden impediments to trade.
C. Voluntary export restraints	**3.** Agreements between nations to restrict trade.
D. Nontariff trade barriers	**4.** Taxes on imports.

9. Complete the statement with GATT or NAFTA: _____ is a worldwide trade agreement, while _____ applies to a single continent.

Summary

This chapter has provided an overview of a market-based economy. In the factor markets, households provide labor and capital to firms in exchange for money. In the product markets, firms provide goods and services to households in exchange for money. In recent years, international trade agreements have lowered the barriers to trade, hastening the move to a global economy. Here are the main points of the chapter:

1. Most people are not self-sufficient but instead specialize to earn income, which they use to buy goods and services from others.

2. A system of international specialization and trade is sensible because people and nations have different opportunity costs of producing goods, giving rise to comparative advantage.

3. The foreign exchange market allows people to exchange one currency for another, facilitating international trade.

4. The free flow of goods can be hampered by barriers to trade, including tariffs, quotas, voluntary export restraints, and nontariff trade barriers. There are many international agreements designed to reduce trade barriers, including GATT, NAFTA, and the European Union.

Key Terms

absolute advantage, 46
Asian Pacific Economic Cooperation (APEC), 58
centrally planned economy, 55
circular flow diagram, 47
comparative advantage, 46
European Union (EU), 58
exchange rate, 50
export, 49

financial liberalization, 53
foreign exchange market, 50
General Agreement of Tariffs and Trade (GATT), 58
glasnost, 56
import, 49
International Monetary Fund, 53
mixed economy, 54
multinational corporation, 52

North American Free Trade Agreement (NAFTA), 58
perestroika, 56
privatizing, 55
protectionist policies, 57
special economic zones, 57
transition, 55
World Trade Organization (WTO), 58
worldwide sourcing, 52

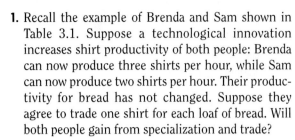

Problems and Discussion Questions

1. Recall the example of Brenda and Sam shown in Table 3.1. Suppose a technological innovation increases shirt productivity of both people: Brenda can now produce three shirts per hour, while Sam can now produce two shirts per hour. Their productivity for bread has not changed. Suppose they agree to trade one shirt for each loaf of bread. Will both people gain from specialization and trade?

2. Consider two financial planners, Phil and Frances. In an hour Phil can either produce one financial statement or answer ten phone calls, while Frances can either produce three financial statements or answer twelve phone calls. Does either person have an absolute advantage in producing both products? Should the two planners be self-sufficient (each producing statements and answering phones) or should they specialize?

3. Professor A is a better teacher than professor B for both an undergraduate course (U) and a graduate course (G). As the chair of the department, you measure teaching performance as the average grade received by students on standardized exams. How would you decide which course the professors should teach? Assume that students in course G will get 90 points if Professor A teaches it or 45 if Professor B teaches it. Students in course U will get 90 points if Professor A teaches it or 60 if Professor B teaches it.

4. Use the notion of comparative advantage to explain why two countries, one of which is less efficient in producing all products, will still find it advantageous to trade.

5. Suppose the prices of goods in Mexico and the United States remain unchanged while the exchange rate increases from 10 pesos per dollar to 20 pesos per dollar. Take the perspective of a U.S. consumer. Are Mexican goods more or less attractive? Take the perspective of a Mexican consumer. Are U.S. goods more or less attractive?

6. Some studies have suggested that industries in countries that receive protection from foreign trade are less efficient than the same industries in other countries that do not receive protection. Can you explain this finding?

7. Web Exercise. Visit the Web site of the Organization of Economic Cooperation and Development (OECD), an international organization of industrialized, market-economy countries (*http://www.oecd.org*). The site has all sorts of data on OECD countries, including data on trade at *http://www.oecd.org/publications/figures/*. Use the data to get figures for imports and exports of goods and services for the following countries: United States, Canada, Germany, France, Japan, and the Netherlands. In which of these countries do exports exceed imports? In which countries do imports exceed exports?

8. Web Exercise. Visit the Fortune Web site (*http://www.pathfinder.com/fortune/fortune500/500list.html*) and get a list of the world's largest corporations. How many corporations in the top 20 are U.S. firms?

9. Web Exercise. Visit the Web site of Accu-Rate Foreign Exchange Corporation (*http://www.accurate.ca/index.html*) to check the most recent exchange rates. If a hotel room in Lisbon costs 4,500 escudos, how much is that in dollars?

Take It to the Net

We invite you to visit the O'Sullivan/Sheffrin page on the Prentice Hall Web site at:
http://www.prenhall.com/osullivan/
for additional World Wide Web exercises for this chapter.

Model Answers to Questions

Chapter-Opening Questions

1. Markets exist because most people are not self-sufficient but instead specialize in producing one or two products and then buy other products from other people.

2. Comparative advantage makes trade between rich and poor nations beneficial for both.

3. The most common forms of protection are quotas, voluntary export restraints, and tariffs.

4. GATT is an international agreement that has lowered trade barriers between the United States and other nations. NAFTA is an international agreement that lowers barriers to trade between the United States, Mexico, and Canada (signed in 1994). The WTO is the new organization that oversees GATT and other international trade agreements.

Test Your Understanding

1. Tim's opportunity cost of one table is one-fifth of a chair, while Carla's opportunity cost of one table is one chair. Carla has a lower opportunity cost of chairs, so she should produce chairs. Tim has a lower opportunity cost of tables, so he should produce tables.

2. The opportunity cost of a financial statement is four phone calls, and the opportunity cost of a phone call is one-fourth of a financial statement.

3. No. If he has a comparative advantage at managerial tasks such as doing the books or marketing, he should hire some workers to wash the cars, allowing him to specialize in the tasks for which he has a comparative advantage.

4. About three-fourths.

5. They transform inputs into outputs—products—and then sell the products.

6. The opportunity cost of wheat is 2 tons of steel in H and 3 tons of steel in T. Therefore, H has a comparative advantage in wheat. The opportunity cost of steel is 1/2 ton of wheat in H and 1/3 ton of wheat in T. Therefore, T has a comparative advantage in steel.

7. More.

8. A4, B1, C3, D2.

9. GATT, NAFTA.

Notes

1. Rone Tempest, "Barbie and the World Economy," *Los Angeles Times*, September 22, 1996, page A1.

CHAPTER

4

Supply, Demand, and Market Equilibrium

In 1998, cigarette makers in the United States signed agreements with all 50 states to settle lawsuits over smoking-related health-care costs. Over the next 25 years, the states will receive $246 billion from the tobacco makers. The agreement includes new restrictions on advertising and marketing of cigarettes, including the elimination of billboard ads, poster ads in buses and trains, and cigarette logos on jackets, T-shirts, and caps. Although the Marlboro man will continue to appear in ads, Joe Camel is retiring. A few weeks after the agreement was announced, the price of cigarettes increased by 40 cents per pack.

As a budget analyst for your state government, you monitor health-care programs dealing with tobacco-related illness. The annual budget for these programs equals the revenue from the tobacco settlement ($80 million per year) plus the revenue collected from the state's cigarette tax ($200 million in the year before the tobacco settlement). Two years after the tobacco settlement, you discover that the revenue from the state is only $250 million, or $30 million less than you expected. What happened? This sounds like a case for the economic detective.

The Determinants of Demand
The Individual Demand Curve
    and the Law of Demand
From Individual to Market Demand

The Supply Curve
The Determinants of Supply
The Marginal Principle and the Output
    Decision
Individual Supply and the Law of Supply
Individual Supply to Market Supply

Market Equilibrium
Excess Demand Causes the Price to Rise
Excess Supply Causes the Price to Drop

Market Effects of Changes in Demand
Increases in Demand
Market Effects of an Increase in Demand
Decreases in Demand
Market Effects of a Decrease in Demand
Normal Versus Inferior Goods

Market Effects of Changes in Supply
Increases in Supply
Market Effects of an Increase in Supply
Decreases in Supply
Market Effects of a Decrease in Supply
Market Effects of Simultaneous Changes
    in Demand and Supply

Applications
Changes in Demand: Population Growth,
    Product Safety, Travel Modes
Changes in Supply: Technology, Weather

Using the Tools

e know that a market is an arrangement that allows buyers and sellers to exchange money and products. In this chapter we use a model of supply and demand—the most important tool of economic analysis—to see how markets work. We can use the model of supply and demand to see how the prices of goods and services are affected by all sorts of changes in the economy, such as bad weather, higher income, technological innovation, taxes, regulation, and changes in consumer preferences. This chapter will prepare you for the applications of supply and demand you'll see in this book. You'll also learn how to be an economic detective, using clues from the market to explain past changes in market prices. The first case for the economic detective is the puzzling revenue shortfall for health-care programs.

We will use the model of supply and demand to explain how a perfectly competitive market operates. A **perfectly competitive market** has a very large number of firms, each of which produces the same standardized product and is so small that it does not affect the market price of the good it produces. The classic example of a perfectly competitive firm is a wheat farmer, who produces a tiny fraction of the total supply of wheat. No matter how much wheat the farmer produces, the market price of wheat won't change.

This chapter includes many applications of supply and demand analysis. Here are some practical questions we answer:

1. **Would there be fewer travel deaths if parents traveling by airplane with infants were required to strap the infants into safety seats?**
2. **Ted Koppel, host of the ABC news program *Nightline*, once suggested that the prices of illegal drugs had fallen because the supply of illegal drugs had increased. Was he correct?**
3. **Some data published in your local newspaper seem to suggest that gasoline consumers violate the law of demand, buying more gasoline at higher prices. Should you be skeptical about the data?**
4. **Over the last few decades the consumption of chicken and turkey has increased. Why?**

Perfectly competitive market: A market with a very large number of firms, each of which produces the same standardized product and is so small that it does not affect the market price of the good it produces.

The Demand Curve

On the demand side of a product market, consumers buy products from firms. The main question concerning the demand side of the market is, How much of a particular product are consumers willing to buy during a particular period? A consumer who is "willing to buy" a particular product is willing to sacrifice enough money to purchase it. The consumer doesn't merely have a desire to buy the good but is willing to sacrifice something to get it. Notice that demand is defined for a particular period, for example, a day, a month, or a year.

The Determinants of Demand

We'll start our discussion of demand with the individual consumer. How much of a product is an individual willing to buy? It depends on a number of variables. Here is a list of the variables that affect a consumer's decision, using the pizza market as an example:

- The price of the product, for example, the price of a pizza
- Consumer income
- The price of substitute goods such as tacos or sandwiches

- The price of complementary goods such as beer or lemonade
- Consumer tastes and advertising
- Consumer expectations about future prices

These variables are the determinants of demand: Together, they determine how much of a particular product an individual consumer is willing to buy. We'll start our discussion of demand with the relationship between the price and quantity demanded, a relationship that is represented graphically by the demand curve.

The Individual Demand Curve and the Law of Demand

The starting point for a discussion of individual demand is a **demand schedule**, a table of numbers that shows the relationship between price and quantity demanded, ceteris paribus (the Latin phrase for "everything else held fixed"). The variables that are held fixed in the demand schedule are the other determinants of demand: income, the prices of substitutes and complements, consumer tastes, advertising, and expectations about future prices. Table 4.1 shows Al's demand schedule for pizza. At a price of $2, Al buys 13 pizzas per month. As the price rises, he buys fewer pizzas: 10 pizzas at a price of $4, 7 pizzas at a price of $6, and so on, down to only 1 pizza at a price of $10.

The **individual demand curve** shows the relationship between the price and the quantity demanded by a consumer, ceteris paribus (everything else held fixed). To draw the curve, we assume that everything else that affects a consumer's demand for pizza (income, prices of substitutes, prices of complementary goods, his tastes, advertising, expectations about future prices) does not change. The only variable that changes is the price of pizza, and we use the numbers from the demand schedule to draw the individual demand curve. Figure 4.1 shows Al's demand curve for pizza.

The demand curve is negatively sloped, reflecting the **law of demand**. This law is not a legal restriction that sends violators to jail, but is a pattern of behavior that we observe in most consumers.

Demand schedule: A table of numbers that shows the relationship between price and quantity demanded by a consumer, ceteris paribus (everything else held fixed).

Individual demand curve: A curve that shows the relationship between price and quantity demanded by a consumer, ceteris paribus (everything else held fixed).

Law of demand: The higher the price, the smaller the quantity demanded, ceteris paribus (everything else held fixed).

LAW OF DEMAND

The higher the price, the smaller the quantity demanded, ceteris paribus (everything else held fixed).

The words "ceteris paribus" provide a reminder that to isolate the relationship between price and quantity demanded, we assume that the other determinants of demand are unchanged. In Al's case we see that as the price of pizza increases, he consumes fewer

Table 4.1   Al's Demand Schedule for Pizzas

Price ($)	Quantity of pizzas per month
2	13
4	10
6	7
8	4
10	1

Figure 4.1
The Individual Demand Curve
According to the law of demand, the higher the price, the smaller the quantity demanded, everything else being equal. Therefore, the demand curve is negatively sloped: when the price increases from $6 to $8, the quantity demanded decreases from 7 pizzas per month (point *d*) to 4 pizzas per month (point *c*).

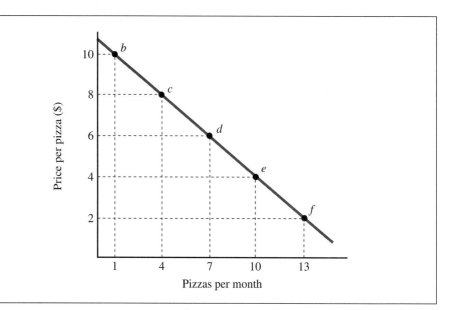

Change in quantity demanded: A change in the amount of a good demanded resulting from a change in the price of the good; represented graphically by movement along the demand curve.

pizzas. A movement along the demand curve is called a **change in quantity demanded**, a change in the quantity a consumer is willing to buy when the price of the good changes. For example, if the price increases from $8 to $10, we move along the demand curve from point *c* to point *b*, and the quantity demanded decreases from 4 pizzas per month to 1 pizza per month.

To see why the law of demand is sensible, think about how Al might react to an increase in the price of pizza.

Substitution effect: The change in consumption resulting from a change in the price of one good relative to the price of other goods.

- **Substitution effect.** The more money Al spends on pizza, the less he has to spend on other products such as tacos, music, books, and travel. The price of pizza determines exactly how much of these other goods he sacrifices to get a pizza. If the price of pizza is $6 and the price of tacos is $1, Al will sacrifice 6 tacos for each pizza he buys. If the price of pizza increases to $8, he'll now sacrifice 8 tacos for each pizza. Given the larger sacrifice associated with buying pizza, he is likely to buy fewer pizzas, substituting tacos for pizza.

Income effect: The change in consumption resulting from an increase in the consumer's real income.

- **Income effect.** Suppose Al has a food budget of $100 per month and buys 10 pizzas at a price of $6 each (a total cost of $60) and spends $40 on other food. If the price of pizza rises to $7 each, the cost of his original food choices will be $110 ($70 for pizza and $40 on other items), well above his $100 food budget. To avoid exceeding his budget, Al must cut back on something and will probably cut back on pizza as well as other items. This is called the income effect because when the price of pizza increases, the purchasing power of Al's income (or budget) decreases, forcing him to consume smaller quantities.

Market demand curve: A curve showing the relationship between price and quantity demanded by all consumers together, ceteris paribus (everything else held fixed).

From Individual to Market Demand

The **market demand curve** shows the relationship between the price of the good and the quantity that all consumers together are willing to buy, ceteris paribus (everything else held fixed). As in the case of the individual demand curve, when we draw the market demand curve, we assume that the other variables that affect individual demand

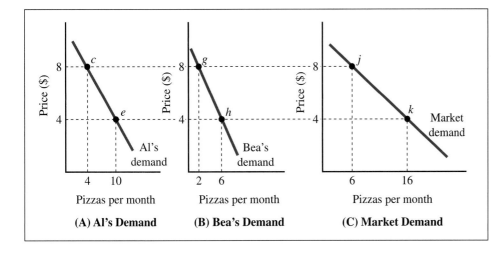

(A) Al's Demand   **(B) Bea's Demand**   **(C) Market Demand**

Figure 4.2
**From Individual
to Market Demand**
The market demand equals
the sum of the demands of
all consumers. In this case
there are only two con-
sumers, so at each price, the
market quantity demanded
equals the quantity
demanded by Al plus the
quantity demanded by Bea.
At a price of $8, Al's quantity
is 4 pizzas (point *c*) and Bea's
quantity is 2 pizzas (point *g*),
so the market quantity
demanded is 6 pizzas (point
j). Each consumer obeys the
law of demand, so the market
demand curve is negatively
sloped.

(income, the prices of substitute and complementary goods, tastes, and price expectations) are fixed. In addition, we assume that the number of consumers is fixed. The market demand curve shows the relationship between price and the quantity demanded by
all consumers, everything else being equal.

Figure 4.2 shows how derive the market demand curve when there are only two
consumers. Panel A shows Al's demand curve for pizza, and panel B shows Bea's
demand curve for pizza. At a price of $8, Al will buy 4 pizzas (point *c*) and Bea will buy
2 pizzas (point *g*), so the total quantity demanded at this price is 6 pizzas (4 + 2). In
panel C, point *j* shows the point on the market demand curve associated with a price of
$8; at this price, the market quantity demanded is 6 pizzas. At a price of only $4, Al buys
10 pizzas and Bea buys 6 pizzas, for a total of 16 pizzas (shown by point *k* on the market demand curve).

The market demand is negatively sloped, reflecting the law of demand. This is sensible because if each consumer obeys the law of demand, consumers as a group will too.
When the price increases from $4 to $8, there is a change in quantity demanded as we
move along the demand curve from point *k* to *j*. The movement along the demand curve
occurs if the price of pizza is the only determinant of demand that has changed.

The Supply Curve

On the supply side of a perfectly competitive market, firms sell their products to consumers. The main question for the supply side of the market is, How much of a particular product are firms willing to sell?

The Determinants of Supply

Here are the variables that affect the decisions of sellers, using the market for pizza as an
example:

- The price of the product, such as the price of pizza

- The cost of the inputs used to produce the product, such as the wage paid to workers, the cost of electricity, and the cost of equipment

- The state of production technology, such as the knowledge used in making pizza

- The number of producers, such as the number of pizzerias

- Producer expectations about future prices

- Taxes or subsidies from the government

These variables are the determinants of supply. Together, they determine how much of a particular product producers are willing to sell. We'll start our discussion of market supply with the relationship between price of a good and quantity of that good supplied, a relationship that is represented graphically by the supply curve.

The Marginal Principle and the Output Decision

A perfectly competitive market has dozens or perhaps hundreds of firms, and we'll start our discussion of the supply curve with an individual firm. Nora's supply curve shows how many pizzas she is willing to produce at each price. Her decision about how many pizzas to produce is based on the marginal principle.

 MARGINAL **PRINCIPLE**

> **Increase the level of an activity if its marginal benefit exceeds its marginal cost; reduce the level of an activity if its marginal cost exceeds its marginal benefit. If possible, pick the level at which the activity's marginal benefit equals its marginal cost.**

Nora's activity is producing pizzas. If the price of pizza is $8, the marginal benefit of producing a pizza is the $8 Nora gets from selling it. In Figure 4.3, when the price is $8, the marginal benefit curve for pizza is horizontal at $8. Recall that marginal cost is the increase in total cost resulting from one more unit. In Figure 4.3 the marginal-cost curve for pizza is positively sloped, indicating that the more pizzas Nora produces, the higher the marginal cost of production.

When the price of pizza is $8, Nora satisfies the marginal principle at point *p*. She produces exactly 300 pizzas because that's the quantity at which the $8 marginal benefit

Figure 4.3

The Marginal Principle and the Output Decision

The marginal benefit curve is horizontal at the market price. To satisfy the marginal principle, the firm produces the quantity at which the marginal benefit equals the marginal cost. An increase in the price shifts the marginal-benefit curve upward and increases the quantity at which the marginal benefit equals the marginal cost.

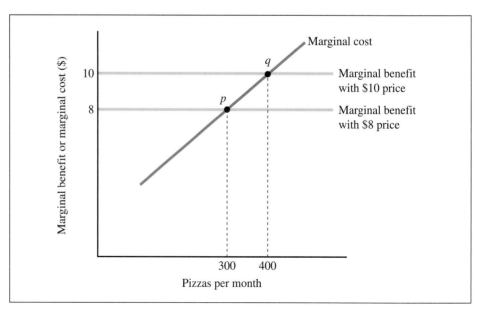

equals the marginal cost of producing pizza. She stops at 300 pizzas because the marginal cost of producing the 301st pizza exceeds the $8 she could get from selling it. For example, if the marginal cost of the 301st pizza is $8.02, she would lose $0.02 on the 301st pizza.

How would Nora react to an increase in the price of pizza? If the price of pizza increased to $10, the marginal benefit of pizza production will increase to $10. At the higher price, it makes sense to produce the 301st pizza because the $10 benefit exceeds the $8.02 cost of producing it. In fact, when Nora applies the marginal principle with the higher price, she will increase production to 400 pizzas because that's the quantity at which the $10 marginal benefit equals the marginal cost. In Figure 4.3 the marginal-benefit curve for a price of $10 intersects the marginal cost curve at 400 pizzas (point *q*).

Individual Supply and the Law of Supply

A firm's **supply schedule** is a table of numbers that shows the relationship between price and the quantity supplied by the individual firm, ceteris paribus (everything else held fixed). The other determinants of supply that are held fixed are input costs, technology, expectations, and government taxes or subsidies. Table 4.2 shows Nora's supply schedule for pizza. At a price of $4, she supplies 100 pizzas per month. As the price rises, she supplies more pizza: 200 pizzas at a price of $6; 300 pizzas at a price of $8, and so on, up to 500 pizzas at a price of $12.

The **individual supply curve** shows the relationship between the price and the quantity supplied by a single firm, ceteris paribus (everything else held fixed). To draw the curve, we assume that everything else that affects the supply of pizza (input costs, technology, price expectations, government taxes and subsidies) does not change. The only variable that changes is the price of pizza, and we use the numbers from the supply schedule to draw a supply curve. Panel A of Figure 4.4 shows Nora's supply curve for pizza.

Nora's supply curve is positively sloped, reflecting the **law of supply**, a pattern of behavior that we observe in producers.

LAW OF SUPPLY

> **The higher the price, the larger the quantity supplied, ceteris paribus (everything else held fixed).**

The words "ceteris paribus" remind us that to isolate the relationship between price and quantity supplied, we assume that the other determinants of supply are unchanged. As the price of pizza increases, Nora produces a larger quantity of pizza. A movement along the supply curve is called a **change in quantity supplied**, a change in the quantity a producer

Supply schedule: A table of numbers that shows the relationship between price and quantity supplied, ceteris paribus (everything else held fixed).

Individual supply curve: A curve that shows the relationship between price and quantity supplied by a producer, ceteris paribus (everything else held fixed).

Law of supply: The higher the price, the larger the quantity supplied, ceteris paribus (everything else held fixed).

Change in quantity supplied: A change in the quantity supplied resulting from a change in the price of the good; represented graphically by movement along the supply curve.

Table 4.2	Nora's Supply Schedule for Pizza
Price ($)	Quantity of pizzas per month
4	100
6	200
8	300
10	400
12	500

Figure 4.4
Individual and Market Supply Curve
(A) Supply of individual firm. Nora supplies 300 pizzas at a price of $8 (point p) but 400 pizzas at a price of $10 (point q).
(B) Market supply. There are 100 identical pizzerias, so the market quantity equals 100 times the quantity supplied by Nora, the typical pizzeria. At a price of $8, Nora supplies 300 pizzas (point p), so the market quantity supplied is 30,000 pizzas (point u).

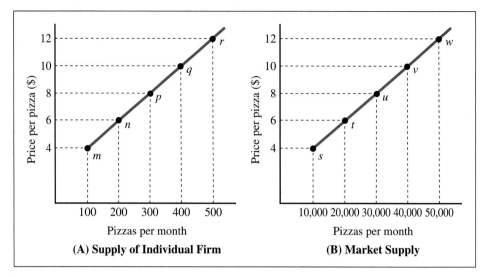

is willing to sell when the price of the good changes. For example, if the price increases from $8 to $10, Nora moves upward along her supply curve from point p to point q, and the quantity supplied increases from 300 pizzas per month to 400 pizzas per month.

Individual Supply to Market Supply

The **market supply curve** for a particular good shows the relationship between the price of the good and the quantity that all producers together are willing to sell, ceteris paribus (everything else held fixed). To draw the market supply curve, we assume that the other variables that affect individual supply are fixed. In addition, we assume that the number of producers is fixed.

Panel B of Figure 4.4 shows the market supply curve when there are 100 producers, each of which has the same individual supply curve as Nora. At a price of $8, Nora supplies 300 pizzas per month (point p), so the 100 firms together produce 30,000 pizzas (300 pizzas per firm times 100 firms), as shown by point u. If the price increases to $10, Nora supplies 400 pizzas (point q), so the quantity supplied by the market is 40,000 (point v).

The market supply curve is positively sloped, reflecting the law of supply. This is sensible because if each firm obeys the law of supply, firms as a group will too. When the price increases from $8 to $10, there is a change in quantity supplied as we move along the market supply curve from point u to point v. The movement along the supply curve occurs if the price of pizza is the only determinant of supply that has changed.

Market supply curve: A curve showing the relationship between price and quantity supplied by all producers together, ceteris paribus (everything else held fixed).

TEST Your Understanding

1. Complete the statement with "increase" or "decrease": When a price increases, the law of demand suggests that the quantity demanded will _____, while the law of supply suggests that the quantity supplied will _____.

2. List the variables that are held fixed in drawing a market demand curve.

3. List the variables that are held fixed in drawing a market supply curve.

Market Equilibrium

When the quantity of a product demanded equals the quantity supplied, this is called a **market equilibrium**. When a market reaches an equilibrium, there is no pressure to change the price. For example, if pizza firms produce exactly the quantity of pizza consumers are willing to buy, there will be no pressure for the price of pizza to change. The equilibrium price is shown by the intersection of the supply and demand curves. In Figure 4.5, at a price of $8, the supply curve shows that firms will produce 30,000 pizzas, which is exactly the quantity that consumers are willing to buy at that price.

Market equilibrium: A situation in which the quantity of a product demanded equals the quantity supplied, so there is no pressure to change the price.

Excess Demand Causes the Price to Rise

If the price is below the equilibrium price, there will be **excess demand** for the product. Excess demand (sometimes called a shortage) occurs when consumers are willing to buy more than producers are willing to sell. In Figure 4.5 at a price of $6, there is an excess demand equal to 17,000 pizzas: Consumers are willing to buy 37,000 pizzas (point *d*), but producers are willing to sell only 20,000 pizzas (point *c*). This mismatch between supply and demand will cause the price of pizza to rise. Firms will increase the price they charge for their limited supply of pizza, and anxious consumers will pay the higher price to get one of the few pizzas that are available.

Excess demand: A situation in which, at the prevailing price, consumers are willing to buy more than producers are willing to sell.

An increase in price eliminates excess demand by changing both the quantity demanded and quantity supplied. As the price increases,

- The market moves upward along the demand curve (from point *d* toward point *e*), *decreasing* the quantity demanded.

- The market moves upward along the supply curve (from point *c* toward point *e*), *increasing* the quantity supplied.

Because quantity demanded decreases while quantity supplied increases, the gap between the quantity demanded and the quantity supplied narrows. The price will continue to rise until excess demand is eliminated. In Figure 4.5, at a price of $8, the quantity supplied equals the quantity demanded.

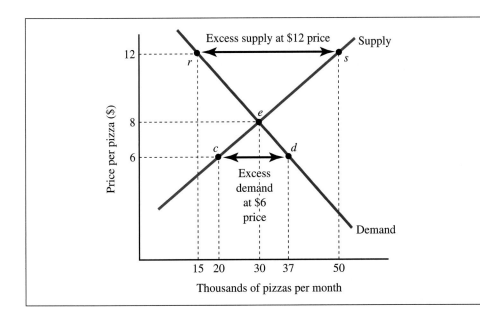

Figure 4.5

Supply, Demand, and Market Equilibrium
At the market equilibrium (point *e*, with price = $8 and quantity = 30,000), the quantity supplied equals the quantity demanded. At a price lower than the equilibrium price ($6), there is excess demand (the quantity demanded exceeds the quantity supplied). At a price above the equilibrium price ($12), there is excess supply (the quantity supplied exceeds the quantity demanded).

In some cases, government creates an excess demand for a good by setting a maximum price (sometimes called a price ceiling). If the government sets a maximum price that is less than the equilibrium price, the result is a permanent excess demand for the good. The most prominent example in the United States is rent control, a maximum price for apartments. During World War II the federal government instituted a national system of rent controls. Although New York City was the only city to retain rent control after the war, rent control returned to dozens of cities in the 1970s. Since then several states have passed laws that have weakened rent control.

Excess Supply Causes the Price to Drop

Excess supply: A situation in which, at the prevailing price, producers are willing to sell more than consumers are willing to buy.

What happens if the price is above the equilibrium price? **Excess supply** (sometimes called a surplus) occurs when producers are willing to sell more than consumers are willing to buy. This is shown by points *r* and *s* in Figure 4.5. At a price of $12, the excess supply is 35,000 pizzas: producers are willing to sell 50,000 pizzas (point *s*), but consumers are willing to buy only 15,000 pizzas (point *r*). This mismatch will cause the price of pizza to fall as firms cut the price to sell their pizza. As the price drops,

- The market moves downward along the demand curve, *increasing* the quantity demanded.

- The market moves downward along the supply curve, *decreasing* the quantity supplied.

Because the quantity demanded increases while the quantity supplied decreases, the gap between quantity supplied and demanded narrows. The price will continue to drop until excess supply is eliminated. In Figure 4.5, at price of $8, the quantity supplied equals the quantity demanded.

The government sometimes creates an excess supply of a good by setting a minimum price (sometimes called a price floor). If the government sets a minimum price that is greater than the equilibrium price, the result is a permanent excess supply. For several decades, the U.S. government set minimum prices for dozens of agricultural products such as corn and dairy products. These agricultural price-support programs ended in 1996. The European Community has price supports (minimum prices) for grains, dairy products, livestock, and sugar, and Japan has price supports for dairy products and sugar.

TEST Your Understanding

4. Complete the statement: The market equilibrium is shown by the intersection of the _____ curve and the _____ curve.

5. Complete the statement with "less" or "greater": Excess demand occurs when the price is _____ than the equilibrium price; excess supply occurs when the price is _____ than the equilibrium price.

6. Complete the statement with "supply" or "demand": A maximum price below the equilibrium price causes excess _____, while a minimum price above the equilibrium price causes excess _____.

Market Effects of Changes in Demand

We've seen that a market equilibrium occurs when the quantity supplied equals the quantity demanded, shown graphically by the intersection of the supply curve and the demand curve. In this part of the chapter, we'll see how changes on the demand side of the market affect the equilibrium price and equilibrium quantity.

Earlier in the chapter we listed the determinants of demand, the variables that determine how much of a particular product consumers are willing to buy. One of the determinants is the price of the product, and the law of demand summarizes the negative relationship between price and quantity demanded. We're ready to take a closer look at the other determinants of demand—income, the prices of related goods, tastes, advertising, and the number of consumers—and see how changes in these variables affect the demand for the product and the market equilibrium.

If any of these other variables change, the relationship between price and quantity—shown numerically in the demand schedule and graphically in the demand curve—will change. That means we will have an entirely different demand schedule and a different demand curve. To convey the idea that changes in these other variables change the demand schedule and the demand curve, a change in any of these variables causes a **change in demand**. In contrast, a change in the price of the good causes *a change in quantity demanded*.

Change in demand: A change in the amount of a good demanded resulting from a change in something other than the price of the good; represented graphically by a shift of the demand curve.

Increases in Demand

We'll start with changes in the pizza market that increase the demand for pizza. An increase in demand means that at each price, consumers are willing to buy a larger quantity. In Figure 4.6 an increase in demand shifts the market demand curve from D_2 to D_3. At the initial price of $8, the quantity demanded increases from 30,000 pizzas (point i) to 48,000 (point j). An increase in demand like the one represented in Figure 4.6 can occur for several reasons, which are listed in the first column of Table 4.3.

- **Increase in income.** Consumers use their income to buy products, and the more money they have, the more money they spend. For a **normal good** there is a positive relationship between consumer income and the quantity consumed.

- **Increase in price of a substitute good.** When two goods are **substitutes**, an increase in the price of the first good causes some consumers to switch to the second good.

Normal good: A good for which an increase in income increases demand.

Substitutes: Two goods that are related in such a way that an increase in the price of one good increases the demand for the other good.

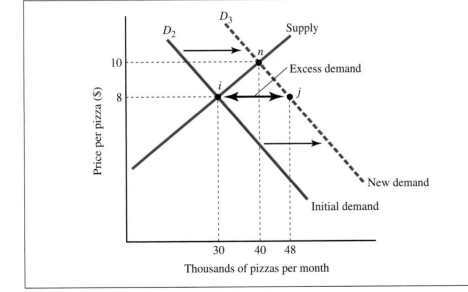

Figure 4.6

Market Effects of an Increase in Demand

An increase in demand shifts the demand curve to the right: At each price, the quantity demanded increases. At the initial price ($8), the shift of the demand curve causes excess demand, causing the price to rise. Equilibrium is restored at point n, with a higher equilibrium price ($10, up from $8) and a larger equilibrium quantity (40,000 pizzas, up from 30,000 pizzas).

Table 4.3 — Changes in Demand Shift the Demand Curve

An increase in demand shifts the demand curve to the right when	A decrease in demand shifts the demand curve to the left when
The good is normal and income increases	The good is normal and income decreases
The good is inferior and income decreases	The good is inferior and income increases
The price of a substitute good increases	The price of a substitute good decreases
The price of a complementary good decreases	The price of a complementary good increases
Population increases	Population decreases
Consumer tastes shift in favor of the product	Consumer tastes shift away from the product
Favorable advertising	
Consumers expect a higher price in the future	Consumers expect a lower price in the future

Tacos and pizzas are substitutes, so an increase in the price of tacos increases the demand for pizzas as some consumers substitute pizza for tacos, which are now more expensive relative to pizza.

Complements: Two goods that are related in such a way that an increase in the price of one good decreases the demand for the other good.

- **Decrease in price of a complementary good.** When two goods are **complements**, they are consumed together as a package, and a decrease in the price of one good decreases the cost of the entire package. As a result, consumers buy more of both goods. Pizza and beer are complementary goods, so a decrease in the price of beer decreases the cost of a beer and pizza meal, increasing the demand for pizza.

- **Increase in population.** An increase in the number of people means that there are more pizza consumers—more individual demand curves to add up to get the market demand curve—so market demand increases.

- **Shift in consumer tastes.** Consumers' preferences or tastes change over time, and when consumers' preferences shift in favor of pizza, the demand for pizza increases.

- **Favorable advertising.** The purpose of an advertising campaign is to shift consumers preferences in favor of a product, so a successful pizza advertising campaign will increase the demand for pizza.

- **Expectations of higher future prices.** If consumers think next month's pizza price will be higher than they had initially expected, they may buy a larger quantity today (and a smaller quantity next month). That means that the demand for pizza today will increase.

Market Effects of an Increase in Demand

We can use Figure 4.6 to show the effects of an increase in demand on the equilibrium price and equilibrium quantity. An increase in the demand for pizza shifts the demand curve to the right, from D_2 to D_3. At the initial price of $8 (the equilibrium price with the initial demand curve), there will be an excess demand, as indicated by points i and j: Consumers are willing to buy 48,000 pizzas (point j), but producers are willing to sell only 30,000 pizzas (point i). Consumers want to buy 18,000 more pizzas than producers are willing to supply, so there is pressure to increase the price.

As the price rises, the excess demand shrinks because the quantity demanded decreases while the quantity supplied increases.

- The market moves upward along the supply curve to a larger quantity supplied.

- The market moves upward along the new demand curve to a smaller quantity demanded.

The supply curve intersects the new demand curve at point n, so the new equilibrium price is $10 (up from $8), and the new equilibrium quantity is 40,000 pizzas (up from 30,000).

Decreases in Demand

What sort of changes in the pizza market will decrease the demand for pizza? A decrease in demand means that at each price, consumers are willing to buy a smaller quantity. In Figure 4.7 a decrease in demand shifts the market demand curve from D_2 to D_1. At the initial price of $8, the quantity demanded decreases from 30,000 pizzas (point i) to 12,000 pizzas (point k). A decrease in demand like the one represented in Figure 4.7 can occur for several reasons, which are listed in the second column of Table 4.3.

- **Decrease in income.** A decrease in income means that consumers have less to spend, so they buy a smaller quantity of each normal good.

- **Decrease in price of a substitute good.** A decrease in the price of a substitute good such as tacos makes pizza more expensive relative to tacos, causing consumers to demand less pizza.

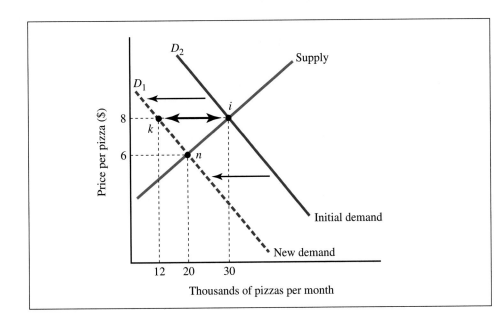

Figure 4.7
Market Effects of a Decrease in Demand
A decrease in demand shifts the demand curve to the left: At each price, the quantity demanded decreases. At the initial price ($8), the leftward shift of the demand curve causes excess supply, causing the price to fall. Equilibrium is restored at point n, with a lower equilibrium price ($6, down from $8) and a smaller equilibrium quantity (20,000 pizzas, down from 30,000 pizzas).

- **Increase in price of a complementary good.** An increase in the price of a complementary good such as beer increases the cost of a beer and pizza meal, decreasing the demand for pizza.

- **Decrease in population.** A decrease in the number of people means that there are fewer pizza consumers, so the market demand for pizza decreases.

- **Shift in consumer tastes.** When consumers' preferences shift away from pizza in favor of other products, the demand for pizza decreases.

- **Expectations of lower future prices.** If consumers think next month's pizza price will be lower than they had initially expected, they may buy a smaller quantity today, meaning the demand for pizza today will decrease.

Market Effects of a Decrease in Demand

We can use Figure 4.7 to show the effects of a decrease in demand on the equilibrium price and equilibrium quantity. The demand for pizza shifts the demand curve to the left, from D_2 to D_1. At the initial price of $8 (the equilibrium price with the initial demand curve), there will be an excess supply, as indicated by points i and k: Producers are willing to sell 30,000 pizzas (point i), but given the lower demand, consumers are willing to buy only 12,000 pizzas (point k). Producers want to sell 18,000 more pizzas than consumers are willing to buy, so there is pressure to decrease the price.

The excess supply means that there is pressure to reduce prices, and as the price falls, the excess supply shrinks because the quantity demand increases while the quantity supplied decreases.

- The market moves downward along the supply curve to a smaller quantity supplied.

- The market moves downward along the new demand curve to a larger quantity demanded.

The supply curve intersects the new demand curve at point n, so the new equilibrium price is $6 (down from $8), and the new equilibrium quantity is 20,000 pizzas (down from 30,000 pizzas).

Normal Versus Inferior Goods

Inferior good: A good for which an increase in income decreases demand.

Up to this point, we've assumed that there is a positive relationship between income and the demand for a particular product such as pizza. The label for such a good is normal good, a label indicating that for most products there is a positive relationship between income and demand. For some goods there is a negative rather than a positive relationship between income and consumption. For an **inferior good** an increase in income decreases demand, shifting the demand curve to the left. In most cases an inferior good is an inexpensive good such as margarine that has an expensive alternative (butter). As income increases, some consumers switch from the inexpensive good to the expensive one, for example, buying less margarine and more butter. As a result, the demand for margarine decreases and the demand curve shifts to the left. Some other examples of inferior goods are potatoes, intercity bus travel, and used clothing.

7. Which of the following go together?

 a. Change in demand

 b. Change in quantity demanded

 c. Change in price

 d. Movement along the demand curve

 e. Shifting the demand curve

 f. Change in income

8. What's wrong with the following statement? "Demand increased because the demand curve shifted."

9. Complete the statement with "right" or "left": An increase in the price of cassette tapes will shift the demand curve for CDs to the _____; an increase in the price of CD players will shift the demand curve for CDs to the

 _____.

10. In the following list of variables, circle the ones that change as we move along the demand curve for pencils, and cross out the ones that are assumed to be fixed: quantity of pencils demanded, number of consumers, price of pencils, price of pens, consumer income.

Market Effects of Changes in Supply

In this part of the chapter, we'll see how changes on the supply side of the market affect the equilibrium price and equilibrium quantity. Earlier in the chapter we listed the determinants of supply, the variables that determine how much of a particular product firms are willing to sell. One of the determinants is the price of the product, and the relationship between price and quantity supplied is shown by the law of supply. We're ready to take a closer look at the other determinants of supply—input costs, technology, the number of firms, and price expectations—and see how changes in these variables affect the supply of the product and the market equilibrium.

If any of these other variables changes, the relationship between price and quantity—shown numerically in the supply schedule and graphically in the supply curve—will change. That means that we will have an entirely different supply schedule and a different supply curve. To convey the idea that changes in these other variables change the supply schedule and the supply curve, a change in any of these variables causes a **change in supply**. In contrast, a change in the price of the good causes *a change in quantity supplied* (defined earlier in the chapter).

Change in supply: A change in the amount of a good supplied resulting from a change in something other than the price of the good; represented graphically by a shift of the supply curve.

Increases in Supply

We'll start with changes in the pizza market that increase the supply of pizza. An increase in supply means that at each price, producers are willing to sell a larger quantity. In Figure 4.8 an increase in supply shifts the market supply curve from S_2 to S_3. At the initial price of $8, the quantity demanded increases from 30,000 pizzas (point *i*) to 45,000 (point *m*). An increase in supply like the one represented in Figure 4.8 can occur for several reasons, which are listed in the first column of Table 4.4.

- **Decrease in input costs.** A decrease in the cost of labor or some other input will make pizza production less costly and more profitable at a given price, so producers will supply more.

Figure 4.8
Market Effects of an Increase in Supply

An increase in supply shifts the supply curve to the right: At each price, the quantity supplied increases. At the initial price ($8), the rightward shift of the supply curve causes excess supply, causing the price to drop. Equilibrium is restored at point *n*, with a lower equilibrium price ($6, down from $8) and a larger equilibrium quantity (36,000 pizzas, up from 30,000 pizzas).

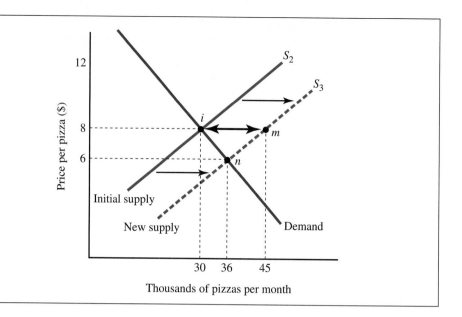

- **Advance in technology.** A technological advance that makes it possible to produce pizza at a lower cost will make pizza production more profitable, so producers will supply more.

- **An increase in the number of producers.** The market supply is the sum of the supplies of all producers, so the larger number of producers, the greater the supply.

- **Expectations of lower future prices.** If firms think next month's pizza price will be lower than they had initially expected, they may be willing to sell a larger quantity today (and a smaller quantity next month). That means that the supply of pizza today will increase.

- **Subsidy.** If the government subsidizes the production of the product (pays firms some amount for each unit produced), the subsidy will make the product more profitable, so firms will produce more.

Table 4.4   Changes in Supply Shift the Supply Curve

An increase in supply shifts the supply curve to the right when	A decrease in supply shifts the supply curve to the left when
The cost of an input decreases	The cost of an input decreases
A technological advance decreases production costs	
The number of firms increases	The number of firms decreases
Producers expect a lower price in the future	Producers expect a higher price in the future
Subsidy	Tax

Market Effects of an Increase in Supply

We can use Figure 4.8 to show the effects of an increase in supply on the equilibrium price and equilibrium quantity. An increase in the supply of pizza shifts the demand curve to the right, from S_2 to S_3. At the initial price of $8 (the equilibrium price with the initial demand curve), there will be an excess supply, as indicated by points i and m: Producers are willing to sell 45,000 pizzas (point m), but consumers are willing to buy only 30,000 (point i). Producers want to sell 15,000 more pizzas than consumers are willing to buy, so there is pressure to decrease the price.

As the price decreases, the excess supply shrinks because the quantity supplied decreases while the quantity demanded increases.

- The market moves downward along the new supply curve to a smaller quantity supplied.

- The market moves downward along the demand curve to a larger quantity demanded.

The new supply curve intersects the demand curve at point n, so the new equilibrium price is $6 (down from $8) and the new equilibrium quantity is 36,000 pizzas (up from 30,000).

Decreases in Supply

What sort of changes in the pizza market will decrease the supply of pizza? A decrease in supply means that at each price, producers are willing to supply a smaller quantity. In Figure 4.9, a decrease in supply shifts the market supply curve from S_2 to S_1. At the initial price of $8, the quantity supplied decreases from 30,000 pizzas (point i) to 14,000 pizzas (point p). A decrease in supply like the one represented in Figure 4.9 can occur for several reasons, which are listed in the second column of Table 4.4.

- **Increase in input costs.** A increase in the cost of labor or some other input will make pizza production more costly and less profitable at a given price, so producers will supply less.

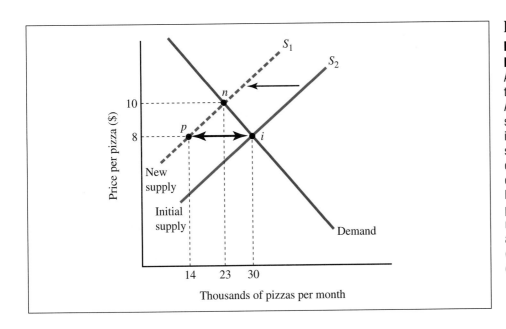

Figure 4.9

Market Effects of a Decrease in Supply
A decrease in supply shifts the supply curve to the left: At each price, the quantity supplied decreases. At the initial price ($8), the leftward shift of the supply curve causes excess demand, causing the price to rise. Equilibrium is restored at point n, with a higher equilibrium price ($10, up from $8) and a smaller equilibrium quantity (23,000 pizzas, down from 30,000 pizzas).

- **A decrease in the number of producers.** The market supply is the sum of the supplies of all producers, so a decrease is the number of producers decreases supply.

- **Expectations of higher future prices.** If firms think next month's pizza price will be higher than they had initially expected, they may be willing to sell a smaller quantity today (and a larger quantity next month). That means that the supply of pizza today will decrease.

- **Tax.** If the government imposes a tax on producers (a firm pays the government some amount for each unit produced), the tax will make the product more costly and less profitable, so firms will supply less.

Market Effects of a Decrease in Supply

We can use Figure 4.9 to show the effects of a decrease in supply on the equilibrium price and equilibrium quantity. A decrease in the supply of pizza shifts the supply curve to the left, from S_2 to S_1. At the initial price of $8 (the equilibrium price with the initial supply curve), there will be an excess demand, as indicated by points i and p: Consumers are willing to buy 30,000 pizzas (point i), but producers are willing to sell only 14,000 pizzas (point p). Consumers want to buy 16,000 more pizzas than producers are willing to sell, so there is pressure to increase the price.

As the price increases, the excess demand shrinks because the quantity demanded decreases while the quantity supplied increases.

- The market moves upward along the demand curve to a smaller quantity demanded.

- The market moves upward along the new supply curve to a larger quantity supplied.

The new supply curve intersects the demand curve at point n, so the new equilibrium price is $10 (up from $8), and the new equilibrium quantity is 23,000 pizzas (down from 30,000).

Market Effects of Simultaneous Changes in Demand and Supply

What happens to the equilibrium price and quantity when both supply and demand increase? It depends on which change is larger. In panel A of Figure 4.10, the increase in demand is larger than the increase in supply, meaning the demand curve shifts by a larger amount than the supply curve. The market equilibrium moves from point i to point d, and the equilibrium price increases from $8 to $9. This is sensible because an increase in demand tends to pull the price up, while an increase in supply tends to push the price down. If demand increases by a larger amount, the upward pull will be stronger than the downward push, and the price will rise.

We can be certain that when supply and demand both increase, the equilibrium quantity will increase. That's because both changes tend to increase the equilibrium quantity. In panel A of Figure 4.10, the equilibrium quantity increases from 30,000 to 44,000 pizzas.

Panel B of Figure 4.10 shows what happens when the increase in supply is larger than the increase in demand. The equilibrium moves from point i to s, meaning that the price falls from $8 to $7. This is sensible because the downward pull on the price resulting from the increase in supply is stronger than the upward pull from the increase in demand. As expected, the equilibrium quantity rises from 30,000 to 45,000 pizzas

What about simultaneous *decreases* in supply and demand? In this case the equilibrium quantity will certainly fall because both changes tend to decrease the equilibrium

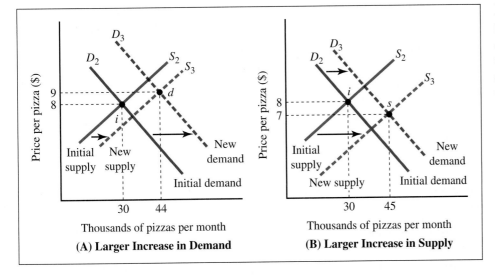

Figure 4.10
Market Effects of Simultaneous Changes in Supply and Demand
(A) Larger increase in demand. If the increase in demand is larger than the increase in supply (if the shift of the demand curve is larger than the shift of the supply curve), both the equilibrium price and the equilibrium quantity will increase.
(B) Larger increase in supply. If the increase in supply is larger than the increase in demand (if the shift of the supply curve is larger than the shift of the demand curve), the equilibrium price will decrease and the equilibrium quantity will increase.

quantity. The effect on the equilibrium price depends on which change is larger, the decrease in demand, which pushes the price downward, or the decrease in supply, which pulls the price upward. If the change in demand is larger, the price will fall because the force pushing the price down will be stronger than the force pulling it up. In contrast, if the decrease in supply is larger, the price will rise because the force pulling the price up will be stronger than the force pushing it down.

TEST Your Understanding

11. Which of the following items go together?

    a. Change in quantity supplied   **d.** Shifting the supply curve

    b. Change in input cost   **e.** Movement along the supply curve

    c. Change in price   **f.** Change in supply

12. An increase in the wage of computer workers will shift the supply curve for computers to the left. True or false? Explain.

13. In the following list, circle the variables that change as we move along the market supply curve for housing, and cross out the variables that are assumed to be fixed: quantity of housing supplied, number of potential consumers, price of wood, price of houses, consumer income.

Applications

We can use the lessons from the pizza market to explore the effects of changes in other markets on equilibrium prices and quantities. Table 4.5 summarizes the effects of changes in demand and supply on equilibrium prices and quantities. When demand changes and the demand curve shifts, price and quantity change in the same direction.

- **Increase in demand.** Both the equilibrium price and the equilibrium quantity increase.

- **Decrease in demand.** Both the equilibrium price and the equilibrium quantity decrease.

Table 4.5 Market Effects of Changes in Demand or Supply

Change in Demand or Supply	Change in Price	Change in Quantity
Increase in demand	Increase	Increase
Decrease in demand	Decrease	Decrease
Increase in supply	Decrease	Increase
Decrease in supply	Increase	Decrease

When supply changes and the supply curve shifts, price and quantity change in opposite directions.

- **Increase in supply.** The equilibrium price decreases, but the equilibrium quantity increases.

- **Decrease in supply.** The equilibrium price increases, but the equilibrium quantity decreases.

Changes in Demand: Population Growth, Product Safety, Travel Modes

How will an increase in enrollment at a university affect the equilibrium price of apartments in the university town? In Figure 4.11, the initial equilibrium is shown by point i, with a monthly rent of $400 per apartment. An increase in university enrollment increases the number of students seeking apartments, shifting the demand for apartments to the right. The new equilibrium is shown by point n, with a price of $600 per apartment. The increase in demand increases the equilibrium price and the equilibrium quantity of apartments.

How does public information about the safety of products affect equilibrium prices and quantities? In 1999 a controversial report suggested that pesticide residue on

Figure 4.11

University Enrollment and Apartment Rent

An increase in university enrollment will increase the demand for apartments in the university town, shifting the demand curve to the right. Equilibrium is restored at point *n*, with a higher price ($600, up from $400) and a larger quantity (4,000 apartments, up from 3,000 apartments).

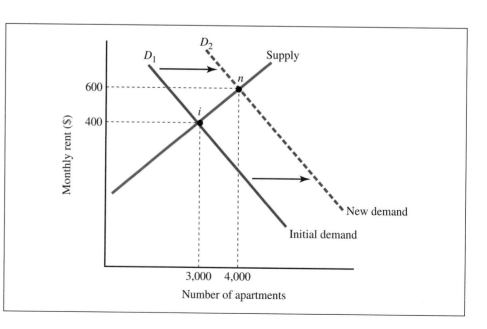

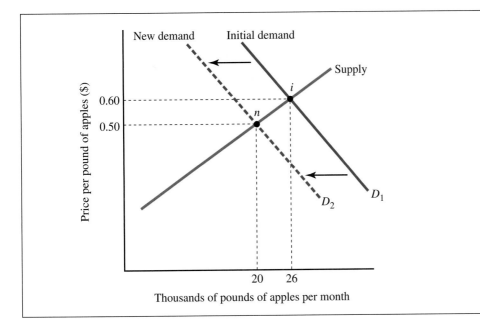

Figure 4.12
Market Effects of Pesticide Residue

A report of pesticide residue on apples decreases the demand for apples, shifting the demand curve to the left. Equilibrium is restored at point *n*, with a lower price ($0.50, down from $0.60) and a smaller quantity (20,000 pounds, down from 26,000 pounds).

apples made them unsafe for infants and small children. Although many experts disputed the report, it decreased the demand for apples. In Figure 4.12, the initial equilibrium is shown by point *i*, with a price of $0.60 per pound and a quantity of 26,000 pounds per month. The pesticide report shifted the demand curve to the left, leading to a new equilibrium at point *n*, with a lower equilibrium price ($0.50) and a smaller equilibrium quantity (20,000 pounds). The decrease in demand decreased the equilibrium price and the equilibrium quantity of apples.

How does an increase in the price of air travel affect automobile travel and highway deaths? For the answer, read "A Closer Look: Infant Airline Seats and Safety."

Changes in Supply: Technology, Weather

How do technological innovations affect equilibrium prices? Recent innovations in electronics have decreased the cost of producing personal computers. In Figure 4.13 the initial equilibrium is shown by point *i*. The decrease in production costs increases the supply of personal computers, shifting the supply curve to the right. The new equilibrium is shown by point *n*: The equilibrium price decreases from $1,000 to $800, and the equilibrium quantity increases from 20,000 to 30,000 computers per month. The personal computer is just one example of the many goods that are made affordable by technological innovations that decreased production costs and prices.

How does poor weather affect equilibrium prices? In 1992, several events combined to decrease the world supply of coffee and increase its price. Poor weather and insect infestations in Brazil and Colombia decreased the coffee-bean harvest by about 40%. In addition, a slowdown by dockworkers at Santos, Brazil's main coffee port, decreased the amount supplied to the world market. In Figure 4.14, the initial equilibrium is shown by point *i*, with a price of $0.60 per pound. The poor weather, insect infestations, and other supply disruptions shifted the supply curve to the left, and the new equilibrium is shown by point *n*. The equilibrium price of coffee increased to $0.72 per pound, and the equilibrium quantity decreased from 30 million to 22 million pounds per month.

Figure 4.13

Technological Innovation and the Computer Market
Technological innovation decreases production costs, increasing supply and shifting the supply curve to the right. The equilibrium price decreases, and the equilibrium quantity increases.

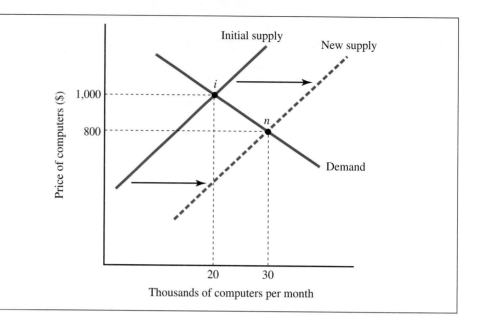

The Economic Detective

We can use the information in Table 4.5 to play economic detective. Suppose we observe changes in the equilibrium price and quantity of a particular good, but we don't know what caused these changes. It could have been a change in demand or a change in supply. We can use the information in Table 4.5 to work backwards, using what we observe about changes in prices and quantities to discover the reason for the changes. We discuss three cases for the economic detective: an increase in the consumption of poultry products, a decrease in the price of illegal drugs, and the budgetary effects of the tobacco settlement.

Figure 4.14

Bad Weather and the Coffee Market
Bad weather decreases the supply of coffee beans, shifting the supply curve to the left. Equilibrium is restored at point *n*, with a higher price ($0.72, up from $0.60) and a smaller quantity (22 million pounds, down from 30 million pounds).

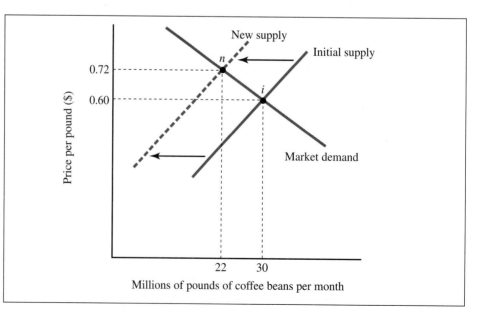

A CLOSER LOOK | Infant Airline Seats and Safety

Should parents traveling by airplane be allowed to hold their infants in their laps? Or should they be required to buy a ticket for each infant and strap them into safety seats? A law requiring separate tickets and seats for infants would generate good news and bad news.

- Good news: Fewer infants would die in airline crashes because infants are safer in their own seats on aircraft.
- Bad news: More people would die in car crashes. A law requiring parents to buy tickets for infants would increase the cost of traveling by air, causing some parents to switch from flying to driving. Driving is actually more dangerous than flying: The number of people injured or killed per 100,000 miles traveled is much higher in cars.

There is an ongoing dispute between two federal agencies over infant safety seats for air travel. Since 1979 the National Transportation Safety Board has recommended that safety seats be mandatory, while the Federal Aviation Administration has used its regulatory authority to prevent such rules. Ultimately, the Congress will resolve this dispute.

The lesson from this example is that consumers respond to changes in prices. An increase in the price of one good (air travel) causes some consumers to switch to a substitute good (highway travel), leading to some unexpected results.

An increase in the price of air travel will cause some consumers to switch to highway travel, which is actually more dangerous.

Source: "Effort Under Way to Revamp Laws on Child Safety," *Oregonian*, March 23, 1997, p. A20.

The Mystery of Increasing Poultry Consumption

Why has the consumption of poultry (chicken and turkey) increased so much over the last several decades? One possibility is that consumers have become more health conscious and have switched from red meat to poultry as part of an effort to eat healthier food. In other words, the demand curve for poultry may have shifted to the right, increasing the equilibrium quantity of poultry. Of course, an increase in demand will increase the price too, so if this explanation is correct, we should also observe higher prices for poultry.

According to the U.S. Department of Agriculture, this popular explanation is incorrect.[1] In fact, the increase in poultry consumption was caused by an increase in supply, not an increase in demand. This conclusion is based on the fact that poultry prices have been decreasing, not increasing. Between 1950 and 1990, the real price of poultry (adjusted for inflation) decreased by about 75%. As shown in Figure 4.15, an increase in supply causes the market equilibrium to shift from point i (price = $2 and quantity = 50 million pounds) to point n (price = $0.80 and quantity = 90 million pounds). The increase in supply decreases the equilibrium price. The supply of poultry increased because innovations in poultry processing decreased the cost of producing poultry products. The lesson here is that we shouldn't jump to conclusions based on limited information. A change in the equilibrium quantity could result from either a change in supply or a change in demand. To draw any conclusions, we need information about both price and quantity.

There may be a grain of truth in the popular explanation. It is possible that both demand and supply increased, shifting both curves to the right. Because the price of poultry decreased, however, we know that the shift of the supply curve (which tends to decrease the price) overwhelmed any shift of the demand curve (which tends to increase the price). Although changes in consumer preferences might contribute to increasing poultry consumption, the changes in consumption were caused largely by changes on the supply side of the market.

The Mystery of Falling Cocaine Prices

Ted Koppel, host of the ABC news program *Nightline*, once said, "Do you know what's happened to the price of drugs in the United States? The price of cocaine, way down, the price of marijuana, way down. You don't have to be an expert in economics to know that when the price goes down, it means more stuff is coming in. That's supply and demand."[2] According to Koppel, the price of drugs dropped because the government's efforts to control the supply of illegal drugs had failed. In other words, the lower price resulted from an increase in supply. According to the U.S. Department of Justice, the quantity of drugs consumed actually decreased during the period of dropping prices.[3] Is Koppel's economic detective work sound?

In this case, both the price and the quantity decreased. As shown in the second row of Table 4.5, when both the price and the quantity decrease, that means demand has decreased. In Figure 4.16 a decrease in demand shifts the demand curve to the left, and

Figure 4.15

The Mystery of Increasing Poultry Consumption

Because the price of poultry decreased at the same time the quantity of poultry consumed increased, we know that the increase in consumption resulted from an increase in supply, not an increase in demand. Innovations in poultry processing decreased production costs, shifting the supply curve to the right.

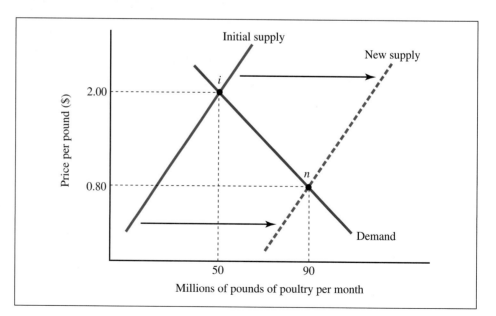

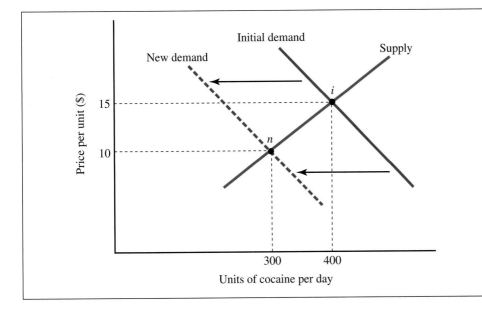

Figure 4.16

The Mystery of Lower Drug Prices
Because the quantity of cocaine consumed decreased at the same time the price of cocaine decreased, we know that the decrease in price resulted from a decrease in demand, not an increase in supply. A decrease in the demand for cocaine decreased the price and decreased the quantity consumed.

the market moves from point i (price = $15 and quantity = 400 units per day) to point n (price = $10 and quantity = 300 units per day). Koppel's explanation (an increase in supply) would be correct if the quantity of drugs increased at the same time that the price decreased. Because the quantity of drugs consumed actually decreased during the period of dropping prices, Koppel's explanation is incorrect. Lower demand—not a failure of the government's drug policy and an increase in supply—was responsible for the decrease in drug prices.

The Tobacco Settlement and Revenue for Health-Care Programs
At the beginning of this chapter, we presented a puzzle for a state budget analyst. The analyst expected the state support for programs dealing with tobacco-related illness to be $280 million per year, including $80 million from the tobacco settlement and $200 million from the state's cigarette tax. In fact, the state provided only $250 million. What happened?

The key to solving this mystery is the fact that the agreement will decrease the quantity of cigarettes purchased. Cigarette producers responded to the agreement by increasing the price of cigarettes by about 40 cents per pack. Consistent with the law of demand, the increase in price decreased the quantity demanded, decreasing the revenue from the cigarette tax. In Figure 4.17 an increase in price from $3.00 to $3.40 causes movement upward along the initial demand curve from point i to point p, decreasing the quantity sold from 80 million to 72 million packs per year. The agreement also required cigarette makers to reduce their advertising and marketing activities. As a result, the demand curve shifted to the left, as shown in Figure 4.17. The cutback in advertising reduced the quantity sold from 72 million packs per year (point p) to 50 million packs per year (point n). The net effect of the agreement is to decrease the quantity of cigarettes sold—and taxed—from 80 million to 50 million packs per year. With a tax of $1 per pack, that means that the state's revenue from the cigarette tax falls from $80 million to $50 million.

For another mystery that can be solved with a few clues and some simple economic analysis, consider the market for amber, a semiprecious material made of fossilized resin

Figure 4.17

The Mystery of the Tobacco Money

The tobacco settlement increases the price of cigarettes from $3.00 to $3.40, causing movement upward along the original demand curve from point *i* to point *p*, decreasing the quantity consumed from 80 million to 72 million packs. The reduction in advertising and marketing shifts the demand curve to the left, reducing the quantity demanded at the new price ($3.40) from 72 million (point *p*) to 50 million packs (point *n*).

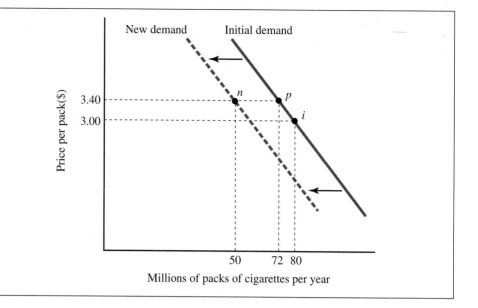

from prehistoric trees. Some pieces of amber contain the preserved remains of plants and animals from millions of years ago—including mosquitoes, which may have feasted on dinosaurs during the Jurassic period. The market price of amber tripled during 1993. Why? See "A Closer Look: Jurassic Park and the Price of Amber." ◆

A CLOSER LOOK   Jurassic Park and the Price of Amber

Scientists who use amber to study fossils and extinct animals were shocked when the price of amber tripled during 1993. Because the equilibrium quantity of amber increased along with its price, the increase in price was caused by an increase in demand, not a decrease in supply. The increase in demand coincided with the release of the movie Jurassic Park, in which scientists use specimens from amber to clone dinosaurs. Many of the people who saw the movie bought amber specimens, and this new consumer demand increased the demand for amber. The demand curve shifted to the right, increasing the equilibrium price and quantity.

Source: Tim Friend, "Dino-Craze Sends Sales of Amber with Insects Buzzing," *USA Today*, June 17, 1993, p. A1.

Amber contains the preserved remains of mosquitoes that feasted on dinosaurs. In 1993 the price of amber tripled.

TEST Your Understanding

14. Complete the statement with "supply" or "demand": If the price and quantity change in the same direction, _____ is changing; if the price and quantity change in opposite directions, _____ is changing.

15. Suppose a freeze in Florida wipes out 20% of the orange crop. How will this affect the equilibrium price of Florida oranges? Defend your answer with a graph.

16. Suppose that between 2000 and 2001, the equilibrium price and the equilibrium quantity of amber both decrease. Draw a supply-demand diagram that explains these changes.

Using the TOOLS

In this chapter you learned how to use two tools of economics—the supply curve and the demand curve—to find equilibrium prices to predict changes in prices and quantities. Here are some opportunities to use these tools to do your own economic analysis.

1. ECONOMIC EXPERIMENT: Market Equilibrium

The simple experiment takes about 20 minutes. We start by dividing the class into two equal groups: consumers and producers.

- The instructor provides each consumer with a number indicating the maximum amount he or she is willing to pay (WTP) for a bushel of apples: The WTP is a number between $1 and $100. Each consumer has the opportunity to buy 1 bushel of apples per trading period. The consumer's score for a single trading period equals the gap between his or her WTP and the price actually paid for apples. For example, if the consumer's WTP is $80 and he or she pays only $30 for apples, the consumer's score is $50. Each consumer has the option of not buying apples. This will be sensible if the best price the consumer can get exceeds his or her WTP. If the consumer does not buy apples, his or her score will be zero.

- The instructor provides each producer with a number indicating the cost of producing a bushel of apples (a number between $1 and $100). Each producer has the opportunity to sell 1 bushel per trading period. The producer's score for a single trading period equals the gap between the selling price and the cost of producing apples. So if a producer sells apples for $20 and his or her cost is only $15, the producer's score is $5. Producers have the option of not selling apples, which is sensible if the best price the producer can get is less than his or her cost. If the producer does not sell apples, his or her score is zero.

Once everyone understands the rules, consumers and producers meet in a trading area to arrange transactions. A consumer may announce how much he or she is willing to pay for apples and wait for a producer to agree to sell apples at that price. Alternatively, a producer may announce how much he or she is willing to accept for apples and wait for a consumer to agree to buy apples at that price. Once a transaction has been arranged, the consumer and producer inform the instructor of the trade, record the transaction, and leave the trading area.

There are several trading periods, each of which lasts a few minutes. After the end of each trading period, the instructor lists the prices at which apples sold during that period. Then another trading period starts, providing consumers and producers another opportunity to buy or sell 1 bushel of apples. After all the trading periods have been completed, each participant computes his or her score by adding the scores from each trading period.

2. Using Data to Draw a Demand Curve

The following table shows data on gasoline prices and gasoline consumption in a particular city. Is it possible to use these data to draw a demand curve? If so, draw the demand curve. If not, why not?

Year	Gasoline Price (per gallon)	Quantity Consumed (millions of gallons)
1999	1.20	400
2000	1.40	300
2001	1.60	360

3. Foreign Farm Workers and the Price of Berries

Current law allows thousands of Mexican workers to work on farms in the United States during harvest season. Suppose a new law outlaws the use of foreign farm workers. Assume that the resulting excess demand for labor increases the wage paid to farm workers by 20%. Use a supply-demand graph to predict the effects of the higher wage on the price of berries.

4. Market Effects of an Import Ban on Shoes

Consider a nation that initially imports half the shoes it consumes. Use a supply-demand graph to predict the effect of a ban on shoe imports on the equilibrium price and quantity of shoes.

5. The Mystery of Free Used Newspapers

In 1987 you could sell a ton of used newspapers for $60. Five years later, you could not sell them at any price. In other words, the price of used newspapers dropped from $60 to zero in just five years. Over this period the quantity of used newspapers bought and sold increased. What caused the drop in price? Defend your answer with a supply-demand graph.

Summary

In this chapter we've seen how supply and demand determine prices. And we saw how to predict the effects of changes in demand or supply on prices. Here are the main points of the chapter.

1. To draw a demand curve, we must be certain the other determinants of demand (consumer income, prices of related goods, tastes, expectations, and number of consumers) are held fixed.

2. To draw a market supply curve, we must be certain the other determinants of supply (input costs, technology, the number of producers, expectations, taxes and subsidies) are held fixed.

3. An equilibrium in a market is shown by the intersection of the demand curve and the supply curve. When a market reaches an equilibrium, there is no pressure to change the price.

4. A change in demand changes price and quantity in the same direction: An increase in demand increases the equilibrium price and quantity; a decrease in demand decreases the equilibrium price and quantity.

5. A change in supply changes price and quantity in opposite directions: An increase in supply decreases price and increases quantity; a decrease in supply increases price and decreases quantity.

Key Terms

Change in demand, 73
Change in quantity demanded, 66
Change in quantity supplied, 69
Change in supply, 77
Complements, 74
Demand schedule, 65
Excess demand, 71
Excess supply, 72

Income effect, 66
Individual demand curve, 65
Individual supply curve, 69
Inferior good, 76
Law of demand, 65
Law of supply, 69
Market demand curve, 66
Market equilibrium, 71

Market supply curve, 70
Normal good, 73
Perfectly competitive market, 64
Substitutes, 73
Substitution effect, 66
Supply schedule, 69

Problems and Discussion Questions

1. Figure 4.A shows the supply and demand curves for CD players. Complete the following statements.

   a. At the market equilibrium (shown by point _____), the price of CD players is _____ and the quantity of CD players is _____.

   b. At a price of $100, there would be excess_____, so we would expect the price to _____ (fill in with increase or decrease).

   c. At a price exceeding the equilibrium price, there would be excess _____ so we would expect the price to _____ (fill in with increase or decrease).

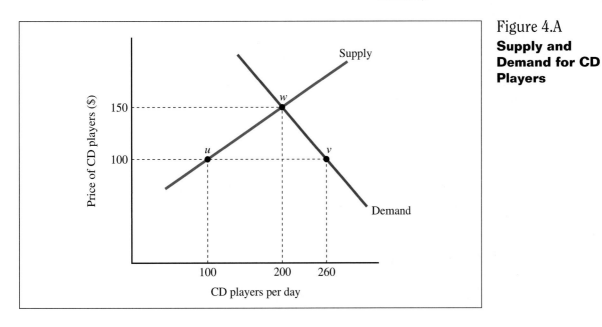

Figure 4.A
Supply and Demand for CD Players

2. The following table shows the quantities of corn supplied and demanded at different prices:

Price per Ton	Quantity Supplied	Quantity Demanded	Excess demand or Excess Supply
$ 80	600	1,200	_____
$ 90	800	1,100	_____
$100	1,000	1,000	_____
$110	1,200	900	_____

   a. Complete the table.

   b. Draw the demand curve and the supply curve.

   c. What is the equilibrium price of corn?

3. Consider the market for personal computers. Suppose that the demand is stable: The demand curve doesn't change. Predict the effects of the following changes on the equilibrium price of computers. Illustrate your answer with a supply and demand diagram.

   a. The cost of memory chips (one component of a computer) decreases.

   b. The government imposes a $100 tax on personal computers.

4. Draw a supply-demand diagram to illustrate the effect of an increase in income on the market for restaurant meals.

5. Suppose that the tuition charged by public universities increases. Draw a supply-demand diagram to illustrate the effects of the tuition hike on the market for private college education.

6. Suppose that the government imposes a tax of $1 per pound of fish and collects the tax from fish producers. Draw a supply-demand diagram to illustrate the market effects of the tax.

7. As summer approaches, the equilibrium price of rental cabins increases and the equilibrium quantity of cabins rented increases. Draw a supply-demand diagram that explains these changes.

8. Suppose that the initial price of a pocket phone is $100 and that the initial quantity demanded is 500 phones per day. Depict graphically the effects of a technological innovation that decreases the cost of producing pocket phones. Label the starting point with an *i* and the new equilibrium with an *n*.

9. You've been hired as an economic consultant to evaluate the nation's airport security systems (metal detectors and machines that allow security people to see what's inside carry-on luggage). Suppose these security systems add $5 to the typical airplane ticket and require 10 minutes of extra time for each passenger. List the questions you will answer in your evaluation.

10. Suppose a freeze in Florida wipes out 20% of the orange crop. How will this affect the equilibrium price of California oranges? Defend your answer with a graph.

11. The Multifiber Agreement sets import quotas for various apparel products—including shirts—coming into the United States. Use a supply-demand graph to show the effects of the shirt quota on the equilibrium price of shirts in the United States.

12. Web Exercise: Visit the Web site of the National Association of Realtors: *(http://www.realtor.com)*. Follow the "Find a Home" instructions and check housing prices for a three-bedroom, two-bath house in several cities, for example, San Francisco, California; Topeka, Kansas; Dallas, Texas; Concord, Massachusetts; and Seattle, Washington. Use supply and demand diagrams to explain why housing prices vary from city to city.

13. Web Exercise: Visit the Web site of eBay, a company that provides on-line auctions *(http://www.ebay.com)*. Suppose you want to buy a traditional 35mm camera. Access the listing of cameras being auctioned and check the most recent bids. Suppose someone develops a digital camera that takes better pictures than the traditional 35mm camera at half the cost. Predict the effects of the new camera on the supply of traditional 35mm cameras and the prices for cameras auctioned on the ebay site.

Take It to the Net

We invite you to visit the O'Sullivan/Sheffrin page on the Prentice Hall Web site at:
http://www.prenhall.com/osullivan/
for additional World Wide Web exercises for this chapter.

Model Answers for Questions

Chapter-Opening Questions

1. As is explained in A Closer Look on page 85, fewer infants would die in airplane crashes, but more people would die in automobile crashes as many parents responded to the higher cost of airline travel by switching to the alternative travel mode.

2. As is explained in one of the Economic Detective exercises, a lower price doesn't necessarily mean that supply has increased. The equilibrium quantity decreased at the same time, so the price drop was caused by a decrease in demand.

3. As is explained in one of the "Using the Tools" exercises, we can't draw a demand curve from a table of price and quantity data unless we know that the other determinants of demand (income, population, prices of substitutes and complementary goods, tastes, advertising) are fixed over the period covered by the data.

4. Innovations in poultry processing decreased the cost of producing poultry products. The resulting increase in supply decreased the equilibrium price, causing consumers to buy more poultry products.

Test Your Understanding

1. decrease, increase

2. Consumer income, the prices of substitute goods, the prices of complementary goods, consumer tastes, advertising, the number of consumers, and price expectations.

3. Input costs, technology, price expectations, number of producers, taxes and subsidies

4. supply, demand

5. less, greater

6. demand, supply

7. One group is a, e, and f; another group is b, c, and d.

8. The statement is incorrect because it confuses the direction of causality. The correct statement is: "The demand curve shifted because demand increased." When something other than the price of the product changes, the relationship between price and quantity changes, causing the demand curve to shift.

9. right, left

10. Circle quantity of pencils demanded and price of pencils. Cross out number of consumers, price of pens, and consumer income.

11. One group is a, c, and e; another group is b, d, and f.

12. True. An increase in the wage increases production cost, so fewer computers will be supplied at each price.

13. Circle quantity of housing supplied and price of houses. Cross out number of consumers, price of wood, and consumer income.

14. demand, supply

15. The supply of oranges decreases, shifting the supply curve to the left. The equilibrium price will increase.

16. The demand decreases, shifting the demand curve to the left (an end to the Jurassic Park fad buying?), decreasing both the price and the quantity.

Using the Tools

2. Using Data to Draw a Demand Curve. It's tempting to use the data in the table to plot three combinations of price and quantity, connect the points with a curve, call it a demand curve. That is not appropriate because we don't know what happened to the other determinants of the demand for gasoline over this period (consumer income, prices of substitutes and complements, tastes, advertising, price expectations). To draw a demand curve with these data, we must have additional data showing that these other variables did not change. If any of these other variables changed, we cannot draw a demand curve.

3. Foreign Farm Workers and the Price of Berries. The higher wage caused by the elimination of foreign farm workers will increase the production costs of berry farmers. The resulting decrease in supply of berries will shift the supply curve to the left. In Figure 4.B, the equilibrium price of berries increases from $0.60 to $0.73.

Figure 4.B

Market Effects of Higher Farm Wages

Reducing the number of foreign farm workers will increase the wage of farm workers, increasing the production costs of berry producers. The supply curve shifts to the left: At each price, a smaller quantity is supplied. Equilibrium is restored at point *n*, with a higher price ($0.73, up from $0.60) and a smaller quantity (16,000 pounds, down from 20,000 pounds).

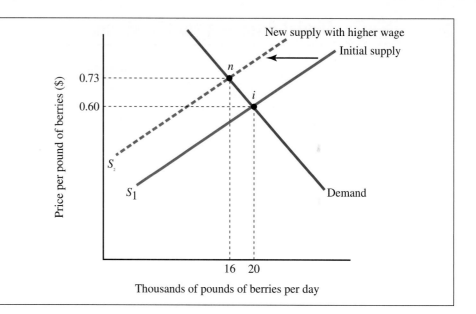

4. Market Effects of an Import Ban. An import ban has the same effect as a decrease in the number of firms in the market: supply decreases, shifting the market supply curve to the left. In Figure 4.C, the free-trade equilibrium is shown by point *f*, and the equilibrium with an import ban is shown by point *b*. The ban on imported shoes increases the price of shoes from $25 to $34.

5. The Mystery of Free Used Newspapers. Between 1987 and 1992 the price and quantity moved in opposite directions, meaning that the decrease in price was caused by an increase in supply. Over this five-year period, hundreds of communities adopted curbside recycling programs. These programs increased the supply of used newspapers, generating an excess supply of used newspapers that decreased the equilibrium price. In Figure 4.D, the increase in supply was so large that the equilibrium price fell to zero.

Figure 4.C

The Market Effects of an Import Ban

A ban on shoe imports decreases the supply of shoes, shifting the supply curve to the left. The free-trade equilibrium is shown by point *f*, and the equilibrium under the import ban is shown by point *b*. The import ban increases the price from $25 to $34 and decreases the quantity from 12 million to 9 million pairs of shoes.

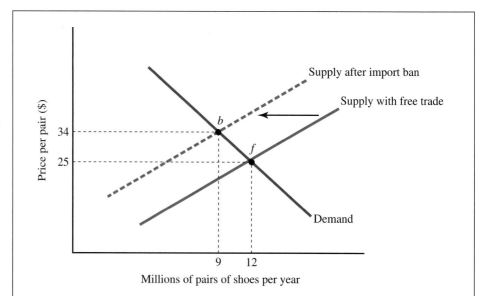

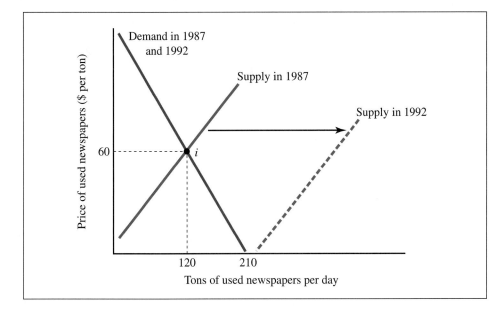

Figure 4.D

The Mystery of Free Used Newspapers

Between 1987 and 1992 the price of used newspapers decreased from $60 per ton to zero, a result of increases in supply caused by the expansion of curbside recycling programs.

Notes

1. Mark R. Weimar and Richard Stillman, Market Trends Driving Broiler Consumption, Livestock and Poultry Situation and Outlook Report LPS-44 (Washington, DC: U.S. Department of Agriculture, Economic Research Service, November 1990).

2. Kenneth R. Clark, "Legalize Drugs. A Case for Koppel," Chicago Tribune, August 30, 1988, sec. 5, p. 8.

3. U.S. Department of Justice, Drugs, Crime, and the Justice System (Washington, DC: U.S. Government Printing Office, 1992), p. 30.

CHAPTER

5

Elasticity: A Measure of Responsiveness

In every large city in the United States, the public bus system runs a deficit: The total revenue from passenger fares is less than the cost of operating the bus system. Suppose your city wants to reduce its bus deficit and has decided to increase bus fares by 10%. Consider the following exchange between two city officials:

Buster: A fare increase is a great idea. We'll collect more money from bus riders, so revenue will increase and the deficit will shrink.

Bessie: Wait a minute, Buster. Haven't you heard about the law of demand? The increase in the bus fare will decrease the number of passengers taking buses, so we'll collect less money, not more, and the deficit will grow.

Who is right? As we'll see in this chapter, we can't predict how an increase in price will affect total revenue unless we know just how responsive consumers are to an increase in price. Like other consumers, bus riders obey the law of demand, but that doesn't necessarily mean that total fare revenue will fall.

Price elasticity of demand: A measure of the responsiveness of the quantity demanded to changes in price; computed by dividing the percentage change in quantity demanded by the percentage change in price.

Price elasticity of supply: A measure of the responsiveness of the quantity supplied to changes in price; computed by dividing the percentage change in quantity supplied by the percentage change in price.

From Chapter 4, we know that the quantity of a product demanded is determined by the price of the product, consumer income, and the prices of related goods. In this chapter, we'll use the concept of elasticity to measure the responsiveness of the quantity demanded to changes in these variables. The **price elasticity of demand** measures the responsiveness of quantity demanded to changes in the price of the product. We say that demand is elastic if a small change in price causes a large change in quantity demanded. Demand is inelastic if the quantity does not change very much as price changes. As we'll see later in the chapter, because the demand for bus service is inelastic, Buster is correct: An increase in the bus fare will increase total revenue. We can also use the concept of elasticity to measure the responsiveness of consumer demand to changes in the other factors that affect demand: consumer income, the price of substitute goods, and the price of complementary goods.

Switching to the supply side of the market, we can use elasticity to measure the responsiveness of the quantity supplied to changes in price. We know from Chapter 4 that an increase in price will increase the quantity supplied, but sometimes the question is, How much more will be supplied at the higher price? The **price elasticity of supply** measures the responsiveness of quantity supplied to changes in price. We say that supply is elastic if a small change in price causes a large change in the quantity supplied. In contrast, if producers are not very responsive, we say that supply is inelastic.

This chapter contains many applications of the concept of elasticity. Here are some practical questions that we answer:

1. **How would a tax on beer affect the number of highway deaths among young adults?**
2. **Why is a bumper crop bad news for farmers?**
3. **If a firm wants to increase its total revenue, should it raise or lower its price?**
4. **Why do policies that limit the supply of illegal drugs increase the number of burglaries and robberies?**
5. **If the demand for a product increases, what information do we need to predict the resulting change in the equilibrium price?**

The Price Elasticity of Demand

When the price of a good decreases, consumers will buy more of it, but how much more will they buy? The price elasticity of demand (E_d) measures the responsiveness of consumers to changes in price. We compute the price elasticity of demand by dividing the percentage change in the quantity demanded by the percentage change in price:

$$E_d = \frac{\text{percentage change in quantity demanded}}{\text{percentage change in price}}$$

As we saw in the appendix to Chapter 1, the simple way to compute the percentage change in a variable is to divide the change in the variable by the initial value of the variable. Suppose the price of milk increases from $2.00 to $2.20. (The appendix to this chapter shows how to compute the price elasticity with the more precise midpoint formula described in the appendix to Chapter 1.)

We can use the numbers shown in Figure 5.1 to compute the price elasticity of demand for milk as follows:

- The percentage change in price equals the change in price (+$0.20) divided by the initial price ($2.00), or +10% (equal to +$0.20 divided by $2.00).

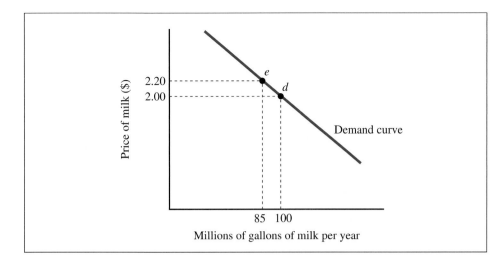

Figure 5.1

Market Demand Curve and Price Elasticity of Demand
A 10% rise in the price of milk (from $2 to $2.20) decreases the quantity demanded by 15% (from 100 to 85), so the price elasticity of demand is 1.50 = 15%/10%.

- The percentage change in quantity demanded equals the change in quantity (−15 million) divided by the initial quantity (100 million), or −15% (equal to −15 million divided by 100 million).

The conventional practice is to ignore any minus signs and compute the price elasticity as follows:

$$E_d = \frac{\text{percentage change in quantity demanded}}{\text{percentage change in price}} = \frac{15\%}{10\%} = 1.5$$

In this example, the price elasticity of demand, E_d, is equal to 1.5.

Why do we ignore the minus sign? The law of demand tells us that price and quantity move in opposite directions, so the percentage change in quantity will always have the opposite sign (+ or −) of the percentage change in price (− or +). In our example, a +10% change in price results in a −15% change in quantity. So to be absolutely precise, the price elasticity should be reported as a negative number. The conventional approach is to report all price elasticities as positive numbers. This means that a large number indicates that the quantity demanded is very elastic, or highly responsive to changes in price. As long as we remember the law of demand, there is no harm in dropping minus signs and reporting all price elasticities of demand as positive numbers.

The responsiveness of consumers to price changes varies from one good to another. An increase in the price of table salt doesn't change the quantity of salt demanded very much, but an increase in the price of a specific brand of corn flakes causes a large reduction in the quantity demanded. We can use the concept of price elasticity of demand to divide goods into three groups:

- **Elastic.** If the price elasticity of demand for a particular good is greater than 1.0, we say that demand is elastic. This is sensible because if the elasticity is greater than 1.0, the percentage change in quantity demanded exceeds the percentage change in price, meaning that consumers are very responsive to changes in price.

- **Inelastic.** If the price elasticity of demand is less than 1.0, consumers are not very responsive to changes in price, and we say that demand is inelastic.

- **Unitary elastic.** If the elasticity equals 1.0, the percentage change in quantity demanded equals the percentage change in price, and we say that demand is unitary elastic.

Elasticity and Substitutes

The price elasticity of demand for a particular good depends on the availability of substitutes. Consider two goods: insulin (a medicine for diabetics) and cornflakes. There are no good substitutes for insulin, so consumers are not very responsive to changes in price: An increase in price doesn't cause a large reduction in the quantity of insulin demanded. In other words, the lack of substitutes for insulin means that the demand is inelastic. In contrast, there are many substitutes for cornflakes, including different types of corn cereal and cereals made from other grains (wheat, rice, and oats). Therefore, a small increase in the price of cornflakes will cause a large decrease in quantity demanded as consumers switch to other types of cereal whose price has not changed. In other words, if substitutes are plentiful, demand is relatively elastic.

Table 5.1 shows the price elasticities of demand for various products. The different elasticities illustrate the importance of substitutes in determining the price elasticity of demand. Because there are no good substitutes for water and salt, it's not surprising that the elasticities are small. For example, the price elasticity of demand for water (0.20) means that a 10% increase in the price of water would decrease the quantity demanded by only 2%:

$$E_d = \frac{\text{percentage change in quantity of water demanded}}{\text{percentage change in price}} = \frac{2\%}{10\%} = 0.20$$

The demand for cigarettes, an addictive good, is also inelastic. The elasticity of 0.30 means that a 10% increase in price would cause a 3% decrease in quantity demanded.

Table 5.1 Price Elasticities of Demand for Selected Products

Product	Price Elasticity of Demand
Salt	0.1
Water	0.2
Coffee	0.3
Cigarettes	0.3
Shoes and footwear	0.7
Housing	1.0
Automobiles	1.2
Foreign travel	1.8
Restaurant meals	2.3
Air travel	2.4
Motion pictures	3.7
Specific brands of coffee	5.6

Sources: Frank Chaloupka, "Rational Addictive Behavior and Cigarette Smoking," *Journal of Political Economy*, August 1991, pp. 722–742; Gregory Chow, *Demand for Automobiles in the United States* (Amsterdam: North-Holland, 1957); David Ellwood and Mitchell Polinski, "An Empirical Reconciliation of Micro and Grouped Estimates of the Demand for Housing," *Review of Economics and Statistics*, vol. 61, 1979, pp. 199–205; H. F. Houthakker and Lester B. Taylor, *Consumer Demand in the United States: Analysis and Projections*, 2nd ed. (Cambridge, MA: Harvard University Press, 1970); John R. Nevin, "Laboratory Experiments for Estimating Consumer Demand: A Validation Study," *Journal of Marketing Research*, vol. 11, August 1974, pp. 261–268; Herbert Scarf and John Shoven, *Applied General Equilibrium Analysis* (New York: Cambridge University Press, 1984).

Because there are no good substitutes for coffee, the demand for coffee is inelastic (0.30). But because different brands of coffee are substitutes for one another, the demand for a specific brand of coffee is very elastic (between 5.6 and 8.9). An elasticity of 5.6 means that a 10% increase in price of a specific brand would decrease the quantity demanded by 56%. The change in quantity is large because consumers can easily switch to other brands.

For another example of the price elasticity of demand, consider the demand for trash disposal. Until recently, most cities charged a fixed monthly fee for trash collection. Under an alternative approach, called pay-to-throw, the more trash a household generates, the higher its trash bill. In 1991, Charlottesville, Virginia, switched 75 households from a fixed monthly fee to a price of $0.80 per 32-gallon bag of trash. The new pricing plan caused the following changes among the households participating in the experiment:[1]

- The volume of trash collected decreased by 37%, to 0.46 bag per person per week. The price elasticity of demand with respect to the volume of trash was 0.23.

- The weight of trash collected decreased by 14%, to 9.37 pounds per person per week. The weight decreased by a small amount because of the "Seattle stomp," a technique that allows a person to pack more trash into each bag. (Seattle had an early experiment in pay-to-throw pricing.) The price elasticity of demand with respect to the weight of trash was 0.08.

- The weight of recyclable materials (collected at no cost to the household) increased by 16%, to 4.27 pounds per person per week.

- Illegal dumping (littering and dumping household trash in commercial dumpsters) is difficult to measure. It appears that it may have increased by about 0.5 pound per person per week.

This study has some lessons for other communities that are considering a pay-to-throw plan: Although the total volume of trash would decrease, the total weight would decrease by a small amount, and illegal dumping would increase.

Other Determinants of Elasticity

We've seen that the availability of substitute goods affects the price elasticity of demand. Several other factors affect the price elasticity of demand:

- **Time.** Because it takes time to change consumption habits and find substitute goods, the more time we give consumers to respond to a price change, the larger their response. When the price of gasoline increases, consumers' immediate response is limited by their inability to immediately buy more fuel-efficient cars or move closer to their workplaces. Eventually, consumers can change cars and relocate, so we would expect a much larger reduction in gasoline consumption in the long run. As time passes, demand becomes more elastic because consumers have more options. For another example of time and price elasticity read "A Closer Look: The Demand for International Telecommunications."

- **Importance in budget.** If a good represents a small part of the budget of the typical consumer, demand for it is relatively inelastic. If the price of pencils increases by 10% (from $0.50 to $0.55), there will be a relatively small decrease in the quantity demanded because the price change is trivial relative to the income of the typical consumer. In contrast, a 10% increase in the price of cars (from $20,000 to $22,000) will generate a much larger response because the change in price is large relative to consumer income. International comparisons of the price elasticity of demand for

The Demand for International Telecommunications

International telecommunication plays a vital role in today's global economy. In the last decade, the prices of international telephone services have dropped considerably; technological innovations have decreased the cost of providing telephone service, and deregulation has increased competition among companies providing the service. How have consumers responded to these lower prices? A study of telephone service between Sweden and the United States suggests that the price elasticity of demand is 0.51 in the short run (one year) and 1.18 in the long run (several years). In other words, a 10% drop in price increases the quantity demanded by 5.1% in the short run and 11.8% in the long run. The demand elasticities for Sweden's other major trading partners—Germany and the United Kingdom—reflected the same pattern, the long-run elasticities being higher than the short-run elasticities.

Source: Peter Hackl and Anders H. Westlund, "Demand for International Telecommunication: Time Varying Price Elasticity," *Journal of Econometrics*, vol. 70, 1996, pp. 243–260.

food suggest that demand is more price-elastic when the good represents a large part of the budget. In wealthy countries such as the United States, Canada, and Germany, the price elasticity of demand for food is around 0.15.[2] In poor countries such as India, Nigeria, and Bolivia, people spend a larger fraction of their budget on food, so they are more responsive to changes in food prices: in these countries the price elasticity is around 0.34.

- **Necessities Versus luxuries.** For necessities such as bread, rice, and potatoes, demand is relatively inelastic. For luxury goods such as restaurant meals and air travel, demand is relatively elastic. This is sensible because it is easier to do without luxury goods.

Elasticity Along a Linear Demand Curve

If a demand curve is linear—a straight line—does that mean that the elasticity of demand is the same at all points on the line? As shown in Figure 5.2, the price elasticity of demand decreases as we move downward along a linear demand curve.

- On the upper part of a linear demand curve, demand is elastic. In moving from point *r* to point *s*, the percentage change in quantity (20% = 2/10) is four times the percentage change in price (5% = 4/80), so the elasticity is 4.0.

- In the middle of a linear demand curve, the price elasticity is unitary elastic. In moving from point *t* to point *u*, the percentage change in quantity (8% = 2/25) equals the percentage change in price (8% = 4/50), so the elasticity is 1.0.

- On the lower part of a linear demand curve, demand is inelastic. In moving from point *v* to point *w*, the percentage change in quantity (5% = 2/40) is one-fourth of the percentage change in price (20% = 4/20), so the elasticity is 0.25.

Why does the price elasticity vary along a linear demand curve? It's tempting to think the elasticity is constant because a straight line has a constant slope. But that's incorrect because elasticity is measured by percentage changes, not absolute changes. As we move downward along the demand curve, we're moving in the direction of larger

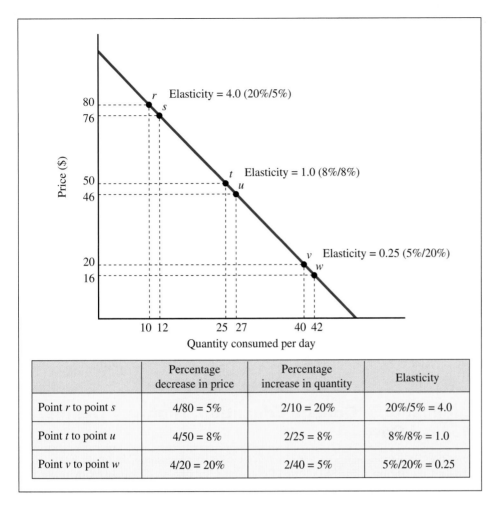

r Elasticity = 4.0 (20%/5%)

t Elasticity = 1.0 (8%/8%)

v Elasticity = 0.25 (5%/20%)

Quantity consumed per day

Figure 5.2
Price Elasticity along a Linear Demand Curve
The price elasticity of demand decreases as we move downward along a linear demand curve. Demand is elastic on the upper half of the demand curve, inelastic on the lower half, and unitary elastic at the midpoint of the demand curve.

	Percentage decrease in price	Percentage increase in quantity	Elasticity
Point *r* to point *s*	4/80 = 5%	2/10 = 20%	20%/5% = 4.0
Point *t* to point *u*	4/50 = 8%	2/25 = 8%	8%/8% = 1.0
Point *v* to point *w*	4/20 = 20%	2/40 = 5%	5%/20% = 0.25

quantities, so the same absolute change in quantity (two units) becomes a smaller percentage change in quantity. Between points *r* and *s*, the percentage change in quantity is 20% (2/10), compared to only 5% (2/40) between points *v* and *w*. At the same time, the movement downward along the curve leads to a larger percentage change in price. As a result, the elasticity becomes smaller and smaller.

TEST Your Understanding

1. Complete the statement: To compute the price elasticity of demand, we divide the percentage change in _____ by the percentage change in _____.

2. Complete the statement: If a 10% increase in price decreases the quantity demanded by 12%, the price elasticity of demand is _____.

3. Explain why the demand for prerecorded audio tapes is more elastic in the long run than in the short run.

4. If we are on the upper portion of the market demand curve and the price increases by 10%, will the quantity demanded decrease by more than 10% or by less than 10%?

Using the Price Elasticity of Demand

The price elasticity of demand is a very useful tool for economic analysis. We know from the law of demand that a decrease in price will increase the quantity demanded, ceteris paribus. If we know the elasticity of demand for a particular good, we can predict how much more of that good will be sold at the lower price. We can also predict whether an increase in price will increase or decrease total spending on the good.

Predicting Changes in Quantity Demanded

We can use the price elasticity of demand to predict what happens to the quantity demanded when the price increases. The formula for the elasticity has three variables: The price elasticity of demand (one variable) equals the percentage change in quantity (the second variable) divided by the percentage change in price (the third variable). If we know two of the three variables, we can compute the third. For example, suppose you run a campus film series and you've decided to increase your admission price by 15%. If you know the elasticity of demand for your movies, you could use the elasticity formula to predict how many fewer tickets you'll sell at the higher price. If the elasticity of demand is 2.0, a 15% price hike will decrease the quantity demanded by 30%:

$$E_d = 2.0 = \frac{\text{percentage change in quantity demanded}}{15\%} = \frac{30\%}{15\%}$$

Applications: College Education, Highway Deaths, Medical Care

How could university officials use the price elasticity of demand? Suppose a university increases its tuition from $4,000 to $4,400 and wants to predict how many fewer students will enroll in the university as a result of the higher price. The price elasticity of demand for higher education is about 1.40, so a 10% increase in tuition will decrease enrollment by 14%:

$$E_d = 1.4 = \frac{\text{percentage change in quantity demanded}}{10\%} = \frac{14\%}{10\%}$$

How would a tax on beer affect highway deaths among young adults? The price elasticity of demand for beer among young adults is about 1.30, and the number of highway deaths is roughly proportional to the group's beer consumption.[3] If a state imposes a beer tax that increases the price of beer by 20%, what will happen to the number of highway deaths among young adults? Using the elasticity formula, we predict that beer consumption will decrease by 26%:

$$E_d = 1.3 = \frac{\text{percentage change in quantity demanded}}{20\%} = \frac{26\%}{20\%}$$

If the number of highway deaths among young adults is proportional to their beer consumption, the number of highway deaths will also decrease by 26%. Of course, if young adults switch from beer to other alcoholic beverages, the number of highway deaths will decrease by a smaller amount.

If the price of medical care increases, how will consumers respond? The rising cost of medical care has forced many nations to take a closer look at programs that subsidize medical care for their citizens. If prices are increased to cover more of the costs of pro-

A CLOSER LOOK   Pricing Medical Care in Developing Countries

Many developing nations subsidize medical care, charging consumers a small fraction of the cost of providing the services. If a nation increased its price of medical care, how would the higher price affect its poor and wealthy households? In Côte d'Ivoire in Africa, the price elasticity of demand for hospital services is 0.47 for poor households and 0.29 for wealthy households. This means that a 10% increase in the price of hospital services would cause poor households to cut back their hospital care by 4.7%, while wealthy households would cut back by only 2.9%. In Peru, the differences between poor and wealthy households are even larger: The price elasticity is 0.67 for poor households but only 0.03 for wealthy households. The same pattern occurs in the demand for the medical services provided by physicians and health clinics. The poor are much more sensitive to price, so when prices increase, they suffer much larger reductions in medical care.

In developing nations, the poor are relatively sensitive to changes in the price of medical care.

Source: Paul Gertler and Jacques van der Gaag, *The Willingness to Pay for Medical Care: Evidence from Two Developing Countries* (Baltimore: Johns Hopkins University Press, 1990).

viding medical care, how will this affect poor and wealthy households? For an answer, read "A Closer Look: Pricing Medical Care in Developing Countries."

Predicting Changes in Total Revenue

If a firm increases the price of its product, will total sales revenue increase or decrease? The answer depends on the price elasticity of demand for the product. If we know the price elasticity, we can determine whether a price hike will increase or decrease the firm's total revenue.

Let's return to the example of the campus film series. Suppose you are thinking about increasing the price of tickets from $4.00 to $4.40. An increase in the ticket price brings good news and bad news:

- **Good news.** You get more money for each ticket sold.

- **Bad news.** You sell fewer tickets.

Your total revenue will decrease if the bad news (fewer tickets sold) dominates the good news (more money per ticket). The elasticity of demand tells us how the good news compares to the bad news. If demand is elastic, consumers will respond to the higher price by purchasing many fewer tickets, so although you will collect more money per ticket, you'll sell so few tickets that your total revenue will decrease. For example, as Table 5.2

Table 5.2 Price and Total Revenue with Elastic Demand

Price	Quantity of Tickets Sold	Total Revenue
4.00	100	$400
4.40	80	$352

shows, if the price elasticity of demand is 2.0, a 10% increase in price will decrease the quantity demanded by 20%, from 100 to 80 tickets. Because the percentage decrease in quantity (the bad news) exceeds the percentage increase in price (the good news), total revenue decreases, from $400 to $352.

In general, an elastic demand means that the percentage change in quantity (the bad news from a price hike) will exceed the percentage change in price (the good news), so an increase in price will decrease total revenue.

We get the opposite result if the demand for the good is inelastic: An increase in price increases total revenue. If demand is inelastic, consumers are not very responsive to an increase in price, so the good news (more money per unit sold) dominates the bad news (fewer units sold). For example, suppose that the campus bookstore starts with a textbook price of $50 and a quantity of 100 books. If the bookstore increases its price by 10% (from $50 to $55 per book) and the elasticity of demand for textbooks is 0.40, the quantity of textbooks sold will decrease by only 4% (from 100 to 96). Therefore, the store's total revenue will be $5,280 ($55 times 96), compared to only $5,000 at the lower price ($50 times 100). In general, an inelastic demand means that the percentage change in quantity will be smaller than the percentage change in price, so an increase in price will increase total revenue.

Table 5.3 summarizes the revenue effects of changes in prices for different types of goods:

- **Elastic demand.** There is a negative relationship between price and total revenue: An increase in price decreases total revenue; a decrease in price increases total revenue.

- **Inelastic demand.** There is a positive relationship between price and total revenue: An increase in price increases total revenue; a decrease in price decreases total revenue.

- **Unitary elastic demand.** Total revenue does not vary with price.

The relationship between elasticity and total revenue provides a simple test of whether demand is elastic or inelastic. Suppose that when a music store increases the price of its CDs, its total revenue from CDs drops. The negative relationship between price and total revenue means that demand for the store's CDs is elastic: Total revenue decreases because consumers are very responsive to an increase in price, buying a much smaller quantity. In contrast, suppose that when a city increases the price it charges for water, the total revenue from water sales increases. The positive relationship between

Table 5.3 Elasticity and Total Revenue

Type of Demand	Value of Price Elasticity of Demand	Change in Quantity Versus Change in Price	Effect of Higher Price on Total Revenue	Effect of Lower Price on Total Revenue
Elastic	Greater than 1.0	Larger percentage change in quantity	Decreases	Increases
Inelastic	Less than 1.0	Smaller percentage change in quantity	Increases	Decreases
Unitary elastic	1.0	Same percentage changes in quantity and price	Does not change	Does not change

price and total revenue suggests that the demand for the city's water is inelastic: Total revenue increases because consumers are not responsive to an increase in price.

We can use Figure 5.3 to reinforce what we've learned about price elasticity and total revenue. Panel A shows a linear demand curve (the same as the one in Figure 5.2), and Panel B shows the total revenue curve associated with the demand curve. We know that demand is elastic along the upper half of a linear demand curve: that means that a decrease in price will increase the quantity sold by a larger percentage amount. As a result, total revenue will increase, as shown by the positively sloped total-revenue curve between points *b* and *c*. In contrast, demand is inelastic along the lower half of a linear demand curve; that means that a decrease in price will increase the quantity sold by a smaller percentage amount. As a result, total revenue will decrease, as shown by the negatively sloped total-revenue curve between points *c* and *d*. The total-revenue curve will reach its maximum at the midpoint of the linear demand curve, where demand is unitary elastic. In Figure 5.3, demand is unitary elastic at point *t* on the demand curve, so total revenue reaches its maximum at $1,250 at point *c* on the total-revenue curve.

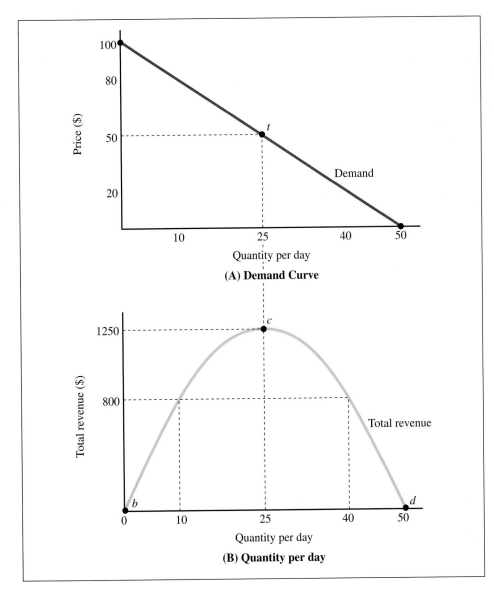

Figure 5.3

Elasticity and Total Revenue
Demand is elastic along the upper half of a linear demand curve, so a decrease in price increases total revenue. Demand is inelastic along the lower half of a linear demand curve, so a decrease in price decreases total revenue. Total revenue reaches its maximum at the midpoint of the demand curve, where demand is unitary elastic.

(A) Demand Curve

(B) Quantity per day

Applications: Transit Deficits, Property Crime

At the beginning of the chapter, we considered the question of whether increasing the price of bus rides would reduce a city's transit deficit. Now we know that to answer the question, we need to know the price elasticity of demand for bus service. The price elasticity in the typical city is 0.33, meaning that a 10% increase in fares will decrease ridership by about 3.3%.[4] Because demand for bus travel is inelastic, the good news associated with a fare hike (more revenue per rider) will dominate the bad news (fewer riders), and total fare revenue will increase. In other words, an increase in fares will reduce the transit deficit.

What's the connection between antidrug policies and property crimes such as robbery, burglary, and auto theft? The government uses search-and-destroy tactics to restrict the supply of illegal drugs. If this approach succeeds, drugs become scarce and the price of drugs increases. Because the demand for illegal drugs is inelastic, the increase in price will increase total spending on illegal drugs. Many drug addicts support their habits by stealing personal property—robbing people, stealing cars, and burglarizing homes—so the increase in total spending on drugs means that drug addicts will commit more property crimes.[5] To support their more expensive drug habits, addicts will commit more burglaries, robberies, and auto thefts.

ECONOMIC
DETECTIVE

The Video Elasticity Mystery

The manager of a video-rental store has asked you to solve a mystery. According to national studies of the video-rental market, the price elasticity of demand for video rentals is 0.80: A 10% increase in price decreases the quantity of videos demanded by about 8%. In other words, the demand for videos is inelastic. Based on this information, the manager of the video store increased her price by 20%, expecting her total revenue to increase. She expected the good news (more money per rental) to dominate the bad news (fewer rentals). When her total revenue decreased instead of increasing, she was puzzled. Your job is to solve this mystery.

The key to solving this mystery is to recognize that the manager can't use the results of a national study to predict the effects of increasing her own price. The national study suggests that if all video stores in the nation increased their prices by 10%, the nationwide quantity of videos demanded would drop by 8%. But when a single video store in a city increases its price, consumers can easily switch to other video stores in the city. As a result, a 10% increase in the price of video rentals at one store will decrease the quantity sold by that store by much more than 8%. The demand facing an individual store is elastic, so an increase in price will decrease total revenue. ◆

TEST Your Understanding

5. Complete the statement: If the price elasticity of demand is 0.60, a 10% increase in price will _____ (fill in with *increase* or *decrease*) the quantity demanded by _____%.

6. If an increase in the price of accordions does not change total revenue from accordion sales, what can we infer about the price elasticity of demand for accordions?

7. Suppose the price elasticity of demand for vanity license plates in the state of Ohio is 2.60. If the state's objective is to maximize its revenue from vanity plates, should it pick a higher price or a lower one?

Other Elasticities of Demand

We've seen that the price elasticity of demand measures the responsiveness of consumers to changes in the price of a particular good. Of course, the demand for a particular product also depends on other variables such as consumer income and the prices of related goods—substitutes and complements. We can use two other elasticities to measure the responsiveness of consumers to changes in these other variables that affect demand.

We saw in Chapter 4 that the demand for a particular product depends in part on the consumer's income. The income elasticity of demand measures the responsiveness of demand to changes in income, indicating how much more or less of a particular product is purchased as consumer income changes. The **income elasticity of demand** is defined as the percentage change in quantity demanded divided by the percentage change in income:

$$E_i = \frac{\text{percentage change in quantity demanded}}{\text{percentage change in income}}$$

Income elasticity of demand: A measure of the responsiveness of the quantity demanded to changes in consumer income; computed by dividing the percentage change in the quantity demanded by the percentage change in income.

For example, if a 10% increase in income increases the quantity of books demanded by 15%, the income elasticity of demand for books is 1.50 (equal to 15%/10%).

We can use the income elasticities of demand for various products to divide the products into different types. If the income elasticity is positive—indicating a positive relationship between income and demand—we say that the good is *normal*. If the income elasticity is negative—revealing a negative relationship between income and demand—we say that the good is *inferior*. Some examples of products with negative income elasticities are intercity bus travel and used clothing. We can divide the set of normal goods into two types. If the income elasticity is greater than 1.0—meaning that the percentage change in quantity demanded exceeds the percentage change in income—we say that the demand for a product is income-elastic. If the income elasticity is less than 1.0—indicating a smaller increase in quantity demanded—we say that demand is income-inelastic.

We saw in Chapter 4 that the demand for a particular product depends in part on the prices of related goods—substitutes and complements. The **cross elasticity of demand** measures the responsiveness of demand to changes in the prices of other goods, indicating how much more or less of a particular product is purchased as other prices change. The cross elasticity is defined as the percentage change in quantity demanded of one good (*X*) divided by the percentage change in the price of a related good (*Y*):

$$E_{xy} = \frac{\text{percentage change in quantity of } X \text{ demanded}}{\text{percentage change in price of } Y}$$

Cross elasticity of demand: A measure of the responsiveness of the quantity demanded to changes in the price of a related good; computed by dividing the percentage change in the quantity demanded of one good (*X*) by the percentage change in the price of another good (*Y*).

As we saw in Chapter 4, two goods are considered substitutes if there is a positive relationship between the quantity demanded of one good and the price of the other good. For example, an increase in the price of bananas increases the demand for apples as consumers substitute apples for the more expensive bananas. For substitute goods, the cross elasticity is positive. In contrast, two goods are considered complements if there is a negative relationship between the quantity demanded of one good and the price of the other. For example, an increase in the price of ice cream increases the cost of apple pie with ice cream, causing consumers to demand fewer apples. For complementary goods, the cross elasticity is negative.

The Price Elasticity of Supply

Let's look at elasticity on the supply side of the market. The price elasticity of supply measures the responsiveness of producers to changes in price. We compute this elasticity by dividing the percentage change in quantity supplied by the percentage change in price:

$$E_s = \frac{\text{percentage change in quantity supplied}}{\text{percentage change in price}}$$

In Figure 5.4, when the price of milk increases from $2.00 to $2.20, the quantity supplied increases from 100 million gallons to 120 million gallons. In other words, a 10% increase in price increased the quantity supplied by 20%, so the price elasticity of supply is 2.0:

$$E_s = \frac{\text{percentage change in quantity supplied}}{\text{percentage change in price}} = \frac{20\%}{10\%} = 2.0$$

Time is an important factor in determining the price elasticity of supply for a product. When the price of a particular product increases, the immediate response is that current producers produce more of the product in their existing production facilities (for example, factories, stores, offices, or restaurants). Although a higher price will certainly induce firms to produce more, the response is limited by the limited capacity of the firms' production facilities. Over time, however, new firms can enter the market and old firms can build new production facilities, so there will be a larger response in the long run. As time passes, supply becomes more elastic because more and more firms have the time to build production facilities and produce more output.

The milk industry provides a good example of the difference between short-run and long-run supply elasticities. The price elasticity of supply over a one-year period is 0.12: If the price of milk increases by 10% and stays there for a year, the quantity of milk supplied will rise by only 1.2%.[6] In the short run, dairy farmers can squeeze a little more output from their existing production facilities. Over a 10-year period, the price elastic-

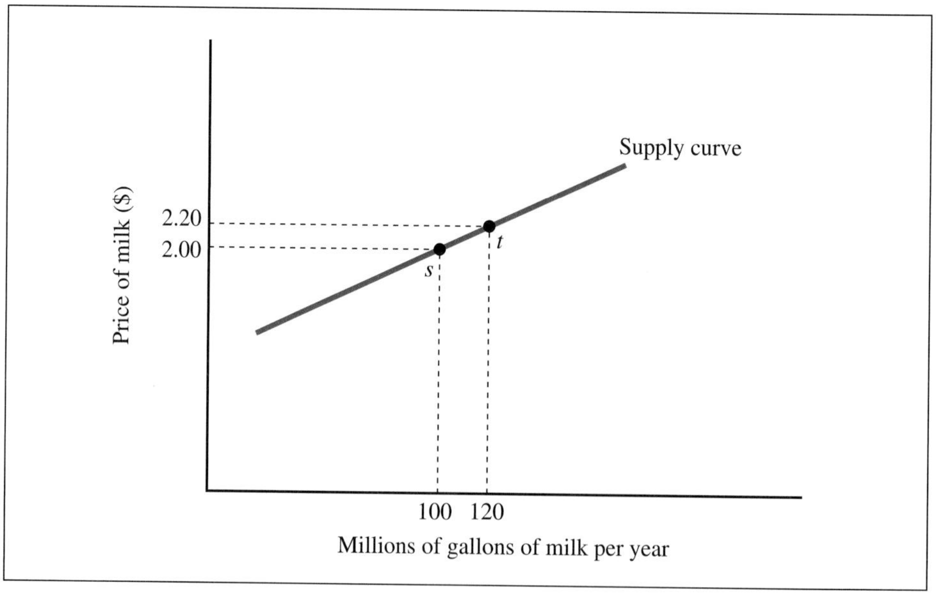

Figure 5.4

Market Supply Curve and Price Elasticity of Supply

A 10% increase in the price of milk (from $2 to $2.20) increases the quantity supplied by 20% (from 100 million gallons to 120 million), so the price elasticity of supply is 2.0 = 20%/10%.

ity is 2.5: The same 10% rise in price will increase the quantity supplied by 25%. In the long run, dairy farmers can expand existing facilities and build new ones, so in the long run, there is a larger response to a higher price.

We can use the price elasticity of supply to predict the effect of price changes on the quantity supplied. For example, suppose that the elasticity of supply is 0.80 and the price increases by 5%. Using the elasticity formula, we would predict a 4% increase in quantity supplied:

$$E_s = 0.80 = \frac{\text{percentage change in quantity supplied}}{5\%} = \frac{4\%}{5\%}$$

As we saw in Chapter 4, many governments establish minimum prices for agricultural products. The higher the minimum price, the larger the quantity supplied, consistent with the law of supply. If we know the price elasticity of supply, we can predict just how much more will be supplied at the higher price. For example, if the minimum price of cheese increases by 10% and the price elasticity is 0.60, the quantity of cheese supplied will rise by 6%:

$$E_s = 0.60 = \frac{\text{percentage change in quantity supplied}}{10\%} = \frac{6\%}{10\%}$$

Predicting Price Changes Using Price Elasticities

When supply or demand changes—when the supply curve or demand curve shifts—we can draw a supply and demand diagram to predict whether the equilibrium price will increase or decrease. In many cases, the simple diagram will show all we need to know about the effects of a change in supply or demand. But what if we want to predict how much a price will increase or decrease? We can use a simple formula to predict the change in the equilibrium price resulting from a change in supply or a change in demand.

In Figure 5.5, an increase in demand shifts the demand curve to the right and increases the equilibrium price. We explained in Chapter 4 that a demand curve shifts as

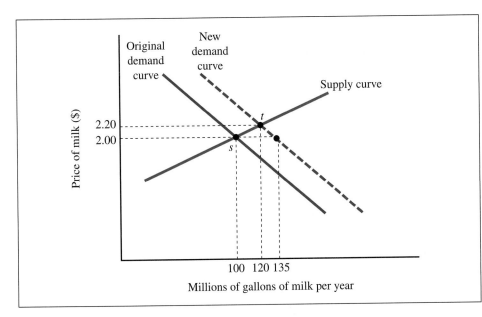

Figure 5.5

Increase in Demand Increases the Equilibrium Price

An increase in demand shifts the demand curve to the right, increasing the equilibrium price. In this case, a 35% increase in demand increases the price by 10%. Using the price-change formula, we have 10% = 35%/(2.0 + 1.5).

a result of a change in something other than the price of the product—for example, a change in income, tastes, or the price of a related good. When demand increases, the immediate effect is excess demand: At the original price ($2.00), the quantity demanded exceeds the quantity supplied by 35 million gallons (135 million − 100 million). As the price increases, both consumers and producers help to eliminate the excess demand: Consumers buy less (the law of demand), and firms produce more (the law of supply). If both consumers and producers are very responsive to changes in price, it will take a small increase in price to eliminate the excess demand. In other words, an increase in demand will cause a small increase in price if both demand and supply are elastic.

Price-change formula: A formula that shows the percentage change in equilibrium price resulting from a change in demand or supply, given values for the price elasticity of supply and price elasticity of demand.

We can use the following **price-change formula** to predict the change in the equilibrium price resulting from a change in demand. We divide the percentage change in demand by the sum of the price elasticities of supply and demand:

$$\text{percentage change in equilibrium price} = \frac{\text{percentage change in demand}}{E_s + E_d}$$

The numerator is the rightward shift of the demand curve in percentage terms. In Figure 5.5, the initial quantity demanded at a price of $2.00 is 100 million gallons (shown by the initial demand curve), while the new quantity demanded at the same price is 135 million gallons (shown by the new demand curve). The change in demand is 35 percent (35/100). The two price elasticities appear in the denominator. This is sensible because if consumers and producers are very responsive to changes in price (the elasticities are large numbers), excess demand will be eliminated with a relatively small increase in price.

We can use a simple example to see how to use the price-change formula. Suppose that demand increases by 35% (the demand curve shifts to the right by 35%). If the supply elasticity is 2.0 and the demand elasticity is 1.5, the predicted change in the equilibrium price is 10%:

$$\begin{aligned}\text{percentage change in equilibrium price} &= \frac{\text{percentage change in demand}}{E_s + E_d}\\[6pt] &= \frac{35\%}{2.0 + 1.5} = 10\%\end{aligned}$$

In Figure 5.5, the equilibrium price increases by 10%, from $2.00 to $2.20. If either demand or supply were less elastic (if either of the elasticity numbers were smaller), the predicted change in price would be larger. For example, if the supply elasticity were 0.25 instead of 2.0, we would predict a 20% increase in price (35%/1.75).

What about the direction of the price change? We know from Chapter 4 that an increase in demand increases the equilibrium price and a decrease in demand decreases the equilibrium price. Therefore, the percentage change in price is positive when the change in demand is positive (when demand increases and the demand curve shifts to the right), and negative when the change in demand is negative (when demand decreases and the demand curve shifts to the left). For example, suppose the demand for a product decreases by 15% (the demand curve shifts to the left by 15%). If the supply elasticity is 1.0 and the demand elasticity is 0.50, the price-change formula shows that the equilibrium price will decrease by 10%:

$$\text{percentage change in equilibrium price} = \frac{\text{percentage change in demand}}{E_s + E_d}$$

$$= \frac{-15\%}{1.0 + 0.5} = -10\%$$

We can use a slightly different version of the price-change formula to predict the change in the equilibrium price resulting from a change in supply. As explained in Chapter 4, a change in supply results from changes in something other than the price of the product—for example, a change in the cost of labor or raw materials, a change in production technology, or a change in the number of firms. The immediate effect of an increase in supply is excess supply: At the original price, the quantity supplied exceeds the quantity demanded. As the price drops, consumers respond by purchasing more, and producers respond by producing less, so the gap between quantity supplied and demanded narrows. If both consumers and producers are very responsive to changes in price, it will take a small decrease in price to eliminate the excess supply. In other words, an increase in supply will cause a small decrease in price if both demand and supply are elastic.

To predict the change in price resulting from a change in supply, we just substitute supply for demand in the numerator of the price-change formula and add a minus sign. The minus sign indicates that there is a negative relationship between the equilibrium price and supply: When supply increases—when the supply curve shifts to the right—the price drops; when supply decreases, the price rises:

$$\text{percentage change in equilibrium price} = -\frac{\text{percentage change in supply}}{E_s + E_d}$$

For example, suppose the supply of milk increases by 10%. If the price elasticity of demand is 0.6 and the price elasticity of supply is 1.4, the equilibrium price will decrease by 5%:

$$\text{percentage change in equilibrium price} = -\frac{\text{percentage change in supply}}{E_s + E_d}$$
$$= -\frac{10\%}{1.4 + 0.6} = -5\%$$

TEST Your Understanding

8. Complete the statement: If a 10% increase in price increases the quantity supplied by 15%, the price elasticity of supply is _____.

9. Suppose the price elasticity of a supply of cheese is 0.80. If the price of cheese rises by 20%, by what percentage will the quantity supplied change?

10. Suppose that the elasticity of demand for chewing tobacco is 0.70 and the elasticity of supply is 2.30. If an antichewing campaign decreases the demand for chewing tobacco by 30%, in what direction and by what percentage will the price of chewing tobacco change?

11. Suppose that the elasticity of demand for motel rooms in a town near a ski area is 1.0 and the elasticity of supply is 0.50. If the population of the surrounding area increases by 30%, in what direction and by what percentage will the price of motel rooms change?

Using the TOOLS

This chapter introduced several new tools of economics, including four different elasticities and a formula that can be used to predict the change in price resulting from a change in supply or demand. Here are some opportunities to use these tools to do your own economic analysis.

1. Projecting Transit Ridership

As a transit planner, you must predict how many people ride commuter trains and how much money is generated from train fares. According to a recent study,[7] the short-run price elasticity of demand for commuter rail is 0.62 and the long-run elasticity is 1.59. The current ridership is 100,000 people per day. Suppose fares increase by 10%.

a. Predict the changes in train ridership over a one-month period (short run) and a five-year period (long run).

b. Over the one-month period, will total revenue increase or decrease? What will happen in the five-year period?

2. Bumper Crops

Your job is to predict the total revenue generated by the nation's corn crop. Last year's crop was 100 million bushels, and the price was $4.00 per bushel. This year's weather was favorable throughout the country, and this year's crop will be 110 million bushels, or 10% larger than last year's. The price elasticity of demand for corn is 0.50.

a. Predict the effect of the bumper crop on the price of corn, assuming that the entire crop is sold this year.

b. Predict the total revenue from this year's corn crop.

c. Did the favorable weather increase or decrease the total revenue from corn? Why?

3. Washington, D.C., Gas Tax

You are a tax analyst for Washington, D.C., and have been asked to predict how much revenue will be generated by the city's gasoline tax. The initial quantity of gasoline is 100 million gallons per month, and the price elasticity of demand for gasoline in the typical large city is 4.0. The tax, which is $0.10 per gallon, will increase the price of gasoline by 5%.

a. How much revenue will the gasoline tax generate?

b. In 1980, tax analysts in Washington, D.C., based their revenue predictions for a gasoline tax on the elasticity of demand for gasoline in the United States as a whole, which is 1.0. Would you expect the national elasticity to be larger or smaller than the elasticity for the typical large city? Would you expect the analysts to overestimate or underestimate the revenue from the gasoline tax?

4. College Enrollment and Housing

Consider a college town where the initial price of apartments is $400 and the initial quantity is 1,000 apartments. The price elasticity of demand for apartments is 1.0, and the price elasticity of supply of apartments is 0.50.

a. Use supply and demand curves to show the initial equilibrium, and label the equilibrium point *i*.

b. Suppose an increase in college enrollment is expected to increase the demand for apartments in a college town by 15%. Use your graph to show the effects of the increase in demand on the apartment market. Label the new equilibrium point *f*.

c. Predict the effect of the increase in demand on the equilibrium price of apartments.

Summary

This chapter deals with the numbers behind the laws of demand and supply. The law of demand tells us that an increase in the price of a product will decrease the quantity demanded, ceteris paribus. If we know the price elasticity of demand for that good, we can determine just how much less of it will be sold at the higher price. Similarly, if we know the price elasticity of supply for a product, we can determine just how much more of it will be supplied at a higher price. Here are the main points of the chapter.

1. The price elasticity of demand—defined as the percentage change in quantity demanded divided by the percentage change in price—measures the responsiveness of consumers to changes in price

2. Demand is relatively elastic if there are good substitutes.

3. If demand is elastic, there is a negative relationship between price and total revenue. If demand is inelastic, there is a positive relationship between price and total revenue.

4. The price elasticity of supply—defined as the percentage change in quantity supplied divided by the percentage change in price—measures the responsiveness of producers to changes in price.

5. If we know the elasticities of supply and demand, we can predict the percentage change in price resulting from a change in demand or supply.

Key Terms

cross elasticity of demand, 109
income elasticity of demand, 109

price-change formula, 112
price elasticity of demand, 98

price elasticity of supply, 98

Problems and Discussion Questions

1. When the price of compact discs (CDs) increased from $10 to $11, the quantity of CDs demanded decreased from 100 to 87. What is the price elasticity of demand for CDs? Is demand elastic or inelastic?

2. Explain why the demand for residential natural gas (gas used for heating, cooling, and cooking) is more elastic than the demand for residential electricity.

3. Would you expect the demand for a specific brand of running shoes to be more elastic or less elastic than the demand for running shoes in general? Why?

4. For each of the following goods, indicate whether you expect demand to be inelastic or elastic, and explain your reasoning: opera, foreign travel, local telephone service, video rentals, and eggs.

5. You observe a positive relationship between the price your store charges for CDs and the total revenue from CDs. Is the demand for your CDs elastic or inelastic?

6. Suppose the price elasticity of demand for a campus film series is 1.40. If the objective of the film society is to maximize its total revenue (price times the number of tickets sold), should it increase or decrease its price?

7. As the head of a state chapter of MADD (Mothers Against Drunk Driving), you are to speak in support of policies that discourage drunk driving. The number of highway deaths among young adults, which is roughly proportional to the group's beer consumption, is initially 100 deaths per year. You have scheduled a news conference to express your support for a beer tax that will increase the price of beer by 10%. The price elasticity of demand for beer is 1.30. Complete the following statement: "The beer tax will decrease the number of highway deaths among young adults by about _____ per year."

8. When the price of paper increases from $100 to $104 per ton, the quantity supplied increased from 200 to 220 tons per day. What is the price elasticity of supply?

9. Suppose that the government restricts logging to protect an endangered species. The restrictions increase the price of wood products and shift the supply curve for new housing to the left by 4%. The initial price of new housing is $100,000, the elasticity of demand is 1.0, and the elasticity of supply is 3.0. Predict the effect of the logging restriction on the equilibrium price of new housing. Illustrate your answer with a graph that shows the initial point (*i*) and the new equilibrium (*f*).

10. **Web Exercise.** Visit the Web site of Roll Back the Beer Tax (www.beertax.com). What are the arguments against beer taxes? Does this site ignore some of the benefits associated with beer taxes? What do you think about beer taxes?

11. **Web Exercise.** Visit the Web site of the Center for Disease Control (*http://www.cdc.gov*). Search for the facts on the price elasticity of demand for cigarettes. How are the estimated elasticities used by policy analysts?

Take It to the Net

We invite you to visit the O'Sullivan/Sheffrin page on the Prentice Hall Web site at:
http://www.prenhall.com/osullivan/
for additional World Wide Web exercises for this chapter.

Model Answers for This Chapter

Chapter-Opening Questions

1. A beer tax will increase the price of beer, decreasing beer consumption. Highway deaths are roughly proportional to beer consumption, so the tax will also decrease highway deaths. The actual change in highway deaths depends on the price elasticity of demand for beer.

2. As shown in "Using the Tools: Bumper Crops," a bumper crop of corn decreases the equilibrium price of corn by a relatively large amount because the demand for corn is inelastic. Although corn farmers will sell more bushels, they will receive much less per bushel, so total revenue will drop.

3. If demand is elastic, the firm should lower its price. If demand is inelastic, the firm should raise its price.

4. The policies increase the price of the illegal drug, which increases total spending on the drug because demand is inelastic. If drug addicts support their habits with property crime, they must commit more crime to support their more expensive habits.

5. The percentage change in demand, the price elasticity of supply, and the price elasticity of demand.

Test Your Understanding

1. Quantity, price.

2. 1.20.

3. An increase in the price of tapes will cause some consumers to buy CD players and switch from tapes to CDs, but this takes some time.

4. On the upper portion, demand is elastic, so quantity will decrease by more than 10%.

5. Decrease, 6.

6. The price elasticity is 1.0 (neither elastic nor inelastic).

7. Demand is elastic, so a decrease in price would increase total revenue.

8. 1.50 = 15%/10%.

9. The quantity supplied will increase by 16%.

10. Using the price-change formula, the price will decrease by 10% = 30%/3.

11. Using the price-change formula, the price will increase by 20% = 30%/1.50.

Using the Tools

1. Projecting Transit Ridership

   a. According to the elasticity formula, ridership will decrease by 6.2% in the short run (a loss of 6,200 riders) and 15.9% in the long run (a loss of 15,900 riders).

   b. Demand is inelastic in the short run, so total revenue will increase. Demand is elastic in the long run, so total revenue will eventually decrease.

2. Bumper Crops

   a. Using the price elasticity formula, to sell an additional 10% of corn, the price must decrease by 20%, to $3.20.

   b. Total revenue is 110 million × $3.20, or $352 million.

   c. Total revenue last year was $400 million, so the bumper crop decreased total revenue. This occurs because demand is inelastic, so the price decreases by a large amount.

3. Washington, D.C. Gas Tax

   a. Using the price elasticity formula, the 5% increase in price will decrease the quantity demanded by 20%, from 100 million gallons to 80 million gallons. The revenue is the tax per gallon ($0.10) × the quantity (80 million gallons), or $8 million.

   b. They will overestimate the revenue from the tax because they will underestimate the change in quantity demanded by the tax. Specifically, they will predict a quantity of 95 million gallons instead of 80 million gallons and revenue of $9.5 million instead of $8 million. Because it is relatively easy to buy gasoline in a nearby city, the demand for gasoline will be relatively elastic at the city level.

4. College Enrollment and Housing

   c. Use the price-change formula to compute the change in the equilibrium price. The price increases by 10% = 15%/(0.50 + 1.0).

Notes

1. Don Fullerton and Thomas Kinnaman, "Household Responses to Pricing Garbage by the Bag," *American Economic Review*, vol. 86, no. 4, 1996, pp. 971–984.

2. Chin-Fun Cling and James Peale, Jr., "Income and Price Elasticities," in *Advances in Econometrics Supplement*, edited by Henri Theil (Greenwich, CT: JAI Press, 1989).

3. Henry Saffer and Michael Grossman, "Beer Taxes, the Legal Drinking Age, and Youth Motor Vehicle Fatalities," *Journal of Legal Studies*, vol. 41, June 1987.

4. Kenneth A. Small, *Urban Transportation Economics* (Philadelphia, PA: Harwood Academic Publishers, 1992).

5. L. P. Silverman and N. L. Sprull, "Urban Crime and the Price of Heroin," *Journal of Urban Economics*, vol. 4, 1977, pp. 80–103.

6. Richard Klemme and Jean-Paul Chavas, "The Effects of Changing Milk Price on Milk Supply and National Dairy Herd Size," *Economic Issues*, University of Wisconsin, June 1985.

7. Richard Voith, "The Long Run Elasticity of Demand for Commuter Rail Transportation," *Journal of Urban Economics*, vol. 30, 1991, pp. 360–372.

Using the Midpoint Formula to Compute Price Elasticity

The midpoint formula (Appendix, Chapter 1) provides a more precise way to compute percentage changes than the formula used in this chapter. Using the midpoint approach, we divide the change in a variable (for example, the change in price) by the average value of the variable (the average price). We can use this approach to compute the price elasticity associated with points d and e in Figure 5.1.

The percentage change in price equals the change (0.20) divided by the average price ($2.10), or 9.52%):

$$\text{percentage change in price} = \frac{\text{change}}{\text{average value}} = \frac{0.20}{(2.00 + 2.20)/2}$$
$$= \frac{0.20}{2.10} = 0.0952 = 9.52\%$$

The percentage change in quantity equals the change (–15) divided by the average quantity (92.5), or –16.22%:

$$\text{percentage change in quantity} = \frac{\text{change}}{\text{average value}} = \frac{-15}{(100 + 85)/2}$$
$$= \frac{-15}{92.5} = -0.1622 = 16.22\%$$

If we plug these percentage changes into the formula for the price elasticity of demand, the computed price elasticity is 1.70:

$$E_d = \frac{\text{percentage change in demand}}{\text{percentage change in price}} = \frac{16.22}{9.52} = 1.70$$

Why is this elasticity different from the elasticity we computed with the simple approach (1.50)? The midpoint approach measures the percentage changes more precisely, so we get a more precise measure of price elasticity. In this case, the percentage changes are relatively small, so the two elasticity numbers aren't too far apart. If the percentage changes were larger, however, the elasticity numbers generated by the two approaches would be quite different, and it would be wise to use the midpoint approach.

CHAPTER 6

Market Efficiency and Government Intervention

Consumer: How much is this radio?
Salesperson: It's $25, complete with headphones.
Consumer: I'll take it. Here's the money.
Salesperson: Thank you.
Consumer: Thank you.

Every day, there are millions of mundane transactions like this one, most of them ending in a double "thank you." Are people being polite, or do they really mean it? The millions of "thank yous" remind us that both people in a voluntary transaction benefit; otherwise, they wouldn't make the trade. In this chapter, we'll see that a market equilibrium—with the quantity demanded equal to the quantity supplied—may generate the largest possible net benefits for buyers and sellers. In other words, the market equilibrium may be efficient. We'll explore the logic behind Adam Smith's metaphor of the invisible hand, the idea that individual buyers and sellers, each acting in his or her own self-interest, *frequently* promote the social interest.

The metaphor of the invisible hand is qualified by the word "frequently." In some markets, buyers and sellers acting in their own self-interest generate outcomes that are contrary to the social interest. We can rule out these sorts of markets by making four assumptions:

1. **Informed Buyers and Sellers.** We'll assume that both buyers and sellers have enough information to make informed decisions about buying and selling.

2. **Perfect Competition.** A perfectly competitive market has a very large number of firms, each of which is so small that it takes the market price as given. Firms are free to enter or exit the market, so whenever there is an opportunity to make a profit—that is, whenever the price of a product exceeds the cost of producing it— firms will enter the market and supply more of the product. The quantity supplied will continue to increase until the opportunity for profit is eliminated, which happens when the price is just high enough to cover the cost of providing the product, but no higher.

3. **No Spillover Benefits.** There is a spillover benefit when part of the benefits from some product go to someone who does not decide how much of the product to consume. For example, if your farm is in a flood plain and another farmer builds a dike to protect low-lying areas, you benefit from that farmer's decision to build a dam. The markets considered in this chapter do not have spillover benefits, meaning that the benefits of consumption are confined to the person who is deciding how much to consume.

4. **No Spillover Cost.** There is a spillover cost when part of the cost of producing some product is borne by someone who does not decide how much of the product to produce. For example, if you live downstream from a paper mill that dumps chemical waste into the river, you bear some of the cost of paper production because it makes the river unsafe for swimming and drinking. In the first part of this chapter, we consider markets without spillover costs, meaning that producers, who decide how much to produce, bear all the costs of production.

As we'll see in the last part of the chapter, when there are spillover costs—for example, water pollution—the market equilibrium will be inefficient, and government can guide buyers and sellers to make choices that promote the social interest. Later in the book, we'll examine the three other reasons for inefficiency: a small number of firms, spillover benefits, and poorly informed sellers and buyers.

This chapter also discusses the effects of government intervention in markets that would otherwise be efficient. We'll see that when government intervenes—controlling the price of the good or the quantity sold—it will prevent some voluntary transactions that would benefit both buyer and seller. For that reason, government intervention causes inefficiency. As we explore the efficiency of markets and the effects of government intervention, we answer the following practical questions:

1. If a college town uses a rent-control policy to cut the monthly rent on apartments, will some students be harmed by the policy?
2. If you want to operate a taxi in New York City, Toronto, or Boston, you must first buy a taxi medallion for over $100,000. Why?
3. Why is there a shortage (excess demand) for human organs for transplanting?
4. Who bears the cost of restrictions on textile imports, and what is the cost per textile job saved?
5. If a factory dumps chemical waste into a river, harming people downstream, what should the government do?

Consumer Surplus and Producer Surplus

We'll start our discussion of market efficiency by showing how to measure the benefits experienced by consumers and producers. We'll start with consumers, exploring the benefits they receive and how to measure them. Then we'll look at the supply side of the market.

The Demand Curve and Consumer Surplus

If you said "thank you" the last time you purchased a product, did you mean it? If you were willing to pay more than the price you actually paid, you received what's called **consumer surplus**. Consumer surplus is the difference between the maximum amount a consumer is willing to pay for a product and the price that he or she pays for the product. For example, if you are willing to pay $21 for a CD that you buy for $10, your consumer surplus is $11.

Let's start our discussion of consumer surplus with another look at the demand curve, which shows how much consumers are willing to pay for a product. Figure 6.1 shows the market demand curve for lawn cutting in a small town. The demand curve shows that no one will pay to have their lawn cut for $25 (point *t*), but the first consumer

Consumer surplus: The difference between the maximum amount a consumer is willing to pay for a product and the price that he or she pays for the product.

ACTIVE GRAPH

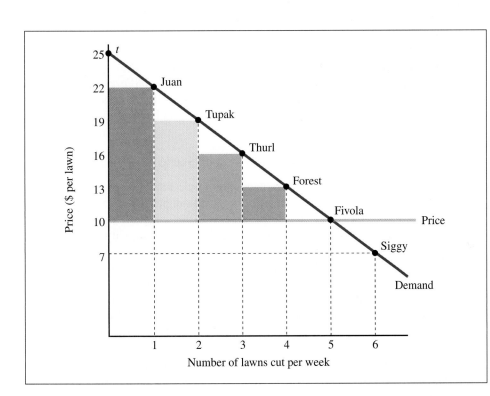

Figure 6.1
Demand Curve and Consumer Surplus
Consumer surplus equals the maximum amount a consumer is willing to pay (shown by the demand curve) minus the price paid. Juan is willing to pay $22, so if the price is $10, his consumer surplus is $12. The market consumer surplus equals the sum of the surpluses earned by all consumers in the market. In this case, the market consumer surplus is $30 = $12 + $9 + $6 + $3 + $0.

The price of a consumer good is less than or equal to the amount the consumer is willing to pay for the good. Consumer surplus measures the bonus or surplus received by the consumer.

(Juan) will pay for a cut if the price drops to $22. This suggests that Juan is willing to pay up to $22 to have his lawn cut, but no more. Moving down the demand curve, the second consumer (Tupak) will pay for lawn cutting when the price drops to $19, suggesting that he is willing to pay up to $19. As we continue to move downward along the demand curve, other consumers are willing to pay less and less for each additional lawn cut.

We can use the demand curve to measure just how much of a net benefit or surplus consumers get. Suppose that the price of a lawn cut is $10, and everyone pays this price. Juan's consumer surplus is $12, the amount he is willing to pay ($22) minus the price. Similarly, Tupak's consumer surplus is $9, equal to the difference between the amount he is willing to pay ($19) and the market price. To compute the total consumer surplus in the lawn-cutting market, we simply add up the surpluses for each of the five consumers who buy lawn cutting at a price of $10. In this example, the market consumer surplus is $30, equal to $12 (Juan) + $9 (Tupak) + $6 (Thurl) + $3 (Forest) + $0 (Fivola). The fifth consumer (Fivola) gets no consumer surplus because the price equals the amount she is willing to pay. The sixth person (Siggy) doesn't have his lawn cut because the amount he is willing to pay is less than the price.

The Supply Curve and Producer Surplus

Producer surplus: The difference between the price a producer receives for a product and the minimum amount the producer is willing to accept for the product.

Like consumers, the people who produce goods and services say "thank you" when they sell their products. This suggests that they too receive a net benefit or surplus from voluntary transactions. **Producer surplus** is the difference between the price a producer receives for a product and the minimum amount the producer is willing to accept for the product. For example, if you are willing to cut someone's lawn for any amount over $4 and you do it for $10, your producer surplus is $6 ($10 – $4). The minimum amount a producer is willing to accept is the marginal cost of producing the product, so producer surplus is the difference between the price and the marginal cost.

Let's start our discussion of producer surplus with another look at the supply curve, which shows the marginal cost of production. Figure 6.2 shows the market supply curve for lawn cutting in a small town. Let's imagine that six people are willing to cut lawns if the price is right. Each potential cutter incurs the same cost for renting a lawn mower but different opportunity costs for their time. The marginal cost for the first producer (Abe) is $2:

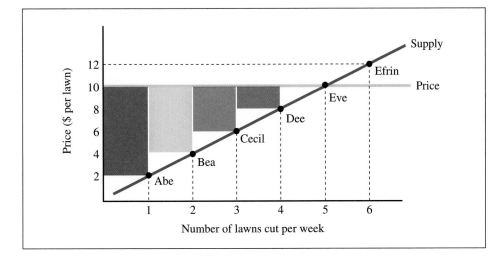

Figure 6.2
Supply Curve and Producer Surplus

Producer surplus equals the market price minus the producer's marginal cost (shown by the supply curve). Abe's marginal cost is $2, so if the price is $10, his consumer surplus is $8. The market producer surplus equals the sum of the surpluses earned by all producers in the market. In this case, the market producer surplus is $20 = $8 + $6 + $4 + $2 + $0.

He incurs a cost of $2, including the cost of renting a mower and the opportunity cost of his time. Therefore, Abe is willing to cut a lawn if he receives at least $2. On the supply curve, if the price is $2, one person—Abe—will cut lawns. Bea has a higher opportunity cost of time and therefore a higher marginal cost ($4): She won't cut a lawn unless she is paid at least $4. If the price is $4, two people—Abe and Bea—will cut lawns. Moving upward along the supply curve, the other potential lawn cutters have even higher marginal costs. The higher the price, the larger the number of people willing to cut lawns.

We can use the supply curve to measure just how much of a net benefit or surplus producers get. If the price of lawn cutting is $10, Abe's producer surplus for the first lawn is $8, the price he receives minus his marginal cost ($2). Similarly, Bea's producer surplus is $6, equal to the difference between the price and her marginal cost ($4). To compute the total producer surplus in the lawn-cutting market, we simply add up the surpluses for each of the five producers who cut lawns at a price of $10. In this example, the market producer surplus is $20, equal to $8 (Abe) + $6 (Bea) + $4 (Cecil) + $2 (Dee) + $0 (Eve). The fifth producer (Eve) gets no producer surplus because the price equals her marginal cost, and the sixth potential producer (Efrin) doesn't cut any lawns because the price is less than his cost.

Market Equilibrium and Efficiency

Figure 6.3 puts the demand and supply curves together to show the equilibrium in the market for lawn cutting. The demand curve intersects the supply curve at a price of $10 per lawn. At this price, five lawns are cut, meaning that there are five buyers and five sellers. The total surplus of a market is the sum of consumer surplus and producer surplus. In Figure 6.3, the consumer surplus is $30 and the producer surplus is $20, so the total surplus of the market is $50. As we'll see in this part of the chapter, the market equilibrium generates the highest possible total surplus. That's why we say that the market equilibrium is efficient: We can't do any better in terms of the total surplus of the market.

Total Surplus Is Lower with a Price Below the Equilibrium Price

To see why the market equilibrium maximizes the total surplus of the market, let's look at the total surplus of the market when the price is less than the equilibrium price. Suppose the government imposes a maximum price of $4 on lawn cutting. As

Figure 6.3

Market Equilibrium and the Total Value of the Market

The total surplus of the market equals consumer surplus (the lightly shaded areas) plus producer surplus (the darkly shaded areas). The market equilibrium generates the highest possible total market value, equal to $50 = $30 (consumer surplus) + $20 (producer surplus).

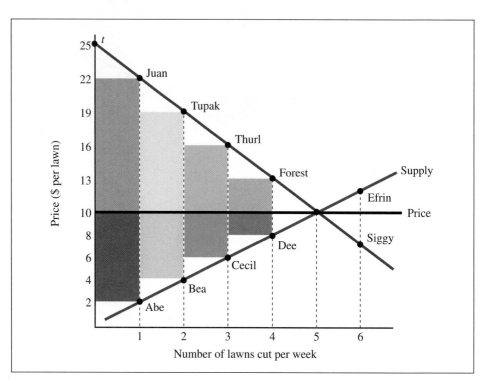

shown in panel A of Figure 6.4, at this price only two people cut lawns, and the producer surplus is shown by the darkly shaded area between the price line and the supply curve. Consumers can buy only as much as producers sell, so the market consumer surplus equals the surpluses for the first two consumers. This is shown as the lightly shaded areas between the price line and the demand curve. Comparing Figure 6.4 to Figure 6.3, we see that the maximum price reduces the total surplus of the market. For the first two lawns, consumers simply gain at the expense of producers. The maximum price also eliminates the surpluses from the third and fourth lawns, so the total surplus decreases.

The maximum price reduces the total surplus of the market because it prevents some mutually beneficial transactions. The third consumer (Thurl) is willing to pay $16 to have his lawn cut, and the third producer (Cecil) is willing to cut a lawn if he is paid at least $6. Thurl is willing to pay more than Cecil requires, so cutting Thurl's lawn would generate a net benefit of $10. If they split the difference, agreeing on a price of $11, each would get a surplus of $5. The maximum price prevents Thurl and Cecil from executing this transaction, so the maximum price decreases the total surplus of the market. The same logic applies to the fourth lawn: The maximum price prevents Forest and Dee from executing a transaction that would generate a net benefit of $5, equal to Forest's willingness to pay ($13) minus Dee's marginal cost ($8).

Total Surplus Is Lower with a Price Above the Equilibrium Price

What would happen if the government imposed a minimum price instead of a maximum price? If the minimum price is $19, as shown in panel B of Figure 6.4, the demand curve indicates that consumers would be willing to buy only two lawn cuts. The total surplus of the market would be the sum of consumer and producer surplus for the first two lawns, the same as it was under the maximum price. The difference between the two

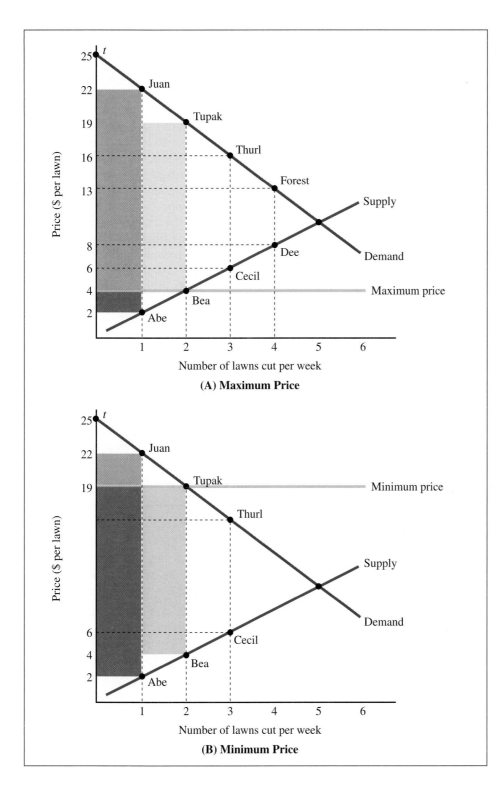

Figure 6.4

A Maximum Price or a Minimum Price Decreases the Total Surplus of the Market

(A) Maximum Price A maximum price of $4 reduces the total value of the market. The first two consumers gain at the expense of the first two producers. The consumer and producer surplus for the third and fourth lawns are lost entirely, so the total value of the market decreases.

(B) Minimum Price A minimum price of $19 reduces the total value of the market. The first two producers gain at the expense of the first two consumers. The consumer and producer surplus for the third and fourth lawns are lost entirely, so the total value of the market decreases.

policies is that under a maximum price, the first two consumers gain at the expense of the first two producers, while under the minimum price, the producers gain at the expense of consumers.

Efficiency and the Invisible Hand

The market equilibrium maximizes the total surplus of the market because it guarantees that all the mutually beneficial transactions happen. Once we reach the market equilibrium at point *e* in Figure 6.3, there are no more transactions that would benefit a buyer and a seller. The demand curve tells us that the potential buyer of the sixth lawn cut (Siggy) is willing to pay only $7, and the supply curve tells us that the potential seller of the sixth lawn cut (Efrin) has a marginal cost of $12. This transaction doesn't happen because the potential buyer is not willing to pay the cost of producing the good.

Our little example of the market for lawn cutting illustrates a general lesson about markets. The typical market has thousands of buyers and thousands of sellers, each acting in his or her own self-interest. If the market is perfectly competitive and has no spillovers, the market reaches the price and quantity that maximizes the total surplus of the market and is therefore efficient. Instead of using a bureaucrat to coordinate the actions of everyone in the market, we can rely on the actions of individual consumers and individual producers, each guided only by self-interest. This is the invisible hand in action.

The experience of the former Soviet Union demonstrates the importance of prices and the power of Adam Smith's ideas embodied in the metaphor of the invisible hand. The Soviet economy was a planned economy in the sense that bureaucrats—not individual producers—decided how much of each good to produce. There were no prices to guide the decisions of producers. When the Soviets discovered a persistent mismatch between what they were producing and what consumers wanted, they asked a team of experts to propose a solution to the problem. The experts told the bureaucrats to figure out the prices that would have occurred if the Soviet economy were a market economy instead of a planned one. Once the bureaucrats had these predicted prices, they could then base their production decisions on the predicted prices. In other words, the experts told the bureaucrats to base their decisions on the prices that would have emerged from a market economy.

TEST Your Understanding

1. Complete the statement: Consumer surplus equals _____ minus _____, while producer surplus equals _____ minus _____.

2. You are willing to pay $2,000 to have your house painted, and Pablo's marginal cost of painting a house is $1,400. If you split the difference, what's your consumer surplus? What's Pablo's producer surplus?

3. Looking back at Figure 6.4, how much is Forest willing to pay for the fourth cut lawn? What is Dee's marginal cost for cutting the fourth lawn? Describe a mutually beneficial transaction that would be blocked by a maximum price of $4.

4. The conclusion that a market equilibrium is efficient is based on four assumptions. What are they?

Government Intervention: Controlling Price

Now that we've seen that a perfectly competitive market without spillovers is efficient, we can discuss the effects of government intervention in such a market. We'll start with government policies that control the price of the product, setting either a maximum price or a minimum price. In each case, if the market is perfectly competitive and has no spillovers, government intervention reduces the total surplus of the market and thus causes inefficiency.

Maximum Prices: Rent Control

We've already seen two different effects of a maximum price. In Chapter 4, we saw that when the government sets a maximum price that is less than the equilibrium price, the result is excess demand for the product. The decrease in price reduces the quantity supplied and increases the quantity demanded, so at the controlled price, consumers want to buy more than producers want to sell. In this chapter, we see from Panel A of Figure 6.4 that a maximum price decreases the total surplus of the market: Some consumers gain at the expense of producers, and the total surplus decreases. Here are some examples of goods that have been or may be subject to maximum prices:

- **Rental housing.** A **rent control** program establishes a maximum monthly rent.

- **Gasoline.** Price controls on gasoline in the 1970s established a maximum price.

- **Medical goods and services.** Some proposals to control medical costs include price controls.

> **Rent control:** A policy under which the government specifies a maximum rent that is below the equilibrium rent.

In all three cases, a maximum price will cause excess demand and reduce the total surplus of the market.

Let's use rent control to discuss some of the subtle effects of a maximum price. As we saw in Chapter 4, a maximum price creates excess demand for the product. Rent control creates a gap between the number of consumers willing to rent housing and the number of apartments available. The excess demand for apartments means that consumers will spend more time searching for apartments. One cost of rent control is the opportunity cost of the extra time spent searching for apartments. Another example of the time cost of a maximum price is price controls for gasoline: Consumers spent hours waiting in line to buy gasoline, using time that could have been spent working, studying, or having fun.

We saw in this chapter that a maximum price is inefficient because it prevents mutually beneficial transactions between potential buyers and sellers. In the case of rent control, many people violate the spirit and the letter of the law by executing transactions of dubious legal merit. Consumers in some rent-control cities pay extra money to property owners to outbid other consumers for scarce apartments. These extra payments are often disguised as nonrefundable security deposits or "key money" (hundreds or thousands of dollars to get the key to the apartment when a consumer signs a lease).

Is rent control good for the poor? Many wealthy and famous people benefit from rent control,[1] suggesting that rent control is a very blunt instrument for helping the poor: You don't have to be poor to qualify for a rent-controlled apartment. As we explain later in the book, the government could use other policies to more effectively improve the economic circumstances of the poor.

Minimum Prices

We've already seen two different effects of a minimum price. In chapter 4, we saw that when the government sets a minimum price that exceeds the equilibrium price, the result is excess supply of the product. The increase in price increases the quantity supplied as producers react to the higher price by producing more. The increase in price also decreases the quantity demanded as consumers react by purchasing less. At the minimum price, producers want to sell more than consumers want to buy.

As shown in Panel B of Figure 6.4, a minimum price of $19 decreases the quantity sold from 5 lawns per hour to 2 lawns per hour. At the minimum price of $19, producers are willing to cut a large number of lawns, but at that price, they would have only two customers. The minimum price produces winners and losers. The winners are the two lucky producers who cut lawns at the higher price, and thus earn larger producer surpluses. The other three producers who would cut lawns at the equilibrium price are losers, as they lose their producer surpluses. Consumers are losers: two consumers still participate in the market, but get smaller surpluses; three consumers drop out of the market, and thus earn no consumer surplus. Because the gains of the winners are less than the losses of the losers, the total surplus of the market decreases.

Government Intervention: Restricting Quantity

What happens when the government controls the quantity of a particular product instead of its price? We'll consider two policies that control quantities. In the domestic economy, many state and local governments limit the number of firms in particular markets by limiting the number of business licenses to operate in those markets. As we saw in Chapter 3, national governments use a wide variety of policies to restrict imports, including import bans, import quotas, tariffs, and voluntary export restraints.

Licensing: Taxi Medallions

You may be surprised to learn the extent of business licensing programs used by state and local governments. There are limits on the number of taxicabs, dry cleaners, tobacco farms, liquor stores, bars selling liquor, appliance repairers, and dog groomers. Some people defend licensing schemes on the grounds that they protect consumers from high prices, low-quality products, and poor service. But studies of licensing show that most licensing programs increase prices without improving the quality of products and service.[2] We can use the licensing of taxis to explain the market effects of licensing. The analysis applies to other markets in which the government uses licenses to limit the number of firms.

Panel A of Figure 6.5 shows the market equilibrium in the taxi market. The demand curve intersects the supply curve at point e. The industry provides 10,000 miles of taxi service per day at a price of $3.00 per mile. Each taxi produces 100 miles of service per day, and there are 100 taxicabs in the market. The total surplus of the market equals the sum of consumer surplus and producer surplus, shown by the area between the demand curve and the supply curve.

Taxi medallion: A license to operate a taxi.

Suppose that the city passes a law requiring each taxicab to have a taxi license—also known as a **taxi medallion**—and limits the number of medallions to 80. The city gives the taxi medallions to the first 80 people who show up at City Hall. In Panel B of Figure 6.5, the vertical line at 8,000 miles of service shows that this policy fixes the quantity of taxi service at 8,000 miles per day (80 taxis times 100 miles per taxi per day). The medallion policy creates an excess demand for taxi service: At the original price ($3.00), the quantity demanded is 10,000 miles, but the city's 80 taxicabs provide only 8,000 miles of service. The market moves upward along the demand curve to point m, where the price is $3.60 per mile of service. The medallion policy increases the price and decreases the quantity of taxi services.

Licensing and Market Efficiency

The medallion policy decreases the total surplus of the taxi market. In Figure 6.5, we see that the total surplus in Panel B is less than the total surplus in Panel A. The medallion policy decreases consumer surplus, a result of the higher price and smaller quantity. Producer surplus could increase or decrease, depending on the shapes of the supply and demand curves. In this example, it actually increases by a small amount. Like other policies such as maximum and minimum prices, the medallion policy decreases the quantity of goods sold, decreasing the total surplus of the market. The producers of the first 8,000

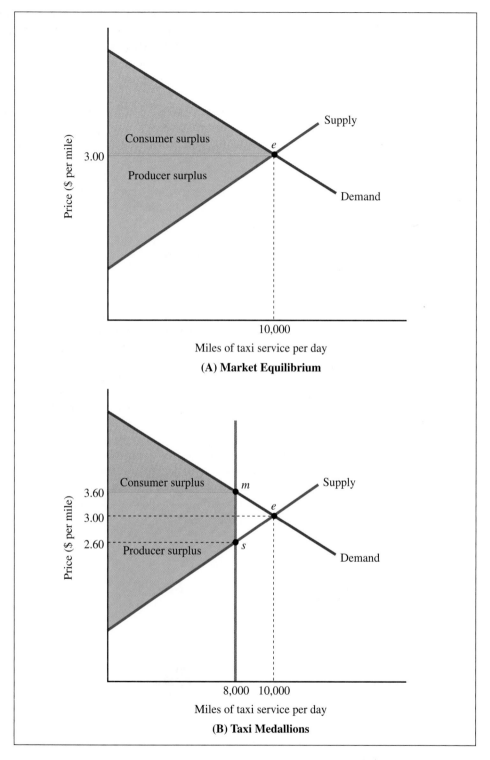

Figure 6.5

The Market Effects of Taxi Medallions
(A) Market Equilibrium The market equilibrium is shown by point *e*, with a price of $3.00 and a quantity of 10,000 miles per day. The total surplus is the area between the demand and supply curves.
(B) Taxi Medallions A medallion policy that fixes the number of taxis at 80 fixes the quantity of taxi service at 8,000 miles per day (100 miles per taxi) and increases the price to $3.60 (point *m*). The producers of the first 8,000 miles gain at the expense of consumers, but the surpluses on between 8,000 and 10,000 miles are lost entirely, so the total surplus decreases.

ACTIVE GRAPH

miles of service gain at the expense of consumers, but the surpluses on between 8,000 and 10,000 miles are lost entirely, so the total surplus of the market decreases.

Another way to see the inefficiency of taxi medallions is to look at the consumers and producers who are excluded from the market. Some of the excluded consumers would gladly pay the cost of providing taxi service. As shown by the points between m and e on the demand curve, many consumers are willing to pay between $3.00 and $3.60 per mile for taxi service. Although there are plenty of drivers who would be willing to provide taxi service at these prices, they can't do so without a medallion. Because the medallion policy prevents these riders and drivers from executing mutually beneficial transactions, the policy causes inefficiency.

Our analysis of taxi medallions applies to any market subject to quantity controls. State and city governments use licensing to limit many small businesses. Some cities limit the number of housing units by limiting the number of permits to build housing. These policies decrease the quantity supplied, increase prices, and cause inefficiency. Although some producers are willing to supply the good at a lower price, the government does not allow them to do so. Sometimes governments go beyond simply reducing the quantity produced, and outlaw markets for some goods. For an example, read "A Closer Look: A Market for Used Human Organs?"

Winners and Losers from Medallions

Who benefits and who loses from the city's medallion policy? The losers are consumers, who pay more for taxi rides. The winners are the people who receive a free medallion and the right to charge an artificially high price for taxi service. In some cities, people buy and sell taxi medallions, and the market value of a medallion reflects the profits it can earn its owner. The market price of a medallion is over $150,000 in New York City, $140,000 in Boston and $100,000 in Toronto.[3] In cities such as Chicago, where medallions are more plentiful, the market price is much lower.

To be a winner in the medallion game, you must have received a medallion free of charge from the government. If you were to buy a medallion at the current market price (say, $100,000), you won't benefit from the medallion policy because the price you pay will be just high enough to offset any profits you'll earn with the medallion. In fact, you would be a big loser if, after you buy a medallion, the city issues more medallions. An increase in the number of medallions—and taxis—will decrease the price and profits of taxi service, decreasing the market price of your medallion. One reason that medallion schemes persist is that the current owners of medallions would lose a lot of money if the government allowed additional taxis to enter the market.

 **A CLOSER LOOK**   A Market For Used Human Organs?

Each year, thousands of Americans die waiting for replacement kidneys, hearts, livers, pancreases, and lungs. In the last decade, improvements in the effectiveness of organ transplants have increased the demand for used human organs. Because the supply hasn't increased along with demand, there are shortages of transplantable organs. In a normal market, the price would rise to eliminate the shortage, but because it is illegal to buy and sell human organs, there is no pricing mechanism to close the gap between the quantity supplied and the quantity demanded. The conventional approach to the organ shortage is to appeal to people's generosity, urging

them to commit their organs to the transplant program. The failure of this approach led Nobel-winning economist Gary Becker to suggest monetary incentives for organ donors. Under his proposal, the federal government would pay organ donors and their survivors and would distribute the organs to hospitals for transplanting. This proposal raises all sorts of ethical questions and has not been embraced by many policy makers or health experts.

Source: Gary S. Becker, "How Uncle Sam Could Ease the Organ Shortage," *Business Week*, January 20, 1997, p. 18.

The Case of the Cheap Pet Salon

After 20 years of dog haircuts, perms, and pedicures, Doug wants to sell his pet-grooming salon. Several months earlier, a similar pet salon sold for $50,000. But Doug hasn't found anyone willing to buy his for more than $20,000. He suspects that the city has quietly increased the number of pet-grooming licenses, and that's why the price of grooming services dropped, pulling down the market price of pet salons like his. According to the local pet-grooming association, the quantity of grooming services (the number of haircuts, perms, and pedicures) has not changed in recent years. Why has the market price of a pet salon decreased so much? Has the city issued more licenses, or is there another explanation?

The key to solving this mystery is the fact that the quantity of grooming service hasn't changed. This means that the city hasn't issued any more licenses. In Figure 6.6, the vertical line at 300 indicates the fixed supply resulting from the city's limit on the number of grooming licenses. An increase in the number of licenses would shift this line to the right and increase the quantity of service. Therefore, the lower prices for grooming services—and lower prices for pet salons—must have been caused by a decrease in the demand for grooming services. The demand curve shifted to the left, decreasing the price of grooming services from $12 to $9. The lower price means that pet salons will be less profitable, meaning that Doug must accept a lower price for his salon. ◆

Import Restrictions

We've seen that the government can control the quantity of a good produced by issuing a limited number of business licenses to producers. Another way to control quantity is to limit the imports of a particular good. Like a licensing scheme, an import restriction increases the market price and decreases the total surplus of the market.

To show the market effects of import restrictions, let's start with an unrestricted market. Panel A of Figure 6.7 shows the market equilibrium in a sugar market when there is free trade. The domestic supply curve shows the quantity supplied by domestic

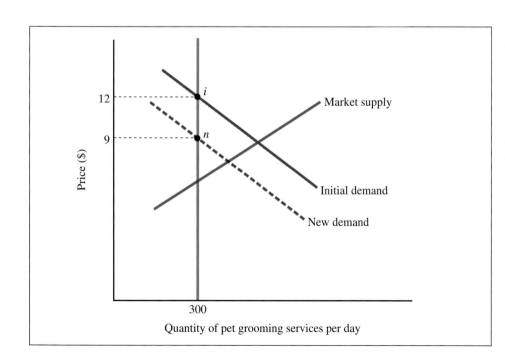

Figure 6.6
Decrease in Demand and the Price of Pet Grooming
If the quantity of grooming services hasn't changed, a decrease in price is a result of a decrease in demand, not an increase in the number of grooming licenses. The decrease in demand decreases the price from $12 to $9. The lower price of grooming services reduces the profits for pet salons, decreasing their market value.

Figure 6.7

The Effects of an Import Ban on Prices, Consumer Surplus, and Producer Surplus
(A) Free Trade with No Domestic Production With free trade, demand intersects the total supply curve at point *i*, with a price of 12¢ and a quantity of 360 million pounds. This price is below the minimum price of domestic suppliers (26¢, as shown by point *m*), so domestic firms do not participate in the market. The total surplus is shown by the shaded areas (consumer and producer surplus).
(B) Import Ban and Domestic Production If sugar imports are banned, the equilibrium is shown by the intersection of the demand curve and the domestic (U.S.) supply curve (point *d*). The price increases to 30¢. Although the ban generates a producer surplus for domestic producers, their gain is less than the loss of domestic consumers.

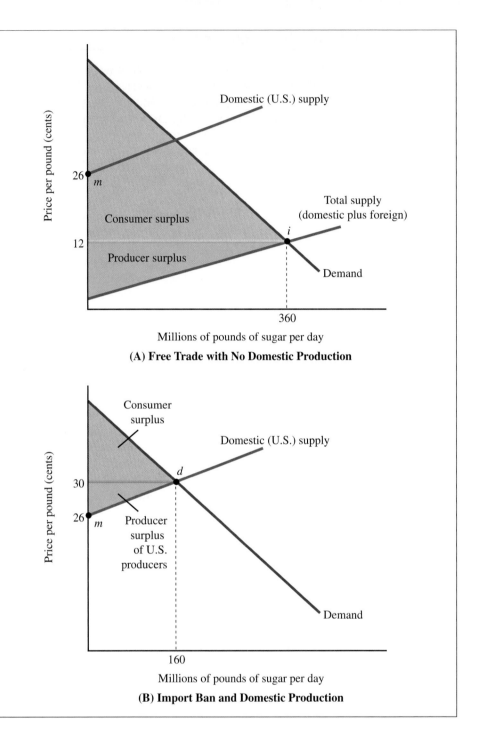

(A) Free Trade with No Domestic Production

(B) Import Ban and Domestic Production

(U.S.) firms at different prices. Looking at point *m*, we see that U.S. firms will not supply any sugar unless the price is at least 26 cents per pound. The total supply curve, which shows the quantity supplied by both domestic and foreign firms, lies to the right of the domestic curve. At each price, the total supply exceeds the domestic supply because foreign firms also supply sugar. Point *i* shows the free-trade equilibrium: The domestic demand curve (showing the demand by U.S. consumers) intersects the total supply curve at a price of 12 cents per pound and a quantity of 360 million pounds per day.

Because this price is below the minimum price for domestic firms, domestic firms do not supply any sugar.

What would happen if the United States banned sugar imports? Foreign suppliers would disappear from the market, so the total supply of sugar would be the domestic supply. In Panel B of Figure 6.7, the new equilibrium is shown by point *d*: The demand curve intersects the domestic supply curve at a price of 30 cents per pound and a quantity of 160 million pounds. The decrease in supply resulting from the import ban increases the price and decreases the quantity, and domestic firms produce all the sugar for the domestic market.

The import ban decreases the total surplus of the market. The shaded areas in the two graphs show the consumer and producer surpluses with and without free trade. The import ban reduces consumer surplus, as shown by the two pink triangles in the two graphs. The ban also eliminates the producer surplus of foreign suppliers (shown by the blue triangle in Panel A of Figure 6.7) and generates a producer surplus for domestic suppliers (shown by the blue triangle in Panel B of Figure 6.7). The import ban causes domestic producers to gain at the expense of domestic consumers. Consumers lose more than domestic producers gain, so the import ban causes a net loss for people in the domestic economy.

Import restrictions are often defended on the grounds that they increase employment in the protected industries. The protection of these jobs increases consumer prices, so there is a trade-off: more jobs in the protected industry, but higher prices for consumers. According to one study, import restrictions in force in 1993 protected 56,464 jobs in the U.S. textile and apparel industries at a cost to consumers of about $178,000 per job, and protected 3,419 jobs in the motor-vehicle industry at a cost of about $271,000 per job.[4]

In many cases, policies that restrict imports are more subtle than an explicit ban. For some examples, read "A Closer Look: International Food Fights."

TEST Your Understanding

5. Why do tenants in rent-control cities voluntarily pay extra money for nonrefundable cleaning deposits and keys?

6. In Figure 6.5, consider a consumer who is represented by a point on the demand curve halfway between point *m* and point *e*. How much is the consumer willing to pay for a mile of taxi service? Consider a producer who is represented by a point on the supply curve halfway between point *s* and point *e*. What is the marginal cost of a mile of taxi service? Describe a mutually beneficial transaction between the consumer and the producer.

7. In Figure 6.7, how much sugar will domestic firms produce at a price of $0.15?

8. Complete the statement with *increases* or *decreases*: An import ban _____ the price of sugar, _____ the quantity of sugar, and _____ the output of the domestic sugar industry.

Spillovers and Market Inefficiency

Up to this point in the chapter, we have assumed that there are no spillovers in consumption or production. As we will see in this last part of the chapter, when there are spillover costs, the market equilibrium will be inefficient and government intervention may be beneficial.

A CLOSER LOOK International Food Fights

In some cases, a country restricts imports indirectly, using rules and regulations to protect domestic firms from foreign competition. Japan requires foreign exporters of fruit to test their goods for the presence of harmful insects and diseases. In a case brought before the World Trade Association (WTO), the United States argued that Japan's quarantine testing system, which can take up to two years to complete, was not justified on scientific grounds. In 1999, the WTO ruled in favor of the United States, directing Japan to revise and simplify its quarantine procedures. The ruling is expected to increase the volume of apples, cherries, peaches, walnuts, and nectarines exported to Japan.

Australia and New Zealand were involved in a similar dispute. Australia claimed that apples imported from New Zealand posed a risk of spreading fireblight to Australian trees. New Zealand responded that the fireblight risk is trivial, estimating that there would be one case of fireblight every 10,000 years. Moreover, claimed the New Zealanders, fireblight was already present in Australia. This case is expected to be decided by the WTO.

Source: "Apple Export Ban Likely to Add Bite to Trade Talks," *Wellington Newspapers Limited*, December 16, 1998, p. 2.

 ## SPILLOVER **PRINCIPLE**

> **For some goods, the cost or benefit of the good are not confined to the person or organization that decides how much of the good to produce or consume.**

In this section, we'll take a brief look at the implications of spillover costs for market efficiency. Later in the book, we'll take a more detailed look at spillovers—including spillover costs and benefits—and discuss several policy responses to them.

Spillover Costs

We can use the cardboard market to illustrate the inefficiency that occurs in a market with spillover costs. Suppose there are several cardboard mills along a river and that a city downstream from the mills draws water from the river for drinking. The city's water-treatment costs depend on how much chemical waste is dumped into the river. For each gallon of chemical waste from cardboard mills, the city's treatment costs increase by $2. There are spillover costs because the decision-makers in the cardboard mills ignore the costs incurred by people in the downstream city. In other words, some of the costs of producing cardboard are external to the firm, where decisions about how much cardboard to produce are made. Another word for spillover is *externality*.

Panel A of Figure 6.8 shows the market equilibrium in the cardboard market. The demand curve intersects the supply curve at point *e*, generating a price of $30 per ton and a quantity of 50 tons per day. The total surplus (the sum of consumer and producer surplus) is shown by the pink and blue triangles, the area between the demand curve and the supply curve. The total pollution cost depends on how much chemical waste is generated, which depends on how much cardboard is produced. If each ton of cardboard generates 5 gallons of waste at a cost of $2 per gallon to the city, the pollution cost per ton of cardboard is $10. In the market equilibrium with 50 tons of cardboard, the total pollution cost is $500, shown as the area of the brown rectangle.

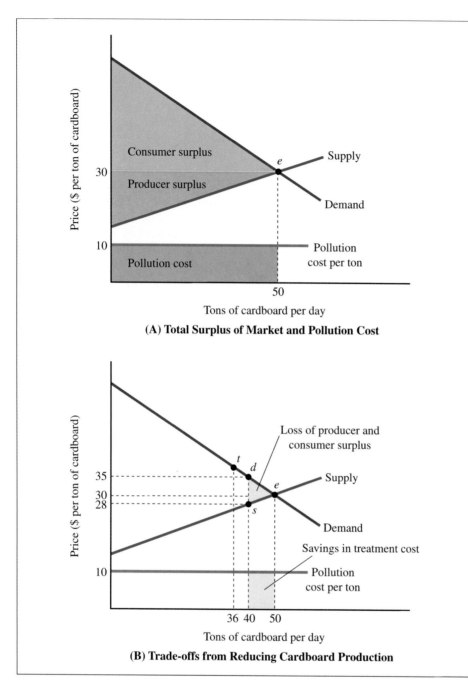

Figure 6.8
Market Inefficiency with Pollution Costs
(A) Total surplus of market and external cost In the market equilibrium, shown by point *e*, the price is $30 per ton and the quantity is 50 tons. The triangles show the total surplus of the market (consumer surplus plus producer surplus). The rectangle shows the total pollution cost.
(B) Trade-offs from reducing cardboard production Reducing the quantity of cardboard generates good news and bad news. The triangle shows the bad news: the loss of consumer and producer surplus. The rectangle shows the good news: the savings in pollution cost. In this case, the good news is greater than the bad news, so reducing the quantity is sensible.

Trade-Offs from Producing Less

What are the trade-offs from reducing the quantity of cardboard? We know that the equilibrium quantity maximizes the sum of consumer and producer surplus, so producing less will decrease the surpluses. Suppose production drops from 50 tons to 40 tons. In Panel B of Figure 6.8, the sum of consumer and producer surplus decreases by an amount shown by the yellow triangle. This is the bad news associated with reducing the quantity of cardboard by 10 tons. If there were no spillovers, there would be no good news from reducing cardboard production to offset this bad news. In the absence of spillovers, it would clearly be inefficient to produce less than the equilibrium quantity.

Because there are spillover costs from cardboard production, however, there is some good news from producing less. For each ton of cardboard not produced, the city's treatment costs decrease by $10. The savings in pollution costs from reducing paper production from 50 to 40 tons is $100 ($10 per ton times 10 tons), shown by the yellow rectangle in Panel B of Figure 6.8. In this case, the good news (savings in pollution costs shown by the rectangle) is greater than the bad news (the reduction of the total surplus of the market, shown by the triangle), so it is sensible to reduce paper production. The rectangle is bigger than the triangle, meaning that the gain of the downstream city exceeds the loss of cardboard consumers and producers.

If cutting cardboard production by 10 tons is a good idea, what about eliminating the cardboard market? Of course, that means the elimination of the consumer and producer surplus of cardboard. This bad news is shown in Panel A of Figure 6.8 as the pink and blue triangles (the total surplus of the market). The good news from eliminating the market would be that the city's treatment costs would decrease by $500 ($10 times 50 tons), shown by the brown rectangle in Panel A of Figure 6.8. The elimination of the cardboard market is not sensible because the bad news (shown by the pink and blue triangles) exceeds the good news (shown by the brown rectangle). In this case, the gain of the downstream city is less than the loss of cardboard consumers and producers.

What is the socially efficient quantity of cardboard? We've seen that the market equilibrium generates too much cardboard, but the elimination of the market would not be sensible. We could use the marginal principle to decide how much to reduce cardboard production.

MARGINAL **PRINCIPLE**

Increase the level of an activity if its marginal benefit exceeds its marginal cost, but reduce the level if the marginal cost exceeds the marginal benefit. If possible, pick the level at which the marginal benefit equals the marginal cost.

In the case of the cardboard, the activity mentioned in the principle is reducing the quantity produced.

We've already seen the benefits and costs of reducing cardboard production as the good news (benefits) and bad news (costs) from producing less. What about the marginal benefits and marginal costs?

- **Marginal benefit:** the savings in treatment cost from reducing cardboard production by one ton.

- **Marginal cost:** the loss in consumer and producer surplus from reducing cardboard production by one ton.

The marginal principle tells us that we should cut cardboard production as long as the $10 savings in treatment cost exceeds the loss of consumer and producer surplus.

Suppose we have already cut production to 40 tons. The question is, starting from 40 tons of cardboard, should we cut cardboard production by one more ton? As shown by point d in Panel B of Figure 6.8, a consumer is willing to pay $35 for the 40th ton, so with a price of $30, the consumer surplus lost would be $5 (equal to $35 − $30). As shown by point s, the marginal cost of producing the 40th ton is $28, so the producer surplus lost by not producing the 40th ton would be $2 (equal to $30 − $28). When the losses in consumer and producer surplus are added, the marginal cost of cutting production from 40 to 39 tons is $7. Because this marginal cost is less than the $10 marginal benefit, it is sensible to cut production from 40 to 39 tons.

There is a simple graphical solution to the problem of finding the quantity of cardboard at which the marginal benefit of cutting back equals the marginal cost. The vertical difference between the demand curve and the supply curve shows the marginal cost of cutting output, the loss of consumer surplus plus the loss of producer surplus. If we find the quantity at which the vertical distance between the demand and supply curves equals the marginal benefit (the $10 savings in treatment cost), we have found the quantity that satisfies the marginal principle. In Panel B of Figure 6.8, this happens at point *t*, with 36 tons of cardboard. Going beyond this point to smaller quantity of cardboard would violate the marginal principle: The marginal benefit (the $10 savings in treatment cost) would be less than the marginal cost (the loss in consumer and producer surplus, as shown by the vertical difference between the demand and supply curves).

Market Effects of a Pollution Tax

We've seen that when there are spillover costs, the market equilibrium is inefficient in the sense that too much of the polluting good is produced. The economic approach to pollution is to force producers to pay for the pollution they generate, just as they pay for labor, raw materials, and machinery. In our cardboard example, the government could impose a pollution tax of $2 for each gallon of waste dumped into the river. The pollution tax internalizes the pollution externality: The tax means that the costs associated with the chemical waste from cardboard are no longer external to the firm (where decisions about how much to produce are made), but internal.

Figure 6.9 shows the market effects of the pollution tax. Because each ton of cardboard generates 5 gallons of chemical waste, a tax of $2 per gallon of waste increases the marginal cost of producing cardboard by $10 per ton ($2 per gallon times 5 gallons per ton). As shown in Figure 6.9, the pollution tax shifts the supply curve for cardboard up by $10. A new equilibrium reached at point *t*, with a price of $37 and a quantity of 36 tons. It's not a coincidence that this is the same point we found to be socially efficient using the marginal principle. When firms bear the full cost of production, including the cost of pollution, the market equilibrium is socially efficient.

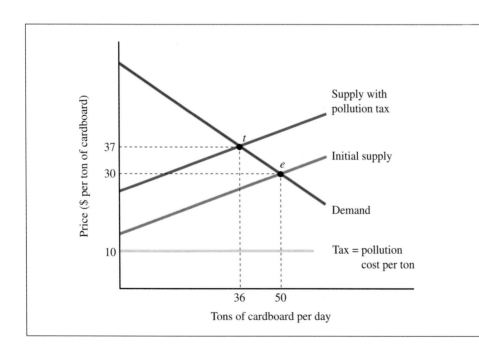

Figure 6.9

The Market Effect of a Tax on Pollution

A pollution tax of $2 per gallon of waste increases the marginal cost of producing cardboard by $10 per ton ($2 per gallon times 5 gallons of waste per ton of cardboard) and shifts the supply curve up by $10. The new equilibrium is shown by point *t*: The price increases from $30 to $37, and the quantity decreases to 36 tons per day.

TEST Your Understanding

9. Suppose the price of cardboard is $30 and a consumer is willing to pay $32 for the 45th ton of cardboard. If the marginal cost of producing the 45th ton is $29 how much consumer and producer surplus would be lost if the 45th ton is not produced?

10. What is the economic approach to pollution?

11. Suppose a new production process reduces the chemical waste per ton of cardboard to 3 gallons. By how much would a tax of $2 per gallon of waste increase the cost of producing a ton of cardboard?

Using the **TOOLS**

In this chapter, we used two of the tools of economics—the supply curve and the demand curve—to study the effect of government intervention in perfectly competitive markets with and without spillovers. Here are some opportunities to use these tools to do your own economic analysis.

1. ECONOMIC EXPERIMENT: Government Intervention

Recall the market-equilibrium experiment from Chapter 4. We can modify that experiment to show the various forms of government intervention in the market. After several trading periods without any government intervention, you can change the rules as follows:

* The instructor sets a maximum price for apples.
* The instructor sets a minimum price for apples.
* The instructor issues licenses to a few lucky producers.
* The instructor divides producers into domestic producers and foreign producers, and some of the foreign producers are excluded from the market.

2. Price Controls for Medical Care

Suppose that in an attempt to control the rising costs of medical care, the national government imposes price controls on visits to physicians. The maximum price for a physician visit is 10% less than the equilibrium price. Assume that the price elasticity of demand for physician visits is 0.60 and the price elasticity of supply is 1.5.

a. By what percentage will the quantity of medical care supplied decrease?

b. By what percentage will the quantity of medical care demanded increase?

c. Illustrate your answer with a graph.

d. What sort of inefficiencies will occur as a result of the maximum price?

e. Would you expect patients and physicians to find ways around the maximum price?

3. Barber Licensing

Consider the market for haircuts in a city. In the initial equilibrium, the price is $6, and the quantity is 200 haircuts per day. The demand curve for haircuts is linear, with 200 haircuts demanded at a price of $6 and 100 haircuts demanded at a price of $12. Initially, there are 20 barbers, each of whom produces 10 haircuts per day. Suppose the city passes a law requiring all barbers to have a license and then issues only 15 barber licenses. Each licensed barber continues to provide 10 haircuts per day.

Predict the new equilibrium price of haircuts and illustrate your answer with a supply-demand diagram.

4. Bidding for a Boston Taxi Medallion

In 1997, there were 1,500 taxi medallions in the city of Boston, and the price of a medallion was $140,000. In 1998, the city announced that it would issue 300 new taxi medallions, auctioning the new medallions to the highest bidders.[5] Even with the new medallions, the number of taxis in the city will still be less than the number that would occur in an unregulated market. If you were interested in entering the taxicab business, how much would you pay for one of these medallions? To compute the new price of a medallion, assume the following: The price elasticity of demand for taxi service is 2.0; the initial price is $5.00 per mile; the cost per mile of taxi service is $4.00 per mile.

Summary

In this chapter, we discussed the efficiency of markets and the consequences of government intervention in perfectly competitive markets. Government intervention in a market without spillovers prevents consumers and producers from executing beneficial transactions, meaning that intervention reduces the total surplus of the market and causes inefficiency. When there are spillover costs, it is sensible to intervene in markets to reduce the quantity produced. Here are the main points of the chapter:

1. The total surplus of a market equals the sum of consumer surplus and producer surplus.

2. In a perfectly competitive market without spillover costs, the market equilibrium maximizes the total surplus of the market, and is therefore efficient.

3. Price controls (a maximum or a minimum price) reduce the total surplus of a market because they prevent mutually beneficial transactions.

4. Quantity controls (licensing or import restrictions) decrease consumer surplus and the total surplus of the market.

5. When there are spillover costs from pollution, the market equilibrium is inefficient, but efficiency can be restored by imposing a tax on pollution.

Key Terms

consumer surplus, 121
producer surplus, 122

rent control, 127

taxi medallion, 128

Problems and Discussion Questions

1. What assumptions do we make to ensure that the market equilibrium in a perfectly competitive market is efficient? For each assumption, provide an example of a good for which the assumption is likely to be violated.

2. According to Ida, "I'm willing to buy a CD player for $50, but I can't find anyone willing to sell me one for that price." Does that mean that the market for CD players is inefficient?

3. Figure 6.A shows a supply curve and a demand curve and several areas between the curves. Identify the areas on the figure that represent the following:

   a. Consumer surplus in the market equilibrium
   b. Producer surplus in the market equilibrium
   c. Total surplus in the market equilibrium
   d. Consumer surplus under a maximum price of $10
   e. Producer surplus under a maximum price of $10

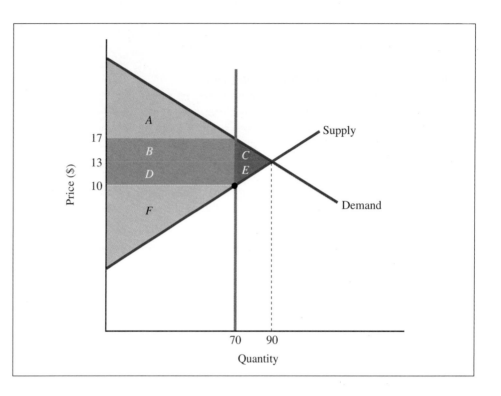

Figure 6.A

Identifying the Surpluses

f. Total surplus under a maximum price of $10

g. Consumer surplus under a maximum quantity of 70

h. Producer surplus under a maximum quantity of 70

i. Total surplus under a maximum quantity of 70

4. Your city just announced a new rent-control program under which the maximum rent on apartments will be 20% below the equilibrium price. The price elasticity of supply of apartments is 0.50.

   a. Use a supply-demand diagram to show the effects of the rent-control program on the rental housing market. The initial price is $300 per month and the initial quantity is 10,000 apartments. Label the initial equilibrium point with an *i* and the point that shows the quantity supplied under rent control with an *s*.

   b. By what percentage will the quantity of apartments increase or decrease?

5. Why are local rent controls (a maximum price on rental housing in a city) more common than a maximum price on food or clothing sold in a city?

6. In the gasoline market, the equilibrium price is $2 and the equilibrium quantity is 100 million gallons per day. Suppose the government sets a maximum price of $1.80. The price elasticity of supply of gasoline is 2.0, and the price elasticity of demand is 1.0.

Draw a graph and show the excess demand for gasoline. Compute the amount of excess demand.

7. In the example in the text of taxi medallions (Figure 6.5), suppose the city announces that it will issue 110 medallions instead of 80. Predict the market price of taxi service and the market price of medallions.

8. Using Figure 6.5 as a starting point, suppose the demand for taxi service decreases and the new demand curve intersects the supply curve at a quantity of 7,000 miles per day. If the government doesn't change the number of medallions, what happens to the price of a medallion?

9. Predict the effect of each of the following policies on the price of the relevant good. Then draw a supply-demand diagram to defend your answer.

   a. Licenses for dry cleaners

   b. Limit on building permits for housing

   c. Import restrictions on clothing

10. Suppose that initially there are no restrictions on importing kiwi fruit. The supply curves are the same as the supply curves for sugar shown in Figure 6.7. The initial price of kiwi fruit is 12 cents per piece. When imports are banned, the equilibrium price increases to 22 cents. Draw a market demand curve consistent with these numbers.

11. Suppose a new production process reduces the chemical waste per ton of cardboard to 3 gallons. Use

a supply-demand diagram to predict the effect of a pollution tax ($2 per gallon of waste) on the price and quantity of cardboard. Compared to the initial situation with 5 gallons of waste per ton, is the price higher or lower? Is the quantity larger or smaller? Explain any differences between the two cases.

12. Suppose that in response to concerns about greenhouse gases and global warming, the government imposes a tax of $0.50 per gallon on gasoline. Use a supply-demand diagram to show the effects of the tax on the gasoline market.

13. Web Exercise. Visit the Web site of the Adam Smith Institute (*www.adamsmith.org.uk*). Access the Policy Division and pick your favorite quote of Adam Smith. Explain the logic behind the quote.

14. Web Exercise. Visit the official Web site for New York City (*http://www.ci.nyc.ny.us/*). Search the site for information on taxi medallions. You should find Web pages that describe what's involved in becoming a medallion owner and provide some data on the price of taxi medallions. Describe the process involved in becoming a taxi medallion owner or report the most recent price of a medallion.

Take It to the Net

We invite you to visit the O'Sullivan/Sheffrin page on the Prentice Hall Web site at:
http://www.prenhall.com/osullivan/
for additional World Wide Web exercises for this chapter.

Model Answers to Questions

Chapter-Opening Questions

1. The rent-control policy decreases the quantity of apartments supplied, forcing some students out of the market.

2. The city limits the number of taxi licenses or medallions, leading to higher taxi prices and large profits for people who own the medallions.

3. It is illegal to buy or sell human organs, so there is no pricing mechanism to close the gap between quantity demanded and quantity supplied.

4. Consumers pay higher prices, and the cost per job saved is about $178,000.

5. Impose a tax equal to the cost per unit of pollution.

Test Your Understanding

1. The willingness to pay, price, price, marginal cost.

2. The price would be $1,700, giving you and Pablo each a surplus of $300.

3. Forest is willing to pay $13, and Dee's marginal cost is $8. If they split the difference, the price would be $10.50, and each would get a surplus of $2.50.

4. No spillover costs, no spillover benefits, perfect competition, informed buyers and sellers.

5. Many consumers are willing to pay more than the controlled price for an apartment, and deposits and

key money allow them to do so and get an apartment they could otherwise not get.

6. The consumer is willing to pay $3.30, and the producer's marginal cost is $2.80. If they split the difference, agreeing on a price of $3.05, each will get a surplus of $0.25.

7. Zero. This is below the minimum domestic price.

8. Increases, decreases, increases.

9. The consumer loses $2 ($32 – $30) and the producer loses $1 ($30 – $29), for a combined loss of $3.

10. Impose a tax on pollution equal to the cost generated by the pollution.

11. The tax increases cost per ton by $6 ($2 per gallon times 3 gallons per ton).

Using the Tools

2. Price Controls for Medical Care

   a. Using the supply elasticity formula, the quantity of doctor visits supplied will decrease by 15%: 1.5 = 15%/10%.

   b. Using the demand elasticity formula, the quantity of doctor visits demanded will increase by 6%: 0.60 = 6%/10%.

   c. In Figure 6.B, the initial equilibrium point (before the maximum price) is shown by point *i*:

Figure 6.B
Maximum Prices for Medical Care

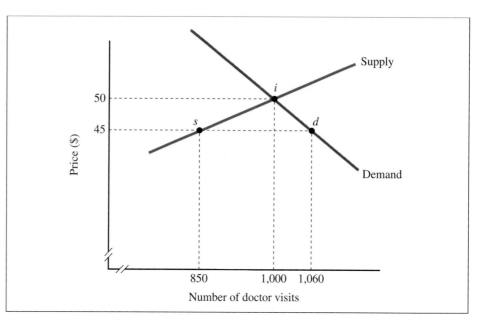

The price is $50 and the quantity is 1,000 visits. The maximum price is $45, so the new quantity supplied is 850 (point *s*), and the new quantity demanded is 1,060 (point *d*).

d. The policy outlaws transactions that would benefit a buyer and a seller and causes a shortage (excess demand) that will increase the time spent waiting for doctors.

e. Perhaps doctors can increase the prices charged for other services (X-rays, stitches, vaccinations, other office procedures).

3. Barber Licensing. See Figure 6.C. If there are 15 licenses, the maximum quantity is 150 haircuts per day. This quantity is halfway between 100 (at which the price is $12) and 200 (at which the price is $6), so the new price is $9.

Figure 6.C
Market Effects of Barber Licenses

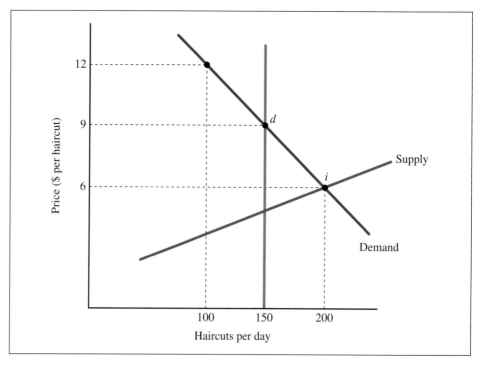

4. Bidding for a Boston Taxi Medallion. The new medallions will increase the quantity of taxi service supplied by 20 percent (300/1,500). The price of taxi service will drop by an amount large enough to increase the quantity demanded by 20 percent. According to the price-elasticity formula from Chapter 5, the price will decrease by 10 percent:

$$E_d = \frac{\text{percentage change in quantity demanded}}{\text{percentage change in price}}$$

$$= 2.0 = \frac{20 \text{ percent}}{10 \text{ percent}}$$

In other words, to close the gap between the quantity supplied and the larger quantity supplied, the price must drop by 10 percent, from $5.00 to $4.50. The profit per mile of service drops from $1.00 (equal to the price of $5.00 minus the cost per mile of $4.00) to $0.50 (equal to $4.50 minus $4.00). Because the price of medallions reflects the profit earned from taxi service, cutting the profit per mile in half will cut the price of a medallion in half as well. Therefore, we expect the price of medallions to drop from $140,000 to $70,000.

Notes

1. William Tucker, "A Model for Destroying a City," *Wall Street Journal*, March 12, 1993, p. A8.

2. J. K. Smith, "An Analysis of State Regulations Governing Liquor Store Licensees," *Journal of Law and Economics*, October 1982, pp. 301–319; David Kirp and Eileen Soffer, "Taking Californians to the Cleaners," *Regulation*, September/October 1985, pp. 24–26; D. W. Taylor, "The Economic Effects of Direct Regulation of Taxicabs in Metropolitan Toronto," *Logistics and Transportation Review*, June 1989, pp. 169–182.

3. Taylor, "The Economic Effects of Direct Regulation of Taxicabs in Metropolitan Toronto."

4. *The Economic Effects of Significant U.S. Import Restraints* (Washington, DC: U.S. International Trade Commission, initial report in 1993; update in 1996).

5. Brown, Laura, "Hub cabbie hopefuls cry: The Russians are Coming!" *Boston Herald*, Dec. 16, 1998, p. 1.

Consumer Choice

During the nineteenth century, some philosophers thought it was possible to measure the utility or satisfaction consumers receive from goods and services. The idea was to hook a person up to some sort of machine, let the person consume a product such as a pie, and then read from the machine's gauges the amount of additional happiness, or utility, generated by the pie. Because such a machine has not been invented, it is impossible to measure utility. Jeremy Bentham, one of these "utilitarians," died in London in 1832. He helped establish University College, London, and his fully clothed skeleton—with a wax head—is kept in a glass case there.

s we saw in Chapter 4, the demand curve shows the relationship between the price of a good and the quantity that a consumer is willing to buy. The demand curve is negatively sloped, reflecting the law of demand: The higher the price, the smaller the quantity demanded, ceteris paribus (everything else held fixed). In this chapter, we use some of the key principles of economics to explain the logic behind the demand curve and the law of demand.

This chapter takes a close look at the consumer's decision-making process. Here are some practical questions we'll answer:

1. **How should a consumer divide his or her income among alternative goods and services?**
2. **Once you pay the admission fee to Disneyland, all the rides are free. Unfortunately, you may wait for two or three hours to get on your favorite ride. Why don't the managers of Disneyland shorten the lines by charging a dollar or two for each ride?**

The Marginal Principle and Individual Demand

Let's consider a hypothetical market for burgers and examine the decisions of Bob, a consumer who has a fixed income of $30 per month to spend on two goods: burgers and tacos. Bob must decide how many burgers and tacos to buy each month. The quantity of burgers he buys is determined by a number of factors, including the price of burgers, the price of tacos, his income, and his tastes or preferences for the two goods.

The individual demand curve in Figure 7.1 shows the quantity of burgers Bob is willing to buy (demand) at each price. To find each point on the demand curve, we pick a price, say $3 per burger, and answer the question "How many burgers is Bob willing to buy at that price?" If the answer is 8 burgers per month, point *b* (with $3 on the price axis and 8 burgers on the quantity axis) is on Bob's demand curve. We can find a different point on the demand curve by choosing a different price, say $2, and asking the same question. If the answer is 11 burgers per month, point *c* is on Bob's demand curve too. We can find other points in the same way.

Figure 7.1

Individual Demand Curve

The individual demand curve is negatively sloped, consistent with the law of demand: The higher the price, the smaller the quantity demanded. If the price of burgers is $3, Bob consumes 8 burgers per month (point *b*). At a price of $2, he consumes 11 burgers per month (point *c*).

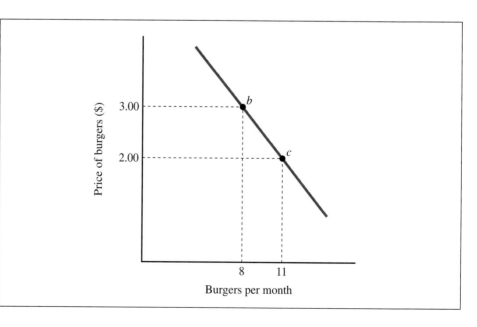

Each point on the individual demand curve is the result of a rational choice by the consumer. When we say "rational," we mean that the consumer considers the benefit and cost of the buying the good, and buys the good only if the benefit exceeds the cost. We can use the marginal principle to show how consumers incorporate benefits and costs into their consumption decisions.

MARGINAL **PRINCIPLE**

> **Increase the level of an activity if its marginal benefit exceeds its marginal cost, but reduce the level if the marginal cost exceeds the marginal benefit. If possible, pick the level at which the marginal benefit equals the marginal cost.**

Bob's activity is buying burgers, so he should pick the quantity of burgers at which the marginal benefit of burgers equals the marginal cost.

Total and Marginal Utility

Before we use the marginal principle, let's think about how to measure the benefit of buying a particular good. A consumer's benefit from a product is the **utility** from the product, defined as the pleasure or satisfaction from consuming the product. Although it's easy to define the benefit, it is difficult to measure: We can't hook Bob up to a satisfaction meter to determine how much happier he is after eating a burger. Nonetheless, suppose we can measure the consumer's benefit as the number of utils generated by the good (a **util** is one unit of utility or satisfaction).

Utility: The satisfaction the consumer experiences when he or she consumes a good.

The **total utility** from a product is defined as the utility or satisfaction from whatever quantity of the product the consumer gets. Panel A of Figure 7.2 shows the relationship between Bob's total utility from burgers and the number of burgers he buys. As the number of burgers increases, Bob's total utility increases, but at a decreasing rate. When Bob buys his first burger, his total utility increases from zero to 26 utils (point u on the total utility curve). When he buys the second burger, his utility increases from 26 to 50 utils (point v), so buying the second burger increases Bob's utility by 24 utils (50 – 26). Buying the second burger increases Bob's total utility, but the second burger adds less utility (24 utils) than the first (26 utils). Moving upward along the curve, the eighth burger increases Bob's utility by only 12 utils (152 minus 140). Eventually, additional burgers actually decrease Bob's utility level, as shown by the points beyond point y on the curve.

Util: A unit of utility.
Total utility: The utility (measured in utils) from whatever quantity of the product the consumer gets.

Panel B of Figure 7.2 shows Bob's marginal-utility curve. **Marginal utility** is defined as the change in utility resulting from buying one additional unit of the good. According to the **law of diminishing marginal utility**, as the consumption of a particular good increases, marginal utility decreases. In panel B of Figure 7.2, the marginal utility drops from 26 utils for the first burger to 24 utils for the second burger down to 12 utils for the eighth burger.

Marginal utility: The change in total utility from one additional unit of the good.
Law of diminishing marginal utility: As the consumption of a particular good increases, marginal utility decreases.

The Marginal Benefit Curve

To use the marginal principle, we must compute the marginal benefit for different quantities of burgers. We're measuring benefits in terms of utility, so the marginal benefit is the same as the marginal utility. Table 7.1 shows Bob's marginal benefits for the fifth through the tenth burgers, with the values of marginal utility drawn from Figure 7.2. The marginal benefit is 18 utils for the fifth burger, 16 utils for the sixth burger, and so on, to 10 utils for the ninth burger.

Figure 7.2

Total and Marginal Utility

In panel A, as the quantity of burgers consumed increases, the utility or satisfaction increases at a decreasing rate. In panel B, as the quantity of burgers increases, the marginal utility (the change in utility from one more burger) decreases. Both curves reflect the law of diminishing marginal utility.

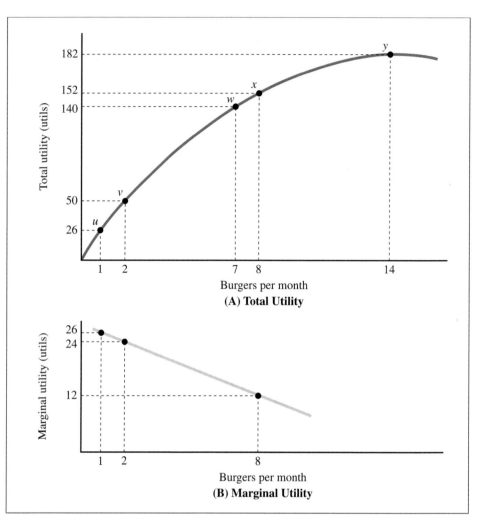

The Marginal Cost Curve

Bob has a fixed budget to spend on burgers and tacos, so for each burger he buys, he sacrifices some tacos. To compute the marginal cost of burgers, we must determine how much utility from tacos he sacrifices by buying a burger rather than some tacos. Table 7.2 shows his marginal utility for different quantities of tacos. For example, the top row shows that starting with 3 tacos, if Bob were to buy and eat one more taco, his total utility would increase by 5 utils. As we move down the table to larger quantities of tacos, the marginal utility decreases, consistent with the law of diminishing marginal utility.

Table 7.1 Marginal Utility of Burgers

Number of burgers	Marginal benefit (utility) of a burger
5	18
6	16
7	14
8	12
9	10

Table 7.2 Marginal Utility of Tacos

Number of tacos	Marginal benefit (utility) of a taco
3	5
6	4
9	3
12	2
15	1

Once we know the marginal-utility numbers for tacos, we can compute the marginal cost of burgers by following these five steps.

1. Pick a quantity of burgers, such as five burgers.

2. Determine how many tacos Bob could consume, given the following:
   - Assumed number of burgers
   - His income
   - The prices of the two goods.

   In our example, Bob's income is $30 and the price of burgers is $3, so if Bob buys five burgers, he spends $15 on burgers, leaving $15 to spend on tacos. The taco price is $1, so if he buys five burgers he can afford 15 tacos.

3. In Table 7.2, find the marginal utility of tacos, given the quantity of tacos computed in step 2. For example, with 15 tacos, the marginal utility of tacos (the extra utility from buying one more taco—the sixteenth taco) is 1 util.

4. Use the prices of the two goods to compute the trade-off between burgers and tacos, that is, the number of tacos sacrificed per burger. If the burger price is $3 and the taco price is $1, the trade-off is three tacos per burger.

5. Compute the marginal cost of a burger by multiplying the marginal utility of tacos (1 util per taco) by the trade-off between tacos and burgers (three tacos per burger). The marginal cost associated with the fifth burger is 3 utils:

   marginal cost of fifth burger = 1 util per taco × 3 tacos sacrificed per burger

This gives us one point on the marginal-cost curve, point *q* in Figure 7.3.

To draw the rest of the marginal-cost curve in Figure 7.3, we simply repeat these steps for different quantities of burgers. For example, if Bob buys six burgers:

- He can afford 12 tacos (spending $18 on burgers leaves $12 for 12 tacos)

- At this quantity of tacos, the marginal utility is 2 utils per taco (from the fourth row of Table 7.2)

- The marginal cost of the sixth burger is 6 utils (2 utils per taco × 3 tacos sacrificed).

This gives us point *s* on the marginal-cost curve, with a marginal cost of 6 utils.

The marginal cost curve is positively sloped. For example, starting with 5 burgers, the marginal cost is 3 utils (point *q*), while starting with 6 burgers, the marginal cost is 6 utils (point *s*). Why does the marginal cost increase as burger consumption increases?

- The more burgers Bob buys, the fewer tacos he can afford.

- The fewer tacos he consumes, the higher the marginal utility of tacos—a result of diminishing marginal utility in reverse.

Figure 7.3

Marginal Principle and Demand

The marginal benefit of burgers equals the marginal cost at eight burgers, so the marginal principle is satisfied at point *m*.

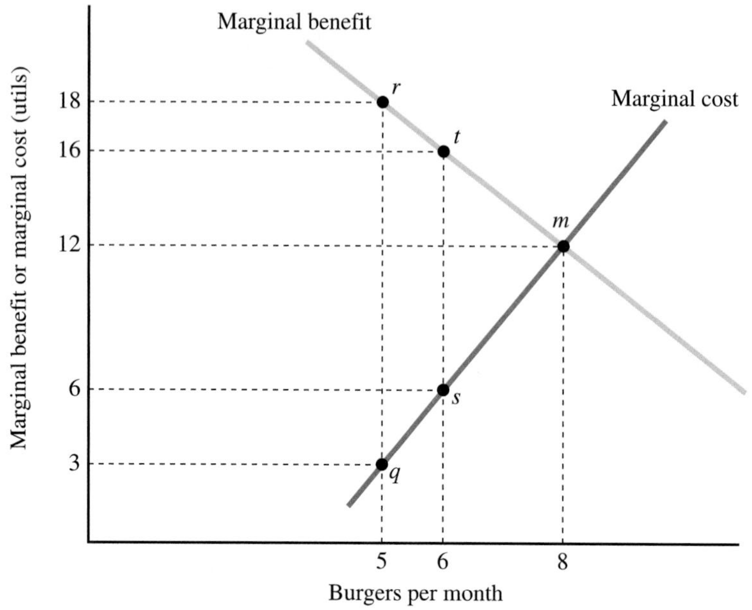

ACTIVE GRAPH

Burgers per month

Quantity	Marginal benefit (utils)	Marginal cost (utils)
5	$18	$3
6	$16	$6
7	$14	$9
8	**$12**	**$12**

If the marginal utility of tacos is higher, for each additional burger Bob consumes, he will sacrifice more taco utility (the marginal utility times the trade-off of three tacos per burger). The marginal cost of a burger is the taco utility sacrificed for an additional burger, so the marginal-cost curve is positively sloped.

Finding a Point on the Demand Curve

Figure 7.3 shows the marginal-benefit curve (the same as the marginal-utility curve) and the marginal-cost curve. The marginal-cost curve intersects the marginal-benefit curve at eight burgers. In other words, to satisfy the marginal principle Bob should buy 8 burgers. For each of the first eight burgers, the extra satisfaction from buying and eating the burger (the marginal benefit) is greater than or equal to the potential satisfaction from the three tacos he could have bought and eaten instead (the marginal cost). For example, the extra satisfaction from the fifth burger is 18 utils, compared to only 3 utils for the tacos he could have bought instead. Similarly, the marginal benefit is greater than the marginal cost for the sixth and seventh burgers; the marginal benefit equals the marginal cost for the eighth burger. Bob stops at eight burgers because the marginal benefit of the ninth burger (10 utils) is less than its marginal cost (15 utils from the tacos he could eat instead).

We've seen that one point on the demand curve satisfies the marginal principle. When the price of burgers is $3, Bob consumes eight burgers because that is the quantity at which the marginal benefit equals the marginal cost. If we repeated this exercise with different prices, we'd find that each point on the demand curve satisfies the marginal principle and therefore is a rational choice, given the price of the good.

Is it possible to measure the utility or satisfaction consumers receive from goods and services? As we saw in the chapter opener, utilitarians in the nineteenth century thought so. Unfortunately for the utilitarians, no one has invented a utility meter, so it is impossible to measure consumer utility. Nonetheless, utility theory is still useful as conceptual framework because it provides some insights into consumer decision-making. As explained in the Appendix to this chapter, economists have developed a different way to analyze consumer choices. This modern approach doesn't require the measurement of utility, but simply requires consumers to compare alternative bundles of goods and services.

The Utility-Maximizing Rule

We can use utility theory to introduce a general rule for consumer decisions. According to the **utility-maximizing rule**, a consumer will maximize his or her utility by picking the affordable combination of consumer goods that makes the marginal utility per dollar spent on one good equal to the marginal utility per dollar spent on a second good. In our example of burgers and tacos, this means that

$$\frac{\text{marginal utility of burgers}}{\text{price of burgers}} = \frac{\text{marginal utility of tacos}}{\text{price of tacos}}$$

Utility-maximizing rule: Pick the affordable combination of consumer goods that makes the marginal utility per dollar spent on one good equal to the marginal utility per dollar spent on a second good.

To get the marginal utility per dollar spent on burgers, we divide the marginal utility of burgers by the amount of money spent on each burger (the price of burgers). For example, the marginal utility of the eighth burger is 12 utils and the price is $3, so the marginal utility for each dollar spent on the eighth burger is 4 utils. Looking back at the numbers in Tables 7.1 and 7.2, we see that Bob's choice of eight burgers and six tacos satisfies the utility-maximizing rule: The marginal utility per dollar spent on tacos is 4 utils per dollar (4 utils for the sixth taco divided by a price of $1), which is the same as the marginal utility per dollar spent on burgers (12 utils for the eighth burger divided by $3). The utility-maximizing rule is consistent with the marginal principle.

To see the logic behind the utility-maximizing rule, let's see what would happen if Bob picked a different combination of burgers and tacos. Would it be wise to pick 5 burgers and 15 tacos? In this case the marginal utility per dollar spent on burgers is 6 utils per dollar (18 utils divided by $3), while the marginal utility per dollar spent on tacos is only 1 util per dollar (1 util divided by $1). In other words, he gets a bigger marginal utility per dollar—or a bigger "bang per buck"—for the money he spends on burgers. Therefore, it would be sensible to spend more money on burgers and less on tacos. To maximize his utility, he should increase his burger consumption as long as an additional burger generates a larger bang per buck (a larger marginal utility per dollar). He should stop at eight burgers and six tacos because the bang per buck of the ninth burger (3.33 utils per dollar) would be less than the bang per buck of tacos (4 utils per dollar).

We've seen how consumers make decisions about how much to buy, given their income and the prices of alternative goods. For a discussion of consumer decisions involving limited time instead of limited money, read "A Closer Look: The Economics of Disneylines."

At Disneyland, you pay an admission fee ($45 for adults, $35 for kids), and once you're in the park, there is no extra charge for rides such as the Pirates of the Caribbean, Splash Mountain, and Indiana Jones' Temple of the Forbidden Eye. With waiting times between one and three hours on the typical day, however, these rides are not free. Each ride has an opportunity cost equal to the time you'll spend in line. Once you're in the park, you don't have to worry about how to spend money on rides, but you must decide how to spend your limited time on them. You'll be helped out by the large signs that list the waiting times for all the rides and attractions.

Why doesn't Disney charge a price for each attraction according to its popularity, with the price of each high enough to reduce the time wasted in lines? Economists have developed three possible explanations:

- People don't like to think about money while they are vacationing. It is not a coincidence that the other examples of this type of pricing—cruise ships, ski resorts, and other theme parks—cater to vacationers.
- Waiting in line validates the consumer's decision. "If all these people are here," the consumer thinks, "I made a great choice to be here."

Part of the cost of a ride at Disneyland is the opportunity cost of time spent waiting in line.

- The lines allow parents to economize on expenses without having to say "No" to their kids. If Disney charged a price high enough to eliminate the lines, a family could spend hundreds of dollars on a day of fun. By forcing kids to wait in line, parents can save money without being held responsible for limiting the fun.

Source: Peter Passell, "Disneyland and the Old USSR: Sharing Something in Common," *New York Times*, April 24, 1996.

TEST Your Understanding

1. Betty bought five books in January, six books in February, and seven books in March. Her utility level from books was 30 utils in January, 45 utils in February, and 54 utils in March. Are these utility numbers consistent with the law of diminishing marginal utility?

2. As a person's consumption of a particular good increases, what happens to the marginal benefit of that good? Relate your answer to the law of diminishing marginal utility.

3. Suppose that Bob initially consumes 6 burgers and 12 tacos. Use the numbers in Tables 7.1 and 7.2 to compute the marginal utility per dollar spent for each good. Which good generates the larger bang per buck?

Using the **TOOLS**

In this chapter, we use some of the key principles of economics to explain the logic behind consumer choice and the law of demand. Here are some opportunities to do your own economic analysis.

1. Consumer Metrics

You are the economist for Consumer Metrics, a consumer research firm that has developed a new device that measures the satisfaction level of a consumer before and after consuming a particular product. At the company's annual holiday party, people ate food and drank punch, and the firm paid for everything. By the end of the party, everything was consumed. Your job is to determine whether the company spent its party budget wisely. If you could hook the new device to the typical person at the party, what information would you collect, and how would you use it? What additional information would you need to determine whether the firm's chosen combination of food and punch maximized the utility of the typical partygoer?

2. Gasoline or Gasohol?

Consider the following statement: "My car can use either gasoline or gasohol (a mixture of methanol and gasoline). I use whatever fuel has a lower price per gallon." Is this a good rule for deciding what type of fuel to use in a car? If not, develop a rule that is consistent with the utility-maximizing rule.

Summary

We've seen that the market demand curve represents the rational decisions of individual consumers. We've also used utility theory to think about how people make consumption decisions. Here are the main points of the chapter.

1. Each point on the demand curve satisfies the marginal principle: The consumer increases the number of units consumed until the marginal benefit equals the marginal cost.

2. To maximize utility, a consumer should pick the affordable combination of goods that makes the marginal utility per dollar spent on one good equal to the marginal utility per dollar spent on a second good.

Key Terms

Problems and Discussion Questions

1. Suppose the price of muffins is $2 and the price of cookies is $1. Use the following table to determine how many muffins Betty will consume, given a budget of $60.

Muffins		Cookies	
Number of muffins	Marginal benefit (utility) of a muffin	Number of cookies	Marginal benefit (utility) of a cookie
5	11	44	6
6	8	46	5
7	5	48	4
8	3	50	3

2. Suppose you have a fixed monthly budget for audio tapes and CDs. The price of CDs is $10, and the price of tapes is $5. Given your current choice of CDs and tapes, your marginal utility of CDs is 60, and your marginal utility of tapes is 15. Are you doing the best you can with your music budget? If not, should you buy more CDs (and fewer tapes) or more tapes (and fewer CDs)? Relate your answer to the marginal principle and the utility-maximizing rule.

3. Suppose you have a fixed budget of $3,000 per year to spend on food and music. The price of food is $1 per pound, and the price of music is $10 per CD. You currently spend $2,400 on food and $600 on music. If you want to determine whether you are spending your money wisely, what questions must you ask yourself?

4. **Web Exercise.** Visit the Web site for the Kelley Blue Book (*http://www.kbb.com*). This site provides pricing information for new and used cars. Consider a Honda Accord LX Sedan with automatic transmission. How does the price of this model vary with age (the model year) and mileage? What's the price for a 1992 model with 90,000 miles? What's the price for a 1992 model with only 80,000 miles? From your perspective, is it worth spending the additional money to get a car with 10,000 fewer miles?

5. **Web Exercise.** Suppose you decide to buy a new digital camera. To get the facts on the alternative cameras, visit the Web site of *Consumers Digest* (*http://www.consumersdigest.com/*). How does this site help consumers to decide between alternative products?

Take It to the Net

We invite you to visit the O'Sullivan/Sheffrin page on the Prentice Hall Web site at:
http://www.prenhall.com/osullivan/
for additional World Wide Web exercises for this chapter.

Model Answers to Questions

Chapter-Opening Questions

1. According to the utility-maximizing rule, the consumer should pick the affordable combination of consumer goods that makes the marginal utility per dollar spent on one good equal to the marginal utility per dollar spent on a second good.

2. "A Closer Look: The Economics of Disneylines," lists three possible explanations: Consumers like to avoid thinking about money on vacations; waiting in lines validates consumers' decisions; lines allow parents to economize on expenses without having to say "No."

Test Your Understanding

1. The marginal utility drops from 15 for the sixth book to 9 for the seventh book, consistent with the law of diminishing marginal utility.

2. The marginal benefit equals the marginal utility, which according to the law of diminishing marginal utility, decreases as consumption increases.

3. For burgers, 5.33 utils per dollar (16 utils divided by $3); for tacos, 2 utils per dollar (2 utils divided by $1). Burgers generate a larger bang per buck.

Using the Tools

1. Consumer Metrics. You could use the device to determine the marginal utility of food (the change in utility or satisfaction from eating the last ounce) and the marginal utility of punch (the change in utility or satisfaction from drinking the last ounce). If you get information on the prices of food and punch (prices per ounce), you could compute the marginal utility per dollar (bang per buck) for both food and punch. To maximize utility, the firm should equate the bang per buck on the two goods.

2. Gasoline or Gasohol? Applying the utility-maximizing rule, utility is the miles driven on a tank of fuel, and marginal utility is the miles per gallon of fuel (mpg). The rule suggests that to maximize utility, a driver should equate the mpg of gasohol divided by the price of gasohol to the mpg of gasoline divided by the price of gasoline. If the consumer picks one fuel or the other, she or he should pick the fuel that has the higher mpg divided by price. For example, suppose the price of gasohol is $1 per gallon and the price of gasoline is $1.25. If gasohol has an mpg of 18 and gasoline has an mpg of 25, gasoline is a better buy: It provides 20 miles per dollar, compared to 18 miles per dollar for gasohol. Although gasoline is more expensive, its higher mpg more than offsets the higher price per gallon. The rule suggested in the quote is misguided because it doesn't take into account differences in mpg.

Consumer Choice Using Indifference Curves

In Chapter 7 we used utility theory to show that each point on the demand curve is the result of a rational choice by the consumer. In this appendix, we use a different model of consumer behavior to explain how the consumer makes this rational choice. The model is based on the notion that the consumer's objective is to maximize his or her utility, given the limitations dictated by his or her income and the prices of consumer goods. In contrast to the old-style utility theory discussed earlier, this modern approach does not require the measurement of utility or satisfaction. It just requires us to determine the rate at which a consumer is willing to trade one good for another. The modern approach is more realistic and useful because a consumer can easily answer the question "How many tacos am I willing to give up to get one more burger?"

The Budget Set and Budget Line

Consider Bob, who has a fixed income of $30 per month, which he spends entirely on two goods: burgers and tacos. Bob must decide how many burgers and tacos to consume each month, given a $3 price per burger and a $1 price per taco.

Bob's ability to purchase burgers and tacos is limited by his income and the prices of the two goods. A consumer's **budget set** is defined as all the combinations of two goods the consumer can afford, given his or her income and the prices of two goods. Bob's budget set

Budget set: A set of points that includes all the combinations of goods that a consumer can afford, given the consumer's income and the prices of the goods.

includes all the combinations of burgers and tacos that he can afford, given his income and the prices of burgers and tacos. In Figure 7A.1, the budget set is shown by the shaded triangle. A consumer's **budget line** shows all the combinations that exhaust his or her budget. In Figure 7A.1 the budget line connects points y and x. At point y, Bob spends his entire budget on tacos, getting 30 tacos ($30 = $1 per taco times 30 tacos); at point x, he spends his entire budget on burgers, getting 10 burgers ($30 = $3 per burger times 10 burgers). If Bob spends some money on each good, he can reach the points between y and x. For example, he could reach point e (eight burgers and six tacos) by spending $24 on burgers and $6 on tacos. The budget set is the shaded area below the budget line.

The slope of the budget line is the market trade-off between burgers and tacos. It shows the rate at which the consumer can trade burgers for tacos, given the market prices of the two goods. Starting from any point on the budget line, if Bob buys one more burger, he uses $3 that he could have used instead to buy three tacos. The market trade-off is equal to the ratio of the two prices, the price of burgers divided by the price of tacos. The slope of the budget line is the negative of the price ratio, –3.0 tacos per burger in our example.

Indifference Curves

We can represent the consumer's preferences or tastes with indifference curves. An **indifference curve** shows the combinations of the two goods that generate the same level of utility or satisfaction. In Figure 7A.2 the indifference curve passing through point e separates the combinations of burgers and tacos into three groups.

- **Superior combinations.** All the combinations above the indifference curve generate more satisfaction (higher utility) than combinations on the curve. Bob would prefer point h to point e or f because he gets more of both goods with point h.

Budget line: The line connecting all the combinations of two goods that exhaust a consumer's budget.

Indifference curve: The set of combinations of goods that generate the same level of utility or satisfaction.

Figure 7A.1
Budget Set and Budget Line
The budget set (the shaded triangle) shows all the affordable combinations of burgers and tacos, and the budget line (with endpoints x and y) shows the combinations that exhaust the budget.

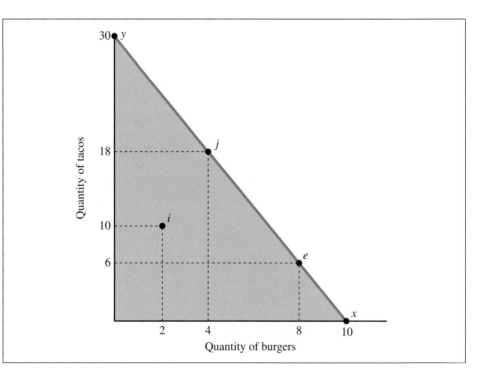

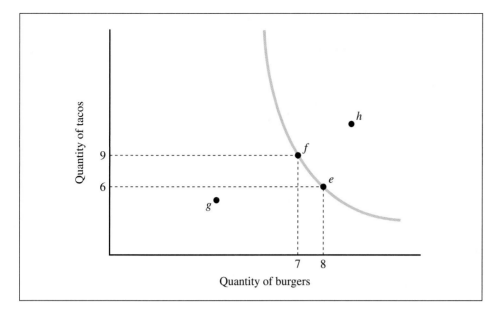

Indifference Curve and the Marginal Rate of Substitution
The indifference curve shows the different combinations of burgers and tacos that generate the same utility level. The slope is the marginal rate of substitution between the two goods (three tacos per burger between points *e* and *f*).

- **Inferior combinations.** All the combinations below the indifference curve generate less satisfaction (lower utility) than do combinations on the curve. Bob would prefer point *e* to point *g* because he gets more of both goods with point *e*.

- **Equivalent combinations.** All combinations along the indifference curve generate the same satisfaction (the same utility) as combination *e*. Bob would be indifferent between combinations *e* and *f*.

An indifference curve shows the subjective preferences of an individual consumer, so indifference curves vary from one consumer to another. Nonetheless, the indifference curves of all consumers share two characteristics: They are negatively sloped, and they become flatter as we move downward along an individual curve.

Why is the indifference curve negatively sloped? If we increased Bob's burger consumption by one burger without changing his taco consumption, his utility would increase. To restore the original utility level, we must take away some tacos. In other words, there is a negative relationship between burgers and tacos, so the indifference curve is negatively sloped. The slope of the curve is the **marginal rate of substitution (MRS)** between the two goods, the rate at which a consumer is willing to substitute one good for another, that is, the subjective trade-off between the two goods. The marginal rate of substitution is the number of tacos we must take from Bob to offset the effect of giving him one more burger. In Figure 7A.2 if Bob starts at point *f* and we give him one more burger, we must take away three tacos to keep him on the same indifference curve. Therefore, the marginal rate of substitution near point *f* is three tacos per burger.

The indifference curve becomes flatter as we move downward along the curve because of diminishing marginal utility. As we move down Bob's indifference curve, burger consumption increases and taco consumption decreases. The marginal rate of substitution decreases for two reasons:

- The larger the number of burgers, the lower the marginal utility of burgers, so we can take away fewer tacos to offset each additional burger.

Marginal rate of substitution (MRS): The rate at which a consumer is willing to substitute one good for another.

- The smaller the number of tacos, the higher the marginal utility of tacos. Therefore, each taco we take away has a larger negative effect on Bob's utility, so we can offset any given increase in utility by taking away fewer tacos.

On the upper portion of the curve, Bob has many tacos and just a few burgers, so he is willing to trade several tacos to get another burger: The MRS is large, and the curve is steep. On the lower portion of the curve, he has many burgers and just a few tacos, so he is not willing to trade very many tacos to get another burger: The MRS is small, and the curve is flat.

An indifference map is a set of indifference curves, each with a different level of utility. Figure 7A.3 shows three indifference curves: C_1, C_2, and C_3. As Bob moves from a point on indifference curve C_1 to any point on C_2, his utility increases. This is sensible because he can get more of both goods on C_2, so he will be better off. In general, Bob's utility increases as he moves in the northeasterly direction to higher indifference curve (from C_1 to C_2 to C_3, and so on).

Maximizing Utility

Bob's objective is to maximize his utility, given his budget and the market prices. Bob can pick from many affordable combinations of burgers and tacos, and he will pick the one that generates the highest level of utility or satisfaction. In graphical terms, Bob will reach the highest indifference curve possible, given his budget set.

In Figure 7A.4, Bob will choose point e (eight burgers and six tacos) and will achieve the utility level associated with indifference curve C_2. Why does he choose point e instead of point i, j, or k?

- **Point i.** Bob doesn't choose this point for two reasons. First, it is not on the budget line, so it does not exhaust his budget: He has some money left over. Second, it is on a lower indifference curve—and generates less utility—than point e.

- **Point j.** Although point j exhausts Bob's budget, j lies on a lower indifference curve than e, so it generates less utility than point e. Starting from point j, Bob could real-

Figure 7A.3

Indifference Map

An indifference map shows a set of indifference curves, with utility increasing as we move northeasterly to higher indifference curves.

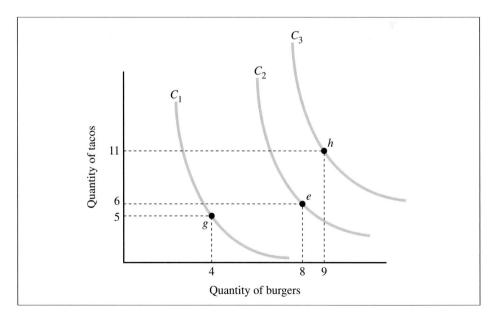

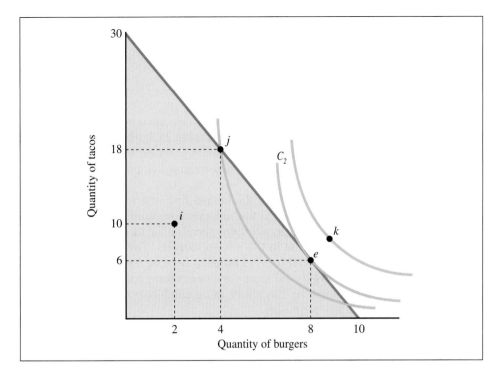

Figure 7A.4

Consumer Maximizes Utility at Tangency of Indifference Curve and Budget Line
To maximize utility, the consumer finds the combination of hamburgers and tacos at which an indifference curve is tangent to the budget line. At the utility-maximizing combination, the marginal rate of substitution equals the price ratio.

locate his budget and buy more burgers and fewer tacos. As he moves down his budget line, he moves to progressively higher indifference curves, ultimately reaching point e on indifference curve C_2.

- **Point k.** Although point k generates a higher utility level than point e (it's on a higher indifference curve), it lies outside Bob's budget set, so he cannot afford it.

At point e, Bob reaches the highest indifference curve possible, given his budget set. The indifference curve touches—but does not pass through—the budget line: The indifference curve is tangent to the budget line. As we saw earlier in the discussion of point j, if Bob tentatively picked a point on the budget line whose indifference curve cuts through the budget line, he could increase his utility by moving along his budget line to a higher indifference curve. For the combination of goods that generates the highest possible utility, the indifference curve is tangent to the budget line.

What is the economic interpretation of the tangency condition? At the point of tangency, the slope of the indifference curve (the MRS) equals the slope of the budget line (the price ratio). Therefore, the consumer's subjective trade-off between the two goods (the MRS) equals the market trade-off (the price ratio). At point e in Figure 7A.4, the MRS (three tacos per burger) equals the price ratio (3.0). At any other combination of burgers and tacos, the MRS would not be equal to the price ratio, so the consumer could reallocate his budget and increase his utility. For example, starting at point j,

- Bob's MRS (the slope of the indifference curve) is 7.0: He is willing to give up seven tacos to get one burger.

- Given the prices of the two goods, the price ratio is 3.0, so Bob must give up only three tacos to get one burger.

To get one more burger (the fifth) Bob must give up only three tacos instead of the seven he is willing to give up, so he his better off buying one more burger and three fewer tacos. He will continue to reallocate his budget until the MRS equals the price ratio (until the slope of the indifference curve equals the slope of the budget line). This occurs at point e, where MRS is equal to three tacos per burger.

Drawing the Demand Curve

We can use the consumer choice model to draw Bob's demand curve for burgers. We've already derived one point on his demand curve: In Figure 7A.4, when the price of burgers is \$3, he consumes eight burgers. To find another point on the demand curve, we change the price of burgers and find the utility-maximizing combination of burgers and tacos associated with the new price.

Figure 7A.5 shows what happens to the budget line when the price of burgers decreases to \$2. The decrease in price tilts the budget line outward. The original vertical intercept (point y) is still in the budget set: If Bob spends his entire budget on tacos, he would be unaffected by the decrease in the price of burgers. The horizontal intercept moves outward from x (10 burgers) to z (15 burgers) because a given budget will buy more burgers. If Bob buys burgers and tacos (he chooses some point between the horizontal and vertical intercepts), he can afford more combinations of the two goods because he spends less money per burger.

How will Bob respond to the lower price of burgers? Given the new budget line and the same set of indifference curves, Bob picks point n, where one of his indifference curves is tangent to the new budget line. In other words, he responds to the decrease in burger price by consuming 11 burgers instead of 8.

In Figure 7A.6, we can draw a second point on the demand curve: When the price is \$2, Bob consumes 11 burgers. We can find other points on the demand curve by repeating this process for other prices: Draw the new budget line and find the point at which an indifference curve is tangent to the new budget line. When we do this, we'll find that the demand curve is negatively sloped, consistent with the law of demand: The lower the price, the larger the quantity demanded.

Figure 7A.5

Consumer's Response to a Decrease in Price
A decrease in the price of burgers tilts the budget line outward. The indifference curve is tangent to the budget line at a larger quantity of burgers (11 burgers instead of 8). This is the law of demand: The higher the price, the smaller the quantity demanded.

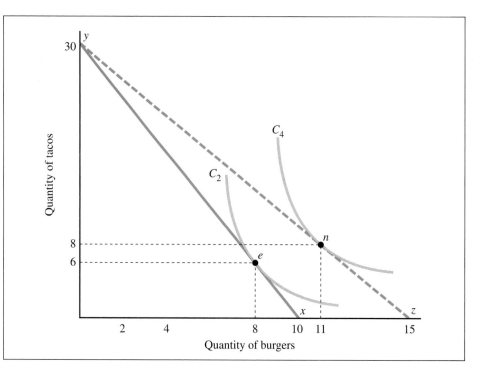

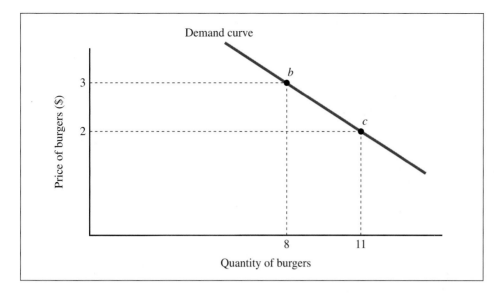

Figure 7A.6
Individual Demand Curve
At a price of $3 per burger, Bob maximizes his utility with 8 burgers (point *e* in Figure 7A.5 and point *b* in Figure 7A.6); at a price of $2 per burger, Bob maximizes his utility with 11 burgers (point *n* in Figure 7A.5 and point *c* in Figure 7A.6).

We've used the consumer choice model to find two points on the individual demand curve. For each price we found the quantity of burgers that generated the highest possible utility level, given the consumer's budget and the price of the other good (tacos). We have drawn a true demand curve because we changed the price of burgers but did not change the consumer's income or the prices of other goods.

 ## Summary

We've used a model of consumer behavior to show how a consumer decides how much of a particular good to consume. The consumer's objective is to maximize his or her utility, given an income and the prices of consumer goods. Here are the main points of the appendix.

1. To maximize utility, the consumer finds the point at which one of her indifference curves is tangent to her budget line.

2. At the utility-maximizing combination of two goods, the marginal rate of substitution (the consumer's subjective trade-off between the two goods) equals the price ratio (the market trade-off).

 ## Key Terms

budget line, 156
budget set, 155

indifference curve, 156

marginal rate of substitution (MRS), 157

1. Consider a person who spends a total of $200 on hats and violets. The price of hats is $20, and the price of violets is $5. Draw a budget line with hats on the horizontal axis and violets on the vertical axis.

   a. What is the slope of the budget line?

   b. Draw a conventional indifference curve (negatively sloped and convex to the origin) that intersects the budget line. Explain why the consumer can reach a higher utility level than the level shown by this indifference curve.

   c. Draw a second indifference curve that shows the highest possible utility level.

   d. Complete the statement: To maximize utility, the consumer finds the combination of hats and violets such that _____ equals 4.

2. Mistletoe, Inc. spent $500 on food and drink for this year's party. At the end of the party, there were no leftovers. The price of food (per ounce) is three times the price of drink. Your task is to figure out whether the firm could have spent the $500 more wisely.

   a. If you could conduct an exit poll as the employees leave the party, what question (only one) would you ask them?

   b. Provide an answer to your question that would suggest the firm should have spent more on food and less on drink.

3. Carla has a fixed budget for a new car and has tentatively decided to buy a car with 80 horsepower (hp) and 100 cubic feet (cf) of interior space. Given the current selection of cars and their prices, the price of horsepower is one-third the price of cubic feet. After some prompting from the used-car salesperson, Carla said, "To get an additional unit of horsepower, I would be willing to sacrifice 2 cubic feet of interior space." Does her tentative choice (80 hp and 100 cf) maximize her utility subject to her auto budget? If not, should she choose an auto with more or less horsepower?

CHAPTER

8

Production and Cost

Your small city is about to replace its aging 800-bed hospital with either a new 800-bed hospital or two new 400-bed hospitals. In a public hearing before the city council, an economic consultant made the following statement: "A big hospital is much more efficient than a small one, so it would be silly to build two 400-bed hospitals rather than a single 800-bed hospital. In fact, the cost per bed of an 800-bed hospital is about one-third of the cost per bed of a 400-bed hospital."

This chapter is about how production cost varies with the size of the production facility and the quantity of output produced in a given facility. Before the city council decides whether to build one or two new hospitals, it should take a careful look at the cost of providing hospital services in large and small hospitals. Similarly, before a firm builds a computer-chip factory, it should compare the production cost per chip in a large factory to the cost per chip in a small one. This chapter also explores how the cost of production varies with the quantity of output produced in a given facility. Before a computer firm decides how many chips to produce in its chip factory, it should take a careful look at the cost of producing different quantities of chips.

In later chapters, we'll use the cost curves discussed in this chapter to explain firms' decisions about whether to enter a market and how much output to produce once they enter. In this chapter, we'll see how to use cost curves to answer the following practical questions:

1. **If the government breaks up a large aluminum producer into two smaller firms, by how much will the average cost of producing a given quantity of aluminum increase?**
2. **Are large trucking firms more efficient than smaller trucking firms? If so, how much more efficient?**
3. **Why is the typical short-run average cost curve shaped like the letter U, while the typical long-run average cost curve is shaped like the letter L?**
4. **Suppose that one electric utility has three times as many customers as another electric utility. Which utility has a higher unit cost of electricity, and how large is the cost difference?**

Introduction

This chapter is about production cost in the short run and long run. Let's start with some definitions of cost and then review the difference between the short run and the long run.

Economic Profit Versus Accounting Profit

Our discussion of the firm's cost is based on the notion of economic cost. You may be surprised to hear that accountants and economists differ in the way they compute the cost of production. As we see in Table 8.1, a firm's total accounting cost equals the firm's **explicit cost**, defined as actual cash payments for inputs. For example, if the firm spends a total of $60,000 per year on labor, materials, rent, and machinery, its explicit cost would be $60,000, and this is the firm's total accounting cost.

Explicit cost: The firm's actual cash payments for its inputs.

The key principle underlying the computation of economic cost is the principle of opportunity cost.

PRINCIPLE OF OPPORTUNITY COST

The opportunity cost of something is what you sacrifice to get it.

Implicit cost: The opportunity cost of nonpurchased inputs.

The firm's total economic cost equals explicit cost plus **implicit cost**. The firm's implicit cost is defined as the opportunity cost of nonpurchased inputs such as the entrepreneur's time or money.

Table 8.1 Accounting Versus Economic Cost

	Accounting Approach	Economic Approach
Explicit cost (purchased inputs)	$60,000	$ 60,000
Implicit: opportunity cost of entrepreneur's time		30,000
Implicit: opportunity cost of funds		10,000
Total cost	$60,000	$100,000

- **Opportunity cost of the entrepreneur's time.** An entrepreneur has less time to pursue other activities, and economic cost includes the opportunity cost of the time spent running the firm. If an entrepreneur could earn $30,000 per year in another job, the opportunity cost of his or her time is $30,000 per year.

- **Opportunity cost of funds.** Many entrepreneurs use their own funds to set up and run their businesses, and economic cost includes the opportunity cost of these funds. If an entrepreneur starts a business with some money withdrawn from his or her bank account, sacrificing $10,000 of interest income per year, the opportunity cost of the funds invested in the firm is $10,000 per year.

In this case, the implicit cost is $40,000 per year, and the **economic cost**—defined as the sum of the explicit and implicit cost—is $100,000. The economic cost is higher because the economist includes implicit cost, but the accountant does not. When we refer to the firm's production cost, we mean the economic cost of production, including both implicit and explicit cost.

Economic cost: Explicit cost plus implicit cost.

Short-Run Versus Long-Run Decisions

In later chapters, we'll see how firms use their cost curves to make two types of decisions:

- A firm that already has a production facility must decide how much output to produce in that facility. This is a short-run decision because one of the factors of production (the facility) is fixed.

- A firm that has decided to enter a market must decide how large a facility to build. Such a firm is making a long-run decision because none of the factors of production are fixed. The firm starts from scratch and can choose a production facility of any size.

In most cases, the long run is the time required for a firm to build a production facility and start producing output. For example, if it takes a firm in the garden-tool business one year to build a factory, the long run for that firm is one year, and the short run is any time less than a year. The long run varies across industries. If it takes one day to get a hot-dog cart and start selling hot dogs, the long run is a day. In contrast, it takes several years to design and build a computer chip factory, so the long run in that industry is several years.

Production and Cost in the Short Run

The short run is defined as a period of time over which at least one input to the production process is fixed. For most firms, the fixed input is its production facility, for example, a factory, store, office, or farm. In the short run, the firm cannot modify its production facility or build a new facility.

As we saw in Chapter 2, the key principle for short-run decision-making is the principle of diminishing returns.

PRINCIPLE OF DIMINISHING RETURNS

Suppose that output is produced with two or more inputs and we increase one input while holding the other inputs fixed. Beyond some point—called the point of diminishing returns—output will increase at a decreasing rate.

A pizzeria experiences diminishing returns because its workers share a fixed production facility: a pizza oven. When the pizzeria adds a worker, each worker becomes less productive because he or she works with a smaller piece of the production facility. As the pizzeria adds more and more workers, output increases at a decreasing rate, meaning the marginal product of labor decreases.

Production and Marginal Product

Consider a firm that produces lawn rakes in a factory equipped with machines and other equipment. The firm's variable input is labor, and the firm's fixed input is its production facility, the equipped factory. As the number of workers increases—and the production facility doesn't change—what happens to the quantity of rakes produced?

Total product curve: A curve showing the relationship between the quantity of labor and the quantity of output produced.

Table 8.2 shows relationship between the number of workers and the number of rakes produced per minute. The firm needs 8 workers to produce one rake per minute, 12 workers to produce 2 rakes per minute, and so on up to 130 workers to produce 10 rakes per minute. Figure 8.1 uses the numbers in Table 8.2 to show the firm's **total product curve**, the relationship between the quantity of labor and the quantity of output produced. Let's look at two different parts of the total product curve, starting with the part between points *d* and *e*.

Table 8.2   Labor Input and Output

Output: Rakes per Minute	Labor: Number of Workers
0	0
1	8
2	12
3	15
4	20
5	27
6	36
7	48
8	65
9	90
10	130

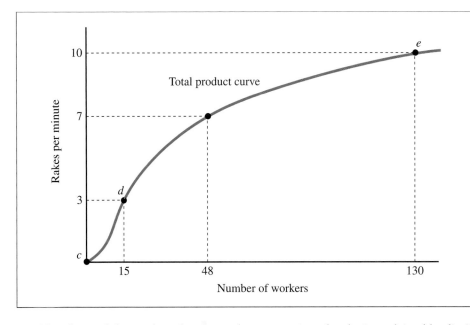

Figure 8.1
Total Product Curve
The total product curve shows the relationship between the quantity of labor and the quantity of output, given a fixed production facility. For the first 15 workers, output increases at an increasing rate: a result of labor specialization. Point *d* is the point of diminishing returns. Beyond this point, adding workers increases output at a decreasing rate.

The shape of the total product curve between points *d* and *e* is explained by diminishing returns. As the number of workers increases beyond 15, the curve becomes flatter; that is, output increases at a decreasing rate. The rake workers share the factory and all the machinery for making rakes, and as the number of workers increases, each worker has a smaller share of the facility. Eventually, adding a worker makes each worker in the factory less productive, so the marginal product of labor decreases and the total product curve becomes flatter. In Figure 8.1, this happens at point *d*, the point of diminishing returns.

To illustrate the notion of diminishing returns, consider the amounts of labor required to produce between 3 and 5 rakes per minute. In Table 8.2, to increase output from 3 to 4 rakes, the firm must increase its workforce from 15 to 20 workers, hiring 5 additional workers. To increase output from 4 to 5 rakes per minute, the firm must increase its workforce from 20 to 27 workers, hiring 7 additional workers. Because of diminishing returns resulting from sharing the production facility, it takes progressively more workers to increase output by one more rake.

What about the total product curve between points *c* and *d*? For a small workforce and a small quantity of output, the slope of the curve increases as the number of workers increases. In other words, the marginal product of labor increases for the first 15 workers. Although this may seem to be contrary to the principle of diminishing returns, remember that the principle says that eventually output will increase at a decreasing rate. So what's different when the firm produces a small quantity of output?

The difference is the possibility of labor specialization. Suppose there are 15 distinct tasks associated with making a rake. If the firm hires only 8 workers, some of the workers will be forced to perform more than one of these tasks. Together, the 8 workers will produce 1 rake per minute. Adding 4 more workers would allow some workers to specialize, each doing one of the 15 tasks. A worker with a single task will spend less time switching between tasks and also will become more skillful in the assigned task. In other words, specialization increases output per worker, so the firm can increase output from 1 to 2 rakes by adding only 4 workers. Adding 3 more workers—bringing the workforce to 15 workers—allows each worker to specialize in a single task, and increases output from 2 to 3 rakes per minute. In this example, there are benefits from specialization for the first 15 workers, so the firm's marginal product increases for the first 15 workers.

Short-Run Total Cost and Short-Run Marginal Cost

Now that we know about the relationship between the quantities of labor and output, we're ready to introduce several of the firm's short-run cost curves. Table 8.3 shows some hypothetical cost data for the rake producer whose total product curve is shown in Figure 8.2. The question is, How does the cost of producing rakes vary as the number of rakes produced *per minute* increases?

There are two types of production cost in the short run: fixed cost and variable cost.

Fixed cost (FC): Cost that does not depend on the quantity produced.

- **Fixed cost (FC)** is defined as the cost that does not vary with the quantity produced. In our example, the fixed cost is the cost of the rake factory, including the cost of the building and all the machinery and equipment inside. We're interested not in the total output of the rake factory over its 30-year life, but in its output per minute. Therefore, we must translate the one-time $100 million expense for the factory into a cost per minute, for example $36 per minute. As shown in the second column in Table 8.3, the fixed cost is $36 per minute, regardless of how much output is produced.

Total variable cost (TVC): Cost that varies as the firm changes its output.

Short-run total cost (STC): The total cost of production in the short run, when one or more inputs (for example, the production facility) is fixed; equal to fixed cost plus variable cost.

- **Variable cost** is defined as a cost that varies with the quantity produced. For example, to produce more rakes, the firm must hire more workers. If we assume that the firm pays each of its workers $1 per minute, the **total variable cost (TVC)** per minute is the same as the number of workers, $8 for one rake, $12 for two rakes, and so on.

The **short-run total cost (STC)** equals the sum of fixed and variable costs. Figure 8.2 shows the three cost curves. The horizontal line shows the fixed cost of $36, and the lower of the two positively sloped curves shows the total variable cost. The third curve shows short-run total cost as the sum of fixed cost and total variable cost. The vertical distance between the STC curve and the TVC curve equals the firm's fixed cost.

Table 8.3 Short-Run Production Costs

(1) Output: Rakes per Minute	(2) Fixed Cost (FC)	(3) Total Variable Cost (TVC)	(4) Short-Run Total Cost (STC)	(5) Short-Run Marginal Cost (SMC)	(6) Average Fixed Cost (AFC)	(7) Short-Run Average Variable Cost (SAVC)	(8) Short-Run Average Total Cost (SATC)
0	36	0	36	—	—	—	—
1	36	8	44	8.00	36.00	8.00	44.00
2	36	12	48	4.00	18.00	6.00	24.00
3	36	15	51	3.00	12.00	5.00	17.00
4	36	20	56	5.00	9.00	5.00	14.00
5	36	27	63	7.00	7.20	5.40	12.60
6	36	36	72	9.00	6.00	6.00	12.00
7	36	48	84	12.00	5.14	6.86	12.00
8	36	65	101	17.00	4.50	8.13	12.63
9	36	90	126	25.00	4.00	10.00	14.00
10	36	130	166	40.00	3.60	13.00	16.60

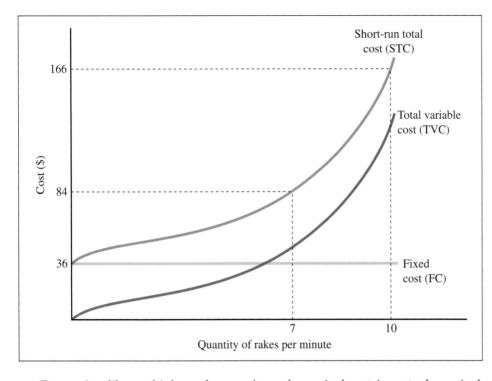

Economists like to think on the margin, and marginal cost is part of marginal thinking. The **short-run marginal cost (SMC)** is defined as the change in short-run total cost resulting from producing one more unit of the good. As shown in the fourth column of Table 8.3, if the firm decides to produce just one rake, its short-run total cost increases from $36 (the fixed cost) to $44, so the marginal cost of the first rake is $8. For the first three rakes, the marginal cost gets smaller and smaller, a result of the benefits of labor specialization. The firm needs eight workers to produce the first rake (a marginal cost of $8), but only four more workers to produce the second rake (marginal cost = $4), and only three more workers to produce the third rake. We saw earlier that specialization leads to increasing marginal productivity; now we know that it also leads to decreasing marginal cost. In Figure 8.3, the short-run marginal-cost curve is negatively sloped for the first three rakes.

Starting with the fourth rake, the short-run marginal cost increases as the number of rakes increases, a result of diminishing returns. Once the benefits of labor specialization are exhausted, diminishing returns set in, and it takes more and more workers to increase output by one rake. To increase output from three to four rakes, the firm needs five additional workers (marginal cost = $5, shown by point *c*). To increase output from four to five rakes, the firm needs seven additional workers (marginal cost = $7, shown by point *d*). Because the firm requires more and more workers to increase production by one unit, the marginal cost of production increases. In Table 8.3 and Figure 8.3, marginal cost increases to $12 for the seventh rake, to $25 for the ninth rake, and so on.

Short-Run Average Cost Curves

It will often be useful to express the firms cost of production as average cost. There are three types of short-run average cost:

- **Average fixed cost (AFC):** fixed cost divided by the quantity produced.

- **Short-run average variable cost (SAVC):** total variable cost divided by the quantity produced.

Short-run marginal cost (SMC): The change in short-run total cost resulting from producing one more unit of the good.

Average fixed cost (AFC): Fixed cost divided by the quantity produced.
Short-run average variable cost (SAVC): Total variable cost divided by the quantity produced.

Figure 8.3

Short-Run Marginal Cost and Short-Run Average Cost

The positively sloped portion of the short-run marginal cost curve (SMC) results from diminishing returns. The short-run average total cost curve (SATC) is U-shaped, a result of spreading fixed cost (which pulls down the average total cost) and diminishing returns (which pulls up the average total cost). The SMC curve intersects each average-cost curve (SAVC and SATC) at the minimum point of the average curve.

Short-run average total cost (SATC): Short-run total cost divided by the quantity of output; equal to AFC plus SAVC.

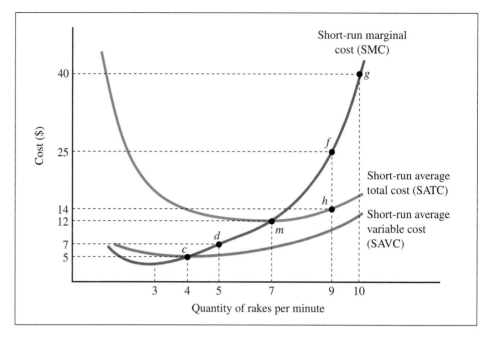

- **Short-run average total cost (SATC):** total cost divided by the quantity produced; equal to the sum of AFC and SAVC.

The last three columns of Table 8.3 show these three types of average cost for our rake producer. To compute AFC, we simply divide the fixed cost by the quantity of rakes produced. In our example, AFC decreases from $36 per rake, to $18 per rake for two rakes, and so on. As output increases, the fixed cost ($36) is spread over more units, so AFC decreases.

To compute SAVC, we divide the total variable cost by the quantity of rakes produced. In Figure 8.3, the SAVC curve is negatively sloped for small quantities of output but positively sloped for larger quantities. The negative slope reflects the benefits of labor specialization when the firm produces a small quantity of output. Adding workers to a small workforce makes workers more productive on average, so the average cost of labor per rake drops. The SAVC curve is positively sloped for large quantities of output, a result of diminishing returns: adding more workers to a large workforce makes workers less productive on average, so the average cost of labor per rake rises.

Why is the SATC curve shaped like a U? At very small quantities of output, the curve is negatively sloped, a result of two forces that work together to pull SATC down as output increases:

- **Spreading the fixed cost.** For small quantities of output, a one-unit increase in output reduces AFC by a large amount because the fixed cost is pretty "thick," being spread over just a few units of output. For example, going from one rake to two rakes decreases AFC from $36 per rake to $18 per rake.

- **Labor specialization.** For small quantities of output, SAVC decreases as output increases, a result of labor specialization that increases worker productivity.

These two forces both pull SATC downward as output increases, so the curve is negatively sloped for small quantities of output.

What happens once the firm reaches the point at which the benefits of labor specialization are exhausted? As the firm continues to increase output, the average variable cost increases, a result of diminishing returns. There is a tug-of-war between two forces;

the spreading of fixed cost continues to pull SATC down, while diminishing returns and rising SAVC pushes SATC up. In other words, the SATC curve could be negatively sloped or positively sloped, depending on the relative strengths of the two forces.

The outcome of the tug-of-war depends on the quantity produced, giving the SATC curve its U shape.

- Intermediate quantities of output (between three and seven rakes per minute). The tug-of-war is won by the spreading of fixed cost, so SATC decreases as output increases. In this case, the decrease in AFC is larger than the increase in SAVC large because the fixed cost isn't too "thin" and diminishing returns are not too strong. As a result, short-run average total cost decreases as output increases.

- Large quantities of output (eight rakes per minute or more). The tug-of-war is won by diminishing returns and rising SAVC, so SATC increases as output increases. In this case, the reductions in AFC are relatively small because the fixed cost is so "thin" already, and diminishing returns are severe. As a result, short-run average total cost increases as output increases.

The Relationship Between Marginal and Average Curves

Figure 8.3 shows the relationship between short-run marginal cost and short-run average total cost. Whenever the marginal cost is less than the average total cost (for fewer than seven rakes), the average total cost is falling. In contrast, whenever the marginal cost exceeds the average total cost (for more than seven rakes), the average total cost is rising. Finally, when the marginal cost equals the average total cost, the average cost is neither rising nor falling (for seven rakes). In other words, the marginal-cost curve intersects the short-run average total cost curve at its minimum point.

We can use some simple logic to explain the relationship between average cost and marginal cost. Suppose that you start the semester with a cumulative GPA of 3.0 (a B average) and enroll in a single course this semester—a history course. If you receive a grade of C in history (2.0 for computing your GPA), your GPA will drop below 3.0. Your GPA decreases because the grade in the "marginal" course (the history course) is less than the "average" grade (the starting GPA) so the marginal grade pulls down your GPA. Suppose that you take an economics class the following semester and get a grade of A (4.0 for computing your GPA). In this case, your GPA will increase because the marginal grade (in economics) is higher than your average (your GPA) so the marginal grade pushes up your GPA. If you were to take a course the following semester and your grade in the course is the same as your GPA, your GPA wouldn't change. To summarize, whenever the marginal grade is less than the average grade, the average will fall; whenever the marginal grade exceeds the average grade average will rise; whenever the marginal grade equals the average grade, the average will not change.

In Figure 8.3, the SATC curve is negatively sloped for the first six rakes. Using the arithmetic of averages, the fact that the average cost is decreasing means that the marginal cost is less than the average cost: the lower marginal cost pulls down the average. In contrast, the SATC curve is positively sloped for eight or more rakes, which means that the marginal cost exceeds the average total cost: the higher marginal cost pulls up the average. If the average total cost is neither increasing nor decreasing, the marginal cost must equal the average total cost. In Figure 8.3, this happens at point m, the minimum point of the SATC curve. Using the same logic, the marginal cost equals the average variable cost at the minimum point of the SAVC curve (point c).

What is the relationship between average variable cost and average total cost? The total cost is the sum of fixed cost and variable cost, so the difference between the average total cost and the average variable cost is the average fixed cost. As output increases, the average fixed cost decreases because the fixed cost is spread over more and more rakes, decreasing the vertical distance between average total cost and average variable cost. In Figure 8.3, as output increases, the vertical distance between SAVC and SATC decreases.

The Cost of Pencils

Mr. Big wants to enter the pencil-making business. He gathered some information from two existing pencil manufacturers: Sharp, Inc. and Pointy, Inc. The two firms have identical production facilities—identical factories and equipment. The two firms also pay the same wage to their workers and pay the same prices for materials. Although Sharp produces 1,000 pencils per minute and Pointy produces 2,000 per minute, each firm has a short-run average total cost of 10 cents per pencil. After building a production facility identical to the ones used by Sharp and Pointy, Mr. Big hired enough workers and bought enough materials to produce 2,500 pencils per minute. Based on the experience of Sharp and Pointy, he expected to produce at an average cost of 10 cents per pencil. After all, he thought, that's the average cost for 1,000 pencils and 2,000 pencils, so it should also be the average cost for 2,500 pencils. Much to his dismay, his average cost was 14 cents per pencil.

We can solve this mystery with a quick look at a typical short-run average total cost curve. In Figure 8.4, the U-shaped SATC curve shows an average cost of 10 cents for both Sharp (1,000 pencils) and Pointy (2,000 pencils). Sharp produces on the negatively sloped portion of the average cost curve, while Pointy produces on the positively sloped portion. In contrast, Mr. Big produces 2,500 pencils at an average cost of 14 cents. Mr. Big thought that because Sharp and Pointy had the same average cost, the average cost curve must be horizontal. He didn't realize that the short-run average cost curve is U-shaped. Along a U-shaped curve, it is possible to have the same average cost for two different quantities of output. Unfortunately for Mr. Big, it's not possible to have the same average cost for three different quantities. ◆

Figure 8.4

The Cost Mystery
Because the short-run average total cost curve is U-shaped, it is possible to have the same short-run average cost at two—but not three—different quantities of output.

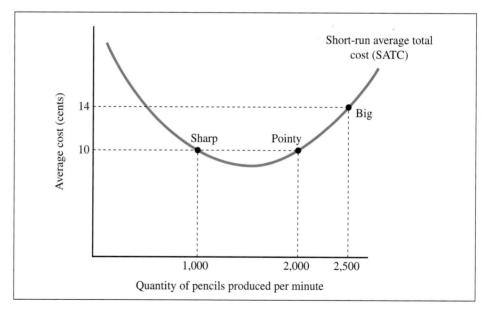

TEST Your Understanding

1. What key principle explains the positively sloped portion of the short-run marginal cost curve?

2. Comment on the following statement: "We're planning on increasing the output of our rubber-chicken factory by 10%. It's obvious that our short-run average total cost will decrease because we'll spread our fixed costs over more chickens."

3. According to the foreman in your chair factory, the short-run marginal cost of chairs is less than the short-run average cost. If you increase your output of chairs, will your short-run average cost increase or decrease?

4. Complete the statement with average or marginal: The short-run marginal cost curve intersects the short-run average cost curve at the minimum point of the _____ cost curve.

Production and Cost in the Long Run

Up to this point, we've been exploring short-run cost curves, which show the cost of producing different quantities of output in a given production facility. Let's turn next to long-run cost curves, which show the production costs in facilities of different sizes. The long run is defined as the period of time over which a firm is perfectly flexible in its choice of all inputs. In the long run, a firm can build a new production facility (factory, store, office, or restaurant) or modify an existing facility.

The key difference between the short run and the long run is that there are no diminishing returns in the long run. Remember that diminishing returns occur because workers share a fixed production facility, so the more workers in the facility, the smaller the piece of the facility available for each worker. In the long run, the firm can expand its production facility as its workforce grows.

Expansion and Replication

Continuing the example of rake production, consider a rake producer that has decided to replace its existing factory with a new one. The firm has been producing seven rakes per minute at a total cost of $84 per minute, or an average cost of $12 per rake. If the firm wants to produce twice as much output per minute in its new facility, what should it do?

One possibility is to simply double the original operation. The firm could build two factories that are identical to the original factory and hire two workforces, each identical to the original workforce. In this case, the firm's total cost will double with its output: each new factory will produce 7 rakes per minute at a cost of $84 per minute, so the firm can produce a total of 14 rakes per minute at twice the cost, $168 per minute. The firm's **long-run total cost** is defined as the total cost of production when the firm is perfectly flexible in its choice of all inputs, and can choose a production facility of any size. Table 8.4 shows the firm's long-run total cost for several different quantities, including 7, 14, and 28 rakes per minute. The replication process means the long-run total cost increases proportionally with the quantity produced, from $84 for 7 rakes per minute, to $168 for 14 rakes per minute, to $336 for 28 rakes per minute.

The firm's **long-run average cost of production (LAC)** is defined as long-run total cost divided by the quantity of output produced. In Table 8.4, the long-run average cost is $12

Long-run total cost: The total cost of production in the long run when a firm is perfectly flexible in its choice of all inputs and can choose a production facility of any size.

Long-run average cost of production (LAC): Long-run total cost divided by the quantity of output produced.

Table 8.4 Long-Run Costs: Total and Average Cost

Output: Rakes per minute	Long-Run Total Cost	Long-Run Average Cost
3.5	$ 70	$20
7	$ 84	$12
14	$168	$12
28	$336	$12

per rake for 7 or more rakes per minute. Because long-run total cost is proportional to the quantity produced, the long-run average cost doesn't change as output increases. In Figure 8.5, the long-run average cost curve is horizontal for 7 or more rakes per minute.

For a firm that wants to double its output in the long run, replication is one option. Another possibility is to build a single larger factory, one that can produce the target quantity of output at a lower cost than would be possible by simply building two factories identical to the original. If so, the long-run average cost of producing the larger quantity (for example, 14 rakes per minute) would be less than $12.

Decrease in Output and Indivisible Inputs

Suppose that instead of expanding its operation, a rake producer wants to reduce its operation, producing half as many rakes per minute as it did in its original operation. Could the firm simply hire half as many workers, build a factory with half the floor area, and fill the factory with half as much machinery and equipment? Perhaps, but there may be a problem with indivisible inputs.

Indivisible input: An input that cannot be scaled down to produce a smaller quantity of output.

An input is **indivisible** if it cannot be scaled down to produce a smaller quantity of output. For example, firms use industrial molds to make multiple copies of the same item, and a firm needs a mold regardless of how many copies it produces. Suppose the rake factory uses an industrial mold to shape plastic into the fan-shaped end of the rake. The firm needs the standard mold, regardless of how many rakes it produces, so cutting

Figure 8.5

Long-Run Average Cost Curve

The long-run average cost curve is negatively sloped for up to seven rakes per minute, a result of indivisible inputs and the effects of labor specialization. If the firm replicates the operation that produces seven rakes per minute, the long-run average cost curve will be horizontal beyond seven rakes per minute.

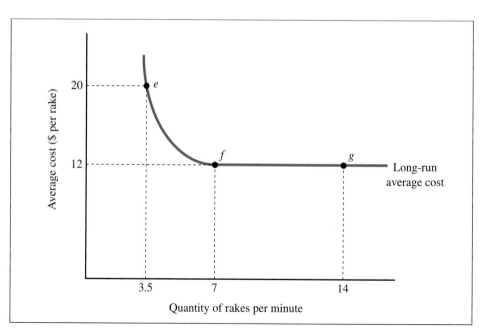

The production of many goods and services involves indivisible inputs, such as this large ship for ocean cargo service.

back from 7 rakes per minute to 3.5 rakes per minute won't affect the cost of the mold, so cutting output in half won't cut the firm's long-run total costs in half.

Table 8.4 shows the implications of indivisible inputs for total and average cost. In the first row, the long-run total cost of producing 3.5 rakes per minute is $70, compared to $84 for 7 rakes per minute. That means the long-run average cost of 3.5 rakes is $20 per rake ($70/3.5), compared to $12 per rake for 7 rakes per minute. In Figure 8.5, the long-run average cost is negatively sloped between points *e* and *f*. In general, if there are indivisible inputs, the long-run average total cost curve will be negatively sloped.

Most production processes have at least one indivisible input. Here are some other examples of firms and their indivisible inputs:

- A railroad company providing freight service between two cities must lay a set of tracks between them. The company cannot scale down the tracks by laying a half set of tracks (a single rail).

- A cable TV firm uses a cable running throughout its territory.

- A computer-chip factory uses "clean rooms" and complex machines and testing equipment.

- A shipping firm uses a large ship to carry TV sets from Japan to the United States.

- A steel producer uses a large blast furnace.

- A hospital uses imaging machines (for X-rays, CAT scans, and MRIs).

- A pizzeria uses a pizza oven.

These indivisible inputs cannot be scaled down to produce a smaller quantity of output. For example, it is impractical to produce a small quantity of steel in a factory with a small blast furnace, just as it is impractical to transport a single TV set across the ocean in a rowboat. For another example of indivisible inputs, read "A Closer Look: Indivisible Inputs and the Cost of Fake Killer Whales."

A CLOSER LOOK | Indivisible Inputs and the Cost of Fake Killer Whales

Sea lions off the Washington coast eat steelhead and other fish, depleting some species threatened with extinction and decreasing the harvest of the commercial fishing industry. Rick Funk, a plastics manufacturer, thinks that a variation on the scarecrow would solve the sea lion problem. Killer whales love to eat sea lions, and Funk says that he could build a life-sized fiberglass killer whale, mount it on a rail like a roller coaster, and then send the whale diving through the water to scare off the sea lions. According to Funk, it would cost about $16,000 to make the first whale. Once the mold is made, however, each additional whale would cost an additional $5,000: It would cost a total of $21,000 for two whales, $26,000 for three whales, and so on.

This little story illustrates the effects of indivisible inputs on the firm's cost curves. The cost of the first whale ($16,000) includes the cost of the mold (the indivisible input). Once the firm has the mold, the additional cost for each whale is only $5,000, so the average cost per whale decreases as the number of whales increases.

How much would it cost to make fake killer whales to scare away sea lions that feast on steelhead and other fish?

Source: Sandi Doughton, "Killer Whale Latest Idea on Sea Lions," *The Oregonian*, January 7, 1995.

Decrease in Output and Labor Specialization

A second reason for higher average long-run costs in a smaller operation is that labor will be less specialized in the small operation. As the number of workers decreases, each worker will be forced to take on more production tasks. Labor productivity will be lower because workers spend more time switching between tasks and will be less proficient because they have less experience at each task. The workers in the smaller rake firm will be less specialized and thus less productive, so the workforce required to produce 3.5 rakes per minute will be more than half the workforce required to produce 7 rakes per minute. When the firm cuts back to only 3.5 rakes per minute, the firm's labor costs will not be cut in half, so the long-run average cost will increase to some amount greater than $12.

Two centuries ago, Adam Smith used the making of sewing pins to illustrate the benefits from specialization.[1]

> A workman . . . could scarce, perhaps with his utmost industry, make one pin a day, and certainly could not make twenty. But the way in which this business is now carried on . . . one man draws out the wire, another straightens it, a third cuts it, a fourth points it, a fifth grinds the top for receiving the head; to make the head requires two or three distinct operations. . . . The . . . making of a pin is, in this manner, divided into about eighteen distinct operations. . . . I have seen a small manufactory of this kind where ten men . . . make among them . . . upward of forty eight thousand pins in a day.

The idea of specialization is summarized in the old saying that a person who is a jack of all trades is a master of none. In a small operation, each worker is a jack of many tasks and is not very productive at any particular task. In a large operation, each worker concentrates on just a few tasks and becomes a master at those tasks.

Economies of Scale

A firm experiences **economies of scale** if its long-run average-cost curve is negatively sloped. In Figure 8.5, the rake producer experiences economies of scale between points e and f. For example, at point e, the long-run average cost of producing 3.5 rakes per minute is $20, compared to $12 for 7 rakes per minute (point f). An increase in output from 3.5 to 7 rakes per minute decreases the long-run average cost of production, so there are some economies (that is, cost savings) associated with scaling up the firm's operation. The economies of scale result from indivisible inputs and the benefits from labor specialization.

Economies of scale: A situation in which an increase in the quantity produced decreases the long-run average cost of production.

Actual Long-Run Average Cost Curves

What does the typical long-run average cost curve look like? Figures 8.6 through 8.9 show the actual long-run average cost curves for several products: electricity generation, aluminum production, truck freight, and hospital services. Each long-run average-cost curve is negatively sloped for small quantities of output and relatively flat (almost horizontal) over a large range of output. In addition, each curve has a slight positive slope for large quantities of output. In other words, these curves are L-shaped. Other studies suggest that the long-run cost curves of a wide variety of goods and services have the same shape.[2]

Why is the typical long-run average cost curve L-shaped? The average-cost curves are negatively sloped for small quantities of output because there are economies of scale resulting from indivisible inputs and labor specialization. The long-run average-cost curves are horizontal over a wide range of output because once a firm reaches a certain scale, long-run total cost increases proportionately with output, reflecting the ability to increase inputs and outputs proportionately.

Minimum Efficient Scale

One way to quantify the extent of scale economies in the production of a particular good is to determine the minimum efficient scale for producing the good. The **minimum efficient scale** is defined as the output at which scale economies are exhausted. In graphical terms, the minimum efficient scale is the quantity at which the long-run average cost

Minimum efficient scale: The output at which the long-run average cost curve becomes horizontal.

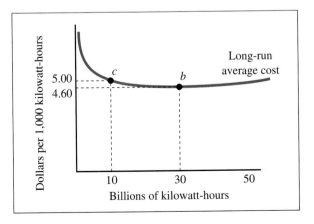

Figure 8.6

Long-Run Average Cost Curve for Electricity Generation

Source: Laurits Christensen and William H. Greene, "Economies of Scale in U.S. Electric Power Generation," *Journal of Political Economy*, vol. 84, 1976, pp. 655–676. Reprinted by permission of The University of Chicago Press.

curve becomes horizontal, for example point *f* in Figure 8.5. If a firm starts out with a quantity of output below the minimum efficient scale, an increase in output will decrease its long-run average cost. Once the minimum efficient scale has been reached, an increase in output no longer decreases the long-run average cost.

Economists have estimated the minimum efficient scale for various industries. In Britain, the minimum efficient scale is 1 million tons of sulfuric acid per year (about 30% of the British market), 9 million tons for steel (about 33% of the British market), 10 million tons of oil per year (10% of the British market), and 300,000 tons of ethylene per year (9% of the British market).[3] In the United States, the minimum efficient scale for automobiles is between 200,000 and 400,000 autos per year.[4] This means that a produc-

Figure 8.7
Long-Run Average Cost Curve for Aluminum Production

Source: Joel P. Clark and Merton C. Flemings, "Advanced Materials and the Economy," *Scientific American*, vol. 255, October 1986, pp. 51–60. Copyright © 1986 by Scientific American, Inc. All rights reserved.

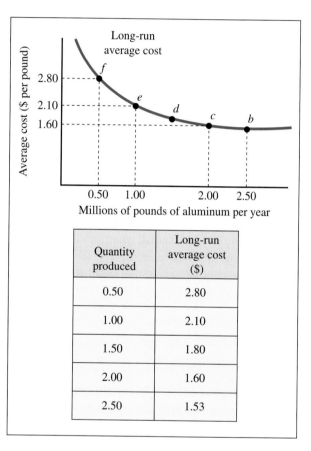

Quantity produced	Long-run average cost ($)
0.50	2.80
1.00	2.10
1.50	1.80
2.00	1.60
2.50	1.53

Figure 8.8
Long-Run Average Cost Curve for Truck Freight

Source: Roger Koenker, "Optimal Scale and the Size Distribution of American Trucking Firms," *Journal of Transport Economics and Policy*, January 1977, p. 62.

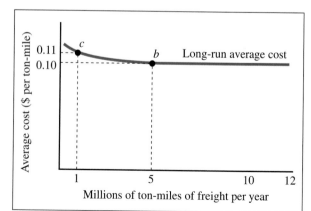

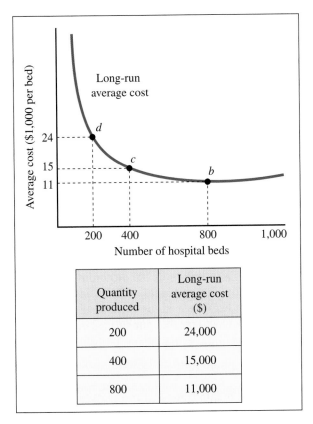

Figure 8.9

Long-Run Average Cost Curve for Hospital Services

Source: Harold A. Cohen, "Hospital Cost Curves with Emphasis on Measuring Patient Care Output," in *Empirical Studies in Health Economics*, edited by Herbert E. Klarman (Baltimore: Johns Hopkins University Press, 1970).

Quantity produced	Long-run average cost ($)
200	24,000
400	15,000
800	11,000

tion facility serving between 3% and 6% of the U.S. market would be large enough to fully exploit the economies of scale in auto production.

The possibility of economies of scale provides one reason why two companies may consider merging into one. There may be cost savings from using production facilities more efficiently, as well as savings in operating cost from combining the purchases of inputs and coordinating shipping operations. For an example, read "A Closer Look: Cost Savings from a Mega-Merger."

Diseconomies of Scale

If a firm's long-run average cost curve is positively sloped, the firm experiences **diseconomies of scale**, meaning that when the firm increases its output, the long-run average cost of production increases. Diseconomies of scale may arise for two reasons:

Diseconomies of scale: A situation in which an increase in the quantity produced increases the long-run average cost of production.

- **Coordination problems.** One of the problems of a large organization is that it requires several layers of management (a bureaucracy) to coordinate the activities of the different parts of the organization. If an increase in the firm's output requires additional layers of management, the long-run average cost curve may be positively sloped.

- **Increasing input costs.** When a firm increases its output, it will demand more of each of its inputs and may be forced to pay higher prices for some of these inputs. An increase in input prices will increase the long-run average cost of production, generating a positively sloped long-run average cost curve.

The long-run cost curves shown in Figures 8.6 through 8.9 suggest that diseconomies of scale are relatively mild. Once we reach a large quantity of output, the long-run average cost curves have a slight positive slope. The studies of other goods and services generate the same sort of L-shaped curves, suggesting that diseconomies of scale are not very severe, at least in the range output firms actually produce. This is sensible because if a firm experienced diseconomies of scale, it could decrease its long-run average cost by decreasing the quantity of output.

The experience of General Motors suggests there are diseconomies of scale in the production of automobiles, largely because of coordination problems.[5] General Motors, which is one-third bigger than Ford and larger than the two largest Japanese automakers combined (Toyota and Nissan), produces automobiles at an average cost that is between $200 and $2,000 higher than the average cost of Ford, Chrysler, and the Japanese. The Saturn project—an independent manufacturing operation with its own production facilities and its own input suppliers—is General Motors' response to these diseconomies of scale. By dividing its production into smaller pieces, General Motors hopes to avoid the high costs resulting from diseconomies of scale.

Firms recognize the possibility of diseconomies of scale and adopt various strategies to avoid them. An example of a firm that adjusts its operations to avoid diseconomies of scale is Minnesota Mining & Manufacturing, also known as 3M. According to Gordon Engdahl, the company's vice president for human resources, "We made a conscious effort to keep our units as small as possible because it keeps them flexible and vital. When one gets too large, we break it apart. We like to say that our success in recent years amounts to multiplication by division."[6]

Application: Hospital Services

At the start of this chapter, an economic consultant claims that the average cost per bed in an 800-bed hospital would be one-third the cost per bed in each 400-bed hospital. The long-run average cost curve shown in Figure 8.9 indicates that the consultant has overstated the scale economies in hospital services. For the 800-bed hospital the long-run average cost is $11,000 per bed (point *b*), compared to a long-run average cost of

A CLOSER LOOK   Cost Savings from a Mega-Merger

When Chrysler and Daimler-Benz merged, they formed DaimlerChrysler AG, one of the world's largest car companies. Officials from the new auto giant predicted that the merger would save about $1.4 billion per year. Some of these savings are expected to come from producing two very different vehicles—the Jeep Grand Cherokee (formerly a Chrysler product) and the Mercedes-Benz M-Class sport-utility vehicle (formerly a Daimler-Benz product)—on the same production line in Graz, Austria. Workers in the Graz plant have assembled Cherokees since 1994 and started producing M-Class vehicles in May of 1999, just five months after the merger took effect.

How will this production arrangement save money? When the demand for M-Class vehicles turned out to be higher than expected,

DaimlerChrysler decided to increase its production of the vehicle. One option was to expand the capacity of the Mercedes M-Class plant in Tuscaloosa, Alabama, but because the Graz plant had excess capacity, it was actually cheaper to convert the Graz assembly line to produce both Cherokees and M-Class vehicles. Company officials also plan to combine the input-purchasing operations and the transport operation of the two vehicles, resulting in substantial cost savings. As an example, the former Chrysler crews in Graz save $59,000 per year by having a nearby Mercedes shop repair their tools rather than shipping them to an independent shop.

Source: Brian Coleman, "A Daimler Factory Shows How a Trans-Atlantic Merger Works," *Wall Street Journal*, March 9, 1999, p. A18.

$15,000 per bed for a 400-bed hospital (point *c*). Although the larger hospital is more efficient, the difference in cost is not as large as the consultant suggested.

Short-Run Versus Long-Run Cost

Why is the firm's short-run average cost curve U-shaped, while the long-run average cost curve is L-shaped? For large quantities of output, the short-run curve is positively sloped because of diminishing returns and the resulting increases in the labor cost per unit of output. In the long run, the firm can scale up its operation by building a larger production facility, so the firm does not suffer from diminishing returns. If there are no diseconomies of scale, the long-run average cost curve will be negatively sloped or horizontal. If the firm experiences some diseconomies of scale, the long-run average-cost curve will eventually be positively sloped, but the short-run average-cost curve will be much steeper.

TEST Your Understanding

5. Draw a line connecting each item on the left with the appropriate item on the right.
   - Diseconomies of scale
   - Economies of scale
   - Indivisible inputs
   - Input specialization
   - Coordination problems

   - Negatively sloped long-run average cost curve
   - Positively sloped long-run average cost curve

6. When you mention that most firms have L-shaped long-run average cost curves, your new boss says, "You're wrong. Haven't you heard of the principle of diminishing returns?" How should you respond?

7. As a child, you recorded the costs of your lemonade stand and drew your long-run average cost curve. Now you work in a computer-chip factory. Would you expect any similarities between the lemonade cost curve and the long-run average-cost curve for the chip factory? Would you expect any differences?

Using the TOOLS

You've learned all about the firm's short- and long-run cost curves. Here are some opportunities to use those curves as graphical tools in your own economic analysis.

1. Production Consultant

A hammer manufacturer has just hired you to advise the firm on its production costs. In your first meeting with production managers, you hear the following statements. Are they true or false? Explain.

a. "If the production process is subject to diminishing returns, the long-run average cost curve will be positively sloped."

b. "At the current output level, this factory is subject to diminishing returns. Therefore, the firm is operating along the upward-sloping portion of its short-run marginal cost (SMC) curve."

c. "At the current output level, this factory is subject to diminishing returns. Therefore, the firm is operating along the upward-sloping portion of its short-run average total cost (SATC) curve."

d. "The short-run average total cost of producing 250 hammers is less than the short-run average cost of producing 260 hammers. Therefore, the short-run marginal cost of 260 hammers is less than the short-run average cost of 260 hammers."

2. Cost of Breaking Up an Aluminum Firm

Consider a large aluminum firm that initially produces two million pounds of aluminum per year. Suppose that an antitrust action breaks up the firm into two smaller firms, each of which produces half as much as the original firm. Use the information in Figure 8.7 to predict the effects on the long-run average cost of producing aluminum.

3. Deregulation and the Cost of Trucking

Consider the market for truck freight, which is currently served by a single regulated firm. If the market is deregulated, several new firms, unconstrained by regulations, will enter the market. At a public hearing on the issue of deregulation, the manager of the regulated firm issued a grim warning to the regulatory authorities: "If you deregulate this market, four or five firms will enter the market and the unit cost of truck freight will at least triple. There are big economies of scale in trucking services, so a single large firm is much more cost-efficient than several small firms would be. If you want firms in your city to pay three times as much for their truck freight, go ahead and deregulate this market." Use the information in Figure 8.8 to comment on this statement.

Summary

In this chapter, we looked at the cost side of a firm, explaining the shapes of the firm's short-run cost curves and long-run cost curves. Here are the main points of the chapter.

1. The positively sloped portion of the short-run marginal cost curve (SMC) results from diminishing returns.

2. The short-run average total cost curve (SATC) is U-shaped because of the conflicting effects of (a) fixed costs being spread over a larger quantity of output and (b) diminishing returns.

3. The long-run average cost curve (LAC) is horizontal over some range of output because replication is an option, so doubling output will no more than double long-run total cost.

4. The long-run average cost curve (LAC) is negatively sloped for small quantities of output because there are indivisible inputs that cannot be scaled down and a smaller operation has limited opportunities for labor specialization.

5. Diseconomies of scale arise if there are problems in coordinating a large operation or higher input costs in a larger organization.

Key Terms

Problems and Discussion Questions

1. Suppose that the indivisible inputs used in the production of shirts have a cost per day of $400. To produce one shirt per day, the firm must also spend a total of $5 on other inputs (labor, materials, and other capital). For each additional shirt, the firm incurs the same additional cost ($5). Compute the average cost for 40 shirts, 100 shirts, 200 shirts, and 400 shirts. Draw the long-run average cost curve for 40 to 400 shirts per day.

2. Consider a firm with the following short-run costs:

Quantity	Variable Cost	Total Cost
1	30	90
2	50	110
3	90	150
4	140	200
5	200	260

   a. What is the firm's fixed cost?
   b. Compute short-run marginal cost, short-run average variable cost, and short-run average total cost for the different quantities of output.
   c. Draw the three cost curves. Explain the relationship between the SMC curve and the SATC curve and the relationship between the SAVC curve and the SATC curve.

3. Given the following relationship between labor input and the quantity produced, compute the marginal product of labor for the different input levels. Then draw the total product curve and the marginal-product curve.

Labor	Output
0	0
1	5
2	11
3	15
4	18
5	19

4. Consider a firm that has a fixed cost of $60 per minute. Complete the following table.

Output	FC	TVC	STC	SMC	AFC	SAVC	SATC
1	___	10	___	___	___	___	___
2	___	18	___	___	___	___	___
3	___	30	___	___	___	___	___
4	___	45	___	___	___	___	___
5	___	65	___	___	___	___	___
6	___	90	___	___	___	___	___

5. Consider a firm that has constant marginal returns. That means that the first worker is just as productive as the second, who is just as productive as the third, and so on. The same is true for all the firm's inputs.
   a. Draw the firm's short-run marginal cost curve.
   b. Explain why this firm's cost curve differs from the short-run marginal cost curve for rake production.

6. Beaverduck Bus Company wants to compute the cost of adding a third daily bus between Eugene and Corvallis. Comment on the following statement of Abby Abacus, the company accountant: "If we add the third bus, our total cost would increase from $700 to $780. Therefore, the marginal cost of the third bus is $260 ($780 divided by 3)."

7. You want to know the short-run marginal cost of producing a Chevrolet Caprice. Comment on the following statement from an analyst in the production department: "The marginal cost of a Caprice, given our current volume, is $12,500. Of course, the actual marginal cost depends on the number of cars produced. The larger the number produced, the lower the unit cost because we will spread out our design and tooling costs over more cars."

8. Explain the difference between diseconomies of scale and diminishing returns. Based on the cost curves you've seen in this chapter, which is more pervasive?

9. Suppose that one firm generates 30 billion kilo-watt-hours of electricity, which is about three times the output of a second electricity firm. Which firm will have a higher cost per kilowatt-hour? Use the information in Figure 8.6 to predict the difference in the average costs of the two firms.

10. Web Exercise. Visit the Web site of the Cooperative Administrative Support Unit (CASU), an organization that helps government agencies reduce their operating costs (*http://www.dol.gov/dol/casu/welcome.html*). What economic concept allows CASU to help government agencies reduce their costs? Check out the details of CASU's "cost per copy" program. Are there economies of scale in photocopying?

11. Web Exercise. Visit the Web site of the Bureau of Labor Statistics (*http://stats.bls.gov/*) and do a keyword search of the site for information on compensation costs. How does the hourly compensation of U.S. workers compare with the compensation of workers in other countries?

Take It to the Net

We invite you to visit the O'Sullivan/Sheffrin page on the Prentice Hall Web site at:
http://www.prenhall.com/osullivan/
for additional World Wide Web exercises for this chapter.

Model Answers to Questions

Chapter-Opening Questions

1. As shown in Figure 8.7, the average cost for the large firm is $1.60 per pound (point *c*), compared to an average cost of $2.10 for each of the small firms.

2. As shown in Figure 8.8, although a larger trucking firm has lower average costs than a small one, the difference is relatively small, except for very small firms.

3. The short-run curve reflects diminishing returns, which pulls up short-run average cost as output increases. There are no diminishing returns in the long run.

4. In Figure 8.6, the larger firm (30 billion kwh) has an average cost that is 8% lower than the smaller firm (10 billion kwh).

Test Your Understanding

1. The principle of diminishing returns.

2. It's not obvious that the short-run average cost will decrease because diminishing returns pull up average cost as the quantity of output increases. If the initial quantity of output is large enough, the bad news associated with increasing output (diminishing returns) will dominate the good news (spreading out the fixed costs), so average cost will increase.

3. If the marginal cost is less than the average cost, the marginal pulls down the average, so the average cost curve is negatively sloped. Therefore, average cost will decrease, at least for small increases in output.

4. Average.

5. Draw lines from "diseconomies of scale" and "coordination problems" to "positively sloped long-run average cost curve." Draw lines from "economies of scale," "indivisible inputs," and "input specialization" to "negatively sloped long-run average cost curve."

6. Diminishing returns occur when we increase output in an existing production facility. The principle of diminishing returns is applicable in the short run, not in the long run. To draw the long-run cost curve, we assume that we can change the size of the production facility.

7. There are some indivisible inputs for the lemonade stand (the pitcher and the sign), just as there are indivisible inputs for the chip factory (testing equipment, clean room). Therefore, both operations will have negatively sloped long-run average cost curves. Of course, the cost of these indivisible inputs is tiny for the lemonade stand and huge for the chip factory. Therefore, the average cost curve for the chip factory will be negatively sloped over a large range of output. If your lemonade stand was a one-person operation, you probably never experienced the benefits from input specialization. In contrast, input specialization will be important in the chip factory.

Using the Tools

1. Production Consultant
   a. False. The principle of diminishing returns is applicable to the short-run cost curves, not the long-run curves.
   b. True. Diminishing returns imply increasing short-run marginal cost.
   c. False. Diminishing returns imply increasing short-run marginal cost but do not imply increasing short-run average cost. If the output is small enough, the spreading of fixed costs will generate a negatively sloped short-run average-cost curve even if there are diminishing returns.
   d. False. The first sentence implies that the short-run average-cost curve is positively sloped. This means that the short-run marginal cost exceeds the short-run average cost.

2. Cost of Breaking Up an Aluminum Firm. In Figure 8.7, the average cost for the large firm is $1.60 per pound (point c), compared to an average cost of $2.10 for each of the small firms.

3. Deregulation and the Cost of Trucking. The cost curve for trucking service in Figure 8.8 suggests that the manager has overstated the effects of deregulation on the average cost of trucking services. Suppose that the regulated firm provides 5 million ton-miles of trucking services per year at an average cost of $0.10 per ton-mile (point b). The entry of five firms would decrease the output per firm to 1 million ton-miles per year, increasing the cost per ton-mile to $0.11 (point c). In other words, deregulation would increase the average cost by only $0.01 per ton-mile.

Notes

1. Adam Smith, *The Wealth of Nations* (New York: The Modern Library, 1937), pp. 4–5.
2. John Johnson, *Statistical Cost Analysis* (New York: McGraw-Hill, 1960).
3. Aubrey Silberson, "Economies of Scale in Theory and Practice," *Economic Journal*, vol. 82, 1972, pp. 369–391.
4. Walter Adams and James W. Brock, "Automobiles," Chapter 4 in *The Structure of the American Economy*, 9th ed., edited by Walter Adams and James W. Brock (Upper Saddle River, NJ: Prentice Hall, 1995).
5. Walter Adams and James W. Brock, "Automobiles."
6. Frederick C. Klein, "At 3M Plants, Workers Have Flexibility, Involvement—And Their Own Radios," *Wall Street Journal*, February 5, 1982, p. 1.

CHAPTER

9

Perfect Competition: Short Run and Long Run

In 1992, Hurricane Andrew struck the southeastern United States, leaving millions of people without electricity for several days. Refrigerators stopped working, and thousands of people suddenly needed a lot of ice to cool and preserve their food. The price of a bag of ice immediately rose from $1 to $5. The same sort of price hikes occurred for chain saws (for clearing downed trees), bottled water, tarpaper (for repairing roofs), and plywood. If you had been the governor of Florida in 1992, what would you have done?

This is the first of 4 chapters exploring the decisions made by firms in different types of markets. Markets differ in the number of firms that compete against one another for customers. At one extreme is a monopoly: a market with a single seller. We'll explore the decisions of a monopolist in the next chapter. In this chapter, we'll look at the other extreme, a **perfectly competitive market**, a market with four features:

Perfectly competitive market: A market with a very large number of firms, each of which produces the same standardized product and takes the market price as given.

- There are many firms.
- The product is standardized or homogeneous.
- Firms can freely enter or leave the market in the long run.
- Each firm takes the market price as given.

The first three features of perfect competition imply the fourth. If there are many firms selling a standardized product, each firm has a tiny fraction of the market, and no matter how much any individual firm produces and sells, the market price won't change. There is no incentive for any firm to cut the price because any firm can sell as much as it wants at the market price. There is no incentive to raise the price because a firm doing so would lose all its customers to other firms selling the standardized product at the market price. A perfectly competitive firm is a price taker: It takes the market price as given. For example, each corn farmer produces a tiny fraction of the total supply of corn, and no matter how much corn one farmer produces, the price of corn won't change.

If you're thinking that the model of perfect competition is not very realistic, you're right. Most firms have some control over their prices. When a firm increases its price slightly, it will certainly sell less, but the quantity sold will probably not go to zero. Although perfect competition is rare, it's a good starting point for the analysis of firms' decisions because a price-taking firm's decision is easy to understand. The firm doesn't have to worry about picking a price; it just decides how much to produce, given the market price. Once you understand this simple case, you will be ready to tackle the more complex decisions of firms that have some control over their prices.

In this chapter, you will see how firms use information on revenues and costs to decide how much output to produce. We'll consider both the short-run and the long-run responses to an increase in price, showing that the law of supply works in both the short run and the long run. Here are some practical questions that we answer:

1. **What information does the firm need to decide how much output to produce?**
2. **If your firm's accountant reports that you are losing money, should you close your business or continue to operate at a loss?**
3. **How did Hurricane Andrew affect prices in the short run and in the long run?**
4. **Health concerns decreased the demand for butter. The price initially dropped but then rose. Why?**

The Short-Run Output Decision

Total revenue: The money the firm gets by selling its product; equal to the price times the quantity sold.

The firm's objective is to maximize its profit, equal to revenue minus cost. A firm's **total revenue** is the money the firm gets by selling its product and is equal to the price times the quantity sold. For example, the total revenue for a farmer who sells 100 bushels of corn at $2 per bushel is $200. We know from Chapter 8 that a firm's total economic cost is the sum of its explicit costs (the firm's actual cash payments for its inputs) and implicit costs (the opportunity costs of nonpurchased inputs such as the entrepreneur's time or money). A firm's **economic profit** equals its total revenue minus its total economic cost. If our corn farmer has an economic cost of $180, the farmer's profit would be $20.

Economic profit: Total revenue minus total economic cost.

Table 9.1 Deciding How Much Output To Produce

Output: Rakes per Minute	Price	Total Revenue	Total Cost	Profit	Marginal Revenue (Price)	Marginal Cost
0	25	0	36	–36	25	0
1	25	25	44	–19	25	8
2	25	50	48	2	25	4
3	25	75	51	24	25	3
4	25	100	56	44	25	5
5	25	125	63	62	25	7
6	25	150	72	78	25	9
7	25	175	84	91	25	12
8	25	200	101	99	25	17
9	25	225	126	99	25	25
10	25	250	166	84	25	40

The Total Approach: Computing Total Revenue and Total Cost

The first approach to deciding how much output to produce involves computing the total revenue and total cost of different quantities of output. Table 9.1 shows the total revenue and total costs of a hypothetical rake producer. As shown in the third column, if the price of rakes is $25 per rake, the firm's total revenue equals $25 times the number of rakes produced, so total revenue increases by $25 for each additional rake produced and sold. The fourth column shows the short-run total costs associated with different quantities of rakes produced. The fifth column shows economic profit, defined as total revenue minus total cost. In this example, profit is maximized when the firm produces either 8 or 9 rakes per minute. In either case, total revenue exceeds total cost by $99. We'll assume that whenever profit is highest for two quantities of output (8 and 9 in this case), the firm produces the larger quantity.

Figure 9.1 shows how to choose the quantity of output that maximizes profit. We're looking for the largest profit, meaning the biggest gap between total revenue and total cost. In this case, profit is maximized when the firm produces either 8 or 9 rakes, with a profit equal to $99.

The Marginal Approach

The other way to decide how much output to produce involves the marginal principle, the general decision-making rule that is one of the key principles of economics.

MARGINAL **PRINCIPLE**

> **Increase the level of an activity if its marginal benefit exceeds its marginal cost, but reduce the level if the marginal cost exceeds the marginal benefit. If possible, pick the level at which the marginal benefit equals the marginal cost.**

Figure 9.1
Using the Total Approach to Choose an Output Level

Economic profit is shown by the vertical distance between the total-revenue curve and the total-cost curve. To maximize profit, the firm chooses the quantity of output that generates the largest vertical difference between the two curves.

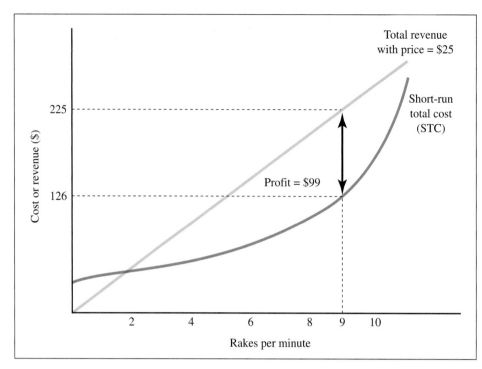

In our example, the firm's activity is producing rakes, so to use the marginal principle, the firm must compute the marginal benefit and the marginal cost of producing different quantities of rakes.

The benefit of producing and selling rakes is the revenue the firm collects. Therefore, the marginal benefit of producing rakes is the **marginal revenue** from rakes: the change in total revenue that results from selling one more rake. As shown in columns two and three in Table 9.1, the perfectly competitive rake firm can sell as much as it wants at the $25 market price, so if the firm sells one more unit of output, its total revenue increases by $25. This means that

Marginal revenue: The change in total revenue that results from selling one more unit of output.

marginal benefit = marginal revenue = market price

The marginal principle tells us that the firm will maximize its profit by choosing the quantity at which marginal revenue (the market price) equals marginal cost:

price = marginal cost

Figure 9.2 illustrates the use of the marginal principle for the firm's output decision. In panel A, the market supply and demand curves represent the collective choices of all rake producers and consumers. The market supply curve intersects the market demand curve at a price of $25. In panel B, the horizontal line shows the market price—the marginal revenue for the perfectly competitive firm. The marginal-revenue line intersects the marginal-cost curve at a quantity of 9 rakes per minute, so that's the quantity that maximizes profit (where marginal revenue equals marginal cost).

To see that an output of 9 rakes per minute maximizes the firm's profit, imagine the firm produced only 4 rakes per minute. Could the firm make more profit by producing 5 rakes instead of 4?

1. From the seventh row of numbers in Table 9.1 and point *d* in Figure 9.2, we know that the marginal cost of the 5th rake is $7.
2. The price of rakes is $25, so the marginal benefit (marginal revenue) is $25.

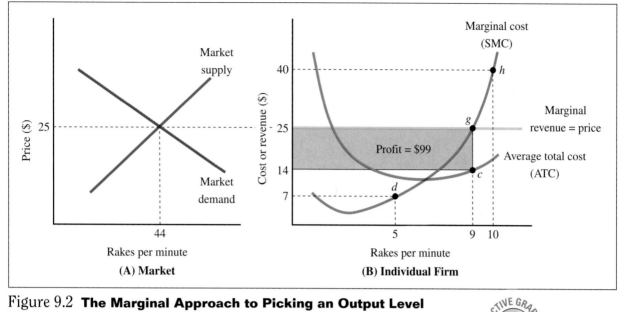

Figure 9.2 **The Marginal Approach to Picking an Output Level**
A perfectly competitive firm takes the market price as given. In panel A, the market supply curve intersects the market demand curve at a price of $25. In panel B, using the marginal principle, the typical firm will maximize profit at point *g*, where the market price ($25) equals the marginal cost. Economic profit equals the difference between price and average cost ($11 = $25 – $14) times the quantity produced (nine rakes per minute), or $99 per minute.

Because the extra revenue from the 5th rake (price = $25) exceeds the extra cost (marginal cost = $7), the production and sale of the 5th rake increases the firm's total profit by $18 (equal to $25 – $7). Therefore, it is sensible to produce the 5th rake. The same logic applies, with different numbers for marginal cost, for the 6th through the 8th rakes. For the 9th rake, marginal revenue equals marginal cost, so the firm's profit doesn't change. To be consistent with the marginal principle, we'll assume that the firm goes to the point at which marginal revenue equals marginal cost. In this case, the firm produces the 9th rake.

The same logic applies for producing any quantity greater than 9 rakes per minute. Imagine the firm produced 10 rakes. Would its profit be higher if it produced one fewer rake (9 rakes instead of 10)? From Table 9.1 and the marginal cost curve in Figure 9.2, we see that the marginal cost of the 10th rake is $40 (point *h*), which exceeds the marginal revenue (the market price) of $25. The 10th rake adds more to cost ($40) than it adds to revenue ($25), so producing the rake decreases the firm's profit by $15 (equal to $40 – $25). The marginal principle suggests that the firm should choose point *g*, with an output of 9 rakes.

Economic Profit

We've seen that the perfectly competitive firm maximizes its profit by producing the quantity at which its marginal revenue (price) equals its marginal cost. How much profit does the firm earn? The firm's economic profit equals its total revenue minus its total cost. The easiest way to compute a firm's total economic profit is to multiply the average profit per unit produced (the gap between the price and the average cost) by the quantity produced:

economic profit = (price – average cost) × quantity produced

In Figure 9.2, the average cost of producing 9 rakes is $14 (point c), so the economic profit is $99:

$$\text{economic profit} = (\$25 - \$14) \times 9 = \$99$$

In Figure 9.2, the firm's profit is shown by the area of the shaded rectangle. The height of the rectangle is the average profit ($11 per rake), and the width of the rectangle is the quantity produced (9 rakes).

The Turnaround Artist

ECONOMIC DETECTIVE

Emilio knows how to turn an unprofitable company into a profitable one. His latest project was a firm that was losing money producing and selling hammers. The firm sold 100 hammers per day at a price of $20 each and lost $500 per day. Emilio showed up at the factory on Monday and told the factory manager to increase production to 101 hammers on Tuesday. After a brief conversation with the factory manager on Wednesday, Emilio gave his advice, collected his fee, and disappeared. One week later, the firm was producing fewer hammers but making a profit of $2 on each hammer. What is Emilio's secret formula for success? What was his advice on Wednesday?

The key to answering these questions is the marginal principle. The purpose of Emilio's experiment was to compute the marginal cost of hammers. He compared the total cost of producing 101 hammers to the total cost of 100 hammers, and must have discovered that the marginal cost of the 101st hammer was greater than the market price ($20). According to the marginal principle, if the marginal cost exceeds the marginal benefit (the price), a decrease in output will increase profit. Emilio's formula for success is the marginal principle. ◆

TEST Your Understanding

1. Explain why a perfectly competitive firm takes prices as given.

2. Complete the statement: A perfectly competitive firm will produce the quantity of output at which _____ equals _____.

3. Suppose the market price of sugar is 22 cents per pound. If a sugar farmer produces 100,000 pounds, the marginal cost of sugar is 30 cents per pound. Is the farmer maximizing profit? If not, should the farmer produce more sugar or less sugar?

The Shut-Down Decision

Consider next the decisions faced by a firm that is losing money. Suppose the market price is so low that the firm's total revenue is less than its total cost, even though the firm used the marginal principle to decide how much to produce. For an unprofitable firm like this one, the question is, Should we continue to operate at a loss or should we shut down? This may seem like a silly question. Why would any firm continue to operate if it is losing money? As we'll see, it will be sensible to operate at a loss if the firm would lose even more money by shutting down.

Figure 9.3 shows the situation faced by an unprofitable firm. Suppose the market price of rakes drops to $9 per rake. If the firm continues to operate, it will produce 6 rakes per minute (shown by point z, where the marginal revenue (the price) equals mar-

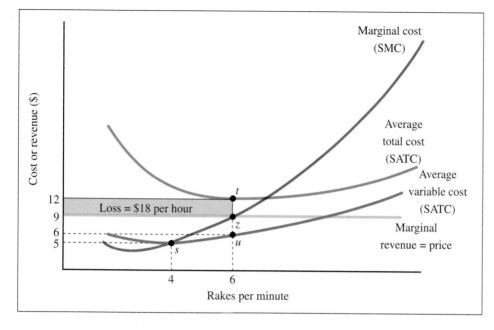

Figure 9.3
Shut-Down Decision
With a price of $9, the marginal principle indicates that the firm should pick point z, producing 6 rakes per minute. The average cost exceeds the price by $3, so the firm loses $18 per minute ($3 per rake times 6 rakes per minute). The average variable cost is $6 per rake, which is less than the $9 price, so total revenue exceeds total variable cost, and it is sensible to continue operating.

ginal cost). The firm's problem is that the average total cost of production ($12, as shown by point t) is less than the price ($9), so economic profit is negative. The average cost exceeds the price by $3, so the firm will lose $18 per minute ($3 per rake times 6 rakes per minute). Should the firm continue to operate at a loss, or shut down?

Total Revenue Versus Total Variable Cost

The firm should continue to operate if the benefit of operating exceeds the cost of operating. The benefit equals the firm's total revenue, or the price times the quantity produced. In Figure 9.3, the firm can sell 6 rakes at a price of $9 per rake, so the total revenue from operating is $54. The firm's cost of operating—as opposed to shutting down—equals the firm's total variable cost. As shown by point u, when the firm produces 6 rakes, its average variable cost is $6 per rake. Therefore, its total variable cost is $36 ($6 per rake times 6 rakes). Because the benefit of operating (total revenue of $54) exceeds the variable cost ($36), it is sensible for the firm to continue to operate.

We can use a shortcut to determine whether total revenue exceeds the total variable cost. Total revenue is the price times the quantity produced, and total variable cost is the average variable cost times the quantity produced. Therefore, if the price exceeds the average variable cost, total revenue will exceed total variable cost. The firm should continue to operate if price exceeds the average variable cost; otherwise, it should shut down.

Operate: price > average variable cost
Shut down: price < average variable cost

In Figure 9.3, the price is $9 and the average variable cost of 6 rakes is $6 per rake, so it is sensible to continue operating, even at a loss.

The firm's **shut-down price** is defined as the price at which the firm is indifferent between operating and shutting down. In Figure 9.3, the shut-down price is $5 (shown by point s). If the market price of rakes drops below the shut-down price, the firm would be better off shutting down. At the shut-down price, marginal cost equals price (the marginal principle) and average variable cost also equals the price (for total revenue to equal total variable cost). Therefore, marginal cost equals average variable cost, and as

Shut-down price: The price at which the firm is indifferent between operating and shutting down.

A firm should shut down an unprofitable facility if its total revenue is less than its total variable cost.

we saw in Chapter 8, that happens at the minimum point of the average variable cost curve. That means that the shut-down price is the minimum average variable cost.

Why Operate an Unprofitable Facility?

If the idea of operating an unprofitable facility is puzzling, think about what would happen if the firm shut down. Although the firm would no longer pay for labor and materials, it would still pay for its idle production facility, for example, a factory full of machinery and equipment. The cost of the production facility is a **sunk cost**, defined as a cost the firm has already paid or has agreed to pay some time in the future. For example, a firm with a $1 million production facility has a sunk cost of $1 million, regardless of whether the firm paid for the facility in the past or will pay for it in the future. What matters is that the firm cannot do anything about this sunk cost.

Sunk cost: The cost a firm has already paid or has agreed to pay some time in the future.

If a firm shuts down its production facility, it will still pay its sunk costs—the cost of the production facility. In our example, the sunk cost is the same as the fixed cost, which is $36 per minute (see the first row of numbers in Table 9.1, where the total cost with zero output is $36). Therefore, the firm will lose $36 per minute if it shuts down. But if the firm operates, it will lose only $18 per minute. Because the firm loses less money if it operates, it is sensible to continue operating.

How long should a firm continue to operate at a loss? Let's think about what happens when the firm must decide whether to build a new production facility. The firm will build a new facility—and produce output to stay in the market—only if the price of rakes exceeds the average total cost of production. In other words, the firm will stay in the market only if the market price is high enough that total revenue is high enough to cover all the costs of production, including the cost of a new facility. Although a firm may operate an existing facility at a loss, it won't replace it if the new facility would be unprofitable too.

TEST Your Understanding

4. Complete the statement with a number: If a lamp producer can sell 40 lamps per day at a price of $20 per lamp, the benefit of operating its production facility is _____ per day.

5. Complete the statement with *operate* or *shut down*: Consider a firm with total revenue of $500, total cost of $700, and variable cost of $400. The firm should _____ its production facility.

6. Complete the statement: A firm that is losing money should continue to operate if the market price exceeds _____.

Short-Run Supply Curves

Now that we've explored the output decision of a price-taking firm, we're ready to show how firms respond to changes in the market price of output. We'll represent the relationship between price and quantity supplied with two short-run supply curves, one for the individual firm and one for the entire market.

The Short-Run Supply Curve of the Firm

The firm's **short-run supply curve** shows the relationship between the market price and the quantity supplied by the firm over a period of time during which one input—the production facility—cannot be changed. In the case of rake producers, the firm's supply curve answers the following question: At a given price of rakes, how many rakes will the firm produce? We have already used the marginal principle and the marginal-cost curve to answer this question for two different prices. At a price of $9, the marginal revenue (price) equals marginal cost when the firm produces 6 rakes per minute; at a price of $25, price equals marginal cost with 9 rakes.

Short-run supply curve: A curve showing the relationship between the price of a product and the quantity of output supplied by a firm in the short run.

The firm's short-run supply curve is the part of the firm's short-run marginal cost curve above the shut-down price. The shut-down price for the rake firm is $5, so as shown in Figure 9.4, the short-run supply curve is the marginal cost curve starting at $5. For any price above the shut-down price, the firm will choose the quantity at which price equals marginal cost, so we can read the firm's quantity supplied from its marginal cost curve. If the price is $12, the firm will supply 7 rakes per minute (point m). As the price increases, the firm responds by supplying more rakes: 8 rakes when the price is $17 and 9 rakes when the price is $25.

What about prices below the shut-down price? If the price drops below the shut-down price, the firm's total revenue will not be high enough to cover its total variable cost, so the firm will shut down and produce no output. In panel A of Figure 9.4, the firm's supply curve starts at point s, indicating that the quantity supplied is zero for any price less than $5. For another example of the short-run supply curve, read "A Closer Look: Supply Decisions of a Corn Farmer."

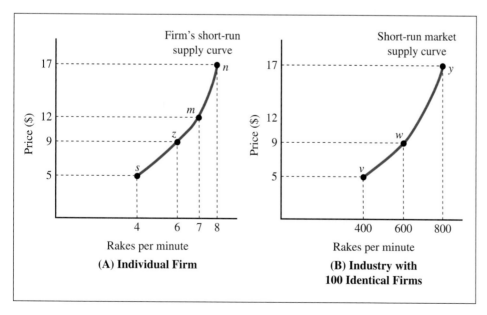

(A) Individual Firm

(B) Industry with 100 Identical Firms

Figure 9.4
Short-Run Supply Curves
In panel A, the firm's short-run supply curve is the part of the marginal-cost curve above the shut-down price ($5). For prices below the shut-down price, the firm shuts down, so the quantity supplied is zero. In panel B, there are 100 firms in the market, so the market supply at a given price is 100 times the quantity supplied by the typical firm. At a price of $9, each firm supplies 6 rakes per minute (point z), so the market supply is 600 rakes per minute (point w).

Supply Decisions of a Corn Farmer

What's the shut-down price for a corn farmer? What's the break-even price? We can answer these questions with the actual short-run cost curves for corn farmers shown in the figure at the right (in 1971 dollars). The break-even or zero-profit price is $0.72 per bushel. At any higher price, the farmer will make a profit. If the price is $1.00, the farmer will produce 53,000 bushels at an average cost of about $0.74 and earn a profit of about $13,780. The shut-down price is $0.44: At prices between $0.44 and $0.72, the farmer will lose money but will continue to operate at a loss because the price exceeds the average variable cost; at prices below $0.44, the farmer will shut down the unprofitable operation.

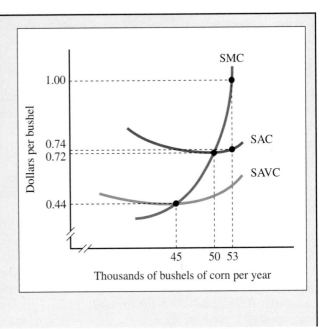

Source: Walter Adams, ed., *The Structure of the American Economy*, 8th ed., (Upper Saddle River, NJ: Prentice-Hall, 1990). Adapted by permission.

The Market Supply Curve

Short-run market supply curve:
A curve showing the relationship between price and the quantity of output supplied by all firms in the short run.

The **short-run market supply curve** shows the relationship between the market price and the quantity supplied by all firms in the short run. Panel B of Figure 9.4 shows the short-run market supply curve when there are 100 identical rake firms. For each price, we get the quantity supplied for the entire market by multiplying the quantity supplied by the typical firm (from the individual supply curve) by 100. At a price of $9, each firm produces 6 rakes (point z), so the market supply is 600 rakes (point w). If the price increases to $17, each firm produces 8 rakes, so the market supply is 800 rakes (point y).

What happens if firms are not identical but instead have different individual supply curves? To compute the market supply in this case, we would add the quantities supplied by the dozens (or hundreds) of firms in the market. The assumption that firms are identical is harmless: It makes it easier to derive the market supply curve from the supply curve of the typical firm, but it does not change the analysis.

TEST Your Understanding

7. Complete the statement: The firm's short-run supply curve shows the relationship between _____ and _____.

8. Suppose that you want to draw the firm's short-run supply curve. What information do you need?

9. Suppose there are 100 identical firms in a perfectly competitive industry. At a price of $22, the typical firm supplies 50 units of output. What is the market quantity supplied at a price of $22?

The Long-Run Supply Curve for an Increasing-Cost Industry

In the long run, firms can enter or leave an industry, and existing firms can modify their facilities or build new facilities. A market reaches a long-run equilibrium when three conditions hold:

1. The quantity of the product supplied equals the quantity demanded.
2. Each firm in the market maximizes its profit, given the market price.
3. Each firm in the market earns zero economic profit, so there is no incentive for other firms to enter the market.

The first two conditions are actually the two conditions for short-run equilibrium, so the only difference between the short run and the long run is that in the long run, economic profit is zero. When a firm earns zero economic profit, its total revenue equals its total economic cost. The total economic cost includes opportunity cost of the firm's inputs, including the entrepreneur. A firm earning zero economic profit stays in business because it isn't losing any money, and the entrepreneur receives a wage equal to the opportunity cost of his or her time.

Figure 9.5 shows a market in long-run equilibrium. The demand curve intersects the short-run market supply curve at a price of $12 and a quantity of 700 rakes per minute (condition 1). There are 100 firms, each of which produces 7 rakes per minute. Each firm maximizes its profit by choosing the quantity at which the marginal revenue (the price) equals the marginal cost, producing 7 rakes per minute (condition 2). At the quantity chosen by each firm, price equals short-run average total cost, so each firm makes zero economic profit (condition 3).

Production Costs and the Size of the Industry in the Long Run

Let's look at the **long-run market supply curve**, which shows the relationship between the market price and the quantity supplied by all firms in the long run, a period long enough that firms can enter or leave the market. Suppose the typical rake firm produces 7 rakes per minute, using a standard set of inputs, including a factory, some workers, and raw materials (wood and plastic). In a perfectly competitive industry, there are no restrictions on entry, so anyone can use the standard set of inputs to produce 7 rakes per minute.

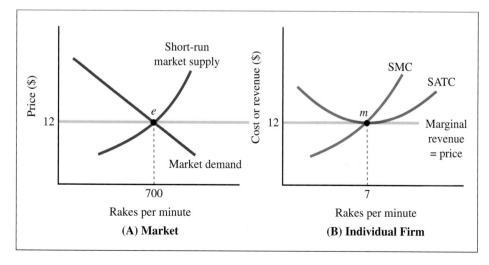

(A) Market   (B) Individual Firm

Long-run market supply curve: A curve showing the relationship between the market price and quantity supplied by all firms in the long run.

Figure 9.5

Long-Run Market Equilibrium
In panel A, the market demand curve intersects the short-run market supply curve at a price of $12. In panel B, given the market price, the typical firm satisfies the marginal principle at point *m*, producing 7 rakes per minute. Because price equals the average cost at the chosen quantity, economic profit is zero, and no other firms will enter the market.

Table 9.2 Industry Output and Average Production Cost

Number of Firms	Industry Output	Rakes per Firm	Total Cost for Typical Firm	Average Cost per Rake
50	350	7	$70	$10
100	700	7	84	12
150	1,050	7	96	14

Table 9.2 shows hypothetical data on the cost of producing rakes. Let's start with the first row, which shows the firm's production costs in an industry with 50 firms and a total of 350 rakes (with 7 rakes per firm). To compute the total cost for the typical firm, we add the cost of the firm's production facility (the cost of the rake factory), the cost of labor, and the cost of materials. In the first row, the total cost of the typical firm producing 7 rakes per minute is $70, and the average cost is $10 per rake ($70 divided by 7 rakes).

Increasing-cost industry: An industry in which the average cost of production increases as the total output of the industry increases; the long-run supply curve is positively sloped.

The rake industry is an example of an **increasing-cost industry**, defined as an industry in which the average cost of production increases as the total output of the industry increases. In the last column of Table 9.2, the average cost is $10 per rake in an industry that produces 350 rakes, $12 per rake in an industry that produces 700 rakes, and so on. The average cost increases as the industry grows for two reasons:

- **Increasing input prices.** As an industry grows, it competes with other industries for limited amounts of various inputs, and this competition drives up the prices of these inputs. For example, suppose that the rake industry competes against other industries for a limited amount of special wood. To get more of that wood to produce more rakes, firms in the rake industry must outbid other industries for the limited amount available, and this competition drives up the price of wood.
- **Less productive inputs.** A small industry will use only the most productive inputs, but as the industry grows, firms may be forced to use less productive inputs. For example, a small rake industry will use only the most skillful workers. As the industry grows, it will have to rely on less skillful workers. As the average skill level of the industry's workforce decreases, the average cost of production increases: In a large rake industry, it will take more hours of labor—and more money—to produce each rake. Another example is the production of agricultural products such as sugar. Because of variation in climate and soil conditions, it is cheaper to grow sugar in some areas than in others. As the quantity of sugar produced increases, growers are forced to produce sugar in areas with higher costs.

Drawing the Long-Run Market Supply Curve

The long-run supply curve tells us how much output will be produced at each price in the long run, when the number of firms in the market can change. Given a market price, we determine the total output of the industry by multiplying the output per firm (7 rakes in our example) by the number of firms in the industry. So the key question for the long-run supply curve is, How many firms will be in the market at that price?

Let's think about the incentive for a firm to enter the market. Economic profit is positive when total revenue exceeds total cost or when price exceeds the average cost. Whenever there is an opportunity to make a profit in a market—whenever the price exceeds average cost—firms will enter the market. Firms will continue to enter a market until economic profit is zero, which happens when the price equals average cost. When economic profit is zero, the firm's revenue is high enough to cover all its costs—including the opportunity cost of all its inputs—but not high enough to cause additional firms to enter the market. Each firm that is already in the market makes just enough money to stay in business, so there is no incentive for new firms to enter the market, and no incentive for existing firms to leave.

As a starting point, suppose the price of rakes is $12. There are no restrictions on entry into the industry, so any firm can use the standard set of inputs to produce 7 rakes per minute. The information in Table 9.2 suggests that there will be 100 firms in the market. To explain why 100 is the correct number, think about what would happen if there were either fewer firms or more firms:

- **Fewer firms.** If there were fewer than 100 firms, the average cost per rake would be less than the $12 price. If there were only 50 firms (producing a total of 350 rakes per minute), the average cost would be only $10 per rake. At that average cost, the profit per rake would be $2 (a price of $12 minus an average cost of $10). Firms would start to enter this profitable market, and entry would continue until the average cost reached the $12 market price. This occurs when there are 100 firms producing a total of 700 rakes.
- **More firms.** If there were more than 100 firms, the average cost per rake would exceed the $12 price. If there were 150 firms (producing a total 1,050 rakes per minute), the average cost would be $14 per rake. Each firm would lose $2 per rake (an average cost of $14 minus a price of $12). Firms would start to leave this unprofitable market, and exit would continue until the average cost dropped to the $12 market price, which occurs when there are 100 firms producing a total of 700 rakes.

To find the number of firms in the market, we find the number of firms at which the average cost per rake equals the $12 market price. If the price equals the average cost, each of the 100 firms makes zero economic profit, so there is no incentive for new firms to enter the market and no incentive for existing firms to leave.

Each point on the long-run supply curve shows the quantity of rakes supplied at a particular price. To find a point on the supply curve, we pick a price and then determine how many rakes the industry will produce at that price. At a price of $12, there will be 100 firms producing 700 rakes, so one point on the supply curve shown in Figure 9.6 is point *h*. To find the other points on the long-run supply curve, we pick other prices and use the data in Table 9.2 to determine the quantity at which price equals the average cost of production. At a price of $10, the quantity is 350 rakes (point *e*), and at a price of $14, the quantity is 1,050 (point *j*).

The long-run supply curve in Figure 9.6 is positively sloped, as it will be for any increasing-cost industry. This is another example of the law of supply. The higher the

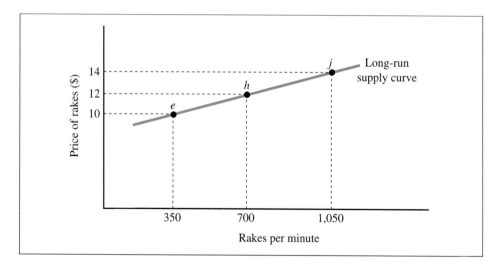

Figure 9.6

Long-Run Market Supply Curve

The long-run market supply curve shows the relationship between the price and quantity supplied in the long run, when firms can enter or leave the industry. At each point on the supply curve, the market price equals the long-run average cost of production. The market supply curve for an increasing-cost is positively sloped.

The supply of rental housing is relatively inelastic because most local governments restrict the amount of land available for building apartments.

price of rakes, the larger the quantity supplied. An increase in the price of rakes makes rake production more profitable, so firms enter the market, increasing the quantity supplied to the market. Firms will continue to enter the market until the average cost per rake reaches the market price. Each firm gets just enough revenue to cover its production costs, so economic profit is zero. For another example of the law of supply, read "A Closer Look: The Supply of Wolfram During World War II."

Examples of Increasing-Cost Industries: Sugar, Rental Housing

The sugar industry is an example of an increasing-cost industry. If the price of sugar is only 11 cents per pound, sugar production is profitable in areas with relatively low production costs, including the Caribbean, Latin America, Australia, and South Africa.[1] At a price of 11 cents, the world supply of sugar equals the amount produced in these areas. As the price increases, sugar production becomes profitable in areas where production costs are higher, increasing the quantity of sugar supplied as these other areas join the world market. For example, at a price of 14 cents per pound, sugar production is profitable in the European Community; and at a price of 24 cents, production is profitable even in the United States. The law of supply works in the world sugar market: The higher the price, the larger the number of areas that produce sugar, so the larger the quantity of sugar supplied.

Another example of an increasing-cost industry is rental housing. Local governments use land-use zoning to restrict the amount of land available for apartments. When housing producers decide to build more apartments, there is fierce competition for the small amount of land zoned for apartments, so the cost of land—and the cost per apartment—increases by a large amount.[2]

TEST Your Understanding

10. Complete the statement: The long-run supply curve shows the relationship between _____ (on the horizontal axis) and _____ (on the vertical axis).

11. Use Table 9.2 to compute the average cost in a 75-firm industry, assuming the total cost of the typical firm in such an industry is $70.

12. Circle the three items in the following list that go together: positively sloped supply curve, horizontal supply curve, increasing-cost industry, increasing average cost of production, constant average cost of production.

A CLOSER LOOK — The Supply of Wolfram During World War II

For an example of the law of supply, let's look at what happened to the supply of wolfram during World War II. Wolfram is an ore of tungsten, an alloy required to make heat-resistant steel for armor plate and armor-piercing shells. During World War II, the United States and its European allies bought up all the wolfram produced in Spain, thus denying the Axis powers (Germany and Italy) access to Spanish wolfram. The idea was to hamper the Axis war effort by denying them a vital input to the production of military equipment and weapons. This buying program was very costly to the Allied powers for two reasons:

- The Allied powers had to outbid the Axis powers for the Spanish wolfram, and the price of wolfram increased from $1,144 per ton to $20,000 per ton.

- Spanish firms responded to the higher prices by supplying more wolfram. Workers poured into the Galatia area in Spain, where they used simple tools to gather wolfram from the widely scattered outcroppings of ore. The quantity of wolfram supplied increased tenfold. Because wolfram miners obeyed the law of supply, the Allied powers were forced to buy a huge amount of wolfram, much more than they had expected.

Source: D. I. Gordon and R. Dangerfield, *The Hidden Weapon* (New York: Harper & Brothers, 1947), pp. 105–116.

Market Equilibrium Revisited

We can use what we've learned about the short-run supply curve and the long-run supply curve to get a deeper understanding of perfectly competitive markets. Let's use the two supply curves to explore the short-run and the long-run effects of a change in demand.

Increase in Demand and the Incentive to Enter

Figure 9.7 shows the short-run effects of an increase in the demand for rakes. Panel A shows what's happening at the market level. Let's start with the initial equilibrium shown by point *e*: The original demand curve intersects the short-run market supply curve at a price of $12 per rake and a quantity of 700 rakes. When demand increases, the market demand curve shifts to the right, and it intersects the supply curve at a price of $17 and a quantity of 800 rakes. In panel B, an increase in price from $12 to $17

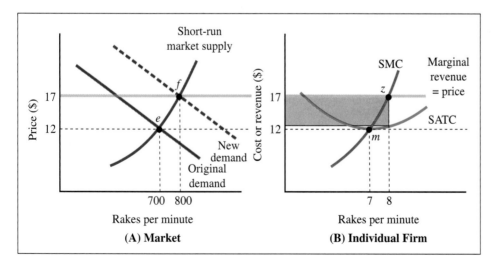

(A) Market

(B) Individual Firm

Figure 9.7

Short-Run Effects of an Increase in Demand

An increase in demand increases the market price to $17, causing the typical firm to produce 8 rakes instead of 7. Price exceeds the short-run average total cost at the chosen quantity, so economic profit is positive. Firms will enter the profitable market.

increases the output per firm from 7 rakes to 8 rakes. At this quantity, the $17 price now exceeds the average total cost, so the typical firm makes an economic profit (shown by the shaded rectangle). At the market level shown in panel A, the new short-run equilibrium has a price of $17 and a quantity of 800 rakes.

This is not a long-run equilibrium because each firm is making a positive economic profit. Firms will enter the profitable market and as they compete for customers, the price of rakes will decrease. New firms will continue to enter the market until the price drops to the point at which economic profit is zero. The question is, How far does the price drop?

The Long-Run Effects of an Increase in Demand

We can use the long-run supply curve to determine the long-run price. In Figure 9.8, the short-run effect of the increase in demand is shown by the move from point e to point f: The price increases from $12 to $17, and the quantity increases from 700 to 800. The new long-run equilibrium is shown by point s, where the new demand curve intersects the long-run supply curve. Starting with a price of $17 (the new short-run equilibrium), firms will continue to enter the market until the price drops to $14 and the quantity is 1,050 rakes per minute. At this price and quantity, each of the 150 firms produces 7 rakes per minute and earns zero economic profit.

Figure 9.8 shows how the price of rakes changes over time. An increase in demand causes a large upward jump in the price (from point e to point f), followed by a slide downward to the new long-run equilibrium price (from point f to point s). In the short run, firms respond to an increase in price by squeezing more output from their existing production facilities. Because of diminishing returns, it is costly to increase output in the short run, so the price increases by a large amount. The higher price causes new firms to enter the market, and as they enter, the price gradually drops to the point at which each firm makes zero economic profit. The long-run supply curve is relatively flat because firms enter the industry and build new factories, so there are no diminishing returns.

Long-Run Supply for a Constant-Cost Industry

As the rake industry expanded, the average cost of production increased, a result of higher input costs. In other words, the rake industry is an increasing-cost industry. In

Figure 9.8

Short-Run and Long-Run Effects of an Increase in Demand

The short-run supply curve is steeper than the long-run supply curve because there are diminishing returns in the short run. In the short run, an increase in demand increases the price from $12 (point e) to $17 (point f). In the long run, firms enter the industry, and the price drops to $14 (point s). The large upward jump in price is followed by a downward slide to the new long-run equilibrium price.

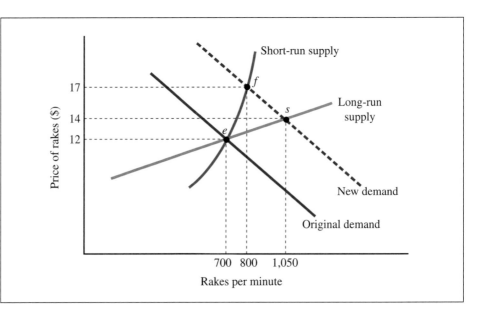

contrast, as a **constant-cost industry** grows, it continues to buy its inputs at the same prices. For this to happen, the industry must be a small part of the relevant input markets, meaning that the expansion of the industry doesn't have a big enough effect on the input market to affect input prices. As a result, the average cost of production for the typical firm doesn't change as the industry grows. In Table 9.2, the rake industry would be a constant-cost industry if the average cost of rakes were constant at $10, regardless of how many rakes were produced.

As an example of a constant-cost industry, consider the taxi industry in a city. As the taxi industry grows, it will use more gasoline, more workers, and more cars, but because the industry is such a small part of the markets for gasoline, labor, and cars, the prices of these inputs won't change. As a result, the average cost of production won't change as the industry grows.

The long-run supply curve for a constant-cost industry is horizontal at the constant average cost of production. If the average cost of taxi service is $3 per mile (including the cost of gasoline, the taxicab, and the driver), the long-run supply curve for taxi service is horizontal at $3, as shown in Figure 9.9. At any lower price, the quantity of taxi service supplied would be zero because no rational firm would provide taxi service at a price less than the average cost of providing the service. At any higher price, firms would enter the taxi industry in droves, and entry would continue until the price dropped to the constant average cost of taxi service ($3).

Hurricane Andrew and the Price of Ice

For an example of the short-run and long-run effects of an increase in demand, let's look at the short-run and long-run effects of a hurricane. In 1992, Hurricane Andrew struck the southeastern United States, leaving millions of people without electricity for several days. Figure 9.10 shows the short- and long-run effects of the hurricane on the price of ice, which was used to cool and preserve food in areas without electricity. Before the hurricane, the market was at point e, with a price of $1 per bag of ice. The long-run supply curve is horizontal, indicating that the ice industry is a constant-cost industry.

In the short run (a day or two), the number of ice suppliers is fixed. The increase in demand caused by the hurricane moved the market from point e to point f, and the price rose to $5 per bag of ice. In the long run, firms responded to the higher price by entering the market. Many people trucked ice from distant locations and sold it from trucks parked on streets and highways. As these firms entered the ice market in the days after

Constant-cost industry: An industry in which the average cost of production is constant; the long-run supply curve is horizontal.

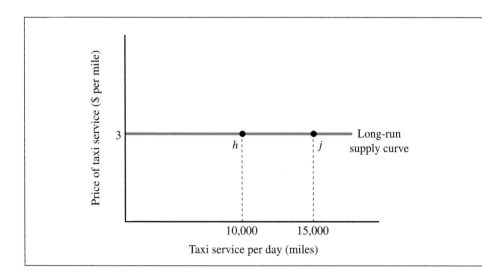

Figure 9.9
Long-Run Supply Curve for a Constant-Cost Industry
In a constant-cost industry, input prices do not change as the industry grows, so the average production cost is constant and the long-run supply curve is horizontal. For the taxi industry, the cost per mile of taxi service is constant at $3, so the supply curve is horizontal at $3 per mile of service.

Figure 9.10

Hurricane Andrew and the Price of Ice

A hurricane increases the demand for ice, shifting the demand curve to the right. In the short run, the supply curve is steep, so the price rises by a large amount. In the long run, firms enter the industry, pulling down the price. Because this is a constant-cost industry, the supply curve is horizontal, and the large upward jump in price is followed by a downward slide back to the original price.

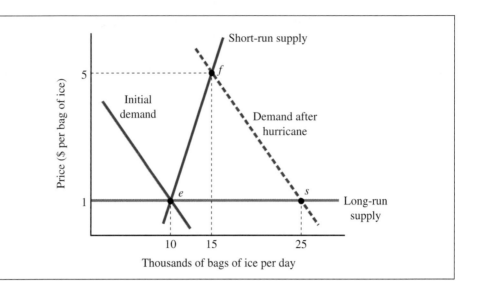

the hurricane, the price of ice gradually dropped, and the market eventually reached the intersection of the new demand curve and the long-run supply curve (point *s*), with a price equal to the prehurricane price.

This pattern of price changes following the hurricane was observed in other markets. Immediately after the hurricane, $200 chain saws were sold for $900, but the price dropped steadily as new roadside firms entered the market. The same sort of price changes occurred for bottled water, tarpaper, and plywood. The basic pattern was a large upward jump in price followed by a downward slide to the long-run equilibrium price.

Public officials are often tempted to pass laws prohibiting what's called *price gouging*, charging high prices for scarce goods after a natural disaster. One effect of such laws is to slow the transition from the short run to the long run. The people who set up roadside stands to sell ice were motivated by the high price. If the price were controlled at $1 per bag, few people would have incurred the large expenses associated with trucking the ice from distant locations and setting up roadside stores. The result would have been less ice and more spoiled food. An alternative to a law regulating prices is to leave prices to the market and help to ease the transition from short run to long run by making it easier for entrepreneurs to enter the market.

ECONOMIC DETECTIVE

Butter Prices

Several years ago, people became concerned about the undesirable health effects of eating butter. The demand for butter dropped, decreasing its price. Some time later, the price of butter started rising steadily, although demand hadn't been changing. After several months of price hikes, the price of butter was getting close to the price observed before demand decreased. According to a consumer watchdog organization, the rising price of butter was evidence of a conspiracy on the part of butter producers. Is there some other explanation for the rising price of butter?

The key to solving this puzzle is the distinction between the short run and the long run. In Figure 9.11, the short-run effect of a decrease in demand is shown by the move from point *e* (price = $2.00) to point *f* (price = $1.44). In the short run, not many firms will leave the market when the price drops, so the decrease in demand will cause a large price drop. Although many of the remaining firms will lose money, they will stay in the market if their total revenue covers their total variable cost. In the long run, however,

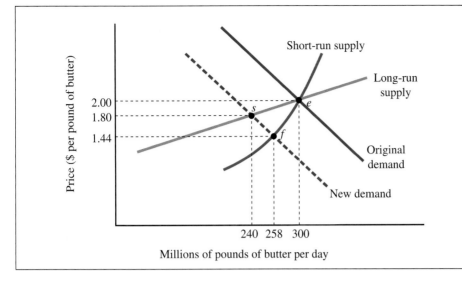

Figure 9.11

The Short-Run and Long Run Effects of a Decrease in the Demand for Butter

The short-run supply curve is steeper than the long-run supply curve because there are diminishing returns in the short run. In the short run, a decrease in demand decreases the price from $2.00 (point *e*) to $1.44 (point *f*). In the long run, firms leave the industry, and the price rises to the new equilibrium price of $1.80 (point *s*).

unprofitable firms will leave the market, causing the price to rise. In Figure 9.11, the new long-run equilibrium is shown by point *s*, with a price of $1.80. The pattern of a large price drop followed by a gradual increase in price is a normal pattern for a perfectly competitive market. ◆

TEST Your Understanding

13. Explain why the short-run supply curve is steeper than the long-run supply curve.

14. Describe the short-run price effect and the long-run price effect of a decrease in the demand for rakes.

15. Under what circumstances would an increase in demand for a particular good not affect the price of the good in the long run?

Using the TOOLS

We've seen how a perfectly competitive firm can use its cost curves to decide how much to produce and whether to continue operating an unprofitable operation. We've also explored the short- and long-run effects of changes in demand. Here are some opportunities to do your own economic analysis.

1. Advice for an Unprofitable Firm

You've been hired as an economic consultant to a price-taking firm that produces shirts. The firm already has a shirt factory, so it is operating in the short run. The price of shirts is $5, the hourly wage is $12, and each shirt requires $1 worth of material. At the current level of output (20 workers and 70 shirts per hour), the firm is losing money: Its total cost exceeds its total revenue. The firm has experimented with different numbers of workers and discovered that 21 workers would produce 72 shirts; 15 workers would produce 60 shirts; and 16 workers would produce 63 shirts. Your job is to tell the firm which of these four options to take:

- **Option 1:** Shut down the unprofitable operation.
- **Option 2:** Continue to produce 70 shirts per hour.
- **Option 3:** Produce more shirts.
- **Option 4:** Produce fewer shirts.

2. Maximizing the Profit Margin
According to the marginal principle, the firm should choose the quantity of output at which price equals marginal cost. A tempting alternative is to maximize the firm's profit margin, defined as the difference between price and short-run average total cost. Use the firm's short-run cost curves to evaluate this approach. Draw the firm's short-run supply curve and compare it to the supply curve of a firm that maximizes its profit.

3. Market Effects of an Increase in Housing Demand
Consider the market for apartments in a small city. In the initial equilibrium, the monthly rent (the price) is $500 and the quantity is 10,000 apartments. Suppose that the population of the city suddenly increases by 24%. The price elasticity of demand for apartments is 1.0. The short-run price elasticity of supply is 0.20, and the long-run price elasticity of supply is 0.50.

a. Depict graphically the short- and long-run effects of the increase in population.

b. By what percentage will the price increase in the short run? (Use the price-change formula from Chapter 5.)

c. By what percentage will the price increase in the long run?

Summary

In this chapter, we explored the decisions made by perfectly competitive firms and the implications of these decisions for the supply side of the market. In the short run, a firm uses the marginal principle to decide how much output to produce. In the long run, a firm will enter a market if the price exceeds the average cost of production. Here are the main points of this chapter:

1. A price-taking firm should produce the quantity of output at which the marginal revenue (the price) equals the marginal cost of production.

2. An unprofitable firm should continue to operate if its total revenue exceeds its total variable cost.

3. The long-run supply curve will be positively sloped if the average cost of production increases as the industry grows.

4. The long-run supply curve is flatter than the short-run supply curve because there are diminishing returns in the short run, but not in the long run.

5. An increase in demand causes a large upward jump in price, followed by a downward slide to the new long-run equilibrium price.

Key Terms

constant-cost industry, 203
economic profit, 188
increasing-cost industry, 198
long-run market supply curve, 197

marginal revenue, 190
perfectly competitive market, 188
short-run market supply curve, 196
short-run supply curve, 195

shut-down price, 193
sunk cost, 194
total revenue, 188

Problems and Discussion Questions

1. In the following table, provide the numbers for marginal cost. Then use the data to draw the short-run supply curve for tables.

Tables per hour	Total cost	Marginal cost
3	120	—
4	155	—
5	200	—
6	270	—

2. The following table shows short-run marginal costs for a perfectly competitive firm:

Output	100	200	300	400	500
Marginal cost	$5	$10	$20	$40	$70

   a. Use this information to draw the firm's marginal-cost curve.

   b. Suppose the shut-down price is $10. Draw the firm's short-run supply curve.

   c. Suppose there are 100 identical firms with the same marginal-cost curve. Draw the short-run industry supply curve.

3. You've been hired by an unprofitable firm to determine whether it should shut down its unprofitable operation. The firm currently uses 70 workers to produce 300 units of output per day. The daily wage (per worker) is $100, and the price of the firm's output is $30. Although you don't know the firm's fixed cost, you know that it is high enough that the firm's total cost exceeds its total revenue. Should the firm continue to operate at a loss?

4. Consider the choices facing an unprofitable (and perfectly competitive) firm. The firm currently produces 100 units per day and sells them at a price of $22 each. At the current output quantity, the total cost is $3,000 per day, the variable cost is $2,500 per day, and the marginal cost is $45.

   a. Evaluate the following statement from the firm's accountant: "Given our current production level, our variable cost ($2,500) exceeds our total revenue ($2,200). We should shut down our production facility."

   b. Illustrate your answer with a graph showing short-run cost curves and the revenue curve of a perfectly competitive firm.

5. Consider the following statement from a wheat farmer to his workers: "The price of wheat is very low this year, and the most I can get from the crop is $35,000. If I paid you the same amount as I paid you last year ($30,000), I'd lose money, because I also have to worry about the $20,000 I paid three months ago for seed and fertilizer. I'd be crazy to pay a total of $50,000 to harvest a crop I can sell for only $35,000. If you are willing to work for half as much as last year ($15,000), my total cost will be $35,000, so I'll break even. If you don't take a pay cut, I won't harvest the wheat." Is the farmer bluffing, or will the farmworkers lose their jobs if they reject the proposed pay cut?

6. Consider a firm that uses the following rule to decide how much output to produce: If the profit margin (price minus short-run average total cost) is positive, the firm will produce more output. Use the firm's short-run cost curves to evaluate this approach. Draw the firm's short-run supply curve and compare it to the short-run supply curve of a profit-maximizing firm.

7. Consider the following data on the relationship between the price of gasoline (in real terms, adjusted for inflation) and the quantity of gasoline sold per day in the city of Ceteris Paribus:

Year	Price	Gallons per Day
1995	1.00	50,000
1996	1.10	53,000

   If possible, draw the industry supply curve and compute the price elasticity of supply.

8. Between 1980 and 1990, the percentage of U.S. households with videocassette recorders (VCRs) increased from 1% to 70%. The rapid growth in the number of VCRs increased the demand for video rentals. Predict the effect of this increase in demand on the price of video rentals in the short run and the long run.

9. Suppose each lamp manufacturer produces 10 lamps per hour. In the following table, fill in a number wherever you see a _____. Then use the data in the table to draw the long-run supply curve for lamps.

Number of Firms	Industry Output	Total Cost for Typical Firm	Average Cost per Lamp
40	_____	$300	$_____
80	_____	$360	$_____
120	_____	$420	$_____

10. Suppose that a new technology decreases the amount of labor time required to produce a particular good. Would you expect all firms eventually to adopt the new technology?

11. Draw a long-run supply curve for haircutting that is consistent with the following statement: "The haircutting industry in our city uses a tiny fraction of the electricity, scissors, and commercial space available on the market. In addition, the industry uses only about 100 of the 50,000 people who could cut hair."

12. Draw a long-run supply curve for pencils and explain why you drew it as you did.

13. Web Exercise. Visit the Web site of Agricultural Weather dot Com (*http://www.agriculturalweather .com*). How might the information available at this Web site be useful to someone involved in the market for Florida orange juice?

14. Web Exercise. Visit the Web site of the Florida Agricultural Statistics Service (*http://www.nass .usda.gov/fl/*). Access the reports provided to get some data on recent trends in the price of some Florida citrus products. Draw a supply-demand graph consistent with the recent changes in prices and quantities.

Take It to the Net

We invite you to visit the O'Sullivan/Sheffrin page on the Prentice Hall Web site at:
http://www.prenhall.com/osullivan/
for additional World Wide Web exercises for this chapter.

Model Answers to Questions

Chapter-Opening Questions

1. To use the marginal principle, the firm needs the price (marginal benefit or marginal revenue) and the marginal cost of production for different levels of output.

2. It would be sensible to shut down if your total revenue is less than your variable cost. Otherwise, it would be sensible to continue operating.

3. Hurricane Andrew increased the demand for goods such as ice, chain saws, and plywood. In the short run, the supply curve for ice is steep, so the price increased by a relatively large amount. Over time, the price dropped as new firms entered the market to supply ice.

4. The large drop in price was a short-run effect, reflecting the steep short-run supply curve. As firms dropped out of the market and production decreased, the price started to rise.

Test Your Understanding

1. The firm is such a tiny part of the market that no matter how much output it produces, it will not affect the market price.

2. Marginal revenue (or price), marginal cost.

3. The farmer is not maximizing profit because the marginal revenue (price) is less than the marginal cost. The farmer should produce less sugar.

4. $800 ($20 per lamp times 40 lamps).

5. Operate.

6. Average variable cost.

7. Price, quantity supplied.

8. You need the short-run marginal cost curve and the shut-down price. If you have the average variable cost curve and the marginal cost curve, you can figure out the shut-down price by finding the price at which the two curves intersect.

9. 5,000 units (50 units per firm times 100 firms).

10. Quantity supplied, price.

11. The average cost per rake is $10 ($70/7 rakes).

12. The related terms are positively sloped supply curve, increasing-cost industry, and increasing average cost of production.

13. There are diminishing returns in the short run, so production costs increase rapidly as a firm increases its output.

14. In the short run, the price would drop by a large amount. Then the price would start to rise. If the rake industry is an increasing-cost industry, the new long-run price would be less than the original price.

15. If the good is produced by a constant-cost industry, one with a horizontal long-run supply curve.

Using the Tools

1. Advice for an Unprofitable Firm. At the current output level (70 shirts), the marginal cost of production is $7 per shirt: To produce one more shirt, the firm must use 0.50 hour of labor, which would cost $6 (half of the hourly wage) and $1 worth of material. Because the marginal cost exceeds the price ($5), the firm is not maximizing its profit.

At an output level of 60 shirts, the marginal cost of production is only $5 per shirt: To produce one more shirt, the firm must use one-third of an hour of labor, which would cost $4 (one-third of the hourly wage) and $1 worth of material. At this quantity of output, the price equals marginal cost, so the firm is maximizing profit. Total revenue ($300 = $5 per shirt × 60 shirts) exceeds variable cost ($240 = $180 for labor [$12 per hour × 15 hours]) plus $60 for materials ($1 per shirt × 60 shirts), so it is sensible to continue to operate, even if total cost exceeds total revenue.

2. Maximizing the Profit Margin. To maximize the profit margin, the firm will choose the quantity that generates the largest possible gap between the price and average cost, and this occurs at the minimum point of the average cost curve. In Figure 9.A, the average total cost curve reaches its minimum point at point *b*, with a quantity of 7 rakes and an average cost of $12. With a price of $17, the firm would produce 7 rakes per minute and earn a profit of $5 per rake or $35 per minute.

As shown in Figure 9.A at a price of $17, the firm would earn more profit by using the marginal principle. The price equals marginal cost with 8 rakes, and profit is $38.40 (an average cost of $12.20 means profit per unit is $4.80). The profit-margin approach is misguided because it looks at only one part of the profit picture: Total profit equals the profit margin times the quantity produced. Although the profit margin will be lower with 8 rakes, total profit will be higher.

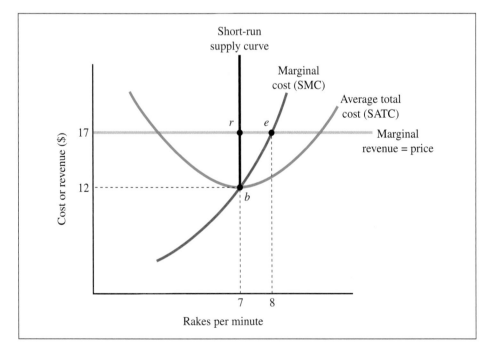

Short-run supply curve

Marginal cost (SMC)

Average total cost (SATC)

Marginal revenue = price

17 · · · · · · · · · *r* · · · · *e*

12 · · · · · · · · · · · · · · *b*

Cost or revenue ($)

7   8

Rakes per minute

Figure 9.A

Short-Run Supply Curve with Maximizing the Profit Margin

A firm that maximizes its profit margin (the difference between price and average cost) will produce the quantity at which average cost is at its minimum. The supply curve is a vertical line starting at the minimum of the average-cost curve.

Figure 9.B

Short- and Long-Run Effects of Population Growth

The initial equilibrium is shown by point *i*. The increase in demand moves the market to point *s* in the short run and to point *f* in the long run.

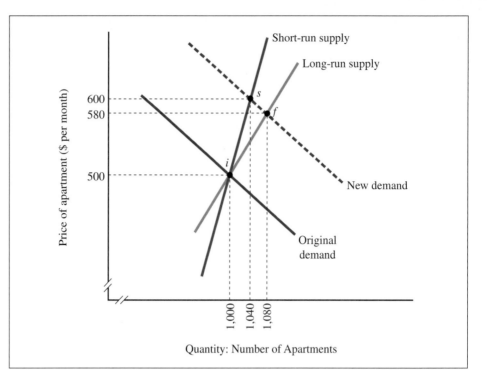

As shown in Figure 9.A, the supply curve is a vertical line starting at the minimum point of the average-cost curve. Suppose the firm will shut down if the profit margin is negative. At any price less than $12, price will be less than average cost, so the profit margin will be negative and the firm will shut down. To maximize the gap between price and average cost, the firm will choose the quantity associated with the minimum point of the average cost curve (7 rakes), regardless of the price of rakes. Therefore, as long as the price exceeds $12, the firm will produce 7 rakes. In contrast, the supply curve of a profit-maximizing firm is the marginal cost curve above the shut-down price.

3. Market Effects of an Increase in Housing Demand
   a. See Figure 9.B.
   b. Use the price-change formula from Chapter 5: percentage change in price = % change in demand/(Es + Ed) = 24/1.20 = 20%.
   c. Percentage change in price = 24/1.50 = 16%.

 **Notes**

1. Frederic L. Hoff and Max Lawrence, *Implications of World Sugar Markets, Policies, and Production Costs for U.S. Sugar*, Agricultural Economic Research Report 543 (Washington, DC: U.S. Department of Agriculture, Economic Research Service, November 1985).

2. Frank De Leeuw and Nkanta Ekanem, "The Supply of Rental Housing," *American Economic Review*, vol. 61, 1971, pp. 806–817.

CHAPTER 10

Monopoly

The Coca-Cola Company recently built a new football scoreboard for a large state university. Now football fans can enjoy the latest in scoreboard graphics as they watch the game. In addition, Coca Cola gave $2.3 million dollars to remodel the university's student center,[1] providing students with a comfortable place to meet, eat, talk, and relax. What explains this outburst of generosity? Does it have anything to do with the fact that Coca-Cola was recently given the exclusive right to sell beverages on campus—a monopoly? Who is really paying for the scoreboard and the student center?

The Monopolist's Output Decision
Total Revenue and Marginal Revenue
The Marginal Principle and the Output Decision
Picking a Quantity and a Price
Formula for Marginal Revenue

The Costs of Monopoly
Monopoly Versus Perfect Competition
Rent Seeking: Using Resources to Get Monopoly Power

Patents and Monopoly Power
Incentives for Innovation
Trade-Offs from Patents
Do the Benefits Exceed the Costs?

Natural Monopoly
Picking an Output Level
Will a Second Firm Enter?
Price Controls for a Natural Monopoly

Using the Tools

211

I n Chapter 9, we explored the decisions made by firms in a perfectly competitive market, a market where there are dozens or perhaps hundreds of firms. This chapter deals with the opposite extreme: a **monopoly**, a market served by a single firm. In contrast with a perfectly competitive or price-taking firm, a monopolist can pick any price it wants. Of course, the higher the price it charges, the smaller the quantity it will sell, because consumers obey the law of demand.

A monopoly occurs when there is one firm and a barrier to entry—a barrier that prevents other firms from entering a market. Here is a list of possible barriers to entry:

Monopoly: A market in which a single firm serves the entire market.

Patent: The exclusive right to sell a particular good for some period of time.

- A **patent** is granted by the government, giving an inventor the exclusive right to sell a new product for some period of time. Under a GATT agreement that took effect in 1995, patents in the United States and other GATT nations are now issued for 20 years from the time the inventor applies for a patent. To receive a patent, the inventor must prove the product is useful and novel (a true innovation, not just a slight modification of an existing product) and must provide a working model. Patent holders in many European countries pay an annual renewal fee for their patents, and the longer an inventor holds a patent, the higher the annual fee. In the United States, there are no renewal fees, so by paying a one-time fee, an inventor can prevent anyone else from selling the product for 20 years.

- In some cases, the government implicitly grants monopoly power by allowing industrial associations to restrict the number of firms in the market. For example, the U.S. government allows sports associations such as the major-league baseball leagues to restrict the number and location of teams.

Franchise or licensing scheme: A policy under which the government picks a single firm to sell a particular good.

- Under a **franchise or licensing scheme**, the government designates a single firm to sell a particular good. Here are some examples of franchise and licensing schemes:
  - Some cities select a single firm to provide off-street parking.
  - The National Park Service picks a single firm to sell food and other goods in Yosemite National Park.
  - The Federal Communications Commission issues licenses for individual radio and television stations.

- In some markets, there are large economies of scale in production (average cost decreases as the firm's output increases), so a single firm will be profitable, but a pair of firms would lose money. A natural monopoly occurs when the entry of a second firm would make price less than average cost, so a single firm serves the entire market.

- As we'll see later in the book, some firms use illegal means to exclude other firms from the market.

To explain how a monopoly works, we'll start with an example of a monopoly that results from a patent. We'll see that a monopolist can use the marginal principle to find the price that generates the highest possible profit. Later in this chapter, we'll explore the policy implications of a natural monopoly. Here are some of the practical questions relating to monopoly that we will answer:

1. **What are the trade-offs associated with patents and other policies that grant monopoly power?**
2. **When the patent on a popular pharmaceutical drug expires, what happens to the price of the drug?**
3. **Should the government allow an electric utility (a monopolist in the market for electricity) to charge any price it wants?**

Because the indivisible inputs required to generate electric power are very costly, there are large economies of scale in power generation.

4. It costs about $5 billion to set up the satellites for a global pocket phone network. How many firms are likely to set up such a network and provide pocket-phone service?

The Monopolist's Output Decision

A monopolist must decide what price to charge and how much output to produce. Like other firms, the monopoly's objective is to maximize profit, defined as the difference between total revenue and total cost. We learned about production costs in an earlier chapter, so we start our discussion with the revenue side of the monopolist's profit picture. Then we show how a monopolist picks a price and a quantity.

Total Revenue and Marginal Revenue

A firm's total revenue—the money it gets by selling its product—equals the price times the quantity sold. Table 10.1 shows how to use a demand schedule (in the first two columns) to compute a firm's total revenue (in the third column). At a price of $16, the firm doesn't sell anything, so its total revenue is zero. To sell 1 unit, the firm must cut its price to $14, so its total revenue is $14. To get consumers to buy 2 units instead of just one, the firm must cut its price to $12. The total revenue associated with selling 2 units is $24. As the price continues to drop and the quantity sold increases, total revenue increases for a while but then starts falling. To sell 5 units instead of 4, the firm cuts its

Table 10.1 Demand, Total Revenue, and Marginal Revenue

Price	Quantity Sold	Total Revenue	Marginal Revenue
$16	0	0	—
$14	1	$14	$14
$12	2	$24	10
$10	3	$30	6
$ 8	4	$32	2
$ 6	5	$30	−2
$ 4	6	$24	−6

price from $8 to $6, and total revenue decreases from $32 to $30. The total revenue associated with selling 6 units is even lower ($24). The top panel in Figure 10.1 shows the relationship between total revenue and the quantity sold.

The firm's marginal revenue is defined as the change in total revenue that results from selling one more unit of output. In Table 10.1, we compute marginal revenue by taking the difference between the total revenue from selling a certain quantity of output (for example, 3 units), and the total revenue from selling one fewer unit of output (for example, 2 units). As shown in the fourth row in the table, the total revenue from selling 3 units is $30 and the total revenue from selling 2 units is only $24, so the marginal revenue from selling the third unit is $6. As shown in the table and in the lower panel of Figure 10.1, marginal revenue is positive for the first 4 units sold. Beyond 4 units, selling an additional unit results in lower total revenue, so marginal revenue is negative. For example, the marginal revenue for the fifth unit is –$2, and the marginal revenue for the 6th unit is –$6.

Table 10.1 and Figure 10.1 illustrate the trade-offs associated with cutting a price to sell a larger quantity. When the firm cuts its price from $12 to $10, there is good news and bad news:

- **Good news.** The firm collects $10 from the new customer (the third), so revenue increases by $10.

- **Bad news.** The firm cuts the price for all its customers, so it gets less revenue from the customers who would have been willing to pay the higher price ($12). Specifically, the firm collects $2 less from each of the two original customers, so revenue decreases by $4.

Figure 10.1

Total Revenue and Marginal Revenue

As the firm cuts its price to sell more output, its total revenue rises for the first 4 units sold, but then decreases for the 5th and 6th units. Therefore, marginal revenue (the change in total revenue from selling one more unit) is positive for the first 4 units and then becomes negative.

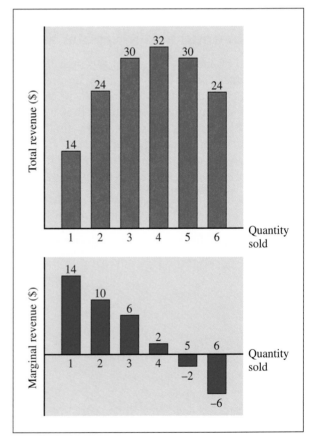

The combination of good news and bad news leads to a net increase in total revenue of only $6, resulting from the $10 gained from the new customer minus the $4 lost on the first two customers. Because of the bad news associated with selling an additional unit of output, a firm's marginal revenue is always less than its price.

Figure 10.2 shows the demand curve and marginal revenue curve for the data shown in Table 10.1. Because the firm must cut its price to sell more output, the marginal revenue curve lies below the demand curve. For example, the demand curve shows that the firm will sell 3 units at a price of $10 (point d), but the marginal revenue for this quantity is only $6 (point i). For quantities of 5 units and greater, marginal revenue is negative because when the firm cuts its price to sell one additional unit, the bad news dominates the good news: The amount the firm loses on its original customers exceeds the amount it gains on the new one, so total revenue drops.

The Marginal Principle and the Output Decision

We use a simple example to explain how a monopolist decides how much output to produce. Sneezy, who holds a patent on a new drug that cures the common cold, must decide how much of the drug to produce and what price to charge for it. These two decisions are related because according to the law of demand, the higher the price, the smaller the quantity demanded. Sneezy can use the marginal principle to choose how much to produce and what price to charge.

MARGINAL **PRINCIPLE**

Increase the level of an activity if its marginal benefit exceeds its marginal cost, but reduce the level if the marginal cost exceeds the marginal benefit. If possible, pick the level at which the marginal benefit equals the marginal cost.

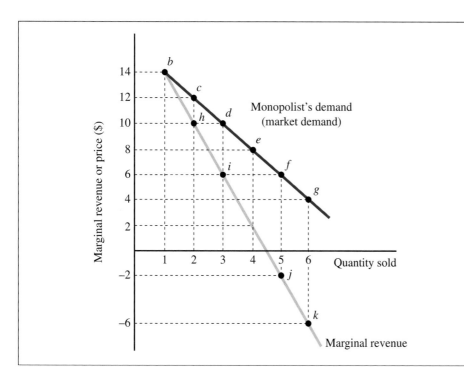

Figure 10.2
Demand Curve and Marginal Revenue Curve
Marginal revenue is equal to the price for the first unit sold, but is less than price for all other units sold. To increase the quantity sold, a firm cuts its price and receives less revenue on the units that could have been sold at the higher price. Therefore, beyond the first unit sold, the marginal revenue curve lies below the demand curve.

Sneezy's activity is producing the cold drug, and he will pick the quantity at which the marginal revenue from selling one more unit (the marginal benefit) equals the marginal cost associated with that unit:

$$\text{marginal revenue} = \text{marginal cost}$$

The first two columns in Table 10.2 show the relationship between the price of the cold drug and the quantity demanded. We can use these numbers to draw the market demand curve, as shown in Figure 10.3. Because Sneezy is a monopolist—the only seller of the drug—the market demand curve shows how much he will sell at each price. The demand curve is negatively sloped, consistent with the law of demand. For example, at a price of $18 per dose, the quantity demanded is 600 doses per hour (point h), compared to 900 doses at a price of $15 (point m).

Like other monopolists, Sneezy must cut his price to sell a larger quantity. Therefore, marginal revenue is less than price, as shown in the third column in Table 10.2. In Figure 10.3 the marginal revenue curve lies below the demand curve. For example, with a price of $18, Sneezy will sell 600 doses (point h), and the marginal revenue for this quantity is $12 (point i). In other words, if he cuts his price by an amount large enough to sell just one more dose, his total revenue would increase by $12. Similarly, with a price of $15, he will sell 900 doses (point m), and the marginal revenue is $6 (point n). Figure 10.3 also shows some of Sneezy's cost curves.

Picking a Quantity and a Price

We're ready to show how a monopolist can use the marginal principle to pick a quantity and price. To maximize his profit, Sneezy should produce the quantity at which the marginal revenue equals marginal cost. By looking at the numbers in Table 10.2, we can see that this happens with a quantity of 900 doses and a price of $15, as shown in the fourth row. In Figure 10.3, the marginal revenue curve intersects the marginal cost curve at point n with a quantity of 900 doses, so that's the quantity that maximizes profit. To get consumers to buy this quantity, the price must be $15 (point m on the demand curve). The average cost of production is $8 per dose (shown by point c), so the profit per dose is $7 ($15 minus $8). Sneezy's profit equals the profit per dose ($7) times the quantity sold (900 doses), or $6,300 per hour.

To show that a price of $15 and a quantity of 900 doses maximizes Sneezy's profit, let's see what would happen if he picked some other quantity. Suppose he decided to pro-

Table 10.2 Using the Marginal Principle to Pick a Price and Quantity

Price (per Dose)	Quantity Sold (Doses)	Marginal Revenue	Marginal Cost	Total Revenue	Total Cost	Profit
$18	600	$12	$4.00	$10,800	$5,710	$5,090
$17	700	$10	$4.60	$11,900	$6,140	$5,760
$16	800	$8	$5.30	$12,800	$6,635	$6,165
$15	900	$6	$6.00	$13,500	$7,200	$6,300
$14	1,000	$4	$6.70	$14,000	$7,835	$6,165
$13	1,100	$2	$7.80	$14,300	$8,560	$5,740
$12	1,200	0	$9.00	$14,400	$9,400	$5,000

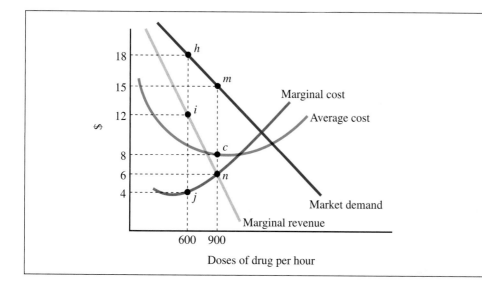

Figure 10.3

Monopolist Picks a Quantity and a Price

To maximize profit, the monopolist picks point *n*, where marginal revenue equals marginal cost. The monopolist produces 900 doses per hour at a price of $15 (point *m*). The average cost is $8 (point *c*), so the profit per dose is $7 (equal to the $15 price minus the $8 average cost) and the total profit is $6,300 (equal to $7 per dose times 900 doses).

duce 599 doses per hour at a price just above $18 (just above point *h* on the demand curve). Could he make more profit by cutting his price by enough to sell one more dose? Sneezy should answer two questions:

- What is the extra cost associated with producing dose number 600? As shown by point *j* on the marginal cost curve, the marginal cost of the 600th dose is $4.

- What is the extra revenue associated with dose number 600? As shown by point *i* on the marginal revenue curve, the marginal revenue is $12.

If Sneezy wants to maximize his profit, he should produce the 600th dose because the $12 extra revenue exceeds the $4 extra cost, so his total profit will increase by $8. The same argument applies, with different numbers for marginal revenue, and marginal cost, for doses 601, 602, and so on, up to 900 doses. Sneezy should continue to increase the quantity produced as long as the marginal revenue exceeds the marginal cost. The marginal principle is satisfied at point *n*, with a total of 900 doses.

Why should Sneezy stop at 900 doses? Beyond 900 doses, the marginal revenue from an additional dose will be less than the marginal cost associated with producing it. Although Sneezy could cut his price and sell a larger quantity, an additional dose would add less to revenue than it adds to cost, so his total profit would decrease. As shown in the fifth row in Table 10.2, Sneezy could sell 1,000 doses at a price of $14, but the marginal revenue at this quantity is only $4, while the marginal cost at this quantity is $6.70. Producing the 1,000th dose would decrease Sneezy's profit by $2.70. For any quantity exceeding 900 doses, the marginal revenue is less than the marginal cost, so Sneezy should produce exactly 900 doses.

Formula for Marginal Revenue

There are two ways to compute a firm's marginal revenue. One way, shown in Table 10.1, involves computing the total revenue from selling two different quantities of output. A second way uses a simple formula that incorporates the good news and bad news associated with cutting prices:

$$\text{marginal revenue} = \text{price} - (\text{quantity} \times \text{slope of demand curve})$$

The first part of the formula's right side shows the good news. When a firm cuts its price by just enough to sell one more unit (the last unit sold), the firm's revenue increases by an amount equal to the new price. Recall that the bad news equals the previous quantity sold (one less than the current quantity) times the price cut. The slope of the demand curve is the change in price divided by the resulting change in quantity. In other words, the slope is the price cut required to sell just one more unit of output. To keep the arithmetic simple, we'll use the current quantity—not the previous quantity—to compute the bad news, so the bad news equals the current quantity times the slope of the demand curve.

We can use our earlier example to show how to use this marginal revenue formula. At point h on Sneezy's demand curve, the price is $18 and the quantity is 600 doses. The slope of the demand curve is $0.01 per dose: If we use points h and m, the rise is $3 (equal to $18 − $15) and the run is 300 doses (equal to 900 − 600), so the slope is $0.01 per dose (equal to $3/300 doses). This means that to sell the 600th dose, Sneezy cuts his price by $0.01. We can plug these values into the marginal revenue formula:

$$\text{marginal revenue} = \text{price} - (\text{quantity} \times \text{slope of demand curve})$$

$$\text{marginal revenue} = \$18 - (600 \text{ doses} \times \$0.01 \text{ per dose}) = \$12$$

This is shown by point i on the marginal revenue curve: At the quantity 600 doses, the marginal revenue is $12. This formula provides an approximate value for marginal revenue because it uses the current quantity (600) instead of the previous quantity (599). If the quantity is large, the one-unit difference between the current quantity and the previous quantity won't matter much, and the formula provides a good approximation of the true marginal revenue.

The Costs of Monopoly

What are the trade-offs—the costs and benefits to society as a whole—associated with a monopoly? This is an important question because in many cases, a monopoly results from government policy. If the costs exceed the benefits, it may be sensible to remove the barriers to entry and allow other firms to enter the market. We discuss the costs of monopoly in this part of the chapter and explore the benefits in the next part.

Monopoly Versus Perfect Competition

How does a monopoly differ from a perfectly competitive market? To show the difference, let's consider an example of an arthritis drug that could be produced by a monopoly or a perfectly competitive industry. Let's take the long-run perspective, a period of time long enough that a firm is perfectly flexible in its choice of inputs and firms can enter or leave a perfectly competitive market.

Consider the monopoly outcome first. Let's assume that the long-run average cost of producing the arthritis drug is constant at $8 per dose. As we saw in Chapter 8, if average cost is constant, the marginal cost equals average cost. In panel A of Figure 10.4, the long-run marginal cost curve is the same as the long-run average cost curve. Given the demand and marginal revenue curves in panel A of Figure 10.4, the monopolist will maximize profit where marginal revenue equals marginal cost (point n), producing 200 doses per hour at a price of $18 per dose. The monopolist's profit is $2,000 per hour (a $10 profit per dose ($18 − $8) times 200 doses).

Consider next the market for the arthritis drug under perfect competition. We're assuming that the arthritis drug industry is a constant-cost industry: Input prices do not

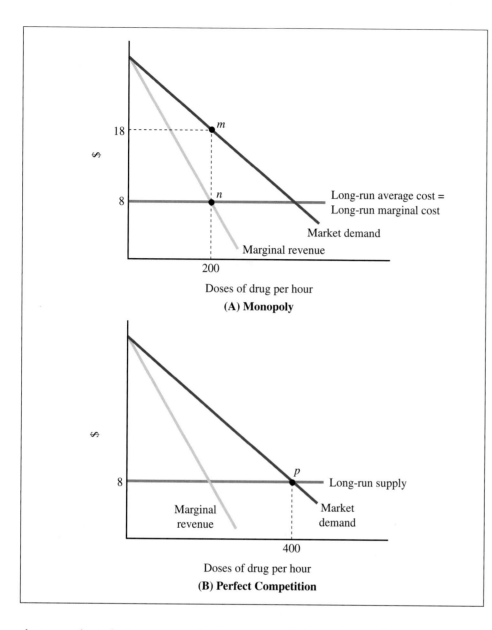

Figure 10.4

Monopoly Versus Perfect Competition
(A) Monopoly The monopolist picks the quantity at which long-run marginal cost equals marginal revenue (200 doses per hour, as shown by point *n*). As shown by point *m* on the demand curve, the price associated with this quantity is $18 per dose.
(B) Perfect Competition The long-run supply curve of a perfectly competitive, constant-cost industry intersects the demand curve at point *p*. The equilibrium price is $8, and the equilibrium quantity is 400 doses per hour.

change as the industry grows, so the long-run market supply curve is horizontal at the long-run average cost of producing the drug ($8 per dose). In panel B of Figure 10.4, the horizontal long-run supply curve intersects the demand curve at point *p*, with an equilibrium price of $8 and an equilibrium quantity of 400 doses per hour. Compared to a monopoly outcome, the perfectly competitive outcome has a lower price ($8 instead of $18) and a larger quantity (400 doses instead of 200).

To examine the social cost of monopoly power, let's imagine that we start with a perfectly competitive market and then switch to a monopoly. Consumers will be worse off under monopoly, and we can use the concept of consumer surplus to determine just how much worse off they are. As we saw in Chapter 6, consumer surplus is shown by the area between the demand curve and the horizontal price line. In Figure 10.5, the monopoly price is $18, so the consumer surplus associated with the monopoly is shown by triangle *C*. In contrast, the perfectly competitive price is $8, so the consumer surplus with perfect competition is shown by the larger triangle consisting of triangle *C*, rectangle *R*,

Figure 10.5

Deadweight Loss from Monopoly

A switch from perfect competition to monopoly increases the price from $8 to $18 and decreases the quantity sold from 400 to 200 doses. Consumer surplus decreases by an amount shown by the areas *R* and *D*, while profit increases by the amount shown by rectangle *R*. The net loss to society is shown by triangle *D* (the deadweight loss of monopoly).

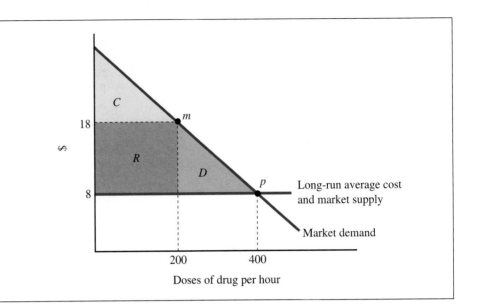

and triangle *D*. In other words, a switch from perfect competition to monopoly decreases consumer surplus by the areas *R* and *D*.

Let's take a closer look at the loss of consumer surplus resulting from a switch to monopoly:

- **Rectangle *R*.** The switch to monopoly increases the price by $10 per dose. Consumers buy 200 doses from the monopolist and pay $10 extra on each of these doses, for a loss of $2,000 per hour.

- **Triangle *D*.** The switch to monopoly decreases the quantity consumed because the price increases and consumers obey the law of demand. Consumers lose consumer surplus on the doses they would have consumed at the lower price. This loss is shown by triangle *D*, with an area of $1,000 (one half the base of the triangle (200 doses) times the height ($10)).

The total loss of consumers is the sum of the areas of rectangle *R* and triangle *D*, or $3,000.

How much better off are firms under perfect competition? Under perfect competition, each firm makes zero economic profit, while a monopolist earns positive economic profit. In Figure 10.5, the monopolist's profit is shown by rectangle *R*: The profit margin is $10 (a price of $18 minus an average cost of $8) and the quantity is 200 doses per hour, for a total profit of $2,000 per hour. The switch to monopoly means that the monopolist gains rectangle *R* at the expense of consumers: They pay an additional $10 per dose, while the monopolist gets a profit of $10 per dose.

Only part of the loss experienced by consumers is recovered by the monopolist, so there is a net loss from switching to monopoly. Consumers lose rectangle *R* and triangle *D*, but the monopolist gains only rectangle *R*. That leaves triangle *D* as the net loss or **deadweight loss from monopoly.** The word *deadweight* indicates that this loss is not offset by a gain to anyone. In contrast, Rectangle *R* is lost by consumers but gained by the monopolist. Consumers lose triangle *D* because in a perfectly competitive market, they would receive some consumer surplus from the 201st through 400th doses, which of course a monopolist would not produce. The lesson is that monopoly is inefficient because, compared to a perfectly competitive market, the monopolist produces less output.

Deadweight loss from monopoly: A measure of the inefficiency from monopoly; equal to the difference between the consumer-surplus loss from monopoly pricing and the monopoly profit.

Rent Seeking: Using Resources to Get Monopoly Power

Another source of inefficiency from a government-sanctioned monopoly is that firms use resources to acquire monopoly power. A firm that gets a monopoly on a particular product will earn a large profit, so firms are willing to spend large sums of money in an effort to persuade the government to erect barriers to entry (licenses, franchises, and industrial associations). In Figure 10.5, a firm would be willing to spend up to $2,000 per hour to get a monopoly on the arthritis drug. One way to get monopoly power is to hire lobbyists to persuade legislators and other policymakers to grant monopoly power. This is known as **rent seeking**.

Rent seeking is inefficient because it uses resources that could be used in other ways. For example, the people employed as lobbyists could instead produce goods and services. In Figure 10.5, if a monopolist spent all its potential profit ($2,000 per hour) on rent-seeking activity, the net loss to society would be areas R and D, not just area D. The classic study of rent seeking found that firms in some industries spent up to 30% of their total revenue to get monopoly power.[2]

At the beginning of this chapter, we saw that Coca-Cola helped a state university to build a new football scoreboard and remodel the student center. Was this an act of generosity? In return for the scoreboard and the remodeled student center, Coca-Cola earned the exclusive right to sell beverages on campus. Just like any monopolist, Coca-Cola will use its monopoly power to charge higher prices for beverages, so the cost of the scoreboard and student center actually comes out of the pockets of students.

Rent seeking: The process under which a firm spends money to persuade the government to erect barriers to entry and pick the firm as the monopolist.

TEST Your Understanding

1. Why is a monopolist's marginal revenue less than its price?

2. Complete the statement with a number: At a price of $15 per CD, a firm sells 80 CDs per day. If the slope of the demand curve is $0.10 per CD, marginal revenue is _____.

3. You want to determine the quantity of output produced by a monopolist. What information do you need, and how would you use it?

4. At a price of $18 per CD, the marginal revenue of a CD seller is $12. If the marginal cost of CDs is $9, should the firm increase or decrease the quantity produced? Should it increase or decrease its price?

Patents and Monopoly Power

Are there benefits associated with a government-sanctioned monopoly? As we'll see, a patent or another entry barrier encourages innovation because the innovator knows he or she will earn monopoly profits on a new product for some specific period of time. If the monopoly profits are large enough to offset the substantial research and development costs of a new product, a firm will develop the product and become a monopolist.

Incentives for Innovation

Let's use the arthritis drug to show why a patent encourages innovation. Suppose that Hanna hasn't yet developed the drug and she computes the potential benefits and costs of developing the drug as follows:

- The cost of research and development would be $14 million.

- The estimated annual profit from a monopoly would be $2 million (in today's dollars).

- Hanna's competitors will need three years to develop and produce their own versions of the drug, so if Hanna isn't protected by a patent, her monopoly will last only three years.

Based on these numbers, Hanna won't develop the drug unless she receives a patent that lasts at least seven years. That's the length of time she needs to recover her research and development costs ($2 million per year times seven years is $14 million). If there is no patent and she loses her monopoly in three years, she will earn a profit of $6 million, which is less than her research and development costs. On the other hand, with a 20-year patent she will earn $40 million, which is more than enough to recover her costs.

Trade-Offs from Patents

Is the patent for Hanna's drug beneficial from the social perspective? The patent grants monopoly power to Hanna, and she responds by charging a higher price and producing less than the quantity that would be produced in a perfectly competitive market (200 doses per hour instead of 400). From society's perspective, 400 doses would be better than 200 doses, but we don't have that choice. Hanna won't develop the drug unless a patent protects her from competition for at least seven years. Therefore, society's choice is between 200 doses (the patent and monopoly outcome) and zero doses. Because 200 doses is clearly better than none, the patent is beneficial from society's perspective.

What about a product that would be developed without the protection of a patent? Suppose Marcus could develop a new drug with a research and development project costing $5 million. If Marcus does not have a patent for his new drug, he would earn monopoly profits of $2 million per year for three years, a total of $6 million. Because his research and development costs are low relative to the monopoly profit, a three-year monopoly will generate enough profit to cover his costs, so he will develop the new drug

There are trade-offs with patents: The monopoly power causes higher prices for consumers but encourages firms to invest in research and development to develop new drugs.

even without a patent. Therefore, if the government issues a 20-year patent, the only effect is to prolong Marcus's monopoly, and that means the patent would be inefficient from society's perspective.

What are the general conclusions about the merits of the patent system? As usual, there are some trade-offs. It is sensible to grant a patent for a product that would otherwise not be developed but not sensible to grant one for a product that would be developed even without a patent. Unfortunately, no one knows in advance whether a particular product would be developed without a patent, so the government can't be selective in granting patents. Therefore, some patents will merely prolong a firm's monopoly power and generate higher prices. There is no consensus among economists on whether the benefits of patents (from the development of new products) exceed the costs (from prolonging monopoly power).

What happens when a patent expires? New firms will enter the market, and the resulting competition for consumers will decrease prices. The transition from monopoly to competition is not always a smooth one, as you'll see in "A Closer Look: Barriers to Generic Drugs."

Do the Benefits Exceed the Costs?

From the efficiency perspective, we cannot make a clear-cut case for or against a government-sanctioned monopoly. As usual, there are both benefits and costs associated with using patents, licenses, franchises, and industrial associations to establish monopolies:

- On the cost side, a monopolist produces less output than a perfectly competitive market, and people also waste resources trying to get and keep monopoly power.

- On the benefit side, a patent or a license increases the payoff from research and development, and firms respond by developing new products.

A CLOSER LOOK   Barriers to Generic Drugs

When the patent for a popular pharmaceutical drug expires, other firms introduce generic versions of the drug. The generics are virtually identical to the original branded drug, but they sell at a much lower price. The producers of branded drugs have an incentive to delay the introduction of generic drugs, and sometimes use illegal means to do so.

In 1999, the Federal Trade Commission (FTC) launched a probe of four large pharmaceutical companies to determine whether they unfairly stifled competition from generic producers. The FTC is investigating allegations that the makers of branded drugs made deals with generic suppliers to keep generics off the market. The alleged practices include cash payments and exclusive licenses for new versions of the branded drug.[3] Eli Lilly and Company announced a deal under which Sepracor, Inc. would have the exclusive right to sell a purified version of Prozac (the antidepressant with annual sales of $2.8 billion). In effect, this deal would extend Lilly's monopoly over the drug for another 15 years. Abbott Laboratories was accused of paying $24 million per year to Ivax Corporation and an undisclosed amount to Novartis AG to delay the launch of their generic versions of Hytrin, Abbott's hypertension drug. Similar allegations of payoffs to generic suppliers have been levied against Hoechst AG in connection with its annual payment of $40 million to Andrx Corporation, which had produced—but not sold—a generic version of Cardizem, Hoechst's heart medication. Another tactic used by the producers of branded drugs is to claim that generics are not as good as the branded drug. Dupont has asserted that generic versions of its Coumadin (a blood thinner) are not equivalent to Coumadin, and may pose risks to patients.

In some cases—when research and development costs are substantial and other firms could quickly imitate a new product—the benefits will dominate the costs, and public policies that support a monopoly are sensible. In other cases, it would be more efficient to eliminate the artificial barriers to entry.

TEST Your Understanding

5. Your city will select a single firm to provide off-street parking. Your long-run average cost is $30 per parking space per day, and you would charge a price of $35 per space per day for a total of 500 spaces. How much would you be willing to pay for the monopoly?

6. Consider the arthritis example. Will Hanna develop the drug without a patent if she will have a monopoly for five years instead of just three years?

7. Critically appraise the following statement: "I just invented a new product. I could do the research and development required to bring the product to the market, but it would cost me $100 million. Once other firms develop imitations of my product, I will earn an annual profit of only $1 million. If I don't have a patent, I would be crazy to develop this product."

8. In the United States, you cannot patent a gambling device such as a slot machine. Can you think of any rationale for this policy?

Natural Monopoly

Up to this point, we have considered a monopoly that results from artificial barriers to entry. In some monopolized markets, a second firm could enter a market, but if it did, both firms would lose money. That's why a single firm serves the entire market in what's called a **natural monopoly**. The classic examples of natural monopolies are public utilities (sewerage, water, and electricity generation) and transportation services (railroad freight and mass transit). We'll use the example of electricity generation to explain why a natural monopoly occurs.

Natural monopoly: A market in which the entry of a second firm would make price less than average cost, so a single firm serves the entire market.

Picking an Output Level

Figure 10.6 shows the long-run average cost curve for electricity generation, using real data from Chapter 8. The curve is negatively sloped and steep, reflecting the large economies of scale associated with generating electric power. These economies of scale occur because the indivisible inputs required to generate power (the power plant or hydroelectric dam) are very costly.

What about the long-run marginal cost of generating electricity? As we learned in Chapter 8, if the average cost of production is decreasing (if the average cost curve is negatively sloped), the marginal cost is less than the average cost. In Figure 10.6, the long-run marginal-cost curve of electricity lies below the long-run average-cost curve.

Figure 10.6 shows how to use the cost curves and revenue curves to pick the output level that maximizes profit. If a single firm—a monopolist—provides electricity, the monopolist's demand curve is the same as the market demand curve: To determine how much electricity the monopolist will sell at a particular price, we look at the market demand curve. The demand curve is negatively sloped, and the marginal-revenue curve lies below the demand curve. The marginal principle is satisfied at point n, with 3 billion

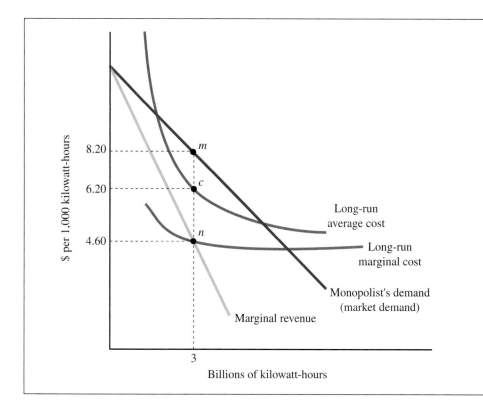

Figure 10.6

Natural Monopolist Uses the Marginal Principle to Pick a Price and Quantity

Because of scale economies in production (indivisible inputs), the long-run average cost curve is negatively sloped. The monopolist chooses point *n* (where marginal revenue equals marginal cost), supplying 3 billion units at a price of $8.20 per unit (point *m*) and an average cost of $6.20 per unit (point *c*). The profit per unit of electricity is $2.00.

ACTIVE GRAPH

units of electricity (thousands of kilowatt-hours). The price associated with this quantity is $8.20 per unit of electricity (shown by point *m*) and the average cost is $6.20 per unit (shown by point *c*), so the profit per unit of electricity is $2.00. The price exceeds the average cost, so the electric company will earn a profit.

Will a Second Firm Enter?

If there are no artificial barriers to entry, a second firm could enter the electricity market. What would happen if a second firm entered the market? In Figure 10.7 the entry of a second firm would shift the demand curve facing the first firm—the former monopolist—to the left, from D_1 to D_2: At each price, the first firm will sell a smaller quantity of electricity because it now shares the market with another firm. For example, at a price of $8.20, the total quantity of electricity sold is 3 billion units, or 1.5 billion units for each firm. In general, the larger the number of firms, the lower the demand curve facing the typical firm. D_2 is the demand curve for the typical firm in a two-firm market, so it is also the demand curve for the potential entrant.

Will a second firm enter the electricity market? The demand curve of the typical firm in a two-firm market lies entirely below the long-run average-cost curve, so there is no quantity at which the price exceeds the average cost of production. No matter what price the typical firm charges, it will lose money. The firm's demand curve lies below the average cost curve because the average cost curve is steep, reflecting the large economies of scale in generating electricity. A second firm—with half the market—would have a very high average cost and wouldn't be able to charge a price high enough to cover its high average cost. Therefore, the second firm will not enter the market, so there will be a single firm, a natural monopoly. For an example of a potential global natural monopoly, read "A Closer Look: A Global Pocket-Phone Monopoly?"

Figure 10.7

**Why Won't a
Second Firm
Enter the Market?**
The entry of a second electricity firm would shift the demand curve facing the typical firm to the left. In this example, after entry, the firm's demand curve lies entirely below the long-run average cost curve. No matter what price the typical firm charges, it will lose money. Therefore, a second firm will not enter the market.

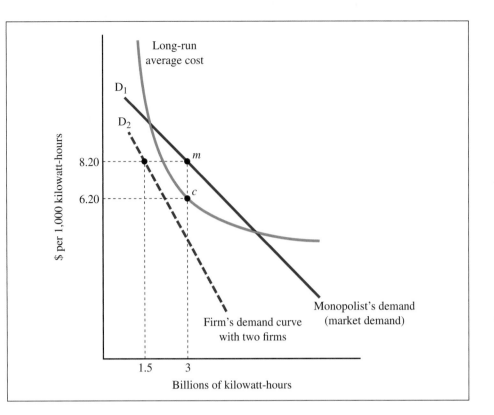

Price Controls for a Natural Monopoly

When a monopoly is inevitable—the case of natural monopoly—the government often sets a maximum price for the monopolist. There are many examples of natural monopolies that are subject to maximum prices. Local governments regulate utilities and firms that provide water, electricity, and local telephone service. State governments use public utility commissions (PUCs) to regulate the electric-power industry.

Let's use the electricity market to explain the effects of government regulation of a natural monopoly. Suppose the government sets a maximum price for electricity and

A CLOSER LOOK   A Global Pocket-Phone Monopoly?

In 1999, Iridium LLC launched a $5 billion global satellite phone system, a constellation of 66 low-orbit satellites that in theory allows phone calls between any two points on the earth's surface.[4] In the first year of operation, the system encountered technical difficulties, and only 20,000 customers signed up for the service. Iridium filed for bankruptcy protection, and it's unclear whether the firm—and its phone system—will survive.

If Iridium can work out its technical problems, the global satellite system is a potential natural monopoly. Given the large cost of setting up the satellite system, there are large economies of scale in pocket-phone communication services. Once the system is in place, the marginal cost of relaying phone signals will be low. If the demand for pocket-phone communication is not large enough to support more than one satellite system, there will be a global natural monopoly. Another possibility is that other firms will launch their own satellites and enter the pocket-phone communication market. This will occur if the demand for pocket phones increases to the point where the market can support more than one $5 billion satellite system.

forces the electric company to serve all the consumers who are willing to pay the maximum price. In other words, the government—not the firm—picks a point on the market demand curve. Under an **average-cost pricing policy**, the government picks the price at which the market demand curve intersects the monopolist's long-run average cost curve. In Figure 10.8, the original average cost curve intersects the demand curve at point *i*, with a price of $5.20 per unit of electricity. Although consumers would prefer a lower price, the electric company would lose money at any price less than $5.20, so lower prices are not feasible.

Average-cost pricing policy: A regulatory policy under which the government picks the point on the demand curve at which price equals average cost.

How will this regulatory policy affect the monopolist's production costs? Under average cost pricing, a change in the monopolist's production cost will not affect its profit because the government will adjust the regulated price to keep the price equal to the average cost. The government will increase the regulated price when the monopolist's cost increases, and decrease the price when its cost decreases. Because there is no reward for cutting its costs and no penalty for higher costs, the monopolist has little incentive to control its cost, so its costs will increase, pulling up the regulated price.

The average-cost policy causes the market to move along the market demand curve in two steps:

- **Downward slide.** Starting from the price and quantity resulting from an unregulated monopoly (point *m*), we slide down the demand curve to point *i* (*i* stands for impossible dream), the point that would occur if regulation did not increase the monopolist's cost.

- **Upward climb.** As the monopolist's cost increases because of regulation, the regulator increases the price to cover the extra costs, so we climb part way back up the market demand curve, from point *i* to point *r*.

Figure 10.8
Regulation Using Average Cost Pricing
Under an average cost pricing policy, the government chooses the price at which the demand curve intersects the average cost curve. Regulation shifts the long-run average cost curve upward, so the government picks point *r*, with a price of $6.00 per unit.

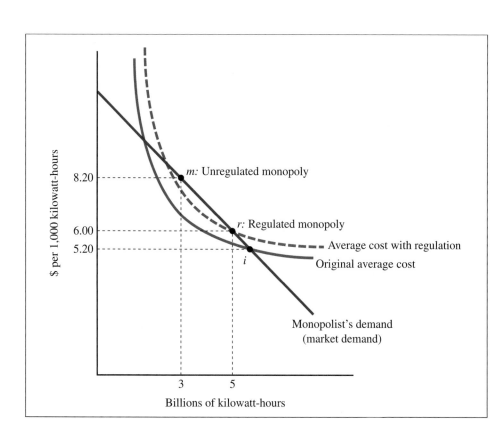

In this example the net effect of this regulatory policy is a lower price of electricity ($6.00 instead of $8.20) and a larger quantity (5 billion units instead of 3 billion units). In other words, the regulatory policy moves the market downward along the market demand curve, from point *m* to point *r*.

ECONOMIC DETECTIVE

A Decrease in Demand Decreases the Price?

When the population of Powerland decreased, the demand for all sorts of goods—including housing, clothing, and electricity—decreased as well. The decrease in the demand for housing decreased the price of housing, consistent with simple supply and demand analysis. In contrast, the price of electricity increased, a result that seems to defy the laws of supply and demand. What explains the puzzling increase in the price of electricity?

The key to solving this mystery is the fact that electricity is a regulated natural monopoly, with prices set by government regulators. The government of Powerland uses an average-cost pricing policy to set the price of electricity: the regulated price equals the average cost of production. Any decrease in the quantity of electricity produced will lead to a higher average cost as the producer moves upward along the negatively sloped average-cost curve. Under average-cost pricing, the higher the average cost, the higher the regulated price. In graphical terms, the demand curve for electricity shifted to the left, so it intersected the negatively sloped average-cost curve at a smaller quantity of electricity and a higher average cost. The regulated price is shown by the intersection of the demand curve and the average-cost curve, so a leftward shift in demand increases the regulated price. ◆

TEST Your Understanding

9. Complete the statement: A natural monopolist picks the quantity of output at which _____ equals _____.

10. Explain the effects of the entry of a second firm on the demand curve facing the original monopolist.

11. Complete the statement with *above* or *below:* A natural monopoly occurs when the long-run cost curve lies entirely _____ the demand curve of the typical firm in a two-firm market.

Using the TOOLS

1. Textbook Pricing: Publishers Versus Authors

Consider the problem of setting a price for an economics textbook. The marginal cost of production is constant at $20 per book. The publisher knows from experience that the slope of the demand curve is $0.20 per textbook: Starting with a price of $48, a price cut of $0.20 will increase the quantity demanded by 1 textbook. For example, here are some combinations of price and quantity:

Price per textbook	$44	$40	$36	$32	$30
Quantity of textbooks	80	100	120	140	150

a. What price will the publisher choose?

b. Suppose that the author receives a royalty payment equal to 10% of the total sales revenue from the book. If the author could choose a price, what would it be?

c. Why do the publisher and the author disagree about the price for the book?

d. Design an alternative author-compensation scheme under which the author and the publisher would choose the same price.

2. Payoff for Casino Approval

In 1996, developers interested in building an American Indian casino in Creswell, Oregon, placed a curious announcement in the local newspaper. If local voters approved the casino, the developers promised to give citizens $2 million per year. Given an adult population of about 1,600, each adult in Creswell would receive a cash payment of $1,250 per year.

a. Why did the developers propose this deal? Why aren't similar deals proposed for new clothing stores, music stores, or auto-repair shops?

b. If the deal goes through and you moved to Creswell, would you expect to get $1,250 per year?

3. Environmental Costs for Regulated Monopoly

The Bonneville Power Administration (BPA) is a regulated monopoly that uses dozens of hydroelectric dams to generate electricity. The dams block the path of migrating fish and thus contribute to the decline of several species of fish. Suppose that BPA spends $100 million to make its hydroelectric dams less hazardous for migrating fish. Who will bear the cost of this program?

 # Summary

In this chapter, we've seen some of the subtleties of monopolies and their pricing policies. Compared to a perfectly competitive market, a monopoly means a higher price, a smaller quantity, and resources wasted in the process of seeking monopoly power. On the positive side, some of the products we use today might never have been invented without the patent system and the monopoly power it grants. Here are the main points of the chapter:

1. Compared to a perfectly competitive market, a market served by a monopolist will have a higher price and a smaller quantity of output.

2. A switch from perfect competition to monopoly decreases consumer surplus by more than it increases profits, so there is a net loss or a deadweight loss to society.

3. Some firms spend money and use resources to acquire monopoly power, a process known as rent-seeking.

4. Patents protect innovators from competition, leading to higher prices for new products but a greater incentive to develop new products.

5. A natural monopoly occurs when there are large-scale economies in production, so the market can support only one firm.

6. Under an average-cost pricing policy, the regulated price for a natural monopoly is equal to the average cost of production.

 # Key Terms

average-cost pricing policy, 227
deadweight loss from monopoly, 220
franchise or licensing scheme, 212

monopoly, 212
natural monopoly, 224

patent, 212
rent seeking, 221

Problems and Discussion Questions

1. Consider a restaurant that charges $10 for all you can eat and has 30 customers at this price. The slope of the demand curve is $0.10 per meal, and the marginal cost of providing a meal is $3. What price will satisfy the marginal principle and maximize the restaurant's profit?

2. The National Park Service grants a single firm the right to sell food and other goods in Yosemite National Park. Discuss the trade-offs associated with this policy.

3. Since 1963, many state governments that outlaw commercial lotteries have introduced state lotteries to raise revenue for state and local governments. In 1994, the net revenue from state lotteries was about $10 billion. Would you expect the state lotteries to have higher or lower paybacks (total prize money divided by the total amount of money collected) than commercial games of chance such as horse racing and slot machines? Explain.

4. Consider the Slappers, a hockey team that plays in an arena with 8,000 seats. The only cost associated with staging a hockey game is a fixed cost of $6,000: The team incurs this cost regardless of how many people attend a game. The demand curve for hockey tickets has a slope of $0.001 per ticket ($1 divided by 1,000 tickets): Each $1 increase in price decreases the number of tickets sold by 1,000. For example, here are some combinations of price and quantity:

Price per ticket	$4	$5	$6	$7
Quantity of tickets	8,000	7,000	6,000	5,000

The owner's objective is to maximize the profit per hockey game (total revenue minus the $6,000 fixed cost).

   a. What price will maximize profit?

   b. If the owner picks the price that maximizes profit, how many seats in the arena will be empty?

   c. Is it rational to leave some seats empty?

5. The government allows professional sports associations (collections of teams) to restrict the number of teams. How do these barriers to entry affect the price of tickets to professional sporting events and the number of tickets sold? If we eliminated these barriers to entry, what would happen to ticket prices and total attendance at sporting events?

6. Consider a natural monopolist. Here are some data on prices and quantities:

Price per unit	$20	$19	$18	$17	$16
Quantity (units)	100	120	140	160	180
Marginal revenue	—	—	—	—	—

   a. Complete the table: For each quantity, use the formula for marginal revenue to compute the marginal revenue.

   b. Draw the monopolist's demand curve and the monopolist's marginal revenue curve.

   c. Suppose that the monopolist's long-run marginal cost is $9. How much output should the monopolist produce?

7. Consider a regulated natural monopoly with an initial price (equal to average cost) of $3 per unit. Suppose the demand for the monopolist's product decreases. What will happen to the price? How does this differ from the effects of a decrease in demand for a product produced in a perfectly competitive market?

8. Consider a monopolist who owns a natural spring that produces water that, according to nearby residents, has a unique taste and healing properties. The monopolist has a fixed cost of installing plumbing to tap the water but no marginal cost. The demand curve for the spring water is linear. Depict graphically the monopolist's choice of a price and quantity. At the profit-maximizing quantity, what is the price elasticity of demand? If the spring were owned by the government, what price would it charge?

9. In the board game "Monopoly," when a player gets the 3rd deed for a group of properties (for example, the 3rd orange property: St. James, New York, and Tennessee Avenues), he or she doubles the rent charged on each property in the group. Similarly, a player who has a single railroad charges a rent of $25, while a player who has all 4 railroads charges a rent of $200 for each railroad. Are these rules consistent with the analysis of monopoly in this chapter?

10. Adam Smith predicted that a monopolist would charge "the highest price which can be got." Do you agree?

11. Suppose the drug company Bristol-Meyers-Squibb announces that it will increase the price of Taxol, the cancer-fighting drug, by 10%. According to a consumer advocate, "The price hike will increase Bristol's total revenue from Taxol by 10%." Do you agree? What is the advocate assuming about the

price elasticity of demand for Taxol? Is this assumption realistic?

12. **Web Exercise.** How much does it cost to get a patent on an invention? To find out, visit the Web site of the U.S. Patent and Trademark Office (*http://www.uspto.gov*). A patent on an invention is called a utility patent. How much does it cost to file for a patent? How much do you pay when it is issued? How much do you pay to maintain your patent?

13. **Web Exercise.** Visit the Web site of the U.S. Postal Service, one of the world's largest government-sanctioned monopolies (*http://www.usps.gov/*). If you access the part of the site with the title "Inside the Postal Service," you can get some facts and figures and read the annual performance plan. List some of the facts and some of the postal service's goals and objectives.

Take It to the Net

We invite you to visit the O'Sullivan/Sheffrin page on the Prentice Hall Web site at:
http://www.prenhall.com/osullivan/
for additional World Wide Web exercises for this chapter.

Model Answers to Questions

Chapter-Opening Questions

1. The bad news is that a monopolist charges a higher price. The good news is that monopoly profits encourage innovation.

2. In response to competition from generic equivalents, the producer of the branded drug usually decreases its price, but the price of the branded drug is still higher than the price of generic drugs.

3. An unregulated monopolist will charge a high price and earns a large profit, so the government often sets a maximum price.

4. The substantial fixed cost means that the market will be able to support only a few firms.

Test Your Understanding

1. To sell one more unit, the monopolist must cut the price. The marginal revenue equals the price minus the revenue lost from selling goods at a lower price to the original customers.

2. MR = $15 – (80 units times $0.10 per unit) = $7.

3. You need the marginal revenue curve and the marginal cost curve. The monopolist will pick the quantity at which the two curves intersect.

4. Marginal revenue exceeds marginal cost, so the firm should increase the quantity produced. To increase the quantity, the firm must cut its price.

5. The profit per space is $5 ($35 – $30), so the daily profit is $2,500 ($5 per space times 500 spaces).

You are willing to pay up to $2,500 per day for the monopoly.

6. If Hanna's monopoly profit lasts five years, she'll earn a total of $10 million, which is still less than the cost of the research and development project ($14 million). She won't develop the drug.

7. It will be sensible to develop the product even without a patent if the inventor maintains his monopoly position long enough. Suppose it takes other firms five years to develop an imitation product and the original inventor earns a profit of $30 million per year. In this case, the monopoly profit will more than cover the costs of research and development.

8. The absence of a patent will discourage innovation in gambling devices. Perhaps this is an indirect way of discouraging gambling.

9. Marginal revenue, marginal cost.

10. The firm's demand curve shifts to the left: At each price, the firm sells a smaller quantity.

11. Below.

Using the Tools

1. Textbook Pricing: Publishers Versus Authors

   a. To maximize profit, the publisher picks the quantity at which marginal revenue equals marginal cost. Using the marginal revenue formula, we can compute the marginal revenue at each price and quantity. Here are the numbers for marginal revenue:

Price	$44	$40	$36	$32	$30
Quantity	80	100	120	140	150
MR	$28	$20	$12	4	0

If the marginal cost is $20, the publisher will pick a price of $40 and a quantity of 100 books.

b. The author's objective is to maximize total revenue (price times quantity), not profit (total revenue minus total cost). From the author's perspective, the marginal cost of selling another textbook is zero, so to satisfy the marginal principle, the author will choose the price at which marginal revenue is zero. In this case, the author would choose a price of $30.

c. They disagree because the authors ignore production costs.

d. If the author received a share of profits instead of a share of revenue, he or she would choose the same price as the publisher.

2. Payoff for Casino Approval

a. The proposal to pay residents a total of $2 million per year is an example of rent seeking. The developers anticipate a profit of at least $2 million per year from their casino monopoly and are willing to pay at least this amount to get the monopoly. There are no such offers of cash for stores and repair shops because the city doesn't regulate entry into these other activities, so there are no monopoly profits and rent seeking.

b. The prospect for a big annual cash payment will attract people to Creswell, so we would expect the population to grow and the per-capita payment to shrink.

3. Environmental Costs for a Regulated Monopoly. The environmental costs will increase the monopolist's costs, and the higher costs will result in a higher regulated price. In graphical terms, the long-run average-cost curve will shift upward, and the demand curve will intersect the cost curve at a higher price. Consumers will bear the costs of environmental protection.

Notes

1. Jeannie Donnelly, "OSU Beverages Will Be Provided Exclusively by Coca-Cola," *The Daily Barometer*, May 27, 1994, p. 1.

2. Richard A. Posner, "The Social Costs of Monopoly and Regulation," *Journal of Political Economy*, vol. 83, 1975, pp. 807–827.

3. Ralph T. King, Jr., "FTC Widens Probe into Generic-Drug Barriers," *Wall Street Journal*, March 9, 1999, page B8.

4. Leslie Cauley, "Iridium's Downfall: The Marketing Tool That Took a Back Seat to Science," *Wall Street Journal*, August 18, 1999, page A1.

Entry and Monopolistic Competition

Tweeter just inherited a lot of money, enough to start her own car-stereo business. Woofer owns the only car-stereo store in town and sells stereos at a price of $230 with an average cost of $200 per stereo, for a profit of $30 per stereo. Should Tweeter use her inheritance to open her own car-stereo store? If she does, will she make a profit of $30 per stereo, just like Woofer?

The Effects of Market Entry
Output and Entry Decisions
Application: Woofer and Tweeter
Entry in the Real World

Monopolistic Competition
Short-Run and Long-Run
  Equilibrium
Trade-Offs with Monopolistic
  Competition
Spatial Differentiation and
  Competition

Using the Tools

Entrepreneur: A person who has an idea for a business and coordinates the production and sale of goods and services, taking risks in the process.

weeter wants to become a successful entrepreneur. An **entrepreneur** comes up with an idea for a business and puts the idea into practice by acquiring a production facility (a factory, store, or office building), buying raw materials, and hiring workers. An entrepreneur takes risks, committing time and money to a business without any assurance that it will be profitable.

Like entrepreneurs around the world, Tweeter has a difficult decision to make. Before she decides whether or not to enter the car-stereo market, she must predict how much she would be able to charge for her car stereos and how much it would cost her to supply them. Before she enters the market, there is a $30 gap between price and average cost, but the gap is likely to shrink when she enters the market. The price will fall as Woofer and Tweeter compete for customers. In addition, Tweeter may have a higher average cost than Woofer. If the price drops below her average cost, Tweeter would lose money, so she would be better off using her inheritance some other way.

In this chapter, we explore how entrepreneurs make decisions about entering a market. We also explain the effects of market entry on consumers and other firms in the market. Here are some practical questions that we answer:

1. **If the entry of a firm into a market would increase the average production cost of firms already in the market, should the government prevent the firm from entering?**

2. **How did the deregulation of trucking services affect the prices and the profits of trucking firms?**

3. **What is likely to happen when Network Solutions, Inc. loses its government-sanctioned monopoly in the market for registering Internet addresses?**

4. **De Beers, the dominant firm in the world diamond market is thinking about etching its logo and a serial number on each of its gems. Why?**

5. **Are video-rental stores likely to disappear in the next few years?**

The analysis in this chapter is based on two assumptions. First, we assume there are no barriers to entry: There are no patents or government licensing programs that limit the number of firms. Second, we assume that firms do not act strategically: Each firm acts on its own, taking the actions of other firms as given. This means that firms already in the market do not conspire to fix prices and do not try to prevent other firms from entering the market.

The Effects of Market Entry

Consider a market served by a single profitable firm, a monopolist. We saw in Chapter 10 that if there are large economies of scale in production, the entry of a second firm would drive the market price below average cost, meaning that each firm would lose money, with its total cost exceeding its total revenue. Because no firm will enter a market where it will lose money, the market will remain a monopoly. In this chapter, we will see that if there are not large economies of scale, additional firms will enter the market, driving down prices and profit.

Output and Entry Decisions

As we saw earlier in the book, a firm in any market can use the marginal principle to decide how much output to produce.

MARGINAL **PRINCIPLE**

> **Increase the level of an activity if its marginal benefit exceeds its marginal cost, but reduce the level of the activity if the marginal cost exceeds the marginal benefit. If possible, pick the level of the activity at which the marginal benefit equals the marginal cost.**

Consider a firm whose activity is producing toothbrushes. The marginal benefit of producing toothbrushes is the marginal revenue from selling one more brush. In Figure 11.1, if a single firm produces toothbrushes, the demand curve facing the firm is the market demand curve. The marginal cost of producing toothbrushes is simply the marginal cost of production.

A firm that is considering entering the toothbrush market must make a long-run decision about what size and type of production facility to build. Therefore, the long-run cost curves—which show production costs for a firm that hasn't committed to a particular production facility—are relevant for the firm's entry decision. In Figure 11.1, the long-run average cost curve is L-shaped, which, as we saw in Chapter 8, is consistent with empirical studies of production costs. If the average cost of production is decreasing (if the average cost curve is negatively sloped), the marginal cost is less than the average cost. In Figure 11.1, the marginal-cost curve lies below the average-cost curve.

As we saw in Chapter 10, the monopolist will maximize profit by picking the quantity at which marginal revenue equals marginal cost. In Figure 11.1, this happens at point n, with a quantity of 300 toothbrushes. From the market demand curve, the price associated with this quantity is $2.00. Given an average cost of $0.90 per toothbrush, the monopolist's profit per unit is $1.10 (equal to $2.00 minus $0.90), so the total profit is $330. Given the large profits in the toothbrush market, will a second firm enter the market?

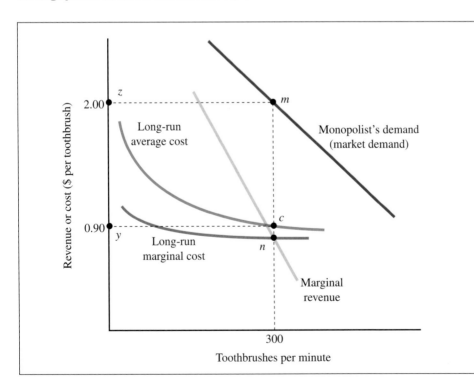

Figure 11.1

Short-Run Equilibrium in Monopolistic Competition: A Single Toothbrush Producer

The single toothbrush producer (a monopolist) picks point n (where marginal revenue equals marginal cost), supplying 300 toothbrushes per minute at a price of $2.00 (point m) and an average cost of $0.90 (point c). The profit per brush is $1.10.

Figure 11.2

Entry Decreases Price and Increases Average Cost

The entry of a second tooth-brush producer shifts the demand curve for the original firm to the left: A smaller quantity is sold at each price. The marginal principle is satisfied at point *x*, so the firm produces a smaller quantity (200 instead of 300 tooth-brushes) at a higher average cost ($1.00 instead of $0.90 per toothbrush) and sells at a lower price ($1.85 instead of $2.00).

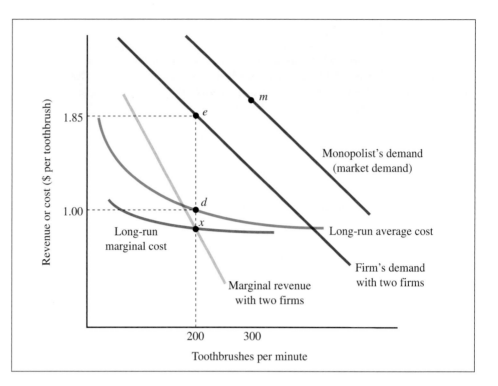

When a second firm enters a market, the demand curve facing the original firm shifts to the left. At any particular price, some consumers will patronize the new firm, so there will be fewer consumers who are willing to purchase toothbrushes from the first firm. In other words, the first firm will sell fewer brushes at each price. In Figure 11.2, the demand curve facing the first firm—the original monopolist—shifts to the left, and profit decreases for three reasons:

1. **The market price drops.** The marginal principle is satisfied at point *x*, so the first firm produces 200 toothbrushes at a price of $1.85 (point *e*). The competition between the two firms causes the price to drop, from $2.00 to $1.85.

2. **The quantity produced by the first firm decreases.** The first firm produces only 200 toothbrushes, down from 300 produced as a monopolist.

3. **The first firm's average cost of production increases.** The decrease in the quantity produced causes the firm to move upward along its negatively sloped average-cost curve to a higher average cost (from $0.90 to $1.00).

The combination of a lower price, a higher average cost, and a smaller quantity means that the first firm earns less profit. The profit rectangle (shown by points *z*, *m*, *c*, and *y* in Figure 11.1) shrinks because the top of the rectangle (determined by the price) sinks, the bottom of the rectangle (determined by the average cost) rises, and the right side of the rectangle (determined by the quantity) moves to the left. In our example, the profit drops from $330 to $170.

What about the second firm? If we assume that the second firm has access to the same production technology as the first firm and pays the same prices for its inputs, the cost curves for the second firm will be identical to the cost curves for the first firm. If the second firm produces the same product as the first firm, the demand curve facing the second firm will be identical to the demand curve facing the first firm. As a result, we can use Figure 11.2 to represent both firms. Each firm produces 200 toothbrushes at an average cost of $1.00 per toothbrush and sells them at a price of $1.85.

Application: Woofer and Tweeter

For an example of the effects of entry on price, cost, and profit, recall Tweeter's entry decision described at the beginning of the chapter. Woofer the monopolist initially sells 10 stereos per day at a price of $230 and an average cost of $200 per stereo. Suppose that if Tweeter enters the market, the price will drop to $225 and her average cost will be $205, so she could earn a profit of $20 per stereo. Although Tweeter's entry squeezes profit from both sides—decreasing the market price and increasing the average cost—there is still some profit to be made, so she will enter the market. Of course, other firms may also enter the market, so Tweeter should not count on making a $20 profit per stereo for very long.

Entry in the Real World

Empirical studies of real markets provide overwhelming evidence that entry decreases market prices and firms' profit.[1] In one study of the retail pricing of tires, a market with only two tire stores had a price of $55 per tire, compared to a price of $53 in a market with three stores, $51 with four stores, and $50 with five stores.[2] In other words, the larger the number of stores, the lower the price of tires.

A recent change in public policy shows what happens when the government eliminates artificial barriers to entry. The Motor Carrier Act of 1980 eliminated the government's entry restrictions on the trucking industry, most of which had been in place since the 1930s. New firms entered the trucking market, and freight prices dropped by about 22%.[3] The market value of a firm's trucking license reflects the profit the firm can earn in the market. As a result of increased competition and lower prices from deregulation, the average value of a trucking license dropped from $579,000 in 1977 to less than $15,000 in 1982.[4] For another example of deregulation, read "A Closer Look: Ending the Monopoly for Internet Registration."

European nations are also deregulating their markets. Until recently, most nations in Western Europe had national monopolies in telecommunication equipment and services. That changed in 1988, when the European Union deregulated telecommunication

A CLOSER LOOK   Ending the Monopoly for Internet Registration

In February 1999, the U.S. government announced plans to end the five-year monopoly held by Network Solutions, Inc. for registering Internet addresses. Network Solutions had an exclusive government contract to register Web addresses (also known as domain names) ending in .net, .org, .edu, and .com. The company registered almost 500,000 domain names in 1996, almost 1 million names in 1997, and almost 2 million names in 1998.[6] The company collected $70 for each address registered and an annual renewal fee of $35 for each address. The real money, however, comes after registration. The firm that registers a company's domain name is in a position to provide other services that help the firm to set up a Web page and start electronic commerce over the Internet.

The government's plan for entry into the Internet registration business restricts entry to five firms. In addition, there are requirements for security and backup measures, $500,000 in liability insurance, and a minimum of $100,000 in liquid assets (cash on hand for needed expenditures). Critics of the plan say that the government is moving too slowly in opening the market to competition. Richard Foreman, the president of Register.com, a potential entrant, said, "This is the intersection of commerce and politics. I'm very excited. Eventually we will be one of the registrars."

markets, starting with the market for data communication in 1990, followed by the market for voice communication in 1998. European and U.S. companies are preparing to enter the deregulated markets, with many of the companies forming transatlantic alliances. For example, Deutsche Telekom and France Telecom have an alliance with Sprint (the third largest U.S. long-distance carrier), while MCI and AT&T each have their own alliances with other European companies. The increase in competition is expected to improve service and decrease prices, perhaps cutting the cost of international calls by as much as 50%.[5]

TEST Your Understanding

1. Complete the statement: A firm picks the quantity of output at which _____ equals _____.

2. Draw a graph showing the effect of the entry of a second firm on the demand curve facing the original firm (a monopolist).

3. Complete the statement with "increases" or "decreases": The entry of an additional firm _____ the profit per unit of output because entry _____ the price and _____ the average cost of production.

4. Suppose that when Tweeter enters the car-stereo market, the price drops by $20 and the average cost increases by $15. Is it sensible to enter the market?

Monopolistic Competition

Now that we know the effects of entry into a monopolized market, let's think about how many firms will actually enter a particular market. The extreme case of market entry is monopolistic competition, a situation in which dozens of firms enter the market. Here are the characteristics of a market that is subject to **monopolistic competition.**

Monopolistic competition: A market served by dozens of firms selling slightly different products.

1. **Many firms.** Because there are relatively small economies of scale, small firms can produce at about the same average cost as large firms. Therefore, even a small firm can cover its costs, and the market can support many firms.

2. **Differentiated product.** The firms sell slightly different products. Product differentiation may be in the form of differences in physical characteristics, location, services, and the aura or image associated with the product.

3. **No artificial barriers to entry.** There are no patents or government regulations preventing firms from entering the market.

What's the logic behind the label *monopolistic competition*? Although it may seem like an oxymoron, there are good reasons for the label. Each firm differentiates its product from the products of other firms in such a way that each firm is the sole seller of a narrowly defined good. For example, each firm in the toothbrush market uses a unique design for its toothbrushes, so each is a monopolist for its unique toothbrush. That's the reason for the word *monopolistic* in monopolistic competition. The *competition* in the label results from the keen competition among firms for customers to buy products that are close but not perfect substitutes. When one firm increases its price, many of its consumers will switch to the products of other firms because they are close substitutes. In other words, the demand for the product of a monopolistically competitive firm is very price elastic: An increase in price decreases the quantity demanded by a relatively large amount because consumers can easily switch to another firm selling a similar product.

Let's take a closer look at the notion of product differentiation, one of the key features of monopolistic competition. Firms in such a market differentiate their products in several ways:

- **Physical characteristics.** A firm can distinguish its products from the products of other firms by offering a different size, color, shape, texture, or taste. For example, toothpastes differ in flavor, color, texture, whitening capability, and alleged ability to fight decay and plaque. Some other examples of goods that are differentiated by their physical characteristics are athletic shoes, dress shirts, appliances, and pens.

- **Location.** Some products are differentiated by where they are sold. Some examples are gas stations, music stores, grocery stores, movie theaters, and ice-cream parlors. In each case, firms sell the same product at different locations.

- **Services.** Some products are distinguished by the services that come with them. For example, some stores provide informative and helpful salespeople, while others require consumers to make decisions on their own. Other examples of services that can differentiate products are home delivery (for appliances and pizza) and free technical assistance (for computer hardware and software).

- **Aura or image.** Some firms use advertising to make their products stand out from a group of nearly identical products. In this case, product differentiation is a matter of perception rather than reality. Some examples are aspirin, designer jeans, and motor oil.

An unusual product-differentiation strategy is being considered by De Beers, the dominant firm in the world diamond market.[7] The demand for diamonds has decreased in recent years, in large part because of the Asian economic crisis. For example, Japan's demand for diamonds, which had tripled in the preceding 15 years, decreased by 20% during 1998. At the same time, new suppliers have entered the market and have not cooperated with De Beers in keeping prices high. The result is lower profits for De Beers and concern that diamonds may eventually become another standardized commodity in the global market, with much lower prices and profits. To differentiate its diamonds, De Beers is experimenting with etching, in script that is invisible to the naked eye, its logo and a serial number on each of its gems. Will customers be willing to pay a premium for a gem from the biggest name in diamonds? We'll see.

Short-Run and Long-Run Equilibrium

We'll use the toothbrush example to illustrate the features of monopolistic competition. The producers of toothbrushes differentiate their products with respect to color, bristle design, handle size and shape, and durability. We saw earlier that after a second firm enters the toothbrush market, both firms still make a profit. Will a third firm enter this lucrative market? The entry of a third firm will shift the demand curve facing each firm farther to the left, decreasing the market price, decreasing the quantity produced per firm, and increasing the average cost per toothbrush. If after the third firm enters the market, profit would still be positive for all three firms, then the third firm will enter the market. This entry process will continue until the entry of one more firm would make the profit of each firm negative.

Because there are no barriers to entering the toothbrush market, firms will continue to enter the market until each firm makes zero economic profit. Figure 11.3 shows the long-run equilibrium from the perspective of the typical firm in a monopolistically competitive market. As more firms enter the market, the market share of the typical firm decreases, so its demand curve shifts to the left. The typical firm satisfies the marginal principle at point g and sells 55 brushes per minute at a price of $1.35 (point h) and an average cost of $1.35. The price equals the typical firm's average cost,

Figure 11.3

Long-Run Equilibrium with Monopolistic Competition: Toothbrushes

In a monopolistically competitive market, new firms will continue to enter the market until economic profit is zero. The typical firm picks the quantity at which its marginal revenue equals its marginal cost (point *g*). Economic profit is zero because the price equals the average cost (shown by point *h*).

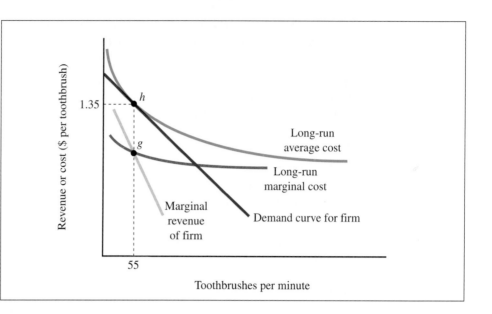

so the typical firm makes zero economic profit. Each firm's revenue is high enough to cover all its costs—including the opportunity cost of all its inputs—but not enough to cause additional firms to enter the market. In other words, each firm makes just enough money to stay in business.

Trade-Offs with Monopolistic Competition

There are some trade-offs associated with monopolistic competition and product differentiation. Let's compare the monopoly outcome (shown in Figure 11.1) with the long-run equilibrium under monopolistic competition (Figure 11.3). There are many more toothbrush producers with monopolistic competition, and that brings good news and bad news:

- **Good news: lower price.** Competition among firms decreases the price of toothbrushes from $2.00 to $1.35.

- **Good news: greater variety.** The large number of toothbrush firms—each selling a toothbrush with a unique design—means more choice for consumers.

- **Bad news: higher average cost.** Each of the firms in the monopolistically competitive market produces less output than the monopolist and has a higher average cost of production: $1.35 per toothbrush, compared to $0.90 for the monopolist.

Given these trade-offs, it's impossible to make a clear-cut case for or against monopolistic competition. Although a market with many brands of toothbrushes has lower prices and more variety, it also has a higher average cost of production because more factories, machinery, and equipment may be used to produce toothbrushes. Looking at the trade-offs from the other perspective, a nation that limited the number of toothbrush firms to one would have a lower average cost of producing toothbrushes, but prices would be higher and consumers would have fewer toothbrush options.

For another example of the trade-offs from monopolistic competition, consider restaurant meals. The typical large city has dozens of Italian restaurants, each of which has a slightly different menu and prepares its food in slightly different ways. In this example, the benefit of product differentiation is variety: Consumers can pick from restaurants offering a wide variety of menus and preparation techniques. Although a city with a single Italian restaurant would have a lower average cost of preparing Italian meals—a result of scale economies in producing meals—there would be less variety for restaurant patrons.

The same logic applies to articles of clothing such as jeans and shirts, which are differentiated according to their fit, color, design, and durability and the aura associated with the label. There is a trade-off between production cost and variety: If we all wore uniforms, the average cost of producing clothing would be lower, but most people prefer to wear a variety of clothes.

Spatial Differentiation and Competition

Some products are differentiated by where they are sold. Your city probably has several music stores, each of which sells a particular CD at about the same price. Everything else being equal, you are likely to purchase CDs from the most convenient store, but if a store across town offers lower prices, you might purchase your CDs there instead. In other words, each music store has a monopoly in its own neighborhood but competes with music stores in the rest of the city.

Figure 11.4 shows the long-run equilibrium in the market for CDs. Because there are no barriers to entering the market, new music stores will enter the market until each music store makes zero economic profit. The typical music store satisfies the marginal principle at point g, selling 70 CDs per hour at a price of $14 per CD (point h) and an average cost of $14 per CD. The price equals the store's average cost, so the typical store makes zero economic profit. Each store's revenue is high enough to cover all its costs—including the opportunity cost of all its inputs—but not enough to cause additional stores to enter the market. In other words, the firm makes just enough money to stay in business.

We saw earlier that there are trade-offs with monopolistic competition. The larger the number of firms, the lower the price and the greater the product variety, but the higher the average cost of production. When firms differentiate their products by offering them at more locations, the benefit of having more firms is that consumers travel

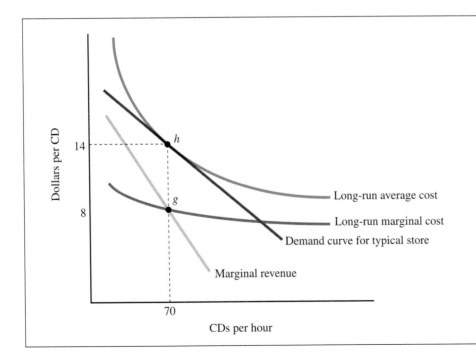

Figure 11.4

Long-Run Equilibrium with Monopolistic Competition: Music Stores

Music stores and other retailers differentiate their products by selling them at different locations. The typical firm chooses the quantity of CDs at which its marginal revenue equals its marginal cost (point g). Economic profit is zero because the price equals average cost (shown by point h).

shorter distances to get the product. If a large metropolitan area had only one music store, the average cost of production would be lower, but prices would be higher and music consumers would spend much more time traveling to buy CDs.

There are many differentiated products that are sold in monopolistically competitive markets. We've seen that CDs from different stores are differentiated according to location or accessibility. This sort of differentiation occurs for other retail products that require consumers to travel, such as groceries, hardware, drugs, dry cleaning, and bank services. Different firms sell essentially the same product at different locations. As explained in "A Closer Look: Good-Bye Video Rental Stores?," the market for video rentals is subject to monopolistic competition, but this may change in the next few years.

ECONOMIC DETECTIVE

How Many Gas Stations?

Consider a city that initially allowed only one gasoline station to operate. When Jane, a staff member of a local employment agency, heard that the city had decided to relax its restrictions and allow more gasoline stations to operate in the city, she decided to identify some unemployed workers who could apply for the new station-manager jobs. She knew that the city's single gas station pumped 20,000 gallons of gasoline per hour and the long-run average cost curve reaches its minimum point with an output of 5,000 gal-

A CLOSER LOOK   Good-Bye Video Rental Stores?

If you enjoy cruising the aisles of your neighborhood video store, you'd better savor your next cruise because you may not have many left. If you don't like cruising, relief is on the way. According to some experts, most of these video stores will disappear in the next five or six years, to be replaced by video-on-demand (VOD), a system that allows consumers to have movies piped into their homes at any time.

The market for video rentals is subject to monopolistic competition. The scale economies associated with renting videos are very small. To supply video rentals, all you need is a set of videos and a cash register. So the typical city can support dozens of video stores. The VOD system, which has been tested in several markets, uses fiber-optic technology to deliver movies on demand, just as a phone system delivers voice signals on demand. In Snohomish County, Washington, Chambers Cable allows its subscribers to pick from a menu of 250 movies.[8] Unlike conventional pay-per-view films, which run continuously, the movies on the VOD system will be controlled by viewers: They will be able to rewind, fast-forward, and pause the movies.

There are substantial fixed costs in setting up the fiber-optic technology: The fiber-optic cable must be

laid throughout a city, so the typical city will be able to support only one or two VOD providers. Dozens of video rental stores could be replaced by one or two VOD firms, probably the local cable-TV company and the local phone company. In other words, a market that is subject to monopolistic competition could be replaced by a monopoly or a duopoly (two firms).

The development of video on demand (VOD) may cause video rental-outlets to disappear.

lons per hour. Therefore, Jane reasoned, the city would soon have a total of four gas stations (20,000 gallons divided by 5,000 gallons per station) and would need three new station managers.

You can imagine Jane's surprise when she discovered that there would be five new gas stations instead of three. She had to scramble to find five unemployed workers to apply for the new manager jobs. Your job is to solve this puzzle. Why did Jane underestimate the number of new gasoline stations?

There are two keys to solving the gas-station puzzle:

- The law of demand means a larger quantity of gasoline sold. The entry of firms will increase competition in the gasoline market, so the market price will drop and the quantity of gasoline demanded will rise. The total quantity of gasoline demanded will exceed the initial quantity of 20,000 gallons per hour.

- Entry means a smaller quantity per gas station. The typical firm operates along the negatively sloped portion of its average cost curve, not the horizontal portion, so we would expect each gas station to pump less than 5,000 gallons per hour.

If the total demand is greater than 20,000 gallons and the output per station is less than 5,000 gallons, there will be more than four stations. For example, suppose that the total quantity demanded rises to 24,000 gallons per hour and each station pumps only 4,000 gallons per hour. In this case, there will be six gas stations (24,000 gallons divided by 4,000 gallons per station) instead of just four. ◆

TEST Your Understanding

5. Explain the logic behind the label *monopolistic competition*. What is monopolistic, and what form does the competition take?

6. Explain the trade-offs associated with monopolistic competition and product differentiation.

7. Suppose each new firm in the car-stereo market in Tweeter's town decreases the price by $5 per stereo and increases the average cost per stereo by $5. How many firms will enter the market?

Using the TOOLS

We've used the tools of economics to explore the firm's entry decision, showing that a firm will enter a market if the price will exceed the average cost of production. Here are some opportunities to use these tools to do your own economic analysis of markets.

1. ECONOMIC EXPERIMENT: Business Licenses

Here is an experiment that shows the effects of entry on prices and average cost. Students play the role of entrepreneurs who must decide whether to enter a market and how much to pay for a business license.

- The class is divided into groups of three to five students. Each group represents a firm that has the option of buying a business license to produce and sell tables.
- The following table shows how the market price, the quantity per firm, and the average cost of production vary with the number of firms in the market.

Number of Firms	Price	Quantity per Firm	Average Cost
1	$20	10	$9
2	$18	9	$10
3	$16	8	$11
4	$14	7	$12
5	$12	6	$13
6	$10	5	$14
7	$8	4	$15

- A business license allows a firm to operate the business for one day. Each license will be auctioned to the highest bidder. Each firm can buy only one license.
- For the first three rounds of the experiment, the instructor auctions up to seven business licenses. The instructor will continue to auction licenses as long as someone bids a positive amount for one of the licenses.
- Once the license auction is complete (everyone who wants to buy a license gets one), each firm can use the table to compute its daily profit:

$$\text{profit} = [(\text{price} - \text{average cost}) \times \text{quantity}] - \text{price of license}$$

- After three rounds of auctioning seven licenses in each round, the instructor auctions only two licenses for rounds four and five.
- At the end of the experiment, we compute the profit of each firm by adding up its profit over the five rounds.

2. How Many Music Stores?

Consider the city of Discville, where zoning laws allow only one music store. The city's music store sells CDs at a price of $20 with an average cost of $12. Suppose the city eliminates its restrictions on music stores, allowing additional stores to enter the market. According to an expert in the music market, "Each additional music store will decrease the price of CDs by $2 per CD and increase the average cost of selling CDs by $1 per CD." How many music stores will enter the market?

3. Opposition to a New Drugstore

The city of Drugville is evaluating a request by a drugstore chain to open a new drugstore in the city. Consider the following statement from a citizen at a public hearing: "The output of the typical drugstore in our city is about 80% of the output at which its long-run average cost is minimized, so the average cost of drugs is higher than the minimum cost. The new drugstore would increase the average cost of production even further, so all our drugstores—including the new one—would be unprofitable, and consumers would pay higher prices for drugs." Assume that the citizen is correct in stating that the typical drugstore produces at 80% of the output at which average cost is minimized. Do the citizen's conclusions (all stores will be unprofitable and consumers will pay higher prices) follow logically from the facts?

4. ECONOMIC EXPERIMENT: Fixed Costs and Entry

Here is an experiment that shows the implications of entry for prices and profits. Students play the role of entrepreneurs who must decide whether to enter the market for lawn cutting. If they decide to enter the market, they must then decide how much to charge for cutting lawns.

- There are eight potential lawn-cutting firms (each represented by one to three students). There are two sorts of costs for firms: a fixed cost per day, and a marginal cost of cutting each lawn. Each firm can cut up to two lawns per day.
- There are 16 potential consumers who are willing to pay different amounts to have their lawns cut.
- The experiment has two stages. In the first stage, each potential firm decides whether to enter the market. The entry decision is sequential: The instructor will go down the list of potential firms, one at a time, and give each firm the option of entering the market. The entry decisions are public knowledge. When a firm enters the market, it incurs a fixed cost of $14.
- Each firm in the market posts a price for lawn cutting, and consumers shop around and decide whether to purchase lawn care at the posted prices. Each trading period lasts several minutes, and each firm can change its posted price up to three times (a total of three prices per trading period).
- A consumer's score in a trading period equals the difference between the amount that he or she is willing to pay for lawn care and the price actually paid.
- A firm's score equals its profit, which is its total revenue minus its total cost (the fixed cost of $14 plus the variable cost equal to $3 per lawn times the number of lawns cut).

Summary

This chapter is about market entry and monopolistic competition. In a monopolistically competitive market, entry continues until each firm in the market makes zero economic profit. Firms can differentiate their products by picking a distinct physical design, level of service, location, or product aura. Here are the main points of the chapter:

1. As firms enter a market, the market price drops because of competition among firms for consumers, and the average cost of production increases because each firm produces less output.

2. In a monopolistically competitive market, firms compete for customers by producing differentiated products.

3. There are some trade-offs associated with monopolistic competition: An increase in the number of firms decreases price and increases variety, but it also increases the average cost of production.

Key Terms

entrepreneur, 234

monopolistic competition, 238

Problems and Discussion Questions

1. Consider the city of Discville, where zoning laws limit the number of video arcades to one. The city's only video arcade has a price of 50 cents per game with an average cost of 34 cents per game. Suppose that the city eliminates its restrictions on video arcades, allowing additional firms to enter the market. According to an expert in the arcade market,

   "Each additional video arcade will decrease the price of games by 2 cents and increase the average cost of providing video games by 3 cents." What is the equilibrium number of video arcades?

2. Jean-Luc owns the only wig store in town and sells 30 wigs per week at a price of $70 per wig with an average cost of $35 per wig. Some experts have

reported the following facts on the wig market: (a) The average cost of wig selling increases by \$2 for every 1-unit decrease in the number of wigs sold. For example, if Jean-Luc sold only 29 wigs per week, his average cost would be \$37. (b) The price of wigs decreases by \$1 for every 1-unit increase in the number of wigs sold: the slope of the market demand curve is \$1. Suppose Sinead opens a second wig store in town and sells her wigs at a price of \$60 each. If Jean-Luc sells wigs at the same price as Sinead, will the profit per firm be positive or negative?

3. The city of Zoneville currently uses zoning laws to restrict the number of pizzerias. Under a proposed law, the restrictions on pizzerias would be eliminated. Consider the following statement by an expert in the pizza industry: "A pizzeria reaches the horizontal portion of its long-run average cost curve at an output of about 1,000 pizzas per day. The city's existing pizzeria sells 3,000 pizzas per day. Based on these facts, I predict that if the city eliminates the restrictions on pizzerias, we will soon have three pizzerias (3,000 pizzas divided by 1,000 pizzas per pizzeria)." If we assume that the expert's facts about production costs are correct, is the expert's conclusion (three pizzerias) correct?

4. A prominent feature of Mao's Communist China was the blue uniform worn by all citizens.
    a. Explain the trade-offs associated with the use of uniforms. What were the benefits, and what were the costs?
    b. Suppose people had a choice among ten types of uniforms rather than being required to wear a single type. Would you expect the benefits of requiring uniforms to decrease by a little or a lot?

5. Consider the "Fixed Cost and Entry" experiment. Suppose the fixed cost per day is \$18 per firm and the marginal cost is \$4. Each firm can cut up to 3 lawns per day. The market demand curve is linear, with a vertical intercept of \$70 and a slope of –\$1

per lawn. Predict the outcome of the experiment, including the equilibrium price, quantity, and number of firms. Explain the reasoning behind your predictions.

6. Under a franchising arrangement, a firm such as McDonald's sells the right to operate retail outlets. Your job is to determine how many franchises McDonald's should sell in Burgerburg.
    a. List the information you need and explain how you would use it.
    b. Provide a numerical example such that McDonald's should sell four franchises.
    c. If you purchase one of the four franchises, would you be better off if McDonald's sold fewer or more franchises? Use your numerical example to defend your answer.

7. Consider a city that issues licenses for pet groomers. Initially, the city does not allow the licenses to be bought and sold. Shortly after an economist joins the city licensing authority, the city decides to allow the licenses to be bought and sold on the open market. Much to the surprise of the licensers, the price of the licenses was zero: No one was willing to pay a positive amount for a pet grooming license.
    a. Explain why the price of grooming licenses is zero.
    b. Illustrate your answer with a supply-demand diagram.

8. Web Exercise. Is the market for outdoor backpacks monopolistically competitive? Visit the Web site of Fog Dog Sports (*http://www.fogdog.com*). Click on the "Outdoor Shop" icon and check how many types of backpacks are available from this site. How are the alternative backpacks differentiated?

9. Web Exercise. Do a Web search using the word "franchising" to find some sites that provide information on franchising opportunities. One possible site is The Franchise Doctor (*http://www.franchisedoc.com/*). What sort of franchising opportunities exist?

Take It to the Net

We invite you to visit the O'Sullivan/Sheffrin page on the Prentice Hall Web site at:
http://www.prenhall.com/osullivan/
for additional World Wide Web exercises for this chapter.

Model Answers to Questions

Chapter-Opening Questions

1. The entry of a firm will increase average cost but will also decrease price and increase the variety of products on the market, so it's not clear that preventing it from entering is sensible.

2. Because many firms entered the market, prices dropped by about 22% and the profit per license decreased.

3. The entry of new firms (initially a maximum of five additional firms) will increase competition and decrease prices.

4. Recent decreases in demand and increases in supply have led to fears that diamonds will become another standard commodity. The purpose of etching the logo and a serial number on each diamond is to differentiate De Beers products from the gems of other suppliers.

5. The VOD system uses fiber-optic technology to deliver movies on demand. There are substantial fixed costs in setting up the fiber-optic technology, so the typical city will be able to support only one or two VOD providers. Dozens of video stores could be replaced by one or two VOD providers.

Test Your Understanding

1. Marginal revenue, marginal cost.

2. The firm's demand curve shifts to the left: At each price, the firm sells a smaller quantity.

3. Decreases, decreases, increases.

4. No. The new price would be $210 per stereo, which would be less than the new average cost of $215 per stereo.

5. Each firm has a monopoly in the sale of its differentiated product, but the firms compete with firms that sell similar products.

6. The larger the number of firms, the lower the price and greater the variety of products. On the other hand, having more firms means less output per firm and a higher average cost.

7. With four firms in the market, the price is $215 per stereo and the average cost is $215 per stereo, so each firm makes zero economic profit.

Using the Tools

2. How Many Music Stores? Based on the information from the expert, we expect two additional music stores to enter the market. The following table shows price and average cost for different numbers of music stores:

Number of stores	1	2	3	4
Price	$20	$18	$16	$14
Average cost	$12	$13	$14	$15

In a 3-store market, price exceeds average cost by $2. In a four-store market, price is $1 less than average cost. Therefore, we would expect three firms in the music market.

3. Opposition to a New Drugstore. In all the examples we have considered, the typical firm operates along the negatively sloped portion of its long-run average cost curve, yet profit is still positive. A firm will enter the market only if it expects to earn a positive profit, so the statement that the new drugstore would make profit negative for all drugstores is puzzling. We know that entry decreases prices as firms compete for customers, so the statement that consumers would pay higher prices is also puzzling.

Notes

1. Leonard W. Weiss, ed., *Concentration and Price* (Cambridge, MA: MIT Press, 1989).

2. Timothy F. Bresnahan and Peter C. Reiss, "Entry and Competition in Concentrated Markets," *Journal of Political Economy*, vol. 99, October 1991, pp. 977–1009.

3. Theodore E. Keeler, "Deregulation and Scale Economies in the U.S. Trucking Industry: An Econometric Extension of the Survivor Principle," *Journal of Law and Economics*, vol. 32, October 1989, pp. 229–253.

4. Thomas Gale Moore, "Rail and Truck Reform—The Record So Far," *Regulation*, November/December 1983.

5. Richard L. Hudson, "European Companies Speed Shift to Phone Competition," *Wall Street Journal*, June 24, 1994, p. B4. Reprinted by permission of the *Wall Street Journal*,

© 1994 Dow Jones & Company, Inc. All Rights Reserved Worldwide.

6. Andres Aajac, "Company Deals with Challengers Intent to Know What's in a Name," *The Oregonian*, March 8, 1999, page E3. KnightRidder/Tribune Services.

7. "De Beers Is It," *Economist*, December 19, 1998.

8. "Chambers Revamps Cable Service," *Seattle Times*, December 21, 1998, p. B1.

Oligopoly and Strategic Behavior

When Paul Allen, one of the billionaire founders of Microsoft, announced the grand opening of the Jimi Hendrix museum in Seattle, there was an outbreak of messages on the Internet chat site dedicated to the rock legend. Four Hendrix fanatics who had been exchanging messages on the chat site for several months decided to travel to Seattle to meet each other and celebrate the opening of the museum. They all flew in for the occasion, and the discussion among the Web pals eventually turned to the cost of their airline tickets. Although each of the four traveled about the same distance to Seattle, they paid very different prices for their airline tickets.

- Katrina is puzzled and upset: "Brian lives in a city that is served by a single airline, and so do I. But Brian paid $370 and I paid $400." Why is the price lower in Brian's city?
- Jason is puzzled and upset too: "Melissa lives in a city that is served by two airlines, and so do I. But Melissa paid $350 and I paid $400." Why is the price higher in Jason's city?

Oligopoly: A market served by a few firms.

Concentration ratio: A measure of the degree of concentration in a market; the four-firm concentration ratio is the percentage of the market output produced by the 4 largest firms.

n this chapter, we explain these puzzling differences in prices. The monopolist in Brian's city could be charging a low price to discourage other firms from entering the market. The two airlines in Jason's city could have a price-fixing scheme under which they do not compete with one another but instead collude and charge the same high price.

This is the fourth chapter on decision-making by firms. In earlier chapters, we looked at perfect competition (many firms selling a homogeneous product), monopoly (a market with a single firm), and monopolistic competition (a market with dozens of firms). In this chapter, we look at an **oligopoly**, a market with just a few firms. Table 12.1 shows the facts on five oligopolies in the United States. The numbers in parentheses are the U.S. market shares of the different companies. For example, Coca-Cola has 45% of the U.S. beverage market, compared to 31% for Pepsi and 14% for Cadbury Schweppes.

Economists use **concentration ratios** to measure the degree of concentration in a market. For example, a four-firm concentration ratio is the percentage of total output in a market produced by the four largest firms. In Table 12.2, the four-firm concentration ratio for cigarettes is 93%, indicating that the largest four firms produce 93% of the cigarettes in the United States. According to one rule of thumb, if the four-firm concentration ratio is greater than 40%, the market is considered an oligopoly.

In this chapter, we explore the decisions of oligopolists and the role of public policy in markets with just a few firms. Here are some of the practical questions we answer:

1. You've probably heard an advertisement that goes like this: "If you buy a stereo from us and find the same stereo for sale somewhere else for a lower price, we'll pay you the difference in price." Does this refund policy lead to higher or lower stereo prices?
2. Suppose two airlines agree to charge the same high price for air travel between two cities. Will this pricing agreement persist?
3. Will the spread of electronic commerce on the Internet lead to higher or lower prices?
4. In the last few years, a new option for college textbooks has emerged: You can now purchase textbooks on the Internet. How will your favorite monopoly—the campus bookstore—respond to competition from Web booksellers?

You may be surprised by the answers to some of these questions. Perhaps you should write down your own answers now and look at them after you've read the chapter.

Table 12.1 Oligopolies in the United States

Beverages	Music	Tobacco	Phone Service	Cars
Coca-Cola (45%)	Universal/Polygram (26%)	Philip Morris (49%)	AT&T/TCI (47%)	General Motors (29%)
Pepsi (31%)	Warner Music (18%)	RJR Nabisco (24%)	Bell Atlantic/GTE (24%)	Ford (25%)
Cadbury Schweppes (14%)	Sony Music (17%)	Brown and Williamson (15%)	SBC/Ameritec (18%)	Chrysler (16%)
	EMI Group PLC (13%)		MCI WorldCom (12%)	
	BMG Entertainment (12%)			

Source: G. Pascal Zachary, "Let's Play Oligopoly!," *Wall Street Journal*, March 8, 1999, p. B1.

Table 12.2 Concentration Ratios in Selected Manufacturing Industries

Industry	Four-Firm Concentration Ratio (%)	Eight-Firm Concentration Ratio (%)
Cigarettes	93	Not available
Guided missiles and space vehicles	93	99
Beer and malt beverages	90	98
Batteries	87	95
Electric bulbs	86	94
Breakfast cereals	85	98
Motor vehicles and car bodies	84	91
Greeting cards	84	88
Engines and turbines	79	92
Aircraft and parts	79	93

Source: U.S. Bureau of the Census, *1992 Census of Manufacturing, Concentration Ratios in Manufacturing* (Washington, DC: U.S. Government Printing Office, 1995).

The key feature of an oligopoly is that firms act strategically. The firms in an oligopoly are interdependent in the sense that they sell similar products and consumers can easily switch from one firm to another. As a result, the actions of one firm affect the profits of other firms in the oligopoly. For example, if one airline cuts its fares, the other airlines in the market will lose customers to the low-price airline unless they cut their prices too. We'll discuss two types of strategies used by oligopolists: price fixing (conspiring to keep prices high) and entry deterrence (preventing additional firms from entering the market).

Most firms in an oligopoly earn economic profit, yet additional firms do not enter the market. An oligopoly—a market with just a few profitable firms—occurs for three reasons:

- **Economies of scale in production.** As you saw in Chapter 10, a natural monopoly occurs when there are relatively large economies of scale in production, so a large firm can produce at a much lower cost than a small firm. In some cases, scale economies are not large enough to generate a natural monopoly but are large enough to generate a natural oligopoly, with a few firms serving the entire market.

- **Government barriers to entry.** As you saw in Chapter 10, government may limit the number of firms in a market by issuing patents or controlling the number of business licenses.

- **Advertising campaign.** In some markets, a firm cannot enter without a substantial investment in an advertising campaign. The result is the same as economies of scale in production: Just a few firms will enter the market.

Cartel Pricing and the Duopolists' Dilemma

One of the virtues of a market economy is that firms compete with one another for customers, and this leads to lower prices. But in some markets, firms cooperate instead of competing with one another. The eighteenth-century economist Adam Smith recognized the possibility that firms would conspire to raise prices: "People of the same trade seldom meet together, even for merriment and diversion, but the conversation ends in a conspiracy against the public, or in some contrivance to raise prices."[1] We'll see that raising prices is not simply a matter of firms getting together and agreeing on higher prices. An agreement to raise prices is likely to break down unless the firms find some way to punish a firm that violates the agreement.

We'll use a market with two firms—a duopoly—to explain the key features of an oligopoly. The basic insights from a duopoly apply to oligopolies with more than two firms. Consider a duopoly in the market for air travel between two hypothetical cities. The two airlines can compete for customers on the basis of price, or they can cooperate and conspire to raise prices. To simplify matters—and to keep the numbers manageable—let's assume that the average cost of providing air travel is constant at $300 per passenger. As shown in Figure 12.1, the average cost is constant, which means that marginal cost equals average cost.

Cartel: A group of firms that coordinate their pricing decisions, often by charging the same price.

A **cartel** is a group of firms that coordinate their pricing decisions, often charging the same price for a particular good or service. In our airline example, the two airlines could form a cartel and choose the price that a monopolist would choose. In Figure 12.1, the demand curve facing a monopolist is the market demand curve, and the marginal-revenue curve intersects the marginal-cost curve at a quantity of 150 passengers per day (point *f*). If the two airlines act as one, they will pick the monopoly price of $400 and split the monopoly output, each serving 75 passengers per day. The average cost is $300, so each airline earns a daily profit of $7,500 (a profit of $100 per passenger × 75 passengers). An arrangement under which the two firms act as one, coordinating their pricing decisions, is also known as **price fixing**. As we'll see later in the chapter, cartels and price-fixing are illegal under U.S. antitrust laws.

Price fixing: An arrangement in which two firms coordinate their pricing decisions.

What would happen if the two firms competed against one another? If they do, each firm faces its own demand curve. The firm's demand is to the left of the market demand curve because consumers are divided between the two firms: At a given price, the number of passengers served by a single firm will be less than the number served by both firms together. In Figure 12.2, panel A shows the perspective of the individual firm. Given the

Figure 12.1

A Cartel Picks the Monopoly Price

Point *c* shows the outcome with a successful price-fixing arrangement (a cartel). The total output is 150 passengers and the price is $400 per passenger, so each firm serves 75 passengers at an average cost of $300 per passenger (shown by point *f*) and earns a profit of $7,500 per day.

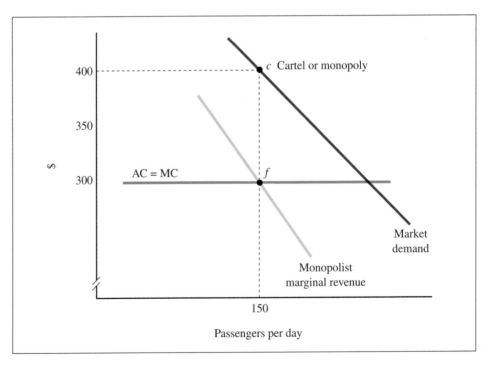

firm's demand curve and marginal-revenue curve, the marginal principle is satisfied at point *c*, where marginal revenue equals marginal cost. Each firm serves 100 passengers at a price of $350 (point *d*). Panel B shows the market perspective: The price is $350, and the quantity is 200 passengers. Given an average cost of $300, each firm earns a profit of $5,000 (equal to $50 per passenger × 100 passengers). When the two firms compete, each earns only $5,000, compared to $7,500 each when they conspire to fix the price.

The Game Tree

Each firm would earn more profit under a price-fixing agreement, but will the firms reach such an agreement? We can answer this question with the help of a **game tree**, a graphical tool that provides a visual representation of the consequences of alternative strategies. Each firm must choose a price for airline tickets, either a high price (the cartel price of $400) or a low price (the duopoly price of $350). Each firm can use the game tree to develop a pricing strategy, knowing that the other firm is also choosing a price.

Game tree: A graphical representation of the consequences of different strategies.

Figure 12.3 shows the game tree for the price-fixing game. Let's call the managers of the airlines Jack and Jill. The game tree has three components:

- The squares are decision nodes. For each square, there is a player (Jack or Jill) and a list of the player's options. For example, the game starts at square X, where Jill has two options: the high price or the low price.

- The arrows show the path of the game from left to right. Jill chooses her price first, so we move from square X to one of Jack's decision nodes, either square Y or square Z. If Jill chooses the high price, we move from square X to square Y. Once we reach

Figure 12.2

Competing Duopolists Pick a Lower Price

At the individual firm (duopolist) level, marginal revenue equals marginal cost at point *c*, so each firm serves 100 passengers at a price of $350 per passenger (shown by point *d* in panel A). Given an average cost of $300 per passenger, each duopolist earns a profit of $5,000. At the market level (panel B), the duopoly outcome has a quantity of 200 passengers (100 passengers per firm × 2 firms) at a price of $350 (point *e*).

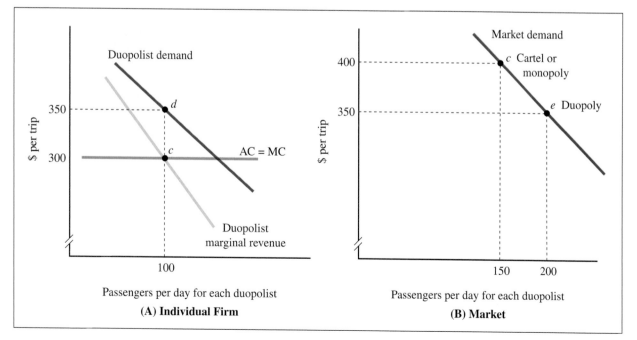

(A) Individual Firm

(B) Market

Figure 12.3

Game Tree for Price-Fixing Game

The path of the game is square X to square Z to rectangle 4: Each firm picks the low price and earns a profit of $5,000. The duopolists' dilemma is that each firm would make more profit if both picked the high price, but neither firm will do so, fearing that the other firm would pick the low price.

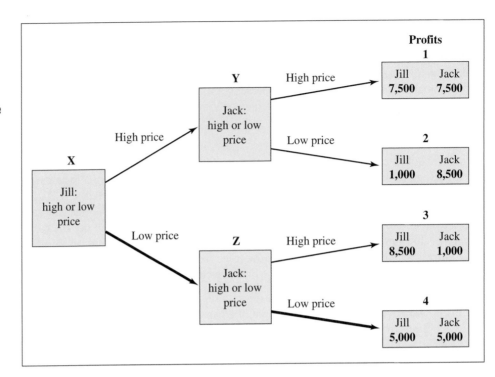

one of Jack's decision nodes, he chooses a price (high or low), and then we move to one of the rectangles. For example, if Jack chooses the high price too, we move from square Y to rectangle 1.

- The rectangles show the profits for the two firms. When we reach a rectangle, the game is over, and the players receive the profits shown in the rectangle.

There is a profit rectangle for each of the four possible outcomes of the price-fixing game.

We've already computed the profits for two profit rectangles. The first rectangle shows what happens when each firm chooses the high price. This is the cartel or price-fixing outcome, with each firm earning $7,500. The fourth rectangle shows what happens when each firm chooses the low price. This is the duopoly outcome, with each firm earning $5,000.

What would happen if the two firms chose different prices? If Jill chooses the low price and Jack chooses the high price, Jill will capture a large share of the market and gain at Jack's expense. In the first column of Table 12.3, Jill serves 170 passengers at a price of $350 each and an average cost of $300 per passenger, so her profit is $8,500 (a $50 profit per passenger × 170 passengers). In the second column, Jack serves only 10 passengers at a price of $400 each and the same average cost, so his profit is $1,000 (a

Table 12.3 Profits When Firms Choose Different Prices

	Jill: Low Price	Jack: High Price
Price	$350	$400
Quantity	170	10
Average cost	$300	$300
Profit per passenger	$50	$100
Profit	$8,500	$1,000

$100 profit per passenger $\times$ 10 passengers). This is shown by rectangle 3 in Figure 12.3: The path of the game is square X to square Z to rectangle 3. The other underpricing outcome is shown by rectangle 2. In this case, Jill chooses the high price and Jack chooses the low price, so Jack gains at Jill's expense. The roles are reversed, and so are the numbers in the profit rectangle.

The Outcome of the Price-Fixing Game

We can predict the outcome of the price-fixing game by a process of elimination. We'll eliminate the rectangles that would require one or both of the firms to act irrationally, leaving us with the rectangle showing the outcome of the game.

- If Jill chooses the high price, we'll move along the upper branches of the tree and eventually reach rectangle 1 or 2, depending on what Jack does. Although Jill would like Jack to choose the high price too, this would be irrational for Jack, because he can make more profit by choosing the low price. Therefore, we can eliminate rectangle 1.

- If Jill chooses the low price, we'll move along the lower branches of the tree, eventually reaching rectangle 3 or 4, depending on Jack's choice. Jack won't choose the high price because then Jill would gain at his expense. Therefore, we can eliminate rectangle 3.

We've eliminated the two rectangles involving a high price for Jack. This means that the low price is a **dominant strategy** for Jack: Regardless of what Jill does, Jack will choose the low price.

There are two rectangles left (2 and 4), and Jill's action will determine which rectangle we'll reach. Jill knows that Jack will choose the low price regardless of what she does, so she can either choose a high price and allow Jack to gain at her expense (rectangle 2) or choose the low price too (rectangle 4). It would be irrational for Jill to allow herself to be underpriced, so we can eliminate rectangle 2. The remaining rectangle shows the outcome of the game: Each person chooses the low price. The thick arrows show the path of the game, from square X to square Z to rectangle 4.

Both firms will be unhappy with this outcome because each could earn a higher profit with rectangle 1. To get there, however, each firm must choose the high price. The **duopolists' dilemma** is that although both firms would be better off if they chose the high price, each firm chooses the low price. Jill won't choose the high price because Jack would underprice her and gain at her expense. Jack won't choose the high price because then Jill would gain at his expense. As we'll see later, the firms can avoid this dilemma, but only if they find some way to punish a firm that underprices. For a description of how one cartel tried to enforce a price-fixing arrangement, read "A Closer Look: Agents Turn Bakers in Battle Against Italian-Bread Cartel."

Dominant strategy: An action that is the best choice under all circumstances.

Duopolists' dilemma: A situation in which both firms in a market would be better off if both chose the high price but each chooses the low price.

The Prisoners' Dilemma

The duopolists' dilemma is similar to the prisoners' dilemma. Consider two people, Bonnie and Clyde, who have been accused of committing a crime. The police give each person an opportunity to confess to the crime, with Bonnie speaking first and Clyde second. The traditional version of the story involves simultaneous decision-making: The two are put in separate rooms, and each makes a choice without the other person knowing what that choice is. The results are the same with sequential or simultaneous decision-making; we'll use the sequential approach to emphasize the similarities to the price-fixing scenario.

The police confront the two criminals with the game tree shown in Figure 12.4. If both confess, each gets 5 years in prison. If neither confesses, the police can convict

A CLOSER LOOK

Agents Turn Bakers in Battle Against Italian-Bread Cartel

For years, law-enforcement officials heard complaints about a small group of bakers trying to corner the Italian-bread market in parts of New York City. Investigators were told that the cartel used threats of violence to control the distribution of fresh Italian bread to small grocery stores in Brooklyn and Staten Island. The cartel eliminated competition and inflated prices.

But investigators found that bakers and store owners were reluctant to cooperate. The only way to get to the heart of the Italian-bread racket, they decided, was to open a bakery themselves. So a team of a half-dozen undercover detectives opened a storefront at 327 West 11th Street in Greenwich Village in early 1993 and called it Louis Basile's. Wearing bakers' whites, they pretended to bake hundreds of loaves of bread each day, taking turns getting up at 3:00 A.M. to drive to New Jersey to buy the real stuff and slipping the loaves into the customized white paper sleeves that are the signature of authentic, fresh Italian bread. Not long after the investigators began trying to sell the bread to neighborhood grocery stores in Manhattan and Brooklyn, they heard from the Association of Independent Bakers and Distributors of Italian Bread. Over drinks at the White Horse Tavern on Hudson Street, investigators say, a detective posing as a baker was told by two members of the association that violence could come to Basile's and its employees if they did not play by association rules.

"The rules involved fixed prices for bread—a system of distribution that forced a store to buy from a single baker," said the Manhattan District Attorney, Robert M. Morgenthau, who announced the indictment of four officials of the association on price-fixing charges. "If a store wanted to shift to another baker, he said, the association had to be consulted and cash paid to the former baker."

Daniel J. Castleman, head of investigations in Mr. Morgenthau's office, said that association members included about 50 bakeries that supplied Italian bread to more than 1,000 small grocery stores and delicatessens in the city. As an example of the association's activity, Mr. Morgenthau cited a decision in 1990 to raise the retail price of bread from 75 cents to 85 cents. Five cents of the increase went to the bakers, and the other five was divided between the bread deliverers and the store owners, he said. "Because the association had a lock on the market, consumers had no choice but to pay the increase," Mr. Morgenthau said. All the association members printed the new price on their bread sleeves, he noted. While Mr. Morgenthau said he could not estimate how much the association and its members profited from illegal operations, Mr. Castleman said the 1990 price increase cost consumers millions of dollars.

Source: Adapted from Seth Faison, "Agents Turn Bakers in Battle Against Italian-Bread Cartel," *New York Times*, July 14, 1994, p. A1. Copyright © 1994 by The New York Times Co. Reprinted by Permission.

them on a lesser charge, and each gets 2 years. If only one confesses and implicates the other, the confessor is rewarded with a 1-year prison sentence and the other gets 10 years. Clyde, who goes second, will confess no matter what Bonnie does, and Bonnie knows this. The rational choice for each person is to confess, so each serves 5 years. Although both criminals would be better off if they both kept quiet, they implicate each other because the police reward them for doing so. There is an incentive for squealing, just as there is an incentive for one duopolist to underprice the other.

Avoiding the Dilemma: Price Matching

The duopolists' dilemma occurs because the two firms are unable to coordinate their pricing decisions and act as one. Each firm has an incentive to underprice the other firm because the low-price firm will capture a larger share of the market and earn a larger profit. One way to avoid this dilemma is to develop a system of price matching.

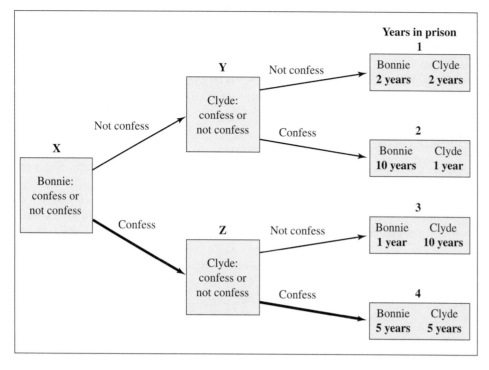

Guaranteed Price Matching

To eliminate the incentive for underpricing, one firm can guarantee that it will match its competitor's price. Suppose Jill places the following advertisement in the local newspaper: "If you buy a plane ticket from me and then discover that Jack offers the same trip at a lower price, I will pay you the difference between my price and Jack's price. If I charge you $400 and Jack's price is only $350, I will pay you $50." This pricing scheme is known as **guaranteed price matching**: Jill guarantees that she will match Jack's price. It is also known as a *meet-the-competition policy*. Jill's promise to match Jack's lower price is credible because she announces it in the newspaper.

How will Jack respond to Jill's price-matching scheme? In effect, Jill tentatively chooses the high price but will instantly switch to the low price if Jack picks the low price. After a $50 refund, Jill's price will be $350, the same as Jack's. Jack will respond to Jill's price-matching scheme in one of two ways:

1. **Choose the high price.** If Jack matches Jill's announced high price, each firm will earn a profit of $7,500 (rectangle 1 in the game tree in Figure 12.3).
2. **Choose the low price.** If Jack tries to underprice Jill, she will switch to the low price, and each will earn a profit of only $5,000 (rectangle 4 in the game tree).

Jack's decision is easy: A pair of high prices is more profitable than a pair of low prices, so he will choose the high price, just like Jill.

Jill's price-matching scheme eliminates the duopolists' dilemma and makes cartel pricing possible, even without a formal cartel. The duopolists' dilemma disappears because underpricing is no longer possible. The motto of the price-matching scheme is "High for one means high for all, and low for one means low for all." It would be irrational for Jack to choose the low price because he knows that Jill would match it. Once the possibility of underpricing has been eliminated, the duopoly will be replaced by an informal cartel, each firm charging the price that would be charged by a monopolist.

Guaranteed price matching: A scheme under which a firm guarantees that it will match a lower price by a competitor; also known as a meet-the-competition policy.

To most people, the notion that guaranteed price matching leads to higher prices is surprising. After all, Jill promises to give refunds if her price exceeds Jack's, so we might expect her to keep her price low to avoid giving out a lot of refunds. In fact, she doesn't have to worry about refunds because she knows that Jack will also choose the high price. In other words, Jill's promise to issue refunds is an empty promise. Although consumers might think Jill's refund policy will protect them from high prices, the policy guarantees that they will pay the high price.

Price Fixing in Cyberspace?

What are the implications of electronic commerce on the Internet for competition and prices? Will the spread of electronic commerce lead to higher or lower prices for consumer goods such as books, CDs, and cameras? The Internet gives consumers an unprecedented opportunity to almost instantly compare the products and prices of different sellers and could promote competition and lead to lower prices. Unfortunately,

Many stores advertise their guaranteed price-matching policies. Focus Camera goes beyond matching a lower price, promising to refund the difference plus 10%. This empty promise promotes price fixing by camera stores.

At **FOCUS CAMERA**, we guarantee you the lowest prices. If you purchase a camera from us and within 30 days find the same camera at a lower price, we'll **REFUND** the difference **PLUS** 10%. For example, if you buy a camera from us for $300 and find it elsewhere for $280, we'll give you $22, making our actual price only $278!

the Internet also gives firms an unprecedented opportunity to engage in price matching to maintain a cartel price.

A firm has an incentive to cut price if the firm could sell more output at the lower price, as consumers switch from rival sellers. But if a rival can instantly respond to a price cut on the Internet, the price-cutting firm won't gain many consumers. That could mean that a firm won't cut its prices in the first place, and a cartel price may persist. The same logic applies to a potential entrant, who might be tempted to enter the market with a price below the cartel price. If the original firms can instantly match the entrant's lower price, the entrant won't sell very much, and the payoff from entering may be so low that the firm won't enter the market.

Application: Different Ticket Prices

At the beginning of this chapter, we saw that Jason paid more for his plane ticket than Melissa did for hers, even though both live in cities that are served by two airlines. The two airlines in Melissa's city may suffer from the duopolists' dilemma: Although they would prefer the high price ($400), they both choose the low price ($350). In contrast, an airline in Jason's city could use a guaranteed price-matching scheme, promising to refund the difference between its price and the price of the other airline. The price-matching scheme eliminates underpricing, so each airline will choose the high price ($400). Jason pays a higher price because the price-matching scheme allows the airlines in his city to engage in cartel pricing (price fixing).

TEST Your Understanding

1. Complete the statement with *e* or *c*: Rectangle 1 in Figure 12.3 is associated with point _____ in Figure 12.2, while rectangle 4 is associated with point _____.

2. Use Figure 12.3 to complete the statement: If each firm picks the low price, the path of the game is square _____ to square _____ to rectangle _____, and each firm earns a profit of _____.

3. Suppose Jack promises that if Jill chooses the high price, he will too. If Jack's objective is to maximize his profit, what will he do after Jill chooses the high price?

4. If you were Jill, would you believe Jack's promises to choose the high price? Which price would you choose?

5. Complete the statement with a number: Suppose that Jack offers plane tickets for $350. Under Jill's price-matching scheme, she would give each of her customers a refund of _____.

6. Have you ever encountered a guaranteed price-matching scheme? If so, did you think it was good news or bad news for consumers? What do you think now?

Repeated Pricing and Retaliation for Underpricing

Up to this point, we've assumed that the price-fixing game is played only once. Each firm chooses a price and sticks with that price for the lifetime of the firm. What happens when two firms play the price-fixing game repeatedly, setting prices over an extended period of time? We'll see that repetition makes price fixing more likely because firms can punish a firm that cheats on a price-fixing agreement.

Retaliation Strategies

Firms use several strategies to maintain a price-fixing agreement. We explore three, all of which involve punishing a firm that underprices the other firm. Continuing the airline example, suppose Jack and Jill choose their prices at the beginning of each month. Jill chooses the cartel price ($400) for the first month and then waits to see what price Jack chooses. Jill could use one of the following schemes to punish Jack if he underprices her:

1. **Duopoly price.** Jill continues to choose the high price until Jack underprices her. Once that happens, she chooses the duopoly price ($350 in our example) for the remaining lifetime of her firm. Jill allows herself to be underpriced only once and then abandons the idea of cartel pricing and accepts the duopoly outcome, which is less profitable than the cartel outcome but more profitable than being underpriced by the other firm.

2. **Grim trigger.** When Jack underprices Jill, she responds by dropping her price to a level at which each firm will make zero economic profit forever. This is called the grim-trigger strategy because grim consequences are triggered by Jack's underpricing.

3. **Tit-for-tat.** Starting in the second month, Jill chooses whatever price Jack chose the preceding month. As long as Jack chooses the cartel price, the cartel arrangement will persist, but if Jack underprices Jill, the cartel will break down. In Figure 12.5, Jack underprices Jill in the second month, so Jill chooses the low price for the third month, resulting in the duopoly outcome. To restore the cartel outcome, Jack must eventually choose the high price, allowing Jill to underprice him for one month. This happens in the fourth month, so the cartel is restored in the fifth month. Although Jack can gain at Jill's expense in the second month, if he wants to restore cartel pricing, he must allow Jill to gain at his expense during the fourth month.

These three pricing schemes promote cartel pricing by penalizing the underpricer. To decide whether to underprice Jill, Jack must weigh the short-term benefit against the long-term cost:

1. The short-term benefit is the increase in profit in the current period. If Jack underprices Jill, he can increase his profit from $7,500 (Jack's profit if both firms pick the high price) to $8,500 (Jack's profit if he chooses the low price and Jill chooses the high price). Therefore, the short-term benefit of underpricing is $1,000.

Grim trigger: A strategy under which a firm responds to underpricing by choosing a price so low that each firm makes zero economic profit.

Tit-for-tat: A strategy under which the one firm in a duopoly starts out with the cartel price and then chooses whatever price the other firm chose in the preceding period.

Figure 12.5

Tit-for-Tat Pricing

Under a tit-for-tat retaliation scheme, the leading firm (Jill, the square) chooses whatever price the other firm (Jack, the circle) chose the preceding month.

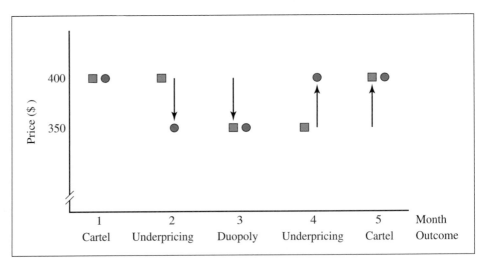

2. The long-term cost is the loss of profit in later periods. Jill will respond to Jack's underpricing by cutting her price, and this decreases Jack's profit. For example, if Jill pulls the grim trigger, Jack will lose the opportunity for a monthly profit of $7,500 for the remaining lifetime of his firm.

If the two firms expect to share the market for a long time, the long-term cost of underpricing will exceed the short-term benefit, so underpricing is less likely. The threat of punishment makes it easier to resist the temptation to cheat on the cartel.

Price Fixing and the Law

Under the Sherman Anti-Trust Act of 1890 and subsequent legislation, explicit price fixing is illegal. It is illegal for firms to discuss their pricing strategies or their methods of punishing a firm that underprices other firms. In one of the early price-fixing cases (Addyston Pipe, 1899), six manufacturers of cast-iron pipe met to fix prices in certain geographical areas. Several months after the Supreme Court ruled that their cartel pricing was illegal, the firms merged into a single firm, so instead of acting like a monopolist, which was illegal, they became a monopolist. Here are some other examples of price fixing:

1. GE/Westinghouse (1961). General Electric and Westinghouse were convicted of fixing prices for electrical generators, resulting in fines of over $2 million and imprisonment or probation for 30 corporate executives.

2. Coca-Cola (1986). The Coca-Cola Bottling Company of North Carolina paid a fine and issued discount coupons to its customers to settle a case involving a conspiracy to fix the prices of soft drinks.

3. Infant formula (1993). The three major producers of infant formula (together serving 95% of the market) paid a total of $200 million to wholesalers and retailers to settle lawsuits claiming that they had conspired to fix prices.

4. Plastic wrap in Japan (1993). A Tokyo court found eight Japanese companies guilty of conspiring to fix the prices of the plastic film used for wrapping food. The companies received fines of $54,000 to $73,000, and 15 executives were given suspended jail sentences of six months to one year.

5. Airline pricing (1994). In an antitrust lawsuit filed in 1992, the U.S. Justice Department alleged that the nation's airlines used advanced price listing to fix airline ticket prices. Before an airline increased its price, it could post a "suggested" price on a central computer and see whether the other airlines would increase their prices. By March 1994, eight of the nation's largest airlines (United Airlines, USAir Group, American Airlines, Delta Airlines, Northwest Airlines, Continental Airlines, Trans-World Airlines, and Alaska Air) had agreed to drop this practice. According to Ann Bingaman of the antitrust division of the Justice Department, advance price listing allowed airlines to fix prices at an artificially high level, costing consumers an extra $1.9 billion for airline tickets.[2]

6. Steel beam pricing in Europe (1994). The European Union Commission fined 16 steel companies a total of 104 million European currency units ($116 million) for conspiring to fix the price of steel beams.

7. Carton board pricing in Europe (1994). The European Union Commission fined 19 manufacturers of carton board a total of 132 million European currency units ($165 million) for operating a cartel that fixed prices at secret meetings in luxury Zurich hotels.

8. Food additives (1996). An employee of Archer Daniels Midland (ADM), a huge food company that likes to call itself "the supermarket to the world," provided audio and video tapes of ADM executives scheming to fix prices. ADM pleaded guilty to the charges of price fixing and was fined $100 million.

Price Leadership

Price leadership: An implicit agreement under which firms in a market choose a price leader, observe that firm's price, and match it.

Because explicit price fixing is illegal, firms often rely on implicit pricing agreements to fix prices at the monopoly level. Under a **price leadership** arrangement, a group of firms selects a firm to serve as a price leader, observes the price chosen by the leader, and then matches it. Such an agreement allows firms to cooperate without actually discussing their pricing strategies.

The problem with an implicit pricing agreement is that it relies on indirect signals that are often garbled and misinterpreted. Suppose that two firms have cooperated for several years, both sticking to the cartel price. When one firm suddenly drops its price, the other firm could interpret the price cut in one of two ways:

1. **Change in market conditions.** Perhaps the first firm has observed a change in demand or production cost and decides that both firms would benefit from a lower price.
2. **Underpricing.** Perhaps the first firm is trying to increase its market share and profit at the expense of the second firm.

The first interpretation would probably cause the second firm to match the lower price of the first firm, and price fixing would continue at the lower price. In contrast, the second interpretation could trigger a price war destroying the price-fixing agreement. Because firms often pull the grim trigger when a more moderate response would be appropriate, implicit pricing agreements are difficult to maintain.

Kinked Demand Curve

Kinked demand model: A model under which firms in an oligopoly match price reductions by other firms but do not match price increases by other firms.

The **kinked demand model** of oligopoly gets its name from its assumptions about how firms in an oligopoly respond when one firm changes its price. Figure 12.6 shows the demand curve facing Kirk, one of three firms in the oligopoly. Suppose each of the three firms starts out with a price of $6, so Kirk sells 30 units of output (point k).

1. If Kirk increases his price, the other two firms will not change their prices. Kirk will have a higher price than the other firms, so his quantity will decrease by a large amount (from 30 to 10 units).
2. If Kirk decreases his price, the other firms will decrease their prices. Kirk will have the same (lower) price as other firms, so his quantity will increase by a small amount (from 30 to 33 units).

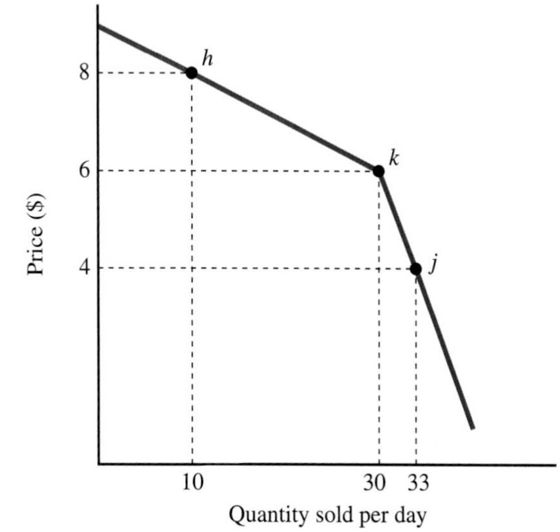

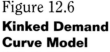

Figure 12.6
Kinked Demand Curve Model

Under the kinked demand model, when one firm increases its price, the other firms don't change their prices, so the quantity sold by the firm will decrease by a large amount. But when one firm decreases its price, the other firms cut their prices too, so the quantity sold by the firm will increase by a small amount.

Price ($)	Quantity demanded
8	10
6	30
4	33

These assumptions mean that the demand curve of the typical firm has a kink at the prevailing price: It is relatively flat (price-elastic) for higher prices because other firms won't match a higher price but relatively steep (price-inelastic) for lower prices because other firms will match a lower price. Once a price has been established, it will tend to persist because there is a large penalty for a firm that picks a higher price (a large decrease in the quantity sold) and a small benefit for a firm that picks a lower price (a small increase in the quantity sold).

The model of kinked demand is really a model of pessimism. Each firm assumes the worst about how its fellow oligopolists will respond to a change in price: The other firms will not go along with a higher price but will match a lower price. Although this model may have some intuitive appeal, there is no evidence that firms really act this way. Starting in 1947, various studies of oligopolies have failed to find compelling evidence to support the kinked-demand model of oligopoly.[3]

TEST Your Understanding

7. Which retaliation strategy, the duopoly price or the grim trigger, provides a greater incentive to maintain cartel pricing? Explain.

8. Suppose that Jack and Jill use a tit-for-tat scheme to encourage cartel pricing and Jill chooses the low price for a single month. How long will the two firms deviate from cartel pricing? Explain.

9. Complete the statement with cost or benefit: If two firms expect to be in the market together for a long time, the _____ of underpricing will be large relative to the _____.

Entry Deterrence by an Insecure Monopolist

You've seen what happens when two duopolists try to act as one, fixing the price at the monopoly level. Now let's think about how a monopolist might try to prevent a second firm from entering its market. In other words, we look at a potential oligopoly. To explain how a monopolist tries to protect a monopoly, we use some of the numbers from our airline example, although we look at a different city with a different cast of characters.

Suppose that Jane initially has a secure monopoly in the market for air travel between two cities. When there is no threat of entry, Jane uses the marginal principle (marginal revenue = marginal cost) to pick a quantity and a price. In Figure 12.7, we start at point *m*, with a quantity of 150 passengers per day and a price of $400 per passenger. Her profit per passenger is $100 ($400 minus the average cost of $300), so her daily profit is $15,000. If Jane discovers that the manager of a second airline is thinking about entering the market, what will she do? Now that she has an **insecure monopoly**, she has two options: She can be passive and allow the second airline to enter the market, or she can try to prevent the second airline from entering.

Insecure monopoly: A monopoly that is faced with the possibility that a second firm will enter the market.

Game Tree for the Entry Game

Let's look first at the passive strategy. By producing a small quantity of output, Jane will leave room in the market for the second airline. If the second airline enters the market,

Figure 12.7

Entry Deterrence and Limit Pricing

Moving downward along the demand curve, point *m* shows the secure monopoly, point *i* shows the insecure monopoly, and point *d* shows the duopoly. Point *h* shows what happens if the insecure monopolist produces a large quantity but a second firm enters anyway.

ACTIVE GRAPH

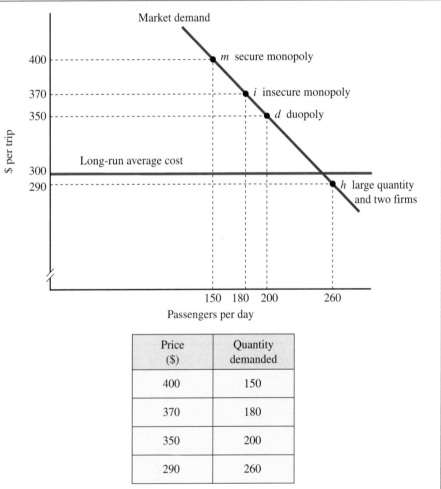

Price ($)	Quantity demanded
400	150
370	180
350	200
290	260

Jane will be forced to cut her price to compete with the new airline for customers. In Figure 12.7, the market will move downward along the demand curve from point m to point d (the duopoly outcome). The price is lower ($350 instead of $400), and Jane will have only 100 passengers per day (half of the 200 passengers served at a price of $350). Her profit per passenger will be $50 ($350 minus the average cost of $300), so her daily profit will be $5,000. In Figure 12.8, the path of the game is square X to square Y to rectangle 1: If Jane is passive, Dick will enter the market and each firm will receive a profit of $5,000.

What must Jane do to prevent Dick from entering the market? One possibility is to buy a large fleet of airplanes and sign labor contracts that force her to hire a large work-force. These actions would commit Jane to serve a large number of passengers at a low price. If Dick enters the market, he will be forced to charge a low price too, and both firms would lose money. This is shown in the lower branches of the game tree in Figure 12.8.

- If Jane produces a large quantity and Dick enters anyway, the total output of the two firms will be very large. In Figure 12.7, the market would move downward along the demand curve to point h, with a price of $290 and a quantity of 260 passengers. Consumers would be happy with this outcome, but the two firms would not: The price would be less than the average cost of each firm, so each firm would lose $1,300 (rectangle 3 in Figure 12.8).

- If Jane produces a large quantity and Dick stays out of the market, the total output of the market will be 180 passengers, as shown by point i in Figure 12.6. Jane's profit would be $12,600 ($70 per passenger × 180 passengers). This outcome is shown by rectangle 4 in Figure 12.8.

The Outcome of the Entry Game

Let's use a process of elimination to predict the outcome of the entry-deterrence game. We've already eliminated rectangle 2: If Jane is passive and chooses a small quantity,

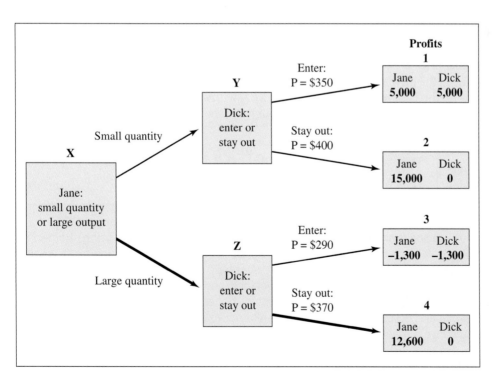

Figure 12.8

Game Tree for the Entry Game
The path of the game is square X to square Z to rectangle 4: Jane chooses a large quantity, so Dick decides to stay out. Jane earns a profit of $12,600, and Dick gets nothing.

Dick will enter. We've also eliminated rectangle 3: If Jane produces a large quantity, Dick would lose money in the market, so he will stay out.

Rectangles 1 and 4 are left, and Jane's action will determine which rectangle we'll reach. If Jane produces a large quantity, she can prevent Dick from entering the market, but is this sensible? Jane's profit from the passive approach (rectangle 1) is lower than the profit from entry deterrence (rectangle 4), so we can eliminate rectangle 1. The remaining rectangle shows the outcome of the game: Jane will maintain her insecure monopoly by producing a large quantity. The thick arrows show the path of the game, from square X to square Z to rectangle 4.

The entry-deterrence game generates a market price that is between the price of a secure monopolist and the duopoly price. Before Dick threatened to enter the market, Jane was a secure monopolist and charged $400 (point m in Figure 12.7). Once Dick threatens to enter the market, point m will no longer be an option because if Jane continues to act like a secure monopolist (choosing a small quantity of output), Dick will enter the market and the price will fall to $350 (point d). Jane can avoid sharing the market by committing herself to produce a large quantity and accepting the lower price associated with an insecure monopolist ($370, as shown by point i).

Limit pricing: A scheme under which a monopolist accepts a price below the normal monopoly price to deter other firms from entering the market.

The strategy of picking a price that is lower than the normal monopoly price to deter entry is known as **limit pricing**. For a discussion of limit pricing by Microsoft Corporation, read "A Closer Look: What's the Monopoly Price for Microsoft Windows?"

Although our example shows that deterrence is the best strategy for Jane, it won't be the best strategy for all monopolists. Suppose Rod could prevent Leah from entering his market but only by increasing his output by a very large amount and thus accepting a much lower price. A low price means a small profit, so the deterrence strategy could generate less profit than simply sharing the market with Leah. In general, entry deterrence will not be profitable if the price required to prevent entry is relatively low.

Applications: Aluminum, Plane Tickets, Campus Bookstores

Between 1893 and 1940, the Aluminum Company of America (Alcoa) had a monopoly on aluminum production in the United States.[5] During this period, Alcoa kept other firms out of the market by producing a large quantity and keeping its price low. Although a higher price would have generated more profit in the short run, other firms would have entered the market, so Alcoa's profit would have been lower in the longer run.

At the beginning of this chapter, we saw that Katrina paid more for her plane ticket than Brian paid for his, even though they both live in cities that are served by a

What's the Monopoly Price for Microsoft Windows?

The Windows operating system from Microsoft, Inc. runs about 90% of the world's personal computers, so it is natural to think that Microsoft has a monopoly in the market for operating systems. According to economist Richard Schmalensee, an expert on oligopoly and monopoly, Microsoft's profit-maximizing monopoly price is between $900 and $2,000. That's the amount Microsoft would charge if it acted like a regular monopolist.[4]

So why does Microsoft charge only $99 for Windows? One possibility is limit pricing. Perhaps Microsoft is an insecure monopolist and picks a low price to discourage entry and preserve its monopoly. If Microsoft charged $2,000 for its operating system, there would be an incentive for other firms to develop alternative operating systems.

single airline. If the monopolist in Katrina's city is secure, meaning that there is no threat that another airline would enter the market, the airline will charge the normal monopoly price of $400. In Brian's city, an insecure monopolist prevents a second airline from entering the market by committing itself to produce a large quantity and accepting a low price. Brian pays a lower price because he buys his ticket from an insecure monopolist.

We can apply the notion of entry deterrence to your favorite monopoly: your campus bookstore. On most college campuses the campus bookstore has a monopoly on the sale of textbooks. Other organizations are prohibited, usually by the state government or the college, from selling textbooks on campus. The recent growth of Internet commerce has given students another option: Order textbooks over the Web and have them shipped by mail, UPS, Federal Express, or Airborne Express. Several Web booksellers charge less than the campus bookstore, and the growth of Web book sales threatens the campus bookstore monopoly. If your campus bookstore suddenly feels insecure about its monopoly position, it could cut its prices to prevent Web booksellers from capturing too many of its customers. If it does this, you will pay lower prices even if you don't patronize the Web seller.

Entry Deterrence and Contestable Markets

We've seen that an insecure monopolist may cut its price to prevent other firms from entering the market. The threat of entry moves the market price closer to the price that would occur in a market with two firms. The same logic applies to a monopolized market that could potentially have many firms: The threat of entry will force the monopolist to charge a price that could be close to the one that would occur in a market with many firms. The mere existence of a monopoly does not mean that it will charge high prices and earn large profits. To protect its monopoly, a monopolist may act like a firm in a market with many firms, picking a low price and earning a small profit.

The threat of entry underlies the theory of market contestability. Firms can enter or leave a **contestable market** without incurring large costs. The few firms in a contestable market will be threatened constantly by the entry of new firms, so prices and profits will be low. In the extreme case of perfect contestability, firms can enter and exit a market at zero cost. In this case, the price will be the same as the price that would occur in a perfectly competitive market, one with dozens of firms. Although few markets are perfectly contestable, many markets are contestable to a certain degree, and the threat of entry tends to decrease prices and profits.

Contestable market: A market in which the costs of entering and leaving are low, so the firms that are already in the market are constantly threatened by the entry of new firms.

BallPoint Pens

ECONOMIC DETECTIVE

In 1945, Reynolds International Pen Corporation introduced a revolutionary product: the ballpoint pen. The new type of pen could be produced with a very simple production technology.[6] For three years, Reynolds earned enormous profits on this innovative product. In 1948, Reynolds stopped producing pens, dropping out of the market entirely. What happened?

The key to solving this mystery is the fact that Reynolds earned enormous profits for a short time. The simple technology of the ballpoint pen could be easily copied by other producers, so the price required to deter entry was very low. The entry-deterring price was so low that it was better for Reynolds to charge a high price and squeeze out as much profit as possible from a short-lived monopoly. Reynolds sold its pens for $16, about 20 times the average production cost ($0.80). By 1948, a total of 100 firms had entered the ballpoint market, and the price had fallen close to the production cost. ◆

Review: Four Types of Markets

This is the fourth of four chapters on decision-making by firms in different market settings. We can use Table 12.4 to review the characteristics of the four types of markets we've discussed in Chapters 9 though 12.

1. **Perfect Competition.** There are very many firms, each selling a standardized or homogeneous product. Each firm is such a small part of the market that the firm takes the market price as given: The demand for the individual firm's product is perfectly elastic.

2. **Monopolistic competition.** There are many firms, each selling a slightly different product. Some examples are restaurants, retail stores, gas stations, and clothing. This contrasts with perfect competition, in which each firm sells a standardized product. Because the products sold by different firms in a monopolistically competitive market are not perfect substitutes, the demand for the firm's product is not perfectly elastic. There are no barriers to entering the market, so there are many firms.

3. **Oligopoly.** There are just a few firms in the market, a result of two sorts of barriers to entry: economies of scale and government policies limit the number of firms in the market. The demand for an individual firm's product is less elastic than it would be in a monopolistically competitive market because there are fewer firms in the oligopoly. Some examples are automobiles, airline travel, and breakfast cereals.

4. **Monopoly.** A single firm serves the entire market. A monopoly occurs when the barriers to entry are very large, which could result from very large economies of scale or a government limit on the number of firms. The demand for a monopolist's product is shown by the market demand curve. Some examples of goods with large scale economies are local phone service and electric power generation. Some examples of monopolies established by government policy are drugs covered by patents and concessions in national parks.

Table 12.4 Characteristics of Different Types of Markets

	Perfect Competition	Monopolistic Competition	Oligopoly	Monopoly
Number of firms	Very large number	Many	Few	One
Type of product	Standardized (homogeneous)	Differentiated	Standardized or differentiated	Unique
Demand faced by individual firm	Price taker: demand is perfectly elastic	Demand is price elatic but not perfectly elastic	Demand is less elastic than demand facing monopolistically competitive firm	Firm faces market demand curve
Entry conditions	No barriers	No barriers	Large barriers from economies of scale or government policies	Large barriers from economies of scale or government policies
Examples	Wheat, soybeans	Toothbrushes, music stores, clothing	Air travel, automobiles, beverages, cigarettes, long-distance phone service	Local phone service, patented drugs

TEST Your Understanding

10. Complete the statement: Suppose that Jane picks a small quantity of output. In Figure 12.8, the path of the game would be square _____ to square _____ to rectangle _____.

11. In Figure 12.8, Jane would prefer rectangle 2 to rectangle 4. Why can't she get to rectangle 2?

12. Why does a secure monopolist charge a higher price than an insecure monopolist does?

Using the **TOOLS**

We've used one of the tools of economics—the game tree—to predict the outcomes of price-fixing and entry-deterrence games. Here are some opportunities to use this tool to do your own economic analysis of markets.

1. ECONOMIC EXPERIMENT: Price-Fixing

Here is a price-fixing or cartel game for the classroom. You'll have an opportunity to conspire to fix prices in a hypothetical market with five firms.

- The instructor divides the class into five groups. Each group represents one of five firms that produce a particular good.
- Each group must develop a pricing strategy for its firm, recognizing that the other groups are choosing prices for their firms at the same time. There are only two choices: a high price (the cartel price) or a low price.
- The profit of a particular firm depends on the price chosen by the firm and the prices chosen by the four other firms. Here is the profit matrix:

Number of High-Price Firms	Number of Low-Price Firms	Profit for Each High-Price Firm	Profit for Each Low-Price Firm
0	5	—	$50
1	4	$20	70
2	3	40	90
3	2	60	110
4	1	80	130
5	0	100	—

1. From the second row, if one of the five firms chooses the high price and the other four firms choose the low price, the high-price firm earns a profit of $20, and each low-price firm earns a profit of $70.

2. The game is played for several rounds. In the first three rounds, the firms make their choices without talking to each other in advance. In the fourth and fifth rounds, the firms discuss their strategies, disperse, and then make their choices.

3. The group's score equals the profit earned by the firm.

2. Advertising and Price Fixing

Consider two sellers of CD players (Cecil and Dee) who suffer from the duopolists' dilemma. Although both Cecil and Dee would be better off if both chose the high price, they both choose the low price. Cecil recently discovered that Dee is planning a big advertising campaign, the purpose of which is to increase her sales at Cecil's expense (without changing her price). Suppose that Cecil has the opportunity to launch his own advertising campaign before Dee starts hers. What sort of advertising campaign should he launch?

3. Entry Deterrence

Your firm sells a very popular children's toy. The manager of another firm is thinking about introducing a similar toy. You have the following facts:

- Your average cost of production is constant at $2 per toy.
- At the current monopoly price of $5 per toy, you sell 120 toys per day.
- You could prevent the entry of the second firm by increasing your output to 150 toys per day and cutting your price to $4 per toy.
- If the second firm enters the market, your price would decrease to $3 per toy, and you would sell only 80 toys per day.

Should you prevent entry of the second firm?

Summary

In this chapter, we've seen that when a few firms share a market, they have an incentive to act strategically. Firms may use cartel pricing or price fixing to avoid competition and keep prices high. If another firm threatens to enter a monopolist's market, the monopolist may cut its price to discourage other firms from entering a market. Here are the main points of the chapter.

1. Each firm in an oligopoly has an incentive to underprice the other firms, so price fixing (also known as cartel pricing) will be unsuccessful unless firms have some way of enforcing a price-fixing agreement.

2. One way to maintain price fixing is a guaranteed price-matching scheme: One firm chooses the high price and promises to match a lower price offered by its competitor.

3. Price fixing is more likely to occur if firms choose prices repeatedly and can punish a firm that chooses a price below the cartel price.

4. To prevent a second firm from entering the market, an insecure monopolist may commit itself to produce a relatively large quantity and accept a relatively low price.

Key Terms

cartel, 252
concentration ratio, 250
contestable market, 267
dominant strategy, 255
duopolists' dilemma, 255

game tree, 253
grim trigger, 260
guaranteed price matching, 257
insecure monopoly, 264
kinked demand model, 262

limit pricing, 266
oligopoly, 250
price fixing, 252
price leadership, 262
tit-for-tat, 260

Problems and Discussion Questions

1. Consider two firms, Speedy and Hustle, that provide land transportation from the downtown area to the airport. The practice of guaranteed price matching is illegal.

- If the two firms act independently (they do not engage in price fixing or any other collusive behavior), each firm will serve 100 passengers per day.

day at a price of $20 per passenger and an average cost of $15 per passenger.

- Under a price-fixing or cartel arrangement, each firm would serve 75 passengers at a price of $28 and an average cost of $18 per passenger.
- If one firm charges $20 and the other firm charges $28, the low-price firm will earn a profit of $900 and the high-price firm will earn a profit of $400.
- Speedy chooses a price first, followed by Hustle.

Draw a game tree for the price-fixing game and predict the outcome.

2. Recall the example of the repeated pricing game between Jack and Jill. Suppose that each firm uses the grim-trigger strategy to punish underpricing. Each person expects to go out of business in one month, meaning that each person is about to choose a price for the last time. Which price will each person choose?

3. Many firms have going-out-of-business sales with remarkable bargains. What insights does the material in this chapter provide about such sales?

4. Consider the example of entry deterrence shown in Figure 12.8. Suppose that just one number changes: If Jane chooses a large quantity and Dick stays out, Jane's profit would be $4,500. All the other numbers are the same as those shown in Figure 12.8. Draw a new game tree and predict the outcome: Will Jane choose a large or a small quantity, and will Dick enter or stay out?

5. On Wa-ki-ki beach, there are two hotels, Weird and Bizarre. The practice of guaranteed price matching is illegal. If the two firms act independently (they do not engage in price fixing or any other collusive behavior), each firm will rent 50 rooms per day at a price of $50 per room and an average cost of $45 per room. Under a price-fixing or cartel arrangement, each hotel would rent 30 rooms per day at a price of $60 and an average cost of $48. If one firm charges $50 and the other firm charges $60, the low-price firm will earn a profit of $500, and the high-price firm will earn a profit of $150. Bizarre picks a price first, followed by Weird.

   a. Suppose each firm must pick a price and maintain its chosen price for the remaining lifetime of the firm. Draw a game tree and predict the outcome.

   b. Suppose the two firms can change their prices daily, and expect to be in business for three more days. Weird announces that he will start with the high price and maintain the price as long as Bizarre does too. If Bizarre undercuts Weird,

however, Weird will pick the low price for the remainder of the game. Predict the outcome of the game.

6. Consider the market for air travel between Madison and Chicago. The long-run average cost is constant at $200 per passenger, and the demand curve is linear, with a slope of –$1 per passenger. A secure monopolist would charge a price of $280 and serve 70 passengers per day. The other possible prices are $260 for an insecure monopolist, $250 for the duopoly outcome, and $180 for the case in which one firm picks a large quantity and a low price but a second firm enters anyway.

   a. Use these numbers to draw two figures, one like Figure 12.7 and a second like Figure 12.8. Provide a complete set of numbers, and briefly explain how you got them. Label any curves you draw, and identify the relevant points on your graph.

   b. Use your second figure to predict the outcome of the entry-deterrence game. What is the price of air travel?

7. In the state of Turnover, the typical car-stereo seller stays in business for one year. In the state of Longtime, the typical car-stereo seller stays in business for five years. Which state is likely to have higher prices for car stereos?

8. Consider the Jack and Jill repeated price game described in the text. Suppose Jill uses the duopoly-pricing strategy, and the two firms expect to be in business for three periods.

   a. In the current period, what are Jack's costs and benefits of underpricing?

   b. Will Jack underprice in the final period? If Jill can predict Jack's behavior in the last period, what will she do? What are the implications for the second period?

9. **Web Exercise.** Visit the Web site of the U.S. Federal Trade Commission to get the facts on the most recent price-fixing cases (*http://www.ftc.gov/*). Click on the Search icon, and do a search of News Releases using the words "price fixing." Write a brief description of three recent price-fixing cases.

10. **Web Exercise.** To check out the competition for your campus bookstore, visit the Web sites of a few Internet book sellers. (Here are some URLs: *http://www.eFollet.com, http://www.Varsitybooks.com,* and *http://www.Bigwords.com.*) How do the prices, including shipping charges, compare to those charged by the campus bookstore? What's the story on renting books instead of buying them?

Take It to the Net

We invite you to visit the O'Sullivan/Sheffrin page on the Prentice Hall Web site at:
http://www.prenhall.com/osullivan/
for additional World Wide Web exercises for this chapter.

Model Answers to Questions

Chapter-Opening Questions

1. It is likely to lead to higher prices because it eliminates the possibility of underpricing. The promise to issue refunds is an empty promise.

2. The price-fixing arrangement is more likely to persist if the airlines pick prices repeatedly over time, giving the airlines the opportunity to punish anyone who cheats on the price-fixing agreement.

3. The Internet gives consumers more opportunities to shop for low prices but also gives rival firms more opportunities to match prices and promote cartel pricing.

4. The growth of the off-campus firms threatens the campus bookstore monopoly, and the bookstore might cut its prices to prevent off-campus booksellers from extending their services to your town.

Test Your Understanding

1. *c, e.*

2. X, Z, 4, $5,000.

3. He will choose the low price and gain at Jill's expense.

4. Jack's promise is not credible because once Jill chooses the high price, he will earn more profit by choosing the low price. Jill should ignore the incredible promise and choose the low price.

5. $50 ($400 − $350).

6. They are common in appliance and electronics stores and in hardware stores. Many grocery stores honor the coupons of other stores. Although these schemes appear to be good news for consumers, they actually facilitate price-fixing and lead to higher prices.

7. The grim trigger makes profit zero, while the duopoly price leaves each firm with a positive profit. The costs of underpricing are higher with the grim trigger, so there is a greater incentive to charge the cartel price.

8. Two months. In the first month, Jill underprices Jack. In the second month, Jill chooses the high price but is underpriced by Jack, who is punishing her for underpricing him in the first month. In the third month, they both choose the high price.

9. Cost, benefit.

10. X, Y, 1.

11. If she chooses a small quantity, Dick will enter.

12. To prevent the entry of a second firm, an insecure monopolist commits itself to produce a large quantity of output and accepts a low price. A secure monopolist doesn't have to worry about other firms entering the market.

Using the Tools

2. Advertising and Price Fixing. The first option is the duopolist strategy. To prevent losing sales to Dee, Cecil could neutralize Dee's advertising campaign with an identical campaign of his own. Cecil and Dee would probably continue to sell about the same quantities at the same prices, but their profits would be lower because the advertising campaign costs money. The second option is a guaranteed price-matching scheme. Cecil could advertise the monopoly price and promise to match any lower price by Dee. If Dee recognizes the opportunity for price fixing, she will also advertise the monopoly price, and both firms will earn more profit.

3. Entry Deterrence. The profit from entry deterrence is $300 per day: Profit is the quantity (150) × the gap between price and average cost ($2 = $4 − $2). The profit from allowing entry is only $80 per day: The profit is the quantity (80) × the gap between price and average cost ($1 = $3 − $2). The deterrence strategy generates a higher price and a larger quantity with no change in average cost, so profits are higher.

Notes

1. Adam Smith, *The Wealth of Nations* (New York: Modern Library, 1994).

2. Sharon Walsh, "Six Airlines to Halt Advance Price Listing," *New York Times News Service*, printed in *The Oregonian*, March 18, 1994, p. B1.

3. George Stigler, "The Kinked Oligopoly Demand Curve and Rigid Prices," *Journal of Political Economy*, vol. 55, 1947, pp. 432–449.

4. "Big Friendly Giant," *The Economist*, January 30, 1999, p. 72.

5. Leonard W. Weiss, *Economics and American Industry* (New York: Wiley, 1963) pp. 189–204.

6. Thomas Whiteside, "Where Are They Now?" *New Yorker*, February 17, 1951, pp. 39–58.

Using Market Power: Price Discrimination and Advertising

The day after his 60th birthday, George took his granddaughter to the movies. He got a $3 senior-citizen discount for admission but paid the full price for popcorn. George's experience raises two questions about the pricing decisions of firms:

- Is a senior-citizen discount an act of generosity or an act of profit maximization?
- If a senior discount is sensible for admission to a movie, why isn't it sensible for popcorn?

 n Chapters 10 through 12, we saw that many firms have market power in the sense that their actions affect market prices. In this chapter, we take a closer look at the behavior of firms with market power. We'll explain why some firms charge different prices for different types of consumers. We'll also explore the firm's decision to advertise, and we'll look at the trade-offs—the costs and benefits—of advertising. Here are some practical questions that we'll answer:

1. **Why do faculty members pay more than students for on-campus movies?**
2. **Why are hardback books so much more expensive than paperback books?**
3. **How does a firm decide how many TV commercials to use?**
4. **Why have the prices of Internet banner advertisements (those bothersome promotional pitches at the top of Web pages) dropped in the last few years?**

Price Discrimination

Price discrimination: The process under which a firm divides consumers into two or more groups and picks a different price for each group.

Up to this point in the book, we've assumed that a firm charges the same price to all its consumers. In some markets, firms divide consumers into two or more groups and charge a different price to each group, a practice known as **price discrimination**. One approach is to offer a discount (resulting in a lower price) to some types of consumers. The firm identifies a group of customers who are not willing to pay the regular price and then offers a discount to people in that group.

Here are some examples of price discrimination with discounts for certain groups of consumers:

- Discounts on airline tickets for travelers who spend Saturday night away from home. An airline passenger who spends a Saturday night away from home is likely to be a tourist, not a business traveler. The typical tourist is not willing to pay as much for air travel as is the typical business traveler.

- Discount coupons for groceries and restaurant food. The typical coupon-clipper is not willing to pay as much as the typical consumer.

- Manufacturers' rebates for appliances. A person who takes the trouble to mail a rebate form to the manufacturer is not willing to pay as much as the typical consumer.

- Senior-citizen discounts on airline tickets, restaurant food, drugs, and entertainment.

- Student discounts on movies and concerts.

The only legal restriction on price discrimination is that a firm cannot use it to drive rival firms out of business.

Price discrimination is not always possible. A firm has an opportunity for price discrimination if three conditions are met:

1. **Market power.** The firm must have some control over its price. Therefore, price discrimination does not occur in a perfectly competitive market, in which each firm takes the market price as given.
2. **Different consumer groups.** Consumers must differ in their willingness to pay for the product or in their responsiveness to changes in price (as measured by the price elasticity of demand).
3. **Resale is not possible.** It must be impractical for one consumer to resell the product to another consumer. As a counterexample, suppose a bar sells drinks to women at a discount price and women can easily resell drinks to men. In this case,

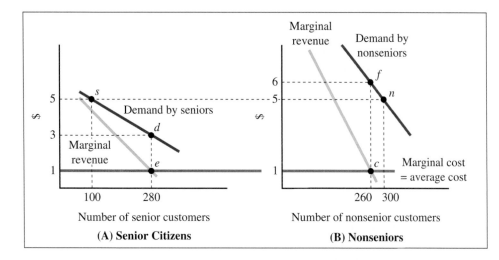

Figure 13.1
**Price
Discrimination**
A firm that picks a single
price of $5 (for both seniors
and nonseniors) reaches
point *n* on the nonsenior
demand curve (300 cus-
tomers) and point *s* on the
senior demand curve (100
customers). Under a price-
discrimination scheme, the
price for nonseniors is $6
(point *f*), and the price for
the seniors is $3 (point *d*).

(A) Senior Citizens

(B) Nonseniors

women are likely to buy extra drinks and sell them to men, so the bar won't sell
many drinks at the regular price and price discrimination won't be profitable. In
general, the possibility of resale causes price discrimination to break down, so a
firm will be better off with a single price.

Senior Discounts in Restaurants

Consider a restaurant whose patrons can be divided into two groups, senior citizens and
others. In Figure 13.1, the demand curve for senior citizens is lower than the demand
curve for other citizens, reflecting the assumption that the typical senior is willing to
pay less than the typical nonsenior.

What happens if the restaurant picks a single price for its meals, charging the same
amount to seniors and nonseniors? Suppose the most profitable single price is $5. If the
average cost of producing meals is constant at $1 per meal, the restaurant will make a
profit of $4 on each meal served. At a price of $5, the restaurant will have 100 senior customers (point *s*) and 300 nonsenior customers (point *n*). As shown in Table 13.1, the
firm gets a profit of $400 from seniors and $1,200 from nonseniors, for a total profit of
$1,600.

Under a price-discrimination scheme, the restaurant will divide its customers into
two groups and offer a lower price to senior citizens. This is sensible because the two

Table 13.1 A Senior Discount Increases Total Profit

	Single Price Policy		Senior Discount	
	Seniors	Nonseniors	Seniors	Nonseniors
Price	$5	$5	$3	$6
Average cost per meal	$1	$1	$1	$1
Profit per meal	$4	$4	$2	$5
Number of meals	100 meals	300 meals	280 meals	260 meals
Profit	$400	$1,200	$560	$1,300
Total profit	$1,600		$1,860	

groups have different demands for restaurant meals, so the restaurant should treat them differently. Panel A of Figure 13.1 shows how to pick a price for senior citizens. The marginal principle (marginal revenue = marginal cost) is satisfied at point e, with 280 senior meals per day. Therefore, the appropriate price for seniors is $3 (point d on the senior demand curve). The profit per senior meal is $2 (the $3 price minus the $1 average cost), and the restaurant's profit from its senior customers is $560 per day ($2 per meal times 280 meals). The senior discount increases the restaurant's profit from its senior customers from $400 to $560.

We can also use the marginal principle to find the appropriate price for nonseniors. In panel B of Figure 13.1, the marginal principle is satisfied at point c, with 260 nonsenior meals per day. Therefore, the restaurant should charge $6 for nonseniors (point f on the demand curve). The profit per nonsenior meal is $5 (the $6 price minus the $1 average cost) and the restaurant's profit from nonseniors is $1,300 per day ($5 per meal $\times$ 260 meals). The higher price for nonseniors increases the restaurant's profits from its nonsenior customers from $1,200 to $1,300.

By treating the two groups of consumers differently, the restaurant can earn more profit. The switch from a single-price policy to price discrimination generates a lower price for seniors and a higher price for nonseniors. The switch in pricing increases the restaurant's profit in both segments of the market, and its total profit increases from $1,600 to $1,860 per day.

Price Discrimination and the Elasticity of Demand

We can use the concept of price elasticity of demand to explain why price discrimination increases the restaurant's profit. Compared to other consumers, senior citizens have more elastic demand for restaurant meals, in part because they have lower income and more time to shop around for low prices. Starting with the single-price policy, the demand for restaurant meals by seniors is elastic, while the demand by nonseniors is inelastic. What are the implications for the switch to the new pricing scheme, with a higher price for nonseniors and a lower price for seniors?

A higher price for nonseniors, who have inelastic demand, increases the restaurant's profit. We know from Chapter 5 that if demand is inelastic, an increase in price will increase total revenue: The good news (more revenue per customer) dominates the bad news (fewer customers). Therefore, an increase in the nonsenior price will increase the revenue from nonseniors. At the same time, the higher price means that the restaurant will serve fewer meals to nonsenior customers, so the restaurant's production costs will decrease. Because the restaurant's nonsenior revenue increases while the cost of serving nonseniors decreases, profit from nonseniors will increase.

A lower price for senior customers, who have elastic demand, increases the restaurant's profit. We know that if demand is elastic, a decrease in price will increase total revenue: The good news (more customers) dominates the bad news (less revenue per customer). At the same time, the lower price means the restaurant will serve more meals to seniors, so the restaurant's total cost will increase. If demand is very elastic, the increase in revenue will more than offset the increase in total cost and the restaurant's profit from senior citizens will increase.

The same logic applies to other cases of price discrimination. A firm will charge a higher price to consumers with relatively inelastic demand. For example, local pharmacies pay up to five times as much as hospitals for common drugs.[1] The demand for drugs by pharmacies is relatively inelastic because pharmacies stock a wide variety of drugs to fill individual prescriptions, and they buy much smaller quantities of each drug. The inelastic demand by pharmacies encourages pharmaceutical firms to discriminate

In the 1980s, the worst place to buy a Korean TV set was Korea, where consumers paid 52% more than their U.S. counterparts paid for identical Korean sets.[2] Why did Korean firms charge their fellow citizens so much more for TV sets?

The Korean firms engaged in price discrimination, selling for a higher price in the market that had relatively inelastic demand. Demand was inelastic in Korea because the firms had a virtual monopoly in the home market: Koreans did not have the option of buying imported TV sets, so they were not very responsive to changes in the price of Korean TV sets. In contrast, the Korean firms competed with dozens of firms in the U.S. market, so demand in the U.S. market was relatively elastic. Korean firms discriminated against their fellow citizens because they had inelastic demand.

As a result of price discrimination by Korean producers, Korean consumers paid 52% more than U.S. consumers for identical TV sets.

against them. For an example of international price discrimination, read "A Closer Look: International Price Discrimination: Korean TV Sets."

Application: Movie Admission and Popcorn

We're ready to answer the two questions in the opening paragraph of the chapter. A senior discount for movie admission is not an act of generosity by a firm, but part of the firm's pricing strategy designed to increase profit. Senior citizens are typically willing to pay less than other citizens for movies, so a theater divides its consumers into two groups—seniors and others—and offers a discount to seniors. This price discrimination in favor of senior citizens increases the theater's profit.

Why don't theaters offer a senior discount for popcorn? Unlike admission to the theater, popcorn can be easily transferred from one customer to another. If senior citizens could buy popcorn at half the regular price, many nonseniors would get seniors to buy popcorn for them, so the theater wouldn't sell as much popcorn at the regular price. Price discrimination for popcorn would not be profitable.

Why Are Hardback Books So Expensive?

ECONOMIC DETECTIVE

Most novels are published in two forms—hardback and paperback—the paperback edition being published and available for sale several weeks or months later than the hardback edition. The cost of producing a hardback book is only about 20% higher than the cost of producing the same book as a paperback, but the price of a hardback book is about three times the price of a paperback book. Why is the price difference so large when the cost difference is so small?

The key to solving this puzzle is the fact that hardback books are published first, followed by the paperback edition. Booksellers use hardbacks and paperbacks to distinguish between two types of consumers: those who are willing to pay a lot and those who are willing to pay a little. The people who are willing to pay the most are eager to read the book as soon as it comes out, so they pay $18 for a hardback book. The people who are willing to pay less are more patient and are willing to wait a few weeks for the $6 paperback version. The pricing of hardback and paperback books is another example of price discrimination, with consumers with less elastic demand paying a higher price. ◆

TEST Your Understanding

1. Why is aspirin sold in airports so much more expensive than aspirin sold in grocery stores?

2. Complete the statement with "increase" or "decrease": Suppose a firm starts with a single price and then switches to a price-discrimination scheme. The firm will _____ the price for the group of consumers with relatively inelastic demand and _____ the group with relatively elastic demand.

3. Many cocktail lounges and bars that have cover charges have lower cover charges for women than for men. Why?

Advertising

In most modern economies, firms spend enormous amounts of money on advertising to increase the demand for their products. In the United States, firms spend about $45 billion each year on television advertisements, and much more on print advertisements in newspapers and magazines. The total spending on Internet advertising is about $3 billion per year and growing rapidly.

Advertising and the Marginal Principle

How do firms decide how much to spend on advertising and where to spend it? Consider a producer of laundry detergent that has decided to advertise on television. The firm can use the marginal principle to decide how many 30-second slots to buy each week.

MARGINAL PRINCIPLE

Increase the level of an activity if its marginal benefit exceeds its marginal cost, but reduce the level if the marginal cost exceeds the marginal benefit. If possible, pick the level at which the marginal benefit equals the marginal cost.

The marginal benefit of advertising depends on how many more boxes of detergent are sold as a result of the TV ad. The second column of Table 13.2 shows the quantities of detergent sold with different numbers of TV ads. If the firm does not advertise, it sells 100,000 boxes. As the number of ads increases, so does the quantity sold: from 110,000 for one ad, to 119,000 for two ads, and so on. The marginal benefit of advertising (shown in the third column) is the change in quantity sold resulting from the last ad times the firm's net revenue (revenue less cost) per unit sold. Let's assume that the net revenue is $1 per box. The first ad increases the quantity sold by 10,000 boxes, so the marginal ben-

Table 13.2   Advertising and the Marginal Principle

Number of Advertisements	Quantity of Detergent Sold (Boxes)	Marginal Benefit (Assuming Net Revenue of $1 per Box)	Marginal Cost
0	100,000		
1	110,000	$10,000	$7,000
2	119,000	$9,000	$7,000
3	127,000	$8,000	$7,000
4	134,000	$7,000	$7,000
5	140,000	$6,000	$7,000
6	145,000	$5,000	$7,000

efit of the first ad is $10,000. Moving down the third column, the marginal benefit decreases to $9,000 for the second ad, $8,000 for the third ad, and so on.

Before we can use the marginal principle, we must determine the marginal cost of advertising. In our example, the marginal cost is simply the price of each 30-second advertising slot. In the last column of Table 13.2, the marginal cost is constant at $7,000 per slot. According to the marginal principle, the firm should buy 4 ads, because that's the number at which the marginal benefit equals the marginal cost. Starting with any smaller quantity, the marginal benefit of another ad exceeds the cost, so an additional ad would increase the firm's profit.

What sort of firms will advertise? For advertising to be profitable, the increase in sales must be large relative to the cost of advertising, meaning that consumers' choices must be sensitive to advertising. Several brands of laundry detergent are close but not perfect substitutes, and advertising causes many consumers to switch from one brand to another. The same is true for pain medications: Advertising causes consumers to switch among Tylenol, Advil, Bayer Aspirin, and Excedrin. Some other examples of heavily advertised products are cough medicines, antacids, and cold remedies. In contrast, there is little to be gained from advertisements for standardized goods such as wheat or notebook paper.

The Prices of Advertising Slots

A firm that has decided to launch an advertising campaign must decide where and when to run the advertisements. A firm advertising on radio or television must decide when to run the ad. A firm advertising in newspapers or on the World Wide Web must decide where to place the ad in the newspaper or on the Web. If the prices were the same for all ad slots (all times and locations), the firm's decision would be simple: Pick the slot that generates the greatest exposure to potential customers.

Of course, the prices of advertising slots vary, being determined by the laws of supply and demand. Advertisers are willing to pay the most for slots that have the biggest audience, so the price for television advertising slots is highest during the most popular programs. The most expensive slots are during major sporting events such as the Super Bowl and the Academy Awards; the least expensive slots are for the early morning hours (3:00 A.M. to 5:00 A.M.), when most consumers are asleep. For an example of how the prices of advertising slots change over time, read "A Closer Look: Internet Banner Advertising."

A CLOSER LOOK | Internet Banner Advertising

How much does it cost to place an advertisement on a Web page? In 1999, the average price of a banner advertisement—a promotional pitch at the top of a Web page—was $35 per 1,000 "impressions," the number of times an advertisement appears on a computer screen as part of a Web page.[3] For example, if the Web page on which your banner ad appeared got 10,000 hits in a week, your advertising bill would be $350.

The price of banner advertisements fell during 1998 and 1999, a result of changes on both sides of the market. The proliferation of Web sites increased the number of sites available for banner ads, and competition among sellers pulled down the price. Some new Web sites even provided free advertising in an attempt to demonstrate their marketing worth to potential clients. On the demand side, the percentage of Web users who click on advertisements—and thus access the advertising information—decreased from 2.5 percent to 0.5 percent. The fewer the clicks, the fewer the consumers seeing the information, so the smaller the benefit of a banner ad in terms of increased sales. As a result, the amount that advertisers were willing to pay for a banner ad dropped.

The Missing Ads for Generic Drugs

ECONOMIC DETECTIVE

The sellers of brand-name pain medication (such as Bayer Aspirin, Tylenol, Advil, Excedrin) spend millions of dollars every year on advertising. The same is true for the manufacturers of brand-name cough syrup and cold medications. But the sellers of generic versions of these products—which are chemically equivalent—do not advertise at all. Why?

The key to solving this mystery is to recognize the difference between the consumers of generics and the consumers of branded products. The potential purchasers of generic drugs recognize the chemical equivalence of generic and branded drugs, so they are sensitive to price and generally pick the product with the lowest price. An advertisement for a generic aspirin wouldn't increase sales by very much. In fact, if a producer of a generic product increased the price of its product to cover the costs of an advertising campaign, the quantity sold might actually decrease. In contrast, the consumers of branded drugs and medications are sensitive to advertising and less sensitive to price, so advertising increases total sales, even if the price of a branded drug increases to cover the cost of advertising.

The Advertisers' Dilemma

Up to this point, we have looked at a firm's decision to advertise in isolation, without considering the possible responses of rival firms. What happens when a second firm selling a competing product has the opportunity to react to the first firm's advertising campaign? In Chapter 12, we used game trees to explore the interdependence of firms concerning pricing and market entry. We can use the same tool to look at interactions concerning advertising. As we'll see, firms might get caught in an advertisers' dilemma: Although each firm would be better off if neither advertised, both firms advertise.

Consider the producers of two brands of aspirin. Each firm must decide whether to spend $7 million on an advertising campaign for its product. In Table 13.3, the first two columns of numbers show what happens if neither firm advertises. Each earns $8 million in net revenue (revenue minus production costs) and spends no money on advertising, so the profit per firm is $8 million. The third and fourth columns of numbers show what happens if each firm spends $7 million on advertising. Net revenue increases from

Table 13.3 Advertising and Profit

	Neither Advertises		Both Advertise		Jack Advertises	
	Jack	Jill	Jack	Jill	Jack	Jill
Net revenue from sales ($ million)	8	8	13	13	17	5
Cost of advertising ($ million)	0	0	7	7	7	0
Profit ($ million)	8	8	6	6	10	5

$8 million to $13 million, a benefit of $5 million. The benefit of advertising ($5 million) is less than the cost ($7 million), so the profit earned by each firm falls, from $8 million to $6 million.

What happens if one firm advertises and the other does not? The last two columns of numbers in Table 13.3 show that advertising is profitable for the advertising firm. If Jack spends $7 million on advertising and Jill spends nothing, Jack's net revenue increases from $8 million to $17 million. The benefit of advertising (a $9 million increase in net revenue) exceeds the $7 million cost, so Jack's profit increases to $10 million ($17 million − $7 million).

Jack's advertising allows him to gain at Jill's expense. Jack's advertising causes some of Jill's consumers to switch to Jack, and Jill's net revenue drops from $8 million to $5 million. Jill's profit falls from $8 million to $5 million.

We can use the data in Table 13.3 to construct a game tree for the advertising game. In Figure 13.2, Jack makes his decision first, followed by Jill.

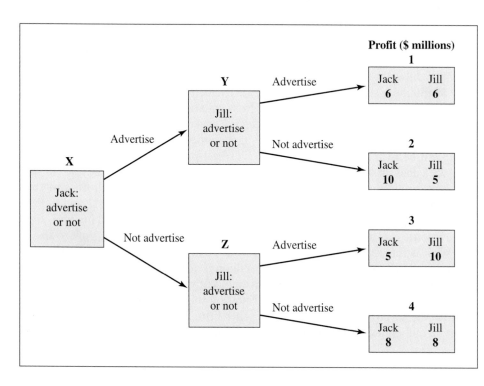

Figure 13.2
Game Tree for Advertisers' Dilemma
Jack moves first, choosing to advertise or not. Jill's best response is to advertise no matter what Jack does. Knowing this, Jack realizes that the only possible outcomes are shown by rectangles 1 and 3. From Jack's perspective, rectangle 1 ($6 million) is better than rectangle 3 ($5 million), so his best response is to advertise too. Both Jack and Jill advertise, and each earns a profit of $6 million.

Some types of advertising are wasteful because the campaign of one firm simply cancels out the campaign of another firm.

- If neither firm advertises, we go from square X to square Z to rectangle 4, and the payoff (profit) is $8 million for each firm.

- If both firms advertise, we go from square X to square Y to rectangle 1, and each firm earns a profit of $6 million.

- If Jack advertises and Jill does not, we go from square X to square Y to rectangle 2, and Jack earns $10 million, while Jill earns $5 million. If the roles are reversed, we end up in rectangle 3, with Jill the advertiser earning $10 million, while Jack earns $5 million.

What is the outcome of this advertising game? Suppose Jack decides to advertise, meaning that we move along the upper branches of the game tree from square X to square Y. Jill will earn $6 if she matches Jack's advertising campaign (rectangle 1) but only $5 million if she does not (rectangle 2). The best response is to match Jack's campaign. If Jack does not advertise, we go from square X to square Z, and Jill chooses between rectangle 3 and rectangle 4. Jill can use advertising to take sales away from her rival Jack, earning a profit of $10 million in the process. If she does not advertise, her profit will be $8 million. To summarize, Jill's best response is to advertise no matter what Jack does. In other words, for Jill, advertising is a dominant strategy.

Jack can figure out that advertising is a dominant strategy for Jill. Knowing this, Jack realizes that the only possible outcomes are shown by rectangles 1 and 3. From Jack's perspective, rectangle 1 ($6 million) is better than rectangle 3 ($5 million), so his best response is to advertise too. Both firms advertise, and each earns a profit of $6.

What is the advertisers' dilemma? Both Jack and Jill would be better off if neither advertised: Each would get a profit of $8 million if neither advertised, compared to $6 million when both advertise. Each firm has an incentive to use advertising to increase its net revenue at the expense of the other. Knowing this, each firm spends $7 million to counter the advertising campaign of the other firm. Stuck in the dilemma, each firm earns $2 million less than it would if neither advertised.

The advertisers' dilemma occurs when advertising causes a relatively small increase in the total sales of the industry but allows a firm that advertises to gain at the expense of firms that don't advertise. In our example, a pair of advertising campaigns costing a total of $14 million increases the industry's net revenue by only $10 million—from $16 million ($8 million each) to $26 million ($13 million each). If the increase in industry net revenue were larger, advertising could benefit both firms. We'll see an example of that type of advertising in the Using the Tools exercise, "Got Milk?"

Trade-Offs from Advertising

What are the trade-offs associated with advertising? There is no doubt that advertising influences consumer choices; otherwise, firms would not spend billions of dollars each year on it. What do firms and consumers get for the billions of dollars worth of resources used for advertising? Let's take a look at some of the issues in the spirited debate over the merits of advertising.

One benefit of advertising is that it helps consumers to make informed decisions. Some advertisements contain factual information about product characteristics, and this information helps consumers to choose among products that are similar but not identical. For example, a car advertisement that discloses the car's fuel efficiency could help a fuel-conscious consumer to make a decision about what car to buy. Advertisements can also help by providing information about where to go to buy a product.

Another benefit is that advertising provides consumers with information on the prices and promotes competition. The market for eyeglasses provides a test of the effects of advertising on prices. Some states outlaw advertising for eyeglasses, while most allow it. One study found that states that outlawed advertising for eyeglasses had eyeglass prices that were 20% higher than prices in states that allowed advertising.[4] Advertising promotes competition by providing new firms with a means of quickly and efficiently spreading information about their products. This encourages firms to enter profitable markets, leading to lower prices.

The game tree shown in Figure 13.2 shows one possible negative aspect of advertising. If the industry's net revenue increases by an amount that is less than the cost of the advertising campaigns, advertising will decrease profit. In this case, the two firms are trapped in an advertisers' dilemma. Because the advertising campaigns cancel out each other, the resources used in the advertising campaigns—workers' time, raw materials, and equipment—are wasted.

On the negative side, some advertisements give the impression that there are real differences between products when there are none. The purpose of some advertising is to establish an image or aura for the product. Many advertisements for beer, soft drinks, cigarettes, and designer jeans don't discuss ingredients and other features of product. Instead, they show people having a wonderful time while drinking, smoking, or wearing the product. The message is that people who use product are more popular and happy, and you too could be more popular and happy if you consumed the product.

We can summarize the trade-offs from advertising as follows: In some cases, advertising campaigns of rival firms simply cancel each other out, so the resources used in the process are wasted. In other cases, the purpose of advertising is to suggest there are differences in products when there are none or to establish an image or aura for the product. On the other hand, advertising can provide information about product characteristics, prices, and locations, and help consumers to make informed decisions. Some types of advertising promote competition and decrease prices.

TEST Your Understanding

4. In Table 13.2, suppose the cost of a 30-second TV ad increases to $9,500. How many ads should the firm use?

5. In Table 13.2, suppose the net revenue per box of detergent decreases to $0.80. How many ads should the firm use?

6. If the percentage of Web users who click on advertisements increased, how would that affect the price of Internet banner ads?

Using the TOOLS

In this chapter, we've seen examples of firms using their market power to increase their profit. Many firms charge different prices to different types of consumers, a practice known as price discrimination. Firms spend billions of dollars each year on advertising, with the idea of increasing the demand for their products and their profit. Here are some opportunities to do your own economic analysis.

1. ECONOMIC EXPERIMENT: Price Discrimination

Here is an experiment that shows how a monopolist—a museum—picks different prices for different consumer groups. Some students play the roles of consumers, and others play the roles of museum managers. Here is how the experiment works:

- The instructor picks a small group of students (three to five) to represent the museum. There is a fixed marginal cost of each museum patron (for ticket-takers, guides, cleanup, and other tasks).
- There are 40 consumers (potential museum patrons), and half the consumers are senior citizens with senior-citizen cards. Each consumer receives a number indicating how much he or she is willing to pay for a trip to a museum.
- In each round of the experiment, each museum posts two prices: one for senior citizens and one for nonseniors. Consumers then decide whether to buy a ticket at the relevant posted price.
- A consumer's score in a particular round equals the difference between his or her willingness to pay and the amount actually paid for a museum admission.
- A museum's score equals its profit, equal to its total revenue minus its total cost ($2 times the number of patrons).
- The experiment is run for five rounds. At the end of the experiment, each consumer computes his or her score by adding up his or her consumer surpluses. The museum's score equals the sum of the profits from the five rounds.

2. Price Discrimination in a Campus Film Series

You manage a campus film series and charge different prices to students and faculty members. The current prices and numbers of viewers are as follows:

	Price	Number of viewers	Slope of demand curve
Students	$3	100	$0.01 per viewer
Faculty	$4	50	$0.10 per viewer

The marginal cost of another viewer is zero. Does the current pricing scheme maximize your total revenue? If not, how should you change your prices?

3. Pricing First-Run Movies and Early Apples

If you see a movie when it first comes out, you pay much more than you would if you waited a month or two for the movie to appear at a second-run movie theater. If you buy apples early in the harvest season, you pay more than you would if you waited until the middle of the harvest season. Are both movies and apples subject to price discrimination?

4. Picking a Web Page for a Banner Ad

You sell books on the Internet, and your net revenue is 20% of total sales revenue. You are looking for a Web page on which to place a banner advertisement and have narrowed your choices to 2 pages with the following characteristics:

	Web Page A	Web Page B
Clicks per 1,000 impressions	50	30
Average income of viewers	$2,000	$5,000
Price per 1,000 impressions	$35	$35

One of every 10 people who actually see your advertisement (after clicking on the banner ad) order some books, and the average order is 2% of the customer's monthly income. Which of the two Web pages should you choose for your banner ad?

5. Advertising with Spillover Benefits: Got Milk?

Bessie and George are milk producers, and each must decide whether to spend $7 million on an advertising campaign. If neither advertises, each will earn $10 million in net revenue from sales (net revenue). If both advertise, each will earn $20 million in net revenue and $13 million in profit ($20 million – $7 million for advertising). If only one producer advertises, that firm will earn $16 million in net revenue, and the other firm will earn $15 million in net revenue. Prepare a game tree like Figure 13.2 (assume that Bessie decides first) and predict the outcome of this advertising game. If there is an advertisers' dilemma, how does it differ from the advertisers' dilemma discussed earlier in the chapter? How might the dairy industry solve this dilemma? (*Hint:* Think white mustaches.)

 ## Summary

In this chapter, we've seen two ways in which firms use their market power to increase their profits. Many firms charge different prices to different types of consumers, a practice known as price discrimination. Firms spend billions of dollars per year on advertising, with the idea of increasing the demand for their products and their profit. Here are the main points of the chapter:

1. To engage in price discrimination, a firm divides its customers into two or more groups and charges lower prices to groups with more elastic demand.

2. Price discrimination is not an act of generosity; it's an act of profit maximization.

3. A firm can use the marginal principle to decide how many advertisements to purchase.

4. Rival firms may get caught in an advertisers' dilemma: Although each would be better off if neither advertised, both advertise.

5. The prices of advertising slots are determined by supply and demand; the most expensive slots are the ones with the greatest exposure to potential consumers.

Key Terms

price discrimination, 276

Problems and Discussion Questions

1. Consider an airline that initially has a single price ($300) for all consumers. At this price, it has 120 business travelers and 80 tourists. The airline's marginal cost is $100. The slope of the business demand curve is –$2 per traveler and the slope of the tourist demand curve is –$1 per traveler. Does the single-price policy maximize the airline's profit? If not, how should it change its prices?

2. Comment on the following statement from a member of a city council: "Several of the merchants in our city offer discounts to our senior citizens. These discounts obviously decrease the merchants' profits, and we should decrease the merchants' taxes to offset their losses on senior-citizen discounts."

3. An advertisement for an early-bird sale at a fabric store notes that people who buy fabric between 6:00 and 7:00 A.M. receive a 40% discount, and people who shop between 7:00 and 8:00 A.M. receive a 20% discount. What is the rationale for such a pricing scheme?

4. Why are senior-citizen discounts common for services such as admission to museums and other entertainment but uncommon for consumer goods such as hardware, appliances, and automobiles?

5. Car companies offer many options on new cars, including automatic transmissions, CD players, leather trim, and heated seats. The markup on these options (the difference between the price consumers pay and the cost incurred by the car company) is higher for leather trim and CD players than it is for automatic transmissions. Why?

6. Your bicycle shop makes a profit of $20 on each bike sold. Advertisements on the local radio station cost $250 per 30-second slot. If you don't advertise, you'll sell 200 bikes per month. The first advertisement will increase sales by 80 bikes (from 200 to 280), and each additional ad will increase bike sales by half as much as the previous ad: The second ad increases sales by 40 bikes, the third increases sales by 20 bikes, and so on. How many radio ads should you purchase?

7. Comment on the following rule for advertising: "You should increase your advertising budget as long as one additional dollar of advertising increases your sales by at least one dollar."

8. Consider two automobile companies that are considering advertising campaigns. If neither firm advertises, each will earn net revenue of $5 million. If each spends $10 million on advertising, each firm's net revenue will be $12 million. If one advertises and the other does not, the firm that advertises will earn $17 million in net revenue, while the firm that does not will earn $1 million. Draw a game tree and predict the outcome. From the industry perspective, do the benefits of advertising exceed the costs?

9. **Web Exercise.** Visit the Web site of CouponNet, an organization that provides information on all sorts of coupons (*http://www.couponnet.com/*). Click on "Coupons" in the main menu to see a list of coupons available through this site and others. Are there any free coupons? You can get packets of coupons mailed to you. How much do firms providing these coupon packs charge?

10. **Web Exercise.** Visit the Web site of the Manitoba Milk Producers (*http://www.milk.mb.ca/*). What sort of promotion does this association do. Why do the producers of milk band together to advertise milk rather than staging individual advertising campaigns?

Take It to the Net

We invite you to visit the O'Sullivan/Sheffrin page on the Prentice Hall Web site at:
http://www.prenhall.com/osullivan/
for additional World Wide Web exercises for this chapter.

Model Answers to Questions

Chapter-Opening Questions

1. Compared to students, faculty members are willing to pay more for campus movies (their demand is less elastic), so a profit-maximizing monopolist will charge them a higher price.

2. Consumers who are eager to read a book are willing to pay more, so they buy the expensive hardback version because it comes out first. People who are willing to pay less wait for the cheaper paperback version a few months later.

3. Using the marginal principle, the firm picks the number of ads at which the marginal benefit (the increase in net sales revenue) equals the marginal cost (the cost per ad).

4. Supply has increased as Web sites have proliferated, and the willingness to pay has decreased because a smaller percentage of people are clicking on the banner ads.

Test Your Understanding

1. People looking for aspirin in airports usually have a headache or expect one. They are willing to pay more than a headache-free grocery shopper: The airport shopper has a less elastic demand. Firms engage in price discrimination, charging a higher price to the group of consumers with the less elastic demand (airport customers).

2. Increase, decrease.

3. If women are willing to pay less than men for admission into a cocktail lounge or bar (they have a more elastic demand), price discrimination may increase the bar's profit. A discounted cover charge works well because the good purchased (admission) cannot be transferred to men.

4. One ad. The marginal benefit of the first ad exceeds the higher marginal cost, but the marginal benefit of the second ad ($9,000) is less than the marginal cost.

5. Two ads. The marginal benefit of the first ad is $8,000, and the marginal benefit of the second ad is $7,200, compared to a marginal cost of $7,000. The marginal benefit of the third ad is only $6,400, which is less than the marginal cost.

6. The price will increase. The more clickers, the greater the consumer exposure to banner ads, so the larger the increase in sales and the more money an advertiser is willing to pay for a banner ad.

Using the Tools

2. Price Discrimination in a Campus Film Series. We can use the formula for marginal revenue (explained in Chapter 10) to compute the marginal revenue for the two types of consumers. At the current prices, the marginal revenue for students is $2 = $3 − (100 viewers × $0.01 per viewer), which exceeds the marginal cost, so you should decrease the price for students. In contrast, the marginal revenue for faculty is −$1 = $4 − (50 viewers × $0.10 per viewer). Marginal revenue is negative, so an increase in price for faculty will increase total revenue.

3. Pricing First-Run Movies and Early Apples. The price pattern for movies is another example of price discrimination. Eager moviegoers are willing to pay a large amount of money for a movie when it first comes out, while patient moviegoers are willing to wait for the movie to appear in a second-run theater at a lower price.

   The price pattern for apples is unlikely to be a case of price discrimination because the apple market is perfectly competitive: Each farmer takes the market price as given. Price discrimination isn't possible unless the firm has some control over its price. The price pattern for apples reflects the forces of supply and demand: Early in the harvest season, there aren't many apples available for sale, so the equilibrium price is relatively high. As supply increases over the course of the harvest season, the price drops. At the end of the season, the price rises again.

4. Picking a Web Page for a Banner Ad. The following table shows how to compute the net benefits for each Web page. If one of ten clickers purchases something, the number of orders (per 1,000 impressions) is 5 for A and 3 for B. If each customer spends 2% of his or her income, the average order is $40 for A and $100 for B. Total revenue equals the number of orders times the amount of the average order, and the net revenue equals 20% of total revenue. The net revenue is $40 for A and $60 for B, so the net benefit for A is $5 and the net benefit for B is $25. B is a better choice.

	Page A	Page B
Clicks per 1,000 impressions	50	30
Income of viewers	$2,000	$5,000
Orders	5	3
Average order	$40	$100
Revenue	$200	$300
Net revenue	$40	$60
Cost per 1,000 impressions	$35	$35
Net benefit	$5	$25

5. Advertising with Spillover Benefits: Got Milk? Figure 13.A shows the game tree. For George (the second mover), not advertising is a dominant strategy. If Bessie advertises, George earns a profit of $15 if he does not advertise, compared to only $13 if he does. If Bessie does not advertise, George earns of profit of $10 if he does not advertise, compared to $9 if he does. Knowing that George will not advertise no matter what she does, Bessie's best response is not to advertise: She earns a profit of $10 if she does not advertise, compared to $9 if she does. The advertisers' dilemma is that each firm would benefit if both firms advertised: Each would earn a profit of $13 million instead of $10 million, but neither will advertise. In this case, there are spillover benefits from advertising, while in the earlier example, the advertising campaign of one firm reduced the net revenue of a nonadvertising firm. An industry association might form to solve this problem by providing general advertising for milk, each firm sharing the cost of the campaign. The next time you see one of those "Got Milk?" advertisements, check to see who pays for it.

Figure 13.A
Game Tree for Advertising with Spillover Benefits

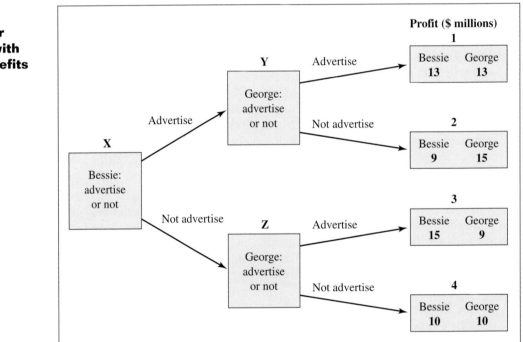

Notes

1. William Comanor and Stuart O. Schweitzer, "Pharmaceuticals," Chapter 7 in *The Structure of the American Economy*, 9th ed., edited by Walter Adams and James W. Brock (Upper Saddle River, NJ: Prentice Hall, 1995).

2. Taeho Bark, "The Korean Consumer Electronics Industry: Reaction to Antidumping Actions," Chapter 7 in *Antidumping: How It Works and Who Gets Hurt*, edited by J. Michael Finger (Ann Arbor, MI: University of Michigan Press, 1993).

3. Andrea Petersen, "Price of Internet Banner Ads Starts to Fall," *Wall Street Journal*, February 24, 1999, p. B8.

4. Benham, Lee, "The Effects of Advertising on the Price of Eyeglasses," *Journal of Law and Economics*, vol. 15, 1972, pp. 337–352.

Controlling Market Power: Antitrust Policy and Deregulation

Dwayne started his company, a small Internet service provider (ISP), a few years ago with some college buddies. After three years of losing money while he worked out the kinks and learned how to market his services, he expects his company finally to earn a modest profit this year. You can imagine his dismay as he reads in the ISP newsletter that corporate giants AT&T and TCI plan to provide Internet access at much faster speeds than is possible along the phone lines used by independent ISPs like Dwayne's. The newsletter urges ISPs to write to their representatives in Washington, D.C. to express their views. The newsletter also urges ISPs to contribute money to support a lobbying effort in the nation's capital. Should Dwayne write a letter and send some money?

his chapter explores two policy issues concerning firms in concentrated markets. We'll start with a look at antitrust policies, which are designed to promote competition in markets dominated by a few large firms. Under federal antitrust rules, the government can break up monopolies into several smaller companies, prevent corporate mergers that would reduce competition, and regulate business practices that tend to reduce competition. The second policy issue is deregulation. We'll discuss recent deregulation of two markets: air travel and telecommunications. In both cases, the government recently reversed a long history of regulation in an attempt to promote competition. Here are some practical policy questions that we answer:

1. **Why did the government prevent the proposed merger between Office Depot and Staples, two office-supply chains?**
2. **What was the government's antitrust case against Microsoft Corporation all about?**
3. **How did the deregulation of air travel affect the price of air travel?**
4. **How will the development of high-speed cable modems affect the markets for Internet access?**

Antitrust Policy

The purpose of antitrust policy is to promote competition among firms, with the idea that competition leads to lower prices and better products. Table 14.1 provides a brief summary of the history of antitrust policy. The first legislation was the Sherman Antitrust Act of 1890, which made it illegal to monopolize a market or to engage in practices that result in a restraint of trade. Because the act did not specify which practices were illegal, it led to conflicting court rulings.

Many of the ambiguities of the Sherman Act were resolved by the Clayton Act of 1914. The Clayton Act outlawed specific practices that discourage competition, including tying contracts (requiring a consumer who buys one product to buy a second product) and price discrimination that reduces competition. The act also outlawed mergers resulting from the purchase of a competitor's stock when such a merger would substantially reduce competition. Also in 1914, the government established the Federal Trade Commission to enforce antitrust laws.

Table 14.1 Brief History of Antitrust Legislation

1890	Sherman Act: Made it illegal to monopolize a market or to engage in practices that result in a restraint of trade.
1914	Clayton Act: Outlawed specific practices that discourage competition, including tying contracts, price discrimination for the purpose of reducing competition, and stock-purchase mergers that would substantially reduce competition.
1914	Federal Trade Commission Act: Established to enforce antitrust laws.
1936	Robinson-Patman Act: Prohibited selling products at "unreasonably low prices" with the intent of reducing competition.
1950	Celler-Kefauver Act: Outlawed asset-purchase mergers that would substantially reduce competition.
1980	Hart-Scott-Rodino Act: Extended antitrust legislation to proprietorships and partnerships.

More recent legislation has clarified and extended antitrust law. The Robinson-Patman Act of 1936 prohibited selling products at unreasonably low prices with the intent of reducing competition, a practice known as predatory pricing. The Celler-Kefauver Act of 1950 closed a loophole in the Clayton Act by outlawing mergers through the purchase of another firm's physical assets (for example, buildings and equipment) when such a merger would reduce competition substantially. The Hart-Scott-Rodino Act of 1980 extended antitrust legislation to proprietorships and partnerships. Before this act, antitrust legislation applied only to corporations.

Two government organizations, the Antitrust Division of the Department of Justice, and the Federal Trade Commission, are responsible for initiating actions against individuals or firms that may be violating antitrust laws. The courts have the power to impose penalties on the executives found to be in violation of the laws, including fines and prison sentences. In some cases, the government seeks no penalties but directs the firm to discontinue illegal practices and take other measures to promote competition.

Breaking Up Monopolies

One form of antitrust policy is to break up a monopoly into several smaller firms. A **trust** is an arrangement under which the owners of several companies transfer their decision-making powers to a small group of trustees, who then make decisions for all the participating firms. Firms in a trust act as a single firm, so an industry that appears to have many firms may in fact be a virtual monopoly.

Trust: An arrangement under which the owners of several companies transfer their decision-making powers to a small group of trustees, who then make decisions for all the firms in the trust.

The label *antitrust* comes from early cases that involved breaking up trusts. The classic example is John D. Rockefeller's Standard Oil Trust, which was formed in 1882 when the owners of 40 oil companies empowered nine trustees to make the decisions for all 40 companies. The trust controlled over 90 percent of the market for refined petroleum products, and the trustees ran it like a monopoly. In 1911, the government ordered the breakup of the Standard Oil Trust. The Supreme Court found that Rockefeller had used "unnatural methods" to maintain his monopoly power and drive his rivals out of business. He coerced railroads to give him special rates for shipping and spied on his competitors. The government broke up Standard Oil into 34 separate companies, including the corporate ancestors to Exxon, Mobil, Chevron, and Amoco.

After the American Tobacco Company bought 30 of its competitors, it controlled 95% of the U.S. cigarette market. The Supreme Court found that American Tobacco maintained its monopoly power by driving rivals out of business and agreeing to exclusive contracts with wholesalers that prevented them from purchasing cigarettes from other companies. The court-ordered breakup in 1911 led to several new companies, including several of today's big cigarette companies: Reynolds, Liggett and Meyers, and P. Lorillard.

In 1982, the government broke up American Telephone and Telegraph (AT&T) into seven regional phone companies. AT&T had used its legal monopoly in local telephone service to prevent competition in the markets for long-distance service and communications equipment. After an eight-year legal battle, AT&T agreed to form seven Regional Bell Operating Companies, transforming "Ma Bell" into seven "Baby Bells." The new AT&T was allowed to compete in the market for long-distance service, where it faced competition from newcomers MCI and Sprint. AT&T was also allowed to operate in the market for communications equipment, where it faced competition from newcomers Mitel and Northern Telecom.

Blocking Mergers

A **merger** occurs when two firms combine their operations. A second type of antitrust policy is to block corporate mergers that would reduce competition and lead to higher

Merger: A process in which two or more firms combine their operations.

prices. We saw in Chapter 11 that as the number of firms in a market increases, competition among firms drives down prices. Because a merger decreases the number of firms in a market, it is likely to lead to higher prices. In 1994, Microsoft tried to purchase Intuit, the maker of Quicken, a personal-finance software package that was a substitute for a similar Microsoft product. The merger would have reduced competition in the personal-finance software market, so the government blocked the merger.

Of course, the government does not oppose all corporate mergers. One possible benefit from a merger is that the new firm could combine production, marketing, or administrative operations and thus produce its products at a lower average cost. In 1997, the Justice Department and the Federal Trade Commission released new guidelines for proposed mergers. The new guidelines allow companies involved in a proposed merger to present evidence that the merger would reduce costs and lead to lower prices, better products, or better service. If the evidence for greater efficiency is convincing, the government might allow a merger that reduces the number of firms in a market. FTC Chairman Robert Pitofsky assessed the effects of the new guidelines as follows:[1]

> *There may be some deals that go through which otherwise would not have. But it won't change the result in a large number of cases [rather it will have] the greatest impact in a transaction where the potential anticompetitive problem is modest and efficiencies that would be created are great.*

The new guidelines will bring the U.S. antitrust rules closer to those of Europe and Canada, and could help U.S. companies compete in those markets.

In recent years, the analysis of proposed mergers has shifted from counting the number of firms in a market to predicting how a particular merger would affect price effects. The data generated by retail checkout scanners provides an enormous amount of information about prices and quantities sold. Using this data, economists can determine how one firm's pricing policies affect the sales of that firm and its competitors. Economists can use this information to predict whether a merger would lead to higher prices. Two recent antitrust cases illustrate how this new approach works.

Wonder Bread

In 1995, Interstate Bakeries (the nation's third largest wholesale baker) tried to buy Continental Baking (the maker of Wonder Bread). Based on grocery-store scanner data, the government concluded that Wonder Bread is a close substitute for Interstate's bread: The demand for Wonder Bread increases when the price of Interstate's bread increases, and vice versa.[2] The scanner data showed that when Interstate increased its price, many consumers switched to Wonder Bread, so their bread money went to Continental instead of Interstate. The substitutability of the two brands discouraged Interstate from increasing its prices.

Figure 14.1 shows the pricing decisions for each firm when each acts independently. Each firm uses the marginal principle, picking the quantity at which the marginal revenue from bread equals the marginal cost. Given a constant marginal cost of $1.00, each firm charges a price of $1.50 and sells 500 loaves per minute. The profit per loaf is $0.50, so the total profit for each firm is $250 ($0.50 per loaf times 500 loaves).

How would a merger affect Interstate's incentives to raise its prices? After a merger, a single company (let's call it Wonderstate) would earn the profits from both brands (Wonder and Interstate) and pick both prices. Suppose Wonderstate increased the price of Interstate bread to $1.60 but kept the price of Wonder bread at $1.50. The price hike would bring bad news and good news for the Wonderstate, the new firm:

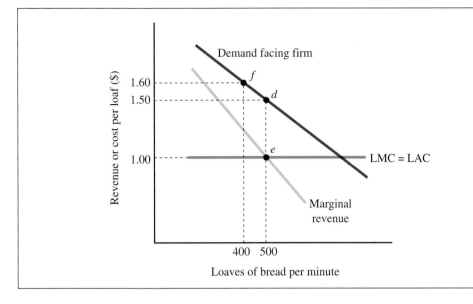

Figure 14.1
The Marginal Principle and Pricing of White Bread
Using the marginal principle, each bread firm picks the quantity at which marginal revenue equals marginal cost. At the profit-maximizing price of $1.50 per loaf, each firm sells 500 loaves and earns a profit of $0.50 per loaf, for a profit of $250.

- **Bad news: Less profit on Interstate Bread.** As shown in Figure 14.1, at the higher price, only 400 loaves of Interstate bread would be sold. As we see by multiplying the new profit per loaf ($0.60) by the new quantity (400 loaves), profit from the Interstate brand would decrease to $240, down from $250.

- **Good news: More profit on Wonder Bread.** Suppose the increase in the price of Interstate Bread increases the quantity of Wonder Bread sold from 500 to 560 loaves per minute. The profit per loaf is still $0.50 per bread, so the profit on Wonder Bread increases to $280, up from $250.

In this case, the good news ($30 more in profit from Wonder Bread) exceeds the bad news ($10 less profit from Interstate Bread), so the price hike for Interstate bread would increase the profit of Wonderstate, the new firm. Before a merger, the good news would be experienced by another firm (the firm making Wonder Bread). A merger means that this good news stays within the larger firm, encouraging that firm to increase prices.

The lesson from this example is that a merger of two firms selling close substitutes may lead to higher prices. That's what the Department of Justice concluded in the case of Interstate Bakeries and Continental Bakery. The government allowed the merger between the two companies but forced Interstate to sell some of its brands and bakeries. For example, Interstate sold the rights to sell its Weber brand bread to Four-S Banking Company. The idea is to ensure that other companies will compete with the new merged company in the market for white bread.

Staples and Office Depot

Pricing data were also used to predict the price effects of a merger between two office-supply chains, Staples and Office Depot, in 1997. Economists with the Federal Trade Commission (FTC) examined the prices and quantities of each item sold by the two chains. With the help of computers, the economists found an interesting pattern: The prices charged by Staples were lower in cities where Office Depot also had a store.[3]

Figure 14.2 shows the economics behind higher prices in cities without an Office Depot. The figure shows Staples' revenue and cost curves for one specific product: file folders. Panel A shows what happens when Staples faces no competition from an Office

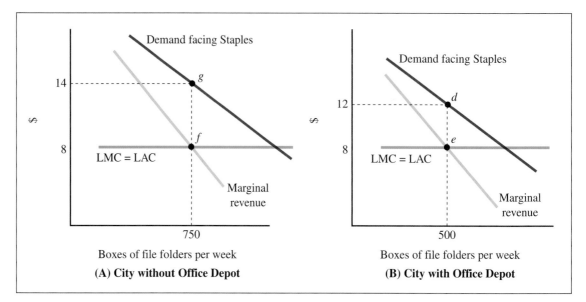

Figure 14.2 **Pricing by Staples Office Supplies in Different Cities**

Using the marginal principle, Staples picks the quantity at which its marginal revenue equals its marginal cost. In a city without a competing firm, Staples picks the monopoly price of $14. In a city where Staples competes with Office Depot, the demand facing Staples is relatively low, so the profit-maximizing price is only $12.

Depot, and panel B shows what happens when it does. The demand curve facing Staples is lower in the city where it faces competition with Office Depot because the two firms share the market. Using the marginal principle, Staples picks the quantity and price where its marginal revenue equals its marginal cost. The profit-maximizing price is $14 in a city without an Office Depot, and $12 in a city with one.

The FTC used this logic to convince the court that the proposed merger of Staples and Office Depot would lead to higher prices. The judge in the case observed that, "direct

Pricing data showed that the prices charged by Staples were lower in cities where Office Depot also had a store. The Department of Justice blocked a proposed merger of the two firms.

A CLOSER LOOK — The Price Effects of Mergers

In 1981, the Federal Trade Commission brought an antitrust suit against Xidex Corporation for its earlier acquisition of two rivals in the microfilm market. By acquiring Scott Graphics, Inc. in 1976 and Kalvar Corporation in 1979, Xidex increased its market share of the U.S. microfilm market from 46% to 71%. As a result, the price of microfilm increased: The price of one type of microfilm (diazo) increased by 11%, and the price of a second type (vesicular) increased by 23%. These price hikes were large enough that Xidex recovered the cost of acquiring its two rivals ($4.2 million for Scott Graphics and $6 million for Kalvar) in less than two years.[6]

This is a classic case of a merger that leads to higher prices and more profits for a dominant firm. To settle the antitrust lawsuit, Xidex agreed to license its microfilm technology—at bargain prices—to other firms. The idea is that if other firms have access to the microfilm technology, the competition between Xidex and the competing firms will decrease the price of microfilm.

---

evidence shows that by eliminating Staples' most significant, and in many markets, only, rival, this merger would allow Staples to increase prices or otherwise maintain prices at an anti-competitive level."[4] Evidence from the companies' pricing data showed that the merger would have allowed Staples to increase its prices by about 13%. By blocking the merger, the FTC saved consumers an estimated $1.1 billion over five years.[5]

In some cases, the government acts after the fact, seeking remedies for an earlier merger that increased prices. For an example, read "A Closer Look: The Price Effects of Mergers."

Check the Yellow Pages

On Katrina's first day on the job as an economist with the Federal Trade Commission, she was put on a team examining a proposed merger between the country's second and fourth largest hardware-store chains. Her job was to predict whether a merger would increase hardware prices. Her boss handed her some disks with checkout scanner data from the second largest chain. Each disk contained scanner data from one small town, listing the prices and quantities of hammers, wrenches, nuts, bolts, rakes, glue, drills, and hundreds of other hardware products. Her boss also gave her the telephone yellow pages for each small town. What can she do with the disks and the yellow pages?

ECONOMIC DETECTIVE

The key to solving this mystery is to recognize the similarity to the case of Staples and Office Depot. A merger of the country's second and fourth largest hardware chains could reduce competition and lead to higher prices. If the scanner data show that prices are lower in some towns, Katrina could look in the yellow pages to see which towns have hardware stores from both chains and which don't. If the towns that are served by both chains have lower prices, the proposed merger would probably decrease competition and increase prices.

Regulating Business Practices

The third type of antitrust policy involves the regulation of business practices. The government may intervene when a specific business practice increases market concentration in an already concentrated market. Among the practices that are subject to scrutiny are price fixing (discussed in Chapter 12), **tying** (forcing consumers of one product to purchase another), and price discrimination that reduces competition.

Tying: A business practice under which a consumer of one product is required to purchase another product.

The Robinson-Patman Act prohibits selling products at "unreasonably low prices" with the intent of reducing competition, a practice known as **predatory pricing**. The idea is that a firm sells a product at a price below its production costs, forcing its rivals to do the same or leave the market. Once the predator's rivals drop out of the market, the firm then charges a monopoly price, well above its production cost. This will be a profitable strategy if the firm can charge the monopoly price for a long enough period to offset the losses it experienced while driving its rival out of business.

Is there a reason to be skeptical about a claim of predatory pricing? Consider a market with two firms, one of which is determined to have the market to itself. By cutting its price below its cost, the firm can drive its competitor out of business, losing perhaps $10 million in the process. If it increases its price next year, there may be nothing to prevent a new firm from entering the market. If so, it would have to cut its price below its cost again to drive the new firm out. The problem with predatory pricing is that it never ends; the firm must repeatedly lose money to drive out an endless series of competitors.

The Microsoft Case

In recent years, the most widely reported antitrust actions have involved Microsoft Corporation, the software giant. Microsoft receives royalties from computer makers that install the Microsoft operating software on their computers. The curious—and illegal—feature of the original arrangement was that Microsoft received a royalty for every computer made by the firm, even if the firm installed other operating systems on some of its computers. This scheme discouraged computer makers from using software from Microsoft's rivals, and the courts declared it illegal in 1994.

In the case of the *United States* v. *Microsoft Corporation*, Judge Jackson found that Microsoft stifled competition in the software industry in several ways:

- Microsoft's contracts with computer manufacturers required them to install Microsoft's Internet Explorer (an Internet browser) on their computers. When Compaq Corporation announced plans to substitute Netscape's Navigator (used at the time by 87% of people browsing the Web) for Internet Explorer (used by only 4% of Web users), Microsoft delivered an ultimatum to Compaq: Install Internet Explorer or lose the license to install the Microsoft operating system.

- Microsoft's contracts with computer manufacturers also prohibited them from altering the Windows desktop by removing Microsoft's desktop links to the Internet.

- Microsoft's bundling of Internet Explorer with Windows 95 and its inclusion as part of Windows 98 involves tying the operating system with the browser.

The judge found that Microsoft used its virtual monopoly in operating system (90% of personal computers use Windows) to gain a monopoly in the browser market.

The judge also concluded that Microsoft used illegal practices to protect its monopoly in the market for operating systems. Like an operating system, a browser can serve as a software platform to run application programs such as word processors, spreadsheets, and graphics programs. If Microsoft succeeded in driving competing browsers out of the market, the browser threat to Windows would disappear.

Here is an excerpt from Judge Jackson's ruling: "In essence, Microsoft mounted a deliberate assault upon entrepreneurial efforts that . . . could well have enabled the introduction of competition into the market for Intel-compatible PC operating systems. (The evidence) does reveal that Microsoft placed an oppressive thumb on the scale of competitive fortune, thereby effectively guaranteeing its continued dominance in the relevant market. More broadly, Microsoft's anticompetitive actions trammeled the competitive process through which the computer software industry generally stimulates innovation . . . ."

In the next stage of the legal process, Judge Jackson will determine what penalties or remedies are appropriate. For the latest on the case, check the Web site for the U.S. Department of Justice (*http://www.usdoj.gov*)

TEST Your Understanding

1. List three types of antitrust policies.

2. Why was the federal government concerned about the merger of Interstate Bakeries and Continental Baking?

3. What are the essential provisions of the new guidelines for corporate mergers?

4. Why might Microsoft want to drive competing browsers out of the market?

Deregulation of Airlines and Telecommunications

In this part of the chapter, we explore the recent deregulation of two markets: air travel and telecommunications. In both cases, the motivation behind deregulation was to increase competition and decrease prices. The Airline Deregulation Act of 1978 eliminated entry restrictions and price controls in the market for air travel. The Telecommunications Act of 1996 eliminated most price controls for cable television and established a framework for entry into the markets for cable television service, local telephone service, and Internet service.

Deregulation of Airlines

Before 1978, the Civil Aeronautics Board (CAB) regulated interstate air travel by limiting entry into the market and controlling prices. About 90% of the markets were monopolized, with prices that were between 30% and 50% higher than the prices that would have occurred in a more competitive environment.[7] The Airline Deregulation Act of 1978 eliminated most of the entry restrictions and price controls, and the CAB eventually disappeared.

In the first few years after deregulation, a large number of firms entered the market, and competition among airlines serving individual markets (individual routes) increased. Since then, many of the firms that entered the market just after deregulation have disappeared. Some firms went out of business, and others merged with other airlines. Some of the airline mergers have led to lower production costs and prices, while others have reduced competition and led to higher prices.[8] Some cities now have a dominant airline, and fares are actually higher than they were before deregulation.[9]

The consensus among economists is that airline deregulation generated net benefits for consumers.[10] On average, fares have decreased by about 33% in real terms since deregulation, and the frequency of service has increased. Several factors contributed to lower prices: competition from incumbent carriers (18% of the savings), competition from Southwest Airlines (31%), competition from other entrants (10%), and improvements in carriers' operating efficiencies (41%).

Deregulation of Telecommunication Services

The Telecommunications Act of 1996 established new rules for firms involved in the transmission of video, voice, and data. The basic idea is to promote competition in the markets for telecommunications services. Several provisions of the act will affect the

Regional Bell Operating Companies (the Baby Bells) that were formed as a result of the breakup of AT&T in 1982. Here are the most important provisions of the act:

- **Local telephone service.** The act opened local telephone service to competition, with the idea that new firms would compete with the Baby Bells for local service. In addition, cable-TV firms might eventually provide telephone service over their cables.

- **Cable-TV service.** Price controls for cable-TV services were eliminated, and telephone companies are to be allowed to enter the market for cable-TV services.

- **Long-distance service.** Once there is sufficient competition for local telephone service, the Baby Bells will be allowed to enter the market for long-distance service.

One purpose of the act is to open local telephone service to real competition. The challenge is to develop a set of rules that would allow new competitors to get access to the copper wires leading into residences. These wires are controlled by the Baby Bells, which of course are not eager to give their new competitors access to their facilities. Although the Federal Communication Commission has developed pricing rules governing access to the copper wires, the rules have been tied up in court for several years. Therefore, there has been little progress in opening up local telephone service to competition. Consequently, the Baby Bells have not been allowed to enter the market for long-distance service.

The inability of the Baby Bells to enter the long-distance market has important implications for the rapidly growing market for Internet services. In the past, Internet service providers (ISPs) have had free access to the copper wires leading into residences. In the typical community, there are several ISPs to choose from, and competition has kept prices low. A new technology (digital subscriber line or DSL) will deliver high-speed access to the Internet over copper wires. This new technology is costly to deploy, and the question is: How much should ISPs pay the Baby Bells to access the new system?

The policy objective is to negotiate an access fee for ISPs that is high enough for the telephone companies to recover the costs of installing and maintaining the system. The Baby Bells would like to enter the market for Internet services themselves but are prohibited from entering any market for long-distance services—for voice or data—until there is more competition in local phone service.

There is a new alternative for accessing the Internet from residences. The development of the high-speed cable modem (with speeds about 50 times faster than the 56K modems that run over phone lines) has made it possible to access the Internet over the cable lines laid by cable TV companies. The cable companies are eager to enter the market for Internet access, and the question for government regulators is whether to require cable companies to grant independent ISPs access to their cables. If not, the independent ISPs will be forced to rely on slower telephone lines and will probably disappear. If the government requires the cable companies to provide access to their cables, the regulators must determine the price to be charged to ISPs. For a preview of the likely political battles, read "A Closer Look: One-Stop Shopping for Telecommunications?"

We can summarize our discussion of deregulation of telecommunications as follows. In the telecommunications market, competition requires rival firms to share facilities (copper wires and cables leading into residences). The challenge for policy makers is to develop a set of pricing rules that allows rival firms to share this facility. Once those rules are in place and households have more options for the transmission of voice, data, and video, we can expect more competition, lower prices, and better service.

A CLOSER LOOK | One-Stop Shopping for Telecommunications?

In June 1998, AT&T Corporation and Tele-Communications Inc. (TCI) announced plans for a $48 billion merger. The transaction would create AT&T Consumer Services, which would provide one-stop shopping for all sorts of telecommunication services, including local and long-distance phone service, wireless communication, high-speed Internet access, and cable-TV service. To provide this bundle of services, the new firm must upgrade the cable network, at a cost of about $1.8 billion.[11]

AT&T/TCI must get the approval of thousands of local cable commissions that oversee cable-TV franchise agreements. The Mt. Hood Cable Regulatory Commission oversees the cable television franchise—currently granted to TCI—in Multnomah County, Oregon. Before the new telecommunications giant can provide its bundle of services in Multnomah County, the commission must agree to transfer cable rights from TCI to AT&T Consumer Services. The commission agreed to transfer the rights if AT&T Consumer Services agreed to let rival Internet service providers share its cable network. AT&T declined the offer and vowed to sue the commission, arguing that the issue of cable access was the responsibility of federal regulators.

TEST Your Understanding

5. Did the deregulation of the airline industry lead to low prices in all cities?

6. Under what conditions will the Baby Bells be allowed to provide long-distance service?

7. What are the competing technologies for Internet access?

Using the TOOLS

In this chapter, we've explored some policy issues concerning firms in concentrated industries. We've explored the incentives for predatory pricing, seen the price effects of mergers, and considered the effects of deregulation on competition and prices. Here are some opportunities to do your own economic analysis.

1. Cost Savings from a Merger

Consider the following statement from a firm that has proposed a merger between two companies: "The two companies could save about $50 million per year by combining our production, marketing, and administrative operations. In other words, we could realize substantial economies of scale. Therefore, the government should allow the merger." In light of the new guidelines concerning mergers, how would you react to this statement?

2. Willingness to Pay for New Airport Gates

Your city is considering an airport expansion project that would increase the number of airport gates and allow additional airlines to serve your city. According to a recent report, the additional competition made possible by the new gates would decrease the average airline fare from $220 to $200 and increase the number of passengers from 400 to 600 per day. The city would borrow money to finance the project, and the daily payment required to pay off the loan (over 20 years) would be $8,100. Is the project worthwhile from the social perspective?

Summary

In this chapter, we've explored two types of policy issues concerning firms in concentrated industries: antitrust policy and deregulation. The purpose of antitrust policy is to promote competition among the few firms in a concentrated market. In the airline industry and the telecommunication industry, deregulation has generated mixed results. Here are the main points of the chapter:

1. Under antitrust policies, the government breaks up some dominant firms, prevents some corporate mergers, and regulates business practices that reduce competition.

2. The modern approach to merger policy doesn't simply look at the number of firms in an industry but uses data on prices and quantities sold to predict the price effects of a merger.

3. In most circumstances, predatory pricing is unprofitable because the monopoly power is costly to acquire and doesn't last very long.

4. The deregulation of the airline industry has led to more competition and lower prices on average but higher prices in some markets.

5. The purpose of the deregulation of the telecommunications industry is to promote competition in phone service, cable television, and Internet access.

Key Terms

merger, 295

predatory pricing, 300

trust, 295

tying, 299

Problems and Discussion Questions

1. Consider a market that is initially served by two firms, each of which charges a price of $10 and sells 100 units of the good. The long-run average cost of production is constant at $9 per unit. Suppose a merger would increase the price to $14 and reduce the total quantity sold from 200 to 150. Compute the consumer loss associated with the merger. How does it compare to the increase in profit? What is the net loss from the merger?

2. Consider an allegation that a firm is engaging in predatory pricing, picking a price below its average cost in an attempt to drive its competitors out of business. Why might you be skeptical about such a claim?

3. The construction project at your city's airport is nearing completion, and your job is to decide how to use the 10 new gates of the airport. The city is currently served by Gotcha Airlines, which has offered the city $20 million to help cover the cost of the airport construction project. In return, the new gates would be designated for the exclusive use of Gotcha.

What trade-offs are associated with accepting Gotcha's offer?

4. As the recently appointed head of the Federal Communications Commission, your job is to develop a set of rules for the use of the cables laid by cable-television companies. You must decide whether the ISPs should have access and, if so, at what price.

5. Web Exercise. Visit the Web site of the U.S. Federal Trade Commission (*http://www.ftc.gov/*). Access the Antitrust/Competition part of the Web Site, and in the Antitrust Menu, open the document *Promoting Competition, Protecting Consumer: A Plain English Guide to Antitrust Laws*. What is the difference between a vertical merger and a horizontal merger? What is a Potential Competition merger and why might the FTC block one?

6. Web Exercise. Visit the Web site of the U.S. Federal Communications Commission (*http://www.fcc.gov/*). Do a search of the site for the latest news and analysis of the issue of broadband Internet access. What is the FCC doing to promote competition in Internet access?

Take It to the Net

Model Answers to Questions

Chapter-Opening Questions

1. Pricing data showed that the prices charged by Staples were lower in cities where Office Depot also had a store, suggesting that competition between the two firms kept prices low. A merger would eliminate the competition, leading to higher prices.

2. The government alleged that Microsoft used its monopoly power in operating systems to try to gain a monopoly in the Internet browser market. In addition, the government alleged that Microsoft tried to dominate the browser market to protect its monopoly in operating systems. A "findings of fact" accepted these allegations.

3. Deregulation decreased prices on average, but increased concentration in some cities led to higher fares in those cities.

4. The high-speed cable modem provides an alternative to slower access along copper wires. Firms employing copper wires will be at a disadvantage, and may lose sales to firms using high-speed cable modems.

Test Your Understanding

1. Breaking up monopolies, blocking mergers, and regulating business practices (price fixing, tying and price discrimination).

2. Scanner data showed that the white breads produced by the two firms were close substitutes. An unregulated merger would have reduced competition and led to higher prices.

3. Companies that are involved in a proposed merger can present evidence that the merger would reduce costs and lead to lower prices, better products, or better service. If the evidence for this is convincing,

the government might allow a merger that reduces the number of firms in a market.

4. If Microsoft succeeded in driving competing browsers out of the market, the browser threat to Internet Explorer would disappear.

5. No. On average, prices decreased, but travelers to and from some cities that are served by only one or two airlines pay higher prices.

6. Sufficient competition in the market for local telephone service.

7. Old copper wire technology, new copper wire technology (ADSL), high-speed cable modems.

Using the Tools

1. Cost Savings from a Merger. The new guidelines allow companies to present evidence that a merger would reduce costs. If the evidence for greater efficiency is convincing, the government might allow a merger that reduces the number of firms in a market. As is shown in the quote from FTC Chairman Pitofsky, the increased efficiency must be large enough to offset concerns about the reduction in competition. The question is whether reduced competition and higher prices might offset the $50 million savings in cost.

2. Willingness to Pay for New Airport Gates. We can compute the gain in consumer surplus resulting from the decrease in price generated by the expansion project (Chapter 7). In Figure 14.A, the gain in consumer surplus is shown by trapezoid *ABCD*, with area equal to $9,000 per day. The area of the shaded rectangle is $8,000 and the area of the shaded triangle is $1,000. The change in consumer surplus exceeds the cost of the project, so the project is worthwhile.

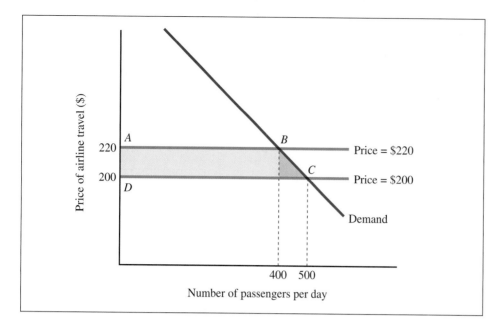

Figure 14.A

Consumer Surplus and Airport Expansion Project
A decrease in price from $220 to $200 increases the consumer surplus by the area of the trapezoid *ABCD*, or $9,000.

Notes

1. John R. Wilke, "New Antitrust Rules May Ease Path to Mergers," *Wall Street Journal*, April 9, 1997, pp. A3–A4.

2. "The Economics of Antitrust: The Trustbuster's New Tools," *The Economist*, May 2, 1998, pp. 62–64.

3. "The Economics of Antitrust: The Trustbuster's New Tools."

4. *Federal Trade Commission v. Staples, Inc.*, 970 F. Supp. 1066 (D.D.C. 1997, Hogan, J).

5. U.S. Federal Trade Commission, *Promoting Competition, Protecting Consumers: A Plain English Guide to Antitrust Laws* (*http://www.ftc.gov/bc/compguide/index.htm*).

6. David M. Barton and Roger Sherman, "The Price and Profit Effects of Horizontal Merger: A Case Study," *Journal of Industrial Economics*, vol. 33, December 1984, pp. 165–177.

7. William G. Shepherd and James W. Brock, "Airlines," Chapter 10 in *The Structure of American Industry*, edited by Walter Adams and James W. Brock (Upper Saddle River, NJ: Prentice Hall, 1995).

8. Clifford Winston, "U.S. Industry Adjustment to Economic Deregulation," *Journal of Economic Perspectives*, vol. 12, no. 3, Summer 1998, pp. 89–110.

9. Paul MacAvoy, *Industry Regulation and the Performance of the American Economy* (New York: W.W. Norton, 1992).

10. Clifford Winston, "U.S. Industry Adjustment to Economic Deregulation," *Journal of Economic Perspectives* vol. 12, no. 3, Summer 1998, pp. 89–110; Alfred E. Kahn, "Airline Deregulation—A Mixed Bag but a Clear Success Nonetheless," *Transportation Law Journal*, vol. 16, 1988, pp. 229–252.

11. Su-Jin Yim, "Bad Reception for AT&T," *The Oregonian*, December 14, 1998, p. C1.

CHAPTER

15

Public Goods, Taxes, and Public Choice

Here is the text from a TV newscast in the year 2070:

Boomer, the 200-meter asteroid on a collision path with the earth, is expected to land at about 10:00 tomorrow morning in the heart of the world's breadbasket, the American Midwest. The energy to be released by the impact will exceed the total explosive yield of all the nuclear weapons on the planet. Although Boomer is much smaller than the asteroid that caused the extinction of the dinosaurs about 65 million years ago, it is large enough to cause significant changes in the world's climate. The collision will generate a stratospheric dust cloud that will inhibit photosynthesis and retard plant growth, resulting in lower agricultural yields throughout the world. According to scientists, the earth's total agricultural output will decrease by about 20% over the next decade, increasing the price of food by about 35%.

Could this catastrophe have been averted? Yes, according to scientists at the National Aeronautics and Space Administration. In 1996, scientists developed the technology for an asteroid-diversion system: Large optical telescopes would detect an asteroid on a collision course with the earth, and an orbiting gossamer mirror of coated polyester would focus a tight beam of sunlight on the asteroid, vaporizing enough of its surface to change its path. In the U.N. debate over the asteroid-diversion system, everyone agreed that the potential benefits of the system would outweigh the costs, but no one was willing to pay for the system. Why couldn't the nations of the world agree on such an important program, one that would have prevented tomorrow's catastrophe?

n this chapter, we'll see that if a particular good generates spillover benefits, government intervention can make beneficial transactions happen. For example, the cost of an asteroid-diversion program is so high that no single person would provide such a program. We will never have such a program—even if its benefits exceed its costs—unless we make a collective decision about what sort of diversion program to develop and how to pay for it. The purpose of government is to help make this sort of collective decision. That hypothetical newscast suggests that some sort of multinational arrangement will be necessary to launch an asteroid-diversion program.

This chapter explores the economic challenges associated with providing—and paying for—goods that generate spillover benefits. We also take a look at some alternative theories on how governments operate. Here are some practical questions that we answer:

1. **Should we eliminate taxes and pay for government programs with voluntary contributions instead?**
2. **Is it sensible to pay landowners to host endangered wildlife such as wolves and spotted owls?**
3. **How will a monthly apartment tax of $80 affect the monthly rent on apartments?**
4. **It often seems that there is little difference between the candidates in an election. Why?**

Overview of Government

In Chapter 3, we discussed the role of government in a market-based economy. In most modern societies, governments provide goods and services, redistribute income, regulate business practices, and regulate international trade. In this chapter, we look at the first of these roles, exploring the rationale for using government to provide goods and services such as education, public safety, national defense, and space exploration. We also explore the effects of taxes on the markets for goods and services.

In the United States, there are three levels of government: federal, state, and local. Figure 15.1 shows the budget breakdown for the three levels of government.

- There are more than 80,000 local governments in the United States, including municipalities (city governments), counties, school districts, and special districts responsible for providing services such as water, fire protection, and libraries. Local governments spend most of their money on education (kindergarten through high school), public welfare and health (payments to poor households and support for public hospitals), highways, and police protection.

- For states, the biggest spending programs are education (including colleges and universities), public welfare, highways, health and hospitals, and corrections (state courts and prisons).

- For the federal government, the biggest spending programs are national defense, programs for the elderly (Social Security and Medicare), and income security (payments to the poor), and interest on the national debt.

Spillover Benefits

In Chapter 6, we saw that a market in which there are neither spillover benefits nor costs is an efficient market. Government intervention in an efficient market can only make it less than efficient. In this chapter, we'll see that a market with spillover benefits is inefficient, so there is an opportunity for government to promote efficiency. Recall the spillover principle.

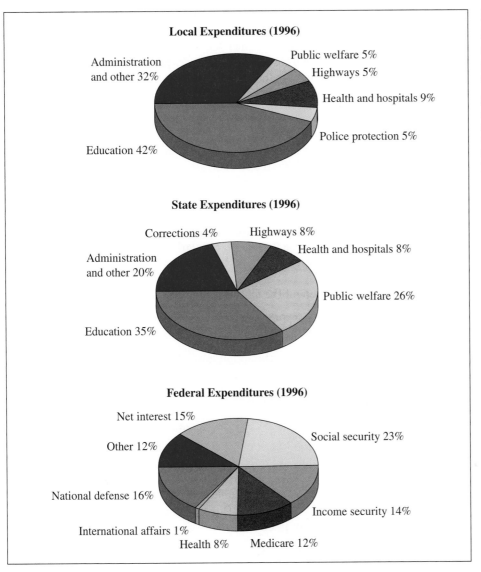

Figure 15.1

Percentages of Government Spending on Various Programs

Sources: Statistical Abstract of the United States, 1998; Economic Report of the President (Washington, DC: U.S. Government Printing Office, 1998).

Local Expenditures (1996)

- Administration and other 32%
- Public welfare 5%
- Highways 5%
- Health and hospitals 9%
- Police protection 5%
- Education 42%

State Expenditures (1996)

- Corrections 4%
- Highways 8%
- Health and hospitals 8%
- Administration and other 20%
- Public welfare 26%
- Education 35%

Federal Expenditures (1996)

- Net interest 15%
- Social security 23%
- Other 12%
- National defense 16%
- International affairs 1%
- Income security 14%
- Health 8%
- Medicare 12%

SPILLOVER **PRINCIPLE**

For some goods, the costs or benefits associated with the good are not confined to the person or organization that decides how much of the good to produce or consume.

To illustrate the idea of spillover benefits, consider a dam built for flood-control purposes. There are 100,000 people in the valley below the dam, and each person gets a $5 benefit from the dam. The total benefit of the dam is $500,000 (equal to 100,000 people times $5 per person), which exceeds the $200,000 total cost of the dam. Because the total benefit exceeds the total cost, the dam should be built. The problem is that no single person will build the dam because the $200,000 cost exceeds his or her $5 personal benefit. In other words, if we rely on the forces of supply and demand, with each person considering only the personal benefits and costs of a dam, no dam will be built.

The government can solve this problem by collecting enough taxes to pay for the dam. Suppose the government offers to build the dam and pay for it with a tax of $2 per person. The tax raises $200,000 in tax revenue ($2 per person times 100,000 people), which is just high enough to pay the $200,000 cost of the dam. Every person will support this proposal because the $2 tax per person is less than the $5 benefit per person. The government can use its taxing power to provide a good that would otherwise not be provided.

Public Goods

Public good: A good that is available for everyone to consume, regardless of who pays and who doesn't.

Private good: A good that is consumed by a single person or household.

The dam is an example of a **public good**, a good that is available for everyone to consume, regardless of who pays and who doesn't. In contrast, a **private good** is consumed by a single person or household. For example, only one person can eat a hot dog. If a government hands out free cheese to the poor, is the free cheese a public good or a private good? Although anyone can get in line for the cheese, only one person can actually consume a particular piece of cheese, so the free cheese is a private good that happens to be available free of charge from the government. Similarly, an apartment in a public housing project can be occupied by a single household, so it is a private good provided by the government.

We can be more precise about the difference between public and private goods:

- Private goods are rival in consumption (only one person can consume the good) and excludable (it is possible to exclude a person who does not pay for the good).

- Public goods are nonrival in consumption (available for everyone to consume) and nonexcludable (it is impractical to exclude people who don't pay).

Here are some other examples of public goods:

National defense	Preservation of endangered species
Law enforcement	Protecting the earth's ozone layer
Space exploration	Income transfers to the poor

If someone refuses to pay for one of these public goods, it would be impractical to prevent that person from consuming the good. One role of government is to use its taxing power to collect money to pay for public goods.

Private Goods with Spillover Benefits

There are some private goods that generate spillover benefits. One example is education, a good that generates two sorts of spillover benefits.

- Workplace spillovers. In most workplaces, people work in groups, and teamwork is important. A well-educated person understands instructions readily and is more likely to suggest ways to improve the production process. When a well-educated person joins a work team, the productivity of everyone on the team increases, leading to higher wages for everyone on the team.

- Civic spillovers. Citizens in a democratic society make collective decisions by voting in elections, and each citizen must live with these decisions. A well-educated person is more likely to vote intelligently, so there are spillover benefits for other citizens.

Because of these spillover benefits from education, the government uses various policies to encourage people to become educated. Local governments provide free education through high school. States subsidize students at public colleges and universities, providing college education at a fraction of the actual cost of the education. In addition, the federal government provides financial aid to students in both public and private schools.

The government subsidizes other goods that generate spillover benefits. For example, many firms use government subsidies to support on-the-job training and education. This is sensible because some of the benefits of education and training go to other firms: When a worker trained by one firm switches to another firm, the second firm also benefits. This is the rationale for subsidizing some types of education and training programs. Another example is research at universities and other nonprofit organizations. If a research project provides knowledge or technology that leads to the development of new products or the improvement of old ones, the benefits from the project spill over onto consumers and producers. This is the rationale for subsidizing basic research in the sciences.

Voluntary Contributions and the Free-Rider Problem

Most public goods are supported by taxes. What would happen if we eliminated taxes and asked people to contribute money to pay for national defense, dams, city streets, and the police? Would people contribute enough money to support these programs at their current levels?

The problem with using voluntary contributions to support public goods is known as the **free-rider problem**. Each person will try to get the benefits of a public good without paying for it, trying to get a free ride at the expense of others who do pay. Of course, if everyone tries to get a free ride, there will be no money to support the public good, so it won't be provided. The flip side of the free-rider problem is the chump problem: No one wants to be the chump—the person who gives free rides to other people—so no one contributes any money. The free-rider problem suggests that if taxes were replaced with voluntary contributions, the government would be forced to cut back or eliminate many programs.

Free-rider problem: Each person will try to get the benefit of a public good without paying for it, trying to get a free ride at the expense of others who do pay.

A Classroom Experiment in Free Riding

Do people really try to get free rides? Or would most people contribute at least some money to support a public good? Here is a classroom experiment that helps to answer this question.

- The instructor selects 10 students at random and gives each student 10 dimes (or play money).

- Each student can contribute money to support a public good by dropping 1, 2, or 3 dimes into a public-good pot. Each student has the option of keeping all the dimes and not contributing anything. The contributions are anonymous; none of the students knows how much the other students contribute.

- For each dime in the pot, the instructor adds 2 dimes. For example, if the students contribute a total of 40 dimes, the instructor adds 80 dimes, for a total of 120 dimes in the pot. The 2-for-1 match represents the idea that the benefits of public goods exceed the costs. In this case, the benefit-cost ratio is 3 to 1.

- The instructor divides the money in the public-good pot equally among the 10 students. For example, if there are 120 dimes in the pot, each student receives 12 dimes.

- Steps 2 through 4 can be repeated 4 or 5 times.

If your instructor does this experiment in your course, you'll see how much money your fellow students contribute to the public good. You'll also see the payoffs earned by students with different contribution strategies.

If your instructor does not do the experiment, you can learn something from the instructions from the experiment by answering the following questions:

- How much would you contribute?

- If your fellow students acted in the same way as you, how much money would you have at the end of 5 rounds?

- If your fellow students acted differently (contributing more or less than you contributed), how much money would you have?

We can change the experiment to mimic the compulsory tax system. The instructor could require each student to contribute three dimes, the maximum amount, each round. Would a switch to a compulsory tax system make the students better off or worse off?

The Mystery of the Three-Clock Tower

Back in the days before the inexpensive wristwatch, most people did not carry their own timepieces. Many towns built clock towers in the center of town so that their citizens could know the time. The towns paid for the clock towers with voluntary contributions from citizens. One town in the northeastern United States built a four-sided tower but put clock faces on only three sides of the tower. To most people, this seems bizarre. If you build a clock tower, why not put clock faces on all four sides?

The key to solving this puzzle is the free-rider problem. It turns out that one of the town's wealthy citizens refused to contribute money to help build the clock tower. The town officials decided that because he did not pay, they should not put a clock face on the side of the tower facing his house. In other words, the citizen tried—unsuccessfully—to get a free ride. The problem is that other citizens on the same side of town also suffered from not seeing the clock. In this case, preventing a free ride by one citizen caused problems for other citizens. ◆

Overcoming the Free-Rider Problem

Many organizations, including public radio and television, religious organizations, and charitable organizations, raise money through voluntary contributions. So it appears that some people overcome their inclination to be free riders and contribute voluntarily to organizations that provide public goods. The successful organizations use a number of techniques to encourage people to contribute, such as the following:

- Give contributors private goods such as coffee mugs, books, musical recordings, and magazine subscriptions. People are more likely to contribute if they get something for it.

- Arrange matching contributions. You are more likely to contribute if you know that your $30 contribution will be matched with a contribution from another person.

- Appeal to people's sense of civic or moral responsibility.

It's important to note, however, that these organizations are only partly successful in mitigating the free-rider problem. Public radio is one of the success stories, but the typical public-radio station gets contributions from fewer than a quarter of its listeners.

TEST Your Understanding

1. Explain why the free-rider problem occurs for public goods but not for private goods.

2. Margie, one of the students participating in the free-rider experiment, thinks in marginal terms and asks the following question: "If I contribute one dime, how will that affect my payoff from the experiment?" Answer her question, assuming that her contribution does not affect the contribution of other students.

3. Suppose Margie uses the marginal principle to make all her decisions. Will she contribute the extra dime?

Applications: Asteroids and Wildlife

Now that we've discussed some of the economic challenges associated with providing public goods, let's think about two unconventional public goods: the diversion of asteroids and the preservation of wolves.

Asteroid Diversion

How do we apply the concepts of public goods to the issue of protecting the earth from catastrophic collisions with asteroids? On average, the earth is hit by a 200-meter asteroid every 10,000 years, by a 2-kilometer asteroid every million years, and by a 10-kilometer asteroid every 100 million years.[1] As was explained at the beginning of the chapter, we have the technology to divert approaching asteroids.

The diversion of asteroids is a public good in the sense that it is available for everyone to consume, regardless of who pays and who doesn't. As with any public good, the key to developing an asteroid-diversion program is to collect money to pay for the program. According to NASA scientists, the program would require several new telescopes, which would cost about $50 million to install and about $10 million per year to operate.[2] The cost of the gossamer mirror or the nuclear weapons required to change the path of the asteroid would be $100 million to $200 million. Although it would be sensible to finance the program with contributions from all earthlings, it may be impossible to collect money from everyone. A more likely outcome is that one or more developed countries will finance their own diversion systems.

Preservation of Wolves

We can also apply the concepts of public goods and free riding to the issue of preserving wildlife. There are some trade-offs associated with preserving wolves and other wildlife in Yellowstone Park. To environmentalists, wolves are a part of the ecosystem, and the purpose of preserving wolves is to maintain the natural ecosystem. Ranchers, whose livestock is often eaten by wolves, consider the wolf a pest that should be eliminated or tightly controlled. In other words, there are costs as well as benefits associated with the preservation of wolves, just as there are costs and benefits associated with other public goods such as dams, fireworks, national defense, and space exploration.

One response to the wolf-preservation problem comes from Defenders of Wildlife, an environmental group in Montana. The organization collects money from its members and uses the money to reward landowners who allow wolves to live on their properties. The host landowner receives a payment of $5,000 for each litter of wolf pups reared on the property.[3] In addition, the organization compensates ranchers for livestock killed

Some organizations treat the preservation of species such as the wolf as a public good.

by wolves. As a result of these programs, ranchers in the Yellowstone area are more likely to support efforts to maintain the wolves as part of the ecosystem of Yellowstone Park. The programs treat preservation as a public good, one that is supported by money collected from the people who benefit from preservation.

Financing Government: Taxes

So far, we've discussed the rationale for government spending programs. The three levels of government—local, state, and federal—raise money to pay for these programs by imposing taxes on all sorts of goods and services. Figure 15.2 shows the revenue sources for the three levels of government:

- The major revenue source for local governments is the property tax. The property tax is a flat percentage of the value of residential, commercial, or industrial property. For example, if the tax rate is 2% and you own a property with a market value of $100,000, your annual tax would be $2,000 (0.02 times $100,000).

- The major revenue sources for the states are sales taxes and individual income taxes. The sales tax is a fixed percentage of the purchase price of a consumer good. A person's state income-tax liability is based on how much he or she earns, with tax rates that typically increase as income increases.

- The major revenue sources for the federal government are individual income taxes and "social insurance and retirement receipts," which are taxes collected to support Social Security, Medicare, and workers' compensation.

In this part of the chapter, we'll look at the market effects of taxes and answer two important questions about taxes. First, who really bears the burden of a tax? As we'll see, it is not necessarily the person who actually pays the tax to the government. Second, is the total burden of a tax equal to the revenue collected by the government? As we'll see, a tax changes people's behavior, so the total burden actually exceeds the revenue collected. We'll start with the issue of who bears the tax burden.

Tax Shifting: Forward and Backward

We can use supply and demand curves to look at the market effects of taxes. Suppose that your city imposes a tax of $80 per apartment and collects the tax from housing firms. You may think the burden of the tax falls exclusively on the housing firm, since that's who mails the check to the government. But some simple supply and demand analysis will

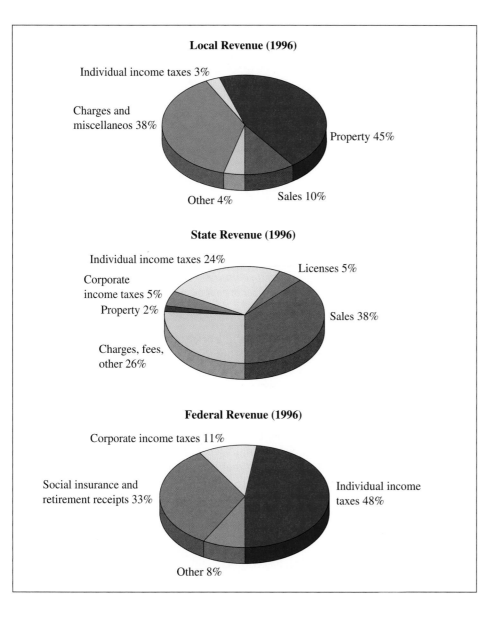

Figure 15.2

Percentages of Government Revenue from Different Sources

Sources: Statistical Abstract of the United States, 1998; Economic Report of the President (Washington, DC: U.S. Government Printing Office, 1998); Census Bureau data at http://www.census.gov/govs/www/.

Local Revenue (1996)

Individual income taxes 3%

Charges and miscellaneos 38%

Property 45%

Other 4%

Sales 10%

State Revenue (1996)

Individual income taxes 24%

Corporate income taxes 5%

Property 2%

Licenses 5%

Sales 38%

Charges, fees, other 26%

Federal Revenue (1996)

Corporate income taxes 11%

Social insurance and retirement receipts 33%

Individual income taxes 48%

Other 8%

show why this is incorrect. The housing firm will charge more for apartments and pay less for its inputs, so the tax will actually be paid by consumers and input suppliers.

Figure 15.3 shows the market effects of an $80 tax on apartments. We saw in Chapter 4 that an increase in the cost of producing a good shifts the supply curve to the left. In a perfectly competitive industry, in the long run, the equilibrium price equals the average cost of production. That means each firm makes just enough money to stay in the market. The original price of $200 was just high enough to cover the monthly cost of providing an apartment. The tax increases the average cost per apartment by $80. Therefore, the $200 original price is now less than the $280 average cost ($200 + $80 tax). At the $200 price, housing firms will lose money on their apartments, so they will withdraw some apartments from the market and build fewer new apartments to replace old ones. As a result, the supply curve will shift to the left: At each price, fewer apartments will be supplied.

The leftward shift of the supply curve increases the equilibrium price of apartments. At the $200 price, there will be an excess demand for apartments, and the price will increase to eliminate the excess demand. In Figure 15.3, the market moves from point *i* to point *f*: The

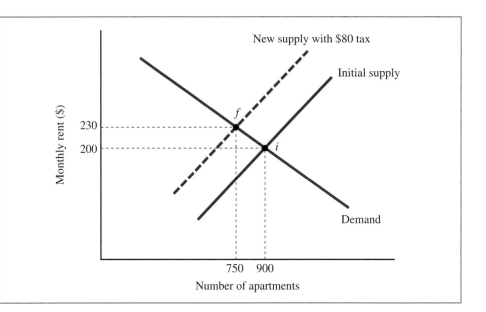

Figure 15.3

Market Effects of an Apartment Tax

A tax of $80 per apartment shifts the supply curve to the left, moving the market equilibrium from point *i* to point *f*. The equilibrium price increases from $200 to $230, and the equilibrium quantity decreases from 900 to 750 apartments.

demand curve intersects the new supply curve at a price of $230, compared to $200 before the tax. In other words, housing firms shift part of the tax forward to consumers, who pay $30 of the $80 tax. Although housing firms pay the entire $80 tax in a legal sense, they get some of the money to pay the tax by charging consumers $30 more for apartments.

The apartment tax also affects the people who supply inputs to the housing industry. The tax decreases the output of the industry, so the industry needs smaller quantities of all the inputs used to produce apartments. Therefore, the tax causes an excess supply of each of the inputs used to produce housing, such as labor and land. To eliminate the excess supplies, input prices drop, meaning that housing firms pay less for their inputs, and part of the $80 tax is shifted backward to input suppliers: Housing firms pay lower wages and less for land. Although housing firms pay the apartment tax in a legal sense, they get some of the money to pay the tax by paying less to workers and landowners.

So who really pays the apartment tax? Although the housing firm actually sends the money to the government, the housing firm collects more money from consumers and pays less money to input suppliers, so consumers and input suppliers indirectly pay the tax. Recall that at every point on the long-run supply curve, economic profit per firm is zero. Each housing firm makes zero profit before and after the tax, so the housing firm doesn't pay the tax in an economic sense. This is possible because the firm shifts part of the tax forward to consumers and shifts the rest of the tax backward to input suppliers.

We can use Figure 15.3 to show just how much of the $80 apartment tax is paid by consumers and how much is paid by input suppliers. After the tax is imposed, the typical apartment owner charges $230 to consumers, pays a tax of $80 to the government, leaving $150 to pay all the people who supply the inputs required to produce the apartment. Before the tax, the apartment owner charged $200 and gave it all to input suppliers. Therefore, the tax makes input suppliers worse off by $50 per apartment ($200 received before the tax minus $150 received after the tax). If we add the $50 burden imposed on input suppliers to the $30 price hike experienced by consumers, we get a total of $80, an amount equal to the apartment tax.

Predicting the Amount of Forward Shifting

How much of a tax will be shifted forward to consumers, and how much will be shifted backward to input suppliers? No one likes to pay taxes, so everyone will try to avoid paying a particular tax by changing his or her behavior. We've already seen that housing firms avoid paying the tax by shifting part of the tax to consumers. Firms can shift the tax forward because they produce fewer apartments, causing an excess demand for apartments that increases the price of apartments. If consumers want to avoid paying too much of the tax, they must change their behavior.

The amount of the tax shifted forward to consumers depends on the price elasticity of demand for the taxed good. If the demand for apartments is inelastic—meaning that consumers are not very responsive to price changes—we need a large price hike to eliminate the excess demand for housing caused by the tax. Therefore, consumers will be hit by a large increase in price, and so they will pay the bulk of the tax. This is shown in panel A of Figure 15.4: Demand is inelastic—the demand curve is steep—and a $5 tax increases the equilibrium price by $4 (from $10 to $14). Consumers pay four-fifths of the tax. In panel B, demand is elastic—the demand curve is nearly flat—and consumers pay a small part of the tax. A $5 tax increases the equilibrium price by only $1 (from $10 to $11), so consumers pay only one-fifth of the tax.

The amount of backward shifting to input suppliers depends on their responsiveness to changes in input prices. We know that a tax on a product causes an excess supply of the inputs used to produce that product, and input prices must drop to eliminate the excess supply. If input suppliers are not very responsive to price changes—meaning that the supply of inputs is very inelastic—a large decrease in input prices will be needed to eliminate the excess supply of inputs. Therefore, input suppliers will pay the bulk of the tax.

Why should we care about tax shifting? An important policy question is, Who actually pays the taxes that support public goods? We've seen that the easy answer—the people who are legally responsibile for paying the tax—is often wrong. A tax increases consumer prices and decreases input prices, so we must look beyond the taxpayer to determine who actually bears the cost of a tax. The subtleties of tax shifting are often missed by the people who design our tax policy and the media folks who report on it.

Applications: Cigarette Tax and Luxury Tax

We can use what we've learned about tax shifting to discuss some recent episodes in tax policy. In 1994, President Clinton proposed an immediate $0.75 per pack increase in the cigarette tax. The tax had two purposes: to generate revenue for Clinton's health-care reform plan and to decrease medical costs by discouraging smoking. Figure 15.5 shows the effects of the proposed tax on the cigarette market. The tax would decrease the supply

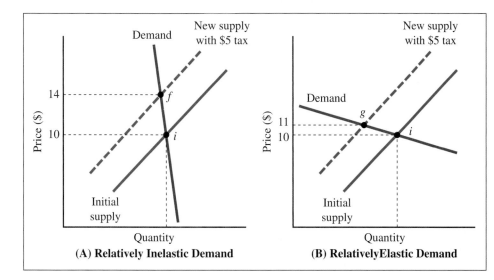

(A) Relatively Inelastic Demand

(B) RelativelyElastic Demand

Figure 15.4

Elasticities of Demand and Tax Effects

If demand is inelastic (panel A), a tax will increase the market price by a large amount, so consumers will bear a large share of the tax. If demand is elastic (panel B), the price will increase by a small amount and consumers will bear a small share of the tax.

Figure 15.5
Market Effects of a Cigarette Tax

A tax of $0.75 per pack of cigarettes shifts the supply curve to the left, moving the market equilibrium from point *i* to point *f*. The equilibrium price increases from $2.00 to $2.45, and the equilibrium quantity decreases.

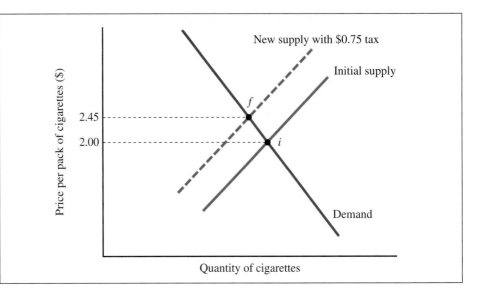

It appears that tobacco farmers and landowners understand the economics of cigarette taxes. Led by a group of representatives and senators from tobacco-growing areas in North Carolina, Kentucky, and Virginia, the Congress scaled back Clinton's proposed tax hike from $0.75 to $0.05. Although the government would collect the tax from cigarette producers, savvy tobacco farmers realized the tax would decrease their income and the price of the land used to grow tobacco. The representatives of tobacco-growing areas, acting on behalf of tobacco farmers and landowners, used their power in Congress to scale back the President's proposed tax hike.

Another lesson on backward shifting comes from a special luxury tax passed by the U.S. Congress in 1990 and repealed a few years later. The idea was to raise money from wealthy consumers by taxing luxury goods such as expensive boats. For example, the luxury tax on a $300,000 boat was $20,000. In fact, the luxury tax was shared by consumers and input suppliers, including people who worked in boat factories and boat yards. The tax decreased the quantity of boats produced, so the boat industry needed fewer workers, leading to layoffs and lower wages for the remaining workers. Although the idea behind the luxury tax was to "soak the rich," the tax actually harmed low-income workers in the boat industry.

The Total Burden of a Tax

We've seen that people respond to a tax by changing their behavior, causing the tax to be shifted to other people. These changes in behavior also have implications for the total burden of a tax. If people change their behavior in response to a tax, the total burden of a tax will exceed the amount of money the government actually collects from the tax. To see why, suppose the government imposes a tax on No. 3 pencils and the tax is large enough that everyone who initially used No. 3 pencils switches to other types of pencils or other writing implements. If no one purchases No. 3 pencils, the tax won't raise any revenue for the government, but the tax generates a burden because some people who would prefer to use No. 3 pencils have switched to other writing implements.

A luxury tax on expensive boats will harm wealthy consumers as well as the people who work in boat factories and boat yards.

We'll use the fish market to explore the total burden of a tax. In Figure 15.6, the initial supply curve for fish is a horizontal line, indicating that the fish market is a constant-cost industry. This means that input prices don't change as the industry grows or shrinks. The demand curve intersects the initial supply curve at point *i*, so the price is $2 per pound and the quantity is 60,000 pounds of fish per day. If the government imposes a tax of $1 per pound of fish, the supply curve will shift upward by $1. In addition to paying $2 for the inputs required to produce one pound of fish, the fish producer must also pay a $1 tax, so the price required to cover all expenses is now $3 instead of $2.

In Figure 15.6, the fish tax increases the equilibrium price of fish from $2 to $3. Why does the price increase by an amount equal to the tax? In a constant-cost industry, input prices are fixed, so there is no opportunity to shift the tax backward onto input suppliers: They get the same prices for their inputs, regardless of how much output is produced. Therefore, consumers bear the full cost of the tax.

ACTIVE GRAPH

Figure 15.6
Total Burden of a Tax
In a constant-cost industry, a tax increases the equilibrium price by the tax ($1 per pound in this example). Consumer surplus decreases by areas *R* and *E*. Total tax revenue is shown by rectangle *R*, so the total burden exceeds tax revenue by triangle *E*, sometimes known as the deadweight loss or excess burden of the tax.

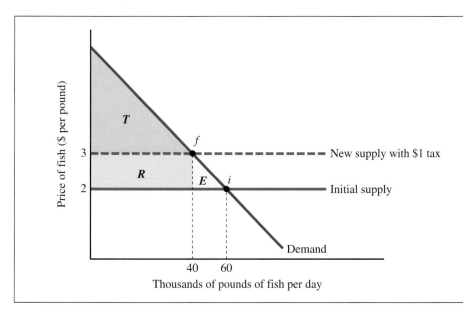

We can use the concept of consumer surplus to determine just how much consumers lose as a result of the tax. Before the fish tax, the consumer surplus is shown by the area between the initial supply curve and the demand curve, or areas T, R, and E. When the price increases to $3, the consumer surplus shrinks to the area of triangle T, so the loss of consumer surplus is shown by rectangle R and triangle E. Let's take a closer look at these two areas:

- Rectangle R shows the extra money consumers must pay for the 40,000 pounds of fish they purchase. The tax increases the price by $1 per pound, so consumers pay an extra $40,000.

- Triangle E shows the loss of consumer surplus on the fish that are not consumed because of the tax. Consumers obey the law of demand, so when the price rises, they cut their purchases, buying 20,000 fewer pounds of fish. As a result, they give up the consumer surplus they would have received on these 20,000 pounds of fish.

How does the total burden of the tax compare to the tax revenue raised by the government? The total tax revenue is the tax per pound ($1) times the quantity consumed (40,000 pounds), or $40,000. This is shown by rectangle R: Part of the loss experienced by consumers is the revenue gain for government. In addition to losing rectangle R, consumers also lose triangle E, so the consumers' total burden of the tax exceeds the tax revenue. Triangle E is sometimes known as the **deadweight loss from taxation** or the **excess burden of a tax**. Because the tax causes consumers to change their behavior—they consume less fish at the higher price—there is a deadweight loss or excess burden.

The essential reason for excess burden is that taxes cause people to change their behavior, making choices to avoid taxes. For another example of changes in behavior in response to taxes, read "A Closer Look: Taxes and December Babies."

Deadweight loss from taxation: The difference between the total burden of a tax and the amount of revenue collected by the government.

Excess burden of a tax: Another name for deadweight loss.

TEST Your Understanding

4. Complete the statement with *right* or *left*: A tax on a particular good shifts the market supply curve to the _____.

5. How will a tax on backpacks affect the equilibrium price and quantity of backpacks?

6. Complete the statement with *excess supply* or *excess demand*: A tax on chairs will initially cause _____ in the market for chairs and _____ in the markets for the inputs used to make chairs.

A CLOSER LOOK Taxes and December Babies

The current tax law includes a tax credit for children: A child born on or before December 31 reduces the household's tax liability in that year and every subsequent year until the child reaches 18. A recent study shows that the higher the tax credit, the larger the percentage of children born in the last week of the year and the smaller the percentage of children born in the first week of the year[4]. It appears that couples time the births of their children to take advantage of the tax credit. The authors estimate that increasing the tax benefit of having a child by $500 raises the probability of having the child in the last week of December by about 27%.

Public Choice

We have discussed the challenges associated with providing and paying for goods that generate spillover benefits. In this part of the chapter, we look at how governments actually operate, exploring four contrasting views of government that have emerged from a field of study known as **public-choice economics**.

Public choice economics: A field of economics that explores how governments actually operate.

Governments Take Actions to Promote Efficiency

The public-interest view of government is based on the idea that governments make the economy more efficient. For example, governments provide public goods, including dams, national defense, and space exploration. Because of the free-rider problem, a system of voluntary contributions for public goods is unlikely to raise enough money to support public goods at the efficient levels. The alternative to voluntary contributions is to give government the power to collect taxes.

Voters Tell Governments What to Do

The second view of government focuses on voters and how they affect government decisions. We vote directly on ballot measures and budget elections, both of which may impose constraints on government. We also vote for people to represent our viewpoints in legislative bodies (city councils, state legislatures, Congress) and in executive positions (mayor, governor, president). The basic idea of a democracy is that the government will take actions that are approved by the majority of citizens. If governments are responsive to voters, the voting public ultimately makes all the important decisions, and the actions of government reflect the preferences of voters.

One result of public choice economics is known as the median-voter rule. According to the **median-voter rule**, the choices made by government will reflect the preferences of the median voter, defined as the voter who splits the voting population into two halves, one half wanting more of something (for example, a larger government budget) and the other half wanting less (a smaller government budget). As we'll see, this rule has some interesting implications for decision-making and politics.

Median-voter rule: A rule suggesting that the choices made by government will reflect the preferences of the median voter.

To see the logic of this rule, consider a state where there are two candidates for governor—Penny and Buck—and the only issue in the election is how much the state should spend on education. Each citizen will vote for the candidate whose proposed education budget is closest to the citizen's preferred budget. Figure 15.7 shows citizens'

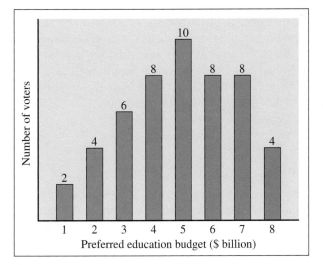

Figure 15.7
Median Voter Rule
If Penny proposes a $3 billion budget and Buck proposes a $7 billion budget, the election will result in a tie. By moving toward the median budget, Penny can increase her chance of being elected. Both candidates will propose a budget close to the $5 billion preferred budget of the median voter.

preferences for education spending, with different preferred budgets on the horizontal axis and the number of voters with each preferred budget on the vertical axis. For example, 2 citizens have a preferred budget of $1 billion, 4 have a preferred budget of $2 billion, and so on. The median budget, which splits the rest of the voters into two equal groups (20 voters on either side), is $5 billion.

Suppose the two candidates start out with very different proposed education budgets. Penny proposes a budget of $3 billion, and Buck proposes $7 billion. The 20 citizens with preferred budgets less than or equal to $4 billion will vote for Penny because her proposed budget is closest to their preferred budgets. Buck's supporters include the 20 citizens with preferred budgets greater than or equal to $6 billion. The two candidates will split the 10 voters with a preferred budget of $5 billion (halfway between the two proposed budgets), so each candidate will get a total of 25 votes, resulting in a tie.

Penny could increase her chance of being elected by increasing her proposed budget. Let's say she proposes $4 billion instead of $3 billion. The voters with a preferred budget of $5 billion will switch to Penny because Penny's $4 billion proposal is now closer to their $5 billion preferred budget than Buck's $7 billion. Penny won't lose any of her other votes, so she will win the election by a vote of 30 (2 + 4 + 6 + 8 + 10) to 20 (8 + 8 + 4). If Buck is smart, he will realize that he could get more votes by moving toward the median budget. For example, if he decreases his proposed budget to $6 billion, the election would result in a tie vote again. Penny and Buck will continue to move their proposed budgets toward the median budget ($5 billion) until they both actually propose budgets that are very close to the median budget.

There are powerful forces pulling the two candidates toward the preferences of the median voter. As long as Penny proposes a smaller budget than Buck, the people with small preferred budgets will continue to vote for her. The benefit of moving toward the median is that she can take some votes from Buck. Similarly, Buck doesn't have to worry about people with large preferred budgets but can concentrate instead on the battle for voters in the middle. The result is that by election day, the 2 candidates have adopted virtually the same position: the position of the median voter. The median-voter rule says that the choices made by government will reflect the preferences of the median voter. In other words, there isn't much of a choice.

The logic of the median-voter result also applies to competition among some types of sellers. Read the "A Closer Look: Are Politicians Like Ice-Cream Vendors?"

It is also possible to "vote with your feet." The economist Charles M. Tiebout suggested that a household's choice of which community to live in is based in part on the tax and spending policies of different communities. Households express their preferences by moving to communities that offer the best package of services and taxes. A community with inefficient public services will experience a loss in population, perhaps causing the local officials to make the public services more efficient.

It is clear that people vote with their ballots and with their feet. In both cases, citizens can express their preferences for public goods, taxes, and public policies. These two sources of citizen power limit the ability of governments to take actions that are inconsistent with the preferences of most voters.

Government Officials Pursue Their Own Self-Interest

Several economists, including Nobel laureate James Buchanan, have suggested a model of government that focuses on the selfish behavior of government officials. According to this view, politicians and bureaucrats pursue their own narrow interests, which of course may differ from the public interest. For example, politicians or bureaucrats may

A CLOSER LOOK | Are Politicians Like Ice-Cream Vendors?

Imagine a one-mile stretch of beach with 120 swimmers and sunbathers distributed evenly along the beach. Suppose each person on the beach will purchase one ice-cream cone. If there are two ice-cream vendors on the beach selling an identical product, where will they locate? The most efficient arrangement would be to divide the beach into two half-mile territories and locate each vendor at the middle of his or her territory. Lefty would be at the quarter-mile mark, and Righty would be at the three-quarter mile mark. Each vendor will sell 60 ice-cream cones. If beach people patronize the closest vendor, this arrangement will minimize the total travel costs of ice-cream patrons.

Is this an equilibrium arrangement? If Lefty were to move to the right—to the half-mile mark, the median location—he would not lose any of his customers to his left but would capture part of Righty's market: Lefty would now be the closest vendor for the people located between the half-mile mark and the five-eighths mark, so he would sell 75 ice-cream cones instead of only 60. Righty would now sell only 45 cones. To protect her market, Righty would move to the median location too. In the equilibrium, both vendors pick the median location, with equal numbers of customers on each side (60 for each vendor). The outcome of the ice-cream vendors' game is the same as the politicians' game. Like the politicians, the vendors have an incentive to move to the median location, so there is no real difference between the two vendors.

gain prestige from starting a new spending program even if the cost of the program exceeds its social benefit. Because voters don't have much information about the costs and benefits of public services, they may not be in a position to evaluate the actions of politicians or bureaucrats and vote accordingly.

The self-interest theory of government explains why voters sometimes approve explicit limits on taxes and government spending. For example, most states have limits on the amount of property taxes that can be raised, and many states also limit total government spending. According to the self-interest theory of government, limitations on taxes and spending are necessary safeguards against politicians and bureaucrats who benefit from larger budgets.

The theory of rent seeking, which we described in Chapter 10, also applies to governments. Many public policies cause one group of citizens to gain at the expense of others, and a citizen group may try to persuade government officials to implement policies that are favorable to members of the group. Resources are expended in the attempts to influence the decisions of politicians and bureaucrats, and from a social point of view, much of this expenditure is wasteful.

Special-Interest Groups Manipulate the Government

Another model of government is based on the idea that small groups of people manipulate government for their own gain. Suppose the total benefit of a dam is less than its total cost, so the project is inefficient, but a few farmers reap large benefits from the dam, while the costs are spread over a million taxpayers. The farmers have a strong incentive to spend time and money to convince policymakers to build the dam. If the tax is only $1 per person, not many taxpayers will make their preferences known to policymakers. If politicians listen to people who express their preferences and contribute money to political campaigns, the inefficient project may be approved. This is an example of a special-interest group (farmers) that manipulates government at the expense of a larger group (all taxpayers). In general, when a few people share the benefit from a project and a large number of people share the cost, government is more likely to approve inefficient projects.

In general, whenever benefits are concentrated on a few citizens but costs are spread out over many citizens, we expect special-interest groups to form. Special-interest organizations often use lobbyists to express their views to government officials and policy makers.

The European Union (EU), with 15 member nations, makes decisions that affect people and firms throughout Europe. As the power of the union has grown, so has the number of lobbyists expressing their points of view. By 1995, there were 10,000 lobbyists trying to influence decision-makers on the European Commission (the executive branch), the Council of Ministers (the representatives of member states), and the European Parliament (popularly elected representatives).[5] The fear of manipulation by lobbyists representing special interests has led some officials to advocate a formal registration process: Each lobbyist would be required to provide a list of his or her clients and the amount of money spent on the behalf of each client. Under another proposal, lobbyists would be issued color-coded entry badges that would allow them to enter only certain parts of the parliament building, limiting their access to officials of the EU.

Which Theory Is Correct?

Which of these theories best describes the actual practices of governments? This is a very difficult question. Economists and political scientists have studied many dimensions of the decision-making processes underlying tax policies and spending policies. There is evidence that people do vote with ballots and with their feet and that these two forms of voting make a difference. There is also evidence that government officials sometimes pursue their own interests and those of special-interest groups. The field of public choice is a very active area of research involving economists and political scientists.

TEST Your Understanding

7. In Figure 15.7, suppose that 32 additional citizens enter the state and each has a preferred budget of $2 billion. How will the new citizens affect the election?

8. Do you think all citizens have the same opportunity to vote with their feet, picking the community that provides the best package of goods and services.

9. In the 1960s and 1970s, many people greeted Vietnam War protesters with signs that read "America: Love It or Leave It." Does your ability to vote with your feet vary with the level of government?

Using the TOOLS

In this chapter, we explain why the government provides public goods. Because of the free-rider problem, we can't rely on voluntary contributions to support public goods and subsidies, so we use taxes to support public programs. Here are some opportunities to do your own economic analysis of public goods and taxes.

1. ECONOMIC EXPERIMENT: Voluntary Contributions

In this voluntary-contribution experiment, students play the role of citizens who have the opportunity to contribute money to support public education. Here is how the experiment works:

- The class is divided into groups of three to five students per group, with each group representing a citizen. Each group starts with $30.

- Each time period each citizen decides how much to contribute to public education. The maximum contribution is $10 per time period. The group records this amount on its report card.
- The instructor computes the total contributions to public education. Each dollar contributed to public education decreases the cost of the city's welfare system and criminal-justice system by $3, so the city's budget savings from the contributions equals the total contributions times 3. The tax refund per citizen equals the budget savings divided by the number of citizens. Here are some examples of contributions and tax refunds for a city with 20 citizens:

Total Contributions	Decrease in Budget	Tax Refund per Citizen
$20	$60	$6
$100	$300	$30
$200	$600	$60

- The experiment is run for five rounds. A group's score for the experiment equals the amount of money it has at the end of five rounds.

2. Stream Preservation

Consider a trout stream that is threatened with destruction by a nearby logging operation. Each of the 10,000 local fishers would be willing to pay $5 to preserve the stream. The owner of the land would incur a cost of $20,000 to change the logging operation to protect the stream.

a. Is the preservation of the stream efficient from the social perspective?

b. If the landowner has the right to log the land any way he wants, will the stream be preserved?

c. Propose a solution to this problem. Describe a transaction that would benefit the fishers and the landowner.

d. Will your proposed solution work?

3. Shifting a Housecleaning Tax

Consider a city where people from poor households clean the houses of rich households. Initially, firms charge households $10 per hour, keep $1 per hour for administrative costs, and pay their workers $9 per hour. Like many luxury goods, the demand for housecleaning service is very elastic. Housecleaning workers are not very responsive to changes in the wage.

a. Use supply and demand curves to show the initial equilibrium in the market for cleaning services (price = $10 per hour; quantity = 1,000 hours of cleaning per week), and label the equilibrium point with an *i*.

b. Suppose the city imposes a tax of $3 per hour of cleaning services, and one-third of the tax is shifted forward to consumers. Use your graph to show the effects of the tax on the housecleaning market. Label the new equilibrium point with an *f*. What is the new price?

c. Is it reasonable that only one-third of the tax is shifted forward? Explain.

d. Suppose that firms continue to keep $1 per hour for administrative costs. Predict the new wage.

e. Who bears the bulk of the housecleaning tax: wealthy households or poor households?

Summary

In this chapter, we've seen that governments can solve the problems caused by spillover benefits. We also saw that taxes affect the prices of consumer goods and inputs, and that we must look beyond the taxpayer to determine who actually bears the cost of a tax. We've also examined three different views on how governments actually operate. Here are the main points of the chapter:

1. If the cost of a particular good exceeds its per capita benefit, that good will not be provided by a market, even if the total benefit of the good exceeds its total cost. We can use government—with its taxing authority—to make a collective decision about whether to provide such a good.

2. A system of voluntary contributions suffers from the free-rider problem: People will voluntarily contribute only a small fraction of the amount that would be generated under a compulsory taxation to pay for the public good.

3. A tax on a good will be shifted forward to consumers and backward to input suppliers.

4. Because a tax causes people to change their behavior, the total burden of the tax exceeds the revenue generated by the tax.

Key Terms

deadweight loss from taxation, 320
excess burden of a tax, 320
free-rider problem, 311

median-voter rule, 321
private good, 310

public choice economics, 321
public good, 310

Problems and Discussion Questions

1. A three-person city is considering a fireworks display. Bertha is willing to pay $100 for the proposed fireworks display; Marian is willing to pay $30; Sam is willing to pay $20. The cost of the fireworks display is $120.
   a. Will any single citizen provide the display on his or her own?
   b. If the cost of the fireworks display is divided equally among the citizens, will a majority vote in favor of the display?
   c. Describe a transaction that would benefit all three citizens.

2. Churches collect substantial sums of money through voluntary contributions. What explains their ability to overcome the free-rider problem at least partially?

3. Suppose the students in the chapter's free-rider experiment make the following agreement: If any single person does not contribute three dimes, all the contributions will be returned, each contributor receiving a refund equal to the amount that he or she contributed. How will this agreement affect the outcome of the experiment?

4. The spotted owl is an endangered creature that lives in old-growth forests. Logging in the old-growth forests destroys the habitat of the owls. Explain how the lessons from the wolf-preservation program might be applied to the issue of preserving the spotted owl.

5. Each of the 80,000 citizens in a particular county would be willing to pay $0.10 to increase the number of wolf litters by one. Each litter of wolves imposes costs on ranchers (from livestock losses) of $5,000.
   a. Is the provision of an additional litter of wolves efficient from the social perspective?
   b. If ranchers have the right to kill any wolves on their property, will an additional litter be protected?
   c. Propose a solution to this problem. Describe a transaction that would benefit the wolf lovers and ranchers.

6. Contributions to organizations such as United Way and the American Cancer Society are tax deductible: For each dollar contributed, a person's tax liability decreases by $0.15 to $0.31. Explain the rationale for this tax policy.

7. Under a special luxury tax passed by Congress in 1990, buyers of expensive cars pay a 10% tax on the portion of the purchase price above $30,000.

    a. Will the luxury car tax be paid exclusively by the wealthy consumers who buy expensive cars?

    b. What information do you need to determine the share of the tax paid by wealthy consumers?

8. In the words of Will Rogers, "The trouble with land is that they're not making it any more." In other words, the supply of land is fixed, and the supply curve is a vertical line.

    a. If the government imposes a tax on land, which side of the market—land consumers or landowners—will pay a larger part of the tax?

    b. Will the land tax generate a deadweight loss?

9. Consider the example of the governor's election shown in Figure 15.7. Suppose 18 new people move into the state and each newcomer has a desired education budget of $9 billion.

    a. Will the two candidates change their proposed education budget? If so, how much will each candidate propose?

    b. How would your answer to part (a) change if each newcomer had a desired budget of $15 billion instead of $9 billion?

10. Consider the market effects of a tax on hotel rooms. The market is perfectly competitive, with an initial equilibrium price of $50 per night and an initial equilibrium quantity of 100 rooms rented out per day. Draw a supply and demand graph such that a $10 tax per room increases the equilibrium price from $50 to $56 and decreases the equilibrium quantity from 100 rooms to 80 rooms. How is the tax divided between consumers and input suppliers?

11. **Web Exercise.** Visit the Web site of the U.S. Department of Treasury (*http://www.ustreas.gov*). Access the most recent annual report, and list the 10 largest expenditure categories. Identify the categories with the most rapid increases in the last few years.

12. **Web Exercise.** Visit the Web site of the Census Bureau that has data on government finance (*http://www.census.gov/govs/www*). Click the link entitled "State and Local Government Finance Estimates, by State" and get the most recent data on your state's tax and expenditures. How does the percentage of your state's revenue from income taxes compare to the percentage shown for all states in Figure 15.2?

Take It to the Net

We invite you to visit the O'Sullivan/Sheffrin page on the Prentice Hall Web site at:
http://www.prenhall.com/osullivan/
for additional World Wide Web exercises for this chapter.

Model Answers to Questions

Chapter-Opening Questions

1. A system based on voluntary contributions would suffer from the free-rider problem, with few people contributing money to support the public good.

2. The payments to host landowners treat preservation as a public good supported by money collected from the people who benefit from preservation.

3. The housing firm will collect more money from consumers (the price of apartments will be higher) and pay less money to input suppliers (the prices of inputs will be lower), so consumers and input suppliers will indirectly pay the tax.

4. A liberal candidate who moves toward the center won't lose the votes of liberal citizens but will gain some votes from moderate citizens. A conservative candidate who moves toward the center won't lose conservative votes but will gain moderate votes. Both candidates are likely to adopt the position favored by the median voter.

Test Your Understanding

1. The producer of a private good collects money from each consumer. If you don't pay, you don't get the good. In contrast, it is impossible to prevent people who don't pay from consuming a public good.

2. If Margie adds a dime to the pot, the instructor adds 20 cents and then divides the 30 cents equally among the 10 students, so Margie gets back 3 cents for every dime she puts in.

3. She will not contribute the extra dime because the marginal benefit (3 cents) is less than the marginal cost (10 cents).

4. Left.

5. The equilibrium price increases and the equilibrium quantity decreases.

6. Excess demand, excess supply.

7. The median voter now has a preferred budget of $3 billion: A total of 38 voters have a lower preferred budget ($1 or $2 billion), and a total of 38 voters have a higher preferred budget. Both candidates will propose the median budget ($3 billion).

8. Low-income households cannot afford housing in many neighborhoods, so they have fewer options. Many suburban communities have zoning policies that limit high-density housing, restricting the choices of low-income households. If there is racial discrimination, minority households will have fewer options.

9. At the local level, the typical metropolitan area has many municipalities to choose from, so foot voting is not very costly. At the national level, voting with your feet means renouncing your citizenship and moving far away, so it is more costly.

Using the Tools

2. Stream Preservation

a. The benefit is $50,000 (10,000 fishers time $5 per fisher), which exceeds the cost of $20,000. Because the benefit exceeds the cost, the preservation of the stream is socially efficient.

b. No. If the landowner is also a fisher, the $20,000 cost exceeds the $5 benefit.

c. The citizens could contribute to a stream-preservation fund to cover the landowner's cost. If each fisher contributed $3 (60% of his or her benefit), together they could raise a total of $30,000. The landowner would be better off by $10,000, and each fisher would be better off by $2.

d. The free-rider problem may make it difficult to raise enough money to pay off the landowner.

3. Shifting a Housecleaning Tax

a. See Figure 15.A.

b. See Figure 15.A. The tax shifts the supply curve to the left, and the new price is $11.

c. We know that demand is very elastic and input suppliers are not very responsive, so a one-third shift is reasonable.

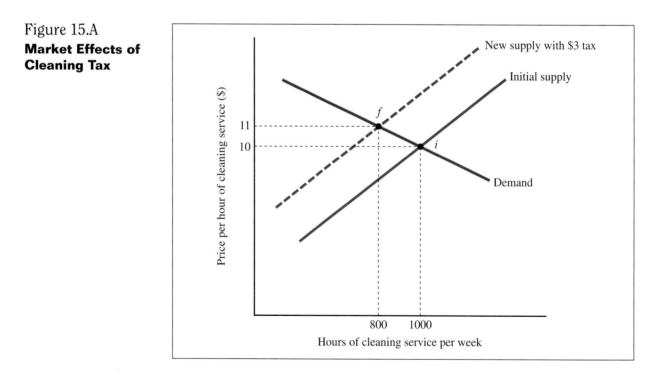

Figure 15.A
Market Effects of Cleaning Tax

d. The firm collects $11 from consumers, pays the $3 tax, and pays its $1 administrative cost, leaving only $7 for workers. The wage decreases from $9 to $7.

e. Workers experience a wage cut of $2 per hour, while consumers pay an additional $1 per hour for cleaning services.

 # Notes

1. Carl Sagan, "A Warning for Us?," *Parade*, June 5, 1994, p. 8; John Boudreau, "Collision Course: Scientists Say There's a Big Asteroid Bang in Our Future," *Washington Post*, April 6, 1994, p. C1.

2. "Mirror Beam Could Deflect Killer Asteroid, Theory Says," *New York Times*, November 9, 1994, p. C6.

3. Terry L. Anderson, "A Carrot to Save the Wolf," *The Margin*, Spring 1992, p. 28.

4. Stacy Dickert-Conlin and Amitabh Chandra, "Taxes and the Timing of Births," *Journal of Political Economy* 107, February 1999, pp. 161–77.

5. Charles Goldsmith, "The EU Is Beset by Swarms of Lobbyists," *Wall Street Journal*, April 14, 1995, p. A6.

Environmental Policy

Under the Climate Control Accord of 1994, electric utilities in the United States agreed to do their part in the battle against global warming. Arizona Public Service provides electricity to the rapidly growing population in the southwestern United States. Although the utility could decrease its emissions of the pollutants responsible for global warming, it would be very costly to do so. Instead, Arizona Public Service paid for projects that will decrease air pollution in India, China, and other developing countries, where pollution abatement costs less than it does in developed countries.[1] In addition, Arizona Public Service paid for a reforestation project in Mexico, which will help in the battle against global warming because forests absorb some of the pollutants responsible for global warming.

his story of Arizona Public Service provides an introduction to recent innovations in environmental policy. Governments around the world are setting pollution targets and letting polluters decide how to meet those targets. This approach contrasts sharply with the traditional regulatory policy under which the government gets involved in the details of pollution abatement. In the case of global warming, Arizona Public Service can meet its pollution-abatement responsibility by paying for abatement projects elsewhere, even projects in other countries. Indeed, our most pressing environmental problems—global warming, the depletion of the ozone layer, and acid rain—cross international boundaries, and so do the solutions.

As we saw in the previous chapter, the government has a role in markets with spillover benefits. In this chapter, we'll see that the government also plays a role in markets with spillover costs.

SPILLOVER **PRINCIPLE**

> **For some goods, the costs or benefits associated with the good are not confined to the person or organization that decides how much of the good to produce or consume.**

One of the lessons from Chapter 6 that if a particular good generates spillover costs, the market equilibrium will be inefficient and a tax on pollution will make the market efficient. In this chapter, we take a closer look at spillover costs, exploring several environmental problems that result from spillover costs and evaluating alternative policies to deal with spillover costs. You've seen the headlines and read the stories about global warming, the hole in the ozone layer, acid rain, and urban smog. Now you'll learn why these problems occur and what we can do about them. Here are some practical questions that we answer:

1. How would a switch from a traditional regulatory policy to a pollution tax affect the price of a polluting good and the amount of pollution?
2. What is a carbon tax, and how would a tax of $100 per ton of carbon affect the equilibrium price of gasoline?
3. Why do we want to protect the ozone layer in the upper atmosphere but get rid of ozone (also known as smog) near the earth's surface?
4. What is the rationale for the cash-for-clunkers program, under which firms buy old cars and destroy them?

Pollution Tax Versus Regulation

As we saw in Chapter 6, the economist's response to a pollution problem is to impose a pollution tax. A pollution tax forces firms to pay for the waste they generate, causing firms to produce less of the polluting good. In this chapter, we'll take a closer look at a firm's response to a pollution tax, showing that a pollution tax also encourages firms to spend money to abate pollution. We'll also look at some alternatives to a pollution tax.

Suppose there are several paper mills along a river and a city downstream from the mills uses the river water for drinking. Each gallon of chemical waste from paper mills increases the city's water-treatment costs by $4. Therefore, the appropriate **pollution tax**, equal to the spillover cost per ton of waste, is $4 per gallon of waste. Assume that each paper mill produces one ton of paper per day.

Pollution tax: A tax or charge equal to the spillover cost per unit of waste.

The Firm's Response to a Pollution Tax

Most polluting firms can control the amount of waste they dump into the environment. For example, a paper firm could install filters and other abatement equipment, or it could switch to raw materials that generate less chemical waste. The first two columns of Table 16.1 show a hypothetical relationship between the volume of waste generated and the cost of producing one ton of paper. For example, the cost per ton is $60 if the firm generates 5 gallons of waste per ton of paper but $61 if the firm generates only 4 gallons of waste per ton of paper. In other words, when the firm decreases its waste by 1 gallon, the production cost per ton increases by $1. As the firm continues to decrease the volume of waste, it becomes progressively more expensive to decrease it further. This makes sense because the firm must use progressively more expensive abatement equipment to decrease the volume of waste. For example, the cost of eliminating the last gallon of waste is $30 ($116 minus $86).

The third and fourth columns of Table 16.1 show the tax cost per ton and the total cost per ton of paper with different volumes of waste. The tax is $4 per gallon of waste, so the tax cost is $20 if the firm generates 5 gallons of waste per ton of paper but only $16 for 4 gallons, $12 for 3 gallons, and so on. The fourth column of Table 16.1 shows the firm's total cost per ton of paper, equal to the sum of the production cost per ton and the tax cost per ton. If the firm generates 5 gallons of waste, the production cost will be $60 and the tax cost will be $20, so the total cost per ton is $80. As the firm continues to decrease the volume of waste, the production cost increases while the tax cost decreases. The total cost per ton initially decreases (from $80 to $77 to $76) but eventually increases, reaching $116 if the firm generates no waste.

How will the typical paper firm respond to a pollution tax? The question for the firm is: Should we continue to generate 5 gallons of waste per ton of paper and pay $20 in pollution taxes or should we spend some money to reduce our waste? In Table 16.1, the total cost per ton is minimized at $76 with 3 gallons of waste. Therefore, the typical firm will decrease its waste from 5 to 3 gallons per ton of paper.

We can use the marginal principle to explain why it is sensible to generate only 3 gallons of waste.

MARGINAL **PRINCIPLE**

> **Increase the level of an activity if its marginal benefit exceeds its marginal cost, but reduce the level if the marginal cost exceeds the marginal benefit. If possible, pick the level at which the marginal benefit equals the marginal cost.**

Table 16.1 Cost per Ton of Paper with Varying Amounts of Pollution

Waste per Ton (Gallons)	Production Cost per Ton	Tax Cost per Ton	Total Cost per Ton
5	$ 60	$20	$ 80
4	$ 61	$16	$ 77
3	$ 64	$12	$ 76
2	$ 71	$ 8	$ 79
1	$ 86	$ 4	$ 90
0	$116	$ 0	$116

In this case, the activity is reducing waste, so the firm should continue to cut its waste as long as the marginal benefit (the $4 savings in taxes) exceeds the marginal cost (the extra production cost from cutting waste by 1 gallon). Starting with 5 gallons of waste, it is sensible to cut back to 4 gallons because the $4 marginal benefit exceeds the $1 marginal cost. Similarly, it is sensible to cut back to 3 gallons because the $4 marginal benefit exceeds the $3 marginal cost. The firm will not cut back to 2 gallons because the $4 marginal benefit is less than the $7 marginal cost.

The Market Effects of a Pollution Tax

We're ready to study the market effects of a pollution tax. Suppose that each firm produces 1 ton of paper per day and has the production costs shown in Table 16.1. Figure 16.1 shows the effects of the $4 pollution tax ($4 per gallon of waste) on the industry supply curve. In a perfectly competitive industry, the equilibrium price equals the average cost of production, so each firm makes just enough money to stay in the market. The original price of $60 per ton was just high enough to cover the cost of producing a ton of paper without the pollution tax. The tax increases the cost of producing paper because the typical firm pays some pollution taxes and incurs some additional costs when it cuts back its pollution from 5 gallons to 3 gallons per ton of paper. Therefore, the $60 price will not be high enough to cover the higher production costs, so some firms will leave the market. As a result, the supply curve will shift to the left: At each price, a smaller quantity of paper will be supplied.

The leftward shift of the supply curve increases the equilibrium price of paper. In Figure 16.1, the market moves from point i to point f, where the demand curve intersects the new supply curve. The price of paper increases from $60 to $68 per ton, and consumers respond to the higher price by decreasing the quantity of paper demanded, from 100 to 80 tons per day. Like other taxes, the pollution tax is partially shifted to consumers in the form of a higher price, and they respond by consuming less paper. When consumers face the full cost of producing paper, they decide to consume less of it.

How does the pollution tax affect the total volume of waste dumped into the river? The volume of waste decreases for two reasons:

Figure 16.1

Market Effects of a Pollution Tax

The pollution tax increases the cost of producing paper, shifting the market supply curve to the left. The equilibrium moves from point i to point f. The tax increases the equilibrium price from $60 to $68 per ton and decreases the equilibrium quantity from 100 to 80 tons per day.

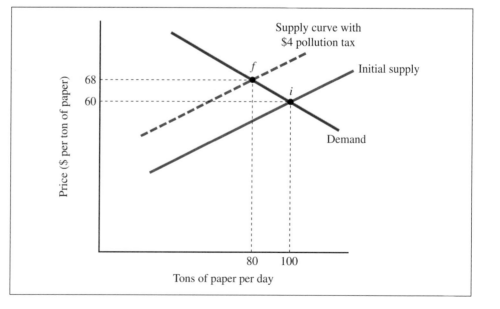

- **Abatement.** There is less waste per ton of paper: 3 gallons instead of 5 gallons per ton.

- **Lower output.** The industry produces less paper: 80 tons instead of 100 tons per day.

In this example, the volume of water pollution decreases from 500 gallons per day (100 tons of paper times 5 gallons per ton) to 240 gallons per day (80 tons of paper times 3 gallons per ton). In general, we can clean up the environment by producing less of a polluting good and generating less waste per unit of the good.

In some cases, it is government rather than industry that generates spillover costs and makes inefficient choices. For an example read "A Closer Look: Spillover Costs from Rock Salt."

Traditional Regulation: Command and Control

An alternative to a pollution tax is a system of regulations that control the amount of pollution generated by each firm. The label for a traditional regulatory policy is a **command-and-control policy.** The government commands each firm to produce no more than a certain volume of pollution and controls the firm's production process by forcing the firm to use a particular pollution-control technology. In our paper example, the government would tell each firm to produce no more than 4 gallons of chemical waste per ton of paper and force each firm to install a particular type of filter to meet the pollution target.

One problem with this approach is that the mandated abatement technology—the control part of the policy—is unlikely to be the most efficient technology. There are two reasons for this:

> **Command-and-control policy:**
> A pollution-control policy under which the government commands each firm to produce no more than a certain volume of pollution and controls the firm's production process by forcing the firm to use a particular pollution-control technology.

 **A CLOSER LOOK** Spillover Costs from Rock Salt

Local governments in many northern states use rock salt to melt ice on streets and highways during the winter. The problem is that rock salt is corrosive: It causes metal objects such as cars and bridges to rust, and it also harms roadside vegetation. According to a study by New York state, each ton of rock salt generates $1,600 worth of damage. An alternative deicer, calcium magnesium acetate (CMA), generates no spillover costs. If all the local governments in Minnesota switched from rock salt to CMA, the total cost of deicing the streets and highways—including corrosion costs—would decrease by about $244 million per year.

Why don't local governments switch from rock salt to CMA? A small local government is concerned only with the budgetary costs of melting the ice on its streets. Local governments use rock salt because it is cheaper, selling for $20 per ton, compared to $400 per ton for CMA.[2] Like a paper mill that ignores the spillover costs of paper production, the local government ignores the spillover costs of rock salt. One solution to this problem is a pollution tax equal to the

spillover cost of rock salt. If the state of Minnesota imposed a tax of $1,600 per ton of rock salt, the net price of rock salt ($1,620) would exceed the price of CMA ($400), so local governments would to switch to CMA.

The rock salt used to melt ice on streets and highways causes corrosion and requires costly repairs for cars and bridges.

- The regulatory policy specifies a single abatement technology for all firms. Because the producers of a polluting good often use different materials and production techniques, an abatement technology that is efficient for one firm is likely to be inefficient for others.

- The regulatory policy decreases the incentives to develop more efficient abatement technologies. The command part of the policy specifies a maximum volume of waste for each firm (for example, 4 gallons per ton), and there is no incentive to cut the volume of waste below the maximum volume. There is a small benefit from developing new technology because there is no payoff from using it. In contrast, a pollution tax provides the right incentives: If the firm develops a new technology that cuts the firm's waste below 4 gallons per ton, the firm will pay less in pollution taxes.

Because a command-and-control policy causes firms to use inefficient abatement technology, the policy will increase firms' costs by a large amount.

Figure 16.2 shows the market effects of a command-and-control policy. Assume that the maximum volume of waste is 4 gallons per ton of paper. This policy increases the cost of producing paper, so it shifts the market supply curve to the left. For the reasons explained earlier, the mandated technology will be less efficient—and more costly—than the technology developed under a pollution tax. That means that the supply shift resulting from the regulatory policy will be larger than the supply shift from the pollution tax. To see this, compare Figure 16.2 with Figure 16.1. The regulatory policy has a larger supply shift even though firms generate more waste (4 gallons per ton instead of the 3 gallons per ton under the tax). In Figure 16.2, the new supply curve intersects the demand curve at point *f*: The price of paper increases to $74, and the quantity of paper decreases to 70 tons per day. The total volume of pollution is 280 gallons per day (70 tons times 4 gallons per ton).

How does the regulation outcome compare to the pollution-tax outcome? Comparing Figure 16.1 with Figure 16.2, we see the following under regulation:

- The price of paper is higher: $74 instead of $68 with the tax.

- The quantity of paper produced is lower: 70 tons per day instead of 80 tons per day with the tax.

Figure 16.2

Market Effects of Command and Control

The command-and-control policy increases the cost of producing paper, shifting the market supply curve to the left. The equilibrium price increases to $74 per ton, and the equilibrium quantity decreases to 70 tons per day. Compared to the pollution-tax policy, the command-and-control policy leads to a higher price and a smaller quantity.

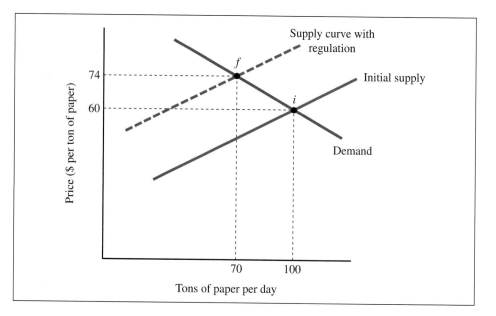

- There is more pollution: 280 gallons per day instead of 240 gallons per day with the tax.

The command-and-control policy generates more pollution at a higher cost to consumers because the mandated abatement technology is inferior—and more costly—than the technology developed under the tax policy.

Another advantage of the tax policy is that it generates tax revenue. The money raised from a pollution tax could be used to cut other taxes or increase spending on public programs. In some European nations—Germany, France, and the Netherlands—the revenue from pollution taxes is used to clean up polluted rivers.

A command-and-control policy does have one advantage over a pollution tax. The response to a command-and-control policy is predictable: The policy specifies how much waste each firm can produce, so we can predict the total volume of waste. In contrast, we don't know how firms will respond to the pollution tax—they could pollute a little or a lot, depending on the tax and the cost of abating pollution—so it is difficult to predict the total volume of waste.

Marketable Pollution Permits

In recent years, policymakers have developed a new approach to environmental policy. Here is how a government runs a system of **marketable pollution permits** works:

- Pick a target pollution level for a particular area.

- Issue just enough pollution permits to meet the pollution target.

- Allow firms to buy and sell the permits.

For example, if the target pollution level in the paper industry is 400 gallons of waste per day, the government would issue a total of 400 permits, each of which entitles a firm to generate 1 gallon of waste per day. The key innovation is that these permits are marketable: Firms can buy and sell the permits. In fact, an environmental group could decrease the amount of pollution by purchasing a permit and then retiring it.

Marketable pollution permits: A system under which the government picks a target pollution level for a particular area, issues just enough pollution permits to meet the pollution target, and allows firms to buy and sell the permits.

Marketable Permits

To explain the effects of marketable pollution permits, let's extend our example of the paper industry to include firms that have higher pollution-abatement costs. Specifically, there are two types of paper mills, each of which produces 1 ton of paper per day:

- Half the paper mills can abate pollution at a low cost, as shown in the second column of Table 16.2. For example, the production cost per ton is $61 with 4 gallons of waste, compared to $60 with 5 gallons of waste.

- Half the paper mills have high abatement costs, as shown in the third column of Table 16.2. For example, if a high-cost firm generates 4 gallons of waste, the cost per ton is $67, compared to $61 for a low-cost firm generating the same volume of waste.

The differences in abatement costs could result from differences in raw materials or production techniques. For some types of raw materials and some production techniques, the cost of abating pollution is relatively high.

Suppose the government issues four marketable permits to each paper mill. If a particular firm wants to generate 5 gallons of waste per day, it can buy a fifth permit from another firm. Of course, a firm that sells one of its permits can generate only 3 gallons of waste per day. Each firm with low abatement cost will sell a permit to a firm with high

Table 16.2 Abatement Costs: Low-Cost Firm Versus High-Cost Firm

Waste per Ton (Gallons)	Production Cost per Ton: Firm with Low Abatement Cost	Production Cost per Ton: Firm with High Abatement Cost
5	$60	$60
4	$61	$67
3	$64	$82
2	$71	$112
1	$86	$172
0	$116	$300

abatement cost. Such an exchange benefits both the buyer and the seller because the buyer is willing to pay more than the seller is willing to accept.

- **Willingness to pay.** Each firm with high abatement cost is willing to pay up to $7 for a permit. If such a firm gets a fifth permit, it can generate 5 gallons of waste per ton and produce a ton of paper for $60, compared to a cost of $67 per ton when the firm has only four permits. Getting a fifth permit saves the firm $7 on the ton of paper it produces, so the firm is willing to pay up to $7 for a permit.

- **Willingness to accept.** Each firm with low abatement cost is willing to accept any amount above $3 for one of its permits. If such a firm gives up one of its four permits, it could generate only 3 gallons of waste, so its production cost for the ton of paper it produces would increase by $3 (from $61 to $64). Giving up a permit costs the firm $3, so the firm is willing to accept any amount greater than $3 for a permit.

The actual price of the permit depends on the negotiating skills of the two firms. A plausible outcome of the bargaining process is a price halfway between the buyer's $7 willingness to pay and the seller's $3 willingness to accept. If the buyer and the seller split the difference, the price will be $5.

Allowing firms to sell their permits decreases the total cost of achieving any abatement target. For each permit sold, a firm with high abatement cost saves $7 in abatement costs. The firm with low abatement cost will have one less permit, so it must abate one more unit pollution, at a cost of $3. For each permit sold, the total cost of abatement decreases by $4, the difference between the $7 cost saved by the high-cost firm and the $3 cost incurred by the low-cost firm.

Why is the total cost of abatement lower with marketable permits? By allowing firms to trade their permits, the government exploits the differences in abatement costs, relying on firms with low abatement cost to do the abatement. As a result, we can achieve the same volume of pollution abatement at a lower cost. In a perfectly competitive market, these cost savings will be passed on to consumers in the form of a lower price of paper.

Experiences with Marketable Permits

The first program of marketable pollution permits, started in 1976 by the U.S. Environmental Protection Agency, allowed limited trading of permits for several airborne pollutants. Trading was later extended to lead in gasoline (in 1985) and the chemicals that are responsible for the depletion of the ozone layer (in 1988). The 1990 Clean Air Act established a trading system for sulfur dioxide, which is responsible for acid rain.

In the early 1990s, a trading system was introduced in the Los Angeles Basin for the pollutants that are responsible for urban smog.

The first pollution permit was sold in 1977, and thousands of exchanges have occurred since then. Here are some examples:

- Duquesne Light Company paid $3,750,000 to Wisconsin Power and Light for the rights to dump 15,000 tons of sulfur dioxide. In this transaction, the price of a ton of sulfur dioxide emissions was $250.

- Mobil Oil Corporation paid $3,000,000 for the rights to dump 900 pounds of reactive vapors per day. Mobile paid this sum to the city of Torrance, California, which had earlier acquired the pollution rights from General Motors.

- A firm in Los Angeles installed a new incinerator that decreased its hydrocarbon emissions by 100 tons per year and offered to sell the rights to emit 100 tons of hydrocarbons for $400,000.

A system of marketable permits may lead to severe pollution in some areas. For example, if you live in Torrance, California, you probably don't like the idea that Mobil Oil will use a marketable permit to generate more pollution at its refinery. You probably don't care that the marketable permit system is more efficient than a command-and-control system that would limit the refinery's pollution to its current level. This "hot spot" problem suggests that the marketable permit system may be inappropriate for pollutants that generate large local effects. Alternatively, the number of permits issued for a particular geographical area could be limited to prevent severe pollution.

The government can use marketable permits to reduce air and water pollution over time. A common practice is to issue marketable permits with a one-year life and then decrease the number of permits issued each year. For example, under an air-quality management plan for the Portland Oregon, metropolitan area, the number of permits will decrease by 10% each year. This approach was also used by the Environmental Protection Agency to phase out lead in gasoline and the chemicals that are responsible for the depletion of the ozone layer.

No Market for Marketable Permits

**ECONOMIC
DETECTIVE**

A state issued some marketable permits for sulfur dioxide emissions to several electricity generators and set up a special marketing office to help firms buy and sell the permits. Most of the permits were given to the utilities with the oldest generating facilities. One year later, none of the permits had been bought or sold. This was puzzling to the state officials and the people in the marketing office. The idea of issuing marketable permits was to get a market going. Your job is to solve this mystery. Why didn't the marketable-permit program work? How could the program be changed to encourage trading?

A careful reading of the description of the permit policy reveals a clue that will help solve this mystery. Old electricity-generating facilities usually have old pollution-abatement technology, so they have higher abatement costs than newer plants. When a utility sells one of its permits, it must reduce its emissions, and this would be costly for old facilities with high abatement costs. By issuing most of the permits to old facilities with high abatement costs, the state inadvertently gave most of the permits to the utilities that had the greatest incentive to keep them. These utilities kept all their permits rather than selling them.

A simple example will show why a utility with high abatement costs will hold onto its permit. Suppose a 1-ton reduction in sulfur dioxide emissions would increase abatement costs by $1,000 in an old facility but by only $200 in a new facility. In this case, the old facility would be willing to accept no less than $1,000 for one of its pollution permits, while a new facility would be willing to pay no more than $200 for a permit. The two utilities can't make a deal because the minimum amount the old facility is willing to accept exceeds the maximum amount the new facility is willing to pay. To encourage trading, the state could redesign its permit policy to spread the permits more evenly among old and new facilities. ◆

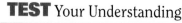

TEST Your Understanding

1. Complete the statement with *low* or *high*: Under a system of marketable pollution permits, a firm with _____ abatement costs will buy permits from a firm with _____ abatement costs.

2. Why will a switch to marketable pollution permits decrease total abatement costs?

3. Looking back at Table 16.2, suppose that for the low-cost firm, the production cost per ton with 3 gallons of waste is $69 (instead of $64). If the government issues four permits per firm, will trading still occur? Explain.

4. Looking back at Table 16.2, suppose that after the high-cost and low-cost firms finish buying and selling permits, an environmental group appears. If the group is willing to pay $10 for each gallon of waste reduction, how many permits will the group purchase?

Global Warming and Public Policy

Now that we've discussed the policy options for dealing with environmental problems, we are ready to discuss some environmental problems. We look at global warming first and then discuss ozone depletion, acid rain, and urban smog.

The Causes of Global Warming

Here is a simple experiment that explains global warming. On a warm day, park your car in a sunny spot, close the windows and wait. Solar energy in the form of visual and ultraviolet light will come through the car windows and heat the air in the car. This is the greenhouse effect: If all the windows are closed, there is no way for the heat to escape, so the temperature in the car (or in a greenhouse) will increase.

The windows of the car are like the earth's atmosphere. Solar energy comes through the atmosphere and heats the air near the earth's surface. Certain types of gases in the atmosphere (called greenhouse gases) trap this heat close to the earth's surface and are beneficial. Without these gases, the earth's surface temperature would be far below freezing, so most forms of life would die off. Unfortunately, we are pumping more of these greenhouse gases into the atmosphere, so the earth's temperature is increasing. Just as rolling up a window in a parked car increases the temperature in the car, increasing the volume of greenhouse gases increases the temperature near the earth's surface.

Carbon dioxide is by far the most important greenhouse gas. To explain why the volume of carbon dioxide is increasing, let's look at the carbon cycles, the movement of carbon between the earth's atmosphere and the plant material on the earth's surface. When a plant grows, it converts carbon dioxide from the atmosphere into carbon and stores this carbon in its tissue. When we burn oil, coal, and gas (the fossilized remains of old plants), the carbon stored in the plant material combines with oxygen to form carbon dioxide, which is released back into the atmosphere. To put it bluntly, plants suck in carbon dioxide, and we blow it back out when we burn plant material. In the last century, we have blown out more carbon than plants have been able to suck in, and the volume of carbon dioxide in the atmosphere has increased by about 25%. By digging up stored carbon and burning it, we've thrown the carbon cycle out of whack, and the resulting increase in greenhouse gases has increased global temperatures.

How does the destruction of tropical rain forests affect the volume of carbon dioxide in the atmosphere? The plants in these forests absorb some of the carbon dioxide we generate when we burn fossil fuels. The destruction of tropical rain forests has two effects:

- If trees and plants are burned to clear the land, the carbon stored in these plants is converted into carbon dioxide.

- Once the forest is cleared, there is less plant material to convert carbon dioxide into stored carbon.

As we'll see later in the chapter, one approach to dealing with global warming is to protect existing rain forests and promote the recovery of damaged forests.

The Consequences of Global Warming

Scientists agree that greenhouse gases are accumulating. The volume of atmospheric carbon dioxide is now about 25% above the preindustrial level, and it is increasing at a rate of about 1.6% per year,[3] so the volume of greenhouse gases will double in about 60 years. Most scientists agree that a doubling of atmospheric carbon dioxide will increase global temperatures, but they don't agree just how large the increase in temperature will be. Because we know so little about how the earth's ecosystems will respond to a rapid increase in carbon dioxide, the actual change in temperature could be small or large. The practical policy question is: Should we wait to find out the consequences of a doubling of atmospheric carbon dioxide or do something now to reduce the accumulation of greenhouse gases?

How would an increase in temperatures affect the earth's environment and the global economy? Most scientists expect total rainfall to increase, with some areas getting more and others getting less. The increase in carbon dioxide will make all plants—crops and weeds alike—grow faster. Overall, the net effect on agriculture is likely to be negative because scientists expect less rainfall in areas with fertile soil and more rainfall in areas with less productive soil. For a discussion of some of the implications of global warming for U.S. agriculture, read "A Closer Look: Would Global Warming Be Good for U.S. Agriculture?"

An increase in global temperatures would also melt glaciers and the polar ice caps, raising sea levels. As a result, a large amount of land currently used for agriculture or living space could be inundated. Of course, we could build dikes to protect low-lying areas, but such protective measures are very expensive. The Netherlands has launched a multibillion-dollar program to increase the height of its sea walls. According to a recent report from the Climate Institute, by the year 2070, much of the metropolitan area in Manila, Philippines, could be under 1 meter of water, and rising sea levels could force the relocation of 3.3 million people in Jakarta, Indonesia.[5]

A Carbon Tax

The economist's response to the accumulation of greenhouse gases is to impose a tax on fossil fuels. The spillover cost of a particular fuel depends on how much carbon dioxide is released into the atmosphere, so the **carbon tax** for a particular fuel would be determined by the fuel's carbon content.

Carbon tax: A tax based on a fuel's carbon content.

According to the conventional view, global warming would be a disaster for U.S. agriculture, with crop losses of about $20 billion per year. This view is based on several studies that study the effects of climatic changes on the U.S. heartland, where we grow cool-weather crops such as corn and wheat.

A recent study challenges this conventional view and suggests that global warming may actually be beneficial for U.S. agriculture.[4] Specifically, the changes in climatic conditions could increase total revenue from crops by about $1.5 billion per year. This new study differs from the older studies in two ways:

- The new study explores the effects of climatic changes on the entire United States, not just the heartland. The crop losses in the heartland will be more than offset by gains in warm-weather crops grown elsewhere (cotton, fruit, vegetables, rice, hay, and grapes).

- The old studies were based on the "dumb farmer" assumption: Farmers were assumed to use the same inputs to grow the same crops, regardless of the climatic conditions. The new study recognizes that farmers will respond to changes in climate by changing the way they grow a given crop (changing seeds, fertilizer, or growing techniques) and switching to crops that are more suited to the new climate.

The old studies generate different conclusions because they ignore the good news from global warming and assume that farmers are inflexible.

Figure 16.3 shows the effects of a carbon tax on the market for coal in China. Coal provides about three-fourths of the primary energy in China and is used in small industrial boilers, household stoves, and room heaters. In contrast, most of the coal consumed in developed countries such as the United States is used to generate electricity. A carbon tax will add to the expenses incurred by coal producers, so some of them will lose money at the initial price, and some suppliers will leave the market. The resulting decrease in the supply of coal will shift the supply curve to the left. In Figure 16.3 the carbon tax leads to a higher price for coal ($42 instead of $35 per ton) and a smaller quantity (78 instead of 100 tons per day).

Figure 16.3
Market Effects of a Carbon Tax on Coal
A carbon tax shifts the supply curve to the left, moving the equilibrium from point *i* to point *t*. A tax of $10 per ton of carbon increases the equilibrium price of coal from $35 per ton to $42 per ton and decreases the equilibrium quantity from 100 to 78 tons per day.

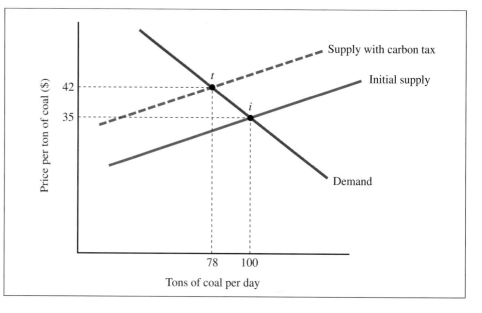

Table 16.3 shows some of the effects of two carbon taxes—a low one and a high one—on the prices of fossil fuels. For example, the high tax would more than double the price of coal (a fuel with a high carbon content), but it would increase the price of gasoline by only 23%.

In Table 16.3, we see that a carbon tax of $100 per ton of carbon would decrease greenhouse emissions by 43%, a result of three types of changes:

- The tax will increase the price of energy and increase the cost of producing energy-intensive goods. Consumers will respond by demanding smaller quantities of these goods, in part by switching to goods produced with less energy.

- Some energy producers will switch to noncarbon energy sources such as the wind, the sun, and geothermal sources.

- Energy producers will improve the efficiency of carbon-based fuels, squeezing out more energy per ton of coal or oil.

One concern about a carbon tax is that it would impose a large burden on the poor. In Table 16.3, we see that the low carbon tax would generate $10 billion per year, while the high tax would generate $125 billion per year. This money could be used to reduce income taxes or payroll taxes, reducing the burden of the carbon tax on the poor.

The Kyoto Agreement and Developing Nations

The United Nations officially recognized the greenhouse effect in 1995, when its International Panel on Climate Change noted that human activity had a "discernible influence" on global temperatures. In 1997, the Kyoto Conference on global warming produced an agreement under which the largest industrial nations, including the United States, pledged to reduce their carbon dioxide emissions to just below the 1990 levels by the year 2008. To meet the pledge, these nations must make large and costly changes in their energy systems.

Table 16.3   Effects of Different Carbon Taxes

	Low Tax	High Tax
Tax per ton of carbon	$5.00	$100.00
Effect on price of coal		
Tax per ton	$3.50	$70.00
Percentage increase	10	205
Effect on price of oil		
Tax per barrel	$0.58	$11.65
Percentage increase	2.8	55
Effect on price of gasoline		
Tax per gallon	$0.014	$0.28
Percentage increase	1.2	23
Percentage reduction in greenhouse emissions	10	43
Total tax revenue per year, U.S. (billions)	$10.00	$125.00

Source: William D. Nordhaus, "Economic Approaches to Greenhouse Warming," in *Global Warming: Economic Policy Responses*, edited by Rudiger Dornbusch and James M. Poterba (Cambridge, MA: MIT Press, 1991).

The developing nations were exempted from the Kyoto deal, over the strenuous objections of the United States and other industrialized nations. As the economies of developing nations grow over the next few decades, they are likely to rely on coal, which is inexpensive and easy to transport, as a major source of energy. Because coal generates about twice as much carbon dioxide as natural gas, the developing nations will produce a large volume of carbon dioxide emissions. The exemption of the developing nations is a stumbling block in the effort to control the accumulation of greenhouse gases.

TEST Your Understanding

5. Use a supply and demand diagram to show the effects of a carbon tax on the market for an energy-intensive good such as aluminum or steel.

6. Explain how a carbon tax would decrease the total volume of greenhouse gases.

7. In Chapter 14, you learned the rationale for subsidizing goods that generate spillover benefits. Does the same sort of reasoning apply to trees?

Other Environmental Problems

The problem of global warming is not the only environmental problem that we face today. There are many other problems, including the depletion of the ozone layer, acid rain, and urban smog. Let's look at each of these problems separately.

Ozone Depletion

A layer of ozone in the upper atmosphere prevents most of the sun's harmful ultraviolet light from reaching the surface of the earth. Ultraviolet light causes living cells to mutate, causing skin cancer and eye disease in humans and the death of marine organisms at the base of the food web. It also disrupts plant growth and hastens the decay of plastics. The ozone layer in the upper atmosphere is essential to life on this planet because it protects us from the harmful effects of ultraviolet light.

A 1991 report suggests that human-made chemicals had depleted the ozone layer by about 3% overall, with a 50% depletion in the atmosphere over Antarctica. The primary culprit is a family of chemicals known as chlorofluorocarbons (CFCs), which were once used in refrigeration, air conditioning, spray products, foam injection, and industrial solvents. When these chemicals reach the upper atmosphere, they act as catalysts, converting ozone into oxygen, which does not block ultraviolet light. The depletion over Antarctica is much greater because the presence of ice crystals accelerates this chemical reaction.

The nations of the world have agreed to stop producing CFCs altogether. Under the Montreal Protocol (of 1990), the production of these chemicals will stop by 2010. Because CFCs take a long time to break down, however, scientists expect the depletion of the ozone layer to continue for at least 50 more years. The ban on CFCs will increase the equilibrium prices of the goods that were produced with these chemicals. For example, refrigerator producers will switch from CFCs to other chemicals that don't harm the ozone layer but are more expensive and less efficient as coolants. The resulting increase in production costs will increase the equilibrium price of refrigerators.

Acid Rain

In the 1970s and 1980s, there were persistent reports of sterile lakes and withering trees in the northeastern United States, eastern Canada, Scandinavia, and Germany. The sulfur dioxide emissions (SO_2) of coal-burning power plants, combined with nitrogen oxides and other chemicals in the atmosphere to form acid rain. The rainfall in the areas downwind from the power plants changed the acidity of soil and water, causing problems for trees, fish, and other forms of aquatic life. Power plants in the eastern and midwestern United States caused acid rain in the northeastern United States and eastern Canada, while power plants in the United Kingdom and Germany caused acid rain in Scandinavia.

The Clean Air Act of 1990 established a system of marketable pollution permits for SO_2. Each utility will receive enough permits to generate between 30% and 50% of the volume of SO_2 it produced 10 years earlier. Overall, the permit system will decrease SO_2 emissions by about 10 million tons per year, a reduction of about 40%. Under the first permit trade, a Wisconsin utility sold permits to the Tennessee Valley Authority at a price of $250 per ton of sulfur dioxide. A report from the National Acid Precipitation Assessment Program (NAPAP) estimated the cost of reducing sulfur dioxide emissions under two alternative systems: one with marketable permits and one with nonmarketable permits. The cost with marketable permits is 15 to 20% lower.[6]

Although the SO_2 permits were expected to sell for about $300 per ton, by 1999 the price was only $140. The price was lower than expected for two reasons:[7]

- **Overinvestment in scrubbers.** One way to reduce the emissions of a power plant is to install scrubbers, which reduce the amount of sulfur that exits the smokestacks. The decisions to install scrubbers were made in 1992, three years before the new policy took effect. Many firms' scrubber decisions were based on an assumed permit price of $300 to $400 per ton. At this price, scrubbing would be cheaper than buying permits, so many utilities installed scrubbers. Once installed, the marginal cost of operating the scrubber equipment is only $65 per ton of SO_2. If a permit has a price

The sulfur dioxide emissions (SO_2) of coal-burning power plants combine with nitrogen oxides and other chemicals in the atmosphere to form acid rain.

of $140 per ton, it is less costly to scrub than to buy a permit. The large investment in scrubbers reduced the demand for permits (used by firms that did not install scrubbers), leading to lower permit prices.

- **Lower price for low-sulfur coal.** The other way to reduce SO_2 emissions is to switch to low-sulfur coal. In the mid-1990s, the price and transport costs of low-sulfur coal dropped, making it less expensive to switch to low-sulfur coal. The resulting decrease in the demand for SO_2 permits decreased their price.

Utilities responded to the lower than expected price of permits by canceling plans for additional investment in scrubber equipment.

Urban Smog: Emissions Standards and Cash for Clunkers

Urban smog is one of our most persistent environmental problems. Smog results from the mixing of several pollutants, including nitrogen oxides, sulfur dioxide, and volatile organic compounds. Another name for smog is ground-level ozone. Although atmospheric ozone is beneficial because it blocks harmful ultraviolet light, ozone is harmful when it comes in contact with living things, as it does at ground level. Smog causes health problems in human beings and animals. It also retards plant growth and decreases agricultural productivity. The Environmental Protection Agency (EPA) has established standards for the concentrations of urban smog. About one-third of the U.S. population lives in areas where the concentrations of smog often exceed the EPA standards.

The automobile is by far the biggest source of the pollutants that lead to smog. We currently use a command-and-control approach to regulate automobile pollution: The Environmental Protection Agency tells automakers what emissions equipment to install in cars. There are several problems with this approach:

- If a car is not properly maintained, the emissions equipment quickly loses its effectiveness. Although many states have inspection programs to monitor emissions equipment, many of the programs are not very effective.

- Many of the cars on the road were built before the emissions controls were implemented, and these cars are responsible for a large share of automobile emissions.

- The emissions equipment does not control the total emissions of the car, just the emissions per mile driven. If people drive more miles in a cleaner car, total emissions can actually increase.

An alternative to the current policy is to levy an annual pollution tax on each car.[8] At the end of the year, a car would be tested to determine the volume of pollution per mile driven. The tax per mile would equal the volume of pollution per mile times a tax per unit of pollution. The annual tax would be computed by multiplying the tax per mile by the number of miles driven in the last year. For example, if a car generated 5 units of pollution per mile and the tax per unit of pollution were $0.01, the tax per mile would be $0.05. If the car were driven 10,000 miles each year, the annual pollution tax would be $500. The pollution tax would encourage people to buy cleaner cars, maintain their emissions equipment, drive less, and use alternative modes of transportation. The tax is consistent with the idea that people should pay the full cost of driving an automobile, including the spillover costs.

One of the problems with the current policy is that it does nothing to decrease the pollution from cars that don't have pollution-control equipment. In 1992, the Environmental Protection Agency (EPA) designed a program that would allow many types of firms to meet their pollution-abatement responsibilities by purchasing and destroying old cars. A disproportionate amount of automobile air pollution comes from cars that were built before modern emissions equipment was required. The EPA has a booklet that shows how much pollution each type of car generates. Under a cash-for-clunkers program, a firm can meet its pollution abatement responsibility by retiring enough cars so the volume of automobile pollution avoided equals the amount the firm would otherwise abate itself. There have been several successful experiments with cash-for-clunkers programs in Los Angeles, Denver, and the state of Texas.

TEST Your Understanding

8. Use a supply-demand diagram to show the effects of a ban on CFCs on the market for refrigerators.

9. Explain how a carbon tax will affect the urban smog problem.

10. The policy of buying and destroying heavy polluting cars is called "Cash for Clunkers," not "Cash for Cars." Why?

Using the **TOOLS**

You've learned about several environmental policies, including a pollution tax, pollution regulations, and marketable pollution permits. Now you can use what you've learned to do your own economic analysis of environmental problems.

1. Market Effects of a Carbon Tax

Consider the market for gasoline. In the initial equilibrium, the price is $2.00 per gallon and the quantity is 100 million gallons. The price elasticity of demand is 1.0, and the price elasticity of supply is 2.0. Suppose the government imposes a carbon tax and the tax is expected to shift the gasoline supply curve to the left by 24%.

a. Use a supply-demand diagram to show the market effects of the carbon tax.

b. Predict the new equilibrium price and quantity of gasoline.

2. Predict the Price of Pollution Permits

Consider the example of marketable pollution permits discussed in this chapter. Suppose that instead of issuing 4 permits to each firm, the government issues only 3 permits to each firm.

a. How much money is a high-cost firm willing to pay to get one additional permit?

b. How much money is a low-cost firm willing to accept in exchange for one of its permits?

c. If firms split the difference between the willingness to pay and the willingness to accept for a permit, what will be the price of a permit?

3. *Hot Rod, Motor Trend,* and Cash for Clunkers

Several car-hobby magazines, including *Hot Rod* and *Motor Trend*, have run editorials in opposition to the cash-for-clunkers program. Why would car-hobby magazines oppose the program? Can you imagine any way to overcome their objections?

4. ECONOMIC EXPERIMENT: Pollution Permits

In the pollution-permit experiment, students play the role of paper firms that buy or sell pollution permits. The experiment, which extends over five trading periods, works as follows:

- The class is divided into groups of three to five students, each group representing a firm that produces 1 ton of paper per period. The instructor provides each firm with data about its cost of production. The cost depends on how much waste the firm generates: The smaller the volume of waste, the higher the production cost. Here is an example:

Gallons of waste	2	3	4
Production cost per ton	$66	$56	$50

- Each firm receives three pollution permits for each of the five trading periods. A firm that does not sell any of its permits to other firms has the right to generate 3 gallons of waste in that period. A firm that sells one of its three permits can generate only 2 gallons of waste, and a firm that buys a permit from another firm can generate 4 gallons of waste.

- At the beginning of each trading period, firms meet in the trading area to buy or sell pollution permits for that day. Each firm can buy or sell one permit per day. Once a transaction has been arranged, the buyer and the seller inform the instructor of the transaction, record the transaction on their report cards, and then leave the trading area.

- In each trading period, we compute the firm's profit with the following equation:

$$\text{profit} = \text{price of paper} - \text{production cost} + \text{revenue from permit sold} - \text{cost of permit purchased}$$

- In each period, a firm will either buy or sell a permit, so we compute the firm's profit with just 3 numbers. For example, using the production-cost numbers from the table shown, if the price of paper is $70 per ton and a firm buys a permit for $5, the firm's profit is

$$\text{profit} = \$70 - \$50 + 0 - \$5 = \$15$$

- If another firm sold a permit for $12, the firm's profit would be $16:
- profit = $70 - $66 + $12 - 0 = $16
- For the fourth and fifth trading periods, several environmental groups have the option of buying pollution permits. Each environmental group is given a fixed sum of money to spend on permits, and the objective is to get as many permits as possible, reducing the total volume of pollution in the process.

Summary

We started this chapter by showing the market effects of a pollution tax. Because a traditional command-and-control policy discourages innovation in pollution abatement technology, it is less efficient—and more costly—than a pollution tax or a system of marketable permits. Here are the main points from the chapter:

1. A pollution tax, which forces firms to pay for pollution, decreases the total volume of pollution because firms produce less of the polluting good and generate less pollution for each unit produced.

2. Compared to a pollution tax, a command-and-control policy is likely to lead to higher consumer prices and more pollution (less abatement).

3. A system of marketable permits is predictable because the government issues just enough permits to reach a target level of pollution. The system

is efficient because the firms with the lowest abatement costs will do the abatement.

4. One approach to the problem of carbon dioxide emissions is a carbon tax.

5. Urban smog is a continuing problem, in part because we use command-and-control policies. An annual pollution tax would be more effective at reducing smog.

Key Terms

carbon tax, 341
command-and-control policy, 335

marketable pollution permits, 337

pollution tax, 332

Problems and Discussion Questions

1. Use a supply-demand graph to show a situation in which the equilibrium quantity of a polluting good is 20 tons but a pollution tax decreases the equilibrium quantity of the good to zero. Is this situation likely to occur?

2. Suppose paper firms have access to the abatement technology shown in the first two columns of Table 16.1 and the government imposes a pollution tax of $8 per gallon of waste.

   a. Compute new values for the third and fourth columns of the table. How much waste will the typical firm generate?

   b. Use a supply-demand diagram to show the market effects of the tax.

   c. Would you expect the volume of pollution to be larger or smaller than the volume generated with the $4 tax (shown in Figure 16.1)?

3. Suppose the government adopts a zero-tolerance pollution policy for the production of paper. In other words, the government requires each paper mill to eliminate all its water pollution. Suppose the paper firms have access to the abatement technology shown in the first two columns of Table 16.1.

   a. What is the production cost per ton under the zero-tolerance policy?

   b. If the government uses a pollution tax to implement its zero-tolerance policy, what is the smallest tax that would cause the typical firm to voluntarily pick zero pollution?

4. To predict the market price of a marketable pollution permit, what information do you need? Explain how you would use this information.

5. Use a supply-demand diagram to show the market effects of a cash-for-clunkers program on the market for used cars.

6. Consider the use of marketable pollution permits for the control of sulfur dioxide emissions from two electric utilities: Old Power and Light (OPL) and Young Power and Light (YPL). The following table shows the production cost for the two utilities with different volumes of sulfur dioxide emissions.

Tons of Sulfur Dioxide	Production Cost for OPL	Production Cost for YPL
10	$1,000	$1,000
9	$1,100	$1,020
8	$1,300	$1,060
7	$1,600	$1,120

   Assume that the government issues 10 marketable pollution permits to OPL and 8 marketable permits to YPL.

   • Will any permits be traded? Explain.

   • Suppose the government had issued 9 permits to YPL and 9 permits to OPL. Will any permits be traded? If so, predict the equilibrium price for a permit.

7. One of the objections to a carbon tax is that it would be regressive: Poor people would pay a large fraction of their incomes for carbon taxes. How could we overcome this objection?

8. You are the economic consultant to a member of Congress. Someone has just introduced a bill that would impose a $50 carbon tax, which will of course affect the market for home-heating oil. Would you expect the entire tax to be paid by con-

sumers? Why or why not? Your job is to determine which side of the market—consumers or input suppliers—will pay the larger part of the tax. What additional information do you need?

9. **Web Exercise.** Visit the Web site for the U.S. Environmental Protection Agency (*http://www.epa.gov*). Search the site for information on electric vehicles. How do the costs of electric cars compare to the costs of gas-powered vehicles? What about performance?

10. **Web Exercise.** Visit the part of the Web site of the U.S. Environmental Protection Agency that describes acid-rain programs (*http://www.epa.gov/docs/acidrain/*). Click on "SO$_2$ Emissions Trading." Imagine that you are a member of an environmental group that wants to buy a pollution permit (an allowance). How would you do it? How much are you likely to pay for a one-ton allowance for SO$_2$? You may have to do some digging—or clicking. *Hint:* Check the auction web pages.

Take It to the Net

We invite you to visit the O'Sullivan/Sheffrin page on the Prentice Hall Web site at:
http://www.prenhall.com/osullivan/
for additional World Wide Web exercises for this chapter.

Model Answers to Questions

Chapter-Opening Questions

1. Figures 16-1 and 16-2 show that compared to a command-and-control policy, a pollution tax generates a lower price of paper, more output, and less pollution.

2. As shown in Table 16.3, a $100 tax on carbon would increase the price of gasoline by $0.28 per gallon.

3. Atmospheric ozone is beneficial because it blocks harmful ultraviolet light. Ozone is harmful when it comes in contact with living things, as it does at ground level.

4. A disproportionate amount of automobile air pollution comes from cars built before modern emissions equipment was required. The cash-for-clunkers program removes these heavy-polluting cars from the road.

Test Your Understanding

1. High, low.

2. Under a system of marketable permits, low-cost firms do most of the abating.

3. No. The low-cost firm is willing to accept any amount greater than $8 (equal to $69 – $61), which exceeds the $7 willingness to pay by the high-cost firm.

4. The group will buy one permit from each low-cost firm (the willingness to accept for one of the firm's three permits is $7 = $71 – $64) and one from each

of the high-cost firms (the willingness to accept for one of the firm's 5 permits is $7 = $67 – 60).

5. The tax will increase production costs, shifting the supply curve to the left. The new supply curve will intersect the demand curve at a higher price and a smaller quantity.

6. Consumers will buy a smaller quantity of the good. Energy producers will switch to noncarbon energy sources and improve the efficiency of carbon fuels.

7. A tree decreases the volume of carbon dioxide in the atmosphere and diminishes the problem of global warming, so there is a spillover benefit. A subsidy internalizes the externality, encouraging people to plant and maintain trees.

8. The tax will increase production costs, shifting the supply curve to the left. The new supply curve will intersect the demand curve at a higher price and a smaller quantity.

9. The tax will increase the price of gasoline, causing people to drive fewer miles and generate smaller volumes of the pollutants that cause urban smog.

10. The word *clunker* suggests an old car in poor repair, which is the sort of car that is likely to be destroyed under the policy.

Using the Tools

1. Market Effects of a Carbon Tax
   a. See Figure 16.A.

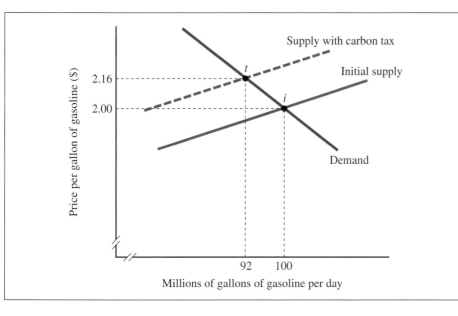

Figure 16.A
**Market Effects
of a Carbon Tax**

b. According to the price-change formula from Chapter 6, the percentage change in price is 8% = % change in demand/$(E_s + E_d)$ = 24%/(2.0 + 1.0). Therefore, the price increases from $2.00 to $2.16 per gallon. According to the formula for demand elasticity, the tax causes the market to move upward along the demand curve, so we can use the formula for the price elasticity of demand to predict the change in quantity: E_d = % change in quantity/% change in price. The percentage change in quantity is 8%: 1.0 = 8%/8%. Therefore, the quantity decreases from 100 million gallons to 92 million gallons.

2. Predict the Price of Pollution Permits

a. A high-cost firm is willing to pay up to $15 for one more permit because a fourth permit would allow the firm to generate 4 gallons (with production cost = $67 for a ton of paper) instead of 3 gallons (production cost = $82 for a ton of paper).

b. A low-cost firm is willing to accept any amount greater than $7 for one of its three permits. If a low-cost firm sold one of its permits, the firm could generate only 2 gallons of waste and its production cost would increase from $64 to $71 per ton of paper.

c. A price of $11 for a permit is halfway between the $15 willingness to pay by the high-cost firm and the $7 willingness to accept by the low-cost firm.

3. *Hot Rod, Motor Trend*, and Cash for Clunkers. The hobby magazines are written for car hobbyists, many of whom like to buy old cars and fix them up—or at least try to fix them. The cash-for-clunkers program will decrease the supply of fix-up cars and increase their price. This will make the car-restoration hobby more expensive, so we can expect fewer people to buy old cars and hobby magazines. One way to overcome this problem would be to use the clunkers program to destroy only the engine of the high-pollution cars, giving hobbyists the opportunity to buy the rest of the car and install a cleaner engine.

Notes

1. Peter Pasell, "For Utilities, New Clean-Air Plan," *New York Times*, November 18, 1994, p. C1; Brad Knickerbocker, "Trading Pollutants Is a Big First Step Toward Cleaner Air," *Christian Science Monitor*, November 22, 1994, p. 12.

2. David Morris, "A Free Market Demands Accurate Prices," *Building Economic Alternatives*, Fall 1990, p. 4.

3. Andrew R. Solow, "Is There a Global Warming Problem?" in *Global Warming: Economic Policy Responses*, edited by Rudiger Dornbush and James M. Poterba (Cambridge, MA: MIT Press, 1991).

4. Robert Mendelsohn, William D. Nordhaus, and Daigee Shaw, "The Impact of Global Warming on Agriculture: A

Ricardian Analysis," *American Economic Review*, vol. 84, no. 4, September 1994, pp. 753–771.

5. Eduardo Lachica, "Asia Faces Increasing Pressure to Act as Global Warming Threatens Its Coasts," *Wall Street Journal*, August 22, 1994, p. A5C.

6. *1990 Integrated Assessment Report* (Washington, DC: U.S. National Acid Precipitation Assessment Program, 1991).

7. Richard Schmalensee, Paul L. Joskow, A. Denn Ellerman, Juan Pablo Montery, and Elizabeth M. Bailey, "An Interim Evaluation of Sulfur Dioxide Emission Trading," *Journal of Economic Perspectives*, vol. 12, 1998, pp. 53–68.

8. Edwin S. Mills and Lawrence J. White, "Government Policies Towards Automobile Emissions Control" in *Approaches to Air Pollution Control*, edited by Anne Frielaender (Cambridge, MA: MIT Press, 1978).

Imperfect Information and Disappearing Markets

Otto is about to buy his first car. He has decided to buy a 10-year-old model X—the same make, model, and model year all of his friends have. According to several consumer magazines, half the model X cars on the road are lemons. A lemon is a car that breaks down frequently and costs a lot to repair. Otto figures that there is a 50% chance he will get a lemon. Before buying, Otto asks his friends about their experiences with their model X cars. To his surprise, 9 of 10 friends purchased cars that turned out to be lemons! Given the conflicting information from the consumer magazines and his friends, Otto doesn't know what to think. Is there a 50% chance of getting a lemon or a 90% chance?

In this chapter, we show why Otto is likely to buy a lemon, just like most of his friends. Although half the model X cars on the road may be high-quality cars, few of the high-quality cars will be offered for sale in the used-car market, so most buyers will get lemons. To understand this, think about who is more likely to sell a used car: the owner of a lemon or the owner of a high-quality car—let's call it a plum. Because people with lemons are more likely to sell their cars, most of the cars for sale will be lemons. Buyers realize this, so they won't be willing to pay very much for used cars, and the price of used cars will be relatively low. The low price makes the owners of the plums even less likely to sell their cars, so the average quality of cars decreases further. In the market equilibrium, most of the used cars on the market are lemons.

We'll see that a market will break down if either buyers or sellers are unable to distinguish between low-quality goods and high-quality goods. As we saw earlier in this book, the model of supply and demand is based on several assumptions. One of the assumptions is that buyers and sellers have enough information to make informed choices. In a world of fully informed buyers and sellers, markets operate smoothly, generating an equilibrium price and an equilibrium quantity for each good. In a world with imperfect information, some goods will be sold in very small numbers or not sold at all.

This chapter explores the effect of imperfect information on several types of markets. Here are some of the practical questions that we answer:

1. **What questions should you ask before joining a commercial dating service?**
2. **Why do some sellers of used cars offer money-back guarantees?**
3. **Why do we rely on volunteer blood donors instead of paying people to donate blood?**
4. **Why do professional baseball pitchers who switch teams spend so much time on the disabled list, nursing their injuries instead of playing?**
5. **The federal government is expected to spend $200 billion to cover the losses incurred by dozens of Saving and Loan Associations (S&Ls). How did the S&Ls get into so much trouble?**

The Mixed Market for Used Cars

The classic example of a market with imperfect information is the market for used cars.[1] Suppose prospective buyers cannot distinguish between low-quality cars (lemons) and high-quality cars (plums). Although a buyer can get some information about a particular car by looking at the car and taking it for a test drive, the information gleaned from this kind of inspection is not enough to determine whether the car is a lemon or a plum. In contrast, the seller (the current owner of a used car) knows from experience whether the car is a lemon or a plum. We say that there is **asymmetric information** in a market if one side of the market—either buyers or sellers—has better information than the other. For example, the sellers of used cars know more about the cars being sold than buyers do. Because buyers cannot distinguish between lemons and plums, there will be a single market: Lemons and plums will be sold together in a mixed market for the same price.

We begin our discussion with an extreme case, a market in which all the cars on the market will be lemons. This extreme case is unrealistic, but it provides a useful starting point for a discussion of the implications of asymmetric information. This extreme case shows that one possibility is the disappearance of the market for the high-quality good. As we'll see later, a more realistic case is a situation in which most—but not all—the used cars are lemons, so there is a small chance that a buyer will get a high-quality car.

Asymmetric information: One side of the market—either buyers or sellers—has better information about the good than the other.

Ignorant Consumers and Knowledgeable Sellers

How much is a consumer willing to pay for a used car that could be either a lemon or a plum? To determine the price in a mixed market—with both high-quality and low-quality goods—we must answer three questions:

1. How much is the consumer willing to pay for a plum (a high-quality car)?
2. How much is the consumer willing to pay for a lemon (a low-quality car)?
3. What is the chance that a used car purchased in the mixed market will be a lemon?

Suppose the typical buyer is willing to pay $4,000 for a plum and $2,000 for a lemon. In addition, the consumer has neutral expectations about the used-car market. That means that the consumer assumes that half the used cars are lemons and the other half are plums, so there is a 50% chance of getting a lemon. How much is the consumer willing to pay for a car that has a 50% chance of being a lemon? A reasonable assumption is that she or he is willing to pay the average value of the two types of cars, or $3,000.

Sellers of used cars are knowledgeable about what they are selling. The current owner of a used car knows from everyday experience whether the car is a lemon or a plum. Given a single market price for all used cars, lemons and plums alike, each current owner must decide whether or not to sell his or her car. We can use the supply curves for lemons and plums to show how many plums and lemons will be supplied at a particular price.

Figure 17.1 shows two hypothetical supply curves: one for plums and another for lemons. The minimum price for plums is $2,500: At any price less than $2,500, no plums

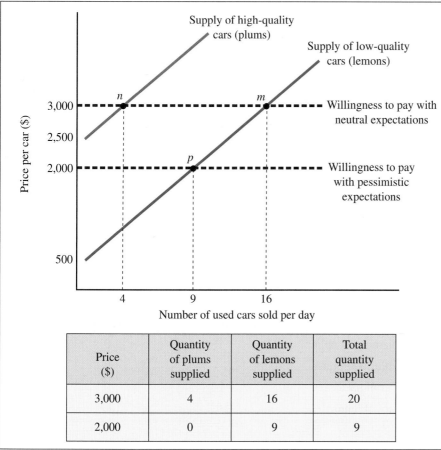

Figure 17.1

Market for Used Cars

If buyers have neutral expectations (assume that there is a 50% chance of getting a lemon), they are willing to pay $3,000 for a used car. At this price, the supply of plums is 4 (point *n*) and the supply of lemons is 16 (point *m*). At a price of $2,000, only lemons will be supplied (9 lemons, as shown by point *p*).

Price ($)	Quantity of plums supplied	Quantity of lemons supplied	Total quantity supplied
3,000	4	16	20
2,000	0	9	9

will be supplied. As shown by the plum supply curve, the number of plums supplied increases with the price of used cars. For example, 4 plums will be supplied at a price of $3,000 (point *n*). The minimum price for lemons is $500: At any price less than $500, no lemons will be supplied. Lemons have a lower minimum price because they are worth less to their current owners. As shown by the lemon supply curve, the number of lemons supplied increases with the price of used cars. For example, 16 lemons will be supplied at a price of $3,000 (point *m*).

Equilibrium in the Mixed Market

Table 17.1 shows two scenarios for our hypothetical used-car market, with numbers consistent with the supply curves shown in Figure 17.1. In the first column we assume that buyers have neutral expectations about the chance of getting a lemon. If buyers assume that half the used cars on the market are lemons and half are plums, the typical buyer will be willing to pay $3,000 for a used car. At this price, 4 plums and 16 lemons will be supplied, so 80% of the used cars (16 of 20) will be lemons. In this case, consumers underestimate the chance of getting a lemon.

What will consumers do when they realize that they've underestimated the chance of getting a lemon? They certainly won't be willing to pay $3,000 for a used car. In general, the greater the chance of getting a lemon, the smaller the amount that consumers are willing to pay. As a result, the price of used cars will decrease. As was explained earlier in the book, a market reaches an equilibrium when there is no pressure to change the price. Therefore, the scenario represented by the data in the first column is not an equilibrium.

Suppose that after observing the outcome in the first column, buyers become very pessimistic. They assume that all the used cars on the market are lemons. Under this assumption, the typical buyer will be willing to pay only $2,000 (the value of a lemon) for a used car. This price is less than the $2,500 minimum price for supplying plums, so plums will disappear from the used-car market. This is shown in Figure 17.1: At a price of $2,000, the quantity of plums supplied is zero, but the quantity of lemons is 9 (point *p*). In other words, all the used cars will be lemons, so consumers' pessimism is justified. Because consumers' expectations are consistent with their actual experiences in the market, the equilibrium price of used cars is $2,000. The equilibrium in the used-car market is shown in the second column of Table 17.1.

Table 17.1 All Used Cars Are Lemons

	Neutral Expectations	Pessimistic Expectations
Assumed chance of lemon	50%	100%
Willingness to pay for lemon	$2,000	$2,000
Willingness to pay for plum	$4,000	$4,000
Willingness to pay for used car	$3,000	$2,000
Number of lemons supplied	16	9
Number of plums supplied	4	0
Total number of used cars	20	9
Actual chance of lemon	80%	100%

In this equilibrium, no plums are bought or sold, so every buyer will get a lemon. The domination of the used-car market by lemons is an example of the **adverse-selection problem**. The uninformed side of the market (buyers in this case) must choose from an undesirable or adverse selection of goods (used cars in this example). The asymmetric information in the market generates a downward spiral of price and quantity: A decrease in price decreases the quantity of plums supplied, decreasing the price further when buyers realize that most of the cars on the market are lemons, which leads to even fewer plums on the market. In the extreme case, this downward spiral continues until all the cars on the market are lemons, so every buyer will get a lemon.

The problem of adverse selection occurs whenever one side of the market has better information than the other side. As explained in "A Closer Look: Should You Join a Commercial Dating Service?," a person who joins a commercial dating service may encounter an adverse selection of companions.

Adverse-selection problem: The uninformed side of the market must choose from an undesirable or an adverse selection of goods.

TEST Your Understanding

1. Complete the statement with *buyers* or *sellers*: There is asymmetric information in the used-car market because _____ cannot distinguish between lemons and plums but _____ can.

2. Suppose the typical consumer is willing to pay $3,000 for a plum and $1,000 for a lemon. If there is a 50% chance of getting a lemon, how much is the consumer willing to pay for a used car?

3. Why do goods of different qualities (such as used cars) sell for the same price, but goods of different sizes (such as apples) sell for different prices?

4. When buyers assume that there is a 40% chance of getting a lemon, 8 lemons and 2 plums are supplied. Is this an equilibrium? Explain.

5. Complete the statement: The fact that a buyer must pick a used car from an undesirable selection of cars is called the _____ problem.

Reviving the High-Quality Market

The disappearance of high-quality cars from our hypothetical market is an extreme—and unrealistic—case. In most used-car markets, some high-quality cars are offered for sale, so there is at least a small chance that a buyer will get a high-quality car. There are some high-quality cars on the market because some plum owners are willing to sell their cars at a low price, a result of changes in their transportation needs or a desire to buy a new car.

Thin Market for Plums

In our earlier example, the market for high-quality used cars disappears because informed suppliers refuse to participate in the mixed market for used cars. Specifically, the $2,500 minimum price for high-quality cars is so high that no plums are supplied at the equilibrium price of $2,000. If the minimum price for plums is lower, say $1,800, some plums will be supplied when the market price is $2,000. Although most of the used cars will be lemons, some lucky buyers will get plums. In this case, we say that asymmetric information generates a **thin market**: Some high-quality goods are sold, but fewer than would be sold in a market with perfect information.

Thin market: A market in which some high-quality goods are sold but fewer than would be sold in a market with perfect information.

A CLOSER LOOK | Should You Join a Commercial Dating Service?

Imagine yourself in 10 years, working 50 hours per week in a high-pressure job that leaves little time to search for a husband, wife, or partner. You could join a commercial dating service, but is it worth the $1,000 price tag?

Our discussion of imperfect information and adverse selection provides a framework for thinking about whether to join a dating service. Here are some questions you should answer before joining:

- Will the dating service provide an adverse selection of potential partners, with a large number of lemons and just a few plums? If a person is willing to pay $1,000 to meet potential partners, what does this mean about that person? Do the clients of dating services have personality problems that make it difficult for them to initiate and maintain relationships with other people? Or are they just too busy to meet new people on their own?

- Given your expectations about the mixture of lemons and plums, is the $1,000 fee worthwhile?

Commercial dating services provide introductions to potential companions.

We can use a simple example to show how we get a thin market for plums. In Table 17.2, consumers assume that there is a 90% chance of getting a lemon (worth $2,000 to the consumer) and a 10% chance of getting a plum (worth $4,000 to the consumer). Let's assume that each consumer is willing to pay $2,200 for a used car under these circumstances. Consumers are willing to pay a little more than the value of a lemon because there is a small chance of getting a plum. Figure 17.2 shows the supply curves for this example: At a price of $2,200, there will be 2 plums (shown by point *s*) and 18 lemons (shown by point *t*). In this case, consumers accurately assess the chance of getting a lemon: 90% of the used cars sold (18 of 20) turn out to be lemons. Therefore, the equilibrium price of used cars is $2,200 and the equilibrium quantity is 20 cars, 10% of which are plums.

Table 17.2 Thin Market for Plums

Assumed chance of lemon	90%
Willingness to pay for lemon	$2,000
Willingness to pay for plum	$4,000
Willingness to pay for used car	$2,200
Number of lemons supplied	18
Number of plums supplied	2
Total number of used cars	20
Actual chance of lemon	90%

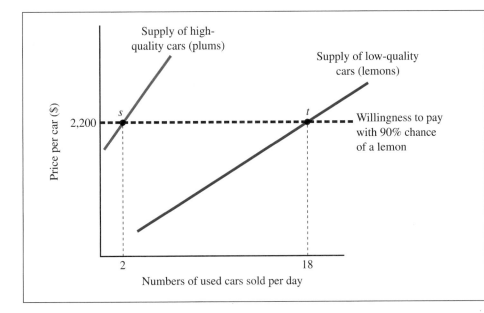

Figure 17.2

**Thin Market
for Plums**

If buyers assume that there is a 90% chance of getting a lemon, they are willing to pay $2,200 for a used car. At this price, the supply of plums is 2 (point *s*) and the supply of lemons is 18 (point *t*), so the actual chance of getting a lemon is 90%, the same as the assumed chance of getting a lemon.

Applications: Otto's Puzzle, the Supply of Blood

This chapter started with Otto's puzzle. Is there a 50% chance of getting a lemon, as suggested by a casual reading of the data from consumer magazines, or a 90% chance, as suggested by the experiences of Otto's friends? As we see in Table 17.2 and Figure 17.2, the answer is 90%. To assess his chances of getting a lemon, Otto should listen to his friends. The price of model X cars is so low that just a few plum owners sell their cars.

For another example of a good with asymmetric information, think about blood used for transfusions. About 30 years ago, a large fraction of the blood used for transfusions in the United States came from paid donors ("commercial" blood). Today, all the blood for transfusions comes from volunteer donors. During the 1960s, Japan made similar changes in its blood supply system, moving from a largely commercial supply to one that relies to a much greater extent on volunteer donors.[2] What explains these shifts away from commercial blood supply in favor of a volunteer supply? The answer is adverse selection.

Hospitals cannot always distinguish between bad blood (from donors with infectious disease such as hepatitis) and good blood. Thirty years ago, 30% of heart-surgery patients contracted hepatitis from tainted blood. According to Dr. Harvey G. Klein, the chief of the department of transfusion medicine at the National Institutes of Health, blood from paid donors was a big factor in the hepatitis problem.[3] The monetary incentives caused a large number of people with "bad" blood to give blood—and be less than completely honest about their health histories. The elimination of paid donors in the last 30 years has decreased the chance of contracting hepatitis during heart surgery to only 2%.

Money-Back Guarantees and Warranties

The domination of the used-car market by lemons provides an opportunity for clever sellers. Buyers are willing to pay $4,000 for a plum, and some plum owners would gladly sell their cars if they could get more than $2,200 for them. This large gap between the willingness to pay and the willingness to accept provides a profit opportunity for clever entrepreneurs who can somehow persuade a skeptical consumer that a particular used car is a plum, not a lemon.

A supplier could identify a particular car as a plum in a sea of lemons by offering one of the following guarantees:

- **Money-back guarantee.** The seller could promise to refund the $3,500 price if the car turned out to be a lemon. Because the car is in fact a plum—a fact known by the seller—the buyer will not ask for a refund, and buyer and seller will be happy with the transaction.

- **Warranties and repair guarantees.** The seller could promise to cover any extraordinary repair costs for one year. Because the car is a plum, there won't be any extraordinary repair costs, so buyer and seller will be happy with the transaction.

Car consumers also have an incentive to get information about the quality of used cars. A consumer who identified a plum could buy the high-quality car for a price below his or her willingness to pay ($4,000). There is a big payoff from information that enables the consumer to distinguish between lemons and plums. It may be rational for a car consumer to hire a mechanic to inspect a particular car for defects.

Lemons Laws

Many states have laws that require automakers to buy back cars that experience frequent problems in the first year of use. For example, under California's Song-Beverly Consumer Warranty Act, also known as the lemons law, auto dealers are required to repurchase vehicles that have been brought back for repair at least four times for the same problem or have been in the mechanic's shop for at least 30 calendar days in the first year following purchase. A vehicle repurchased under the lemons law must be fixed before it is sold to another customer and must be identified as a lemon with a stamp on the title and a sticker on the car that says "lemons law buyback."

Do state lemons law work? Mr. Reynoso, a Los Angeles dental technician purchased a used 1996 Astro van for $22,000. He didn't find out until much later that the vehicle had been repurchased by the dealer under the lemons law after the original owner had brought the van in for repairs 44 times in just a few months.[4] Four years earlier, the California Department of Motor Vehicles claimed that General Motors, the maker of the Astro van, had violated the lemons law by reselling lemons to consumers without identifying them as lemons. GM paid $330,000 to settle those charges, but it didn't admit to any wrongdoing. Mr. Reynoso's experience led to a class-action lawsuit against General Motors.

Another problem with enforcing these laws is that lemons can cross state lines without a paper trail. For example, a Dodge Caravan with a leaky roof was bought and repurchased under state lemons laws three times in three different states: Virginia, Minnesota, and Illinois.[5] The interstate commerce in lemons has led to new laws requiring the branding of lemons on vehicle titles to follow the car when it crosses state lines.

TEST Your Understanding

6. When buyers assume that there is a 70% chance of getting a lemon, 7 lemons and 3 plums are supplied. Is this an equilibrium? Explain.

7. Explain why it would not be rational for a lemon owner to offer a buyer a money-back guarantee.

8. Suppose that the minimum price of plums decreases. Would you expect the market to become "thinner" or "thicker"?

9. Explain why there are profit opportunities in a thin market.

Applications

The most important lesson of this chapter is that if one side of a market cannot distinguish between high- and low-quality goods, the mixed market will be dominated by low-quality goods. The adverse-selection problem is caused by imperfect information. Let's look at three other examples of mixed markets that suffer from the adverse-selection problem: used baseball pitchers, malpractice insurance, and medical insurance.

Used Baseball Players

Professional baseball teams compete with each other for players. After six years of play in the major leagues, a player has the option of becoming a free agent and offering his services to the highest bidder. A player is likely to switch teams if the new team offers him a higher salary than his original team. One of the puzzling features of the free-agent market is that pitchers who switch teams are more prone to injuries than pitchers who don't. On average, pitchers who switch teams spend 28 days per season on the disabled list; pitchers who do not switch teams spend only 5 days per season on the disabled list.[6] This doesn't mean that all the switching pitchers are lemons: Many of them are injury-free and are terrific additions to their new teams. But on average, the switching pitchers spend five times longer recovering from injuries.

This puzzling feature of the free-agent market for baseball players is explained by asymmetric information and adverse selection. Because the coaches, physicians, and trainers from the player's original team have interacted with the player on a daily basis for several years, they know from experience whether he is likely to suffer from injuries that prevent him from playing. In contrast, the new team has much less information: Its physicians can examine the pitcher, but a single exam is not the same as several years of daily experience with the pitcher. Suppose the market price for pitchers is $1 million per year and a pitcher who is currently with the Chicago Cubs is offered this salary by

Baseball pitchers who switch teams are more prone to injuries than those who don't switch.

another team. If the Cubs think the pitcher is likely to spend a lot of time next season recovering from injuries, they won't try to outbid another team for the pitcher; they will let the pitcher switch teams. But if the Cubs think the pitcher will be injury-free and productive, he will be worth more than $1 million to the Cubs, so they will outbid other teams and keep the pitcher. In general, an injury-prone pitcher is more likely to switch teams: Like the used-car market, there are many "lemons" on the used-pitcher market. The market for baseball players playing other positions (outfield, infield) does not suffer from the adverse selection, perhaps because the injuries that affect their performance are easier for a potential new team to detect.

Although you may think it's bizarre to compare baseball pitchers to used cars, people in baseball don't think so. They recognize the similarity between the two markets. Jackie Moore, who managed a free-agent camp where teams looking for players can see free agents in action, sounds like a used-car salesman:[7] "We want to get players off the lot. We want to cut a deal. How many camps can you go into where you can look at a player and take him home with you?"

Malpractice Insurance

So far, we've discussed markets in which sellers have better information than buyers, but what happens when buyers are better informed than sellers? Consider the market for insurance. A person who buys an insurance policy knows much more about his or her risks and needs for insurance than the insurance company knows. For example, when you buy an auto-insurance policy, you know more than your insurance company about your driving habits and your chances of getting in an accident. We'll see that insurance markets suffer from the adverse-selection problem: Insurance companies must pick from an adverse or undesirable selection of customers.

Let's look at the market for malpractice insurance. To keep things simple, suppose there are only two types of physicians: careful and reckless. On average, the cost of settling malpractice suits against careful doctors is $4,000 per doctor per year, while the cost of settling malpractice suits against reckless doctors is $30,000 per doctor per year. If the doctor is insured, these costs are paid by an insurance company. Uninsured physicians will have to pay these costs themselves. Suppose insurance companies cannot distinguish between careful doctors and reckless doctors, but each doctor knows whether he or she is careful or reckless. This means that there is asymmetric information in the insurance market: Buyers (physicians) have better information than sellers (insurance companies).

If insurance companies cannot distinguish between careful doctors and reckless doctors, there will be a mixed market and a single price for malpractice insurance. Suppose all insurance companies are initially neutral in their expectations about what type of doctors will buy malpractice insurance. Insurance companies assume that half the doctors who buy insurance are careful and half are reckless. If the typical insurance company gets equal numbers of careful doctors and reckless doctors, the average cost of providing insurance will be $17,000 per doctor. Therefore, if the insurance company charges $17,000 per year for insurance and its expectations about the mixture of careful doctors and reckless doctors are correct, the company's total revenue will cover its total cost. In other words, the company will earn zero economic profit.

The expectations of the insurance company are unlikely to be realized. At a price of $17,000, none of the careful physicians will buy malpractice insurance. They won't buy it because the premium is over four times the average cost of settling malpractice suits against a careful doctor, so malpractice insurance is not a very good deal for them. A careful doctor would rather take the risk, knowing that he or she will pay an average of $4,000 per year to settle malpractice suits. This is the adverse-selection problem:

Insurance companies get an undesirable (adverse) selection of doctors. To ensure zero economic profit, the price of insurance must increase to $30,000, the average cost of serving the reckless physicians.

In this example, careful physicians do not buy malpractice insurance because insurance companies are unable to distinguish between careful doctors and reckless doctors. The reckless doctors in the mixed market increase the cost of providing insurance and increase the price of insurance. In fact, insurance companies try to identify careful doctors and offer them lower insurance rates. When a doctor applies for an insurance policy, the insurance company gathers information about the doctor and the history of his or her medical practice. Although these actions help insurance companies to distinguish between careful and reckless physicians, they are by no means perfect, so the adverse-selection problem persists.

Pricing Health Insurance

Our discussion of adverse selection provides some insights into recent changes in the pricing of medical insurance. Until recently, most insurance prices were based on **community rating**. In a given community or metropolitan area, every firm paid the same price for the medical insurance for its employees, with the price equal to the average cost of providing medical coverage to the entire community. A firm providing medical coverage to its employees through an insurance company would pay the insurance company an amount equal to the number of employees times the community price.

Most insurance companies now use **experience rating** to set their prices. Under this system, they charge different prices to different firms, depending on the past medical bills of the firm's employees. A firm whose employees have low medical bills pays a low price for its employees' insurance. The switch from community rating to experience rating occurred when insurance companies were able to identify employers with low medical costs. Eventually, most insurance companies switched to experience rating.[8]

Experience rating gives firms an incentive to decrease the health costs of their workers. Firms are more likely to invest in safety and health programs for their workers. Firms will also make a greater effort to avoid hiring applicants with health problems. Under experience rating, a firm that hires a worker with above-average medical costs will soon face an increase in the price of its insurance. Among the workers who might suffer as a result are older workers and the disabled.

Community rating: In a given community or metropolitan area, every firm pays the same price for medical insurance.

Experience rating: Each firm pays a different price for medical insurance, depending on the past medical bills of the firm's employees.

Moral Hazard

Does insurance affect people's risk-taking behavior? Insurance causes people to take greater risks because part of the cost of an undesirable outcome will be borne by the insurance company. Here are some examples of people taking greater risks because they have insurance:

- Irma could buy a fire extinguisher for her kitchen. If she had to pay for any property damage caused by a fire, she would definitely buy a fire extinguisher. But because her homeowner's insurance covers property damage from fires, she doesn't buy a fire extinguisher.

- Harry decides how carefully to drive his car. If he had to pay for any repairs resulting from a collision, he would drive very carefully. But his auto insurance covers all repair costs, so he drives recklessly.

- Flo can either fly on a commercial airline or hitch a ride with her pilot friend in a 4-seat airplane. Traveling in small airplanes is much riskier, and if Flo dies in an airplane crash, her family would lose the income she would otherwise earn. If she didn't have life insurance to offset these income losses, she wouldn't take the risk of harming her family in that way. But because her family would collect $1 million in life insurance, she is willing to take the risk.

Moral hazard problem: Insurance encourages risky behavior.

The **moral hazard problem** is that insurance encourages risky behavior. More precisely, moral hazard occurs when an insured party takes an unobserved action (not observed by the insurer) that affects the probability of the event that triggers payment from the insurer. For example, Harry's unobserved action is reckless driving, which increases the probability of a collision, an event that triggers payment from his auto-insurance company.

The moral-hazard problem is pervasive. The availability of fire insurance decreases investment in fire-prevention programs and other investment that reduces the risk of fire. Collision insurance increases risky behavior on the roads. The availability of life insurance encourages risky activities such as flying small airplanes, parachuting, and bungee jumping. For an example of a very costly moral hazard problem in the banking industry, read "A Closer Look: Moral Hazard from Deposit Insurance."

ECONOMIC
DETECTIVE

Bicycle Theft Insurance

At Wheeler State University, 1 out of every 10 bicycles was stolen in 1998. When a group of young entrepreneurs discovered that no one on campus had bicycle-theft insurance, they decided to go into the insurance business, offering one-year theft insurance for $15 per bike. They sold 100 policies in 1999 and expected 10 of their 100 customers (10% of them) to lose their bicycles to theft. The entrepreneurs figured that their total revenue would more than cover the cost of replacing 10 bicycles, leaving a tidy profit. By the end of 1999, a total of 20 insured bicycles had been stolen, and the students lost a bundle of money on their little enterprise. What happened?

A CLOSER LOOK Moral Hazard from Deposit Insurance

Suppose you deposit $10,000 in a Savings and Loan (S&L) and a year later the S&L goes bankrupt. The Federal Deposit Insurance Corporation (FDIC) insures the first $100,000 of your deposit, so if the S&L goes bankrupt, you'll still get your money back. The federal deposit insurance law was enacted in 1933 in response to the bank failures of the Great Depression.

Deposit insurance for S&Ls causes a moral hazard problem. If you know you will get your money back no matter what happens to the S&L, you may deposit your money in the S&L without evaluating the S&L's performance and the riskiness of its investments. If you and other depositors don't monitor the bank's performance, an S&L with a very risky investment strategy will continue to attract deposits because the depositors don't face any risk. That

means the manager of an S&L will be more likely to take on risky investments, knowing that if the investments don't pay off and the S&L goes bankrupt, the federal government will bear the cost, paying off all the depositors. Recognizing this moral-hazard problem, the federal government historically limited S&Ls to relatively safe investments.

In the 1980s, the federal government loosened some of the restrictions on S&L investments, and the managers of S&Ls started taking on very risky investments, including high-risk commercial mortgages and junk bonds. When these risky investments failed, many S&Ls that had invested heavily in these high-risk investments went into bankruptcy. The government bailed out the failed S&Ls, at a total cost to taxpayers of about $200 billion.

The key to solving this puzzle is the fact that the 10% theft rate occurred in 1998, when no one had theft insurance. When the entrepreneurs offered theft insurance, they expected the same theft rate. Because of moral hazard, however, the students who bought theft insurance were less careful in protecting their bikes from theft, perhaps using less secure locks or leaving their bikes on campus overnight. As a result, the theft rate for insured bikes was 20%, not 10%. The entrepreneurs lost money because they did not anticipate that insurance would increase risk-taking. ◆

TEST Your Understanding

10. Your favorite baseball team just announced that it signed two pitchers from the free-agent market. What's your reaction?

11. Complete the statement with numbers: Suppose that the average annual malpractice cost is $40,000 for reckless doctors and $2,000 for careful doctors. If half the insured doctors are reckless, the insurance company will earn zero economic profit if the price of insurance is _____. If careful doctors are not willing to pay any more than $5,000 for insurance, the price required for zero economic profit is _____.

12. Many professional athletes purchase insurance against career-ending injuries. Would you expect the insured players to act differently from those who don't have insurance?

Using the TOOLS

We've seen what happens when one side of the market—either buyers or sellers—has better information than the other side. In a market for a used good, sellers know more than buyers, and the market will be dominated by low-quality goods. In an insurance market, buyers know more than sellers, and the market will be dominated by high-risk consumers. Here are some opportunities to do your own economic analysis of markets with asymmetric information.

1. ECONOMIC EXPERIMENT: Lemons

In this experiment, students play the role of consumers purchasing used cars. Over half the used cars on the road (57%) are plums, and the remaining cars (43%) are lemons. Each consumer offers a price for a used car and then rolls a pair of dice to find out whether he or she gets a lemon or a plum. In general, rolling a big number is good news: To get a plum, you need to roll a big number. The higher the price you offer, the smaller the number you must roll to get a plum. Here is how the experiment works:

- Each consumer tells the instructor how much he or she is offering for a used car and then rolls the dice.
- The instructor tells the consumer whether the number she rolled is large enough to get a plum. If the number is not large enough, she gets a lemon.
- The consumer's score equals the difference between the maximum amount she is willing to pay for the type of car she got ($1,200 for a plum and $400 for a lemon) and the price she actually paid. For example, if Otto offers $500 and gets a plum, his score is $700. If Carla offers $600 and gets a lemon, her score is –$200.
- The instructor announces the result of each transaction to the class.
- There are three to five buying periods. At the end of the last trading period, each consumer adds up his or her surpluses.

2. Rising Insurance Rates

At a large state university, an insurance company provides group medical coverage for university employees. When the company discovered that some of the younger employees had switched to insurance companies with lower rates, the company increased its rates. This is puzzling because you might think that the insurance company would drop its rates to prevent other employees from switching to other companies. Indeed, the rate hike caused more employees to switch. Did the insurance company act irrationally?

3. Purchasing a Fleet of Used Cars

You are responsible for buying a fleet of 10 used cars for your employees and must pick either brand B cars or brand C cars. For your purposes, the two brands are identical except for one difference: Based on your market experience with the two brands, you figure that 50% of B cars are lemons and only 20% of C cars are lemons. You are willing to pay $1,000 for a known lemon and $3,000 for a known plum. If the price of B cars is $1,800 and the price of C cars is $2,200, which brand of car should you pick?

4. State Auto Insurance Pool

Consider a state in which automobile drivers are divided equally into two types of drivers: careful and reckless. The average annual auto-insurance claim is $400 for a careful driver and $1,200 for a reckless driver. Suppose the state adopts an insurance system under which all drivers are placed in a common pool and allocated to insurance companies randomly. An insurance company cannot refuse coverage to any driver it is assigned, but a driver who is unhappy with the insurance company has the option of being reassigned (randomly) to another insurance company. By law, each insurance company must charge the same price to all its customers. Predict the price of auto insurance under two alternative policy scenarios:

a. Auto insurance is mandatory.

b. Auto insurance is voluntary.

5. ECONOMIC EXPERIMENT: Bike Insurance

This experiment shows the effect of asymmetric information on the market for bicycle insurance. Consider a city with two types of bike owners; some face a relatively high probability of bike theft, and others face a relatively low probability of bike theft. Bike owners know from experience whether they face a high probability or a low probability of theft, but the insurance company cannot distinguish between the two types of owners. For the city as a whole, 20% of bicycles are stolen every year. Here is how the experiment works:

- The class is divided into small groups, each of which represents an insurance company that must pick a price at which the firm will offer bike theft insurance. The insurance company must pay $100 for each insured bike that is stolen.

- The instructor has a table showing, for each price of bike insurance, how many owners of each type (high probability and low probability) will purchase insurance. Using the numbers supplied by the instructor, each insurance company can compute its total revenue (the price per bike insured times the number of insured bikes), the number of bikes stolen, and the company's total replacement cost.

- The group's score for a trading period equals the company's profit, which is the total revenue less the total replacement cost for stolen bikes.

- The experiment runs for several trading periods, and a group's score equals the sum of its profits over these trading periods.

Summary

In this chapter, we've seen what happens when one of the assumptions underlying most supply and demand analysis—that people make informed decisions—is violated. If either buyers or sellers don't have reliable information about a particular good or service, the market will suffer from the adverse-selection problem. The uninformed side of the market picks from an adverse selection of goods or customers. Here are the main points of the chapter:

1. If one side of the market cannot distinguish between high-quality and low-quality goods, both types of goods will be sold in a mixed market at the same price.

2. The markets for many used goods suffer from the adverse-selection problem because sellers have better information than buyers.

3. If sellers of high-quality goods have a relatively low minimum price, some high-quality goods will be sold, but most of the goods will be of low quality.

4. Insurance markets suffer from adverse selection because buyers have better information than sellers.

5. Insurance encourages risky behavior because part of the cost of an unfavorable outcome will be paid by an insurance company.

Key Terms

adverse-selection problem, 357
asymmetric information, 354

community rating, 363
experience rating, 363

moral hazard problem, 364
thin market, 357

Problems and Discussion Questions

1. Use the notion of adverse selection to explain a classic quip from Groucho Marx: "I won't join any club that is willing to accept me as a member."

2. The following table shows some scenarios for different used-car markets. Which markets are in equilibrium? Graph each equilibrium, using Figure 17.1 as a model.

	Scenario A	Scenario B	Scenario C
Assumed chance of lemon	60%	80%	95%
Willingness to pay for used car	$6,000	$5,000	$4,500
Number of lemons supplied	70	40	90
Number of plums supplied	30	10	10
Total number of used cars	100	50	100

3. You are thinking about buying a used camera at a price of $60. You are willing to pay $20 for a lemon and $100 for a plum. Under what circumstances

would it be wise to buy a used camera? Are these circumstances likely to occur? Explain.

4. Suppose that both buyers and sellers of used cars are ignorant: No one can distinguish between lemons and plums. Would you expect the market to be dominated by lemons?

5. Suppose that a new lie detector is 100% accurate. Discuss the implications for the adverse-selection problem in the used-car market.

6. When a person applies for life insurance, the insurance agent asks the applicant about his or her occupation. Why should this matter to the insurance company?

7. Scientists have recently developed new genetic tests that could be used by an insurance company to determine whether a potential customer is likely to develop certain diseases. Discuss the trade-offs associated with allowing insurance companies to use these tests.

8. On the campus of Bike University, half the bikes are expensive (replacement value = $100), and half are cheap (replacement value = $20). There is a 50% chance that any particular bike—expensive or

cheap—will be stolen in the next year. Suppose a firm offers bike-theft insurance for $40 per year: The firm will replace any insured bike that is stolen. If the firm sells 20 insurance policies, will the firm make a profit? Explain.

9. In a given year, there is a 10% chance that a fire in Ira's warehouse will cause $100,000 in property damage. If Ira spent $5,000 on a fire-prevention program, the probability of a fire would drop to zero. If Ira doesn't have fire insurance, will he spend the money on the prevention program? If he has an insurance policy that covers 80% of the property damage from a fire, will he spend the money on the prevention program? At what coverage rate (40%, 50%, 60%, 70%), will Ira be indifferent about spending money on the prevention program?

10. As Kira tries to decide whether or not to do a bungee jump, she asks to make one phone call. If there is a moral hazard problem, whom will she call?

11. Web Exercise. Visit the Web site of Carfax (*http://www.carfax.com*) and check out the sample reports. What sort of deception occurs in the market for used cars? How much does it cost to get a report on a used car you are considering buying? Do you think the information is worth the price?

12. Web Exercise. Visit the Web site of the Red Cross (*http://www.redcross.org/*) and get the facts on donating blood. Click on "Want to Help?" and then "Give Blood." Are you eligible to give blood? Where would you go to donate blood?

Take It to the Net

We invite you to visit the O'Sullivan/Sheffrin page on the Prentice Hall Web site at:
http://www.prenhall.com/osullivan/
for additional World Wide Web exercises for this chapter.

Model Answers to Questions

Chapter-Opening Questions

1. Will the service generate an adverse selection of dates? Given your expectations of the mix of lemons and plums, is the service worth the fee you would pay?

2. They are trying to distinguish their high-quality cars from low-quality cars.

3. Hospitals cannot always distinguish between bad blood (from donors with infectious disease such as hepatitis) and good blood. Monetary incentives for blood caused a large number of people with "bad" blood to give blood—and be less than completely honest about their health histories.

4. Like the used-car market, the used-pitcher market has asymmetric information: the pitcher's original team has more information than the new team. A team is more likely to be outbid by another team for a pitcher's services, if the pitcher has health problems that make him worth less to the original team.

5. As explained in "A Closer Look: Moral Hazard from Deposit Insurance," the problem was caused by fed-

eral deposit insurance, which encouraged the managers of S&Ls to take on very risky investments. When these risky investments failed, many S&Ls that had invested heavily in these high-risk investments went into bankruptcy.

Test Your Understanding

1. Buyers, sellers.

2. $2,000, the average value of the two types of cars.

3. It is easy to determine the size of an apple but not easy to determine the quality of a car.

4. No: 80% of the used cars are lemons, meaning consumers underestimate the chance of getting a lemon.

5. Adverse-selection.

6. Yes: 70% of the cars are lemons.

7. The buyer will eventually return the car and get a full refund, perhaps after putting a lot of miles on it or abusing it.

8. Thicker: The lower the minimum price, the larger the quantity supplied at each price, so the more plums in the market.

9. There will be a large gap between the amount a buyer is willing to pay for a true plum and the amount a plum owner is willing to accept.

10. You may be skeptical about the new player because free-agent pitchers who switch teams spend a long time on the disabled list. Before reading this chapter, you might have been more optimistic about the pitchers.

11. $21,000 (the average of the two cost figures), $40,000 (the cost for reckless doctors).

12. Insured athletes are likely to spend less effort in avoiding injuries, knowing that the insurance company will compensate them for a career-ending injury.

Using the Tools

2. **Rising Insurance Rates.** The medical costs of younger employees are usually lower than the average medical cost for all university employees. When the youngsters switched to a different insurance company, the average age—and the average medical costs—of the original insurance company increased. The insurance company increased its rates to cover its higher costs, fully anticipating that this would cause other low-cost employees to switch to other companies. The insurance company faced a progressively more adverse selection of customers, and the higher price of medical insurance reflects the adverse selection.

3. **Purchasing a Fleet of Used Cars.** The following table shows how to compute the benefits and costs of the two brands. For brand B, you expect half the cars to be lemons and half to be plums, so the total value of a brand B fleet is $20,000 (5 lemons together worth a total of $5,000 and 5 plums together worth a total of $15,000). At a price of $1,800, the total cost of a B fleet is $18,000 ($1,800 per used car × 10 cars). Therefore, the value of a B fleet exceeds its cost by $2,000. We can do the same computations for the C fleet. The only difference is that you would get 2

lemons and 8 plums with a C fleet. The value of a C fleet exceeds its cost by $4,000, so the C fleet is a better deal. Although you pay $400 more per C car, the extra cost is more than offset by the smaller number of lemons in the C fleet.

	Brand B	Brand C
Number of lemons	5	2
Value of lemons	$5,000	$2,000
Number of plums	5	8
Value of plums	$15,000	$24,000
Total value of fleet	$20,000	$26,000
Total cost of fleet	$18,000	$22,000
Surplus (value – cost)	$2,000	$4,000

4. **State Auto Insurance Pool**
   a. Under the pooling policy, there will be a single mixed market and a single price for auto insurance. If auto insurance is mandatory, the pooling policy will increase the price to $800—the average cost per driver for each insurance company.
   b. If auto insurance is voluntary, the long-run equilibrium price will exceed $800 and may even approach $1,200. If insurance companies initially have neutral expectations about the mixture of careful drivers and reckless drivers, the price of insurance will be $800 per driver. If this price exceeds the maximum price of some careful drivers, they will drop out of the market, so more than 50% of the insured drivers are reckless. Given the larger percentage of reckless (high cost) drivers, insurance companies will lose money at a price of $800 per driver, so they will increase the price. The price of insurance will increase until the insurance company's expectations about the mixture of careful drivers and reckless drivers are realized. If all the careful drivers drop out of the market, the price of insurance will increase to $1,200, the cost per reckless driver.

Notes

1. George Akerlof, "The Market for 'Lemons': Quality Uncertainty and the Market Mechanism," *Quarterly Journal of Economics*, August 1970, pp. 488–500.

2. Alvin W. Drake, Stan N. Finkelstein, and Harvey M. Sapalsky, *The American Blood Supply* (Cambridge, MA: MIT Press, 1982).

3. Oz Hopkins Koglin, "U.S. Blood 'Extremely Safe' as Volunteer Donors Cut Risks," *The Oregonian*, November 7, 1994, p. B1.

4. Kathryn Kranhold, "Lawsuit Accuses General Motors of Violating State Lemon Law," *Wall Street Journal*, Oct 1, 1997.

5. Andrea Adelson, "Pushing Lemons over State Lines," *New York Times*, August 27, 1996, p. C1.

6. Kenneth Lehn, "Information Asymmetries in Baseball's Free Agent Market," *Economic Inquiry*, vol. 22, January 1984, pp. 37–44.

7. Chris Sheridan, "Free Agents at End of Baseball's Earth," Associated Press, printed in *Corvallis Gazette-Times*, April 15, 1995, p. B1.

8. Henry J. Aaron, "Issues Every Plan to Reform Health Care Financing Must Confront," *Journal of Economic Perspectives*, vol. 8, no. 3, Summer 1994, pp. 31–43.

CHAPTER

18

The Labor Market

Recent reports on the earnings of college graduates have made the jobs of college recruiters easier:[1]

- In 1972, the typical college graduate earned 43% more than a high-school graduate.
- In 1997, the typical college graduate earned 78% more than a high-school graduate.

These facts raise two questions: First, why do college graduates earn so much more than high-school graduates? Second, why did the earnings gap almost double during the last 25 years?

n this chapter, we use a model of supply and demand to answer these and other practical questions about the labor market. You may be surprised by the answers. Here are some of the other issues that we address:

1. If the wage increases, will an individual work more hours or fewer hours?
2. If a worker switches from a relatively safe factory job to a job in a steel mill, by how much will his or her wage increase?
3. Why do women, on average, earn only about 75% as much as men?
4. How have companies such as Nike and Disney responded to allegations that their products are produced in foreign sweatshops with dreadful working conditions and low wages?
5. In 1913, Henry Ford increased the wage of his autoworkers from $3 per day (the wage paid by other automakers) to $5. Was he being generous or was he trying to maximize his profit?

The Demand for Labor

We can use supply and demand curves to show how wages are determined and show how public policies affect wages and employment. We'll start with the demand side of the labor market, looking first at how an individual firm can use the key principles of economics to decide how many workers to hire.

Labor Demand by an Individual Firm in the Short Run

Consider a perfectly competitive firm that produces rubber balls. Because this firm is perfectly competitive, it takes the price of its output and the prices of its inputs as given. Because it hires a tiny fraction of the workers in the labor market, it takes the market wage as given and can hire as many workers as it wants at that wage. In addition, the firm produces a tiny fraction of the rubber balls sold in the market, so it takes the price of its output as given. Let's say the price of rubber balls is $0.50.

Consider the firm's hiring decision in the short run, defined as the period during which at least one input—for example, the factory—cannot be changed. We can use two of the key principles of economics to explain the firm's hiring decision. Recall the marginal principle:

MARGINAL **PRINCIPLE**

> **Increase the level of an activity if its marginal benefit exceeds its marginal cost, but reduce the level if the marginal cost exceeds the marginal benefit. If possible, pick the level at which the marginal benefit equals the marginal cost.**

This firm's activity is hiring labor to produce rubber balls, and the firm will pick the quantity of labor at which the marginal benefit of labor equals the marginal cost of labor. The firm can hire as many workers as it wants at the market wage, so the marginal cost of labor equals the hourly wage. If the wage is $8 per hour, the extra cost associated with one more hour of labor—the marginal cost—is $8, regardless of how many workers the firm hires.

What is the marginal benefit of labor? The firm hires labor to produce balls, so the marginal benefit equals the monetary value of the balls produced with an additional hour of labor. Table 18.1 shows how to compute the marginal benefit associated with different quantities of labor. The first two columns show the relationship between the number of workers and the quantity of balls produced. As the number of workers increases, the number of balls increases, but at a decreasing rate, consistent with the principle of diminishing returns.

PRINCIPLE OF DIMINISHING RETURNS

Suppose that output is produced with two or more inputs and we increase one input while holding the other inputs fixed. Beyond some point—called the point of diminishing returns— output will increase at a decreasing rate.

Because of diminishing returns, the marginal product of labor (the change in output from one additional worker) decreases as the number of workers increases, from 26 for the first worker, to 24 for the second worker, and so on.

The marginal benefit of labor equals the **marginal revenue product of labor (MRP)**, defined as the extra revenue generated by one additional worker. To compute the MRP, we multiply the marginal product of labor by the price of output ($0.50 per ball in this example):

$$MRP = price\ of\ output \times marginal\ product$$

Marginal revenue product of labor (MRP): The extra revenue generated from one more unit of labor; equal to price of output times the marginal product of labor.

Figure 18.1 shows the marginal revenue product curve. Because the marginal product drops as the number of workers increases, the MRP curve is negatively sloped, falling from $11 for the third worker (point n) to $8 for the fifth worker (point m), and so on.

A firm can use its MRP curve to decide how much labor to hire at a particular wage. In Figure 18.1, the marginal-cost curve is horizontal at the market wage ($8). The perfectly competitive firm takes the wage as given, so the marginal-cost curve is also the labor-supply curve faced by the firm. The marginal principle is satisfied at point m, where the marginal cost equals the marginal revenue product. The firm will hire 5 workers because for the first 5 workers, the marginal benefit (the MRP) is greater than or equal to the marginal cost (the $8 wage). It would not be sensible to hire another worker because the additional revenue from the 6th worker ($6) would be less than the $8 additional cost of that worker. If the wage increases to $11, the firm will satisfy the marginal principle at point n, hiring only 3 workers.

Table 18.1 The Marginal Principle for Labor Decision

Number of Workers	Balls per Hour	Marginal Product	Price per Ball	Marginal Benefit = Marginal Revenue Product	Marginal Cost when Wage = $8
1	26	26	$0.50	$13	$8
2	50	24	0.50	$12	$8
3	72	22	0.50	$11	$8
4	92	20	0.50	$10	$8
5	108	16	0.50	$8	$8
6	120	12	0.50	$6	$8
7	128	8	0.50	$4	$8
8	130	2	0.50	$1	$8

Figure 18.1
The Marginal Principle and the Firm's Demand for Labor
Using the marginal principle, the firm picks the quantity of workers at which the marginal benefit (the marginal revenue product of labor) equals the marginal cost (the wage). The firm's short-run demand curve for labor is the marginal revenue product curve.

ACTIVE GRAPH

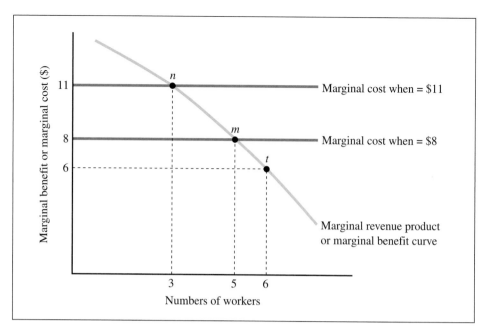

The MRP curve is also the firm's **short-run demand curve for labor**, which shows the relationship between the wage and the quantity of labor demanded in the short run, the period when the firm cannot change its production facility. The demand curve answers the following question: At each wage, how many hours of labor does the firm want to hire? We've already used the MRP curve to answer this question for two different wages ($11 and $8), and we can do the same for any other wage. Because the MRP curve is a marginal-benefit curve and the firm uses the marginal principle to decide how much labor to hire, the MRP curve is the same as the firm's demand curve. If you pick a wage, the MRP curve tells you exactly how much labor the firm will demand.

What sort of changes would cause the demand curve to shift? To draw the labor demand curve, we hold fixed the price of the output and the productivity of workers. Therefore, an increase in the price of output will increase the MRP of workers, shifting the entire demand curve to the right: At each wage, the firm will hire more workers. Similarly, if workers become more productive, the increase in the marginal product of labor will increase the MRP and shift the demand curve to the right. Conversely, a decrease in price or labor productivity would shift the demand curve to the left.

Market Demand in the Short Run

To draw the short-run market demand curve for labor, we add the labor demands of all the firms that use a particular type of labor. In the simplest case, all firms are identical, and we simply multiply the number of firms by the quantity of labor demanded by the typical firm. If there were 100 firms and each hired 5 workers at a wage of $8, the market demand for labor would be 500 workers. Similarly, if the typical firm hired 3 workers at a wage of $11, the market demand would be 300 workers.

What About Labor Demand in the Long Run?

Recall that in the long run, firms can enter or leave the market and firms already in the market can change all their inputs, including their production facilities. The **long-run demand curve for labor** shows the relationship between the wage and the quantity of labor demanded over the long run, when the number of firms in the market can change and firms in the market can modify their production facilities.

Although there are no diminishing returns in the long run, the market demand curve is still negatively sloped. As the wage increases, the quantity of labor demanded decreases for two reasons:

- The **output effect**. An increase in the wage will increase the cost of producing balls, and firms will pass on at least part of the higher labor cost to their consumers: Prices will increase. According to the law of demand, firms will sell fewer balls at the higher price, so they will need less of all inputs, including labor.

Output effect: The change in the quantity of labor demanded resulting from a change in the quantity of output produced.

- The **input-substitution effect**. An increase in the wage will cause the firm to substitute other inputs for labor. At a wage of $4, it may not be sensible to use much machinery in the ball factory, but at a wage of $20, it may be sensible to mechanize the factory, using more machinery and fewer workers.

Input-substitution effect: The change in the quantity of labor demanded resulting from a change in the relative cost of labor.

The output effect reinforces the input-substitution effect, so the market demand curve is negatively sloped.

The notion of input substitution applies to other labor markets as well. For the most graphic examples of factor substitution, we can travel from a developed country such as the United States, Canada, France, Germany, or Japan to a less developed country in South America, Africa, or Asia. Wages are much lower in the less-developed countries, so production tends to be more labor intensive. In other words, labor is less costly relative to machinery and equipment, so labor is substituted for these other inputs. Here are some examples:

- **Mining.** U.S. firms use huge earth-moving equipment to mine for minerals, while many firms in less-developed countries use thousands of workers, digging by hand.

- **Furniture.** Firms in developed countries manufacture furniture with sophisticated machinery and equipment, while many firms in less-developed countries make furniture by hand.

- **Accounting.** Accountants in developed countries use computers and sophisticated software programs, while some accountants in less-developed countries use simple calculators and ledger paper.

Short-Run Versus Long-Run Demand

How does the short-run demand curve for labor compare to the long-run demand curve? There is less flexibility in the short run because firms cannot enter or leave the market, and firms in the market cannot modify their production facilities. As a result, the demand for labor is less elastic in the short run. That means the short-run demand curve is steeper than the long-run demand curve. You may recall that we used the same logic to explain why the short-run supply curve for a product (lawn rakes) was steeper than the long-run supply curve for the product.

TEST Your Understanding

1. The coach of a professional basketball team wants to hire a new player for $3 million per year. Under what circumstances would it be sensible to hire the player?

2. Complete the statement with *increase* or *decrease*: According to the output effect, a decrease in the wage will _____ production costs, so the price of output will _____. The quantity of output produced will _____, so the demand for labor will _____.

3. Explain the input-substitution effect associated with a decrease in the wage.

The Supply of Labor

The labor supply curve answers the following question: How many hours of labor will be supplied at each wage? When we speak of a labor market, we are referring to the market for a specific occupation in a specific geographical area. Consider the supply for nurses in the city of Florence. The supply question is, How many hours of nursing services will be supplied at each wage? To answer, we must think about how many nurses are in the city and how many hours each nurse works.

The Individual Decision: How Many Hours?

Let's start with an individual's decision about how many hours to work. The decision to work is a decision to sacrifice some leisure time: Each hour of work reduces leisure time by one hour. Therefore, the demand for leisure is the flip side of the supply of labor. The price of leisure time is the income sacrificed for each hour of leisure, that is, the hourly wage.

We know from Chapter 4 that an increase in the price of a good has two effects: a substitution effect and an income effect. An increase in the wage—the price of labor—has the following effects on the demand for leisure:

- **Substitution effect.** The worker faces a trade-off between leisure time and consumer goods such as music, books, food, and entertainment. For each hour of leisure time Leah takes, she loses 1 hour of work time, and her income drops by an amount equal to the wage. Therefore, she has less money to spend on consumer goods. For example, if the wage is $8 per hour, each hour of leisure decreases the amount of income available to spend on consumer goods by $8. When the wage increases to say $10, Leah will sacrifice more income—and consumer goods—for each hour of leisure. Given the larger sacrifice of consumer goods per hour of leisure time, she will demand less leisure time. That means that she will work more hours and earn more money for consumer goods. In other words, as the wage increases, she will substitute income—and the consumer goods it buys—for leisure time.

- **Income effect.** For most people, leisure is a normal good in the sense that the demand for leisure increases as real income increases. An increase in the wage increases Leah's real income in the sense that she can afford more of all goods, including leisure time. Suppose Leah has a total of 100 hours per week to divide between leisure and work. At a wage of $10, she works 36 hours and has 64 hours of leisure. She also earns $360 ($10 per hour × 36 hours of work) and spends that amount on consumer goods. If her wage increases to $15, her real income increases because she can have more consumer goods *and* more leisure time. For example, if she worked only 30 hours, she could buy $450 worth of consumer goods ($15 per hour × 30 hours) and have 70 hours of leisure (100 hours per week – 30 hours of work). The increase in real income causes Leah to consume more of all goods, including leisure time. That means that an increase in real income causes her to demand more leisure and supply less labor.

For the demand for leisure, the income and substitution effects of an increase in the wage work in opposite directions: The substitution effect decreases the desired leisure time, while the income effect increases the desired leisure time. Therefore, we can't predict whether an increase in the wage will cause Leah to demand more leisure time (supply less labor) or less leisure (supply more labor).

A simple example will show why we can't predict a worker's response to an increase in the wage. Suppose each nurse initially works 36 hours per week at an hourly wage of $10 and the wage increases to $12. Here are three reasonable responses to the higher wage:

1. **Lester works fewer hours.** If Lester works 30 hours instead of 36 hours, he gets 6 hours of extra leisure time and still earns the same income per week ($360 = 30 hours × $12 per hour).

2. **Sam works the same number of hours.** If Sam continues to work 36 hours per week, he gets an additional $72 of income ($2 per hour × 36 hours) and the same amount of leisure time.

3. **Maureen works more hours.** If Maureen works 43 hours instead of 36 hours, she sacrifices 7 hours of leisure time but earns a total of $516, compared to only $360 at a wage of $10 per hour.

Empirical studies of the labor market confirm that each of these responses is reasonable. When the wage increases, some people work more, others work less, and others work about the same amount.[2] In most labor markets, the average number of hours per worker doesn't change very much as the wage changes because the increases in work hours from people like Maureen are nearly offset by decreases in work hours from people like Lester.

The Market Supply Curve

Now that we know how individual workers respond to changes in wages, we're ready to consider the supply side of the labor market. The **market supply curve for labor** shows the relationship between the wage and the quantity of labor supplied. In Figure 18.2, the market supply curve for labor is positively sloped, consistent with the law of supply: The higher the wage (the price of labor), the larger the quantity of labor supplied. An increase in the wage affects the quantity of nursing supplied in three ways:

Market supply curve for labor: A curve showing the relationship between the wage and the quantity of labor supplied.

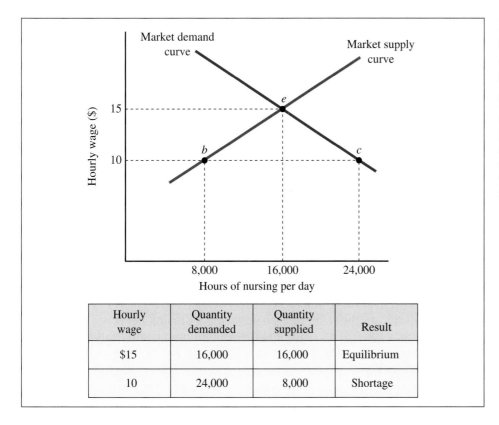

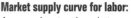

Figure 18.2

Supply, Demand, and Market Equilibrium
At the market equilibrium (point *e*, with wage = $15 per hour and quantity = 16,000 hours), the quantity supplied equals the quantity demanded, so there is neither excess demand for labor nor excess supply of labor.

Hourly wage	Quantity demanded	Quantity supplied	Result
$15	16,000	16,000	Equilibrium
10	24,000	8,000	Shortage

1. **Change in hours per worker.** When the wage increases, some nurses will work more hours, while others will work fewer hours, and others will work the same number of hours. We don't know for certain whether the average number of work hours will increase, decrease, or stay the same, but the change in the average number of hours is likely to be relatively small.

2. **Occupational choice.** An increase in the nursing wage will cause some workers to switch from other occupations to nursing and motivate more new workers to pick nursing over other occupations.

3. **Migration.** Some nurses in other cities will move to Florence to earn the higher wages offered there.

The second and third effects reinforce one another, so an increase in the wage causes movement upward along the market supply curve. If the wage of Florence nurses increases from $10 to $15 per hour, the quantity of nurses supplied increases from 8,000 hours per day (point *b*) to 16,000 hours per day (point *e*). Although individual workers may not work more hours as the wage increases, the supply curve is positively sloped because an increase in the wage changes workers' occupational choices and causes migration.

Market Equilibrium

We're ready to put supply and demand together to think about equilibrium in the labor market. A market equilibrium is a situation in which there is no pressure to change the price of a good or service. Figure 18.2 shows the equilibrium in the market for nurses. The supply curve intersects the demand curve at point *e*, so the equilibrium wage is $15 per hour, and the equilibrium quantity is 16,000 hours of nursing per day. At this wage, there is neither an excess demand for labor nor an excess supply of labor, so the market has reached an equilibrium.

How would a change in the demand for nurses affect the equilibrium wage of nurses? We know from Chapter 4 that a change in demand causes the equilibrium price and the equilibrium quantity to move in the same direction: An increase in demand increases the equilibrium price and quantity, while a decrease in demand decreases the equilibrium price and quantity. For example, suppose that the demand for medical care increases. Nurses help provide medical care, so an increase in the quantity of medical care demanded will shift the demand curve for nurses to the right: At each wage, firms will demand more hours of nursing services. As shown in Figure 18.3, an increase in demand increases the equilibrium wage and the equilibrium quantity of nursing services.

How would a change in supply of nurses affect the equilibrium wage of nurses? We know from Chapter 4 that a change in supply causes price and quantity to move in opposite directions: An increase in supply decreases the equilibrium price but increases the equilibrium quantity, while a decrease in supply increases the equilibrium price but decreases the equilibrium quantity. Suppose a new television program makes nursing look like an attractive occupation, causing a large number of youngsters to become nurses rather than accountants, lawyers, or doctors. The supply curve for nurses will shift to the right: At each wage, more nursing hours will be supplied. The equilibrium wage will decrease, and the equilibrium quantity will increase. For another example of the market effects of a change in supply, read "A Closer Look: Nannies Versus Au Pairs."

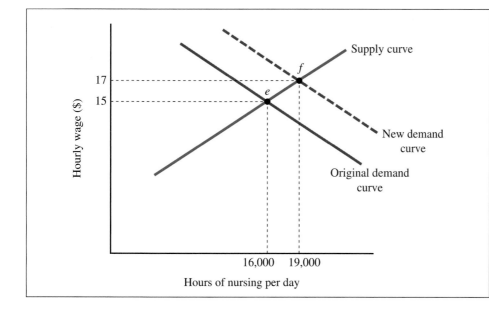

Figure 18.3

Market Effects of an Increase in Demand for Labor
An increase in the demand for nursing services shifts the demand curve to the right, moving the equilibrium from point *e* to point *f*. The equilibrium wage increases from $15 to $17 per hour, and the equilibrium quantity increases from 16,000 hours to 19,000 hours.

TEST Your Understanding

4. Your objective is to earn exactly $120 per week. If your wage decreases from $6 to $4 per hour, how will you respond?

5. Each worker in a certain occupation works exactly 40 hours per week, regardless of the wage. Does this mean that the market supply curve for the occupation is vertical (a fixed quantity, regardless of the wage)?

6. Complete the following: A decrease in the supply of nurses will _____ the equilibrium wage and _____ the equilibrium quantity of nursing services.

A CLOSER LOOK   Nannies Versus Au Pairs

In 1992, the Network of American Nanny Agencies (NANA) asked the U.S. Congress to impose strict limits on the number of European women participating in cultural exchange programs. Why? Each year about 8,000 European women participate in the au pair program, coming to the United States for 1-year stints to learn about the country, improve their English, and provide child care. NANA claimed the au pairs provide unfair competition and depress the wages of domestic nannies.[3]

How would the elimination of the au pair program affect the wage of nannies? As shown in the Figure, the supply curve for child-care services would shift to the left: At each wage, fewer workers would provide child-care services. As a result, the equilibrium wage for child-care workers would

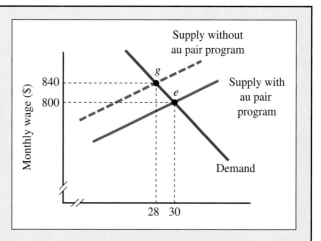

increase, from $800 per month to $840 per month in this example.

Explaining Differences in Wages and Income

Now that we know how the equilibrium wage for a particular occupation is determined, we're ready to explain why wages vary from one job to another. Let's think about why some occupations pay more than others, why women earn less than men, and why college graduates earn more than high-school graduates.

Why Do Wages Differ Across Occupations?

There is substantial variation in wages across occupations. Most professional athletes earn more than medical doctors, who earn more than college professors, who earn more than janitors. We'll see that the wage for a particular occupation will be high if the supply of workers in that occupation is small relative to the demand for those workers. This is shown in Figure 18.4, where the supply curve intersects the demand curve at a high wage.

The supply of workers in a particular occupation could be small for four reasons:

1. **Few people with the required skills.** To play professional baseball, people must be able to hit balls thrown at them at about 90 miles per hour. The few people who have this skill are paid a lot of money because baseball owners compete with one another for skillful players bidding up the wage. The same logic applies to other professional athletes, musicians, and actors. The few people who have the skills required for these occupations are paid high wages.

2. **High training costs.** The skills required for some occupations can only be acquired through education and training. For example, the skills that are required of a medical doctor can be acquired in medical school, and legal skills can be acquired in law school. If it is costly to acquire these skills, a relatively small number of people will become skilled, and they will receive high wages. The higher wage compensates workers for their training costs.

3. **Undesirable job features.** Some occupations are dangerous, and only a relatively small number of people are willing to work in dangerous occupations. The workers with the greatest risk of losing their lives on the job are lumberjacks, boiler-

Figure 18.4

Supply Is Low Relative to Demand
If supply is low relative to demand—because few people have the skills, training costs are high, or the job is undesirable—the equilibrium wage will be high.

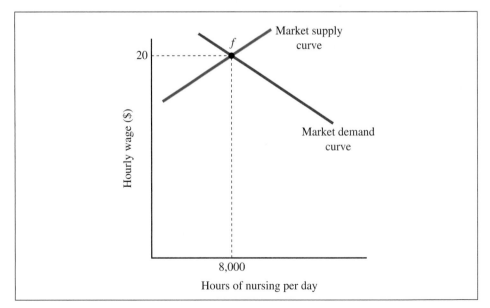

makers, taxicab drivers, and mine workers. The workers who choose dangerous occupations receive high wages, so they are compensated for the danger associated with their jobs. The same logic applies to other undesirable job features. For example, wages are higher for jobs that are stressful or dirty or that force people to work at odd hours.

4. **Artificial barriers to entry.** As we'll see later, government and professional licensing boards restrict the number of people in certain occupations, and labor unions restrict their membership. These supply restrictions increase wages.

For some facts on wages in dangerous jobs, read "A Closer Look: High Wages for Steelworkers."

Gender and Racial Discrimination

Why do women, on average, earn less than men? In the United States, the typical woman earns about 75% as much as the typical man. The gender gap is smaller in European nations but much larger in Japan.

Why is the gender gap so large? Part of the gender gap is explained by differences in skills and productivity. On average, women in many occupations have less education and less work experience, so they are less productive and are paid less. Another reason for the wage gap is occupational discrimination: Women have been denied access to many occupations, causing them to flood a small number of female-dominated occupations such as teaching, nursing, and clerical work. Given the plentiful supply of workers in these female-dominated occupations, wages are low compared to the wages in male-dominated occupations. Given the distribution of men and women in different occupations in the 1990s, about half of female workers would have to change occupations to achieve equal gender representation in all occupations.[5]

What about differences in earnings by race? In 1995, black males who worked full time earned 73% as much as their white counterparts earned,[6] while black females earned 86% as much as their white counterparts. Hispanic males earned 62% as much as white males, while Hispanic females earned 73% as much as white females.[6] For both males and females, part of the earnings gap is caused by differences in productivity: On average, whites have more education and work experience, so they are paid higher wages. Part of the wage gap is caused by racial discrimination. Some black and Hispanic workers are paid lower wages for similar jobs, and others are denied opportunities to work in some high-paying jobs.

How much of the earnings gap is caused by discrimination? A recent study suggests that racial discrimination decreases the wages of black men by about 13 percent.[7] Another study[8] shows that black-white earnings differences have decreased over the last few decades and that the differences are now small enough that "most of the disparity in

 **A CLOSER LOOK** High Wages for Steelworkers

Why do steelworkers earn more than other manufacturing workers? Studies of the labor market have shown that more dangerous jobs pay higher wages.[4] Let's compare the wage for a very safe manufacturing job to the wage in a steel mill. Each year, 1 in 10,000 steelworkers is killed on the job. To compensate for the higher risk of getting killed on the job, steelworkers receive a wage premium of 3.7%, or about $700 per year.

earnings between blacks and whites in the labor market of the 1990s is due to the differences in skills they bring to the market, and not to discrimination within the labor market."

Why Do College Graduates Earn Higher Wages?

In 1997, the typical college graduate earned 78% more than the typical high-school graduate. Over the last 25 years, this wage gap, or "college premium," has almost doubled. There are two explanations for the college premium.

The first explanation is based on supply and demand analysis. A college education provides the skills necessary to enter certain occupations, so a college graduate has more job options than a high-school graduate. Both high-school grads and college grads can fill jobs that require only a high-school education, so the supply of workers for these low-skilled jobs is plentiful, and the equilibrium wage for these jobs is low. In contrast, there is a smaller supply of workers for jobs that require a college education, so the wages in these high-skill jobs are higher than the wages for low-skilled jobs. This is the **learning effect** of a college education: College students learn the skills required for certain occupations.

Learning effect: The increase in a person's wage resulting from the learning of skills required for certain occupations.

The second explanation of the college premium requires a different perspective on college and its role in the labor market. Suppose certain skills are required for a particular job but an employer cannot determine whether a prospective employee has these skills. For example, most managerial jobs require the employee to manage his or her time efficiently, but it is impossible for an employer to determine whether a prospective employee is a good manager of time. Suppose that these skills are also required to complete a college degree. For example, to get passing grades in all your classes, you must be able to use your time efficiently. When you get your college degree, firms will conclude that you have some of the skills they require, so they may hire you instead of an equally skilled high-school graduate. This is the **signaling effect** of a college education: A person who completes college provides a signal to employers about his or her skills. This second explanation suggests that colleges simply provide a testing ground where students can reveal their skills to potential employers.

Signaling effect: The increase in a person's wage resulting from the signal of productivity provided by completing college.

The most important factor in doubling the college premium over the last 25 years is technological change. Changes in technology have increased the demand for college graduates relative to the demand for other workers. In all sectors of the economy, firms are switching to sophisticated machinery and equipment that require highly skilled workers. The share of jobs that require the skills of a college graduate has increased steadily, increasing the demand for college graduates and increasing their wages. Another factor in the growing college premium is the pace of technological change. Workers with more education can more easily learn new skills and new jobs, so firms are willing to pay more for college graduates.

TEST Your Understanding

7. Complete the statement with *demand* or *supply*: The wage for a particular occupation will be low if _____ is small relative to _____.

8. The wages of police officers vary from city to city. What could explain the wage differences?

9. In some countries, it is customary to tip restaurant waiters. What are the implications for the wages paid to waiters?

10. Would you expect people who work between midnight and 8:00 A.M. to earn higher or lower wages than people who work from 9:00 A.M. to 5:00 P.M.? Explain.

Public Policy and Labor Markets

We can use the model of the labor market to show the effects of public policies on wages and employment. We'll look at two policies: the minimum wage and occupational licensing. Each of these policies affects one side of the labor market—supply or demand—leading to changes in the equilibrium wage and total employment.

Effects of the Minimum Wage

In 1997, the federal minimum wage was $5.15 per hour. Figure 18.5 shows the effects of a minimum wage on the market for restaurant workers. The market equilibrium is shown by point *e*: The supply of restaurant workers equals demand at a wage of $4.70 and a quantity of 50,000 worker hours per day. Suppose a minimum wage is established at $5.15 per hour. At this wage, the quantity of labor demanded is only 49,000 hours (point *d* on the demand curve). In other words, the minimum wage decreases the quantity of labor used by restaurants by 1,000 hours per day.

What are the trade-offs associated with the minimum wage? From the perspectives of restaurant workers and restaurant diners, there is good news and bad news:

- **Good news for some restaurant workers.** Some workers keep their jobs and receive a higher wage ($5.15 per hour instead of $4.70 per hour).

- **Bad news for some restaurant workers.** Some workers lose their jobs. If the typical workday for restaurant workers is 5 hours, the loss of 1,000 hours of restaurant work per day translates into a loss of 200 jobs.

- **Bad news for diners.** The increase in the wage increases the cost of producing restaurant meals, increasing the price of meals.

There are winners and losers from the minimum wage: Workers who keep their jobs gain at the expense of other workers and at the expense of diners.

In recent years, there has been growing concern in the United States about poor working conditions and low wages for foreign workers who produce products for U.S. consumers. For a discussion of this issue, read "A Closer Look: Foreign Sweatshops and Codes of Conduct."

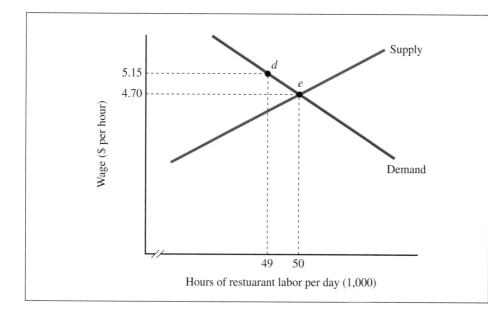

Figure 18.5

The Market Effects of a Minimum Wage
The market equilibrium is shown by point *e*: The wage is $4.70 per hour, and the quantity of labor is 50,000 labor hours per day. A minimum wage of $5.15 per hour decreases the quantity of labor demanded to 49,000 hours per day. Although some workers receive a higher wage, others lose their jobs or work fewer hours.

Several widely publicized reports have documented poor working conditions and low wages in foreign factories that produce shoes, clothing, and toys for U.S. corporations. In 1996, a report revealed that part of Wal-Mart's Kathie Lee Collection was produced in Honduras by people working 20 hours per day for 31 cents per hour.[9] Similar reports suggested that goods sold by Nike, Disney, and Mattel were produced in overseas sweatshops. Some human-rights activists have organized protests to publicize what they consider unethical business practices and have organized consumer boycotts.

The corporations have responded to the uproar by monitoring the firms that produce their goods and establishing codes of conduct for foreign suppliers.[10] The Council on Economic Priorities, an interest group in New York, inspects workplaces and awards the "Social Accountability 8000" to businesses that meet its criteria for wages and working conditions. The Apparel Industry Partnership, a group that includes social activists and apparel firms, is developing a code of conduct for apparel producers. The group was pleased to see the results of a survey suggesting that three-fourths of America's shoppers would be willing to pay higher prices for clothes and shoes bearing a "No Sweat" label. Some companies have hired accounting firms such as Price Waterhouse Coopers to audit their foreign suppliers. On campus, the United Students Against Sweatshops is developing a code of conduct for companies that produce products bearing university logos.

The efforts to monitor the labor practices of foreign suppliers raise several questions:

- How will better working conditions and higher wages affect the cost of producing the products and their prices?
- How will consumers respond to the higher prices?

- How much more are consumers willing to pay for "No Sweat" products?
- Will firms selling "No Sweat" products lose customers to firms selling products produced in factories that don't meet the codes of conduct?

Corporations with overseas production facilities responded to the uproar over sweatshops by monitoring the foreign firms that produce the goods for the corporations and establishing codes of conduct for foreign suppliers.

Occupational Licensing

In some occupations, the number of workers is limited by government-sanctioned licensing boards. A licensing board establishes requirements for working in a particular occupation. For example, a person may be prohibited from working in an occupation unless she or he (1) completes a given educational program, (2) passes an examination, (3) has a certain amount of work experience, and/or (4) has lived in a particular area for some time. Among the workers who are subject to occupational licensing are physicians, dentists, beauticians, plumbers, and pharmacists. In the United States, there are over 1,500 occupational licensing boards.[11]

Occupational licensing is controversial. In principle, the licensing requirements are designed to protect consumers from incompetent workers. However, occupational licensing has been criticized on three grounds:

1. **Weak link between performance and licensing requirements.** In many cases, the licensing requirements seem arbitrary, and there is a weak link between the requirements and the likely performance of the worker.

2. **Alternative means of protection.** There are other ways to protect consumers from incompetent workers. The government could provide consumers with information about the past performance of workers. Or consumers can spread the word about workers' performance, just as they spread the word for other goods and services. Of course, the dissemination of information will work better for some occupations (for example, plumbers and beauticians) than they do for others (such as doctors).

3. **Entry restrictions.** The licensing requirements increase the cost of entering the occupation, decreasing the supply of workers and increasing the wage paid to workers subject to occupational licensing.

Figure 18.6 shows the market effects of occupational licensing for retail pharmacists. Most of the drugs dispensed by retail pharmacists have already been prepared for use by drug companies, so the principal tasks for a retail pharmacist are counting pills and pasting labels on bottles. To be licensed as a retail pharmacist, a worker can complete a 5-year baccalaureate or a 6-year doctorate. The market equilibrium with this educational requirement is shown by point *e* in Figure 18.6: The wage of retail pharmacists is $15 per hour.

What would be the market effects of increasing the educational requirement for retail pharmacists? In 1991, three labor organizations representing over 170,000 pharmacists proposed changes in the licensing of pharmacists, changes that would force all new pharmacists to complete the 6-year doctorate program.[12] The increase in the edu-

Figure 18.6

The Market Effects of Occupational Licensing
Occupational licensing increases the cost of entering an occupation, shifting the supply curve to the left. An increase in the required education for pharmacists increases the equilibrium wage from $15 to $17 and decreases the equilibrium quantity from 32,000 to 24,000 hours of pharmacist labor.

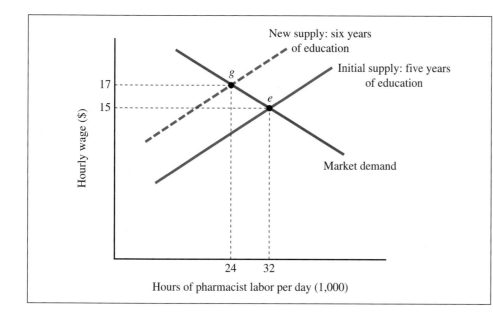

cation requirement (from 5 years to 6) would increase the cost of entering the occupation, shifting the supply curve to the left: At every wage, fewer pharmacist hours would be supplied. In Figure 18.6, the market would move from point *e* to point *g*, increasing the equilibrium wage to $17. In addition, the increase in the wage would increase the cost of producing and selling drugs, increasing the price of drugs. The general lesson is that occupational licensing increases wages, increases production costs, and increases prices.

If occupational licensing leads to higher prices, why does it persist for workers such as plumbers, beauticians, and retail pharmacists? Perhaps it persists because consumers believe that licensing protects them from incompetent and unscrupulous workers and because consumers are willing to pay higher prices for this perceived protection. Or perhaps the workers who receive higher wages are better organized than consumers and are therefore more effective in influencing public policy. This could be another example of public policy that benefits special-interest groups at the expense of the general public.

TEST Your Understanding

11. Imelda works 20 hours per week in a shoe store and is paid the minimum wage. When the government increases the minimum wage by $1, she rejoices, saying, "I will be better off by $20 per week." Is her calculation correct?

12. Comment on the following statement: It's silly to suggest that an increase in the minimum wage will decrease the quantity of labor demanded by fast-food restaurants. It's impossible to substitute machines for workers, so the restaurants will hire the same number of workers at the higher wage.

13. Complete this statement with *increases* or *decreases*: Occupational licensing increases the cost of entering an occupation, so it _____ supply, _____ the wage, and _____ the price of goods produced by the licensed occupation.

Labor Unions

We've used a simple model of labor supply and labor demand to explain differences in wages. Our analysis is based on the assumption that workers take the market wage as given. A **labor union** is an organized group of workers, the objectives of which are to increase job security, improve working conditions, and increase wages and fringe benefits.

A Brief History of Labor Unions in the United States

As shown in Figure 18.7, about one-sixth of all workers in the United States belong to a union, down from about one-third of workers 40 years ago. Among private-sector workers, the unionization rate is less than 10%, while over 37% of public-sector workers belong to unions. There are two types of labor unions:

- A **craft union** includes workers from a particular occupation, for example, plumbers, bakers, or electricians.

- An **industrial union** includes all types of workers from a single industry, for example, steelworkers or autoworkers.

There are also umbrella organizations that include many individual unions. The largest of these "unions of unions" is the AFL-CIO (the American Federation of Labor–Congress of Industrial Organizations).

Labor union: An organized group of workers; the objectives of the organization are to increase job security, improve working conditions, and increase wages and fringe benefits.

Craft union: A labor organization that includes workers from a particular occupation, for example, plumbers, bakers, or electricians.

Industrial union: A labor organization that includes all types of workers from a single industry, for example, steelworkers or autoworkers.

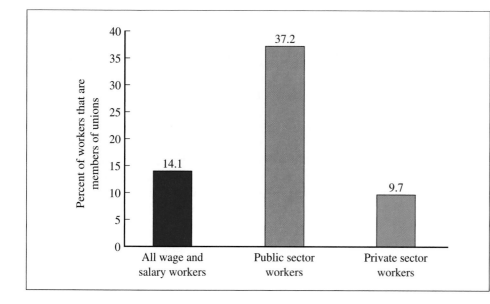

Figure 18.7
Unionization Rates in the United States, 1997
Overall, 14% of all wage and salary workers are members of unions. Over 37% of public-sector workers are members of unions.

Source: Statistical Abstract of the United States, 1998.

Let's take a brief look at the history of labor organizations in the United States. In the nineteenth century, there were all sorts of craft unions, and the main umbrella organizations were the Knights of Labor (founded in 1869) and the AFL (founded in 1881). The CIO (formed in 1931) was a collection of industrial unions that represented semi-skilled workers in mass production, including workers in the automobile, rubber, and steel industries. The CIO merged with the AFL in 1955. The most important recent trend has been the expansion of unions serving workers in the public sector. In the last 30 years, the number of government workers in unions and employee associations has more than doubled.

Labor unions get their power to influence labor markets from the states and the federal government. Let's take a brief look at the most important pieces of labor legislation:

- The Wagner Act (1935) guaranteed workers the right to join unions and required each firm to bargain with a union formed by a majority of its workers. The National Labor Relations Board (NLRB) was established to enforce the provisions of the Wagner Act.

- The Taft-Hartley Act (1947) gave government the power to stop strikes that "imperiled the national health or safety" and gave the states the right to pass right-to-work laws. These laws, which are currently in force in 21 states, outlaw union shops, defined as workplaces where union membership is required as a condition of employment.

- The Landrum-Griffin Act (1959) was a response to allegations of corruption and misconduct by union officials. This act guaranteed union members the right to fair elections, made it easier to monitor union finances, and made the theft of union funds a federal offense.

Labor Unions and Wages

One goal of a union is to increase the wages of its members, and there is evidence that unions raise the wages of union workers. One study of unions concluded that unionized workers earn 20% to 30% more than nonunion workers doing the same work.[13] Let's look at three ways in which a union could try to increase the wages of its members.

One approach is to organize workers and negotiate a higher wage. Suppose workers in a particular industry form an industrial union and agree on a union wage that exceeds the equilibrium wage. Like a minimum wage imposed by a government, a wage negotiated by a union means that some workers will earn higher wages but other workers who are willing to work will not have the opportunity to work. To deal with this problem, the union can reduce the number of workers by restricting membership or can share the smaller number of jobs among its members.

Another way in which a union can increase the wage of its members is to promote the products produced by union workers. You've probably seen advertisements encouraging people to buy products with the union label. The demand for labor is a derived demand, so an increase in the demand for a final good will increase the demand for labor used to produce that good, increasing the equilibrium wage. This approach can be used together with a negotiated union wage to prevent an excess supply of labor at the union wage.

A third approach—which may or may not increase wages—is to impose work rules that increase the amount of labor required to produce a given quantity of output. One example of featherbedding is a minimum crew size, which forces a firm to hire more workers than it needs to perform a particular task. For example, the typical unionized airline hires three workers to guide an airplane into the gate, while nonunion airlines use only two workers. In the past, railroad unions forced railroads to use firemen (whose job is to shovel coal) on diesel-powered engines, which don't use coal.

Featherbedding may or may not increase the demand for labor. Although featherbedding forces the firm to use more labor per unit of output, it also decreases the quantity of output. A firm suffering from featherbedding hires workers it doesn't need, so its production costs will be higher than it would be without featherbedding. Firms increase their prices to cover these extra production costs, and consumers respond by purchasing less output. Therefore, the direct effect of featherbedding (that is, the increase in the amount of labor required for a given quantity of output) will be at least partly offset by a decrease in output. The demand for labor is derived from the demand for the final good, so featherbedding may actually decrease the demand for labor, decreasing the wage and total employment.

A different approach to managing union employment comes from Volkswagen A.G., Europe's largest automaker. In 1993, Volkswagen got its labor unions to switch to a 4-day, 28-hour workweek, down from a 5-day, 36-hour workweek. If workers hadn't accepted the shorter workweek and lower pay, Volkswagen would have eliminated 30,000 of its 100,000 jobs in Germany. In other words, the switch to the shorter workweek preserved 30,000 union jobs in the automobile industry.[14] Some analysts suggest that shorter workweeks for union workers will become more common as European unions grapple with lower demand for their workers.

Do Labor Unions Increase Productivity?

We've seen that unions lead to higher wages and work rules that are designed to decrease labor productivity. In other words, there are some costs associated with labor unions. Could unions increase productivity?

Unions may increase productivity by facilitating communication between workers and managers. If a worker is unhappy with his or her job, one option is to quit. From the firm's perspective, this is costly because the firm loses an experienced worker and must train a new one. A dissatisfied worker who belongs to a union has a second option: The worker can use the union as an intermediary to discuss job issues with managers. This sort of communication can solve problems before they become so severe that the worker quits. There is evidence that firms whose workers are in unions have lower turnover rates, in part because they facilitate communication between workers and managers.[15] These lower turnover rates lead to lower training costs and a more experienced workforce.

Other Imperfections in the Labor Market

So far, our analysis of the labor market has been based on two key assumptions: First, there is perfect information in the labor market. Second, employers take the market wage as given. Let's see what happens when these assumptions are not satisfied.

Imperfect Information and Efficiency Wages

What happens when workers have better information than their employers? Workers differ in their skill levels and the amount of effort they exert on the job. Employers cannot always distinguish between skillful and unskillful workers or between hard workers and lazy workers. In other words, there is asymmetric information in the labor market.

We know from our discussion of the market for used cars that asymmetric information causes high-quality and low-quality goods to be sold in a mixed market at a single price. Suppose there are 2 types of workers:

- Low-skill workers, whose marginal revenue product = $100 per day

- High-skill workers, whose marginal revenue product = $200 per day

The employer cannot distinguish between these two types of workers and offers a single wage, realizing that it will probably hire some workers of each type.

What is the appropriate wage? Suppose the opportunity cost of high-skill workers is $130 and a firm offers a wage of $110. Because the wage is less than the opportunity cost of high-skill workers, only low-skill workers will apply for jobs. The firm will lose money because the $110 wage exceeds the $100 marginal revenue product of the low-skill workers. To get some high-skill workers, the employer must pick a wage that exceeds the $130 opportunity cost of high-skill workers. As the firm increases its wage, it will attract more high-skill workers, and the average productivity of its workforce will increase. Depending on the responses of the two types of workers to the higher wage, a firm could make more profit by offering a higher wage. This is known as **paying efficiency wages**: The firm pays a higher wage to increase the average productivity of its workforce.

Another reason for paying relatively high wages is to encourage employees to work hard. Firms realize that their employees can vary their work efforts, from working hard to hardly working (shirking). To encourage their employees to work hard, employers fire workers who are caught shirking. The penalty associated with being fired will be much greater if the firm pays a wage above the worker's opportunity cost. For example, suppose a worker could earn $80 per day in another job. If the firm pays its workers $100 per day, a worker who is fired—and then immediately gets a job with another firm—would take a pay cut of $20 per day. This is another example of paying efficiency wages: By increasing the wage, the firm increases the work effort of its employees and increases the average productivity of its workforce.

Paying efficiency wages: The practice of a firm paying a higher wage to increase the average productivity of its workforce.

Higher Wages at Ford Motor Company

ECONOMIC DETECTIVE

In the early days of the automobile industry, the prevailing wage for autoworkers was $3 per day. The assembly-line jobs were repetitive and tedious, and the turnover rate of workers was very high. When Henry Ford decided to increase the daily wage for his workers from $3 to $5, most observers were baffled. They figured that Ford's labor costs would be almost twice as high as those of his rivals, so he would lose a lot of money and

People were baffled when Henry Ford increased the daily wage for his assembly workers from $3 to $5.

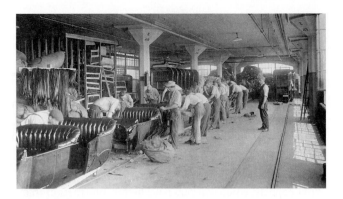

quickly go out of business. The wage hike appeared to be a great act of generosity but very bad business. You can imagine their surprise when Ford's profit doubled from $30 million to $60 million. How was this possible? How can higher wages lead to higher profits?

The key to solving this puzzle is the concept of efficiency wages. When Ford raised the wage, the average productivity of Ford workers increased by about 50%, a result of several changes in the workforce:[16]

- The pool of job applicants improved, so Ford could choose better workers.

- Fewer workers were fired for shirking.

- Fewer workers quit voluntarily.

- The rate of absenteeism was cut in half.

In the words of Henry Ford, "There was no charity in any way involved. . . . The payment of five dollars a day for an eight-hour day was one of the finest cost cutting moves we ever made." ◆

Monopsony Power

Monopsony: A market in which there is a single buyer of an input.

We've assumed that each employer is such a small part of the labor market that it takes the market wage as given. The labor-supply curve faced by the firm is horizontal at the market wage. Although this is true for many labor markets, in some markets there is a single employer. For example, if your city has a single hospital, there will be a single employer of surgical nurses. This is the case of **monopsony**: There is a single buyer of a particular input.

A monopsonist faces a positively sloped market supply curve of labor. If the monopsonist hires more workers, it must pay a higher wage to attract them away from other activities. In Figure 18.8, the firm can hire 7 workers at a wage of $10 (point *c*) and 8 workers at a wage of $12 (point *d*). The firm's **marginal labor cost** (also known as *marginal factor cost*) is defined as the increase in total labor cost from hiring one more worker. When the firm decides to hire 8 workers instead of 7, its total labor cost increases from $70 per hour ($10 per worker per hour × 7 workers) to $96 per hour ($12 per worker per hour × 8 workers), an increase of $26. Therefore, the firm's marginal labor cost for the 8th worker is $26 (shown by point *e* in Figure 18.8).

Marginal labor cost: The increase in total labor cost resulting from hiring one more worker. (Also known as *marginal factor cost.*)

As shown in Figure 18.8, the marginal labor cost exceeds the hourly wage. The reason is that when the firm increases the wage to hire one more worker, the firm must increase the wage for all of its workers. To hire the 8th worker, the firm pays $12 to the new worker but also pays an extra $2 for each of the 7 workers who were willing to work at the $10 wage. We compute the marginal labor cost as follows:

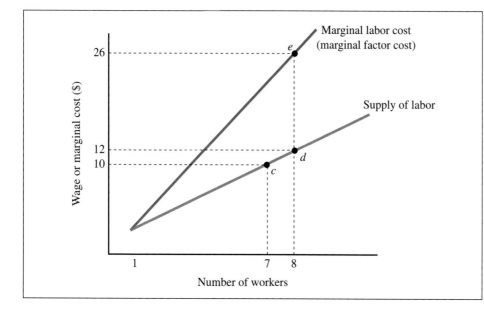

Figure 18.8
The Supply of Labor and Marginal Labor Cost for a Monopsonist
To hire more workers, the monopsonist must pay a higher wage, so the marginal labor cost exceeds the wage. To hire the 8th worker, the firm increases the wage from $10 to $12. The marginal labor cost for the 8th worker is $26, equal to $12 paid to the 8th worker plus $14 extra money paid to the 7 original workers, each of whom receives $2 more per hour.

marginal labor cost = wage paid to new worker + (change in wage × quantity of original workers)

$$\$26 \quad = \quad \$12 \quad + \quad (\$2 \times 7)$$

In this case, the marginal labor cost is $26, including $12 for the new worker and $14 for the original workers.

Figure 18.9 shows how a monopsonist decides how many workers to hire. Using the marginal principle, the firm chooses the quantity of labor at which the marginal benefit of labor equals the marginal cost of labor. The marginal labor cost curve intersects the marginal revenue product curve (the marginal benefit curve) at point *m*, so the firm

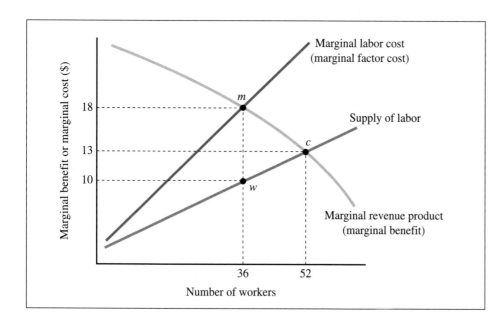

Figure 18.9
The Hiring Decision of a Monopsonist
The monopsonist chooses point *m*, where the marginal benefit of labor (the marginal revenue product) equals the marginal labor cost. The supply curve indicates that to hire 36 workers, the monopsonist must pay a wage of $10 (point *w*).

Table 18.2   Monopoly versus Monopsony

Monopoly	Monopsony
Single seller of output	Single buyer of input
High price of output	Low price of input
Small quantity of output	Small quantity of input

hires 36 workers. As shown by the supply curve, if the firm wants to hire 36 workers, it must pay a wage of $10 per hour (shown by point w).

How does the monopsony outcome compare to the perfectly competitive outcome? Any firm that hires workers—either a monopsonist or perfect competitor—will continue to hire more workers until the marginal cost equals the marginal benefit (the marginal revenue product). For a perfectly competitive firm, the marginal cost is simply the wage. For a monopsonist, the marginal cost is the marginal labor cost, which exceeds the wage because the monopsonist must increase its wage to hire more workers. The monopsonist will hire fewer workers because its higher marginal cost equals the marginal benefit at a smaller quantity of labor. A monopsonist will hire fewer workers than would be hired by a collection of perfectly competitive firms, each of which takes the market wage as given.

You may have noticed the similarity between a monopsonist and a monopolist. A monopolist (a single seller) uses its market power to increase the price of output, while a monopsonist (a single buyer) uses its market power to decrease the wage or other input prices. The monopolist produces an artificially small quantity of output, while the monopsonist hires an artificially small quantity of a particular input such as labor. Table 18.2 summarizes the key features of a monopolist and a monopsonist.

What is the role of a labor union in a labor market with a single buyer? Monopsony leads to an artificially low wage, and a union leads to an artificially high wage. A market with both a union and a monopsonist will have a wage somewhere between the two extremes, depending on the bargaining power of the two sides. It may be sensible to counteract market power on the demand side of the market (a monopsony) with market power on the supply side (a union).

TEST Your Understanding

14. Explain how an increase in the wage can increase the average productivity of the firm's workforce.

15. Suppose a union's objective is to maximize total employment in a certain occupation, and it cannot affect the demand for labor. The firms in the market take the wage as given. What should the union do?

16. Suppose a union's objective is to maximize the total income of nurses (total money spent by firms on nurses). At the current wage, the price elasticity of demand for nurses is 1.5. Should the union increase or decrease the union wage? Explain.

17. Complete the statement with *high* or *low*: A monopolist sells its output at a relatively _____ price, while a monopsonist buys its inputs at a relatively _____ price.

Using the **TOOLS**

We've seen how to use supply and demand curves to explain differences in wages and to predict the effects of public policy on the equilibrium wage and employment. We've also seen the effects of unions and the rationale for paying a wage above the equilibrium wage. Here are some opportunities to do your own economic analysis.

1. Market Effects of Immigration

In the initial equilibrium, the wage for farmworkers is $5 per hour. The elasticity of supply of farmworkers is 2.0, and the elasticity of demand for farmworkers is 1.0. Suppose that immigration increases the supply of farmworkers by 12%: The supply curve shifts to the right by 12%.

a. Predict the effect of immigration on the wage paid to farmworkers: By how much will the wage increase or decrease?

b. How will immigration affect the cost of producing food and the equilibrium price of food?

2. Effects of a Nurses' Union

Suppose that the nurses in the city of Florence form a union and that to work as a nurse, you must belong to the union. The nurses do not allow new nurses to join the union, so the supply of nurses decreases by 3% per year as old nurses retire. As shown in Figure 18.2, before the union is formed, the equilibrium wage is $15 and the equilibrium quantity is 16,000 hours per day.

a. Depict graphically the effect of forming the union on the nursing market.

b. If the price elasticity of demand for nursing is 1.5, by what percentage will the wage of nursing increase each year?

3. Demand for Newskids

Consider the market for newspaper delivery kids in Kidsville. Each newskid receives a piece rate of $2 per subscriber per month and has a fixed territory that initially has 100 subscribers. The price elasticity of demand for subscriptions is 2.0. Suppose the new city council of Kidsville passes a law that establishes a minimum piece rate of $3 per subscriber per month. As a result, the publisher increases the monthly price of a subscription by 20%. How will the new law affect the monthly income of the typical newskid?

4. Equilibrium with Efficiency Wages

Consider a labor market with asymmetric information: Each worker knows his or her marginal revenue product, but firms cannot distinguish between low-skill and high-skill workers. Each low-skill worker has an opportunity cost of $80 and a marginal revenue product of $100, and each high-skill worker has an opportunity cost of $130 and a marginal revenue product of $200. The workforce is divided equally between the two types of workers. Your job is to predict the equilibrium wage in the market given that each firm takes the price as given and earns zero economic profit. Try the following wages: (a) $90, (b) $100, (c) $140, (d) $150, (e) $170.

Summary

We've seen how wages are determined in perfectly competitive labor markets and why wages differ from one occupation to another. We've also explored the effects of various market imperfections—public policies, unions, and imperfect information—on wages and employment. Here are the main points of the chapter:

1. The wage in a particular occupation will be relatively high if supply is small relative to demand. This will occur if (a) few people have the skills required for the occupation, (b) training costs are high, or (c) the job is dangerous or stressful.

2. College graduates earn more than high-school graduates because a college education provides new skills and allows people to reveal their skills to employers.

3. There are trade-offs with a minimum wage or a union wage: Some workers earn higher income, but others lose their jobs.

4. Occupational licensing increases the wage of the licensed occupation and increases the price of the good produced by that occupation.

5. A firm that increases its wage may increase the average productivity of its workers and increase its profit.

Key Terms

craft union, 386
industrial union, 386
input-substitution effect, 375
labor union, 386
learning effect, 382

long-run demand curve for labor, 374
marginal labor cost, 390
marginal revenue product of labor (MRP), 373
market supply curve for labor, 377

monopsony, 390
output effect, 375
paying efficiency wages, 389
short-run demand curve for labor, 374
signaling effect, 382

Problems and Discussion Questions

1. You are an economic consultant to a city that just imposed a payroll tax of $1 per hour of work. This payroll tax is paid by workers through a payroll deduction: For each hour of work, the employer deducts $1 and sends the money to the city government. The initial wage (before the tax) is $10, and total employment is 20,000 hours per day. Use a graph to show the effect of the tax on the equilibrium wage and employment.

2. We discussed the response of Lester, Sam, and Maureen to an increase in the wage. Which person's response is closest to your own? If your wage increased, would you work more hours, fewer hours, or about the same number of hours?

3. Critically appraise the following statement from Mr. Chuckles: "The law of supply says that an increase in price increases the quantity supplied. A decrease in the income tax rate will increase the worker's net wage, so each worker will work more hours. As a result, the revenue from the income tax will increase."

4. Consider two markets for carpenters: the city of Portland and the United States. Draw two supply curves for carpenters: one for the city of Portland and one for the United States. In which market would you expect a more elastic supply of carpenters?

5. The advocates of higher salaries for teachers point out that most teachers have college degrees and that teaching children is an important job.

   a. Why aren't teachers' salaries higher, given the importance of the job and the education required?

   b. Suppose a new law requires that teachers are paid the same hourly wage as college graduates who work in business. Predict the effects of this law on the market for teachers.

6. Comment on the following: "There is no substitute for an airline pilot: Someone has to fly the plane. Therefore, an increase in the wage of airline pilots will not change the number of pilots used by the airlines."

7. Suppose a new government program improves worker safety in coal mines. Use a graph to predict the effect of the program on the equilibrium wage for coal workers.

8. Under some occupational licensing laws, licensed members of an occupation write licensing exams. An example is the bar exam for licensing lawyers. How might this practice limit entry into an occupation?

9. One response to the gap in wages between men and women is a policy called comparable worth, under which the government specifies a minimum wage for some occupations, typically the occupations with a disproportionate number of women. Evaluate the merits of a such a policy. What are the trade-offs?

10. **Web Exercise.** Visit the Web site of the U.S. Census Bureau (*http://www.census.gov*), and download the report "Money Income in the United States." How do the average earnings of women with bachelor's degrees compare to those of female high-school dropouts and women with masters' degrees? Do the same comparisons for men.

11. **Web Exercise.** Visit the Web site of the U.S. Bureau of Labor Statistics (*http://www.bls.gov/*). Do a keyword search of the site to get some information on the bureau's projections of employment in different occupations. Try the following: "occupational + employment + projections." Which occupations are expected to grow most rapidly in coming years? Which are expected to grow slowly?

Take It to the Net

We invite you to visit the O'Sullivan/Sheffrin page on the Prentice Hall Web site at:
http://www.prenhall.com/osullivan/
for additional World Wide Web exercises for this chapter.

Model Answers to Questions

Chapter-Opening Questions

1. When the wage increases, some people work more hours, others work fewer hours, and others work about the same number of hours.

2. As shown in "A Closer Look: High Wages for Steelworkers," the worker's income would increase by about 3.7%.

3. The gender gap results from differences in skills and productivity as well as occupational discrimination.

4. As shown in "A Closer Look: Foreign Sweatshops and Codes of Conduct," U.S. corporations have developed codes of conduct and hired firms to audit their foreign suppliers.

5. Henry Ford described the wage hike as "one of the finest cost cutting moves we ever made."

Test Your Understanding

1. If the marginal revenue product of the new player exceeds $3 million. If the player increased attendance and increased the revenue from ticket sales by $4 million, it would be sensible to hire the player.

2. Decrease, decrease, increase, increase.

3. As the wage decreases, labor will become less expensive relative to other inputs, so the firm will substitute labor for other inputs.

4. You will work 30 hours per week instead of 20 hours.

5. No. An increase in the wage will increase the number of workers because of changes in occupational choices and migration.

6. Decrease, increase.

7. Demand, supply.

8. Wages are higher in cities where police officers face a greater chance of being killed on the job.

9. Waiters in tipping countries will have lower wages than waiters in nontipping countries.

10. Working between midnight and 8:00 A.M. disrupts sleeping and eating patterns and a person's social life. Because of these undesirable consequences, we expect workers on the midnight to 8:00 A.M. shift to receive higher wages than workers on the day shift.

11. Imelda's statement could be incorrect for three reasons: (1) She may lose her job as a result of the

higher minimum wage; (2) if she keeps her job, her employer may ask her to work fewer hours per week; (3) as a consumer, she will pay higher prices for the goods produced by minimum-wage workers, partly offsetting any increase in income she may receive.

12. There are opportunities to substitute machinery for workers, as shown by the switch to "smart" cash registers (the pictures on the buttons speed up money collection; beaming the information to the kitchen speeds up the process of filling orders and collecting money) and automated cooking machines (burgers on tracks). In addition, there is the output effect: The increase in cost will increase price, so restaurants will sell less food and thus need fewer workers.

13. Decreases, increases, increases.

14. The firm will attract better applicants, and workers are less likely to shirk.

15. Total employment is maximized at the intersection of supply and demand, so the union should do nothing, letting the market reach the equilibrium.

16. If demand is elastic, a decrease in price will increase total expenditures (total revenue, total income). Therefore, the union should decrease its wage.

17. High, low.

Using the Tools

1. **Market Effects of Immigration.** Immigration will shift the supply curve to the right, decreasing the equilibrium wage. We can use the price-change formula for an increase in supply (explained in Chapter 5) to predict the change in the equilibrium wage (the price of labor):

   a. The wage will decrease from $5.00 to $4.80 per hour.

   b. The cost of producing food will decrease, so the price of food will decrease.

2. **Effects of a Nurses' Union**

   a. The union causes movement upward along the market demand curve as the number of nurses decreases by 3% per year.

   b. The quantity of labor decreases by 3% per year. To compute the resulting change in price, we can use the formula for price elasticity of demand. To be consistent with an elasticity of 1.5, a 3% decrease in quantity generates a 2% increase in the wage.

3. **Demand for Newskids.** The elasticity of demand is 2.0, so a 20% increase in price will decrease the quantity demanded by 40%: A price elasticity of 2.0 means the percentage change in quantity is 2 times the percentage change in price. In other words, the number of subscribers per newskid will decrease from 100 to 60. The income of the typical newskid will decrease from $200 ($2 per subscriber × 100 subscribers) to $180 ($3 per subscriber × 60 subscribers). This is the output effect in action.

4. Equilibrium with Efficiency Wages

   a. Wage = $90. Each firm will get all low-skill workers, each with marginal revenue product (MRP) = $100. Each firm will make a profit, so this is not an equilibrium. Competition among the firms will bid up the wage.

   b. Wage = $100. Each firm will get all low-skill workers, each with MRP = $100. Each firm will make zero economic profit, so this is an equilibrium wage.

   c. Wage = $140. Each firm will get half low-skill workers and half high-skill workers, so the average MRP = $150. Each firm will make a profit, so this is not an equilibrium. Competition among the firms will bid up the wage.

   d. Wage = $150. Each firm will get half low-skill workers and half high-skill workers, so the average MRP = $150. Each firm will make zero economic profit, so this is an equilibrium.

   e. Wage = $170. Each firm will get half low-skill workers and half high-skill workers, so the average MRP = $150. Each firm will lose money, so this is not an equilibrium.

 **Notes**

1. W. Michael Fox and Beverly J. Fox, "What's Happening to Americans' Income?" *The Southwest Economy*, Federal Reserve Bank of Dallas, Issue 2, 1995, pp. 3–6; U.S. Bureau of the Census, Current Population Reports, P60-200, *Money Income in the United States: 1997* (Washington, DC: U.S. Government Printing Office, 1998).

2. Mark Killingsworth, *Labor Supply* (New York: Cambridge University Press, 1983).

3. Brent Bowers, "Nanny Agencies Say Threat from 'Au Pairs' Isn't Kid Stuff," *Wall Street Journal*, May 28, 1992, p. B1.

4. Craig Olson, "An Analysis of Wage Differentials Received by Workers on Dangerous Jobs," *Journal of Human Resources*, vol. 16, Spring 1981, pp. 167–85.

5. Suzanne Bianchi and Daphne Spain, "Women, Work, and Family in America," *Population Bulletin*, vol. 51, no. 3, 1998, pp. 2–48.

6. U.S. Department of Labor, *Employment and Earnings* (Washington, DC: U.S. Government Printing Office, 1996).

7. William Darity and Patrick Mason, "Evidence on Discrimination in Employment: Codes of Color, Codes of Gender," *Journal of Economic Perspectives*, vol. 12, no. 2, 1998, pp. 63–90.

8. James Heckman, "Detecting Discrimination," *Journal of Economic Perspectives*, vol. 12, no. 2, 1998, pp. 101–116.

9. "Stamping Out the Sweatshops: Dress Code," *The Economist*, April 19, 1997.

10. "Sweatshop Wars," *The Economist*, February 27, 1999.

11. Werner Hirsch, *Law and Economics: An Introductory Analysis*, 2nd ed. (San Diego, CA: Academic Press, 1988), pp. 347–350.

12. Lawrence J. McQuillan, "Pharmacists' Proposal Will Raise Costs of Medicine," *The Margin*, Spring 1993, p. 52.

13. Richard B. Freeman and James Medoff, *What Do Unions Do?* (New York: Basic Books, 1985).

14. Ferdinand Protzman, "VW Plan for 4-Day Workweek Is Adopted," *New York Times*, November 26, 1993, p. D11; Tyler Marshall, "VW, Unions, OK 20% Reduction in Work Week," *Los Angeles Times*, November 26, 1993, p. A1; "Worldwire," *Wall Street Journal*, July 8, 1994, p. A5.

15. Freeman and Medoff, *What Do Unions Do?*

16. J. R. Lee, "So-Called Profit Sharing System in the Ford Plant," *Annals of the American Academy of Political and Social Science*, May 1915, pp. 297–310; David Halberstam, *The Reckoning* (New York: William Morrow, 1986), pp. 91–92; Daniel M. G. Graff and Lawrence H. Summers, "Did Henry Ford Pay Efficiency Wages?" *Journal of Labor Economics*, vol. 5, 1987, pp. 557–86.

CHAPTER

19

Economic Challenges: Poverty, Aging, and Health Care

Ethena Jones just graduated with an honors degree in computer engineering and is pleased with the high salary she will earn at her new job. But she wonders about her classmates from high school who did not go to college, especially the ones living in poverty. She also wonders whether her older brother, who recently lost his job, will be able to afford health insurance. She is concerned about her parents, who are near retirement age. Is the Social Security trust fund about to run out of money, and how might that affect her parents?

Poverty and Public Policy
Who Are the Poor?
What Causes Poverty?
Anti-poverty Programs

The Aging of Society
The Social Security System
The Coming Financing Crisis
Challenge: Financing the Elderly

Health Care
Problems with Our Health-Care System
Challenge: Reforming the System

Using the Tools

n this chapter, we discuss three economic challenges that confront the United States and other developed countries. Poverty is a persistent and vexing problem, and the growing frustration with traditional welfare policies—involving assistance for all poor families—led to a new welfare system that requires work in exchange for time-limited assistance. A second economic challenge is dealing with an aging population. In the next century, the proportion of the population over 65 years of age will increase sharply, requiring changes in the way we support the elderly population. A third economic challenge is dealing with the rising costs of health care. As health-care costs increase, it becomes more difficult to support the elderly and the poor—both large consumers of health care—and more difficult for all of us to maintain the same level of health care.

We explore the policy choices we will face as we try to deal with these issues in the twenty-first century. We first look at the possible causes of poverty and the policy options available to reduce poverty. We then turn to the problems generated by the aging of the population and the high costs of providing adequate health care. As you read this chapter, you will see that the fundamental problem in economics—scarcity of resources—is still with us. Here are some of the practical questions that we answer in this chapter.

1. **Is poverty more prevalent among senior citizens or children?**
2. **Why is homelessness more prevalent in some cities?**
3. **What are the trade-offs—the advantages and disadvantages—of privatizing Social Security?**
4. **Why does the cost of health care continue to rise?**

Poverty and Public Policy

In every society, some people do not earn enough income to provide what most of us consider a reasonable amount of food, clothing, housing, medical care, and other goods. In this part of the chapter, we explain the causes of poverty and discuss antipoverty policies.

Who Are the Poor?

Household: A group of related family members and unrelated individuals who live in the same housing unit.

Poverty budget: The minimum amount the government estimates that a family needs to avoid being in poverty; equal to 3 times the minimum food budget.

A **household** is a group of related family members and unrelated persons who live in the same housing unit. According to the U.S. government, a household is considered poor if its total income is less than the amount required to satisfy its minimum needs. The government computes a household's minimum needs or the **poverty budget** by estimating a minimum food budget and multiplying the minimum food budget by three. For example, in 1997, the poverty budget was $12,802 for a three-person household and $16,400 for a four-person household. A household whose income is less than the official poverty budget is considered poor.

Figure 19.1 shows the poverty rates for various groups. The poverty rate equals the percentage of people in a particular group who live in households below the official poverty line. The overall poverty rate in the U.S. is 13.3%, and poverty rates differ sharply by groups:

- Race. The poverty rates for blacks and Hispanics are over twice as high as the rate for whites. The poverty rate for Asian-Americans is 14%.

- Family type. The poverty rate for female-headed households is about six times the rate for two-parent households.

Figure 19.1

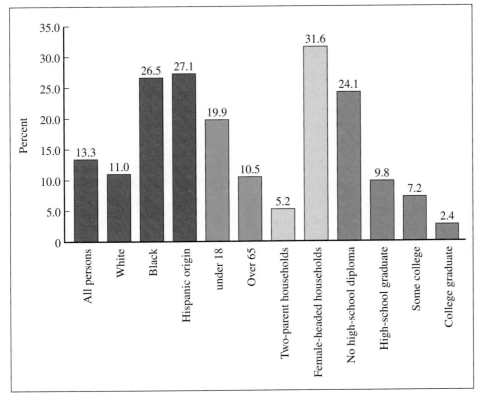

Poverty Rates for Different Population Groups
Poverty rates are highest among racial minorities, children, and people with low educational attainment.

Source: U.S. Bureau of the Census, Current Population Reports, Series P60-201, *Poverty in the United States, 1997*. (Washington, DC: U.S. Government Printing Office, 1998).

- **Age.** One of the recent successes in the battle against poverty was the decrease in poverty among the elderly. The poverty rate for the elderly dropped from 35% in 1959 to 10.5% in 1997, largely as a result of increased Social Security benefits. In contrast, the poverty rate for children is almost 20%.

- **Education.** The poverty rate of high-school dropouts is over twice the poverty rate for high-school graduates and over 8 times the poverty rate of college graduates.

What Causes Poverty?

To put it simply, poverty results from the failure of the adults in a household to earn enough money to provide for the household's basic needs. Some adults are unable to work because of health problems, disabilities, or age. Others have limited work options because they are responsible for raising small children. A common perception is that most poor adults don't work, but this is incorrect. More than half of poor households have someone who works at least part-time, and one in five poor households has a full-

The poverty rate for children is about twice the poverty rate for senior citizens.

time, year-round worker.[1] For the working poor, the problem is low wages and part-time employment, not the lack of a job. For example, a four-person household with one full-time worker will be below the poverty line if the worker's wage is less than $8.20 per hour, well above the minimum wage.

There are many reasons for poverty. It is difficult to disentangle the factors that cause poverty, and economists have not reached a consensus about which of these factors is the most important.

- **Inadequate education.** As shown in Figure 19.1, the poverty rate for high-school dropouts is about ten times the poverty rate for college graduates. Workers who do not complete high school lack many of the basic skills needed in the workplace. Therefore, they are less likely to be employed, and if they are employed, they earn low wages.

- **Racial segregation.** In most cities in the United States, racial minorities—especially blacks—are concentrated in the central cities, far from jobs in suburban areas. Many poor households don't own cars, and mass-transit systems are ill-equipped for commuting from the central city to the suburbs. A recent study shows that young black adults are much worse off in segregated cities: They earn less income, have lower high-school graduation rates, are more likely to be idle (neither working nor attending school), and are more likely to become single mothers.[2] The more segregated the city, the more prevalent are these adverse outcomes.

- **Weak economy.** Because the poor are usually less productive than other workers, they are the last hired and the first fired. They are the last hired when the economy grows rapidly and are the first to lose their jobs when the economy slows down.

- **Racial and gender discrimination in the labor market.** Although white workers earn more than minority workers and men earn more than women, most of the differences in wages are explained by differences in hours worked, education, and work experience. Part of the difference results from racial and gender discrimination: Whites are paid more than equally productive blacks; men are paid more than equally productive women. The size of the discrimination penalty has been shrinking over time, and there is some disagreement about the actual size of the penalty.

- **Single parenthood.** As shown in Figure 19.1, the poverty rate among female-headed households is about six times the poverty rate for two-parent families.

How have recent changes in production technology affected the wages of the least educated and least productive workers? Recent advances in technology have decreased the demand for these workers for two reasons: First, the new technology allowed firms to replace many low-skilled workers with "smart machines." Second, the least educated workers do not have the skills required to work in firms that produce and use the new technology. As a result, the demand for low-skilled workers has fallen, resulting in lower wages. As an illustration, the wage for a job that required the use of a computer is about 19% higher than the wage for a similar job that does not require a computer.[3]

Anti-poverty Programs

As we saw in Chapter 15, the federal government and the states spend billions of dollars on programs designed to reduce poverty. Spending on anti-poverty programs accounts for about 14% of the federal budget, 32% of state budgets, and 5% of local-government budgets. This money is spent on job-training programs, cash assistance, and transfers of goods and services such as food stamps and medical care.

In August 1996, President Clinton signed into law the Personal Responsibility and Work Opportunity Reconciliation Act of 1996, a comprehensive welfare-reform plan. The plan abolished the traditional anti-poverty program for poor families (Aid to Families with Dependent Children, or AFDC) and thus eliminated the entitlement of poor families to receive cash assistance. The federal government now provides block grants to the states, and the states are responsible for designing and implementing programs to move most poor adults from welfare dependence to employment. The new program, called Temporary Assistance to Needy Families (TANF), has the following restrictions:

- After a maximum of 24 months of assistance (consecutive or nonconsecutive), a recipient must participate in work activities, defined as employment, on-the-job training, work experience, community service, vocational training, or child-care services for individuals providing community service. Single parents must participate at least 30 hours per week, and two-parent families must participate at least 35 hours per week. There are exceptions to this rule for the parents of very young children.

- After a total of 60 months of cash assistance (consecutive or nonconsecutive), assistance is stopped. States can allow exceptions to this rule, with the restriction that no more than 20% of the state's recipients exceed the 60-month limit.

The states are responsible for implementing welfare reform. Florida's reform law—known as Work and Gain Economic Self-Sufficiency (WAGES)—provides an example of one state's response to the new welfare law. The program gives temporary assistance to poor families with children and provides parents with work opportunities and support services. This is a work-first program: When a person applies for assistance, he or she is immediately referred for employment. Unless exempted, each recipient must participate in work activities to the full extent of the federal guidelines. For a family of three, the maximum cash assistance is $303 per month, which is less than one-third of the poverty budget for a family of three. Cash assistance is limited to 24 consecutive months in any 60-month period, and no recipient will receive payments for more than 48 months.

How will welfare reform affect the markets for low-skilled labor? The switch from a traditional welfare system to a program requiring work in exchange for time-limited assistance will increase the number of low-skilled people in the labor market. As shown in Figure 19.2, an increase in the number of low-skilled workers shifts the labor supply

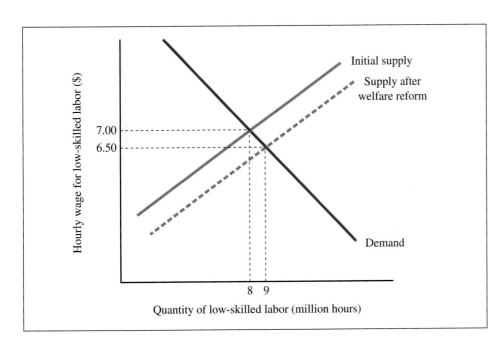

Figure 19.2
The Effects of Welfare Reform on the Market for Low-Skilled Labor
The welfare-reform program requires welfare recipients to join the workforce. The resulting increase in supply of low-skilled workers will decrease the equilibrium wages for low-skilled workers.

curve to the right: At each wage, more hours of labor are supplied. In this example, the wage drops from $7.00 to $6.50 per hour, and the quantity of labor increases. The actual effects of welfare reform on wages and employment will be determined by the elasticity of supply of low-skilled labor and the elasticity of demand for low-skilled labor. A recent study estimates that the wages for the least educated and lowest-skilled workers (high-school dropouts and the least productive high-school graduates), could drop by about 6%.[4] In general, low-skilled women will suffer the largest losses in earnings and wages because they are the workers who will face the most additional competition as many former welfare recipients join the workforce.

**ECONOMIC
DETECTIVE**

Wages of College Graduates and High-School Dropouts

During the 1980s and 1990s, the supply of both college graduates and high-school dropouts increased, with a larger increase in the supply of college graduates. Given the larger increase in supply of college graduates, we would expect the wage of college graduates to decrease relative to the wage of high-school dropouts. Yet the relative wage of college graduates actually increased. Use a supply and demand diagram to solve this mystery.

Figure 19.3 shows how to solve this puzzle. In each market, the supply curve shifted to the right, with a larger shift in the market for college graduates. At the same time, the demand curve for college graduates shifted to the right, a result of technological change that caused employers to demand more workers with the skills required to produce and use new technology. The increase in demand was larger than the increase in supply, so the wage for college graduates increased. In the market for high-school dropouts, the

Figure 19.3 Changes in Equilibrium Wages for High-School Dropouts and College Graduates
Between 1980 and 2000, the supply of college graduates increased by more than the supply of high-school dropouts. Because the demand for low-skilled labor decreased, the wage for high-school dropouts decreased. The demand for high-skilled labor increased, more than offsetting the increase in supply of college graduates, so the wage of college graduates increased.

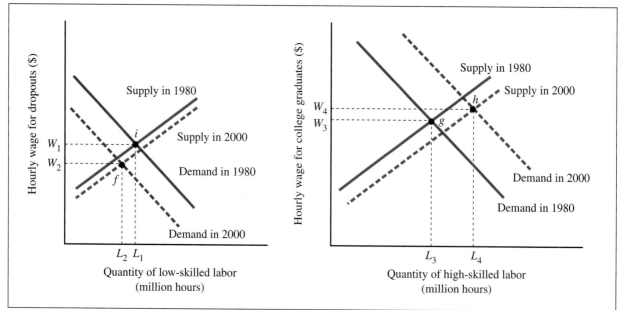

demand curve for low-skilled labor decreased. The combination of increase in supply and decrease in demand resulted in lower wages for high-school dropouts. Because the college wage increased and the dropout wage decreased, the relative wage of college graduates increases. ◆

TEST Your Understanding

1. Which of the following statements are true, and which are false?

   a. The poverty rate among the elderly exceeds the poverty rate among children.

   b. Most poor households have at least one part-time worker.

   c. A single parent can avoid poverty by getting a full-time job at the minimum wage.

2. How does the government determine the poverty budget for a three-person household?

3. Why is the poverty rate low when the economy is growing rapidly, and why does it increase when the economy slows down?

A CLOSER LOOK | The Homeless

An extreme version of the problems experienced by the poor is homelessness. The McKinney Homeless Assistance Act of 1987 defines a homeless person as someone who sleeps (1) outside, (2) inside in places not intended for sleeping (e.g., the lobby of a public building), or (3) in housing shelters (places providing temporary housing). On a given night in the United States, the homeless population is between 250,000 and 350,000. About three-fourths of the homeless are single men, and 15% are children.[5]

Most homeless adults have suffered serious economic and social difficulties. About half are high-school dropouts, and about one in five has spent some time in a mental hospital. About one in three homeless people has spent some time as a patient in a chemical-dependency program. Over half of the homeless have spent time in jail (a short period for misdemeanor violations), and about one-quarter have spent time in prison (longer periods for felony violations). About one in five homeless people has attempted suicide.

What causes homelessness? From an economic perspective, a person will be homeless if his or her income is low enough relative to the price of housing

that it is not sensible—or not even possible—to purchase housing services. The homeless rate varies considerably across metropolitan areas, the highest rates being in cities where low-quality housing is expensive, job growth is slow, welfare payments are low, and the percentage of the mentally ill in institutions is low.[6]

One factor in the growth of the homeless population in the last few decades was the loss of low-quality housing in large cities. Historically, many of the poor lived in boarding houses, rooming houses, and residential hotels (also known as single-room occupancy units, or SROs). This housing had small living quarters, shared bathrooms, and limited kitchen facilities, but it was affordable for most pensioners and day laborers. During the 1970s and 1980s, much of the SRO stock was eliminated, a result of urban renewal and conversion to other uses. Many of the hotels and large houses that were used for boarding or rooming houses have been renovated for higher-income households. Nationwide, over 1 million SRO units were lost during the 1970s and 1980s. The loss of SROs contributed to the homeless problem by decreasing the supply of low-quality housing and increasing its price.

The Aging of Society

In 1950, there were seven people aged 24 to 64 (prime working age) for every person 65 years and older. By 1990, that ratio had fallen to 4.8. Current projections indicate that by the year 2030, there will be only 2.8 people of working age for every person over retirement age. This dramatic change in the age distribution of our population will force us to reexamine many of our social programs.

These changes are not occurring only in the United States. Many countries around the world, both developed and developing countries, are facing an aging population in the future. Figure 19.4 presents projections of the **dependency ratio**, defined as the ratio of the population over 65 years of age to the population between 20 and 65, in Japan and the United States. As the diagram indicates, by the year 2050, the United States is projected to have a dependency ratio of 37%, while Japan is projected to have a much higher dependency ratio of 60.1%. This means that in the year 2050, Japan will have only 1.66 (1/0.601) people between the ages of 20 and 65 for every person over the age of 65.

Dependency ratio: The ratio of the population over 65 years of age to the population between 20 and 65.

The Social Security System

As we saw earlier in this chapter, the poverty rate among the elderly is much lower than the poverty rate for other age groups. The reason for this low rate of poverty is the Social Security system. Started in 1935 during the depths of the Great Depression, the **Social Security** system provides retirement and health benefits to the elderly. It is one of our most popular social programs and has widespread support throughout the entire political system.

Social Security: A government program that provides retirement, survivor, and disability benefits.

The Social Security system is complex and has many different provisions. Here is a basic overview:

- Over 92% of the civilian workforce is included in the Social Security system today. (Not all employment is covered by Social Security, and there are minimum earning requirements.)

Figure 19.4

Dependency Ratios for Japan and the United States

The dependency ratio is the ratio of the population over 65 years to the population between 20 and 65 years.

Source: Congressional Budget Office.

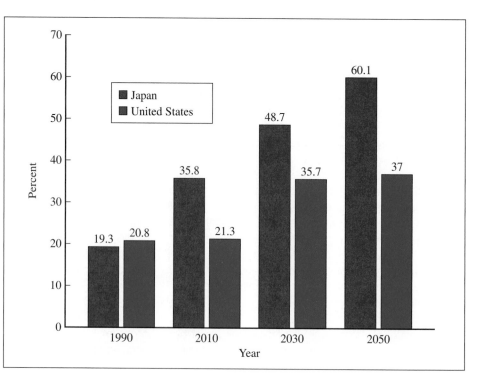

- Workers who are included in Social Security receive either retirement benefits at the age of 65 or reduced benefits at the age of 62.

- A recipient with a dependent wife, husband, or child receives 50% more than a recipient without dependents.

- If a worker dies, survivor benefits are provided to the family.

- Social Security also provides disability payments for workers who suffer from an illness that prevents them from working for a minimum of a year.

In addition to these retirement provisions, the other major part of the Social Security system is **Medicare**, health coverage for the elderly. Medicare consists of both hospital insurance and supplementary medical insurance for doctor services and other services outside the hospital. Medicare hospital benefits are provided automatically to workers and their married partners when they reach the age of 65. Supplementary medical insurance is voluntary and requires monthly payments, which are typically only about one-quarter of the cost of equivalent private insurance. Widows and widowers of deceased workers are also covered at the age of 65.

Medicare: A government program that provides health benefits to people over 65 years of age.

The Social Security system (except for supplementary medical insurance) is financed through flat payroll taxes on both employees and employers. Each contributes one-half the total tax. For all parts of the system except the hospital portion of Medicare, there is a yearly maximum amount (or "cap") beyond which a worker does not contribute in a given year.

The retirement benefits, survivor benefits, and disability benefits that Social Security pays are determined by an average of the wages the worker earned during employment. The Social Security system calculates a replacement rate for each worker, which is the fraction of their average wage they will receive. Replacement rates are higher for workers who earned lower wages. Therefore, the Social Security system redistributes income to retirees who had low wages and away from retirees who had higher wages. Despite the fact that the system is financed with a flat payroll tax, the system as a whole redistributes income toward low-wage workers. As a result, the system is viewed as a **social insurance** system, a program that takes care of those who have had bad luck, possess low skills, or experience misfortunes.

Social insurance: A system that compensates individuals for bad luck or low skills.

The Coming Financing Crisis

From nearly the beginning of the Social Security system, the payroll taxes paid by employees and employers in any given year paid for the benefits received by retirees in that same year. Thus, the payments that an employer and an employee made did not go into an account earmarked for that worker's retirement. Instead, these dollars were paid out immediately to current recipients. This type of financing mechanism is called a **pay-as-you-go** system.

Pay-as-you-go: A system that uses revenue collected this year to pay for benefits paid to recipients this year.

In the early days of the Social Security system, pay-as-you-go worked quite well. As long as the elderly population is small relative to the working population, it does not take a high level of payroll taxes to finance retirements. Throughout much of its history, retirees under Social Security received vastly more in benefits than they paid in taxes. In fact, the first recipient paid $22 in Social Security taxes, lived to the age of 99, and collected $20,000 in benefits.[7] The easy times for Social Security are behind us for two reasons:

- As we will see later in the chapter, medical costs have risen rapidly, and they are expected to continue rising. Rising medical costs increase the costs of Medicare.

- As the average age of the population increases, there will be fewer workers for each retiree.

Given rising medical costs and an aging population, it will be costly to continue providing the same level of payments to the recipients of Social Security and Medicare. How high must payroll taxes go to support the system at its current benefit levels? Projections far into the future are risky, but a typical estimate is that the combined employer-employee payroll tax rates, now 15.3%, may have to rise to about 26%.[8] Income taxes and other taxes come on top of these payroll taxes. Assuming that federal and state income taxes stay in the same range, this would mean the average worker could easily face total taxes between 50% and 60% of his or her income. While some European countries have tax rates this high, such rates would bring about a dramatic change in our fiscal system.

Challenge: Financing the Elderly

What are the options for dealing with the problem of supporting an aging population? There are three possible approaches.

1. Preserve Future Benefits but Invest More Today

If we increased our rate of investment today, we could increase the living standards of the next generation. With higher living standards, the next generation would be better able to bear the burden of financing Social Security and Medicare payments. We could view this as a generational compact or deal: Workers today will provide the next generation with higher living standards by consuming less and investing more, as long as the next generation provides Social Security and Medicare benefits to the members of the current generation when they retire.

Although this may seem like a reasonable bargain, higher living standards for future generations will not reduce the tax rates they face. As increased investment by today's generations raises real income over time, retirement benefits will rise because they are largely determined by wages near retirement. If current generations save more, they will receive larger retirement benefits. Total tax rates for the average worker in future generations could still range between 50% and 60%. Looking back, will future workers remember their bargain? Or will they just be dissatisfied with the high rates of taxation? Raising the standard of living for future generations does nothing to alleviate the redistribution between generations that will occur if the system is not changed.

2. Cut Benefits

A second possibility is to reduce benefits. Obviously, reducing benefits for current retirees or those nearing retirement would be perceived as unfair. However, it is possible to cut future benefits. For example, the retirement age is already scheduled to be increased in the twenty-first century, and further increases are possible. In addition, unlike private retirement plans, Social Security benefits are currently fully adjusted for inflation. Reducing the inflation adjustment could provide considerable long-run savings.

But we should not underestimate the degree of difficulty in even making these changes. Retirement ages, for example, have drifted down in recent years from an average age of 65 to 62. Workers anticipating an earlier retirement will not want to see benefits held off until a later age. Similarly, many elderly people worry that they will not have sufficient assets and that their only benefits will be from Social Security. If these benefits are not protected against inflation, will the elderly be forced into poverty?

3. Privatize the Entire System

A third—perhaps shocking—alternative would be to make the benefits received by any person depend directly on his or her own contribution. In other words, we could privatize the entire system. The government would require everyone to make at least a minimum contribution, but each contributor would be free to direct his or her funds among an approved set of alternatives. On retirement, the contributor could draw on his or her accumulated savings. Chile recently replaced its pay-as-you-go system with a fully funded privatized system.

Proponents of a privatized system point to several advantages. First, it would alleviate future workers from the burden of paying excessive taxes. Second, workers could invest their savings in the stock market. Historically the rate of return in the stock market has been high enough that money invested there would generate a more generous retirement plan than provided by the same amount of money put into the Social Security System. Third, total saving and investment in the economy are likely to increase as workers save for their own retirements rather than simply waiting to receive Social Security benefits as in the current system.

Nonetheless, there are some disadvantages to replacing our current system. First, there are transition problems. Consider a woman who is now 50 years old and anticipates retiring in 15 years. During her working career, she did not save very much because she knew that she would receive Social Security; so during all her working years, she paid taxes that financed the retirement of others. If we suddenly privatized the system, she would have only 15 years to save for her retirement, which is not sufficient time to set aside funds for her old age. Clearly, we would not think this was fair and would have to design some transition system that would supplement her savings. Still, she gets a raw deal: In the past, she paid for others to retire, and now she must pay for part of her own retirement as well. There is no way to escape this problem. During a transition, some groups in society will have to pay both for their own retirement and for the retirement of others.

Second, full privatization of the Social Security system would effectively end our current system of social insurance. Under the current system, if the breadwinner in the household dies, the family receives survivor benefits. Under full privatization, these benefits would not be available unless the government created a new program. Similarly, if a worker made a series of poor investments with his or her retirement funds and then died, would the widow or widower live in poverty?

The funding of Social Security and Medicare will be debated on a large scale as we enter the twenty-first century. In 1996, an advisory council to the Social Security Administration reported on alternative solutions to the challenges of funding future benefits. Their report discussed several options, including partial or total privatization as well as investing some of the payroll taxes in the stock market. The group had to confront the issues we've raised, including the role of the Social Security system in providing social insurance as well as difficult transition issues. As you can see, some fundamental aspects of the nature of our society are at stake in this debate.

TEST Your Understanding

4. Because Social Security is financed by a flat payroll with a cap, it redistributes income from low-wage earners to high-wage earners. True or false? Explain.

5. Explain why the age distribution in a society matters for a pay-as-you-go system.

6. List two advantages and two disadvantages of privatizing the Social Security system.

Health Care

In recent years, the rising cost of health care for the poor and elderly has caused budgetary problems for the federal and state governments. At the same time, workers and businesses in the private sector find themselves struggling to afford health care. In the last part of the chapter, we look at our health-care system and the challenges we face in controlling costs and providing care.

Problems with Our Health-Care System

Despite the availability of the latest technology, many social scientists believe that our health system has serious difficulties. Over the last 40 years, real spending per person on medical care has risen at a rate of over 4% a year. Such rapid growth has meant that we are devoting an increasing fraction of our resources to health care. From 1960 to 1997, the share of total income devoted to health care rose from 6% to 14%. As shown by Figure 19.5, compared to other developed countries, the United States spends a much higher fraction of its total income on health care. The United Kingdom, for example, devotes 6.7% of its total income to health care, and Japan spends 7.3% of its total income.

In principle, there is no reason why such a high level of spending in the United States might not be worthwhile. But most observers believe that much of our spending is not worthwhile. In making spending decisions, we should be guided by the marginal principle.

 MARGINAL **PRINCIPLE**

> **Increase the level of an activity if its marginal benefit exceeds its marginal cost, but reduce the level if the marginal cost exceeds the marginal benefit. If possible, pick that level at which the marginal benefit equals the marginal cost.**

Figure 19.5

Health Expenditure as Percent of Total Income (Gross Domestic Product), 1997

The United States spends a relatively large fraction of total income on health care.

Source: OECD Health Data, 1998.

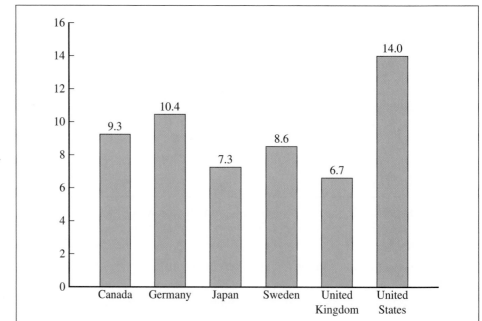

In the health sector, we constantly violate the marginal principle: We make expenditures of little marginal value that have substantial marginal costs. For example, studies suggest that as many as one-fourth of common medical procedures for the elderly have costs that exceed the benefits.[9] The violation of the marginal principle is partly a result of the fact that physicians have traditionally been trained to heal the sick, not to make economic decisions. Another factor is the temptation to use new technology, regardless of its cost. Many patients and physicians choose high-cost treatments even when their advantage over lower-cost treatments is minimal.

Traditional health-care insurance does not provide physicians an incentive to control costs. Under a traditional insurance policy, insurance companies pay for any treatment. If doctors and hospitals are fully reimbursed for their expenses, they have little incentive to discourage patients from getting expensive care even if the marginal benefit of that care is extremely low. In recent years, many employers have required their employees to join health-maintenance organizations (HMOs), in which physicians are paid a fixed amount per patient regardless of the treatments that are actually provided. Under this type of system, doctors and hospitals have an incentive to contain costs. Because they are paid a fixed amount per patient, their profits increase as they reduce their costs. A health system in which HMOs and similar organizations compete for patients is commonly known as **managed competition**.

Managed competition: A health system in which organizations such as HMOs compete for patients.

A second problem caused by the health-care insurance system is that many people are not insured. Insurance companies want to avoid providing insurance to people who have a high risk of large medical bills. If an insurance company is providing insurance to the employees of a large firm, it probably has a good idea of the total risk it faces because the employees of the large firm are likely to be a typical cross section of the labor force. But if it offers insurance policies to individuals, those at high risk (whom the insurance company cannot easily distinguish from those at low risk) will have the greatest incentives to purchase the policies. The insurance companies recognize this problem and charge high rates for individual policies or to small firms. Because of these high costs, many individuals and workers in small firms do not buy insurance.

In 1998, about 42 million people (about 16% of the population) were not covered by health insurance. Almost all the elderly are covered through Medicare, and many of the poor are covered under Medicaid. Most U.S. workers receive their health insurance through their employers. The uninsured are the people and their families who do not receive insurance through their employers, are unemployed or between jobs, or are poor but do not qualify for Medicaid in their state. People who do not have health insurance obtain care for emergencies but fail to receive routine, and less costly, preventive care.

Challenge: Reforming the System

It appears that there is little chance of an immediate, radical, sweeping reform of the health system. During 1993–1994, the Clinton administration tried to provide universal coverage, in part by requiring all firms to provide health insurance to their employees. This plan was soundly defeated because of its sheer complexity and the difficulties of developing policies to subsidize small firms so that they could provide insurance to their employees. However, as the costs of health care continue to grow and large numbers of people remain uninsured, there will be pressures for change. Let's look at some of the key issues that will be debated in the twenty-first century.

1. Work Toward Universal Coverage

The problem of so many uninsured people does not show any signs of improving. Although the defeat of the Clinton health plan probably means that universal coverage cannot be achieved by requiring employers to provide health insurance for all workers,

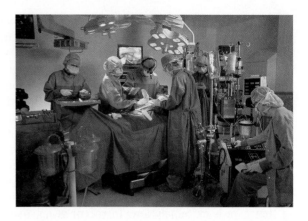

Complex and expensive heart operations are commonplace today.

there may be other solutions. Stanford health economist Victor Fuchs has suggested a voucher plan in which everyone would receive a health voucher to purchase insurance.[10] The difficulty with any voucher plan is that new taxes would be necessary to finance it. While it would be possible to raise rates on existing taxes to finance such a plan, most European countries that provide universal coverage have a value-added tax, essentially a national sales tax. Clearly, introducing a new tax or raising existing tax rates to finance a voucher plan would be very controversial and would require a broad political consensus that health reform is absolutely necessary.

2. Reform Medicare

Some politicians and policymakers have suggested that managed competition needs to be introduced into Medicare to provide incentives to reduce costs. This would be a major departure from the current system because few of the elderly are currently enrolled in HMOs. Because Medicare expenses directly affect the federal budget, politicians are keenly aware of the need to reduce costs and have been discussing this option, despite resistance among the elderly, who want to ensure that the treatment they would receive from HMOs matches the quality of their current care.

3. Reform Insurance Markets

How can we ensure that everyone has access to some type of health insurance? What types of new laws or regulations are needed to address some of the problems in the market for insurance? Several states have experimented with plans to require insurance companies to provide broad coverage, that is, coverage to more firms and their workers. This approach has been difficult to implement because large firms that provide insurance to their own employees are, by federal law, exempt from state insurance laws.

Even with laws that require broad coverage, some economists believe subsidies would be required to entice many of the uninsured to purchase insurance. Many young and healthy people would rather take their chances and hope they stay healthy rather than pay for health insurance.

4. Manage Technological Change

How can we benefit from technological advance in medicine without bankrupting our society? Can the private market handle this problem? Or should the government play an active role in evaluating advances in medical technology? Fuchs proposed a small tax on health providers to fund a private institute devoted to assessing new medical technologies. Ideally, this institution would be able to uncover the technological advances for which marginal benefits truly exceed marginal costs.

7. Explain how to use the marginal principle to guide our choice of medical technology.

8. Why is the price of medical insurance for employees of a large firm lower than the price of medical insurance for an individual?

9. What is universal coverage? Why is it so difficult to achieve?

Using the **TOOLS**

In this chapter, we've explored some of the policy challenges associated with poverty, Social Security, and the health-care system. Here are some opportunities to do your own economic analysis.

1. Welfare Reform and Wages of Low-Skilled Labor

Consider the market for low-skilled labor in a large metropolitan area. The initial wage is $6.00 per hour, and the initial quantity is 100 million hours per day. The elasticity of supply of labor for the market is 0.20, and the elasticity of demand is 1.0. Suppose welfare reform increases the supply of low-skilled labor in the city by 6%. Predict the effects of welfare reform on the equilibrium wage and equilibrium quantity of low-skilled labor. How does welfare reform affect the weekly pay of a low-skilled worker who worked 40 hours per week before the reform and continues to work 40 hours per week?

2. Chile's Transition to a Private Pension System

When Chile made the transition from a pay-as-you-go social security system to a private system, it had a very young population. Compared to the United States, the ratio of working-age people to retirees was three times as high. How did the age structure in Chile make it easier to move to a private system?

3. Evaluating Medical Technology

Suppose new technology enables patients of heart surgery to return to work one week earlier. The new technology is as safe as the old technology but very expensive. Hospitals and patients both want to use this new technology, and you must decide whether to allow Medicare to reimburse them. What information do you need before you make your recommendation?

Summary

We explored three policy issues that the United States and other countries will face in the twenty-first century. We will continue to grapple with poverty. At the same time, the aging of the population and the continued escalation of the cost of health care will pose new and difficult challenges. Here are the main points of the chapter.

1. The main causes of poverty are inadequate education, racial segregation, a weak economy, racial and gender discrimination in the labor market, and single parenthood.

2. Dramatic changes in the age distribution of the population—fewer workers per retiree—will force

many countries to modify programs for the elderly. In the United States, reform efforts have focused on the Social Security system, with proposals to cut benefits or privatize the system.

3. Compared to other developed countries, the United States spends a much larger fraction of its income on health care. The decisions to spend money on health care often violate the marginal principle.

4. About 16% of people in the United States are not covered by health insurance, and given the failure of recent proposals for universal coverage, there is no sign that the problem of the uninsured will be solved soon.

Key Terms

dependency ratio, 406
household, 400
managed competition, 411

Medicare, 407
pay-as-you-go, 407
poverty budget, 400

social insurance, 407
Social Security, 406

Problems and Discussion Questions

1. During the 1980s, the wages of older less-educated workers (those in their 40s) increased relative to the wages of young less-educated workers (those in their 20s). Explain why this could occur.

2. Suppose that the birth rate begins to fall. How would this affect a pay-as-you-go social security system?

3. Suppose state governments increased the funding for state colleges and universities, allowing the nationwide college enrollment to increase by 20%. Predict the effect of the increase in enrollment on the wage of college graduates relative to the wage of high-school graduates.

4. Explain why an HMO might encourage pregnant women to have regular appointments with their doctors.

5. What is a disadvantage of having employers provide health insurance?

6. Why might replacing a pay-as-you-go system with private pensions increase total savings?

7. Web Exercise. Visit the Web site of the U.S. Census bureau for the latest facts on poverty rates (*http://www.census.gov/hhes/www/poverty.html*). Click on "Poverty in the United States" and then "State Poverty Rates" to check the poverty rate in your state. How does it compare to the national average?

8. Web Exercise. Visit the Web site of the Social Security Administration (*http://www.ssa.gov*) and access the on-line publications site (*http://www.ssa.gov/pubs*) to find publications that help you answer the following questions:

   a. What are the current tax rates for Social Security and Medicare?

   b. How much does your employer pay in Social Security and Medicare taxes?

   c. How is the money raised through these taxes used?

Take It to the Net

We invite you to visit the O'Sullivan/Sheffrin page on the Prentice Hall Web site at:
http://www.prenhall.com/osullivan/
for additional World Wide Web exercises for this chapter.

Model Answers to Questions

Chapter-Opening Questions

1. The poverty rate for children (19.9%) is higher than the poverty rate for senior citizens (10.5%).

2. The homeless rate is highest in cities where low-quality housing is expensive, job growth is slow, welfare payments are low, and the percentage of the mentally ill in institutions is low.

3. Privatizing Social Security may increase savings and investment in the economy. On the other hand, it would provide less protection for people who, because of bad luck or low skills, have low income.

4. Technological change has offered many opportunities for improving health care. However, society has not weighed the benefits from medical advances against their costs. The result has been continuing increases in costs.

Test Your Understanding

1. Statements (a) and (c) are false. Children have a higher poverty rate (a) and the minimum wage is not high enough to avoid poverty (c). Statement (b) is true.

2. The government estimates the food budget for the household and multiplies by 3.

3. Low-skilled workers are the last hired when the economy is growing and the first fired when the economy slows down.

4. False. The benefit structure redistributes income because the replacement rates are higher for lower-wage workers.

5. The age structure matters because the more workers per senior citizen, the lower the required tax rate.

6. Advantages: higher rates of return on investment and increased saving for society. Disadvantages: costs of making the transition and a weakening of the social-insurance aspects of the system.

7. The marginal principle tells us to adopt a new technology if its marginal benefit exceeds its marginal cost.

8. For a large firm, the average medical expense per employee will be close to the average expense for the entire U.S. labor force. If insurance is offered to individuals, people with the highest medical expenses have the greatest incentive to purchase the insurance.

9. Under universal coverage, all workers would be enrolled in medical insurance plans. The Clinton plan for universal coverage was defeated because of the difficulty of developing policies to subsidize the insurance costs of small firms.

Using the Tools

1. **Welfare Reform and Wages of Low-Skilled Labor.** The supply curve shifts to the right by 6%. Use the formula for predicting price changes from changes in supply (Chapter 5): The percentage change in the price (the wage) is $5\% = 6\% / (0.20 + 1.0)$. The wage drops by 5%, from $6.00 to $5.70 per hour. Use the formula for the price elasticity of demand to predict the change in quantity of hours worked as we move downward along the market demand curve; the change in quantity is 5%. For a worker who initially worked 40 hours per week, welfare reform decreases weekly income from $240 to $228.

2. **Chile's Transition to a Private Pension System.** During any transition period from a pay-as-you-go system, it will be necessary to provide support for the retired and those near retirement. Managing this transition is easier if there is a young population because the necessary tax rate will be lower as more workers will be contributing.

3. **Evaluating Medical Technology.** You need to compare the marginal benefit of the new technology to its marginal cost. The marginal benefit is the value of returning people to work one week earlier. The marginal cost is the extra cost of this procedure over the original procedure. If there are no other considerations, the new technology should be used only if its marginal benefit exceeds its marginal cost.

Notes

1. U.S. Bureau of the Census, Current Population Reports, Series P60-201, *Poverty in the United States, 1997.* (Washington, DC: U.S. Government Printing Office, 1998).

2. Cutler, David M., and Edward L. Glaeser. "Are Ghettos Good or Bad?," *Quarterly Journal of Economics* 1997, pp. 827–872.

3. Alan B. Kreuger, "How Computers Have Changed the Wage Structure: Evidence from Microdata, 1984–1989," *Quarterly Journal of Economics*, vol. 108, 1993, pp. 33–60.

4. Holzer, Harry J., "Employer Demand, AFDC Recipients, and Labor Market Policy," Institute for Research on Poverty Discussion Paper No. 1115-96, 1996.

5. Burt, Martha R., *Over the Edge: The Growth of Homelessness in the 1980s* (New York: Sage, 1992).

6. Honig, Marjorie, and Randall K. Filer, "Causes of Intercity Variation in Homelessness," *American Economic Review*, vol. 83, 1993, pp. 248–255.

7. "Your Stake in the Fight," *Consumer Reports*, September 1981, pp. 503–510.

8. For estimates of future tax rates, see Henry Aaron, Barry Bosworth, and Gary Burtless, *Can America Afford to Grow Old?* (Washington, DC: Brookings Institution, 1989).

9. For a discussion of inefficient spending in the health care system, see David Cutler, "Cutting Costs and Improving Health Care," in *The Problem That Won't Go Away*, edited by Henry Aaron (Washington, DC: Brookings Institution, 1996), pp. 250–265.

10. Victor Fuchs, "Economics, Values, and Health Reform," *American Economic Review*, March 1996, pp. 1–26.

CHAPTER 20

Measuring a Nation's Production and Income

Last week, Sally heard a business news reporter on television say, "GDP soared in the fourth quarter, and income hit an all time high." This sounded like good news. But she was not quite sure what it really meant. She also wondered whether these economic statistics somehow also reflected her concerns about traffic, pollution, and the quality of life.

This chapter begins your study of **macroeconomics**: the branch of economics that deals with any nation's economy as a whole. Macroeconomics focuses on the economic issues—unemployment, inflation, growth, trade, and the gross domestic product—that are most often discussed in newspapers, on the radio, and on television.

Macroeconomics: The branch of economics that looks at the economy as a whole.

Macroeconomic issues are at the heart of political debates. All presidential candidates must learn a quick lesson in macroeconomics. Once elected, a President learns that the prospects for reelection will depend on how well the economy performs during his or her term of office. If the voters believe that the economy has performed well, the President will be reelected: otherwise, the President will not likely be reelected. Democrats such as Jimmy Carter, as well as Republicans such as George Bush, have failed in their bids for reelection because of the voters' economic concerns. Bill Clinton survived a personal scandal in part because of the superb performance of the U.S. economy while he was President.

Macroeconomic events profoundly affect our everyday lives. For example, if the economy fails to create enough jobs, workers will become unemployed throughout the country, and millions of lives will be disrupted. Similarly, slow economic growth will mean that living standards will not increase rapidly in the future. By contrast, if prices for all goods start increasing rapidly, some people will find it difficult to maintain their lifestyles.

This chapter and the next will introduce you to the concepts you need to understand macroeconomics. In this chapter, we will explain how economists and government statisticians measure the income and production for an entire country. The next chapter will discuss unemployment and inflation. Both chapters will explain the terms that are often used when economics is reported in the media.

Macroeconomics focuses on two basic issues. One focus is on long-run economic growth. We need to understand what happens during the long run to understand what factors are behind the rise in living standards in modern economies. Today, in the United States, living standards are much higher than they were for our grandparents; and our living standards are much higher than those of millions of people throughout the globe.

The other focus of macroeconomics is fluctuations in economic performance. Although living standards have improved over time, the economy has not grown smoothly. There are periods when the economy appears to malfunction and no longer grow as rapidly. A recession is a period when the economy fails to grow for at least six consecutive months. During these periods, not enough jobs are created, and large numbers of workers become unemployed. At other times, unemployment may not be a problem, but we become concerned that the prices of everything that we buy seem to increase rapidly. In later chapters, we will study these fluctuations in detail.

Before we can study growth and fluctuations, we need to have a basic vocabulary and understanding of some key concepts. We begin with production and income because these are the most fundamental concepts. Every day, men and women go off to work, where they produce or sell merchandise or provide services, then return home with paychecks at the end of the week or month. The income that they earn allows them to purchase the goods and services necessary to conduct modern life. This chapter steps back from these individual details and looks at the economy as a whole. From the perspective that looks at the entire economy, we will be able to construct measures that can tell us how quickly the entire economy is growing or whether it has failed to grow. We will also be able to measure the total income generated in the economy and how this income flows back to workers and investors. These measures are critical for understanding how many people find jobs and whether their living standards are rising or falling.

After reading this chapter, you will be able to answer the following questions:

1. **How are production and income related?**
2. **What is the gross domestic product?**
3. **When prices change, how do we measure real income?**
4. **Do increases in gross domestic product necessarily translate into improvements in the welfare of citizens?**

As we learn the answers to these questions, we will build the necessary foundation for studying macroeconomics.

Production, Income, and the Circular Flow

Let's begin with the circular flow introduced in Chapter 3. We use the circular flow to make a very simple but fundamental point: Production generates income.

In the simple economy depicted in Figure 20.1, there are only households and firms, which make transactions in both factor markets and product markets. In the factor markets, the households supply inputs to production. The primary inputs are labor and capital—what economists call *factors of production*. Households supply labor by working for firms, and households supply capital—buildings, machines, and equipment—to the firms. In the factor markets, households are paid by the firms for supplying these factors: wages for their work and interest, dividends, and rents for supplying capital. The households then take their income and purchase the goods and services produced by the firms in the product markets. The payments the firm receives from the sale of its products are used to pay for the factors of production. The important part of this diagram is that production generates income; corresponding to the production of goods and services in the economy are flows of income to households.

For example, consider a manufacturer of computers. At the same time the computer manufacturer produces and sells new computers, it also generates income

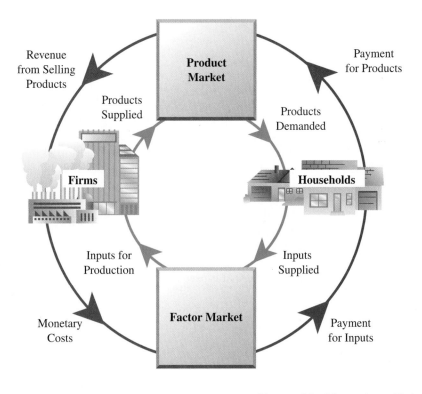

Figure 20.1
Circular Flow
The circular flow diagram shows how production of goods and services generates income for households and how households purchase goods and services produced by firms.

through its production. The computer manufacturer pays wages to workers, perhaps pays rent on office and factory buildings, and pays interest on borrowed money. Whatever is left over after paying for the cost of production is the firm's profit, which is income to the owners of the firm. Wages, rents, interest, and profits are all different forms of income.

In another example, your taxes pay for a school district to hire principals, teachers, and other staff to provide educational services to the students in your community. These educational services are considered production in the modern economy. At the same time, the principals, teachers, and staff all earn income through their employment with the school district. The school district may also rent buildings where classes are held and pay interest on borrowed funds.

Our goal is to understand both sides: the production in the economy and the generation of income in the economy. We begin with understanding how to measure the production for the entire economy.

Measuring Gross Domestic Product

To measure the production of the entire economy, we need to combine an enormous array of goods and services, from new computers to professional basketball games. We can add computers to basketball games, much as we can really add apples and oranges if we are interested in the total monetary value of an apple harvest and an orange harvest. Our goal is to summarize the total production of an entire economy into a single number, which we call the gross domestic product.

Gross domestic product (GDP): The total value of all the goods and services produced in an economy in a given year.

The most common measure of the total output of an economy is **gross domestic product (GDP)**, the total market value of all the final goods and services produced within an economy in a given year. All the words in this definition are important. Let's analyze each part of this definition.

"Total market value" means that we take the quantity of goods produced and multiply them by their respective prices and then add up the totals. If an economy produced 2 cars at $15,000 per car and 3 computers at $3,000 per computer, the total value of these goods and services would be

$$(2 \text{ cars} \times \$15,000/\text{car}) + (3 \text{ computers} \times \$3,000/\text{computer}) = \$39,000$$

The reason we multiply the goods by their prices is that we cannot simply add together the number of cars and the number of computers. Using prices allows us to express the value of everything in a common unit of measurement—in this case dollars. (In countries other than the United States, we would express the value in terms of the local currency.) This is how we add apples and oranges together: by finding out what is the value of both the apples and the oranges (as measured by what you would pay for them) and adding them up in terms of their prices.

"Final goods and services" in the definition of GDP means those goods and services that are sold to ultimate, or final, purchasers. For example, the 2 cars that were produced would be final goods if they were sold to households or to a business. However, in producing the cars, the automobile manufacturer bought steel that went into the body of the cars. This steel would not be counted as a final good or service in GDP. It is an example of an **intermediate good**, a good that is used in the production process; therefore it is not a final good or service.

Intermediate goods: Goods used in the production process that are not final goods or services.

The reason we do not count intermediate goods as final goods is to avoid double-counting. The price of the car already reflects the price of the steel that is contained in it. We do not want to count the steel twice. Similarly, the large volumes of paper used by an accounting firm are also intermediate goods because they become part of the final product delivered by the accounting firm to its clients.

The final words in our definition of GDP are "in a given year." GDP is expressed as a rate of production, that is, as so many dollars per year. In 1998, for example, GDP in the United States was 8,551 billion dollars. Goods produced in prior years, such as used cars, are not included in GDP this year.

Because we measure GDP using the current prices for goods and services, GDP will increase if prices increase, even if the physical amount of goods that are produced remains the same. Suppose that next year the economy again produces 2 cars and 3 computers, but in the following year, all the prices in the economy have doubled: The price of cars is $30,000, and the price of computers is $6,000. GDP in the following year will also be twice as high, or $78,000—(2 cars × $30,000/car) + (3 computers × $6,000/computer)—even though quantity produced is the same as during the prior year.

Let's apply the reality principle, one of our five basic principles of economics:

REALITY **PRINCIPLE**

What matters to people is the real value of money or income— its purchasing power—not the face value of money or income.

We would like to have another measure of total output in the economy that does not increase just because prices increase. For this reason, economists have developed the concept of **real GDP**, a measure of GDP that takes into account price changes.

Later in this chapter, we explain how real GDP is calculated. The basic idea is simple. When we use current prices to measure GDP, that is what we call **nominal GDP**. Nominal GDP can increase for one of two reasons: Either the production of goods and services has increased or the prices of those goods and services has increased.

To explain real GDP, we need first to look at a simple example. Suppose an economy produced a single good: computers. In year 1, 10 computers were produced, and each sold for $1,000. In year 2, 12 computers were produced, and each sold for $1,100. Nominal GDP would be $10,000 in year 1 and $13,200 in year 2. Nominal GDP would have increased by a factor of 1.32.

We can measure real GDP by calculating GDP using year 1 prices as a measure of what was produced in year 1 *and* also what was produced in year 2. In year 1, real GDP would be 10 computers × $1,000/computer = $10,000; and in year 2, it would be 12 computers × $1,000/computer = $12,000. Real GDP in year 2 is greater than real GDP in year 1 by a factor of 1.2. The key idea is that we construct a measure using the same prices for both years and thereby take price changes into account.

Figure 20.2 plots real GDP for the U.S. economy for the years 1930–1998. The data for real GDP are constructed so that nominal GDP and real GDP are set equal for a single year, in this case 1992. For both earlier and later years, the data for real GDP take into account changes in prices and thus measure movements in real output only.

The graph shows that real GDP has grown substantially over this period. This is what economists call **economic growth**: sustained increases in the real production of an economy over a long time. Later, in Chapter 23, we will study economic growth in detail. We will also look carefully at the behavior of real GDP over shorter periods, during which real GDP can rise and fall. Decreases in real GDP cause great disruption and lead to a loss of jobs and unemployment.

Real GDP: A measure of GDP that adjusts for changes in prices.

Nominal GDP: The value of GDP in current dollars.

Economic growth: Sustained increases in the real production of an economy over a period of time.

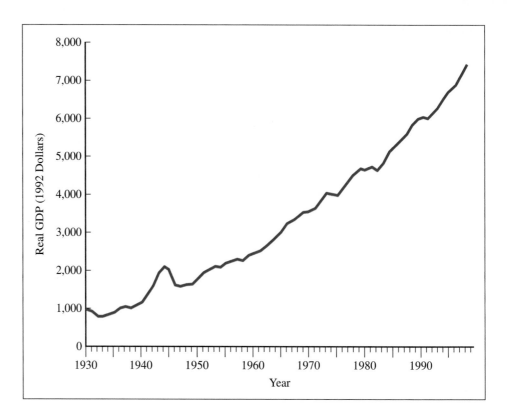

Figure 20.2
U.S. Real GDP, 1930–1998

Who Purchases GDP?

To gain further insight into gross domestic product, let's look at its components. Economists divide GDP into four broad categories, each corresponding to different types of purchasers represented in GDP:

1. Consumption expenditures: purchases by consumers.
2. Private investment expenditures: purchases by firms.
3. Government purchases: purchases by federal, state, and local governments.
4. Net exports: net purchases by the foreign sector, or domestic exports minus domestic imports.

Before discussing these categories, let's look at some data for the U.S. economy to get a sense of the size of each of these four components. Table 20.1 shows the figures for GDP for the second quarter of 1999. (A quarter is a three-month period; the second quarter runs from April through June.) In the second quarter of 1999, GDP was $8,893 billion, or

Table 20.1 Composition of U.S. GDP, Second Quarter 1999
(billions of dollars expressed at annual rates)

GDP	Consumption Expenditures	Private Investment Expenditures	Government Purchases	Net Exports
8,893	6,148	1,427	1,544	–226

Source: U.S. Department of Commerce.

approximately $8.9 trillion. To get a sense of the magnitude, consider that the U.S. population is approximately 268 million people, making GDP per person approximately $29,231.

Consumption Expenditures

Consumption expenditures are purchases by consumers of currently produced goods and services, either domestic or foreign. These purchases include TV sets, VCRs, automobiles, clothing, hair-styling services, jewelry, movie tickets, food, and all other consumer items. We can break down consumption into durable goods, nondurable goods, and services. **Durable goods** last for a long time, such as automobiles or refrigerators. **Nondurable goods**, such as food, last for a short time. **Services** reflect work done in which people play a prominent role in delivery (such as a dentist filling a cavity); they range from haircutting to health care. Services are the fastest-growing component of consumption. Overall, consumption spending is the most important component of GDP, constituting about 68% of total purchases.

Private Investment Expenditures

Private investment expenditures in GDP consist of three components:

1. First, there is spending on new plants and equipment during the year. If a firm builds a new factory or purchases a new machine, that is included in GDP. Purchasing an existing building or buying a used machine does not count in GDP because the goods were not produced during the current year.

2. Second, newly produced housing is included in investment spending. The sale of an existing home to a new owner is not counted because the house was not built in the current year.

3. Finally, if firms add to their stock of inventories, the increase in inventories during the current year is included in GDP. If a hardware store had $1,000 worth of nuts and bolts on its shelves at the beginning of the year and $1,100 at the year's end, its inventory investment would be $100 ($1,100 − $1,000). The $100 increase in inventory investment is included in GDP.

We call the total of new investment expenditures **gross investment**. During the year, some of the existing plant, equipment, and housing will deteriorate or wear out. This wear and tear is called **depreciation**. If we subtract depreciation from gross investment, we obtain **net investment**. Net investment is the true addition to the stock of plant, equipment, and housing in a given year.

Make sure you understand this distinction between gross investment and net investment. Consider the $1,427 billion in total investment spending for second quarter of 1999, a period in which there was $943 billion in depreciation. That means that there was only ($1,427 − $943) = $484 in net investment by firms in that year. 66% of gross investment went to make up for depreciation of existing capital.

Warning: When we discuss measuring production in the GDP accounts, we use *investment* in a different way than when we use *investment* in the sense we have come to understand it. For an economist, investment in the GDP accounts means purchases of new final goods and services by firms. In everyday conversation, we may talk about investing in the stock market or investing in gold. Buying stock for $1,800 on the stock market is a purchase of an existing financial asset; it is not the purchase of new goods and services by firms. So that $1,800 does not appear anywhere in GDP. The same is true of purchasing a gold bar. In GDP accounting, *investment* denotes the purchase of new capital. Be careful not to confuse the common usage of *investment* with the definition of *investment* as we use it in the GDP accounts.

Consumption expenditures: Purchases of newly produced goods and services by households.

Durable goods: Goods that last for a long period of time, such as appliances.

Nondurable goods: Goods that last for shorter periods of time, such as food.

Services: Work done in which people play a prominent role in delivery, ranging from haircutting to health care.

Private investment expenditures: Purchases of newly produced goods and services by firms.

Gross investment: Actual investment purchases.

Depreciation: The wear and tear of capital as it is used in production.

Net investment: Gross investment minus depreciation.

Government Purchases

Government purchases: Purchases of newly produced goods and services by all levels of government.

Government purchases are the purchases of newly produced goods and services by federal, state, and local governments. They include any goods that the government purchases plus the wages and benefits of all government workers (paid when the government purchases their services as employees). The majority of spending in this category actually comes from state and local governments: $1,010 billion of the total $1,544 billion in 1999.

This category does not include all the spending by governments. It excludes **transfer payments**; these are funds paid to individuals but are not associated with the production of goods and services. For example, payments for Social Security, welfare, and interest on government debt are all considered transfer payments and are not included in government purchases in GDP. The reason they are excluded is that nothing is being produced in return for the payment. But wage payments to the police, postal workers, and the staff of the Internal Revenue Service are all included because they do correspond to services that are currently being produced.

Transfer payments: Payments from individuals from governments that do not correspond to the production of goods and services.

Because transfer payments are excluded from GDP, a vast portion of the budget of the federal government is not part of GDP. In 1999, the federal government spent approximately $1,806 billion, of which only $533 billion (about one-third) was counted as federal government purchases. Transfer payments are important, however. They affect both the income of individuals and their consumption and savings behavior. They also affect the size of the federal budget deficit, which we will study in a later chapter. At this point, keep in mind the distinction between government purchases—which are included in GDP—and total government spending or expenditure—which may not be included.

Net Exports

Net exports: Exports minus imports.

The United States has an open economy; that means that the United States trades with other economies. Recall from Chapter 3 that imports are goods we buy from other countries and exports are goods made here and sold to other countries. **Net exports** are total exports minus total imports. In Table 20.1, we see that net exports in the second quarter of 1999 were –$226 billion. Net exports were negative because our imports exceeded our exports.

In creating a measure of GDP, we try to measure the goods produced in the United States. Consumption, investment, and government purchases include all purchases by

Spending on new bridges, such as San Francisco's Golden Gate bridge is included as government purchases in the National Income Accounts.

consumers, firms, and the government, whether or not the goods were produced in the United States. But purchases of foreign goods by consumers, firms, or the government should be subtracted when we calculate GDP because these goods were not produced in the United States. At the same time, we must add to GDP any goods produced here and sold abroad. For example, supercomputers made in the United States and sold in Europe should be added to GDP. By including net exports as a component of GDP, we correctly measure U.S. production by adding exports and subtracting imports.

For example, suppose someone in the United States buys a $25,000 Toyota made in Japan. If we look at final purchases, we will see that consumption spending rose by $25,000 because a consumer made a purchase of a consumption good. Net exports fell by $25,000, however, because the value of the import was subtracted from total exports. Notice that total GDP did not change with the purchase of the Toyota. This is exactly what we want in this case, because there was no U.S. production.

Now suppose that the United States sells a car for $18,000 to a resident of Spain. In this case, net exports would increase by $18,000 because the car was a U.S. export. GDP would also be a corresponding $18,000 higher because this sale represents U.S. production.

For the United States in the second quarter of 1999, net exports were –$226 billion dollars. In other words, in that quarter, the United States bought $226 billion more goods from abroad than it sold abroad. When we buy more goods from abroad than we sell, we have a **trade deficit**. A **trade surplus** occurs when our exports exceed our imports.

Figure 20.3 shows the U.S. trade surplus as a share of GDP from 1950 to 1998. While at times the United States had a trade surplus, in the 1980s the United States ran a trade deficit that often exceeded 3% of GDP. What are the consequences of such large trade deficits?

When the United States runs a trade deficit, U.S. residents are spending more on goods and services than they are currently producing. Although the United States does sell many goods abroad (e.g., supercomputers, movies, records, and CDs), it buys even more goods and services from abroad (e.g., Toyotas, VCRs, German machine tools).

Trade deficit: An excess of imports over exports.

Trade surplus: An excess of exports over imports.

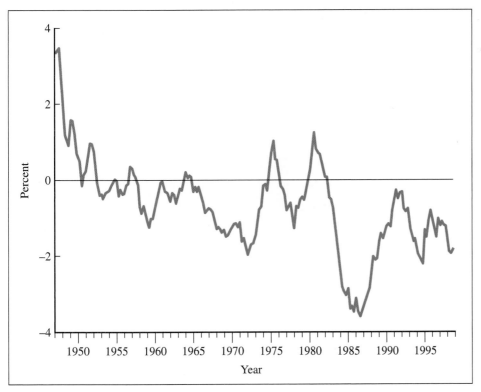

Figure 20.3
U.S. Trade Balance as a Share of GDP, 1950–1998

The result is that the United States is forced to sell some of its assets to individuals or governments in foreign countries. Here is how it works: When U.S. residents buy more goods abroad than they sell, they give up more dollars for imports than they receive in dollars from the sale of exports. These dollars given up to purchase imports end up in the hands of foreigners, who can use them to purchase U.S. assets such as stocks, bonds, or real estate. In the early 1990s, Japanese investors bought many assets in the United States. This should not have been terribly surprising because we had been running large trade deficits with the Japanese. They were willing to sell us more goods than we were selling to them, and therefore, they accumulated U.S. dollars with which they could purchase U.S. assets.

It is the total trade surplus with all the other countries that determines the amount of foreign assets that a single country will acquire. If a country ran a trade surplus with one country and an equally large trade deficit with another, it would not add to its stock of foreign assets. Figure 20.4 shows the trade surplus as a percent of GDP for a variety of other countries. For these countries, Canada had the largest trade surplus as a share of GDP, followed by Japan. As you can see, the United States was not alone in running a trade deficit. In later chapters, we study how trade deficits can affect a country's economy.

TEST Your Understanding

1. What are the four components of GDP?

2. The circular flow describes the process by which GDP generates _____, which is spent on goods.

3. What part of government spending is excluded from GDP because it does not correspond to goods or services being produced currently?

4. What is the difference between gross investment and net investment?

5. Define *net exports*.

Figure 20.4
Trade Balance as a Percent of GDP, 1997

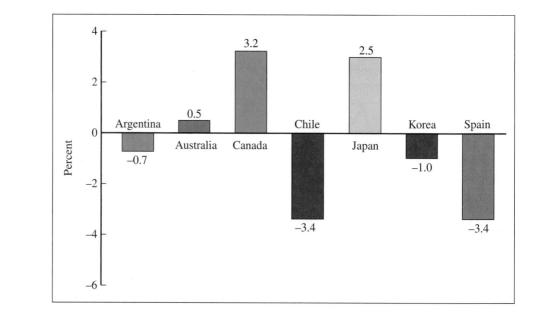

Who Gets the Income?

Recall from the circular flow that when GDP is produced, income is created. The income that flows to the private sector is called **national income**. To measure national income, economists first make three adjustments to GDP.

First, we add to GDP the net income earned by U.S. firms and residents abroad. To make this calculation, we add to GDP any income earned abroad by U.S. firms or residents and subtract any income earned in the United States by foreign firms or residents. For example, we add the profits earned by U.S. multinational corporations that are sent back to the United States but subtract the profits from multinational corporations operating in the United States that are sent back to their home countries. The result of these adjustments is the total income earned worldwide by U.S. firms and residents. This is called the **gross national product (GNP)**. For the United States, the actual difference between GDP and GNP is very small. But as "A Closer Look: GDP Versus GNP," demonstrates, the differences are large for some countries.

The second adjustment that we make on the way to calculating national income is to subtract depreciation from GNP. Recall that depreciation is the wear and tear on plant and equipment that occurred during the year. In a sense, our income is reduced because our buildings and machines are wearing out. When we subtract depreciation from GNP, we reach **net national product (NNP)**, where "net" means after depreciation.

The third and last adjustment we make to reach national income is to subtract **indirect taxes**, which are sales taxes or excise taxes on products. If a store sells you a product for $1.00 and the sales tax is $0.08, your total bill is $1.08. However, only $1.00 of that purchase goes to the store to pay wages, rent, interest, and maybe even some profit to the owners. The remainder, $0.08, goes to the government; it is not part of private-sector income.

After making all three adjustments, we reach national income. Table 20.2 shows these adjustments (ignoring a few minor items) for the second quarter of 1999.

National income is divided among five basic categories: compensation of employees (wages and benefits), corporate profits, rental income, proprietor's income (income of unincorporated business), and net interest (interest payments received by households from business and from abroad). Table 20.3 presents U.S. data for the second quarter of 1999. Approximately 71% of all national income goes to workers in the form of wages and benefits. For most of the countries in the world, wages and benefits are the largest part of national income.

National income: Net national product less indirect taxes.

Gross national product (GNP): GDP plus net income earned abroad.

Net national product (NNP): GNP minus depreciation.

Indirect taxes: Sales and excise taxes.

A CLOSER LOOK | GDP Versus GNP

For most countries, the distinction between what they produce within their borders, GDP, and what their citizens earn, GNP, is not that important. For the United States, the difference between GDP and GNP is typically just two-tenths of 1%. In some countries, the differences are much larger. Turkey, for example, sends to Germany as "guest workers" many of its people, who send back to their families money that is included in the calculation of Turkey's GNP. For Turkey, foreign earnings in 1997 accounted for nearly 4.7% of GNP or total worldwide income. The country of Kuwait earned vast amounts of income from its oil riches, which it invested abroad. Earnings from these investments are included in Kuwait's GNP; in 1997, those earnings constituted over 17% of the total income in Kuwait.

What is the best measure of a country's status in the world: its production or its earnings?

Source: International Monetary Fund, *International Financial Statistics*, 1999; World Bank, *World Development Indicators*, 1999.

Table 20.2 From GDP to National Income, Second Quarter 1999 (billions of dollars)

Gross domestic product	8,893
plus net income from abroad =	
Gross national product	8,788
minus depreciation =	
Net national product	7,846
minus indirect taxes (and other adjustments) =	
National income	7,265

Source: U.S. Department of Commerce.

Value added: The sum of all the income (wages, interest, profits, and rent) generated by an organization.

One way to measure national income is to look at the **value added** of each firm in the economy. Economists define the value added of a firm as the sum of all the income—wages, profits, rents, and interest—that it generates. By adding up the value added for all the firms in the economy (plus nonprofit and governmental organizations), we can calculate national income. Consider a simple example.

Suppose an economy consists of two firms: an automobile firm that sells its cars to consumers and a steel firm that sells only to the automobile firm. If the automobile company sells a car for $16,000 to consumers and purchases $6,000 worth of steel from the steel firm, the auto firm has $10,000 remaining—its value added—which can then be distributed as wages, rents, interest, and profits. If the steel firm sells $6,000 worth of steel but does not purchase any inputs from other firms, its value added is $6,000, which is paid out in the form of wages, rents, interest, and profits. Total value added in the economy from both firms is $16,000 ($10,000 + $6,000), which is the sum of wages, rents, interest, and profits for the entire economy, because there are only these two firms in the entire economy.

As this example illustrates, we measure the value added for a typical firm by starting with the value of its total sales and subtracting the value of any inputs it purchases from other firms. The amount of income that remains is the firm's value added, which is then distributed as wages, rents, interest, and profits. In calculating national income, it is important to include all the firms in the economy, even the firms that produce intermediate goods.

Personal income: Income (including transfer payments) received by households.

In addition to national income, which measures the income earned in a given year by the entire private sector, we are sometimes interested in determining the total payments that flow directly into households, a concept known as **personal income**. Households

Table 20.3 Composition of U.S. National Income, Second Quarter of 1999 (billions of dollars)

National income	7,265
Compensation of employees	5,166
Corporate profits	869
Rental income	168
Proprietor's income	598
Net interest	464

Source: U.S. Department of Commerce.

do not receive all the profits earned by firms in any given year because a portion is typically retained by firms for their investments. In addition, households receive transfer payments from the government. Personal income includes labor income, transfer payments, and any income from investments paid to individuals. The amount of personal income that households keep after paying taxes is called **personal disposable income**.

Personal disposable income:
Personal income after taxes.

In summary, we can look at GDP from two sides: We can ask who buys the output that is produced, or we can ask who gets the income that is created through the production process. From the spending side, we see that nearly 70% of GDP consists of consumer expenditures. From the income side, we see that nearly three-fourths of national income is paid in wages and benefits.

TEST Your Understanding

6. What do we add to GDP to reach GNP?

7. What is the largest component of national income?

8. Complete the statement with *households* or *firms*: Personal income and personal disposable income refer to payments ultimately flowing to _____.

Real Versus Nominal GDP

Output in the economy can increase from one year to the next. And prices can rise from one year to the next. Realizing that, we need a measure of output that reflects actual increases in production, separate and apart from any price changes that may have occurred in the economy during the year. Recall that we defined nominal GDP as GDP measured in current prices, and we defined real GDP as GDP adjusted for price changes. Now we take a closer look at how real GDP is measured in modern economies.

Let's start with a simple economy in which there are only two goods, cars and computers, produced in the years 2004 and 2005. The data for this economy, the prices and quantities produced for each year, are shown in Table 20.4. The production of cars and the production of computers increased, but the production of computers increased more rapidly. The price of cars rose, while the price of computers remained the same.

Let's first calculate nominal GDP for this economy in each year. Nominal GDP is the total value of goods and services produced in each year. Using the data in the table, we can see that nominal GDP for the year 2004 is:

$$(4 \text{ cars} \times \$10,000/\text{car}) + (1 \text{ computer} \times \$5,000/\text{computer}) = \$45,000$$

Similarly, nominal GDP for 2005 is $75,000.

Now we'll find real GDP. To compute real GDP, we calculate GDP using constant prices. What prices should we use? For the moment, let's use the prices for the year

Table 20.4 GDP Data for a Simple Economy

| Year | Quantity Produced | | Price | |
	Cars	Computers	Cars	Computers
2004	4	1	$10,000	$5,000
2005	5	3	12,000	5,000

2004. Because we are using 2004 prices, real GDP and nominal GDP for 2004 are both equal to $45,000. For 2005, real GDP is

$$(5 \text{ cars} \times \$10,000/\text{car}) + (3 \text{ computers} \times \$5,000/\text{computer}) = \$65,000$$

Note that real GDP for 2005, which is $65,000, is less than nominal GDP for 2005, which is equal to $75,000. The reason real GDP is less than nominal GDP here is because prices of cars rose between 2004 and 2005, and we are measuring GDP using 2004 prices. We can measure real GDP for any other year simply by calculating GDP using constant prices.

We now calculate the growth in real GDP for this economy between 2004 and 2005. Because real GDP was $45,000 in 2004 and $65,000 in 2005, real GDP grew by

$$(\$65,000 - \$45,000)/\$45,000 = .444$$

which equals 44.4%. This is an average of the growth rates for both goods, cars and computers.

We can also use the data in Table 20.4 to measure the changes in prices for this economy. The basic idea is that the differences between nominal GDP and real GDP for any year arise only because of changes in prices. Thus, by comparing real GDP and nominal GDP, we can measure the changes in prices for the economy. In practice, we do this by creating an index, called the **GDP deflator**, which measures how prices change over time. Because we are calculating real GDP using year 2004 prices, we will set the value of this index equal to 100 in the year 2004, which we call the base year. To find the value of the GDP deflator for the year 2005 (or other years), we use the following formula:

value of GDP deflator in 2005 = 100 × [(nominal GDP in 2005)/(real GDP in 2005)]

Using this formula, we find that the value of the GDP deflator for 2005 is

$$100 \times (\$75,000/\$65,000) = 100 \times 1.15 = 115$$

Since the value of the GDP deflator is 115 in 2005 and was 100 in the base year of 2004, this means that prices rose by 15% ([(115 − 100)/100] = .15 or 15%) between the two years. Note that this 15% is an average of the price changes for the two goods, cars and computers.

Up until 1996, the Commerce Department, which produces the GDP figures, used these methods to calculate real GDP and measure changes in prices. It chose a base year and measured real GDP by using the prices in that base year and also calculated the GDP deflator, just as we did, by taking the ratio of nominal GDP to real GDP. Today, the Commerce Department calculates real GDP and the price index for real GDP using a more complicated method. In our example, we measured real GDP using 2004 prices. But we could have also measured real GDP using prices from 2005. If we did, we would have come up with slightly different numbers both for the increase in prices between the two years and for the increase in real GDP. To avoid this problem, the Commerce Department today uses a **chain index**, a method for calculating price changes based on taking an average of price changes using base years from neighboring years (that is, 2004 and 2005 in our example). If you look in the newspapers today or at the data produced by the Commerce Department, you will see real GDP measured in *chained-dollars* and a *chain-type price index* for GDP.

GDP deflator: An index that measures how the price of goods included in GDP change over time.

Chain index: A method for calculating changes in prices that includes an average of price changes using base years from neighboring years.

GDP as a Measure of Welfare

GDP is our best measure of the value of output produced by an economy. But it is not a perfect measure. There are several recognized flaws in the construction of GDP of which you need to be aware. Because of these flaws, we should be cautious if we want to interpret GDP as a measure of our economic well being. First, GDP ignores transactions that do not take place in organized markets. The most important example is services, such as cleaning, cooking, and providing free child care, that are performed in the home. Because these services are not transferred through markets, GDP statisticians cannot measure them. This has probably led us to overestimate the growth in GDP. In the last three decades, there has been a big increase in the percentage of women in the labor force. Since more women are now working outside the home, there is naturally a demand for more meals in restaurants, more cleaning services, and more paid child care. All this new demand shows up in GDP, but the services that were provided earlier—when they were provided free—did not show up in earlier GDP. This naturally overstates the true growth in GDP.

Second, GDP ignores the underground economy, where transactions are not reported to official authorities. These transactions can be legal, but people don't report the income they have generated, because they want to evade paying taxes on that income. For example, waiters and waitresses may not report all their tips, and owners of flea markets may make under-the-table cash transactions with their customers. There are also illegal transactions that result in unreported income, such as profits from the illegal drug trade.

In the United States, the Internal Revenue Service estimated in the early 1990s that about $100 billion in federal income taxes from the underground economy were not collected each year. If the average federal income tax rate in the country is about 20%, this means approximately $500 billion ($100/0.20) in income escapes the GDP accountants from the underground economy every year, about 7% of GDP at the time.

Third, GDP does not value changes in the environment that arise through the production of output. Suppose a factory produces $1,000 of output but pollutes a river and lowers the river's value by $2,000. Instead of recording a loss to society of $1,000, GDP will show a $1,000 increase. This is an important limitation of GDP accounting as a measure of our economic well-being because changes in the environment are important. In principle, we can make adjustments to try to correct for this deficiency.

The growth in GDP is exaggerated because the cost of restaurant meals includes cooking services that were previously performed at home and not counted in GDP.

The U.S. Department of Commerce, which collects the GDP data, had a project to try to account for environmental changes. In 1994, it released a report on the first phase of the study, in which it focused on the value of mineral resources (oil, gas, coal, etc.) in the United States. The government first measured proven reserves of minerals from 1958 to 1991: those reserves of minerals that can be extracted, given current technology and current economic conditions. They decrease when minerals are extracted and increase when new investments (such as oil wells or mines) are made.

The question the Commerce Department asked was whether the stock of proven reserves had been depleted—that is, depreciated—over time. If it had been depreciated, the reduction in the value of the stock of minerals should be subtracted from GDP to measure national income correctly. It is important to note that this calculation focuses only on proven reserves, not the total stock of minerals in the earth. The reason the Commerce Department counts only proven reserves is that some mineral deposits are simply too expensive to extract under current economic conditions. Changes in proven reserves alone correspond most closely to changes in our current economic well-being.

It turned out that the Commerce Department found that these adjustments had very little affect on measures on national income. But mineral stocks are only part of our environment. These methods can be extended to include renewable resources, such as forests and fish, although the data may not be as accurate as the data for minerals. A much more challenging task would be to value changes in clean air and clean water. Has our environment improved or deteriorated as we experienced economic growth? Finding the answer to this question will pose a real challenge for the next generation of economic statisticians.

Using the **TOOLS**

In this chapter, we looked closely at how we measure a nation's production and how we measure its income. Here's an opportunity to test your understanding of the key concepts.

1. Nominal GDP Versus Real GDP
Economists observed that in one country nominal GDP increased two years in a row, but real GDP fell over the same two years. How can this have occurred? Construct a numerical example to illustrate this possibility.

2. Fish and National Income
Suppose you were worried that national income did not adequately take into account the depletion of the stock of fish in the economy. Describe how you would advise the Commerce Department to take this into account in their calculations.

3. Transfer Payments Versus Government Employment
In Economy A, the government puts on the payroll as government employees workers who cannot find jobs for long periods, but these "employees" do no work. In Economy B, the government does not hire any long-term unemployed workers; instead, it just gives them cash grants. How do the GDP statistics compare between the two, otherwise identical economies?

Summary

In this chapter, we explored how economists and government statisticians measure our national income and production. Developing meaningful statistics for an entire economy is difficult. As we have seen, statistics can convey useful information—if they are used with care. Here are some of the main points to remember in this chapter:

1. The circular flow helps represent the idea that the production of GDP also generates income.
2. GDP is the value of all final goods and services produced in a given year.
3. GDP is divided into consumption, investment, government purchases, and net exports.
4. National income is obtained from GDP by adding net income from abroad, then subtracting depreciation and indirect taxes.
5. Real GDP is calculated by using constant prices. The Commerce Department now uses methods that take an average using base years from neighboring years.
6. GDP does not include nonmarket transactions, the underground economy, or changes to the environment.

Key Terms

chain index, 430
consumption expenditures, 423
depreciation, 423
durable goods, 423
economic growth, 421
GDP deflator, 430
government purchases, 424
gross domestic product (GDP), 420
gross investment, 423
gross national product (GNP), 427

indirect taxes, 427
intermediate goods, 420
macroeconomics, 418
national income, 427
net exports, 424
net investment, 423
net national product (NNP), 427
nominal GDP, 421
nondurable goods, 423
personal income, 428

personal disposable income, 429
private investment expenditures, 423
real GDP, 421
services, 423
trade deficit, 425
trade surplus, 425
transfer payments, 424
value added, 428

Problems and Discussion Questions

1. Should we care more about the growth of nominal GDP or real GDP?

For Problems 2–4, use the following data:

| | Quantities Produced | | Prices | |
	CDs	Tennis Rackets	$/CD	$/Tennis Rackets
Year 2004	100	200	20	110
Year 2005	120	210	22	120

2. Calculate real GDP using prices from 2004. By what percent did real GDP grow?
3. Calculate the value of the price index for GDP for 2005 using 2004 as the base year. By what percent did prices increase?
4. Repeat Problem 2 but use prices from 2005.

5. Suppose someone told you that the value of a price index in a country was 115. Is this information, by itself, useful?
6. A student once said, "Trade deficits are good because we are buying more goods than we are producing." What is the downside to trade deficits?
7. Consumer durables depreciate over time. In your household, which consumer goods have substantial depreciation? Can you estimate the value of depreciation in a given year for consumer goods in your household?
8. A publisher buys paper, ink, and computers to produce textbooks. Which of these purchases is included in investment spending?
9. Air quality in Los Angeles deteriorated in the 1950s through 1970s and then improved in the 1980s and 1990s. How could a change in air quality like this be incorporated into our measures of national income?

10. When we calculate value added, we add up the value created in all organizations, even those producing intermediate goods. Can you explain why this does not cause double-counting?

11. In the 1980s and 1990s, computers were rapidly introduced into the economy. The prices of computers fell rapidly over time during this period. Suppose that in calculating real GDP, the Commerce Department used a single base year, one in which computer prices were still at their earlier, high levels. What distortions would using this base year cause to measures of real GDP and to changes in prices?

12. Web Exercise. Go to the Webs site for the Federal Reserve Bank of St. Louis (*http://www.stls.frb.org /fred/*). Find the data for nominal GDP, real GDP in chained dollars, and the chain price index for GDP.

   a. Calculate the percentage growth for nominal GDP since 1990 until the most recent year.

   b. Calculate the percentage growth in real GDP since 1990 until the most recent year.

   c. Finally, calculate the percentage growth in the chain price index for GDP over this same period and compare it to the difference between your answers to (a) and (b).

13. Web Exercise. Search the Web for articles on the underground economy. You might want to start with the National Center for Policy Analysis (*http: //www.ncpa.org*). What are some of the different ways in which economists try to measure the size of the underground economy?

Take It to the Net

We invite you to visit the O'Sullivan/Sheffrin page on the Prentice Hall Web site at:
http://www.prenhall.com/osullivan/
for additional World Wide Web exercises for this chapter.

Model Answers to Questions

Chapter-Opening Questions

1. Production also generates income in an economy.
2. GDP is the value of all final goods and services produced in an economy.
3. We use constant prices to measure real GDP.
4. GDP is not a perfect measure of true economic welfare.

Test Your Understanding

1. The four components of GDP are consumption, investment, government spending, and net exports.
2. Income.
3. Transfer payments are excluded.
4. The difference is depreciation.
5. Net exports are exports minus imports.
6. We add net income earned abroad.
7. The largest component is compensation of employees.
8. Households.

Using the Tools

1. Nominal GDP Versus Real GDP. Real GDP can fall, but prices rise sufficiently to make nominal GDP increase. Any example with very large increases in prices will work.

2. Fish and National Income. Follow the same procedure for mineral wealth. First, estimate (at appropriate prices) the value of all the fish in the sea at the beginning of the year and the end of the year. Then calculate the change in the value of the stock of fish. If the value of the stock of fish has decreased, this is similar to depreciation, and the decrease in value should be subtracted from GDP to obtain national income. If the value of the stock of fish has increased, the increase in value should be added to national income. Note that there may be problems with national boundaries. Whose GDP is affected if the stock of fish declines in the middle of the Atlantic or Pacific oceans?

3. Transfer Payments Versus Government Employment. In Economy A, GDP would be higher because the government employees would count as government purchases of goods and services. They would not be part of GDP in Economy B because they are just transfer payments.

21

Unemployment and Inflation

Could the Internet solve all our unemployment problems? Let's suppose the following: Every employer posted every job vacancy on the Internet, and everyone seeking a job posted his or her qualifications on the Internet. The government, or perhaps some private company, organized these postings by geographical area and the type of the job. Would information made available in this way reduce unemployment down to zero? Would this really work?

n this chapter, we look at unemployment and inflation, two key concepts in macroeconomics. Unemployment and inflation are at the heart of all macroeconomic policy. Losing a job is one of the most stressful experiences a person can suffer. For the elderly, the fear that the purchasing power of their wealth will evaporate with inflation is also a source of deep concern.

In this chapter, we examine how economists define unemployment and inflation and the problems in measuring them. Once we have a basic understanding of what unemployment is and what inflation is, we will be able to investigate further their causes and consequences.

After studying this chapter, you will be able to answer the following questions:

1. **What is unemployment? Why can't it be driven down to zero?**
2. **What demographic groups suffer the most unemployment? Can the unemployment statistics tell us the answer?**
3. **What is the Consumer Price Index and how is it related to the cost of living?**
4. **How accurately can we measure inflation in the economy? If we don't do a good job, what impact does our inaccuracy have?**

What Is Unemployment?

One of the reasons we want to avoid poor economic performance is that it imposes costs on individuals and society. If the economy fails to create enough jobs, many individuals will not find work, causing hardship for them and their families. Recall from Chapter 20, that one of the key issues for macroeconomics is understanding economic fluctuations—the ups and downs of the economy. During periods of poor economic performance, such as economic recessions when real GDP declines, unemployment rises sharply and becomes a cause of public concern. During times of good economic performance and rapid economic growth, unemployment is reduced but does not disappear. Our first task is to understand how economists and government statisticians measure unemployment and then learn to interpret what they measure.

Definitions

Let's begin with some definitions.

Unemployed: People who are looking for work but do not have jobs.

Employed: People who have jobs.

Labor force: The employed plus the unemployed.

The **unemployed** are those individuals who do not currently have a job but who are actively looking for work. The phrase *actively looking* is critical. Individuals who looked for work in the past but are not looking currently are not counted as unemployed. The **employed** are individuals who currently have jobs. Together, the unemployed and employed comprise the **labor force**.

$$\text{labor force} = \text{employed} + \text{unemployed}$$

The unemployment rate is the number of unemployed divided by the total labor force; it represents the percentage of the labor force unemployed and looking for work:

$$\text{unemployment rate} = \text{unemployed/labor force}$$

Labor force participation rate: the fraction of the population that is over 16 years of age that is in the labor force.

Finally, we need to understand what is meant by the **labor force participation rate**, defined as the labor force divided by the population 16 years and older. It represents the fraction of the population 16 years and older that is in the labor force:

$$\text{labor force participation rate} = \text{labor force/population 16 and over.}$$

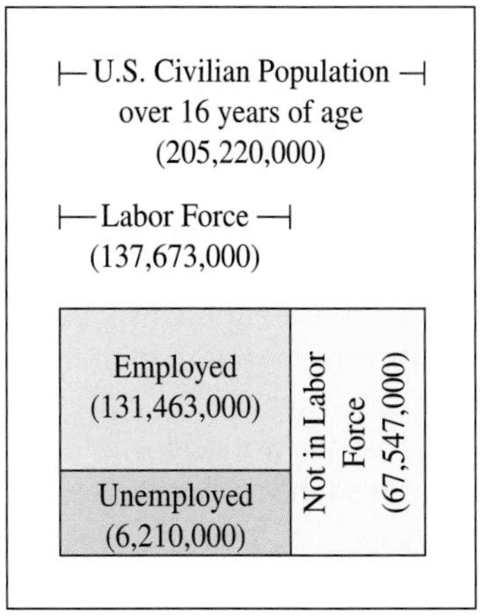

Figure 21.1

```
├── U.S. Civilian Population ──┤
       over 16 years of age
          (205,220,000)

├── Labor Force ──┤
     (137,673,000)

┌─────────────────┬─────────┐
│                 │         │
│   Employed      │ Not in  │
│  (131,463,000)  │ Labor   │
│                 │ Force   │
├─────────────────┤(67,547,000)│
│   Unemployed    │         │
│   (6,210,000)   │         │
└─────────────────┴─────────┘
```

Unemployment Data, 1998

Source: Economic Report of the President (Washington, DC: U.S. Government Printing Office, 1999).

To illustrate these concepts, suppose that an economy consists of 200,000 individuals 16 years and older, of whom 122,000 are employed and 8,000 are unemployed. In this example, the labor force is 130,000 (122,000 + 8,000) people. The labor force participation rate is 0.65, or 65% (130,000/200,000). The unemployment rate is 0.0615, or 6.15% (8,000/130,000).

Figure 21.1 helps to put these definitions into perspective for the U.S. economy. The large box is the total population 16 years and older, which in 1998 was comprised of 205,220,000 individuals. This population is divided into two groups: those in the labor force and those outside the labor force. For this year, the labor force participation rate was 67.1%. Within the labor force, there were 131,463,000 employed and 6,210,000 unemployed.

Table 21.1 contains some international data on unemployment for 1999. Notice the sharp differences between countries; for example, the Netherlands had a 3.2% unemployment rate, while Spain had an unemployment rate of 16.1%.

Table 21.1 Unemployment Rates Around the World, 1999

Country	Unemployment Rate (%)
United States	4.3
Belgium	12.7
Sweden	6.4
France	11.2
Italy	12.0
Spain	16.1
United Kingdom	6.0
Netherlands	3.2
Japan	4.9
Australia	7.2

Source: The Economist, September 11, 1999.

Issues in Measuring Unemployment

Recall that we defined the unemployed as those people who are looking for work but do not currently have jobs. With that in mind, let's take a closer look at our measures of unemployment.

It is relatively straightforward in principle to determine who is employed: Just count the people who are working. What is more difficult is to distinguish between those who are unemployed and those who are not in the labor force. How are these two groups distinguished? Each month, the Bureau of Labor Statistics directs its staff to interview a large sample of households. It asks about the employment situation of all members of households 16 years and older. If someone in a household is not working, the interviewer asks whether the person is actively looking for work. If so, he or she is classified as unemployed; but if the unemployed person is not actively looking for work, that person is classified as not being in the labor force.

Obviously, it is difficult for an interviewer to determine whether someone is truly looking for work. Without knowing whether someone in the household actually made any effort to look for a job during the time before the interview, the interviewer must rely on good-faith responses to the questions.

What about those people who were looking for work sometime in the recent past but did not find any opportunities and have stopped looking? These people are considered **discouraged workers**. They are not included in the official count of the unemployed.

The Bureau of Labor Statistics (BLS) has long recognized that it is difficult to distinguish between people who are unemployed, and people who are unemployed and not in the labor force. In 1994, the BLS interviewers changed the way they asked questions to avoid biasing responses in the direction of not being in the labor force. Studies revealed these changes did not have much effect on the overall unemployment rate but did raise the unemployment rate somewhat for older workers.

To add to difficulties in measurement and interpreting what is measured, some workers may hold a part-time job but prefer to work full time. Other workers may hold jobs far below their capabilities. Workers in either of these situations are called **underemployed**. It is very difficult for the government to distinguish between employed and underemployed workers.

Another fact about unemployment that we have to understand is that different groups of people suffer more unemployment than other groups. Table 21.2 contains some unemployment statistics for selected groups for January 1999. Adults have substantially lower unemployment rates than teenagers. Minorities have higher unemployment rates, African-American teenagers having extremely high unemployment rates. On average, men and women have roughly the same unemployment rates, but the unemployment rates for married men and married women are lower than unemployment rates of women who maintain families alone.

These relative differentials among unemployment rates do vary somewhat as GDP rises and falls. Teenage and minority unemployment rates often rise very sharply during poor economic times. In better times, there is typically a reduction of unemployment for all groups. Nonetheless, teenage and minority unemployment remains high at all times.

Types of Unemployment

We can divide unemployment into three basic types. By studying each type separately, we can gain insight into some of the causes of each type of unemployment.

The unemployment rate is closely tied to the overall fortunes of the economy. Unemployment rises sharply during periods when real GDP falls and decreases when real GDP grows rapidly. During periods of falling GDP, firms will not want to employ as many workers as they do in good times because they are not producing as many goods and ser-

Discouraged workers: Workers who left the labor force because they could not find jobs.

Underemployed: Workers who hold a part-time job but prefer to work full time or hold jobs that are far below their capabilities.

Table 21.2 Selected U.S. Unemployment Statistics, Unemployment Rates for January 1999 (in percent)

Total	4.3
Males 20 years and older	3.4
Females 20 years and older	3.7
Both sexes, 16–19 years	15.5
White	3.8
African American	7.8
White, 16–19 years	13.0
African American, 16-19 years	29.8
Married men	2.3
Married women	2.8
Women maintaining families	6.3

Source: Bureau of Labor Statistics, U.S. Department of Labor, 1999.

vices. Firms will lay off or fire some current workers and will be more reluctant to add new workers to their payrolls. The result will be fewer workers with jobs and rising unemployment. Economists call the unemployment that accompanies fluctuations in real GDP **cyclical unemployment**. Cyclical unemployment rises during periods when real GDP falls or grows at a slower than normal rate and decreases when the economy improves.

Unemployment occurs even during periods when the economy is growing. Since 1970, for example, the unemployment rate in the United States has not fallen below 4% of the labor force. Unemployment that is not associated with economic fluctuations is either frictional unemployment or structural unemployment.

Frictional unemployment is the unemployment that occurs naturally during the normal workings of an economy. It can occur for a variety of reasons. People change jobs, move across the country, get laid off from their current jobs and search for new opportunities, or take their time after they enter the labor force to find an appropriate job. Suppose that when you graduate from college, you take six months to find a job that you like. During the six months in which you are looking for a good job, you are among those unemployed who make up frictional unemployment. Searching for a job, however, makes good sense. It would not be wise to take the first job you were offered if it had low wages, poor benefits, and no future.

The chapter opening story raised the possibility that the Internet could help to reduce unemployment down to zero, as firms could post help-wanted advertisements and workers could indicate interest in seeking employment. As we think about the nature of search and frictional unemployment, we can see that mere exchanges of information would not reduce frictional unemployment down to zero. Some workers, for example, would prefer to continue searching for jobs in their own area rather than moving across country to seek another job. Firms would also want to scrutinize employees very carefully because hiring and training a worker is costly. Improving information flows could even have a perverse effect of informing workers of other opportunities in the economy and thereby lead to more workers quitting their current jobs and seeking other employment.

Structural unemployment occurs because of a mismatch between the jobs that are available and the skills of workers who are seeking jobs. Workers with low skills may not find

Cyclical unemployment: the component of unemployment that accompanies fluctuations in real GDP.

Frictional unemployment: The part of unemployment associated with the normal workings of the economy, such as searching for jobs.

Structural unemployment: The part of unemployment that results from the mismatch of skills and jobs.

opportunities for employment. If the government requires employers to pay wages, taxes, and benefits that exceed the contribution of these workers, firms will not be likely to hire them. Similarly, workers whose skills do not match the employment opportunities in their area may be unemployed. Aerospace engineers in California will not find jobs in their area if the aerospace industry relocates to Alabama.

The line between frictional unemployment and structural unemployment is sometimes hard to draw. Suppose a highly skilled steelworker is laid off because his company shuts down its plant in his area and moves to a new plant overseas. The worker would like to find a comparable job, but only low-wage, unskilled work is available in his town. Jobs are available but not his kind of job, and the steel company will never return. Is this person's unemployment frictional or structural? There really is no correct answer. You might think of the steelworker as experiencing either frictional or structural unemployment. In practice, it does not matter, either to the steelworker or to the economist, whether this episode of unemployment is frictional or structural.

Suspicious Unemployment Statistics

Suppose that after a long period of high unemployment, government statisticians noticed that the labor force was smaller than it was before the spell of unemployment. Is there any reason you might be suspicious of these numbers? As an economic detective, you may have good reasons to be suspicious of these numbers. During the period of high unemployment, some workers may have become discouraged and dropped out of the labor force. They may return to the labor force when economic conditions improve. ◆

Natural rate of unemployment: The level of unemployment at which there is no cyclical unemployment.

Full employment: The level of employment that occurs when the unemployment rate is at the natural rate.

Total unemployment in an economy is composed of cyclical, frictional, and structural unemployment. The level of unemployment at which there is no cyclical unemployment is called the **natural rate of unemployment**. The natural rate of unemployment consists of only frictional unemployment and structural unemployment. The natural rate of unemployment is the economist's notion of the rate unemployment should be, when there is **full employment**. It may seem strange to think that workers can be unemployed when the economy is at full employment. But economists choose to consider the economy to be at full employment when there is no cyclical unemployment, although there is frictional and structural unemployment. The economy needs some frictional unemployment to operate efficiently: it is the unemployment that exists so that workers and firms find the right matches.

In the United States today, economists estimate that the natural rate of unemployment is between 4.0% and 5.5%. The natural rate of unemployment can vary over time and will differ across countries. In Europe, for example, estimates of the natural rate of unemployment place it between 7% and 10%. In a later chapter, we explore why the natural rate of unemployment is higher in Europe than in the United States and why the natural rate of unemployment can vary over time in the same country.

The actual unemployment rate can be higher or lower than the natural rate of unemployment. During a period in which the real GDP fails to grow at its normal rate, there will be positive cyclical unemployment, and actual unemployment can far exceed the natural rate of unemployment. For example, in the United States in 1983, unemployment exceeded 10% of the labor force. A more extreme example occurred in 1933 during the Great Depression, when the unemployment rate reached 25%. On the other hand, when the economy grows very rapidly for a long period, actual unemployment can fall below the natural rate of unemployment. With sustained rapid economic growth, employers will be aggressive in hiring workers. During the late 1960s, unemployment rates fell below 4%; the natural rate of unemployment was estimated to be over 5% at that time. In this case, cyclical unemployment was negative.

The desperate economic times of the Great Depression drove many of the unemployed to sell apples on the street, as this man did in "Hobo Jungle" in New York City.

Just as a car will overheat if the engine is overworked, so the economy will overheat if economic growth is too rapid. At low unemployment rates, firms will find it difficult to recruit workers, and competition among firms will lead to increases in wages. As wages increase, increases in prices soon follow. The sign of this overheating will be a general rise in prices for the entire economy, which we commonly call inflation. As we discuss in later chapters, when the actual unemployment rate falls below the natural rate of unemployment, inflation will increase.

TEST Your Understanding

1. How do economists measure the unemployed?
2. Previously unemployed individuals who have stopped looking for work are called _____ workers.
3. The three types of unemployment are cyclical, frictional, and _____.
4. The natural rate of unemployment consists solely of _____ and _____ unemployment.

The Consumer Price Index and the Cost of Living

Suppose you moved to France and began to work. You received your first paycheck, which was in francs, the French currency. The actual number of francs written on the check would not mean much to you initially. What you would like to know is what goods and services your paycheck could buy. Was this a fat paycheck or a thin one? Should you celebrate your first paycheck with a 5-course gourmet dinner or head for the nearest inexpensive café?

Even in our own country, where we feel we have a reasonable sense of what a dollar can buy, we do know that the value of a dollar—what it purchases—varies over time. In 1976, a new starting professor of economics was paid $15,000. In 1999, a new starting professor at the same university was paid $55,000. Prices, of course, had risen in those 23 years. Which starting professor had the best deal?

These examples are illustrations of one of our five principles of economics, the reality principle:

REALITY **PRINCIPLE**

> **What matters to people is the real value of money or income—its purchasing power—not the face value of money or income.**

Consumer Price Index (CPI):
A price index that measures the cost of a fixed basket of goods chosen to represent the consumption pattern of individuals.

Economists have developed a number of different measures to track the cost of living over time. The best known of these measures is the **Consumer Price Index (CPI)**.

The CPI is widely used by both government and the private sector to measure changes in prices facing consumers. The CPI is an index that measures changes in a fixed *basket of goods*—a collection of items chosen to represent the purchasing pattern of a typical consumer. We first find out how much this basket of goods costs in a given year, called the base year. We then ask how much it costs in other years and measure changes in the cost of living relative to this base year. The CPI index for a given year, say year K, is defined as

$$\text{CPI in year } K = (\text{cost of basket in year } K/\text{cost of basket in base year}) \times 100$$

Suppose a basket of goods costs $200 in the base year of 1992 and $250 in 1997. First, the value for the CPI in 1992 (the base year) is

$$\text{CPI in 1992} = (200/200) \times 100 = 100$$

The CPI in 1992 is 100. The way that the CPI is constructed its value in a base year will always be 100. Now let's calculate the value of the CPI for 1997:

$$\text{CPI in 1997} = (250/200) \times 100 = 125$$

The CPI in 1997 is 125. The CPI rose from 100 in 1992 to 125 in 1997 in this example, a 25% increase in average prices over this 5-year period.

Here is how you would use this information. Suppose you had $300 in 1992. How much would you need to be able to have the same standard of living in 1997? The answer is given by multiplying the $300 by the ratio of the CPI in 1997 to the CPI in 1992:

$$\$300 \times (125/100) = \$375$$

You need $375 in 1997 just to maintain what was your standard of living in 1992. This is the type of calculation that economists do to evaluate changes in living standards over time.

How do we actually calculate the CPI in practice? Each month, the Bureau of Labor Statistics sends its employees out to sample prices for over 90,000 specific items around the entire country. Figure 21.2 shows the broad categories that are used in the CPI and the importance of each category in household budgets. Rent and food and beverages account for 44% of total spending by households.

Figure 21.2
Components of the CPI

Source: Bureau of Labor Statistics Handbook (Washington, DC: U.S. Government Printing Office, 1992).

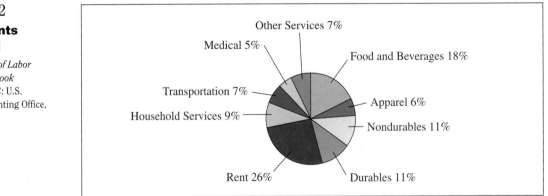

The CPI Versus the Chain Index for GDP

In Chapter 20, we discussed measuring nominal GDP and real GDP. We also mentioned that since 1996, the Commerce Department has used a chain index (replacing the GDP deflator) to measure changes in prices for goods and services included in GDP. The chain index for GDP and the CPI are both measures of average prices for the economy, yet they differ in several ways.

First, the CPI measures the costs of a typical basket of goods for consumers. It includes goods produced in prior years (such as older cars) as well as imported goods. The chain price index for GDP does not measure price changes from either used goods or imports. The reason that the chain index for GDP does not include used or imported goods is that it is based on the calculation of GDP, which measures only goods and services produced currently in the United States.

Second, unlike the chain price index for GDP, the CPI asks how much a fixed basket of goods costs in the current year compared to the cost of those same goods in a base year. Because consumers will tend to buy less of goods whose prices have risen, the CPI will tend to overstate true changes in the cost of living. For example, if the price of steak rises, consumers may switch to chicken and spend less on steak. But if the current basket of goods and services in the CPI includes steak, the CPI thinks the share of higher-priced steak in the basket is the same as the share of steak before its price increase; the CPI does not allow the share of steak in the index to decrease.

Problems in Measuring Changes in Prices

Most economists believe that in reality all the indexes—the chain index for GDP and the CPI—overstate actual changes in prices. In other words, the increase in prices is probably less than the reported indexes tell us. The principal reason for this overstatement is that we have a difficult time measuring quality improvements. Suppose that the new computers sold to consumers become more powerful and more efficient each year. Further, suppose that the dollar price of a new computer remains the same each year. Even though the prices remain the same, the computers in later years are of much higher quality. If we looked simply at the prices of computers and did not take into account the change in quality, we would say there was no price change for computers. But in later years we are getting more computer power for the same price. If we failed to take the quality change into account, we would not see that the price of computer power has fallen.

Government statisticians do try to adjust for quality when they can. But quality changes are so common in our economy and products evolve so rapidly that it is impossible to keep up with all that is occurring. As a result, most economists believe that we overestimate the inflation rate by between 0.5% and 1.5% each year. This overstatement has important consequences. Some government programs, such as Social Security, automatically increase payments when the CPI goes up. Some union contracts also have **cost-of-living adjustments** or automatic wage changes based on the CPI. If the CPI overstates increases in the cost of living, the government and employers might be overpaying Social Security recipients and workers for changes in the cost of living, as "A Closer Look: Costly Biases in the Price Indexes?" explains.

Cost-of-living adjustments:
Automatic increases in wages or other payments that are tied to a price index.

Inflation

We have now looked at two different price indexes: the chain price index used for calculating real GDP and the Consumer Price Index. Using either price index, we can calcu-

Costly Biases in the Price Indexes?

Each year, the federal government increases Social Security payments to the elderly by the rate of increase of prices as measured by the Consumer Price Index. The reason for this adjustment is to make sure that the elderly, whose other income tends to be fixed, do not suffer too much from changes due to increases in the cost of living. But as we have seen, the CPI does not fully account for quality changes, so that true increase in prices is less than the increase as measured by the CPI. Because Social Security payments are increased by the CPI, we overcompensate the elderly for price changes and actually increase their benefits in real terms.

How much extra are we paying the elderly because of the bias in the CPI? Economists believe that the CPI overstates actual price increases by between 0.5% and 1.5% a year. Assume that the figure is 1%. According to the Congressional Budget Office, if we reduced this adjustment for Social Security by 1%, it would save $42 billion dollars over a 5-year period! As you can tell, not accounting for technical change is a costly bias in our price indexes.

Defenders of the elderly claim this is a misleading argument. While the CPI may overstate price increases in general, it probably understates the rate of price increases facing the elderly. The elderly consume more medical care than do average citizens in the United States, and prices for medical care have increased faster than other prices in the economy. Regardless of which side of the debate we favor, it is evident that many tax dollars depend on precise calculation of the CPI.

Inflation rate: The percentage rate of change of the price level in the economy.

late the percentage rate of change of the index. The percentage rate of change of a price index is the **inflation rate**:

$$\text{inflation rate} = \text{percentage rate of change of a price index}$$

Here is an example. Suppose that a price index in a country was 200 in 1998 and 210 in 1999. Then the inflation rate between 1998 and 1999 was

$$\text{inflation rate} = (210 - 200)/200 = .05 = 5\%$$

The country experienced a 5% inflation rate.

It is important to distinguish between the price level and the inflation rate. In everyday language, people sometimes confuse the *level of prices* with inflation. You might hear someone say that inflation is high in San Francisco because rents on apartments are high, but this is not a correct use of the term *inflation*. Inflation refers not to the level of prices, whether they are high or low, but to their percentage change. If rents were high in San Francisco but remained constant between 2 years, there would be no inflation in rents there during that time.

To gain some historical perspective, Figure 21.3 plots a price index for GDP from 1875 to 1998 for the United States. As you can see from the figure, from 1875 to the period just before World War I, there was virtually no change in the price level. The price level rose during World War I, fell after the war ended, and also fell sharply during the early 1930s. However, the most pronounced feature of the figure is the sustained rise in prices beginning around the 1940s. Unlike the earlier periods, in which the price level did not have a trend, after 1940 the price level increased sharply. By 1995, the price level had increased by a factor of 12 over its value in 1940.

Taking a closer look at the period following World War II, Figure 21.4 plots the inflation rate, the percentage change in the price index, for 1950–1998 for the United States. In the 1950s and 1960s, the inflation rate was frequently less than 2% a year. The infla-

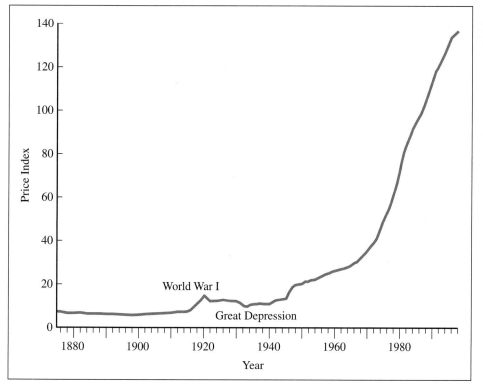

Figure 21.3
Price Index of U.S. GDP, 1875–1998

Source: R. J. Gordon, *Macroeconomics* (N.Y.: Harper Collins 1993), U.S. Department of Commerce.

tion rate was a lot higher in the 1970s, reaching nearly 12% per year. In recent years, the inflation rate has subsided, and in 1999, it was again less than 2% a year. Prices rarely fall today but as "A Closer Look: Deflations and Depressions" shows, prices have actually fallen quite sharply at times in U.S. history.

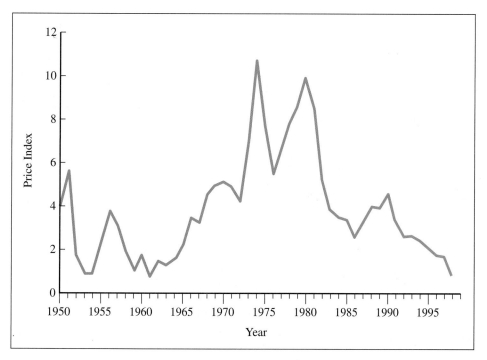

Figure 21.4
U.S. Inflation Rate, 1950–1998, Based on Chain Price Index

Source: U.S. Department of Commerce.

Deflations and Depressions

If you were born after 1952, you have never lived in a year without the price level rising, that is, without inflation. You might think it would be great if prices fell and we experienced what economists call a deflation. It may surprise you that we think you should hope that never happens.

During the Great Depression, the United States underwent a deflation, with the average level of prices falling 33% between 1929 and 1933. Wages fell along with prices during this period. The biggest problem caused by a deflation is that people cannot pay their debts. Imagine that you owe $40,000 for your education and expect to be able to pay it off over several years if you earn $20,000 a year. If a

massive deflation caused your wages to fall to $10,000, you might not be able to pay your $40,000 debt, which doesn't fall with deflation. You would be forced to default on your loan, as millions of people did during the Great Depression.

When people fail to pay interest and principal on their loans, banks get into trouble because they are no longer earning any money. In the 1930s, banks failed in the United States and throughout the world, including Austria, Hungary, Czechoslovakia, Romania, Poland, and Germany. These bank failures helped to make the Great Depression a worldwide phenomenon.

TEST Your Understanding

5. The value of a price index in the base year is _____.

6. Economists believe that the CPI tends to underestimate the increase in the cost of living over time. True or false? Explain.

7. Unlike the CPI, the chain price index for GDP does not include used goods or _____ goods.

8. If a price index is 50 in 1998 and 60 in 1999, the rate of inflation between the two years is _____.

Looking Ahead

With this basic vocabulary of macroeconomics, we can begin to explain and you can begin to understand how the overall economy works. Here is a preview of what's ahead.

In macroeconomics, we develop models and tools to help us analyze the economy as we try to understand it. The types of models often depend on the topics or questions we want to address. For some purposes, it will be useful to analyze the economy without considering business cycles or economic fluctuations; that is, we will want to look at the economy when it is operating at or near full employment. For example, when we study economic growth or look at the causes of extremely high inflation rates, it is easier to analyze the problem by assuming that the economy is operating at full employment. In these cases, we do not significantly improve our understanding by considering economic fluctuations. As in all areas of economics, we can understand the issues more clearly if we focus on the essential aspects of a problem and not on all the details. As a useful shorthand, we call the study of the economy when it operates at or near full employment **classical economics**.

Classical economics: A school of economic thought that provides insights into the economy when it operates at or near full employment.

At other times, we will be concerned with business cycles, economic fluctuations, and sharp changes in unemployment rates. For these issues, we want to understand how the economy can deviate from full employment. As another useful shorthand, we will call the study of business cycles and economic fluctuations that we develop **Keynesian economics** (after John Maynard Keynes, who made fundamental contributions to macroeconomics). Our understanding of economic fluctuations today has progressed substantially since Keynes's initial writings and incorporates many different perspectives, including those of economists who were highly critical of Keynes. Our use of the term *Keynesian economics* is therefore just convenient shorthand for our study of economic fluctuations.

Keynesian economics: A school of economic thought that provides insights into the economy when it operates away from full employment.

In this book, we use insights from both classical economics and Keynesian economics and integrate them into our story of how the macroeconomy works. In particular, we will see that the factors stressed by Keynes and the tradition that followed him are useful for understanding the behavior of the economy in the short run, when the economy can be far away from full employment. However, in the long run, there are forces pushing the economy back to full employment. When the economy reaches full employment, the insights from classical economics become valuable.

Sometimes the words *classical* and *Keynesian* are used to refer to two different schools of economic thought. Classical economists, though recognizing that economic fluctuations do occur (and often developing their own theories of fluctuations), believe that the economy has a strong tendency to return to full employment. They therefore place great importance on studying the behavior of the economy at or near full employment.

Keynesian economists believe that the economy returns to full employment only slowly, if at all, and emphasize the role of economic fluctuations. In this book, we draw freely on the ideas of both schools because both have important perspectives that we need to understand the full range of macroeconomic phenomena. As we will see, one of the principal disagreements among macroeconomists is about precisely how strong the forces are that push the economy back to full employment.

Using the TOOLS

1. Government Employment and the Unemployment Rate
Suppose the government hires workers who are currently unemployed but does not give them any work to do. What will happen to the measured unemployment rate? Is this an accurate reflection of the underlying economic situation?

2. Starting Salaries for Young Professors
The starting salary for a new assistant professor was $15,000 in 1976 and $55,000 in 1999. The value of the CPI for 1999 was 164.3 compared to 55.6 in 1976. In which year did a newly hired professor earn more in real terms?

3. Interpreting World Unemployment Statistics
A student looking at Table 21.1 argues that Spain must have very high cyclical unemployment compared to Japan because Spain's unemployment rate is so high. Explain why the student may not be correct.

4. Apartment Vacancies and Unemployment
In a major city, the vacancy rate for apartments was approximately 5%, yet substantial numbers of individuals were searching for new apartments. Can you explain why this occurs and relate it to unemployment?

Summary

In this chapter, we continued our introduction to the basic concepts of economics and explored the definition and nature of both unemployment and inflation. We also looked at the complex issues involved in measuring unemployment and inflation. Here are some of the key points to remember:

1. The unemployed are individuals who do not have jobs but are actively seeking employment.
2. The three types of unemployment are cyclical, frictional, and structural.
3. Unemployment rates vary across groups. It is often difficult to distinguish between the unemployed and discouraged workers who were once unemployed but stopped looking for work.
4. Economists measure changes in the cost of living through the Consumer Price Index, which is based on the cost of purchasing a standard basket of goods and services.
5. We measure inflation as the percentage change in the price level.
6. Economists believe that most price indices overstate true inflation because they fail to capture quality improvements.
7. Sometimes, we want to study the behavior of the economy when it operates at or near full employment. The study of the economy at full employment is known as classical economics. At other times, we want to study economic fluctuations, which are the subject of what we call Keynesian economics. In this book, we draw freely on the insights of both approaches to macroeconomic problems.

Key Terms

classical economics, 446
consumer price index (CPI), 442
cost-of-living adjustments, 443
cyclical unemployment, 439
discouraged workers, 438
employed, 436

frictional unemployment, 439
full employment, 440
inflation rate, 444
Keynesian economics, 447
labor force, 436
labor force participation rate, 436

natural rate of unemployment, 440
structural unemployment, 439
underemployed, 438
unemployed, 436

Problems and Discussion Questions

1. Here are some data for an economy:
   - 10 million individuals 16 years and older
   - 5.5 million employed
   - 0.5 million unemployed

   Calculate the labor force, the labor force participation rate, and the unemployment rate for this economy.

2. Sometimes at the beginning of an economic boom, total employment increases sharply but the unemployment rate does not fall. Why might this occur?

3. In inner cities, minority youths have high unemployment rates. Many economists believe that the unemployment picture is worse than the statistics portray. What could be the basis for this belief?

4. Suppose the government decided that housewives and househusbands should be counted as employed because they perform important services. How do you think this change would affect our measure of the labor force, the labor force participation rate, and the unemployment rate? (You may want to construct a numerical example.)

5. Why is the natural rate of unemployment always positive?

6. When oil prices increased sharply in the 1970s, some businesses were affected more adversely than others. Explain why some economists believe that the oil price increase led to higher frictional unemployment.

7. A country reports a price index of 55 in 1990 and 60 in 1991. What is the inflation rate between 1990 and 1991?

8. A job paid $3,000 in 1960. The CPI in 1960 was 29.3 compared to 164 in 1999. In 1999, what salary would be comparable to 1960's $3,000 in real terms?

9. An economy has 100,000,000 people employed, 8,000,000 unemployed, and 4,000,000 discouraged

workers. What is the conventional measure of the unemployment rate? What would be the best alternative measure that takes into account discouraged workers?

10. Critically evaluate the following statement: "Tokyo is an expensive place to live. They must have a high inflation rate in Japan."

11. **Web Exercise.** Go to the data section of the Web site for the Bureau of Labor Statistics (*http://stats. bls.gov*). Contrast the change in the price indexes from 1960 to the present for the overall CPI with the change in some of its components such as food and beverage and medical care services. What are some of your findings?

12. **Web Exercise.** Use the Web to find articles about the difficulties in precisely measuring changes in prices in the economy. You might want to start with the Boskin report which can be found on the history page of the Social Security Administration (*http://www.ssa/gov/history/repstud.html*). On the basis of your reading, what do you consider to be the most important problem?

Take It to the Net

We invite you to visit the O'Sullivan/Sheffrin page on the Prentice Hall Web site at:
http://www.prenhall.com/osullivan/
for additional World Wide Web exercises for this chapter.

Model Answers to Questions

Chapter-Opening Questions

1. The unemployed are individuals without jobs and actively seeking work. The unemployment rate cannot be driven down to zero because of natural frictions in the labor market.

2. Teenagers and minorities have the highest unemployment rates.

3. The Consumer Price Index is a price index that is used to measure changes in the cost of living.

4. Because of changes in the quality of goods and other factors, we cannot measure inflation perfectly and probably tend to overestimate the true inflation rate. This will have financial implications if payments are linked to changes in measured prices.

Test Your Understanding

1. The unemployed are individuals who are not employed but are actively looking for work.

2. Discouraged.

3. Structural.

4. Frictional and structural.

5. 100.

6. False. The CPI overestimates the increase in the cost of living over time for two reasons. It does not fully take into account technological change and assumes that the quantities of goods consumed do not decrease as prices increase.

7. Imported.

8. 20%.

Using the Tools

1. Government Employment and the Unemployment Rate. If the government hires an individual, that individual is an employee and no longer unemployed. The unemployment rate would fall. But the underlying economic reality has not changed: The individual is not producing any goods or services.

2. Starting Salaries for Young Professors. Starting salaries were higher in 1999. The 1999 equivalent of the 1976 salary of $15,000 is $15,000 × (164.3/55.6) = $44,325, which is less than the actual salary of $55,000 for 1999.

3. Interpreting World Unemployment Statistics. Spain could have higher frictional unemployment or structural unemployment than Japan. Without detailed knowledge of an economy, we cannot tell how much of unemployment is cyclical, frictional, or structural.

4. Apartment Vacancies and Unemployment. Owners of apartments naturally want to choose reliable renters, while at the same time, prospective tenants want to find the best apartments. This results in a process of search, just like in the labor market. Apartment vacancies are analogous to job vacancies and apartment seekers are analogous to the unemployed.

CHAPTER

22

Classical Economics: The Economy at Full Employment

John Maynard Keynes referred to his predecessors as classical economists. He believed that they lacked his insights about macroeconomics. Perhaps that's why classical economics slipped into disrepute for many years. Today, many economists are proud to call themselves classical economists. We'll explain the power of the classical approach to macroeconomics in this chapter.

We will explain how the amount of capital and labor determine GDP when an economy is producing at full employment. The study of how the economy operates at full employment is commonly known as **classical economics**. As you will see, classical economics is based on the principle that prices adjust in a natural way to bring the markets for goods and labor into equilibrium.

Classical economics: A school of economic thought that provides insights into the economy when it operates at or near full employment.

The classical economists believed that there are strong forces pushing the economy back to full employment after shocks that caused excessive unemployment. Although they did not deny that the economy could experience booms or busts, classical economists believed that booms and busts were temporary and that the economy would return naturally to full employment.

There are several reasons for studying classical economics. First, there are issues in macroeconomics concerning the long run, that we should know about. Here are a few examples: Suppose the government increases spending for several years to fight a war or to rehabilitate our cities. What effects will this have on the level of consumption or investment in the economy? Or suppose we are concerned about low wages in the economy. What public policy actions can we take to raise the level of wages in the economy in the long run? The classical model that we develop in this chapter provides the tools to answer these questions.

Supply-siders: Economists who emphasize the role of taxation for influencing economic activity.

Second, many of today's debates in economics can best be analyzed with the tools of classical economics. For example, economists and politicians debate the effects of taxes on the level of work effort and output in the economy. One school of economists, known as **supply-siders**, made this the basis of their analysis of the economy. The tools of classical economics can help us to understand some of these debates.

Third, the tools of classical economics are used by a new school of economic thought—real business cycle theory—to explain why there are economic booms and recessions.

When the economy is at full employment, that does not mean there are no unemployed workers. Recall the distinction between frictional, structural, and cyclical unemployment. Frictional unemployment occurs naturally in the labor market as workers search for jobs. Structural unemployment arises from a mismatch of skills and jobs. Cyclical unemployment is the part of unemployment that rises and falls with economic fluctuations. Cyclical unemployment can be positive, when unemployment exceeds the natural rate during a recession, or negative when unemployment is less than the natural rate during a boom. Full employment corresponds to zero cyclical unemployment; that means that when the economy is at full employment, the only unemployment is frictional and structural.

Here are issues that we can address with the tools we develop in this chapter:

1. How does increased immigration affect wages and the level of output in the economy?
2. What are the benefits of increased investment?
3. What happens to wages, employment, and GDP if employers must pay higher taxes for hiring labor?
4. If our governments spend more, does this mean we must have a lower level of consumption or investment in our economy?

In the classical model, wages and prices are assumed to adjust freely and quickly to all changes in demand and supply. It is precisely this flexibility in wages and prices that distinguishes the classical model from the Keynesian models that we examine in later chapters. You must keep this assumption and this distinction in mind as we develop the classical model in this chapter.

The Aggregate Production Function for the Economy

One of the most extremely simplified assumptions in macroeconomics is the aggregate production function. As a reminder, a function is just a convenient way to describe the relationship between variables. The **aggregate production function** explains the relationship of the total inputs used throughout the economy to the total level of production in the economy or GDP. We assume that there are only two factors of production: capital and labor. The **stock of capital** comprises all the machines, equipment, and buildings in the entire economy. **Labor** consists of the efforts of all the workers in the economy. We write the aggregate production function as

$$Y = F(K, L)$$

where Y is total output, or GDP, K is the stock of capital, and L is the labor force.

What the math says in words is that total output is produced from both capital and labor. The aggregate production function $F(K, L)$ tells us how much output is produced from the inputs to production, K and L. More inputs of either capital or labor lead to increased output.

The stock of capital that a society has at any point in time is given to us by its past investments in new plants and equipment. Investments taken today will have no or little immediate effect on the total stock of machines, equipment, and buildings in existence today. It takes time for investment to change the stock of capital. In this chapter, most of our discussion will assume that the stock of capital is fixed at a constant level, which we call K^*. But there will be a few places where we will stray from that assumption to consider what happens when there are changes in the stock of capital. We promise to let you know where we are straying from the assumption of fixed capital.

With the stock of capital fixed at the constant level K^*, only variations in the amount of labor can change the level of output in the economy. Figure 22.1 plots the relation-

Aggregate production function: Shows how much output is produced from capital and labor.

Stock of capital: The total of all the machines, equipment, and buildings in the entire economy.

Labor: The total effort of all employed workers in an economy.

Figure 22.1

Relationship between Labor and Output with Fixed Capital
With capital fixed, output increases with labor input but at a decreasing rate.

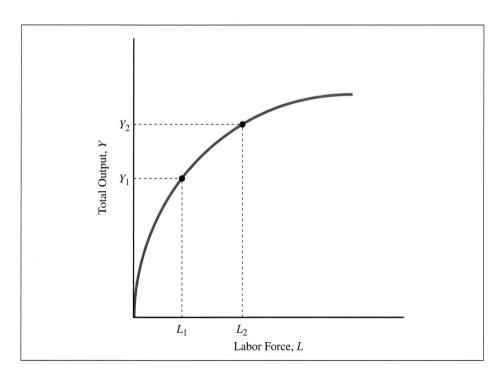

ship between the amount of labor used in an economy and the total level of output with a fixed stock of capital. Because the amount of labor can be changed over a short period, resulting in a corresponding change in output, also within a short time, this diagram is called the **short-run production function**.

Figure 22.1 shows that as labor inputs are increased from L_1 to L_2, output increases from Y_1 to Y_2. The relationship between output and labor shown here reflects the principle of diminishing returns.

Short-run production function:
Shows how much output is produced from varying amounts of labor when the capital stock is held constant.

PRINCIPLE OF DIMINISHING RETURNS

> **Suppose that output is produced with two or more inputs and that we increase one input while holding the other inputs fixed. Beyond some point—called the point of diminishing returns— output will increase at a decreasing rate.**

To explain what diminishing marginal returns means, look at the data in Table 22.1 from a typical production function. The table shows the amount of output that can be produced from different amounts of labor inputs while the stock of capital is held constant at some amount. (We don't care what amount, as long as it is constant.) First, notice that as the amount of labor increases, so does the amount of output produced. Second, as output increases, it increases at a diminishing rate. For example, as labor input increases from 3 to 4 labor units, output increases by 5 output units, from 10 to 15 output units. But as labor input increases from 4 to 5 labor units, output only increases by 4 output units, from 15 to 19 output units. The rate of output dropped from 5 output units per additional unit of labor input to 4 output units per additional unit of labor input, and that's diminishing returns.

What happens if the stock of capital increases, say, from K^* to K^{**}? Figure 22.2 shows that when the stock of capital increases, the entire short-run production function shifts upward. At any level of labor input, more output can be produced than before the stock of capital was increased. As we add more capital, workers become more productive and can produce more output. That's why the production function curve is higher for more capital. For example, an office has five staff members who must share one copier. They will inevitably waste some time waiting to use it. Adding a copier will enable the staff to be more productive. The benefit of additional capital is a higher level of output from any level of labor input.

Table 22.1 Output and Labor Output

Y (Output)	L (Labor Input)
10	3
15	4
19	5
22	6

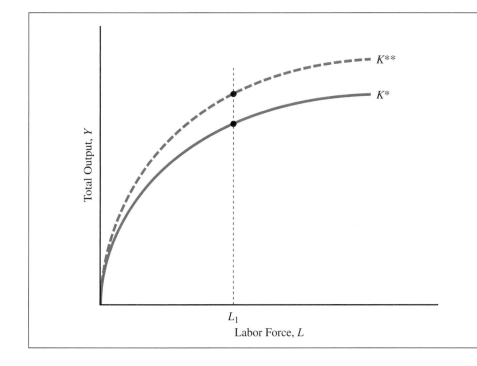

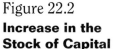

Figure 22.2
Increase in the Stock of Capital
When capital increases from K* to K** the production function shifts up. At any level of labor input, the level of output increases.

TEST Your Understanding

1. What is an aggregate production function?

2. Complete the statement with *increases* or *decreases*: With the stock of capital fixed, output increases with labor input but at a rate that _____.

3. Complete the statement with *upward* or *downward*: An increase in the stock of capital shifts the production function _____.

The Demand and Supply for Labor

We've just seen that with the amount of capital fixed, the level of output in the economy will be determined exclusively by the amount of labor employed. Now we'll see how the amount of employment in an economy is determined by the demand and supply for labor.

On the basis of what you already know about supply and demand from Chapter 4, you should be able to see what Figure 22.3 represents with respect to the demand and supply for labor for the entire economy. Firms hire labor to produce output and make profits. The amount of labor they will hire depends on the **real wage**: the wage rate paid to employees adjusted for changes in prices. To understand the demand for labor, we use the marginal principle:

Real wage: The wage paid to workers adjusted for changes in prices.

MARGINAL **PRINCIPLE**

> **Increase the level of an activity if the marginal benefit exceeds its marginal cost, but reduce the level if the marginal cost exceeds the marginal benefit. If possible, pick the level at which the marginal benefit equals the marginal cost.**

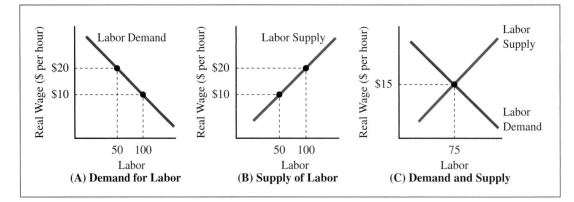

Figure 22.3 **Demand for and Supply of Labor**

The marginal benefit that a firm receives from hiring an additional worker is the value of the extra output that results when that additional worker is hired. The marginal cost of the worker is the real wage a firm pays to hire the additional worker. The firm will continue to hire additional workers as long as the marginal benefit from an additional worker exceeds the marginal cost of that additional worker. For example, if the real wage is $20 per hour, a firm will continue to hire additional workers as long as the marginal benefit from an additional hour of work exceeds $20 and will continue hiring only until the marginal benefit from an additional hour equals $20.

If the real wage falls, the marginal cost of labor falls. As the cost falls, the firm will again hire additional labor—again, only until the marginal benefit again equals marginal cost. For example, suppose the real wage is $20 per hour and the marginal benefit from an extra hour of work is $20. Let's say the wage falls $10 per hour. Then, the marginal benefit to the firm will exceed the wage. The firm will respond by hiring more labor until the marginal benefit from hiring an additional worker equals $10.

As the real wage falls, firms will hire more labor. The labor demand curve in Figure 22.3 is therefore downward sloping. In panel A, we see that as the real wage falls from $20 to $10 per hour, the firm will increase the amount of its labor from 50 to 100 workers.

The labor supply curve is based on the decisions of workers. They must decide how many hours they want to work and how much leisure they want to enjoy. Changes in wages have two different effects on workers' decisions about those wants.

First, an increase in the real wage will make working more attractive and raise the opportunity cost of not working. Called the **substitution effect**, this increase leads to workers to supply more hours of labor. This is called the substitution effect because workers want to substitute work for leisure. Second, a higher wage raises a worker's income for the amount of hours that he or she is currently working. As income rises, a worker may choose to enjoy more leisure hours and work fewer hours. This is known as the **income effect** because as workers have more income, they can afford to have more leisure time.

The substitution effect and the income effect work in opposite directions. In principle, a higher wage could lead workers to supply either more or fewer hours of work. In our analysis, we assume that the substitution effect dominates, so a higher wage rate will lead to increases in the supply of labor. In panel B of Figure 22.3 we see that 50 people would like to work at $10 per hour, but $20 per hour motivates 100 people to want to work.

Panel C puts the demand and supply curves together. At a wage of $15 per hour, the amount of labor that firms want to hire—75 workers—will be equal to the number who want to work—75 workers. This is the labor market equilibrium: The quantity

Substitution effect: An increase in the wage rate increases the opportunity cost of leisure and leads workers to supply more labor.

Income effect: An increase in the wage rate raises a worker's income at the current levels of hours of work and may lead to more leisure and a decreased supply of labor.

The capital equipment in this modern plant allows workers to produce high levels of output.

demanded for labor equals the quantity supplied. Together, the demand and supply curves determine the level of employment in the economy and the level of real wages.

When firms increase their capital stock, they find that the marginal benefit from hiring workers increases because each worker becomes more productive with the additional capital. For example, suppose that the marginal benefit of an additional hour of work is initially $15, and an increase in the supply of capital raises it to $20. Firms will want to hire additional workers at the existing wage until the marginal benefit again equals the marginal cost.

Because the demand for labor increases at any real wage, the labor demand curve shifts to the right. Panel A of Figure 22.4 shows the effects of an increase in labor demand. The new market equilibrium moves from E to E'. Real wages increase, and the amount of labor employed in the economy increases as well. Having more capital in the economy is beneficial for workers.

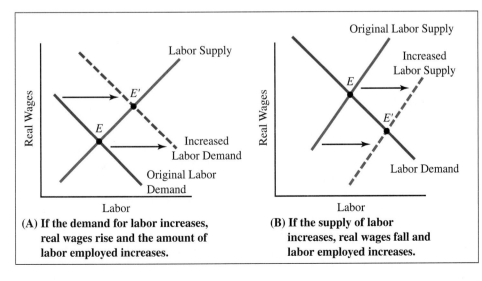

Figure 22.4
Shifts in Demand and Supply

(A) If the demand for labor increases, real wages rise and the amount of labor employed increases.

(B) If the supply of labor increases, real wages fall and labor employed increases.

We also can analyze the effect of an increase in the supply of labor that might come, for example, from immigration. If the population increases, we would expect that more people would want to work at any given wage. This means that the labor supply curve would shift to the right. Panel B of Figure 22.4 shows that with an increase in the supply of labor, the labor market equilibrium moves from E to E'. Real wages have fallen, and the amount of labor employed has increased. Workers who were employed before the increase in labor supply suffer because real wages have fallen—all wages, including theirs.

We can now see why currently employed workers might be reluctant to favor increased immigration. The additional supply of labor will tend to decrease real wages. Our model also explains why workers would like to see increases in the supply of machines and equipment as long as full employment can be maintained. The increased supply of capital increases labor demand and leads to higher real wages.

The Case of Asian Wages and Employment

Suppose you were told that in one Asian country, both wages and employment increased. As an economic detective, would you start looking for factors that increased labor demand or factors that increased the supply of labor? To solve this mystery, you want to look for factors that increased the demand for labor. Increases in the demand for labor will increase both real wages and employment. ◆

Finally, our model can also help us understand the very different behavior of real wages in the United States and Europe during the 1980s and 1990s. Although GDP grew at roughly the same rate in the United States and Europe, in the United States there was a substantial increase in new jobs, while in Europe very few jobs were created. In both places, the labor demand curve shifted to the right as the stock of capital increased. However, the labor supply in the United States grew at a faster rate than the labor supply in Europe. The supply curve for labor shifted to the right more in the United States than in Europe. We would expect that this would mean higher employment growth but slower growth in real wages in the United States. This is precisely what happened. Real wages in Germany rose by over 12% from 1980 to 1990; in the United States, real wages (excluding fringe benefits) fell by 6%. Over the same period, industrial employment grew by 22% in the United States but did not grow at all in Germany.

TEST Your Understanding

4. Labor market equilibrium occurs at a real wage at which the quantity demanded for labor equals the quantity _____ of labor.

5. Explain why the demand curve for labor is negatively sloped and the supply curve for labor is positively sloped.

6. Complete the statement with *right* or *left*: An increase in the amount of capital in the economy will shift the demand for labor curve to the _____, leading to higher real wages and employment.

7. Complete the statement with *right* or *left*: Increased immigration is likely to lead to a shift in the labor supply curve to the _____.

8. Draw the supply and demand graphs to illustrate the differences in employment and wage growth between Europe and the United States in the 1980s.

Labor Market Equilibrium and Full Employment

We now show exactly how much output the economy can produce when it is operating at full employment—a big objective of this chapter. We'll put the short-run production function in a context with the demand and supply for labor. Together, they will give us a model that will help us to achieve our objective as well as help us to understand how taxes on employers affect the level of output.

Figure 22.5 brings the model of the labor market together with the short-run production function. Panel B depicts equilibrium in the labor market, which we saw in Figure 22.3. The demand and supply for labor determine the real wage rate W^* and identify the level of employment L^*. Panel A plots the short-run production function. With the level of employment determined at L^* in panel B, we move upward to panel A and use that level of employment to determine the level of production is Y^*. **Full-employment output** is the level of output that is produced when the labor market is in equilibrium. It is also known as *potential output* because a meaningful measure of an economy's long-run productive potential will need to have the labor market in equilibrium. How do economists typically measure the level of full employment output, or potential output?

Full-employment output: The level of output that results when the labor market is in equilibrium. (Also known as *potential output*.)

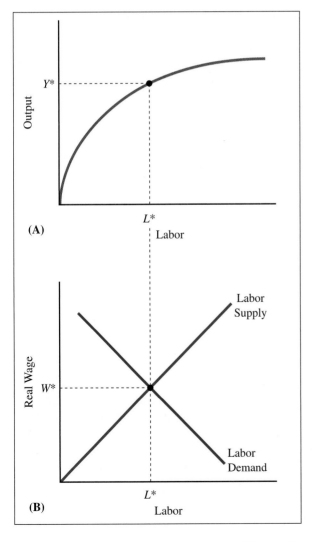

Figure 22.5
Determining Full Employment Output
Panel B determines the equilibrium level of employment at L^* and the real wage rate at W^*. Full employment output in panel A is Y^*.

They start with an estimate of what the unemployment rate would be if cyclical unemployment were zero—that is, if the only unemployment were due to frictional or structural factors. In the United States, estimates of the natural rate in recent years have varied between 4.0% to 5.5%. Economists then estimate how many workers will be employed and use the short-run production function to determine potential output. In a worldwide economy, there may be many additional things to consider in measuring full employment, as "A Closer Look: Global Production and Potential Output," explains.

The level of potential output in an economy increases as the supply of labor increases or the stock of capital increases. An increase in the supply of labor, perhaps from more liberal immigration, would shift the labor supply curve to the right and lead to a higher level of employment in the economy. With a higher level of employment, the level of full employment output will increase. An increase in the stock of capital will increase the demand for labor. As labor demand increases, the result will be higher wages and increased employment. Higher employment will again raise the level of full employment output

Applications of the Classical Model

The classical model is used extensively in macroeconomics to analyze a wide range of issues.

Many politicians and economists have argued that high tax rates have hurt the U.S. economy and reduce the level of output and production. We will use the classical model to explore the logic of these claims.

We will also see how the classical model can be used to explain booms and recessions—fluctuations in output. This will allow us to understand the fundamental idea of an influential school of economic thought: real business cycle theory.

Taxes and Potential Output

We use the classical model in Figure 22.6 to study the effects of a tax paid by employers for hiring labor, such as the taxes they pay for workers' Social Security. Economists use similar arguments to study a variety of taxes, including personal and corporate income taxes. A tax on labor will make labor more expensive and raise the marginal cost of hiring

 **A CLOSER LOOK** Global Production and Potential Output

When government statisticians and business economists try to estimate potential output, they look at how firms are using their plant and equipment as well as the rate of unemployment. If factories are fully using all their plant and equipment, the economy is producing at its potential. But with U.S. firms manufacturing products throughout the world, some economists argue that traditional notions of capacity are obsolete.

For example, in 1994, the "big three" automobile manufacturers—Ford, Chrysler, and General Motors—had the capacity to produce 14 million vehicles at plants within the United States. However, by using plants in Canada and Mexico, another 4.5 million vehi-

cles could be produced. The automobile manufacturers plan their production on a global basis and could meet a U.S. demand for 18.5 million vehicles from their North American operations.

When do we reach potential output for the big three: at 14 million or 18.5 million vehicles? Economists try to pinpoint potential output by determining the level of demand for cars at which automobile manufacturers sharply raise their prices, because that's the level of output where they cannot easily produce any more cars. But as production becomes increasingly global, it is becoming more and more difficult to estimate potential output.

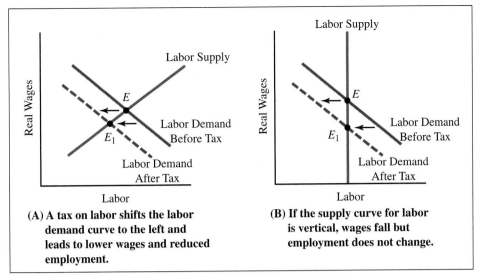

Figure 22.6
Effects of Employment Taxes

ACTIVE GRAPH

(A) A tax on labor shifts the labor demand curve to the left and leads to lower wages and reduced employment.

(B) If the supply curve for labor is vertical, wages fall but employment does not change.

workers. For example, let's say that there is no tax on labor, and suddenly a 10% tax is imposed. An employer who had been paying $10 an hour for workers will now find that labor costs $11 an hour. Since the marginal cost of hiring workers has gone up but the marginal benefit has not changed, employers will respond by hiring fewer workers at any given wage. In panel A of Figure 22.6, the labor demand curve shifts to the left, reflecting the tax as the increased cost of labor. As the demand curve shifts to the left, the market equilibrium moves from E to E_1. The result is lower real wages and lower employment.

As we have just seen, higher taxes lead to less employment. With reduced employment, potential output in the economy will be reduced as the economy moves to a lower level of output on the short-run production function. Higher taxes therefore lead to lower output. The size of the reduction in output depends critically on the slope of the labor supply curve. The slope of the labor supply curve indicates how sensitive labor supply is to changes in real wages. Panel B in Figure 22.6 shows the effect of the same tax with a vertical labor supply curve. A vertical labor supply curve means that workers will supply the same amount of labor regardless of the wage. For example, a single parent might work a full 40 hours a week regardless of the wage. His or her supply curve will be vertical. If other workers in the economy put in the same hours regardless of the wage, the supply curve for labor in the economy will be vertical. In panel B, we see that with a vertical supply curve, the tax will reduce wages but have no effect on employment and therefore no effect on output.

This example illustrates that taxes can affect wages and output. In both cases, either output or wages were lowered when the tax was imposed. However, the extent of the decline in output depends on the slope of the labor supply curve. To understand the effects of taxes on output, we need information about the slope of the labor supply curve.

There have been many studies of labor supply. Most show that full-time workers do not change their hours worked very much when wages change. There is some evidence that part-time workers or second earners in a family are more sensitive to changes in wages and do vary their labor supply when wages change. But the bulk of the evidence suggests that the supply curve for the economy as a whole is close to vertical. This implies that it is more likely higher taxes will reduce wages and not have pronounced effects on output.

The entire area of taxation and economics is an active branch of economics research. Economists such as Martin Feldstein of Harvard University, have studied how many different types of taxes affect employment, savings, and production. Economists use models to try to measure these effects, just as we did for the employment tax. "A Closer Look: The Laffer Curve and Capital Gains," highlights one controversial policy debate about taxation.

Real Business Cycle Theory

Fluctuations in economic activity can result from a variety of causes. Here are some examples: A developing country that is highly dependent on agriculture can lose its cash crop to a prolonged drought. According to economic historian Stanley Lebergott, the nineteenth century U.S. agricultural-based economy was devastated by grasshopper invasions in North Dakota in 1874 to 1876 and by the boll weevil migration from Mexico to Texas in 1892. Sharp increases in the price of oil can hurt economies that use oil in production, as was the case throughout the world in both 1973 and 1979. Wars can devastate entire regions of the world, and natural disasters, such as earthquakes or floods, can cause sharp reductions in GDP.

Major shifts in technology can also cause economic fluctuations. Consider some economic developments, starting with the early nineteenth century. There were large investments in textile mills and steam power. The birth of the steel industry and railroads dominated the last half of the century. At the end of the nineteenth century, new industries arose that were based on chemical manufacturing, electricity, and the automobile. It is inconceivable that the vast change in technology that led to the creation of

Laffer curve: A relationship between tax rates and tax revenues that illustrates that high tax rates may not always lead to high tax revenues if high tax rates discourage economic activity.

A CLOSER LOOK   The Laffer Curve and Capital Gains

Is it possible for a government to cut tax rates yet still raise more revenue? That's a politician's dream: People would face lower tax rates, yet there would be more money for politicians to spend. Economist Arthur Laffer argued in the late 1970s that there was a strong possibility that we could do this in the U.S. economy, and his views influenced many politicians at that time.

Here is an example of what is called the **Laffer curve**. Suppose a government imposed extremely high tariffs (taxes) on imported goods, tariff rates so high that no one could afford to import any goods whatsoever. If this were the case, the government would not collect any revenue from the tariffs. But, if the government cut the rates and individuals began to buy imported goods, the government would start to collect some tariff revenue. This is the Laffer curve in action: lower taxes (tariffs) leading to higher government revenues.

Virtually all economists today believe this argument does *not* apply to broad-based income taxes or payroll taxes. For these taxes, cutting rates will simply reduce the revenues that the government collects. But there are some taxes for which this claim is plausible.

Let's say that you buy a share of stock, which then rises in price. Then you sell it. You will pay a tax, known as the *capital gains tax*, on the difference between your original purchase price and your selling price. Many economists believe that cutting the tax rate for capital gains will actually lead to more total tax revenue. They argue that the individual does not have to sell a stock that has increased in value. If the capital gains tax burden is too large, the individual could simply hold onto the stock. If the capital gains tax rate is cut, more individuals will be induced to sell their stocks, and total revenues will increase.

Many economists do believe that in the short run, cutting capital gains tax rates will increase revenue as enough individuals will sell their stocks. But there is more dispute about the longer-run consequences. Tax revenues may increase now as individuals sell their stocks but only at the expense of fewer sales of stocks (and revenue) in the future. This remains a very active area of economics research.

these new industries would not have profound effects on the economy, particularly because these changes in technology often came in short bursts.

Economic fluctuations can also occur because a number of small shocks all hit the economy at the same time. For example, a country that primarily produces tea might face a sudden shift of consumer preferences throughout the world to coffee. Or a series of small improvements to technology could cause output to rise among worldwide producers of tea.

One school of economic thought, known as **real business cycle theory**, emphasizes that shocks to technology can have a big part in causing economic fluctuations. Led by Edward Prescott of the University of Minnesota, real business cycle economists have developed new models that integrate shocks to technology into the classical model we have been discussing.

The idea behind real business cycle theory is simple: Changes in technology will usually change the level of full employment or potential output. For example, if there is a significant technological improvement, it will enable the economy to increase the level of both actual and potential output. Similarly, if there are adverse technological developments (such as would occur if the Internet were to crash, for example) or adverse shocks to the economy, output and potential output will fall.

Figure 22.7 gives a simple example of how the real business cycle theory works. Suppose an adverse technological shock occurred, decreasing the demand for labor. The demand curve for labor would shift to the left, and the labor market equilibrium would move from E to E_1. The result would be a lower level of employment and lower real wages. Total GDP would fall both because employment would be low and because the economy would be less productive than before from the adverse technological shock.

The real business cycle school of thought has been influential with some academic economists but is generally viewed as controversial. Critics of the real business cycle theory find it difficult to understand how many of the post–World War II recessions could be explained by adverse changes in technology. In addition, it does not provide an explanation of unemployment. In the real business cycle model, the labor market is in equilibrium and the quantity demanded for labor equals the quantity supplied. At the equilibrium wage, the quantity of labor demanded equals the quantity of labor supplied, and everyone who seeks employment finds employment. Proponents of the real business

Real business cycle theory:
An economic theory that emphasizes how shocks to technology can cause fluctuations in economic activity.

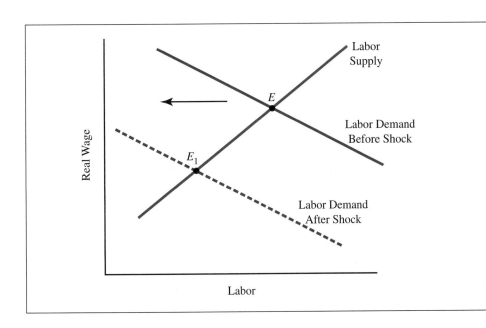

Figure 22.7
Effects of an Adverse Technology Shock
An adverse shock to the economy shifts the labor demand curve to the left and leads to lower wages, reduced employment, and reduced output.

cycle model counter that other types of economic models can be used to explain unemployment, but the real business cycle can still explain fluctuations in employment. So far, real business cycle theory has not had an impact on current macroeconomic policy. However, real business cycle theory is an active area of research, and its methods and approach, grounded in classical economics, influence professional research today.

The Division of Output Among Competing Demands

Our model of full employment is based entirely on the supply of factors of production. The demand for and supply of labor determine the real wage and total employment in the economy. Together, labor and the supply of capital determine the level of output through the production function. And that means that in a full-employment economy, total GDP is determined by the supply of factors of production.

Full-employment GDP must be divided among competing demands in the economy. From the previous two chapters, you know that economists think of GDP as being composed of consumption, investment, government purchases, and net exports, which we denote as $C + I + G + NX$. In this section, we first discuss how different societies' total GDP is composed. Because governments, for many different reasons, increase their level of spending, we would like to know how increased government spending would affect other types of spending. We will see how increases in government spending must reduce other types of expenditures when the economy is operating at full employment. This phenomenon is called **crowding out**.

Crowding out: Reductions in consumption, investment, or net exports caused by an increase in government purchases.

Some Comparative Data

Countries divide GDP among its competing demands in very different ways. Table 22.2 presents data on the percent of GDP in alternative uses for five countries in 1997. Recall that consumption (C), investment (I), and government purchases (G) refer to total spending by residents of that country. Net exports (NX) is the difference between exports (sales of goods to foreign residents) and imports (purchases of goods abroad). If a country has positive net exports (Japan, France, Singapore, and Germany), it is selling more goods in other countries than it is buying from other countries. If a country has negative net exports (United States), it is buying more goods than it is selling to other countries.

Let's make one more point: These data are from the *International Financial Statistics*, which is published by the International Monetary Fund (IMF). In these statis-

Table 22.2 Alternative Uses of GDP for 1997 (percent of total GDP)

	C	I	G	NX
Japan	61	28	10	1
United States	68	15	18	−1
France	60	16	20	4
Singapore	41	36	9	14
Germany	57	23	19	1

Source: International Monetary Fund, *International Financial Statistics*, 1999.

tics, government purchases include only government consumption (such as military spending or wages for government employees). Government investment (such as spending on bridges or roads) is included in the investment category (I).

Table 22.2 reveals considerable diversity among countries. The United States consumes 68% of its GDP, a higher fraction than any of the other countries. Singapore consumes only 41% of its GDP. The United States also invests a much smaller fraction of GDP than do the other countries. Singapore invests 36% of GDP and Japan invests 28%, whereas the United States invests only 15%. Japan and Singapore have a smaller fraction of GDP devoted to government consumption than do Germany, France, and the United States. Finally, the countries differ in the size of net exports relative to GDP.

This wide diversity challenges economists to explain these differences. Some economists have suggested that Japan has a high savings rate, that is, a relatively low percent of GDP devoted to consumption, because it has a relatively fast-growing population, and young adults tend to be a high-saving part of the population. Other economists have suggested that high payroll taxes in Singapore reduce workers' incomes and their ability to consume. But not all economists accept these explanations, and there are no obvious, purely economic reasons why the United States, France, and Germany should exhibit such different behavior.

Crowding Out in a Closed Economy

We know that government spending is part of GDP. Let's say that GDP is given and government increases its spending. What happens in a country that increases its government purchases within a fixed GDP? Because the level of full employment output is given by the supply of factors in the economy, an increase in government spending must come at the expense of other uses of GDP. Another way of looking at this: increased government spending crowds out other demands for GDP. This is an example of the principle of opportunity cost:

PRINCIPLE OF OPPORTUNITY COST

The opportunity cost of something is what you sacrifice to get it.

At full employment, the opportunity cost of increased government spending is some other component of GDP.

To understand crowding out, let's first consider what will happen when government spending increases in an economy without international trade. An economy without international trade is called a **closed economy**. In a closed economy, full employment output is divided among just 3 different demands: consumption, investment, and government purchases. We can write this as

> output = consumption + investment + government purchases
>
> $$Y = C + I + G$$

Closed economy: An economy without international trade.

Because we are considering an economy at full employment, the supply of output (Y) is fixed. Increases in government spending must reduce—that is, crowd out—either consumption or investment; in general, both are affected.

Figure 22.8
Increased Government Spending Crowds Out Consumption

Source: U.S. Department of Commerce.

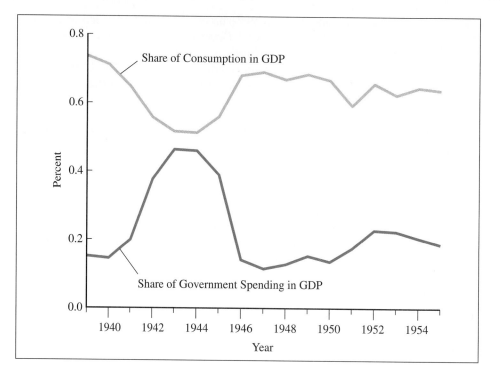

For example, crowding out occurred in the United States during World War II as the share of government spending in GDP rose sharply. Figures 22.8 and 22.9 show that at the same time the share of government spending increased, the shares of consumption and investment spending in GDP decreased.

Figure 22.9
Increased Government Spending Also Crowds Out Investment

Source: U.S. Department of Commerce.

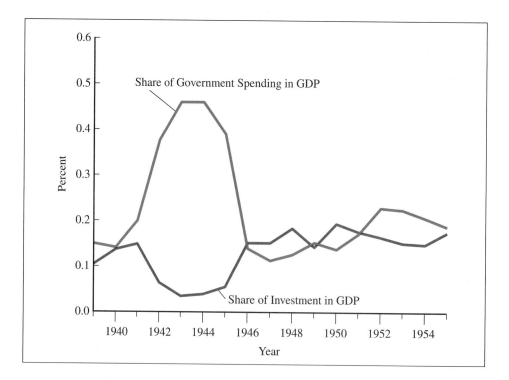

Crowding Out in an Open Economy

In an **open economy**, an economy with international trade, full-employment output is divided among 4 uses: consumption, investment, government purchases, and net exports (exports – imports):

open economy: An economy with international trade.

$$Y = C + I + G + NX$$

In an open economy, increases in government spending need not crowd out either consumption or investment. Increased government spending could lead to reduced exports and increased imports. Therefore, what could instead get crowded out is net exports.

Here is how this might happen: Suppose the U.S. government began buying domestic goods to use for some governmental purpose. Let's say these are goods that consumers would have purchased but now cannot. If consumers want to maintain their consumption level despite the goods no longer being available because the government's got them, they could purchase goods previously sold abroad (exports) and purchase goods sold by foreign countries (imports). The result would be a decrease in the amount of goods exported and an increase in imports, that is, a decrease in net exports. In practice, increases in government spending in an open economy would crowd out consumption, investment, and net exports.

Crowding In

Governments do not always increase spending. Sometimes, they decrease it. When the government cuts spending and the level of output is fixed, some other type of spending will be crowded in, or increase. In a closed economy, consumption or investment or both could increase. In an open economy, net exports could increase as well. As an example, after a war, we might see increases in consumption, investment spending, or net exports as they replace military spending.

The nature of changes in government spending will have some affect on the type of spending that is crowded out (or crowded in). If the government built more public swimming pools, households would most likely cut back on their own spending on backyard pools. If the government spent less on mail service, businesses and households would most likely spend more.

TEST Your Understanding

9. When the economy operates at full employment, an increase in government spending must crowd out consumption. True or false? Explain.

10. In an open economy, increases in government spending can crowd out consumption, investment, or _____.

11. Compared to other countries, does the United States have a relatively high or low share of consumption spending in GDP?

Using the TOOLS

In this chapter, we developed several tools, including labor demand, labor supply, and the short-run production function. Using these tools, we developed a model of potential output. Here are four problems that test and extend your understanding of the tools developed in this chapter.

1. Payroll Tax for a Health Program

To finance a health care program, the government places a 10% payroll tax on all labor that is hired.

a. Show how this shifts the demand for labor.

b. If the labor supply function is vertical, what are the effects on real wages, output, and employment? Explain why economists say that labor bears the full burden of the tax in this case.

c. If the labor supply were horizontal, what would be the effects on wages, output, and employment?

2. Too Quick a Conclusion?

A journalist noticed that wages had fallen and wrote that the quantity of labor demanded must have fallen. Do you think he may have jumped to a premature conclusion? What key piece of evidence would help you to determine whether he was right or wrong?

3. Twin Deficits

In the early 1980s in the United States, government spending increased and taxes decreased, resulting in government budget deficits. Soon, a trade deficit emerged. These two deficits—government budget and trade deficits—were called the twin deficits. Explain how the spending increases and tax cuts that caused the budget deficit might cause a trade deficit to emerge. (Hint: Think about crowding out in the open economy.)

4. Would a Subsidy for Wages Necessarily Increase Employment?

Suppose the government paid a subsidy to firms for hiring workers; that is, it paid them an amount for every worker they hired. Using supply and demand diagrams, show how this could possibly lead to higher wages but no increase in employment. Under what circumstances would employment increase the most?

Summary

In this chapter, we analyzed the classical model of full employment. In this model, the level of GDP is determined by the supply of factors of production, labor, and capital. We focused on how the economy operates when it is at full employment; in later chapters, we consider economic fluctuations. Here are the main points from this chapter:

1. Full employment or potential output is the level of GDP produced from a given supply of capital when the labor market is in equilibrium. Potential out-

put is fully determined by the supply of factors of production in the economy.

2. Increases in the stock of capital raise the level of full-employment output and real wages.

3. Increases in the supply of labor will raise the level of full-employment output but lower the level of real wages.

4. The classical model has many applications. Many economists use it to study the effects of taxes on

potential output. Others have found it useful in understanding economic fluctuations.

5. At full employment, increases in government spending must come at the expense of other components of GDP. In a closed economy, either consumption or investment must be crowded out. In an open economy, net exports can be crowded out as well. Decreases in government spending will crowd in other types of spending.

Key Terms

aggregate production function, 453
classical economics, 452
closed economy, 465
crowding out, 464
full-employment output, 459

income effect, 456
labor, 453
Laffer curve, 462
open economy, 467
real business cycle theory, 463

real wage, 455
short-run production function, 454
stock of capital, 453
substitution effect, 456
supply-siders, 452

Problems and Discussion Questions

1. Economists who are interested in the damage that taxation can do to the economy often discuss the labor market in Europe, where there are high payroll taxes and employment growth has been low. Why are they interested in this case?

2. Suppose economist A claims that the natural rate of unemployment is 4%, while economist B claims that it's 5%. Which economist will estimate a higher value for potential output?

3. Explain why labor unions might be interested in limiting the employment of young workers.

4. Some economists have argued that while immigration does not have a major impact on the overall level of wages, it does increase the wage gap between high school graduates and college graduates. Can you explain the wage gap?

5. Studies have shown that U.S. towns near the border with Mexico have lower wages than towns farther away. Can you explain why?

6. Let's say the labor supply curve is close to vertical. Explain why cutting payroll tax rates will not increase the total revenue the government receives from the payroll tax.

7. Draw a graph to show how a real business cycle economist would explain an economic boom. According to real business cycle theory, how do real wages behave during recessions and booms?

8. Some Japanese economists have argued that we should limit the use of our credit cards in the

United States to increase our rate of investment. Explain why they say this.

9. At one time, labor economists found that married women had relatively flat labor supply curves, which are very sensitive to real wages. Do you believe that married women still have relatively flat labor curves today?

10. In some societies, it is a custom for the bride's family to give a gift having very large monetary value to the family of the groom. How might this affect the savings rate in those societies?

11. Suppose that a country has very limited opportunities for successful investment projects but that the population has a high savings rate. Explain why this country is likely to have a large trade surplus.

12. Web Exercise. Go to the Web site for the Congressional Budget Office (*http://www.cbo.gov*) and find a study that explores the effects of taxation on economic behavior and on total tax revenue.

13. Web Exercise. Edward Prescott is one of the leaders of the real business cycle school. Several of his influential papers are on the Web site of The Federal Reserve Bank of Minneapolis (*http://research.mpls.frb.fed.us/research/economists/ecp.html*). Read his article "Theory Ahead of Measurement." What is the key message he is trying to convey?

We invite you to visit the O'Sullivan/Sheffrin page on the Prentice Hall Web site at:
http://www.prenhall.com/osullivan/
for additional World Wide Web exercises for this chapter.

Model Answers for This Chapter

Chapter-Opening Questions

1. Increased immigration will typically lower real wages while increasing the level of output in the economy.

2. Increased investment will mean a higher capital stock in the future. The higher stock of capital will allow a higher standard of living.

3. If employers are required to pay higher taxes for hiring labor, wages will fall; typically, employment and GDP will fall as well. As the chapter explains, the amount that employment and GDP fall depends on how sensitive labor supply is to real wages.

4. In a closed economy (not open to trade) operating at full employment, increased government spending must lead to reduced spending on either consumption or investment. In an open economy (which allows for trade), higher government spending could lead to a reduction in net exports.

Test Your Understanding

1. An aggregate production function shows the relationships between inputs and outputs in the economy.

2. Decreases.

3. Upward.

4. Supplied.

5. The demand curve slopes downward because when wages are lower, the firm will want to hire more labor. The supply curve slopes upward because at higher wages, more people will seek employment.

6. Right.

7. Right.

8. Draw 2 graphs in which the demand curve shifts equally to the right in both but the supply curve shifts more to the right in the graph for the United States.

9. False. Investment could also be crowded out.

10. Net exports.

11. It is high.

Using the Tools

1. Payroll Tax for a Health Program
   a. The tax will shift the labor demand curve to the left. At any wage, the employer's cost is 10% greater. The employer will hire less labor at any wage, since labor has become more expensive.
   b. The demand for labor shifts to the left, lowering the real wage. Since the labor supply curve is vertical, the amount of labor supplied does not change, nor does total output. Labor bears the full burden of the tax because wages fall by the total amount of the tax.
   c. If the supply of labor were horizontal, the decrease in labor demand would not reduce real wages but would reduce employment. Full-employment output would fall as well.

2. Too Quick a Conclusion? The piece of evidence you would like to have is the change in the quantity of employment. If the quantity of employment fell along with wages, the demand curve shifted to the left and the demand of labor fell. But if the quantity of employment increased along with the fall in wages, this is best explained by an increase in the supply of labor, that is, a rightward shift in the labor supply curve.

3. Twin Deficits. The increase in government spending would crowd out net exports. The tax cut would also lead to higher consumer spending on imports. The result is less exports and more imports, or a trade deficit.

4. Would a Subsidy to Wages Necessarily Increase Employment? A subsidy is the reverse of a tax. A subsidy for hiring labor would shift the firm's demand curve to the right. If the supply of labor were vertical (that is, not sensitive to the real wage), the subsidy would raise wages but not employment. The subsidy would be most effective in raising employment if the supply curve for labor were relatively flat.

23

Why Do Economies Grow?

To understand what economic growth means, consider how the typical American lived in 1783, seven years after the Declaration of Independence was written. According to economic historian Stanley Lebergott, an average U.S. home at that time had no central heat, one fireplace, no plumbing, no hot water, and toilets that were outdoor shacks surrounding a hole in the ground. The lack of plumbing meant that hygiene was not like it is today: Well into the nineteenth century, a typical farmer took a bath once a week. Houses had no electricity or gas; a solitary candle provided light at night. There were no refrigerators, no toasters, or any appliances. Bedrooms contained no furniture other than a bed (with no springs); two people slept in what we now consider a single bed. For women, things were particularly hard. They were expected to bake over half a ton of bread a year, kill chickens, and butcher hogs, as well as prepare all vegetables. Canned foods were not readily available until a century later. And you really don't want to hear about medical "science" in those days.[1]

ur living standards are dramatically different today because there has been a remarkable growth in GDP per person. Growth in GDP is perhaps the most critical aspect of a country's economic performance. Over long periods, there is no other way to raise the standard of living in an economy.

With the tools developed in this chapter, here are some questions we can answer:

1. **What countries have the highest living standards today?**
2. **Do countries with high savings rates have faster rates of GDP growth?**
3. **Do trade deficits help or hinder economic growth?**
4. **What factors determine technological progress?**

The chapter begins by looking at some data from both rich and poor countries over the last 30 years. We will see how GDP per capita (meaning per person—every man, woman, and child) compare over this period.

We then look at how growth occurs. Economists believe that there are two basic mechanisms that increase GDP per capita over the long term. One is **capital deepening**, increases in an economy's stock of capital—its total stock of plant and equipment—relative to its workforce. **Technological progress** is the other mechanism by which economies can grow. To economists technological progress specifically means that an economy operates more efficiently, producing more output, but without using any more inputs. In other words, the economy gets more output without any more capital or labor. Technological progress does occur and is a key element of economic growth. We examine different theories of the origins of technological progress and discuss how to measure its overall importance for the economy.

Finally, we discuss in detail the role of education and investments in human beings in fostering economic development.

The appendix to this chapter contains a simple model of capital deepening known as the Solow model. It shows how increases in capital per worker lead to economic growth. It will also allow us to better understand the role of technological progress in sustaining economic growth.

Capital deepening: Increase in the stock of capital per worker.

Technological progress: An increase in output without increasing inputs.

The Diversity of Economic Experience

Throughout the world, there are vast differences in standards of living and in rates of economic growth. To understand these differences, we first need to look at the concepts and the tools economists use to study economic growth. With these concepts and tools, we will be equipped to understand the data that measures economic growth.

Measuring Economic Growth

From earlier chapters, we know that real GDP measures in constant prices the total value of final goods and services in a country. Since countries differ in the size of their populations, we want to know what is a country's real GDP per person, or its **real GDP per capita**.

Real GDP per capita typically grows over time. A convenient way to describe the changes in real GDP per capita is growth rates. The **growth rate** of a variable is the percentage change in that variable from one period to another. For example, calculate the growth rate of real GDP from year 1 to year 2. Suppose real GDP was 100 in year 1 and 104 in year 2. The growth rate of real GDP is

Real GDP per capita: Gross domestic product per person adjusted for changes in prices. It is the usual measure of living standards across time and between countries.

Growth rate: The percentage change of a variable.

$$
\begin{aligned}
\text{growth rate, } \textbf{in percent} &= [(\text{GDP in year 2} - \text{GDP in year 1}) \,/\, \text{GDP in year 1}] \times 100 \\
&= [(104 - 100) \,/\, 100] \times 100 \\
&= [4 \,/\, 100] \times 100 \\
&= [0.04] \times 100 = 4\% \text{ per year}
\end{aligned}
$$

Real GDP grew by 4% per year.

If we know the growth rate and the initial value for GDP, we can also calculate the value for the next period, assuming that the past growth rate continues into the next period. Here is the simple formula that links the growth rate, g, and the values of GDP for one period and the following period:

$$\text{GDP year 2} = (1 + g) \times \text{GDP year 1}$$

GDP in the second year is the product of GDP in the first year times the sum of 1 plus the growth rate.

Example: If the growth rate for GDP were 0.04 (that is, 4% per year) and GDP in year 1 were 100, then

$$\text{GDP year 2} = (1 + 0.04)(100)$$
$$= 104$$

We can apply the formula for growth rates between longer periods.

Suppose an economy started at a level of 100 in year 1 and grew at a rate g for two periods.

From the first year to the second year, output would be $(1 + g)(100)$.

From the second and to the third year, output would again grow by $(1 + g)$. To calculate output in the third year, we need to multiply $(1 + g)$ times output in the second year:

$$(1 + g)[(1 + g)(100)] = (1 + g)^2(100)$$

Example: If the economy grew at 4% per year for two years, then in the second year real GDP would be $(1 + 0.04)(100)$, or 104. In the third year, real GDP would be $(1.04)[(1.04)(100)] = 108.2$.

We can use this idea repeatedly if the economy grows at the same rate for several years. If the economy started at 100 and grew at rate g for n years, then the formula for real GDP after n years would be

$$\text{GDP } [n \text{ year later}] = (1 + g)^n(100)$$

Example: The economy starts at 100 and grows at a rate of 4% a year for 10 years. Output after 10 years will be

$$\text{GDP } [10 \text{ years later}] = (1 + 0.04)^{10}(100) = (1.04)^{10}(100) = (1.48)(100)$$
$$= 148$$

which is nearly 50% higher than in the first year.

Here's a rule of thumb to help you understand the power of growth rates. Suppose you know the growth rate of real GDP and it is constant, but you want to know how many years it will take until the level of real GDP doubled. The answer is given by the **rule of 70**:

$$\text{years to double} = 70/(\text{percentage growth rate})$$

Rule of 70: If an economy grows at x percent per year, output will double in $70/x$ years.

Example: For an economy that grew at 5% a year, it would take

$$70/5 = 14 \text{ years}$$

for real GDP to double. (In case you were curious, the rule of 70 is derived by using the mathematics of logarithms.)

Making comparisons of real GDP across countries is difficult. Every country has its own currency and its own price system. In the United States, we quote prices in dollars, the French use francs, the British use pounds, and the Israelis use shekels. In addition, consumption patterns are different across countries. For example, because land is scarce in Japan, people live in much smaller spaces than do residents of the United States.

Fortunately, a team of economists led by Robert Summers and Alan Heston of the University of Pennsylvania has devoted decades to developing methods for measuring real GDP across countries. They have published statistics that take into account the difficulties in comparing real GDP across countries with different currencies and different consumption patterns. Their methods are designed to measure true variations in the cost of living across countries.

How do they do it? Teams of economists collect vast amounts of data on prices of comparable goods in all countries. They try to ensure that the goods are of identical quality, but if not, they make appropriate adjustments, such as making allowances for the different size and quality of automobiles. They then use the prices of all these goods in different countries to express the GDP of each country in U.S. prices.

Consider a simple example: Suppose, in the United States 1 gallon of milk costs $2.00, while in Germany 1 gallon of milk costs 4.0 marks (the currency of Germany). With respect to a gallon of milk, $2.00 in the United States is equivalent to 4.0 marks in Germany, and $0.50 is equivalent to 1 mark ($2.00/4 marks = $0.50/mark). If German consumers spend 10 million marks on milk in a given year, that amount is equivalent to spending $5 million (10 million marks × $0.50/mark) in U.S. prices. German consumption of milk is then $5 million measured in U.S. currency.

We can do similar calculations for all final goods and services in Germany, calculating for each good, one at a time. Each calculation converts German purchases of a good or service in marks to an equivalent amount in U.S. dollars. Adding up all the final goods and services gives us German GDP in U.S. prices. If we do these calculations using constant U.S. prices (say, from 1997), we obtain measures of real German GDP in constant U.S. dollars. Most economists view this method, which uses vast amounts of price data and proceeds on a commodity-by-commodity basis, as the best method for comparing standards of living across countries.

Exchange rate: The rate at which one currency trades for another.

According to these measures, the country with the highest level of income in 1997 was Luxembourg; its real GDP per capita was $33,119. The United States was second; its

A CLOSER LOOK   Why Switzerland is Not Number One

Every so often, an economist will say that the U.S. per capita GDP has fallen far behind that of other countries; usually, Switzerland is the example. Here is how that economist might argue: In 1997, GDP per capita in Switzerland was 52,252 Swiss francs. The **exchange rate**—the rate at which one currency trades for another—between the U.S. dollar and the Swiss franc in that year was 1.46 Swiss francs per dollar. If we use this exchange rate, Swiss GDP per capita in U.S. dollars is $35,789 (52,252 Swiss francs/1.46 Swiss francs per dollar). This is nearly 25% higher than the 1997 U.S. GDP per capita of $29,010.

This calculation is misleading, because it is wrong to use the exchange rate between the two currencies to translate Swiss GDP to U.S. dollars. As we will discuss in a later chapter, exchange rates are deter-mined in financial markets and reflect the demand and supply for goods that are traded between countries as well as financial flows—such as the purchases of stocks and bonds—between countries. Exchange rates do not reflect the value of the goods that determine living standards—such as housing—but are not traded. Moreover, the Swiss francs are also more expensive because Switzerland tries to attract foreign funds through its efficient and secure banking system.

If we use methods that account for both goods that are traded and those that are not, Switzerland has a GDP per capita today that is about 90% that of the U.S. GDP per capita. This is a very high level by world standard but still less than the GDP per capita of the United States.

real GDP per capita was $29,010. It is important to use the methods of Heston and Summers to compare living standards across countries, as "A Closer Look: Why Switzerland Is Not Number One," explains.

Growth Rates and Patterns of Growth

Table 23.1 lists real GDP per capita for 1997 and average annual growth rate of real GDP per capita between 1960 and 1997 for 11 countries. Japan, with a GDP per capita of $24,070, follows the United States. Not far behind are France, Italy, and the United Kingdom. More representative of typical countries were Mexico and Costa Rica, with GDPs per capita in 1997 of $8,370 and $6,650, respectively. This is less than one-third of GDP per capita in the United States. The very poor countries have extremely low GDP per capita. India, for example, had a GDP per capita of $1,670—6% of the GDP per capita of the United States.

In the third column of Table 23.1, notice the differences in growth rates. Consider Japan. In 1960 Japan had a GDP per capita that was one-half France's and one-fourth the United States' GDP per capita. But Japan's GDP per capita grew at 4.87% per year, compared to 2.09% for the United States and 2.76% for France. To place Japan's growth rate for this period into perspective, recall the rule of 70. If an economy grows at an average annual rate of x percent a year, it takes $70/x$ years for output to double. In Japan's case, per capita output was doubling every $70/4.87$ years, or approximately every 14 years. At this rate, from the time someone is born to the time that person reaches the age of 28, living standards have increased by a factor of four—an extraordinary rate of growth.

One question economists ask is whether poorer countries can close the gap between their level of GDP per capita and the GDP per capita of richer countries. Closing this gap is called **convergence**. To converge, poorer countries have to grow at more rapid rates than richer countries are growing. Since 1960 Japan, Italy, and France all have grown more rapidly than the United States and have narrowed the gap in per capita incomes.

Convergence: The process by which poorer countries catch up with richer countries in terms of real GDP per capita.

For a more extensive look at the evidence, Figure 23.1 plots for 16 currently developed countries the average growth rate from 1870 to 1979 versus the level of GDP in 1870. The line through the points slopes downward, which means that countries with higher levels of GDP in 1870 grew more slowly than countries with lower levels of GDP;

Table 23.1 GDP per Capita and Economic Growth

Country	GDP per Capita in 1997 Dollars	Average per Capita Growth Rate, 1960–1997 (%)
United States	$29,010	2.09
Japan	24,070	4.87
France	22,030	2.76
Italy	20,290	3.10
United Kingdom	20,730	2.10
Mexico	8,370	2.31
Costa Rica	6,650	2.42
Pakistan	1560	1.05
Zimbabwe	2,350	1.48
India	1,670	1.76
Zambia	960	−1.30

Source: World Bank Development Indicators, 1999.

Cell phones are a sign of economic growth throughout the entire world.

in other words, there was a tendency for countries with lower levels of initial income to grow faster and thus catch up. Depending on which countries we look at, there seems to have been convergence among the currently developed countries.

If we compare the less developed countries to the advanced industrial countries, the picture is not so clear. While Pakistan grew at a faster rate than the United States, its neighbor India grew only 1.76% per year and fell farther behind advanced economies. In

Figure 23.1
Countries with Lower Income in 1870 Grew Faster

Source: M. Obstfeld and K. Rogoff, *Foundation of International Macroeconomics* (Cambridge, MA: MIT Press, 1996), Table 7.1.

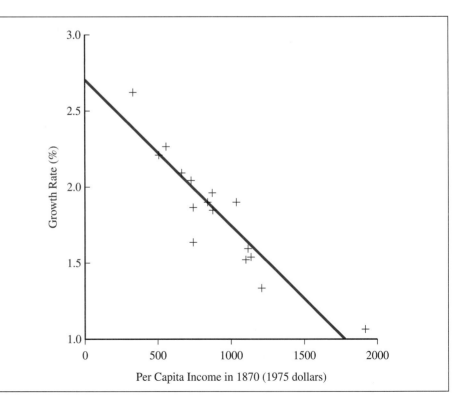

Africa GDP per capita fell substantially in Zambia, while in Zimbabwe GDP per capita grew at a slower rate than the U.S. rate.

Economists who have studied the process of economic growth in detail find weak evidence that poorer countries are closing the gap in per capita income with richer countries. On average, it does not appear that poorer countries grow at substantially higher rates than richer countries are growing. Although there are some success stories, such as Japan and other Asian economies, including Hong Kong and Singapore, there are also economies such as Zambia's that have regressed.

The rule of 70 reinforces how important are small differences in economic growth. A per capita GDP growth rate of 5% a year means that the living standard doubles in 14 years. With only 1% growth, doubling would take 70 years.

TEST You Understanding

1. What measure of output do we use to measure living standards across countries with populations of different sizes?

2. How would we convert spending on TV sets in France to U.S. dollars?

3. Economists who have studied economic growth find only weak evidence for convergence. True of false? Explain.

4. At a 2% annual growth rate in GDP per capita, how many years would it take for GDP per capita to double?

Capital Deepening

One of the most important mechanisms of economic growth economists have identified is increases in the amount of capital per worker: capital deepening.

In Chapter 22, we studied the effects of an increase in capital in a full-employment economy. Figure 23.2 shows the effects on output and real wages. For simplicity, the supply of labor is assumed not to be affected by real wages and is drawn as a vertical line. The additional capital shifts the production function upward because more output can be produced from the same amount of labor. In addition, firms increase their demand for labor because the marginal benefit from employing labor will increase.

Panel B shows how the increase in capital raises the demand for labor and increases real wages. As firms increase their demand and compete for the fixed supply of labor, they will bid up real wages in the economy. In panel A, we show how the increase in the amount of capital in the economy shifts the production function upward and allows more output to be produced for any level of labor input. With a given supply of labor, increases in the stock of capital both raise real wages and lead to increases in output.

An economy is better off with an increase in the stock of capital. With additions to the stock of capital, workers will enjoy higher wages, and total GDP in the economy will increase. Workers are more productive because each worker has more capital at his or her disposal.

But how does an economy increase its stock of capital per worker?

Saving and Investment

Let's begin with the simplest case: an economy with a constant population, producing at full employment, that has no government or foreign sector. In this simple economy, output can be purchased only by consumers or by firms. In other words, output consists solely of consumption and investment. At the same time, this output generates an

Figure 23.2

Increase in the Supply of Capital

An increase in the supply of capital will shift the production function upward and increase the demand for labor. Real wages will increase form W^* to W^{**}, and potential output will increase from Y^* to Y^{**}.

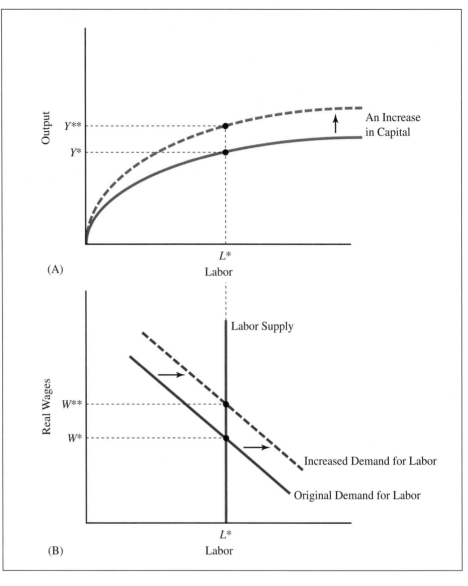

(A)

(B)

Saving: Total income minus consumption.

amount of income that is equivalent to the amount of output. Any income that is not consumed we call **saving**. In this economy, saving must equal investment. Here's why: By definition, consumption plus saving equals income:

$$C + S = Y$$

but at the same time income—which is equivalent to output—also equals consumption plus investment:

$$C + I = Y$$

Thus, saving must equal investment:

$$S = I$$

This means that whatever consumers decide to save goes directly into investment.

Next, we need to link the level of investment in the economy to the stock of capital in the economy. The stock of capital depends on two factors. The stock of capital increases with any gross investment spending but decreases with any depreciation. (Recall that *gross* means "before taking depreciation into account.") For example, suppose the stock of capital at the beginning of the year is $100. During the year, if there were $10 in gross investment and $4 in depreciation, the capital stock at the end of the year would be $106 (= $100 + $10 − $4).

It may be helpful to picture this as being like a bathtub. The level of water in a bathtub (the stock of capital) depends on the flow of water into the bathtub through the input faucet (gross investment) minus the flow of water out of the bathtub down the drain (depreciation). As long as the flow in exceeds the flow out, the water level in the bathtub (the stock of capital) will increase.

Higher saving, which leads to higher gross investment, will therefore tend to increase the stock of capital available for production. As the stock of capital grows, however, there typically will be more depreciation, because there is more capital to depreciate. It is the difference between gross investment and depreciation, which is net investment, that ultimately determines the change in the stock of capital for the economy and therefore the level of real wages and real output. In our example net investment is $10 − $4 = $6.

Population Growth, Government, and Trade

So far we've considered the simplest economy. Let's consider a more realistic economy with population growth, government, and trade.

First, consider the effects of population growth. A larger labor force will allow the economy to produce more total output. However, with a fixed amount of capital and an increasing labor force, the amount of capital per worker will be less. With less capital per worker, output per worker will also tend to be less because each worker has fewer machines to use. This is an illustration of the principle of diminishing returns.

PRINCIPLE OF DIMINISHING RETURNS

> **Suppose that output is produced with two or more inputs and that we increase one input while holding the other inputs fixed. Beyond some point—called the point of diminishing returns— output will increase at a decreasing rate.**

Consider India, which has the world's second largest population, approaching one billion people. Although India has a large labor force, the amount of capital per worker is low. With sharp diminishing returns to labor, per capita output in India will tend to be low.

The government can affect the process of capital deepening in several ways through its policies of spending and taxation. Suppose the government taxed its citizens so that it could fight a war, pay its legislators higher salaries, or give foreign aid to needy countries. The higher taxes will reduce total income. If consumers save a fixed fraction of their income, total private saving (savings from the nongovernmental sector) will fall. In these cases the government is not investing the funds it collects, putting those funds into capital formation. Instead, it is draining from the private sector saving that would have been used for capital deepening. The overall result is a reduction of total investment in the economy and less capital deepening. In these examples the government is taxing the private sector to engage in consumption spending, not investment.

Now suppose the government took all the tax revenues and invested them in valuable infrastructure such as roads, buildings, and airports. Suppose consumers were saving 20% of their incomes. If the government took a dollar in taxes, private saving would fall by 20 cents, but government investment would increase by $1. The net result is an increase in total social saving (private plus government) of 80 cents. This would promote capital deepening: In this case the government is taxing its citizens to provide investment.

Finally, the foreign sector can affect capital deepening. An economy can run a trade deficit and import investment goods to aid capital deepening. The United States, Canada, and Australia built their vast railroad systems in the nineteenth century by running trade deficits (selling less goods and services to the rest of the world than they were buying, financing this gap by borrowing) to enable them to purchase the large amount of capital needed to build their rail networks. In these cases, the large trade deficits were valuable for the economy. They enabled growth to occur at more rapid rates through the process of capital deepening. Eventually, these economies had to pay back the funds that were borrowed from abroad by running trade surpluses, selling more goods and services to the rest of the world than they would buy. But since economic growth raised GDP and the wealth of the economy, they could afford to pay back the borrowed funds. Therefore, this was a reasonable strategy for these countries to follow.

Not all trade deficits promote capital deepening, however. Suppose a country ran a trade deficit because it wanted to buy more consumer goods. The country would be borrowing from abroad, but there would be no additional capital deepening, just additional consumption spending. When the country was forced to pay back the funds, there would be no additional GDP to help foot the bill. Society will be poorer in the future when it must pay the bill for what it consumes now—its current consumption.

Limits to Capital Deepening

There are inherent limits to growth through capital deepening. To understand these limits, let's recall that the stock of capital increases only when there is positive net investment. Remember that net investment equals gross investment minus depreciation. Gross investment depends on the rate of saving in the economy. Depreciation depends on the total stock of capital that the economy has in place.

As the economy accumulates capital and the stock of capital increases, there will be an increase in the total amount of depreciation of capital in the economy. We show, in the appendix to this chapter, that as the stock of capital increases, the economy eventually reaches a point where gross investment equals depreciation. At this point, net investment becomes zero and the stock of capital will no longer increase.

Therefore, there is a limit to growth through capital deepening as depreciation eventually catches up to the level of gross investment. While a higher rate of saving can increase the level of real GDP, eventually the process of growth through capital deepening comes to a halt. However, it takes time—decades—for this point to be reached. Capital deepening can be an important source of economic growth for a long time.

TEST Your Understanding

5. Explain why saving must equal investment if we are not taking into account the government sector or the foreign sector.

6. If everything else is held equal, how does an increase in the size of the population affect total and per capita output?

7. If the private sector saves 10% of its income and the government raises taxes by $200 to finance public investments, by how much will total investment—private and public—increase?

8. If a country runs a trade deficit to finance increased current consumption, it will have to reduce consumption in the future to pay back its borrowings. True or false? Explain.

The Key Role of Technological Progress

The other mechanism affecting economic growth is technological progress. Economists use the term technological progress in a very specific way: It means that an economy operates more efficiently by producing more output without using any more inputs.

In practice, technological progress can take many forms. The invention of the light bulb made it possible to read and work indoors at night; the invention of the thermometer assisted doctors and nurses in their diagnoses; and the invention of disposable diapers made life easier at home. All these examples—and you could provide many more—enable society to produce more output without more labor or more capital. With higher output per person, we enjoy a higher standard of living.

Technological progress can be thought of as the birth of new ideas. These new ideas enable us to rearrange our economic affairs and make us more productive. Not all technological innovations are necessarily major scientific breakthroughs; some are much more mundane. Good commonsense ideas from the workers or managers of a business allow it to make more effective use of its capital and labor and to deliver a better product to its consumers at the current price—this is also technological progress. As long as there are new ideas, inventions, and new ways of doing things, the economy can become more productive and per capita output can increase.

How Do We Measure Technological Progress?

If someone asked you how much of the increase in your standard of living were due to technological progress, how would you answer?

Robert Solow, a Nobel laureate in economics from the Massachusetts Institute of Technology, developed a method for measuring technological progress in an economy. As is usual with good ideas, his theory was simple. It was based on the idea of a production function.

You know from Chapter 22 that the production function links inputs to outputs:

$$Y = F(K, L)$$

where output (Y) is produced from capital (K) and labor (L), which are linked through the production function F. What Solow did was include in the production function some measure of technological progress, A:

$$Y = F(K, L, A)$$

Increases in A represent technological progress. Higher values of A mean that more output is produced from the same level of inputs K and L. If we could find some way to measure A, we could estimate how much technological progress affected output.

Solow noted that over any period, we can observe increases in capital, labor, and output. Using these, we can measure technological progress indirectly. We first ask how much of the change in output can be explained by contributions from the changes in the amount of inputs—capital and labor—that are used. Whatever growth we cannot explain must have been caused by increases in technological progress. The method that Solow developed for determining the contributions to economic growth from increased capital, labor, and technological progress is called **growth accounting**.

Following this basic approach, Table 23.2 contains a breakdown of the sources of growth for the U.S. economy for 1929 to 1982. Figure 23.3 shows the relative contributions of the sources of growth based on these data. Over 1929 to 1982 total output grew at a rate of nearly 3%. Because capital and labor growth are measured at 0.56% and 1.34%, respectively, the remaining portion of output growth, 1.02%, must be due to technological progress. That means that approximately 35% of output growth comes directly from technological progress.

Growth accounting: A method to determine the contribution to economic growth from increased capital, labor, and technological progress.

Figure 23.3

Percentage Contributions to Real GDP Growth

Source: Data from Edward F. Denison, *Trends in Economic Growth 1929–82* (Washington, DC: The Brookings Institution, 1985).

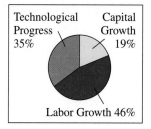

Technological Progress 35%

Capital Growth 19%

Labor Growth 46%

Table 23.2 Sources of Real GDP Growth, 1929–1982
(average annual percentage rates)

Due to capital growth	0.56
Due to labor growth	1.34
+ technological progress	1.02
Output growth	2.92

Source: Edward F. Denison, *Trends in Economic Growth 1929–82*
(Washington, DC: The Brookings Institution, 1985).

Growth Accounting: Two Examples

Growth accounting is a useful tool for understanding different aspects of economic growth. Here are two examples of how economists use growth accounting.

Singapore and Hong Kong

Singapore and Hong Kong have both had phenomenal post–World War II economic growth. From 1980 to 1985 each grew at a rate of approximately 6% a year. But a closer examination, by Alwyn Young of the University of Chicago, revealed that the sources of growth in each were very different.[2] In Singapore nearly all the growth was accounted for by increases in labor and capital. In particular, the ratio of investment to GDP reached as high as 43% in 1983.

Hong Kong had a much lower investment rate—approximately 20% of GDP—and technological progress made an important contribution. This meant that the residents of Hong Kong could enjoy the same level of GDP but consume, not save, a higher fraction of GDP. Residents of Hong Kong were enjoying higher consumption than residents of Singapore were, despite the similarity in growth rates.

The difference in the sources of economic growth between Singapore and Hong Kong may also have important implications for future growth. As we explained a moment ago, there are natural limits to growth through capital deepening. Singapore increased its GDP by increasing its labor inputs and increasing its stock of capital. Eventually, Singapore will find it difficult to keep increasing inputs to production. Economic leaders became concerned that unless they managed to increase their rate of technological progress, their long-term growth prospects would not be strong.

In Hong Kong, there is a different concern. Now that Hong Kong is part of China, residents hope the Chinese will allow them to continue to maintain their free and open economy in which technological progress has flourished. Technological progress has been the driving force for growth in Hong Kong, where there is a strong desire to maintain the system that produced technological innovation.

**ECONOMIC
DETECTIVE**

Labor productivity: Output per
hour of work.

Explaining the Slowdown in Labor Productivity

One of the common statistics reported about the U.S. economy is **labor productivity**. Defined as output per hour of work, labor productivity is a simple measure of how much a typical worker can produce given the amount of capital in the economy and the state of technological progress. Since 1973, there has been a slowdown in the growth of labor productivity in the United States and other countries in the world. Table 23.3 shows U.S. productivity growth for different periods since World War II. The table shows productivity growth slowed in the late 1960s and then during the oil price shocks of the 1970s and

Table 23.3 U.S. Annual Productivity Growth, 1947–1998

Years	Annual Growth Rate (%)
1947–1955	2.9
1955–1968	2.5
1968–1973	1.5
1973–1980	0.4
1980–1986	1.1
1986–1994	1.0
1994–1998	1.4

Source: Economic Report of the President (Washington, DC: U.S. Government
Printing Office, 1999).

has not fully recovered to its prior levels. Productivity growth in the United States is
approximately 1.4% today, compared to growth rates over 2% in the 1950s and 1960s.

Similar patterns have been observed in other countries. Zvi Grilliches, a Harvard
economist and expert on productivity, compared the growth of output per hour in the
manufacturing for 12 countries over different periods.[3] If we use his data and compare
the periods 1960 to 1973 and 1979 to 1986, we find that productivity growth slowed in
11 of 12 countries. In Japan, it fell from 10.3% to 5.6%; in Canada, it fell from 4.5% to
1.4%. Only the United Kingdom exhibited any increase in productivity growth over
those periods, and that increase was only from 4.3% to 4.4%.

The slowdown in productivity growth has also meant slower growth in real wages
and in GDP in the United States since 1973. Figure 23.4 plots real hourly earnings for
U.S. workers; it shows that real hourly earnings have fallen since 1973. Total compensa-

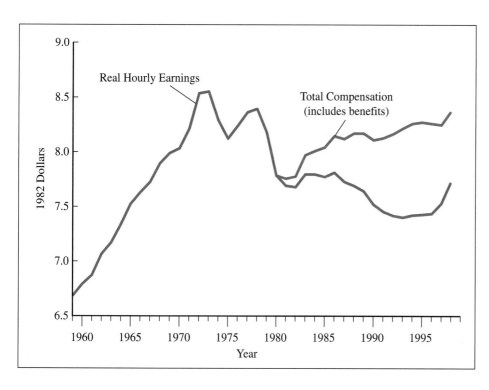

Figure 23.4
Real Hourly Earnings and Total Compensation in the United States

Source: Economic Report of the President (Washington, DC: U.S. Government Printing Office, 1999), Tables B47 and B48.

tion, which includes employee benefits such as health insurance, did continue to rise through the 1980s as employees received lower wages but higher benefits. But the rate of growth of total compensation was less than the growth of real hourly earnings in the pre-1973 period.

The decrease in the growth of labor productivity was the primary factor behind this pattern of real wages, because wages can rise with a growing labor force only if output per worker continues to increase. What can explain this decrease in the growth rate? Economists are not short of possible answers. The factors, they say, are declines in the education and skills of the workforce, lower levels of investment and thus a lower level of capital, less spending on infrastructure (such as highways and bridges), and the belief that managers of companies are more concerned with producing short-term profits than long-term profits, among lots of other economic and sociological factors as well.

Growth accounting has been used to narrow the range of plausible explanations. Using growth accounting methods, economists typically find that the slowdown in labor productivity, in the United States and abroad, cannot be explained by reduced rates of capital deepening. Nor can they be explained by changes in the quality or experience of the labor force. Either a slowdown in technological progress or other factors that are not directly included in the analysis, such as higher worldwide energy prices, must be responsible for the slowdown. Moreover, since the slowdown has been worldwide, it's possible that factors that affect all countries (such as higher energy prices) are responsible rather than factors specific to a single country. Dale Jorgenson, a Harvard economist, has conducted extensive research attempting to link higher energy prices to the slowdown in productivity growth. Not all economists accept this view, however, and the productivity slowdown remains a bit of a mystery. ◆

Yet another mystery surrounding productivity has baffled many economists. Since the late 1980s, firms have invested heavily in computers and, more broadly, in advanced information technology. By 1996, nearly 40% of all equipment investment has been in information technology. Despite this introduction of modern technology, we have yet to see the gains in terms of productivity. There are several explanations for the failure of productivity growth to increase despite this rapid investment in new technology.

First, it may take much longer, decades maybe, before new technology is used in ways that really increase our output. Paul David, an economic historian who teaches at Oxford and Stanford, has noted that it took nearly 40 years after the electric dynamo began to be used in the 1880s before there were significant productivity gains in the economy.[4]

Second, and related to the first, is that at the current time, computers may be useful, but they have not revolutionized our lives as did the introduction of electricity, automobiles, or the airplane. Although computers may allow us to process information rapidly, for many people computers are just a gadget.

Third, it may be that computers have improved productivity but we are failing to measure it. Economists find it difficult to measure the quality of outputs in the service industries, where much of the investment in computers has occurred. For example, most of us now obtain cash from cash machines without waiting in long lines inside a bank. We also communicate much more rapidly through e-mail. Yet these increases in convenience are difficult to measure in conventional GDP accounting.

What Causes Technological Progress?

Because technological progress is an important source of growth, we want to know how it occurs and what government policies can do to promote it. Economists have identified a variety of factors that may influence the pace of technological progress in an economy.

Research and Development in Fundamental Science

One way to induce more technological progress in an economy is to pay for it. If the government or large firms employ workers and scientists to advance the frontiers in physics, chemistry, and biology, their work can lead to technological progress in the long run. Figure 23.5 presents data on the spending on research and development as a percent of GDP for each of seven major countries for 1995. Although the United States spends the most in total on research and development, as a percent of GDP it spends somewhat less than Japan. Moreover, a big part of U.S. spending on research and development is in defense-related areas, unlike in Japan. The United States has the highest percentage of scientists and engineers in the labor force in the world.

But not all technological progress is "high tech." An employee of a soft-drink company who discovers a new and popular flavor for a soft drink is engaged in technological progress, just as scientists and engineers are.

Monopolies That Spur Innovation

The radical notion that monopolies spur innovation was put forth by economist Joseph Schumpeter. In his view a firm will try to come up with new products and more efficient ways to produce products only if it reaps a reward. The reward a firm seeks is high profit from its innovations. And high profit can be obtained only if the firm is the sole seller or monopolist for the product. Other firms will try to break its monopoly through more innovation, a process Schumpeter called **creative destruction**. By allowing firms to compete to be monopolies, society benefits from increased innovation.

Creative destruction: The process by which competition for monopoly profits leads to technological progress.

Governments do allow temporary monopolies for new ideas by issuing patents. A patent allows the inventor of a product to have a monopoly until the term of the patent expires, which in the United States is now 20 years. With a patent, we tolerate some monopoly power (the power to raise prices that comes with limited competition) in the hope of spurring innovation.

A related idea, which is becoming increasingly important in modern society, is the need to protect intellectual property rights. Publishers of both books and computer software face problems of unauthorized copying, particularly in some developing countries.

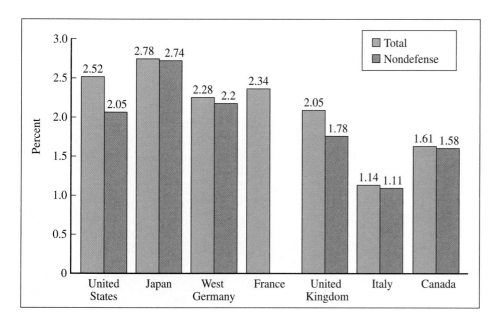

Figure 23.5
Research and Development as a Percentage of GDP, 1995.

Source: National Patterns of R&D Resources Washington, DC: National Science Foundation/SRS (1997).

While the residents of those countries clearly benefit from inexpensive copied software or books, the producers of the software and books in the developed countries will face reduced incentives to enter the market. Large and profitable firms with secure domestic markets may continue to produce despite unauthorized copying, but other firms may be discouraged. The United States has put piracy and unauthorized reproduction among its top agenda items in recent trade talks with several countries.

The Scale of the Market

Adam Smith stressed that the size of a market was important for economic development. In larger markets there are more incentives for firms to come up with new products and new methods of production. Just as Schumpeter suggested, the lure of profits guides the activities of firms, and larger markets enable firms the opportunity to make larger profits. This provides another rationale for free trade. With free trade, markets are larger, and there is more incentive to engage in technological progress.

Induced Innovations

Some economists have emphasized that innovations come about through inventive activity designed specifically to reduce costs. This is known as induced innovation. For example, during the nineteenth century in the United States, the largest single cost in agriculture was wages. Ingenious farmers and inventors came up with many different machines and methods to cut back on the amount of labor required.

Education and the Accumulation of Knowledge

Education can contribute to economic growth in two ways. First, increased knowledge and skills can be a form of investment in human beings that complements our investments in physical capital, as we will see in the next section. Second, education can enable the workforce in an economy to use its skills to develop new ideas or to copy ideas or import them from abroad. Consider a developing country today. In principle, it has at its disposal the vast accumulated knowledge of the developed economies. If it could find a way to tap into this knowledge, it could more quickly and easily adapt their technological progress to its own economies. But this probably requires a broad and skilled workforce—one reason why many developing countries send their best students to educational institutions in developed countries.

For many years, economists who studied technological progress typically did so independently of economists who studied models of economic growth. But starting in the mid-1980s, several economists, including Nobel laureate Robert E. Lucas of the University of

The rate of return to elementary school education in Africa probably exceeds the rate of return to investment in machines and buildings.

Chicago and Paul Romer, now of Stanford University, began to develop models of growth that contained technological progress as essential features. Their work helped to initiate what is known as **new growth theory**, which accounts for technological progress within a model of economic growth. In this field, economists study, for example, how incentives for research and development, new product development, or international trade interact with the accumulation of physical capital. It enables economists to address policy issues, such as whether subsidies for research and development are socially justified and whether policies that place fewer taxes on income earned from investment will spur economic growth or increase economic welfare. Current research in economic growth now takes place within a broad framework that includes explanation of technological progress.

All growth theory today is "new growth theory."

New growth theory: Modern theories of growth that try to explain the origins of technological progress.

Human Capital

Increasing knowledge and skills can be considered a form of **human capital**—an investment in human beings. Many economists, including Nobel laureate Gary Becker of the University of Chicago have studied this in detail.

Human capital: Investment in education and skills.

A classic example of human capital is the investment a student makes to attend college. The costs of attending college consist of the direct out-of-pocket costs (tuition and fees) plus the opportunity costs of forgone earnings. The benefits of attending college are the higher wages and more interesting jobs offered to college graduates as compared to high school graduates. Individuals decide to attend college because these benefits exceed the costs, and it is a rational economic decision. A similar calculation faces a newly graduated doctor who must decide whether to pursue a specialty. Will the forgone earnings of a general physician (which are quite substantial) be worth the time spent learning a specialty that will eventually result in extra income? Investments in health and nutrition can be analyzed within the same framework.

Human capital theory has two implications for understanding economic growth.

First, not all labor is equal. When economists measure the labor input in a country, they must adjust for differing levels of education. These levels of education reflect past investments in education and skills; individuals with higher educational levels will, on average, be more productive.

Second, health and fitness also affect productivity. In developing countries, economists have found that there is a strong correlation between the height of individuals and the wages that they can earn in the farming sector. At the same time, increases in income through economic growth have led to sharp increases in height and weight as "A Closer Look: Our Tiny Ancestors," explains.

Human capital theory can also serve as a basis for important public policy decisions. Should a developing country invest in capital (either public or private) or in education? The poorest developing countries lack many things: good sanitation systems, effective transportation systems, and capital investment for agriculture and industry. However, the best use of investment funds may not be for bridges, sewer systems, and roads but for human capital and education. Studies demonstrate that the returns from investing in education are extremely high in developing countries. The gains from elementary and secondary education, in particular, often exceed the gains from more conventional investments. In developing countries, a person having an extra year in school can often raise his or her wages by 15% to 20% a year.

The returns to investing in the education of females in developing countries are often higher than those for men. This is particularly true in the poorest countries, where female literacy rates are often less than 10%. Women's health in developing countries is closely tied to their education. Education promotes not only productivity but basic social develop-

As you may have seen in a museum, men and women have grown taller and heavier in the last 300 years. As an example, an average American male adult today stands at approximately 5'10", nearly 4.5 inches taller than the typical Englishman in the late eighteenth century. Body weights are also substantially higher today. According to Nobel laureate Robert Fogel of the University of Chicago, the average weight of English males in their thirties was about 134 pounds in 1790—20% below today's average. A typical Frenchman in his thirties at that time weighed only 110 pounds!

Fogel has argued that these lower weights and heights reflected inadequate food supplies and chronic malnutrition. Not only did lower food supplies lead to smaller physical stature, they also led to a higher incidence of chronic disease. Fogel estimated that the chronic malnutrition caused by limited food supplies at those times limited labor productivity. In France, 20% of the labor force lacked enough physical energy to put in more than 3 hours of light work a day. A high percentage of workers in the society were too frail and ill to contribute much to national output.

Economic growth produced a "virtuous" circle. It increaed food supplies, enabling workers to become more productive and increase GDP even more.

ment as well. For these reasons, the World Bank has focused attention on the crucial role that increased female education can play in promoting economic development.

As you see, human capital analysis is a valuable tool for understanding economic growth.

TEST Your Understanding

9. Technological progress means that we produce more output without using any additional inputs. True or false? Explain.

10. Explain how economists estimate the contribution of technological change to the growth of output.

11. Who invented the theory of creative destruction?

12. Define *human capital*.

Using the **TOOLS**

In this chapter, we studied what affects economic growth. Here are some opportunities to do your own economic analysis.

1. Shorten the Length of Patents?
A group of consumer activists claim that drug companies earn excessive profits because of the patents they have on drugs. The activists advocate cutting to five years the length of time that a drug company can hold a patent. They argue this will lead to lower prices for drugs because competitors will enter the market after the five-year period. Do you see any drawbacks to this proposal?

2. Capital Deepening
Which of the following will promote economic growth through capital deepening?

a. Higher taxes used to finance universal health care

b. Increased imports to purchase new VCRs for consumers

c. Increased imports to purchase supercomputers for industry

3. Future Generations
Some economists say that economic growth involves a trade-off between current generations and future generations. If a current generation raises its saving rate, what does it sacrifice? What will be gained for future generations?

4. Will the Poorer Country Catch Up?
Suppose one country has a GDP that is one-eighth the GDP of its richer neighbor. But the poorer country grows at 10% a year, while the richer country grows at 2% a year. In 35 years, which country will have a higher GDP? (Hint: Use the rule of 70.)

Summary

In this chapter, we explored the mechanisms of economic growth. Although economists do not have a complete understanding of what leads to growth, they regard increases in capital per worker, technological progress, and human capital as key factors. In this chapter we discussed these factors in detail. Here are the main points to remember:

1. There are vast differences in per capita GDP throughout the world. There is debate about whether poorer countries in the world are converging in per capita incomes to richer countries.

2. Economies grow through two basic mechanisms: capital deepening and technological progress. Capital deepening is an increase in capital per worker. Technological progress is an increase in output with no additional increases in inputs.

3. Ongoing technological progress will lead to sustained economic growth.

4. A variety of theories try to explain the origins of technological progress and determine how we can promote it. They include spending on research and development, creative destruction, the scale of the market, induced inventions, and education and the accumulation of knowledge.

5. Investments in human capital are an important component of economic growth.

Key Terms

capital deepening, 472
convergence, 474
creative destruction, 485
exchange rate, 473
growth accounting, 481

growth rate, 472
human capital, 487
labor productivity, 482
new growth theory, 487

real GDP per capita, 472
rule of 70, 473
saving, 478
technological progress, 472

Problems and Discussion Questions

1. If a country's GDP grows at 3% per year, how many years will it take for GDP to increase by a factor of four?

2. The growth rate of real GDP per capita equals the growth rate of real GDP minus the growth rate of the population. If the growth rate of population is 1% per year, how fast must real GDP grow for real GDP per capita to double in 14 years?

3. Describe briefly how we can compare GDP per capita in the United Kingdom with GDP per capita in the United States even though the British measure GDP using their own currency, pounds.

4. Explain why the expansion of markets from free trade can lead to increased technological innovation.

5. If we cannot measure every invention or new idea, how can we possibly measure the contribution to growth of technological progress?

6. Even with a high savings rate, there is a natural limit to capital deepening. Why is there a limit?

7. Suppose a government places a 10% tax on incomes and spends half of the money from taxes on investment and half on a public consumption good such as military parades. Individuals save 20% of their income and consume the rest. Does total investment (public and private) increase or decrease in this case?

8. The United States ran large trade deficits during the 1980s and 1990s. How would you determine whether these trade deficits led to increased or decreased capital deepening?

9. Economic historians have found that the average height of individuals in both the United States and the United Kingdom fell during the mid-nineteenth century before rising again. This was a period of rapid industrialization as well as migration into urban areas and foreign immigration. Incomes appeared to continue to rise. What factors do you think might account for this fall in height and how would it affect your evaluation of economic welfare during the period?

10. Most law students tend to be in their twenties and thirties, rather than in their forties. Explain this phenomenon, using the idea of investment in human capital.

11. Web Exercise. The Web site for the National Bureau of Economic Research (*http://www.nber.org*) contains links to online data, including the Penn World Tables. Using these links, compare the relative growth performance for real GDP of Italy, Great Britain, and France (or other countries) over a period of your choice.

12. Web Exercise. Using the Web site for the World Bank (*http://www.worldbank.org*), prepare a short paper on prospects and barriers for economic growth in Africa.

Take It to the Net

We invite you to visit the O'Sullivan/Sheffrin page on the Prentice Hall Web site at:
http://www.prenhall.com/osullivan/
for additional World Wide Web exercises for this chapter.

Model Answers for This Chapter

Chapter-Opening Questions

1. Countries with the highest standard of living today include the United States, Luxembourg, Japan, and Germany.

2. Countries with higher savings rates can grow faster for some period of time, although the growth of per capita income in the long run is determined by the rate of technical progress.

3. A trade deficit that is used to finance investment can lead to higher growth; however, a trade deficit that is used to finance consumption will allow higher consumption now but will reduce consumption in the future.

4. Technological progress depends on a number of factors, including research and development, the process of creative destruction, the scale of the market, induced innovations, and education and the accumulation of knowledge.

Test Your Understanding

1. We use per capita real GDP.

2. Use the prices of identical TV sets in both countries to obtain an "exchange rate" for TV sets. Use this exchange rate to convert French spending on TV sets to U.S. dollars.

3. True. Developing countries have not caught up to developed countries.

4. It would take 35 years (70/2).

5. Output is divided into consumption and investment. Output also equals income. Income is either consumed or saved. Therefore, saving must equal investment.

6. Total output increases, while per capita output falls.

7. $180. Government investment is $200; but with a saving rate of 10%, the $200 in taxes reduces private saving (and private investment) by $20.

8. True. Without using the trade deficit to increase investment, consumption must fall in the future.

9. True. Technological progress means more output without additional inputs.

10. The contribution from technological progress is estimated by determining how much of the growth in output cannot be explained by the growth in inputs.

11. Joseph Schumpeter.

12. Human capital includes investments in education and skills.

Using the Tools

1. Shorten the Length of Patents? The drawback to the proposal is that the shorter patent life will reduce the incentive of drug companies to invest in the discovery of new drugs. As Schumpeter emphasized, firms need incentives in the form of monopoly profits to engage in long-term research. However, prices are clearly higher as long as a single firm has a patent.

2. Capital Deepening. Only c, increased imports to purchase supercomputers for industry, adds to capital deepening. The others will not increase the stock of capital.

3. Future Generations. A country that increases its saving rate must cut back on its consumption. The long-run benefit will be a higher stock of capital for future generations. The current generation, however, will have to make a sacrifice, in terms of reduced consumption, to provide the additional capital. Therefore, there will be a trade-off in consumption between the present generation and future generations.

4. Will the Poorer Country Catch Up? After 35 years, GDP in the initially poorer country will exceed the GDP of its slower growing neighbor. Because the poorer country grows at 10% a year, the rule of 70 implies that its GDP doubles every seven years. In 35 years, its GDP will have doubled five times. This means that its GDP will have grown by a factor of 32 over the 35-year period. According to the rule of 70, the richer country, growing at 2% a year, will only double its GDP in 35 years. This implies that the country that was poorer initially will have a higher level of GDP after 35 years, even though it started at one-eighth the level of the richer country. To see this, suppose that the poorer country had a GDP of 1 and the richer country had a GDP of 8. After 35 years, the initially poorer country would now have a GDP of 32, while the initially richer country would have a GDP of 16.

 **Notes**

1. Stanley Lebergott, *The Americans* (New York: W.W. Norton, 1984), pp. 65–68.

2. Alwyn Young, "A Tale of Two Cities: Factor Accumulation and Technical Change in Hong Kong and Singapore," in *NBER Macroeconomic Annual 1992*, edited by Olivier Blanchard and Stanley Fischer (Cambridge, MA: MIT Press 1992); pp. 1–53.

3. Zvi Grilliches, "Productivity Puzzles and R&D: Another Nonexplanation," *Journal of Economic Perspectives*, vol. 2, Fall 1988, pp. 9–21.

4. Paul David, "The Dynamo and the Computer: An Historical Perspective on the Modern Productivity Paradox," *American Economic Review*, May 1990, pp. 355–61.

A Model of Capital Deepening

Here's a simple model showing the links among saving, depreciation, and capital deepening. Developed by Nobel laureate Robert Solow of the Massachusetts Institute of Technology, the Solow model, will help us understand more fully the critical role technological progress must play in economic growth. In using it, we rely on one of our basic principles of economics to help explain the model as well as make a few simplifying assumptions. We assume constant population and no government or foreign sector. In the chapter we discussed the qualitative effects of population growth, government, and the foreign sector on capital deepening. Here we focus solely on the relationships among saving, depreciation, and capital deepening.

Figure 23A.1 plots the relationship in the economy between output and the stock of capital, holding the labor force constant. Notice that output increases as the stock of capital increases but at a decreasing rate. This is an illustration of the principle of diminishing returns.

PRINCIPLE OF DIMINISHING RETURNS

> **Suppose output is produced with two or more inputs and we increase one input while holding the other inputs fixed. Beyond some point—called the point of diminishing returns—output will increase at a decreasing rate.**

Increasing the stock of capital while holding the labor force constant will increase output, but at a decreasing rate.

As Figure 23A.1 indicates, output increases with the stock of capital. But what causes the stock of capital to increase? The capital stock will increase as long as gross

Figure 23A.1
Diminishing Returns to Capital
Holding labor constant, increases in the stock of capital increases output but at a decreasing rate.

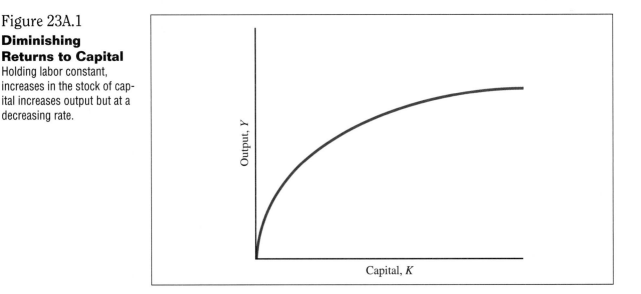

investment exceeds depreciation. Therefore, we need to determine the level of gross investment and the level of depreciation to see how the capital stock changes over time.

Recall that without government or a foreign sector, saving equals gross investment. Thus, to determine the level of investment, we need to specify how much of output is saved and how much is consumed. We will assume that a fraction s of total output (Y) is saved. For example, if $s = 0.20$, then 20% of GDP would be saved and 80% would be consumed. Total saving will be sY, the product of the saving rate and total output.

In panel A of Figure 23A.2, the top curve is total output as a function of the stock of capital. The curve below it represents saving as a function of the stock of capital. Because saving is a fixed fraction of total output, the saving curve is a constant fraction of the output curve. If the saving rate is 0.2, saving will always be 20% of output for any level of the capital stock. Total saving increases in the economy with the stock of capital, but at a decreasing rate.

To complete our model, we need to determine depreciation. Let's say the capital stock depreciates at a constant rate of d per year. If $d = 0.03$, the capital stock would depreciate at 3% a year. If the capital stock were 100 at the beginning of the year, depreciation would equal 3. Total depreciation can be written as dK, where K is the stock of capital.

Panel B of Figure 23A.2 plots total depreciation as a function of the stock of capital. The larger the stock of capital, the more total depreciation there will be. Because the depreciation rate is assumed to be constant, total depreciation as a function of the stock of capital will be a straight line through the origin. Then if there is no capital, there will be no depreciation, no matter what the depreciation rate.

If the depreciation rate is 3% and the stock of capital is 100, depreciation will be 3; if the stock of capital is 200, the depreciation rate will be 6. Plotting these points will give a straight line through the origin.

We are now ready to see how the stock of capital changes:

$$\text{change in the stock of capital} = \text{savings} - \text{depreciation}$$
$$= sY - dK$$

The stock of capital will increase—the change will be positive—as long as total saving in the economy exceeds depreciation.

Figure 23A.3 shows how the Solow model works by plotting output, saving, and depreciation all on one graph. Suppose the economy starts with a capital stock K_0. Then total saving will be given by point A on the saving schedule. Depreciation at the capital stock K_0 is given by point B. Because A lies above B, total saving exceeds depreciation and the capital stock will increase. As the capital stock increases, there will be economic growth through

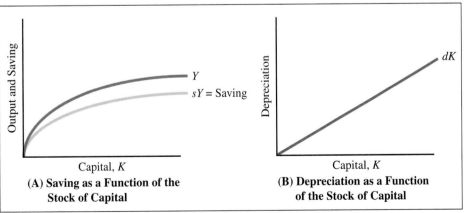

Figure 23A.2

Saving and Depreciation as Functions of the Stock of Capital

(A) Saving as a Function of the Stock of Capital

(B) Depreciation as a Function of the Stock of Capital

Figure 23A.3

Basic Growth Model

Starting at K_0, saving exceeds depreciation. The stock of capital increases. This process continues until the stock of capital reaches its long-run equilibrium at K^*.

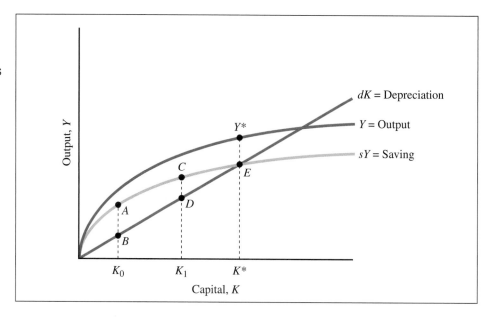

capital deepening. With more capital per worker in the economy, output is higher and real wages increase. The economy benefits from the additional stock of capital.

Using the diagram, we can trace the future for this economy. As the stock of capital increases, we move to the right. When the economy reaches K_1, total saving is at point C and total depreciation is at point D. Because C is still higher than D, saving exceeds depreciation and the capital stock continues to increase. Economic growth continues. Eventually, after many years, the economy reaches capital stock K^*. The level of output in the economy now is Y^*, and the saving and depreciation schedules intersect at point E. Because total saving equals depreciation, the stock of capital no longer increases. The process of economic growth through capital deepening has stopped.

In this simple model, the process of capital deepening must eventually come to an end. As the stock of capital increases, output increases but at a decreasing rate because of diminishing returns. Because saving is a fixed fraction of output, it will also increase but also at a diminishing rate. On the other hand, total depreciation is proportional to the stock of capital. As the stock of capital increases, depreciation will always catch up with total saving in the economy. It may take decades for the process of capital deepening to come to an end. But as long as total saving exceeds depreciation, the process of economic growth through capital deepening will continue.

What would happen if a society saved a higher fraction of its output? Figure 23A.4 shows the consequences of a higher saving rate. Suppose the economy were originally saving at a rate s_1. Eventually, the economy would reach E_1, where saving and depreciation meet. If the economy had started to save at the higher rate s_2, saving would exceed depreciation at K_1 and the capital stock would increase until the economy reached K_2. At K_2 the saving line again crosses the line representing depreciation. Output is higher than it was initially, but the process of capital deepening stops at this higher level of output.

If there is ongoing technological progress, economic growth can continue. If technological progress raises GDP, saving will increase as well, because saving increases with GDP. This will lead to a higher stock of capital. In Figure 23A.5 technological progress is depicted as an upward shift of the saving function. The saving function shifts up because saving is a fixed fraction of output and we have assumed that technological progress has raised the level of output.

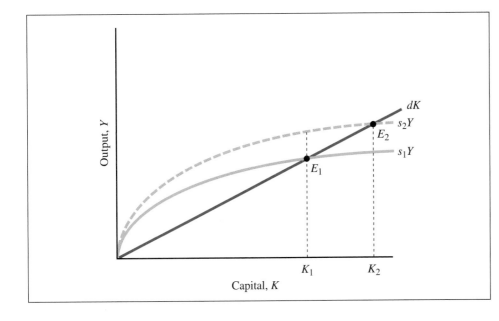

Increase in the Saving Rate
A higher saving rate will lead to a higher stock of capital in the long run. Starting from an initial capital stock of K_1, the increase in the saving rate leads the economy to K_2.

With a higher level of saving, the stock of capital will increase. If the stock of capital were originally at K_0, the upward shift in the saving schedule will lead to increases in the stock of capital to K_1. If there are further gains in technological process, capital deepening will continue.

Technological progress conveys a double benefit to a society. Not only does the increased efficiency directly raise per capita output, it also leads to additional capital deepening. Therefore, output increases for two reasons.

Let's summarize the basic points of the Solow model:

1. Capital deepening, an increase in the stock of capital per worker, will occur as long as total saving exceeds depreciation. As capital deepening occurs, there will be economic growth and increased real wages.

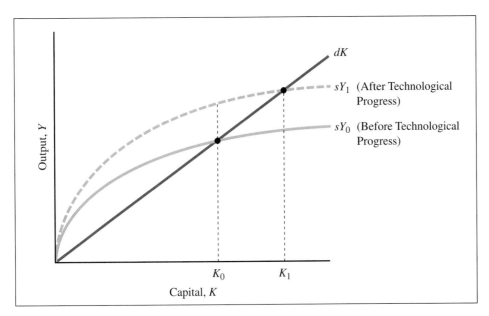

Figure 23A.5

Technological Progress and Growth
Technological progress shifts up the saving schedule and promotes capital deepening.

2. Eventually, the process of capital deepening will come to a halt as depreciation catches up with total saving.

3. A higher saving rate will promote capital deepening. If a country saves more, it will have a higher output. But eventually, the process of economic growth through capital deepening alone comes to an end, even though this may take decades to occur.

4. Technological progress not only directly raises output but allows capital deepening to continue.

It is possible to relax our assumptions and allow for population growth, government taxes and spending, and the foreign sector. In more advanced courses these issues are treated in detail, but the underlying message is the same. There is a natural limit to economic growth through capital deepening. Technological progress is required to ensure that per capita incomes grow over time.

TEST Your Understanding

1. What two factors determine how the stock of capital changes over time?

2. Why does capital deepening come to an end?

3. Does a higher saving rate lead to a permanently higher rate of growth?

Using the **TOOLS**

1. Germany and Japan After World War II
Much of the stock of capital in the economies of Japan and Germany was destroyed during World War II. Both economies had high saving rates after the war ended. Use the Solow model to explain why after the war, growth in those economies was higher than that in the United States.

2. Faster Depreciation
Suppose a society switches to equipment that depreciates rapidly. Use the Solow model to show what will happen to the stock of capital and output if the rate of depreciation increases.

Model Answers for the Appendix

Test Your Understanding
1. The factors are gross investment and depreciation.
2. Depreciation eventually catches up with saving.
3. No. A higher saving rate will raise the level of output, but eventually, capital deepening and economic growth comes to an end.

Using the Tools
1. Germany and Japan after World War II. Both Germany and Japan started after World War II with a low capital stock and a high saving rate. Both would be expected to have high rates of capital deepening. The United States, however, would be closer to the long-run position, in which capital deepening would cease in the absence of technological progress.

2. Faster Depreciation. If the rate of depreciation increases, the line from the origin that gives total depreciation will rotate to the left. This will reduce the stock of capital.

CHAPTER

24

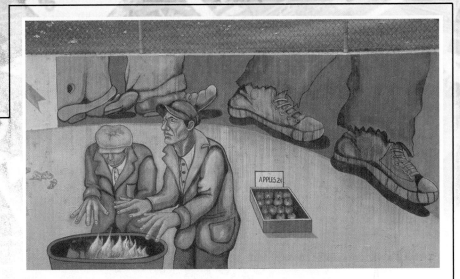

Aggregate Demand and Aggregate Supply

During the Great Depression of the 1930s, nearly one-fourth of the U.S. labor force was unemployed. Unemployed workers could not buy goods and services. Factories were shut down because there was little or no demand for their products. As factories shut down, more workers became unemployed. More factories shut down. How could this destructive chain of cause and effect be stopped and turned around? We'll see how as we begin our study of economic fluctuations.

conomies do not always operate at full employment, nor do they always grow smoothly. At times, real GDP grows below its potential or falls steeply, as it did in the Great Depression. Recessions and excess unemployment occur when real GDP falls. At other times, GDP grows too rapidly, and unemployment falls below the natural rate of unemployment. When real GDP grows too fast, the result is an increase in the rate of inflation. Real GDP growth that is too slow and real GDP growth that is too fast are examples of **economic fluctuations**, movements of GDP away from potential output. Economic fluctuations, also called **business cycles**, are the subject of this part of the book.

Economic fluctuations: Movements of real GDP above or below normal trends.

Business cycles: Another name for economic fluctuations.

After studying this chapter, you will be able to answer the following questions:

1. **How do we define a recession?**
2. **Why doesn't the economy always operate at full employment?**
3. **Why can a sharp decrease in government spending cause a recession?**
4. **How do changes in the demand for goods and services affect prices and output in the short run and in the long run?**

Let's begin by getting familiar with the terms we use when we talk about economic fluctuations.

During the Great Depression, there was a failure in coordination. Factories would have produced more output and hired more workers if there had been more demand for their products. If that had happened, the additionally employed workers would have been able to demand and afford to buy the additional goods that the factories produced.

Insufficient demand for goods and services was a key problem, identified by John Maynard Keynes, during the Great Depression. Since then, economists have viewed real GDP as determined by demand in the short run, when these coordination problems are most pronounced. We will make clear that the short run in macroeconomics is the time when prices do not fully adjust to changes in demand. In the next several chapters, we examine **Keynesian economics**; we will be analyzing models based on the idea that demand determines output in the short run.

Keynesian economics: A school of economic thought that provides insights into the economy when it operates away from full employment.

In this chapter, we develop tools for analyzing economic fluctuations in both the short run and the long run. We introduce the aggregate demand and aggregate supply curves, which will assist us in understanding some aspects of business cycles. The aggregate demand and aggregate supply curves will set the stage for our investigations of economic fluctuations in later chapters.

Business Cycles and Economic Fluctuations

To begin our study of economic fluctuations, let's look at data on real GDP at the end of the 1980s and the early 1990s. Figure 24.1 plots real GDP for the United States from 1988 to 1992. Notice that in mid-1990, real GDP begins to fall. A **recession** is a period when real GDP falls for six or more consecutive months. Economists talk more in terms of quarters of the year—consecutive three-month periods—than in terms of months. So they would say that when real GDP falls for two consecutive quarters, that's a recession. The date at which the recession starts, when output starts to decline, is called the **peak**; and the date at which the recession is considered to have begun to end, when output starts to increase again, is called the **trough**. In Figure 24.1 we see the peak and trough of the recession. After a trough, the economy enters a recovery period.

Recession: Six consecutive months of negative economic growth.

Peak: The time at which a recession begins.

Trough: The time at which output stops falling in a recession.

Since World War II, the United States has experienced nine recessions. Table 24.1 contains the dates of the peaks and troughs of each recession as well as the percent decline in real GDP from each peak to each trough. The sharpest decline in output occurred during the recession from 1973 to 1975, which started as a result of a sharp

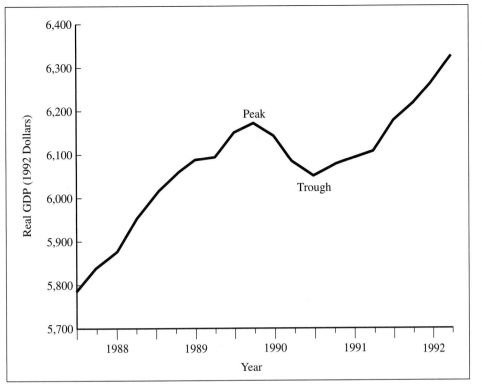

Figure 24.1
The 1990 Recession

Source: U.S. Department of Commerce.

rise in worldwide oil prices. Since 1982, there has been only one recession in the United States, and the recession that began in July 1990 was mild relative to the other recessions after World War II. There have been other periods of economic downturns—20 of them from 1860 up to World War II. Not all of these were particularly severe, and in some, unemployment hardly changed. However, there were economic downturns, such as those in 1893 and 1929, that were severe.

Depression is the common term for a severe recession. In the United States, the Great Depression refers to 1929–1933, the period when real GDP fell by over 33%. It created the most severe disruptions to ordinary economic life in the United States during the

Depression: The common name for a severe recession.

Table 24.1   Nine Postwar Recessions

Peak	Trough	Percent Decline in Real GDP
November 1948	October 1949	1.5
July 1953	May 1954	3.2
August 1957	April 1958	3.3
April 1960	February 1961	1.2
December 1969	November 1970	1.0
November 1973	March 1975	4.9
January 1980	July 1980	2.5
July 1981	November 1982	3.0
July 1990	March 1991	1.4

twentieth century. Throughout the country and in much of the world, banks closed, businesses failed, and many people lost their jobs and their life savings. Unemployment rose sharply. In 1933, over 25% of people who were looking for work failed to find jobs.

Although the United States has not experienced a depression since that time, other countries have. During the late 1980s and 1990s, several Asian countries and several Latin American countries suffered severe economic disruptions that were true depressions.

Although the definition of recessions focuses on the behavior of real GDP, other important economic measures follow the behavior of output. In particular, unemployment rises sharply during recessions. Figure 24.2 plots the unemployment rate for 1965 to 1996. The periods of recessions are marked on the graph with shaded bars. As you can see in the graph, unemployment rises sharply during recessions. For example, during the 1990 recession, the unemployment rate rose from 5.5% to 7.5% before beginning to turn downward.

The relationship between changes in real GDP and corresponding changes in unemployment is called **Okun's law**. To understand Okun's law, we first need to remember that potential GDP typically grows over time. We call the average rate of potential GDP the *trend* rate of growth. Here is Okun's law: For every percentage point that real GDP grows faster than the normal rate of increase in potential output, the unemployment rate falls by 1/2 of a percentage point. For example, suppose the trend rate of growth of real GDP is 3% per year and the current unemployment rate is 5% of the total labor force. If real GDP then grows at 4% for a year (1 percentage point above trend), the unemployment rate will fall by 1/2 of a percentage point, to 4.5%. If real GDP grew at only 2% per year (1 percentage point below trend), the unemployment rate would rise to 5.5%. Okun's law provides a link between real GDP growth and the unemployment rate.

Okun's law: A relationship between changes in real GDP and the unemployment rate.

Figure 24.2

The Unemployment Rate During Recessions

Shaded bars are recessions according to NBER (National Bureau of Economic Research) business cycle reference dates.

Source: Bureau of Labor Statistics, Department of Labor.

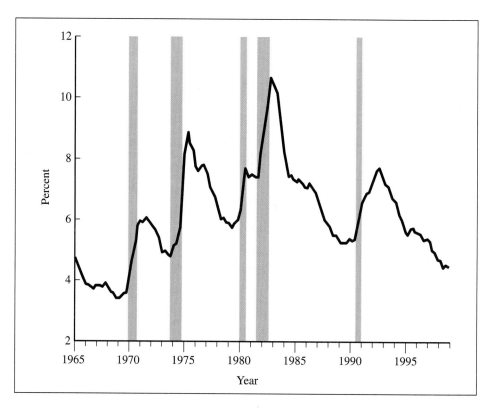

Other economic measures also rise and fall along with real GDP. Both investment spending and consumption spending rise and fall along with increases and decreases in real GDP. The prices of shares of stocks also tend to rise and fall as real GDP goes up and down. We use the term **procyclical** to describe economic measures that move in conjunction with real GDP. Thus, investment spending, consumption spending, and prices of stocks are all procyclical. Economic measures that fall as real GDP rises are known as **countercyclical**. Unemployment, for example, is countercyclical.

Procyclical: Economic measures moving in the same direction as real GDP.

Countercyclical: Economic measures moving in the opposite direction of real GDP.

Be sure you understand that when economists say "business cycle," they are not referring to a regularly recurring cycle, such as phases of the moon, the rotation of the seasons, or the appearance of the 17-year locusts. There are no fixed time intervals between recessions, as you can see in Table 24.1. During the 1960s and the 1990s, there were long periods without economic downturns. Yet there were two back-to-back recessions in the early 1980s.

Moreover, recessions tend to be unpredictable. After a recession has occurred, we can sometimes pinpoint its possible causes: either external shocks to the economy (such as sharp increases in the world price of oil) or changes in economic policy (such as sharp decreases in government spending). And the stock market always plunges sharply during recessions. But the wise men and women of Wall Street never anticipate the precise timing of an economic downturn.

Although we have focused on recessions, don't forget that a sustained period during which economic growth is too rapid can also damage the economy. Although an economy can operate for a time beyond its level of potential output, if output stays above potential output for too long a time, it will also be disruptive to the economy. When real GDP grows faster than its trend rate of growth, unemployment will fall. When the unemployment rate falls sufficiently below the natural rate of unemployment, the result will be an increase in the inflation rate for the economy.

This is why good economic policy tries to avoid both unnecessary downturns and recessions as well as prolonged booms that reduce unemployment below the natural rate. Whether we have become more successful in recent years in reducing economic fluctuations is a subject of current debate as we discuss in "A Closer Look: Have Business Fluctuations Become Less Severe?"

 **A CLOSER LOOK** Have Business Fluctuations Become Less Severe?

Until about 15 years ago, nearly all economists believed that the U.S. economy had become much more stable after World War II. However, University of California at Berkeley economist Christina Romer challenged this perception. Romer argued that economic historians had to rely on incomplete data and had used statistical methods that had exaggerated economic fluctuations before World War II. Her own estimates suggested that business fluctuations had not been reduced substantially in the postwar era.

Romer's initial work triggered a reexamination of this entire issue. Today, economic historians recognize that these matters are quite complex. For example, the period from 1901 to 1930 (coming after a major recession at the end of the nineteenth century and before the Great Depression of the 1930s) was a remarkably stable period, comparable to our post–World War II experience. But was the Great Depression unprecedented in U.S. history? Whether we should include the Great Depression in our comparisons raises the question, was this a singular and unprecedented event (which should therefore be excluded) or simply a very large recession in an unstable world? Understanding whether fluctuations have been dampened is important in interpreting whether our economic policies and institutions have become more effective in reducing economic fluctuations.

TEST Your Understanding

1. A recession occurs when growth is negative for _____ months in a row.
2. Since the unemployment rate rises when output falls, we say that unemployment is _____.
3. The highest level of output before a recession is known as the _____.
4. After a business cycle trough, the _____ phase begins.

Sticky Prices and Demand-Side Economics

Why do recessions occur? In Chapter 22, we discussed how real, adverse shocks to the economy could cause economic downturns. We also outlined the theory of real business cycles, which focuses on how shocks to technology cause economic fluctuations. Now we examine another approach to understanding economic fluctuations.

John Maynard Keynes and many economists since have identified difficulties in coordinating economic affairs as providing the starting point for understanding fluctuations in economic activity.

Normally, the price system is the mechanism that coordinates what goes on in an economy, even in a complex economy. In microeconomics, we learn that the price system helps to coordinate who does what, what resources to use, how much to make, from whom to buy, and so on, so that the economy produces as efficiently as possible. Prices give the correct signals to all producers in the economy so that resources are used efficiently and without waste. If consumers decide to consume fresh fruit rather than chocolate, the price of fresh fruit will rise and the price of chocolate will fall. The economy will produce more fresh fruit and less chocolate on the basis of these price signals. On a day-to-day basis, the price system works silently in the background, matching the desires of consumers with the output from producers.

But the price system does not always work instantaneously. If prices are slow to adjust, then the proper signals are not given quickly enough to producers and consumers. Demands and supplies will not be brought immediately into equilibrium, and coordination can break down.

In modern economies, some prices are very flexible, while others are not. Arthur Okun, the economist who came up with Okun's law, distinguished between *auction prices*, prices that adjust on a nearly daily basis, and *custom prices*, prices that adjust slowly. Prices for fresh fish, vegetables, and other food products are examples of auction prices—They typically are very flexible and adjust rapidly. Prices for industrial commodities such as steel rods or machine tools are custom prices and tend to adjust slowly to changes in demand. As shorthand, economists often refer to slowly adjusting prices as *sticky prices* (just like a door that won't open immediately but sometimes gets stuck).

Wages, the price of labor, adjust very slowly. Workers often have long-term contracts that do not allow employers to change workers' wages at all during a given year. Union workers, university professors, high-school teachers, and employees of state and local governments are all groups whose wages adjust very slowly. As a general rule, there are very few workers in the economy whose wages change quickly. Perhaps movie stars, athletes, and rock stars are the exceptions; their wages rise and fall with their popularity. But they are far from the typical worker in the economy. Even unskilled, low-wage workers are often protected from decreases in their wages by minimum wage laws.

For most firms, the most important cost of doing business is wages. If wages are sticky, firms' overall costs will be sticky as well. This means that firms' product prices

Prices for industrial commodities adjust slowly to changes in demand.

will remain sticky. Sticky wages causing sticky prices get in the way of the economy's ability to coordinate economic activity, and bring demand and supply into balance.

Because prices and wages are sticky over short periods, prices do not fully do the job of bringing demands and supplies into balance over short periods of time.

Typically, firms such as automobile manufacturers and steel firms let demand determine the level of output in the short run. To understand this idea, consider an automobile firm that buys material from a steelmaker on a regular basis. Because the auto firm and the steel producer have been in business with one another for a long time and have an ongoing relationship, they have negotiated a contract that keeps steel prices fixed in the short run.

Suppose that the automobile company's cars suddenly become very popular. The firm needs to expand production, so it needs more steel. Under their agreement, the steel company would meet this higher demand for its product and sell more steel—without raising its price—to the automobile company. So the production of steel is totally determined in the short run by the demand from automobile producers, not by price.

But, what if the firm discovered that it had produced an unpopular car and needed to cut back on its planned production? The firm would require less steel. Under the agreement, the steelmaker would supply less steel but not reduce its price. Again, demand, not price, determines steel production in the short run.

Similar agreements between firms, both formal and informal, exist throughout the economy. Typically, in the short run, firms will meet changes in the demand for their products by adjusting production with only small changes in the prices they charge their customers.

What we have just illustrated for an input such as steel applies in the same way to workers as inputs to production. Suppose that the automobile firm hires union workers under a contract that fixes their wages for a specific period. If the economy suddenly thrives at some point during that period, the automobile company will employ all the workers and perhaps require some to work overtime. If the economy stagnates at some point during that period, the firm will lay off some workers, using only part of the union labor force. In either case, wages will not change during the period of the contract.

Over longer time, prices do change. Suppose the automobile company's car remains popular for a long time. The steel company and the automobile company will adjust the price of steel on their contract to reflect this increased demand. These price adjustments only occur over long periods; in the short run, demand, not prices, determines output, and prices are slow to adjust. The **short run in macroeconomics** is the period when prices do not change or don't change very much. In the macroeconomic short run, demand determines output.

In the long run, prices adjust fully to changes in demand. But over short periods, both formal and informal contracts between firms mean that changes in demand will be reflected primarily in changes in output, not prices. We will use the term *Keynesian economics* to mean that demand determines output in the short run.

Short run in macroeconomics: The period of time in which prices do not change very much.

Aggregate Demand and Aggregate Supply

We now develop the graphical tool known as the aggregate demand and aggregate supply model. We consider aggregate demand and aggregate supply to understand how output and prices are determined in both the short run and in the long run. We will be able to do that because we will consider two types of aggregate supply curves: one for the long run and one for the short run.

Aggregate Demand

Aggregate demand curve: The relationship between the level of prices and the quantity of real GDP demanded.

The **aggregate demand curve** plots the total demand for GDP as a function of price level. (Recall that the price level is the average level of prices in the economy, as measured by a price index.) For each price level, we ask what the total quantity demanded will be for all goods and services in the economy. In Figure 24.3, the aggregate demand curve is downward sloping. As the price level falls, the total quantity demanded for goods and services increases. To understand what the aggregate demand curve represents, we must first learn why it is downward sloping, and then we must learn what factors shift it.

The Slope of the Aggregate Demand Curve

Let's consider the supply of money in the economy. We discuss the supply of money in detail in later chapters, but for now, just think of the supply of money as being the total amount of currency (cash plus coins) held by the public and the value of all deposits in checking accounts in the economy. If you have $100 in cash and $900 in your checking account, you have $1,000 of money.

As the price level or average level of prices in the economy changes, so does the purchasing power of your money. This is an example of the reality principle:

REALITY **PRINCIPLE**

What matters to people is the real value or purchasing power of money or income, not the face value of money or income.

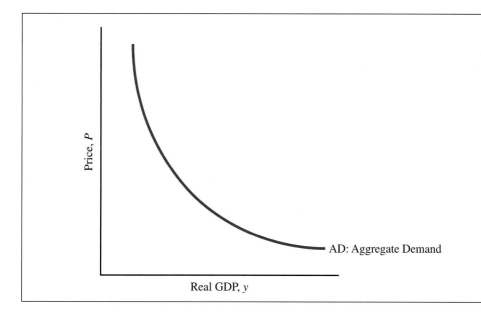

Figure 24.3
Aggregate Demand
The aggregate demand curve plots the total demand for real GDP as a function of the price level. The aggregate demand curve slopes downward, indicating that aggregate demand increases as the price level falls.

The change in the purchasing power of money will affect aggregate demand—the total demand for all goods and all services in the economy.

As the price level falls, the purchasing power of money will increase, and your $1,000 can purchase more goods and services. As the price level falls, increasing the purchasing power of money, people find that they are wealthier. With increased wealth, people want to increase their spending on goods and services. And so the quantity demanded for goods and services will increase as the price level falls. This means that the aggregate demand curve is downward sloping.

When the price level increases, the real value of money decreases, reducing wealth and thus reducing the total demand for goods and services. And so as the price level increases, total demand for goods and services in the economy decreases.

The increase in spending that occurs because the real value of money increases when the price level falls is known as the **wealth effect**. This is one reason the aggregate demand curve slopes downward. Lower prices lead to higher levels of wealth. Higher levels of wealth increase spending on total goods and services.

There are two other reasons why the aggregate demand curve is downward sloping: one has to do with interest rates, and the other has to do with international trade.

First, consider the interest rate effect. With a given supply of money in the economy, a lower price level will lead to lower interest rates. As interest rates fall, the demand for investment goods in the economy (both investment by firms and consumer durables by households) will increase. We'll explain this in detail in later chapters.

Second, consider the effects from international trade. In an open economy, a lower price level will mean that domestic goods become cheaper relative to foreign goods, so the demand for domestic goods will increase. Moreover, as we will see, lower interest rates will affect the exchange rate to make domestic goods become relatively cheaper than foreign goods. The wealth effect, the interest rate effect, and the effects from international trade reinforce one another, leading to the downward sloping aggregate demand curve in Figure 24.3.

Wealth effect: The increase in spending because the real value of money increases when the price level falls.

Factors That Shift the Aggregate Demand Curve
Different factors can shift the aggregate demand curve. At any price level, an increase in aggregate demand means that total demand by all sectors of the economy for all the

goods and services contained in real GDP has increased, and the curve shifts to the right. Factors that decrease aggregate demand will shift the aggregate demand curve to the left. At any price level, a decrease in aggregate demand means that total demand for the goods and services contained in real GDP has decreased.

Let's look at the key factors that shift the aggregate demand curve:

1. Changes in the supply of money. An increase in the supply of money in the economy will increase aggregate demand and shift the aggregate demand curve to the right. We know that an increase in the supply of money will lead to higher demand by both consumers and firms. At any given price level, a higher supply of money will mean more consumer wealth and an increased demand for goods and services. A decrease in the supply of money will decrease aggregate demand and shift the aggregate demand curve to the left. (We will discuss the money supply and aggregate demand further in later chapters.)

2. Changes in taxes. A decrease in taxes will increase aggregate demand and shift the aggregate demand curve to the right. Lower taxes will increase income available to households and increase their spending on goods and services. Aggregate demand will increase as taxes are decreased. For opposite reasons, increases in taxes will decrease aggregate demand and shift the aggregate demand curve to the left. (We will discuss taxes and aggregate demand further in the next chapter.)

3. Changes in government spending. An increase in government spending will increase aggregate demand and shift the aggregate demand curve to the right. Because the government is a source of demand for goods and services, higher government spending naturally leads to an increase in total demand for goods and services. Similarly, decreases in government spending will decrease aggregate demand and shift the curve to the left. (We will discuss government spending and aggregate demand further in the next chapter.)

4. Other factors. Any change in demand from households, firms, or the foreign sector will also change aggregate demand. For example, if the Japanese economy expands very rapidly and the Japanese buy more U.S. goods, our aggregate demand will increase. Similarly, if firms become optimistic about the future and increase their investment spending, aggregate demand will also increase.

When we discuss factors that shift aggregate demand, we must not include any changes in the demand for goods and services that arise from movements in the price level. Changes in aggregate demand that accompany changes in the price level are already included in the curve and do not shift the curve. The increase in consumer spending that occurs from the wealth effect when the price level falls is included in the curve and does not shift the curve.

Both Figure 24.4 and Table 24.2 summarize our discussion. Decreases in taxes, increases in government spending, and increases in the supply of money all shift the aggregate demand curve to the right. Increases in taxes, decreases in government spending, and decreases in the supply of money shift it to the left. In general, any increase in demand (not brought about by a change in the price level) will shift the curve to the right. Decreases in demand shift it to the left.

Aggregate Supply

The **aggregate supply curve** depicts the relationship between the level of prices and real GDP. We will develop two different aggregate supply curves: one corresponding to the long run and one to the short run.

The Classical Aggregate Supply Curve

First we'll consider the aggregate supply curve for the long run, that is, when the economy is at full employment; it is also called the **classical aggregate supply curve**. In previous

Aggregate supply curve: The relationship between the level of prices and the quantity of output supplied.

Classical aggregate supply curve: A vertical aggregate supply curve. It reflects the idea that in the long run, output is determined solely by the factors of production.

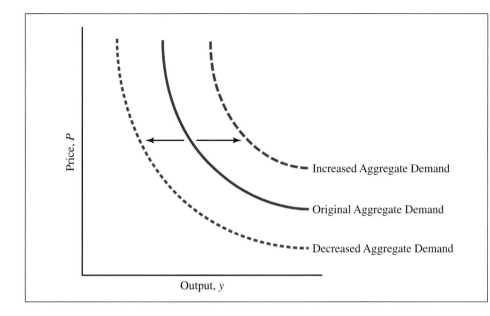

Figure 24.4
Shifting Aggregate Demand
Decreases in taxes, increases in government spending, and an increase in the supply of money all shift the aggregate demand curve to the right. Higher taxes, lower government spending, and a lower supply of money shift the curve to the left.

chapters, we saw that the level of full-employment output y^* depends solely on the supply factors—capital and labor—and the state of technology. These are the fundamental factors that determine output in the long run, that is, when the economy operates at full employment.

The level of full-employment output does not depend on the level of prices in the economy. Because the level of full-employment output does not depend on the price level, we can plot the classical aggregate supply curve as a vertical line (unaffected by the price level), as in Figure 24.5.

We combine the aggregate demand curve and the classical aggregate supply curve in Figure 24.6. Given an aggregate demand curve and an aggregate supply curve, their intersection determines the price level and level of output. At that intersection point, the total amount demanded will just equal the total amount supplied. The position of the aggregate demand curve will depend on the level of taxes, government spending, and the supply of money. The level of full-employment output determines the classical aggregate supply curve.

An increase in aggregate demand (perhaps brought about by a tax cut or an increase in the supply of money) will shift the aggregate demand curve to the right as in Figure 24.6. With a classical aggregate supply curve, the increase in aggregate demand will raise prices but leave the level of output unchanged. In general, shifts in the aggregate demand curve when we have a classical supply curve do not change the level of output in

Table 24.2   Factors That Shift Demand

Factors That Increase Aggregate Demand	Factors That Decrease Aggregate Demand
Decrease in taxes	Increase in taxes
Increase in government spending	Decrease in government spending
Increase in money supply	Decrease in money supply

Figure 24.5

Classical Aggregate Supply

In the long run, the level of output y^* is independent of the price level.

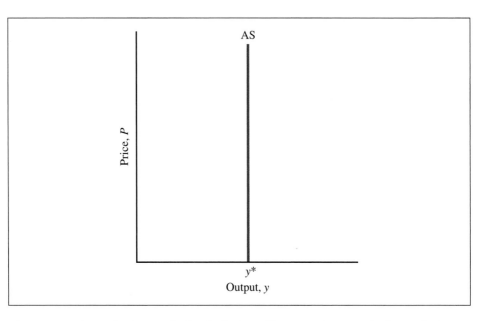

the economy but only change the level of prices. That is, an increase in demand when we have a classical supply curve will only raise the average level of prices in the economy but not change the level of real output.

This is the main long-run result from the classical model. In the long run, output is determined solely by the supply of capital and the supply of labor. As our model of the aggregate demand curve with the classical aggregate supply curve indicates, changes in demand will affect only prices, not the level of output.

The Keynesian Aggregate Supply Curve

In the short run, prices are sticky (slow to adjust), and output is determined primarily by demand. We can use the aggregate demand curve combined with a **Keynesian aggregate supply curve** to illustrate this idea. Figure 24.7 shows a relatively flat Keynesian aggregate

Keynesian aggregate supply curve: A relatively flat supply curve. It reflects the idea that prices do not change very much in the short run and that firms adjust production to meet demand.

ACTIVE GRAPH

Figure 24.6

Aggregate Demand and Classical Aggregate Supply

Output and prices are determined at the intersection of AD and AS. An increase in aggregate demand leads to a higher price level.

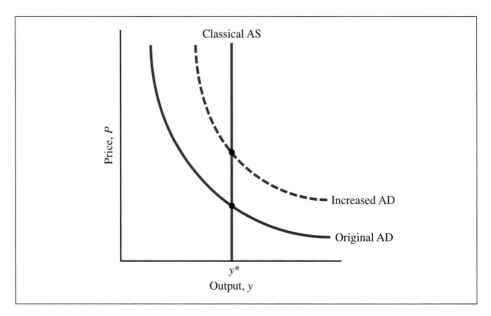

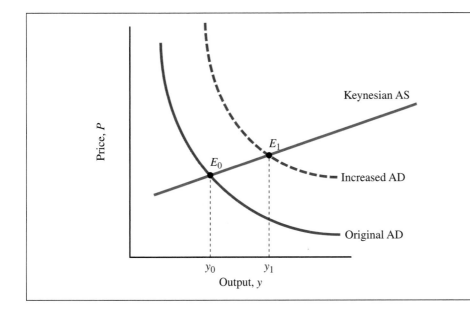

Figure 24.7

Aggregate Demand and Keynesian Aggregate Supply
With a Keynesian aggregate supply curve, shifts in aggregate demand lead to changes in output but small changes in prices.

ACTIVE GRAPH

supply curve (AS). The Keynesian aggregate supply curve is relatively flat because in the short run, firms are assumed to supply all the output demanded, with small changes in prices. We previously discussed that with formal and informal contracts, firms will supply all the output that is demanded with only relatively small changes in prices. The Keynesian aggregate supply curve has a small upward slope. As they supply more output, firms may have to increase prices somewhat if, for example, they have to pay higher wages to obtain more overtime from workers or pay a premium to obtain some raw materials.

As we just explained, the Keynesian supply curve is relatively flat because at any point in time, firms are assumed to supply all the output demanded with relatively small changes in prices. However, the entire Keynesian supply curve can shift upward or downward as prices adjust to their long-run levels, as we shall see later in this chapter. Our description of the aggregate supply curve is consistent with evidence about the behavior of prices in the economy. Most studies find that changes in demand have relatively little effect on prices within a few quarters. Thus, the aggregate supply curve can be viewed as relatively flat within a limited time. However, changes in aggregate demand will ultimately have an effect on prices.

The intersection of the AD and AS curves at point E_0 determines the price level and the level of output. Because the aggregate supply curve is flat, aggregate demand primarily determines the level of output. In Figure 24.7, as aggregate demand increases, the new equilibrium will be at a slightly higher price, and output will increase from y_0 to y_1.

It is important to realize and understand that the level of output where the aggregate demand curve intersects the Keynesian aggregate supply curve need not correspond to full-employment output. Firms will produce whatever is demanded. If demand is very high, output may exceed full-employment output; if demand is very low, output will fall short of full-employment output. Because prices do not adjust fully over short periods of time, the economy need not always remain at full employment or potential output. Changes in demand will lead to economic fluctuations with sticky prices and a Keynesian aggregate supply curve. Only in the long run, when prices fully adjust, will the economy operate at full employment.

Figure 24.8

Supply Shock
An adverse supply shock, such as an increase in the price of oil, will shift up the AS curve. The result will be higher prices and a lower level of output.

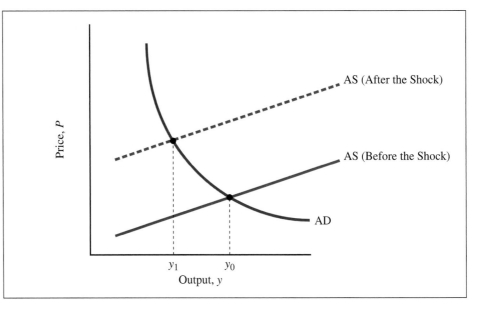

Supply Shocks

Up to this point, we have been exploring how changes in aggregate demand affect output and prices in the short run and in the long run. However, even in the short run, it is possible for external disturbances to hit the economy and cause the Keynesian aggregate supply curve to move. **Supply shocks** are external events that shift the aggregate supply curve.

Supply shocks: External events that shift the aggregate supply curve.

The most important illustrations of supply shocks for the world economy are the sharp increases in the price of oil that occurred in 1973 and again in 1979. When oil prices increased sharply, firms no longer sold all the goods and services that were demanded at the current price—meaning the price before the increases in oil prices. Because oil was a key input to production for many firms in the economy, the additional costs of oil reduced the profits of firms. To maintain their profit levels, firms raised the prices of their products.

Figure 24.8 illustrates a supply shock that raises prices. The Keynesian aggregate supply curve shifts up with the supply shock because firms will supply their output only at a higher price. The shift of the AS curve raises the price level and lowers the level of output from y_0 to y_1. Adverse supply shocks can therefore cause a recession (a fall in output) with increasing prices. This situation corresponds closely to the events of 1973, when higher oil prices led to both a recession and rising prices for the economy.

Favorable supply shocks, such as falling prices, are also possible. In this case the Keynesian aggregate supply curve will shift down. As "A Closer Look: Favorable Supply Shocks," indicates, this happened to the United States in the 1990s.

Did Higher Taxes Cause the Recession?

ECONOMIC DETECTIVE

The economy went into a recession. The political party that was in power blamed an increase in the price of world oil and food. Opposing politicians blamed a tax increase that the party in power had enacted. On the basis of aggregate demand and aggregate supply analysis, what evidence should you look at to try to determine what caused the recession?

A CLOSER LOOK Favorable Supply Shocks

During the 1970s, the world economy was hit with a series of unfavorable supply shocks, raising prices and lowering output. These shocks included a spike (a sudden steep increase) in the price of oil in 1973, another in 1979 when producers of oil reduced their supplies to the market, and increases in the prices of many agricultural commodities.

In the 1990s, things were different—pleasantly different. Between 1997 and 1998, the price of oil on the world market fell from $22 a barrel to less than $13 a barrel. The result was that gasoline prices, adjusted for inflation, were lower than they had ever been in our lifetimes. This not only meant cheaper vacations and commuting, it also had positive macroeconomic effects. Favorable supply shocks allowed output to rise and prices to fall simultaneously—the best of all worlds. These favorable shocks allowed the U.S. economy to grow rapidly and reduced unemployment without incurring risks of increased inflation.

To determine whether increases in world prices for oil and food or tax increases caused the recession, you need to look at what happened to domestic prices in the economy. If prices rose sharply while output fell, then supply shocks (increases in world oil and food prices) caused the recession. However, if prices fell while output fell, tax increases probably were the culprit. ◆

Output and Prices in the Short Run and in the Long Run

Up to this point, we have examined how aggregate demand and aggregate supply determine output and prices both in the short run and in the long run. You may be wondering how long is the short run and how short is the long run. Here is a preview of how the short run and the long run are connected.

In Figure 24.9, we show the aggregate demand curve intersecting the Keynesian aggregate supply curve at E_0 at an output level y_0. We also depict the classical aggregate supply curve in this figure. The level of output in the economy, y_0, exceeds the level of potential output y_p. In other words, this is a boom economy: Output exceeds potential. Because the economy is producing at a level beyond its long-run potential, the level of unemployment will be very low. This will make it difficult for firms to recruit and retain workers. They will also find it more difficult to purchase needed raw materials and other inputs for production. As firms compete for labor and raw materials, there will be a tendency for both wages and prices to increase over time.

Increasing wages and prices will shift the Keynesian aggregate supply curve upward. Figure 24.10 illustrates this graphically; the dashed lines indicating how the Keynesian aggregate supply curve shifts upward over time. As long as the economy is producing at a level of output that exceeds potential output, there will be continuing competition for labor and raw materials that will lead to continuing increases in wages and prices. In the long run, the Keynesian aggregate supply curve will keep rising until it intersects the aggregate demand curve at E_1. At this point, the economy reaches the long-run equilibrium—precisely the point where the aggregate demand curve intersects the classical aggregate supply curve.

The lesson here is that adjustments in wages and prices take the economy from the short-run Keynesian equilibrium to the long run classical equilibrium. In later chapters,

Figure 24.9

The Economy in the Short Run

In the short run, the economy produces at y_0 which exceeds potential output y_p.

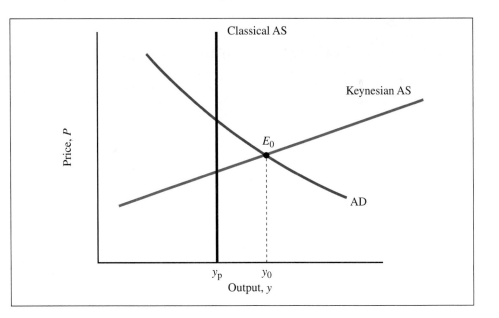

we will explain in detail how this adjustment occurs, and we will show how changes in wages and prices can steer the economy back to full employment in the long run.

Looking Ahead

The aggregate demand and aggregate supply models in this chapter provide an overview of how demand affects output and prices in both the short run and the long run. The next several chapters explore more closely how aggregate demand determines output in the short run. We expand our discussion of aggregate demand to see in detail how such realistic and important factors as spending by consumers and firms, government policies on taxation and spending, and foreign trade affect the demand for goods and services. We will also study the critical role that the financial system and monetary policy

Figure 24.10

Adjusting to the Long Run

With output exceeding potential, the AS curve shifts upwards as depicted by the dotted lines. The economy adjusts to the long run equilibrium at E_1.

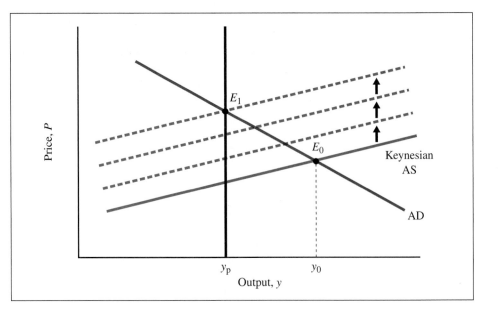

play in determining demand. We will see the critical role government plays in determining aggregate demand through its control of taxes, spending, and the supply of money.

Finally, we will study in more depth in later chapters how the aggregate supply curve shifts over time and can lead the economy back to full employment. From this, we will be able to study in detail how the economy recovers both from recessions and the inflationary pressures generated by economic booms. At the conclusion of our studies, we will have a complete model that we can use to analyze the full behavior of the economy in the short run and in the long run and can address key economic policy issues.

TEST Your Understanding

5. Name three factors that shift the aggregate demand curve to the right.

6. A decrease in the price level shifts the aggregate demand curve to the right. True or false? Explain.

7. Complete the statement with *vertical* or *horizontal*: The classical aggregate supply curve is _____.

8. Suppose the supply of money increases. How do prices and real GDP change in both the classical and Keynesian worlds?

Using the TOOLS

In this chapter, we explored the nature of economic fluctuations and developed the tools of aggregate demand and aggregate supply. Take this opportunity to test your skills using the tools we developed in this chapter.

1. Counting Recessions
Consider the data for the fictitious economy of Euroclive:

Year and Quarter	2000:1	2000:2	2000:3	2000:4	2001:1	2001:2	2001:3
Real GDP	195	193	195	196	195	194	198

How many recessions occurred in the economy over the time indicated?

2. Rationales for Sticky Wages
Think of some group of workers (for example, federal workers) that has sticky wages. Explain why sticky wages may provide economic benefits for both workers and employers.

3. Frugal Consumers
Suppose households become nervous about the future and decide to increase their saving and decrease their consumption spending. How will this shift the aggregate demand curve? Use the Keynesian aggregate supply curve to figure out what will happen to prices and output in the short run. Use the classical aggregate supply curve to determine what will happen to prices and output in the long run.

4. Stagflation
Suppose oil prices suddenly increase and the economy is hit by an adverse supply shock. What will happen to the price level and real GDP? Why is this sometimes called *stagflation*?

Summary

We examined the nature of business cycles and economic fluctuations and provided the foundation for studying short-run, demand-side economics. We also developed aggregate demand and aggregate supply as tools to help us analyze what is happening or has happened in the economy. Here are the main points to remember in this chapter:

1. Recessions occur when real output falls for two quarters.

2. Unemployment rises during recessions; other economic measures rise and fall with real GDP.

3. Economists think of GDP as being determined primarily by demand factors in the short run.

4. The aggregate demand curve depicts the relationship between the price level and total demand for real output in the economy. The aggregate demand curve is downward sloping because of the wealth effect, an interest rate effect, and an international trade effect.

5. Decreases in taxes, increases in government spending, and increases in the supply of money all increase aggregate demand and shift the aggregate demand curve to the right. Increases in taxes, decreases in government spending, and decreases in the supply of money all decrease aggregate demand and shift the aggregate demand curve to the left. In general, anything (other than price movements) that increases the demand for total goods and services will increase aggregate demand.

6. The aggregate supply curve depicts the relationship between the price level and the level of output firms supply in the economy. Output and prices are determined at the intersection of the aggregate demand and aggregate supply curves.

7. The classical aggregate supply curve is vertical because, in the long run, output is determined by the supply of factors of production. The Keynesian aggregate supply curve is fairly flat because, in the short run, prices are largely fixed and output is determined by demand.

8. Supply shocks can shift the Keynesian aggregate supply curve even in the short run.

9. The Keynesian aggregate supply curve shifts in the long run, restoring the economy to the full employment equilibrium.

Key Terms

aggregate demand curve, 504
aggregate supply curve, 506
business cycles, 498
classical aggregate supply curve, 506
countercyclical, 501
depression, 499

economic fluctuations, 498
Keynesian aggregate supply curve, 508
Keynesian economics, 498
Okun's law, 500
peak, 498

procyclical, 501
recession, 498
short run in macroeconomics, 504
supply shocks, 510
trough, 498
wealth effect, 505

Problems and Discussion Questions

1. What can be misleading about the term *business cycle?*

2. Explain intuitively why the unemployment rate is countercyclical.

3. To compare how deeply recessions affected the economies of two different countries, we might use the following measures:

   a. The number of recessions

   b. The proportion of time each economy was in a recession

   c. The magnitude of the worst recession

   Draw several diagrams that show economies experiencing recessions. Use these diagrams to illustrate how these measures convey different features of recessions.

4. Explain why the aggregate demand curve is downward sloping.

5. Give an example of a good or service whose prices are sticky. What factors tend to make its price sticky?

6. Explain why the classical aggregate supply curve is vertical and why the Keynesian supply curve is horizontal.

7. Suppose that in the classical model, there was a new higher level of full-employment output. What would happen to the level of prices in the economy?

8. In the short run, what happens to the unemployment rate if aggregate demand suddenly falls?

9. Suppose the economy is at full employment and aggregate demand falls. Show the effects on output and prices in the short run. Also show how the Keynesian aggregate supply curve adjusts over time to bring the economy to the long-run equilibrium.

10. Use aggregate demand and aggregate supply diagrams to show the effects of "favorable" supply shocks.

11. **Web Exercise.** Is the U.S. trade balance (export minus imports) procyclical or countercyclical? Use the World Wide Web to find data of the trade balance and GDP to explore this answer. A good place to start might be the Web site of the Federal Reserve Bank of St. Louis (*http://www.stls.frb.org/fred/*). You might also want to explore this issue for other countries.

12. **Web Exercise.** How are movements in the stock market related to business cycles? Use the Web site in question 11 or your own source to answer this question.

Take It to the Net

We invite you to visit the O'Sullivan/Sheffrin page on the Prentice Hall Web site at:
http://www.prenhall.com/osullivan/
for additional World Wide Web exercises for this chapter.

Model Answers to Questions

Chapter-Opening Questions

1. A recession occurs when real GDP declines for two consecutive quarters.

2. Because wages and prices are slow to adjust, the economy may not always operate at full employment.

3. In the short run, output is largely determined by demand. Therefore, a sharp decrease in government spending could cause a recession.

4. In the short run, changes in the demand for goods and services primarily affect output. In the long run, changes in demand for goods and services primarily affect prices.

Test Your Understanding

1. Six.

2. Countercyclical.

3. Peak.

4. Recovery.

5. Increases in government spending, decreases in taxes, and increases in the supply of money.

6. False. Changes in prices are movements along the aggregate demand curve, not shifts of the curve.

7. Vertical.

8. In the classical model, an increase in the money supply will raise prices but not change output. In the Keynesian model, an increase in the supply of money will increase output but not change prices very much.

Using the Tools

1. Counting Recessions. There was only one recession in Euroclive, the peak of which was in 2000:4. Although output did fall in 2000:2, the decline was only for one quarter. The decline beginning in 2001:1 lasted for two quarters.

2. Rationales for Sticky Wages. It would be inconvenient and costly for employers and employees to renegotiate wages every day. Conflicts over wages would certainly arise. To keep the peace, wages are adjusted only periodically.

3. Frugal Consumers. The decrease in consumption spending is a decrease in the demand for total goods and services—therefore, a decrease in aggregate demand. The aggregate demand curve shifts to the left. In the short run, output falls and prices decrease slightly. In the long run, prices fall and output returns to full employment.

4. Stagflation. If the Keynesian aggregate supply curve shifts upward, the result will be a lower level of output and higher prices. This is sometimes called stagflation because the falling output means that the economy is stagnating and the rising prices mean that the inflation rate will rise.

Keynesian Economics and Fiscal Policy

In early 1999, the Internal Revenue Service began to issue refund checks for individuals who had overpaid their income taxes during the previous year. Refunds were substantially higher than refunds the year before. The higher refunds were primarily due to tax credits for children and educational expenses that the Congress had enacted in 1998.

A number of economic forecasters predicted that consumer spending, such as for family vacations, would increase as a result of these higher refund payments. They predicted further that the increase in consumer spending would bolster growth in real GDP for at least the first few quarters.

Why should increased income tax refunds generate higher real GDP growth? How can we explain the reasoning of the economic forecasters?

ewspaper and television stories about the economy tend to focus on what causes the changes in short term real GDP. For example, it is common to read about how changes in economic conditions in Europe or Asia or changes in government spending or taxation will affect near-term economic growth. To understand these stories, we need to understand the behavior of the economy in the short run. To do that, we will get help from John Maynard Keynes.

In this chapter, we explore Keynes's idea that spending determines output or GDP, at least over short periods. In macroeconomics, the short run is the period during which prices do not change or change very little. Until prices adjust in the long run, the demand for goods and services determines the level of GDP. Producers will supply, in the short run, all the output that is demanded. This was Keynes's point: In the short run, the level of GDP is determined primarily by demand.

We start this chapter with the simplest case: a model of the behavior of the economy in the short run that ignores the role of the government and the foreign sector. We then bring government and the foreign sector into our model and illustrate how it works with examples of what really happens.

We also introduce the Keynesian cross, a graph that we will use as an analytical tool. The Keynesian cross enables us to understand how demand determines output in the short run and how changes in demand change output. We also use simple formulas that help to reinforce the ideas behind the demand-side models. The appendix to the chapter shows how these formulas are derived.

With the tools in this chapter, you will be able to answer the following questions:

1. **Why do governments cut taxes to increase economic output?**
2. **Why is the U.S. economy more stable today than it was prior to World War II?**
3. **If consumers become more confident about the future of the economy, can that confidence lead to faster economic growth?**
4. **If a government increases spending by $10 billion, could total GDP increase by more than $10 billion?**
5. **If a country stops buying our exports, could that drop in exports lead to a recession?**

The Simplest Keynesian Cross

Let's begin with the simplest model of how demand determines output in the short run. The simplest model is a graph with the demand for goods and services represented on the vertical axis, output (y) represented on the horizontal axis, and a 45° diagonal line, as shown in Figure 25.1, representing a key relationship between demand and output. From any point on that 45° diagonal line, the distance leftward over to the vertical axis is equal to the distance downward to the horizontal axis. That's simple graphical math: From any point on the diagonal, the vertical distance and horizontal distance measured to the axes are equal—a key fact that you must understand and remember as we proceed.

Understanding what the diagonal represents, we can start to build a simple demand-side model. Let's start by assuming that neither the government nor the foreign sectors exist. Only consumers and firms can demand output: Consumers demand consumption goods, and firms demand investment goods. We make things even simpler, assuming that consumers and firms each demand a fixed amount of goods. Let consumption demand be an amount C and let investment demand be an amount I. Total demand will be $C + I$.

In the short run, demand determines output:

$$\text{output} = \text{demand}$$

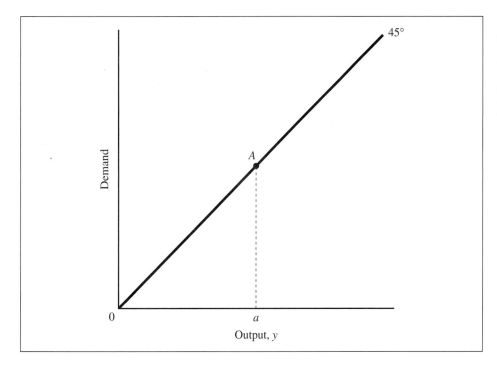

Figure 25.1
The 45° Line
Any point on the 45° line corresponds to the same vertical and horizontal distances. The distance 0*a* equals the distance *Aa*.

In this case,

$$\text{output} = \text{demand} = C + I$$

Figure 25.2 can help us to understand how output—the level of real GDP—is determined. On the demand-output diagram, we superimpose the line representing demand, $C + I$, which is a horizontal line, because both C and I are fixed amounts. Because total demand is fixed at $C + I$, it does not depend on output.

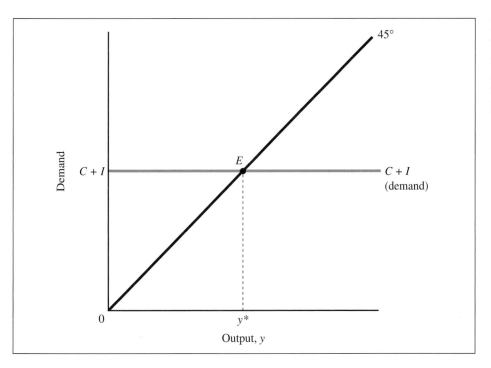

Figure 25.2
The Keynesian Cross
At equilibrium output y^*, total demand Ey^* equals output $0y^*$.

Equilibrium output: The level of GDP at which the amount of demand for output equals the amount that is produced.

Equilibrium output is at y^*, the level of output at which the demand line crosses the 45° line. They cross at point E, where output measured on the horizontal axis equals demand by consumers and firms measured on the vertical axis. How do we know this? Because point E is on the 45° line; therefore, the vertical distance Ey^* equals the horizontal distance $0y^*$. Recall that the vertical distance is total demand and that the horizontal distance is the level of output. Therefore, at output y^*, total demand equals output.

What would happen if the economy were producing at a higher level of output, such as y_1 in Figure 25.3? At that level of output, more goods and services are being produced than consumers and firms are wanting and buying. Goods that are produced but not purchased will pile up on the shelves of stores. Firms will react to this by cutting back on production. The level of output will fall until the economy reaches y^*, as indicated by the leftward arrow in Figure 25.3.

If the economy were producing at a lower level of output, y_2, demand would exceed total output. When demand exceeds output, firms find that the demand for consumption and investment goods is greater than their current production. Inventories disappear from the shelves of stores, and firms face increasing backlogs of orders for their products. Firms respond by stepping up production, so GDP increases back to y^*, as indicated by the rightward arrow in Figure 25.3.

Table 25.1 also helps to illustrate the process that determines equilibrium output. The table shows, with a numerical example, what happens to production when demand does not equal output.

Demand (consumption plus investment) equals 100 billion dollars. In the first row, we see that if current production is only 80 billion, stocks of inventories will be depleted by 20 billion, so firms will increase output to restore their inventory levels. In the second row, production is at 120 billion, creating an excess of inventories of 20 billion, and firms will cut back production. In the last row, demand equals output: Neither inventories nor production changes.

Be sure you remember that in the short run, the equilibrium level of output occurs where total demand equals production. If the economy were not producing at that level,

Figure 25.3
Equilibrium Output
Equilibrium output (y^*) is determined at E, where demand intersects the 45° line. If output were higher (y_1), it would exceed demand and production would fall. If output were lower (y_2), it would fall short of demand and production would rise.

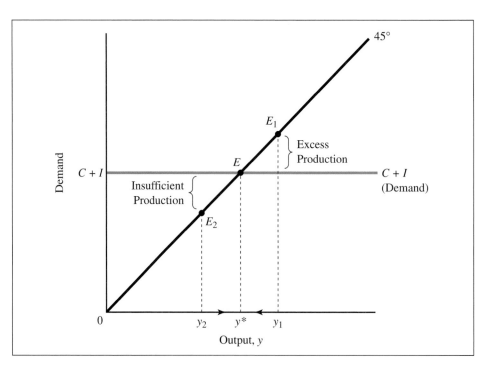

Table 25.1   Adjustments to Equilibrium Output

$C + I$	Production	Inventories	Direction of Output
100	80	Depletion of inventories of 20	Output increases
100	120	Excess of inventories of 20	Output decreases
100	100	No change	Output stays constant

we would find either that the demand for goods was too great relative to production or that there was insufficient demand relative to production. In either case, the economy would rapidly adjust to reach the equilibrium level of output.

The Consumption Function and the Multiplier

Consumer Spending and Income

We now start to make our model more realistic. Economists have found that consumer spending depends on the level of income in the economy. When consumers have more income, they want to purchase more goods and services. The relationship between consumer spending and income is known as the **consumption function**:

$$C = C_a + by$$

where consumption spending C has two parts. The first part, C_a, is a constant and is independent of income. This means that much of consumption spending does not depend on the level of income. For example, all consumers, regardless of their current income, will have to purchase some food. Economists call this **autonomous consumption spending**. The second part, by, represents the part of consumption that is dependent on income. It is the product of a fraction b, called the **marginal propensity to consume (MPC)**, and the level of income y in the economy. The MPC (or b in our formula) tells us how much consumption spending will increase for every dollar that income increases. For example, if $b = 0.6$, then for every \$1 that income increases, consumption increases by \$0.60.

In our simple economy, output (or real GDP) is also equal to the income that flows to the households. As firms produce output, it is paid to the households as income (wages, interest, profits, and rents). We can therefore use the symbol y to represent both output and income.

We plot a consumption function in Figure 25.4 . The consumption function is a line that intersects the vertical axis at C_a, the level of autonomous consumption spending; autonomous consumption must be greater than zero, so the line does not pass through the zero point on the origin. Its slope equals b, the marginal propensity to consume. Although output is plotted on the horizontal axis, remember that it is also equal to income, so income rises dollar for dollar with output. That is why we can plot the consumption function (which depends on income) on the same graph that determines output.

The marginal propensity to consume (the slope of the line) is always less than one. A consumer who receives a dollar of income will spend part of it and save the rest. The fraction that the consumer spends is given by his or her MPC. The fraction that the consumer saves is determined by his or her **marginal propensity to save (MPS)**. The sum of the marginal propensity to consume and the marginal propensity to save is always equal to one. For example, if the MPC is 0.8, then the MPS must be 0.2. When a consumer receives an additional dollar, he or she spends \$0.80 and saves the remaining \$0.20.

Consumption function: The relationship between the level of income and consumption spending.

Autonomous consumption spending: The part of consumption that does not depend on income.

Marginal propensity to consume (MPC): The fraction of additional income that is spent.

Marginal propensity to save (MPS): The fraction of additional income that is saved.

Figure 25.4
Consumption Function
The consumption function relates desired consumer spending to the level of income.

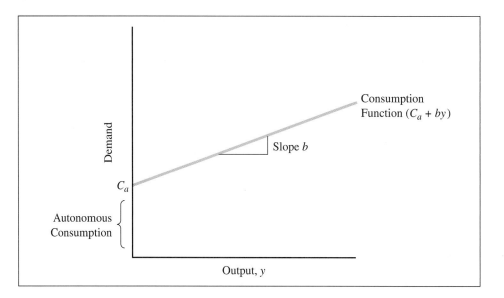

Changes in the Consumption Function

The consumption function is determined by the level of autonomous consumption and by the MPC. The level of autonomous consumption can change, and so can the MPC. Changes in either shift the consumption function to another position on the graph. A higher level of autonomous consumption but no change in MPC will shift the entire consumption function upward and parallel to its original position. Why it shifts upward should be clear: because increased autonomous consumption is represented as a higher intercept on the vertical axis. We show an increase in autonomous consumption in panel A of Figure 25.5.

A number of factors can cause autonomous consumption to change. Here are two:

- Increases in consumer wealth will cause an increase in autonomous consumption. (Wealth consists of the value of stocks, bonds, and consumer durables—consumer goods that last a long time, such as automobiles and refrigerators. Wealth is not the same as income; income is the amount of money earned during a period, such as in a given year.) Nobel laureate Franco Modigliani has emphasized that increases in stock prices, which raise consumer wealth, will lead to increases in autonomous

Figure 25.5
Movements of the Consumption Function

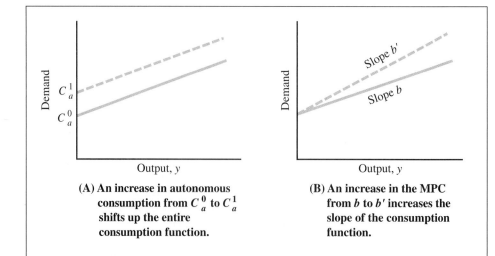

(A) An increase in autonomous consumption from C_a^0 to C_a^1 shifts up the entire consumption function.

(B) An increase in the MPC from b to b' increases the slope of the consumption function.

consumption. Conversely, a sharp fall in stock prices would lead to a decrease in autonomous consumption.

- Changes in consumer confidence will shift the consumption function. Increases in consumer confidence will increase autonomous consumption. Forecasters pay attention to consumer confidence, based on household surveys; consumer confidence is reported regularly in the financial press.

A change in the marginal propensity to consume will cause a change in the slope of the consumption function. We show an increase in the MPC in panel B of Figure 25.5, where we assume that autonomous consumption is fixed. As the MPC increases, the consumption function rotates upward, counterclockwise; that means that the consumption function line gets steeper.

Several factors can change the MPC. Here are two:

- Consumers' perceptions of changes in their income affect their MPC. If consumers believe that an increase in their income is permanent, they will consume a higher proportion of the increased income than they would if they believed the increase was temporary. As an example, consumers will spend a higher proportion of a permanent salary increase than they would spend of a one-time bonus. Similarly, studies have shown that consumers save—not spend—a high proportion of one-time windfall gains, such as lottery winnings.

- Changes in tax rates change the slope of the consumption function, as we will see later in this chapter.

Determining GDP

Using the consumption function, we are now ready to show how real GDP is determined. We assume that GDP is ultimately determined by demand (as before). We continue to assume that investment spending, I, is a constant with respect to changes in income. The only difference between what we did in the preceding section and what we are about to do here is that we now recognize that consumption increases with the level of income.

Figure 25.6 shows how GDP is determined. We first plot the consumption function, C, as before: a sloping line graphically representing that consumption spending is a function of income. Because we are assuming that investment is constant at all levels of income, to graphically get the $C + I$ line, we can simply add vertically the constant level of investment I to the consumption function. Doing this gives us the $C + I$ line, representing total spending in the economy. This line is upward sloping because consumption spending increases with income. At any level of income, we now know the level of total spending, $C + I$.

The level of equilibrium output, y^*, occurs where the spending line $C + I$ crosses the 45° diagonal line. At this level of output, total spending equals output. At any other level of production, spending will not equal output and the economy will adjust back to y^*, for the same reasons and in the same way as in the corresponding example in the preceding section.

In the appendix to this chapter, we show that the equilibrium output in this simple economy is

equilibrium output = (autonomous consumption + investment)/(1 – MPC)

or, in the mathematical terms representing those words,

$$y^* = (C_a + I)/(1 - b)$$

Figure 25.6

Determining GDP
GDP is determined where the $C + I$ line intersects the 45° line. At that level of output, y^*, desired spending equals output.

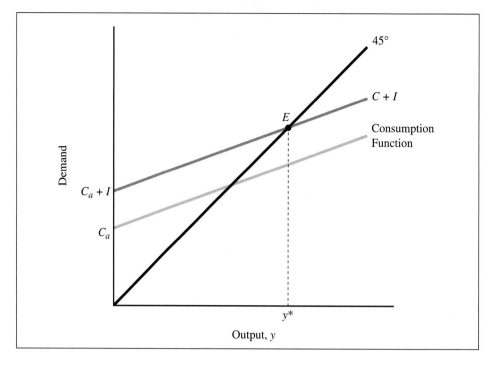

From this relationship and the numerical values for C_a, b, and I, we can calculate equilibrium output. Suppose that

$$C_a = 100$$

$$b = 0.6$$

$$I = 40$$

(This means that the consumption function is $C = 100 + 0.6y$). Then, using our formula for equilibrium output, we have

$$y^* = (100 + 40)/(1 - 0.6)$$

$$= 140/0.4$$

$$= 350$$

Savings and Investment

Equilibrium output can be determined in another way, which highlights the relationship between savings and investment. To understand this relationship, recall that in an economy without taxation or government, the value of output, or production (y), equals the value of income. Households receive this income and either consume it (C), save it (S), or some of both. Realizing that, we can say that savings equals output minus consumption or, in mathematical terms,

$$S = y - C$$

In our simple economy, output is determined by demand, $C + I$, or

$$y = C + I$$

If we subtract consumption from both sides of this equation, we have

$$y - C = I$$

But we just saw that the left side, $y - C$, equals savings, S, so we have

$$S = I$$

Thus, equilibrium output is determined at the level of income where savings equal investment.

The level of savings in the economy is not fixed; it changes, and how it changes depends on the real GDP. To illustrate this, let's return to the previous example in which the consumption function is $C = 100 + 0.6y$. Because $S = y - C$, savings is

$$S = y - (100 + 0.6y)$$

$$S = -100 + 0.4y$$

This is the savings function for this example. A **savings function** describes the relationship between savings and income. In this example's savings function, the marginal propensity to save is 0.4. That means that for every dollar y increases, savings increase by $0.40.

In our previous example, investment $I = 40$, and equilibrium income was 350. Let's check that savings does equal that level of investment. Plugging in the value of equilibrium output (or income) into the savings function, we get

Savings function: The relationship between the level of income and the level of savings.

$$S = -100 + 0.4(350)$$

$$S = -100 + 140$$

$$S = 40$$

So savings equals investment at the level of equilibrium output.

TEST Your Understanding

1. Explain why equilibrium output occurs where the demand line crosses the 45° line.

2. What happens if the level of output exceeds demand?

3. What is the slope of the consumption function called?

4. Complete the statement with *upward* or *downward*: An increase in autonomous consumption will shift the consumption function _____.

5. In our simple model, if $C = 100 + 0.8y$ and $I = 50$, equilibrium output will be _____.

6. If the MPC is 0.7, the marginal propensity to save must be _____.

The Multiplier

In all economies, investment spending fluctuates. We can use the model we developed that determines output in the short run to see what happens if there are changes in investment spending. Suppose investment spending originally was I_0 and increased to I_1, an increase that we will call ΔI (the symbol Δ, the Greek capital letter delta, is universally used to represent change). What happens to equilibrium output?

Figure 25.7 shows how equilibrium output is determined at the original level of investment and at the new level of investment. The increase in investment spending shifts the $C + I$ curve upward by ΔI. The intersection of the $C + I$ curve with the 45° line shifts from E_0 to E_1. GDP increases from y_0 to y_1 by the amount Δy.

The figure shows that the increase in GDP—that is, the amount Δy—is greater than the increase in investment—the amount ΔI—or $\Delta y > \Delta I$.

This is a general result; the increase in output always exceeds the increase in investment. The increase in output divided by the increase in investment is called the **multiplier** for investment. Because output increases more than the initial increase in investment, the multiplier is greater than 1.

The basic idea of how the multiplier works in an economy is simple. Let's say that a computer firm invests $10 million in building a new plant. Initially, total spending in the economy increases by this $10 million paid to a construction firm. The construction workers and owners of the construction firm then spend part of the income they are paid. Suppose the owners and workers spend $8 million on new automobiles. Producers of these automobiles will expand their production because of the increase indicated by this demand. In turn, workers and owners in the automobile industry will earn an additional $8 million in wages and profits. They, in turn, will spend part of this additional income, let's say $6.4 million, on televisions and other goods and services. And the workers in the production of the televisions and those other goods and services will earn additional income, and so on, and so on.

Table 25.2 shows how the multiplier works in detail. In the first round, there is an initial increase of investment spending of $10 million. This additional demand leads to an initial increase in GDP and income of $10 million. Assuming that the MPC is 0.8, the $10 million of additional income will increase consumer spending by $8 million. Round 2 begins with this $8 million increase in consumer spending. Because of this increase in demand, GDP and income increase by $8 million. At the end of round 2, consumers will have an additional $8 million; with a MPC of 0.8, consumer spending will therefore increase by 0.8×8 million, or $6.4 million. The process continues in round 3 with an increase in consumer spending of $6.4 million. It continues, in diminishing amounts,

Multiplier: The ratio of changes in output to changes in spending. It measures the degree to which changes in spending are "multiplied" into changes in output.

ACTIVE GRAPH

Figure 25.7
Multiplier
When investment increases by ΔI from I_0 to I_1, equilibrium output increases by Δy from y_0 to y_1. The change in output (Δy) is greater than the change in investment (ΔI).

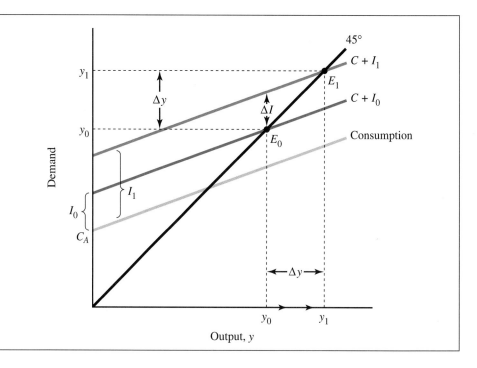

Table 25.2 The Multiplier in Action

Round of Spending	Increase in Demand	Increase in GDP and Income	Increase in Consumption
1	$10	$10	$ 8
2	8	8	6.4
3	6.4	6.4	5.12
4	5.12	5.12	4.096
5	4.096	4.096	3.277
⋮	⋮	⋮	⋮
Total	50 million	50 million	40 million

Note: All figures for increases indicate millions of dollars.

through subsequent rounds. If we add up the spending in all the (infinite) rounds, we will find that the initial $10 million of spending leads to a $50 million increase in GDP and income. In this case, the multiplier is 5.

The multiplier also works in reverse. Suppose that consumers become pessimistic, cutting back on autonomous consumption by $10 million. Demand for GDP falls by $10 million, which means that output and income fall by $10 million. Consumers then cut back their spending further because their incomes have fallen. What happens is the reverse of what we just described for the multiplier working in the positive direction. If the MPC were 0.8, total spending would fall by $50 million.

We show how to derive the formula for a simple multiplier in the appendix to this chapter:

$$\text{multiplier} = 1/(1 - \text{MPC})$$

Suppose the MPC = 0.8; then the multiplier would be $1/(1 - 0.8)$, or 5.

Notice that the multiplier increases as the MPC increases. If MPC = 0.4, the multiplier = 1.67; if the MPC = 0.6, the multiplier = 2.5. To see why the multiplier increases as the marginal propensity to consume MPC increases, think back to our examples of the multiplier. The multiplier occurs because the initial increase in investment spending increases income, which leads to higher consumer spending. With a higher MPC, the increase in consumer spending will be greater, since consumers will spend a higher fraction of the additional income they receive as the multiplier increases. With this extra spending, the eventual increase in output will be greater, and therefore so will the multiplier.

Government Spending and Taxation

Keynesian Fiscal Policy

We now make our model more realistic, bringing in government spending and taxation, therefore making the model useful for understanding economic policy debates. In those debates, we often hear recommendations for increasing government spending to increase GDP or cutting taxes to increase GDP. As we will explain, both the level of government spending and the level of taxation, through their influence on the demand for goods and services, affect the level of GDP in the short run.

Using taxes and spending to influence the level of GDP in the short run is known as **Keynesian fiscal policy**. As we discussed in Chapter 22, changes in taxes can also affect the

Keynesian fiscal policy: The use of taxes and government spending to affect the level of GDP in the short run.

supply of output in the long run through the way taxes can change incentives to work or invest. However, in this chapter, we concentrate on the role of taxes and spending in determining demand for goods and services and, hence, output, in the short run.

Let's look first at the role government spending plays in determining GDP. Government purchases of goods and services are a component of spending:

$$\text{Total spending including government} = C + I + G$$

Increases in government purchases, G, shift the $C + I + G$ line upward, just as increases in investment I or autonomous consumption do. If government spending increases by $1, the $C + I + G$ line will shift upward by $1.

Panel A of Figure 25.8 shows how increases in government spending affect GDP. The increase in government spending from G_0 to G_1 shifts the $C + I + G$ line upward and increases the level of GDP from y_0 to y_1.

As you can see, changes in government purchases have exactly the same effects as changes in investment or changes in autonomous consumption. The multiplier for government spending is also the same as for changes in investment or autonomous consumption:

$$\text{multiplier for government spending} = 1/(1 - \text{MPC})$$

For example, if the MPC were 0.6 and the multiplier were 2.5, a $10 billion increase in government spending would increase GDP by $25 billion. The multiplier for government spending works just like the multiplier for investment or consumption. An initial increase in government spending raises GDP and income. The increase in income, however, generates further increases in demand as consumers increase their spending.

Now let's consider taxes. We need to take into account that government programs affect households' **disposable personal income**—income that ultimately flows back to households and to consumers after subtraction from their income of any taxes paid and after addition to their income of any transfer payments they receive (such as Social Security, unemployment insurance, or welfare). If the government takes $10 net out of every $100 you make, your income after taxes and transfer payments is only $90.

Here's how we include taxes and transfers into the model: We make consumption spending depend on income after taxes and transfers, or $y - T$, where T is net taxes (taxes paid to government minus transfers received by households). For simplicity, we'll just refer to T as taxes, but remember that it is taxes less transfer payments. The consumption function with taxes is

$$C = C_a + b(y - T)$$

If taxes increase by $1, after-tax income will decrease by $1. Since the marginal propensity to consume is b, this means that consumption will fall by $b \times \$1$, and the $C + I + G$ line will shift downward by $b \times \$1$. For example, if b is 0.6, a $1 increase in taxes will mean that consumers will have a dollar less of income and will therefore decrease consumption spending by $0.60.

Panel B of Figure 25.8 shows how an increase in taxes will decrease the level of GDP. As the level of taxes increases, the demand line will shift downward by $b \times$ (the increase in taxes). Equilibrium income will fall from y_0 to y_1.

The multiplier for taxes is slightly different than the multiplier for government spending. If we cut government spending by $1, the $C + I + G$ will shift downward by $1. However, if we increase taxes by $1, consumers will cut back their consumption by only $b \times \$1$. Thus, the $C + I + G$ line will shift downward by slightly less than $1, or $b \times \$1$. For example, if $b = 0.6$, the demand line would shift down vertically only by $0.60.

Disposable personal income:
The income that flows back to households, taking into account transfers and taxes.

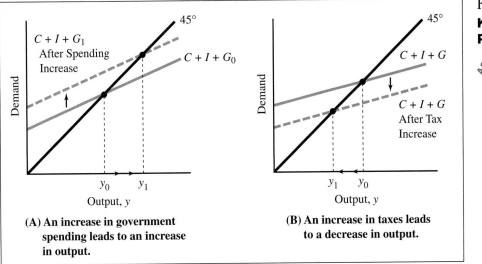

Figure 25.8
Keynesian Fiscal Policy

(A) An increase in government spending leads to an increase in output.

(B) An increase in taxes leads to a decrease in output.

Since the demand line does not shift by the same amount with taxes as it does with government spending, the formula for the tax multiplier is slightly different. Here's the formula for the tax multiplier; in the appendix, we show how to derive it:

$$\text{tax multiplier} = -b/(1-b)$$

The tax multiplier is negative because increases in taxes decrease disposable personal income and lead to a reduction in consumption spending. If the MPC = 0.6, the tax multiplier will be $-0.6/(1-0.6) = -1.5$.

Notice that the tax multiplier is smaller (in absolute value) than the government-spending multiplier, which for the same MPC is 2.5. The reason the tax multiplier is smaller is that an increase in taxes first reduces income of households by the amount of the tax. However, because the MPC is less than 1, the decrease in consumer spending is less than the increase in taxes.

Finally, you may wonder what would happen if we increased both government spending and taxes by an equal amount at the same time. Because the multiplier for government spending is larger than the multiplier for taxes, equal increases in both government spending and taxes will increase GDP. Economists call the multiplier for equal increases in government spending and taxes *the balanced budget multiplier* because equal changes in government spending and taxes will not unbalance the budget. In the appendix, we show that the balanced budget multiplier in our simple model is always equal to 1. For example, if spending and taxes are both increased by $10 billion, then GDP will also increase by $10 billion.

Let's look at several examples of how we can use fiscal policy, altering taxes and government spending to affect GDP. In all these examples, suppose that GDP is $6,000 billion, the marginal propensity to consume is 0.6, the government-spending multiplier is $1/(1-0.6) = 2.5$, and the tax multiplier is $-0.6/(1-0.6) = -1.5$.

1. Suppose policymakers want to increase GDP by 1%, or $60 billion. By how much do policymakers have to increase government spending to meet this target? Since the multiplier for government spending is 2.5, we need to increase government spending by only $24 billion. With a multiplier of 2.5, the $24 billion increase in government spending leads to an increase in GDP of $60 billion ($24 billion $\times$ 2.5 = $60 billion).

2. Suppose policymakers wanted to use tax cuts rather than government spending increases to increase GDP by $60 billion. How large a tax cut would be necessary? Since

the tax multiplier is –1.5, we need to cut taxes by $40 billion. The $40 billion tax cut times the multiplier will lead to the objective, a $60 billion increase in GDP (–$40 billion × –1.5 = $60 billion).

3. Finally, if policymakers wanted to change taxes and government spending by equal amounts, so as to not affect the federal budget, how large a change would be needed to increase GDP by $60 billion? Since the balanced budget multiplier is 1, both government spending and taxes must be increased by $60 billion.

The models that we are using are very simple and leave out important factors. Nonetheless, the same basic principles apply in real situations. Here are three examples of real Keynesian fiscal policy from the 1990s:

1. In 1993, the three members of the President's Council of Economic Advisers wrote a letter to President Clinton stating that they thought the cuts in government spending being proposed at the time were $20 billion too large. The economic model the council members used had a multiplier for government spending of approximately 1.5. With this multiplier, the decrease in GDP from the $20 billion spending cut would be ($20 billion × 1.5) = $30 billion. This was approximately 0.5% of GDP. If, in the absence of these cuts, GDP was expected to grow at 3% a year, the President's advisers estimated that with these cuts, GDP would grow at only 2.5% a year. However, the advice of the council members came too late to influence the policy decisions.

2. During 1994, the U.S. government urged the Japanese to increase Japanese public spending and cut taxes to stimulate their economy. The Japanese came up with a plan and presented it to U.S. policymakers. U.S. policymakers evaluated the effects of this plan by using multiplier analysis. The United States thought that this plan did not provide enough fiscal stimulus and urged the Japanese to take more aggressive actions. Several years later, the Japanese did adopt a more aggressive plan.

3. During the late 1990s, the Chinese economy came under pressure from the economic downturn in Asia and its own attempts to reform and restructure the economy. To prevent a severe economic slowdown, the Chinese engaged in active Keynesian fiscal policy. The government decided to increase its spending on domestic infrastructure, including roads, rails, and urban facilities.

We use special terminology to describe government actions taken to effect changes in the economy. Government policies that increase total demand and GDP are called **expansionary policies**. Government policies that decrease total demand and GDP are **contractionary policies**. Tax cuts and government spending increases are examples of expansionary policies. Tax increases and government spending cuts are examples of contractionary policies.

When a government increases its spending or cuts taxes to stimulate the economy, it will increase the government's **budget deficit**; the difference between its spending and its tax collections. For example, suppose the budget were initially balanced (government spending equaled taxes received) and the government increased its spending. The government would then be running a budget deficit—government spending exceeding taxation. To pay for its additional spending, the government would have to borrow money by selling government bonds, which are government IOUs, to the public. Traditional Keynesian models assume that this borrowing has no significant effects on the economy.

Although Keynesian models are very simple and leave out many factors, like all models, they illustrate some important lessons:

- An increase in government spending will increase the total demand for goods and services.

Expansionary policies: Government policy actions that lead to increases in output.
Contractionary policies: Government policy actions that lead to decreases in output.
Budget deficit: The difference between a government's spending and its revenues from taxation.

- Cutting taxes will increase the after-tax income of consumers and will also lead to an increase in the total demand for goods and services.

In the short run, the level of GDP is determined primarily by the demand for goods and services.

TEST Your Understanding

7. If the MPC is 0.4, what is the government spending multiplier?

8. Using taxes and government spending to control the level of GDP in the short run is known as Keynesian _____ policy.

9. An increase in government spending of $10 billion will shift the $C + I + G$ line upward by _____ and increase GDP by this amount times the government spending multiplier.

10. If the MPC is 0.8, by how much will GDP decrease if taxes are increased by $10 billion?

11. If economic advisers fear that the economy is growing too rapidly, what fiscal policies should they recommend?

Keynesian Fiscal Policy in U.S. History

The elements of Keynes theory were developed in the 1930s, but it took a long time before economic policy decisions were based on Keynesian principles. Many people associate Keynesian fiscal policy in the United States with actions taken by President Franklin Roosevelt during the 1930s. But this is a misleading view, as "A Closer Look: Fiscal Policy in the Great Depression," explains.

Although Keynesian fiscal policy was not deliberately used during the 1930s, the growth in military spending at the onset of World War II increased total demand in the economy and helped to pull the economy out of its long decade of poor performance.

 **A CLOSER LOOK** Fiscal Policy in the Great Depression

The Great Depression in the United States lasted throughout the 1930s and did not really end until the beginning of World War II in the early 1940s. It was during this period that Keynesian economics was born. According to Keynesian economics, expansionary fiscal policy—tax cuts and increased government spending—could pull the economy out of recession or depression. Was Keynesian fiscal policy actually used during the Great Depression?

According to E. Cary Brown, a former economics professor at the Massachusetts Institute of Technology, "Fiscal policy, then, seems to have been an unsuccessful recovery device in the 'thirties—not because it did not work, but because it was not tried." During the 1930s, politicians did not believe in Keynesian fiscal policy, largely because they feared the consequences of government budget deficits. According to Brown, fiscal policy was expansionary only during 2 years of the Great Depression: 1931 and 1936. In those years, Congress voted for substantial payments to veterans, over the objections of Presidents Herbert Hoover and Franklin Roosevelt. Although government spending increased during the 1930s, so did taxes, resulting in no net fiscal expansion.

Source: Adapted from E. Cary Brown, "Fiscal Policy in the Thirties: A Reappraisal," *American Economic Review*, vol. 46, December 1956, pp. 863–868.

But to see Keynesian fiscal policy in action, we need to turn to the 1960s. It was not until the presidency of John F. Kennedy during the early 1960s that Keynesian fiscal policy came to be accepted.

Walter Heller, the chairman of the President's Council of Economic Advisors under John F. Kennedy, was a forceful advocate of Keynesian economics. From his perspective, the economy was operating far below its potential, and a tax cut was the perfect medicine to bring the economy back to full employment. When Kennedy entered office, the unemployment rate was 6.7%. Heller believed that the unemployment rate at full employment was approximately 4%. He convinced Kennedy of the need for a tax program to stimulate the economy, and Kennedy put forth an economic program that was based largely on Keynesian principles.

Two other factors led the Kennedy administration to support the tax cut: First, tax rates were extremely high at the time. The top individual tax rate was 91%, compared to about 40% today. The corporate tax rate was 52%, compared to 35% today. Second, Heller convinced Kennedy that even if a tax cut led to a federal budget deficit (the gap between federal spending and taxes), it was not a problem. In 1961, the federal deficit was less than 1% of GDP, and future projections indicated that the deficit would disappear as the economy grew because of higher tax revenues.

The tax cuts were enacted into law in February 1964, after Lyndon Johnson became President following Kennedy's assassination. The tax cuts included permanent cuts in tax rates for both individuals and corporations. Estimating the actual effects that the tax cuts had on the economy is difficult; to have a valid comparison, we need to estimate how the economy would have behaved without the tax cuts. However, the economy grew at a rapid rate following the tax cuts. From 1963 to 1966, both real GDP and consumption grew at rates exceeding 4%. We cannot rule out the possibility that the economy could have grown this rapidly without the tax cuts. Nonetheless, the rapid growth during this period suggests that the tax cuts had the effect, predicted by Keynesian theory, of stimulating economic growth. (Some economists would argue that supply-side factors, such as lower marginal tax rates, could also have stimulated growth.)

The next major use of Keynesian theory in economic policy occurred in 1968. As the Vietnam War began and military spending increased, unemployment fell to very low levels. From 1966 to 1969, the overall unemployment rate fell below 4%. Policymakers

President Kennedy proposed tax cuts to stimulate the economy.

became concerned that the economy was overheating and that this would lead to a higher inflation rate for the economy. In 1968, a temporary tax surcharge of 10% was enacted to reduce total demand for goods and services. The 10% surcharge was a tax on a tax, so it raised the taxes paid by households by 10%. The surcharge was specifically designed to be temporary and was scheduled to expire within a year.

The surcharge did not decrease consumer spending as much as economists had initially estimated. Part of the reason was that the tax increase was temporary. Economists who have studied consumption behavior have noticed that consumers often base their spending on an estimate of their long-run average income or **permanent income**, not on their current income.

For example, consider a salesman who usually earns $50,000 a year, although his income in any single year might be higher or lower than $50,000. On the basis of his permanent income, he consumes $45,000, for an MPC of 0.9 of his permanent income. If his income in one year is higher than average, say $55,000, he may still consume $45,000, as if he earned his normal $50,000, and save the rest.

The temporary, one-year tax surcharge did not have a major effect on the permanent income of households. Because their permanent income was not decreased very much by the tax surcharge, households that based their consumption decisions on their permanent income would be expected to maintain their prior level of consumption. Instead of reducing consumption, they would simply reduce their saving for the period that the surcharge was in effect. It appears that this is what consumers did, resulting in a smaller decrease in demand for goods and services than economists anticipated.

During the 1970s, there were many changes in taxes and spending but no major changes in overall fiscal policy. There was a tax rebate and other tax incentives in 1975 following the recession in 1973. However, these tax changes were mild.

The tax cuts enacted during 1981 at the beginning of the first term of President Ronald Reagan were significant. However, they were not proposed on Keynesian grounds, to increase aggregate demand. Instead, the tax cuts were justified on the basis of improving economic incentives and increasing the supply of output. As we discussed in Chapter 22, taxes can have important effects on the supply of labor, saving, and economic growth. Proponents of the 1981 tax cuts emphasized these effects and not increases in aggregate demand. Nonetheless, the tax cuts did appear to increase consumer demand and helped the economy recover from the back-to-back recessions in the early 1980s.

By the mid-1980s, large government budget deficits began to emerge. Policymakers became concerned with those growing budget deficits. As deficits grew and became the focus of attention, there was no longer interest in using Keynesian fiscal policy to manage the economy. While there were government spending and tax changes in the 1980s and 1990s, few of them were justified solely by Keynesian thinking.

Permanent income: An estimate of a household's long-run average level of income.

Automatic Stabilizers

With a slight addition to our basic model, we can explain one of the important facts in U.S. economic history. Figure 25.9 plots the rate of growth of U.S. real GDP from 1871 to 1998. It is apparent from the graph that the U.S. economy has been much more stable after World War II than before. The reason is that government taxes and transfer payments (such as unemployment insurance and welfare payments) grew sharply after the war. These taxes and transfer payments can automatically reduce fluctuations in real GDP and thereby stabilize the economy. We say that taxes and transfers act as **automatic stabilizers** for the economy.

Here is how the automatic stabilizers work. When income is high, the government collects more taxes and pays out less in transfer payments. Because the government is taking funds out of the hands of consumers, there will be reduced consumer spending.

Automatic stabilizers: Taxes and transfer payments that stabilize GDP without requiring policymakers to take explicit actions.

Figure 25.9
**Growth Rate
of U.S. GDP,
1871–1998**

Source: Angus Maddison,
*Dynamic Forces in Capitalist
Development* (New York: Oxford
University Press, 1991) and the
U.S. Department of Commerce,
Bureau of Economic Analysis,
1999.

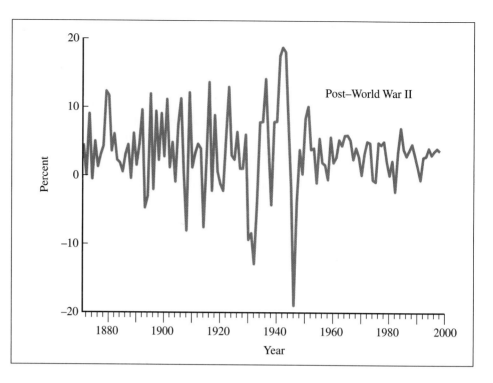

On the other hand, when output is low (such as during recessions), the government collects less taxes and pays out more in transfer payments, increasing consumer spending because the government is putting funds into the hands of consumers. The automatic stabilizers prevent consumption from falling as much in bad times and from rising as much in good times. This stabilizes the economy without any need for decisions from Congress or the White House.

To see how automatic stabilizers work in our model, we must take into account that the government levies income taxes by applying a tax rate to the level of income. To sim-

*This Internal Revenue Service
worker in Austin, Texas is an inte-
gral part of a process to stabilize
the U.S. economy.*

plify, suppose there were a single tax rate of 0.2 (in percent, 20%) and income were $100. The government would then collect $0.2 \times \$100 = \$20$ in taxes.

In general, we can view the total taxes collected by the government T as a product of the tax rate, t, and output, y:

$$T = ty$$

Consumer's after-tax income will be

$$(y - ty) = y(1 - t) = (1 - t)y$$

If consumption depends on after-tax income, we have the following consumption function:

$$C = C_a + b(1 - t)y$$

This is the consumption function with income taxes. The only difference between the consumption function with income taxes and the consumption function without income taxes is that the marginal propensity to consume is adjusted for taxes, and so

$$\text{Adjusted MPC} = b(1 - t)$$

The reason for this adjustment is that consumers keep only a fraction $(1 - t)$ of their income; the rest, t, goes to the government. When income increases by $1, consumers' after-tax incomes increase by only $\$1 \times (1 - t)$, and of that $\$(1 - t)$, they spend a fraction b.

Raising the tax rate therefore lowers the MPC adjusted for taxes. Figure 25.10 shows the consequences of raising tax rates. With a higher tax rate, the government takes a higher fraction of income, and less is left over for consumers. Recall that the slope of the $C + I + G$ line is the marginal propensity to consume. Raising the tax rate lowers the adjusted MPC and reduces the slope of this line. The $C + I + G$ line with taxes intersects the 45° line at a lower level of income. Output falls from y_0 to y_1.

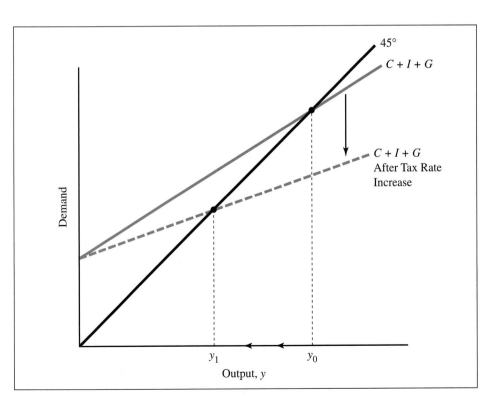

Figure 25.10
Increase in Tax Rates
An increase in tax rates decreases the slope of the $C + I + G$ line. This lowers output and reduces the multiplier.

Remember that a smaller marginal propensity to consume also leads to a lower value for the multiplier. As tax rates increase and the adjusted MPC falls, the multiplier will decrease. A smaller multiplier means that any shocks, such as shocks to investment, will have less of an impact on the economy.

Now that we have introduced income taxes into our model, we can see how automatic stabilizers work. Since World War II, taxes and transfer payments in the United States have increased sharply. As we have seen, higher tax rates will lower the multiplier and make the economy less susceptible to shocks. With higher taxes and transfers payments, there is a much looser link between fluctuations in disposable personal income and fluctuations in GDP. Because disposable personal income is more stable, consumption spending is also more stable. Thus, there is a smaller multiplier, and the economy is more stable.

It is important to emphasize that automatic stabilizers work silently in the background, doing their job without requiring explicit action by policymakers. Total tax collections rise and fall with GDP without requiring that policymakers change tax rates. The fact that the automatic stabilizers work without any laws being enacted is particularly important at times when it is difficult to obtain a political consensus for taking any action and policymakers are reluctant to use Keynesian fiscal policy as a deliberate policy tool.

Other factors contribute to the stability of the economy. We explained how consumers base their spending decisions in part on their permanent income, not just on their current level of income. If households base their consumption decisions partly on their permanent or long-run income, they will not be very sensitive to changes in their current income. If their consumption does not change very much with current income, the marginal propensity to consume out of current income will be small, which will make the multiplier for investment or autonomous consumption spending small as well. When consumers base their decisions on long-run factors, not just on their current level of income, the economy tends to be stabilized.

Exports and Imports

With international trade becoming an increasingly important economic and political issue, it is critical to understand how exports and imports affect the level of GDP. Two simple modifications of our model will allow us to understand how exports and imports affect GDP in the short run.

Exports and imports affect GDP through their influence on how the world beyond the United States demands goods and services produced in the United States. An increase in exports means that there's an increase in the demand for goods produced in the United States. An increase in imports means that there's an increase in foreign goods purchased by U.S. residents. Importing goods rather than purchasing them from our domestic producers reduces the demand for U.S. goods. For example, if we in the United States spend a total of $10 billion on all automobiles but we imported $3 billion in automobiles, then only $7 billion is spent on U.S. automobiles.

To get a clearer picture of the effects on GDP from exports and imports, let's for the moment ignore government spending and taxes. In the appendix, we present a complete model with both government and foreign countries to whom we sell our exports and from whom we buy our imports. To modify our model to include the effects of exports and imports, we need to take two steps:

1. Add exports, X, to other sources of spending as another source of demand for U.S. goods and services. We assume that the level of exports (foreign demand for U.S. products) is given.

2. Subtract imports, M, from total spending by U.S. residents. We will assume that imports, like consumption, increase with the level of income.

Consumers will import more goods as income rises. We can write this as

$$\text{imports} = M = my$$

where m is a fraction known as the **marginal propensity to import**. We subtract this fraction from b, the overall marginal propensity to consume, to obtain the MPC for spending on domestic goods, $b - m$. For example, if $b = 0.8$ and $m = 0.2$, then for every \$1 that GDP increases, total consumption increases by \$0.80 but spending on domestic goods increases only by \$0.60 because \$0.20 is spent on imports. The MPC in this example, adjusted for imports is $(0.8 - 0.2) = 0.6$.

Figure 25.11 shows how equilibrium output is determined in an open economy, that is, an economy that engages in trade with the rest of the world. We plot total demand for U.S. goods and services on our graph and find the level of equilibrium income where it intersects the 45° line. The total demand line has an intercept on the vertical axis of $C_a + I + X$, which is the sum of autonomous consumption, investment, and exports. The slope of the line is $b - m$, which is the MPC adjusted for imports. Equilibrium output is the value of output where the demand line for U.S. goods crosses the 45° line.

Let's examine an application of the model that we just developed. Suppose the Japanese decide to buy another \$5 billion worth of goods from the United States. What will happen to U.S. domestic output? Panel A of Figure 25.12 shows the effect of an increase in exports. The demand line will shift vertically upward by the increase in exports (ΔX). This will increase equilibrium income from y_0 to y_1.

The increase in income will be larger than the increase in exports because of the multiplier effect. This multiplier is based on the MPC adjusted for trade. For example, if $b = 0.8$ and $m = 0.2$, the adjusted MPC ($b - m$) is 0.6 and the multiplier will be $1/(1 - 0.6) = 2.5$. Therefore, a \$5 billion increase in exports will lead to a \$12.5 billion increase in GDP.

Now, suppose that U.S. residents become more attracted to foreign goods, and as a result, our marginal propensity to import increases. What happens to GDP? Panel B of Figure 25.12 depicts the effect of an increase in imported foreign goods. The adjusted

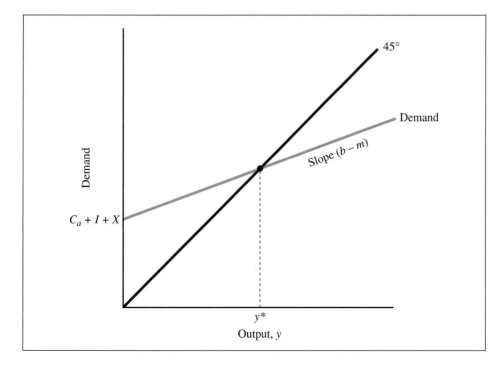

Figure 25.11

Determining Output in an Open Economy

Output is determined where the demand for domestic goods equals output.

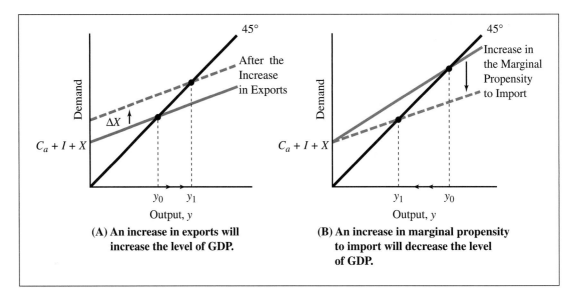

Figure 25.12 **Increase in Exports and Imports**

MPC ($b - m$) will fall as the marginal propensity to import increases. This reduces the slope of the demand line, and output will fall from y_0 to y_1.

We can now understand why our domestic political leaders are eager to sell our goods abroad. Whether it is electronics or weapons, increased U.S. exports will increase U.S. GDP and reduce unemployment in the short run. At the same time, we can also understand why politicians will find "buy American" policies attractive in the short run. To the extent that U.S. residents buy U.S. goods rather than imports, output will be higher.

The Netherlands's Multiplier

Some economists have argued that the multiplier for government spending in the Netherlands is smaller than the multiplier for government spending in the United States. As an economic detective, can you explain this difference? (Hint: Imports and exports are a higher fraction of GDP in the Netherlands.)

The Netherlands is a small country and highly dependent on foreign trade. It has a high marginal propensity to import, which makes its adjusted MPC ($b - m$) low. A low adjusted MPC will make the multiplier low as well. Thus, the multiplier for fiscal policy in the Netherlands is less than the fiscal policy multiplier for the United States because the Netherlands has a higher marginal propensity to import. ◆

A Final Reminder

It is important to emphasize that all the models in this chapter are based on short-run considerations. Policies appropriate for the short run are not necessarily appropriate for the long run. In this chapter, we have seen that an increase in desired consumption spending will raise equilibrium output in the short run. But in our chapter on long-run growth, we saw that higher saving (lower consumption) would increase output in the long run. The models in this chapter are designed only to analyze short-run fluctuations in output. They are not designed for advising what should be long-run policy. In the next several chapters, we continue our study of short-run models by including interest rates and monetary policy as determinants of demand. Later, we will see how changes in wages and prices lead the economy from the short run to the long run.

Using the **TOOLS**

In this chapter, we developed the graphical tools and the mathematical formulas to analyze Keynesian economics. Here is an opportunity to do your own economic analysis.

1. ECONOMIC EXPERIMENT: Estimating the Marginal Propensity to Consume

For this experiment, each class member is asked to fill out the following table. Given a certain monthly income, how would you spend it and how much would you save? The top row of each column gives you the monthly disposable income. How would you allocate it each month among the various categories of spending in the table and savings? Complete each column in the table. The sum of your entries should equal your disposable income at the top of each column.

Monthly Disposable Income	$1,250	$1,500	$1,750	$2,000
Expenditures and Savings				
Food				
Housing				
Transportation				
Medical				
Entertainment				
Other expenses				
Savings				

After you have filled out the chart, compute the changes in your savings and total consumption as your income goes up. What is your marginal propensity to save (MPS)? What is your marginal propensity to consume (MPC) over your total expenditures? Graph your consumption function.

2. Estimating Changes to Output

a. Suppose $C = C_a + 0.6y$; a shock decreases C_a by $10 billion. By how much will GDP decrease?

b. An economy has a MPC = 0.6. By how much will a $10 billion increase in government purchases increase GDP? By how much will a $10 billion increase in taxes decrease GDP?

3. A Shock to Consumption

We can think of a shock to consumption as a change in autonomous consumption C_a. Economic historian Peter Temin argued that the Great Depression was caused by a negative shock to consumption. Use the graphs in this chapter to show how a negative shock to consumption can lead to a fall in output.

4. Tax Refunds and Consumer Spending

We opened the chapter with a discussion of how some economic forecasters predicted that consumption and GDP would increase because of higher refunds on income taxes. Evaluate the reasoning of these forecasters under the following different assumptions:

a. Taxpayers were not aware that they would receive refunds until they had completed their income tax statements.

b. Taxpayers did know that they would receive refunds but, as consumers, based their spending decisions solely on their current level of income.

c. Taxpayers did know that they would receive refunds and, as consumers, based their consumption decisions on their long-run permanent income.

In this chapter, we explained the logic of Keynesian economics: The demand for goods and services determines GDP in the short run. We also discussed the role that government spending and taxes play in determining output. Finally, we showed how the level of exports and imports can affect the economy in the short run. Here are this chapter's main points:

1. The level of GDP in the short run is determined by the total demand for goods and services.

2. Consumption spending consists of two parts: One part is independent of income (autonomous consumption); the other part depends on the level of income.

3. An increase in spending will typically lead to a larger increase in GDP: This effect is called the multiplier.

4. In the short run, increases in government spending lead to increases in GDP; increases in taxes lead to decreases in GDP.

5. Keynesian fiscal policies were used aggressively in the 1960s to manage the economy. Concerns about budget deficits limit the use of these policies.

6. Higher tax rates reduce fluctuations in GDP caused by shocks to spending.

7. Increases in exports lead to increases in GDP; increases in imports lead to lower GDP.

Key Terms

automatic stabilizers, 533
autonomous consumption spending, 521
budget deficit, 530
consumption function, 521
contractionary policies, 530

disposable personal income, 528
equilibrium output, 520
expansionary policies, 530
Keynesian fiscal policy, 527
marginal propensity to consume (MPC), 521

marginal propensity to import, 537
marginal propensity to save (MPS), 521
multiplier, 526
permanent income, 533
savings function, 525

Problems and Discussion Questions

1. Consider an economy in which $C = 200 + 0.5y$ and $I = 200$.
   a. Find equilibrium income.
   b. What is the multiplier for investment spending for this economy?
   c. What is the savings function?
   d. What is the level of savings at the level of equilibrium income?

2. A country wishes to increase its GDP by 100. The marginal propensity to consume is 0.8.
   a. Using the government spending multiplier, by how much should government spending be increased?
   b. Using the tax multiplier, by how much should taxes be decreased?

3. A country has a marginal propensity to consume of 0.6 and a tax rate of 0.15. How much of an increase in investment would be needed to raise GDP by 150?

4. In an open economy, the marginal propensity to consume is 0.9, and the marginal propensity to import is 0.3. How much of an increase in exports would be necessary to raise GDP by 200?

5. Explain why in the model in this chapter, a higher tax rate leads to a lower multiplier for the economy. Does that mean that raising the tax rate is good for the economy in the model in this chapter?

6. John Maynard Keynes once suggested that the reason the economy of ancient Egypt prospered was because the government had a systematic project of building pyramids.
   a. Explain the logic of Keynes' argument.
   b. What are the modern equivalent of pyramids?
   c. How would a classical economist respond to Keynes' argument?

7. a. Suppose clothing stores anticipate a good season and add substantially to inventories in their stores? What will happen to GDP?

b. Suppose economists see inventories suddenly increasing. Does this necessarily mean that there are increases in demand?

8. Sometimes the newspapers state that if the economies of Europe and Japan grow rapidly, this will increase the growth of real GDP in the United States. Using our model with exports and imports, explain the logic of this argument.

9. During the 1970s, President Gerald Ford proposed that taxes be decreased but, to avoid increasing the government budget deficit, government spending should be decreased by the same amount. What happens to GDP if taxes and government spending are both decreased by the same amount?

10. Why could a collapse of the stock market lead to reduced consumer spending?

11. Using the idea of automatic stabilizers, explain why states with more generous unemployment insurance programs will experience smaller fluctuations in output.

12. Web Exercise. As we have seen in this chapter, changes in consumer spending can have powerful effects on the economy. While many factors, including income and wealth affect consumer spending, general consumer confidence may also be a factor. For many years, the University of Michigan has published an index of consumer sentiment. Using the business/fiscal data on the Web site for the Federal Reserve Bank of St. Louis (*http://www.stls.frb.org/fred*), explore the relationships between changes in consumer sentiment and consumer spending for the periods preceding several postwar recessions.

13. Web Exercise. Although John Maynard Keynes is best known today for his book *The General Theory of Employment, Interest and Money*, he wrote several other books as well. Use the Web to find information about some of Keynes's other well-known books. You may want to start with the Web sites for "The London School" (*http://www.thefirmament.com/London*) or from Time Magazine's list of the most important people in the twentieth century (*http://www.pathfinder.com/time/time100*). What were his other writings about?

Take It to the Net

We invite you to visit the O'Sullivan/Sheffrin page on the Prentice Hall Web site at:
http://www.prenhall.com/osullivan/
for additional World Wide Web exercises for this chapter.

Model Answers to Questions

Chapter-Opening Questions

1. Cutting taxes that consumers pay leads to higher consumer spending which increases demand and, in the short run, increases output.

2. The U.S. economy is more stable today because of automatic stabilizers.

3. Increased consumer confidence can lead to higher consumer spending, which will lead to higher GDP in the short run.

4. An increase in government spending of $10 billion will lead to an increase of GDP of more than $10 billion because of the multiplier.

5. Because exports are a component of the demand for an economy's goods and services, a reduction in exports could cause a recession.

Test Your Understanding

1. At the point where the demand line crosses the 45° line, demand equals output.

2. If production exceeds demand, inventories will pile up and firms will cut production.

3. It is the MPC.

4. Upward.

5. 750.

6. 0.3.

7. The multiplier is 1.67.

8. Fiscal.

9. $10 billion.

10. GDP will decrease by $40 billion. (The tax multiplier is –4.)

11. Increase taxes or cut government spending.

Using the TOOLS

2. Estimating Changes to Output

  a. In this case, the multiplier is $1/(1 - 0.6) = 2.5$. Therefore, output will fall by $25 billion.

  b. With an MPC = 0.6, the multiplier is 2.5 $[1/(1 - 0.6)]$. An increase in government spending of $10 billion will lead to an increase in GDP of $25 billion. With an MPC = 0.6, the tax multiplier is -1.5. Thus GDP will fall by $15 billion from a $10 billion increase in taxes.

3. A Shock to Consumption. A decrease in autonomous consumption will shift down the vertical intercept of the $C + I + G$ line. This will lead to a fall in output. A large enough fall could cause a major fall in output.

4. Tax Refunds and Consumer Spending

  a. If the tax refunds were not expected and consumers base their spending on current income, then consumer spending should increase, increasing GDP.

  b. The same would be true if they anticipated the refund but still based their spending on the current value of income (which was increased by the refund).

  c. If they had anticipated the refund and also based their spending on their long-run income, there would be no change in consumption spending. In this case, the tax refund would not change their long-run income and thus would not change their spending decisions.

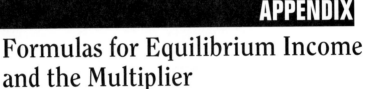

APPENDIX

Formulas for Equilibrium Income and the Multiplier

In this appendix, we do three things:

- Derive a simple formula for calculating equilibrium output for the simplest economy in which there is no government spending nor taxes.

- Derive the multipliers for the economy without government.

- Derive equilibrium output with both government and the foreign sector.

To derive the formula for equilibrium output, we use simple algebra in the following steps:

1. We know that equilibrium output occurs where output equals demand, and we know that demand = $C + I$, therefore,

$$\text{output} = \text{demand, and demand} = C + I$$

$$\text{output} = C + I$$

2. Next, we substitute the symbol y for output; more important, we substitute for the consumption function, $C = (C_a + by)$:

$$y = (C_a + by) + I$$

3. Collect all terms in y on the left side of the equation:

$$y - by = C_a + I$$

4. Factor the left side:

$$y(1 - b) = C_a + I$$

5. Divide both sides by $(1 - b)$:

$$y^* = (C_a + I)/(1 - b)$$

where y^* means the equilibrium level of output.

This is the formula for equilibrium output in the text.

Now let's find the multiplier for investment in this simple economy. To do that, we use the formula we just derived and calculate the equilibrium income at one level of investment, which we call the original level, and then calculate the equilibrium income at some other level of investment, which we call the new level. (We will "calculate" in general terms, not in specific numerical quantities.) What we will get is a formula for the change in output that results from the changes in investment.

For the original level of investment at I_0, we have

$$y_0 = (C_a + I_0)/(1 - b)$$

For a new level of investment at I_1, we have

$$y_1 = (C_a + I_1)/(1 - b)$$

The change in output Δy is the difference between the two levels of output that occur at each level of investment:

$$\Delta y = y_1 - y_0$$

Substituting for the levels of output, we have

$$\Delta y = (C_a + I_1)/(1 - b) - (C_a + I_0)/(1 - b)$$

Because the denominator in both expressions is the same $(1 - b)$, we can put the numerators over that common denominator:

$$\Delta y = [(C_a + I_1) - (C_a + I_0)]/(1 - b)$$

$$\Delta y = (I_1 - I_0)/(1 - b)$$

Finally, because $(I_1 - I_0)$ is the change in investment, ΔI, we can write

$$\Delta y = \Delta I/(1 - b)$$

or

$$\Delta y/\Delta I = 1/(1 - b)$$

Therefore, because the multiplier is the ratio of the change in income to the change in investment spending, we have

$$\text{the multiplier} = \Delta y/\Delta I = 1/(1 - b)$$

Here is another way to derive the formula for the multiplier. This way helps to illustrate its underlying logic. Suppose investment spending increases by $1. Because spending determines output, output will rise by $1. However, because consumption depends on income, consumption will increase by the marginal propensity to consume times the change in income. This means that as output rises by $1, consumption will increase by $(b \times \$1)$. Because spending determines output, this additional increase in consumer demand will cause output to rise further $(b \times \$1)$. But again, as output and income increase, consumption will increase by MPC times the change in income, which in this case will be $b \times (b \times \$1)$ or $b^2 \times \$1$. As we allow this process to continue, the total change in output will be

$$\Delta y = \$1 \times (\$1 \times b) \times (\$1 \times b^2) \times (\$1 \times b^3)\ldots$$

or

$$\Delta y = \$1 \times (1 + b + b^2 + b^3 + \ldots)$$

The term in parentheses is an infinite series whose value is equal to $1/(1 - b)$. Substituting this value for the infinite series, we have the expression for the multiplier:

$$\Delta y = \$1 \times 1/(1 - b)$$

Now we introduce government spending and taxes. Government spending is another determinant of demand, and consumption spending depends on after-tax income, so consumption equals $C_a + b(y - T)$. Following the same steps we used for equilibrium output without government, we do the same, but now with government:

$$\text{output} = \text{demand} = (C + I + G)$$

$$y = C_a + b(y - T) + I + G$$

We first collect all terms in y on the left and leave the other terms on the right:

$$y - by = C_a - bT + I + G$$

We then factor the left side:

$$y(1 - b) = C_a - bT + I + G$$

We then divide both sides by $(1 - b)$:

$$y^* = (C_a - bT + I + G)/(1 - b)$$

Using this formula and the method outlined above, we can find the multiplier for changes in government spending, taxes and the multiplier for changes in taxes:

$$\text{government spending multiplier} = 1/(1 - b)$$

$$\text{tax multiplier} = -b/(1 - b)$$

The multiplier for an increase in government spending is larger than the tax multiplier for a reduction in taxes in the same amount as an increase in government spending. Government spending increases total demand directly. Reductions in taxes first affect consumers' incomes. Because consumers will save a part of their income increase from the tax cut, not all of the tax cut is spent. Therefore, the tax multiplier is smaller (in absolute value) than the government spending multiplier.

As we explained in the text, because government spending has a larger multiplier than taxes, equal increases in government spending and taxes, called balanced budget increases, will increase total output. For equal dollar increases in both taxes and government spending, the positive effects from the spending increase will outweigh the negative effects from the tax increase. To find the balanced budget multiplier, just add the government spending and tax multipliers:

balanced budget multiplier = government spending multiplier + tax multiplier

$$= 1/(1 - b) + -b/(1 - b)$$

$$= (1 - b)/(1 - b)$$

$$= 1$$

The balanced budget multiplier equals 1; a \$10 billion increase in both taxes and government spending will increase GDP by \$10 billion.

Finally, we derive equilibrium output with both government spending, and taxes, and the foreign sector. First, recall that equilibrium output occurs where output equals demand. We now must include demand from both the government sector and the foreign sector. Demand from the foreign sector is exports minus imports:

$$\text{output} = \text{demand} = (C + I + G + X - M)$$

Consumption depends on disposable income:

$$C = C_a + b(y - T)$$

and imports depend on the level of output:

$$M = my$$

Substitute the equations for consumption and imports into the equation where output equals demand:

$$y = C_a + b(y - T) + I + G + X - my$$

Collect all terms in y on the left and leave the other terms on the right:

$$y - (b - m)y = C_a - bT + I + G + X$$

Factor the left side:

$$y[1 - (b - m)] = C_a - bT + I + G + X$$

Divide both sides by $[1 - (b - m)]$:

$$y^* = (C_a - bT + I + G + X)/[1 - (b - m)]$$

This is the expression for equilibrium income with government in an open economy. It can be used, following the method we outlined, to calculate multipliers in the open economy.

Using the TOOLS

1. Find the Multiplier
An economy has a marginal propensity to consume $b = 0.6$ and a marginal propensity to import $m = 0.2$. What is the multiplier for government spending for this economy?

2. The Effects of Taxes and Spending
Suppose the economy has a marginal propensity to consume $b = 0.4$. The government increases its spending by \$2 billion and raises taxes by \$1 billion. What happens to equilibrium income?

3. Savings and Taxes
When there are taxes, savings is defined as disposable income minus consumption or $S = (y - T) - C$. In an economy with government but no foreign sector—a closed economy—equilibrium income is determined where output equals demand or $y = C + I + G$. Show that we can also determine equilibrium income using the relationship $S + T = I + G$.

4. Working with a Model
An economy has

$$C = 100 + 0.5(y - T)$$

$$I = 50$$

$$G = 50$$

$$T = 20$$

a. Find equilibrium income.

b. What is the multiplier for government spending?

c. Find the savings function.

d. What are the level of savings when the economy is in equilibrium?

e. Show that at equilibrium, $S + T = G + I$.

Model Answers to Questions

Using the Tools

1. Find the Multiplier. Since $b = 0.6$ and $m = 0.2$, the marginal propensity to consume adjusted for taxes is 0.4. The multiplier is $1/(1 - 0.4)$, or 1.67. Alternatively, you could use the last formula in the appendix to derive the multiplier explicitly.

2. The Effects of Taxes and Spending. The government spending multiplier in this case is $1/(1 - 0.4)$, or 1.67. The tax multiplier is $-0.4/(1 - 0.4)$, or -0.67. Thus, equilibrium income will increase by (\$2 billion $\times$ 1.67) $-$ (\$1 billion $\times$ 0.67) $=$ \$2.67 billion.

3. Savings and Taxes. First, $y - T - C = S$ or $y - C = S + T$. Second, $y = C + I + G$ or $y - C = I + G$. Thus, $S + T = I + G$.

4. Working with a Model

   a. $y = 100 + 0.5 (y - 20) + 50 + 50$, which yields $y = 380$.

   b. The multiplier is $1/0.5 = 2$.

   c. The savings function is $S = (y - T) - [100 + 0.5 (y - T)]$, or $S = -100 + 0.5(y - T)$.

   d. At the equilibrium income of 380 and with $T = 20$, $S = 80$.

   e. In this case, substituting in $S + T = I + G$ yields 80 $+ 20 = 50 + 50$ or $100 = 100$.

CHAPTER

26

Investment and Financial Intermediation

Ordinary people have always been deeply suspicious of Wall Street. Does all that financial wheeling and dealing—the mergers, the leveraged buyouts, the trading of one kind of security for another, and the speculation—make the U.S. economy more productive? Or do all those financiers live off the hard work of the citizens of the United States? And don't they cost ordinary workers when mergers of large corporations result in downsizing and layoffs?

Surely, financiers, on Wall Street or anywhere in the world are interested in making money. Some are seriously greedy. And mistakes have been made on the stock exchanges and in corporate boardrooms throughout the world. But what happens in the financial markets of the world does contribute to the economies of the world. Financial markets make it easier for economies to invest in the future.

n this chapter, we study the role of investment in the economy and the part that institutions such as banks and savings and loans (often called S&Ls) play in facilitating that investment. In the previous chapter, we assumed that the level of investment was constant. You are about to see the factors that govern investment decisions and how financial markets make it easier for an economy to invest.

In this chapter, you will develop some insight into investment and finance. For example, you will discover how to answer these kinds of questions:

1. **Why does investment spending depend on interest rates? Does it depend also on other factors?**
2. **Why do businesses and homeowners want to borrow in inflationary times, when interest rates are high?**
3. **How can banks and other financial institutions make risk seem to vanish?**
4. **Why would most investments in the economy not occur if there were no financial institutions?**
5. **Why do runs on healthy and profitable banks, which occur when depositors all try to get their money out of banks at the same time, rarely happen today?**

An investment, broadly defined, is an action today that has costs today and provides benefits in the future. A firm that builds a new plant today incurs costs today and will earn revenues in the future. College students incur costs to attend school now to earn higher income in the future. A government spends money for a few years to build a dam to have a source of hydroelectric power for many years into the future. These are examples of investments. Notice that we're using the term *investment* in a broader sense than we did in Chapter 20 when we discussed private domestic investment in the GDP accounts. Here an investment is an action taken by any party, such as a college student, that has costs today and provides benefits in the future.

To understand how investment decisions are made, we need to learn about interest rates. To understand how interest rates influence those decisions you need to learn the distinction between nominal interest rates and real interest rates:

Nominal interest rates: Interest rates quoted in the financial markets.

Real interest rate: The nominal interest rate minus the inflation rate.

- **Nominal interest rates** are the rates actually charged in the market.

- **Real interest rates** are nominal rates that are adjusted for inflation by subtracting the inflation rate—a concept that we will explain later in this chapter.

Financial intermediaries: Organizations that receive funds from savers and channel those funds to investors.

Financial institutions such as banks, savings and loans, and insurance companies play a role in making it easier for an economy to invest. These organizations receive funds from savers and channel savers' fund to investors. You will see that these institutions—called **financial intermediaries**—help to reduce the risks and costs associated with investment and allow a greater volume of investment to occur in the economy.

Investment: A Plunge into the Unknown

Let's look again at the definition of investment: actions today that have costs today and provide benefits in the future. Looking at it again, we can see that investments are trade-offs that occur over time: Firms or individuals incur costs today in the hope of future gain. The phrase "hope of" is an important aspect of investment decisions. That simply means that payoffs occurring in the future cannot be known with certainty. Investments are a plunge into the unknown.

Consider a few examples: When an automobile firm builds a new plant because it anticipates increased future demand for its cars, it is taking a gamble. Suppose the model in the future proves to be unpopular or the economy goes into a recession and

A high-rise building is a risky venture for its investors who are betting that the office space will be needed in the future.

consumers cut back their purchases of all cars. By building a new plant when it was not needed, the firm will have made an investment decision that didn't pay off in the future. Suppose a government builds nuclear plants, then citizens decide that they are unsafe and force the plants to be closed. The government would have wasted resources on this investment.

Firms and individuals are regularly revising their estimates of the future—because it is uncertain. Sometimes, they're optimistic, deciding to increase their investment spending; other times, they're pessimistic, cutting back on investment spending. These changes in outlook can occur suddenly and may lead to sharp swings in investment spending. John Maynard Keynes said these sharp swings were often irrational, reflecting, perhaps, our most basic, primal instincts. He often referred to what he called the animal spirits of investors.

To estimate future events, firms will look carefully at current developments. If economic growth is currently sluggish, firms may project that it will be sluggish in the future as well. If there is an upsurge in economic growth, firms may become optimistic, increasing their investment spending. Investment spending tends to be closely related to the current pace of economic growth. One theory of investment spending, known as the **accelerator theory**, emphasizes the role of expected growth in real GDP on investment spending. When real GDP growth is expected to be high, firms anticipate that their investments in plant and equipment will be profitable and therefore increase their total investment spending.

Projections for the future and investors' current animal spirits are both likely to move in conjunction with real GDP growth. For these reasons, we would expect that

Accelerator theory: The theory of investment that says that current investment spending depends positively on the expected future growth of real GDP.

investment spending would be a volatile component of GDP. As Figure 26.1 indicates, this is the case.

Figure 26.1 plots total investment spending as a share of U.S. GDP from 1976 to 1998. There are two things we need to be sure you see in this figure:

- Over this period, the share of investment in GDP ranged from a low of nearly 11% to a high of nearly 18%—a dramatic difference of seven percentage points of GDP.

- These swings in investment spending often occur over short periods. During periods of recessions, investment spending falls sharply. Investment spending is highly **procyclical**, meaning that investment spending increases during booms and falls during recessions.

Procyclical: A component of GDP is procyclical if it rises and falls with the overall level of GDP.

Although investment spending is procyclical, there are often differences among different types of investment. Figure 26.2 shows that two important components of investment—nonresidential structures and producers' durable equipment—behaved differently during the last U.S. recession and recovery. Although both types of investment fell in 1991, investment in structures such as new factories was slow to recover. Because structures last a long time, firms needed to be sure that the recessionary period had really ended before resuming their normal levels of investment. Firms did not hesitate as long to purchase new equipment. Spending on equipment recovered rapidly and by 1992 had reached its prerecession level.

Although investment spending is a much smaller component of GDP than consumption, it is much more volatile than consumption. It is therefore important for understanding fluctuations in real GDP. Recall that changes in investment are amplified by the multiplier. If the multiplier is 1.5 and investment spending initially falls by 1% of GDP, then GDP will fall by 1.5%. If the fall in GDP makes firms more pessimistic, they may cut investment even further. This further cut in investment will lead to still further

Figure 26.1

Investment Spending as a Share of U.S. GDP, 1970–1998
Shaded areas indicate recessions according to NBER business cycle reference dates.

Source: Economic Report of the President, yearly.

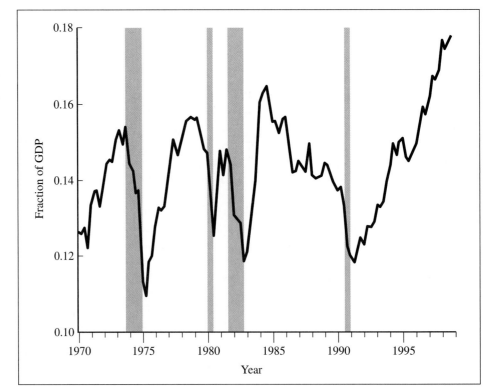

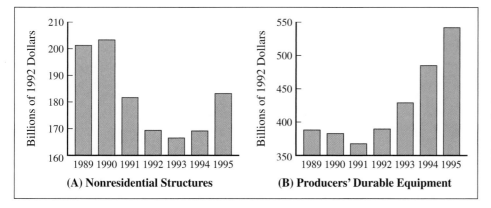

Figure 26.2

Investment in Structures and Equipment in the Early 1990s

Source: Data from *Economic Report of the President* (Washington, DC: U.S. Government Printing Office, yearly).

reductions in GDP. A small initial fall in investment can trigger a much larger fall in GDP. Nobel laureate Paul Samuelson expressed these interactions with his **multiplier-accelerator model**. In this model, a downturn in real GDP leads to a sharp fall in investment, which further reduces GDP through the multiplier for investment spending.

Investment spending is not affected only by psychology or expectations about real GDP growth in the future. Because investments are really trade-offs—something in the present traded for something in the future—the terms affecting what is the trade-off between the present and the future are also important. The terms affecting trade-offs between the present and the future are interest rates, as we shall see next.

> **Multiplier-accelerator model:** A model in which a downturn in real GDP leads to a sharp fall in investment, which triggers further reductions in GDP through the multiplier.

Nominal Interest Rates and Real Interest Rates

If you deposit $100 in a bank and the interest rate the bank pays is 6% a year, at the end of one year you will have $106 ($100 × 1.06). Here are some other familiar examples of interest rates: If you borrow money for college tuition from a bank, the bank will require you to pay the funds back with interest. If a hardware store borrows money from a bank to purchase its inventory, the store will have to pay the funds back to the bank with interest. If you buy from the government or a corporation a $1,000 bond for one year at a 6% annual interest rate, you will receive $1,060 ($1000 × 1.06) next year from the issuer. Remember that a **bond** is a promise to pay money in the future. In buying the bond, you have loaned your $1,000 to the issuer, who has promised to repay it with interest.

> **Bond:** A promise or IOU to pay money in the future in exchange for money now.

The interest rates quoted in the market—that is, at savings and loans, or banks for bonds—are called nominal interest rates. These are the actual rates that individuals and firms pay or receive when they borrow money or lend money. There are many different interest rates in the economy, as "A Closer Look: A Variety of Interest Rates," illustrates.

When there is inflation, the dollar costs of borrowing or lending will not reflect the true costs. To provide an accurate measure of the costs of borrowing or lending, we need to apply the reality principle and make adjustments for changes in prices.

REALITY **PRINCIPLE**

What matters to people is the real value of money or income—its purchasing power—not the face value of money or income.

Distinguishing between nominal interest rates and real interest rates is how economists account for inflation in their measurements of the costs of borrowing and lending.

A CLOSER LOOK   A Variety of Interest Rates

There are many different interest rates in the economy. Loans vary by their riskiness and by their maturity (the length of the loan). Riskier loans and loans for longer maturities typically have higher interest rates.

Figure 26.3 depicts movements in three interest rates during 1998: 30-year fixed-rate mortgages (30-year loans to homeowners with a constant rate), 30-year Treasuries (loans to the U.S. government for 30 years), and 6-month Treasuries (loans to the U.S. government for 6 months).

Notice that the 30-year mortgage rates are higher than the rates on 30-year Treasuries: That's because homeowners are less likely to pay back their loans than the U.S. government is. Interest rates on 6-month Treasuries are less than interest rates on 30-year Treasuries, illustrating the fact that longer-term loans generally carry higher interest rates.

The real rate of interest is defined as the nominal interest rate minus the inflation rate:

$$\text{real rate} = \text{nominal rate} - \text{inflation rate}$$

If the nominal rate of interest is 6% per year and the inflation rate is 4% during the year, the real rate of interest is 2% (6% − 4% = 2%) over that year.

To understand what the real rate of interest means, consider this example. You have $100, and there is 4% annual inflation. It's not hard to figure out that next year you will

Figure 26.3
Interest Rates on Mortgages and Government Securities
Mortgage rates plotted weekly. Bond yields are weekly averages of daily data.

Source: Federal Reserve Bank of St. Louis.

need $104 to have the same purchasing power then that you have today. Let's say you deposit today $100 in a bank that pays 6% annual interest. At the end of the year, you have $106 ($100 × 1.06).

Let's calculate your real gain. After 1 year, you have increased your holdings by $6, starting with $100 and ending with $106. But taking into account the $4 you need to keep up with inflation, your gain is only $2 ($6 − $4). The real rate of interest you earned, the nominal rate adjusted for inflation, is 2% or $2, on the original $100 deposit.

A similar calculation applies to firms or individuals who borrow money. Suppose a firm borrows $100 at a 10% annual interest rate when there is 6% inflation during the year. The firm must pay back $110 at the end of the year ($100 × 1.10). But the borrower will be paying back the funds with dollars whose value has been reduced because of inflation. Since there was 6% inflation during the year, the lender would have to receive $106 (or 6 extra dollars) just to keep up with inflation over the year. There is only a $4 gain ($10 − $6). Thus, the real rate of interest to the borrower is just 4%, or $4 on the original $100 loan, correcting for the effects of inflation.

We defined the real interest rate as the nominal interest rate minus the actual inflation rate. When firms or individuals borrow or lend, they do not know what the rate of inflation will actually be. Instead, they must form an expectation—an estimate—of what they believe the inflation rate will be in the future. For a given nominal interest rate, we can define the **expected real interest rate** as the nominal rate minus the expected inflation rate. The expected real interest rate is the rate at which borrowers or lenders expect to make transactions.

Expected real interest rate: The nominal interest rate minus the expected inflation rate.

It is difficult to determine expected real rates of interest that are precise because we never know exactly what inflation rates people anticipate. One common approach to measuring expectations of inflation is to assume that individuals' expectations are based on the recent past. In Table 26.1, we present estimates of the expected real rate of interest based on this idea and data for a few developed countries from *The Economist* magazine. In the 2nd column, we show interest rates on 3-month loans; in the third column, we show the inflation rate over the last 3 months. The last column shows estimates of the expected real rate of interest in each country by subtracting the inflation rate from the interest rate. Our assumption is that people expect the inflation rate that prevailed in the last 3 months to continue unchanged for the next 3 months. As you can see, both nominal and expected real interest rates differ among developed economies.

Table 26.1   Expected Real Rates of Interest (percent per year)

Country	3-Month Interest Rate	Inflation Rate over Last 3 Months	Expected Real Rate of Interest
Australia	4.85	1.70	3.15
Canada	4.68	2.60	2.08
Denmark	3.02	2.20	0.82
Switzerland	1.21	0.90	0.31
United States	5.33	2.20	3.13

Source: The Economist, September 25, 1999, pp. 122–23.

TEST Your Understanding

1. Investment is a smaller component of GDP than consumption, but it is a more stable component. True or false? Explain.

2. Investment spending is very procyclical, moving in conjunction with GDP. True or false? Explain.

3. Complete the statement with *real* or *nominal*: The rate of interest that you earn in the bank is known as a _____ or dollar rate of interest.

4. With 6% annual inflation, a nominal rate of interest of 10% per year means a real rate of interest of _____% per year.

Investment Spending and Interest Rates

To understand the link between investment spending and interest rates, here's a simple example. A firm can invest $100 today in a project and receive $104 one year from today. There is no inflation: A dollar today and a dollar next year have the same purchasing power. Figure 26.4 depicts this investment. A cost is incurred in today and the return occurs in one year later. Should the firm make this investment?

To decide whether to invest the $100, the firm should take into account the principle of opportunity cost.

PRINCIPLE OF OPPORTUNITY COST

The opportunity cost of something is what you sacrifice to get it.

We have to look at the $100 the firm would give up today to get $104 one year from today. What we look at is how that $100 could have been used for other purposes. Suppose the annual interest rate in the economy were 3%. The firm could lend the $100 at 3% and receive $103 in one year. The interest rate prevailing in the economy provides a measure of the opportunity cost of the investment.

In this case, the firm would not be too smart lending the $100 at 3% annual interest return. The investment is the smart thing to do. The firm will earn a net return of $4

Figure 26.4

Typical Investments
A typical investment, in which a cost of $100 incurred today yields a return of $104 next year.

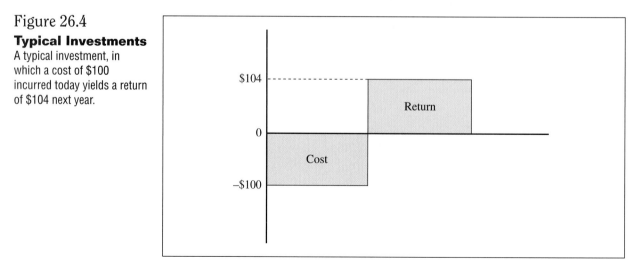

($104 – $100) from the investment project, whereas the return from lending the $100 would have been only $3. Because the net return from the investment exceeds the opportunity cost of the funds, the firm is better off investing.

What if the annual interest rate in the economy were 6%? Lending the $100 would return $6—the opportunity cost that could be earned by lending instead of investing in the project. The return on the investment of $4 would be less than the opportunity cost of $6. The firm would be better off making a loan of the $100, not investing it. The higher lending interest rate makes the difference as to which is the more profitable use of the $100.

There are millions of investment projects that can be undertaken, nearly all providing different returns from any other. Consider the array of investments A through E in Table 26.2. At a market interest rate of 2% per year, only investment A is unprofitable. All the other investments have a return greater than the opportunity cost of the funds. If the interest rate in the market increased to 4%, both A and B would be unprofitable. Investment C would join A and B as being unprofitable at an interest rate of 6%; D would become unprofitable if the market interest rate increased to 8%. If interest rates exceeded 9%, all the investments would become unprofitable.

Firms will compare the net return on an investment with the opportunity cost of that investment, and they will invest as long as the net return exceeds the opportunity cost. As market interest rates rise, there will be fewer profitable investments. The total level of investment spending in the economy will decline as market interest rates increase. Figure 26.5 depicts the negative relationship—graphically represented as the downward-sloping line—between interest rates and investment.

Real investment spending is inversely related to the real interest rate. To understand why, let's return to our example in which a $100 investment today would yield a $104 return in one year, the interest rate was 3%, and there was no inflation. Because there was no inflation, nominal interest rates and real interest rates were the same. In this case, the firm looked at the real net return on the investment of $4 which is a real return of 4% from the investment, compared it to the real rate of interest of 3%, and decided that the investment was profitable.

Now suppose that the return from the investment project and the real interest rate in the economy are the same—3% per year—but there is 2% annual inflation. Also suppose that the inflation rate increases to 5%: the real rate of interest of 3% plus the inflation rate of 2%. The investment project will still cost $100, but it will pay a return of $100 plus $6 = $106 in one year. The extra $2 arises because of the 2% inflation: When the firm sells its product on the market, it will earn 2% more because of the rise in prices in the economy.

The firm will compare its nominal or dollar net return of 6% to the opportunity cost of 5% and find that the investment will be more profitable than making the loan. Because

Table 26.2   Returns on Investment

Investment	Cost	Return
A	$100	$101
B	$100	$103
C	$100	$105
D	$100	$107
E	$100	$109

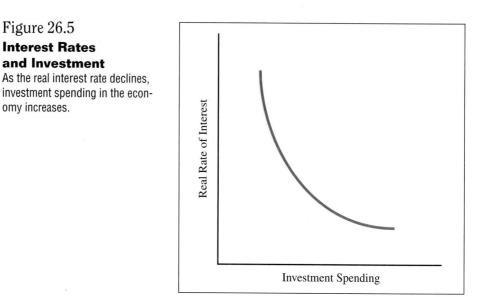

Figure 26.5

**Interest Rates
and Investment**
As the real interest rate declines, investment spending in the economy increases.

both the nominal net return and nominal interest rates in the economy increase by the rate of inflation of 2%, the firm faces the identical situation as if there were no inflation.

You can see now that investment spending is negatively related to real interest rates. That's why nominal interest rates are not a good indicator of the true cost of investing. If nominal interest rates are 10% but inflation is 9%, the real rate of interest is 1%. If a firm had a project that paid a real net return greater than 1%, it would want to undertake this investment. Inflation would increase the nominal net return and the nominal interest rate equally. The firm makes its investment decisions by comparing its expected real net return from investment projects to the real rate of interest.

During the 1970s, homeowners in California understood this logic. They bought homes even though they had to borrow from the bank at interest rates exceeding 10%. They were willing to borrow at such high rates because they had seen housing prices rise by more than 10% and were projecting this rise in prices to continue in the future. For example, if they expected housing prices to rise by 12% a year, they could earn a 2% annual return just by borrowing at 10% and watching their homes appreciate in value at 12%. (They would earn this return only when they sold their home.) They calculated that their real interest rate was –2%. This caused a housing boom in California that lasted until housing prices stopped rising at such high rates.

**ECONOMIC
DETECTIVE**

The Case of High Interest Rates and Investment

Some journalists were puzzled that a country with high inflation had high interest rates but also has high levels of investment spending. As an economic detective, can you explain this phenomenon?

To resolve the mystery, you need to distinguish between real and nominal interest rates. Investment spending depends negatively on real interest rates. However, if there are high levels of inflation, real interest rates could be low, while nominal interest rates remain high. ◆

Economists have incorporated these insights about interest rates and investment into theories of aggregate investment spending. In addition to interest rates, they have also considered other factors, including taxes and the stock market.

Here are two of the key theories: In the **neoclassical theory of investment**, pioneered by Dale Jorgenson of Harvard University, real interest rates and taxes play a key role in determining investment spending. Jorgenson used his theory to analyze the responsiveness of investment to a variety of tax incentives, including investment tax credits that are subsidies to investment. The **Q-theory of investment**, originally developed by Nobel laureate James Tobin of Yale University, looks a bit different from the neoclassical theory on its surface. The Q-theory states that investment spending increases when stock prices are high. If a firm's stock price is high, it can issue new shares of its stock at an advantageous price and use the proceeds to undertake new investment. Recent research has shown a close connection between the Q-theory and neoclassical theory and has highlighted the key role that real interest rates and taxes play in the Q-theory as well.

> **Neoclassical theory of investment:** A theory of investment that says that both real interest rates and taxes are important determinants of investment.
>
> **Q-theory of investment:** The theory of investment that links investment spending to stock prices.

TEST Your Understanding

5. Complete the statement with *increases* or *decreases*: As real rates of interest increase in the economy, real investment spending _____.

6. Complete the following statement with *real* or *nominal*: Both the _____ rate of interest and the _____ return on investment increase with the inflation rate.

7. The _____ cost of funds is the interest that can be earned by lending the funds.

8. If a project costs $100 today and pays a nominal return of $107 next year, what is the nominal annual interest rate at which the project should still be undertaken?

How Financial Intermediation Facilitates Investment

Investment spending in an economy comes from savings. When households earn income, they consume part of it and save the rest. These savings are the source of funds for investment.

Why Financial Intermediaries Emerge

Households save for different reasons than the ones firms have for investing. A typical household might be saving for the children's education or for financial security in later life. Such households do not want their savings, usually considered "life savings" to be subject to risk. And they want their savings to be readily accessible—what economists call **liquid**—in case of financial emergencies. Funds deposited in a bank account, for example, provide a source of liquidity for households; these funds can be obtained at any time.

> **Liquid:** Easily convertible to money on short notice.

Firms and business managers who make investments in the economy are typically risk-takers. They are gambling that their vision of the future will come true and make them vast profits. They need funds that must be tied up for a long time. For example, an entrepreneur who wants to build skyscrapers or large casinos may need financing for several years before they can start building their projects, and years after that before those projects begin to produce profits.

Suppose individual entrepreneurs had to obtain funds directly from individual savers. First, the entrepreneur would have to negotiate with thousands of savers to obtain sufficient funds for a large-scale project. These negotiations would be costly. Second, the savers would face extraordinary risks if they loaned all their funds to a single entrepreneur who had a risky project to undertake. Not only would all their funds be tied up in a single project, they would also have difficulty monitoring investor's decisions. How would they know that the entrepreneur would not run off with the money? Finally, this investment would not be liquid. If the funds were tied up in a major project, households would not be able to get access to them in case of emergencies.

In these circumstances, households would demand extraordinarily high interest rates to compensate them for the costs of negotiation, risk, and lack of liquidity. High interest rates would make it impossible for an entrepreneur to make a profit; no profit from a project means no investors in the project. Society would not be able to turn its savings to profitable investment projects. Figure 26.6 depicts this dilemma. How can society solve it?

Society needs institutions that can reduce costs, monitor investments, reduce risks, and provide liquidity. Fortunately, there are such institutions—the financial intermediaries.

Financial intermediaries are banks, savings and loans, insurance companies, money market mutual funds, and many other types of financial institutions. These institutions accept funds from savers and make loans to businesses and individuals. For example, a local bank accepts deposits from savers and uses the funds to make loans to local businesses. Savings and loan institutions will accept deposits in savings accounts and use these funds to make loans, often for housing. Insurance companies accept premium payments from individuals in exchange for the protection provided by the insurance payments. Then insurance companies lend the premiums received to earn returns from investments so that they can pay off the insurance claims of individuals. Figure 26.7 shows how financial intermediaries create a valuable link between savers and investors.

These institutions pool the funds of savers. By pooling funds and making loans to individual businesses, financial intermediaries reduce the costs of negotiation, such as businesses trying to negotiate terms with each individual investor. They also acquire expertise in both evaluating and monitoring investments. Some financial intermediaries, such as banks, provide liquidity to households. In normal circumstances, not all households converge on a bank to take out their money at the same time. Because that doesn't happen and is not expected to happen, the bank can lend most of its funds to businesses and still have funds on hand to meet emergency withdrawals by depositors.

By pooling funds and gaining expertise, financial intermediaries can reduce costs and provide liquidity. But how do they reduce risk? Financial intermediaries reduce risk by diversification, that is, by not putting all their eggs in one basket.

Risk can be reduced by investing in a large number of projects whose returns, although uncertain, are independent of one another. By independence, we mean that the return from one investment is unrelated to the return on another investment. Consider

Figure 26.6
Savers and Investors

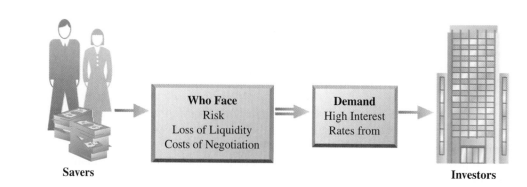

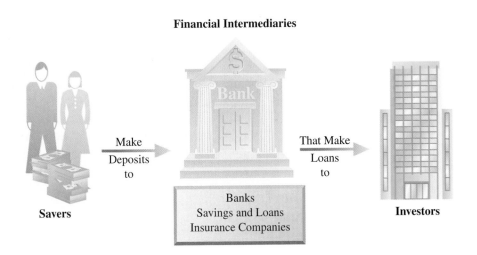

Financial Intermediaries

Savers — Make Deposits to → Banks / Savings and Loans / Insurance Companies — That Make Loans to → Investors

Figure 26.7
**Financial
Intermediaries**

a bank investing in a large number of projects that altogether produce an average return of 8% annually. Each project alone is risky and could pay either a higher or a lower return than 8%. As long as the returns on these projects are independent, the number of projects with higher returns will be matched by an equal number of projects with lower returns. Some of those projects will have good fortune; others will have bad luck. By investing in a large number of projects, the bank can be confident that it will earn an 8% return on all of them as a group.

Financial intermediaries reduce risk in this way. Using the funds that they receive from households' savings, financial intermediaries invest in a large number of projects. Every household has a small stake in many projects. No one household would be able to do this. But if many households deposit their funds in financial intermediaries, the financial intermediaries can invest in a wide range of projects and reduce risk for the households.

Other financial intermediaries reduce risks in related ways. A fire insurance company accepts premiums from many individuals and uses the funds to make investments. Since not all houses will burn down in the same year, the insurance company knows that it will have a stable source of funds for its investments. Banks also benefit from risk reduction when they accept deposits. While some individual depositors may want to withdraw funds on a given day, banks can be confident that not all depositors will come in to withdraw on the same day.

Diversification in insurance works well only when companies insure events that are independent. Some events are not independent and therefore cannot easily be insured. For example, an insurance company would be unwise to provide earthquake insurance for just the Los Angeles area. If an earthquake did occur, the firm would be faced with making many payments to its clients who suffered loss. In somewhat the same way, even bank loans are not fully independent. During a recession, many firms will be operating unprofitably all at the same time, and they will have difficulties meeting their loan obligations to their banks.

When Financial Intermediation Malfunctions

Financial intermediation can sometimes go wrong. When it does, the economy suffers. Important examples of the failure of financial intermediation include commercial bank failures during the Great Depression, the savings and loans crisis of the 1980s in the United States, and a similar crisis in Japan in the 1990s.

During the 1930s in the early days of the Great Depression, many banks in the United States, particularly in rural areas, provided farmers or local businesses loans that

Depositors gathered anxiously outside as banks closed during the Great Depression.

turned out not to be profitable. This worried depositors, and rumors started that banks would soon be closing their doors and depositors would lose all their funds. This triggered runs on the banks—all depositors panicking to withdraw their deposits simultaneously.

No bank, profitable or unprofitable, can survive a run. As financial intermediaries, banks make profits by lending out their deposits. They never keep 100% of these deposits on hand. That's how the runs on banks closed thousands of healthy banks and destroyed the entire banking system in large parts of the United States. Many farmers and businesses could no longer find a source of loans. This failure in the financial system worsened the severity of the Great Depression.

To prevent this from happening again, the U.S. government began to provide deposit insurance for banks and savings and loans. This insurance guarantees that the government will provide you with funds up to $100,000 even if your bank fails. Since everyone knows their deposits are secure, runs on banks no longer occur.

During the Great Depression, bank failures occurred throughout the world. In 1931, a panic broke out after the collapse of Creditanstalt, Austria's largest bank. Banking panics occurred throughout other countries in Europe, including Belgium, France, Germany, Italy, and Poland. Studies have shown that the countries with the most severe banking panics were hardest hit by the Depression. Today, most countries have some form of deposit insurance intended to prevent panics.

Ironically, deposit insurance indirectly helped to create the savings and loan crisis in the United States during the 1980s. In the early 1970s, savings and loan institutions made mortgage loans to households at low interest rates. In the late 1970s, nominal interest rates rose sharply as inflation increased. The savings and loans were in trouble: They had to pay high interest rates to attract deposits, but they were earning interest at low rates from their past investments. Many S&Ls went bankrupt.

The government tried to assist the saving and loan industry by reducing the regulations that restricted the range of their investments and allowing them to make investments other than housing in the hope that they would gain more profits. Depositors were not concerned because their savings were insured. Savings and loans soon became aggressive investors in speculative real estate and other risky projects. Unfortunately, many investment projects collapsed, and the government was forced to provide funds to the many savings and loans at a cost of nearly $100 billion to taxpayers. Depositors' savings, don't forget, were protected through deposit insurance up to a certain amount. So most depositors did not suffer directly from the collapse of their savings and loan institutions, but taxpayers did.

Should the Government Force Socially Responsive Investment?

Like other profit-making institutions, financial intermediaries do not deliberately make loans to depressed areas or to poor communities. They make their decisions on lending based on the opportunity to earn as much money as possible.

Both federal and state governments often have other goals for financial intermediaries. Many states require that state pension funds invest a large fraction of their assets in projects within their respective states, to promote jobs in those states. At the federal level, banking laws require that financial institutions make a percentage of loans within their local region. Some groups that promote the interest of low-income individuals argue that these laws should go much further, requiring investment in projects that bring benefits to distressed neighborhoods and benefit the poor.

These laws may sound reasonable, but they impose a cost. Pension funds that are forced to invest large amounts of funds within the state will earn lower returns and face higher risks because they cannot more fully diversify their investments. Future pension recipients pay the price for these restrictions. Similarly, banks that are required to lend locally may be less profitable and more risky as a result of these restrictions. Some economists believe that if governments want to solve social problems, they should pay for solutions directly and not make investors pay the price.

Japan suffered from similar problems in the 1990s. By 1995, seven of the eight largest mortgage lenders in Japan went bankrupt during falling real estate markets. The Japanese government chose to use taxpayer funds, equivalent to nearly 13 billion U.S. dollars, to rescue these companies and prevent further disruptions in the financial market.

From these examples, you can see that there are reasons why financial intermediation does not always work. There is a continual debate on the role government should play in investment decisions for the economy. "A Closer Look: Should the Government Force Socially Responsive Investment?," discusses one aspect of this debate.

Using the **TOOLS**

In this chapter, we studied investment and financial intermediation and examined the factors that affect firms' investment decisions. Here's an opportunity to do your own economic analysis.

1. ECONOMIC EXPERIMENT: Diversification
This classroom exercise illustrates the power of diversification. Your instructor will describe the game and how to participate. To take part in this exercise, you need to recall a simple lesson from basic statistics: If you flip a coin many times, the fraction of heads that results approaches 1/2 as you increase the number of flips.

You are offered a chance to play this game in which you receive a payoff according to the following formula:

$$payoff = \$10 + \$100 \text{ (number of heads/number of tosses} - 0.5)$$

In this game, you first get $10, but you either win or lose additional funds, depending on whether the fraction of heads that comes up exceeds 1/2.

To help you understand what's going on in this game, suppose you toss the coin only once. Here, the outcome depends only on whether the coin comes up either heads or tails:

$$\text{Heads:} \quad \$10 + \$100\,(1/1 - 0.5) = \$60$$

$$\text{Tails:} \quad \$10 + \$100\,(0/1 - 0.5) = -\$40$$

If the one coin toss comes up heads, you win $60; if it comes up tails, you lose $40 dollars.

The game does have a positive expected payoff or return. The expected or average payoff for this game is the probability of getting a head (1/2) times $60 if a head results plus the probability of getting a tail (1/2) times $40 if a tail results. This is

$$\text{expected payoff} = (0.5)\$60 + (0.5)(-\$40) = \$10$$

On average, if you toss the coin many times, this game would pay $10. But this game is risky if you are allowed to toss the coin only once. Now that you understand the game, answer the following question:

- Would you play this game if limited to only one toss?

Now suppose you were free to toss the coin 1,000 times and received 450 heads. If that happened, your payoff would be

$$\$10 + \$100\,(450/1000 - 0.5) = \$5$$

- Would you play if you could toss the coin 1,000 times?
- a. Did a higher percentage of the class agree to play the game with 1,000 tosses? How does this illustrate the principle of diversification?
- b. If you toss the coin 1,000 times, what is the expected payoff?
- c. If you toss the coin 1,000 times and receive heads fewer than 400 times, you will lose money. What do you think is the probability of this occurring?

2. Animal Spirits
Use the $C + I + G$ diagram from Chapter 25 to show the effects of increased "animal spirits" that leads to higher investment in the economy.

3. Brazilian Economics
During the early 1990s, interest rates in Brazil were typically at double-digit levels, but firms were investing in a large number of projects. Does this make economic sense? If so, in what way?

4. Understanding Banks
How can a bank invest in illiquid loans (say, lend depositors' savings to home buyers over 25 years) and still provide liquid deposits (provide depositors with their savings when they ask for it)?

Summary

We discussed investment spending, interest rates, and financial intermediation. You saw that investment spending is volatile, rising and falling sharply with real GDP, and depends on expectations about the future. We also explained why investment spending also depends inversely on real interest rates. Finally, we examined how financial intermediaries channel funds from savers to investors, reduce interest rates and promote investment. Here are the main points of this chapter to keep in mind:

1. Investments incur costs today, to provide benefits in the future.

2. Investment spending is a volatile component of GDP because expectations of the future can be volatile and investment decisions are made with an eye to the ever-changing future.

3. Investment spending depends inversely on real interest rates.

4. Financial intermediaries reduce risk and costs of making investments through their expertise and through pooling the funds of savers.

Key Terms

accelerator theory, 549
bond, 551
expected real interest rate, 553
financial intermediaries, 548

liquid, 557
multiplier-accelerator model, 551
neoclassical theory of investment, 557
nominal interest rates, 548

procyclical, 550
Q-theory of investment, 557
real interest rate, 548

Problems and Discussion Questions

1. The components of investment spending in the national income accounts include plant and equipment, housing, and inventories. Give a reason why spending in each of these categories is likely to be volatile.

2. "When real interest rates are high, so is the opportunity cost of funds." What does this statement mean?

3. "If the real interest rate were zero, it would be a financially sound decision to level the Rocky Mountains so that automobiles and cars would save on gas mileage." Putting aside ecological concerns, why is this statement true?

4. Traditionally, savings and loan institutions made loans only for housing. At one point, this was viewed as a safe way of doing business. Explain why making loans only for housing may be very risky.

5. If the inflation rate is 10% over the year and annual interest rates are 9%, would you invest in a project that only paid an annual real return of 1%?

6. Explain why some insurance companies have been interested in national programs for insurance for floods, earthquakes, and hurricanes.

7. A business borrows at a 10% annual interest rate from a bank and expects 8% annual inflation. What is the real interest rate and the nominal interest rate facing this borrower?

8. Why does it make sense for individual investors to invest in mutual funds (which invest in a wide range of stocks), rather than in just a few individual companies?

9. Why do many investors put their funds in investments in countries throughout the world, not just investments in the United States?

10. While deposit insurance protects depositors savings and prevents runs on banks, it can motivate banks to take excessive risks in the loans they make. Explain why.

11. Web Exercise. Search the Web to find the current values for interest rates on short-term and long-term government bonds, the prime rate, and long-term corporate bonds. You may want to start with the data Web site for Federal Reserve Bank of St. Louis (*http://www.stls.frb.org/fred*). Try to account for the differences in these rates.

12. Web Exercise. In the chapter, we discussed how equipment and structures behaved during the last recession. Use the Federal Reserve Bank of St. Louis data Web site (*http://www.stls.frb.org/fred*) to find out how investment in residential housing behaved over the 1990–91 recession.

Take It to the Net

We invite you to visit the O'Sullivan/Sheffrin page on the Prentice Hall Web site at:
http://www.prenhall.com/osullivan/
for additional World Wide Web exercises for this chapter.

Model Answers to Questions

Chapter-Opening Questions

1. Interest rates represent the opportunity cost of an investment. The higher the opportunity cost, the less investment. Investment also depends on other factors such as expectations, taxes, and the expected growth of the economy.

2. Borrowing depends on the real interest rate, which is the market interest rate, which is the nominal interest rate adjusted for inflation. In inflationary periods, there may be a high nominal interest rate but a low real interest rate.

3. Diversification of independent risks makes it possible for financial intermediaries to reduce risk.

4. Without financial institutions, it would be too costly for individuals to make loans directly to firms.

5. Federal deposit insurance prevents the runs on banks that occurred during the Great Depression.

Test Your Understanding

1. False. Investment is more volatile than consumption.

2. True. Investment rises and falls with GDP.

3. Nominal.

4. 4%.

5. Decreases.

6. Nominal, nominal.

7. Opportunity.

8. The highest rate is 7%.

Using the Tools

1. Economic Experiment: Diversification

   a. A higher percentage of the class should agree to play the game if students could toss the coin 1,000 times rather than a single time. That's because the expected payoff of 1000 tosses is the same $10 as the expected payoff of a single toss, but the risk is much less.

   b. If a coin is tossed 1,000 times, the probability of fewer than 400 heads is less than 1 in a million.

2. Animal Spirits. The increase in investment will lead to a vertical shift in the $C + I + G$ demand line. This will lead to higher output.

3. Brazilian Economics. While nominal interest rates were at double-digit levels in Brazil during that period, inflation was also at double-digit levels. Real interest rates were substantially lower, which is why firms still wanted to undertake investment projects.

4. Understanding Banks. Using basic statistics, a bank can estimate that only a fraction of its depositors will ask for withdrawals on any given day. Therefore, the bank can allocate a large fraction of the deposits to illiquid loans.

Money, the Banking System, and the Federal Reserve

As long as there has been paper money, there have been counterfeiters. In 1023, China formed a government agency to print paper money; by 1107, they had begun to print money in three colors to thwart counterfeiters. In 1998, the U.S. Treasury introduced a new $20 bill, using modern technology to make life difficult for counterfeiters. The portrait of Andrew Jackson is slightly off-center, and imbedded in the paper is a plastic thread, invisible to the unaided human eye, that glows green under ultraviolet light. The new $20 bills are also printed with a special ink that looks green when viewed directly but changes to black when viewed from side to side. These are ingenious technological marvels. But the institution of money is even a greater marvel.

he term *money* has a special meaning for economists, so we'll look carefully at how they define money and the role that it plays in the economy.

The supply of money in the economy is determined primarily by the banking system and the actions of the Federal Reserve, our nation's central bank. We will see how the Federal Reserve, operating through the banking system, can create and destroy money. We will also study how the Federal Reserve operates and who controls it.

The supply of money is very important for the economy's performance. In our discussion of aggregate demand, we indicated how increases in the supply of money increase aggregate demand. In the short run, when prices are largely fixed, increases in the money supply will raise total demand and output. In the long run, continuing money growth leads to inflation. Therefore, changes in the supply of money have important effects on both output and prices: how much is produced, the cost of producing output, and what will be the prices of what is produced. In this chapter, we explain in detail how the supply of money in the economy is determined.

After reading this chapter, you should be able to answer the following questions:

1. **Why do all societies have some form of money?**
2. **Why do banks play a special role in our economy?**
3. **Can banks really create money through computer entries?**
4. **When the Federal Reserve uses its special powers to buy and sell government bonds, how do buying and selling government bonds affect the supply of money in the economy?**
5. **Why is the chairman of the Federal Reserve one of the most powerful people in the country?**

What Is Money?

Let's first discuss the definition and role of money and then see how it is measured in the U.S. economy.

Definition of Money

Money: Anything that is regularly used in exchange.

Economists define **money** as anything that is regularly used in economic transactions or exchanges. Let's consider some examples of money used in that way.

We use money regularly, every day. In an ice-cream store, we hand the person behind the counter some dollar bills and coins, and we receive an ice-cream cone. This is an example of an economic exchange: One party hands over currency—the dollar bills and the coins—and the other party hands over goods and services (the ice-cream cone). Why do the owners of ice-cream stores accept the dollar bills and coins in payment for the ice cream? The reason is that they will be making other economic exchanges with the dollar bills and coins they accept. Suppose they take the currency they receive from selling the ice cream and pay their supplier with it. The ice-cream cones cost $1.50 each, and 100 ice-cream cones are sold in a day. The seller then has $150 in currency. If the ice cream costs the seller $100, the seller pays $100 of the currency received and keeps $50 for other expenses and profits.

In the real world, transactions are somewhat more complicated. The ice-cream store will take the currency it receives each day and deposit it into an account at its local bank. It will typically pay its suppliers with a check drawn on its account at that local bank. This is another example of an economic exchange: The ice-cream supplier sells ice cream to the store in exchange for a check.

Why does the supplier accept a check? The supplier can use the check to make further transactions. The supplier can deposit the check in his or her own bank account and then either withdraw currency from this account or write checks on it.

In these examples, what is money? Recall the definition of money: anything that is regularly used in economic transactions or exchanges. Clearly, currency is money because it was used to purchase ice cream. Checks are also money because they are used to pay the supplier.

At other times and in other societies, different items have been used as money. In some ancient cultures, precious stones were used in exchanges; therefore, those stones constituted money. In more recent times, gold bars have served as money. During World War II, prisoners of war did not have currency, but they did have rations of cigarettes. The cigarettes began to be used for exchanges among the prisoners and played the role of money in the prison camps.

Three Properties of Money

Regardless of what money is in a particular society, it serves several functions, all related to making economic exchanges easier. Here we discuss three key properties of money.

1. Money Serves as a Medium of Exchange

As our examples illustrate, money is accepted in economic exchanges; that is, it serves as a **medium of exchange**. Suppose money did not exist and you had a car you wanted to sell to buy a boat. You could look for a person who had a boat and wanted to buy a car and then trade your car directly for a boat. This would be an example of **barter**: trading goods directly for goods.

But there are obvious problems with barter. Suppose local boatbuilders were interested in selling boats but not interested in buying your car. Unless there were a **double coincidence of wants**—that is, unless you wanted to trade a car for a boat and the boat owner wanted to trade a boat for your car—this economic exchange could not occur. The probability of a double coincidence of wants occurring is very, very tiny. Even if a boat owner wanted a car, he or she might want a different type of car than yours.

By serving as a medium of exchange, money solves this problem. A car owner can sell the car to anyone who wants it and receive money in return. With that money, the car owner can then find someone who owns a boat and purchase the boat for money. The boat owner can use the money in any way he or she pleases. With money, there is no need for a double coincidence of wants. This is why money exists in all societies: It makes economic transactions much easier.

Medium of exchange: The property of money that exchanges are made through the use of money.

Barter: Trading goods directly for goods.

Double coincidence of wants: The problem in a system of barter that one person may not have what the other desires.

2. Money Serves as a Unit of Account

Money also provides a convenient measuring rod when prices for all goods are quoted in money terms. A boat may be listed for sale at $5,000, a car at $10,000, and a movie ticket at $5.00. All these prices are quoted in money. We could in principle quote everything in terms of movie tickets. The boat would be worth 1,000 tickets, and the car would be worth 2,000 tickets. But since we are using money (and not movie tickets) as a medium of exchange, it is much easier if all prices are expressed in terms of money. We say that money is used as a **unit of account**, and all we mean by that is that prices are quoted in terms of money. This also makes it easier to conduct economic transactions, since there is a standard unit—whether that unit is movie tickets or the more convenient unit of dollars—in which to do so.

Unit of account: The property of money that prices are quoted in terms of money.

3. Money Serves as a Store of Value

If you sell your car to purchase a boat, you may not be able to purchase the boat immediately. In the meantime, you will be holding the money you received from the sale of the car. Ideally, during that period, the value of the money should not change. What we are referring to here is the function of money to be a **store of value**.

Store of value: The property of money that it preserves value until it is used in an exchange.

Money is actually a somewhat imperfect store of value because of inflation. Suppose inflation is 10% a year, which means that all prices rise 10% each year. Let's say you sold a tennis racket for $100 to buy 10 CDs worth $100 but that you waited a year to buy them. Unfortunately, at the end of the year, during which there was 10% inflation, the 10 CDs now cost $110 ($100 × 1.10), or $11 each. With your $100, you can now buy only 9 CDs and get $1 in change. Money has lost some of its stored value.

As long as inflation is low and you do not hold money for a long time, the loss in the purchasing power of money will not be a major problem. But as inflation rates increase, money becomes less useful as a store of value.

TEST Your Understanding

1. Money solves the problem of double coincidence of wants that would regularly occur under a system of _____.

2. Why is money only an imperfect store of value?

3. What is the problem associated with the double coincidence of wants?

4. Because we measure all prices in monetary units, money serves as a unit of account. True or false? Explain.

5. Why are checks included in the definition of money?

Measuring Money in the U.S. Economy

In the United States and other modern economies, there are typically several different ways in which economic transactions can be carried out. In practice, this leads to different definitions of money.

M1: The sum of currency in the hands of the public plus demand deposits plus other checkable deposits.

The most basic measure of money in the United States is called **M1**. Table 27.1 contains the components of M1 and their size for July 1999, and Figure 27.1 shows their relative percentages.

The first part of M1 is currency that is held by the public, that is, all currency held outside of bank vaults. The next two components are deposits in checking accounts, called *demand deposits*. Until the 1980s, checking accounts did not pay interest, and a new category, entitled *other checkable deposits*, was introduced in the early 1980s to describe checking accounts that did pay interest. Today, this distinction is not as meaningful because many checking accounts pay interest if the account balance is sufficiently high. Finally, travelers' checks are included in M1 because they are regularly used in economic exchanges.

Let's take a closer look at the amount of currency in the economy. Since there are approximately 260 million people in the United States, the $487 billion of currency

Table 27.1 Components of M1, July 1999

Currency held by the public	$487 billion
Demand deposits	$361 billion
Other checkable deposits	$241 billion
Travelers' checks	$8 billion
Total of M1	$1,097 billion

Source: Federal Reserve Bank of St. Louis.

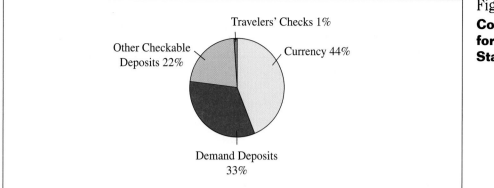

Figure 27.1
Components of M1 for the United States

Travelers' Checks 1%

Other Checkable Deposits 22%

Currency 44%

Demand Deposits 33%

amounts to over $1,873 in currency for every man, woman, and child in the United States. Do you and your friends each have $1,873 of currency?

Most of the currency in the official statistics is not used in ordinary commerce in the United States. Much of it is held abroad by wealthy people who want U.S. currency in case of emergencies or who use it to keep their wealth out of sight of their own governments and tax authorities. Some of it circulates in other countries along with their local currencies. Currency is also used in illegal transactions such as the drug trade. Few dealers of illegal drugs open bank accounts that could be inspected by international law authorities.

The United States is not the only country that has a large amount of currency per capita outstanding, as "A Closer Look: Lots of Currency," explains.

M1 does not include all the assets that are used to make economic exchanges. Economists also use a somewhat broader definition of money known as **M2**, which includes assets that are sometimes used in economic exchanges or can be readily turned into M1. M2 consists of all the assets in M1 plus several other assets such as deposits in money market mutual funds. These are funds in which individuals can invest; they earn interest and can be used to write checks over some minimum amount. Deposits in savings accounts are also included in M2. While deposits in savings accounts cannot gener-

M2: M1 plus other assets, including deposits in savings and loans and money market mutual funds.

Currency held by the public is part of the official money supply.

A CLOSER LOOK | Lots of Currency

The economist Case M. Sprenkel has noted that other developed countries besides the United States have large amounts of currency per capita outstanding. In 1992, for example, while the United States had $1,096 of currency per person, measured in dollars, the Japanese had $2,228 per person and the Swiss had $3,116 per person. Austria, Belgium, Germany, Spain, and Sweden all had per capita currency holdings larger than those of the United States. British currency holdings per person, by contrast, were less than half of per capita money holdings in the United States.

What can explain these differences? There probably are some cultural differences. The Japanese traditionally carry more currency and use it frequently for gifts. There are even automated teller machines in Japan that press money to remove its wrinkles. But cultural preferences are not sufficient explanation.

After all, why should the British hold so much less currency than the Belgians?

Sprenkel believed that much of the currency of the countries with large currency holdings per capita was actually held abroad, in developing countries whose domestic currencies did not provide good stores of value. As he put it, "The Argentinean taxi driver or the Algerian bellhop would like to have the American tourist or businessman's dollars, but would also appreciate the Italian's lire or the Japanese's yen if that is who is arriving." Currencies from developed countries are likely to be better stores of value than currencies in many developing countries.

Source: Case M. Sprenkel, "The Case of the Missing Money," *Journal of Economic Perspectives*, Fall 1993, pp. 175–84 (quotation from p. 177).

ally be used directly in exchanges, they can be converted to M1 and then used in exchanges. In July 1999, M2 totaled $4,541 billion.

Economists use different definitions of money because it is not always clear which assets are used primarily as money—that is, which assets are used for economic exchanges—and which are used primarily for saving and investing. For example, consider money market mutual funds, which came into existence only in the late 1970s. Although people can use these funds to write checks and engage in economic transactions, many people use them in other ways. Some may have their wealth temporarily invested in these funds in anticipation of moving their wealth into the stock market. Others may use them to earn interest while avoiding the risks of the stock market or bond market. Sometimes, money market mutual funds are used like regular checking accounts; other times, they are used like savings accounts. If they are used like checking accounts, they should be in M1; but if they are used like savings accounts, they should be part of M2. Economists keep an eye on both M1 and M2 because they often do not know precisely how money market accounts are used.

TEST Your Understanding

6. About one-third of M1 consists of _____.

7. Complete the statement with *M1* or *M2*: Economists use _____ to measure the amount of money that is regularly used in transactions.

8. Which is greater: M1 or M2?

9. How do you explain the fact that the total amount of currency divided by the U.S. population is approximately $1,873?

10. Why are money market mutual funds hard to classify?

Banks as Financial Intermediaries

Now let's see what part banks play in the creation of the supply of money. In Chapter 26, we discussed how financial intermediaries help to bring savers and investors together. By using their expertise and the powers of diversification, financial intermediaries reduce risk to savers and allow investors to obtain funds on better terms. Commercial banks operate precisely in this manner.

A typical commercial bank will accept funds from savers in the form of deposits, for example, in a checking account. The bank does not leave all these funds idle; if it did, it could never make a profit. Instead, the bank turns the money around and makes loans to businesses. A local hardware store might need a $100,000 loan to purchase its inventory. To make this loan, the bank would pool deposits from many savers. It will make other loans as well, reducing its risk through diversification.

It will be easier to understand how banks work if we examined a simplified **balance sheet** for a commercial bank. A balance sheet shows how banks raise money and where the money goes.

Balance sheets have two sides: one for assets and one for liabilities. **Liabilities** are the source of funds for the bank. If you open a checking account and deposit your funds in that account, the bank is liable for returning these funds to you. Your deposits are liabilities to the bank.

Assets are the uses of these funds. Assets generate income for the bank. Loans are examples of a bank's assets because a borrower must pay interest to the bank.

The difference between a bank's assets and its liabilities is its **net worth**:

$$\text{net worth} = \text{assets} - \text{liabilities}$$

If a bank has $1,000 of assets and $900 of liabilities, it has a net worth of $100. When a bank is started, its owners must place their own funds into the bank. These funds are the bank's initial net worth. If a bank makes profits, its net worth increases; if it loses money, its net worth decreases.

In Figure 27.2, we show the assets and liabilities of a hypothetical bank. On the liability side, the bank has $2,000 of deposits. The net worth of the bank is $200. This is entered on the liability side of the balance sheet because it is also a source of funds. The total source of funds is therefore $2,200—the deposits in the bank plus its net worth.

On the asset side, the bank holds $200 in **reserves**; these are assets that are not lent out. Banks are required by law to hold a specific fraction of their deposits as reserves and not make loans with it; this fraction of deposits is called **required reserves**. Banks may choose to hold additional reserves beyond what is required; these are called **excess reserves**. A bank's reserves are the sum of its required and excess reserves. Reserves can be either cash kept in a bank's vaults or deposits with the Federal Reserve. Banks do not earn any interest on these reserves.

In our example, the bank is holding 10% of its deposits, or $200, as reserves. The remainder of the bank's assets consists of loans. In this case the bank makes $2,000 in loans.

By definition, total assets will always equal liabilities plus net worth. Balance sheets must always balance.

Balance sheet: An account for a bank which shows the sources of its funds (liabilities) as well as the uses for the funds (assets).
Liabilities: The sources of funds for a bank, including deposits.

Assets: The uses of the funds of a bank, including loans and reserves.
Net worth: The difference between assets and liabilities.

Reserves: The fraction of banks' deposits that are set aside in either vault cash or as deposits at the Federal Reserve.
Required reserves: The fraction of banks' deposits that banks are legally required to hold in their vaults or as deposits at the Fed.
Excess reserves: Any additional reserves that a bank holds above its required reserves.

Assets	Liabilities
$ 200 Reserves	$2,000 Deposits
$2,000 Loans	$ 200 Net Worth
Total: $2,200	Total: $2,200

Figure 27.2
Balance Sheet for a Bank

The Process of Money Creation

To understand the role that banks play in determining the supply of money, let's suppose that someone walks into the First Bank of Hollywood and deposits $1,000 in cash to open a checking account. Because currency held by the public and checking deposits are both included in the supply of money, the total money supply has not changed. The money supply did not change because the cash deposit of currency into the checking account reduced the currency held by the public by precisely the amount that the deposit in the checking account increased.

However, banks do not keep in their vaults all the cash they receive. For a bank to make a profit, it must make loans. Let's assume that banks are required to keep 10% of deposits as reserves and hold no excess reserves. That means that the **reserve ratio**—the ratio of reserves to deposits—will be 0.1. The First Bank of Hollywood will keep $100 in reserves and make loans totaling $900. The top panel in Figure 27.3 shows the change in the bank's balance sheet after it has made its loan.

Reserve ratio: The ratio of reserves to deposits.

Suppose the First Bank of Hollywood loaned the funds to an aspiring movie producer. The bank opens a checking account, with a balance of $900, for the producer, who needs the funds to buy equipment. The producer buys the equipment from a supplier who accepts payment in the form of a $900 check, and deposits the check in the Second Bank of Burbank. The next panel in Figure 27.3 shows what happens to the balance sheet of the Second Bank of Burbank. Liabilities increase by the deposit of $900. The bank must hold $90 in reserves (10% of the $900 deposit) and can lend out $810. Suppose that it lends the $810 to an owner of a coffeehouse and opens a checking account with a balance of $810 for her. She then purchases coffee costing $810, paying with a check to the supplier, who deposits the $810 check into the Third Bank of Venice.

The Third Bank of Venice receives a deposit of $810. It must keep $81 in reserves and can lend out $729. This process continues throughout the Los Angeles area with new loans and deposits. The Fourth Bank of Pasadena will receive a deposit of $729, hold $72.90 in reserves, and lend out $656.10. The Fifth Bank of Compton will receive a deposit of $656.10 as the process goes on.

The original $1,000 cash deposit has created checking account balances throughout Los Angeles. What total amount of checking account balances has been created? Adding up the new accounts in all the banks (even the ones we have not named), we have

$$\$1,000 + \$900 + \$810 + \$729 + \$656.10 + \ldots = \$10,000$$

How did we come up with this sum? It's from the following simple formula, which we derive in the appendix to this chapter:

total increase in checking account balance throughout all banks
$$= (\text{initial cash deposit}) \times (1/\text{reserve ratio})$$

In our example, the reserve ratio is 0.1, so the increase in checking account balances is 1/0.1, or 10 times the initial cash deposit. The initial $1,000 deposit led to a total increase in checking account balances throughout all banks of $10,000.

Recall that the money supply, M1, is the sum of deposits at commercial banks plus currency held by the public. Therefore, the change in the money supply, M1, will be the change in deposits in checking accounts plus the change in currency held by the public. Notice that we referred to "change," meaning increase or decrease. Here's why: In our example,

Figure 27.3

Process of Deposit Creation: Changes in Balance Sheets

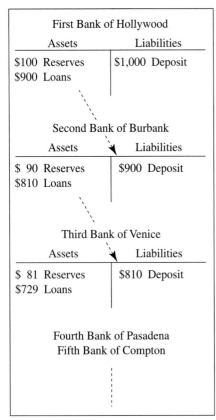

First Bank of Hollywood

Assets	Liabilities
$100 Reserves	$1,000 Deposit
$900 Loans	

Second Bank of Burbank

Assets	Liabilities
$ 90 Reserves	$900 Deposit
$810 Loans	

Third Bank of Venice

Assets	Liabilities
$ 81 Reserves	$810 Deposit
$729 Loans	

Fourth Bank of Pasadena
Fifth Bank of Compton

deposits increased by $10,000, but the public (as represented by the person who made that first deposit at the First Bank of Hollywood) holds $1,000 less of currency because the person deposited the currency in the bank. Therefore, the money supply, M1, increased by $9,000 ($10,000 − $1,000). No single bank lent out more than it had in deposits. Yet for the banking system as a whole, the money supply expanded by a multiple of the initial cash deposit.

The term *1/reserve ratio* in the formula is called the **money multiplier**. It tells us what the total increase in checking account deposits would be for any initial cash deposit. Recall the multiplier for government spending in our demand-side models: An increase in government spending led to larger increases in output through the multiplier. The government spending multiplier arose because additional rounds of consumption spending were triggered by an initial increase in government spending. In the banking system, an initial cash deposit triggers additional rounds of deposits and lending by banks. This leads to a multiple expansion of deposits.

As of 1999 in the United States, banks were required to hold 3% reserves against checkable deposits up to $47.8 million and 10% on all checkable deposits exceeding $47.8 million. Since large banks would face a 10% reserve requirement on any new deposits, you might think, on the basis of our formula, that the money multiplier would be approximately 10.

However, the money multiplier for the United States is between 2 and 3, much smaller than the value of 10 implied by our simple formula. The primary reason is that our formula assumed that all loans made their way directly into checking accounts. In reality, people hold part of their loans as cash. The cash that people hold is not available for the banking system to lend out. The more money people hold in cash, the lower the amount of money they deposit, creating fewer deposits, thus decreasing the money multiplier. The money multiplier would also be less if banks held excess reserves. We can represent these factors in a money multiplier ratio, but it will not be as simple as the one we introduced here.

The money creation process also works in reverse. Suppose you go to your bank and ask for $1,000 in cash from your checking account. The bank must pay you the $1,000. Its liabilities fall by $1,000, but its assets must also fall by $1,000. Withdrawing your $1,000 means two things at the bank: First, if the reserve ratio is 0.1, the bank will reduce its reserves by $100. Second, your $1,000 withdrawal minus the $100 reduction in reserves means that the bank has $900 less to lend out; hence, it will reduce its loans by $900. With fewer loans, there will be fewer deposits in other banks. The money multiplier working in reverse decreases the money supply.

You may wonder how a bank goes about reducing its outstanding loans. If you had borrowed from a bank to invest in a project for your business, you would not want the bank phoning you, asking for its funds, which are not lying idle but are invested in your business. Banks do not typically call in loans from outstanding borrowers. Instead, if banks cannot tap into their excess reserves when their customers want to withdraw cash, they would have to make fewer new loans. In these circumstances, a new potential borrower would find it harder to obtain a loan from the bank.

Up to this point, our examples have always started with an initial cash deposit. However, suppose that Paul receives a check from Freda and Paul deposits it into his bank. Paul's bank will eventually receive payment from Freda's bank. When Paul's bank does receive payment, the bank will initially have an increase in both deposits and reserves, just as if a cash deposit were made. Because Paul's bank has to hold only a fraction of the deposits as reserves, it will be able to make loans with the remainder.

However, there is one crucial difference between this example in which one individual writes a check to another and our earlier example in which an individual makes a cash deposit: When Paul receives the check from Freda, the money supply will not be

Money multiplier: An initial deposit leads to a multiple expansion of deposits. In the simplified case, increase in deposits = (initial deposit) × (1/reserve ratio).

changed. Here's why it won't: When Freda's check is deposited in Paul's bank, the money supply will begin to expand, but when Freda's bank loses its deposit, the money supply will start to contract. The expansions and contractions offset each other when private citizens and firms write checks to one another.

TEST Your Understanding

11. Banks are required by law to keep a fraction of their deposits as _____.

12. Define net worth.

13. Why does a bank prefer to make loans rather than keep reserves?

14. If the reserve ratio is 0.2 and a deposit of $100 is made into a bank, the bank will lend out _____.

15. If the reserve ratio is 0.2, the simplified money multiplier will be _____.

16. Why is the actual money multiplier much smaller than in our simple formula?

The Role of the Federal Reserve in the Money Creation Process

Banks can expand the money supply only if new reserves come into the banking system. When private citizens and firms write checks to one another, there will be no net change in the supply of money in the system. Because the total amount of reserves in the system is unchanged, the money supply cannot expand. There is one organization, however, that has the power to change the total amount of reserves in the banking system: the Federal Reserve.

Open Market Operations

The Federal Reserve (the Fed) can increase or decrease the total amount of reserves in the banking system through either of the following operations:

- In **open market purchases**, the Federal Reserve buys government bonds from the private sector.

- In **open market sales**, the Fed sells government bonds to the private sector.

open market purchases: The Fed's purchase of government bonds, which increases the money supply.
open market sales: The Fed's sales of government bonds to the public, which decreases the money supply.

To understand how the Fed can increase the supply of money, let's trace what happens after an open market purchase. Suppose the Federal Reserve purchases $1 million worth of government bonds from the private sector. The Fed writes a check for $1 million and presents it to the party who sold the bonds. The Federal Reserve now owns those bonds.

The party who sold the bonds has a check written on the Federal Reserve for $1 million. He deposits this check in his bank. The bank credits his account in the amount of $1 million because it has the check for $1 million written against the Federal Reserve.

Here is the key to how that increases the supply of money: Checks written against the Federal Reserve count as reserves for banks. As soon as the bank presents the check to the Federal Reserve, the bank will have $1 million in new reserves. If the reserve requirement is 10%, the bank must keep $100,000 in reserves, but it can make loans for $900,000. And so the process of money creation begins. Open market purchases increase the money supply.

The Federal Reserve has powers that ordinary citizens and even banks do not have. The Fed can write checks against itself to purchase government bonds without having any explicit "funds" in its account for the purchase. Banks accept these checks because they count as reserves for the bank.

As you might expect, open market sales will decrease the supply of money. Suppose the Federal Reserve sells $1 million worth of bonds to a Wall Street firm. The firm will pay for the bonds with a check for $1 million drawn on its bank and give this check to the Federal Reserve. The firm now owns the bonds.

The Federal Reserve presents this check to the Wall Street firm's bank. The bank must either hand over $1 million in cash or, more likely, reduce its reserve holding with the Federal Reserve by $1 million. (Banks keep accounts with the Fed, and in this case, the Fed would reduce the bank's account balance by $1 million.) Because the bank's reserves have fallen, it must decrease its loans to increase reserves to their required levels. And so, the process of money destruction begins. Open market sales decrease the money supply.

In summary, if the Federal Reserve wishes to increase the money supply, it buys government bonds from the private sector—called open market purchases. If the Fed wishes to decrease the money supply, it sells government bonds to the private sector—called open market sales.

Other Tools

Open market operations are by far the most important way in which the Federal Reserve changes the supply of money. There are two other ways in which the Fed can change the supply of money:

- Change the reserve requirement.

- Change the discount rate.

If the Fed wishes to increase the supply of money, it can reduce banks' reserve requirements. Banks would then only need to hold a smaller fraction of their deposits as reserves and could make more loans, expanding the money supply. To decrease the supply of money, the Federal Reserve could raise reserve requirements.

Although changing reserve requirements can be a strong tool, the Federal Reserve does not use it very often because it is disruptive to the banking system. Suppose a major bank whose clients were multinational corporations held exactly 10% of its deposits as reserves and the remainder as loans. If the Federal Reserve suddenly increased its reserve requirement to 20%, the bank would be forced to call in or cancel many of its loans. Its multinational clients would not like this! For these reasons, the Fed today does not make sharp changes in reserve requirements. In the past, the Fed did change reserve requirements sharply; when it did, the results were extremely disruptive to banks and their customers.

The Fed will lend banks reserves at an interest rate called the **discount rate**. Suppose a major customer comes to the bank and asks for a loan. Unless the bank could find an additional source of funds, it would have to refuse to make the loan. Banks are reluctant to turn away major customers. They first try to borrow reserves from other banks through the **federal funds market**, a market in which banks borrow or lend reserves to each other. If the federal funds rate seemed too high to the bank, it could borrow directly from the Federal Reserve at the discount rate.

By changing the discount rate, the Federal Reserve can influence the amount of borrowing by banks. If the Fed raised the discount rate, banks would be discouraged from borrowing reserves because it has become more costly to borrow. Lowering the discount rate will induce banks to borrow additional reserves.

In principle, the Federal Reserve could use the discount rate as a tool independent of monetary policy: lowering the discount rate to expand the money supply and raising the discount rate to reduce the money supply. In practice, the Fed keeps the discount rate close to the federal funds rate to avoid large swings in borrowed reserves by banks. Changes in the discount rate, however, are quite visible to financial markets. Partici-

Discount rate: The interest rate at which banks can borrow from the Fed.

Federal funds market: The market in which banks borrow and lend reserves to one another.

pants in the financial markets often interpret these changes as revealing clues about the Fed's intentions for future monetary policy.

The media typically describes the Federal Reserve as setting the federal funds rate. In fact, the Fed does conduct monetary policy by setting targets for the federal funds rate. Once it has set those targets, it uses open market operations to keep the actual funds rate on target.

TEST Your Understanding

17. Complete the statement with *increases* or *decreases*: When the Federal Reserve buys bonds, it _____ the money supply.

18. Complete the statement with *sale* or *purchase*: An open market _____ will lead to a reduction of reserves in banks.

19. Who borrows and lends in the federal funds market?

20. What is the discount rate?

The Structure of the Federal Reserve

The Federal Reserve System was created in 1913 after a series of financial panics in the United States. Financial panics can occur when there is bad news about the economy or about the health and vitality of financial institutions that causes concern among individuals doing business in the financial markets. During these panics, depositors became fearful that they would not be able to withdraw their account balances if they delayed, so they started to withdraw their funds immediately. This meant that banks could no longer make loans to businesses, resulting in severe economic downturns. Congress created the Federal Reserve System to be a **central bank**, serving as a banker's bank. One of the Fed's primary jobs was to serve as a **lender of last resort**. If there was a panic in which depositors wanted to withdraw their funds, the Federal Reserve would be there to lend funds to banks, thereby reducing some of the adverse consequences of the panic.

All countries have central banks. The German central bank is known as the Bundesbank. In the United Kingdom, the central bank is the Bank of England. Central banks serve as lenders of last resort to the banks in their countries and provide the levers through which they change their money supply.

Congress was aware that it was creating an institution with vast powers, so it deliberately created a structure in which, at least on paper, it attempted to disperse power away from the financial centers (e.g., New York) to the rest of the country. To understand the structure of the Federal Reserve today, keep in mind it has three distinct subgroups: Federal Reserve Banks, the Board of Governors, and the Federal Open Market Committee.

The United States was divided into 12 Federal Reserve districts, each of which has a **Federal Reserve Bank**. These district banks provide advice on monetary policy, take part in decision-making on monetary policy, and provide a liaison between the Fed and the banks in their districts.

Figure 27.4 is a map of the United States, identifying geographically each of the 12 Federal Reserve Banks. At the time the Fed was created, economic and financial power in this country was concentrated in the East and the Midwest. This is no longer true. What major Western city does not have a Federal Reserve Bank?

The **Board of Governors of the Federal Reserve** is the true seat of power over the monetary system. Headquartered in Washington, D.C., the seven members of the board are appointed for staggered 14-year terms by the President and must be confirmed by the Senate. The chairperson of the Board of Governors serves a four-year term. As the princi-

Central bank: A banker's bank; an official bank that controls the supply of money in a country.

Lender of last resort: A central bank is the lender of last resort, the last place, having failed all others, that banks in emergency situations can obtain loans.

Federal Reserve Banks: One of 12 regional banks that are an official part of the Federal Reserve System.

Board of Governors of the Federal Reserve: The seven-person governing body of the Federal Reserve system in Washington, D.C.

Figure 27.4
Federal Reserve Banks of the United States

pal spokesperson for monetary policy in the United States, what the chairperson says, or might say, is carefully observed or anticipated by financial markets throughout the world.

Decisions on monetary policy are made by the **Federal Open Market Committee (FOMC)**. The FOMC is a 12-person board consisting of the seven members of the Board of Governors, the president of the New York Federal Reserve bank plus the presidents of four other regional Federal Reserve Banks. (Presidents of the regional banks other than New York serve on a rotating basis; the seven nonvoting bank presidents attend the meetings and provide their views). The chairperson of the Board of Governors also serves as the chairperson of the FOMC. The FOMC makes the actual decisions on changes in the money supply. Its members are assisted by vast teams of professionals at the Board of Governors and at the regional Federal Reserve Banks. The structure of the Federal Reserve System is depicted in Figure 27.5.

The chairperson of the Board of Governors is also required to report to Congress on a regular basis. Although the Federal Reserve operates with independence from the U.S. Treasury, it is a creation of Congress. The U.S. Constitution gives Congress the power to

Federal Open Market Committee (FOMC): The group that decides on monetary policy; it consists of the seven members of the Board of Governors plus five of 12 regional bank presidents on a rotating basis.

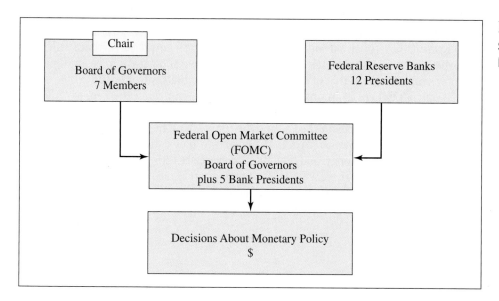

Figure 27.5
Structure of the Federal Reserve

A CLOSER LOOK — Politics and Power: Who Controls the Bankers?

Federal Reserve Bank presidents help to determine monetary policy through their participation in the Federal Open Market Committee. These presidents are chosen by the directors of their banks. At each bank, six of the directors are elected from the member banks in their district, and three are appointed by the Board of Governors.

Some members of Congress have worried about the participation of the bank presidents on the FOMC, particularly because they have tended to be more conservative than members of the Board of Governors. While members of the Board of Governors are nominated by the President and confirmed by the Senate, bank presidents are neither appointed by elected officials nor confirmed by the Senate.

Although the Board of Governors does influence their selection, they represent an independent voice for the member banks in their district and the financial community. Should these bank presidents play such an important role in the determination of monetary policy?

Supporters of the current system argue that the Fed's district bank presidents provide perspectives that are not apparent outside the narrow confines of Washington, DC and that they are in closer touch than the Board of Governors with business developments in their regions. Opponents claim that allowing the bank presidents to vote gives the financial elite in our country too much power in the design of monetary policy. The current system has been in place since 1935, and Congress is unlikely to change it in the near future.

"coin money and regulate the value thereof." In practice, the Fed takes its actions first and later reports its actions to Congress. The chairperson of the Federal Reserve often meets with members of the executive branch to discuss economic affairs.

On paper, the powers of monetary policy appear to be spread throughout the government and the country. In practice, however, the Board of Governors and especially the chairperson have the real control. The Board of Governors operates with considerable independence. Presidents and members of Congress can bring political pressures on the Board of Governors, but 14-year terms provide some insulation from external pressures.

Countries differ in the degree to which the central bank is independent of political authorities. In both the United States and Germany, the central banks operate with considerable independence of elected officials. In other countries, the central bank is part of the treasury department of the government and potentially subject to more direct political control.

There is a lively debate among economists and political scientists as to whether more independent central banks (with less external political pressure) have less inflation. Even if there is an advantage to an independent central bank, there still is an important issue: In a democratic society, why should we allow there to be an important and powerful institution that is not directly subject to the control by the people or our elected officials? There is an ongoing debate over the control of the Fed, as "A Closer Look: Politics and Power: Who Controls the Bankers?," indicates.

Why should we care about the Fed and the supply of money? In this chapter, we have discussed the role that money plays in the economy, how commercial banks play a key role in the creation of money, and how the Fed exercises ultimate control of the money supply. In the next chapter, we will see that the Fed can also determine short-term interest rates and thereby influence the level of economic activity. It is precisely this power over the economy that makes the Fed such a subject of public interest.

Using the **TOOLS**

In this chapter, we studied the money creation process as it works through the banking system. Take this opportunity to do your own economic analysis.

1. ECONOMIC EXPERIMENT: Money and the Store of Value

This experiment demonstrates that goods that are more effective stores of value can become the medium of exchange. There are three types of individuals (A, B, C) and three types of goods in the economy (1, 2, 3). Type A consumes good 1; Type B consumes good 2; and Type C consumes good 3. No type produces the good it consumes: Type A produces Good 2; Type B produces Good 3; and Type C produces Good 1. Here is how the game works: In the first period, individuals start with 1 unit of the good they produce and are randomly paired with other individuals. They can either engage in trade or not. If they successfully trade for the good they are allowed to consume, they consume it immediately and earn 100 points. At that time, they also costlessly produce 1 unit of their good for the next round of play. If individuals do not trade, they must store their goods. They lose 10 points for storing good 1, lose 20 points for storing good 2, and lose 30 points for storing good 3. The game proceeds for several periods, and the individual with the most points wins. What good do you think emerges as the medium of exchange?

2. Bad Loans to South America

During the 1980s, U.S. banks made loans to South American countries. Many of these loans turned out to be worthless. How did this affect the assets, liabilities, and net worth of these banks?

3. Reserve Requirements as a Tax

Left on their own, most banks would reduce their reserve requirements far below 10%. Consequently, banks view reserve requirements as a "tax" on their holdings of deposits. Explain how a 10% reserve requirement could be viewed as a 10% tax.

4. High-Powered Money

Economists define high-powered money as the reserves at banks plus the currency held by the public. The Federal Reserve is often said to control the stock of high-powered money. Does the stock of high-powered money change when:

a. Currency is deposited into a bank?

b. A bank makes a loan?

c. The Federal Reserve buys government bonds?

Summary

We began this chapter examining the role money plays in the economy and how economists define *money*. We then took a closer look at banks as financial intermediaries. We saw how banks can create money through deposit creation. And we learned how the Federal Reserve can control the supply of money through open market purchases and sales and other policies. Here are the main points you should remember from this chapter:

1. Money consists of anything that is regularly used in making exchanges, that is, buying and selling goods and services. In modern economies, money consists primarily of currency and deposits in checking accounts.

2. Banks are financial intermediaries that earn profits by accepting deposits and making loans. Deposits,

which are liabilities of banks, are included in the money supply.

3. Banks are required by law to hold a fraction of their deposits as reserves, either in cash or in deposits with the Federal Reserve. Total reserves consist of required reserves plus excess reserves.

4. If there is an increase in reserves in the banking system, the supply of money will expand by a multiple of the initial deposit. This multiple is known as the money multiplier.

5. The Federal Reserve's primary tool for increasing or decreasing the total amount of reserves in the banking system is through open market purchases of government bonds (which increase reserves) or open market sales (which decrease reserves).

6. The Federal Reserve can also change the supply of money by changing reserve requirements or changing the discount rate.

7. Decisions about the supply of money are made at the Federal Open Market Committee (FOMC), which includes the seven members on the Board of Governors and the president of the New York Federal Reserve Bank, as well as four of the 11 other regional bank presidents, who serve on a rotating basis.

Key Terms

assets, 571
balance sheet, 571
barter, 567
Board of Governors of the Federal Reserve, 576
central bank, 576
discount rate, 575
double coincidence of wants, 567
excess reserves, 571
federal funds market, 575

Federal Open Market Committee (FOMC), 577
Federal Reserve Banks, 576
lender of last resort, 576
liabilities, 571
M1, 568
M2, 569
medium of exchange, 567
money, 566

money multiplier, 573
net worth, 571
open market purchases, 574
open market sales, 574
required reserves, 571
reserve ratio, 572
reserves, 571
store of value, 567
unit of account, 567

Probelms and Discussion Questions

1. Why are travelers' checks classified as money?

2. Both insurance companies and banks are financial intermediaries. Why do macroeconomists study banks more intensively than insurance companies?

3. What is the opportunity cost to a bank of holding excess reserves?

4. If a customer took $2,000 in cash from a bank and the reserve ratio was 0.2, by how much would the supply of money be eventually reduced?

5. If the Federal Reserve undertakes an open market sale of $2 million and the reserve ratio is 0.15, by how much will the money supply decrease?

6. If banks hold excess reserves, how will this affect the money multiplier?

7. Explain the mechanism through which an increase in the discount rate affects the money supply.

8. Occasionally, some economists or politicians suggest that the Secretary of Treasury become a member of the Federal Open Market Committee. How do you think this would affect the independence of the Federal Reserve.

9. Suppose the Federal Reserve purchased gold or foreign currency. How would this purchase affect the domestic money supply? (Hint: Think about open market purchases of government bonds.)

10. The Federal Reserve has traditionally conducted its open market operations through the purchase and sale of government bonds. In principle, could the Federal Reserve conduct monetary policy through the purchase and sale of stocks on the New York Stock Exchange? Do you see any potential drawbacks to such a policy?

11. In 1992, the state of California ran out of funds and could not pay its bills. It issued IOUs, called warrants, to its workers and suppliers. Only large banks and credit unions accepted the warrants. Should these warrants be viewed as money?

12. Web Exercise. Go to the Web site of the Federal Reserve (*http://www.federalreserve.gov*) and read the minutes from the last Open Market Committee meeting. What decisions did they make with regard to open market operations? What other items of business were on their agenda that day?

13. Web Exercise. Go to the data Web site of the Federal Reserve Bank of St. Louis (*http://www.stls.frb.org/fred*). Look carefully at the components of M1 and M2 over the last 10 years. What trends do you see?

Take It to the Net

We invite you to visit the O'Sullivan/Sheffrin page on the Prentice Hall Web site at:
http://www.prenhall.com/osullivan/
for additional World Wide Web exercises for this chapter.

Model Answers to Questions

Chapter-Opening Questions

1. All societies have money because it makes it much easier to conduct trade.

2. Banks play a special role in our economy because the liabilities of banks are part of the supply of money.

3. The banking system as a whole can create money through the process of multiple expansion. However, this depends on the actions of the Federal Reserve.

4. When the Federal Reserve purchases bonds from the public, it increases reserves in banks and leads to an increase in the supply of deposits and loans. When the Federal Reserve sells bonds to the public, the supply of loans and deposits decreases.

5. The chairman of the Federal Reserve is the most powerful person in the Federal Reserve System, which determines the supply of money in the economy.

Test Your Understanding

1. Barter.

2. Inflation makes money an imperfect store of value.

3. Without money, you would need to find someone who had the good that you wanted to buy and also wants to trade for the good that you have.

4. True. Money serves as a unit of account because prices are quoted in terms of money.

5. Checks are counted as money because they are regularly used in economic exchanges.

6. Currency held by the public.

7. M1.

8. M2 is greater.

9. A "typical" person in the United States does not hold this amount of currency. Some currency is held abroad, and some is held for illegal purposes.

10. Money market mutual funds are used both for making transactions and savings.

11. Reserves.

12. Net worth is assets minus liabilities.

13. Banks do not earn interest on reserves, but they do on loans.

14. $80.

15. 5.

16. The simplified formula does not take into account that individuals hold some cash from their loans.

17. Increases.

18. Sale.

19. Banks borrow and lend.

20. The discount rate is the interest rate at which banks can borrow from the Fed.

Using the Tools

1. Economic Experiment: Money and the Store of Value. As the experiment should reveal, good 1 should emerge as the most likely medium of exchange.

2. Bad Loans to South America. Bad loans will reduce the assets of a bank. Because they do not change the liabilities of a bank (its deposits), the net worth of the bank must also fall along with the value of its

assets. If the net worth of a bank falls too far, the bank can be closed.

3. **Reserve Requirements as a Tax.** Because a bank earns no interest on reserves, the reserve requirement acts as a tax. Suppose the bank held no reserves at all and could earn 20% interest on loans. A 10% reserve requirement means that the bank could only earn 20% interest on 90% of its deposits. This is equivalent to a tax of 10%.

4. **High-Powered Money.** The stock of high-powered money changes only when the Federal Reserve buys a government bond. In this case, the total of reserves plus currency increases. If the public deposits currency in the bank, currency held by the public falls but the currency held by the bank (which counts as reserves) increases. When a bank makes a loan, the total reserves in the banking system do not change.

Formula for Deposit Creation

To show how to derive the formula for deposit creation, let's use the example in the text. We showed that with 10% held as reserves, a $1,000 deposit led to total deposits of

$$\$1,000 + \$900 + \$810 + \$729 + \$656.10 + \ldots$$

Let's find the total sum of all these deposits. Because each bank successively had to hold 10% in its reserves, that means that each successive bank received only 0.9 of the deposits of the prior bank. Therefore, we can write the total for the deposits in all the banks as

$$\$1,000 \times (1 + 0.9 + 0.9^2 + 0.9^3 + 0.9^4 + \ldots)$$

We need to find the sum of the terms in parentheses. Using a formula for an infinite sum,

$$1 + b + b^2 + b^3 + b^4 + \ldots = 1/(1 - b)$$

the expression becomes

$$1 + 0.9 + 0.9^2 + 0.9^3 + 0.9^4 + \ldots = 1/(1 - 0.9) = 1/0.1 = 10$$

Therefore, the total increase in deposits will be

$$\$1,000 \times 10 = \$10,000$$

To derive the general formula, note that if the reserve ratio is r, the bank will lend out $(1 - r)$ per dollar of deposits. Following the steps we just outlined, we find the infinite sum will be $1/[1 - (1 - r)] = 1/r$ or 1/reserve ratio. Therefore, in general, we have the formula

increase in checking account balances = (initial deposit) $\times$ (1/reserve ratio)

Monetary Policy in the Short Run

Many of us make decisions that are directly affected by what we think the Federal Reserve will do with respect to interest rates. Consider these examples:

- Your college cannot offer you the full scholarship you hoped for but is offering you a loan. Before you can accept it, you must know the interest rate that will be charged during your college career.
- Your sister would like to own her own home rather than rent an apartment. Her banker has offered her two options for a loan. One is a mortgage that has a constant interest rate for the entire length of the mortgage; it's called a fixed-rate mortgage. The other is a variable-rate mortgage: The starting interest rate is lower than the fixed-rate mortgage, but it will increase or decrease with the general level of interest rates in the economy. If she believes that interest rates will rise in the near future, your sister will take the fixed-rate option; if she believes that interest rates will not change, she will take the variable-rate loan. Your sister needs to know what the Federal Reserve plans to do with interest rates.

 n this chapter, we will learn why everyone is so interested in what the Federal Reserve is about to do. In the short run, when prices don't have enough time to change, so we consider them temporarily fixed, the Federal Reserve can influence the level of interest rates in the economy. When the Federal Reserve lowers interest rates, investment spending and GDP increase. When the Fed increases interest rates, that will reduce investment spending and GDP. It is this power of the Fed to affect interest rates in the short run that will influence your decision to accept the loan. It also explains why your sister wants to know what the Fed will do about interest rates in the near future.

After reading this chapter, you will be able to answer the following questions:

1. **Why do short-term interest rates rise after the Federal Reserve makes open market sales?**
2. **Why do the prices of bonds usually fall when the Federal Reserve raises interest rates?**
3. **How does the housing and the construction industry respond after the Federal Reserve decides to increase the money supply?**
4. **Why might the Fed refuse to lower interest rates even if everyone agrees the economy is in a slump?**

The Federal Reserve influences the level of interest rates in the short run by changing the supply of money through open market operations: selling or buying bonds in the open market. We will explain in this chapter how interest rates are determined in the short run by the supply and demand for money:

- The supply of money is determined largely by the Federal Reserve.

- The demand for money comes from the private sector. Using two principles of economics, *opportunity cost* and the *reality principle*, we will explain the factors that determine the demand for money.

- Putting demand for money and supply of money together, we will see how interest rates are determined in the short run.

Changes in interest rates affect total spending and output in the economy. For example, an open market purchase of bonds, increases the money supply, which leads to lower interest rates and increased investment spending. A higher level of investment spending will ultimately lead to a higher level of GDP. Here is the sequence of events to keep in mind as you read this chapter:

open market purchases	→	increase in money supply	→	fall in interest rates	→	rise in investment spending	→	increase in GDP

We have already seen that the Fed's open market purchases of bonds increase the money supply, increases in the money supply decrease interest rates, decreased interest rates increase investment spending, and higher investment spending leads to higher levels of GDP. From the preceding chapters, all but the link between the money supply increase and falling interest rates should be familiar to you. In this chapter, we add that link to the sequence.

This sequence also works in reverse: The Fed's open market sales of bonds will reduce the money supply, raise interest rates, and lower investment and GDP.

In this chapter, we also discuss how monetary policy works in an open economy: an economy with international trade.

The Fed has immense power, but there are limits to the extent it can effectively control the economy. As we have discussed, in the long run, increases in the money supply affect only prices, not the level of output. In this chapter, we explore the limits of the Fed's monetary policy and fiscal policy in the short run.

Model of the Money Market

We begin by learning the factors that determine the public's demand for money. Once we understand what affects the demand for money, we can see how actions taken by the Federal Reserve determine interest rates in the short run.

The Demand for Money

Let's think of money as simply one part of wealth. Suppose your total wealth is valued at $1,000. In what form will you hold your wealth? Should you put all your wealth into the stock market? Or perhaps into the bond market? Or should you hold some of your wealth in money, that is, currency and checking accounts?

If you invest your wealth in assets such as stocks or bonds, you earn income on your investment. Stocks pay dividends and increase in value; bonds pay interest. If you hold your wealth in currency or a checking account, you receive either no interest or very low interest. Holding your wealth in the form of money means that you sacrifice some potential income.

Money does, however, provide valuable services. It facilitates transactions. If you go to a grocery store to purchase some cereal, the store will accept currency or a check, but you won't be able to pay for your cereal with your stocks and bonds. People hold money primarily for this basic reason: Money makes it easier to conduct transactions. Economists call this reason for holding money the **transactions demand for money**.

To understand the demand for money, we rely on the principle of opportunity cost.

Transactions demand for money: The demand for money based on the desire to facilitate transactions.

PRINCIPLE OF OPPORTUNITY COST

> **The opportunity cost of something is what you sacrifice to get it.**

If you hold more of your wealth in terms of money, it makes it easier to conduct everyday business. But when you hold money, you sacrifice income by not investing that amount in assets (such as stocks and bonds) that earn returns.

The opportunity cost of holding money is the return that you could have earned by holding your wealth in other assets. We measure the opportunity cost of holding money by the interest rate. Suppose that the interest rate available to you on a long-term bond is 6% per year. If you hold $100 of your wealth in the form of this bond, you earn $6 a year. If you hold currency instead, you earn no interest. So the opportunity cost of holding $100 in currency is $6 per year or 6% per year.

As interest rates increase in the economy, the opportunity cost of holding money also increases. Economists have found that as the opportunity cost of holding money increases, the public demands less money. The quantity demanded of money will decrease with an increase in interest rates.

In Figure 28.1, we draw a demand for money curve, M^d, as a function of the interest rate. At higher interest rates, individuals will want to hold less money than they will at lower interest rates because the opportunity cost of holding money is higher. As interest rates rise from r_0 to r_1, the quantity demanded of money falls from M_0 to M_1.

Figure 28.1
Demand for Money
As interest rates increase
from r_0 to r_1, the quantity of
money demanded falls from
M_0 to M_1.

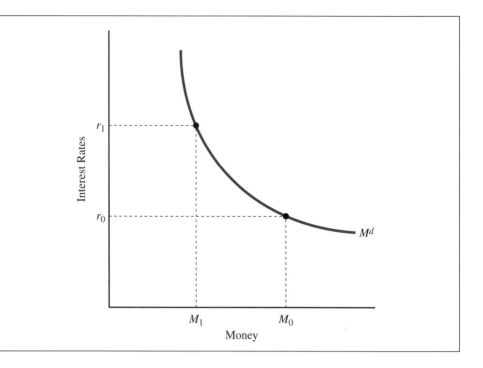

The demand for money also depends on two other factors. One is the overall price level in the economy. The demand for money will increase as the level of prices increases. If prices for your groceries are twice as high, you will need twice as much money to purchase them. The amount of money people typically hold during any time period will be closely related to the dollar value of the transactions that they make. This is an example of the reality principle in action.

REALITY **PRINCIPLE**

What matters to people is the real value of money or income—its purchasing power—not the face value of money or income.

The other factor that influences the demand for money is the level of real GDP or real income. It seems obvious that as income increases, individuals and businesses will make more purchases. As real GDP increases, individuals and businesses will be making more transactions. To facilitate these transactions, they will want to hold more money.

Figure 28.2 shows how changes in prices and income affect the demand for money. Increases in money demand will shift the money demand curve to the right. Panel A shows how the demand for money shifts to the right as the price level increases. At any interest rate, people will want to hold more money as prices increase. Panel B shows how the demand for money shifts to the right as real GDP increases. At any interest rate, people will want to hold more money as real GDP increases. These graphs both show the same result. An increase in prices or an increase in real GDP will increase money demand.

Traditionally, economists have identified other motives besides transactions for individuals or firms to hold money. If you hold your wealth in the form of property, such as a house or a boat, it is costly to sell the house or boat on short notice if you need to obtain funds. These forms of wealth are *illiquid*, meaning that they are not easily transferable into money. If you hold your wealth in currency or checking accounts, you do

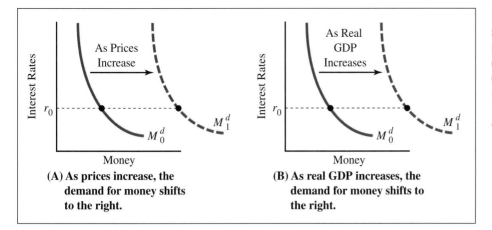

Figure 28.2
Shifting the Demand for Money
Changes in prices and real GDP shift the demand for money.

ACTIVE GRAPH

(A) As prices increase, the demand for money shifts to the right.

(B) As real GDP increases, the demand for money shifts to the right.

not have this problem. Economists recognize that individuals have a **liquidity demand for money**: People want to hold money to be able to make transactions on quick notice.

Individuals may also wish to hold some types of money—particularly savings accounts and assets contained in M2—that pay interest but are less risky than holding stocks or bonds. Over short periods, individuals may not wish to hold stocks or bonds because prices of stocks and bonds might fall. Holding your wealth in a savings account avoids the risk of falling stock or bond prices. The demand for money that arises because it is safer than other assets is called the **speculative demand for money**.

The demand for money, in practice, will be the sum of transactions, liquidity, and speculative demands. As we continue, keep in mind that the demand for money will depend positively on the level of income and prices and negatively on interest rates.

Liquidity demand for money:
The demand for money that represents the needs or desires of individuals or firms to make purchases on short notice without incurring excessive costs.

Speculative demand for money:
The demand for money that reflects holding money over short periods is less risky than holding stocks or bonds.

Interest Rate Determination

Combining the supply of money, determined by the Fed, with the demand for money, determined by the public, we can see how interest rates are determined in the short run in a demand and supply model of the money market.

Figure 28.3 depicts a model of the money market. The supply of money is determined by the Federal Reserve, and we assume for simplicity that it is independent of interest rates. We represent this independence by a vertical supply curve for money, M^s.

ACTIVE GRAPH

Figure 28.3
Equilibrium in the Money Market
Equilibrium in the money market occurs at an interest rate of r^* at which the quantity of money demanded equals the quantity of money supplied.

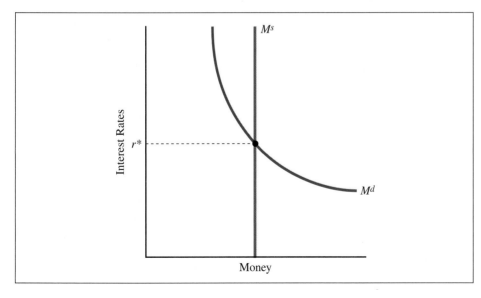

In the same graph, we draw the demand for money M^d. Market equilibrium occurs where the demand for money equals the supply of money, at an interest rate of r^*.

At this equilibrium interest rate, r^*, the quantity of money demanded by the private sector equals the quantity of money supplied by the Federal Reserve. What happens if the interest rate is higher than r^*? At a higher interest rate, the quantity of money demanded would be less than the fixed quantity supplied; the result would be an excess supply of money. In other markets, excess supplies cause the price to fall. It's the same here. The "price of money" in the market for money is the interest rate. The interest rate would fall and return to the equilibrium value, r^*. If the interest rate were below r^*, the demand for money would exceed the fixed supply: There would be an excess demand for money. As in other markets when there are excess demands, the price rises. Here, the "price of money," or the interest rate, would rise until it reached r^*.

As you see, money market equilibrium follows the same logic as any other economic equilibrium.

We can use this simple model of the money market to understand the power of the Federal Reserve. Suppose the Federal Reserve increased the money supply through an open market purchase of bonds. In panel A of Figure 28.4, an increase in the supply of money shifts the money supply curve to the right, leading to lower interest rates. A decrease in the money supply through the Fed's open market sale of bonds, as depicted in panel B of Figure 28.4, will decrease the supply of money, shifting the money supply curve to the left, increasing interest rates.

We can also think of the process from the perspective of banks. Recall our discussion of money creation through the banking system. After the Fed's open market purchase of bonds, banks will find that they have additional reserves and will want to make loans. To entice businesses to borrow, banks will lower the interest rates they charge on their loans. After an open market purchase of bonds by the Fed, interest rates will fall throughout the entire economy.

Now we understand why potential new homeowners—as well as businesspeople and politicians—want to know what the Federal Reserve is likely to do in the near future. The Fed exerts direct control over interest rates in the short run. If the Fed decides interest rates should be lower, it buys bonds in the open market to increase the supply of money. If it wants higher interest rates, it sells bonds in the open market to decrease the money supply.

In the short run, the Federal Reserve determines interest rates. The Fed affects interest rates to influence the level of GDP and inflation in the economy.

Figure 28.4
Federal Reserve and Interest Rates
Changes in the supply of money will change interest rates.

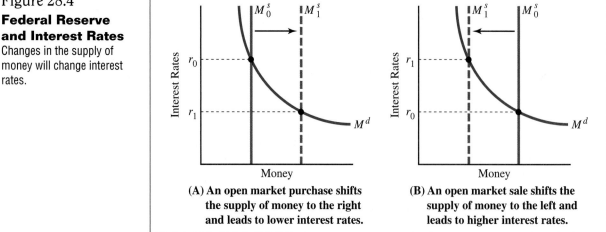

(A) An open market purchase shifts the supply of money to the right and leads to lower interest rates.

(B) An open market sale shifts the supply of money to the left and leads to higher interest rates.

The Mystery of Increasing Interest Rates and Economic Recovery

ECONOMIC DETECTIVE

Economists have often noticed that as an economy recovers from a recession, interest rates start to rise. Some observers have felt that this was mysterious because they believed that higher interest rates were associated with lower output. Using the demand and supply for money diagram, explain why interest rates can rise during an economic recovery.

The key to understanding the mystery is that the increase in income that occurs during the recovery will increase the demand for money. As the demand for money increases while the supply of money remains fixed, interest rates will rise. Thus, we expect to see rising interest rates during a period of economic recovery. ◆

Bond Prices and Interest Rates

When interest rates rise in the economy, bond prices fall. To see why, you first must recall that bonds are promises to pay money in the future. If you own a bond, you are entitled to receive payments from it in the future. Why do the prices of bonds move in the opposite direction from interest rates?

For a bond that promises to pay money one period in the future, there is a simple formula that mathematically represents the relationship between interest rates and bond prices:

$$\text{price of bonds} = \text{promised payment}/(1 + \text{interest rate})$$

The price of a bond is the promised payment divided by 1 plus the interest rate. Suppose the promised payment next year were $106 and the interest rate were 6% per year. The price of the bond would be

$$\text{price of bond} = \$106/1.06 = \$100$$

In this case, the bond would cost $100.

There is an easy way to understand this formula. If you had $100 today and invested it at a 6% annual interest rate, you would have $106 at the end of next year. Therefore, a bond that promises to pay you $106 dollars next year is worth exactly $100 today if you can invest at 6% per year. So it makes sense that the price of the bond will be the $100 amount you would be willing to pay today for the $106 promised payment next year. The formula shows that bond prices change in the opposite direction from changes in interest rates: Bond prices rise when interest rates fall, and bond prices fall when interest rates rise.

To really understand that, let's consider two examples:

- Suppose that the promised payment is still $106 but the interest rate falls from 6% to 4% per year. Using the formula, the price of the bond is $106/1.04, or $101.92. The price of the bond rose because, at the lower interest rate, you would need $101.92 today to invest at 4% per year to have $106 next year.

- Suppose that interest rates rose from 6% to 8% per year. The price of the bond would fall to $106/1.08, or $98.15. The reason the price of the bond fell is that you need only $98.15 to invest at 8% per year to have $106 next year. As interest rates rose, the price of the bond fell.

In financial markets, there are many types of complex bonds that pay different sums of money at different times in the future. However, all bonds, no matter how complex or simple, promise to pay money in the future. As interest rates rise, investors need less money for the promised payments in the future, so the price of bonds falls. As interest rates fall, investors need more money for the promised payments. Therefore, prices of bonds will rise as interest rates fall. The same logic that applied to simple one-period bonds applies to more complex bonds.

There is another way to understand why when bond prices change in one direction, interest rates will change in opposite directions. We know that when the Federal Reserve buys bonds in the open market, interest rates fall. But think about what the Federal Reserve is doing when it conducts the open market purchase. The Federal Reserve is buying bonds from the public. As it buys bonds, it increases the demand for bonds and raises their price. Thus, prices of bonds rise as interest rates fall.

Similarly, interest rates rise following an open market sale of bonds by the Fed. When the Fed conducts an open market sale, it is selling bonds, increasing the supply of bonds in the market. With an increase in the supply of bonds, the price of bonds will fall. Thus, prices of bonds fall as interest rates increase.

Because the Federal Reserve can change interest rates and bond prices in the short run, you can now see why Wall Street firms typically hire Fed watchers (often former officials of the Federal Reserve) to try to predict what the Fed will do. If a Wall Street firm had an inside scoop that the Fed would surprise the market and lower interest rates, the firm could buy millions of dollars of bonds for itself or its clients and make a vast profit as bond prices subsequently rose.

The Federal Reserve is aware of the importance of its deliberations and strives for secrecy. Sometimes it even calls on the law for help. In September 1996, some newspapers reported that they had learned that eight regional bank presidents favored interest rate increases at the next meeting. The Federal Reserve called in the Federal Bureau of Investigation to explore whether there were leaks to the press. (As it turned out, the Fed did not raise interest rates that month.)

We can use our understanding of the relationship between bond prices and interest rates to explain a puzzling phenomenon about the bond market. "A Closer Look: Why Is Good News for the Economy Bad News for the Bond Market?," explains this phenomenon using the tools we have developed.

TEST Your Understanding

1. How do we measure the opportunity cost of holding money?

2. Complete the statement with "increase" or "decrease": The quantity of money demanded will _____ as interest rates increase.

3. Complete the statement with "increase" or "decrease": Both increases in the price level and increases in real GDP will _____ the demand for money.

4. What will happen to interest rates if the Fed sells bonds on the open market?

5. If interest rates are 3% per year, what will be the price of a bond that promises to pay $109 next year?

Interest Rates, Investment, and Output

To show how the Fed's actions affect the economy, we expand our short-run, demand model of the economy to include money and interest rates. Our model will have three related graphs representing the following relationships:

A CLOSER LOOK | Why Is Good News for the Economy Bad News for the Bond Market?

You may have heard on television or read in the newspaper that prices in the bond market often fall in the face of good economic news, such as an increase in real output. Are the markets perverse? Why is good news for the economy bad news for the bond market?

We can understand the behavior of the bond market by thinking about the demand for money. When real GDP increases, the demand for money will increase. As the demand for money increases, the money demand curve will shift to the right. From our model of the money market, we know that increased money demand will increase interest rates. Bond prices move in the opposite direction from interest rates. Therefore, good news for the economy is bad for the bond market.

High GDP growth may also lead to expectations of higher inflation in the future. These expectations will tend to push up nominal interest rates as investors try to protect themselves against future inflation. Higher interest rates will mean lower bond prices, which is bad news for the bond market.

Finally, despite the good news in the economy, stock prices still can fall as well. As interest rates on bonds rise, it becomes more attractive to own bonds rather than stocks, so the demand for stocks falls. The result may be lower stock prices. Sometimes, however, stock prices increase in the face of good news if the good news leads investors to think that profits (and thus future dividends from holding the stock) will be very high in the future.

1. The supply and demand for money, which determines interest rates in the economy.

2. An investment function, which shows that investment spending decreases when interest rates increase, and vice versa.

3. A model in which the demand-side $C + I + G + NX$ line and the 45° line intersect at the level of output where total demand equals total production.

In this expanded short-run demand model, here's what happens:

- The rate of interest is determined in the money market.

- The rate of interest, in turn, determines the level of investment in the economy.

- Knowing the level of investment, we can find the level of output at which total demand for goods and services equals total output.

Figure 28.5 shows how the model works. In panel A we have the demand and supply for money, which determines the rate of interest, r_0. In panel B, we plot investment as a decreasing function of the interest rate. At the interest rate r_0, we find that investment spending will be I_0. In panel C, we show how the level of demand $C + I_0 + G + NX$ determines equilibrium output at y_0 using our familiar 45° line graph. The level of investment spending that we use in the 45° line graph is the same level of investment that we find from the two other panels.

Before illustrating how monetary policy works in this model, we should note that consumption as well as investment can depend on interest rates. Spending on consumer durables, such as automobiles or refrigerators, will also depend negatively on the rate of interest. Consumer durables are really investment goods for the household: If you buy an automobile, you incur the cost today and receive benefits (the ability to use the car) in the future. As interest rates rise, the opportunity costs of investing in the automobile will rise. Consumers will respond to the increase in the opportunity cost by purchasing fewer cars. In the rest of this chapter, we discuss how changes in interest rates affect investment but keep in mind that purchases of consumer durables will be affected as well.

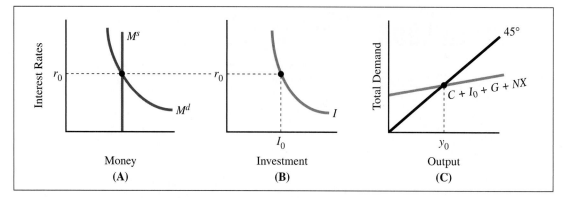

Figure 28.5 **Demand-Side Model with Money**
In panel A, the demand and supply for money determines the interest rate r_0. At this interest rate, panel B shows investment spending at I_0. Finally, in panel C, output is determined where the total demand line, with investment at I_0, intersects the 45° line.

Monetary Policy

Through its actions, the Federal Reserve can change the level of output in the short run. How does it? Consider an open market purchase. The Fed buys government bonds from the public, increasing the supply of money. With an increase in the supply of money, interest rates fall. As we explained in Chapter 26, lower interest rates stimulate additional investment spending. Output, or GDP, increases by the multiplier.

Figure 28.6 shows how an open market purchase of bonds by the Fed works. In panel A, the supply of money increases from M_0^s to M_1^s and interest rates fall from r_0 to r_1. In panel B, investment spending increases from I_0 to I_1 by the increment ΔI. In panel C, the increase in investment spending shifts the total demand line upward by the same incremental amount ΔI. GDP increases from y_0 to y_1, increasing by the increment Δy.

An open market sale of bonds by the Fed works precisely in reverse. In an open market sale, the Fed sells bonds to the private sector, reducing the money supply. Interest rates increase in the money market. With higher interest rates, firms reduce their investment spending. The decrease in investment spending decreases the total demand for goods and services in the economy. The reduced demand for goods and services leads to a reduction in GDP. We can represent this entire sequence of events:

Figure 28.6 **Open Market Purchase**
An open market purchase increases the supply of money, decreases interest rates, and increases the level of output.

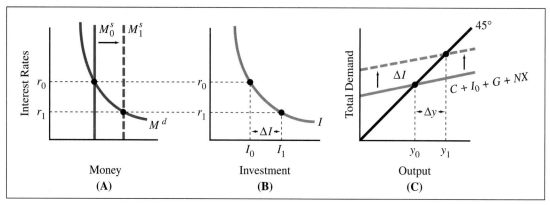

open market sale	$\rightarrow$	decrease in money supply	$\rightarrow$	rise in interest rates	$\rightarrow$	fall in investment spending	$\rightarrow$	decrease in GDP

Stop here for a moment, and think of the sequence of events by which the Federal Reserve can affect the level of GDP in the short run. It all starts in the financial markets. By buying and selling government bonds, the Federal Reserve can change the supply of money and the level of interest rates. In making their investment decisions, firms and individuals are influenced by the level of interest rates. Finally, changes in the demand for goods and services will affect the level of GDP in the short run. The sequence of events may be a bit indirect, but it is powerful.

The Federal Reserve can also influence the level of output through other tools, such as changes in reserve requirements or changes in the discount rate, discussed in Chapter 27. Actions that the Federal Reserve takes to influence the level of GDP are known as **monetary policy**.

Monetary policy: The range of actions taken by the Federal Reserve to influence the level of GDP or the rate of inflation.

This expanded short-run demand model can be used to understand why bank failures are harmful to the economy. During the Great Depression, there were severe bank failures throughout the world. How did these affect the level of GDP? Because deposits are part of the money supply, bank failures reduce the supply of money. As banks closed, they could no longer make loans; and as loans decreased, so did the amount of deposits into other banks. Bank failures therefore led to a contraction of the money supply. The effects of bank failures are similar to the effects of an open market sale of bonds by the Fed. This decrease in the supply of money will reduce the level of output in the economy. And when banks fail, there is less financial intermediation in the economy. Less financial intermediation makes the economy less efficient, which further reduces investment spending. Some economists believe that bank failures were the reason why the Great Depression was so severe in the United States.

Monetary Policy in an Open Economy

We have been discussing monetary policy without taking into account international trade or international movements of financial funds across countries. Once we bring in these considerations, we will see that monetary policy operates through an additional route.

Suppose the Federal Reserve conducts an open market purchase of bonds, lowering U.S. interest rates. As a result, investors in the United States will be earning lower interest rates and will seek to invest some of their funds abroad. To invest abroad, they will need to sell dollars and buy foreign currency of the country where they intend to invest. This will affect the **exchange rate**: the rate at which one currency trades for another currency. As investors sell their dollars to buy foreign currency, the exchange rate, which is the value of the dollar from the perspective of the U.S. investor, will fall. A fall in the exchange rate or a decrease in the value of a currency is called **depreciation**. Lower U.S. interest rates will cause the dollar to depreciate, which means that it declines in value.

Exchange rate: The rate at which one currency trades for another in the market.

Depreciation: A fall in the exchange rate or a decrease in the value of a currency.

The lower value of the dollar will mean that U.S. goods become cheaper on world markets. Suppose that the exchange rate were 2 German marks to the dollar, meaning you received 2 German marks for every dollar. If a U.S. machine tool sold for $100,000, the machine tool would cost the Germans 200,000 marks. Suppose the value of the dollar fell, so you received only 1 mark for each dollar. The same machine tool would cost the Germans only 100,000 marks. The lower value of the dollar makes U.S. goods cheaper to foreigners. Foreign residents will want to buy more U.S. goods as they become less expensive to foreign residents. So the U.S. exports more to foreign countries.

That's the good news about the lower value of the U.S. dollar. The bad news is that the lower value of the dollar will make it more expensive for U.S. residents to buy foreign

In an open economy, monetary policy will affect the level of imports, such as these cars.

goods. If the exchange rate were 2 German marks to the dollar and a German car cost 60,000 marks, the car would cost a U.S. resident $30,000. If the exchange depreciates to 1 mark per dollar, the same car will cost $60,000. As the U.S. exchange rate falls, imports become more expensive, and U.S. residents tend to import fewer goods.

As we have seen, as the U.S. dollar exchange rate falls, U.S. goods become cheaper and foreign goods become more expensive. The United States will export more goods and import fewer goods. Because exports increase and imports decrease, net exports will increase. The increase in net exports increases the demand for U.S. goods and increases GDP in the short run. We can represent this sequence of events:

| open market purchase | → | increase in money supply | → | fall in interest rates | → | fall in exchange rate | → | increase in net exports | → | increase in GDP |

The three new links in the sequence are from interest rates to exchange rates, from exchange rates to net exports, and from net exports to GDP.

This sequence also works in reverse. If the Fed raises interest rates, investors from around the world will want to invest in the United States. As they buy dollars, the U.S. dollar exchange rate will increase, and the dollar will increase in value. An increase in the value of a currency is called **appreciation**. The appreciation of the dollar will make U.S. goods more expensive to foreigners and make imports cheaper for U.S. residents. Suppose the exchange rate appreciates to 3 marks to the dollar. That machine tool will increase in price to the Germans to 300,000 marks, while the German car will fall in price to U.S. residents to $20,000.

When U.S. interest rates increase, we expect exports to decrease and imports to increase, decreasing net exports. The decrease in net exports will decrease the demand for U.S. goods and lead to a fall in output in the short run.

Appreciation: A rise in the exchange rate or an increase in the value of a currency.

Here is the expanded sequence of events:

open market sale → decrease in money supply → rise in interest rates → rise in exchange rate → decrease in net exports → decrease in GDP

To summarize, an increase in interest rates will reduce both investment spending (including consumer durables) and net exports. A decrease in interest rates will increase investment spending and net exports. Monetary policy is even more powerful in an open economy than in a closed economy.

TEST Your Understanding

6. Complete the statement with "higher" or "lower": When the Federal Reserve sells bonds on the open market, it leads to _____ levels of investment and output in the economy.

7. Complete the statement with "sale" or "purchase": To increase the level of output, the Fed should conduct an open market _____ of bonds.

8. What are all the events in the sequence from an open market purchase to a change in output in a closed economy?

9. Complete the statement with "appreciate" or "depreciate": An increase in the supply of money will _____ a country's currency.

10. Explain how monetary policy works in an economy that is open to trade.

Stabilization Policy and Its Limitations

Now that we have brought money into our expanded short-run demand model, we can see that the government has two different types of tools to change the level of GDP in the short run: The government can use either fiscal policy—changes in the level of taxes or government spending—or monetary policy—changes in the supply of money and interest rates—to alter the level of GDP.

If the current level of GDP is below full employment or potential output, the government can use **expansionary policies** such as tax cuts, increased spending, or increases in the money supply to raise the level of GDP and reduce unemployment.

If the current level of GDP exceeds full employment or potential output, the economy will overheat, and the rate of inflation will increase. To avoid this, the government can use **contractionary policies** to reduce the level of GDP back to full employment or potential output.

Both expansionary policies and contractionary policies are examples of **stabilization policies**, actions to move the economy closer to full employment or potential output.

On paper, this sounds simple. In practice, it is difficult—very difficult—for two big reasons. First, there are lags, or delays, in stabilization policy. Lags arise because decision-makers are often slow to recognize and respond to changes in the economy, and monetary policies and fiscal policies take time to operate. The other reason, alas, is that economists simply do not know enough about the economy to be accurate in all their forecasts.

Expansionary policies: Policies that aim to increase the level of GDP.

Contractionary policies: Policies that aim to decrease the level of GDP.

Stabilization policy: Policy actions taken to bring the economy closer to full employment or potential output.

Lags

Poorly timed policies can magnify economic fluctuations. Suppose that (1) GDP was currently below full employment but would return to full employment on its own within one year and (2) stabilization policies took a full year to become effective. If policymakers tried to expand the economy today, their actions would not take effect until a year from now. One year from now, the economy would normally, by itself, be back at full employment. But one year from now, if stabilization policies were enacted, the economy would be stimulated unnecessarily, and output would exceed full employment.

Figure 28.7 illustrates the problem caused by lags. Panel A shows an example of successful stabilization policy. The solid line represents the behavior of GDP in the absence of policies. Successful stabilization policies can dampen (reduce in magnitude) economic fluctuations, lowering output when it exceeds full employment and raising output when it falls below full employment. This would be easy to accomplish if there were no lags in policy. The dashed curve shows how successful policies can reduce economic fluctuations.

Panel B shows the consequences of ill-timed policies. Again, assume that policies take a year before they are effective. At the start of Year 1, the economy is below potential. If policymakers engaged in expansionary policies at the start of Year 1, the change would not take effect until the end of Year 1. This would raise output even higher above full employment. Ill-timed stabilization policies can magnify economic fluctuations.

Inside lags: Lags in implementing policy.

Outside lags: The time it takes for policies to work.

Where do the lags in policy come from? Economists recognize two broad classes of lags: inside lags and outside lags. **Inside lags** are the lags in implementing policy; **outside lags** refer to the time it takes for policies to actually work. To help you understand them, imagine that you are steering a large ocean liner and you are looking out for possible collisions with hidden icebergs. The time it takes you to spot an iceberg, communicate this information to the crew, and initiate the process of changing course is the inside

Figure 28.7

Possible Pitfalls in Stablization Policy

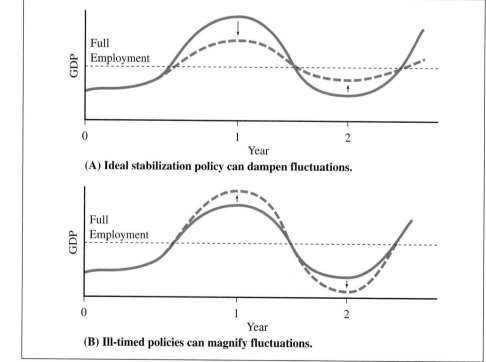

(A) Ideal stabilization policy can dampen fluctuations.

(B) Ill-timed policies can magnify fluctuations.

lag. Because ocean liners are large and have lots of momentum, it will take a long time before your ocean liner begins to turn; this is the outside lag.

Inside Lags

Inside lags occur for two basic reasons. One reason is that it takes time to identify and recognize a problem. For example, the data available to policymakers may be poor and conflicting. Some indicators of the economy may look fine; others may appear worrisome. It often takes from several months to a year before it is clear that there is a serious problem with the economy.

A good example of this problem occurred during the 1990 recession. Today, we date the beginning of the recession from July 1990, a month before Iraq invaded Kuwait. After the invasion, there was some concern that higher oil prices and the uncertainty of the political situation would trigger a recession. However, Alan Greenspan, the chairman of the Federal Reserve, testified before Congress as late as October 1990 that the economy had not yet slipped into a recession. Not until that December did Greenspan declare that the economy had entered into a recession. Yet, looking back, we now know that a recession had started five months earlier.

Another example of an inside lag occurred at the beginning of the Great Depression. Although the stock market crashed in October 1929, we know through newspaper and magazine accounts that business leaders were not particularly worried about the economy for some time. Not until late in 1930 did the public begin to recognize the severity of the depression.

The other reason for inside lags is that once a problem has been diagnosed, it still takes time before any actions can be taken. This problem is most severe for fiscal policy in the United States. Any changes in taxes or spending must be approved by both houses of Congress and by the President. In recent years, the political system has been preoccupied with fights about the size and role of government. In this environment, it is difficult to obtain a consensus for tax or spending changes in a timely manner.

For example, soon after he was elected, President Bill Clinton proposed a stimulus package as part of his overall budget plan. This stimulus package contained a variety of spending programs and was designed to increase the level of GDP and avoid the risks of a recession. However, his plan was attacked as wasteful and unnecessary government spending, and it did not survive. As it turned out, the stimulus package was not necessary, as the economy grew rapidly in the next several years. Nonetheless, this episode illustrates how difficult it is to conduct an active fiscal policy. Monetary policy is not subject to the same long inside lags. Smaller groups such as the Federal Open Market Committee (FOMC) can more easily reach consensus. The FOMC meets eight times a year and can decide on major policy changes at any time. It can even give the chairperson of the Board of Governors some discretion between meetings.

Outside Lags

Both monetary policy and fiscal policy are subject to outside lags, the time it takes for policy to be effective. Consider monetary policy: The Federal Reserve can increase the money supply to rapidly lower interest rates, but firms must change their investment plans before monetary policy can be effective.

To gain some perspective on the outside lags for monetary policy, we can examine the results from several **econometric models**. Econometric models are mathematical versions of the models we have studied that use data to attempt to replicate the behavior of the economy. For example, one part of an econometric model of the economy could consist of a consumption function with numerical values for autonomous consumption and the marginal propensity to consume. Economists use economic theory and statistical methods to build an econometric model.

Econometric models: Mathematical computer-based models that economists build to capture the actual dynamics of the economy.

Figure 28.8

Fall in GDP from 1 Percentage Point Increase in Interest Rates—Results from Four Econometric Models

Source: Glenn Rudebusch, "What Are the Lags in Monetary Policy?" *Federal Reserve Bank of San Francisco Weekly*, February 3, 1995.

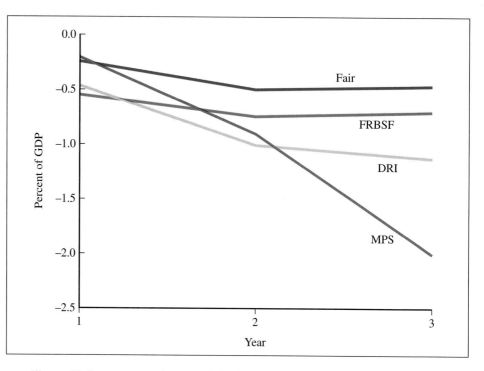

Figure 28.8 presents estimates of the lags in monetary policy from four different econometric models of the economy. These models provide different estimates of the effects of monetary policy. This is understandable, as they were built by different organizations and individuals that relied on different interpretations of macroeconomic theory and used different statistical methods to build their models.

In Figure 28.8, we show for each of these models the effects on real GDP of a 1 percentage point increase in short-term interest rates (from 4% to 5% annual interest) after 1, 2, and 3 years. (The data for Figure 28.8 are given in Table 28.1.) That is, with each model, we calculate what would happen to real GDP if we raised short-term interest rates by 1 percentage point and then display the results graphically. As we can see from the graph, after 1 year, the models predict that GDP would fall between 0.25% and 0.5%. This means that if GDP growth were 3.0% per year before interest rates were increased, the models predict that GDP would grow at a rate between 2.5% and 2.75% per year. At least for the first year, the predictions of the four models are similar.

However, the models differ sharply in their predictions for later years. The MPS model (used at the Board of Governors at the Fed) has GDP falling by 2% after three years, while the Fair model (developed by Yale economist Ray Fair) shows only a 0.5% fall in output after three years. The predictions from the other two models, DRI (Data Resources) and

Table 28.1   Fall in GDP from a 1 Percentage Point Increase in Interest Rates (percent)

Year	Model			
	DRI	Fair	FRBSF	MPS
1	0.47	0.24	0.55	0.20
2	1.00	0.49	0.74	0.90
3	1.13	0.46	0.70	2.00

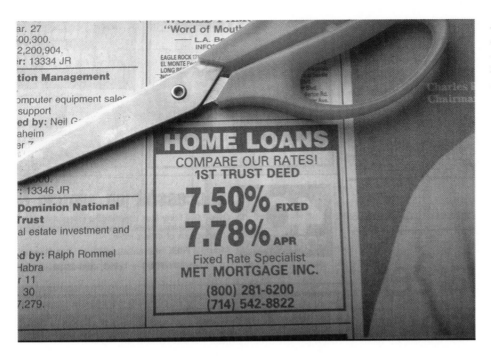

FRBSF (Federal Reserve Bank of San Francisco), fall in between. As Figure 28.8 suggests, the outside lag for monetary policy can be long and is also uncertain.

Fiscal policy is also subject to outside lags. If taxes are cut, individuals and businesses must change their spending plans to take advantage of the cuts; it will take some time before any effects of the tax cuts will be felt in the economy. It will also take some time before increases in spending will raise GDP. Although fiscal policy has a much longer inside lag than monetary policy, its outside lag is shorter. For example, the MPS model predicts that an increase in government spending will increase GDP by its maximum effect after just six months.

Forecasting Uncertainties

What makes the problem of lags even worse is that economists are not very accurate in forecasting what will happen in the economy. For example, a classic problem that policymakers face when the economy appears to be slowing down is knowing whether the slowdown is temporary or will persist. Unfortunately, stabilization policy cannot be effective without accurate forecasting. If economic forecasters predict an overheated economy and the Federal Reserve adopts a contractionary policy, the result could be disastrous if the economy weakened before the policy took effect. Today, most economic policymakers understand these limitations and are cautious in using activist policies.

Looking Ahead

The demand-side models that we developed in this chapter can be used to understand the behavior of the economy *only in the short run*, when prices do not change. Monetary policy can affect output in the short run when prices are largely fixed, but in the long run, changes in the money supply only affect inflation. The Federal Reserve cannot control real interest rates in the long run. In the next part of the book, we explain how prices change over time and how the economy makes the transition by itself from the short run to the long run.

Using the **TOOLS**

In this chapter, we developed the money demand curve, which enabled us to understand how interest rates are determined. We integrated money demand, money supply, and investment spending into a complete demand-side model of the economy. Here is an opportunity to use the tools developed in this chapter.

1. Interest Rates on Checking Accounts

During the 1980s, banks started to pay interest (at low rates) on checking accounts for the first time. Given what you know about opportunity costs, how would interest paid on checking accounts affect the demand for money?

2. Pegging Interest Rates

Suppose the Federal Reserve wanted to fix, or "peg," the level of interest rates at 6% per year. Using a simple supply and demand diagram, show how increases in money demand would change the supply of money if the Federal Reserve pursued the policy of this fixed interest rate. Use your answer to explain this statement: "If the Federal Reserve pegs interest rates, it loses control of the money supply."

3. Nominal Interest Rates and the Demand for Money

We know that investment spending depends on real interest rates. Yet the demand for money will depend on nominal interest rates, not on real interest rates. Can you explain why money demand should depend on nominal rates?

4. The Presidential Praise and Blame Game

Presidents like to take credit for good economic performance. If there are lags in policies, explain why presidents may not deserve all the credit (or blame) for economic policies.

Summary

This chapter brought money and monetary policy into a demand-side model of the economy for the short run. The Fed can control the level of interest rates by open market purchases or sales of bonds. Changes in interest rates will in turn affect investment and output. In an open economy, exchange rates and net exports are also affected by interest rates. We also discussed that there are limits to how successful the results of stabilization policy can be. Here are the main points of the chapter:

1. The demand for money depends negatively on the interest rate and positively on the level of prices and real GDP.

2. The level of interest rates is determined in the money market by the demand for money and the supply of money.

3. To increase the level of GDP, the Federal Reserve buys bonds on the open market. To decrease the

level of GDP, the Federal Reserve sells bonds on the open market.

4. An increase in the money supply will decrease interest rates, increase investment spending, and increase output. A decrease in the money supply will increase interest rates, decrease investment spending, and decrease output.

5. In an open economy, a decrease in interest rates will depreciate the exchange rate and lead to an increase in net exports. An increase in interest rates will appreciate the exchange rate and lead to a decrease in net exports.

6. Both lags in economic policies and economists' uncertainties about the economy make successful stabilization policy extremely difficult in practice.

Key Terms

appreciation, 594
contractionary policies, 595
depreciation, 593
econometric models, 597
exchange rate, 593

expansionary policies, 595
inside lags, 596
liquidity demand for money, 587
monetary policy, 593
outside lags, 596

speculative demand for money, 587
stabilization policy, 595
transactions demand for money, 585

Problems and Discussion Questions

1. Give another example from your own experience of the liquidity demand for money.

2. If a bond promised to pay $110 next year and the interest rate was 5% per year, what would be the price of the bond?

3. If you strongly believed that the Federal Reserve were going to surprise the markets and raise interest rates, would you want to buy bonds or sell bonds?

4. Explain why interest rates are sometimes called the price of holding money.

5. If investment spending became less sensitive to interest rates, how would this reduced sensitivity affect the strength of monetary policy?

6. Refrigerators and clothing are to some extent, durable. Explain why the decision to purchase a refrigerator is likely to be more sensitive to interest rates than the decision to buy clothing.

7. In an open economy, changes in monetary policy affect both interest rates and exchange rates. Comparing the United States and the Netherlands, in which country would monetary policy have a more significant effect on GDP through changes in exchange rates?

8. Explain why interest rates usually fall in a recession.

9. It has been suggested that the President of the United States be given the authority to temporarily increase or decrease taxes. How would this affect

the inside lag for fiscal policy? Do you think it is a wise policy?

10. Some members of the Board of Governors have looked at changes in prices of commodities such as gold or copper for early warning signs of inflation. What policies would they recommend if they saw the price of gold beginning to rise? Can you think of any reasons not related to the general inflation rate why the price of gold might start to increase?

11. Web Exercise. The Federal Reserve uses both econometric models as well as other more general information about the economy to make decisions about monetary policy. To see what some of this general information looks like, go to the Web site for the Federal Reserve Open Market Committee (*http://www.federalreserve.gov/fomc*) and read the report of the Beige Book (a briefing book named for the color of its cover). What type of information is provided in the Beige Book?

12. Web Exercise. As international trade becomes more important, monetary policy becomes more heavily influenced by developments in the foreign exchange markets. Go to the Web page of the Federal Reserve (*http://www.federalreserve.gov*) and read some recent speeches given by Fed officials. Do international considerations seem to affect policy-makers in the United States today?

Take It to the Net

We invite you to visit the O'Sullivan/Sheffrin page on the Prentice Hall Web site at:
http://www.prenhall.com/osullivan/
for additional World Wide Web exercises for this chapter.

Model Answers to Questions

Chapter-Opening Questions

1. When the Federal Reserve sells bonds on the open market, the money supply decreases. Given the demand for money, this raises interest rates.

2. The price of bonds is inversely related to interest rates. Because bonds are promises to pay money in the future, these promises are worth less today when interest rates rise.

3. If the Fed increases the supply of money, interest rates will fall. Lower interest rates will lead to more production of housing and increased construction.

4. It takes time for lowered interest rates to stimulate the economy. If the Federal Reserve believed that a slump was only temporary, it would be reluctant to reduce interest rates for fear of creating too much demand at the time when the economy recovered.

Test Your Understanding

1. We use the interest rates to measure the opportunity cost of holding money because the alternative to holding money is holding assets that pay interest.

2. Decrease.

3. Increase.

4. Interest rates will increase.

5. The price will be $109/1.03 = $105.83.

6. Lower.

7. Purchase.

8. An increase in the money supply will lower interest rates, raise investment, and raise output.

9. Depreciate.

10. An increase in the money supply will lower interest rates, depreciate the exchange rate, raise net exports, and raise output.

Using the Tools

1. Interest Rates on Checking Accounts. When interest is paid on checking accounts, it lowers the opportunity costs of holding wealth in these accounts, since you earn interest on the checking account. With a lower opportunity cost, the demand for money will increase.

2. Pegging Interest Rates. Start with a graph showing the demand for money and the supply of money, where the equilibrium interest rate is 6% per year. An increase in the demand for money will shift the demand curve to the right and raise interest rates above 6%. To prevent this from occurring, the Federal Reserve must increase the supply of money. Similarly, a decrease in the demand for money will lower interest rates below 6% unless the Federal Reserve decreases the demand for money. In either case the Federal Reserve will lose control of the supply of money. If there are shifts in the demand for money, the Federal Reserve cannot control interest rates and control the supply of money, both at the same time.

3. Nominal Interest Rates and the Demand for Money. The nominal interest rate measures the opportunity cost of holding money. If you hold money you earn no interest. If you invest in a bond you earn the nominal rate of interest.

4. The Presidential Praise and Blame Game. Lags make it difficult to tell whether a president is truly responsible for economic developments. If there is a two-year lag in the effects of policies, the performance of the economy for a new president during the first half of his or her term is largely determined by his or her predecessor.

CHAPTER

29

From the Short Run to the Long Run

In the long run, we are all dead.

John Maynard Keynes, *A Tract on Monetary Reform*

I don't try to forecast short-term changes in the economy. The record of economists in doing that justifies only humility.

Milton Friedman

One of the great debates in macroeconomics centers on short-run versus long-run considerations for macroeconomic policy. Up to here, we have discussed separately the economics of the long run—classical economics—and the economics of the short run—Keynesian economics. Now we'll explain how the economy evolves from the short run to the long run. The relationship between the short run and the long run is one of the most important concepts in modern macroeconomics.

These are some of the questions we answer in this chapter:

1. **When do wages in all sectors of the economy rise or fall together?**
2. **Why does expanding the money supply raise output in the short run but only lead to higher prices in the long run?**
3. **Why does the Federal Reserve "remove the punch bowl from the party" and what does this mean?**
4. **Why might tax cuts have beneficial effects for the economy now but have harmful effects in the future?**

Definitions

To begin to understand how the short run and the long run are related, let's return to what we mean by the long run and short run in macroeconomics.

Long Run

In the long run, when prices are flexible, the level of GDP is determined by the demand and supply for labor, the stock of capital, and technological progress. In the long run, the economy operates at full employment. With the supply of output fixed at what can be produced at full employment, any increases in government spending must come at the sacrifice of some other use of the output. We also saw in Chapter 24 that increases in the supply of money (or any other increase in aggregate demand) increase only the level of prices and not the level of output in the long run.

Short Run

In the short run, when prices are primarily fixed, the level of GDP is determined by the total level of demand for goods and services. Increases in the supply of money lower interest rates, stimulate investment, and increase GDP. Increases in government spending or cuts in taxes will also lead to increases in GDP.

Should economic policy be guided by what is expected to happen in the short run or what is expected to happen in the long run? To answer this question, we need to know two things:

1. How does what happens in the short run determine what happens in the long run?
2. How long is the short run?

In Chapter 24, we explained how in the short run, wages and prices are sticky and do not change immediately in response to changes in demand. Over time, wages and prices adjust, and the economy reaches its long-run equilibrium. Short-run, Keynesian economics applies to the period when wages and prices do not change—at least not substantially. Long-run, full-employment economics applies after wages and prices have largely adjusted to changes in demand.

Wage and Price Adjustments

Wages and prices change every day. If the demand for roller blades rises at the same time as there's a fall in the demand for tennis rackets, we would expect to see a rise in the price of roller blades and a fall in the price of tennis rackets. Wages in the roller blade industry would tend to increase; wages in the tennis racket industry would tend to fall.

Sometimes, we see wages and prices in all industries rising or falling together. For example, prices for steel, automobiles, food, and fuel may all rise together. Why? Wages and prices will all tend to increase together during booms when GDP exceeds its full-employment level or potential output. Wages and prices will fall together during periods of recessions when GDP falls below full employment or potential output.

If the economy is producing at a level above full employment, firms will find it increasingly difficult to hire and retain workers. Unemployment will be below its natural rate. Workers will find it easy to obtain a job and easy to change jobs. To attract workers to their firms and to prevent their own workers from quitting, firms will have to raise wages to try to outbid firms looking to hire workers. As one firm raises its wage, other firms will have to raise their wages even higher to attract workers.

For most firms, wages are the largest cost of production. As their labor costs increase, they have no choice but to increase the prices of their products. As prices rise, workers know that they need higher dollar or nominal wages to maintain their real wage. This is an illustration of the reality principle:

REALITY **PRINCIPLE**

What matters to people is the real value of money or income—its purchasing power—not the face value of money or income.

This process by which rising wages cause higher prices and higher prices feed higher wages is known as a **wage-price spiral**. It occurs when the economy is producing at a level of output that exceeds the potential output of the economy.

When the economy is producing below full employment or potential output, the process works in reverse. Unemployment will exceed the natural rate, and there will be excess unemployment. Firms will find that it is easy to hire and retain workers and that they can offer less than other firms to hire skilled workers. As all firms cut wages, the average level of wages in the economy falls. Because wages are the largest component of costs, prices start to fall as well. In this case, the wage-price spiral works in reverse.

Table 29.1 summarizes our discussion of unemployment, output, and changes in wages. The changes in wages and prices that occur when the economy is not producing at full employment are typically changes away from a trend in inflation. Suppose the economy had been experiencing 6% annual inflation. If output exceeds full employment, prices will rise at a faster rate than 6% per year. If output is less than full employment, prices will rise at a slower annual rate than 6%. For the rest of this chapter, we ignore ongoing inflation. We return to the topic of ongoing inflation in the next chapter.

In summary, when output exceeds potential output, wages and prices throughout the economy will rise above previous inflation rates. If output is less than potential output, wages and prices will fall relative to previous inflation rates.

Wage-price spiral: Changes in wages and prices causing more changes in wages and prices.

Table 29.1 Unemployment, Output, and Wage and Price Changes

When unemployment is below the natural rate...	When unemployment is above the natural rate...
Output is above potential	Ouptut is below potential
Wages and prices rise	Wages and prices fall

Aggregate Demand, Aggregate Supply, and Adjustment

The transition between the short run and the long run is easy to understand. If GDP is higher than potential output, the economy starts to overheat, and wages and prices increase. This increase in wages and prices will push the economy back to full employment.

Using aggregate demand and aggregate supply, we can illustrate graphically how the economy moves from a short-run equilibrium to the long run. First, let's review the graphical representations of aggregate demand and aggregate supply.

Aggregate demand curve: The relationship between the price level and the quantity of real GDP demanded.

Classical aggregate supply curve: The vertical aggregate supply curve at full employment.

Keynesian aggregate supply curve: The horizontal aggregate supply at the current level of prices.

1. **Aggregate demand.** The **aggregate demand curve** represents real output—the total demand for all goods and services—on the horizontal axis for any level of prices on the vertical axis.

2. **Aggregate supply.** There are two aggregate supply curves. The **classical aggregate supply curve**—showing the long-run aggregate supply—is represented as a vertical line at the full-employment level of output. The **Keynesian aggregate supply curve**—showing the short-run aggregate supply—is represented as a flat curve; it is flat because, as economists typically find, changes in demand lead to only small changes in prices over short periods.

Figure 29.1 shows an aggregate demand curve and the two aggregate supply curves. In the short run, output and prices are determined where the aggregate demand curve intersects the Keynesian aggregate supply curve—the short-run aggregate supply curve—at point A. This corresponds to a level of real output y_0 and a price level P_0.

In the long run, the level of prices and output is given by the intersection of the aggregate demand curve and the classical aggregate supply curve—the long-run aggregate supply curve—at point D in the diagram. Output is at full employment y_F, while prices are at P_F. How does the economy move from point A in the short run to point D in the long run?

At point A, the current level of output y_0 exceeds the full employment level of output y_F. With output exceeding full employment, the unemployment rate is below the natural rate. Firms find it difficult to hire and retain workers, and the wage-price spiral

Figure 29.1

Aggregate Demand and Aggregate Supply

The aggregate demand curve *AD* intersects the Keynesian aggregate supply curve at point *A* and the classical aggregate supply curve at point *D*.

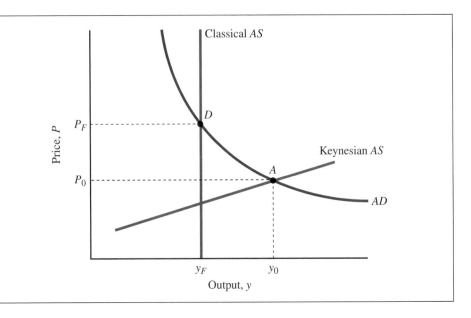

begins. As the level of prices increases, the Keynesian aggregate supply curve shifts upward over time. The Keynesian aggregate supply curve shifts upward because increases in wages raise costs for firms. Firms paying higher costs must charge higher prices for their products or they would lose money, become unprofitable, and go out of business.

This shift in the Keynesian aggregate supply curve will bring the economy to long-run equilibrium, as shown in Figure 29.2. The economy initially starts at point A, where output exceeds full employment. As prices rise, the aggregate supply curve shifts upward from AS_0 to AS_1. The aggregate demand curve and the new aggregate supply curve intersect at point B. This corresponds to a higher level of prices and a lower level of real output. But that lower level of output still exceeds full employment. Wages and prices will continue to rise, shifting the Keynesian aggregate supply curve upwards. At point C, the aggregate supply curve AS_2 intersects the aggregate demand curve at a higher level of price and lower level of output than where AS_1 intersected the aggregate demand curve. As the aggregate supply curve continues to shift upward, it will intersect the aggregate demand curve at higher levels of prices and lower levels of output.

Eventually, the aggregate supply curve will shift to AS_3, and the economy will reach point D, the intersection of the aggregate demand curve and the classical aggregate supply curve—the long-run aggregate supply curve. At this point, the adjustment stops; the economy is at full employment, and the unemployment rate is at the natural rate. With unemployment at the natural rate, the wage-price spiral ends. The economy has made the transition to the long run. Note that the result is predicted by the classical model: Prices are higher, and output returns to full employment.

If the current level of output is below full employment, wages and prices will fall to return the economy to its long-run equilibrium at full employment, shown graphically in Figure 29.3. The economy starts at point A, a level of output below full employment. With unemployment above the natural rate and excess unemployment, the level of wages and prices will fall. As the aggregate supply curve shifts from AS_0 to AS_1, the economy moves from point A to point B, closer to full employment. The process ends when the aggregate supply curve shifts to AS_2 and the economy returns to full employment at point D. This is how an economy recovers from a recession or a downturn.

ACTIVE GRAPH

Figure 29.2
Shifts in the Keynesian Aggregate Supply
As prices rise in the economy, the Keynesian aggregate supply curve shifts upwards. The economy moves from point A to point B. The process continues until the economy reaches the long-run equilibrium point at D.

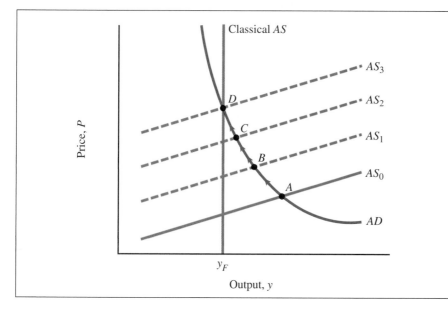

Figure 29.3

Returning to Full Employment

If the initial level of output is less than full employment, wages and prices will fall. As the aggregate supply curve shifts downwards, the economy returns to full employment at point *D*.

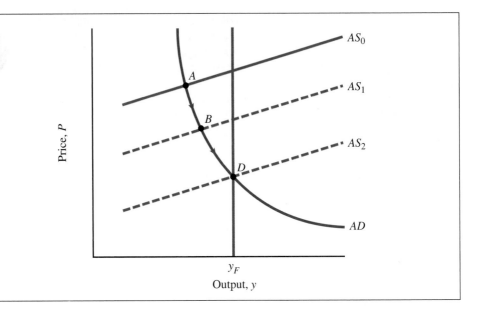

In summary, the economy will eventually return to full employment:

- If output exceeds full employment, prices will rise and output will fall back to full employment.

- If output is less than full employment, prices will fall as the economy returns to full employment.

TEST Your Understanding

1. Wages and prices will increase when unemployment exceeds the natural rate. True or false? Explain.

2. In what direction does the Keynesian aggregate supply curve move if the economy's actual output is below full-employment output?

The Speed of Adjustment and Economic Policy

How long does it take to move from the short run to the long run? Economists disagree on the answer. Some estimate that it takes the U.S. economy two years, some say six years, and others say somewhere in between. Because the adjustment process is slow, there is room, in principle, for policymakers to step in and guide the economy back to full employment.

Suppose the economy were operating below full employment at point *A* in Figure 29.4. One alternative for policymakers would be to do nothing, allowing the economy to adjust itself, with falling wages and prices, until it returns by itself to full employment, point *D*. This may take several years. During that time, the economy will experience excess unemployment and a level of real output below potential.

Another alternative would be to use expansionary policies (open market purchases, increases in government spending, or tax cuts) to shift the aggregate demand curve to

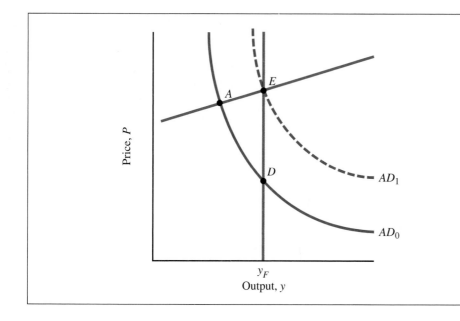

Figure 29.4

Using Economic Policy to Fight a Recession
Rather than letting the economy naturally return to full employment at point D, we can increase aggregate demand from AD_0 to AD_1 to bring the economy to full employment at point E.

the right. In Figure 29.4, we show how expansionary policies could shift the aggregate demand curve from AD_0 to AD_1 and move the economy to full employment, point E. Notice here that the price level is higher at point E than it would be at point D.

Demand policies can also be used to prevent a wage-price spiral from emerging if the economy is producing at a level of output above full employment. Rather than letting an increase in wages and prices bring the economy back to full employment, we can reduce aggregate demand. Either contractionary monetary policy (open market sales) or contractionary fiscal policy (cuts in government spending or tax increases) can be used to reduce aggregate demand and the level of GDP until it reaches potential output.

Expansionary policies and demand policies are stabilization policies, which look simple on paper or on graphs. In practice, the lags and uncertainties that we discussed in Chapter 28 make the task difficult. For example, suppose we are in a recession and decide to increase aggregate demand through expansionary monetary policy. With the lags in monetary policy, it takes time for the aggregate demand curve to shift to the right. In the meantime, the adjustment that occurs during a recession (falling wages and prices) has begun to shift the Keynesian aggregate supply curve downward. It is conceivable that if the adjustment were fast enough, the economy would be restored to full employment before the effects of the expansionary monetary policy were actually felt. When the expansionary monetary policy actually kicks in and the aggregate demand curve finally shifts to the right, the additional aggregate demand would increase the level of output so that it exceeded the full employment level, leading to a wage-price spiral. In this case, our economic policy would have destabilized the economy.

Active economic policies are more likely to destabilize the economy if the adjustment is quick enough. Economists who believe that the economy adjusts rapidly to full employment generally oppose using monetary or fiscal policy to try to stabilize the economy. Economists who believe that the economy adjusts slowly are more sympathetic to using monetary or fiscal policy to stabilize the economy.

It is possible that the speed of adjustment can vary over time, making decisions about policy even more difficult. As an example, economic advisers for President George Bush had to decide whether the economy needed any additional stimulus after the recession of 1990. Based on the view that the economy would recover on its own, only some minor steps were taken. The economy recovered completely at the very end of the Bush administration but too late for his reelection prospects.

Up to this point, we have assumed that the economy could always recover from a recession without active policy, although it might take a long time. Keynes expressed doubts about whether a country could recover from a major recession without active policy. He feared that falling prices could hurt business. Japan's recession in the 1990s illustrates some of the difficulties raised by Keynes, as "A Closer Look: Japan's Bumpy Road to Recovery," explains.

A Closer Look at the Adjustment Process

We have explained that changes in wages and prices restore the economy to full employment in the long run. But exactly how does this happen? We can explain using the short-run model from Chapter 28.

In Figure 29.5, we show the three graphs that make up the model: the money market, the investment schedule, and the 45° line demand diagram. From these diagrams, we know the following:

- The demand and supply for money determine interest rates.

- Interest rates determine the level of investment spending in the economy.

- Investment spending—along with consumption, government spending, and net exports—determines the level of GDP.

A CLOSER LOOK | Japan's Bumpy Road to Recovery

Japan's rapid post–World War II economic growth came to a halt around 1992, and by 1993–1994, the country was suffering from a recession. Inflation started to fall as the economy entered the recession. By 1995, inflation had nearly disappeared from the economy, and wholesale prices had fallen for several years.

Yet the reduction in inflation caused problems for the economy. Real estate prices fell nearly 50% starting in 1990. Large banks that were major investors in real estate lost vast sums of money, and became reluctant to make loans for other investments. Inflation rates were lower than business and household borrowers had anticipated. This raised the burden of debt for both businesses and households and made them more reluctant to purchase goods and services. With fewer loans from banks for new investment and reluctant households and firms, aggregate demand for goods and services was weak.

For a number of years, the United States urged Japan to increase its public spending as one way to begin to stimulate the economy. The Japanese gov-

ernment resisted for a long time because it did not want to expand the public sector and was worried about government budget deficits. Instead, Japan preferred to let the adjustment process run its course. However, the road to recovery was too bumpy, and Japan finally did engage in expansionary fiscal policy in 1998.

While the lights may have been bright in Tokyo, Japan experienced difficult times in the 1990s.

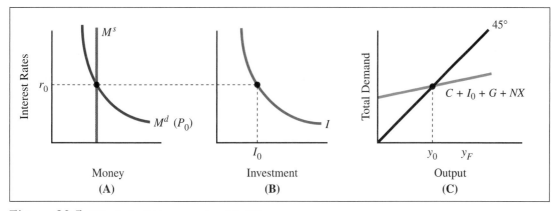

Figure 29.5 Model of Demand with Money
At the current price level P_0, the economy is producing at a level of output y_0 that is below full employment y_F.

The part of this diagram that we want to focus on here is money demand. Recall the reality principle:

REALITY **PRINCIPLE**

> **What matters to people is the real value of money or income—its purchasing power—not the face value of money or income.**

According to this principle, the amount of money that people want to hold depends on the price level. If prices are cut in half, you need to hold only half as much money to purchase the same goods and services. Decreases in the price level will cause the money demand curve to shift to the left.

In Figure 29.5, the price level is P_0. At that price level, interest rates are at r_0, investment spending is at I_0, and the economy is producing at y_0. At y_0, output is below full employment. With output below full employment, actual unemployment will exceed the natural rate of unemployment, so there will be excess unemployment. Wages and prices will start to fall.

The fall in the price level will decrease the demand for holding money. In Figure 29.6, as the price level decreases from P_0 to P_1, the demand for money shifts to the left.

Figure 29.6 Returning to Full Employment
When output is below full employment, the price level falls. This reduces the demand for money and lowers interest rates. Lower interest rates increase investment and stimulate spending. The economy returns to full employment.

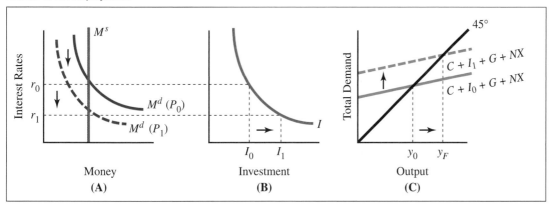

Interest rates fall from r_0 to r_1, and the falling interest rates increase investment spending from I_0 to I_1. As the level of investment spending in the economy increases, the total demand line shifts upward, raising the level of output in the economy.

What we have just described continues until the economy reaches full employment. As long as actual output is below the economy's full employment level, prices will continue to fall. A fall in the price level reduces money demand and interest rates. Lower interest rates stimulate investment spending and push the economy back toward full employment.

All of this works in reverse if current actual output exceeds the economy's potential output. In this case, the economy is overheating and wages and prices rise. A higher price level will increase the demand for money and raise interest rates. Higher interest rates will decrease investment spending and reduce the level of output. All this continues until the economy returns to full employment.

Can you now see why changes in wages and prices restore the economy to full employment? The key to seeing why is that (1) changes in wages and prices will change the demand for money and interest rates and (2) changes in interest rates affect investment and the level of GDP in the economy.

We can also use the graphical model that we just developed to see another potential problem with the natural adjustment process. If an economy is in a recession, interest rates will fall, restoring the economy to full employment. But it's not impossible that at some point, interest rates may become so low that they become zero. Nominal interest rates cannot go far below zero, because investors would rather hold money (which pays a zero rate) than hold a bond that promises a negative return. Suppose, however, that as interest rates approach zero, the economy is still in a slump. The adjustment process then has nowhere to go.

This appears to be what happened in Japan in the 1990s. Interest rates on government bonds were zero. Prices continued to fall. But the fall in prices, by itself, could not restore the economy to full employment. Policymakers have limited options in this case. Normal monetary policy will not work because nominal interest rates cannot fall any further. In principle, fiscal policy can still be effective in restoring the economy to full employment.

Long-Run Neutrality of Money

An increase in the money supply has a different effect on the economy in the short run than it does in the long run. In Figure 29.7, we show the effects of expansionary monetary policy in both the short run and the long run. In the short run, as the supply of money increases, the economy moves from the original equilibrium at point E to point A, with output above potential. But in the long run, the economy returns to point B at full employment but at a higher price level than at E. How is it that the Federal Reserve can change the level of output in the short run but affect prices only in the long run? Why is the short run different from the long run? We can use the model of demand with money to understand this issue.

Figure 29.8 can help us to understand some answers to these questions. The economy starts at full employment y_F. Interest rates are at r_F, and investment spending is at I_F. Suppose the Federal Reserve increases the money supply from M^s_0 to M^s_1. In the short run, the increase in the supply of money will reduce interest rates to r_0. The level of investment spending will increase to I_0. The increased demand for output will raise output above full employment to y_0. All this occurs in the short run. The single-headed arrows in Figure 29.8 show these movements.

However, now output exceeds full employment, and wages and prices will start to increase. As the price level increases, the demand for money will increase. This will start

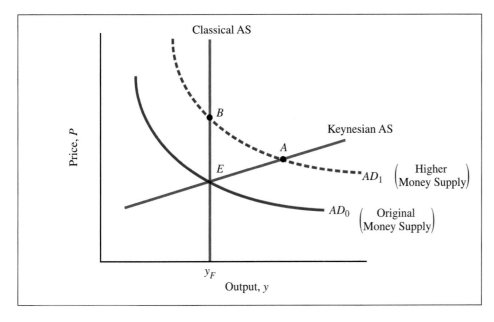

Figure 29.7

Monetary Policy in the Short run and the Long Run
As the Fed increases the supply of money, the aggregate demand curve shifts from AD_0 to AD_1. The economy moves to point A. In the long run, the economy moves to point B.

to increase interest rates. Investment will start to fall as interest rates increase, leading to a fall in output. The double-headed arrows in Figure 29.8 show the transition as prices increase. As long as output exceeds full employment, prices will continue to rise, money demand will continue to increase, and interest rates will continue to rise. Where does this process end? It ends only when interest rates return to their original level of r_F. At that level of interest rates, investment spending will have returned to I_F. This is the level of investment that provides the total level of demand for goods and services that keeps the economy at full employment.

Notice that when the economy returns to full employment, the levels of real interest rates, investment, and output are precisely the same as they were before the Fed increased the supply of money. The increase in the supply of money had no effect on real interest rates, investment, and output. Economists call this the **long-run neutrality of money**. In other words, in the long run, changes in the supply of money are neutral with respect

Long-run neutrality of money: An increase in the supply of money has no effect on real interest rates, investment, or output in the long run.

Figure 29.8 Neutrality of Money
Starting at full employment, an increase in the supply of money will initially reduce interest rates from r_F to r_0, raise investment spending from I_F to I_0, and increase output above full employment from y_F to y_0 (single-headed arrows). As wages and prices increase, the demand for money increases, restoring interest rates, investment, and output to full employment (double-headed arrows).

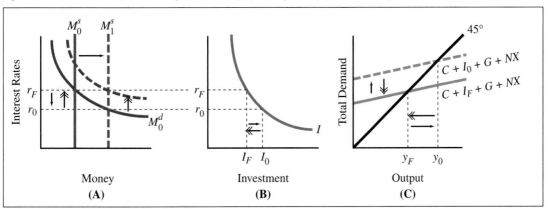

to real variables in the economy. In the long run, increases in the supply of money have no effect on real variables, only on prices.

To better understand the idea of the long-run neutrality of money, consider this thought experiment: Suppose one morning the government announced that we would replace all our normal green currency with blue currency. Every green dollar bill would be replaced by 2 blue dollars. What would happen to prices that are now quoted in blue currency? You should easily be able to see that if all wages and prices in blue dollars doubled, everything would essentially be the same as before. Although everyone has twice as many blue dollars as they formerly had of green dollars, blue dollar prices are twice as high as green dollar prices were, so the purchasing power of blue money is the same as it was for green money. Moreover, because wages and prices have doubled, real wage rates will be the same as before. This currency conversion will have no effect on the real economy and will be neutral.

This example points out how, in the long run, it really does not matter how much money is in circulation because prices will adjust to the amount of nominal money available. Whether additional money comes from an open market purchase or a currency conversion, such as from green to blue money, it will be neutral in the long run.

Money is not neutral in the short run, however. In the short run, changes in the supply of money do affect interest rates, investment spending, and output. The Fed does have strong powers over real GDP, but those powers are ultimately temporary. In the long run, all the Fed can do is to determine the level of prices in the economy.

Now we can understand why the job of the Federal Reserve had been described by William McChesney Martin, Jr., a former Federal Reserve chairman, as "taking the punch bowl away at the party." The punch bowl at the party is monetary policy: It can increase output or give the economy a brief high. But if the Federal Reserve is worried about increases in prices in the long run, it must take the punch bowl away. If the Federal Reserve continues to increase the supply of money in the economy, the result will be continuing increases in prices, or inflation.

TEST Your Understanding

3. What happens to the demand for money and interest rates as the price level increases in the economy?

4. If output is below full employment, we expect wages and prices to fall, money demand to decrease, and interest rates to fall. True or false? Explain.

5. An increase in the money supply will have no effect on the interest rate in the long run. True or false? Explain.

Crowding Out in the Long Run

Keynesian economists often advocate increased government spending to stimulate the economy. Critics of Keynesian economics say increases in spending provide only temporary relief and ultimately harm the economy because government spending will "crowd out" investment spending. In Chapter 22 on classical economics, we discussed the idea of **crowding out**. We can use the model now to understand it in more detail.

Crowding out: The reduction of investment (or other component of GDP) in the long run caused by an increase in government spending.

In Figure 29.9, the economy starts at full employment, and government spending is increased from G_0 to G_1, say, to stimulate the economy. In panel C, we see that the total demand line ($C + I + G_0 + NX$) shifts upward (the single-headed arrow), and output increases in the short run, just as the Keynesian demand models claim. However, now the economy is operating above full employment, and wages and prices begin to

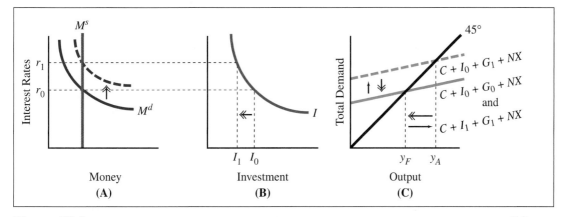

Figure 29.9 **Crowding Out in the Long Run**

Starting at full employment, an increase in government spending from G_0 to G_1 shifts up the total demand line and raises output above full employment (single-headed arrows). As wages and prices increase, the demand for money increases, raising interest rates from r_0 to r_1 and reducing investment from I_0 to I_1. The economy returns to full employment but with a higher level of interest rates and a lower level of investment spending (double-headed arrows).

ACTIVE GRAPH

increase. The increase in the price level raises both the demand for money and the level of interest rates. Higher interest rates reduce the level of investment. As investment spending falls, the level of output returns to the economy's full employment output level. The double-headed arrows in Figure 29.9 show the final adjustment of the economy following the increase in government spending. Interest rates increase to r_1, and investment spending falls to I_1 in the long run.

The increase in government spending had no long-run effect on the level of output. Instead, the increase in government spending displaced, or crowded out, investment spending. The increase in government spending led to a higher level of interest rates, which reduced the incentives for investment in the economy. As we have discussed, the economy adjusts in the long run to the equilibrium predicted by the classical model. In this case, higher government spending crowds out investment spending. This reduction in investment will have further effects on the economy. As we saw in earlier chapters, a reduction in investment spending will reduce capital deepening and lead to lower levels of real income and wages in the future.

A similar argument applies to tax cuts. Tax cuts initially will increase consumer spending and lead to a higher level of GDP. In the long run, however, adjustments in wages and prices restore the economy to full employment. Interest rates will rise during the adjustment process. The increase in interest rates will crowd out investment. In the long run, the increase in consumption spending will come at the expense of lower investment spending, less capital deepening, and lower levels of real income and wages in the future. That is why tax cuts have different effects on income in the long run than they do in the short run.

The idea of crowding out should not be difficult to understand. Because the economy ultimately returns to full employment in the long run, a higher level of government spending must come at the expense of some other component of spending. In Figure 29.9, we showed how investment spending would be crowded out. In other situations, it is possible for consumption or net exports to be crowded out along with investment spending. Keynesian demand policy will increase GDP but only in the short run.

Decreases in government spending (such as a cut in military spending) will lead to increases in investment in the long run, which we call **crowding in**. Initially, a decrease in government spending will cause a decrease in real GDP. But as prices fall, the demand

Crowding in: The increase of investment (or other component of GDP) in the long run caused by a decrease in government spending.

for money will decrease, and interest rates will fall. Lower interest rates will crowd in investment as the economy returns to full employment. In the longer run, the higher investment spending will raise living standards through capital deepening.

Crowding out and crowding in provide examples of this chapter's theme: The short-run effects of policy will generally differ from the long-run effects. Just as an increase in the money supply will increase output only in the short run, changes in government spending have different effects in the short run than they do in the long run.

Political Business Cycles

Political business cycle: The effects on the economy of using monetary or fiscal policy to stimulate the economy before an election to improve reelection prospects.

Using monetary policy and fiscal policy in the short run to improve a politician's reelection prospects may generate what is known as a **political business cycle**.

Here is how a political business cycle might work. About a year or so before an election, a politician might use expansionary monetary policy or fiscal policy to stimulate the economy and lower unemployment. If voters respond favorably to lower unemployment, the incumbent politician may be reelected. After reelection, the politician faces the prospect of higher prices or crowding out. To avoid this, the politician may engage in contractionary policies. The result is a classic political business cycle: Because of actions taken by politicians for reelection, the economy booms before an election but then contracts after the election. Good news comes before the election, and bad news comes later.

The evidence is not clear that the classic political business cycle always occurs. There are episodes that fit what we just described, such as President Nixon's reelection campaign in 1972. However, there are also counterexamples, such as President Carter's deliberate attempt to reduce inflation at the end of his term. According to the theory, Carter would not have adopted policies with adverse consequences just before the election. Although the evidence on the classic political business cycle is mixed, there may be links between elections and economic outcomes. More recent research has investigated the systematic differences that may exist between political parties and economic outcomes. All this research takes into account both the short- and long-run effects of economic policies.

 Using the **TOOLS**

In this chapter, we developed a model showing the transition from the short run to the long run. Take this opportunity to deepen your understanding of the ideas and tools in this chapter.

1. Economic Policies and Supply Shocks

a. In Chapter 24, we discussed supply shocks: sudden increases in the prices of commodities such as oil or food. These shocks shift the Keynesian aggregate supply curve. For example, an increase in oil prices will shift the Keynesian aggregate supply curve upward because firms' costs have risen and firms must charge higher prices to avoid losing money. Suppose that the economy is operating at full employment and foreign countries raised the world price of oil. Assuming that policymakers do not take any action, describe what will happen to prices and output in the short run and in the long run.

b. Suppose the Federal Reserve decided that it wanted to offset any adverse effects on output. What actions could it take? What would happen to the price level if the Fed used monetary policy to fight unemployment?

c. Economists say that supply shocks create a dilemma for the Federal Reserve that shocks to demand (for example, from investment) do not create. Explain why economists say this, using your answer to part (b) and the aggregate demand and supply diagram.

2. Understanding Japanese Fiscal Policy

During the early 1990s, the Japanese were suffering from a recession. Some economists prescribed expansionary fiscal policy. The finance ministry agreed to income tax cuts—but only if national sales taxes were increased several years later. Explain the logic of the finance ministry, using your understanding of the short-run effects and the long-run effects of fiscal policy. What was the finance ministry trying to prevent?

3. Optimistic Firms in the Long Run

Suppose the economy were operating at full employment and firms became increasingly optimistic about the future. They increase their investment spending; graphically, that means that their investment schedule shifts to the right. What happens to real GDP in the short run? Describe what happens to interest rates, investment, and real GDP in the long run. How is the investment boom self-correcting?

Summary

This chapter explained how the economy makes the transition from the short run to the long run. It also highlighted why monetary and fiscal policies have different effects in the short run than the effects they have in the long run. Understanding the distinction between the short run and the long run is critical to evaluating economic policy. Here are the main points to remember from this chapter:

1. When output exceeds full employment, wages and prices rise faster than their past trends. If output is less than full employment, wages and prices fall relative to past trends.

2. The price changes that occur when the economy is away from full employment push the economy back to full employment. Economists disagree on the length that this adjustment process takes; estimates range from two years to six years.

3. If the economy is operating below full employment, falling wages and prices will reduce money demand and lower interest rates. The fall in interest rates will stimulate investment and lead the economy back to full employment.

4. The reverse occurs when output exceeds full employment. Increases in wages and prices will increase money demand and interest rates. As investment spending falls, the economy returns to full employment.

5. In the long run, increases in the supply of money are neutral; that is, increases in the money supply do not affect real interest rates, investment, nor output.

6. Increases in government spending will raise real interest rates and crowd out investment in the long run. Decreases in government spending will lower real interest rates and crowd in investment in the long run.

7. To improve their chances of being reelected, politicians can potentially take advantage of the difference between the short-run effects and the long-run effects of economic policies.

Key Terms

aggregate demand curve, 606
classical aggregate supply curve, 606
crowding in, 614

crowding out, 615
Keynesian aggregate supply curve, 606
long-run neutrality of money, 613

political business cycle, 616
wage-price spiral, 605

Problems and Discussion Questions

1. When the unemployment rate fell to 4% in 1998, some economists became concerned that inflation would increase. Explain their concern.

2. Economists who believe that the transition from the short run to the long run occurs rapidly do not generally favor using active stabilization policy. Use the aggregate demand and aggregate supply graphs to illustrate how active policy, with a rapid adjustment process, could destabilize the economy.

3. During an economic boom, interest rates rise. Investment spending typically increases in the beginning of the boom and then declines. Can you explain why this pattern of economic activity occurs?

4. Suppose inflation, which had been steady at 2% per year for the past five years, suddenly increased to 2.5% per year. (There were no supply shocks.) Use the aggregate demand and aggregate supply graphs to illustrate this. What policies are appropriate to keep the wage-price spiral from accelerating?

5. Countries that have high money growth for long periods do not grow more rapidly than countries with low money growth. Why?

6. Explain why advocates for the housing industry (an industry very sensitive to interest rates) might want to advocate lower government spending for the long term.

7. Use the model in this chapter to explain how tax cuts for consumers will eventually lead to higher interest rates and crowd out investment spending in the long run.

8. The adjustment process can run into problems if interest rates are driven close to zero and the economy remains below full employment. Draw a money demand curve and an investment schedule to illustrate this possibility.

9. At one time in 1998, nominal interest rates on short-term Japanese government debt were slightly negative. Some foreign-owned banks also paid negative rates on yen deposits. Daniel L. Thornton, an economist at the St. Louis Federal Reserve Bank, argued that even though cash paid a zero rate of interest, banks could still attract funds with negative rates because there were costs to holding cash. What are some of these costs? How negative do you think interest rates could actually go?

10. Some economists estimate that the adjustment process takes up to six years to restore an economy back to full employment. What do you think makes the process so slow? (Hint: Think of the factors that cause lags in monetary policy.)

11. **Web Exercise.** During the Great Depression in the United States, some interest rates became close to zero. Search the historical database at the Web site of the National Bureau of Economic Research (*http://www.nber.org*) to find out how low interest rates actually became and when they were at their lowest.

12. **Web Exercise.** Use the Web site for the Federal Reserve Bank of St. Louis (*http://www.stls.frb.org/ fred*) to find historical data on unemployment rates. Use these data to explore whether unemployment behaves differently in the first two years of a presidential term compared to the final two years. Are there any systematic differences in unemployment between Democratic and Republican presidencies?

Take It to the Net

We invite you to visit the O'Sullivan/Sheffrin page on the Prentice Hall Web site at:
http://www.prenhall.com/osullivan/
for additional World Wide Web exercises for this chapter.

Model Answers to Questions

Chapter-Opening Questions

1. Wages and prices will rise together when the economy is operating at a level of output that exceeds full employment. Conversely, they will fall (relative to trend) when the output level of the economy is below full employment.

2. In the short run, the higher demand from lower interest rates will raise output. But because prices rise when output exceeds full employment, the only long-run effect is higher prices.

3. The Federal Reserve is responsible for preventing inflation from emerging or increasing. This may require high interest rates to reduce output at a time when the economy is producing at too high a level.

4. Tax cuts stimulate consumer demand and lead to higher output in the short run. In the long run, increased consumer spending will crowd out investment spending. Lower investment means a lower capital stock in the future and reduced future output.

Test Your Understanding

1. False. Wages and prices decrease when unemployment exceeds the natural rate.

2. The curve moves downward.

3. Money demand increases, interest rates increase.

4. True. This sequence of events occurs when output is below full employment.

5. True. Money is neutral in the long run.

Using the Tools

1. Economic Policies and Supply Shocks

   a. A supply shock shifts the Keynesian aggregate supply curve upward. Prices will rise and output will fall in the short run. With output below full employment, prices will fall. The economy will return to full employment at the initial price level.

   b. The Federal Reserve could increase the supply of money (such as through open market purchases) and shift the aggregate demand curve. The price level would remain at the higher level.

   c. Unlike shocks to aggregate demand, if the Fed tries to offset the effects of an adverse supply shock on output or on unemployment, the price level will remain permanently higher.

2. Understanding Japanese Fiscal Policy. The Japanese finance ministry was worried about crowding out of investment in the long run. They hoped that the income tax cut would stimulate spending in the short run and pull the economy out of a recession. Later, however, they wanted to reduce consumer spending so that it would not displace investment spending.

3. Optimistic Firms in the Long Run. With an investment boom, real GDP would increase with the additional investment spending. However, as output exceeds full employment, prices would rise, leading to increased money demand and interest rates. The higher interest rates would cut back on investment, lowering real GDP.

CHAPTER

30

The Dynamics of Inflation and Unemployment

In the early 1980s, the Federal Reserve in Washington, D.C., began to receive some unusual packages. Large crates of boards and timber were being unloaded on the steps of the marble building that houses the Federal Reserve. Why were these forest products being dumped at the door of the Fed?

The timber was sent by representatives of the housing industry throughout the country. At that time, the Federal Reserve was trying to fight inflation. During the late 1970s, the inflation rate had increased substantially, and most policymakers believed that inflation had to be reduced. The Federal Reserve was cutting back on the growth of the money supply, and interest rates rose sharply. In 1981, the prime rate of interest—the rate banks charged on short-term loans to their best customers—rose to over 18% per year.

With interest rates at these levels, the housing industry was seriously affected. It became increasingly difficult for anyone to afford to take out a loan to buy a house. The construction of new housing and new office buildings came to a halt. Workers in the construction industry were laid off, and many firms went bankrupt. Boards and logs were sent to the Federal Reserve in protest.

wo themes that we've been stressing separately will now be integrated:

- In the short run, changes in money growth affect real output and real GDP.
- In the long run, the rate of money growth determines the rate of inflation and not real GDP.

This chapter brings these two themes together.

Our economic policy debates often concern inflation and unemployment. We will look at the relationships between inflation and unemployment, examining macroeconomic developments in the United States in the 1980s and 1990s. We also explore why heads of central banks typically appear to be strong enemies of inflation.

Although the United States had serious difficulties fighting inflation in the 1970s and 1980s, other countries have, at times, had much more severe problems with inflation. We study the origins of extremely high inflationary periods and their links to government budget deficits. And we'll take a close look at how unemployment and inflation impose costs on a society.

In this chapter, we address these questions:

1. **Why do countries with lower rates of money growth have lower interest-rate levels than countries with higher rates of money growth?**
2. **Why is the relationship between lower unemployment and higher inflation only temporary?**
3. **Why are the heads of central banks (such as the Chairman of the Board of Governors of the Federal Reserve) typically very conservative, in that they prefer to risk increasing unemployment rather than risk increasing the inflation rate?**
4. **Why do countries with large budget deficits often suffer from massive inflation?**
5. **Why do societies deliberately increase unemployment to reduce the rate of inflation? Is the pain of increased unemployment worth the benefit of reduced inflation?**

Money Growth, Inflation, and Interest Rates

An economy can, in principle, produce at full employment with any inflation rate. There is no "magic" inflation rate that is necessary to sustain full employment. To understand this point, consider the long run when the economy operates at full employment. As we have seen, in the long run, money is neutral. If the Federal Reserve increases the money supply at 5% a year, there will be 5% annual inflation; that is, prices in the economy will rise by 5% a year.

Nominal wages: Wages in dollars.

Let's think about how this economy looks. The **nominal wages**—wages in dollars—of workers are all rising at 5% a year. However, because prices are also rising at 5% a year, **real wages**—wages adjusted for changes in purchasing power—remain constant.

Real wages: Nominal or dollar wages adjusted for changes in purchasing power.

Some workers may feel cheated by the 5% inflation. They might believe that without the inflation they would experience real wage increases, because their nominal wages are rising by 5% a year. Unfortunately, they are wrong. They suffer from what economists call **money illusion**, a confusion of real and nominal magnitudes. Here's the source of the illusion: The only reason their nominal wages are rising by 5% a year is the general 5% inflation. If there were no inflation, their nominal wages would not increase at all.

Money illusion: Confusion of real and nominal magnitudes.

Expectations of inflation: The beliefs held by the public about the likely path of inflation for the future.

After a time, everyone in the economy would begin to expect that the 5% annual inflation would continue. Economists say that in this situation, individuals hold **expectations of inflation**. These expectations affect all aspects of economic life. For example, automobile producers will on average expect their prices to be 5% higher next year. They will also expect their costs—labor and steel, for example—to increase by 5% a year. Workers would begin to understand that their 5% increases in wages would be matched by a 5% increase in the prices of the goods they buy. Continued inflation becomes the normal state of affairs. Expectations of inflation become ingrained in decisions made in all aspects of life.

When the public holds expectations of inflation, real and nominal rates of interest will differ. Recall that the nominal interest rate—the rate quoted in the market—is equal to the real rate of interest plus the expected inflation rate. So if inflation is 5% a year, nominal rates will exceed real rates by 5%.

In Chapter 29, you saw that in the long run, the real rate of interest does not depend on monetary policy because money is neutral; that is, changes in the supply of money do not affect real variables in the long run. However, nominal rates of interest depend on the rate of inflation, which in the long run is determined by the growth of the money supply. Monetary policy therefore does affect the nominal interest rate in the long run. If Country A and Country B had the same real rate of interest but Country A had a higher inflation rate, then Country A would also have a higher nominal interest rate. As Nobel laureate Milton Friedman pointed out, countries with higher money growth typically have higher nominal interest rates than the nominal interest rates in countries with lower money growth rates—and that's because of the differences in inflation across the countries.

Money demand will also be affected by expectations of inflation. If the public expects 6% inflation a year, then the public's demand for money will also increase by 6% a year. Recall the reality principle:

REALITY **PRINCIPLE**

What matters to people is the real value of money or income—its purchasing power—not the face value of money or income.

Using this principle, we can say that the public cares about the real value of its transactions. When prices rise at 6% a year, so does the value of transactions, such as your purchases at the grocery store. The public will need to hold 6% more money each year for these transactions. As long as the Fed allows the supply of money to increase by 6%, the demand for money and supply of money will grow at the same rate. With money's demand and supply both growing at the same rate, real interest rates and nominal interest rates will remain constant.

In the short run, however, changes in the growth rate of money will affect real interest rates. To continue with our example, suppose the public expects 6% annual inflation and both the money supply and money demand grow at 6% a year. Now let the Fed suddenly decrease the annual growth rate of money to 4% while the public continues to expect 6% annual inflation. Because money demand grows at 6% but the money supply grows at only 4%, the growth in the demand for money will exceed the growth in the supply of money. Because demand grows faster than supply, the result will be an increase in both real interest rates and nominal interest rates. Higher real rates of interest will reduce investment spending by firms and reduce consumer durable spending by households. With reduced demand for goods and services, real GDP will fall and unemployment will rise. The reduction in the growth rate of the money supply is contractionary.

In the long run, however, the economy will eventually adjust to the lower rate of money growth. Output will return to full employment through the adjustment process described in Chapter 29. Because money is neutral in the long run, the real rate of interest will return to its previous value. In the long run, inflation will fall to 4% per year, the rate of growth of the money supply. Because the real rate of interest has returned to its original value and inflation has fallen, nominal interest rates will also fall.

This basic pattern fits U.S. history in the late 1970s and early 1980s. At that time, the Federal Reserve sharply decreased the rate of growth of the money supply, and interest rates rose. By 1981, interest rates on three-month Treasury bills rose to over 14% from 7% in 1978. The economy went into a severe recession, with unemployment exceeding 10%. By the mid-1980s, however, the economy returned to full employment with lower interest rates and lower inflation rates. By 1986, Treasury bill rates were below 6%.

This is an example in which the long-run effects of policy actions differ from their short-run effects. In the short run, a policy of tight money, meaning slower money growth, raised interest rates. But in the long run, reduced money growth led to reduced inflation and lower interest rates.

TEST Your Understanding

1. The expected real rate of interest is the nominal interest rate minus the expected inflation rate. True or false? Explain.

2. Explain why, in the long run, an inflation rate of 10% per year will lead to an increase in the demand for money of 10% per year.

Expectations and the Phillips Curve

One of the key regularities in U.S. economic data is that inflation increases when economic activity booms and unemployment falls below its natural rate. Similarly, the rate of inflation falls when the economy is in a recession and unemployment exceeds the natural rate. This relationship between unemployment and inflation is known as the **expectations Phillips curve**.

Expectations Phillips curve: The relationship that describes the links between inflation and unemployment, taking into account expectations of inflation.

The expectations Phillips curve is a refined version of the adjustment mechanism for the economy that we described in Chapter 29. There, we discussed how prices and wages rise if output is above potential output and unemployment is below the natural rate. Wages tend to rise during boom periods as firms compete for workers, and prices rise along with wages. Similarly, prices fall when output is below potential, and unemployment exceeds the natural rate. During recessions, high levels of unemployment lead to falling wages and prices.

However, once we take ongoing inflation into account, we need to modify this story slightly: Wages and prices can change, for two reasons: First, just as before, wages and prices will tend to rise during booms and fall during recessions. Second, workers and firms will have expectations of ongoing inflation. Both workers and firms will raise their nominal wages and prices to the extent that they expect ongoing inflation, to maintain the same level of real wages and real prices.

If the economy is operating at full employment, wages and prices will rise at the rate of inflation expected by workers and firms. If unemployment exceeds the natural rate, the high level of unemployment will put downward pressure on wages and prices, and inflation will fall relative to what was expected. Similarly, if unemployment were below the natural rate, employers would bid aggressively for workers, and wages and prices would rise faster than what was expected previously.

According to the expectations Phillips curve, unemployment varies with *unanticipated inflation*. When unemployment is below the natural rate, the actual inflation rate is higher than what was expected. Similarly, when unemployment is above the natural rate, actual inflation is lower than what was anticipated. When the unemployment rate is at the natural rate, the actual inflation rate equals the expected or anticipated inflation rate. Table 30.1 provides a summary of the key points about the expectations Phillips curve.

The expectations Phillips curve was introduced into the economics profession in the late 1960s by Edmund Phelps of Columbia University and Nobel laureate Milton Friedman, then at the University of Chicago. Friedman argued that when the inflation rate suddenly increases, it is likely that some of this sudden increase was not fully anticipated. Actual inflation will then exceed expected inflation. Workers will see their *nominal wages* increase with the inflation, but because they do not fully expect this sudden inflation, they will think that their *real wages* have increased. With higher perceived real wages, potential workers will accept more jobs, and consequently, unemployment will fall below the natural rate. That's why we will often see an association between increases in the inflation rate and a decrease in the unemployment rate.

After workers recognize that the inflation rate is higher, they will incorporate this higher inflation rate into their expectations of inflation. They will no longer confuse a higher nominal wage with a higher real wage. Unemployment will then return to its natural rate. Thus, there is no permanent relationship between the level of unemployment and the level of inflation.

Similarly, if the inflation rate falls, at least part of this fall may be unexpected. If inflation is less than expected, workers will believe that their real wages have fallen because their nominal wage will not be increasing as fast as their expectations of inflation. With lower perceived real wages, potential workers will accept fewer jobs and the unemployment rate will increase. Once they recognize that inflation is lower than expected, they will no longer be confused. Unemployment will again return to the natural rate. Thus, a decrease in the inflation rate is likely to be associated with temporary increases in unemployment.

Friedman's work forced the economics profession to pay careful attention to the process by which the public forms expectations of inflation. Although it has been over 30 years since Friedman first outlined his theory, there are still many different approaches to analyzing how expectations are formed. As we discuss later in the chapter, some economists believe that workers and firms form expectations taking into account the full array of information available in the economy. Other economists, however, believe workers and firms rely more on simple rules of thumb to form their expectations. Since predictions from economic models will depend on how workers and firms form expectations, this has been an important area of economic research.

The expectations Phillips curve differs from initial attempts to explain the relationship between inflation and unemployment. In the late 1950s, an engineer named A.W. Phillips noticed that there seemed to be a negative relationship between the level of inflation and unemployment in British data. He found lower unemployment to be associated with higher inflation. This relationship became known as the Phillips curve. In the early 1960s, Nobel laureates Paul Samuelson and Robert Solow found a similar relationship between unemployment and the level of the inflation rate in the United States. However, these original studies examined periods of history when there was no significant underly-

Table 30.1 Expectations and Business Fluctuations

	Unemployment	Inflation
Boom	Unemployment below the natural rate	Inflation higher than expected
Recession	Unemployment above the natural rate	Inflation lower than expected

ing inflation and did not take into account expectations of inflation. As we have seen, once we take expectations of ongoing inflation into account, the expectations Phillips curve, the relationship between inflation and unemployment, becomes a bit more complex.

U.S. Inflation and Unemployment in the 1980s

We can use the expectations Phillips curve to help describe the patterns of inflation and unemployment in the 1980s. For the sake of this discussion, we will rely on Friedman's generalization that sudden increases in inflation are partly unanticipated and thus are accompanied by lower unemployment. Conversely, temporarily higher unemployment is associated with decreases in inflation.

When President Jimmy Carter took office at the beginning of 1977, the inflation rate was approximately 6.5% per year, and unemployment exceeded 7% of the labor force. By 1980, however, annual inflation had risen to 9.4%. There were two reasons for this increase: One, unemployment had been steadily reduced during the Carter administration, falling below 6% by 1979. Because the natural rate of unemployment was close to 6% of the labor force, this led to an increase in the annual inflation rate. The other reason: There was an oil shock in 1979 that also contributed to higher inflation.

Fears of even higher inflation led President Carter to appoint a well-known inflation fighter, Paul Volcker, as the chair of the Federal Reserve. Volcker immediately began to institute a tight money policy, and interest rates rose sharply by 1980. When President Ronald Reagan took office, he supported Volcker's policy. Eventually, high real interest rates took their toll, and unemployment rose to over 10% by 1983. As actual unemployment exceeded the natural rate of unemployment, the inflation rate fell, just as was predicted by the expectations Phillips curve. By 1986, the inflation rate fell to approximately 2.7% per year with unemployment at 7% of the labor force. The severe recession had done its job in reducing the inflation rate.

Figure 30.1

Dynamics of Inflation and Unemployment, 1986–1993

Source: Data from *Economic Report of the President* (Washington, DC: U.S. Government Printing Office, yearly)

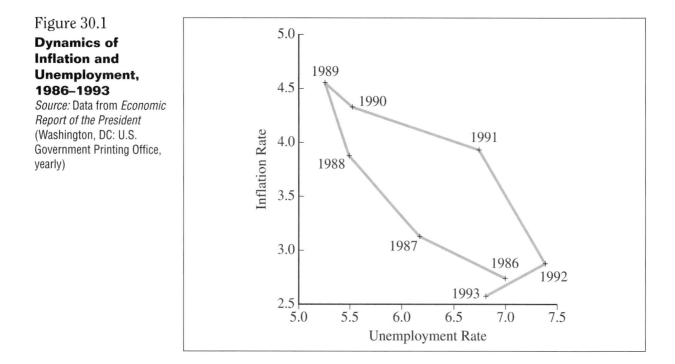

However, as we can see in Figure 30.1, after 1986 the unemployment rate began to fall again. As actual unemployment fell below the natural rate of unemployment, inflation began to increase again. By 1989, annual inflation had risen to 4.5%. This led the Fed to raise interest rates, thereby reducing output and increasing unemployment, to bring down the inflation rate. By 1992, the actual unemployment rate had increased to 7.4% of the labor force, and by 1993, annual inflation had again been brought down below 3%.

President George Bush suffered the consequences of this episode of fighting inflation. By the time he took office in 1989, actual unemployment was below the natural rate of unemployment, inflation had been rising, and the Fed was about to start slowing the economy. Although the rate of inflation was eventually reduced, the recovery back to full employment came too late in his term to be fully appreciated by the voters, and he lost his bid for reelection.

Shifts in the Natural Rate of Unemployment

Up to this point, we have assumed that the natural rate of unemployment is a constant, say, for example, 5% of the labor force. If actual unemployment falls below this constant rate, then inflation will tend to increase. Similarly, if the actual unemployment exceeds 5%, inflation will then fall.

But as you will see next, the natural rate of unemployment can shift over time. At the beginning of the 1990s in the United States, most economists believed that the natural rate of unemployment was in the 5% to 6% range. By the late 1990s, the actual unemployment rate had fallen to almost 4% of the labor force. If the natural rate of unemployment had been in the 5% to 6% range, we would have expected to see an increase in the inflation rate. But, in fact, the inflation rate continued to fall during the late 1990s. This continued drop in inflation suggests that the natural rate of unemployment had fallen. Of course, it is possible that special one-time factors, such as lower world oil prices, may have contributed to the decrease in the inflation rate over this period. But by the late 1990s, many economists had begun to believe that the natural rate of unemployment had decreased.

What factors can shift the natural rate of unemployment? Economists have identified three basic factors that can shift the natural rate of unemployment:

- **Demographics.** The composition of the work force can change to increase the natural rate. For example, we know teenagers have higher unemployment rates than adults. If changes in population lead to a higher percentage of teenagers in the labor force, we would expect the natural rate of unemployment to increase.

- **Institutional changes.** Changes in laws, regulations, and economic institutions can influence the natural rate of unemployment. Suppose the government decreased the length of time during which it made payments to workers who were unemployed. We would then expect that the unemployed would return to work more rapidly and the natural rate of unemployment would decrease. Many economists believe that institutional changes were responsible for the sharp increase in the natural rate of unemployment in Europe as "A Closer Look: Europe's Increase in the Natural Rate," explains.

- **The state of the economy.** Some economists believe the economic performance of the economy itself may influence the natural rate of unemployment. Suppose the economy goes into a long recession. During that time, many young people may not be able to find jobs and fail to develop a strong work ethic. Other workers may lose some of their skills during a prolonged period of unemployment. Both factors could lead to longer-term unemployment and an increase in the natural rate of unemployment.

A CLOSER LOOK Europe's Increase in the Natural Rate

In 1977, a doctoral student in economics at the Massachusetts Institute of Technology completed a thesis that tried to explain why unemployment rates in Europe were below unemployment rates in the United States. Before that time, unemployment rates in Europe were typically in the 2% to 3% range, while U.S. unemployment rates were 4% to 5%.

How times have changed! Now the United States is the envy of Europe. While our natural rate is currently in the neighborhood of 4% to 5.5%, in Europe the natural rate has risen to between 8% and 11%. Because unemployment disproportionately affects the young and less skilled, unemployment has also become a social crisis in Europe. What changed in the last two decades?

Studies of European unemployment cite a variety of different factors. One of the most important is that labor markets in Europe are less flexible than in the United States and unions are more powerful. Strong unions can maintain high wages for workers even during bad economic times, at the expense of the unemployed. European employers also face more restrictions on firing workers, which makes them reluctant to

High unemployment led to many demonstrations in Europe in the 1990s.

hire them in the first place. Finally, European countries are much more generous than the United States in paying unemployment insurance. Eventually, these factors caught up with the Europeans and led to the sharp increase in the natural rate.

Source: Charles Bean, "European Unemployment: A Survey," *Journal of Economic Literature*, vol. 32, June 1994, pp. 573–619.

TEST Your Understanding

3. If inflation increases faster than expected, will the actual unemployment rate be above or below the natural rate of unemployment?

4. Will a sustained boom tend to increase or decrease the natural rate of unemployment?

Credibility and Inflation

Why are the heads of central banks (such as the chair of the Board of Governors) typically very conservative and constantly warning about the dangers of inflation? The basic reason is that these monetary policymakers can influence expectations of inflation. Expectations of inflation will influence actual behavior. For example, workers will want higher nominal wages if they anticipate inflation. If policymakers are not careful, they can actually make it difficult to fight inflation in a society.

Consider an example. A large union is negotiating wages for workers in the auto and steel industries. If the union negotiates a very high nominal wage, other unions will follow, negotiating for and winning high wages. Prices will inevitably rise. Because of these wage settlements, the Fed will begin to see inflation emerge. The Fed had been keeping the money supply constant. What are the Fed's options?

We depict the Fed's dilemma in Figure 30.2. By setting a higher nominal wage, the union shifts the aggregate supply curve from AS_0 to AS_1. The Fed then has a choice:

- Keep the money supply and aggregate demand at AD_0. The economy will initially fall into a recession.

- Increase the money supply and raise aggregate demand from AD_0 to AD_1. This will keep the economy at full employment but lead to higher prices.

The actions of the union will depend on what its leaders expect the Fed to do. If they believe that the Fed will not increase aggregate demand, their actions will trigger a recession, and the union leaders are aware their actions will trigger a recession. They may be reluctant to negotiate a high wage. If they do not increase nominal wages, the economy will remain at full employment and there will be no increase in prices. But if union leaders believe that the Fed will increase aggregate demand, the union has nothing to lose and will increase the nominal wage. The result will be higher prices in the economy.

As this example illustrates, expectations about the Fed's determination to fight inflation will affect behavior in the private sector. If the Fed is credible or believable in its desire to fight inflation, it can deter the private sector from taking aggressive actions that drive up prices. This is the reason the heads of central banks are conservative, preferring to take the risks of increasing unemployment rather than risking an increase in inflation. For example, having a conservative chair of the Fed, someone who strongly detests inflation, sends a signal to everyone in the economy that the Fed will be unlikely to increase the money supply, regardless of what actions are taken in the private sector.

New Zealand took a different approach to ensure the credibility of its central bank. Since 1989, the central bank has been operating under a law that specifies that its only goal is to attempt to maintain stable prices, which, in practice, requires it to keep inflation between zero and 2% a year. This policy sharply limits the central bank's ability to stabilize real GDP, but it does signal to the private sector that the central bank will not be increasing the money supply, regardless of the actions taken by wage setters or unions.

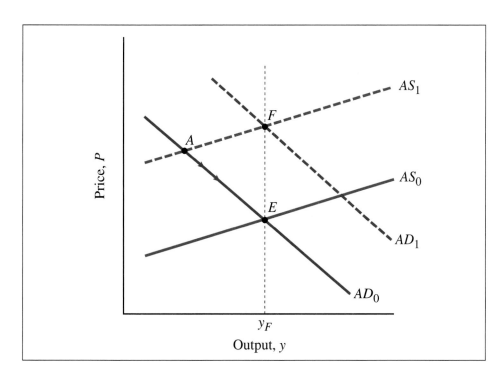

Figure 30.2
Choices for the Fed
If workers push up their nominal wages, the aggregate supply curve will shift from AS_0 to AS_1. If the Fed keeps aggregate demand constant at AD_0, a recession will occur at A, and the economy will eventually return to full employment at E. If the Fed increases aggregate demand, the economy remains at full employment at F but with a higher price level.

Our example suggests that with a credible central bank, a country can have lower inflation without experiencing extra unemployment. Some political scientists and economists have suggested that central banks that have true independence from the rest of the government, and are therefore less subject to political influence, will be more credible in their commitment to fighting inflation.

There is some evidence to support this conjecture. Figure 30.3 plots an index of independence against average inflation rates from 1955 to 1988 for 16 countries. The points appear to lie along a downward-sloping line, meaning that more independence is associated with lower inflation. Germany and Switzerland, the countries with the most independent central banks, had the lowest inflation rates. This same study found no association between GDP growth and central bank independence.

As our discussion illustrates, it's necessary to understand how expectations affect central bank behavior to be able to understand the behavior of output and prices for the economy. As we have noted, economists have paid increasing attention to the role of expectations in many different areas of economics. They have recognized that people develop their expectations in complex ways that take into account the information they have available.

Rational expectations: The economic theory that analyzes how people form expectations in such a manner that, on average, they forecast the future correctly.

In the 1970s, a group of economists led by Nobel laureate Robert E. Lucas, Jr., from the University of Chicago developed the theory of **rational expectations**, which analyzes how firms and individuals may base their expectations on all the information available to them. According to the theory of rational expectations, individuals form their expectations such that, on average, they anticipate the future correctly. Although they may make mistakes in specific instances, on average their expectations are rational or correct. The theory of rational expectations has been used extensively in many areas of economics, including the example with the union and the Fed that we just discussed. In that example, the theory of rational expectations implies that the union will, on average, anticipate whether the Fed will adopt a policy of expanding the money supply in the face of wage increases. A credible Fed, therefore, will tend to deter wage increases. Although not all economists believe that the public is fully rational in economic affairs, insights from this theory have heavily influenced economic research in many different areas.

Figure 30.3
Inflation versus Central Bank Independence

Source: Data from Alesina and Summers, "Central Bank Independence and Macroeconomic Performance," *Journal of Money, Credit, and Banking,* May 1993.

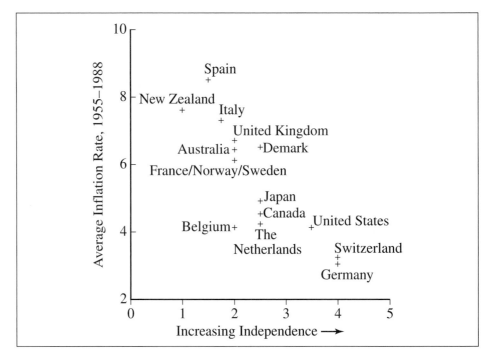

Expectations play a significant role in almost all areas of economics. For example, as we have seen, both lenders and borrowers must form expectations about future inflation rates in setting nominal interest rates. There are many other examples as well. Prices of stocks of firms will depend on investors' expectations about future dividends that the firm will pay. Even your decision to buy a home or rent will depend on your expectation about the future prices of homes. If you believe that home prices will rise sharply in the future, you will be more likely to buy a home and earn a profit from the investment. Economists study how expectations are formed in all these markets, whether they are rational or not, and how expectations influence actual market outcomes.

Inflation and the Velocity of Money

Countries sometimes experience stunning inflation rates. For example, in a period of 15 months from August 1922 to November 1923, the price level in Germany rose by a factor of 10 billion! To explain these extremely high inflation rates and to provide more insight into the links between money growth and inflation, we now introduce a concept that is closely related to money demand: the velocity of money.

The **velocity of money** is defined as the ratio of nominal GDP to the money supply:

$$\text{velocity of money} = \text{nominal GDP/money supply}$$

Velocity of money: Nominal GDP divided by the money supply. It is also the rate at which money changes hands or turns over during the year.

One useful way to think of velocity is that it is the number of times that money must change hands, or turn over, in economic transactions during a given year to purchase nominal GDP.

To understand this, consider a simple example. Suppose that nominal GDP in a country is $5 trillion per year and the money supply is $1 trillion. Then the velocity of money in this economy will be

$$\text{velocity} = \$5 \text{ trillion per year/\$1 trillion}$$
$$= 5 \text{ per year}$$

In this economy, the $1 trillion money supply has to change hands or turn over an average of 5 times a year to purchase the $5 trillion of nominal GDP.

If the money supply turns over 5 times in one year, this means that people are holding each dollar of money for 365 days/5 = 73 days a year. If velocity is very high, individuals turn over money very quickly and do not hold money for a very long time on average. If velocity is low, they turn over money slowly and hold onto money for a longer period of time.

To further understand the role of money and velocity, let's rewrite the definition of velocity as

$$\text{money supply} \times \text{velocity} = \text{nominal GDP}$$
$$\text{or}$$
$$M \times V = P \times y$$

where M is the money supply, V is the velocity of money, P is a price index for GDP, and y is real GDP. This equation is known as the equation of exchange or the **quantity equation**. On the right side, $P \times y$ is nominal GDP, the product of price index and real GDP. This is the total value of spending. On the left side, the money supply, M, is multiplied by V, the velocity of money.

Quantity equation: The equation that links money, velocity, prices, and real output. In symbols, we have $M \times V = P \times y$.

The quantity equation links the money supply and velocity to nominal GDP. If velocity is predictable, we can use the quantity equation and the supply of money to predict nominal GDP. But it's not that easy; the velocity of money does vary over time. For example, in the United States between 1959 and 1999, the velocity of M2 (the measure of the money supply that includes currency, demand deposits, saving accounts, and deposits in money market mutual funds) varied between 1.4 and 2.0. In other words, the total amount of M2 held by the public turned over between 1.4 and 2.0 times a year to purchase nominal GDP for each year during this period.

The basic quantity equation can be used to derive a closely related formula for understanding inflation in the long run:

$$\text{Growth rate of money} + \text{growth rate of velocity}$$
$$= \text{growth rate of prices} + \text{growth rate of real output}$$

Growth version of the quantity equation: An equation that links the growth rates of money, velocity, prices, and real output.

We will call this the **growth version of the quantity equation**. Here is how to use this formula: Suppose that money growth is 10% a year, the growth of real output is 3% a year, and velocity has zero growth (it is constant). Then the rate of growth of prices, which is the inflation rate, is

$$10\% + 0\% = \text{growth rate of prices} + 3\%$$
$$7\% = \text{growth rate of prices} = \text{inflation}$$

Inflation will be 7% a year. This formula allows for real economic growth and for growth in velocity. For example, if velocity grew during this period at the rate of 1% a year, the inflation rate will be 1% higher, or 8% (10 + 1 − 3) a year.

There is a definite link between increases in the growth of money and the rate of inflation. Inflation was lowest in the 1950s, when money growth was lowest. It was also highest in the 1970s, when money growth was highest. The link is not perfect because real GDP and velocity grew at different rates during the decades. But years of economic research have revealed that sustained increases in money growth will lead to inflation.

The links between money growth and inflation are particularly dramatic when money growth is extremely high. But what leads countries to vast increases in their money supply?

TEST Your Understanding

5. Complete this statement with *real* or *nominal*: The velocity of money is equal to _____ GDP divided by the money supply.

6. If the growth of the money supply is 6% a year, velocity decreases by 1%, and there is no growth in real GDP, what is the inflation rate?

Budget Deficits and Hyperinflations

The inflation rates observed in the United States in the last 40 years are insignificant compared to some of the inflation rates around the world throughout history. Economists call very high inflation rates—over 50% per month, which is approximately 13,000% per year—**hyperinflation**. One of the first studies of hyperinflations was conducted by Phillip Cagan of Columbia University. Table 30.2 presents selected data from his study.

Hyperinflation: An inflation rate exceeding 50% per month.

Greece, Hungary, and Russia are three countries that have had hyperinflation. According to the data in Table 30.2, for a period of one year, Greece had a monthly inflation rate of 365%. A monthly inflation rate of 365% per month means the price level rises by a factor of 4.65 each month. (If the price level rises by 4.65, its percent increase is (4.65 − 1)/1 = 3.65, or 365%.) To get a sense of what this means, suppose that we had inflation of this magnitude in the United States. At the beginning of the month, $1 could buy a large order of French fries. Because prices are rising by a factor of 4.65 each month, by

Table 30.2 Some Classic Hyperinflations

Country	Dates	Monthly Rate of Inflation	Monthly Rate of Money Growth	Approximate Increase in Velocity
Greece	November 1943 to November 1944	365%	220%	14.00
Hungary	August 1945 to July 1946	19,800%	12,200%	333.00
Russia	December 1921 to January 1924	57%	49%	3.70

Source: Adapted from Phillip Cagan, "The Monetary Dynamics of Hyperinflation," in *Studies in the Quantity Theory of Money*, edited by Milton Friedman (Chicago: University of Chicago Press, 1956) p. 26.

the end of the month it would take $4.65 to buy the same order of French fries, and one dollar by the end of the month would be worth only 1/4.65 = 0.215, or 21.5 cents.

After two months, a dollar would be worth only (0.215) × (0.215) = 0.046 of its original value, or 4.6 cents. Suppose this continues month after month. After one year, a dollar bill would be worth only 1 millionth of 1 cent! In hyperinflations, money does not hold its value very long.

In Hungary after World War II, prices rose by 19,800% each month. The hyperinflation in Russia in the early 1920s seems moderate by comparison: prices rose by 57% per month.

On the basis of the quantity theory, we suspect that these hyperinflations must have all been caused by money growth. We can see this in the data. For example, in Greece, the monthly inflation of 365% was accompanied by 220% money growth. In Hungary, the monthly inflation of 19,800% was caused by 12,200% money growth.

The value of money deteriorates sharply during hyperinflations. Money no longer serves as a good store of value. In these extreme circumstances, we expect that people will not want to hold money very long but will immediately try to spend it. In other words, we expect the velocity of money to increase sharply during hyperinflations. This is precisely what happens.

The last column of Table 30.2 shows how velocity increases during hyperinflations. In the hyperinflation in Greece, velocity increased by a factor of 14. In the hyperinflation in Hungary, velocity increased by over 333 times.

Hyperinflations have also occurred in recent times. Table 30.3 presents data on three hyperinflations during the 1980s—in Bolivia, Argentina, and Nicaragua, all averaging about 100% per month.

Table 30.3 High Inflations in the 1980s

Country	Year	Rate of Inflation Yearly	Rate of Inflation Monthly	Monthly Money Growth Rate
Bolivia	1985	1,152,200%	118%	91%
Argentina	1989	302,200%	95%	93%
Nicaragua	1988	975,500%	115%	66%

Source: International Financial Statistics Yearbook, 1992. (Washington, DC: International Monetary Fund).

During hyperinflations, money no longer works very well in facilitating exchange. Because prices are changing so fast and unpredictably, there is typically massive confusion about the true value of commodities. Different stores may be raising prices at different rates, and the same commodities may sell for radically different prices. Everyone spends all their time hunting for bargains and finding the lowest prices, a process that becomes very costly in human terms. No country can easily live very long with hyperinflations. Governments are forced to put an end to hyperinflation before it totally destroys their economies.

The cause of all hyperinflations is excessive money growth. But why do governments allow the money supply to grow so fast and cause these economic catastrophes? The answer lies in understanding how some governments finance their deficits—the gap between government spending and revenues.

A government deficit must be covered in some way. If a government wants to spend $1,000 but is collecting only $800 in taxes, where can it get the needed $200? One option is to borrow the $200 from the public. The government will then issue government bonds—IOUs—to the public for $200. In the future, the government will have to pay back the $200 plus interest on the bonds.

An alternative to borrowing from the public is to print $200 worth of new money. All governments have the ability to run the printing presses and come up with $200 in new currency.

In principle, governments could use a mix of borrowing funds from public and printing money as long as the deficit is covered:

government deficit = new borrowing from the public + new money created

During Germany's hyperinflation in the 1920s, it was cheaper to start a fire with currency than it was to purchase wood for kindling.

Now we are in a position to understand how hyperinflations originate. Consider Hungary after World War II. Its economy was destroyed by the war, and its citizens were demanding government services. The government had limited ability to collect taxes because of the poor state of the economy, but it gave in to the demands from its citizens for spending at levels that far exceeded what it could collect. The result was a large deficit. Then the government faced a problem: How would this large deficit be financed? No individuals or governments wanted to buy bonds or IOUs from Hungary (that is, lend Hungary money) because its economy was in such poor shape that it would be unlikely to pay off any debts in the near future. Without an option to borrow, Hungary resorted to printing money at a massive rate. The result was hyperinflation.

Hyperinflations always occur in countries that have large deficits but cannot borrow and are forced to print new money. For example, Argentina in the 1980s had large state-run firms that consistently lost vast sums of money. Because Argentina had a history of past inflations, it could not borrow easily and resorted to printing money. Large, money-losing state enterprises and limited ability to borrow combined to bring money creation and hyperinflation.

To stop hyperinflations, it is necessary to eliminate the government deficit, which is the fundamental cause. Either taxes must be increased or spending must be cut, both of which cause some economic pain. There is no other remedy. Once the deficit has been cut and the government stops printing money, the hyperinflation will end. Without money growth to feed it, hyperinflation will quickly die of starvation.

Economists who traditionally emphasized the role that the supply of money played in determining nominal income and inflation were often called **monetarists**. The most famous monetarist is Nobel laureate Milton Friedman, who studied complex versions of the quantity equation and explored the role of money in all aspects of economic life. Friedman had many influential students, such as Philip Cagan, who is best known for his work on hyperinflations. They, along with other monetarist economists, did pioneering research on the link between money, nominal income, and inflation. Today, most economists agree with the monetarists that, in the long run, inflation is caused by growth in the money supply.

Monetarists: Economists who emphasize the role of money in determining nominal income and inflation.

The Costs of Unemployment and Inflation

While we can understand why societies cannot tolerate hyperinflations, it is less clear what problems occur with what may be considered more ordinary inflation rates. Why do societies deliberately create recessions and unemployment for the purpose of lowering the rate of inflation? In this section, we take a closer look at the costs of unemployment and inflation to better understand the options facing policymakers.

Costs of Unemployment

When there is excess unemployment—actual unemployment above the natural rate of unemployment—both society and individuals suffer economic loss. From a social point of view, excess unemployment means that the economy is no longer producing at its potential. The resulting loss of resources can be very large. For example, in 1983, when the unemployment rate averaged 9.6%, typical estimates of the shortfall of GDP from potential were near 6%. Simply put, this meant that society was wasting 6% of the total resources at its disposal.

That social loss translates into reduced income and lower employment for individuals. When unemployment increases, more workers are fired or laid off from their existing jobs, and individuals seeking employment find fewer opportunities available. To families with fixed obligations such as mortgage payments, the loss in income can bring immediate hardships. **Unemployment insurance**, payments received from the government

Unemployment insurance: Payments received from the government upon becoming unemployed.

upon becoming unemployed, can cushion the blow to some degree, but unemployment insurance is typically only temporary and does not replace a worker's full earnings.

The effects of unemployment can also linger into the future. As we noted, workers who suffer from a prolonged period of unemployment are likely to lose some of their skills. For example, an unemployed stockbroker might be unaware of the latest developments and trends in financial markets. This will make it more difficult for him or her to find a job in the future. Economists who have studied the high rates of unemployment among young people in Europe point to the loss of both skills and good work habits (such as coming to work on time) as key factors leading to long-term unemployment.

The costs of unemployment are not simply financial. In our society, a person's status and position are largely associated with the type of job the person holds. Losing a job can impose severe psychological costs. Some studies, for example, have found that increased crime, divorce, and suicide rates are associated with increased unemployment.

Costs of Inflation

Anticipated inflation: Inflation that is expected.

Unanticipated inflation: Inflation that is not expected.

Economists typically separate the costs of inflation into two categories. One includes costs associated with fully expected or **anticipated inflation**. The other includes the costs associated with unexpected or **unanticipated inflation**. Although inflation causes both types of costs, it is convenient to discuss each case separately.

Anticipated Inflation

Let's consider the costs of anticipated inflation first. Suppose the economy had been experiencing 4% annual inflation for many years and everyone was fully adjusted to it. Workers knew that nominal wage increases of 4% each year were not real wage increases because prices will rise by 4% over the year. Investors earning a 7% annual rate of interest on their bonds knew that their real return would be only 3% after adjusting for inflation.

Menu costs: Costs of inflation that arise from actually changing prices.

Even in this case, inflation still has some costs. First, there are the actual physical costs of changing prices, which economists call **menu costs**. Restaurant owners, catalog producers, and any other business that must post prices will have to incur costs to change their prices because of inflation. Economists believe that these costs are relatively small for the economy.

Second, people will hold less real cash balances when there is inflation. The cost of holding money is its opportunity cost, which is best measured by the nominal rate of interest. Because an increase in inflation will raise the nominal rate of interest, it will raise the cost of holding cash or checking accounts that do not pay interest. People will respond by holding less cash at any one time. If they hold less cash, they must visit the bank or their ATM more frequently because they will run out of cash sooner. Economists use the term **shoe-leather costs** to refer to the additional wear and tear necessary to hold less cash. Economists who have estimated these costs find that they can be large, as much as 1% of GDP.

Shoe-leather costs: Costs of inflation that arise from trying to reduce holdings of cash.

In practice, our tax system and financial system do not fully adjust even to fully anticipated inflation. It is difficult for the government and businesses to change their normal rules of operation when inflation changes. As an example, consider the tax system. Our tax system is based on nominal income, not real income. Suppose the yearly inflation rate is 3%, nominal interest rates are 7% per year, and you have $100 in a savings account. At the end of the year, you will have earned $7. Your income taxes will be based on the full $7, not on $4, which is your earnings adjusted for inflation. This can make a considerable difference. If your tax rate is 50%, you pay $3.50 in taxes, giving you a nominal return after taxes of 3.5% on your original $100 [($7 − $3.50)/$100]. Taking into account the 3% inflation, your real return is only 0.5% (3.5 − 3).

Now suppose that there is no inflation, there is a 4% real rate of return, and the tax rate is 50%. Your taxes will be $2, which, in the absence of inflation, will give you a higher real return after taxes of 2% [($4 − 2)/$100]. Inflation lowered your real after-tax return because the tax system is based on nominal income, not real income. This increase in taxes was not a deliberate action of the legislature; it is solely a creature of inflation.

There are other examples of how inflation interacts with taxation. In the United States before 1986, inflation could have pushed you into a higher tax bracket—for example, from 15% to 28%—with the result that the government took a higher fraction of your income. Since 1986, tax brackets have been adjusted for inflation, eliminating this particular problem. Even today, however, you pay taxes when you sell a stock whose price has increased solely because of inflation even if the real value of the stock did not increase. The government can also lose from inflation as well. Homeowners can deduct from their taxes, their nominal interest payments on their mortgages, not their real interest payments. Higher inflation gives homeowners more deductions and lowers their income tax bills.

Many financial markets are also not fully adjusted for inflation. For example, some states have **usury laws**, or ceilings on interest rates. These ceilings are on nominal rates, not real rates. At times of high inflation, some lenders may require nominal rates above the usury ceilings to provide them with an adequate real return. If they cannot lend at rates above the ceiling, the market may actually disappear.

Usury laws: Laws that do not allow interest rates to exceed specified ceilings.

The column in Table 30.4 on anticipated inflation summarizes our discussion. If the economy can adjust fully to inflation, the only costs of fully anticipated inflation are the small menu costs and shoe-leather costs. But if institutions such as the tax system do not adjust, there will be other costs, such as distortions in the tax system, as well.

Unanticipated Inflation

The last column in Table 30.4 shows the costs of unexpected or unanticipated inflation. The first cost of unanticipated inflation is arbitrary redistributions of income. Suppose the public had been accustomed to 4% annual inflation but inflation reaches 6%. Who would gain and who would lose? Lenders would lose, and borrowers would gain. If lenders and borrowers agreed to a real rate of interest of 3% and expected 4% inflation, the nominal rate would have been 7%. However, with 6% inflation, the real rate actually paid would fall to 1%. Borrowers would rejoice, and lenders would despair.

Anyone making a nominal contract to sell a product would lose. For example, workers who set nominal wages based on expected inflation would earn a lower real wage. Buyers with nominal contracts, such as firms setting nominal wages, would gain. These are unfair redistributions of income, or transfers, caused by unanticipated inflation.

These redistributions eventually impose real costs on the economy. Consider an analogy. Suppose you live in a very safe neighborhood where no one locks their doors. If a rash of burglaries (transfers between you and the crooks) starts to occur, people will invest in locks, alarms, and more police. You and your community will incur real costs to prevent these arbitrary redistributions.

Table 30.4 Costs of Inflation

	Anticipated Inflation	Unanticipated Inflation
Institutions do not adjust	Distortions in the tax system, problems in financial markets	Unfair redistributions
Institutions adjust	Cost of changing prices, shoe-leather costs	Institutional disintigration

The same is true for unanticipated inflation. If a society experiences unanticipated inflation, individuals and institutions will change their behavior. For example, potential homeowners will not be able to borrow for long periods at fixed rates of interest but will be required to accept loans whose rates can be adjusted as inflation rates change. This imposes more risk on homeowners. If unanticipated inflation becomes extreme, individuals will spend more of their time trying to profit from inflation rather than working at productive jobs. As inflation became more volatile in the late 1970s in the United States, many people devoted their time to speculation in real estate and commodity markets to try to beat inflation. The economy becomes less efficient when people take actions based on beating inflation. Latin American countries that have experienced high and variable inflation rates know all too well these costs from inflation.

When inflation becomes a problem, some societies have tried to index nominal contracts, that is, adjust the nominal amounts for inflation. For example, if you had an indexed wage of $10.00 an hour and there was 15% inflation, your wage would rise to $11.50 to compensate you for the inflation ($10.00 × 1.15 = $11.50). The U.S. government has now joined other countries in providing indexed bonds to protect investors from inflation.

In practice, countries find that indexing is not a perfect solution to the problems caused by inflation. There are three reasons:

1. Some policymakers worry that indexing lowers the resolve to fight inflation and therefore could lead to higher inflation.
2. We know that price indices are far from perfect and are extremely difficult to construct when prices are increasing rapidly.
3. Some economists believe that indexing builds inflation into the economic system and makes it difficult to reduce inflation. If price increases automatically lead to wage increases, it becomes difficult to stop wage-price spirals. In 1995, for example, Brazil began to dismantle its very extensive system of indexing precisely for this reason.

Although Table 30.4 is useful for discussing the different costs of inflation, it is important to note that it is not easy to distinguish anticipated inflation from unanticipated inflation. Most inflations are a mixture of the two. Moreover, in all countries, institutions can adjust to inflation only partially. Thus, all the costs outlined in Table 30.4 may apply to any episode of inflation.

These costs are compounded as inflation rises. Studies have shown that as inflation rises, both anticipated inflation and unanticipated inflation increase. At high inflation rates, these costs grow rapidly, and at some point, policymakers are forced to engineer a recession to reduce the inflation rate. Although unemployment and recessions are quite costly to society, they sometimes become necessary in the face of high inflation.

Using the **TOOLS**

In this chapter, we examined how inflation becomes embedded into expectations and the problems in taming inflation. Take this opportunity to do your own economic analysis.

1. ECONOMIC EXPERIMENT: Money Illusion
Economists say that people suffer from money illusion if their behavior is influenced by nominal changes that are also not real changes. Consider the following scenarios and be prepared to discuss them in class:

a. Erin bought an antique clock for $100. Two years later, Betsy bought an identical clock for $121. Meanwhile, there had been inflation each year at 10%. Both Erin and Betsy sell their clocks to other collectors. Erin sold hers for $130; Betsy sold hers for $133. Who profited more in their transactions?

b. Bob and Pete are classic comic book traders. A year ago, Bob and Pete each bought the same comic book for $10. Bob sold his a couple of days later for $20. Pete waited a year and sold his for $21. If inflation last year was 6%, who made the better deal?

2. Short-Term Versus Long-Term Interest Rates

To stop inflation, a central bank cut back sharply on the rate of money growth. When it cut back, short-term nominal interest rates rose, but long-term interest rates (the rates on 30-year government bonds) did not change. After one month during which the central bank continued its tight money policy and short-term rates remained high, long-term rates began to fall. Explain the different behavior of short-term nominal interest rates and long-term nominal interest rates. (Hint: Long-term nominal interest rates will reflect expectations of inflation in the long run.)

3. Tax Indexation

An economy has two income tax brackets for individuals: a tax rate of 10% for the first $30,000 of income and a tax rate of 20% for any income exceeding $30,000.

a. A family earns $40,000. How much tax does it pay?

b. Suppose prices double and the family earns $80,000. How much tax does the family pay?

c. How does the tax as a percentage of income change with the increase in prices? How could the tax system be fixed to ensure that the percentage of income that goes to the tax collector does not change with the level of prices?

4. Public Pronouncements and Fed Officials

When Alan Blinder, a Princeton University professor of economics, was appointed vice-chair of the Federal Reserve in 1994, he gave a speech to a group of central bankers and monetary policy specialists. In that speech, he repeated one of the lessons in this chapter: In the long run, the rate of inflation is independent of unemployment and depends only on money growth; in the short run, lower unemployment can raise the inflation rate. Blinder's speech created an uproar in the financial press. He was attacked by some commentators as not being sufficiently vigilant against inflation. Use the idea of credibility to explain why an apparently innocent speech would cause such an uproar in the financial community.

Summary

In this chapter, we explored the role expectations of inflation plays in the economy and how societies deal with inflation. Interest rates, as well as changes in wages and prices, both reflect expectations of inflation. These expectations depend on the past history of inflation and on expectations about central bank behavior. To reduce inflation, policymakers must increase actual unemployment above the natural rate of unemployment. We also looked at the ultimate causes of hyperinflations. Finally, we discussed the costs of unemployment and inflation and why policymakers sometimes deliberately cause recessions to reduce the rate of inflation. Here are main points to remember from this chapter:

1. In the long run, higher money growth leads to higher inflation and higher nominal interest rates.

2. A decrease in the growth rate of money will initially lead to higher real interest rates and higher nominal interest rates. Real interest rates will eventually return to their prior levels. Nominal interest rates will be permanently decreased with the decrease in inflation.

3. The rate of inflation increases when actual unemployment falls below the natural rate of unemployment; the rate of inflation decreases when actual unemployment exceeds the natural rate of unemployment. Economists explain this relationship by the expectations Phillips curve.

4. Monetary policymakers need to be cautious in their statements and pronouncements because what they say can influence expectations of inflation. Conservative central bankers can dampen expectations of inflation.

5. The quantity equation and the growth version of the quantity equation show the relationship between money, velocity, and nominal income.

6. Governments sometimes print new money to finance large portions of their budget deficits. When they do, the result is rapid inflation.

7. The costs of unemployment include the loss of output for society and economic and psychological hardships for individuals.

8. The costs of inflation arise from both anticipated and unanticipated inflation. In practice, both types of costs rise with the inflation rate.

Key Terms

anticipated inflation, 636
expectations of inflation, 622
expectations Phillips curve, 624
growth version of the quantity equation, 632
hyperinflation, 632

menu costs, 636
monetarists, 635
money illusion, 622
nominal wages, 622
quantity equation, 631
rational expectations, 630

real wages, 622
shoe-leather costs, 636
unanticipated inflation, 636
unemployment insurance, 635
usury laws, 637
velocity of money, 631

Problems and Discussion Questions

1. Interpret the following statement: "High interest rates are the evidence of loose monetary policy, not tight monetary policy."

2. If a business borrows funds at 10% per year, the business has a 40% tax rate, and the annual inflation rate is 5%, what are the real after-tax costs of funds to the business?

3. Are workers or firms more likely to have more accurate information about the future course of inflation?

4. Some economists argue that the natural rate of unemployment did not really decrease in the United States in the late 1990s, but there were temporary factors that kept the inflation from rising. How would you go about determining whether the natural rate of unemployment decreased in the late 1990s in the United States?

5. If the government increases the rate at which it injects money into the economy, individuals and firms will hold onto money for shorter periods. Can you explain this?

6. If the growth rate of money is 10% per year, annual inflation is 7%, and the growth rate of velocity is 1% per year, what is the growth rate of real output?

7. Some economists argue that foreign aid can reduce both the likelihood and the severity of hyperinflations. Explain this argument.

8. How do you think the Internet and on-line shopping would affect the menu costs from inflation?

9. Discuss this quote: "Most businesses are debtors. They will therefore benefit from inflation."

10. Many people find owning their home an attractive investment during times of inflation. Interest payments for the house can be deducted from income before calculating income taxes. When a house is sold at a price that has risen through inflation, most of the profit from owning it is free of tax. Why does an increase in inflation increase the attractiveness of owning a house? Why do people often buy larger houses during periods of high inflation than they normally would?

11. **Web Exercise.** In the 1990s, the U.S. Treasury introduced bonds that were indexed to inflation. Go to the Web site for the Bureau of the Public Debt (*http://www.publicdebt.treas.gov/sec/seciis.htm*) and read about these bonds. Search the Web (or other sources) and compare the interest rates on 30-year Treasury bonds that are indexed for inflation with those that are not. What factors can explain the difference in interest rates?

12. **Web Exercise.** Since teenagers and younger workers tend to have higher unemployment rates than older workers, some economists have argued that changes in the age composition of the labor force can partly explain shifts in the natural rate. Using the Web site for the Bureau of Labor Statistics (*http://stats.bls.gov*), find information on the age composition of the labor force today and compare it to ten years ago.

Take It to the Net

We invite you to visit the O'Sullivan/Sheffrin page on the Prentice Hall Web site at:
http://www.prenhall.com/osullivan/
for additional World Wide Web exercises for this chapter.

Model Answers to Questions

Chapter-Opening Questions

1. Countries with lower rates of money growth will have lower inflation rates than countries with higher money growth. Nominal interest rates (which reflect inflation) will also be lower.

2. In the long run, actual unemployment returns to the natural rate of unemployment, and inflation is largely determined by money growth. Therefore, lower unemployment will lead to higher inflation, but actual unemployment will return to the natural rate of unemployment.

3. It is prudent to have conservative heads of central banks because the private sector will then be less tempted to aggressively raise wages and prices.

4. Budget deficits must be financed by either issuing debt or creating money. When deficits are very large, it is difficult to issue debt, so money is created, causing massive inflation.

5. Inflation imposes real costs on the economy, which is why societies sometimes cause recessions to reduce inflation. However, there are costs to unemployment as well, and these costs need to be balanced against the costs of inflation.

Test Your Understanding

1. True. To find the expected real interest rate, subtract the expected inflation rate from the nominal rate of interest.

2. This is an application of the reality principle. If prices rise, people will want to hold more money to make transactions.

3. When inflation is higher than expected, actual unemployment will be below the natural rate of unemployment.

4. A sustained boom will tend to lower the natural rate of unemployment.

5. Nominal.

6. Use the growth version of the quantity equation: 6 − 1 = inflation + 0. Inflation is thus 5% per year.

Using the Tools

1. Economic Experiment: Money Illusion

   a. As you discuss this in class, first recognize that with 10% inflation, the $100 dollars that Erin paid for the clock was the same as the $121 Betsy paid for the clock two years later. Since Betsy then sold her clock for more than Erin, she made the best deal on the transaction in real terms.

   b. While Pete sold his comic book for $21 and Bob sold his for $20, Pete sold his a year later. With 6% inflation, Bob made the better deal in real terms.

2. Short-Term Versus Long-Term Interest Rates. Short-term interest rates rose because of the increase in the real rate of interest. Because it took a while before inflation fell, expectations of inflation in the near term did not change. However, the

market did expect inflation to fall over the long term. This drop in long-term expected inflation meant that nominal interest rates did not have to rise with tighter money. Indeed, they fell as market participants foresaw lower inflation.

3. Tax Indexation
   a. The family pays $5,000 in taxes ($3,000 on the first $30,000 plus $2,000 on the next $10,000).
   b. Now the family pays $13,000 in taxes ($3,000 on the first $30,000 plus $10,000 on the next $50,000).
   c. In the first case, the family pays 12.5% of its income in taxes. In the second case, the family pays 16.3%, although their real income before taxes was the same in both cases. To prevent inflation from leading to higher tax burdens, the level at which the higher rate takes effect should be adjusted, or indexed, for the price level. If the level of income at which the 20% rate took effect was raised to $60,000, then the family will pay $10,000 in taxes or 12.5% of their income.

4. Public Pronouncements and Fed Officials. The financial markets reacted negatively to Blinder's comments because they perceived that it signaled he was soft on inflation. A conservative central banker will typically not even mention that lower unemployment could increase inflation because that might leave the impression that they might not be aggressive in fighting inflation.

CHAPTER 31

Current Issues in Macroeconomic Policy

Your elderly uncle draws you aside at a family gathering. "So, I hear you're studying economics," he says. "You know, this country has been going downhill ever since President Roosevelt started deficit spending. We're governed by incompetents. Inflation nearly wiped me out in the 1970s. But that recession in the 1980s really did me in. All these politicians—they just want to get reelected. They have totally abandoned good policies. And the taxes I pay are eating me alive. Do they teach you that in college these days?"

You start to respond, but you are saved by the bell—the dinner bell.

Should We Balance the Federal Budget?
Some Background
The Debates

Should the Federal Reserve Aim for Zero Inflation?
Some Background
The Debates

Should Tax Policy Be Designed Solely for Growth?
Some Background
The Debates

Using the Tools

As a student and citizen you are inevitably drawn into economic debates. Sometimes, debates revolve around simple factual issues. For example, when was the last time inflation was below 3%? But in most cases, the debates are complex. They are a mixture of facts, theories, and opinions. Value judgements play a large role in economic debates. Your views on the proper role of tax policy, for example, will depend on whether you believe that low income earners should receive a higher share of national income. And your views on the size of government will depend on whether you believe that individuals or the government should play a larger role in economic affairs.

In previous chapters, you learned the basic vocabulary of economics and studied different theories of the economy. Now we can address some of the key policy issues in macroeconomics. We will focus on three issues in macroeconomics, which are at the center of many other related economic debates. After reading this chapter, you should have an informed opinion on these three issues:

1. **Should the government balance its budget?**
2. **Should the Federal Reserve aim for zero inflation?**
3. **Should fiscal policies be designed solely to promote economic growth?**

Unlike the chapter opening questions in other chapters, there are no simple answers to these questions. But these questions do trigger fundamental economic debates.

Should We Balance the Federal Budget?

Some Background

Deficit: The excess of total expenditures over total revenues.

Surplus: The excess of total revenues over total expenditures.

Government expenditure: Spending on goods and services plus transfer payments.

Government debt: The total of all past deficits.

Before we begin to consider the answers to that question, let's define some terms: Governments run a **deficit** when they spend more than they currently receive in revenues from either taxes or fees. A **surplus** occurs when revenues exceed spending. Governments run a balanced budget when revenues equal spending—purchases of goods and services or transfer payments. Recall that purchases of goods and services are included in GDP, but transfer payments—such as Social Security, welfare payments, and interest on the federal debt—are not included in GDP. To measure total spending by the government, we must include transfer payments and spending on goods and services. We use **government expenditure** to include transfer payments and purchases of goods and services. The **government debt** is the total of all its deficits. For example, if a government initially had a debt of $100 billion and then ran deficits of $20 billion next year, $30 billion the year after that, and $50 billion during the third year, the government's total debt at the end of the third year would be $200 billion (the initial $100 debt plus the successive yearly deficits of $20 + $30 + $50 = $200, all numbers in billions). If a government ran a surplus, it would decrease its total debt. For example, suppose the debt were $100 billion and the government ran a surplus of $10 billion. With the surplus of $10 billion, the government would buy back $10 billion of debt from the private sector, thereby reducing the remaining debt to $90 billion.

The fiscal picture for the federal government has changed a lot during the last several years. Beginning in the 1980s and through most of the 1990s, the federal budget ran large deficits—"deficits as far as the eye can see," according to David Stockman, the director of the Office of Management and Budget in President Reagan's administration. Stockman's eyes, however, did not accurately see developments in the late 1990s. In fiscal year 1998 (which began on October 1, 1997, and ended September 30, 1998), the federal government ran a surplus of $69 billion, the first time there had been a surplus in 30 years. Table 31.1 contains the forecasts for the budget surplus by the Congressional Budget Office (CBO) for

Table 31.1 Forecasts for the Budget Surplus, 1999–2009

Year	1999	2000	2001	2002	2003	2004	2005	2006	2007	2008	2009
Billions of dollars	120	161	193	246	247	266	286	334	364	385	413
Percent of GDP	1.4	1.7	2.0	2.5	2.4	2.4	2.5	2.8	2.9	3.0	3.1

Source: The Economic and Budget Outlook: An Update, July 1, 1999 (Washington DC: Congressional Budget Office).

fiscal years 1999 through 2009 in terms of dollars and as a percentage of GDP. As you can see, the budget surplus is predicted to grow to 3.1% of GDP by 2009.

The federal government surpluses will reduce the outstanding stock of government debt held by the public. Since GDP will be growing over this period, the stock of debt relative to GDP, which is the standard way to measure the effects of debt in an economy, will also decline. According to the CBO projections, the ratio of debt to GDP will fall to below 7% by the year 2009. This is very low by historical standards. Figure 31.1 depicts the debt to GDP ratio from 1791 to 1998. As you can see, except for the period in the 1980s, the ratio rises sharply during wars and falls during peacetime. By historical standards, we will have a relatively low debt to GDP ratio for the next decade.

In preparing these forecasts, the analysts at the CBO must make a number of assumptions. They first need to forecast economic growth; to do that, they assume that real GDP growth proceeds smoothly, without a recession. They also need to make assumptions, projecting what will be government spending over a future number of years. These projections assume that the Congress and the President adhere to strict limits on spending increases for items that are directly under their control. If the economy experiences a recession and the politicians do not control spending, the surpluses may never materialize.

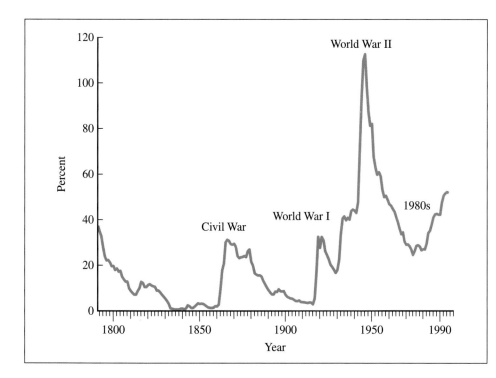

Figure 31.1

Federal Debt as a Percent of GDP, 1791–1998

Sources: Economic Report of the President (Washington, DC: U.S. Government Printing Office, yearly); *Historical Statistics of the United States* (Westport, CT: Greenwood Press, 1993); Thomas Senior Berry, *Estimated Annual Variations in Gross Domestic Product 1789–1909* (Richmond, VA: Bostwick Press, 1968).

These figures also include revenues and expenditures of the Social Security system. Over this period, the Social Security system is expected to run a surplus: Taxes on Social Security exceed spending. Some economists have argued that Social Security should not be included in these calculations because the taxes will ultimately be necessary to pay Social Security recipients.

However, even without including the surplus in Social Security the government budget still shows a surplus—although a smaller one—from 1999 to 2009. Over a longer horizon, there are pressures that lead to forecasts of higher deficits. As our society grows older, expenditures on the elderly for both Social Security and medical care will increase. It's those increasing expenditures that are causing the CBO to predict emerging deficits and increases in the debt-to-GDP ratio to over 50% by 2050 and to 129% by 2060. These long-term estimates are highly speculative, but they do indicate that deficit concerns will not disappear, despite the rosy short-term projections.

What options do we have in the face of the projected near-term surpluses? There are three basic options, among others that fall somewhere between the basic options:

1. Do nothing and let the budget surplus reduce our national debt automatically.
2. Eliminate the budget surplus by increasing government spending on needed programs.
3. Eliminate the budget surplus by cutting federal taxes for individuals and corporations.

Should we reduce our national debt or use the surplus to increase spending or cut taxes? Let's take a look at the debates over the national debt.

The Debates

1. Do Deficits Lead to Inflation?

If a government runs a deficit, it is spending more money than it is taking in, and the gap must be covered in some way. If a government is spending $2,000 but is collecting only $1,600 in taxes, where can it get the $400 needed to fill the gap? One option would be to borrow the $400 from the public in return for government bonds (in effect IOUs). In the future, the government would have to pay back the $400 plus any interest on the bonds. Another way to cover the gap is simply to print $400 worth of new money.

In principle, governments could use a mix of borrowing money and printing money, as long as the total covers its deficits:

government deficit = new borrowing from the public + new money created

In the United States, the Treasury Department always issues government bonds to finance the deficit. The Federal Reserve, however, has the option of buying existing government debt (including the new issues). If the Federal Reserve does purchase the government's bonds, it takes the government debt out of the hands of the public and creates money through its purchase. Economists call the purchase by a central bank of newly created government debt **monetizing the deficit**. If governments finance deficits by creating new money, the result will be inflation. In the United States, we finance only a very small portion of our deficits by creating money. For example, between 1992 and 1993, the Federal Reserve purchased only $15 billion of a government deficit of approximately $270 billion for that period. The remainder of the debt was financed by issuing new government bonds to the public.

Monetizing the deficit: Purchases by a central bank of newly issued government bonds.

If a country has no options other than creating money to finance its deficits, those deficits will inevitably cause inflation. As we discussed in Chapter 30, hyperinflations occur when economies run large deficits and monetize them. Germany and Russia after World War I, Bolivia and Argentina in the 1980s, and the Ukraine in the 1990s are just some of the countries that have had massive inflations through monetizing their deficits. However, large, stable countries that can borrow from the public, such as the United Kingdom, the United States, and Japan, do not have to monetize their deficits. For these countries, deficits do not have to lead inevitably to inflation.

2. Is Government Debt a Burden on Future Generations?

The national debt (another commonly used term for total government debt) can pose two different burdens for society, both of which fall on future generations. First, a large debt can reduce the amount of capital in the economy and thereby reduce future incomes and real wages. Second, a large national debt will mean that future generations will have to pay higher taxes to finance the interest on the debt.

An economy increases its capital stock through the savings of individuals and institutions. These savings flow into capital formation. For example, savers who purchase new stock issued by a company provide the funds that allow the company to invest in plants and equipment. Savers hold the shares of stock as assets.

When governments run deficits and increase their national debt, they finance their deficits by selling bonds to the public. These bonds must be bought by the same individuals and the same institutions that are saving in the economy. This means that the savers will be saving both by buying stock in companies and by buying government bonds. Savers will hold both shares of stock and government bonds as assets, let's say, for their retirement. Further, let's say that all savers' total level of savings in the economy is given, that is, desired savings are $1,000. Now the government needs to finance a $200 deficit, so it sells $200 in new bonds. That means that only $800 is available for savings in new shares. The $200 in government bonds to finance the deficit crowds out $200 in new shares.

The result of government deficits is that less savings are available to firms for investment. As we discussed in earlier chapters, reduced saving will ultimately reduce the stock of private capital, such as new factories and equipment, in society. There will be less capital deepening. With lower capital per worker, real incomes and real wages will be lower.

The second burden of the national debt on future generations is the additional taxes they must pay toward servicing the debt; that is, future generations will be paying interest on the national debt. These interest payments arise because we borrowed in the past and ran up a large debt. Just like your college loans, the bill eventually comes due—even for the national debt.

Some economists say that these interest payments are not a real burden because we owe the national debt to ourselves. Let's first imagine a circumstance in which this would really be true. Today, the national debt is just over $14,000 per person in the United States. Suppose we all owned this debt equally, that is, all taxpayers actually had in their possession $14,000 in government bonds. In this case, the taxes we pay to service the debt would come right back to us as interest payments. It would go out of one pocket into the other and not pose any burden.

In reality, we do not equally share in owning the national debt. Some of it is held by foreigners. A high proportion of it is held by older, wealthy individuals or institutions, which at one point loaned money to the government and now want to be paid back. All working people must pay taxes to service the debt, but they do not earn all the interest. This is a price we pay for running deficits in the past.

Moreover, even if we shared equally in owning the national debt, it would still pose a burden if we held the debt at the expense of holding capital. Here's what we mean by that burden: From an individual point of view, a saver earns a return from holding either government bonds or private capital. But from a social point of view, if society holds bonds rather than capital, the stock of capital available for use in production will be smaller and our living standards will be reduced correspondingly.

Ricardian equivalence: The proposition that it does not matter whether government expenditure is financed by taxes or debt.

Some economists do not believe that government deficits, resulting in government debt, impose a burden on a society. These economists believe in **Ricardian equivalence**, the proposition that it does not matter whether government expenditure is financed by taxes or financed by issuing debt. To understand the case for Ricardian equivalence, consider this example. A government initially has a balanced budget. It then cuts taxes and issues new debt to finance the deficit left by the reduction in taxes. Everyone understands that the government will have to raise taxes in the future to service the debt, so everyone increases his and her savings to pay for the taxes that will be increased in the future. If saving rises sufficiently, the public—everyone—would be able to purchase the new debt without reducing funds for investment. Since investment does not decline, there will be no burden of the debt.

As you can see, Ricardian equivalence requires that savings by the private sector increase when the deficit increases. Do savers behave this way? It is actually difficult to provide a definite answer because many other factors must be taken into account in any empirical study of saving. However, it appears that during the early 1980s, savings decreased somewhat when government deficits increased. This is precisely opposite to what Ricardian equivalence predicts. Nonetheless, the evidence on this topic is mixed, and it is an area of active research today.

Generational accounting: Methods that assign the tax burden of debt and other programs to different generations.

A recent, alternative approach to analyzing deficits, highlights the role of transfers between generations as "A Closer Look: Generational Accounting," explains.

A CLOSER LOOK | Generational Accounting

An increased government debt means that future generations must pay higher interest payments to service the increased debt. But interest is not the only financial burden that governments can impose on future generations. Consider an example. Suppose the government invents a new program that promises everyone over the age of 65 a retirement pension (largely free of tax) and subsidized medical care. These benefits are to be paid through payroll taxes on workers. It does not show up as an official government deficit, but it's not hard to see that this program would pose a burden on future generations who must pay for it.

This is precisely the situation we face today. Social Security and Medicare, programs that promise retirement and health benefits to retirees in the United States, are financed through payroll taxes on current workers, not the past contributions of the retirees.

Laurence Kotlikoff, an economist at Boston University, has developed a new way to measure the full burden on future generations from all government programs, not just government deficits. His approach, called **generational accounting**, provides estimates of the burdens on future generations from all the past actions taken by the government. His study indicates bad news for future generations: In the era since World War II, we have promised large benefits for future retirees that will have to be paid by future generations. According to one of Kotlikoff's estimates, male workers born today would have to hand over nearly 80% of their income to pay for all these benefits! If future workers resist this high rate of taxation, the benefits must decline.

If the government raised the retirement age or cut back on promises of future medical care, this would reduce the burden on future generations of workers without showing up in the official deficit statistics. Kotlikoff's main point is that we should not become obsessed by one single number called the deficit. Other government programs can have profound effects on the burden on future generations.

Kotlikoff's numbers have been criticized because they rely on a number of special assumptions. For example, he assumes that spending programs will not be changed in the future and that the entire burden of financing these programs will fall on the newly born. Neither of these outcomes will necessarily occur. Nonetheless, Kotlikoff provides a valuable warning about our current trends in spending and the potential burden that may fall on future generations.

3. Do Politicians Use Deficits to Increase the Size of Government?

Nobel laureate James Buchanan has argued that because people are less aware of deficits than they are aware of taxes, financing government expenditure through deficits, rather than through taxes, will inevitably lead to higher government spending. While this argument may seem plausible, it faces two difficulties. First, throughout recent U.S. history, spending by state and local governments grew much faster than federal spending. State and local governments face many more restrictions in borrowing than the federal government faces when it borrows. Second, why would the federal government start running surpluses, as we did in the late 1990s, if deficits were so favored by the politicians?

4. Can Deficits Be Good for an Economy?

At times, deficits can be good for a country. They can provide cushion for the economy during economic downturns by stimulating private-sector spending in bad times. Governments may also deliberately create deficits to pull the economy out of a recession.

We encountered both of these ideas in Chapter 25, on Keynesian economics. The increase in the deficit during economic downturns shows the automatic stabilizers of the economy in action, putting additional income into the hands of the public during bad economic times. This additional income allows people to avoid drastic cuts in their consumption spending. Because total spending does not fall as much, the severity of recessions is decreased.

How do automatic stabilizers work? As incomes fall during a recession, so do tax payments. Moreover, transfer payments such as welfare and food stamps rise. Because government spending increases while tax revenues fall, the deficit must rise. Figure 31.2 plots the deficit as a percent of GDP and the unemployment rate for the period 1970 to 1998. Because increases in the unemployment rate signal bad economic times, we expect the deficit to rise and fall along with the unemployment rate. This is precisely what Figure 31.2 shows.

The deficit can also change if the government tries to stabilize the economy through fiscal policy. For example, if a government engages in expansionary fiscal pol-

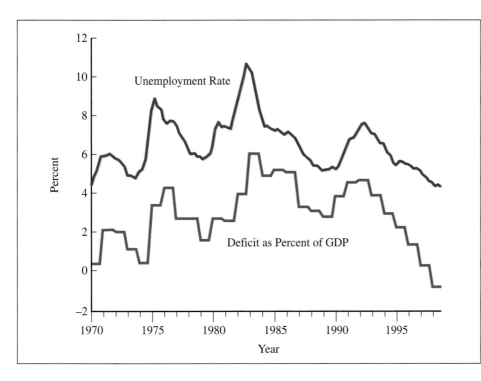

Figure 31.2

U.S. Deficit and Unemployment Rate, 1970–1998

Source: Data from U.S. Department of Commerce and *Economic Report of the President* (Washington, DC: U.S. Government Printing Office, yearly).

icy, by cutting taxes or increasing spending to pull the economy out of a recession, the result will be to increase the deficit. However, during a recession, this may be the appropriate means to steer the economy back to full employment.

The existence of automatic stabilizers and the use of expansionary fiscal policy during recessions suggest that we should not worry about short-run government deficits. Over short time periods, deficits can help the economy to cope with shocks, such as oil price increases or a collapse in the stock market, that may hit the economy. They give the government some room to maneuver out of a recession. Most economists believe that automatic stabilizers have reduced economic fluctuations during the twentieth century.

Professor Robert Barro of Harvard University has also pointed out that deficits can play a role in tax smoothing. Suppose that there is a large, temporary increase in government spending, such as might occur during a war. The government could either finance the war by running a deficit and issuing debt or raise taxes to keep the budget in balance. Barro has argued that it is more efficient to keep tax rates relatively constant than to raise them sharply and then lower them later. Temporarily raising tax rates to very high levels, could cause distortions in economic behavior that we would like to avoid. Thus, by running deficits and only gradually raising taxes later to service the debt, we avoid creating excess distortions in the economy.

5. How Would a Balanced Budget Amendment Really Work?

For many years, there were strong efforts to enact a constitutional amendment to balance the federal budget. The current budget surpluses have dampened (at least for now) interest in this constitutional reform. In early 1995, Congress came very close to passing a balanced budget amendment, sending it back to the states for ratification. It passed in the House of Representatives but failed by a single vote in the Senate. How would a balanced budget amendment actually work?

Many different budgetary constitutional amendments have been proposed. They all require that after a phase-in period, Congress propose in each fiscal year a budget in which total revenues (excluding borrowing) cover total expenditures. The amendments also have various escape clauses—for example, to allow borrowing during wartime. Some amendments also allow Congress to suspend the requirement to propose a balanced budget for other reasons, such as during a recession when deficits naturally emerge. Finally, some versions of the amendment would limit the rate of spending increases to the growth rate of GDP.

Proponents of the balanced budget amendment say that it will finally exert discipline on the federal government, preventing large deficits in peacetime, such as occurred in the 1980s. We can thus avoid the adverse effects of deficits: reduced capital formation and a shift in the burden of taxation to future generations.

Critics of a balanced budget amendment point to many different problems, such as the following:

- There may not be enough flexibility to deal with recessions. Under some versions of the amendment, unless three-fifths of Congress votes to suspend requirements, the government would have to cut expenditures or raise taxes during a recession. This would make the recession worse and limit the ability of the government to use fiscal policy to stabilize the economy.

- The Constitution is not the right mechanism to try to enforce complicated budget rules. As various interested parties challenge the actions of Congress, the courts would become heavily involved in federal budget matters.

- Congress could devise special budgets to get around the requirement, for example, by taking some types of spending "off budget," which means simply not counting it as part of the official budget.

- Congress could also find nonbudgetary ways to carry out the policies that it desires. For example, it could issue more regulations or impose mandates or requirements on business or other governments to carry out its will.

TEST Your Understanding

1. If a government runs a surplus, will it increase or decrease the outstanding stock of debt?

2. Proponents of Ricardian equivalence are primarily concerned about deficits crowding out the stock of capital. True or false? Explain.

3. Explain how deficits can lead to inflation.

Should the Federal Reserve Aim for Zero Inflation?

Some Background

In Chapter 30, we examined some of the costs of inflation, including the following:

- Menu costs, the costs firms had to incur to change posted prices

- Shoe-leather costs, the costs individuals and firms must pay as they try to find ways to economize on holding money

- Distortions in our tax system and financial system from not adjusting our accounts for inflation

- Arbitrary redistributions between debtors and creditors from unanticipated inflation

By the late 1990s, the rate of inflation had fallen to roughly between 2% and 3%. This suggested to some economists that the time was right to avoid all the costs of inflation and bring the inflation rate down to zero and keep it there. A zero inflation rate would mean complete price stability. To achieve zero inflation, the Fed would have to take two actions: First, it would have to use monetary policy to bring the inflation rate to zero from a positive level. Second, it would need to commit to a policy of keeping inflation at zero and not have any other goals.

The Debates

1. How Costly Is It to Reduce Inflation?

You saw in Chapter 30 that to reduce inflation usually requires actual unemployment to rise above the natural rate of unemployment. That means reducing inflation will have a temporary cost in terms of higher unemployment. How large is this cost?

In the United States, economists who study this problem have developed a rough rule of thumb: When actual unemployment exceeds the natural rate of unemployment by 1 percentage point for one year, the inflation rate falls by 0.5 percentage points per year. The following example illustrates this simple rule of thumb. The natural rate of unemployment is 5% of the labor force and the inflation rate is 3% per year. To bring the inflation rate down to zero would require that the unemployment rate exceed the natural rate by 6 percentage points. If this is spread over a three-year period, the unemployment rate for those three years would have to be 7%. Those numbers mean that we would need to create a mild recession to bring the inflation rate down to zero.

Some economists would argue that unemployment would not have to increase as much if the Federal Reserve was credible in its commitment to reducing inflation. As we discussed in Chapter 30, if workers can adjust their expectations (and the contracts that they made in the past based on their expectations), it might be possible to reduce inflation with a smaller increase in unemployment. However, on the basis of past U.S. experience, our rule of thumb works reasonably well.

One complicating factor in measuring the costs of reducing inflation is that the burden of increased unemployment would not be evenly spread across the economy. The increased unemployment will be concentrated among a small fraction of the labor force, who will experience true hardship. In many cases, these workers will be young, unskilled, and from minority populations that already experience high unemployment rates.

The costs of this unemployment need to be measured against the permanent gains from reducing the inflation rate. There is not a consensus, however, on the actual benefits of reduced inflation. For example, there are no precise measures of the increased menu costs that arise at higher inflation rates.

Some economists argue that with zero inflation, the economy will be less able to adjust to adverse aggregate demand shocks, because workers do not want to see their wages cut in absolute terms. For example, if investment spending suddenly falls, the adjustment process requires that nominal wages fall as well to restore the economy to full employment. When there is ongoing inflation, there is no need for wages literally to fall; all wages need to do is to increase less rapidly than the ongoing inflation rate. But with zero inflation, wages actually have to fall. If workers resist this fall in wages, the adjustment mechanism that restores the economy back to full employment may not function efficiently. If we take this argument seriously, we should never try to reduce inflation below 2% to 3% to have sufficient wage flexibility.

Even if we were determined to commit to price stability, there are legitimate questions about what the term *stable prices* really means. As we have discussed, it is very difficult to measure changes in prices accurately when there is significant technological change in the economy. If, as many economists believe, our price indexes overstate the true inflation rate, 2% annual inflation may in reality be true price stability. If so, it would seem particularly foolish to engineer a recession to bring inflation to zero.

2. Should Monetary Policy Target Only Inflation?

Suppose we do reduce the inflation rate to zero. Should monetary policy then focus exclusively on maintaining price stability?

Some economists argue quite strongly that the Fed should have only one goal: price stability. We have learned that in the long run, monetary policy can influence only the level of prices, not the level of employment. Having the Fed worry about other factors—unemployment or the exchange rate—will distract the Fed from its mission. Preoccupation with other goals can easily lead the Fed astray and lead to long-run inflationary pressures building in the economy.

Moreover, if the Fed were committed to the single goal of price stability, it would have enhanced credibility. As we have seen, if the Fed is credible, the private sector will become more responsive to changes in economic policy. Credible policies decrease the need for active monetary policies.

Having a single goal would also help to keep the Fed free from political pressures. Such political pressures might include attempts to stimulate the economy to favor the reelection prospects of incumbents or to give a temporary boost to financial markets.

However, other economists would strongly object to having the Fed concentrate solely on price stability. In the United States, the President and the Congress have not used active fiscal policy as a stabilization tool for decades. While there are automatic fiscal stabilizers, they are often not sufficient to cushion the economy in the face of shocks. In practice, only monetary policy is available as a tool to stabilize output and prevent deep recessions from emerging. If monetary policy is geared solely to price stability and fiscal policy is not used, how can we stabilize the economy? Critics of stabilization policy, of course, believe that not using monetary policy to try to stabilize the economy would actually improve our economic performance. In their view, attempts to stabilize the economy have done more harm than good over the years. In previous chapters, we discussed the difficulties in conducting stabilization policy. These include lags, uncertainties about the strength and timing of policies, and difficulties in estimating the natural rate of unemployment. Whether or not you believe that these difficulties are insurmountable will affect your beliefs about the desirability of using monetary policy to stabilize output and not just maintain price stability.

One recent view is that the Fed should not deliberately set out to bring inflation to zero but should take advantage of favorable shocks. In 1996, a new phrase about monetary policy hit the financial pages: *opportunistic disinflation*. Several economists at the Federal Reserve put forth the idea that the Fed should not deliberately create excess unemployment to reduce inflation. Rather, it should wait for favorable opportunities, such as favorable supply shocks or unforeseen recessions, and use its monetary tools to ensure that these outcomes lead to permanently lower inflation. If the Fed followed this policy for a long period, it would eventually reduce inflation.

Although this seems like a sensible policy, its mere appearance in the newspapers worried some inflation hawks in the financial markets. They wondered whether this policy would mean that the Fed would no longer be as committed to fighting inflation as in the past. If not, the Fed could lose much of the credibility it had gained in recent years, which would make its job even more difficult in the future. To reassure financial markets, officials at the Fed noted that this was just a study, and their views on fighting inflation had not changed.

TEST Your Understanding

4. Why are the costs of reducing inflation temporary but the benefits permanent?

5. Explain why zero inflation implies stable prices.

6. Give two arguments in favor of the Fed solely targeting price stability.

Should Tax Policy Be Designed Solely for Growth?

Some Background

As we discussed in earlier chapters, the United States is a country with a low savings rate. This hurts our long-run growth prospects because our investment spending is limited by our own savings and savings from abroad that arise through current account deficits. Many factors—not purely economic—contribute to our low saving rate. For example, colleges will reduce the financial aid for students whose families have saved for college, thereby reducing the incentive of families to save for themselves. Many of our welfare programs also provide disincentives for individuals to save, as they reduce benefits for families that have saved in the past. The U.S. tax system also discourages savings.

In the United States, we tax income as people earn it and also tax the returns from any savings as those returns are earned. Suppose that you earn $100 and face a tax rate of 20%; you keep $80 after taxes. Now suppose that you save $50 and invest it at a 10% rate for a year. At the end of the year, you will earn an additional $5 (10% × $50) but will get to keep only $4 because the government will take $1 in taxes (20% × $5). You will have paid the government $21 in total: $20 on the $100 you earned plus $1 on your $50 savings. If you did not save at all, you would pay only $20 in taxes, not $21.

Not all tax systems work this way. Tax systems that are based on consumption do not penalize individuals who save. Sales taxes in the U.S. and value-added taxes abroad are familiar examples of **consumption taxes**. It is also possible to create a consumption tax from an income tax by exempting the returns from savings from taxes, just as we do with tax-exempt bonds issued by state and municipal governments. The key feature of consumption taxation is that you do not face any additional taxes if you decide to save more of your income.

In the United States, there are some other methods to save that have reduced taxes on savings. In addition to tax-exempt bonds, they include IRAs (individual retirement accounts) as well as other saving vehicles, such as 401K, 403B, and Keogh plans. However, all of these plans come with restrictions and limitations on their use.

Consumption taxes: Taxes which are based on the consumption, not the income, of individuals.

The Debates

Proponents claim that taxes based on consumption will increase total savings and be more equitable. Let's explore these claims.

1. Will Consumption Taxes Lead to More Savings?

There is no question that consumption taxes provide more incentives to save because the return from savings increases. However, there is no guarantee that these extra incentives will produce more savings. As we discussed with respect to taxes and supply of labor, taxes have both *substitution* effects and an *income* effect. Reducing the tax rate on savings provides direct incentives for increased savings, through the substitution effect. On the other hand, with lower tax rates on savings, individuals have more wealth, and the income effect will lead them to consume more, which means that they save less. Whether savings increase or decrease when tax rates are cut, ultimately must be settled by careful research.

Although there has been much research on the effects of taxation on saving, it is far from conclusive. It is true that individuals will allocate their savings to tax-favored investments over investments that are not favored. For example, individuals will put their funds into IRAs. What is not clear is whether the funds that flow into IRAs are literally new savings—meaning reduced consumption—or merely transfers from other accounts, such as conventional savings accounts, which do not have the same tax advantages. Disentangling these effects is a difficult issue, and it remains an active area of ongoing research.

The corporate tax system also creates other disincentives for savings and investment. Suppose you purchase a share of stock in a corporation. When the corporation earns a profit, it pays taxes at the corporate tax rate. When the corporation pays you a dividend for holding the stock, you must pay taxes on the dividend income that you receive. Corporate income is taxed twice: once when it is earned and again when it is paid out. Some economists have argued that the corporation tax leads to less efficient investment because it forces capital into other sectors of the economy, such as real estate, that do not suffer from this double-taxation.

2. Are Consumption Taxes Fair?

The basic idea behind a consumption tax seems fair. Individuals should be taxed on what they take from the economy's total production—that is, what they consume—not on

Should taxes be based on consumption?

what they actually produce. If an individual produces a lot but does not consume the proceeds from what he or she produced, and instead plows it back into the economy for investment, that individual is contributing to the growth of total output and should be rewarded, not punished. Individual A earns $50 and consumes it all; individual B earns $100 but consumes only $40. Who should pay more?

In practice, moving to a consumption tax system, for example by exempting the return from savings from the income tax, would have a major impact on the distribution of income in the economy. It is the wealthy and high-income individuals who save the most and earn income through interest, dividend, rents, and capital gains. Table 31.2 provides some data from the Congressional Budget Office over a 10-year period to illustrate this point for one type of income: capital gains, the profits earned from the sale of stocks, bonds, real estate or other assets. As you can see from Table 31.2, taxpayers with annual income exceeding $200,000 earned over half of the capital gains over this period. Capital assets are highly concentrated among the wealthy in the economy.

If capital gains and other types of capital income were not included for calculating taxes, total tax revenue would fall, and the government would have to raise tax rates—on everyone—to maintain the same level of spending. Excluding capital income from taxation does have its costs.

Another complication is inherited wealth. Suppose someone inherits $100 million dollars from his or her parents, invests it at 5% per year, and lives comfortably on $5 million a year. Should that individual be exempt from tax on the inheritance income?

Table 31.2 Share of Capital Gains by Income

Income Class	Share of Capital Gains
$10,000–20,000	2.6%
$20,000–30,000	2.9%
$30,000–40,000	4.4%
$40,000–50,000	3.4%
$50,000–75,000	9.0%
$75,000–100,000	8.5%
$100,000–200,000	15.7%
$200,000 and over	56.8%

Source: Congressional Budget Office, *Perspective on the Ownership of Capital Assets and the Realization of Capital Gains*, May 1997. (Based on a 10-year average. Excludes category reporting negative income.)

3. Are There Other Means to Increase Savings?

Even if tax incentives did increase private savings, that is no guarantee that total savings—public savings plus private savings—would increase. Suppose that expanding an existing IRA program cost the taxpayers $5 billion in lost revenue but led to $4 billion in increased private saving. Total savings, public plus private, would fall by $1 billion because of the loss of revenue.

This suggests that we should think more broadly about the sources of saving for the economy. Any policies that reduce the federal deficit or increase the surplus will lead to increases in total savings unless they adversely affect private savings. Cuts in government spending or increases in taxes (that do not hurt private savings) will lead to an increase in total savings for the economy.

TEST Your Understanding

7. Give an example of savings that you can make, completely free of tax.

8. Why would switching to a consumption tax not necessarily increase total savings?

9. Explain why dividends from stock are taxed twice.

Using the **TOOLS**

In this chapter, we explored several policy issues using a variety of different tools. Take this opportunity to do your own economic analysis.

1. Debt and Deficits in Belgium

Here are some data for Belgium in 1989:

GDP	**6160 billion Belgian francs**
Debt	**6500 billion Belgian francs**
Deficit	**380 billion Belgian francs**
Interest rate on bonds	**8.5 percent**

Use these data to answer the following questions:

a. What are the deficit/GDP ratio and debt/GDP ratio? How do these ratios compare to the same ratios in the United States today? To what period in U.S. history does the debt/GDP ratio in Belgium correspond?

b. Approximately how much of the budget in Belgium is devoted to interest payments on the debt? If Belgium could wipe out its debt overnight, what would happen to its current budget deficit?

2. Unemployment and Reducing Inflation to Zero

A country that has a natural rate of 4% unemployment is currently at the natural rate of unemployment. Annual inflation rate is 4%.

a. Using the simple rule of thumb that inflation falls by 0.5% when the unemployment rate exceeds the natural rate by 1 percentage point for the year, describe a path for the unemployment rate that will bring the inflation rate to zero.

b. Suppose the country had a more favorable rule of thumb: Inflation fell by 1 percentage point when the actual unemployment rate exceeded the natural rate of unemployment by 1 percentage point for one year. Describe a path for unemployment that would result in zero inflation in this case.

3. IRAs and Zero Tax Rate

With an IRA, you get to deduct the amount you contribute from your current taxable income, invest the funds free from tax, but then pay taxes on the full amount you withdraw. Suppose your tax rate is 50% and you initially deposit $2000 in an IRA. The proceeds double in seven years to $4000; in seven years when you retire, you pay taxes on the $4000 at your 50% rate.

Show that this is the same outcome if you were free from all taxes (a zero tax rate), invested $1000 for seven years and doubled your initial investment.

Summary

In this chapter, we explored three topics that are the center of macroeconomic policy debates today. Here are the key points to remember:

1. A deficit is the difference between expenditures and revenue. The government debt is the sum of all past deficits.

2. Deficits can be financed through either borrowing or money creation. Money creation leads to inflation.

3. Deficits can be good for the country. Automatic stabilizers and expansionary fiscal policy both work through the creation of deficits.

4. The national debt involves two burdens: The national debt can reduce the amount of capital in an economy, leading to lower levels of income. And the national debt can raise taxes on future generations.

5. Reducing inflation down to zero would require that actual unemployment exceed the natural rate of unemployment for some period.

6. If the Fed's only goal was to maintain price stability, there would be few tools left for active stabilization policy.

7. A consumption tax would increase the incentives for private savings. However, it is not clear that total savings would necessarily increase, and there would be concerns about the fairness of this form of taxation.

Key Terms

consumption taxes, 654
deficit, 644
generational accounting, 648

government debt, 644
government expenditure, 644
monetizing the deficit, 646

Ricardian equivalence, 648
surplus, 644

Problems and Discussion Questions

1. A county has outstanding debt of $10 million. The interest rate on the debt is 10% per year. Expenditures (other than interest payments) are $1 billion, and taxes are $1 billion. What is the debt at the end of next year?

2. In the previous example, suppose that the inflation rate was 5% per year. By how much did the real burden of the debt increase?

3. Why are government deficits more serious in countries with limited abilities to borrow from the private sector?

4. How is a decrease in the age at which workers are eligible for Social Security similar to an increase in the government deficit?

5. In what ways could a balanced budget requirement limit the ability of the government to conduct fiscal policy? Do you think this is a serious loss?

6. In the United States, many states have balanced budget requirements. Is the state experience relevant for the federal government?

7. An economist suggests that what matters for financial markets is a stable inflation rate, not a zero inflation rate. As long as inflation is stable, all individuals can take this into account in their actions. What are the costs associated with a stable 2% inflation rate? Do you believe that it is easier or more difficult to stabilize inflation at 2% rather than at zero?

8. Some economists believe that the Federal Reserve should follow strict rules for the conduct of monetary policy. These rules would require the Fed to make adjustments to interest rates based on information that is fully available to the public, information such as the current unemployment rate and the current inflation rate. What do you see as the pros and cons of such an approach?

9. Suppose the government launches a new program that allows individuals to place funds up to $2000 into a tax-free account. Do you believe that this will have a significant effect on national savings?

10. Evaluate this quote: "Since high-income individuals save more, any tax policies that favor savings will also help the wealthy at the expense of the poor."

11. **Web Exercise.** The Web site for the Congressional Budget Office (*http://www.cbo.gov*) contains their projections for future budget surpluses and deficits as well as options for increasing the surplus. Using this site, find some options that you think are desirable that would have a significant effect on increasing the budget surplus.

12. **Web Exercise.** Have you ever thought that it would be easy to cut government spending or raise taxes to improve the surplus? Now is your chance to find out. Play the National Budget Simulation game hosted on the Web site of the Graduate School of Public Policy at UC Berkeley (*http://garnet.berkeley.edu:3333/budget/budget.html*). What changes can you make to really improve the deficit without disrupting the functions of government?

Take It to the Net

We invite you to visit the O'Sullivan/Sheffrin page on the Prentice Hall Web site at:
http://www.prenhall.com/osullivan/
for additional World Wide Web exercises for this chapter.

Model Answers to Questions

Test Your Understanding

1. Decrease.

2. False. Proponents of Ricardian equivalence do not believe that deficits crowd out capital.

3. Inflation arises when deficits are monetized by the central bank.

4. The increase in unemployment to bring down the inflation rate is the cost, and it is only temporary. However, the temporary increase in unemployment does lead to a permanent reduction in the inflation rate.

5. Because inflation is the rate of change of prices, zero inflation means no change in prices, which means price stability.

6. The Fed can only control inflation in the long run, and it is not effective in stabilizing output.

7. Individual Retirement Accounts.

8. There are both income effects and substitution effects.

9. The income is taxed at the corporate level and then again at the individual level.

Using the Tools

1. Debt and Deficits in Belgium

   a. The deficit/GDP ratio is 6.2%, and the debt/GDP ratio is 106%. The debt/GDP ratio resembles what the debt/GDP ratio was in the United States during World War II.

   b. With a debt of $6,500 and an interest rate of 0.085, interest payments are approximately $6,500 \times 0.085 = \$552$. Because the budget deficit is $380, if the debt disappeared, the budget would have a surplus of $172.

2. Unemployment and Reducing Inflation to Zero

   a. Actual unemployment must rise by 8 percentage points above the natural rate of unemployment. If this occurs over four years, unemployment will be 6% for four years.

   b. In this case, actual unemployment must rise by only four percentage points above the natural rate of unemployment. If this occurs over four years, unemployment will be 5% for four years.

3. IRAs and Zero Tax Rate. With the IRA, you deposit $2,000 and get a reduction of taxes of $1,000, so your initial investment is only $1,000. You withdraw $4,000 from the IRA after seven years, but pay a 50% tax, so your net proceeds are $2,000. This is the identical outcome to investing $1,000 tax-free for seven years and doubling your initial investment.

CHAPTER

32

International Trade and Public Policy

Vilfredo Pareto had been in the mediation business for over 20 years, but he had never confronted a dispute as complex as this one. Seated around the table were three people, each representing one of the interests in the country's apparel industry and each wanting to do something about the country's restrictions on apparel imports. Vilfredo's job was to develop a new trade policy that would make everyone happy. To kick off the session, he let each representative make a brief statement. The consumer representative was first:

"These trade restrictions increase the price of clothing and cost the typical family about $400 per year. If we eliminate the restrictions, the total savings for consumers—that's the savings for the entire nation—would be $400 million per year."

The representative of apparel workers spoke next:

"The elimination of these import restrictions would decrease employment in the apparel industry by 10,000 jobs. What would you do with all the people who lose their jobs?"

Then the representative of the country's high-technology industry spoke:

"Many countries have trade restrictions on computers, semiconductors, and medical equipment in part to retaliate for our country's restrictions on apparel imports. If we eliminated our apparel restrictions, we could export more computers, semiconductors, and medical equipment."

After doing some quick calculations, Vilfredo had a solution:

"The trade restrictions cost consumers $400 million per year and save 10,000 jobs. This means that there is a cost of $40,000 per apparel job saved, which exceeds the average wage of apparel jobs ($30,000). I propose the following plan, which should make everyone happy. First, eliminate the trade restrictions, saving each family about $400 per year. Next, impose a temporary—let's say, two-year—tax of $300 per family, and use the revenue from this tax to pay the salaries of the 10,000 displaced workers for two years. During this two-year period, these workers will enroll in training programs to prepare them for jobs in the high-technology industry."

Benefits from Specialization and Trade
Production Possibilities Curve
Comparative Advantage and the Terms of Trade
The Consumption Possibilities Curve
The Employment Effects of Free Trade

Protectionist Policies
Import Ban
Quotas and Voluntary Export Restraints
Price Effects of Quotas and VERs
Tariffs
Responses to Protectionist Policies

Rationales for Protectionist Policies
To Shield Workers from Foreign Competition
To Nurture Infant Industries
To Help Domestic Firms Establish Monopolies in World Markets

Recent Policy Debates and Trade Agreements
Are Foreign Producers Dumping Their Products?
Do Trade Laws Inhibit Environmental Protection?
Does Trade Cause Inequality?
Recent Trade Agreements

Using the Tools

rom this simple example, you can see that international trade policy is not simple. The United States restricts the imports of many goods, including apparel. Restrictions protect jobs in the domestic industries; restrictions increase domestic consumer prices; and restrictions often lead to retaliatory trade restrictions that harm domestic exporters. One lesson from this chapter is that free trade could, in principle, make everyone better off. The challenge for policymakers is to develop a set of policies that accomplish that goal—or come as close as possible to accomplishing it.

In this chapter, we discuss the rationale for international trade, and we explore the effects of policies that restrict trade. Here are some of the practical questions that we answer:

1. **What are the trade-offs associated with free trade? Who wins? Who loses?**
2. **Why is a tariff (a tax on an imported good) superior to an import quota?**
3. **Why might a firm's export price be less than its domestic price? The domestic price is the price in the domestic market.**
4. **Do trade laws inhibit environmental protection?**
5. **Does trade increase income inequality?**

Benefits from Specialization and Trade

If your nation produced everything it consumed, it would not be dependent on any other nation for its economic livelihood. If you were put in charge of your nation, would you pursue such a policy of national self-sufficiency? Although self-sufficiency may sound appealing, it would be better to specialize in some products and trade some of those products with other nations for products that your nation doesn't produce. You saw in Chapter 3, that specialization and exchange can make both parties better off. In this chapter, we use a simple example to explain the benefits of specialization and international trade between two nations.

Let's say there are two nations, each produces computer chips and shirts, and each nation consumes computer chips and shirts. Table 32.1 shows the daily output of the two goods for the two nations, Shirtland and Chipland. In a single day, Shirtland can produce a maximum of either 108 shirts or 36 computer chips, while Chipland can produce a maximum of either 120 shirts or 120 computer chips. The last two rows of the table show the opportunity costs of the two goods. Recall the principle of opportunity cost:

PRINCIPLE OF OPPORTUNITY COST

The opportunity cost of something is what you sacrifice to get it.

Table 32.1 Output and Opportunity Cost

	Shirtland	Chipland
Shirts produced per day	108	120
Chips produced per day	36	120
Opportunity cost of shirts	1/3 chip	1 chip
Opportunity cost of chips	3 shirts	1 shirt

In Chipland, there is a one-for-one trade-off of shirts and chips: The opportunity cost of one shirt is one chip, and the opportunity cost of one chip is one shirt. In Shirtland, people can produce three times as many shirts as chips in a given amount of time: The opportunity cost of one chip is three shirts; that is, by producing one chip, we sacrifice three shirts; conversely, the opportunity cost of one shirt is one-third of a chip.

Production Possibilities Curve

Let's start by seeing what happens if each nation is self-sufficient. Each nation can use its resources (labor, land, buildings, machinery, equipment) to produce its own shirts and its own chips. The **production possibilities curve** shows all the feasible combinations of the two goods, assuming that the nation's resources are fully employed. This curve, which we discussed in earlier chapters, provides a sort of menu of production options. To keep things simple, we assume that the curve is a straight line, indicating a constant trade-off between the two goods. As shown by Shirtland's production possibilities curve in Figure 32.1, the following combinations of chips and shirts are possible.

Production possibilities curve: A curve showing the combinations of two goods that can be produced by an economy, assuming that all resources are fully employed.

1. **All shirts and no chips: point r.** If Shirtland uses all its resources to produce shirts, it will produce 108 shirts per day.
2. **All chips and no shirts: point t.** If Shirtland uses all its resources to produce chips, it will produce 36 chips per day.
3. **Equal division of resources: point h.** Shirtland could divide its resources between shirts and chips to produce daily 54 shirts and 18 chips.

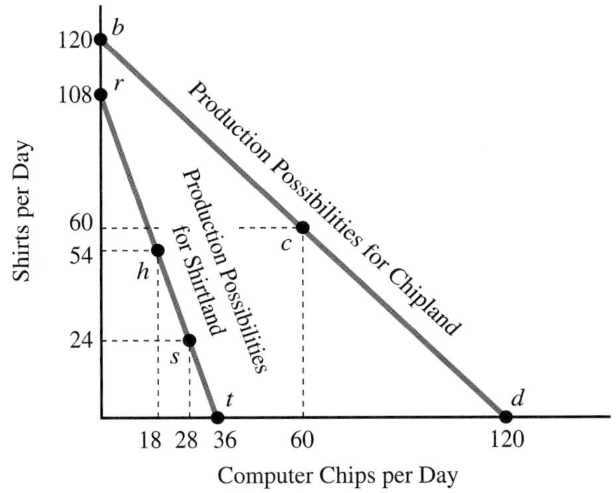

Figure 32.1

Production Possibilities Curve
The production possibilities curve shows the combinations of two goods that can be produced with a nation's resources. For Chipland, there is a one-for-one trade-off between the two goods. For Shirtland, the trade-off is three shirts for every computer chip. In the absence of trade, Shirtland picks point *s* (28 chips and 24 shirts), and Chipland picks point *c* (60 chips and 60 shirts).

Shirtland Possibilites

Point	Shirts	Chips
r	108	0
h	54	18
s	24	28
t	0	36

Chipland Possibilities

Point	Shirts	Chips
b	120	0
c	60	60
d	0	120

All the other points on the line connecting points *r* and *t* are also feasible. One option is point *s*, with 28 chips and 24 shirts. The slope of the curve is the opportunity cost of computer chips: one chip per three shirts. Figure 32.1 also shows the production possibilities curve for Chipland. This nation can produce daily 120 shirts and no chips (point *b*), 120 chips and no shirts (point *d*), or any combination of chips and shirts between these two points. In Chipland, the trade-off is one shirt per computer chip: The opportunity cost of a chip is one shirt, so the slope of the production possibilities curve is 1.0.

Each nation could decide to be self-sufficient in chips and shirts. In other words, each nation could pick a point on its production possibilities curve and produce everything it wants to consume. For example, Shirtland could pick point *s*, producing daily 28 chips and 24 shirts, and Chipland could pick point *c*, producing daily 60 chips and 60 shirts. In the language of international trade, this is a case of **autarky**, or self-sufficiency (in Greek, *aut* means "self" and *arke* means "to suffice").

Comparative Advantage and the Terms of Trade

Would the two nations be better off if each nation specialized in the production of one good and traded with the other nation? To decide which nation should produce a particular good, we need to figure out which nation has a lower opportunity cost for that good. As you saw in Chapter 3, the nation with the lower opportunity cost has a **comparative advantage** in producing that good.

1. Chips produced in Chipland. The opportunity cost of one chip is one shirt in Chipland, and the opportunity cost of one chip is three shirts in Shirtland. Chipland has a comparative advantage in the production of chips. Because Chipland sacrifices fewer shirts to produce one chip, Chipland should produce chips.

2. Shirts produced in Shirtland. The opportunity cost of one shirt is one chip in Chipland, and the opportunity cost of one shirt is 1/3 of a chip in Shirtland. Shirtland has a comparative advantage in the production of shirts. Shirtland sacrifices fewer chips to produce one shirt, so Shirtland should produce shirts.

Trade will make it possible for people in each specialized nation to consume both goods. At what rate will the two nations exchange shirts and chips? To determine the **terms of trade**, let's look at how much Shirtland is willing to pay to get one chip and how much Chipland is willing to accept to give up one chip.

1. To get one chip, Shirtland is willing to pay up to three shirts. That's how many shirts it would sacrifice if it produced its own chip: Shirtland's opportunity cost of one chip is three shirts. For example, if the nations agree to exchange two shirts per chip, Shirtland could rearrange its production, producing one less chip but three more shirts. After exchanging two of the newly produced shirts for one chip, Shirtland will have the same number of chips but one additional shirt.

2. To give up one chip, Chipland is willing to accept any amount greater than one shirt: Chipland's opportunity cost of one chip is one shirt. For example, if the nations agree to exchange two shirts per chip, Chipland could rearrange its production, producing one more chip and one less shirt. After it exchanges the newly produced chip for two shirts, Chipland will have the same number of chips but one additional shirt.

There is an opportunity for mutually beneficial trade because the willingness to pay—three shirts by Shirtland—exceeds the willingness to accept—one shirt by Chipland. It's possible the two countries will split the difference between the willingness to pay and the willingness to accept, exchanging two shirts per chip.

Autarky: A situation in which each country is self-sufficient, so there is no trade.

Comparative advantage: The ability of one nation to produce a particular good at an opportunity cost that is lower than the opportunity cost of another nation in producing the same good.

Terms of trade: The rate at which two goods will be exchanged.

The Consumption Possibilities Curve

A nation that decides to specialize and trade, will not be limited to the options shown by its own production possibilities curve. The **consumption possibilities curve** shows the combinations of two goods (computer chips and shirts in our example) that a nation can consume when it specializes in one good and trades with another nation.

Figure 32.2 shows the consumption possibilities curve for our two nations, assuming that they exchange two shirts per chip.

Consumption possibilities curve: A curve showing the combinations of two goods that can be consumed in a nation when that nation specializes in producing a particular good and trades with another nation.

- In panel A, Chipland will specialize in chips, the good for which it has a comparative advantage, so it produces 120 chips (point *d*). Given the terms of trade, Chipland can exchange 40 chips for 80 shirts, leading to point *x* on the consumption possibilities curve.

- In panel B, Shirtland specializes in shirts (point *r*) and can exchange 80 shirts for 40 chips, leading to point *y* on its consumption possibilities frontier.

How do the outcomes with specialization and trade compare to the autarky outcomes? Chipland moves from point *c* (autarky) to point *x*, so trade increases the consumption of each good by 20 units. Shirtland moves from point *s* to point *y*, so this nation consumes 12 additional chips and 4 additional shirts.

In Figure 32.2, each consumption possibilities curve lies above the nation's production possibilities curves, meaning that each nation has more options about how much to consume under specialization and trade. In most cases, a nation picks a point on the consumption possibilities curve that provides more of each good.

The Employment Effects of Free Trade

You've now seen that trade allows each nation to consume more of each good. But we haven't yet discussed the effects of trade on employment. Under free trade, each nation will begin to specialize in a single good, causing considerable changes in the country's employment in different industries. In Chipland, the chip industry doubles in size—output increases from 60 to 120 chips per day—while the shirt industry disappears.

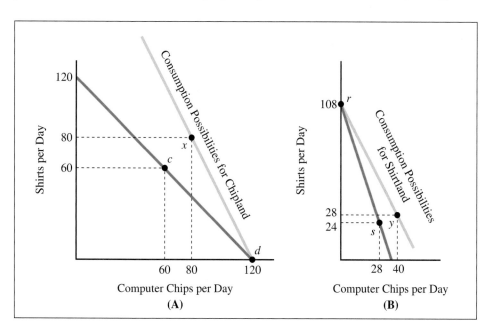

Figure 32.2

Consumption Possibilities Curve

The consumption possibilities curve shows the combinations of computer chips and shirts that can be consumed if each country specializes and trades. In panel A, Chipland produces 120 chips and trades 40 of these chips to Shirtland for 80 shirts. In panel B, Shirtland produces 108 shirts and trades 80 of these shirts to Chipland for 40 chips.

Workers and other resources will leave the shirt industry and move to the chip industry. In Shirtland, the flow is in the opposite direction: Workers and other resources move from the chip industry to the shirt industry.

Is free trade good for everyone? Switching from self-sufficiency to specialization and trade increases consumption in both nations, so on average, people in each nation will benefit from free trade. Some people will be harmed by free trade. In Chipland, people in the shirt industry will lose their jobs when the shirt industry disappears. Some workers can easily move into the expanding computer-chip industry; for these workers, free trade is likely to be beneficial. Other shirt workers will be unable to make the move to the chip industry; they will be forced to accept lower-paying jobs or face unemployment. Free trade is likely to make these displaced workers worse off.

There is a saying, "Where you stand on an issue depends on where you sit." In our example, a worker sitting at a sewing machine in Chipland is likely to oppose free trade because that worker is likely to lose his or her job. A worker sitting at a workstation in a computer-chip fabrication facility is likely to support free trade because the resulting increase in computer-chip exports will generate more employment opportunities in the industry.

TEST Your Understanding

1. Use Figure 32.1 to complete the following statements with numbers: If Chipland starts at point *c* and decides to produce 10 more chips, it will produce _____ shirts. If Shirtland produces only 10 chips, it will produce _____ shirts.

2. In nation H, the opportunity cost of tables is five chairs, while in nation B, the opportunity cost of tables is only one chair. Which country should produce tables, and which should produce chairs?

3. Nations H and B split the difference between the willingness to pay for tables and the willingness to accept. What are the terms of trade?

4. List the two bits of information you need to draw the consumption possibilities curve for a particular nation.

5. In Figure 32.2, suppose the nations agree to exchange one shirt for each chip. Will the consumption possibilities curve for Chipland still be above its production possibilities curve?

Protectionist Policies

Now that you know the basic rationale for specialization and trade, we can explore the effects of public policies that restrict trade. We will consider four common import-restriction policies: an outright ban on imports, an import quota, voluntary export restraints, and a tariff.

Import Ban

To show how an import ban affects the market, let's start with an unrestricted market—no import ban. Figure 32.3 shows the market for shirts in Chipland, a nation with a comparative advantage in computer chips, not shirts. The domestic supply curve shows the quantity of shirts supplied by firms in Chipland. Looking at point *m*, we see that Chipland firms will not supply any shirts unless the price is at least $17 per shirt. The total supply curve for shirts, which shows the quantity supplied by both domestic firms

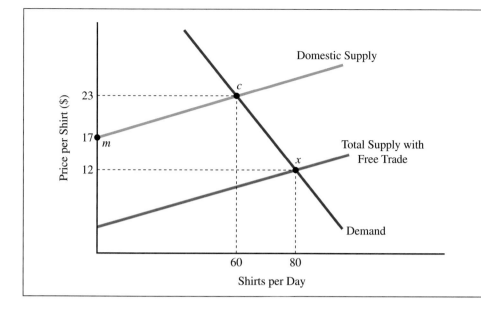

Figure 32.3
Effects of an Import Ban
In the free-trade equilibrium, demand intersects the total supply curve at point *x*, with a price of $12 and a quantity of 80 shirts. If shirt imports are banned, the equilibrium is shown by the intersection of the demand curve and the domestic supply curve (point *c*). The price increases to $23.

and foreign firms (in Shirtland), lies to the right of the domestic supply curve. At each price, the total supply of shirts exceeds the domestic supply because foreign firms supply shirts too. Point *x* shows the free-trade equilibrium: The demand curve from domestic residents intersects the total supply curve at a price of $12 per shirt and a quantity of 80 shirts. Because this price is below the minimum price for domestic firms, domestic firms produce no shirts, and all the shirts in Chipland are imported from Shirtland.

What will happen if Chipland bans imported shirts? Foreign suppliers will disappear from the shirt market, so the total supply of shirts will be the domestic supply. In Figure 32.3, point *c* shows the equilibrium when Chipland bans imported shirts: The domestic demand curve intersects the domestic supply curve at a price of $23 per shirt and a quantity of 60 shirts. In other words, the decrease in supply resulting from the import ban increases the price and decreases the quantity of shirts.

Quotas and Voluntary Export Restraints

An alternative to an import ban is an **import quota**, defined as a limit on the amount of a good that can be imported. An import quota is a restrictive policy that falls between free trade and an import ban: Imports are decreased but not eliminated. Price falls between the price with free trade ($12 per shirt, as in our example) and the price with an import ban ($23 per shirt).

Figure 32.4 shows the effect of an import quota. Starting from the free-trade equilibrium at point *x*, an import quota will shift the total supply curve to the left: At each price there will be a smaller quantity of shirts because foreign suppliers cannot supply as many owing to the import limitation. The total supply curve when there is an import quota will lie between the domestic supply curve and the total supply curve under free trade. In the case of an import quota, the equilibrium occurs at point *q*, where the demand curve intersects the total supply curve, reflecting the import limitation. The $20 price per shirt with the import quota exceeds the $17 minimum price of domestic firms, so domestic firms supply 22 shirts (point *e*). Under a **voluntary export restraint (VER)**, an exporting nation voluntarily decreases its exports in an attempt to avoid more restrictive trade policies. A VER has the same effect as an import quota, which is illegal under the rules of the World Trade Organization (WTO), an organization with over 130 member nations that oversees the General Agreement on Tariffs and Trade and other interna-

Import quota: A limit on the amount of a good that can be imported.

Voluntary export restraint (VER): A scheme under which an exporting country voluntarily decreases its exports.

Figure 32.4

Market Effects of a Quota, a VER, or a Tariff

An import quota shifts the supply curve to the left. The market moves upward along the demand curve to point *q*, which is between point *x* (free trade) and *c* (an import ban). We can reach the same point with a tariff that shifts the total supply curve to the same position.

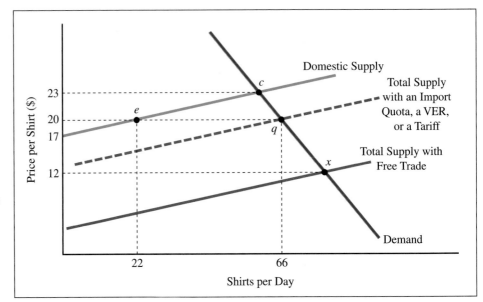

tional agreements. Although VERs are legal under WTO rules, they violate the spirit of international trade agreements. Like a quota, a VER increases the price of the restricted good, allowing domestic firms to participate in the market.

A quota or a VER produces winners and losers. The winners include foreign and domestic shirt producers. In our example, foreign firms can sell shirts at a price of $20 instead of $12 each. In some cases, the government issues import licenses to some citizens, who can then buy shirts from foreign firms at a low price, such as $12, and sell the shirts at the higher domestic price, $20. In addition, the import restrictions allow domestic shirt firms to participate in the market, generating benefits for the firms and their workers. The losers are consumers, who pay a higher price for shirts.

Price Effects of Quotas and VERs

We know that consumers pay higher prices for goods that are subject to protectionist policies, but how much more? In the United States, voluntary export restraints for Japanese automobiles in effect in 1984 increased the price of a Japanese car by about $1,300 and increased the price of a domestic car by about $660.[1] In 1990, U.S. consumers incurred a total cost of $70 billion as a result of the nation's protectionist policies, about $270 per person per year.[2] The largest costs resulted from protectionist policies for apparel (about $84 per person) and textiles (about $13 per person).

Many European nations used VERs to limit their domestic market shares of Japanese automobiles. Figure 32.5 shows the cost of these policies in terms of their effects on the price of Japanese automobiles in several nations. For example, in France, the VERs increased the price of Japanese automobiles by 35%, compared to a 1% increase in price in Germany and a 55% higher price in Italy.

Tariffs

Tariff: A tax on an imported good.

An alternative to a quota or a VER is an import **tariff**, which is a tax on an imported good. We know from our earlier discussion of the market effects of taxes that a tax shifts the supply curve to the left and increases the equilibrium price. In Figure 32.4, suppose the tariff shifts the total supply curve, so it intersects the domestic demand curve at point *q*.

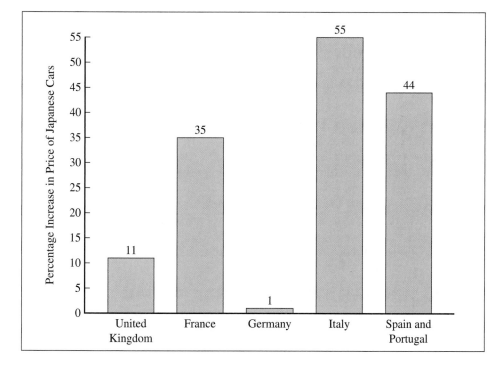

Figure 32.5
Price Effects of VERs for Japanese Cars
Many European nations use VERs to limit the number of Japanese cars imported. The VERs increase the price of Japanese cars.

Source: Alasdair Smith and Anthony J. Venables, "Cost of Voluntary Export Restraints in the European Car Market," Chapter 10 in *International Trade and Trade Policy*, edited by Elhanan Helpman and Asaaf Razin (Cambridge, MA: MIT Press, 1991).

In other words, we reach the same point we reached with the quota: Consumers pay the same $20 price per shirt, and domestic firms produce the same quantity: 22 shirts.

There is one fundamental difference between a quota and a tariff. An import quota allows importers to buy shirts from foreign suppliers at a low price, say, $12 per shirt, and sell them for $20 each, the artificially high price. In other words, importers make money from the quota. Under a tariff, the government gets the money, collecting $8 per shirt from foreign suppliers. Citizens in Chipland will prefer the tariff to the quota because the government can use the revenue from the tariff to cut other taxes or expand public programs.

Responses to Protectionist Policies

A restriction on imports is likely to cause further restrictions on trade. For example, if Chipland bans shirt imports, the shirt industry in Shirtland may call for retaliation in the form of a ban of computer chips from Chipland. A trade war of this sort could escalate to the point at which the two nations return to self-sufficiency. If that happened, we could see the result by looking back at Figure 32.2: Chipland would move from point x to point c, and Shirtland would move from point y to point s. This sort of retaliatory response is common. Because it is, we know that the protection of one industry in a nation is likely to harm that nation's export industries. Chipland's shirt industry, if protected from imports, may grow, but at the expense of its computer-chip industry.

There are many examples of import restrictions that led to retaliatory policies that decreased trade substantially. Here are a few:

1. **Smoot-Hawley tariff of 1930.** When the United States increased its average tariff to 59%, its trading partners retaliated with higher tariffs. The trade war decreased international trade and deepened the worldwide depression of the 1930s.[3]
2. **Chicken tariff of 1963.** The European Economic Community (EEC, the predecessor of the European Union) imposed a large tariff on frozen chickens from the

United States, cutting U.S. imports in half. The United States retaliated by increasing its tariffs on expensive brandies (from France), potato starch (from Holland), and light trucks (from Germany).[4]

3. **Pasta tariff of 1985.** The United States imposed tariffs on pasta from the EEC, and the EEC retaliated by increasing its tariffs on lemons and walnuts from the United States.[5]

The threat of retaliatory policies may persuade a nation to loosen its protectionist policies. In 1995, the United States announced that it would impose 100% tariffs on Japanese luxury cars (with total sales of $6 billion per year) if Japan didn't ease its restrictions on imported auto parts. Just hours before the tariffs were to take effect, the two nations reached an agreement that was expected to increase the sales of U.S. auto parts to Japanese firms by about $9 billion per year.[6]

Import restrictions also create an incentive to smuggle goods. The restrictions create a gap between the cost of purchasing the restricted goods abroad and the price of goods in the protected economy, so there is a profit to be made from smuggling.

NAFTA and the Giant Sucking Sound

ECONOMIC DETECTIVE

The North American Free Trade Agreement (NAFTA), which took effect in January 1994, will gradually phase out tariffs and other trade barriers between the United States, Canada, and Mexico. In the debates over the effects of NAFTA on trade between the United States and Mexico, economists predicted that NAFTA would increase both imports from Mexico and exports to Mexico. This is sensible because NAFTA decreases the tariffs and trade barriers of both nations. Because the pre-NAFTA tariffs between the United States and Mexico were low—about 4%—no one expected any dramatic changes in trade patterns. Instead, the expectation was for moderate growth in both imports and exports.

Table 32.2 provides some trade data for the United States and Mexico for the years surrounding the NAFTA agreement. Several observers, including two presidential candi-

NAFTA helps promote the growth of foreign investment in Mexico.

Table 32.2 Trade Data for the United States and Mexico

Year	U.S. Imports from Mexico (billions)	U.S. Exports to Mexico (billions)	Exchange Rate: Pesos per Dollar	U.S. Trade Surplus (+) or Deficit (−) with Mexico (billions)
1993	$40	$42	3.12	$+2
1994	$49	$51	3.11	$+2
1995	$62	$46	5.33	$−16

Source: U.S. Department of Commerce, *Statistical Abstract of the United States, 1996* (Washington, DC: U.S. Government Printing Office, 1996).

dates, used the figures for 1993 and 1995 to claim that NAFTA was responsible for turning the small $2 billion trade surplus in 1993 into the huge $16 billion trade deficit in 1995. One candidate suggested that NAFTA caused a "giant sucking sound" as jobs moved from the United States to Mexico.

Who is right? The economists who predicted that NAFTA would cause moderate growth in both imports and exports, or the presidential candidates?

The clues that we need to solve this puzzle are shown in the fourth column of Table 32.2. The exchange rate in 1994 was about the same as it was in 1993, so in the first year of NAFTA, imports and exports grew at nearly the same rate, about 22%, as predicted by economists. The following year was different: The exchange rate of the dollar for the peso rose from 3.11 to 5.33 pesos per dollar. As we saw in Chapter 3, an increase in the exchange rate—more pesos per dollar—will make U.S. goods more expensive for Mexican consumers, so U.S. exports to Mexico will drop. At the same time, Mexican goods will become less expensive for U.S. consumers, so U.S. imports from Mexico will rise. According to Table 32.2, that's exactly what happened: Imports increased by $13 billion, and exports dropped by $5 billion. This suggests that the U.S. trade deficit with Mexico was caused by the devaluation of the peso, not by NAFTA. ◆

TEST Your Understanding

6. Complete the following statement: If a country bans the importation of a particular good, the market equilibrium is shown by the intersection of the _____ curve and the _____ curve.

7. Complete the statement with *above* or *below*. The equilibrium price under an import quota is _____ the price that occurs with an import ban and _____ the price that occurs with free trade.

8. From the perspective of consumers, which is better: a tariff or a quota?

9. Under the quota system underlying Figure 32.4, what fraction of the shirt market is supplied by domestic firms?

Rationales for Protectionist Policies

What are the rationales for protectionist policies such as an import ban, an import quota, a voluntary restraint, or a tariff? We will discuss three possible motivations for policies that restrict trade:

1. To shield workers from foreign competition
2. To nurture infant industries until they mature
3. To help domestic firms establish monopolies in world markets

To Shield Workers from Foreign Competition

One of the most basic arguments for protectionism is that it protects workers in industries that would be hurt by trade. Suppose that relative to the United States, nations in the Far East have a comparative advantage in producing textiles. If the United States reduced existing tariffs for the textile industry, domestic manufacturers could not compete. They would have to close their factories and lay off workers. In an ideal world, the laid-off workers would take new jobs in other sectors of the economy. In practice, this is difficult. Many workers don't have the skills to work in other sectors, and obtaining these skills takes time. Moreover, the textile industry is heavily concentrated in the southeastern part of the United States. Politicians from that region will try to keep tariffs in place to prevent the temporary unemployment and changes in employment patterns that free trade would cause. The result of this protection is less efficient production, higher prices, and lower consumption for the United States. For a discussion of the trade-offs between job protection and consumer prices, read "A Closer Look: The Cost of Protecting Jobs."

To Nurture Infant Industries

During World War II, the United States built hundreds of boats, called Liberty Ships, for the Navy. As more and more of these ships were built, each required fewer hours to complete because workers learned from their experiences, acquiring knowledge during

A CLOSER LOOK | The Cost of Protecting Jobs

What is the trade-off between protecting domestic jobs and higher prices for consumers? As shown in the table, protectionist policies for textiles and apparel imposed an annual cost of over $10 billion and saved 56,464 jobs, for a cost per job of $177,759, which is over eight times the average wage in the industry. The cost per job was even higher for dairy products, motor vehicles, sugar, and meat.

Industry Protected	Annual Cost (millions)	Jobs Protected	Cost per Job
Textiles and apparel	$10,037	56,464	$177,759
Dairy products	$1,013	2,038	$497,056
Motor vehicles	$925	3,419	$270,547
Sugar	$661	1,663	$404,776
Meat	$185	45	$4,111,111
Nonrubber footwear	$147	1,316	$111,702

Source: Update of *The Economic Effects of Significant U.S. Import Restraints* (Washington, DC: U.S. International Trade Commission, initial report in 1993; update in 1996).

the production process. Engineers and economists call this phenomenon **learning by doing**. To learn a new game, such as Ping-Pong, you learn by doing. At first, you may find it difficult to play, but your skills improve as you go along.

Tariffs and other protectionist policies are often defended on the grounds that they protect new industries, or **infant industries**, that are in the early stages of learning by doing. A tariff shields a young industry from the competition of its more mature rivals. After the infant industry grows up, the tariff can be eliminated because the industry is able to compete.

In practice, infant industries rarely become competitive with their foreign rivals. During the 1950s and 1960s, many Latin American countries used tariffs and other policies to protect their young manufacturing industries from foreign competition. Unfortunately, the domestic industries never became as efficient as foreign suppliers, and the Latin American countries that tried this policy suffered.

Another problem with protecting an infant industry is that once an industry is given tariff protection, it is difficult to take such protection away. For an interesting discussion of the merits of protecting an industry from "unfair" competition, read "A Closer Look: Protection for Candle Makers."

> **Learning by doing:** Knowledge gained during production, resulting in increases in productivity.

> **Infant industry:** A new industry that is protected from foreign competitors.

To Help Domestic Firms Establish Monopolies in World Markets

If the production of a particular good has very large-scale economies, the world market will support only a few firms. A nation might be tempted to adopt policies to capture the monopoly profits for itself. Suppose the commercial aircraft industry can support only one large firm; if two firms enter the industry, both will lose money. A nation that decides to get into this industry could agree to provide financial support to a domestic firm to guarantee that the firm will make a profit. With such a guarantee, the domestic firm will enter the industry. Knowing this, a foreign firm will be reluctant to enter, so the domestic firm will capture the monopoly profit.

 **A CLOSER LOOK** Protection for Candle Makers

In response to the spread of protectionism, the French economist Frédéric Bastiat (1801–1851) wrote the following fictitious petition, in which French candle makers ask for protection from "unfair" competition:

> We are suffering from the intolerable competition of a foreign rival, placed, it would seem, in a condition so far superior to ours for the production of light, that he absolutely inundates our national market at a price fabulously reduced. The moment he shows himself, our trade leaves us—all of our customers apply to him; and a branch of native industry, having countless ramifications, is all at once rendered completely stagnant. This rival. . . is not other than the sun.
>
> What we pray for is, that it may please you to pass a law ordering the shutting up of all windows, sky-lights, dormerwindows, curtains, blinds, bull's eyes; in a word all openings, holes, chinks, clefts, and fissures, by or through which the light of the sun has been in use to enter houses, to the prejudice of the meritorious manufactures with which we. . . have accommodated our country—a country which, in gratitude, ought not to abandon us now. . .
>
> Does it not argue to the greatest inconsistency to check as you do the importation of coal, iron, cheese, and goods of foreign manufacture, merely because. . . their price approaches zero, while at the same time you freely admit, and without limitation, the light of the sun, whose price is during the whole day at zero?

Source: Frédéric Bastiat, *Economics Sophisms* (Edinburgh: Oliver & Boyd, 1873), pp. 49–53.

One example of this is the Airbus, an airplane that is produced in Europe. Several European countries provided large subsidies for firms producing the Airbus. These subsidies allowed the Airbus firms to underprice some of their rivals in the United States, and at least one U.S. manufacturer of commercial airplanes was forced out of business. What could go wrong with these monopoly-creation policies? If both nations subsidize their domestic firms, both firms will enter the market and lose money. The taxpayers in both countries will then have to pay for the subsidies. And there is the possibility a nation may pick the wrong industry to subsidize. Together, the British and French subsidized an airplane known as the Concorde to provide supersonic travel between Europe and the United States. Although the Concorde captured the market, the market was not worth capturing. The Concorde lost money because it was very costly to develop, and people are not willing to pay a very large premium for supersonic travel.

TEST Your Understanding

10. Comment on the following statement: If we eliminated our textile tariffs, the dislocated workers could easily switch to other jobs.

11. Explain the infant-industry argument.

12. List the two problems associated with subsidizing an industry in the hope of establishing a worldwide monopoly.

Recent Policy Debates and Trade Agreements

We're now ready to discuss three recent policy debates concerning international trade:

1. Are foreign producers dumping their products?
2. Do trade laws inhibit environmental protection?
3. Does trade cause income inequality?

We also discuss some recent trade agreements that have lowered trade barriers and increased international trade.

Are Foreign Producers Dumping Their Products?

Dumping: A situation in which the price a firm charges for a product in a foreign market is lower than either the price it charges for that product in its home market or the product's production cost.

While tariff rates have been reduced in recent years, a number of trade controversies remain. One of these is the rules for dumping. A firm is **dumping** when the price it charges in a foreign market is either lower than the price it charges in its home market or lower than its production cost. Dumping is illegal under international trade agreements; hundreds of cases of alleged dumping are presented to WTO authorities each year. Here are some recent cases in which the WTO concluded that dumping had occurred: Hong Kong VCRs sold in Europe; Chinese bicycles sold in the United States; Asian TV sets sold in Europe; steel from Brazil, India, Japan, and Spain sold in the United States; U.S. beef sold in Mexico; and Chinese computer disks sold in Japan and the United States. Under the current provisions of the WTO, a nation can impose antidumping duties on products that are being dumped.

Why would a firm dump—charge a low price in the foreign market? The first reason is price discrimination. If a firm has a monopoly in its home market but faces strong competition in a foreign market, the firm will naturally charge a higher price in the home market. The foreign price looks low, but only because we compare it to a very high monopoly price in the home market. The firm uses its monopoly power to discriminate against consumers in its home market, so the problem is in the home market, not the foreign market.

To illustrate how international price discrimination works, let's look at the case of Korean VCRs.[7] In the 1980s there were only three firms, all Korean, selling VCRs in Korea, but there were dozens of firms selling VCRs in Europe. The lack of competition in Korea generated very high prices for Korean consumers: They paid much more than European consumers for identical Korean VCRs. Korean firms used their market power to discriminate against Korean consumers. When international trade authorities concluded that Korean firms were dumping VCRs in Europe, the Korean firms responded by cutting prices in their home market. They did not increase their prices in Europe—much to the dismay of European producers and the delight of European consumers.

The second reason for dumping is predatory pricing: cutting prices in an attempt to drive rival firms out of business. The predatory firm sets its price below its production cost. The price is low enough that both the predator and its prey (a firm in the foreign market) lose money. After the prey goes out of business, the predator increases its price to earn monopoly profit. This is also known as *predatory dumping*.

Although the rationale for antidumping laws is to prevent predatory dumping, it is difficult to determine whether low prices are the result of predatory pricing or price discrimination. Many economists are skeptical about how frequently predatory pricing actually occurs; they suspect that many nations use their antidumping laws as protectionist policies in disguise. Because WTO rules limit tariffs and quotas, some nations may be tempted to substitute antidumping duties for these protectionist policies.

Do Trade Laws Inhibit Environmental Protection?

In recent trade negotiations, a new player—environmental groups—appeared on the scene. Starting in the early 1990s, environmentalists began to question whether policies that liberalized trade could harm the environment. The issue that attracted their attention was the killing of dolphins by tuna fishers.

Anyone who catches tuna with a large net will also catch the dolphins that swim with the tuna, and most of the captured dolphins will die. In 1972, the United States outlawed the use of tuna nets by U.S. ships. A short time later, ships from other nations, including Mexico, began netting tuna and killing dolphins. The United States responded with a boycott of Mexican tuna caught with nets, and the Mexican government complained to an international trade authority that the tuna boycott was an unfair trade barrier. The trade authority agreed with Mexico and forced the United States to remove the boycott.

Under current WTO rules, a country can adopt any environmental standard it chooses, as long as it does not discriminate against foreign producers. For example, the United States can limit the exhaust emissions of all cars that operate in the United States. As long as emissions rules apply equally to all cars, domestic and imports, the rules are legal according to the WTO. An international panel upheld U.S. fuel efficiency rules for automobiles on this principle.[8]

The tuna boycott was a violation of WTO rules because killing dolphins does not harm the U.S. environment directly. For the same reason, the United States could not ban imported goods that are produced in factories that generate air or water pollution in other countries. It is easy to understand why WTO rules do not allow countries to restrict trade on the basis of the methods that are used to produce goods and services. Countries differ in the value they place on the environment. For example, a poor nation may be willing to tolerate more pollution if it means attaining a higher standard of living.

If trade restrictions cannot be used to protect the dolphins and deal with other global environmental problems, what else can we do? International agreements have been used for a variety of different environmental goals, from limiting the harvest of whales to eliminating the chemicals that deplete the ozone layer. These agreements are difficult to reach, and some nations will be tempted to use trade restrictions to pursue environmental goals. If they do, they will encounter resistance because WTO rules mean that a nation can pursue its environmental goals only within its own borders.

Trade disputes about environmental issues are part of a larger phenomenon of trade issues intersecting with national regulations. At one time, most trade disputes were simply matters of protecting domestic industries from foreign competition. Agriculture, textile, and steel were frequently beneficiaries of protection in many different countries throughout the world. But in recent years, there has been a new breed of trade disputes that revolve around social issues and the role of government regulation.

As an example, the European Union intended to ban hormone-treated beef. While this was motivated in part by a desire to keep out U.S. imports and protect European farmers, it also reflects the nervousness of European citizens about technology. After all, Europe banned all hormone-treated beef, not just imports from the United States. Shouldn't a country have the right to pursue this policy, even if it is not based on the best science? While the costs of the policy would be fairly straightforward in terms of higher prices for beef products, the benefits, in terms of potential safety, are much more difficult to ascertain. Similar issues will arise as genetically modified crops become more commonplace. As a world trading community, we will have to decide at what point we allow national policy concerns to override principles of free trade.

Does Trade Cause Inequality?

Inequality in wages has been growing in the United States since 1973. Wages of skilled workers have risen faster than the wages of unskilled workers. World trade has also boomed since 1973. Could there be a connection between increased world trade and income inequality?

Trade theory suggests a link between increased trade and increased wage inequality. Here is how they might be linked: Suppose the United States produces two types of goods: one using skilled labor (say, airplanes) and one using unskilled labor (say, textiles). The United States is likely to have a comparative advantage in products that use skilled labor; developing countries are likely to have a comparative advantage in products that use unskilled labor. An increase in world trade will increase both exports and imports. An increase in U.S. exports means that we'll produce more goods requiring skilled labor, so the domestic demand for skilled labor will increase, pulling up the wage of skilled labor in the United States. At the same time, an increase in U.S. imports means that we'll import more goods produced by unskilled labor, so the domestic demand for unskilled labor will decrease, pulling down the wage of unskilled labor in the United States. As a result, the gap between the wages of the two types of workers will increase.

Economists have tried to determine how much trade has contributed to growing wage inequality. As usual, there are other factors that make such a determination difficult. It is difficult, for example, to distinguish between the effects of trade and the effects of technical progress. Technical change, such as the rapid introduction and use of computers, will also tend to increase the demand for skilled workers and decrease the demand for unskilled workers. Economists have noted, however, that the exports of goods using skilled labor and the imports of goods using unskilled labor have both increased, just as the theory predicts. At least some of the increased wage inequality is caused by international trade.

One response to this undesirable side effect of trade is to use trade restrictions to protect industries that use unskilled workers. Another approach is to ease the transition to an economy with a larger fraction of skilled jobs. In the long run, workers will move to industries that use skilled workers, so they will eventually earn higher wages. The government could facilitate this change by providing assistance for education and training.

Recent Trade Agreements

In the last few decades, there has been considerable progress in lowering the barriers to international trade. Here are some examples of international trade agreements:

1. North American Free Trade Agreement (NAFTA). Took effect in 1994 and is being implemented over the following 15 years. The agreement will eventually eliminate all tariffs and other trade barriers among Canada, Mexico, and the United States. NAFTA may soon be extended to other nations in the Western Hemisphere.

2. World Trade Organization (WTO). Has more than 130 member nations and oversees the General Agreement on Tariffs and Trade and other international trade agreements. There have been eight rounds of tariff negotiations, lowering tariffs among the member nations. For example, between 1930 and 1995, the average tariff in the United States has dropped from about 59% to about 5%. The last full set of negotiations, the so-called Uruguay round, completed in 1994, decreased tariffs by about one-third their prior levels. WTO promotes trade in other ways: It has eliminated many import quotas, reduced agricultural subsidies, and outlawed restrictions on international trade in services such as banking, insurance, and accounting.

3. European Union (EU). Designed to remove all trade barriers within Europe and create a single market. Fifteen nations have joined.

4. Asian Pacific Economic Cooperation (APEC). In 1994, the leaders of 18 Asian nations signed a nonbinding agreement to reduce trade barriers among their nations.

These agreements have reduced trade barriers and increased international trade. For example, the Uruguay round was expected to increase the volume of world trade by at least 9% and perhaps as much as 24%.[9]

TEST Your Understanding

13. What is dumping?

14. What restrictions do WTO rules place on a nation's environmental policies?

15. Consider a nation having a comparative advantage in the production of goods using unskilled labor. What types of workers will benefit from increased trade, and what types of workers will lose?

Using the TOOLS

In this chapter, we've discussed the trade-offs associated with protectionist policies and have used supply and demand curves to show the market effects of protectionist policies. Here are some opportunities to do your own economic analysis.

1. ECONOMIC EXPERIMENT: Protectionist Policies

Recall the market-equilibrium experiment from Chapter 4. We can modify the experiment to show the effects of protectionist policies on equilibrium prices and quantities. On the supply side of the market, there are domestic apple producers and foreign apple producers; the domestic producers have higher unit costs. After several trading periods without any government intervention, you can change the rules as follows:

a. Apple imports are banned: Foreign producers cannot participate in the market.

b. There is a tariff (a tax on imports) of $5 per bushel.

2. Incentives for Smuggling

If a country bans imports, smugglers may try to penetrate its markets. Suppose Chipland bans shirt imports, causing some importers to bribe customs officials, who "look the other way" as smugglers bring shirts into Chipland. Your job is to combat shirt smuggling. Use the information in Figure 32.3 in this chapter to answer the following questions:

a. Suppose importers can sell their shirts on the world market at a price of $12 per shirt. How much is an importer willing to pay to get customs officials to look the other way?

b. What sort of change in trade policy would make your job easier?

3. Vilfredo Pareto and Import Restrictions

This chapter opened with a narrative about a policy scheme under which the restrictions on apparel imports would be eliminated. Would you expect all three people to be happy with this scheme? If not, how would you modify the scheme to make them all happy?

4. Ban on Shoe Imports

Consider a country that initially consumes 100 pairs of shoes per hour, all of which are imported. The price of shoes is $40 per pair before a ban on importing them. Depict graphically the market effects of a ban on shoe imports.

Summary

In this chapter, we discussed the benefits of specialization and trade, and we explored the trade-offs associated with protectionist policies. There is a basic conflict between consumers, who prefer free trade because free trade decreases prices, and workers in the protected industries, who want to keep their jobs. Here are the main points of the chapter:

1. If one country has a comparative advantage vis-a-vis another country in producing a particular good (a lower opportunity cost), specialization and trade will benefit both countries.

2. An import ban or an import quota increases the prices of the restricted good and shifts resources from a domestic export industry into the protected domestic industries.

3. Because the victims of protectionist policies often retaliate, the protection of a domestic industry may harm an exporting industry.

4. A tariff (a tax on imports) generates revenue for the government, while an import quota—a limit on imports—generates revenue for foreigners or importers.

5. In principle, the laws against dumping are designed to prevent predatory pricing. In practice, it is difficult to prove predatory pricing, and the laws are often used to shield a domestic industry from competition.

6. Under WTO rules, each country may pursue its environmental goals only within its own borders.

7. International trade has contributed to the widening gap between the wages of low-skilled and high-skilled labor.

Key Terms

autarky, 664
comparative advantage, 664
consumption possibilities curve, 665
dumping, 674

import quota, 667
infant industry, 673
learning by doing, 673
production possibilities curve, 663

tariff, 668
terms of trade, 664
voluntary export restraint (VER), 667

Problems and Discussion Questions

1. In one minute, Country B can produce either 1,000 TVs and no computers or 500 computers and no TVs. Similarly, in one minute, country C can produce either 2,400 TVs or 600 computers.
   a. Compute the opportunity costs of TVs and computers for each country. Which country has a comparative advantage in producing TVs? In producing computers?
   b. Draw the production possibilities curves for the two countries.

2. In country U, the opportunity cost of a computer is 10 pairs of shoes. In Country C, the opportunity cost of a computer is 100 pairs of shoes.
   a. Suppose the two countries split the difference between the willingness to pay for computers and the willingness to accept computers. Compute the terms of trade, that is, the rate at which the two countries will exchange computers and shoes.
   b. Suppose the two countries exchange one computer for the number of shoes dictated by the terms of trade you computed in part (a). Compute the net benefit from trade for each country.

3. In Figure 32.2, suppose the two countries trade 35 computer chips for 70 shirts. For each country, compute the amounts of chips and shirts consumed.

4. Consider two countries, Tableland and Chairland, each capable of producing tables and chairs.
   Chairland can produce the following combinations of chairs and tables:
   • All chairs and no tables: 36 chairs per day
   • All tables and no chairs: 18 tables per day
   Tableland can produce the following combinations of chairs and tables:
   • All chairs and no tables: 40 chairs per day
   • All tables and no chairs: 40 tables per day

   In each country, there is a fixed trade-off of tables for chairs.
   a. Draw the two production possibilities curves, with chairs on the vertical axis and tables on the horizontal axis.
   b. Suppose that each country is initially self-sufficient and each country divides its resources equally between the two goods. How much does each country produce and consume?
   c. Which country has a comparative advantage in tables? Which has a comparative advantage in chairs?
   d. If the two countries split the difference between the buyer's willingness to pay for chairs and the seller's willingness to accept, in terms of chairs per table, what are the terms of trade?
   e. Draw the consumption possibilities curves.
   f. Suppose each country specializes in the good for which it has a comparative advantage, and they exchange 14 tables for some quantity of chairs. Compute the consumption bundles—bundles means the consumption of tables and chairs—for each country.

5. The current approach to restricting automobile imports is to use voluntary export restraints. Evaluate the wisdom of this approach and propose an alternative policy.

6. Evaluate this comment: "If a country bans imports, smuggling is inevitable. We should welcome smuggling because it improves consumer welfare."

7. The European Union is committed to eliminating most of the trade barriers among its 15 member nations. What types of people will benefit? Which types will lose?

8. What is the cost to consumers for each motor-vehicle job protected by import restrictions? In your

opinion, is protecting these jobs worthwhile at this cost? If not, how much should we as a society be willing to pay for each job that is protected?

9. Suppose the president of a nation proposes to switch from a system of import quotas to a system of tariffs, with the idea that the switch would not affect the quantity of goods imported. Who will be in favor of the switch? Who will oppose it? Would you expect the proponents and the opponents to have the same political influence on the president?

10. Suppose residents of one nation are very fearful of biotechnology and they pass a law prohibiting the sale of all genetically altered foods in their country. Another nation, which produces these foods, claims that this law is an unfair trade barrier. In your view, should the first nation be allowed to prevent these

imports, even if there is no scientific basis for their claim?

11. **Web Exercise.** Go to the Web site for the World Trade Organization (*http://www.wto.gov*) and explore some of the ongoing trade disputes. Pick one or two of these disputes and find additional background information, such as newspaper stories, on the Web. Use this information to understand the nature of the controversy.

12. **Web Exercise.** Go to the Web site for the U.S. Trade Representative (*http://www.ustr.gov*), which is an office within the executive branch of the government. From the Web site, what are some of the key trade issues for the U.S. government today?

Take It to the Net

We invite you to visit the O'Sullivan/Sheffrin page on the Prentice Hall Web site at:
http://www.prenhall.com/osullivan/
for additional World Wide Web exercises for this chapter.

Model Answers to Questions

Chapter-Opening Questions

1. The winners are the domestic nation's consumers, who pay lower prices, and the domestic nation's workers in export industries. The losers are people in the domestic nation who lose their jobs as imports replace domestically produced goods.

2. A tariff generates revenue for the government; a quota generates profits for importers.

3. First, if a firm has a monopoly in its home market but faces strong competition in a foreign market, the firm will naturally charge a higher price in the home market (price discrimination). Second, a firm may be engaging in predatory pricing, the practice of cutting prices in an attempt to drive rivals out of business.

4. Under current WTO rules, a country cannot adopt any environmental standard that discriminates against foreign producers. For example, the United States cannot impose an import ban on goods that

are produced in polluting factories in other nations. This rule means that global environmental issues must be resolved with international agreements, not trade restrictions.

5. Although trade increases income inequality, it is unclear just how much of the recent increase in inequality can be attributed to the expansion of trade.

Test Your Understanding

1. 50, 78 (108 – 30).

2. Nation B should produce tables, and nation H should produce chairs.

3. Three chairs per table: Nation H is willing to pay five chairs, and nation B is willing to accept one chair.

4. We need to know the maximum output of the good for which the nation has a comparative advantage and the terms of trade.

5. No. The consumption curve will be the same as the production curve.

6. Demand, domestic supply.

7. Below, above.

8. If a quota and a tariff led to the same price for a good, consumers would be indifferent between them. However, as citizens, they should prefer the tariff which provides revenue to the government, allowing the government to either increase expenditure or reduce taxation.

9. Domestic firms supply 22 units, which is one-third of the total quantity (66).

10. This is false. Some workers do not have the skills to work in other sectors, and it takes time to obtain new skills.

11. It takes some time for a new industry to learn by doing, so it may be sensible to protect a young industry when it is vulnerable to competition from foreign firms.

12. If two nations subsidize firms in the same industry, each nation could lose money. In addition, a nation might pick the wrong industry to subsidize.

13. A foreign firm is dumping when it sells a product in another country at a price below the price it charges in its own market. It is difficult to determine whether dumping is occurring, and many countries used dumping laws as a disguised form of protectionism.

14. A nation's environmental laws must not discriminate against imported goods. The laws must apply equally to imports and domestic goods.

15. The wage of unskilled labor will increase; the wage of skilled labor will decrease.

Using the Tools

2. Incentives for Smuggling

   a. Importers are willing to pay a bribe up to $11 per shirt (the difference between the equilibrium price with the import ban and the world price).

   b. If the import ban were replaced by a tariff of $11 per shirt, the smuggling problem might diminish, although there would still be an incentive to smuggle shirts to avoid the tariff.

3. Vilfredo Pareto and Import Restrictions. Consumers would gain $400 per family per year from lower apparel prices and pay $300 per year in additional taxes for two years. The net gain would be $100 per year for the first two years and $400 per year thereafter. The apparel workers would receive a temporary payment equal to their wages for two years. To make them better off, we must be sure that they find jobs in other industries within two years. The high-technology people will be better off if the retaliatory trade barriers are lifted.

4. Ban on Shoe Imports. In Figure 32.A we move from point x (price = $20 per pair; quantity = 100 pairs) to point c (price = $30 per pair; quantity = 70 pairs).

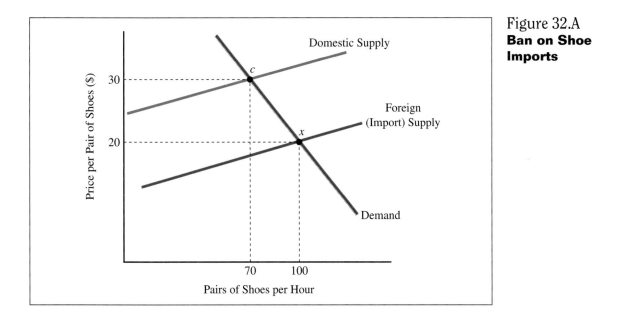

Figure 32.A
Ban on Shoe Imports

Notes

1. *A Review of Recent Developments in the U.S. Automobile Industry Including an Assessment of the Japanese Voluntary Restraint Agreements* (Washington, DC: U.S. International Trade Commission, February 1985).

2. Gary C. Hufbauer, Diane T. Berliner, and Kimberly A. Elliot, *Measuring the Cost of Protectionism in the United States* (Washington, DC: Institute for International Economics, 1994).

3. Charles Kindleberger, *The World in Depression, 1929–1939* (London: Allen Lane, 1973).

4. John A. C. Conybeare, *Trade Wars* (New York: Columbia University Press, 1987).

5. Conybeare, *Trade Wars*.

6. Helene Cooper and Valerie Reitman, "Averting a Trade War, U.S. and Japan Reach Agreement on Autos," *Wall Street Journal*, June 29, 1995, p. 1.

7. Taeho Bark, "The Korean Consumer Electronics Industry: Reaction to Antidumping Actions," Chapter 7 in *Antidumping: How It Works and Who Gets Hurt*, edited by J. Michael Finger (Ann Arbor, MI: University of Michigan Press, 1993).

8. "GATT Panel Supports U.S.," *New York Times*, October 1, 1994, p. A49.

9. Norman S. Fieleke, "The Uruguay Round of Trade Negotiation: An Overview," *New England Economic Review*, May/June 1995.

The World of International Finance

Today, the world currency markets are always open. When foreign exchange traders in New York City are sound asleep at 3:00 A.M., their counterparts in London are already on their phones and computers at 8:00 A.M. In Tokyo, it's 6:00 P.M., and the day is just ending. By the time Tokyo traders return home after their long commutes, the New York traders are back at work. The currency markets keep working even when mere human beings rest.

I n this world market, all currencies are traded 24 hours a day. The value of every currency depends on news and late-breaking developments throughout the world. News from Singapore, South Africa, or Sweden can easily affect the price at which currencies trade, for example, the price of U.S. dollars in terms of Japanese yen. The U.S. Secretary of the Treasury utters a casual remark that might or might not have something to do with currency exchange, and it reverberates instantly throughout the world. Modern communications—fax, e-mail, cell phones, video-conferencing, and satellite transmissions—accelerate the process.

How do changes in the value of currencies affect the U.S. economy? In this chapter, we explain the links between exchange rates and the performance of the economy. Understanding this will help you to interpret the often complex news from abroad. For example, if the value of the dollar starts to fall against the Japanese yen, what does it mean? Is this good news or bad news?

After reading this chapter, you should be able to answer the following questions:

1. **If U.S. interest rates increase, how will this affect the exchange rate between U.S. dollars and German marks? What will increasing interest rates in the United States do to the cost of a summer trip to Europe?**
2. **If the dollar increases in value against the Japanese yen, how will the increase affect the balance of trade between the United States and Japan?**
3. **Why do governments intervene in the foreign exchange market by buying and selling currencies?**
4. **Why have a group of European countries adopted a common currency?**
5. **How do international financial crises emerge?**

How Exchange Rates Are Determined

In this section, we examine how the value of a currency is determined in world markets. We then look at the factors that can change the value of a currency.

What Are Exchange Rates?

Let's start by reviewing some key concepts introduced in Chapter 3. To conduct international transactions between countries with different currencies, it is necessary to exchange one currency for another. The **exchange rate** is defined as the rate at which we can exchange one currency for another. Suppose a U.S. songwriter sells the rights of a hit song to a Japanese producer. The U.S. songwriter agrees to accept $50,000. If the exchange rate between U.S. dollars and Japanese yen is 100 yen per dollar, it will cost the Japanese producer 5,000,000 yen to purchase the rights to the song. Because international trade occurs between nations with different currencies, the exchange rate—the price at which one currency trades for another currency—is a crucial determinant of the trade in goods and assets.

An increase in the value of a currency is called an **appreciation**. If the exchange rate between the dollar and the yen increases from 100 yen per dollar to 110 yen per dollar, one dollar will purchase more yen. Because the dollar has increased in value, we say that the dollar has appreciated against the yen.

A **depreciation** is a reduction in the value of a currency. If the exchange rate falls to 90 yen per dollar, we get fewer yen for each dollar, so we say that the dollar has depreciated against the yen.

Throughout this chapter, we measure the exchange rate in units of foreign currency per dollar, that is, as 100 yen per dollar or 2 marks per dollar. We can think of the exchange rate as the price of dollars in terms of foreign currency. If the dollar appreciates from 100

Exchange rate: The rate at which one currency can be exchanged for another.

Appreciation: An increase in the value of a currency.

Depreciation: A decrease in the value of a currency.

yen per dollar to 110 yen per dollar, the price of dollars in terms of yen has increased, that is, the dollar has become more expensive in terms of yen. An appreciation of the dollar, therefore, is an increase in the price of dollars in terms of yen. Similarly, a depreciation of the dollar against the yen is a decrease in the price of dollars in terms of yen.

Be sure you understand that if the dollar appreciates against the yen, the yen must depreciate against the dollar. If we get more yen in exchange for the dollar, each yen will trade for fewer dollars. If the dollar appreciates from 100 to 110 yen per dollar, 100 yen will exchange for $0.91 rather than $1.00. Similarly, if the dollar depreciates against the yen, the yen must appreciate against the dollar. If we get less yen per dollar, each yen will exchange for more dollars. If the dollar depreciates from 100 yen to 90 yen per dollar, 100 yen will exchange for $1.11 rather than $1.00.

The exchange rate enables us to convert prices in one country to values in another country. A simple example illustrates how an exchange rate works. If you want to buy a cuckoo clock from Germany, you need to know what a clock would cost. You call the store in Germany; you are told that the clock sells for 300 German marks. The store owners live in Germany and want to be paid in German marks. To figure out what it will cost you in dollars, you need to know the exchange rate between marks and dollars. If the exchange rate is 2 marks per dollar, the clock would cost you $150:

$$300 \text{ marks}/2 \text{ marks per dollar} = \$150$$

If the exchange rate is 3 marks per dollar, the clock would cost only $100. The exchange rate allows you to convert the value of the clock (or any other good or service) from marks (or any other currency) to dollars.

Supply and Demand

How are exchange rates determined? The exchange rate between U.S. dollars and German marks is determined in the foreign exchange market, the market in which dollars trade for German marks. To understand this market, we can use simple supply and demand analysis.

In Figure 33.1, we plot the demand and supply curves for dollars in exchange for German marks. On the vertical axis, we have the exchange rate, e, in marks per dollar: e will measure how many marks trade for one dollar. For example, if you receive 2 marks per dollar, then $e = 2$ marks/dollar. If e increases, 1 dollar buys more marks, and the

Figure 33.1
Demand for and Supply of Dollars
Market equilibrium occurs where demand equals supply.

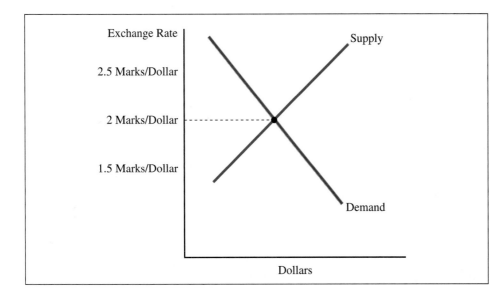

price of dollars in terms of marks has increased. For example, if *e* increases from 2 marks/dollar to 2.5 marks/dollar, the dollar has become more valuable—meaning that it has appreciated—against the mark. Similarly, if the exchange rate falls to 1.5 marks/dollar, the dollar has depreciated in value against the mark, and the price of dollars in terms of marks has decreased.

Be sure you see both sides of the same exchange coin: If the dollar appreciates against the mark, then the mark depreciates against the dollar. If the exchange rate increases from 2 to 2.5 marks/dollar, a single mark falls in value from $0.50/mark to $0.40/mark:

$$(2.5 \text{ marks/dollar} = 1/(2.5) \text{ dollars/marks} = 0.4 \text{ dollars/mark} = \$0.40/\text{mark})$$

Figure 33.1 shows the supply and demand curves for dollars in exchange for marks. The supply curve is the quantity supplied of dollars in exchange for marks. Individuals or firms that want to buy German goods or assets will need to exchange dollars for marks. For example, to invest in the German stock market, a U.S. investor must first trade dollars for marks because German sellers of stocks or bonds want to be paid in their own currency. We have defined the exchange rate as marks per dollar, so an increase in the exchange rate means that each dollar exchanges for more marks and marks become cheaper relative to dollars. The supply curve is drawn under the assumption that as marks become cheaper, total spending on German goods and assets will increase. Therefore, the supply curve is upward sloping: As the value of the dollar increases, more dollars will be supplied to the currency market in exchange for marks.

The demand curve represents the quantity demanded of dollars in exchange for marks. Individuals or firms in Germany that want to buy U.S. goods or assets must trade marks for dollars. For example, to visit Disneyland, a German family must exchange marks for dollars. As the exchange rate falls, dollars become cheaper in terms of marks. This makes U.S. goods and assets less expensive for German residents because each German mark buys more U.S. dollars. As U.S. goods and assets become cheaper, we assume that more German residents will want to trade marks for dollars. Therefore, the demand curve is downward sloping: Total demand for dollars will increase as the price of the dollar falls, or depreciates, against the mark.

Equilibrium in the market for foreign exchange occurs where the demand curve intersects the supply curve. In Figure 33.1, this occurs at an exchange rate of 2 marks/dollar. At this price, the willingness to trade dollars for marks just matches the willingness to trade marks for dollars. The foreign exchange market is in balance.

Changes in Demand or Supply

Changes in demand or changes in supply will change equilibrium exchange rates. In Figure 33.2, we show how an increase in demand, a shift of the demand curve to the right, will increase, or appreciate, the exchange rate. U.S. dollars will become more expensive relative to German marks as the price of U.S. dollars in terms of marks increases.

Two factors will shift the demand curve for dollars: First, higher U.S. interest rates will lead to an increased demand for dollars. With higher returns in U.S. markets, investors throughout the world will want to buy dollars to invest in U.S. assets. The other factor, lower U.S. prices, will also lead to an increased demand for dollars. For example, if prices at Disneyland fell, there would be an overall increase in the demand for dollars because more tourists would want to visit Disneyland.

Figure 33.3 shows the effects of an increase in the supply of dollars, a shift in the supply curve to the right. An increase in the supply of dollars will lead to a fall, or depreciation, of the value of the dollar against the mark. What will cause the supply of dollars to increase? Again, the same two factors: interest rates and prices. Higher German inter-

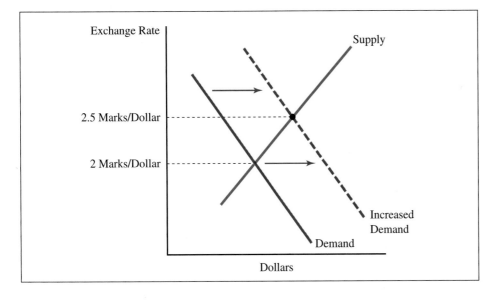

Figure 33.2

Shifts in Demand for Dollars
An increase in the demand for dollars will increase (appreciate) the exchange rate. Higher U.S. interest rates or lower U.S. prices will increase the demand for dollars.

est rates will lead U.S. investors to purchase German bonds or other interest-paying assets. Purchasing German bonds will require U.S. investors to supply dollars for marks, which will drive down the exchange rate for dollars. Lower German prices will also lead to an increase in the supply of dollars for marks.

Let's summarize the key facts about the foreign exchange market, using German marks as our example:

1. The demand curve for dollars represents the demand for dollars in exchange for marks. It is downward sloping. As the dollar depreciates, there will be an increase in the quantity demanded of dollars in exchange for marks.

2. The supply curve for dollars is the supply of dollars in exchange for marks. It is upward sloping. As the dollar appreciates, there will be an increase in the quantity supplied of dollars in exchange for marks.

3. Increases in U.S. interest rates and decreases in U.S. prices will increase the demand for dollars, leading to an appreciation of the dollar.

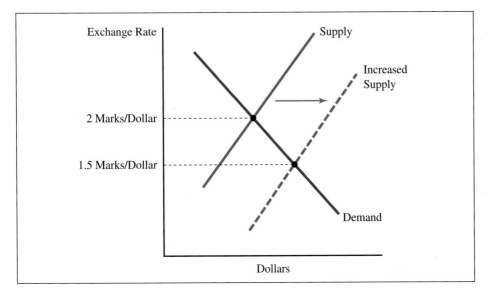

Figure 33.3

Shifts in the Supply of Dollars
An increase in the supply of dollars will decrease (depreciate) the exchange rate. Higher German interest rates or lower German prices will increase the supply of dollars.

4. Increases in German interest rates and decreases in German prices will increase the supply of dollars in exchange for marks, leading to a depreciation of the dollar.

TEST Your Understanding

Use demand and supply analysis to determine whether the dollar will appreciate or depreciate against the mark in each of these cases.

1. Banks cut interest rates in Germany.

2. Interest rates fall in the United States.

3. Annual inflation increases from 4% to 6% in the United States.

4. The German inflation rate falls from 5% to 3% per year.

Real Exchange Rates and Purchasing Power Parity

As our examples of German cuckoo clocks and Disneyland indicate, changes in market exchange rates can affect the demand for a country's goods and services. However, we have been assuming that the prices of cuckoo clocks and trips to Disneyland do not change. In general, prices change over time, and we need to adjust the exchange rate determined in the foreign exchange market to take into account changes in prices. This is an application of the reality principle.

REALITY **PRINCIPLE**

What matters to people is the real value of money or income—its purchasing power—not the face value of money or income.

Real exchange rate: The market exchange rate adjusted for prices.

Economists have developed a concept that adjusts the market exchange rates for changes in prices. It is called the real exchange rate. The **real exchange rate** is defined as the price of all U.S. goods and services relative to all foreign goods and services, expressed in a common currency. We measure it by expressing U.S. prices for goods and services in foreign currency and comparing them to foreign prices. Here is the formula for the real exchange rate:

real exchange rate = (exchange rate × U.S. price index)/foreign price index

We can use this formula to help us understand the factors that change the real exchange rate. First, an increase in U.S. prices will raise the real exchange rate. When foreign prices and the exchange rate are held constant, an increase in U.S. prices will raise the relative price of U.S. goods. Second, an appreciation of the dollar, when prices are held constant, will also raise the price of U.S. goods relative to foreign goods. And if foreign prices fall, U.S. goods will become more expensive as well.

Be sure to understand the real exchange rate because it takes into account changes in a country's prices. Suppose that country A had an inflation rate of 20% while country B had no inflation. Moreover, the exchange rate of country A fell, or depreciated, 20% against the currency of country B. In this case, there would be no change in the real exchange rate between the two countries. Although prices in country A would have increased by 20%, its currency would be 20% cheaper. From the point of view of residents of country B, nothing has changed at all; it would still cost them the same price in their currency to buy goods in country A.

Economists have found that a country's net exports (exports minus its imports) will decrease when its real exchange rate increases. For example, if the U.S. real exchange rate increases, the prices of U.S. goods will increase relative to foreign goods. This will reduce U.S. exports because our goods will have become more expensive; it will also increase imports to the United States because foreign goods will have become cheaper. As a result of the decrease in U.S. exports and the increase in U.S. imports, net exports will decline.

Figure 33.4 plots an index of the real exchange rate for the United States against net exports for the 1980s, a decade in which there were large changes in net exports and in the real exchange rate. The index is based on an average of real exchange rates with all U.S. trading partners; it's called a **multilateral real exchange rate**. Notice that when the multilateral real exchange rate increased, U.S. net exports fell. Net exports increased after 1984 as the real exchange rate began to decrease.

Real exchange rates vary over time, as shown in Figure 33.4. But for goods traded easily across countries (such as gold bars), we would expect the price to be the same when expressed in a common currency. For example, the price of gold bars sold in France should be nearly identical to the price of gold bars sold in New York. If the price were higher in France, demand would shift to New York, raising the price in New York and lowering the price in France until the prices were equal.

The tendency for easily tradable goods to sell at the same price when expressed in a common currency is known as the **law of one price.** Metals, agricultural commodities, computer chips, and other tradable goods follow the law of one price.

If all goods were easily tradable and the law of one price held exactly, exchange rates would reflect no more than the differences in the way the price levels are expressed in the two countries. For example, if a basket of goods in France costs 3,000 francs and the identical basket costs $1,000 in the United States, an exchange rate of 3 francs/dollar would make the costs the same in either currency.

Multilateral real exchange rate: An index of the real exchange rate with a country's trading partners.

Law of one price: The theory that goods that are easily tradable across countries should sell at the same price, expressed in a common currency.

Figure 33.4
Real Exchange Rate and Net Exports in the United States, 1980–1990

Source: Data from *International Financial Statistics* (International Monetary Fund) and *Economic Report of the President* (Washington, DC: U.S. Government Printing Office, yearly).

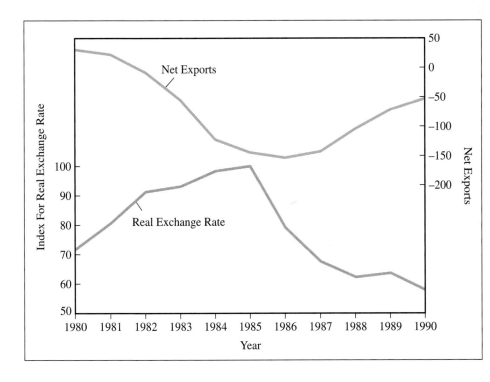

According to one theory of how market exchange rates are determined, market exchange rates simply reflect differences in the overall price levels between countries. This theory is known as **purchasing power parity**. In our France–United States example, the theory of purchasing power parity predicts a market exchange rate of 3 francs/dollar. At that exchange rate, French and U.S. goods would sell for the same price if their products were expressed in a common currency.

Research has shown that purchasing power parity does not hold precisely. An example of this has been created by *The Economist* magazine, which measured the price of a Big Mac throughout the world and checked to see whether the law of one price held. Table 33.1 contains the results for selected countries.

Big Macs sell for widely different prices around the globe compared to the $2.43 they go for in the United States. They are a bargain in Hong Kong at $1.32 but expensive in Israel at $3.44. The price in Japan of $2.44 is nearly the same as the price in the United States.

Table 33.1 also contains the market exchange rate predicted by the theory of purchasing power parity. To obtain this exchange rate, divide the price of Big Macs in the foreign country by the dollar price. For example, in Israel the purchasing power exchange rate is

5.72 shekels/dollar (13.9 shekels/$2.43 = 5.72 shekels per dollar)

At this exchange rate, the Big Mac in Israel would cost the same as in the United States. The actual value for the shekel in April 1999 when these prices were computed was 4.04 shekels/dollar, so the Big Mac was more expensive in Israel.

Clearly, purchasing power parity does not give accurate predictions for exchange rates. The reason is that many goods are not traded across countries. For example, housing and services (such as haircuts) are not traded across countries. The law of one price does not hold for nontraded goods, which make up approximately 50% of the value of production in an economy. There is some truth to purchasing power parity because exchange rates do reflect differences in the price level between countries. But as the Big Mac example shows, purchasing power parity is not a reliable guide to exchange rate levels when nontraded goods must be considered.

Economists have successfully used purchasing power parity theory in other settings. Countries that had been experiencing hyperinflation but then brought the inflation to a halt

Table 33.1 The Big Mac Around the World

Country	Price of a Big Mac in Local Currency	Price of a Big Mac in Dollars	Predicted Purchasing Power Exchange Rate (Foreign Currency per Dollar)	Actual Exchange Rate (Foreign Currency per Dollar)
United States	2.43 dollars	$2.43		
United Kingdom	1.90 pounds	$3.07	1.28	1.61
Hong Kong	10.2 HK dollars	$1.32	4.20	7.75
Israel	13.9 shekels	$3.44	5.72	4.04
Mexico	19.9 pesos	$2.09	8.19	9.54
Singapore	3.20 Singapore dollars	$1.85	1.32	1.73
Japan	294 yen	$2.44	121	120

Source: Data from *The Economist*, April 3, 1999, p. 66.

often need assistance in setting an appropriate exchange rate. Purchasing power parity provides a reasonable guide in such cases. Problems associated with nontraded goods are negligible compared to the vast increases in the price level caused by the hyperinflation.

TEST Your Understanding

5. What is the key difference between the real exchange rate and the market exchange rate? Why should we care?

6. Explain why gold bars sell for the same price around the world but Big Macs do not.

The Current Account and the Capital Account

Economists find it useful to divide international transactions into two types: One is called the current account, and the other is called the capital account. A country's **current account** is the sum of its

- net exports (exports minus imports),
- net income received from investments abroad, and
- net transfer payments from abroad (such as foreign aid).

Current account: The sum of net exports (exports minus imports) plus net income received from investments abroad plus net transfers from abroad.

If a country has a positive current account, we say that its current account is in surplus; if it has a negative current account, we say that its current account is in deficit. If the income from investments abroad and net transfer payments is negligible, the current account becomes equivalent to a country's net exports.

We measure a country's transactions in existing assets on its capital account. The **capital account** is defined as the value of the country's net sales (sales less purchases) of assets. If the United States sold $100 billion net in assets, its capital account would be $100 billion. If the value on the capital account is positive, we say that the country has a surplus on the capital account. Similarly, if the value on the capital account is negative, we say that it has a deficit on the capital account.

Capital account: The value of a country's sales less purchases of assets. A sale of a domestic asset is a surplus item on the capital account, while a purchase of a foreign asset is a deficit item on the capital account.

Here is a simple rule for understanding transactions on both the current account and on the capital account: Any action that gives rise to a demand for foreign currency is a deficit item on the current account or on the capital account. Any action that gives rise to a supply of foreign currency is a surplus item on the current account or on the capital account.

Let's apply this rule to the current account and the capital account, taking the point of view of the United States.

1. Current account. A U.S. import is a deficit (negative) item on the current account because we need to demand foreign currency to acquire the import. On the other hand, with a U.S. export, foreign currency is supplied to the United States in exchange for dollars, so it gives rise to a surplus (positive item) on the current account. Income from investments abroad and net transfers received are treated like exports because they result in a supply of foreign currency for dollars. Summarizing, we have

$$U.S. \text{ current account surplus} = U.S. \text{ exports } - U.S. \text{ imports}$$
$$+ \text{ net income from foreign investments}$$
$$+ \text{ net transfers from abroad}$$

2. Capital account. The purchase of a foreign asset by a U.S. resident gives rise to a deficit (negative) item on the capital account because it requires a demand for foreign currency. (You can think of the purchase of a foreign asset as importing assets.) On the other hand, a purchase of a U.S. asset by a foreign resident leads to a supply of foreign currency and a surplus (positive) item on the current account. (This can be thought of as exporting assets.) Summarizing, we have

$$\text{U.S. capital account surplus} = \text{foreign purchases of U.S. assets}$$
$$- \text{U.S. purchases of foreign assets}$$

The current account and the capital account of a country are linked by a very important identity:

$$\text{current account} + \text{capital account} = 0$$

The current account plus the capital account must sum to zero.

The current account and the capital account must sum to zero because any excess demand for foreign currency that arises from transactions in goods and services—that means we're looking at the current account—must be met by an excess supply of foreign currency arising from asset transactions—the capital account. For example, if the United States had a current account deficit of $50 billion, it would have an excess demand of foreign exchange of $50 billion. This excess demand could be met only by a supply of foreign exchange from $50 billion of net purchases of U.S. assets. The $50 billion net purchase of U.S. assets is a $50 billion surplus on the U.S. capital account. So the current account deficit is offset by the capital account surplus.

Let's look at this from a slightly different angle. Consider again the case in which the United States is running a current account deficit because imports from abroad exceed exports. (For simplicity, transfers and income earned from investments abroad are both zero.) The current account deficit means that, on net, foreign residents and their governments are the recipients of dollars because they have sold more goods to the United States than they have purchased.

What do they do with these dollars? They can either hold them or use them to purchase U.S. assets. In either case, foreign residents and their governments have acquired U.S. assets, either dollars or other U.S. assets. The value of these assets is the U.S. current account deficit. Because a sale of a U.S. asset to a foreign resident is a surplus item on the U.S. capital account, the value of the capital account will be equal to the negative of the value of the current account. So from this perspective also, the current account and the capital account must sum to zero.

If a country runs a current account surplus, it acquires foreign exchange. It can either keep the foreign exchange or use it to buy foreign assets. In either case, its purchases of net foreign assets will equal its current account surplus. Because the capital account is the negative of the purchases of net foreign assets, the current account and capital account will again sum to zero.

Since 1982, the United States has run a current account deficit every year. This means that the United States has run a capital account surplus of equal value for these years as well. Because a capital account surplus means that foreign nations acquire a country's assets, the United States has reduced its net holding of foreign assets. In 1986, the U.S. Department of Commerce estimated that the United States had a **net international investment position** of $136 billion, meaning that U.S. holdings of foreign assets exceeded foreign holdings of U.S. assets by $136 billion. Because of its current account deficits, the U.S. net international investment position fell every year. By 1997, it was –$1,223 billion, meaning that foreign residents owned $1,223 billion more U.S. assets than U.S. residents owned foreign assets. You may have heard the United States referred to as a net debtor; this is just another way of saying that the U.S. net international investment position is negative.

Net international investment position: Domestic holdings of foreign assets minus foreign holdings of domestic assets.

Table 33.2 shows the current account and capital account for the United States for 1997. The current account is made up of the balance in goods, services, net investment income, and net transfers. In 1997, all elements of the current account but the service component were negative. The capital account includes net increases in U.S. holdings abroad (negative entries in the capital account) and foreign holdings of U.S. assets (positive entries in the capital account). Because the current account and capital account data are collected separately, there is a statistical discrepancy. Once we include this statistical discrepancy, the current account and the capital account sum to zero.

The capital account is defined to include purchases and sales of assets by governments as well as private individuals. As you will see next, governments often buy or sell foreign exchange to influence the exchange rate for their currency.

Fixing the Exchange Rate

When a country's exchange rate appreciates—increases in value—it has 2 distinct effects:

1. The increased value of the exchange rate makes imports less expensive for the residents of the country where the exchange rate appreciated. For example, if the U.S. dollar appreciates against the French franc, French wines will become less expensive for U.S. consumers. U.S. consumers would like an appreciated dollar, because it would lower their cost of living.

2. The increased value of the exchange rate makes U.S. goods more expensive on world markets. A U.S. exchange appreciation will increase imports, such as French wine, but decrease exports, such as California wine.

Since exports decrease and imports increase, net exports (exports minus imports) will decrease.

When a country's exchange rate depreciates, there are 2 distinct effects:

- For example, if the U.S. dollar depreciated against the Japanese yen, Japanese imports would become more expensive in the United States, thereby raising the U.S. cost of living.

Table 33.2 U.S. Current Account and Capital Account, 1997 (billions)

Current account	
Goods	–197
Services	87
Net investment income	–5
Net Transfers	–40
Total on Current account	–155
Capital account	
Increases in U.S. holdings abroad	–478
Increases in foreign holdings in U.S.	733
Total on Capital account	255
Statistical discrepancy	–100
Sum of current account, capital account, and statistical discrepancy	0

Source: Economic Report of the President (Washington, DC: U.S. Government Printing Office, 1999).

- At the same time, U.S. goods would become cheaper on world markets. With exports increasing and imports decreasing, net exports would increase.

Sometimes countries do not want their exchange rate to change. They may want to avoid sharp increases in their cost of living from an exchange rate depreciation, or they may want to avoid a reduction in net exports through an exchange rate appreciation. To prevent the value of the currency from changing, governments can enter the foreign exchange market to try to influence the price of foreign exchange. Economists call these efforts to influence the value of foreign exchange **foreign exchange market intervention**.

In the United States, the Treasury Department has the official responsibility for foreign exchange intervention, though in conjunction with the Federal Reserve. In other countries, governments also intervene in the foreign exchange market.

To influence the price at which one currency trades for another, governments have to affect the demand or supply for that currency. For example, to increase the value of its currency, a government must increase the demand for its currency; to decrease the value of its currency, a government must increase the supply of its currency.

In Figure 33.5, we show how governments can fix, or peg, the price of a currency. Suppose the U.S. and German governments want the exchange rate to be 2 marks/dollar. The price at which demand and supply are equal, however, is currently 1.5 marks/dollar. To raise the price of dollars, the governments need to increase the demand for dollars. To do this, either government—the United States or Germany—or both can go into the market for foreign exchange and sell marks in exchange for dollars. This will shift the demand curve for dollars to the right until the price of dollars rises to 2 marks/dollar.

In the other direction, if the free market price exceeded 2 marks/dollar, the governments would have to buy marks in exchange for dollars. By selling dollars in exchange for marks, they would increase the supply of dollars and the exchange rate would fall.

Note that to lower the price of dollars, which raises the value of the mark, the U.S. government has to buy marks in exchange for dollars. The U.S. government therefore acquires and accumulates marks anytime it tries to raise the price of marks. On the other hand, the U.S. government must sell some of the marks it has accumulated, to raise the price of dollars, which lowers the value of the mark. What would happen if the United States had no marks to sell? The United States could borrow marks from the German government or persuade Germany to sell marks for dollars.

Foreign exchange market intervention: The purchase or sale of currencies by governments to influence the market exchange rate.

Figure 33.5

Intervention to Raise the Price of Dollars

To increase the price of dollars, the U.S. government sells marks in exchange for dollars. This shifts the demand curve for dollars to the right.

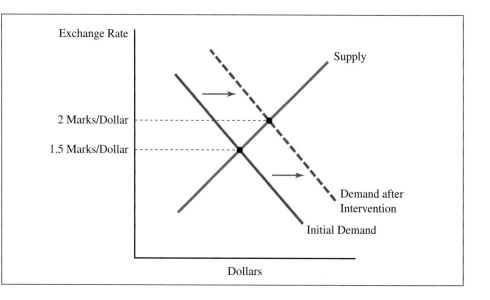

Fixed Versus Flexible Exchange Rates

Next, we discuss two different types of exchange rate systems. Then we take a brief look at the U.S. history on exchange rate policy and developments in exchange rates in the world today.

Fixed Exchange Rates

Whether you are in California, New York, or Indiana, all prices are quoted in dollars. No one asks whether your dollar came from San Francisco or Miami. Within the United States, a dollar is a dollar. Suppose, though, that every state in the United States had its own currency. There might be a California dollar (with a picture of the Golden Gate Bridge), an Oregon dollar (showing pictures of tall trees), and a Florida dollar (showing Disney World, of course). In principle, these dollars might trade at different rates, depending on the supply and demand of one state's dollar relative to the supply and demand for another state's dollar. For example, in one year, the Texas dollar might be worth more than the Michigan dollar, trading for 1.2 Michigan dollars.

Think how much more complicated it would be to do business if each state had different currencies. To buy goods from a mail-order company in Maine, you would have to find out the exchange rate between your state's dollar and the Maine dollar. Any large business operating in all 50 states would be overwhelmed by trying to keep track of all exchange rate movements across the states. The economy would become less efficient as individuals and businesses focused all their attention on exchange rates.

These same ideas apply across nations. Wouldn't it be nice if all countries either used the same currency or fixed their exchange rates against one another so that no one would have to worry about exchange rate movements? Currency systems in which governments try to keep constant the values of their currencies against one another are called **fixed exchange rate** systems.

In a typical fixed exchange rate system, one country stands at the center, and other countries fix, or peg, their exchange rates to the currency of this center country. Each other country must intervene in the foreign exchange market, if necessary, to keep its exchange rate constant. A government will have to intervene if, at the fixed exchange rate, the private demand and supply for its currency are not equal.

Suppose the supply of a country's currency exceeds the demand at the fixed exchange rate. An excess supply of a country's currency at the fixed exchange rate, is known as a **balance of payments deficit**. A balance of payments deficit will occur whenever there is a deficit on the current account that is not matched by net sales of assets to foreigners by the private sector. (For example, a current account deficit of $100 billion with net sales of assets to foreigners of only $80 billion would mean that there is an excess supply of $20 billion.) With an excess supply of a country's currency in the currency market, that currency would fall in value without any intervention. To prevent the currency from depreciating in value and to maintain the fixed exchange rate, the government must sell foreign exchange—that means sell foreign currency—and buy its own currency. As you saw in our discussion of foreign exchange intervention, if a country sells foreign exchange, its holdings of foreign exchange will fall. So you can see that when a country runs a balance of payments deficit, it will decrease its holdings of foreign exchange.

It's also very possible that the demand for a country's currency exceeds the supply of its currency at the fixed exchange rate. An excess demand for a country's currency at the fixed exchange rate is known as a **balance of payments surplus**. A balance of payments surplus arises when there is a current account surplus that is not matched by net purchases of foreign assets by the private sector. With an excess demand for a country's currency, it

Fixed exchange rates: A system in which governments peg exchange rates between currencies.

Balance of payments deficit: Under a fixed exchange rate system, a situation in which the supply of a country's currency exceeds the demand for the currency at the current exchange rate.

Balance of payments surplus: Under a fixed exchange rate system, a situation in which the demand for a country's currency exceeds the supply of its currency at the current exchange rate.

would rise in value without any intervention. To prevent the currency from appreciating in value and to maintain the fixed exchange rate, the government must buy foreign exchange—buy foreign currency—and sell its own currency. Because it is buying foreign exchange, its holdings of foreign exchange will increase. From this discussion, you should be able to see that when a country runs a balance of payments surplus, it will increase its holding of foreign exchange.

Under a fixed exchange rate system, countries that run persistent balance of payments deficits or balance of payments surpluses must take corrective actions. If domestic policy actions—such as changing taxes, changing spending, or changing the supply of money—do not cure the problem, it will eventually become necessary to change the level at which the exchange rate is fixed. A country that faces a balance of payments deficit can lower the value at which the currency is pegged to increase its net exports; this is called a **devaluation**. Conversely, a country that faces a balance of payments surplus can increase the value at which its currency is pegged and reduce its net exports; this is called a **revaluation**.

Devaluation: A decrease in the exchange rate in a fixed exchange rate system.
Revaluation: An increase in the exchange rate in a fixed exchange rate system.

The U.S. Experience with Fixed and Flexible Exchange Rates

After World War II, the countries of the world operated under a fixed exchange system known as Bretton Woods, after the town in New Hampshire where the representatives of each nation met and agreed to adopt this system. The United States operated at the center of this system: All countries fixed or pegged their currencies against the U.S. dollar.

The Bretton Woods system lasted until the early 1970s when the world abandoned it and went to the current system—a **flexible exchange rate system**—in which free markets primarily determine exchange rates. What that means is that the exchange rate of a currency is determined by the supply and demand for it.

Flexible exchange rates: A currency system in which exchange rates are determined by free markets.

If a fixed exchange rate system makes it easier to trade, why did it break down in the early 1970s? Fixed exchange rate systems provide benefits, but they require countries to maintain similar economic policies—especially to maintain similar inflation rates and interest rates.

To understand this, suppose the exchange rate between the United States and Germany were fixed, but the United States had an annual inflation rate of 6% compared to 0% inflation in Germany. Because prices in the United States would be rising by 6% per year, the U.S. real exchange rate against Germany would also be increasing at 6% per year. This difference in their real exchange rates over time would cause a trade deficit to emerge in the United States as U.S. goods became more expensive on world markets. As long as the differences in inflation continued and the exchange rate remained fixed, the U.S. real exchange rate would continue to appreciate, and the U.S. trade deficit would grow even worse. Clearly, this course of events could not continue.

In the late 1960s, inflation in the United States began to exceed inflation in other countries, and a U.S. balance of payments deficit emerged. In 1971, President Nixon surprised the world and devalued the U.S. dollar against the currencies of all the other countries. This was a sharp departure from the rules underlying Bretton Woods, in which the United States was at the center of the system and other countries were supposed to make adjustments, if necessary, against the dollar. Nixon hoped that a one-time devaluation of the dollar would alleviate the U.S. balance of payments deficit and maintain the underlying system of fixed exchange rates.

However, the U.S. devaluation did not stop the U.S. balance of payments deficit. Germany tried to maintain the mark's fixed exchange rate with the U.S. dollar by purchasing U.S. dollars in the foreign exchange market. What Germany was doing was importing inflation from the United States. With the U.S. balance of payments deficit continuing, Germany was required to buy U.S. dollars to keep the mark from appreciating. Germany bought U.S. dollars with German marks. Those German marks were then put into circulation. The German supply of marks in Germany increased. The increase in marks raised the inflation rate in Germany.

Private-sector investors, moreover, knew that Germany did not wish to run persistent trade surpluses and import U.S. inflation. They bet that Germany would revalue the mark against the dollar—that is, raise the value of the mark against the dollar. These speculators bought massive amounts of German assets, trading dollars for marks to purchase them. Their actions forced the German government to buy even more dollars. The flow of financial capital into Germany was so massive that the German government eventually gave up all attempts to keep its exchange rate fixed to the dollar, letting its exchange rate be determined in the free market. This was the end of the Bretton Woods system.

Exchange Rate Systems Today

The flexible exchange rate system has worked well enough since the breakdown of Bretton Woods. World trade has grown at a rapid rate. Moreover, the flexible exchange rate system has managed to handle many diverse situations, including two major oil shocks, large U.S. budget deficits in the 1980s, and large current account surpluses by the Japanese.

During the Bretton Woods period, many countries placed restrictions on flows of financial capital, for example, by not allowing their residents to purchase foreign assets or by limiting foreigners' purchases of domestic assets. By the 1970s, these restrictions began to be eliminated, and private-sector transactions in assets grew rapidly. With massive amounts of funds being traded in financial markets, it becomes very difficult to fix, or peg, an exchange rate.

Nonetheless, countries whose economies are closely tied together might want the advantages of fixed exchange rates. One way to avoid some of the difficulties of fixing exchange rates between countries is to abolish individual currencies and establish a single currency. This is precisely what a group of European countries decided to do. Their plan is to have a single currency throughout Europe and a single central bank to control the supply of the currency. The common currency has been named the **euro**. "A Closer Look: The Euro," provides more details on this system. With a single currency, European countries hope to capture the benefits of a large market, such as the market within the United States.

Euro: The common currency in Europe.

The United Kingdom initially decided to remain outside this European single-currency system. Its currency, like the U.S. dollar and the Japanese yen, will float against each of those currencies and the euro. Many other countries have tied their exchange rate to either the dollar or the yen. Some economists believe that the world will eventually settle into three large currency blocs: the euro, the dollar, and the yen.

Managing Financial Crises

Hardly a year goes by without some international financial crisis. In 1994, Mexico experienced a severe financial crisis. In 1997, the Asian economic crisis began. How do these crises originate? What policies can be taken to prevent or alleviate them?

Let's first consider the Mexican case. During the late 1980s and early 1990s, Mexico decided to fix, or peg, its exchange to the U.S. dollar. Mexico's goal was to signal to investors throughout the world that it was serious about controlling inflation and would take the necessary steps to keep its inflation rates in line with the United States. Mexico also opened up its markets to let in foreign investors. Mexico seemed to be on a solid path to development.

A CLOSER LOOK | The Euro

January 1, 1999, was the day that the euro, the new common European currency made its debut. On that day, Austria, Belgium, Finland, France, Germany, Ireland, Italy, Luxembourg, Netherlands, Portugal, and Spain irrevocably fixed their exchange rates to the euro. By 2002, euro notes and coins will be introduced. Until then, the national currencies of these countries can circulate along with the euro. After July 1, 2002, national currencies will disappear. French francs, German marks, Italian lire, and other currencies will have ceased to exist.

A European central bank will manage the monetary affairs for the single currency. It will play a role similar to the role the Federal Reserve Bank plays in the United States. The countries in the European Union will no longer be able to conduct their own independent monetary policy. With monetary policy gone, fiscal policy will be their only remaining tool for macroeconomic stabilization policy.

Not all the European countries joined this system. Fearing a possible loss of independence, the United Kingdom, Denmark, and Sweden decided not to join this system initially. Greece would have liked to join, but it did not meet some of the EU's fiscal criteria necessary to join. Economists will carefully watch this experiment unfold in the twenty-first century.

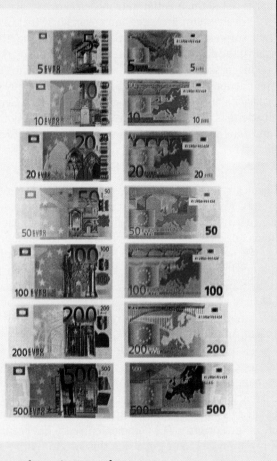

Different denominatons of euro notes.

However, in some sense, the policies proved to be too successful in encouraging foreign investment. As funds poured into the country, the demand for goods increased, and prices started to rise. This rise in prices caused an increase in Mexico's real exchange rate, and the rise in the real exchange rate caused a large trade deficit to emerge. From January 1988 to February 1994, the real exchange rate for Mexico with the United States (the price of Mexican goods relative to U.S. goods) increased by 67%.

Initially, the trade deficit did not cause any difficulties for the Mexican government. Because foreign investors were willingly trading foreign currencies for Mexican pesos to buy Mexican securities, the government in Mexico did not have any problem maintaining its pegged exchange rate with the United States. Although the Mexicans were importing more than they were exporting, they could obtain the necessary dollars to finance this trade imbalance from foreign investors who were purchasing Mexican securities. The government did not have to intervene in the foreign exchange market to keep the price of the peso constant against the dollar. In other words, Mexico did not have a balance of payments deficit.

But then, internal political difficulties arose in Mexico. Following an assassination of a political candidate and a rural uprising, foreign investors started to pull their funds out of Mexico. At this point, the Mexican government made a crucial mistake. Instead of trying to reduce its trade deficit by taking steps to reduce prices, it allowed the trade deficit to continue. Moreover, both the government and the private sector began to find that they had to borrow in dollars because foreign investors thought Mexico might be forced to devalue the peso. If a devaluation did occur, any lender in pesos would suffer a loss because the debt would be repaid at a lower exchange rate. Consequently, Mexican borrowers were forced to borrow in loans denominated in dollars.

Eventually, more political turmoil caused investors to pull out their funds, selling pesos for dollars. The Mexican central bank spent nearly $50 billion buying these pesos in an effort to keep the exchange rate constant. The $50 billion was not enough. Mexico ran out of dollars. Because it could no longer buy pesos to maintain the exchange rate, Mexico had to devalue, putting the peso more in line with its market value.

The devaluation created even more turmoil because the government and the private sector had borrowed billions in dollars. When the peso was devalued against the dollar, the burden of these debts measured in pesos increased sharply, so more pesos were needed to pay the dollar-denominated debts. Mexico faced the prospect of massive bankruptcies and the potential collapse of its economy.

To prevent a financial collapse that could easily have spread to many other developing countries, the U.S. government (along with other international financial institutions) arranged for Mexico to borrow dollars with an extended period for repayment. This allowed Mexican banks and corporations to avoid bankruptcies and prevented a major disaster. In 1996, the Mexican government was able to pay off nearly three-fourths of the loan from the United States.

The Asian crisis had a similar flavor. Economic growth had been remarkable in Asia for over 20 years, improving to a great extent the standard of living of millions of people. In the early 1990s, several Asian countries began to open up their capital markets to foreign investors and began to borrow extensively from abroad. Billions of dollars poured into Asia. In many cases, there was little financial supervision, and many of the investments proved to be unwise. Companies in both Thailand and South Korea began to lose money. Domestic investors and world investors suddenly became pessimistic and began pulling their funds out of South Korea and Thailand, among other Asian countries. The withdrawal of funds forced devaluations of currencies throughout Asia. Because many businesses had borrowed in dollars, the devaluations raised the burden of the debt and further deepened the crisis, taking its toll on other countries, including Indonesia, Malaysia, and Hong Kong. The International Monetary Fund attempted to help restore the health of these economies' financial systems, but in many cases, their policies were ineffective. The countries that undertook fiscal reforms were the quickest to recover. As "A Closer Look: Unnecessary Crisis?," indicates, some economists believe that the entire Asian crisis was an example of market overreaction and could have been avoided by bolder action.

These examples highlight many of the ingredients of a financial crisis. With our vast global capital markets, funds can move quickly from country to country, and economic policies sometimes do not keep pace with changing political and economic developments. It can be extremely difficult to maintain a fixed exchange rate in this environment. The flow of funds, moreover, is often so large that financial failures could cause major global disruptions in trade and commerce. The major countries of the world are searching for a reliable set of rules and institutional mechanisms to assist in financial crises. Historically, the International Monetary Fund has played a key role in assisting countries that run into financial difficulties. However, in Mexico, the sums were so large that the United States was forced to take the lead in resolving its situation. In Asia, the International Monetary Fund did not have this backing from the United States, and it

A CLOSER LOOK   Unnecessary Crisis?

Some economists believe that the Asian crisis could have been avoided if major countries and international agencies had taken stronger action, such as large loans. Although some problems were emerging in Asia, these economists believed that the economies in Asia were fundamentally sound. However, they had borrowed extensively, and their short-term debts exceeded the foreign exchange reserves they had on hand. That made the countries *illiquid* (not having enough currency on hand) but not *insolvent* (bankrupt). In some ways, their situation was analogous to banks that never keep enough currency on hand to meet the immediate demands of their depositors.

Pursuing the banking analogy, these economists argue that the world needs a lender of last resort to prevent these crises from emerging. Such a lender (backed by the world's financial powers) could prevent unnecessary crises. However, other economists and world leaders are skeptical that such a lender would routinely be able to outguess the private markets in assessing the underlying health of the world economies. Moreover, the sums involved are so large in today's market that they could produce unacceptable risks for major financial powers.

was less successful. As world capital markets continue to grow, governments throughout the world will almost surely be tested through new and often unpredictable financial crises. They will need to anticipate and react to rapid changes in the economic and political environment to maintain a stable financial environment for trade.

Using the **TOOLS**

In this chapter, we developed several tools, including the demand and supply for foreign exchange, and the real exchange rate. Take this opportunity to do your own economic analysis.

1. ECONOMIC EXPERIMENT: Determining Exchange Rates

In this experiment, you will see how exchange rates are determined. The class is divided into two groups. One group will be buying a fixed number of German marks. The other group will be selling a fixed number of German marks. Each buyer will have a maximum price that he or she is willing to pay. Each seller will have a minimum price that he or she is willing to accept. Trade will take place in several rounds. In each round, buyers and sellers will meet individually and either negotiate a trade or not. If a trade results, the results will be reported to the instructor and then announced to the class. After each round, the instructor announces the prices at which German marks were traded. After several rounds, what happens to the prices?

2. The Real Exchange Rate Between Germany and the United States

Consider the following data for the United States and Germany:

Year	Germany GDP Deflator	U.S. GDP Deflator	Market Exchange Rate
1980	85.7	76.0	2.49 marks/dollar
1990	113.4	119.6	2.12 marks/dollar

a. By what percent did the dollar depreciate against the mark over this period?

b. Using the formula for the real exchange rate,

$$\text{real exchange rate} = (\text{exchange rate} \times \text{U.S. price index})/\text{foreign price index}$$

compute the real exchange rate for 1980 and for 1990.

c. By how much did the real exchange rate change over this period? Compare your answer to part (a).

3. Exchange Rate Depreciation and the Returns from Investing

A newspaper headline said, "Foreign Investors Fear Dollar Depreciation: U.S. Interest Rates Rise."

a. Suppose you were a German citizen and had invested in a 1-year U.S. bond that yielded 6% per year. The bond cost $1,000 and paid $1,060 at the end of the year. At the time you bought the bond, the exchange rate was 2 marks/dollar. How many marks did the bond cost? If the exchange rate remained at 2 marks/dollar when you received your payment, how many marks would you have? What would be your percentage return in marks for the year?

b. Suppose the dollar fell against the mark during the year from 2 marks to 1.5 marks/dollar. At the end of the year, how many marks would you have? What would be your percentage return in marks for the year?

c. Using your answers to parts (a) and (b), explain the newspaper headline.

4. Pressures on the Bank of England

During the late 1980s, the United Kingdom had fixed exchange rates with other countries in Europe, including Germany. To fight inflationary pressures after East Germany and West Germany were reunited, the German central bank raised interest rates sharply.

a. Let's figure out why the United Kingdom had to raise interest rates along with Germany. First, if the United Kingdom did not raise interest rates, what would investors do with their funds? Second, what effect would this movement of funds have had on the British pound? To prevent these changes in the British pound, what would the British central bank have had to do?

b. In fact, speculators in foreign exchange believed that the Bank of England would not raise interest rates. Why did speculators sell British pounds in massive amounts? Why did this force the British government to abandon its fixed exchange rate with Germany?

Summary

In this chapter, we examined the world of international finance. You saw how exchange rates are determined in markets and how governments can influence these markets. You also learned how the real exchange rate affects the trade deficit. Behind the complex world of international financial transactions are these few simple ideas:

1. Exchange rates are currently determined in foreign exchange markets by supply and demand.

2. The real exchange rate—the market exchange rate adjusted for prices—is the relative price of a country's goods and services on world markets.

3. The current account and the capital account are related as follows:

- The current account is equal to net exports plus net income from existing investments abroad and net transfers from abroad.

- The capital account is the value of a country's sales less purchases of assets.

- The sum of the current account plus the capital account is zero.

4. Governments can attempt to change the value of currencies by buying or selling currencies in the foreign exchange market. Purchasing a currency will raise its value; selling a currency will decrease its value.

5. A system of fixed exchange rates can provide a better environment for business but requires that countries keep their inflation rates and interest rates within narrow limits.

Key Terms

appreciation, 684
balance of payments deficit, 695
balance of payments surplus, 695
capital account, 691
current account, 691
depreciation, 684
devaluation, 696

euro, 697
exchange rate, 684
fixed exchange rates, 695
flexible exchange rates, 696
foreign exchange market
    intervention, 694
law of one price, 689

multilateral real exchange
    rate, 689
net international investment
    position, 692
purchasing power parity, 690
real exchange rate, 688
revaluation, 696

Problems and Discussion Questions

1. Using demand and supply analysis to assist you, what are the effects on the exchange rate between the British pound and the Japanese yen from:
   a. an increase in Japanese interest rates
   b. an increase in the price of British goods
   c. an increase in British interest rates

2. Let's estimate the exchange rate between the United States and the imaginary country of Oz. Your only information is that a Big Mac costs $2.50 in the United States and 30 ozzies in Oz. What is your estimate of the exchange rate between the dollar and the ozzie?

3. Suppose that a South American country saw its exchange rate depreciate 10% against the dollar and that prices in that country rose 12% while prices in the United States did not change. What happened to the real exchange rate between the South American country and the United States?

4. A country had exports of $20 billion, imports of $25 billion, net transfers from abroad of –$15 billion, and –$12 billion of net income from foreign investments. What is the country's balance on the current account?

5. A country ran a current account deficit last year (measured in dollars) of $25 billion. What was its balance on the capital account?

6. Suppose the United States reported that the U.S. Treasury had increased its holdings of foreign currencies from last year. What does this tell you about the foreign exchange policies in which the United States had engaged during the last year?

7. There are rumors that there is about to be a military coup in an Eastern European country. Explain what you think will happen to the country's exchange rate.

8. What would be required before all the countries of the world could enter into a fixed exchange rate system? Do you think it is feasible?

9. Why did inflation in Mexico lead to a rise in the real exchange rate between Mexico and the United States?

10. Explain why apartments rent for different prices around the world while gold bars sell for the same price (measured in a common currency).

11. When a country depreciates its currency, initially its competitiveness in world markets increases. Then why are countries often reluctant to depreciate their currencies?

12. Until the early 1980s, Japan had required its large insurance companies to invest all their vast holdings in Japanese securities. At the prompting of the United States, Japan relaxed the restrictions and allowed the companies to invest anywhere in the world. What effect do you think this had on the yen/dollar exchange rate and the trade balance between the two countries?

13. **Web Exercise.** What are the key policy issues facing the European Central Bank? Go to the Web site of the European Central Bank (*http://www.ecb .int/about/about.htm*). Outline the three most important issues that are currently being debated.

14. **Web Exercise.** Use the Web to find data for a U.S. price index, a Japanese price index, and the yen/dollar exchange rate. You might start with the Web site for the Federal Reserve Bank of St. Louis (*http://www.stls.frb.org/fred*) for U.S. prices and the yen/dollar exchange rate and the Web site for the Japan Statistical Yearbook (*http://www.stat .go.jp/1431.htm*) for data on Japan. What has happened to the real exchange rate between the United States and Japan over the last 10 years?

Take It to the Net

We invite you to visit the O'Sullivan/Sheffrin page on the Prentice Hall Web site at:
http://www.prenhall.com/osullivan/
for additional World Wide Web exercises for this chapter.

Model Answers for this Chapter

Chapter-Opening Questions

1. An increase in U.S. interest rates will raise the value of the dollar against the German mark. This increase in value of the dollar against the mark will decrease the cost for U.S. residents of a summer trip to Europe.

2. If the dollar increases in value against the Japanese yen, it will make our exports more expensive and Japanese imports less expensive. This dollar increase against the yen will reduce our trade balance with Japan.

3. Governments intervene in the market for foreign exchange because they prefer to have a different exchange rate than the one that would come from pure market transactions.

4. Many European countries have adopted a single currency because they believe that a single large market with no worries of exchange rate changes will reduce the costs of trade.

5. Financial crises emerge when private investors suddenly wish to withdraw funds from a country and, as a result, disrupt current financial arrangements.

Test Your Understanding

1. The dollar will appreciate.
2. The dollar will depreciate.
3. The dollar will depreciate.
4. The dollar will depreciate.
5. The nominal exchange rate is the market exchange rate; the real exchange rate adjusts for changes in the prices. The trade balance is related to the real exchange rate, not the market exchange rate.

6. Gold bars are easily transported and, unlike Big Macs, are not largely made and sold with nontraded goods.

Using the Tools

2. The Real Exchange Rate Between Germany and the United States
   a. The dollar fell by 14.8% [(2.12 − 2.49)/2.49 = 0.148].
   b. The real exchange rate increased from 2.208 to 2.236.
   c. Using the formula for the real exchange, we find that the real exchange rate was 2.208 in 1980 and 2.236 in 1990. That is an increase of 1.3% from 1980 to 1990. Although the dollar depreciated, prices rose more in the United States than in Germany, so the real exchange rate actually increased.

3. Exchange Rate Depreciation and the Returns from Investing
   a. At 2 marks/dollar, the bond costs 2,000 marks and pays 2,120 marks, for a 6% return.
   b. If the dollar fell to 1.5 marks/dollar, at the end of the year you would only have (1,060)(1.5) = 1,590 marks, and your return on your 2,000-mark investment would be −20.5%.
   c. If the dollar falls, returns measured in marks will decrease and foreign investors will find dollar investments less attractive. To keep investors

from withdrawing funds from the United States, interest rates would have to increase.

4. Pressures on the Bank of England

 a. If the British did not raise interest rates, investors would have sold British securities to buy German securities. This would have depreciated the pound. The British government would have been forced to sell marks for pounds, decreasing the money supply and raising British interest rates.

 b. If speculators believed that Britain would not raise interest rates, the British pound would fall against the mark. To profit from the fall in the pound, speculators would sell pounds and buy German marks. The massive selling of pounds would require either massive purchases of pounds or higher interest rates. The British were not willing to do this, so they let the pound's value be determined in the market.

Glossary

Absolute advantage: The ability of one person or nation to produce a particular good at a lower absolute cost than that of another person or nation.

Accelerator theory: The theory of investment that says current investment spending depends positively on the expected future growth of real GDP.

Adverse-selection problem: The uninformed side of the market must choose from an undesirable or adverse selection of goods.

Aggregate demand: The relationship between the level of prices and the quantity of real GDP demanded.

Aggregate production function: Shows how much output is produced from capital and labor.

Aggregate supply: The relationship between the level of prices and the quantity of output supplied.

Anticipated inflation: Inflation that is expected.

Appreciation: An increase in the value of a currency.

Asian Pacific Economic Cooperation (APEC) organization: An organization of 18 Asian nations that attempts to reduce trade barriers between their nations.

Assets: The uses of the funds of a bank, including loans and reserves.

Asymmetric information: One side of the market—either buyers or sellers—has better information about the good than the other.

Autarky: A situation in which each country is self-sufficient, so there is no trade.

Automatic stabilizers: Taxes and transfer payments that stabilize GDP without requiring policymakers to take explicit action.

Autonomous consumption: The part of consumption that does not depend on income.

Average-cost pricing policy: A regulatory policy under which the government picks the point on the demand curve at which price equals average cost.

Average fixed cost (AFC): Fixed cost divided by the quantity produced.

Balanced budget: The situation in which total expenditures equals total revenues.

Balance of payments deficit: Under a fixed exchange rate system, a situation in which the supply of a country's currency exceeds the demand for the currency at the current exchange rate.

Balance of payments surplus: Under a fixed exchange rate system, a situation in which the demand for a country's currency exceeds the supply of the currency at the current exchange rate.

Balance sheet: An account for a bank that shows the sources of its funds (liabilities) as well as the uses for the funds (assets).

Barter: Trading goods directly for other goods.

Board of Governors of the Federal Reserve: The seven-person governing body of the Federal Reserve system in Washington, DC.

Bond: A promise or IOU to pay money in the future in exchange for money now.

Budget deficit: The difference between a government's spending and its revenues from taxation.

Budget line: The line connecting all the combinations of two goods that exhaust a consumer's budget.

Budget set: A set of points that includes all the combinations of two goods that a consumer can afford, given the consumer's income and the prices of the two goods.

Business cycles: Another name for economic fluctuations.

Capital: See **physical capital**; see **human capital**.

Capital account: The value of a country's sales less purchases of assets. A sale of a domestic asset is a surplus item on the capital account, while a purchase of a foreign asset is a deficit item on the capital account.

Capital deepening: Increases in the stock of capital per worker.

Carbon tax: A tax based on a fuel's carbon content.

Cartel: A group of firms that coordinate their pricing decisions, often by charging the same price.

Central bank: A banker's bank; an official bank that controls the supply of money in a country.

Centrally planned economy: An economy in which a government bureaucracy decides how much of each good to produce, how to produce the goods, and how to allocate the products among consumers.

Ceteris paribus: Latin meaning "other things being equal."

Chain index: A method for calculating changes in prices that uses data from neighboring years.

Change in demand: A change in the amount of a good demanded resulting from a change in something other than the price of the good; represented graphically by a shift of a demand curve.

Change in quantity demanded: A change in the amount of a good demanded resulting from a change in the price of the good; represented graphically by a movement along a demand curve.

Change in quantity supplied: A change in the amount of a good supplied resulting from a change in the price of the good; represented graphically by a movement along a supply curve.

Change in supply: A change in the amount of a good supplied resulting from a change in something other than the price of the good; represented graphically by a shift of the supply curve.

Classical aggregate supply curve: A vertical aggregate supply curve. It reflects the idea that in the long run, output is determined solely by the factors of production.

Classical economics: A school of thought that provides insights into the economy when it operates at or near full employment.

Closed economy: An economy without international trade.

Command-and-control policy: A pollution-control policy under which the government commands each firm to produce no more than a certain volume of pollution and controls the firm's production process by forcing the firm to use a particular pollution-control technology.

Community rating: In a given community or metropolitan area, every firm pays the same price for medical insurance.

Comparative advantage: The ability of one person or nation to produce a good at an opportunity cost that is lower than the opportunity cost of another person or nation.

Complements: Two goods for which an increase in the price of one good decreases the demand for the other good.

Concentration ratio: A measure of the degree of concentration in a market; the four-firm concentration ratio is the percentage of output produced by the four largest firms.

Constant-cost industry: An industry in which the average cost of production is constant, so the long-run supply curve is horizontal.

Consumer Price Index (CPI): A price index that measures the cost of a fixed basket of goods chosen to represent the consumption pattern of individuals.

Consumer surplus: The difference between the maximum amount a consumer is willing to pay for a product and the price the consumer pays for the product.

Consumption expenditures: Purchases of newly produced goods and services by households.

Consumption function: The relationship between the level of income and consumption spending.

Consumption possibilities curve: A curve showing the combinations of two goods that can be consumed when a nation specializes in a particular good and trades with another nation.

Consumption taxation: A system of taxation which is based on the consuption, not the income, of individuals.

Contestable market: A market in which the costs of entering and leaving are very low, so the firms in the market are constantly threatened by the entry of new firms.

Contractionary policies: Government policy actions that lead to decreases in output.

Convergence: The process by which poorer countries "catch up" with richer countries in terms of real GDP per capita.

Cost-of-living adjustments: Automatic increases in wages or other payments that are tied to a price index.

Countercyclical: Moving in the opposite direction of real GDP.

Craft union: A labor organization that includes workers from a particular occupation, for example, plumbers, bakers, or electricians.

Creative destruction: The process by which competition for monopoly profits leads to technological progress.

Cross elasticity of demand: A measure of the responsiveness of the quantity demanded to changes in the price of a related good; computed by dividing the percentage change in the quantity demanded of one good (X) by the percentage change in the price of another good (Y).

Crowding in: The increase of investment (or other component of GDP) in the long run caused by a decrease in government spending.

Crowding out: The reduction in investment (or other component of GDP) in the long run caused by an increase in government spending.

Current account: The sum of net exports (exports minus imports) plus income received from investments abroad plus net transfers from abroad.

Cyclical unemployment: The component of unemployment that accompanies fluctuations in real GDP.

Deadweight loss from monopoly: A measure of the inefficiency from monopoly; equal to the difference between the consumer surplus loss from monopoly pricing and the monopoly profit.

Deadweight loss from taxation: The difference between the total burden of a tax and the amount of revenue collected by the government; also known as excess burden.

Deficit: The excess of total expenditures over total revenues.

Demand curve: See *individual demand curve*; see *market demand curve*.

Demand schedule: A table of numbers that shows the relationship between price and quantity demanded by a consumer, ceteris paribus (other things being equal).

Dependency ratio: The ratio of the population over 65 years of age to the population between 20 and 65.

Depreciation: The wear and tear of capital as it is used in production.

Depression: The common name for a severe recession.

Devaluation: A decrease in the exchange rate to which a currency is pegged in a fixed rate system.

Diminishing returns: As one input increases while the other inputs are held fixed, output increases but at a decreasing rate.

Discount rate: The interest rate at which banks can borrow from the Fed.

Discouraged workers: Workers who left the labor force because they could not find jobs.

Diseconomies of scale: A situation in which an increase in the quantity produced increases the long-run average cost of production.

Disposable personal income: The income that flows back to households, taking into account transfers and taxes.

Dominant strategy: An action that is the best choice under all circumstances.

Double coincidence of wants: The problem in a system of barter that one person may not have what the other desires.

Dumping: A situation in which the price a firm charges in a foreign market is lower than either the price it charges in its home market or the production cost.

Duopolists' dilemma: A situation in which both firms would be better off if they both chose a high price but each chooses a low price.

Durable goods: Goods that last for a long period of time, such as household appliances.

Econometric models: Mathematical computer-based models that economists build to capture the actual dynamics of the economy.

Economic cost: Explicit costs plus implicit costs.

Economic fluctuations: Movements of GDP above or below normal trends.

Economic growth: Sustained increases in the real production of an economy over a period of time.

Economic profit: Total revenue minus the total economic cost.

Economics: The study of the choices made by people who are faced with scarcity.

Economies of scale: A situation in which an increase in the quantity produced decreases the long-run average cost of production.

Employed: People who have jobs.

Entrepreneur: A person who has an idea for a business and coordinates the production and sale of goods and services, taking risks in the process.

Entrepreneurship: Effort used to coordinate the production and sale of goods and services.

Equilibrium output: The level of GDP at which the demand for output equals the amount that is produced.

Euro: The common currency in Europe.

European Union (EU):   An organization of European nations that has reduced trade barriers within Europe.

Excess burden of a tax: Another name for deadweight loss from taxation.

Excess reserves: Any additional reserves that a bank holds above required reserves.

Exchange rate: The rate at which currencies trade for one another in the market.

Expansionary policies: Government policy actions that lead to increases in output.

Expectations of inflation: The beliefs held by the public about the likely path of inflation for the future.

Expectations Phillips curve: The relationship that describes the links between inflation and unemployment, taking into account expectations of inflation.

Expected real interest rate: The nominal interest rate minus the expected inflation rate.

Experience rating: Each firm pays a different price for medical insurance, depending on the past medical bills of the firm's employees.

Explicit costs: The firm's actual cash payments for its inputs.

Export: A good produced in the home country (for example, the United States) and sold in another country.

External benefit: Another term for spillover benefit.

External cost: Another term for spillover cost.

Factors of production: Labor and capital used to produce goods and services.

Federal funds market: The market in which banks borrow and lend reserves to and from one another.

Federal Open Market Committee (FOMC): The group that decides on monetary policy; it consists of the 7 members of the Board of Governors plus 5 of 12 regional bank presidents on a rotating basis.

Federal Reserve Banks: One of 12 regional banks that are an official part of the Federal Reserve System.

Financial intermediaries: Organizations that receive funds from savers and channel them to investors.

Financial liberalization: The opening of financial markets to participants from foreign countries.

Fiscal year: The calendar on which the federal government conducts its business, which runs from October 1 to September 30.

Fixed costs: Costs that do not change as the level of activity changes.

Fixed exchange rates: A system in which governments peg exchange rates.

Flexible exchange rates: A currency system in which exchange rates are determined by free markets.

Foreign exchange market: A market in which people exchange one currency for another.

Foreign exchange market intervention: The purchase or sale of currencies by governments to influence the market exchange rate.

Franchise or licensing scheme: A policy under which the government picks a single firm to sell a particular good.

Free-rider problem: Each person will try to get the benefit of a public good without paying for it, trying to get a free ride at the expense of others who do pay.

Frictional unemployment: The part of unemployment associated with the normal workings of the economy, such as searching for jobs.

Full employment: The level of employment that occurs when the unemployment rate is at the natural rate.

Full-employment or potential output: The level of output that results when the labor market is in equilibrium.

Game tree: A graphical representation of the consequences of different strategies.

General Agreement on Tariffs and Trade (GATT): An international agreement that has lowered trade barriers between the United States and other nations.

Generational accounting: Methods that assign the tax burden of debt and other programs to different generations.

Government debt: The total of all past deficits.

Government expenditure: Spending on goods and services plus transfer payments.

Government purchases: Purchases of newly produced goods and services by all levels of government.

Grim trigger: A strategy under which a firm responds to underpricing by choosing a price so low that each firm makes zero economic profit.

Gross domestic product (GDP): The total market value of all the final goods and services produced within an economy in a given year.

GDP deflator: An index that measures how the price of goods included in GDP changes over time.

Gross investment: Actual investment purchases.

Gross national product (GNP): GDP plus net income earned abroad.

Growth accounting: A method to determine the contribution to economic growth from increased capital, labor, and technological progress.

Growth rate: The percentage rate of change of a variable.

Growth version of the quantity equation: An equation that links the growth rates of money, velocity, prices, and real output.

Guaranteed price matching: A scheme under which a firm guarantees that it will match a lower price by a competitor; also known as a meet-the-competition policy.

Household: A group of related family members and unrelated individuals who live in the same housing unit.

Human capital: The knowledge and skills acquired by a worker through education and experience and used to produce goods and services.

Hyperinflation: An inflation rate exceeding 50% per month.

Implicit costs: The opportunity cost of nonpurchased inputs.

Imports: A good produced in a foreign country and purchased by residents of the home country (for example, the United States).

Import quota: A limit on the amount of a good that can be imported.

Income effect for price change: The change in consumption resulting from an increase in the consumer's real income.

Income effect for wage change: An increase in the wage rate raises a worker's real income, increasing the demand for leisure.

Income elasticity of demand: A measure of the responsiveness of the quantity demanded to changes in consumer income; computed by dividing the percentage change in the quantity demanded by the percentage change in income.

Increasing-cost industry: An industry in which the average cost of production increases as the industry grows, so the long-run supply curve is positively sloped.

Indifference curve: A curve showing the set of combinations of goods that generate the same level of utility or satisfaction.

Indirect taxes: Sales and excise taxes.

Individual demand curve: A curve that shows the relationship between price and quantity demanded by an individual consumer, ceteris paribus (everything else held fixed).

Individual supply curve: A curve that shows the relationship between price and quantity supplied by an individual firm, ceteris paribus (everything else held fixed).

Indivisible input: An input that cannot be scaled down to produce a small quantity of output.

Industrial union: A labor organization that includes all types of workers from a single industry, for example, steelworkers or autoworkers.

Infant industry: A new industry that is protected from foreign competitors.

Inferior good: A good for which an increase in income decreases demand.

Inflation rate: The percentage rate of change of the price level in the economy.

Input-substitution effect: The change in the quantity of labor demanded resulting from a change in the relative cost of labor.

Insecure monopoly: A monopoly faced with the possibility that a second firm will enter the market.

Inside lags: Lags in implementing policy.

Intermediate good: Goods used in the production process that are not final goods or services.

International monetary fund: An organization that works closely with national governments to promote financial policies that facilitate world trade.

Invisible hand: The term that economists use to describe how the price system can efficiently coordinate economic activity without central government intervention.

Keynesian aggregate supply curve: A relatively flat horizontal supply curve. It reflects the idea that prices do not change very much in the short run and that firms adjust production to meet demand.

Keynesian economics: A school of economic thought that provides insights into the economy when it operates away from full employment.

Keynesian fiscal policy: The use of taxes and government spending to affect the level of GDP in the short run.

Kinked demand model: A model under which firms in an oligopoly match price reductions by other firms but do not match price increases.

Labor: Human effort, including both physical and mental effort, used to produce goods and services.

Labor force: The employed plus the unemployed.

Labor-force participation rate: The fraction of the population over 16 years of age that is in the labor force.

Labor productivity: Output produced per hour of work.

Labor union: An organized group of workers; the objectives of the organization are to increase job security, improve working conditions, and increase wages and benefits.

Laffer curve: A relationship between tax rates and tax revenues that illustrates that high tax rates may not always lead to high tax revenues if high tax rates discourage economic activity.

Law of demand: The lower the price, the larger the quantity demanded, ceteris paribus (other things being equal).

Law of diminishing marginal utility: As the consumption of a particular good increases, marginal utility decreases.

Law of one price: The theory that goods easily tradeable across countries, should sell at the same price, expressed in a common currency.

Law of supply: The higher the price, the larger the quantity supplied, ceteris paribus (other things being equal).

Learning by doing: Knowledge gained during production that increases productivity.

Learning effect: The increase in a person's wage resulting from the learning of skills required for certain occupations.

Lender of last resort: A central bank is the lender of last resort, the last place, all others having failed, from which banks in emergency situations can obtain loans.

Liabilities: The sources of funds for a bank, including deposits of a financial intermediary.

Limit pricing: A scheme under which a monopolist accepts a price below the normal monopoly price to deter other firms from entering the market.

Liquid: Easily convertible to money on short notice.

Liquidity demand for money: The demand for money that represents the needs and desires individuals or firms can fill on short notice without incurring excessive costs.

Long run: A period of time long enough that a firm can change all the factors of production, meaning that a firm can modify its existing production facility or build a new one.

Long-run average cost (LAC): Long-run total cost divided by the quantity of output produced.

Long-run demand curve for labor: A curve showing the relationship between the wage and the quantity of labor demanded over the long run, when the number of firms in the market can change and firms already in the market can modify their production facilities.

Long-run neutrality of money: An increase in the supply of money has no effect on real interest rates, investment, or output in the long run.

Long-run market supply: A curve showing the relationship between the market price and quantity supplied by all firms in the long run.

Long-run total cost: The total cost of production in the long run when a firm is perfectly flexible in its choice of all inputs and can choose a production facility of any size.

M1: The sum of currency in the hands of the public plus demand deposits plus other checkable deposits.

M2: M1 plus other assets, including deposits in savings and loans and money market mutual funds.

Macroeconomics: The branch of economics that looks at a nation's economy as a whole.

Managed competition: A health system in which organizations such as HMOs compete for patients.

Marginal benefit: The extra benefit resulting from a small increase in some activity.

Marginal cost: The additional cost resulting from a small increase in some activity.

Marginal labor cost (marginal factor cost): The increase in total labor cost resulting from hiring one more worker.

Marginal product of labor: The change in output from one additional worker.

Marginal propensity to consume (MPC): The fraction of additional income that is spent.

Marginal propensity to import: The fraction of additional income that is spent on imports.

Marginal propensity to save (MPS): The fraction of additional income that is saved.

Marginal rate of substitution (MRS): The rate at which a consumer is willing to substitute one good for another.

Marginal revenue product of labor (MRP): The extra revenue generated from one more unit of labor; equal to price of output times the marginal product of labor.

Marginal utility: The change in utility from one additional unit of the good.

Market: An arrangement that allows buyers and sellers to exchange things. A buyer exchanges money for a product, while a seller exchanges a product for money.

Market demand curve: A curve showing the relationship between price and quantity demanded by all consumers together, ceteris paribus (other things being equal).

Market equilibrium: A situation in which the quantity of a product demanded equals the quantity supplied, so there is no pressure to change the price.

Market supply curve: A curve showing the relationship between price and quantity supplied by all producers together, ceteris paribus (other things being equal).

Market supply curve for labor: A curve showing the relationship between the wage and the quantity of labor supplied.

Marketable pollution permits: A system under which the government picks a target pollution level for a particular area, issues just enough pollution permits to meet the pollution target, and allows firms to buy and sell the permits.

Median-voter rule: A rule suggesting that the choices made by government will reflect the preferences of the median voter.

Medicare: A government program that provides health benefits to those over 65 years of age.

Medium of exchange: The property of money that exchanges are made through the use of money.

Menu costs: Costs of inflation that arise from actually changing prices.

Merger: A process in which two or more firms combine their operations.

Microeconomics: The study of the choices made by consumers, firms, and government, and how these decisions affect the market for a particular good or service.

Minimum efficient scale: The output at which the long-run average cost curve becomes horizontal.

Mixed economy: A market-based economic system under which government plays an important role, including the regulation of markets, where most economic decisions are made.

Monetarists: Economists who emphasize the role of money in determining nominal income and inflation.

Monetary policy: The range of actions taken by the Federal Reserve to influence the level of GDP or the rate of inflation.

Monetizing the deficit: Purchases by a central bank of newly issued government bonds.

Money: Anything that is regularly used in exchange.

Money illusion: Confusion of real and nominal magnitudes.

Money multiplier: An initial deposit leads to a multiple expansion of deposits. In the simplified case increase in deposits = (initial deposit) × (1/reserve ratio).

Monopolistic competition: A market served by dozens of firms selling slightly different products.

Monopoly: A market in which a single firm serves the entire market.

Monopsony: A market in which there is a single buyer of an input.

Moral hazard problem: Insurance encourages risky behavior.

Multilateral real exchange rate: An index of the real exchange rate with a country's trading partners.

Multinational corporation: An organization that produces and sells goods and services throughout the world.

Multiplier: The ratio of changes in output to changes in spending. It measures the degree to which changes in spending are "multiplied" into changes in output.

Multiplier-accelerator model: A model in which a downturn in real GDP leads to a sharp fall in investment, which triggers further reductions in GDP through the multiplier.

National income: Net national product less indirect taxes.

Natural monopoly: A market in which the entry of a second firm would make price less than average cost, so a single firm serves the entire market.

Natural rate of unemployment: The level of unemployment at which there is no cyclical unemployment.

Natural resources: Things created by acts of nature and used to produce goods and services.

Negative relationship: A relationship in which an increase in the value of one variable decreases the value of the other variable.

Neoclassical theory of investment: A theory of investment that says both real interest rates and taxes are important determinants of investment.

Net exports: Exports minus imports.

Net international investment position: Domestic holdings of foreign assets minus foreign holdings of domestic assets.

Net investment: Gross investment minus depreciation.

Net national product (NNP): GNP less depreciation.

Net worth: The difference between assets and liabilities.

New growth theory: Modern theories of growth that try to explain the origins of technological progress.

Nominal GDP: The value of GDP in current dollars.

Nominal interest rates: Interest rates quoted in the market.

Nominal value: The face value of a sum of money.

Nondurable goods: Goods that last for short periods of time, such as food.

Normal good: A good for which an increase in income increases demand.

North American Free Trade Agreement (NAFTA): An international agreement that lowers barriers to trade between the United States, Mexico, and Canada (signed in 1994).

Okun's law: A relationship between changes in real GDP and the unemployment rate.

Oligopoly: A market served by a few firms.

Open economy: An economy with international trade.

Open market purchases: The Fed's purchase of government bonds, which increases the money supply.

Open market sales: The Fed's sales of government bonds to the public, which decreases the money supply.

Opportunity cost: What you sacrifice to get something.

Output effect: The change in the quantity of labor demanded resulting from a change in the quantity of output.

Outside lags: The time it takes for policies to work.

Patent: The exclusive right to sell a particular good for some period of time.

Pay-as-you-go: A system that uses revenue collected this year to pay for benefits to recipients this year.

Paying efficiency wages: The firm's practice of paying wages to increase the average productivity of its workers.

Peak: The time at which a recession begins.

Perfectly competitive market: A market with a very large number of firms, each of which produces the same standardized product and takes the market price as given.

Permanent income: An estimate of a household's long-run average level of income.

Personal disposable income: Personal income after taxes.

Personal income: Income (including transfer payments) received by households.

Physical capital: Objects made by human beings and used to produce goods and services.

Political business cycle: The effects on the economy of using monetary or fiscal policy to stimulate the economy before an election to improve reelection prospects.

Pollution tax: A tax or charge equal to the spillover cost per unit of waste.

Positive relationship: A relationship in which an increase in the value of one variable increases the value of the other variable.

Poverty budget: The minimum amount the government estimates that a family needs to avoid being in poverty; equal to three times the minimum food budget.

Predatory pricing: A pricing scheme under which a firm decreases its price to drive a rival out of business, and increases the price when the other firm disappears.

Price ceiling: A maximum price; transactions above the maximum price are outlawed.

Price change formula: A formula that shows the percentage change in equilibrium price resulting from a change in demand or supply, given the values for the price elasticity of demand and the price elasticity of supply.

Price discrimination: The process under which a firm divides consumers into two or more groups and picks a different price for each group.

Price elasticity of demand: A measure of the responsiveness of the quantity demanded to changes in price; computed by dividing the percentage change in quantity demanded by the percentage change in price.

Price elasticity of supply: A measure of the responsiveness of the quantity supplied to changes in price; computed by dividing the percentage change in quantity supplied by the percentage change in price.

Price fixing: An arrangement in which two firms coordinate their pricing decisions.

Price floor: A minimum price; transactions below the minimum price are outlawed.

Price leadership: An implicit agreement under which firms in a market choose a price leader, observe that firm's price, and match it.

Price level: An average of all the prices in the economy as measured by a price index.

Price-support program: A policy under which the government specifies a minimum price above the equilibrium price.

Principle: A simple truth that most people understand and accept.

Private good: A good that is consumed by a single person or household.

Private investment expenditures: Purchases of newly produced goods and services by firms.

Privatizing: The process of selling state firms to individuals.

Procyclical: Moving in same direction as real GDP.

Producer surplus: The difference between the market price of a product and the minimum amount a producer is willing to accept for that product; alternatively, the difference between the market price and the marginal cost of production.

Production possibilities curve: A curve showing the combinations of two goods that can be produced by an economy, assuming that all resources are fully employed.

Protectionist policies: Rules that restrict the free flow of goods between nations, including tariffs (taxes on imports), quotas (limits on total imports), voluntary export restraints (agreements between governments to limit exports), and nontariff trade barriers (subtle practices that hinder trade).

Public choice economics: A field of economics that explores how governments actually operate.

Public good: A good that is available for everyone to consume, regardless of who pays and who doesn't.

Purchasing Power Parity: A theory of exchange rates, stating that the exchange rate between two currencies is determined by the price levels in the two countries.

Q-theory of investment: The theory of investment that links investment spending to stock prices.

Quantity equation: The equation that links money, velocity, prices and real output. In symbols, we have $M \times V = P \times y$.

Rational expectations: The economic theory that analyzes how people form expectations in such a manner that, on average, they forecast the future correctly.

Real business cycle theory: The economic theory that emphasizes how shocks to technology can cause fluctuations in economic activity.

Real exchange rate: The market exchange rate adjusted for prices.

Real GDP: A measure of GDP that controls for changes in prices.

Real GDP per capita: Gross domestic product per person adjusted for changes in prices. It is the usual measure of living standards across time and between countries.

Real interest rate: The nominal interest rate minus the inflation rate.

Real value: The value of a sum of money in terms of the quantity of goods the money can buy.

Real wage: The wage paid to workers adjusted for changes in prices.

Real wages: Nominal or dollar wages adjusted for changes in purchasing power.

Recession: Six consecutive months of negative economic growth.

Rent control: A policy under which the government specifies a maximum rent that is below the equilibrium rent.

Rent seeking: The process under which a firm spends money to persuade the government to erect barriers to entry and pick the firm as the monopolist.

Required reserves: The fraction of banks' deposits that banks are legally required to hold in their vaults or as deposits at the Fed.

Reserve ratio: The ratio of reserves to deposits.

Reserves: The fraction of banks' deposits set aside in either vault cash or as deposits at the Federal Reserve.

Revaluation: An increase in the exchange rate in a fixed exchange system.

Ricardian equivalence: The proposition that it does not matter whether government expenditure is financed by taxes or by debt.

Saving: Total income minus consumption.

Savings Function: The relationship between the level of income and the level of savings.

Scarcity: A situation in which resources are limited and can be used in different ways, so we must sacrifice one thing for another.

Services: Reflect work done in which people play a prominent role in delivery, ranging from haircutting to health care.

Shoe-leather costs: Costs of inflation that arise from trying to reduce holdings of cash.

Short run: A period of time over which one or more factors of production is fixed; in most cases, a period of time over which a firm cannot modify an existing facility or build a new one.

Short-run average total cost (SATC): Short-run total cost divided by the quantity of output, equal to AFC plus AVC.

Short-run average variable cost (SAVC): Variable cost divided by the quantity produced.

Short-run demand curve for labor: A curve showing the relationship between the wage and the quantity of labor demanded in the short run, the period when the firm cannot change its production facility.

Short run in macroeconomics: The period of time that prices do not change very much.

Short-run marginal cost (SMC): The change in total cost resulting from producing one more unit of the good in the short run.

Short-run market supply curve: A curve showing the relationship between price and the quantity of output supplied by all firms in the short run.

Short-run production function: Shows how much output is produced from varying amounts of labor, holding the capital stock constant.

Short-run supply curve for a firm: A curve showing the relationship between the price of a product and the quantity of output supplied by a firm in the short run.

Shut-down price: The price at which the firm is indifferent between operating and shutting down.

Signaling effect: The increase in a person's wage resulting from the signal of productivity provided by completing college.

Slope: The change in the variable on the vertical axis resulting from a one-unit increase in the variable on the horizontal axis.

Social insurance: A system that compensates individuals for bad luck, low skills, or misfortunes.

Social Security: A government program that provides retirement, survivor, and disability benefits.

Speculative demand for money: The demand for money that reflects holding money over short periods is less risky than holding stocks or bonds.

Spillover: A cost or benefit experienced by people who are external to the decision about how much of a good to produce or consume.

Stabilization policy: Policy actions taken to bring the economy closer to full employment or potential output.

Stock of capital: The total of all the machines, equipment, and buildings in the entire economy.

Store of value: The property of money that it preserves value until it is used in an exchange.

Structural unemployment: The part of unemployment that results from the mismatch of skills and jobs.

Substitutes: Two goods related in such a way that an increase in the price of one good increases the demand for the other good.

Substitution effect for price changes: The change in consumption resulting from a change in the price of one good relative to the price of other goods.

Substitution effect for wage changes: An increase in the wage rate increases the opportunity cost of leisure and leads workers to demand less leisure and supply more labor.

Sunk cost: The cost a firm has already paid—or has agreed to pay some time in the future.

Supply curve: See **individual supply curve**; see **market supply curve**.

Supply schedule: A table of numbers that shows the relationship between price and quantity supplied, ceteris paribus (other things being equal).

Supply shocks: External events that shift the aggregate supply curve.

Supply-siders: Economists who emphasize the role of taxation for influencing economic activity.

Surplus: The excess of total revenues over total expenditures.

Tariff: A tax on an imported good.

Taxi medallion: A license to operate a taxi.

Technological progress: An increase in output without increasing inputs.

Terms of trade: The rate at which two goods will be exchanged.

Thin market: A market in which some high-quality goods are sold, but fewer than would be sold in a market with perfect information.

Tit-for-tat: A strategy under which the one firm in a duopoly starts out with the cartel price and then chooses whatever price the other firm chose in the preceding period.

Total product curve: A curve showing the relationship between the number of workers and the quantity of output produced.

Total revenue: The money the firm gets by selling its product; equal to the price times the quantity sold.

Total surplus of a market: The sum of the net benefits experienced by consumers and producers; equal to the sum of consumer surplus and producer surplus.

Total utility: The utility (measured in utils) from whatever quantity of the product the consumer gets.

Total variable cost (TVC): Cost that varies as the firm changes the quantity produced.

Trade deficit: The excess of imports over exports.

Trade surplus: The excess of exports over imports.

Transactions demand for money: The demand for money based on the desire to facilitate transactions.

Transfer payments: Payments to individuals from governments that do not correspond to the production of goods and services.

Transition: The process of shifting from a centrally planned economy toward a mixed economic system, with markets playing a greater role in the economy.

Trough: The time at which output stops falling in a recession.

Trust: An arrangement under which the owners of several companies transfer their decision-making powers to a small group of trustees, who then make decisions for all the firms in the trust.

Tying: A business practice under which a consumer of one product is required to purchase another product.

Unanticipated inflation: Inflation that is not expected.

Underemployed: Workers who hold a part-time job but prefer to work full time or hold jobs that are far below their capabilities.

Unemployed: People who are looking for work but do not have jobs.

Unemployment insurance: Payments received from the government upon becoming unemployed.

Unemployment rate: The fraction of the labor force that is unemployed.

Unit of account: The property of money that prices are quoted in terms of money.

Usury laws: Laws that do not allow interest rates to exceed specified ceilings.

Util: One unit of utility.

Utility: The satisfaction or pleasure the consumer experiences when he or she consumes a good, measured as the number of utils.

Utility-maximizing rule: Pick the affordable combination of consumer goods that makes the marginal utility per dollar spent on one good equal to that of a second good.

Value added: The sum of all the income (wages, interest, profits, rent) generated by an organization.

Variable: A measure of something that can take on different values.

Variable costs: Costs that vary as the quantity produced changes.

Velocity of money: Nominal GDP divided by the money supply. It is also the rate at which money turns over during the year.

Voluntary export restraint (VER): A scheme under which an exporting country voluntarily decreases its exports.

Wage-price spiral: Changes in wages and prices causing more changes in wages and prices.

Wealth effect: The increase in spending that occurs because the real value of money increases when the price level falls.

World Trade Organization (WTO): An organization that oversees GATT and other international trade agreements.

Worldwide sourcing: The practice of buying components for a product from nations throughout the world.

Photo Credits

Answers to Odd Problems and Discussion Questions

Chapter 1

1. Buying a used car: It is difficult to determine the quality of the car.

   Providing health insurance: It is difficult to determine whether the customer will have large or small medical expenses.

3. The number of lectures attended, the hours of sleep the night before the exam.

5. Move along, shift.

Appendix to Chapter 1

1. a. See Figure S.1.
   b. The slope is $5.
   c. The monthly bill will increase by $15.

3. 10%, –2%, 6%.

5. The number of burglaries will decrease by 4.

Chapter 2

1. The statement ignores the opportunity cost of the time spent in college.

3. The marginal cost is the cost of equipping and paying one more officer. The officer would presumably decrease crime, and the marginal benefit is determined by the reduction in

crime resulting from the additional officer. If you can measure the marginal cost and the marginal benefit, you should continue to hire officers until the marginal benefit equals the marginal cost.

5. In the long run, the firm can modify its production facility or build a new one.

7. Eventually, we expect output to increase at a decreasing rate because more and more workers share the espresso machine.

9. Salaries increased faster than the price of consumer goods.

Chapter 3

1. Brenda could specialize in bread. Instead of producing one shirt for herself, Brenda could use the time it would take to produce 1 shirt to produce 2 loaves of bread. If she then trades one loaf of bread for one shirt, she will have one loaf of bread left over. She gets the same number of shirts and one extra loaf of bread. Sam could specialize in shirts. Instead of producing one loaf of bread for himself, Sam could use the time it would take to produce a loaf of bread to produce two shirts. If he trades one shirt for one loaf of bread, he will have the same amount of bread but one extra shirt.

3. Professor A has a comparative advantage in the graduate course: He is twice as productive as Professor B in that course (90/45), but only 1.5 times as productive in the undergraduate course (90/60). Looking at this another way, the total performance (score in the undergraduate course plus the score in the graduate course) is 150 when Professor A teaches the graduate course and Professor B teaches the undergraduate course (90 in G plus 60 in U), compared to only 135 when Professor A teaches the undergraduate course and Professor B teaches the graduate course.

5. Mexican goods are now less costly and therefore more attractive. An American who wants to buy a good that costs 5 pesos must spend $0.25 to get the pesos to pay for the good (5 pesos times the price of $0.05 per peso), compared to $0.50 before (5 pesos times the price of $0.10 per peso). From the perspective of a Mexican consumer, American goods are now more costly and therefore less attractive. A Mexican who wants to buy a good that costs $1 must spend 20 pesos to get the dollar to pay for the good ($1 divided by the price of $0.05 per peso), compared to only 10 pesos before ($1 divided by the price of $0.10 per peso).

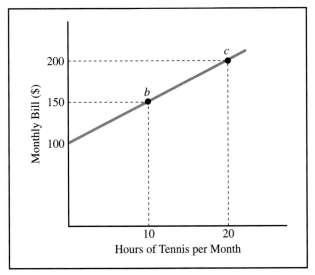

Figure S.1 **Relationship Between Hours of Tennis and the Monthly Tennis Club Bill**

Chapter 4

1. a. w, $150,200 per day.
   b. demand, increase.
   c. supply, decrease.
3. a. The cost of producing computers will decrease, so the production of computers will be more profitable, so firms will supply more of them. The supply curve will shift to the right, decreasing the equilibrium price.
   b. The tax increases the production cost, shifting the supply curve to the left and increasing the equilibrium price.
5. Education at private and public schools are substitutes, so the tuition hike will shift the demand for private education to the right, increasing the equilibrium price and quantity.
7. If price and quantity both increase, we know from Table 4.1 that demand has increased. We shift the demand curve to the right, increasing the price and quantity.
9. How many people switch to automobile travel as a result of the higher cost of air travel? How does the shift to automobile travel affect the number of injuries and deaths on the highways? Does the airport security system reduce the number of injuries and deaths related to air travel? If so, how many lives are saved and how many injuries are avoided?
11. The supply curve for shirts shifts to the left, increasing the equilibrium price and decreasing the equilibrium quantity.

Chapter 5

1. The price elasticity is 1.30 = the percentage change in quantity (13%) divided by the percentage change in price (10%). Demand is elastic.
3. Each brand has many substitute goods (all the other brands), so the demand for a specific brand will be more elastic than the demand for running shoes in general.
5. Inelastic: An increase in price increases total revenue, while a decrease in price decreases total revenue.
7. Use the elasticity formula: The 10% increase in the price of beer will decrease the quantity of beer consumed by 13%, decreasing the highway death rate by the same percentage. Therefore, the number of highway deaths will decrease by 13 (13% of 100).
9. Use the price-change formula: The predicted change in price is 1% = 4%/(1 + 3). In the graph, we shift the supply curve to the left, so the restrictions increase the price from $100,000 to $101,000 and decreases the equilibrium quantity.

Chapter 6

1. We assume that buyers and sellers have enough information to make informed choices and that there are no spillover benefits nor spillover costs. The assumption of informed choices is likely to be violated in the case of used cars: buyers don't know the quality of the car. The assumption of no spillover benefits is likely to be violated for national defense, space exploration, public radio, and education. The assumption of no spillover costs is likely to be violated for goods that generate pollution such as paper, transportation (auto and bus), and electricity.

3. a. A + B + C
   b. D + E + F
   c. A + B + C + D + E + F
   d. A + B + D
   e. F
   f. A + B + D + F
   g. A
   h. B + D + F
   i. A + B + D + F
5. The supply of clothing to an individual city is much more elastic than the supply of housing, so price controls would decrease the quantity of clothing supplied by a larger amount. In addition, everyone would have to wait in line to get clothing. In contrast, people who occupy rent-controlled apartments don't have to find a new apartment every week, so they avoid most of the queuing and search costs and provide political support for rent control.
7. In the market equilibrium, there are 100 taxis and the price of taxi service is $3, which is just high enough to cover the cost of providing taxi service. If the government issues more than 100 medallions, no one will use the extra medallions, and the medallion policy will have no effect on the market: The price of taxi service will be $3, and the price of a medallion will be zero.
9. For parts (a) and (b), as in the case of taxi medallions, the quantity restrictions will increase the equilibrium price and decrease the equilibrium quantity. For part (c), the import restrictions shift the market supply curve to the left, increasing the equilibrium price and decreasing the equilibrium quantity.
11. With only 3 gallons of waste per ton of cardboard, the pollution tax increases the production cost per ton by $6 (instead of $10), so the supply curve shifts by a smaller amount. Compared to the case with 5 gallons per ton, the 3-gallon case generates a lower equilibrium price and a larger equilibrium quantity.

Chapter 7

1. Betty will consume 6 muffins. If Betty chooses 6 muffins, the marginal benefit is 8 utils (from the muffin table). Given a budget of $60, she would have $48 left to spend on cookies, meaning that she could buy 48 cookies at $1 each. If she consumes 48 cookies, the marginal utility of cookies is 4 utils per cookie (from the cookie table). Given the prices ($2 per muffin and $1 per cookie), she sacrifices 2 cookies for each muffin, so the marginal cost of muffins is 8 utils (2 cookies per muffin times 4 utils per cookie). The marginal benefit of muffins equals the marginal cost, so the best she can do is 6 muffins and 48 cookies.
3. What is the marginal utility of a dollar spent on food? What is the marginal utility of CDs? Your current choice maximizes your utility if the marginal utility of CDs is ten times the marginal utility of food.

Appendix to Chapter 7

1. The vertical intercept of the budget line is 40 violets, and the horizontal intercept is 10 hats.

a. The slope is the price of hats divided by the price of violets, or 4.0.

b. An indifference curve that intersects the budget line is not the highest (most northeasterly) possible indifference curve.

c. The second indifference curve should be tangent to the budget line.

d. marginal rate of substitution.

3. Carla's MRS is 2.0, which exceeds the price ration of 1/3. Therefore, she should pick an auto with more horsepower and less interior space.

Chapter 8

1. The average cost is $15 for 40 shirts, $9 for 100 shirts, $7 for 200 shirts, and $6 for 400 shirts.

3.

Labor	Output	Marginal Product
0	0	
1	5	5
2	11	6
3	15	4
4	18	3
5	19	1

5. There are no diminishing returns, so marginal cost is constant.

7. The $12,500 figure includes some of the fixed cost of production (design and tooling costs), so it is an average cost, not a marginal cost.

9. As shown in Figure 8.6, the average cost for the large generator is $4.60 (point *b*), compared to an average cost of $5.00 for the small generator (point *c*).

Chapter 9

1.

Tables per hour	Total cost	Marginal cost
3	120	—
4	155	35
5	200	45
6	270	70

3. If the firm continues to operate its facility, its total revenue will be $9,000 = $30 times 300 units of output. This is the benefit of operating the facility. The cost of operating the facility is the variable cost, which equals labor cost ($7,000 = the $100 wage times 700 workers). Total revenue exceeds variable cost, so it is sensible to continue operating the facility, even though it is losing money.

5. The manager is bluffing. His total revenue ($35,000) exceeds the *variable cost* ($30,000 for the farm workers). The $20,000 paid for seed and fertilizer was incurred months ago, and it is a sunk cost that will be ignored in the decision about whether to harvest the crop. Because his

total revenue exceeds his variable cost, the farmer will harvest the crop even if the workers don't accept a wage cut.

7. We cannot draw a supply curve or complete the price elasticity of supply because we cannot be certain that the other variables that affect the supply of gasoline (the price of inputs, technology) did not change over this period.

9.

Number of firms	Industry output	Total cost for typical firm	Average cost per lamp
40	400	$300	$30
80	800	$360	$36
120	1,200	$420	$42

We have 3 points on the long-run supply curve: At a price of $30, the quantity is 400 lamps; at a price of $36, the quantity is 800 lamps; at a price of $42, the quantity is 1,200 lamps.

11. Because the industry uses such tiny amounts of the relevant inputs, the prices of these inputs won't change as the industry grows. Therefore, the average cost per haircut does not depend on the quantity of haircuts. The long-run supply curve is horizontal, for example, at a constant cost of $10 per haircut.

Chapter 10

1. To maximize profit, the restaurant will pick the quantity at which marginal revenue equals marginal cost. Using the marginal-revenue formula, we can compute the marginal revenue at each price and quantity:

Price	$10	$9	$8	$7
Quantity	30	40	50	60
Marginal revenue	$7	$5	$3	$1

Marginal revenue equals marginal cost at a price of $8 and a quantity of 50 meals.

3. On average, the payback per dollar spent on these lottery games is about 50¢. In other words, for every $100 spent by players, the state pays $50 in prizes. The commercial gambling games have much higher paybacks: The payback per dollar is 81¢ for horse racing and 89¢ for slot machines. The lottery games have lower paybacks because each state has a monopoly on lottery games: The state outlaws commercial lotteries. If the state allowed other organizations to offer lottery games, the competition between commercial and state lottery games would increase the payback from lottery games.

5. The artificial barrier to entry will generate higher prices and a smaller quantity demanded. If we eliminated the barriers, there would be more teams, and ticket prices would fall, increasing total attendance.

7. A decrease in demand shifts the demand curve to the left, and the new demand curve will intersect the negatively sloped long-run average-cost curve at a smaller quantity and a higher average cost (price). The loss of scale economies will cause the regulated price to rise.

9. Monopoly power increases prices in the game of Monopoly, consistent with the conclusions in this chapter.

11. The consumer advocate is assuming that the demand for the drug is perfectly inelastic, so an increase in price does not have any effect on the quantity demanded. This is unrealistic and is inconsistent with the law of demand.

Chapter 11

1. The following table shows price and average cost for different numbers of arcades. Price exceeds average cost for the first 4 arcades, so the equilibrium number of arcades is 4.

Number of arcades	1	2	3	4	5
Price	50¢	48¢	46¢	44¢	42¢
Average cost	34¢	37¢	40¢	43¢	46¢

3. There are two logical errors in the expert's statement. First, the entry of firms will decrease the market price, and the market will move downward along the market demand curve. Therefore, the total quantity of pizzas demanded will exceed 3,000 (the quantity associated with the monopoly price). Second, as shown in all the examples in this chapter, we expect the typical firm to operate along the negatively sloped portion of its average-cost curve, not the horizontal portion. In other words, we expect each firm to produce fewer than 1,000 pizzas per day. These two observations suggest that there will be more than 3 pizzerias. For example, if the decrease in price increases the quantity demanded to 4,000 and each store produces only 800 pizzas per day, there will be 5 pizzerias (4,000 divided by 800).

5. A firm that cuts 3 lawns will have a total cost of $30 ($18 in fixed cost + $12 in variable cost (3 lawns times $4 per lawn), or an average cost of $10 per lawn. In equilibrium, the price will be equal to average cost, which happens with a quantity of 60 lawns. Dividing the 60 lawns cut by 3 lawns per firm, there will be 20 firms in equilibrium.

7. The city must have issued a sufficiently large number of licenses that entry continued to the point where economic profit reached zero. In graphical terms, the demand curve facing the typical firm is tangent to the negatively sloped average-cost curve: Average cost equals price, so economic profit is zero and no one is willing to pay anything for a license.

Chapter 12

1. See Figure S.2. The profit per firm under the duopoly outcome is $500 (a profit of $5 per passenger times 100 passengers). The profit per firm under the cartel is $750 (a profit of $10 per passenger times 75 passengers). Each firm will pick the low price. The path of the game is X to Z to rectangle 4.

3. One reason for low prices at these sales is that there is no punishment for underpricing the other firm. Any prior arrangement for cartel pricing would evaporate when one firm knows that it will soon go out of business.

5. If both firms pick the high price, each will get a profit of $360. If both pick the low price, each will get a profit of

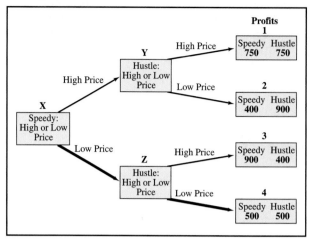

Figure S.2 **Game Tree for Airporter Price-Fixing Game**

$250. For each firm, picking the low price is the dominant strategy.

If firms pick prices each day, Bizarre weighs the benefit of undercutting ($140 on the day of undercutting) against the cost (the difference between the high-price profit ($360) and the low-price profit ($250) times the number of days remaining after the undercutting. On the first day, the cost is $220, which exceeds the benefit of $140. Assuming that Bizarre is not savvy enough to think about the end game (the last day), she will not undercut Weird.

7. The longer the time both firms will be in the market, the greater the opportunity for punishing a firm that undercuts, so the more likely price fixing will work. Longtime is more likely to have price fixing that keeps prices high.

Chapter 13

1. The marginal revenue for business travelers is MR = $300 − 2.0 × 120 = $60, which is less than the marginal cost, so the airline should increase the price for business travelers. The marginal revenue for tourists is MR = $300 − 1.0 × 80 = $240, which is greater than the marginal cost, so the airline should decrease the price for tourists.

3. This price-discrimination scheme is based on the notion that bargain hunters are early birds. The large discounts for early fabric purchases attract consumers who would otherwise not buy fabric at the regular price.

5. Car companies use price discrimination in their option pricing. They have higher markups on options that have relatively inelastic demand.

7. As shown in Table 13.2, the marginal benefit of advertising equals the change in quantity times the net revenue per unit. In contrast, the statement in the questions suggest that the marginal benefit is the increase in total revenue.

Chapter 14

1. Consumer surplus decreases by $700. For the 150 that are units sold at the higher price, consumers lose an amount equal to the change in price ($4) times the quantity con-

sumed (150), or $600. In addition, the price hike reduces the quantity consumed, and the loss of consumer surplus for the 151st through the 200th units is equal to the change in price ($4) times the change in quantity (50 units) times 1/2, or an additional $100. The total profit of the firms increases from $200 ($1 per unit times 200 units sold) to $750 ($5 per unit times 150 units). The increase in profit ($550) is less than the loss of consumer surplus ($700), so the net loss for society is $150.

3. Giving the gates to Gotcha will allow the airline to maintain its monopoly power and continue to charge higher prices than would occur if there was competition.

Chapter 15

1. a. No. Bertha is willing to pay the most ($100), but she is willing to pay less than the cost ($120).
   b. No. The cost per citizen will be $40, so Bertha is the only one who is willing to pay more than the cost per capita.
   c. Suppose each citizen pays $10 less than his or her willingness to pay: Bertha pays $90; Marian pays $20; Sam pays $10. This scheme raises $120 and benefits each citizen.

3. The free-rider problem disappears because if any person does not contribute, the public good won't be provided. This money-back guarantee makes it more likely that everyone will contribute and get 30¢ at the end of the experiment.

5. a. The benefit is $8,000 (80,000 citizens times $0.10 per person), which exceeds the cost of $5,000. Since the benefit exceeds the cost, the provision of the additional litter is socially efficient.
   b. No. The benefit to the rancher ($0.10) is less than the cost ($5,000).
   c. The citizens could contribute to a wolf-preservation fund to provide the rancher with enough money to offset the cost of a litter of wolves. For example, if each citizen contributed $0.07 (70% of his or her benefit), they could raise a total of $5,600. By paying this amount to the landowner who hosts the wolf litter, the rancher would be better off by $600, and each of the citizens would be better off by $0.03.

7. a. No. Part of the tax will be shifted backward onto input suppliers, including laborers who work in auto factories and dealerships.
   b. The price elasticity of demand for automobiles and the responsiveness of input suppliers to changes in input prices.

9. a. The median voter now has a desired budget of $6 billion, so each candidate will propose a budget very close to $6 billion.
   b. The answer will not change because the median voter is still the person with the $6 billion budget.

Chapter 16

1. See Figure S.3. The market equilibrium is shown by point *i*: The demand curve intersects the supply curve at 20 units per day. The pollution tax shifts the supply curve by such a large amount that the supply curve lies entirely above the demand curve. For this to occur, the spillover cost from the

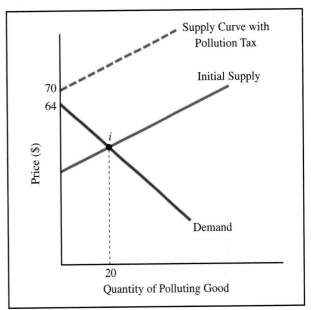

pollutant must be very high, the cost of abatement must be very high, and the demand for good must be relatively low.

3. a. From Table 16.1, the production cost per ton with zero pollution is $116.
   b. The marginal cost associated with going from 1 gallon to 0 gallons is $30. For firms to make this choice, the marginal benefit of abatement (the tax savings) must be at least $30.

5. The supply curve will shift to the left as some of the cars are destroyed. The equilibrium price will increase, and the equilibrium quantity will decrease.

7. We could adjust other taxes to mitigate any undesirable effects on the poor. For example, we could decrease the sales tax rate or adjust the income tax rates.

Chapter 17

1. Suppose Groucho wants to join a social club to associate with people who are richer than he is, and he assumes that other people join clubs for the same reasons. A club will invite him to join only if he would increase the average income of the club. In other words, Groucho will be invited to join only groups in which most people are poorer than he is, clubs with an adverse selection of people. The same reasoning applies if Groucho wants to associate with people who are wittier than he is and he assumes that other people feel the same way. A club that asks him to join will have an average wit level that is less than his, so he will be forced to interact with dimwits.

3. Suppose you're willing to pay the average value of the 2 types of cameras ($60) for a 50% chance of getting a plum. If you expect a greater than 50% chance of getting a plum,

it will be wise to buy a used camera. Given the adverse-selection problem, your chance of getting a plum is likely to be less than 50%.

5. The detector eliminates the imperfect information problem, so the 2 types of used cars will be sold in separate markets, with one price for lemons ($2,000 in our example) and another price for plums ($4,000). There is no adverse selection because each buyer knows exactly what type of car he or she will get.

7. Like the lie detector, the genetic tests eliminate the adverse selection problem, this time for insurance companies. The insurance companies will charge higher prices to those who are likely to contract the diseases and lower prices to those who are not. This may strike many people as unfair.

9. If Ira doesn't have fire insurance, he will spend money on the prevention program because the benefit is the avoidance of an expected loss of $10,000 (a 10% chance of losing $100,000), which exceeds the $5,000 cost. If he has an insurance policy covering 80% of the loss, the benefit is the avoidance of an expected loss of $2,000 (a 10% chance of losing $80,000). The benefit is less than the $5,000 cost, so he won't spend money on the program. Ira will be indifferent with a coverage rate of 50%. In this case, the benefit is the avoidance of an expected loss of $5,000 (a 10% chance of losing $50,000), which is equal to the cost.

Chapter 18

1. The payroll tax shifts the supply curve to the left: At every price, a smaller quantity is supplied. The leftward shift of the supply curve increases the equilibrium wage to a wage above $10.

3. Some people will work fewer hours, so they will pay less in taxes: They pay a lower rate on fewer hours. Other people will work the same number of hours and pay less in taxes too: They pay a lower rate on the same number of hours. Even a person who works more hours could pay less in taxes: If the increase in hours is small relative to the decrease in the hourly tax rate, the tax bill (hours times the tax rate) will actually decrease. The only people who will pay more in taxes are the workers who increase their hours by an amount that is large relative to the decrease in the hourly rate.

5. a. The supply of teachers is large relative to demand, so wages are relatively low. This could result from the psychological rewards from teaching, the work hours, or the free summer time.

   b. This is effectively a minimum wage for teachers, and it has the same effect as a minimum wage for any occupation: The increase in the wage will decrease the quantity demanded, so some teachers will lose their jobs.

7. Let's assume that the program is paid for by government, not coal companies. The program will increase the supply of coal workers, shifting the supply curve to the right. The equilibrium wage will decrease.

9. Like a minimum wage, a comparable-worth policy that increases wages in some occupations will decrease the quantity of labor demanded, so fewer workers will be hired.

In addition, higher wages lead to higher production costs and output prices, so consumers will be harmed. An alternative policy is to break down the barriers that have discouraged women from choosing certain occupations.

Chapter 19

1. Perhaps the high-school education received 25 to 35 years ago by workers who are now in their 40s was superior to the education received 5 to 15 years ago by workers who are now in their 20s.

3. This policy will increase the supply of college graduates, increasing competition for jobs requiring a college education. As a result, we would expect lower wages for college graduates and a smaller gap between the wages of college graduates and high-school graduates (smaller than we would otherwise observe).

5. If health care is provided by the employer, there may be problems when workers change jobs.

Chapter 20

1. If we are interested in the increase in the production of goods and services, we should be interested in the growth of real GDP. If we also care about the increase in prices, we should be interested in the growth of nominal GDP.

3. We calculate the value of the goods produced in 2004 using the prices in 2004 and 2005. For 2004, the value of production is $24,000. For 2005, the value of production is $26,200. The value of production (attributable all to price changes) rose by 9.2%. If the price index for 2004 was 100, the price index for 2005 would be 1.092.

5. No, because you need to compare the price index in one year to a value in another year.

7. Refrigerators are an example of a good that depreciates. If a refrigerator costs $2,000, lasts for 10 years, and depreciates evenly over 10 years, the yearly depreciation would be $200.

9. Deterioration in air quality should be subtracted from NNP to arrive at national income. Improvements to air quality should be added.

11. If the Department of Commerce used a base year in which computer prices were high, it would overstate the growth of real GDP and understate the growth of overall prices.

Chapter 21

1. The labor force is 6 million (employed plus unemployed); the labor force participation rate is 60% (labor force divided by population 16 years and older); the unemployment rate is 8.3% (unemployed divided by labor force).

3. This belief is based on the idea that with high unemployment rates, there are likely to be discouraged workers.

5. There will always be frictional and structural unemployment.

7. The inflation rate is 11% [(60 − 55)/55].

9. The conventional unemployment rate is 7.4% (8 million/108 million). An alternative measure would add the discouraged workers to total unemployment. This would also increase the labor force by the same amount. The alternative unemployment measure would be 10.7% (12 million/112 million).

Chapter 22

1. The economists believe that high payroll taxes are the cause of high unemployment and slow employment growth.

3. With a reduction of the supply in young workers, overall wages would rise for union members.

5. Towns near the border with Mexico have more migration and hence a larger supply of labor. The result is lower wages.

7. The graph would show the demand curve for labor shifting to the right as technology improves in the economy. According to this theory, real wages therefore rise during booms and fall during recessions.

9. Today, many more women work full time and provide support for their families. The labor supply for these women is not likely to be very sensitive to changes in wages and thus is more likely to look like that of men.

11. With limited opportunities for domestic investment, savings will flow abroad. This is accomplished through a trade surplus.

Chapter 23

1. It will double in 23.3 years (70/3) and increase by a factor of 4 in 46.6 years.

3. We collect price data on many commodities in the United Kingdom and the United States in their own currencies. We then use the "exchange rate" for each commodity to calculate expenditures in dollars.

5. We measure it through growth accounting. We ask how much growth can be explained by increases in labor and capital. The remainder is attributed to technological progress.

7. Public investment increases by 5% (one-half of 10%). Private savings and investment falls by 2% (20% of 10%). Thus, total investment (public and private) increases.

9. Although income may have been increasing during this period, the fall in height suggests that basic nutrition and overall welfare may have been decreasing. This perhaps could be accounted for by rapid increases in the population of cities and the stresses of urban life in this period.

Chapter 24

1. The term *cycle* could be misleading if we think of regular, reoccurring cycles. Business cycles do not fit this pattern.

3. Draw a line representing the trend in output. Then draw a pattern of actual output. The number of recessions will be the number of times the output line falls below the trend line. The proportion of the time the economy is in a recession will be the fraction of time the output line is below trend. The magnitude of the worst recession is the farthest the output line falls below trend.

5. Rents on apartments are sticky with month-long or year-long leases. They are sticky because it is costly to move and change apartments.

7. As the classical aggregate supply curve moved to the right, prices would fall.

9. When aggregate demand fails, the aggregate demand curve shifts to the left, and prices and output fall. In the long run, the Keynesian aggregate supply curve falls to restore the economy to full employment.

Chapter 25

1. a. 800
   b. 2
   c. $S = 0.5y - 200$
   d. 200

3. The multiplier is 2.04. Therefore, investment spending needs to rise by 73.5.

5. No. Raising tax rates will also lower GDP.

7. a. GDP will rise.
   b. No. Inventories could rise because demand falls short of the expectations of producers.

9. GDP will fall because of the balanced budget multiplier.

11. More generous unemployment insurance programs put more funds into the economy in bad times and less in good times. This stabilizes consumption spending and output.

Chapter 26

1. Plant and equipment spending are governed in part by expectations of changes in GDP, which can be volatile. Housing will depend on interest rates. Inventories will be volatile because they depend on changes in demand over very short periods of time.

3. The statement is true because, with a zero rate of interest and thus no opportunity cost for invested funds, the savings in gas would ultimately pay for the costs of leveling the mountain.

5. Yes. The real cost of funds is –1%.

7. The nominal rate is 10%; the real rate is 2%.

9. This is an example of diversification, which reduces risk.

Chapter 27

1. They are accepted in exchange.

3. The opportunity cost of excess reserves is the income that could be earned by lending the reserves.

5. $13.3 million (the multiplier is 1/0.15 = 6.6).

7. An increase in the discount rate will lead banks to reduce their borrowed reserves from the Fed, and the supply of money will fall.

9. It would increase the supply of money. Any purchases by the Fed will increase reserves in banks and lead to an expansion of the supply of money.

11. They were not fully equivalent to money because they were accepted in exchange only by large banks and credit unions and not, for example, by stores or by individuals.

Chapter 28

1. You may have an opportunity to buy a rare CD at a music store and need cash on hand. You could not buy the CD with a bond.

3. You would want to sell bonds because bond prices would fall as interest rates rose.

5. It would weaken monetary policy because changes in interest rates would have less of an impact on investment.

7. Trade is more important for the economy of the Netherlands than for that of the United States. Therefore, monetary policy would have more of an effect through exchange rates in the Netherlands.

9. This would shorten the inside lag for fiscal policy. But it would give the President more political power at the expense of Congress. This could be used wisely or abused.

Chapter 29

1. They worried that unemployment had fallen below the natural rate.

3. Interest rates rise because of an increase in money demand during an economic expansion. Investment first rises because of the accelerator effect at the beginning of an expansion and falls, for the same reason, as the GDP slows down at the end of the expansion.

5. Money is neutral in the long run.

7. Tax cuts will lead to higher consumer spending. This crowds out investment in the long run through higher interest rates.

9. It is costly to guard and store large sums of money. However, interest rates are unlikely to fall too far below 0%, only perhaps a few tenths of 1 percent.

Chapter 30

1. High interest rates in the long run result from high inflation rates. High inflation rates occur only when there is rapid growth in the money supply.

3. Typically, firms have better access to information than workers.

5. If the government increases the money supply at a faster rate, inflation will rise. The rise in inflation will raise interest rates and the cost of holding money. Therefore, people will hold money for shorter periods of time.

7. With increased foreign aid, the government has less need to print money to finance a deficit.

9. It is true that businesses are debtors and would benefit initially from inflation that was not anticipated. However, the costs of inflation do affect businesses as well as individuals.

Chapter 31

1. The interest on the debt is $1 billion. The budget deficit (spending + interest − taxes) is $1 billion. Therefore, the debt at the end of the year is $11 billion.

3. They are more likely to need to print money, which causes rapid inflation.

5. It could induce a government to take contractionary actions during economic downturns. This could be serious if there are not sufficient escape mechanisms.

7. With a stable 2% inflation rate and full institutional adjustment, there are both menu costs and shoe-leather costs. It may be more difficult to maintain a commitment to a 2% inflation rate than to zero inflation or price stability.

9. It depends on whether individuals really increase their savings (by cutting consumption) or just shift existing funds into the tax free accounts.

Chapter 32

1. a. In Country B, the opportunity cost of 1 computer is 2 TVs, and the opportunity cost of 1 TV is 1/2 of a computer. In Country C, the opportunity cost of 1 computer is 4 TVs, and the opportunity cost of 1 TV is 1/4 of a computer. Country B has the comparative advantage of producing computers, and Country C the comparative advantage of producing TVs.

   b. The production possibility curves are straight lines for both countries, the slope being the opportunity costs and the intercepts being the maximum level of production of each good.

3. Chipland produces 120 chips and exchanges them for 70 shirts, ending up with 85 chips and 70 shirts. Shirtland produces 108 shirts and exchanges 70 of them for 35 chips, ending up with 35 chips and 35 shirts.

5. If the VERs were replaced with a tariff, the government would collect revenue. Under VERs, the importers earn large profits.

7. Consumers will benefit because prices will decrease. As each nation shifts its production to the goods for which it has a comparative advantage, workers in expanding industries will benefit, while workers in other industries will lose. The challenge for policymakers is to facilitate this transition.

9. Taxpayers will favor the shift because they will earn revenue. The firms importing goods will lobby against this because they will lose the profits they earn from the quotas. Firms may be more effective in lobbying than taxpayers because the losses are concentrated among a few firms, but the benefits are spread widely across taxpayers.

Chapter 33

1. a. The yen will appreciate.
   b. The pound will depreciate.
   c. The pound will appreciate.

3. The real exchange rate for the South American country would rise against the dollar because the percentage increase in the prices of its goods was less than the percent depreciation of its exchange rate.

5. −$25 billion.

7. This will lead to investors wishing to sell the currency and a depreciation of the exchange rate.

9. With a fixed exchange rate, the increase in Mexican prices (at a faster rate than U.S. prices increased) led to a rise in the cost of Mexican goods relative to U.S. goods or an appreciation in Mexico's real exchange rate.

11. Countries are often reluctant to depreciate their currencies because it will lead to a rise in price of imported goods and also hurt its ability to borrow money over the long run.

Index